A History of
Modern Europe

A HISTORY OF
MODERN EUROPE

From the Renaissance to the Present

JOHN MERRIMAN

Yale University

W. W. NORTON & COMPANY
New York · London

The text of this book is composed in Adobe Fairfield Medium
with the display set in Weiss Titling.
Composition by Compset Inc.
Manufacturing by Courier, Westford. Four-color illustrations printed by NEBC.
Book design by Charlotte Staub.
Cover illustration: *The Harbor of Middelburg*, c. 1625, by Adriaen van der Venne.
Rijksmuseum, Amsterdam.
Frontispiece: Detail from *Market Day in a Flemish Town* by Sebastian Vrancx.
Rijksmuseum, Amsterdam.

Library of Congress Cataloging-in-Publication Data
Merriman, John M.
    A history of modern Europe: from the Renaissance to the present/
John Merriman
          p.   cm.
    Includes bibliographical references and index.
    1. Europe—History—1492–   I. Title.
D228.M485   1996
940.2—dc20   95-50028

Acknowledgments and copyrights continue on p. 1433, which serves as a continuation of the copyright page.

ISBN 0-393-96885-5

W. W. Norton & Company, Inc., 500 Fifth Avenue, New York, N.Y. 10110
                                              http://web.wwnorton.com
W. W. Norton & Company Ltd., 10 Coptic Street, London WC1A 1PU

1 2 3 4 5 6 7 8 9 0

For Laura Merriman and
Christopher Merriman

Contents

PART TWO   STATEMAKING

PART FIVE THE AGE OF MASS POLITICS

MAPS

PREFACE

Why a new history of modern Europe? The collapse of communism in 1989–1990 and the break-up of the Soviet Union have redrawn the map of Central and Eastern Europe. A reconfigured Europe calls for a new history. This survey of modern European history explores the roots of the economic and political problems that continue to beset Western and Eastern Europe. For example, it shows how the simmering ethnic tensions that burst into bloody civil war in Bosnia after the disintegration of Yugoslavia echoed the quarrels that eroded the stately Habsburg monarchy a century earlier. To convey an understanding of the complex tensions that still exist in Europe, this survey offers balanced coverage of Russia and Eastern Europe, as well as of the West.

Not only recent events but recent scholarly initiatives suggest that this is the time for a new synthesis. For example, the text draws on the exciting studies in the social history of ideas, approaches that stand at the intersection of intellectual, social, and cultural history. It explains how artistic patronage during the Renaissance and the Golden Age of Dutch culture reveals some of the social foundations of art. Recent studies on the family economy, village and neighborhood life, and the changing structure of work have all enriched this book's account of the transformation of European society from an overwhelmingly peasant society into an increasingly urban and industrial world. The account of the emergence of mass politics in the nineteenth century draws on recent studies of popular culture and the symbolism and power of language.

I have adopted a narrative framework with the goals of both telling a story and analyzing the central themes of the European experience. Each chapter of A History of Modern Europe can be read as part of a larger, interconnected story. Moreover, this book stresses the dynamics of economic, social, and political change.

The story of the emergence of modern Europe and its influence in the world is first of all peopled with extraordinary characters, well known and unknown. The text brings the past to life, presenting portraits of men and women who have played major roles in European history: religious reformers such as Martin Luther and Jean Calvin; Queen Elizabeth I, who solidified the English throne, and Maria Theresa, who preserved the Habsburg monarchy; King Louis XIV of France and Tsar Peter the Great, two monarchs whose reigns exemplified the absolute state; great thinkers like Kepler and Voltaire; Napoleon, both heir to the French Revolution and despot in the tradition of absolute rulers; and the monstrous Adolf Hitler and Joseph Stalin. But ordinary men and women have also played a significant role in Europe's story, and they are in this book as well, making their own history. These chapters thus evoke the lives of both leaders and ordinary people in periods of rapid economic and political change, revolution, and war.

Of the central themes in our story, the politics of states and of peoples is the first important one. The growth of strong, centralized states helped shape modern Europe. Medieval Europe was a maze of overlapping political and judicial authorities. In 1500, virtually all Europeans defined themselves in terms of family, village, town, neighborhood, and religious solidarities. Dynastic states consolidated and extended their territories while increasing the reach of their effective authority over their own people. Great Powers emerged. Then, with the rise of nationalism in the wake of the French Revolution and the Napoleonic era, demands of ethnic groups for national states encouraged the unification of Italy and Germany and stirred unrest among Croats, Hungarians, and Romanians, who were anxious for their own national states. Ordinary people demanded freedom and political sovereignty, with revolution both a reflection of and a motor for political change. The emergence of liberalism in the nineteenth century and then the quest for democratic political structures and mass politics have transformed Europe, beginning in Western Europe. Even the autocracies of Russia and Central and Eastern Europe were not immune to change, and there the quest for democracy still continues.

While discussing dynastic rivalries and then nationalism, the book also considers how wars themselves have often generated political and social change. French financial and military contributions to the American War of Independence further accentuated the financial crisis of the monarchy of France, helping spark the French Revolution. French armies of military conscripts, replacing the professional armies of the age of aristocracy, contributed to the emergence of nationalism. The defeat of the Russian army by the Japanese in 1905 brought political concessions that helped prepare the way for the Russian Revolution of 1917. The German, Austro-Hungarian, Ottoman, and Russian empires disappeared in the wake of the bloodbath of World War I; the economic and social impact of that war generated political instability, facilitating the emergence of fascism and communism.

Like politics, religion has also been a significant factor in the lives of Europeans and in the quest for freedom in the modern world. Catholicism was a unifying force in the Middle Ages; European popular culture for centuries was based on religious belief. However, religion has also been a frequently divisive force in modern European history; after the Reformation in the sixteenth century, states extended their authority over religion, while religious minorities demanded the right to practice their own religion. Religious (as well as racial and cultural) intolerance has scarred the European experience, ranging from the expulsion of Jews and Muslims from Spain at the end of the fifteenth century, to Louis XIV's abrogation of religious toleration for Protestants during the seventeenth century, to the horror of the Nazi Holocaust during World War II. While religion has become less politically divisive in modern Europe, endemic religious conflict in Northern Ireland and the bloody civil war in Bosnia recall the ravaging of Central Europe during the Thirty Years' War.

The causes and effects of economic change are a third thread that weaves through the history of modern Europe. The expansion of commerce in the early modern period, which owed much to the development of means of raising investment capital and obtaining credit, transformed life in both Western and Eastern Europe. The Industrial Revolution, which began in England in the eighteenth century and spread to continental Europe in the nineteenth, was related to a rise in population and agricultural production but also manifested significant continuities with the past, and drew on technology that had been in place for centuries. It ultimately changed the ways Europeans worked and lived.

Europe's interaction with the rest of the world is a fourth major theme that runs through this history. Europe cannot be studied in isolation. Europeans, to be sure, have learned from Muslim, Asian, and African cultures. Through commercial contact, conquest, intellectual, religious, and political influence, and, finally, decolonization, the European powers and cultures have affected the histories of non-Western peoples.

European history remains crucial to understanding the contemporary world. The political, religious, economic, and global concerns that affect Europe and the world today can best be addressed by examining their roots and development. At the same time, the study of European history in itself can enrich our lives, as we contemplate not only the distressing failures and appalling tragedies of the past, but also the exhilarating triumphs that have been part of the European experience.

ACKNOWLEDGMENTS

When I was about ten or eleven in Portland, Oregon, I decided to write a history of the world, country by country, beginning with Albania. Surrounding myself with books, I reached the F's or G's, five or ten pages for each country, before giving up. Lawrence Robinson of Jesuit High School in Portland, Oregon, rekindled my interest in history, at a time when my passionate devotion to basketball and baseball overwhelmed everything else. I also owe a debt of thanks to Albert Feuerwerker and Gerhard Weinberg, in whose courses I learned a great deal when I was a somewhat floundering undergraduate at the University of Michigan. In graduate school, still at Michigan, Charles Tilly, now at the New School for Social Research, first encouraged me to keep my eye on the dynamics of economic, social, and political change, and their effect on ordinary people. This I have tried to do. And I have also always believed that meaningful detail and color reveal the rich texture of the past, and that history can be vivid and compelling. I have tried to write this history with that in mind. Bertolt Brecht's poem "A Worker Reads History" poses questions that I still think are important to answer:

> Who built the seven gates of Thebes?
> The books are filled with the names of kings.
> Was it kings who hauled the craggy blocks of stone?
> And Babylon, so many times destroyed,
> Who built the city up each time? In which of Lima's houses,
> The city glittering with gold, lived those who built it?
> In the evening, when the Chinese wall was finished
> Where did the masons go? Imperial Rome
> Is full of arcs of triumph. Who reared them up? Over whom
> Did the Caesars triumph? Byzantium lives in song,
> Were all her dwellings palaces? And even in Atlantis of the legend
> The night the sea rushed in,
> The drowning men still bellowed for their slaves.

Young Alexander conquered India.
He alone?

Caesar beat the Gauls,
Was there not even a cook in his army?
Philip of Spain wept as his fleet
Was sunk and destroyed. Were there no other tears?
Frederick the Great triumphed in the Seven Years War. Who
Triumphed with him?

Each page a victory,
At whose expense the victory ball?
Every ten years a great man,
Who paid the piper?

So many particulars.
So many questions.

While writing this book, I have necessarily accumulated a good many debts to colleagues and friends. At Yale, Roberto González-Echevarria, Ivo Banac, Mark Micale, Lee Wandel, Henry Hyder, Vincent Moncrief, Linda Colley, Robin Winks, Geoffrey Parker, David Underdown, David Marshall, Richard Brodhead, Piotr Wandycz, Laura King, and, above all, Mark Steinberg and David Bell, shared their knowledge and expertise. I also want to thank Jeffrey Burds of the University of Rochester, Harold Selesky of the University of Alabama, Laura Englestein of Princeton University, Leslie Page Moch of Michigan State University, John Lynn of the University of Illinois, Richard Stites of Georgetown University, David Cannadine of Columbia University, Jim Boyden of Tulane University, Paul Hanson of Butler University, Michael Burns and Robert Schwartz of Mount Holyoke College, Thomas Kaiser of the University of Arkansas, Christopher Johnson of Wayne State University, Louise Tilly of the New School for Social Research, Paul Monod of Middlebury College, Peter McPhee of the University of Melbourne, Judy Coffin of the University of Texas, Austin, John Sweets of the University of Kansas, General (ret.) Harold Nelson, David Large of Montana State University, Kathleen Nilan of Arizona State University, Elinor Accampo of the University of Southern California, Jim McClain of Brown University, Alan Forrest of York University, George Behlmer of the University of Washington, Mary Jo Maynes of the University of Minnesota, Thomas Head of Washington University, Jonathan Dewald of the University of Buffalo, Johan Åhr of Muhlenberg College, as well as Margaret McLane, Jan Albers, Martha Hoffman-Strock, Daryl Lee, Tom Maulucci, Mark Lawrence, and Michael Levin. I would also like to thank Daniel Orlovsky of Southern Methodist University, and Max Oberfus of Washington University, Mary O'Neal of the University of Washington, and a number of anonymous readers.

For much of the time I have been working on this book, I was Master of Branford College at Yale. At Branford, my former assistant and long-time friend Larue Brion made it possible for me to do both. I also want to thank Betsy McCauley and Jerri Cummings in the Department of History at Yale. My colleague Jonathan Spence completed his splendid history of modern China, also with W.W. Norton and Co., in remarkably good time, showing me that a long survey could not only be started, but finished.

I want to thank Christopher and Lois Johnson, Ted and Joby Margadant, Roberto and Isabel González-Echevarria, Bob Schwartz and Marietta Clement, Dick and Cindy Brodhead, Steven Kaplan, Edward Rohrbach, David Bushnell and Karla Klarin, Jeanne Innes and John Innes, Yves and Colette Lequin, Maurice and Marie-Claude Garden, and Victoria Johnson, all good friends who have wondered politely when these two volumes would finally be finished. I hope they will enjoy the result. Many of these chapters were written and revised in Balazuc in the Ardèche in France. To Guy Larochette and Marie-Elise Hilaire, Thierry and Carole Lacharay, Jacques and Catherine Imbertèche, Max and Doris Brioude, Huguette Laroche, Pierre Soares, Lucien and Catherine Mollier, and Hervé and Françoise Parain, among others, and in Collioure, to Jean and Gila Serreau and Philippe Calmus and Corinne Mouchard, *amitiés*.

I have nothing but the greatest admiration for W.W. Norton and Co., very special publishers to whom I am indebted. At Norton, Ruth Mandel resourcefully and imaginatively suggested illustrations and relentlessly tracked down those on which we decided. Bonnie Hall, Adam Dunn, Claire Acher, and Neil Hoos helped with photo research; Roberta Flechner did an excellent job laying out the book; Tim Holahan took care of many details that made production-time work sessions at Norton both useful and enjoyable. David Lynch and Joan Rosenblatt read the galleys and caught a number of errors.

Donald Lamm, chairman of the board and former president of W.W. Norton and Co., embodies the best in publishing. He has helped make Norton a very special place. Don first proposed this project to me. As preliminary discussions moved along, Steve Forman took up editorial responsibility. He has not only been a wonderful editor, but also a friend. Sandy Lifland's deft, skillful, and patient work as developmental editor has contributed greatly to the book. It has also been a great privilege and pleasure to work with her.

Peter Gay read chapters with his usual care and skill; as always, we lunched and laughed, debated and discussed. For more than two decades, I have valued his friendship, and that of Ruth Gay.

Carol Merriman has also read and edited every chapter with a keen eye. She has tolerated with patience and good humor the almost constant presence of this book, along with other projects, in our lives for a decade, as well as my usual quirks and growing obsessiveness. The writing of these volumes has been part of the young lives of Laura Merriman and Christopher Merriman, certainly more than each might have preferred as they grew older. I dedicate this book to them in appreciation and with much love.

Balazuc (Ardèche), France
December 1995

A History of
Modern Europe

PART ONE

FOUNDATIONS

As Europe emerged from the Middle Ages, the foundations for a dynamic era of trading, global discovery, and state-building developed that would affect the lives of both rich and poor alike for centuries. During the Italian Renaissance, which lasted from about 1330 to 1530, humanists rediscovered texts from classical Greece and Rome. Renaissance artists and scholars celebrated the beauty of nature and the dignity of mankind, helping shape the intellectual and cultural history of the modern world. Moreover, after a period when almost all of Western Europe adhered to one religion, abuses in the Church would lead to cries for reform that would not be stilled until most of Europe was divided between Protestants and Catholics. Religious conflict and wars would tear Europe apart, leading to reform in the Church but leaving permanent religious divisions where once there had been near-uniformity of belief and worship.

CHAPTER 1

MEDIEVAL LEGACIES AND TRANSFORMING DISCOVERIES

Jacob Fugger (1455–1525) was one of the sons of a weaver who settled in the southern German town of Augsburg late in the fourteenth century. At age fourteen, he joined his brothers as a trader in spices, silks, and woolen goods. He traded, above all, with the Adriatic port of Venice, where Fugger learned double-entry bookkeeping (keeping track of business credits and debits), which was then unknown in the German states. Jacob Fugger soon proclaimed himself "merchant by the grace of God" and amassed a vast fortune, which he used to loan sizable sums to various rulers in Central Europe. At times he counted an annual return of 50 percent or more. Someone wrote of Fugger that "his name is known in every kingdom and every region, even among the heathens. Emperors, kings, princes, and lords sent emissaries to him; the pope hailed him and embraced him as his own dear son; the cardinals stood up when he appeared." When asked if he wanted to retire, Jacob Fugger replied that he intended to go on making money until he dropped dead.

The family history of the Fuggers intersected with economic growth and statemaking in Central Europe. The Fuggers emerged as the wealthiest and most influential of the international banking families that financed warring states, answering the call of the highest bidder. In 1519, the Fuggers helped Charles V become Holy Roman emperor by providing funds with which the ambitious Habsburg could bribe electors. The Fuggers raised and transported the money that made possible imperial foreign policy. Loaning money to ambitious rulers, as well as popes and military entrepreneurs, the Fugger family rose to princely status and facilitated the consolidation of territorial states and the emergence of a dynamic economy not only in the Mediterranean region but also in the German states and Northwestern Europe by helping merchants and manufacturers find credit for their enterprises.

3

(Left) Jacob Fugger, merchant-banker and creditor of rulers and popes, traded *(right)* with the port of Seville, stepping-off point for colonization of the New World.

Both the emergence of stronger sovereign states and the growth of trade and manufacturing ultimately changed the face of Europe. The stronger states, as well as the expanding economy, contributed to a sense that many Europeans had in 1500 of living in a period of rebirth and revitalization. In Italy, the cultural movement we know as the Renaissance was still in bloom, and was beginning to reach across the Alps into Northern Europe. The Genoese explorer Christopher Columbus' voyages to the New World were causing a great stir in Spain and the Mediterranean region. A chorus of criticism of abuses within the Catholic Church could be heard in some places, particularly in the German states.

Although famine, disease, and war (horsemen of the apocalypse) still trampled their victims across Europe, there were other significant changes as well. Substantial population growth occurred in the late fifteenth and sixteenth centuries. Europe's population stood at about 70 million in 1500 and perhaps 90 million in 1600 (well less than a third of that today). These gains overcame the horrific loss of one-third of the European population caused by the Black Death (the bubonic plague) in the mid-fourteenth century. The expansion of the population brought a recovery in European commerce, particularly in the Mediterranean region and in England and Northwestern Europe, where the Fuggers and other merchant-bankers were financing new industry and trade. Towns multiplied and their merchants grew more prosperous, building elegant houses near markets.

The emergence of sovereign monarchical states also had its roots in the late medieval period (1350–1500). England and France were two precocious states that stood as exceptions amid the territorial fragmentation that characterized medieval Europe. They foreshadowed the emergence of even stronger states during the sixteenth and particularly the seventeenth centuries and the European state system itself in the early modern period.

Finally, the pace of change was quickened by several inventions that would help shape the emergence of the modern world. Gunpowder, first used in China and adopted by Europeans in the fourteenth century, made warfare more deadly, gradually eliminating the heavily armed knight. The invention of printing in the mid-fifteenth century engendered a cultural revolution first felt in religious life, with the Bible and other religious texts now more widely available to be read and debated. And the compass, first used to determine direction by Chinese and Mediterranean navigators in the eleventh or twelfth century, now helped guide European exploration across the oceans.

CONTINUITIES FROM THE MEDIEVAL PERIOD

During the medieval period, England and France emerged as sovereign states. Furthermore, smaller territories also began to coalesce into larger units and rulers began to consolidate and extend their authority. European society took on the shape it would exhibit through 1789, with three orders—clergy, nobles, and peasants— standing in relationships of mutual obligation to each other. Material well-being would remain at a subsistence level for most peasants but would start to improve as commercial trade across greater distances began to rise in the eleventh century. Moreover, small-scale textile manufacturing would grow, as would towns, particularly in Italy and Northwestern Europe during the twelfth and thirteenth centuries.

The Fragmentation of Europe

With the collapse of the Roman Empire in the fifth century, Europe experienced an influx of new peoples. From the east came the Magyars (Hungarians), who settled in Central Europe, where they were converted to Christianity. From Scandinavia came the so-called Northmen (or Norse or Vikings), who reached Ukraine, and who for the most part became Christians. The Arabs invaded Europe in the eighth century, subsequently expanding their influence into North Africa and Spain. The Mongols poured into what is now Russia and Ukraine, sacking Kiev in the 1230s, before their empire began to collapse in the fifteenth century. This multitude of influences contributed to both the political and cultural fragmentation of Europe.

In 1500, Europe was a maze of about 1,500 fragmented states. Economic, political, and judicial institutions were overwhelmingly local. Territories and cities were subject to a confused array of overlapping jurisdictions. Paris, one of five cities in Europe with more than 100,000 inhabitants, was dotted with enclaves of ecclesiastical authority. The city-states of Italy and trading towns of northern Germany were among cities that managed to preserve their independence from territorial rulers. Town residents hoped that town walls would protect them against bandits and disease (during times of plague and epidemics) and would preserve their autonomy.

Villages or, within towns, parishes, formed the universe for most Europeans. Local loyalties, and those to churches, took precedence over those to the state, the effective reach of which in many places remained quite limited. For example, in the late fifteenth century, an entire Balkan village claimed responsibility for the murder of its lord. Many villages were, for all intents and purposes, virtually self-governing; village councils, for example, established which crops would be planted on common land and set the date plowing was to begin. Such councils coexisted with seigneurial authority (that of lords). England, for example, consisted of thousands of relatively small rural communities, interspersed with towns and a handful of major cities.

Europe stood at the crossroads between civilizations and religions. After the collapse of the Roman Empire, Christendom itself had been split between the Roman Catholic Church and the Eastern Orthodox Church following the Great Schism between the two churches in 1054. The claim by the bishop of Rome—the pope—to authority over all Eastern Christians (as well as a festering doctrinal dispute over the nature of the Holy Trinity) led to the break, culminating in the pope's excommunication of the patriarch of Constantinople. By 1500, the Eastern Orthodox Church held the allegiance of most of the people of Russia and the Balkans. The Roman Catholic and Orthodox worlds met in the eastern part of Central Europe, with Poland, Bohemia, and Hungary looking to the West.

The Catholic Church, as an alternate source of allegiance and power claiming to be a universal state (with its own language, Latin), presented a potential impediment to state authority. As both the Church and the monarchies became more centralized, conflict between them became inevitable. The Church itself had been a centralized religious authority since the Roman Empire, the collapse of which left the papacy in Rome independent of secular rule. After the middle of the eleventh century, the popes were elected by the cardinals, each of whom had been appointed by previous popes. Bishops and abbots pledged obedience to the pope in return for tenure over abbey lands and ecclesiastical revenues.

In the Ottoman Empire, religious and political sovereignty rested in the same person, the sultan. In contrast, rulers of territorial states in Europe had succeeded in making themselves largely autonomous from Church authority. Although the Church was wealthy and powerful (owning about 25 percent of the land of Catalonia and Castile, about 33 percent in Bohemia, and perhaps 65 percent in southern Italy), princes were unwilling to let the Church impinge on their secular authority, even though ecclesiastical leaders in many cases crowned them. During the fourteenth and fifteenth centuries, rulers refused to allow ecclesiastical tribunals in their territories. The pope also commanded his bishops and other clergy to be loyal to the rulers of secular states.

Muslims continued to challenge both Roman and Eastern Orthodox Christendom. During the medieval period, Western Christians had attempted to win back lands conquered by Muslims, especially seeking to recapture and hold Jerusalem in the Crusades. In 1204, believing the Eastern Orthodox religion to be heresy, the Crusaders conquered the Eastern Orthodox Byzantine Empire, which had extended from eastern Italy to the Black Sea's eastern end. In doing so, Western Christians eliminated the most effective barrier against Islam. In the fourteenth century, the Ottoman Turks (who were Muslims) conquered two-thirds of Anatolia, much of the Balkan peninsula, and Greece. During the fourteenth and early fifteenth centuries, the Byzantine Empire (which was Greek in culture and Eastern Orthodox Christian in religion) was reduced to a small area straddling the straits between Asia and Europe, which included its capital, Constantinople (modern Istanbul), and some surrounding areas. Finally, the Ottoman Turks captured Constantinople after a lengthy siege in 1453, and by 1481, the Ottoman Turkish Empire extended to the Danube River in Central Europe. Roman Catholic Europe for the next several centuries would view Islam as a perpetual threat to its religion and culture.

Europe thus confronted a huge semicircle of states under direct or indirect Turkish control. The Western powers, which had launched Christian crusades against the Muslims, now were forced into a series of defensive wars against the threat of Islam, which Christians believed represented the "scourge of God." The Venetians constructed fortifications along the Adriatic coast against the Turks in the fifteenth and sixteenth centuries.

Part of Europe's fragmentation was due to its three systems of law. The legal concepts, principles, and procedures of civil law evolved from Roman law, which was based on the rational interpretation of written law applied to human affairs. Civil laws were decreed and thereby sanctioned by rulers, whose authority stemmed in part from their right to make or impose laws. The development of civil law, then, was conducive to the development of sovereign states by closely associating the power of rulers of states with the force of law. Canon law, established by the pope for the Western Church, codified in Latin the canons of Church councils and the revealed authorities of the Bible and Church fathers. As in civil law, canon law helped affirm the authority of rulers, that is, the pope, by closely linking the law to the authority of the ruler, whose subjects owed him personal allegiance.

Customary, or common law, was a codification of established custom, implying a constant reference to decisions taken earlier by judges. It was the usual mode of law in all areas where Roman law was not used. In Western Europe, customary law developed out of the customs of feudalism, a set of reciprocal economic, social, and political relationships that encouraged decentralized power structures.

In England, where common law unified the customary law for the whole land, laws were overseen by local courts, which contributed to the decentralization of royal authority. Unlike Roman law, which helped shape the sense that the ruler was a sovereign lawgiver who could override custom, customary law helped corporate groups (such as guilds) or individuals assert their interests and rights by establishing precedents that, at least in principle, could override the ruler's intervention in the legal process.

Although French customary law also evolved from feudal laws, French kings exploited differences in laws in their kingdom as they gradually increased their influence and authority. In this way, the Parlement of Paris emerged as a royal court to arbitrate among local laws, while in much of southern France, a unified (if not always written) code based on Roman law existed.

Europe's political fragmentation was accompanied by cultural fragmentation, reinforced by the many languages spoken. Latin, the language of culture, was still spoken in university towns (thus the "Latin Quarter" in Paris). Distances and difficulties in travel and communication were also imposing. It sometimes took months for mail to arrive. Yet, upon receiving a letter from another town, a Spanish scholar enthused, "If it had been a trout it would still have been fresh." The fastest galleys, which were rowed by slaves (slavery had been wiped out in Northern Europe, but still existed in some of the Mediterranean countries), could travel more than 100 miles per day. Nonetheless, the shortest time from Madrid to Venice was twenty-two days, and the longest, in bad weather, was four times that.

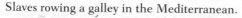

Slaves rowing a galley in the Mediterranean.

The poor man, the artisan, and the lord in late fifteenth-century miniatures.

Some merchants anxiously awaited cargoes that never arrived. Mediterranean storms could come quickly: one of them sank 100 small ships filled with grain.

The Structure of Society

Medieval society was roughly divided into three social groups: the clergy who prayed and cared for souls; nobles who governed and fought; and peasants, the vast proportion of the population, who labored. Burghers, town residents whose entrepreneurial activity made possible the economic dynamism of medieval Europe, were, despite their increasing importance, outside this classical typology.

The clergy were technically the first estate in France. Everywhere, they had many roles, serving as priests, teachers, judges, nurses, landlords, and chaplains. But they could only be tried in ecclesiastical (Church) courts and, in the evolution of the modern state, their status as a class apart would come into question. The secular clergy ministered to the population as a whole. Most of the lower clergy were as poor as their parishioners, but bishops generally were from noble families. The regular clergy included hundreds of thousands of monks and nuns living in monasteries and convents according to strict religious rules, in principle cut off from the outside world by their vows (and in many places legally considered dead!).

Nobles owned most of the land, with their status and income stemming from this land ownership, as well as from their military function. Noble titles connoted superiority of birth, and noble families usually intermarried. Nobles were in principle not to work, but rather to stand ready to defend their monarch, their own interests, or family honor.

Peasants, who made up about 85 percent of the population of Europe in 1500, lived in villages or in small settlements on the lands of the lords, dependent on the latter for protection in exchange for labor. Peasants had no legal status, with the exception of those (for the most part in Western Europe) who owned some land. In some places, they were considered barely better than animals by the lords who oppressed them and the clergy who told them their lot in life was to suffer in anticipation of heavenly rewards.

At least a fifth of the European population lived in extreme poverty. For ordinary laborers, three-quarters of their earnings went to purchase food, mainly bread. Towns and cities were crowded with poor people struggling to get by. Pope Sixtus V complained of vagrants in Rome "who fill with their groans and cries not only public places and private houses but the churches themselves; they provoke alarms and incidents; they roam like brute beasts with no other care than the search for food." The poor also wandered everywhere their feet could carry them, begging and sometimes stealing. Whereas poor beggars from within communities were tolerated, townspeople and villagers alike feared the poor outsider, particularly the gypsy. But acts of charity, encouraged by the Catholic Church, which viewed such acts as essential for salvation, helped many poor people survive.

During the fifteenth century, rebellions—generally protests against new tax impositions—remained small. Such rebels often asked for a return to "ancient rights." But banditry was pervasive. Nobles and urban artisans in medieval times even sometimes placed themselves at the head of bandit bands, particularly in regions where state power was weak (for example,

This early sixteenth-century print shows fishing, plowing, drawing water, the slaughtering of pigs, and beggars begging, all of which made up typical village life.

between Venice and Turkey, or in the Pyrenees, or between the Papal States and the Kingdom of Naples). Wandering minstrels, some of whom were blind, sang the deeds of Balkan bandits. The story of Robin Hood, the English bandit and popular hero, had its counterparts in a good many places.

Feudalism

Feudalism (a term first used by lawyers in Italy in the twelfth century) developed during the ninth and tenth centuries in response to the collapse of the authority of territorial rulers. Between about A.D. 980 and 1030, law and order had broken down in much of Europe, violence becoming the norm. This insecure time (of which contemporaries were keenly aware) had been characterized by warfare between clans and between territorial lords, attended by retinues of armed men, as well as the ravages of predatory bands.

Under feudalism, rulers and powerful lords imposed obligations of loyalty and military service on "vassals," who received, in exchange, use of lands (called fiefs) to which, at least in principle, the lords retained rights, as well as the subsequent protection of heirs under the same conditions, although a vassal had to pay the lord a fee upon inheriting an estate. Vassals also agreed to fight for their lord so many days a year and to ransom the lord if he was captured. For their part, lords adjudicated disputes between vassals. Vassals could join together to oppose a king who failed to meet his obligations; likewise, a king or lord could punish a vassal who neglected his obligations to his lord. Elaborate ceremonies featuring solemn oaths, sworn before God and blessed by churchmen, specified mutual obligations of lord and vassal. "You are mine," said one powerful lord in Aquitaine in what is now southwestern France to a lesser lord, "to do my will."

Despite some decline of royal rights throughout the period, and an increase in the power of great lords, there remained a crucial difference between a king and a prince. Kings received sacred anointment from ecclesiastical authority, and therefore claimed to rule "by the grace of God" even when, as in the case of the early Capetian monarchs of France, they were incapable of coercing the great lords and their families. While swearing to protect vassals and peasants, even the greatest lords avoided using the language associated with kingship. No one was ever anointed duke or count.

Feudalism developed in the context of an overwhelmingly agricultural economy, where great estates were in the possession of rulers or lords. The lord would keep part of the estate for himself (his domain) and would divide the rest among peasants, who would pay for the use of the land with services or in kind (payment in crops, animals, or some other commodity). In return, lords would offer protection. Peasants worked the lands of the lords, giving to the latter not only their labor, but most of what they produced. They were also obligated to mill their grain, brew their beer, and

Peasants at work defer to richly dressed nobles. Note the peasant tipping his hat to his lord.

bake their bread (and pay to do so) on the lord's estates. Thus, feudalism was a system in which the more powerful extracted revenue or services from the weak. Many lords also maintained judicial rights over their vassals and peasants.

Feudalism would finally disappear in the monarchical states in the late fourteenth century with the emergence of stronger state structures and the reimposition of the authority of the Roman Catholic Church in much of Europe. Thus, feudal relationships dissolved as the strength of rulers increased and noble independence declined in the stronger states. The granting of more noble titles by rulers in itself reflects the revived strength of the state. Gradually, royal courts usurped noble judicial authority in some places. Furthermore, economic development contributed to the continued growth of a money economy (payment in specie or in coin minted by rulers), which increasingly made feudalism obsolete. Some of the signs of an emerging money economy, above all, in Western Europe, included the ebbing of military and service obligations to rulers and lords, and the shift to cash payment by peasants to lords, instead of payment in service, crops, or animals.

The Black Death of the mid-fourteenth century itself helped sound the death knell of feudalism in Western Europe by decimating at least a third of the population. As wages rose because of a shortage of labor in the murderous wake of the Black Death, peasants were able to improve their legal status. The plague had also killed many lords. When lords tried to reimpose feudal relationships, some spectacular rebellions occurred, particularly from 1378 to 1382. The resentment of royal troops (along with the imposition of new taxes) contributed to peasant rebellions in Flanders (1323–1328), northern France (the Jacquerie of 1358), and the Peasants' Revolt in England in 1381. There was also unrest among the urban poor (as demonstrated by the revolt of the Ciompi in Florence; see Chapter 2), as ordinary people resisted attempts to return to the *status quo ante*. States took advantage of the chaos by assessing new taxes, such as the hearth tax. By increasing their authority, the monarchies of Western Europe gradually brought to a close the feudal era. Yet, remnants of feudalism (the existence of serfs, who were peasants legally bound to the land that they worked) remained in Eastern Europe and Russia until the nineteenth century.

The Subsistence Economy

Agriculture lay at the base of the European economy. Farming was the principal activity of between 85 to 95 percent of the population. Land was the most prized possession, a principal determinant of status. Wealthy people probably made up 10 to 15 percent of the population. For most, wealth depended on the possession of great estates (known in England as manors).

Peasants were constantly engaged in a protracted and more often than not losing battle against nature. Much land was of poor quality, hilly, rocky, or marshland that could not be farmed. In most of Europe, small plots, poor and exhausted soil, and traditional farming techniques continued to limit yields. Peasants scratched out a living, using horses, cattle, oxen, and mules (where peasants were prosperous enough to own such beasts), or more often, their own hard labor. Steep slopes had to be cleared and terraced by hand (the traces of terracing today provide a glimpse of the struggles of poor peasants in earlier times). Peasants plowed with hand "swing" plows. The "three-field system" left about a third of all land fallow (unplanted) in order that part could replenish itself during the growing

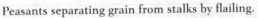

Peasants separating grain from stalks by flailing.

season. This mode of agricultural production itself necessitated sizable landholdings, and could not have worked on small peasant plots. Furthermore, villages held some land in common, probably granted originally by lords. This was economically wasteful, but nonetheless for centuries offered the landless poor a necessary resource for survival. And under the best of circumstances, peasants had to save about one-fifth to one-eighth of their seed for replanting the following year.

Peasants also had to pay part of what meager benefits they managed to extract from the land to lords, by virtue of the latter's status and ownership of land. Lords increasingly found it more advantageous to rent out plots of land, and gradually many commuted labor services to cash, which they spent on goods, including luxuries, available at expanding markets and fairs. These included silk, cotton, and some spices that traders brought from the Levant (countries bordering on the eastern Mediterranean). Peasants (like other social groups) also had to tithe (give 10 percent of their revenue) to the Church. These tithes had traditionally been in kind, but were increasingly monetized during the late Middle Ages. In a fundamentally subsistence economy, this left the rural poor—that is, most families—with little to eat.

Yet, even with the rise in population, lords in the thirteenth century faced frequent shortages of labor, and were forced to grant favorable terms to peasants. In this way, many peasants in Western Europe succeeded in purchasing their freedom, transforming their obligations into rents paid to the lords. Nonetheless, even free peasants still had to pay feudal dues to

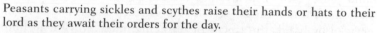

Peasants carrying sickles and scythes raise their hands or hats to their lord as they await their orders for the day.

lords and for the right to mill grain, brew beer, or bake bread, monopolies that the lords retained.

Serfdom began to disappear in France and southern England in the twelfth century, and by 1500 serfdom remained only in parts of eastern France. Peasants were free to move about, although they still owed dues and fees to lords, and, in France, remained under the lord's jurisdiction. Rulers had reason to encourage the movement toward a free peasantry in Western Europe, because free peasants could be taxed, whereas serfs (who were legally attached to the land they worked) were entirely dependent on the lords who owned the land. In Western Europe, the free peasantry reflected the growth in the authority of rulers and a relative decline in that of nobles. In the West, most peasant holdings were increasingly protected by custom and by civic law.

In Eastern and Central Europe, by way of contrast, peasants were rapidly losing their freedom during the sixteenth century, becoming serfs as landowners sought to assure themselves of a stable labor supply. This in itself was a sign that nobles were carving out territorial domination virtually independent from that of kings and other rulers.

Many people were constantly on the move in Europe. Peddlers, artisans, and agricultural laborers were obliged to travel in search of work. Shepherds moved distances of up to 500 miles with their sheep from the plains to summer pastures of higher elevations, and back again in the fall ("transhumance"). Hundreds of thousands of rural people migrated seasonally from the Pyrenees, Alps, and other mountainous regions to undertake construction work in towns, or to follow the harvest. Or people moved in the hope of simply staying alive. The roads, particularly during years of dearth, seemed full of vagabonds and beggars.

Most poor families survived by eating bread and not much else. For peasants, meat was something that lords and burghers ate, fruit was rare, vegetables poor, and bread, soup, and perhaps peas and beans the stuff of life. In southern France, grain made from chestnuts (which were themselves eaten in many forms) served as "the bread of the poor."

Yet, European agriculture was not totally stagnant. Considerable agricultural progress occurred in medieval Europe. Innovations such as three-field rotation, the use of mills, and metal harvesting implements were introduced at that time, although not adopted by all peasants until much later. Once adopted, these methods would remain basically the same until the era of mechanization in the nineteenth century, although a good many refinements contributed to subsequent progress, including the arrival of new crops brought from the New World by Columbus and his successors.

Free peasants contributed to the rise in agricultural production, which, however modest, was sufficient to feed a growing population. Not all peasants were desperately poor. Many could survive (and a minority did quite well) when famine, disease, and war left them alone, selling in the nearest market what produce they had left over after replanting, dues, and other

The medieval innovation of the three-field system allowed for the renewal of one field by leaving it fallow for a season.

obligations were paid up for that year. Many lords became market-oriented farmers in response to increased population. This in itself increased agricultural production.

The growth in the European population during the medieval period depended on these modest increases in agricultural yields. In England, Flanders, northern France, and Sicily (as well as North Africa), grain was intensively cultivated for the market. Urban growth encouraged cash-crop farming, enriching larger landlords, merchants, and wealthy peasants. There were, to be sure, areas of prosperous agriculture, such as the rich valley of the Po River in central Italy, and the plains of Valencia near the southern coast of Spain. Landowners brought more land under cultivation, cleared forests, drained marshes and swamps, and where possible, irrigated arid fields. Free peasants moved toward the eastern frontiers of Europe in search of land, which they brought under cultivation. Agricultural growth, which had been steady until the beginning of the fourteenth century, slowed down until the mid-fifteenth century because of the population losses due to the bubonic plague. But once the population began to grow again, plots that had been abandoned during the Black Death now were plowed once more. In general, too, farming techniques and tools improved during the fifteenth century. The Mediterranean lands, in particular, produced olives and wine, as well as wheat. Beer (made from cereal grains and hops) was a drink limited to Northern Europe, particularly the German states, England, and Scandinavia.

Religion and Popular Culture

Religion maintained a great hold over the lives of most Europeans in 1500, permeating everyday life. The Church, its faith and learning preserved during the so-called Dark Ages, viewed itself as an institution necessary for the salvation of souls and a unifying force in Europe. This gave the clergy great importance as counselors and distributors of the sacraments (above all, penance, the forgiveness of sins), without which Christians believed that salvation could not be achieved. Western Christendom was interlocked with Western civilization, although Muslim and Jewish heritages remained strong in Spain and Turkish-controlled areas. One of Europe's major and most traveled routes took pilgrims from many countries to the shrine of Santiago de Compostella in northwestern Castile.

In many parts of Europe, Jews, some of whom were moneylenders and peddlers, remained outcasts, although in general they did not live apart from the Christian population until the fifteenth century, when they were forced to do so by civil and ecclesiastical authorities. The popes forced Jews in Rome to wear distinctive badges; Venice established the first "ghetto" in 1516. Many Jews, forbidden to enter certain trades, were forced to wander in search of towns "where their weary feet could rest."

Religious themes and subjects permeated virtually all medieval art and much of its music. In the twelfth century, the magnificent Gothic cathedrals, houses of God reaching toward Heaven, began to be built. The construction of these churches often lasted as long as a century, absorbing enormous resources, and were paid for by gifts, large and small, from people of all walks of life. Church bells tolled the hours (clocks would remain novelties until the end of the sixteenth century).

Christianity shaped a general system of belief and values that defined the way most people viewed themselves and the world in which they lived. Thus, the Church blessed oaths of fealty sworn by vassals to lords and rulers, and took an important role in the rites of passage (birth, marriage, death) that marked the lives of peasants and nobles alike. The Italian Renaissance (see Chapter 2), to be sure, rediscovered the dignity of humanity, but it did so within the context of Christian belief.

The clergy had enormous moral authority in village life. When preachers passed through villages, peasants and penitents waited long into the night to have them hear their confessions. Most people believed that saints could intercede with God on behalf of people who prayed to them.

Religious holidays interspersed the calendar year. Thus, popular religious festivals played an important part in daily life in Europe. While ordinary people did not participate in elite culture, elites participated in popular culture, which, to a great extent, had been shaped by Christianity. Likewise, Jewish popular culture reflected a cultural interchange between ordinary people and elites.

Storytellers, whether amateur or professional, kept oral traditions of popular culture alive at a time when most people were illiterate. The most accomplished storytellers passed on their tales during evening gatherings, when villagers, principally women, gathered together to darn, tell stories, and keep warm. Many of these stories and tales reflected the fatalism of societies in which most people died relatively young.

There was much of which to be afraid. Most people believed in magic and the presence of the supernatural on earth. By such views, sorcerers or saints could intervene between people and the bad luck that might befall them. Primitive healers were believed to stand between disease and survival. They could maintain an equilibrium in the community. People believed that rubbing certain saints' images could bring good fortune. When the wine harvest failed in some parts of France, villagers whipped the statue saints that had failed them. People believed that it was a good sign to encounter a wolf, deer, or bear, that a stork landing on a house assured its occupants of wealth and longevity, that meeting a white-robed monk in the morning was a bad omen, a black-robed one a good one, that a crow cawing over the house of someone sick meant death was on its way, and that a magpie announced a cure. Such beliefs helped peasants cope with a world in which droughts, harvest failures, accidents, as well as a myriad of fatal illnesses, could bring personal and family catastrophe.

The belief in the supernatural translated into a belief that conjurers, "cunning folk" and witches could determine earthly events. Many people in need turned to sorcerers before they turned to God. Later, particularly in the seventeenth century, tens of thousands of people were executed for sorcery. Magic might, it was commonly believed, help expectant parents determine the sex of their child. Likewise, a cunning man might discover the identity of a thief by placing papers with names inside little clay balls; the guilty party's name would be the first to unravel inside a bucket of water. If an accused murderer were forced to touch the body of the victim, it was believed that blood would rush from the corpse if he or she were guilty.

Festivals marked the cycles of the year, with time still largely governed by the agricultural calendar. At the beginning of Lent, young men in some places in Western Europe carried brands of blazing straw and frolicked to ensure the village of agricultural and sexual fertility. Carnival was the highlight of the year for most people in early modern Europe, particularly in the Mediterranean region where it can be sunny and relatively warm even in February. There was more to Carnival than simply fun, as people ate and drank as at no other time, tossing flour, eggs, and fruit at each other and playing games, and much more (a disproportionate number of babies were conceived during that magic time). Carnival also stood the world on its head, if only briefly. The poor acted out the misdeeds of the wealthy in elaborate plays that were both ritualized and spontaneous. Ordinary people could poke fun at the powerful in elaborately staged farces

A peasant village carnival.

and parades by dressing up as and spoofing the behavior of judges, nobles, and clergymen. Liberated, however briefly, from their station in life by festivity and disguise, they crowned their own "kings" and "queens" of Carnival.

THE EMERGENCE OF EARLY MODERN EUROPE

The late Middle Ages brought some significant economic, social and political changes that helped shape the emergence of early modern Europe. Following the devastation of the Black Death, Europe's population slowly revived and then grew. More land was brought into cultivation, providing a somewhat greater supply of food. However, the balance between life and death was precarious indeed; famine, disease, and war still intervened frequently and murderously to check population growth.

At the same time, the continent's trade and manufacturing developed rapidly, particularly that in the Mediterranean region and in Northwestern Europe. Prosperous banking families provided capital for traders and manufacturers, as they did for states, and basic mechanisms for the transfer of credit evolved. The Mediterranean region, particularly the Italian city-states, was the center of commerce; trade with Asia and the Middle East developed at a rapid pace. At the same time, towns grew in size, and their merchants became more prosperous, especially in northern and central Italy and in the Low Countries, reflecting the importance of trade and textile manufacturing on urban growth. The growing prosperity of the entrepreneurial elite of many towns, more numerous and larger in Western

Europe than in Eastern Europe and Russia, reflected their relative independence from territorial rulers. One of the characteristics of this relatively favored status was the proliferation of guilds and other organizations that reflected the dynamism of medieval urban, economic, social, and political life.

Yet, at the same time, much of the modern state system was already in place. During the 1350–1450 period, the kingdoms of France, Spain, England, Scotland, Denmark, Norway, Sweden, and Hungary emerged, as rulers consolidated and extended their authority over their territories, eroding the independence of feudal lords and ecclesiastical authorities. Most of the small territorial units were in the German states or in Italy. France and England were sovereign states. The Iberian Peninsula was divided between Castile and Aragon—joined through the marriage of Queen Isabella and King Ferdinand in 1469, forming contemporary Spain—and Portugal. The basic layout of three Scandinavian states already existed. And important states of Central Europe (Poland-Lithuania, Hungary, and Bohemia) were already reasonably well defined. Even the Swiss cantonal federation had emerged.

A Rising Population

Europe's population had almost doubled between 1000 and 1300, rising from about 40 million to perhaps 75 million people. But early in the fourteenth century, the population began to decline, probably because of rampant disease. Then, in the middle of the century, the Black Death ravaged Europe, killing between a third and half of the European population. A bacillus spread by fleas carried by black rats, the plague reached Constantinople from Asia in 1347. It then tore through the Italian peninsula, Spain, and France in 1348, Austria, Switzerland, the German states, the Netherlands, and England in 1349, and Scandinavia and Poland in 1350. Victims died horrible deaths, some in a few days, others lingering in agony, but not for long. Some villages were completely abandoned, as people tried to flee its path. In vain, states and cities tried frantically to prevent the arrival of travelers, fearful that they were carriers of the dread disease.

For the next century, births and deaths remained balanced (with higher mortality rates in cities wiping out increased births in the countryside). Europe only began to recover during the second half of the fifteenth century, thanks to a lull in epidemics and the absence of destructive wars. However, the population did not reach the level it had been at in 1300 until about 1550, or somewhat earlier, when it began to rise rapidly, particularly in towns and in Northern Europe (see Table 1-1).

Europeans remained perpetually vulnerable to disaster and death. Epidemics almost routinely took huge tolls in Europe. Plague was the worst of these, but influenza, typhus, malaria, typhoid, and smallpox also carried off many people, particularly the poor, who invariably suffered from in-

TABLE 1-1. THE EUROPEAN POPULATION IN THE SIXTEENTH AND
SEVENTEENTH CENTURIES (IN MILLIONS)

	1500	1600
Spain and Portugal	9.3	11.3
Italian states	10.5	13.3
France	16.4	18.5
Low countries*	1.9	2.9
British Isles	4.4	6.8
Scandinavia	1.5	2.4
German states	12.0	15.0
Switzerland	0.8	1.0
Balkans	7.0	8.0
Poland	3.5	5.0
Russia	9.0	15.5

*Currently Belgium, the Netherlands, and Luxembourg.
Source: Richard Mackenney, *Sixteenth-Century Europe: Expansion and Conflict* (New York: Macmillan 1993), p. 51.

adequate nutrition. Moreover, Europeans looked to the heavens not only in prayer but also to watch for the bad weather that could ruin harvests, including rainy periods that brought flooding. Famine still killed regularly, a natural disaster that checked population growth, killing off infants, children, and old people in the greatest numbers. "Nothing new here," a Roman wrote in the mid-sixteenth century, "except that people are dying of hunger."

Life, for most people, was short. Life expectancy was about twenty years and, once one had made it out of infancy and childhood alive, perhaps forty years. Infants born in Paris could expect to live to only twenty-three years of age (a figure that includes infant mortality, and that therefore underestimates the average span of life for those surviving infancy). About a fifth of all babies born died before they reached their first birthday. In France, only about half of the children lived past the age of ten. Women lived longer than men, but many died during childbirth. Of 100 children born, less than half lived to age twenty and only about a fifth celebrated a fortieth birthday. Christ, who died at age thirty-three, was not considered to have died young.

The balance between life and death was precarious. In most towns, deaths outnumbered births almost every year. Prosperous families had more children than the poor (the opposite pattern of today). The exposure and abandonment of newly born infants was common. Furthermore, couples may have been practicing birth control, with careful sexual abstention one possible reason for relatively low rates of reproductivity. The fact that one partner often died prematurely also served as a check on population. So, too, did the fact that most couples married relatively late. In Shakespeare's great play *Romeo and Juliet,* Juliet, who marries at the age of fourteen, was not at all representative of most brides. Most English men married at between twenty-six and twenty-nine years of age, women between twenty-four and twenty-six years.

The choice of a marriage partner was important for economic reasons (although in parts of Western Europe, up to a fifth of women never married). In any social stratum, marriages were often arranged—that is, parents played a major and often determining role in choosing partners for their children. For families of means, particularly nobles, the promise of a sizable dowry counted for much. Yet, some evidence suggests that by the end of the sixteenth century the inclinations of bride and groom among English families were sometimes difficult to ignore. For the poor, marriage could increase the chances of improving one's situation or even just getting by. Thus, a young woman whose family could provide a dowry, however modest, or who had a skill, was an attractive prospective spouse, as was a young man with a trade.

Wives remained legally subservient to their husbands, although in what has been called the poor household "economy of makeshifts" their role as managers of income and as workers gave them some degree of equality. Sexual infidelity, while common, also ran against the grain of a popular sense of justice, which placed a premium on loyalty and mutual obligation between marriage partners and between parents and children. Such liaisons might also jeopardize the system of inheritance and the protection of family property by leading to the appearance of unanticipated offspring, in an age when contraceptive techniques were rudimentary and not well known. Still, about a fifth of English brides were pregnant at the time of their wedding, as sexual relations between couples expecting to marry were very common.

Kinship and neighborhood solidarities defined the lives of ordinary people. In some places—for example, the south of France—extended families were common, that is, parents and sometimes other relatives lived with couples. In England, however, the nuclear family (a couple and their children) was the most common household. When children of the lower classes began their working lives—usually at the age of fourteen or fifteen, or earlier for some apprentices—their obligations to their parents did not cease. Often, however, they left home in search of work, rarely, if ever, to return. The poor turned to family and neighbors for help in bad times, as well as for help with harvests, if they owned some land.

One of the consequences of the rise in Europe's population was the inflation that characterized the sixteenth century, particularly its last decades. It seemed to one Spaniard that "a pound of mutton now costs as much as a whole sheep used to." Between 1500 and 1600, the price of wheat rose by 425 percent in England, 650 percent in France, and 400 percent in Poland. The expanding population brought price rises before the arrival of silver from Latin America, a cause of continued inflation during the second half of the century. An English author at mid-century insisted that "the principal cause is the engrossing of things into a few men's hands." A larger population also put pressure on the value of land. The rapid rise in rents led a mid-fifteenth-century Englishman to denounce rich landlords as "men without conscience, men utterly devoid of God's fear, yea men that live as though there were no God at all. . . . They take our houses over our heads, they buy our grounds out of our hands, they raise our rents. . . ."

An Expanding Economy

One of the hallmarks of medieval society had been the marked expansion of trade and manufacture that began in the eleventh century. This occurred after several centuries in which commerce was at a standstill, when virtually all wealth was closely tied to the land and outside markets were extremely limited. During the twelfth and thirteenth centuries, merchants greatly increased the amount of products carried on land routes and in the low galley-ships that hugged the Mediterranean coastline, more confident than ever before that their goods would find purchasers. Rivers like the Rhône and Rhine were essential trade arteries. In the markets of Flanders and northern France, olive oil, fruit, and wine from the Mediterranean region were exchanged for timber, cereals, and salted fish from the Baltic region.

With the expansion in commercial activity, a money economy slowly developed. Yet, trade and barter remained important, particularly for peasants, most of whom were part of a subsistence economy. Currency still did not penetrate some mountainous regions.

The late Middle Ages brought a significant rise in the availability of credit to states and entrepreneurs. In particular, Italian merchants advanced capitalist techniques during the thirteenth century in their trade with the Near East. Some merchants were no longer itinerant travelers, but rather sedentary entrepreneurs able to raise capital and extend (and obtain) credit. They also developed bills of exchange (see Chapter 5), an order drawn upon an agent to pay another merchant money at a future date, perhaps in another country and in another currency.

To raise capital, merchants borrowed from banking families, other merchants (or merchant-banking families who did both), moneylenders, or formed temporary partnerships. Here and there, then, businesses began to work on a commission basis, and some entrepreneurs specialized in transporting goods. They began to keep registers of profits and losses, using double-entry bookkeeping.

Banking families in Venice and other Italian city-states were already well established in the thirteenth century. The powerful merchant-banking families influenced rulers by loaning kings and popes alike vast sums. On a smaller scale, moneylenders still played an important part in rural economies. Territorial rulers and great lords increasingly required a healthy treasury or at least good credit.

Bankers sitting behind their *banco* (counter) doing business.

The greater availability of credit facilitated a commercial boom in the sixteenth century. By 1500, with new mechanisms of credit, coin or money no longer necessarily had to be carried from place to place in order to purchase goods. At the same time, merchants and manufacturers were able to control the distribution of more products, and merchant-manufacturers could put various stages of production under their control. Yet, the multiplicity of states hindered commerce. Even within France, on the Loire River and its tributaries more than 200 tolls were collected in 120 different spots.

The sixteenth century also brought a marked increase in manufacturing, which in some regions may have multiplied by 500 percent. The extraction of iron, copper, and silver quadrupled, for example in Central Europe. Large-scale manufacturing was limited to mining and textiles, as well as to arms manufacturing and shipbuilding.

The production of textiles, whether for large, distant markets or only for local consumption, dominated the manufacturing economy. The manufacture of silk, techniques for which had been imported from China into Europe by Arabs in the tenth century, centered in the Italian states. It spread during the second half of the fifteenth century across the Alps to the German states, France, and Spain, which produced raw silk and no longer depended on imports from Asia and Persia.

The manufacture of cloth spread rapidly in Tuscany, northern France, Flanders, and the Netherlands. The woolens industry of Flanders, which had developed during the medieval period, boomed, centered in the towns of Ypres, Ghent, and Bruges. England, which continued to export wool to the continent, became a major producer of woolen goods in the fourteenth century, forming a base for English industrialization and for London's prosperity as an exporter of manufactured goods. However, Antwerp first emerged as Europe's most important center of trade.

Urban merchants and artisans were organized into guilds, which regulated production and distribution, thus protecting, at least in principle, guild members and consumers. The structure of craft production was organized hierarchically. Apprentices who learned their craft became journeymen and, if all went well, could eventually become masters, joining a masters' guild, and employing journeymen and training apprentices. Most cloth was finished in towns by craft artisans. Through the guilds, masters could preserve the quality of work within their particular trades and, at the same time, the reputations of their town.

During the sixteenth century, a period of great economic dynamism, the gap between rich and poor probably grew, particularly as the massive inflation of that period, pushed by population increase, reduced the value of wages. During the fourteenth and fifteenth centuries, it had become increasingly difficult for journeymen to become independent master craftsmen. Early in the sixteenth century, some German journeymen refused to work for masters who paid them less than they desired or had been used to receiving. Tensions between employers and workers probably intensified during the sixteenth century as a whole.

Many craftsmen avoided restrictions on their work by working outside the walls of cities or in the countryside. In this way, they avoided guild monopolies and guild specifications on wages and piece rates. Likewise, merchant-capitalists who owned raw materials put out spinning, weaving (sometimes renting out looms), and other work into the countryside, where labor was even cheaper. Rural production spread rapidly in northern Italy, the Netherlands, northern France, and England between 1450 and 1550. Hundreds of thousands of peasants produced woolen or linen yarn or wove it into cloth; then urban workers dyed, bleached, or shrunk the cloth, which merchants then sold. This "cottage industry" (also sometimes called "domestic industry") would remain an important part of the manufacturing process well into the nineteenth century.

Merchant-capitalists put out spinning, weaving, and other work into the countryside in cottage (domestic) industry. Here a woman is spinning in her home.

As they grew richer, some merchant families purchased land and noble titles. Merchants therefore became important figures in every state. Many nobles resented the ennoblement of commoners, following the old saying, "the king could make a nobleman, but not a gentleman." In the mid-sixteenth century, a French noble heaped scorn on "the infinity of false noblemen, whose fathers and ancestors wielded arms and performed acts of chivalry in grain-shops, wine-shops, draperies, mills and farmsteads; and yet when they speak of their lineage they are descended from the crown, their roots spring from Charlemagne, Pompey, and Caesar." The rising importance of merchants reflected the fact that, with continued economic growth, the possession of money, the ability to acquire credit, to draw up a bill of exchange, and entrepreneurial skill were gradually becoming more important than the military might and distinguished birth of nobles.

The Growth of Towns

The growth of towns, particularly during the twelfth and thirteenth centuries, reflected and accentuated increased economic development and security in medieval Europe. Fortified stone ramparts, gates, and towers gave each town visible characteristics. A "bourgeois" or "burgher" was technically someone who lived in a town. Towns were the residence of most courts (including municipal courts), hospitals, and fraternal associations, such as religious confraternities, as well as guilds. Administrative and religious buildings were the cornerstones of the medieval towns. Most towns had a relatively large number of clergy living within their walls, ministering to the needs of the population, or, in the case of some convents or monasteries, living a cloistered existence.

Most major towns in Europe were founded before 1300, although new ones were added. The physical development of towns still followed the outlines of original Roman settlements (for example, Leicester in northern England, the German town of Trier, and Narbonne in southern France). In Poland, about 200 new towns were created between 1450 and 1550, adding to the 450 already in existence.

In Italy, Venice, Florence, Genoa, Milan, and Pisa became independent city-states in about 1100, free to establish their domination over surrounding towns and villages. The decline of the Byzantine Empire and the inability of the Holy Roman Empire to establish its authority throughout Italy prevented the development of large territorial states. The prosperity of the city-states, too, impeded the creation of a single Italian state, or even a peninsula divided into two or three major political units. Freed of feudal overlords, the dynamism of these city-states underlay the Renaissance (see Chapter 2). Venetian and Genoese merchants sent trading fleets carrying goods to and from the Levant and beyond, as well as along the spice routes to China (visited by the Italian adventurer Marco Polo during his long voyage from 1275 to 1292), India, and Central Asia.

In Northern Europe, as well, the growth of cities and towns was linked to the expansion of commerce and long-distance trade. In northern Germany, independent trading cities were enriched by the Baltic grain trade, as Polish landowners, like their Hungarian and Bohemian counterparts, concentrated agricultural development on the production of grain for export to the Dutch Netherlands and other Western countries. Lübeck and Hamburg, among other northern German trading cities, formed the Hanseatic League, which at first was a federation against banditry. Its towns began to thrive in the mid-twelfth century, establishing networks of trade that reached from London all the way to Novgorod. The Polish port of Gdansk had its own currency, fleet, army, and diplomats. Likewise, some towns in southern Germany formed leagues to resist territorial lords and protect trade routes. The fairs held outside the towns of Champagne in northern France, as well as Lyon at the confluence of the Saône and Rhône Rivers, and Beaucaire on the Rhône in Provence, served as trading points between Northern Europe and Mediterranean merchants. The market function of trading towns swelled their populations; merchants and small manufacturers catered to the needs of the local population. Market towns also reflected the fact that the European economy remained closely tied to the land, as landowners, particularly in regions of commercialized agriculture, marketed their produce.

Medieval Europe boasted major urban centers of learning, dominated by Church teaching. Paris (theology), Montpellier (medicine), and Bologna (Roman law) were major university centers. Oxford and Cambridge Universities were founded in the thirteenth century. Universities existed not in the sense that we know them today. Rather, the term referred to a common, corporately organized body of students or masters in one town. By 1500, dozens of towns had universities. And, in turn, literacy (limited to a small proportion of the population in the best of circumstances) rose faster in towns than in the countryside, as the equivalent of secondary education shifted from rural monasteries to urban church or grammar schools.

Northern Italy and the Low Countries had the densest networks of towns. However, town dwellers remained a relatively small minority of the population, no more than about 15 percent of the population. Only about 2 percent of the European population lived in towns larger than 40,000. In 1500, only about 6 percent of Europeans lived in towns of more than 10,000 people. Most towns were small: in the German states, only about 200 of 3,000 towns had more than 10,000 residents. Only Constantinople, Naples, Milan, Paris, and Venice had more than 100,000 inhabitants.

Town governments were dominated by oligarchies of rich merchants, guild masters, and property owners (in Italian towns, nobles were part of these oligarchies). Despite the fact that many peasants still lived in towns ("agro-towns"), working fields outside town walls during the day and returning home before the gates slammed shut at nightfall, town and country seemed in some ways worlds apart.

Municipal Liberties

A contemporary saying went "town air makes free" (for example, no town person in Western Europe could be a serf). Towns formed a type of corporation, with residents purchasing freedom from taxes and paying rulers and lords dues as necessary. To some extent, then, towns within the feudal context stood as zones of freedom, because their residents were in most cases not bound by service obligations to landowners. These towns were independent or semi-autonomous because of their purchase of exemptions from the authority of the rulers of territorial states. In such cases, councils, not territorial lords or rulers, made decisions that affected the lives of residents. Towns could also loan money to kings waging war against recalcitrant vassals or other rulers, including popes.

Urban freedoms had to be won and maintained from lords. Urban oligarchs jealously guarded pretensions of municipal independence against noble and monarchical claims. Cities and towns felt pressure from rulers who tried to expand to attain revenue and political consolidation. Towns purchased charters of exemption from taxes in exchange for the payment of lump sums. In some cases, rulers actively sought alliances with towns against nobles, sworn enemies of towns. Where territorial rulers were weak, as in Italy and the German states, towns obtained the greatest degree of freedom. By contrast, towns developed less rapidly in areas where rulers and nobles exercised strong authority.

Traditions of municipal liberties would leave a significant heritage in Western Europe, ultimately shaping the emergence of constitutional forms of government. Whereas social relationships in the countryside were largely defined by personal obligations, in towns these were replaced by collective rights through guilds and other associations. In England, northern France, the Netherlands, Flanders, and Switzerland, urban medieval confraternities and other voluntary associations would spur a democratizing impulse within trading towns as they struggled to maintain their independence from rulers and rural nobles. Lacking the associational infrastructure of many towns in Western Europe, however, Eastern European towns were not able to stem the tide of the increasing power of nobles and, in the case of Russia, the state. As the Muscovite state expanded its authority, the tsars ran roughshod over urban pretensions. Towns in the East extracted none of the special charters of rights that characterized towns in the West. Russian rulers considered towns their personal property, and the residents of towns owed service to their territorial lords.

The Emergence of Sovereign States

Although hardly anyone used the term "state" to denote a political entity, by 1500 the largest monarchical states (see Map 1.1) were taking on some of the characteristics of the modern state, despite significant limits on the

MAP 1.1 EUROPE IN 1500   Europe in 1500 was a maze of fragmented states although sovereign monarchical states were beginning to emerge.

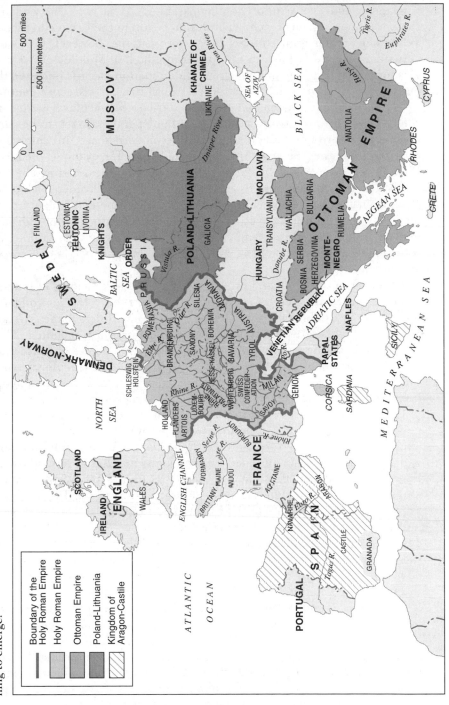

authority of their rulers. During the sixteenth century, France, Spain, and England would evolve into "new monarchies." What was "new" about them was their growing reach, an evolution begun in the late medieval era. While monarchies grew stronger in Western Europe, however, they were actually weakened in Eastern Europe during the late Middle Ages. Struggles for power, civil war, and the growing domination of lords hindered the emergence of strong states there at least until the late sixteenth century.

Sovereign states emerged in Europe during the medieval period as rulers moved toward greater authority and independence. Yet, to be sure, these states were not "nation-states" in the modern sense, in which citizens feel that they belong to a nation by being, for example, Spanish, French, or Italian. Such "imagined national communities," defined by ethnic bonds and cultural and linguistic traditions, would only develop beginning in the late eighteenth century and the nineteenth century. In medieval Europe, rulers governed a complex of territories, semi-independent towns, feudal vassals, and corporate institutions such as guilds that were largely independent of the crown, exchanging personal and or corporate privileges for loyalty.

Yet, between the tenth and fifteenth centuries, the kingdoms of France, England, and Spain grew into sovereign states, as their rulers consolidated their states by establishing their primacy over rivals. Rulers made laws and imposed administrative unity to a degree that was unprecedented. They asserted their authority, but not domination, over the nobles of the territories they claimed. Royal authority directly touched more subjects than ever before. Rulers could raise and command armies, mint money, impose taxes, summon advisers, and appoint officials to represent their will.

The French kings, their territories clustered around Paris, had little real power during the medieval period. Until the mid-fifteenth century, the kings of England held Normandy, Brittany, Maine, Anjou, and Aquitaine, and the counts of Flanders held wealthy lands in what is now northern France and southern Belgium. During the Hundred Years' War, French kings raised the funds and armies necessary to expel the English from France (with the exception of the Channel port of Calais). During the last half of the fifteenth century, the French kings ended the *de facto* independence of the large, prosperous provinces, which were technically fiefs of the crown. In 1482, the crown of France absorbed Burgundy, whose powerful dukes were related to the kings of France, and a decade later the regent for Charles VIII (ruled 1483–1498) invaded Brittany, adding it to France. Through timely royal marriages and warfare, the French monarchs established the foundations for a stronger, more centralized monarchy.

England, too, emerged as a stronger monarchical state during the late medieval period, but with significant differences from its continental counterparts. The vassals of King John (ruled 1199–1216) and the people of London had rebelled against more taxes to finance his attempt to recover continental territories lost to France. In 1215, they forced him to sign the Magna Carta, the "great Charter of Liberties." John agreed to impose major taxes only with the permission of a "great council," representative of the barons and to cease hiring mercenaries when his barons refused to fight. Later in the century, King Edward I (ruled 1272–1307) summoned barons, bishops, and representatives from England's major towns in the hope of obtaining their agreement to provide funds for another war against the king of France. From that "parley," or "parliament," came the tradition in England of consultation with leading subjects and the origins of an English constitutional government that constrained royal authority.

In Central Europe, the Holy Roman Empire was not really a sovereign state. It dated from 962, when German nobles had elected a ruler. By the end of the thirteenth century, the principle that the Holy Roman emperor would be elected, and not designated by the principle of hereditary, had been established. Considering themselves the successors of the Roman Empire, the Holy Roman emperors saw themselves as the protectors of the papacy and of all of Christendom, which involved the emperor in the stormy world of Italian politics.

The Holy Roman Empire encompassed 300 semi-autonomous states, ranging from several large territories to a whole host of smaller states, principalities, and free cities that carried out their own foreign policy and fought wars. The emperor could not levy taxes or raise armies outside of his own hereditary estates. German princes consolidated their own power into many independent and semi-independent territorial states, in what became known as "German particularism." The Holy Roman emperors were unable to consolidate their authority and were increasingly unable to enforce their will outside of the boundaries of their hereditary estates.

The Austrian Habsburgs, the ruling house in the German Alpine hereditary lands, had gradually extended their territories in the fourteenth and fifteenth centuries between the Danube River, the Adriatic Sea, and the Little Carpathian Mountains. Beginning in 1438, when the first Habsburg was elected Holy Roman emperor, until 1740 (when the male line was extinguished), only Habsburgs held the ruling title of Holy Roman emperor. Smaller states, such as the thirteen cantons of Switzerland, struggled to maintain their autonomy against rising Austrian power.

Developing State Structures

The growth of bureaucracies was one means by which rulers consolidated more effective power. Rulers had always had some kind of council, but the importance of their advisers grew in the fourteenth and fifteenth centuries. Chanceries, treasuries, and courts of law represented bureaucratization. Serving as royal officials, some humble men of talent began to reach positions of influence within states.

Rulers still earned revenue from their own lands. But in order to meet the expenses of their states, rulers drew income from taxation, sale of offices (posts in the service of the monarch that were often both lucrative and prestigious), government bonds, and confiscation of land from recalcitrant nobles. (Like other rulers, popes also centralized administration and finances, virtually selling posts.) Rulers also imposed taxes on salt, wine, and other goods, impositions from which nobles and churchmen were exempt. States themselves in the sixteenth century became the great collectors and distributors of revenue. Moreover, the gradual growth of public debt was another sign of the increased power of states. Royal dependency on the loans of merchant-bankers enriched the latter, providing more capital for their ventures.

As they consolidated their realms in the fifteenth century, rulers could offer lords noble titles and offices (lucrative positions within their households or as officials). Thus, with the strengthening of sovereign states, which in part entailed the loss of some noble judicial rights and the right to have armies of retainers, nobles depended more on monarchies for power and honor. More of them came to court and served as royal officials. Furthermore, the sale of offices, especially in France and Spain, ultimately encouraged loyalty to the throne.

Royal courts now adjudicated property disputes, although kings now less frequently dispensed justice themselves. Royal courts gradually eroded noble jurisdiction over the king's subjects. Yet, in France and many of the German states, nobles retained rights of justice over peasants.

Rulers, surrounded by courtiers and councils, became more grand. One of the signs of the ascension of monarchical power was that thrones became hereditary, as rulers worked to consolidate their authority and territories. As people were quite apt to die young, such arrangements, which varied throughout Europe, mattered a great deal.

In the fifteenth century, regular channels for diplomacy emerged among the states of Europe. The Italian city-states were the first to exchange permanent resident ambassadors. By the middle of the fifteenth century, Florence, Milan, Venice, and the kingdom of Naples all routinely exchanged ambassadors, who provided news and other information but also represented the interests of their states. States sent diplomatic representatives to the courts of friend and rival alike.

Limits to State Authority

Significant constraints, however, still limited the authority of rulers. We have seen that the privileges of towns, established through the purchase of royal charters of financial immunity, tempered royal power. Some regions (for example, Navarre in Spain), nominally incorporated into realms, nonetheless maintained autonomy through representative institutions. And, to be sure, distance and physical impediments such as mountains and vast plains also prevented the effective extension of royal authority.

Even more important, there existed the tradition that assemblies of notable subjects who counseled the king had rights, and had to be consulted. In the thirteenth century, rulers had convoked assemblies of notable subjects to explain their policies and to ask for their help and, in doing so, had strengthened and publicized their rule. Because they depended on those whom they convoked to provide military assistance when they required it, they also heard grievances. From this, parliaments, assemblies, diets, and estates developed, representing (depending on the place) nobles, clergy, towns, and, in several cases, everyone else.

Early in the sixteenth century, an Italian exile told the king of France what the monarch would need to attack the duchy of Milan: "three things are necessary: money; more money; and still more money." The most powerful states—France, Habsburg Austria, and Spain—could raise sizable armies with relative ease. But, to meet the extraordinary expenses of wartime, they increasingly borrowed money from wealthy banking families. Rulers also utilized subsidies from friendly powers, imposed special taxes and forced loans, and, especially in Spain and France, sold offices. Sixteenth-century inflation would make wars even more expensive.

Royal levies to finance warfare through direct taxation could only be imposed with the consent of those taxed. The dialogue between rulers and assemblies, and the strength and weakness of such representative bodies, would define the emergence and nature of modern government in the European states.

The princes of the German states had to ask assemblies of nobles for the right to collect excise taxes. Estates dominated entirely or predominantly by nobles in Poland-Lithuania, Bohemia, and Hungary balanced royal authority. In Bohemia, the rights of towns partially balanced noble prerogatives. Rulers could suspend decisions of those "sovereign" bodies, yet such assemblies could not be completely ignored.

The prerogatives of nobles and churchmen also impeded royal authority. Nobles and churchmen successfully resisted royal taxes, which fell on the poor (the vast majority of the population), whom no one represented. Nobles still had to be convinced or coerced to provide armies. Kings became, at least in principle, supreme judges (though not for the clergy, as ecclesiastics were generally tried in Church courts), royal courts offering litigants and petitioners a final appeal.

The struggle between rulers and the popes dated to the late eleventh century, when the popes and Holy Roman emperors had struggled for primacy, particularly over the contested right of lay rulers to appoint bishops and invest them with signs of spiritual authority (the lay investiture crisis, c. 1060–1122). Yet, the clergy generally taught obedience to secular as well as ecclesiastical rulers. Furthermore, in the late medieval period, kings were able to further consolidate their power when popes granted the rulers of France, Spain, and some German towns certain rights over the clergy, including that of naming bishops.

TRANSFORMING DISCOVERIES

The use of gunpowder would transform warfare from "chiefly a matter of violent housekeeping" between lords and vassals to sometimes massive struggles between dynastic rivals. Warfare would became more pervasive in the early modern period because of dynastic quarrels between rulers as they sought to consolidate their territories. The enhanced ability of the rulers of the largest sovereign states to command resources would swell the size of armies, whose ranks would be increasingly filled by mercenaries. Yet, despite so much fighting, there would be surprisingly few major changes in national boundaries between 1450 and the beginning of the Thirty Years' War in 1618.

The invention of printing also led to major change in the late Middle Ages. Common religious texts, most notably the Bible, could be printed in large quantities and could reach more people than ever before. Other texts, religious and nonreligious in nature, helped expand the horizons of Europeans.

European horizons expanded in another significant way, as well. Beginning in the late fifteenth century, explorers sailed across the oceans, conquering colonies, above all, in the Americas. After being on the defensive

Theodore Galle's *Nova reperta* ("new discoveries") celebrates the discovery of the New World and forms of the new technology (gunpowder, the compass, the clock, the saddle with stirrups).

against Arab and Turkish Muslims, Europeans now went on the offensive. During the next century, they would lay claim to more than half of the world's surface.

Gunpowder, Warfare, and Armies

Although kings still depended on nobles to raise armies and to command on the battlefield, the face of battle was transformed in the late medieval period. Invented in China, gunpowder was brought to Europe in the thirteenth century by the Arabs. First used in battle in the early fourteenth century, gunpowder could propel arrows and, increasingly, lead bullets. Gunpowder soon became the explosive for a new weapon, the musket, which could be standardized in caliber and ammunition and for which clockmakers could produce spring-driven wheel locks of quality for a firing mechanism.

Gradually replacing the use of lances and the crossbow and longbow in battle, the musket eroded the role of the noble as privileged warrior since nobles could now be more easily shot off their horses by muskets than unseated by the lances of other nobles or brought down by arrows. Thus, the musket reduced the role of cavalry in battle as well as the advantage of the heavily armored noble knight and the place of swords. Cavalrymen now wore light armor and, while they might well carry a lance, they also sometimes were armed with pistols. Yet, pikemen remained essential to any army; their thirteen-foot-long weapons, made of a long wooden handle topped by a sharp iron point, protected the infantry while soldiers reloaded. Furthermore, the furious attack of pikemen could tear apart the rows of riflemen firing and then kneeling to reload.

Artillery also transformed warfare. Exploding shells could kill and wound many people at once. At the battle of Novara (1513) in northern Italy, artillery fire killed 700 men in three minutes. Deadly bombardments during pitched battles also had a devastating effect on the morale of the enemy. Cannon replaced rams on warships. The sleek galleys that raced along the coast of the Mediterranean during the warm summer months gave way to ships large enough to transport heavy cannon. Solidly forged cannon could last as long as a century. Requiring skilled gunners and reliable shells, artillery also accentuated the scientific dimension in the technology of warfare, making it easier to storm fortified castles and towns. The threat from enemy artillery forced the construction of expanded and more solid fortifications around towns, which again left the defense with a solid advantage in warfare. Sieges lasted longer than ever before. This in itself weighed heavily upon the civilian population of the besieged towns, for civilians who risked being sent unceremoniously through the gates to take their chances as they could, were deemed "useless mouths" to feed during a siege. Furthermore, the victorious armies, frustrated by long sieges, sometimes slaughtered the surviving civilian population.

Although frontier garrisons, artillery units, and the king's household guards were virtually the only true standing, or permanent armies, the size of armies during wars increased in size during the late fifteenth and the sixteenth centuries. During the Hundred Years' War, major battles were fought with between 7,000 and 15,000 troops on each side. During the struggles between the Austrian Habsburg and French Valois dynasties on the Italian peninsula in the fifteenth and sixteenth centuries, armies reached 25,000 in size with the addition of more infantry. In France, some nobles began to serve not as obligated vassals, but as paid volunteers. Some nobles still had private armies, but served their kings as commanders and cavalrymen.

Mercenaries, the original "free lances" increasingly replaced feudal levies (and urban militias, where they existed) in armies mobilized by rulers to defend or expand their territorial interests. "Noah's ark armies" might include Albanians, Englishmen, Scots, Greeks, Poles, and especially Swiss pikemen, who were known for both their defensive and offensive abilities, often winning battles through their relentless and ferocious attacks. Mercenaries received modest, though irregular, pay and expected acceptable rations and the opportunity to pillage. Assuming these conditions were met, they seem to have deserted far less frequently than soldiers recruited by states from their native population.

Yet, most states had some kind of conscription, whether formalized, affecting men between the ages of fifteen and sixty, or simply amounting to the dragooning of men when war approached. Loyal nobles, royal officials, and paid recruiters provided soldiers. Peasants made up more than three-quarters of armies, as they did the European population, followed by urban laborers and craftsmen. Criminals also ended up in armies, often as the price of their release from prison or from execution, though they might well carry with them forever a branded letter as part of their sentence (such as the letter "V" for the French word *voleur*—thief).

Conditions of military service were difficult at best. In addition to barely adequate lodging and food, infractions of rules were dealt with harshly, including the infamous and often fatal "running the gauntlet" through troops lined up on both sides armed with sticks or swords. Commanders dispensed justice without trial or appeal; sentences were carried out immediately. Heads impaled on pikes for several days at the entry to a camp left a lasting impression.

Except for royal guards, artillery units, and other specialized forces, uniforms were rare in any army, although most armies and even regiments sported some identifying symbol such as an armband or cross or other symbol attached to a tunic: the English red cross, the barred cross of Lorraine, or the lion of Lyon.

Epidemics and disease—dysentery and typhoid, among others—carried off far more than did wounds received in battle. But casualty figures were also alarming, however inaccurately kept. The wounded often died from inadequate—even for the time—medical treatment and from neglect.

The Printing Press and the Power of the Printed Word

The invention and spread of printing in the fifteenth century in some ways marked the end of the medieval period (see Map 1.2). Before its invention, monks and scribes had copied books on parchment sheets; one copy of the Bible required about 170 calfskins or 300 sheepskins. The development of woodblock printing and paper had occurred in China in the eighth century; both reached Europe from the Arab world via Spain in the thirteenth century. The manufacture of paper facilitated the copying of manuscripts by replacing parchment, which was very expensive. Paper more readily accommodated merchants, officials, and scholars. But the process of copying itself remained slow. Cosimo de' Medici, the Florentine banker and patron of Renaissance art, hired 200 scribes who filled his library by copying 200 volumes (most of which had religious themes) in two years' time.

All this changed in the fifteenth century when Flemish craftsmen invented a kind of oil-based ink. This and the innovation of a wooden handpress made possible the invention of movable metal type in the German

MAP 1.2 SPREAD OF PRINTING THROUGH EUROPE, 1450–1508   Towns and dates at which printing shops were established throughout Europe, increasing the number of books produced and read.

Cathedral town of Mainz in about 1450 by, among several others, Johann Gutenberg (c. 1395–1468), whose printed Latin Bibles of stunning beauty are treasured today.

Printing shops began to spread in the 1460s to other German towns, reaching the Italian states, Bohemia, France, and the Netherlands by the end of the decade, and Spain and England in the 1470s (see Map 1.2). By the beginning of the sixteenth century, more than 6 million books had been printed, with the average edition running between 200 to 1,000 copies—the latter figure about the average printing of a scholarly publication in the United States today.

Books provided scholars with identical ancient and medieval texts to discuss and critique. Accounts of discoveries and adventures in the New World filtered across Europe from Spain, England, and France. The number of scholarly libraries—which were really just private collections—grew rapidly. New professions developed: the librarian, the bookseller, the publisher, to say nothing of the various trades involved with the printing and publishing process, from typesetters to editors. Moreover, with the greater dissemination of knowledge came an increase in the number of universities, rising from twenty in 1300 to about seventy in 1500.

More people learned how to read, although literate individuals remained far in the minority. In Florence and other prosperous cities, the rate of literacy may have been relatively high, although in the Italian city-states as a whole it is unlikely that more than 1 percent of workers and peasants could read and write. The literate population of the German states in 1500 was about 3 or 4 percent. But among the upper classes many more people developed the habit of reading, as the Bible and other books and even dictionaries could be purchased, discussed, and debated.

Printing made censorship considerably more difficult. Furthermore, not all that was published pleased lay and ecclesiastic leaders. No longer could destroying one or two manuscripts suffice to root out an idea. Thus, Pope Alexander VI warned in a bull in 1501: "The art of printing is very useful insofar as it furthers the circulation of useful and tested books; but it can be very harmful if it is permitted to widen the influence of pernicious works. It will therefore be necessary to maintain full control over the printers so that they may be prevented from bringing into print writings which are antagonistic to the Catholic faith or which are likely to cause trouble to believers."

Exploration and Conquest of the New World

By the last decade of the fifteenth century, the inhabitants of the Iberian Peninsula already had several centuries of navigational and sailing accomplishments behind them. The Portuguese had captured a foothold on the Moroccan coast in 1415, beginning two centuries of expansion. Early in the fifteenth century, they began to explore the west coast of Africa and had taken Madeira and the Azores islands in the Atlantic. Their goal was to break Muslim and Venetian control of European access to Asian spices and silk.

King Ferdinand and Queen Isabella of Spain had initially rejected the request of the Genoese cartographer and merchant Christopher Columbus (1451–1506), who sought financial backing for an ocean voyage to reach the Indies. Columbus, the son of a weaver, wanted to carry the word of God to Asia. In 1492, he convinced the Spanish sovereigns to give him their full support; the royal couple feared that Portuguese vessels might be the first to cross the oceans to reach the great wealth of Asia.

Late in 1492, Columbus set sail with three ships. He believed the earth was a perfect sphere, and since Africa stood in the way of a voyage sailing to the East, he thought it possible to reach the Orient by sailing west across the Atlantic Ocean, which he believed to be quite narrow. His small fleet reached not Asia but rather the small Caribbean island of San Salvador in the Americas. He then also reached Cuba and finally Hispaniola (now the Dominican Republic and Haiti) in the Americas. "What on earth have you come seeking so far away?" he was asked. "Christians and spices," he replied, but he also probably believed that he would find gold, and asked the Indians he encountered on the shore in sign language if

The Portuguese arrive in Japan in 1542.

they knew where some could be found. Columbus was impressed with the beauty of Hispaniola (although he remained convinced that he had discovered islands near India) and the "docility" of the indigenous people. Yet, in the absence of gold, he suggested that the crown could make Hispaniola profitable by selling its people as slaves. Columbus, whose greatest contribution was to find a way across the sea using the trade winds, made three subsequent voyages of discovery, the last in 1502, when his mind was deteriorating.

Portugal, a much poorer state than Spain, struggled to defend its fledgling empire and trade routes against Spanish encroachments. In 1498, Vasco da Gama (c. 1469–1524) reached India; the cargo of spices he brought back to Lisbon paid for his costly expedition sixty times over. The Portuguese maritime route stretched around the coast of Africa across the Indian Ocean to the South China Sea. This route could now compete with overland spice and silk routes that had long linked Europe to the markets of the East. An Indonesian ruler remarked of the Portuguese adventurers, "The fact that these people journey so far from home to conquer territory indicates clearly that there must be very little justice and a great deal of greed among them." This had made them "fly all over the waters in order to acquire possessions that God did not give them."

In 1493, Pope Alexander VI divided the non-Christian world into zones for Spanish and Portuguese exploration and exploitation (see Map 1.3). He awarded Portugal all of sub-Saharan Africa and Asia; Spain, the pope's ally, received most of the Americas, although Portugal claimed Brazil, which became the largest colony in the Americas. But the practical problems of drawing boundaries down the middle of oceans with primitive navigational instruments resulted in zones of contested territory. No one asked the indigenous populations what they thought.

Soon more and more Spanish explorers reached the Americas. Vasco Núñez de Balboa (c. 1475–1519) established Spanish sovereignty over what is now Panama. The island of Cuba, in turn, fell to the Spanish, and then served as a staging point for the conquest of Mexico by Hernando Cortés (1485–1547), which opened a new chapter in European expansion. Cortés, after landing on the coast of Mexico in 1519, went to see the Aztec emperor, Montezuma, who sent him away, although he later sent him gifts of gold and silver. Determined to conquer Mexico, Cortés formed alliances with Montezuma's non-Aztec peoples, who naively hoped that Cortés might help them achieve their independence. The Spanish adventurer then conquered Mexico with no more than sixteen horses and six hundred soldiers, but with 100,000 native American allies. Further south, Francisco Pizarro (c. 1476–1541) led his men in the conquest of the Inca Empire in Peru. Although the Incas were a culturally rich people, they had never seen iron or steel weapons before, nor did they have draft animals. When Pizarro's horses lost their shoes in Peru and there was no iron available to replace them, he had them shod in silver.

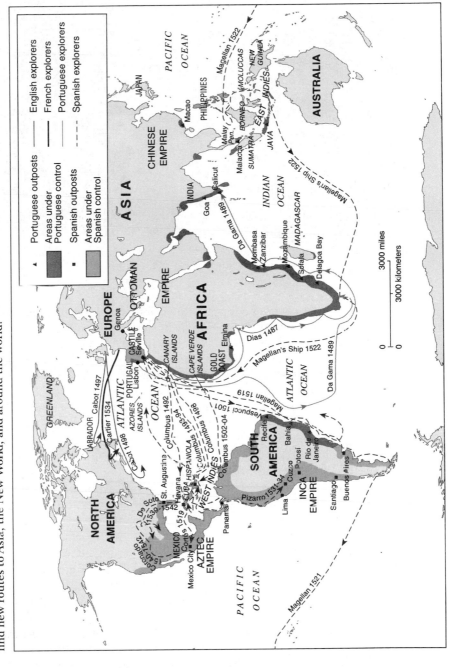

MAP 1.3 EXPLORATION AND CONQUEST, 1492–1542 Pope Alexander VI divided the non-Christian world into zones for Spanish and Portuguese exploration and exploitation. Portuguese, Spanish, French, and English explorers set out to find new routes to Asia, the New World, and around the world.

The first meeting between Hernando Cortés and Aztec Emperor Montezuma in 1519.

The victory of the conquistadors (conquerors) was the victory of steel over stone-bladed wooden swords. Moreover, the surprise element of cannon and guns also contributed to their victory in the Americas as in Southeast Asia, where a witness to a Portuguese attack in 1511 reported, "the noise of the cannon was as the noise of thunder in the heavens and the flashes of fire of their guns were like flashes of lightning in the sky: and the noise of their matchlocks was like that of ground-nuts popping in the frying-pan." In addition to their ability to kill, guns had a shock effect, except in China, where gunpowder had been discovered.

Steeped in tales of crusading chivalry and conquest, the conquerors who followed Columbus to the Americas set out looking for adventure and wealth. Cortés, for example, was the son of a poor Castilian noble family. "We came here to serve God and the king," said one, "but also to get rich." Unlike Columbus, most conquerors died young, far from home, their dreams of wealth shattered by the harsh realities of life in what seemed to them a strange and often inhospitable world. Ferdinand Magellan (c. 1480–1521), the Portuguese-born explorer, was killed by angry islanders on a Pacific beach. His crew nonetheless circumnavigated the globe, having proven that a southwest passage to India did exist and returning in 1522 to Seville.

Not only did many of the conquistadors die in the Americas, many times more of the native people they encountered also died as a result of contact with the Europeans. At one point during his conquests, Cortés and his small army had to fight their way out of the Mexican city of Tenochtitlán, then larger than any other European city except Constantinople. But as the Spanish departed temporarily, the smallpox they had brought with them began to decimate the Indians, bringing massive death on the heels of military conquest. The indigenous population of Mexico fell from about 25 million—or more—in 1520 to perhaps as little as 1 million in 1600. The native population of Peru fell from about 7 million in 1500 to half a million little more than a century later. Other European diseases, including measles, typhus, smallpox, and bubonic plague, also decimated the native population. In Guatemala, a Mayan Indian kept a chronicle of the ravages of European disease among his people: "Great was the stench of the dead. After our fathers and grandfathers succumbed, half of the people fled to the fields. The dogs and vultures devoured the bodies. The mortality was terrible. Your grandfather died, and with him died the sons of the king and his brothers and kinsmen. So it was that we became orphans, oh my sons! So we became when we were young. All of us were thus. We were born to die."

In turn, the Indians gave syphilis, a much less deadly disease (which may have originated in Asia) to the Spanish. It spread with Spanish mercenaries who had fought in Naples two years after Columbus' voyage to America (the French called syphilis "the Neapolitan disease," while the Neapolitans referred to it as "the French disease").

There were other, more beneficial exchanges between the Old and New World. Before the arrival of Europeans, there were no domesticated animals larger than the llama and alpaca in the Americas, and little animal protein in the Indian diet. Spaniards brought horses and cattle with them, as well as cats and dogs. Sheep had accompanied Columbus in 1493 on his second journey. Pigs also were carried on the relatively small ships of discovery and conquest. Taking up little room on board ship, they not only could be eaten but provided the additional benefit of manure for farming once the explorers had gone ashore. The 350 pigs brought to Cuba by Columbus had multiplied to over 30,000 by 1514. But they ate their way through much forest land and also eroded the indigenous agricultural terrace system, upsetting the ecological balance of conquered lands.

Every year the Spanish galleons returned with more riches, as if "the hand of God was guiding them." The Spaniards returned home with tobacco, potatoes, new varieties of beans, chocolate, chili peppers, potatoes, and tomatoes (not until the early eighteenth century, however, could the first European recipes with tomato sauce be found in Italy). They brought back to Europe Indian maize, which they planted and which provided feed for farm animals. These crops had significant, positive effects on European demography, leading to the availability of more food and accompanying population increase. In turn, the Spaniards planted wheat, barley, rice, oats, fruit trees, and bananas in their colonies. By 1600, most of the important food plants of Eurasia and Africa were cultivated in the Spanish Americas.

In 1565, a Spanish galleon completed global transoceanic trade by sailing across the Pacific Ocean from Manila to unload cinnamon on the coast of Mexico. Thereafter, Spanish ships returned with silver, which could purchase silks, porcelain, spices, jade, and mother-of-pearl, which Chinese junks carried to the Philippines, and which oceangoing ships carried to Acápulco. Shipping routes led from Seville, which had been part of Moorish Andalusia until the Castilian reconquest, to the Caribbean Sea and to the ports of Vera Cruz in Mexico and Cartagena in Colombia. They supplied the American colonists with European goods, and on the return route carried Mexican and Peruvian silver that replenished the coffers of European princes and merchants. Saluting Acápulco in 1604, Spanish poet Bernardo de Balbueña wrote, "In thee Spain is joined with China, Italy with Japan, and ultimately a whole world in disciplined commerce." All four continents, Europe, Asia, Africa, and America, moved closer together in reciprocal economic relationships that represented the beginnings of a globalization of trade.

Not only did the Europeans seek to trade with the people in the New World, they also sought to acquire permanent territories as well. Thus, Spanish legal documents affecting the new colonies, drawn up in Spain, declared that Indians would keep all lands they already held, but that all other territories henceforth belonged either to the crowns of Spain or were to be divided up among the conquerors as booty. The conquistadors built new towns, placing the church, town hall, and prison around a central marketplace (*plaza*).

In return for the pope's blessing of the colonial enterprise, missionaries began to arrive hoping to convert the Indians to Christianity. The harsh reality of the colonial experience for the natives, however, was largely untempered by the good intentions of some of the missionaries. "For this kind of people," snapped a Portuguese priest in Brazil in 1563, "there is no better way of preaching than the sword and the rod of iron." However, at least in principle, the missionary impulse remained strong: one monk argued that souls being lost to Satan by Martin Luther's Reformation (see Chapter 3) were being balanced by conversions in the Americas.

An early sixteenth-century Spaniard humanist wrote of Columbus that he "sailed from Spain . . . to mix the world together and give to those strange lands the form of our own." Europeans sought to impose their culture on the peoples they conquered, although Christian teaching made only limited headway in India and virtually none in China. Unlike its view of Muslims, the Church did not consider Indians infidels, but rather as childlike innocents. "Are these Indians not men?," asked a Dominican priest in Santo Domingo in a sermon to shocked colonists in 1511, "Do they not have rational souls? Are you not obliged to love them as you love yourselves?" A papal pronouncement depicted the Indians as "true men . . . capable not only of understanding the Catholic faith, but also, according to our information, desirous of receiving it." In the 1590s, a Franciscan friar boasted that he had built over 200 churches and baptized more than 70,000 Indians. Where Christianity was successful, as it ultimately was in much of Latin America, Christian belief sometimes merged with local religious deities, customs, and shrines to create a distinctive form of Christianity.

Obligatory labor service, enforced more than occasionally by brutality, at first formed the relationship between rulers and the ruled. The Church and the crown periodically tried to protect the Indians against the harsh treatment accorded them by many of their Spanish countrymen in the name of profit. Bishop Bartolomé de Las Casas (1474–1566), whose father had accompanied Columbus on his second voyage to the Americas and who had himself been a conquistador before becoming a priest, spoke out against the treatment of Indians. He saluted the "marvelous government, laws, and good customs" of the Mayas, whom he wanted placed under the authority of the Church.

As the Indian population was depleted through disease, overwork, and brutality, the Spanish looked for new sources of labor. By the fifteenth century, Portuguese traders along the coast of West Africa had begun to make profits selling Africans as domestic servants in Lisbon or as sugar plantation workers in the Portuguese Atlantic islands. The slave-trading network was based on chieftains and traders in African kingdoms, merchants in Seville and Lisbon, settlers in Mexico and Peru, and Brazilian sugar growers. Domestic slavery still existed in Italy, Spain, and Muscovy in the sixteenth century, as well as in the Arab world, and some Indians in the New World also had slaves. The Spaniards believed that Africans could better survive the brutally difficult work and hot climate of America. By 1600, 275,000 black slaves had been transported to Europe and America, and five times that many would be shipped in the next century.

Gradually, more Spanish settlers arrived to populate the American colonies, including small traders, shoemakers, blacksmiths, swordsmiths, and masons. In Paraguay, the governor asked that no lawyers be allowed to emigrate, "because in newly settled countries they encourage dissension and litigation." In Mexico, Spaniards asked that "his Majesty be pleased not to suffer any scholars or men of letters to come into this country, to throw us into confusion with their learning, quibbling and books." By the mid-sixteenth century, about 150,000 Spaniards had crossed to America and by the end of the century, about 240,000 Spaniards had migrated there, and about the same number of Portuguese had gone to Asia. Most of these emigrants never returned to the Old World.

In 1552, a Spanish official wrote Charles V that the discovery of the East and West Indies was "the greatest event since the creation of the world, apart from the incarnation and death of Him who created it." But Michel de Montaigne (1533–1592), a French writer who had met Indians brought back from Brazil, offered another view in 1588, when he observed that "So many goodly cities ransacked and razed; so many nations destroyed and made desolate; so infinite millions of harmless peoples of all sexes, states, and ages, massacred, ravaged and put to the sword; and the richest, the fairest and the best part of the world topsiturvied, ruined and defaced for the traffic of pearls and pepper."

CONCLUSION

The economic and political structures of early modern Europe drew on the dynamism of the medieval period. Demographic vitality finally overcame the catastrophic losses brought by the Black Death. Within Europe, commerce and artisanal manufacturing expanded. Mediterranean traders roamed as far as the Middle East and even Asia. And, although much of Central Europe and the Italian peninsula remained a hodgepodge of small states, rulers in France, England, and Spain had consolidated their authority, as sovereign monarchical states began to emerge.

Above all, three salient movements of change brought the Middle Ages to an end. The first was the Renaissance, or cultural rebirth, engendered by the rediscovery of classical texts, which began in the mid-fourteenth century in the Italian city-states (see Chapter 2). The commercial prosperity of Florence, above all, but also of Venice and other independent city-states made possible this period of extraordinary accomplishment in literature and painting. Significantly, the High Renaissance ended with an invasion of Italy by the king of France, a fact that itself reflects the domination of the emerging monarchies. Thus began a period of warfare in Italy, much of it fought on the peninsula, between Spain and France, both states considerably stronger than the Italian city-states that tried to resist them. Second, as we have seen, was the exploration and colonization of the New World, which would ultimately help end the Mediterranean Sea's role as the center of European prosperity, and which also followed Spain's emergence as a power (see Chapters 5 and 6). The third was the Reformation (see Chapter 3), which, beginning in the second decade of the sixteenth century, challenged the unity of the Roman Catholic Church. Reflecting the influence of Renaissance humanism in Northern Europe, reformers rejected both the pope's authority and Church doctrine itself. Whereas at the beginning of the sixteenth century there was one Christian religion in Western and Central Europe, by 1600 several Protestant religions had established themselves in parts of Europe. Thus, by 1500, in the waning years of the Renaissance, the stage had been set for the trends that would shape early modern Europe.

CHAPTER 2

THE RENAISSANCE

In 1508, Pope Julius II called Michelangelo from Florence to the papal city of Rome. His intention was that the artist paint frescoes on the ceiling of the new Sistine Chapel, a ceremonial chapel next to the papal residence in the Vatican. With some reluctance (since he considered himself primarily a sculptor), Michelangelo agreed to undertake the work. He signed a contract that would pay him 3,000 ducats and began work that very day in May.

During long, difficult years of intense creativity, Michelangelo often lay on his back, staring at the ceiling (still the best position from which to study his masterpieces), before climbing up the scaffolding to work. His frescoes, depicting Creation, Original Sin, the Flood, and the ancestors of Christ, are a triumph of religious painting. Nonetheless, Pope Julius II— perhaps alone—was so dissatisfied with Michelangelo's work on the Sistine Chapel ceiling that he ordered painters to cover with fig leaves certain parts of the nude figures in *The Last Judgment* frescoes. As a result, Michelangelo left Rome in disgust. He left behind him what is arguably the most beautiful pictorial ensemble in Western painting.

Michelangelo's work represents the epitome of art during the Renaissance, a time of cultural rebirth. From about 1330 to 1530, the city-states of the Italian peninsula emerged as the intellectual and artistic centers of Europe. It was a period during which classical texts were rediscovered, thereby reviving the ideas, architecture, arts, and values of ancient Greece and Rome. By celebrating the beauty of nature and the dignity of mankind, Renaissance artists and scholars helped shape the intellectual and cultural history of the modern world. During the fifteenth century, Michelangelo, as well as Leonardo da Vinci and many other Renaissance sculptors and painters, enjoyed the patronage of wealthy families and produced some of the immortal works of the European experience. From about 1490 to 1530, Rome was the center of a final period of artistic innovation, the High Renaissance, during which time the popes, including Julius II, commissioned paintings, sculptures, and churches.

Yet, weakened by internal political turmoil, the Italian city-states were ravaged by foreign invaders beginning in 1494. Unable to resist French in-

The city-states of Renaissance Europe were the most urbanized part of the Western world. Pictured here is the Loggia dei Lanzi, the principal gathering place in Florence.

vasion and then Spanish domination, after 1530 the city-states were no longer able to support artistic glories, and the Renaissance ended in a mood of discouragement.

THE CITY-STATES OF THE ITALIAN PENINSULA

The city-states were the fundamental political unit of the Italian peninsula, the most urbanized part of the Western world. However the vast majority of the population of the Italian peninsula still lived in the countryside. In 1200, there were several hundred independent city-states on the Italian peninsula; gradually, however, that number was reduced, as many were absorbed as subject territories by more powerful city-states. A century later, at least twenty-three cities in the northern and central parts of the peninsula had populations of more than 20,000. It was within these city-states that the achievements of the Renaissance took place.

Thriving Economies

The economic prosperity and social dynamism of the city-states made the cultural achievements of the Renaissance possible. The city-states had become independent and prosperous because of the expansion of commerce during the eleventh and twelfth centuries. The Italian peninsula formed a natural point of exchange between East and West. The vibrant, prosperous, cosmopolitan traders of the city-states used their situation well.

The survival of Roman law and roads were significant legacies from the Roman Empire. Intensively studied in the twelfth and thirteenth centuries, Roman law provided a framework for order and the development of political life within the Italian city-states. Moreover, the Roman Empire had depended on a network of largely autonomous cities and towns, particularly in the plains of the northern part of the peninsula. These had been linked by a system of roads, unrivaled in Europe, all of which, as the saying goes, did indeed eventually lead to Rome.

Although the people of the Italian peninsula had suffered the ravages of the Black Death and the other epidemics of the fourteenth and fifteenth centuries, the ensuing economic recession of the fourteenth century, which led to declines in manufacturing and population in the central Italian region of Tuscany, did not affect much of the northern part of the peninsula as severely, and it still prospered. Drawing its wool from England and Spain, Florence's textile industry employed about 30,000 workers. The finished Florentine cloth and woolen goods were then traded throughout the lands of the Mediterranean, Burgundy, Flanders, England, and as far as Asia. Agriculture thrived in the broad river valleys of Tuscany and Lombardy. The production of grains, vegetables, and wine, aided by the drainage of swamps and marshes and by irrigation, not only fed the urban population, but also provided an agricultural surplus that could be invested in commerce and manufacturing. Aided by the proximity of Mediterranean trade routes, international trade and small-scale manufacturing brought prosperity to ambitious Italian merchants.

The development of banking during the early fourteenth century helped finance internal trade and international commerce. By the first years of the fifteenth century, the Church's condemnation of usury no longer was taken to apply to banking, as long as the rates of interest were not considered excessive. Florence's gold florin became a standard currency in European trading centers, and the bankers of that city, with agents in Avignon and many other cities throughout the trading network, were central to European commerce and monarchical and papal finances. Unlike traders elsewhere in Europe, Florentine merchants had broad experience with bills of exchange and deposit, which provided credit to purchasers. There were, however, risks to such loans. In the fifteenth century, the king of England forced Florentine merchants to loan him money, or else be ex-

A view of the Republic of Venice, major Adriatic port.

pelled from his realm and lose all their assets there. But he defaulted on the loans after his invasion of France failed during the Hundred Years' War, and several major merchant Florentine companies went into bankruptcy.

Venice and Genoa were also major trading and banking cities, as well as centers of shipbuilding and insurance. Each city had long traded with the East Indies and the Far East. Merchants hedged their bets on whether their shipments would fall victim to the sudden Mediterranean storms, to roving pirates, or to some other mishap on the overland route through Central Asia. The merchants carried fine woolens and linen from the Italian peninsula and Northern Europe, as well as metals, to the East. They returned with cotton, silk, and, above all, spices, including pepper, cinnamon, nutmeg, ginger, and sugar, which arrived via Alexandria or Constantinople from the East Indies to awaken the palates of Europeans of means. Both commercial powers used towns in Crimea as intermediary points for trade from Muscovy, Persia, India, and China (see Map 2.1).

Merchant capitalism eroded the power of the nobility by expanding the ranks and influence of townsmen. The wealth and status of urban merchants—although nobles also engaged in trade—allowed them to dominate the oligarchies that ruled the city-states. Prosperity increased the strong sense of municipal identity and pride; the political theorist Niccolò Machiavelli insisted, "I love my native city more than my own soul."

Social Structure

The social structure of the Italian city-states resembled that of other urban centers of trade and manufacturing in England, France, Flanders, and

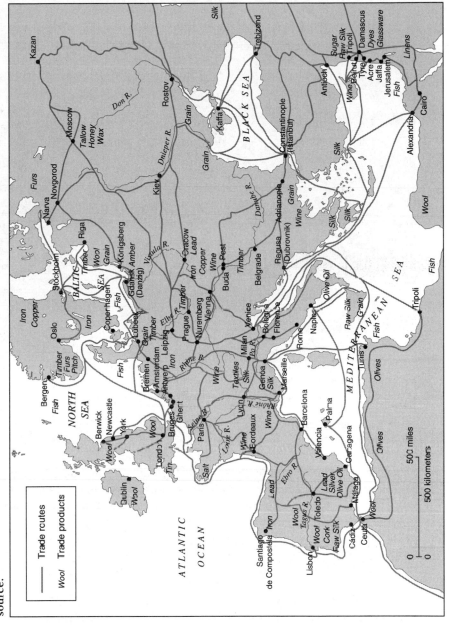

MAP 2.1 REACH OF TRADE DURING THE FIFTEENTH CENTURY   Major trade routes, both by land and by sea led from the Italian city-states of Venice, Genoa, and Florence, as well as from the North and Baltic areas. The Italian city-states formed a natural point of exchange between East and West. Products that were traded are shown at their source.

The *popolo grasso*, or fat people, are shown here lining the streets to view a horse that has returned from winning a race at the Palio.

Holland. In the city-states, the *popolo grasso,* or "fat people," were the elite, including nobles, wealthy merchants, and manufacturers. The *medi-ocri* were the middling sort, including smaller merchants and master arti-sans. The *popolo minuto,* or "little people," made up the bulk of the urban population. In cities, artisans and laborers were burdened by high taxes on consumption. Urban elites owned much of the richest land of the hinter-land, which was worked by tenant farmers, sharecroppers, and agricul-tural laborers, as well as by peasant landowners. In the northern and central part of the Italian peninsula, most peasants were free to be miser-ably poor, while in the southern part many still owed obligations to their lords.

The "fat people" of the city-states comprised no more than 5 percent of the population. The great patricians assumed the status of princes of their cities, whether as dukes, cardinals, or, in the case of Rome, as the pope himself. Although social differences remained sharp in Italian city-states, as everywhere, commercial wealth made possible some degree of social mobility, above all in Florence, the wealthiest city. New families, enriched by commerce, rose into the ruling elite, although opportunities to do so had declined noticeably by the end of the fifteenth century.

An elaborate and highly ritualized etiquette based upon mutual flattery maintained social distance. The wealthiest families became even richer despite the recession that extended throughout much of the fourteenth and fifteenth centuries; their prosperity made them even more eager not to be taken for anyone else of more modest station. Thus, one of the powerful dukes of Milan insisted that his wife be called *Illustrissima,* or the "Illustrious One." Flattery and subservience could be found in every greeting, and in every letter penned to a prince: "Nothing in the world pleases me more than your commands," and the ominous "I live only insofar as I am in your excellency's graces," which was sometimes true enough.

Urban patriarchs dominated their cities through power and patronage. They dispensed titles, privileges, and cash as they pleased. The duke of Ferrara affirmed his power by going door to door once a year to "beg" on behalf of the poor, an inversion of reality that served to define his authority and the subordination of everyone else. But princes and patriarchs also ruled through intimidation, occasionally eliminating enemies with astonishing cruelty.

Renaissance Political Life

The originality of the Italian city-states during the Renaissance lay not only in their remarkable artistic accomplishments but also in their precociously innovative forms of political structure. The organization of some of the city-states into constitutional republics was closely linked to the cultural achievements of the Renaissance. Nonetheless, there was nothing democratic about the city-states of Renaissance Italy, for the elites had brutally crushed the popular uprisings of artisans and shopkeepers that occurred in Siena and a number of other towns during the fourteenth century.

Fourteenth- and fifteenth-century republics were constitutional oligarchies dominated by the most powerful families who filled the executive bodies, legislative or advisory councils, and special commissions that governed each city-state. The percentage of male citizens enjoying the right to vote ranged from about 2 percent in fifteenth-century Venice to 12 percent in fourteenth-century Bologna, the former percentage seeming most representative of the restricted nature of political rights in Renaissance Italy. Venice, Siena, Lucca, and Florence (at least until the waning days of domination by the powerful Medici family) were the most stable oligarchic republics of Renaissance Italy; Genoa, Bologna, and Perugia

MAP 2.2 CITY-STATES IN RENAISSANCE ITALY, 1494 The city-states were the fundamental political unit of the Italian peninsula; their number was reduced as many of them were absorbed by the more powerful city-states.

went back and forth between republican and despotic governments (see Map 2.2).

Some of the other city-states became outright hereditary despotisms (*signori*) run by a single family. Milan, a despotism under the control of the Visconti family, had grown prosperous from metallurgy and textile manufacturing. Francesco Sforza, a *condottieri* (mercenary of common origins), who had married the illegitimate daughter of the last Visconti duke in 1447, helped overthrow the republic less than three years later. Sforza imposed his family's rule with the support of Milanese nobles. The

Sforza family thereafter skillfully played off rivalries between other powerful families, sometimes sanctioning their will with sheer force. The duke of Milan tolerated a council of 900 men drawn from the city's leading citizens, but he appointed magistrates and officials—and in general ruled—as he pleased. Likewise, princely families, such as the Este family of Ferrara and the Gonzaga of Mantua, ran the smaller city-states.

By contrast, Venice, an energetic, prosperous Adriatic port city of lagoons and canals built on a number of small islands, remained a republic. Its constitution offered a balance of political interests: the doge, an official elected for life by the Senate, served as an executive authority whose prerogatives were not that far from those of a monarch. The Great Council, consisting of about 2,500 enfranchised patricians, elected the Senate, which represented the nobility, an increasing number of whom were ennobled merchants living in elegantly decorated houses facing the canals. No one represented the poor, more than half the population of Venice.

Like the monarchies beyond the Alps, the Italian city-states developed small, efficient state bureaucracies, as the despots or oligarchs (a few men or families running the government) of each city improved the effectiveness of state administration. Thus, Florence and Venice had special committees responsible for foreign affairs and commerce. Many offices were sold or filled by members of the leading families linked by marriages. Personal relations between powerful families, for example, between the Medicis and the Sforza, facilitated diplomacy. The Medici engaged financial specialists for the management of the fiscal policies of their city and their family, although the latter, to the detriment of Florence, almost always took precedence ("Better a city ruined," said Cosimo de' Medici, "than lost.").

The *condottieri* were central to the political and military situation in Italy. A military ethos permeated the courts of the Italian princes. The young prince learned military exercises, including jousting (horseback combat with long lances that could occasionally be deadly) and began to hunt, often using falcons. Some dukes hired themselves and their private armies out to the highest bidders, such as powerful Italian princes, the king of France, or the Holy Roman emperor.

Renaissance princes and oligarchs surrounded themselves with an imposing retinue of attendants. The court of Urbino, not particularly wealthy compared to some of the others, employed a staff of 355 people. This number included 45 counts of the duchy, 17 noblemen of various pedigrees, 22 pages, 5 secretaries, 19 chamber grooms, 5 cooks, 19 waiters, 50 stable hands, and 125 servants and jacks-of-all-trades, including the *galoppini*, who galloped around on a variety of errands.

Florence, Milan, Venice, Naples, and the Papal States were as aggressive as France and the other monarchies beyond the Alps, dominating weaker neighbors through force, intimidation, and alliances, picking them off one by one, as in checkers. When they were not battling each other, Florence and Venice combined to limit Milanese control to Lombardy, while establishing their own authority over their respective regions. Venice controlled territory from the Alps to the Po River. Genoa, bitterly divided between merchant factions and nobles living in the hills above the Mediterranean port, struggled to maintain its autonomy because it lay physically exposed to more powerful Milan and the kingdom of France.

The Papal States, which bordered Tuscany east of the Apennines and to their south, functioned like any other city-state. The pope, too, was a temporal, as well as a spiritual, prince. He was elected for life by cardinals, the highest bishops of the Church, who were, in turn, appointed by the pope. Like monarchs and urban oligarchs, popes had to contend with the ambitious nobles of the Papal States. They, too, conspired and sought alliances against other city-states. But despite the prediction of the Tuscan poet Dante Alighieri (1265–1321) that a new imperial civilization would arise on the Italian peninsula, the eternal city was only the peninsula's eighth largest city in the late fourteenth century, ruled by a beleaguered papacy amid distant echoes of past temporal glories. The city-states were increasingly freed from the authority and interference of the papacy. This began with the "Babylonian Captivity" (1309–1378), when the popes lived in Avignon under the direct influence of the king of France and, for a time, a rival pontiff claimed authority from Rome (see Chapter 3). The declining role of the papacy in temporal Italian affairs further aided the rise of Florence, Milan, and Venice.

Florence: Anatomy of a Renaissance City

Florence was the cradle of the Italian Renaissance, fulfilling Dante's dream that it become a great civilizing city. Indeed, early in the Renaissance, the language of the region, Tuscan, emerged as the "courtly language" used by an increasing number of educated Italians beyond Tuscany.

The walled city dominated its rich hinterland of gentle hills and prosperous plain. The Arno River, which flows through Florence, though occasionally turbulent after heavy spring rain, was navigable from the Mediterranean port of Pisa except during the summer months. In 1406, Florence conquered Pisa, another center of textile production, once a worthy challenger of Genoa for maritime trade but now divided into quarreling factions. This window on the sea aided Florentine commerce, enabling the city to become a maritime power.

Several other factors contributed to Florence's success in becoming the center of the revival of classical learning. Roman law and Latin remained the foundation of training of Florentine ecclesiastics, lawyers, and notaries. Although the influence of the Church remained strong, the Medici rulers encouraged a cultural movement that had strong secular elements. Both Christian and secular traditions, then, infused Florentine civic life.

The combination of a dynamic craft tradition and an economy closely tied to the production of luxury goods made Florence receptive to artistic

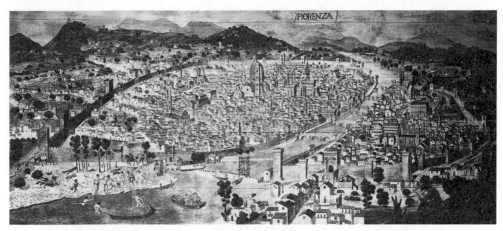

A drawing of Florence in about 1490. Note the Duomo in the center.

innovation. The city honored the accomplishments of its citizens—including cultural achievements. Lastly, Florence's reputation as a relatively educated city helped attract talented newcomers from rural Tuscany and other regions. It had many schools, including a university, and boasted a rate of literacy probably unmatched in Europe. In the fifteenth century, at least 8,000 children in a population of 100,000 attended church and civic schools, as well as private academies. It was also said that even laborers could recite Dante's verses by heart.

The bell tower of the Palazzo Vecchio, the government building completed early in the fourteenth century, watched over the dynamic center of international banking, commerce, and the manufacture of cloth, woolens, silk, and jewelry. By the middle of the fourteenth century, Florence had become the fifth largest city in Europe. Before the plagues of the 1340s, about 100,000 people lived there. After falling by half, Florence's population revived during the next half-century, equaling that of London and Seville, but not its rivals, Venice and Naples, each of which then had at least 100,000 inhabitants.

Most Florentine neighborhoods remained relatively heterogeneous in social composition. But increasingly grand patrician palaces were physically set off and protected from the crowded street and the anonymity of medieval buildings that stretched along in rows. Fancy, flamboyant dress also distinguished the wealthy people from those of lesser means. So did the unprecedented quest by patrician families for elegant crafted furnishings, such as chimney pieces, chests, and sideboards, and other objects, including candlesticks and bird cages. Covered balconies and top-floor terraces opened onto the streets. More modest and poor families lived not far away, yet a world apart, piled into small, sparsely furnished rooms in buildings up to five stories tall, some standing next to small cottages, lining winding streets and narrow lanes.

A Florentine council in session.

Wealthy merchants, the *grandi,* governed Florence with the support of merchants, lawyers, and craftsmen of more modest means. Organized into seven major guilds, the merchants and manufacturers, particularly the cloth merchants, kept the fourteen lesser guilds (whose members included artisans and shopkeepers) in a subordinate position. The guilds elected the nine members of government, the *Signoria,* which administered the city. The *Signoria* proposed laws and conducted foreign affairs. Its members led the processions through the narrow streets during the various religious holidays. Two assemblies, the Council of the People and the Council of the Commune, served as a legislature. Citizens wealthy enough to pay taxes elected the 600 to 700 members of these councils, which met as needed to approve the decisions of the *Signoria.*

During the fifteenth century, while Florence maintained its leading role in shaping the culture of the Renaissance, the business of government went on in the palaces of the wealthiest citizens of Florence. The elite feared that the poor would revolt as they had in 1378 in the revolt known as the Ciompi, or "the wooden shoes," because many of the laborers could only afford wooden shoes. Suffering from economic hardship and aided by disgruntled members of the lower guilds, the cloth workers had risen up in a bloody insurrection in the hope of expanding the guild system already in power. The possibility of another uprising of the poor thereafter remained in the memory of the "fat people," causing them to keep the workers in a position of resentful subservience.

Timely marriages, and thus alliances, between wealthy families reinforced status and power. A poor choice of allies could bring disaster. New families, some of which had moved to Florence from other parts of Tuscany, managed to enter the ranks of the wealthy ruling families. Families enriched by good economic fortune replaced those for whom recent years had not been so good.

The renewal, then, of the Florentine elite with new families provided continuity within change, despite no small degree of political turbulence in the fifteenth century. The crowning cultural achievements of the Renaissance were not only rooted in Florence's prosperity but also in the relative social and political stability within that innovative city-state.

In 1434, Cosimo de' Medici (1389–1464) and his family seized control of Florentine political life. The family drew its great wealth from banking and the manufacture and commerce of textiles. Supported by a few patrician families, Cosimo banished prominent members of the most powerful rival clans. The Medici now controlled the offices of government. They manipulated the electoral process masterfully, using their wealth to curry support. Cosimo reflected the marketplace toughness of his family.

Florentine nobles generally accepted Medici mastery because stability contributed to prosperity. Wealthy families continued to conspire against each other, even as Florence warred against Venice, but the powerful families remained staunchly patriotic, devoted to their city. Nonetheless, some Florentine nobles continued to oppose the Medici. In the Pazzi conspiracy of 1479, Lorenzo the Magnificent (1449–1492), Cosimo's grandson, sur-

Lorenzo de' Medici (the Magnificent).

vived an assassination attempt during Mass in the cathedral. Several hours later, four of the enemies of the Medici were hanging upside down from a government building, including the archbishop of Pisa. Lorenzo composed verses to be placed under their heads and commissioned Sandro Botticelli (c. 1445–1510) to paint them as they swung. Renaissance culture and the often violent political world of the city-states here converged.

The establishment of a Council of Seventy, which elected committees assigned responsibility for domestic and foreign affairs, helped the Medici tighten their grip on the reins of the Florentine republic. Lorenzo extended the family's banking interests and its influence with the pope in Rome. Among the many honors bestowed on the Medici family, Lorenzo considered the papal nomination of his thirteen-year-old son to the rank of Church cardinal "the greatest achievement of our house."

A DYNAMIC CULTURE

Economically and intellectually dynamic, Florence emerged as the center of the Renaissance. As Florence solidified its leading position on the Italian peninsula, its people rediscovered and celebrated classical learning. While glorifying antiquity, Renaissance poetry, prose, and painting emphasized the dignity of the individual, made in the image and likeness of God. It gradually moved civilized concepts like beauty and virtue away from theological constraints.

The Rediscovery of Classical Learning

The Tuscan poet Petrarch (Francesco Petrarcha, 1304–1374) was among the earliest and most influential of those who rediscovered and celebrated the classics of Latin antiquity. Petrarch, the son of a Florentine notary, learned Latin from a monk who inspired the boy to pursue his fascination with the classical world, which he came to view as a lost age. As a young man, Petrarch lived in Avignon, an international community of lawyers and churchmen at the papal court. There he copied ancient works from the manuscripts and books these men had brought with them. Petrarch and his friends searched far and wide for more classical manuscripts. They uncovered the *Letters to Athens* of the Roman orator and moralist Marcus Tullius Cicero (106–43 B.C.), among other texts, stored in the cathedral of Verona. The study of Cicero led Petrarch to see in classical philosophy a guide to life based on experience.

Petrarch's successors found and copied other classical manuscripts. Among them were classical literary commentaries, which provided humanists with a body of information about the authors in which they were interested. Scholars brought works of classical Greek authors, including the playwright Sophocles, from Constantinople and from the libraries of

Agnese world map.

Detail from Benozzo Gozzoli's *Procession of the Magi* (1459–1460).

Raphael's *Madonna di Foligno* (1512).

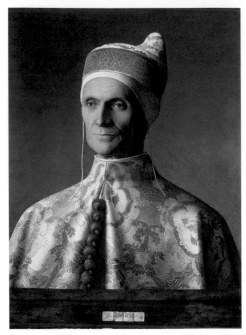

Leonardo da Vinci's *Mona Lisa* (1503–1507).

Giovanni Bellini's *Doge Leonardo Loredano* (1502).

Sandro Botticelli's *The Birth of Venus* (c. 1482).

Titian's *Bacchus and Ariadne* (1522).

Michelangelo's *Fall of Man*, from the ceiling of the Sistine Chapel.

Albrecht Dürer's *Self-Portrait*
(1500).

Gaulli's *The Triumph of the Name of Jesus,*
fresco painted on the ceiling of the Gesú
Church of the Jesuits in Rome.

Pieter Bruegel the Elder's *The Peasants' Wedding* (1568).

Mount Athos. Knowledge of Greek texts (as well as certain Arabic and Hebrew texts) spread slowly through Italy after the arrival of a number of Greek teachers from Constantinople.

The development of printing (see Chapter 1), following its invention by a German, Johann Gutenberg, permitted the diffusion of a variety of histories, treatises, biographies, autobiographies, and poems. Printing increased the knowledge of classical texts and the development of textual criticism itself. Many Renaissance scholars considered Cicero to represent the model of the purest classical prose (although others considered him too long-winded), and by 1500 more than 200 editions of his works had been printed in Italy, including his influential *On Oratory* and his letters. Libraries were established in many of the city-states, including Florence, Naples, and Venice, the last major city-state to turn toward antiquity, and provided scholars with common texts for study.

From Scholasticism to Humanism

The Romans had used the concept of *humanitas* to describe the combination of wisdom and virtue that they revered. The term came to refer to studies that were intellectually liberating, the seven liberal arts of antiquity: grammar, logic, arithmetic, geometry, music, astronomy, and rhetoric (the art of expressive and persuasive speech or discourse). Medieval scholasticism was a system of thought in which clerics applied reason to philosophical and theological questions. Those teachers and students who shifted their focus from the scholastic curriculum—law, medicine, and theology—to the curriculum of Latin grammar, rhetoric, and metaphysics became known as "humanists." They considered the study of the "humanities" to be essential for educating a good citizen.

Renaissance humanists believed that they were reviving the glory of the classical age. They considered their era greater than any since the Roman

(Left) Petrarch. *(Right)* Humanist educator and his charges.

Empire. They believed the Italian peninsula, although divided by political units, dialects, and by the Apennine Mountains, shared a common, special culture.

Venerating classical civilization, the humanists turned their backs on medieval scholasticism, which they believed was composed of irrelevant theological debates on revealed religion and encouraged the ascetic withdrawal of men and women from the world. Scholastics celebrated the authority of Church texts and revered the saint, the monk, and the knight. Petrarch rejected idle philosophic speculation or even knowledge that seemed irrelevant to mankind. He mocked scholastics: they can tell you "how many hairs there are in the lion's mane . . . with how many arms the squid binds a shipwrecked sailor. . . . All these things or the greater part of it is wrong. . . . And even if they were true, they would not contribute anything to the blessed life. What is the use, I pray you, of knowing the nature of beasts, birds, fishes and serpents, and not knowing, or spurning the nature of man, to what end we are born, and from where and whither we pilgrimage."

The humanists proclaimed the writers of antiquity to be heroes worthy of emulation. Although virtually all humanists accepted Christianity, and clerical religious culture persisted intact, humanism stood as an alternative approach to knowledge and culture. Humanists believed that a knowledge of the humanities could civilize mankind, teaching the "art of living." Petrarch insisted that the study of classical poetry and rhetoric could infuse daily life with ethical values.

Unlike the scholastics, humanists believed that it was not enough to withdraw into philosophy. Petrarch rediscovered the classical ideal that the philosopher, or humanist, was a wise man who could govern. Cicero had written that what made an individual great was not the gifts of good fortune, but the use to which he put them. The poet and orator had been a prominent figure in the political life of the Roman Republic, which had confronted threats to its survival. The active life, including participation in public affairs, had formed part of his definition of true wisdom. From the literature of the Greek and Roman past, humanists looked for guides to public life in their own city-states. The first half of the fifteenth century is often referred to as the period of "civic humanism" because of the influence of humanists and artists on the city-states themselves. Like the classic writers of ancient Rome, Renaissance writers were concerned with wisdom, virtue, and morality within the context of the political community. Humanists wrote boastful histories of the city-states, philosophical essays, stirring orations, and flattering biographies, as well as poetry, eagerly imitating classical styles.

The Renaissance and Religion

In rediscovering classic texts and motifs, the Renaissance remained closely linked to religion. Dante's *Divine Comedy* (1321), an allegorical poem, provides the quintessential expression of medieval thought by its demonstration of the extraordinary power that theology exerted on educated thought and literature. In his voyage through Hell, Purgatory, and Heaven, Dante encounters historical figures respectively suffering terrible agonies for their sins, waiting expectantly for admission into Heaven, or reaping the benefits of having lived a good life. Renaissance humanists could reject medieval scholasticism without turning their backs on the Church. Indeed, they claimed that they were searching for the origins of Christianity in the classical world from which it had emerged.

Although not the first to do so, humanists took classic texts, which were pagan, and ascribed to them meanings prophetic of Christianity. For example, the long epic *Aeneid,* written by Virgil (70–19 B.C.), had been commissioned by the Roman Emperor Augustus in the hope that it would offer the most favorable image of himself and of the empire, that is, of fulfilling the divine mandate to bring peace and civilization to the world. The hero of the *Aeneid,* Aeneas, personifies the ideal qualities of a Roman citizen, wanting to fulfill his patriotic duties, seeking glory for the empire but never for himself. The humanists transformed Aeneas's journey into an allegory for the itinerary of the Christian soul, appropriating antiquity into theology by viewing it as a foreshadowing of the true religion.

The place of the Church in Italian life therefore remained strong during the Renaissance, the relative decline in the papacy's temporal power notwithstanding. There was thus considerable continuity between the medieval period and the Renaissance in matters of religion. There were at least 264 bishops in Italy, as many as in the rest of the Christian world. In 1427, Florence had more than 1,400 clerics out of a population of 38,000 living in ecclesiastical institutions. Religious festivals dotted the calendar. The colorful Venetian water processions of elaborately decorated gondolas, jousting, boat races, and the annual horse race *(palio)* sponsored by rival neighborhoods in Siena still bear witness to the playful but intense festivity of the Renaissance city-states, a festivity that gave ritualized religious expression to civic and political life.

The Renaissance Man and Woman

Renaissance literature and poetry, preoccupied with nature, beauty, and reason, placed the individual at the forefront of attention. Renaissance writers praised mankind as "heroic" and "divine," rational and prudent, rather than intrinsically unworthy by virtue of being stained by original sin, as Church theologians held. This, too, represented a revival of the classic vision of the moral greatness of the individual and his or her ability to discover truth and wisdom.

By this view, the lay person could interpret morality through the ancient texts themselves, without the assistance of the clergy. Once someone had learned to read Latin and Greek, neither ecclesiastical guidance nor formalized school settings were necessary for the accumulation of wisdom.

Universities in general remained under the influence of the theological debates of scholasticism, although the universities of Florence, Bologna, and Padua gradually added humanist subjects to their curricula. Relatively few humanists emerged from the universities, which remained training grounds for jurists, doctors, and clerics.

"These studies are called liberal because they make man free," a humanist wrote; they are humane "because they perfect man . . . those studies by which we attain and practice virtue and wisdom; that education which calls forth, trains and develops those highest gifts of body and of mind, which ennoble man." The young Giovanni Pico della Mirandola (1463–1494) exclaimed, "O highest and most marvelous felicity of man! To him it is granted to have whatever he chooses, to be whatever he wills." Pico described the individual as an independent and autonomous being who could make his own moral choices and become, within the context of Christianity, "the molder and sculptor of himself."

Niccolò Machiavelli (1469–1527), too, found personal fulfillment in the study of the classics. He had been employed in the Florentine chancery, serving as a diplomat. Purged when the Medici overthrew the republic in 1512, he took up residence in the countryside. Machiavelli complained that his days consisted of mundane exchanges with rustics. But "when evening comes I return home and go into my study. On the threshold I strip off my muddy, sweaty, workday clothes, and put on the robes of court and palace, and in this graver dress I enter the antique courts of the ancients and am welcomed by them, and there again I taste the food that alone is mine, and for which I was born. And I make bold to speak to them and ask the motives of their actions, and they, in their humanity, reply to me. And for the space of four hours I forget the world, remember no vexation, fear poverty no more, tremble no more at death: I pass indeed into their world." Machiavelli evoked the exhilaration of the individual discovering the joys of antiquity.

The development of the autobiography in literature reflected the celebration of the individual, however much the genre was limited to public people and the image that they sought to present of themselves, revealing virtually nothing of private life. In the first half of the fifteenth century, the portrait and the self-portrait emerged as artistic genres; princes, oligarchs, courtiers and other people of wealth joined Christ, the Virgin Mary, and popular saints as subjects of painting.

A growing sense of what it meant to be "civilized" arose in the Italian city-states and highlighted the place of the individual in society. The Italian patrician may have been cleaner and more perfumed than people elsewhere in Europe, and certainly claimed to be so. Books on good conduct and manners emerged. The writer Baldassare Castiglione (1478–1529) urged the person of taste to show that "whatever is said or done has been done without pains and virtually without thought" as if correct behavior had become part of his or her very being. Women, he contended, should obtain a "knowledge of letters, of music, of painting, and . . . how to dance and be festive."

Castiglione's *The Courtier* (1528) described the ideal courtier, or attendant at a court, as someone who had mastered the classics and several languages, and who could paint, sing, write poetry, advise and console his prince, as well as run, jump, swim, and wrestle. The idea of a "universal person" had existed for some time, although, of course, not everyone had the leisure or resources to study and learn about so many subjects. One example of such a "universal person" was Leon Battista Alberti (1402–1472), a humanist, architect, mathematician, athlete, and papal secretary. But, to be sure, only the scholar who benefited from sufficient patronage, or someone with considerable financial means could become a "Renaissance man."

Some Renaissance humanists were actively hostile to science because as a form of knowledge it did not necessarily focus on mankind. Yet, although he was not a humanist and could not read Latin, Leonardo da Vinci (1452–1519), painter, scientist, architect, military engineer, and philosopher became the epitome of the "Renaissance man" in the view of later ages. The illegitimate son of a notary from a Tuscan village, he was apprenticed to a Florentine painter at the age of twelve. Following acceptance into the master's guild in Florence, he remained in the workshop of his master until moving in 1482 to Milan, where he enjoyed the patronage of the Sforza family. Taking the title "Painter and Engineer of the Duke of Milan," Leonardo taught students in his workshop and undertook scientific studies of anatomy in which he depicted, among other things,

Drawings by Leonardo da Vinci.

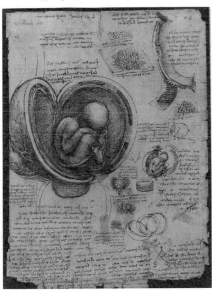
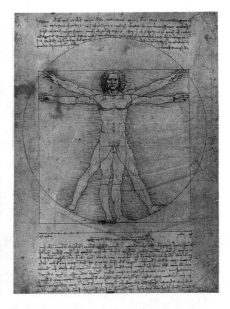

bird wings. His drawings were the first modern scientific illustrations. Leonardo began compiling his prodigious notebooks, in which he jotted down his ideas, perceptions, and experiences. He also sculpted an equestrian monument, designed costumes for theatrical performances, worked as a military engineer, and decorated palaces. In 1500, Leonardo returned to Florence, then went back to Milan six years later, beckoned by the governor of Francis I, king of France. When the Milanese freed themselves from French hegemony, he went south to Rome, where Pope Leo X (pope 1513–1521) provided him with a salary. In 1516, the French king brought Leonardo to his château on the Loire at Amboise, where he sketched court festivals, and served as something of a Renaissance jack-of-all-trades before his death in 1519.

If the Renaissance is often said to have "discovered" mankind in general, this meant, for the most part, men. The Church considered women to be sinful daughters of Eve. Legally, women remained subject to men; they could own property, and make their wills, but could not sell property without their husbands' permission. Both rich and poor families continued to value boys more than girls; poor families were far more likely to abandon female babies or to place them in the care of a distant wet nurse. Many families viewed girls as a liability because of the necessity of providing a dowry, however large or small, for their marriage. Some families of means pushed daughters off into convents. Because of the strict gender division within the Church, women there could aspire not only to holiness and sainthood, but also to leadership in a world of women. Life in a convent left them free to study.

Yet, some patricians educated their girls as well as boys in the humanities. Some girls studied letters, orations, and poems with tutors. But only a small number of women went on to write because they could not enter learned professions. Three alone were well known to contemporaries, including Isotta Nogarola, a fifteenth-century humanist from Verona who abandoned secular life for quiet religious contemplation and scholarship. She apologized for the weakness of women's nature in explaining the fall of mankind in the Garden of Eden, modestly believing that she fell short of "the whole and perfect virtue that men attain."

The Renaissance did not bring about any significant loosening in the restrictions placed on women. In the Italian city-states, women had less of a role in public life than they had enjoyed in the courts of medieval Europe. Women presided over social gatherings, but for the most part in a ritualized, decorative role. Overall, the Renaissance era may even have reduced women's social and personal options. If Renaissance authors idealized love and women, chastity and submission to one's husband remained the reality. If the education of young women clashed with a father's plans for his daughter to marry, the latter won out without discussion. The role of women continued to be to serve their husbands or, in some cases, their lovers. Men's feelings were the focus of considerable attention by Renaissance writers, women's usually were assumed to be unimportant. To be sure, women in large, powerful families like the Sforza, Este, and Gonzaga exerted influence and were patrons to artists. Yet, the subjects they commissioned artists and sculptors to portray were essentially the same as those of their male counterparts and, in patriarchal households, their husbands made the decisions.

RENAISSANCE ART

When the German painter Albrecht Dürer (1471–1528) visited Venice on one of his two trips to the northern Italian peninsula, he was surprised and delighted by the fact that there artists enjoyed considerably more status than in his native Nuremburg: "Here," he wrote, "I am a gentleman, at home a sponger."

Just as the prestige of the artist soared during the Renaissance, remarkable artistic accomplishments mark that special period's place in history. These have endured. Great works of Renaissance architecture, painting, and sculpture are still studied with awe by specialists and appreciated by millions of people each year.

Architecture

Despite the Renaissance concept of the "ideal city" of architectural harmony, reflected in the first treatises on architecture, Florence, Siena, Perugia, and other Italian cities retained their medieval cores, which had developed around their markets and around which stood the town hall

The Pitti Palace in Florence in both the palace and surrounding gardens.

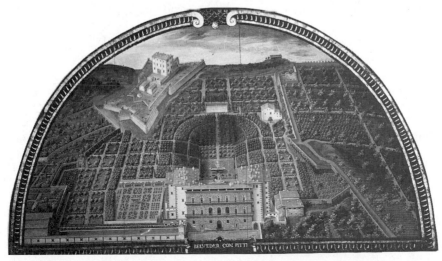

and other public buildings. But during the fifteenth century, their narrow streets and alleyways became interspersed with splendid buildings and dotted with works of art commissioned by wealthy families.

Florence, for example, underwent a building boom during the fifteenth century. Construction of its elegant residences stimulated the economy, providing employment to skilled artisans—brickmakers, masons, roofers, tilers, carpenters, sculptors, cabinetmakers, joiners, and decorative artists, including the talented goldsmiths of Tuscany, sculptors, and painters, as well as day laborers. Renaissance architecture emphasized elegant simplicity, an expansion of the simple rustic fronts that had characterized medieval building. Renaissance architects combined plain white walls with colorful, intricate arches, doors, and window frames. In the fifteenth century, expensive palaces of monumental proportions with columns, arches, and magnificent stairways were considered sensible investments, because they could, if necessary, later be sold at a profit.

Like writers and painters, Renaissance architects looked to antiquity for models. Filippo Brunelleschi (1377–1446) first applied theories of classical architecture to the Foundling Hospital in Florence, the earliest building constructed in Renaissance style. Fourteenth-century architects planned churches in the form of circles, the shape they thought was in the image of God, with no beginning and no end. But they may also have drawn on Rome's Pantheon temple, classical and round. After going to the papal city to study the ruins of classical architecture, Brunelleschi solved daunting technical problems to construct the vast dome, or cupola, of that city's cathedral (Duomo). The magnificent structure, completed in 1413 after work lasting more than a century, reflects the architect's rejection of northern Gothic architectural style, with its pointed arches, vaulting, and flying buttresses that counterbalanced slender vertical columns. Inspired by excavations of classical ruins and the rebuilding of Rome in the late fifteenth century, architects began to copy classical styles closely, adding Corinthian columns, which were tall with ornate capitals and great sweeping arches.

Patronage and the Arts

Renaissance art could not have flourished without the patronage of wealthy, powerful families, though commissions by guilds and religious confraternities were not uncommon. Artists, as well as poets and musicians, were eager, like Leonardo, to be invited into a patrician's household, where there were few or no expenses, and there was time to work. Lesser artists painted coats of arms, tapestries, the prince's pets—dogs and falcons—and even the faces of playing cards.

Some humanists not fortunate enough to be given the run of the palace of a powerful patrician found posts as state secretaries, because they could draft impressive official correspondence, and they tutored the children

Pope Leo X brought to his court artists and musicians. This portrait was done by Raphael.

of patrician families. A few worked as papal courtiers. Such humanists penned orations, scrupulously imitating Cicero, for formal state receptions, clamorous festivals, and funerals, written to awe listeners of all classes. The Medici Pope Leo X, who composed and played music himself, brought to his court a number of distinguished artists and musicians, as well as humanists whom he employed as officials and envoys. At the same time, the genres of wit and satire developed and became part of the ribald and "sharp-tongued" life of the political and social world of the city-state. "Rest be granted by the devil to Pope Sixtus," went one "eulogy" upon the latter's death in 1484, "Friend to Satan, enemy to Christ." The biting, somewhat pornographic satires and lampoons of Pietro Aretino (1492–1556), who enjoyed in succession the patronage of a banker, a cardinal, the duke of Mantua, the Medici of Florence, and then a Venetian doge and nobleman, spared neither secular nor ecclesiastical leaders from mocking jokes and rhymes. Aretino attacked social climbers and the venality of offices in the city-states with particular venom. He spared the one person he referred to as divine—himself.

As the classical texts posited the ideal that the active life included playing a salutary role in one's community, families of means held that they should demonstrate wisdom by making good use of their riches, as they developed their knowledge of the humanities. Commissioning works of art seemed to confirm moral leadership, and therefore the right to govern; in the words of a prosperous Florentine merchant, they "serve the glory of God, the honor of the city, and commemorate myself." Wealthy families also used art to reflect the image that they wished to give of themselves, for example, commissioning portraits to impress the family of a prospective spouse. Portraiture glorified the subject who sat before the artist.

The Medici of Florence, the greatest of the secular patrons of the arts, commissioned buildings, paid for the elaborate decoration of chapels and altarpieces, and restored monasteries. Although wags suggested that he may have been more interested in the expensive bindings of books he purchased than in their contents, Cosimo de' Medici, though himself not a scholar, collected manuscripts and even read some of them. The wealthy banker spent much of his time overseeing the construction of fine palaces and churches. Michelangelo (1475–1564), who designed the Medici tombs in the church of Saint Lorenzo in Florence, was but one sculptor who enjoyed the favor of the Medici. In 1504, he began work on a mural in the city hall commissioned for the city, alongside another undertaken by Leonardo da Vinci.

The long economic recession of the fifteenth century may have actually contributed to the arts. Finding insufficient profits in commerce and manufacturing for their money, patrician families spent considerable sums on paintings and sculpture. This may, in turn, have accentuated the recession by turning productive capital away from economic investments. At the same time, so the argument goes, the recession offered families of means more time to devote to the life of the mind and to culture.

The ruling families of some smaller states were especially lavish in their patronage of the arts. The Gonzaga family of Mantua, for example, carried their enthusiasm for a self-referential courtly life to an extreme that probably was unmatched. To emphasize their might, the Gonzaga brought dwarfs to their court, which was greater in pretension than in might.

The Gonzagas of Mantua. Note the dwarf in the foreground.

Venetian envoys arrived to find the syphilitic marquis in 1515 lying on a couch in his favorite room, attended by his favorite dwarf, who was attired in gold brocade. Nearby stood three pages, and three greyhounds as well, while the walls were covered with paintings of favorite pets and favorite people, and of the duke himself.

Patrons of the arts often specified not only the subject of the work commissioned but certain details as well, requiring, for example, that specific saints be depicted. The size of the work of art and its price of course had to be specified, including the cost of blue pigment or gold for paintings and bronze or marble for sculptures. Cherubs cost more. Although one of the dukes of Ferrara paid for his paintings by the square foot, increasingly patrons paid the artist for his time—and thus his skill—as well as for the materials he used. The contract for a work of art might specify whether it was to be completed by the artist himself, or if assistants from the master's workshop could be employed for certain parts. Patrons sometimes appeared on the canvas, as in the case of *The Adoration of the Magi* (1426), by Tommaso di Giovanni Masaccio (1401–1428), which includes portraits of the notary who commissioned the painting and his son. Conversely, patricians occasionally commissioned artists to humiliate their enemies, as when a painter in Verona was paid to sneak up to the walls of a rival palace and paint obscene pictures.

Renaissance Artists

Because of its basis in the craft tradition, in the medieval world painting had been considered a "mechanical" art. This made the status of the artist ambiguous, because he sold his own works and lacked the humanist's education. Michelangelo's father tried to discourage his son from becoming a sculptor, an art that he identified with stone cutting. Michelangelo himself sometimes signed his paintings "Michelangelo, sculptor," as if to differentiate himself from a mere painter. Yet, in his treatise on painting (1435), Alberti, irritated by contemporary insistence that painting was a "mechanical art," insisted that the artist was no longer a craftsman but a practitioner of a "high art."

Of the artists whose social origins are known, the majority had fathers who were urban shopkeepers or artisans, most often in the luxury trades. Next—surprisingly—in number came the sons of nobles, perhaps reflecting the relative decline in noble fortunes during the Renaissance. Next came the children of merchants and educated professionals such as notaries, lawyers, and officials. Some artists, like Raphael (1483–1520), were sons of artists. A good many others had been apprentice artisans. Only a handful were the sons of peasants.

The contemporary association between craftsmen and painters was appropriate, because, like the former, artists entered a period of apprenticeship. But in contrast, architects and composers lacked such formal training. The architect Brunelleschi belonged to the guild of silk manufacturers and goldsmiths. Composers were usually trained to be musical performers and simply began to write music on their own.

The painters' guild of Venice seems typical of the way in which artists learned their skills. The guild required five years of apprenticeship, followed by two years of journeyman status, requirements similar to those by which silversmiths, shoemakers, cabinetmakers, and other craftsmen were trained. The painters' guilds resembled other craft guilds in that the members were considered brothers in work who passed through life's great hurdles together. They shared not only varying degrees of skill and training but the solidarity of craftsmen as well. Some masters had sizable workshops, where apprentices trained and often lived together, sometimes working on the same paintings (which is one reason it is difficult to authenticate some canvases). If there were no prominent female artists during the Renaissance, at least until well into the sixteenth century, it was because women could neither become apprentices nor attend universities.

By the beginning of the sixteenth century, the artist's status in general had risen so much that a Venetian painter dared propose that only those "noble both by birth and money" be allowed to paint. Michelangelo, Leonardo, Raphael, and Titian (Tiziano Vecellio, c. 1490–1576) lived as gentlemen, the last knighted by Charles V, Holy Roman emperor. Some artists were crowned with laurels—thus the designation of "poet laureate"—by their adoring city-states.

Indeed, artists claimed that they deserved more esteem than a craftsman. Leonardo praised the painter, sitting "at his ease in front of his work, dressed as he pleases, and moves his light brush with the beautiful colors . . . often accompanied by musicians or readers of various beautiful works." In addition to a degree of self-promotion, the artist's quest for beauty and God helps explain the rise of some artists of the Renaissance period from practitioners of a "mechanical art," to the description of Michelangelo offered by a Portuguese painter, "In Italy, one does not care for the renown of great princes: it's a painter only that they call divine." Of course, not all painters ascended to such heights. Yet, for all the ambiguity of the artist's position, less than that of the humanist and still sometimes considered a craftsman, during the Renaissance the status of the artist rose.

Painting and Sculpture

The rediscovery of antiquity, nature, and mankind transformed European painting. Renaissance artists reflected the influence of the Neo-Platonists. In the late fifteenth and early sixteenth centuries, the Neo-Platonists appropriated Plato's belief that eternal ideas—such as beauty, truth, and goodness—existed beyond the realm of everyday life. Humanists believed that the mind could transcend human nature and come to understand these eternal ideas. The artist could reproduce the beauty of the soul through imagination and in doing so reach out to God. To Dante, art was "the grandchild of God." For Michelangelo, beauty "lifts to heaven hearts that truly know."

Artists sought to achieve the representation of beauty in a realistic way by using the proportions created by God in the universe. It was the supreme compliment to say of a Renaissance painter that his work had surpassed nature in beauty. Leonardo put it this way: "Painting . . . compels the mind of the painter to transform itself into the mind of nature itself and to translate between nature and art."

During the Renaissance, nature ceased to be mere background. Painters now faithfully depicted the beauty of mountains, rocks, and gardens for their own sake. Naturalism was heightened by the removal of the kind of pretty detail that embellished medieval art. It can first be seen in the memorable figures of the frescoes (paintings on plaster) of Giotto di Bondone (c. 1266–1337) in the chapels of Holy Cross Church in Florence. These figures, particularly their facial expressions, reflect humanity, deeply personal emotion, and naturalism, unseen since the classical age. The fame of Giotto, who is usually considered the first great painter of the Renaissance, spread rapidly throughout much of Italy and his style greatly influenced his successors.

Objects of everyday life, reflecting a greater preoccupation with realistic depiction, increasingly appeared in paintings. Take, for example, Raphael's painting of the pudgy Pope Leo X, staring off into space while fiddling with a magnifying glass with which he has been examining a book (see p. 69).

Beauty could be portrayed with extraordinary richness, as in the work of Botticelli, or it could be depicted simply. Raphael, who admired and learned from Michelangelo, eight years his senior, wrote of trying to paint a beautiful woman, "I use as my guide a certain idea of the beautiful that I carry in my mind." Raphael's figures reflect a softness and inner beauty that contrast with the powerful, stirring subjects of the tempestuous Michelangelo. Reflecting Neo-Platonist influence, Titian early in the sixteenth century strove to bring the viewers of his paintings closer to the idea of the eternal form of female beauty that he sought to represent with his depictions of Venus.

The Greeks and Romans believed that the painter and sculptor understood and portrayed the soul in reproducing the human face. Leonardo's famous *Mona Lisa* (1503–1507), with its mysterious, confident half-smile, is a compelling illustration of this undertaking. "Movements of the soul," wrote Alberti early in the fifteenth century, "are recognized in movements of the body." Leonardo contended that the depiction of certain gestures indicated the soul or the character of the artist's subject. The painter had to be able to reveal the emotions and passions of the figures he depicted.

Renaissance artists used a large repertoire of stylized portrayals of emotion, the meaning of which was immediately recognized by virtually all viewers of painting. The Florentine Masaccio intended his extraordinary fresco *The Expulsion of Adam and Eve from Eden* (c. 1427) to represent the tortured souls, as well as bodies, of those biblical figures. We see Adam covering his eyes with his fingers in anguish, a truly gripping rendition of Adam and Eve's crushing sense of loss and grief as they leave the Garden of Eden. Likewise, certain colors symbolized status, or hierarchy, even if some of the routine associations of the medieval period (gold for piety, for example) had passed. Violet was often a color of reverence, white that of charity, red of fire, and gray of earth. Clear colors, intense light and splendid proportion were combined in representations of Christ. Deep coloring, more subtle and natural than the blues and golds of medieval painting, enriched the canvas.

Medieval and Byzantine painters offered unlifelike images on a flat space; linear forms were arranged in order of importance, accompanied by symbols easily identifiable to the viewer. The Renaissance development of perspective, through which parallel lines recede from the surface and seem to converge on the vanishing point, facilitated the realistic presentation of figures and movement. Renaissance artists believed that naturalism

Masaccio *(Left) The Expulsion of Adam and Eve from Eden* (c. 1427). *(Right)* Masaccio's *Trinity* (1425).

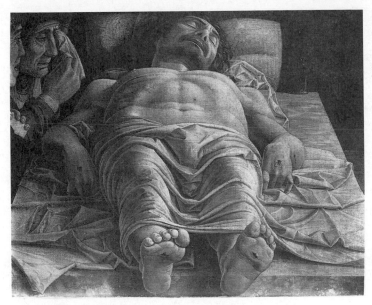

Andrea Mantegna's *The Dead Christ* (*c.* 1506).

could only be achieved through the use of perspective. Masaccio first applied the mathematical laws of perspective to painting in his revolutionary *Trinity* (1425), which makes a two-dimensional surface seem to be three-dimensional. The mastery of light contributed to innovative uses of space; for example, through the technique of foreshortening, proportionally contracting depth so as to give the viewer the illusion of projection or extension into space. In his realistic *The Dead Christ* (*c.* 1506), Andrea Mantegna (*c.* 1430–1506) utilized this technique, pioneered by Masaccio. This shortcut allowed the artist to create the visual impression of a three-dimensional body on a flat surface. Here one sees Christ's legs receding into space, drawing the viewer toward the physical presence of Christ's body. Florentine artists, in particular, used perspective to develop high relief and silhouette, presenting rounded figures on the canvas surface by effective use of tones and shades.

This mastery of perspective by the naturalist painter Masaccio and, above all, the sculptor Donatello (*c.* 1386–1466), who lived much longer and produced much more, helped Renaissance painters choose difficult, complicated themes and treat them with a more complex realism. Donatello utilized perspective to achieve dramatic action through gradations of relief. In *The Feast of Herod* (*c.* 1417), sculpted in bronze for the stone basin in the Siena Baptistery, Donatello captures the shocked reaction of the king and guests as John the Baptist's head is presented to Herod, proportioning unaware musicians in the background through relief and cen-

Donatello's *The Feast of Herod* (c. 1417).

tral perspective. In Leonardo's painting *The Last Supper* (c. 1495–1498), the disciples crowd along the table. The perspective of the ceiling and the sight of Christ centered on the canvas by his presence before the window immediately attracts the viewer's eye, which then falls on the apostles gathered along the table. Here Leonardo identifies Judas, not by leaving him without a halo nor by placing him alone on the other side of the table from Christ, but by painting him as the only figure in shadow.

To Leonardo, painting was the highest form of science and was based on "what has passed through our senses." He asserted "The scientific and true principles of painting first determine" the components of painting: "darkness, light, color, body, figure, position, distance, nearness, motion, and rest." The work of Michelangelo, who attended Latin grammar school, reflects a mastery of mathematics, anatomy, and optics. Animals, birds, and inanimate objects also took on a lifelike quality based upon the discovery of proper proportions.

The quest for the natural representation of beauty led some artists to depict the human body in nude form, which some took to be a more natural and expressive form borrowed from classical paganism. Botticelli's *The Birth of Venus* (c. 1482) represents this trend. Michelangelo believed that the depiction of the human body in sculpture was the ultimate test of human expression. He stripped the body so that its beauty could be better appreciated in its realism, as in his *David* (c. 1501–1504).

Religious, public, and private life overlapped, as the people of Renaissance Italy sought religious meanings in everything they saw. Art with religious subjects also served a teaching function for the Church. In many

Leonardo da Vinci's *The Last Supper* (*c.* 1495–1498).

patrician houses, a religious image could be found in every room. Devotional images, known as *ex votos*, were often erected in public spaces to fulfill a vow made to a saint in times of danger or illness. Patricians commissioned paintings with religious themes to realize similar vows. Moreover, the splendid tombs sculpted for patricians and popes may have reflected a preoccupation with glorifying the individual, but they nonetheless also emphasized eternal salvation.

Religious themes continued to dominate painting, accounting for perhaps nine of every ten paintings; the Virgin Mary was the most popular figure, followed by Christ and the saints (above all, Saint John the Baptist, the patron saint of Florence). The visualization of certain episodes in the life of Christ or of the martyrdom of Saint Sebastian were intended to stimulate piety and encourage morality. Thus, artists took on a role similar to preachers, whose orations evoked a powerful emotional response.

Classical symbolism abounded in Renaissance painting and influenced the depiction of religious themes, incorporating images drawn from pagan Rome. Artists used details about history or mythology that patrons insisted grace their canvases. Some of the classical gods stood as Renaissance symbols of moral or physical qualities. Michelangelo modeled his Christ in *The Last Judgment* (1536–1541) on a classical portrayal of the god Apollo. Mantegna, then the premier painter of northern Italy, drew upon his meticulous study of Roman archaeology.

Yet, along with scenes from classical mythology, paintings with secular themes increased in number, notably portraits of famous men or of wealthy patricians, but also of more ordinary people as well. Aretino, who

Detail from Michelangelo's *The Last Judgment* (1536–1541).

criticized everything, found fault with the democratization of the portrait, despite the fact that he was the son of a shoemaker, saying, "It is the disgrace of our age that it tolerates the portraits even of tailors and butchers." The growing popularity of secular subjects may have reflected a reaction against the power and venality of the clergy. Her well-heeled friends winked and joined in the laughter when Isabella of Mantua dressed one of her dwarfs as a bishop to greet a visiting dignitary; she ordered another to parody the Mass for the amusement of the audience.

High Renaissance Style

During the period of the High Renaissance (1490–1530), the prestige of artists reached its highest level, and the greatest were revered as geniuses. At the same time, the city-states of Italy lost much of their economic and political vitality and faced French invasion and then Spanish domination. In the midst of economic decline as well as internecine political warfare, artists no longer enjoyed the lavish patronage of wealthy patrician families. Instead, the Church became their patron.

The papacy inspired the monumentalism of the High Renaissance. Besieged in the first two decades of the sixteenth century by denunciations of the sale of indulgences—the purchase of the remission of some punishment in Purgatory for one's sins or for those of some family member—the papacy sought to assert forcefully its authority and image. Papal commissions in Rome were one attempt to recover public confidence and made possible the artistic achievements of the High Renaissance. Following excavations beginning in the 1470s that heightened interest in the ancient Roman Empire, Raphael himself oversaw the reconstruction of ancient Rome and personally supervised excavations of the Roman Forum. Influenced by and more dependent on the Church, the canvases of the painters of the High Renaissance became even larger as they became less concerned with rational order and more with achieving a powerful visual response in their viewers through large canvases.

Some humanists now began to claim that the papacy was the heir to the glories of classical Rome. Popes took names that echoed the Roman Empire. Julius II (pope 1503–1513) ordered a medal struck that read "Julius Caeser Pont[ifex]. II," a term that meant "high priest" in classical Rome. Wide boulevards and spaces were forged to accommodate waves of pilgrims descending upon the city.

Leonardo's *Last Supper* is perhaps the first example of the style of the High Renaissance, or what is sometimes called the Grand Manner. Mannerism (a term from the Italian word for style), which particularly characterized the 1520s, is marked by heightened scale, exaggerated drama, and the submersion of detail to a total emotional effect, reflecting the climate of the times. Donato Bramante (1444–1514), who rebuilt St. Peter's Basilica in Rome, in the "grand manner" of the High Renaissance, capped it with a grand dome in the style of Byzantium.

Painters of the High Renaissance increasingly presented large, ambitious, complex, and sometimes even bizarre canvases. Mannerism's imaginative distortions and sense of restlessness offered an unsettling vision in tune with new uncertainties. Mannerism marked something of a reaction against the Renaissance ideal of attaining classical perfection. Thus, some painters ignored the rules of perspective and rationalism, perhaps reflecting the frightening instability of the time. Nature faded into the background again; emotionalism, as well as mysticism and illusionism, won out over classicism. Toward the end of his career, Michelangelo's work reflected this influence. His majestic marble *Moses* (1515), sculpted for the tomb of Pope Julius II, has an immensely prominent head, with an exaggerated facial expression. It reflects Michelangelo's tragic vision of human limitations, including his own. Raphael and Titian presented human figures who seem almost empowered by divine attributes but who nonetheless retain their humanity. Moreover, Titian's mannerist paintings are known for their intense coloring, as in the unsettling *Bacchus and Ariadne* (1522). Raphael's *Madonna di Foligno* (1512) shows the Virgin sitting triumphantly on a cloud, surrounded by adoring saints.

THE END OF THE RENAISSANCE

Late in the fifteenth century, the Italian city-states entered a period of economic and political decline, making the peninsula more vulnerable to foreign invasion. Subsequently, some of the battles between Spain and France, Europe's two dominant powers, were fought on the Italian peninsula. The exploration and gradual colonization of the Americas, first by Spain, and the increase in trade and manufacturing in Northwestern Europe, helped move the economic and cultural vigor toward the Atlantic

Ocean, to Spain and Northwestern Europe, most notably, England, France, and the Dutch Netherlands (see Chapter 6).

Economic Decline

The economic decline of the northern Italian city-states during the second half of the fifteenth century undermined the material base of Renaissance prosperity, indeed the economic primacy of the Mediterranean region. The Italian city-states lost most of their trading routes with Asia. The Turks conquered Genoese trading posts in the Black Sea, the traditional merchant route to Asia, and the Aegean Sea. Turkish domination reduced Genoa's once mighty commercial network to trade centered on the Aegean island of Chios. Of the Italian city-states, Venice alone continued to prosper. After the Ottoman conquest of Constantinople in 1453, merchants in Venice concluded a deal with the Turks by which they received a monopoly on trade with the East, leaving the other city-states without access to their traditional Asian markets. Venice's economy soon diversified with small-scale manufacturing, however, particularly as the Turkish threat to its interests mounted in the eastern Mediterranean and Venetian galleys no longer could venture into the Black Sea.

Merchants of the Italian city-states sought alternatives. The Genoese established a trading post in the Muslim city of Málaga on the south coast of the Iberian Peninsula, although this made them dependent on local Muslim middlemen. Castile's conquest of Gibraltar and Málaga at the end of the century made transport between the Mediterranean and Atlantic ports safer for Christian vessels. Genoese and Florentine merchants undertook exploratory voyages down the west coast of Africa in search of a new route to Asia. But most such vessels never returned. The Portuguese thereafter took up the quest for a southern route to Asia, after acquiring the Atlantic Ocean islands of Madeira, Cape Verdes, and the Azores, which could be used as bases. Portuguese fleets began to monopolize the spice trade with India and beyond after Bartholomew Dias (c. 1450–1500) in 1487 first rounded the Cape of Good Hope, the southern tip of Africa. From then on, Portuguese crews knew how to reach the Indian Ocean, and then Calcutta, on the southwest coast of India.

The Florentine silk and woolen industries, long prosperous, now faced stiff competition from French and Dutch producers and merchants in Northwestern Europe. The dazzling prosperity of the great Italian merchant families ebbed. The economy of Europe and world commerce itself was changing. Portuguese, Spanish, English, and Dutch traders looked to the New World for new products and significant profits. Christopher Columbus, the Genoese explorer, asked an Italian duke to risk funds for his voyages of exploration in 1492, but he refused. Columbus then gained the support of King Ferdinand and Queen Isabella of Spain (see Chapter 1). The rapid growth of Portuguese and then Spanish trade, first down the coast of Africa and then, after 1492, across the Atlantic Ocean to the New World, accentuated the rise of the Atlantic economy. Competition from the larger sailing ships of England, Holland, and Portugal overwhelmed Florence and Genoa and then, more gradually, Venice.

Foreign Invasion

As long as the Italian peninsula remained free from the intervention of France and Spain or other powers, the city-states could continue to prosper while fighting each other and casting wary glances toward the Ottoman Empire as it expanded its influence in the Mediterranean. But the city-states, divided by economic interests and with a long tradition of quarreling among themselves, became increasingly vulnerable to the expansion of French interests.

Threats to the Italian peninsula mounted from France and the Turks. France had adhered to an alliance of Milan and Florence against Venice, signed in 1451. But the three city-states recognized the threat the aggressive French monarchy posed to the peninsula. Furthermore, following the capture of Constantinople in 1453, Turkish ships now appeared more frequently in the Adriatic Sea. It seemed imperative to end the wars between two leagues of city-states. The Peace of Lodi (1454), signed by Florence, Milan, and Venice, established a new political order. Helping discourage Turkish or French aggrandizement, the peace brought four decades of relative peace, which saw some of the crowning artistic glories of the Renaissance.

The establishment of this Italian League formalized this balance of power—it was already called that—between the strongest city-states. Whenever one or two of the states became aggressive—as when Venice and the Papal States attacked Ferrara—the others joined together to restore the status quo. Such wars were fought for the most part by mercenaries, imported and organized by *condottieri* paid for the task. For the moment, Milan's strong army served as a barricade against French invasion.

Perhaps accentuated by the ebbing of prosperity, political life within the city-states deteriorated. In Florence, the Medici despotism faced opposition from republicans. In the 1480s, Perugia had become a warring camp, torn between two rival families. In 1491, 130 members of one faction were executed on a main square and hanged from poles for all to see. Then, in repentance, the oligarchs erected thirty-five altars on that same square, and ordered priests to say Mass for three days in atonement. In a number of the city-states, some patrician families tried to outdo each other in their violence, crushing their opponents within their cities with brutality, then praying over the bodies. Vengeance, like corruption, seemed endemic. The leading Florentine families faithfully attended church, even as they undertook murders of vengeance in defense of family honor. Considerable tension, then, remained between two parallel codes of conduct, one religious, the other defined by family loyalties.

The Italian peninsula became a battleground for the dynastic ambitions and rivalries of the French kings and the Holy Roman emperors, powerful rulers who could mobilize considerably larger armies than those of the city-states. The absorption of the wealthy and strategically important Duchy of Burgundy into the Holy Roman Empire accentuated the struggle between the Habsburg dynasty and Charles VIII (ruled 1483–1498) of France. The latter decided to press his dubious claim to the throne of Naples, encouraged by the Sforza family of Milan, the enemy of Naples. In response, Naples allied with Florence and Pope Alexander VI (pope 1492–1503), himself a Florentine member of the Borgia family, against Milan.

In 1494, Charles VIII invaded the Italian peninsula with an army of 30,000 men. His French cavalry, Swiss mercenary infantry, and Scottish bowmen tore through northern Italy. In Florence, the Medici ruler offered Charles some Florentine possessions in exchange for leaving. This angered Florentine republicans, who drove the Medici from power in 1494 (after sixty years of rule), backed by the army of France. The new government, establishing the Great Council as a legislative assembly, contributed to the city's artistic splendors by commissioning works of art that symbolized republican independence and ideals. Leonardo and Michelangelo painted scenes of Florentine military victories for the meeting hall of the Great Council. Seven years later, the city government commissioned Michelangelo's great statue *David*. Michelangelo's conscious imitation of a Donatello bust of the same name from early in the fifteenth century referred back to the republic's successful resistance to challenges at that time.

Meantime, Charles' army moved toward Naples, devastating everything in its path. It marched into the city to cheers from Neapolitans who opposed the harsh taxes to which they had been subject by their rulers. But an anti-French coalition that included King Ferdinand of Aragon—whose dynastic territories included Sicily, Venice, the Papal States—and the Holy Roman emperor rallied to defeat the French force. Although the French army left the Italian peninsula, the city-states' troubles had only just begun.

In Florence, Girolamo Savonarola (1452–1498), a charismatic Dominican monk who had predicted the French invasion, opposed both the Medici in Florence and the papacy on grounds that both were worldly and corrupt. He had welcomed Charles VIII of France as "an instrument in the hands of the Lord who has sent you to cure the ills of Italy," including the sinfulness of the Florentines. With the Medici driven from power, Savonarola took virtual control of the Florentine republic. His denunciation of abuses within the Church led to his excommunication by Pope Alexander VI. Savonarola also incurred the enmity of patrician families by appealing for support to all ranks of Florentine society. With the pope's blessing, his enemies first hanged and then burned him—the penalty for heresy—in 1498.

The burning of Girolamo Savonarola in Florence.

The next year, Louis XII (ruled 1498–1515), the new French king, invaded the Italian peninsula, intent on making good his claim on the duchy of Milan. He did so with the support of the corrupt Pope Alexander VI, who wanted French assistance as he tried to solidify papal territorial claims, as well as to look after the extended interests of his children. To encourage the French king, the pope annulled Louis' marriage, so that he could marry his predecessor's widow, thereby keeping Brittany within his domains. When Julius II, who had been a bitter enemy of his predecessor, became pope in 1503, he drove the powerful Borgia family from Rome. Then the dissolute pope set about trying to restore temporal holdings taken from the Papal States by Venice and its allies, constructing an alliance against the Venetians and becoming the last pope to lead his troops into the field of battle. That year the Spanish army defeated the French army and the Habsburgs absorbed the kingdom of Naples. Milan remained a fief of Louis XII until French forces were forced from the city in 1512. Three years later, French troops overwhelmed Swiss mercenaries and returned, until the Lombardy city became a Spanish possession in 1535.

Machiavelli

A mood of vulnerability and insecurity spread through the Italian peninsula as the city-states battled each other. Peasants, crushed by taxes and hunger, ever more deeply resented the rich. In turn, wealthy people were increasingly suspicious of the poor, viewing them as dangerous monsters capable of threatening social order.

The devoted Florentine Machiavelli was among those people seeking to understand why the once proud independent city-states of Italy now seemed virtually helpless before the invasion of foreign powers. The son of a lawyer and educated in the classics, Machiavelli found a position as a diplomat and chancery official of the republican government of Florence. The turmoil in Florence led him to write his *Histories* in 1494, which described the decline of the city-states.

Machiavelli's view of politics reflects his experience living in Florence during these tumultuous decades. Influenced by his experience in government, Machiavelli, who had served as a Florentine diplomat at the court of the king of France and in Rome, believed himself to be a realist. He considered war a natural outlet for human aggression. But he also preferred the resolution of disputes by diplomacy. Machiavelli believed that the absence of "civic virtue" accounted for the factionalism within and rivalries between the city-states. By civic virtue (not the same thing as Christian virtue in the sense of distinguishing between and acting on the difference between right and wrong), Machiavelli meant the effective use of military force.

In 1512, the Medicis overthrew the Florentine Republic, returning to power with the help of the papal army and that of Spain. Following the discovery of a plot, of which he was innocent, against the Medici patriarchs, Machiavelli was forced into exile on his country estate outside of the city. Florence had changed. A Medici supporter wrote one of the family heads: "Your forefathers, in maintaining their rule, employed skill rather than force; you must use force rather than skill." The Medici commissioned works of art which suggested that the "golden age" had returned once again.

A year later, Machiavelli wrote *The Prince* (1513). In it he reflected on the recent history of the Italian peninsula and offered a pessimistic assessment of human nature, marked by his belief that a strong leader—the prince—could arise out of strife. By making his subjects afraid of him, the prince could end political instability and bring about a moral regeneration that Machiavelli believed had characterized antiquity. Drawing on Cicero, he studied the cities of the Roman Republic and the Roman Empire. Machiavelli can be considered the first political scientist, because his works reflect a systematic attempt to draw general, realistic conclusions from his understanding of the recent history of the Italian city-states. This preoccupation with the past in itself reveals the influence of the Renaissance.

Machiavelli put his faith in political leadership. Regardless of whether the form was monarchical or republican, Machiavelli believed that the goal of government should be to bring stability to the city. A sense of civic responsibility could only be re-established through "good laws and insti-

The pensive Niccolò Machiavelli.

tutions," but these, for Machiavelli, depended completely on military strength. He called on the Medici to drive away the new barbarians. Machiavelli's *The Art of War* (1521) expressed hope that the brutish mercenaries who had devastated the Italian peninsula would give way to soldier-citizens who would restore virtue. But for the Italian city-states, it was too late.

Machiavelli's invocation of "reasons of state" as sufficient justification for political action and as a political principle in itself, and his open admiration of ruthless rulers, would leave a chilling legacy. While it is unlikely that Machiavelli had a sense of the state in the impersonal, modern sense of the term, he did hold that "good arms make good laws."

The Decline of the City-States

Thus, for much of the first thirty years of the sixteenth century foreign armies battled each other and alliances formed by the city-states. The army of France in Italy reached 32,000 men by 1525, that of Spain 100,000 soldiers. Only Venice could resist the two great powers. In 1521, the first war between King Francis I of France and Holy Roman Emperor Charles V broke out. The latter's armies decimated the French at Pavia in 1525, carting the French king off to Madrid, where he remained until his family paid a ransom. In 1527, Charles V's mercenary army, angry for lack of pay, sacked Rome. By the Peace of Cambrai (1529), France gave up claims to Naples and Milan. But with the exception of Venice, the Italian city-states were in one way or another dependent upon Charles V, Holy Roman emperor, as the Spanish army repulsed new French invasions.

The long wars drained the city-states of financial resources and men, devastating some of the countryside. Nobles, whose political power had been diminished by the wealthy merchants of the fourteenth and fifteenth centuries, took advantage of the chaos to return to prominence in some cities. Patrician families struggled to maintain their authority against newcomers, including wealthy merchants who had married into poorer noble lines and who began to ape the styles of nobles. The Medici, after having once again been expelled by republicans, reconquered their city in 1530 after a siege of ten months. But in Florence, too, the Renaissance was over.

Changing artistic style had already begun to reflect the loss of Renaissance self-confidence that accompanied the devastating impact of the French invasion. For example, Botticelli seemed to abandon the serenity and cheerful optimism that characterized the Renaissance. To his painting *Mystical Nativity*, completed in 1500, Botticelli added an anxious inscription: "I Sandro painted this picture at the end of the year 1500 in the troubles of Italy . . . after the time according to the eleventh chapter of St. John in the second woe of the Apocalypse in the loosing of the devil for three and a half years. Then he will be chained in the twelfth chapter and we will see him trodden down as in this picture." Botticelli thereafter became preoccupied with suffering and the Passion of Christ, reflecting the fact that the High Renaissance was more closely tied to ecclesiastical influence. The deteriorating political situation, combined with the expansion of Spanish influence after 1530, made it more difficult for artists to find patronage in the Italian city-states.

Soon in Italy only Venice, the city of Titian, remained a center of artistic life. Machiavelli, who died in 1527, the year Charles V's troops pillaged Rome, sensed that the humiliation of the Italian city-states by foreign armies brought to a close a truly unique period in not only the history of Italy but in Western civilization. Of the great figures of the High Renaissance, only Michelangelo and Titian lived past 1530.

Impulses Elsewhere

The cultural glories of the Renaissance ebbed even as different kinds of discoveries by Europeans opened up wider appreciation of new possibilities for mankind. Columbus' cross-Atlantic voyages were signs that the economic and cultural vitality of Europe was shifting away from the Mediterranean to Spain and, to a lesser extent, England. The economic interests of these states would increasingly be across the Atlantic Ocean. The mood of optimism associated with the Renaissance seemed to have moved to Central and Northern Europe as Italy lapsed into a considerably less happy period. Many humanists and artists began to emigrate north of the Alps to lands considered by most cultured Italians to have been barbarian only in the last century. Now new universities in Northern Europe beckoned them.

Other dramatic changes had already begun to occur across the Alps. Relentless calls for reform led to a schism within the Church: the Reformation. In Northern Europe, the Dutch monk and humanist Erasmus expressed the exhilaration many men of learning felt when he wrote, "the world is coming to its senses as if awakening out of a deep Sleep."

CHAPTER 3

THE TWO REFORMATIONS

After paying a handsome sum to Pope Leo X in 1515, Albert of Hohenzollern received a papal dispensation (exemption from canon law) that enabled him to become archbishop of Mainz, a lucrative and prestigious ecclesiastical post. Otherwise, under canon law, the twenty-three-year-old Albert would have been ineligible due to his age (archbishops were supposed to be at least thirty years old) and because he already drew income from two other ecclesiastical posts. As part of his payment to the pope and in order to repay the large sum of money loaned to him by the Fugger banking family, the new archbishop authorized the sale of the St. Peter's indulgence, which would release a sinner from punishment for his sins. John Tetzel, a Dominican friar who was in charge of the sale of papal indulgences in the archbishopric of Mainz, was commissioned to preach the indulgence. Half of the proceeds were to go to the papacy, and half to Albert and the Fuggers. In his tour of parishes, Tetzel emotionally depicted the wailing of dead parents in Purgatory, pleading with their children to put coins in the box so that they could be released from their suffering.

The sale of indulgences, particularly their commercial use to allow clergymen to obtain multiple posts, had drawn increasing criticism in some of the German states. Indeed, no other ecclesiastical financial abuse drew as much passionate opposition as did indulgences. More than this, the Roman papacy itself faced considerable opposition in the German states, as the pope had appointed foreigners to many key ecclesiastical posts and had attempted to force the German states to provide him with money for a war against the Turks. The young German monk Martin Luther was among those denouncing Tetzel, the sale of indulgences, and the role of the Roman papacy in the German states.

This opposition to the papacy created a schism that tore Christendom apart beginning in the second decade of the sixteenth century. Originating in the German states and Switzerland, a movement for religious reform

(*Left*) A criticism of the sale of indulgences using the analogy of Christ driving the money changers out of the Temple. (*Right*) The pope selling indulgences in the Temple.

began to spread across much of Europe, in part reflecting the influence of Renaissance humanism in Northern Europe. Reformers rejected the pope's authority and Church doctrine itself. The movement for reform, or of "protest," came to be called the "Reformation." It led to the establishment of many "Protestant" denominations within Christianity. The followers of the German priest Martin Luther became Lutherans, while those of the Frenchman Jean Calvin in Switzerland became known as Calvinists. King Henry VIII established the Protestant Church of England. Under attack from many sides, the Roman Catholic Church undertook a Counter-Reformation, also known as the Catholic Reformation, which sought to reform some aspects of ecclesiastic life, while reaffirming the basic tenets of Catholic theology and belief in the authority of the pope.

By 1600, the pattern of religious adherence had largely been established for the future in Europe. Catholicism remained the religion of the vast majority of people living in Spain, France, Austria, Poland, the Italian states, Bavaria, and other parts of the southern German states. Protestants dominated England and much of Switzerland, the Dutch Netherlands, Scandinavia, and the northern German states. Wars fought in the name of religion broke out within and between European states, beginning in the late sixteenth century and culminating in the Thirty Years' War (1618–1648). These conflicts shaped the next century of European history, with religious divisions affecting the lives of millions of people.

THE NORTHERN RENAISSANCE

Until the middle of the fifteenth century, the Renaissance had been limited to the Italian peninsula. Northern Europe enjoyed very little of the economic and cultural vitality of the Italian city-states. The country estates of noble families were rarely centers of learning. The future Pope Pius II claimed in the mid-fifteenth century that "Literature flourishes in Italy and princes there are not ashamed to listen to, and themselves to know, poetry. But in Germany princes pay more attention to horses and dogs than to poets—and thus neglecting the arts they die unremembered like their own beasts." France and the German states also lacked the Italian peninsula's network of city-states, whose wealthy merchant and banking families patronized humanists and artists.

But in about 1460, Renaissance humanism began to influence scholars in Northern Europe. As in Italy, humanism changed the way many people thought about the world. Humanists were interested in morality and ethics, as well as in subjecting texts to critical scrutiny. Therefore, debates over religion, and the Bible itself, attracted their attention. Humanists began to criticize Church venality and corruption, and the seeming idleness of monastic life. They also called into question scholasticism and its influence on religious theology, as well as criticizing parts of religious practice that they considered illogical and therefore superstitious. The spread of humanism in Northern Europe was gradual, often influencing isolated scholars. In the beginning, it posed no immediate threat to the Church; humanists could not imagine organized religion beyond Roman Catholicism. But the cumulative effect of the Northern Renaissance, and humanism in particular, helped engender a critical spirit that by the first decades of the sixteenth century directly began to challenge Church practices and then doctrine.

Northern Art and Humanism

The Northern Renaissance, which began in the late fifteenth century, reflected considerable Italian influence. Italian ambassadors, envoys, and humanists brought Renaissance art and humanistic thought to Northern Europe. Yet, much of the artistic creativity in Northern Europe, particularly Flanders, emerged independent of Italian influence. Like the Italian city-states, the Dutch Netherlands, which had a well-developed network of trading towns, had wealthy urban families who patronized the arts. Lacking the patronage of the Church, which so benefited Florentine and other Italian painters, Flemish painters did few church frescoes (which a generally wet climate also discouraged). They emphasized decorative detail, such as that found in illuminated manuscripts, more than the spatial harmonies of Italian art. Dutch and Flemish painters favored realism more

Dürer's *Four Horsemen of the Apocalypse* (c. 1497–1498).

than Italian Renaissance idealism in their portrayal of the human body. They began to break away from religious subject matter and Gothic use of dark, gloomy colors and tones. In contrast to Italian painting, intense religiosity remained an important element in Flemish and German painting, and it was relatively rare to see a depiction of nudes.

Albrecht Dürer's visits to Italy reflect the dissemination and influence of the Italian Renaissance beyond the Alps. Born the son of a Nuremberg goldsmith, Dürer was apprenticed to a book engraver. As a young man, Dürer seemed irresistibly drawn to Italy as he wrestled with how to depict the human form. During two visits to Venice—in 1494 and 1505–1506—he sought out Italian painters, studying their use of mathematics in determining and representing proportion.

Many of the Italian envoys to Northern Europe had studied the classics and carried on diplomacy with oratorical and writing skills learned by reading Cicero and other Roman authors. Literary societies, academies, and universities contributed to the diffusion of Renaissance ideals in Northern Europe. Some nobles now sent their children to humanist schools or employed humanists as tutors, as did a number of wealthy urban bourgeois. Italian artists and scholars found employment in northern courts. Leonardo da Vinci, Renaissance artist and scientist, was employed by King Francis I of France and died in the château of Amboise on the

Loire River. Kings and princes hired humanists to serve as secretaries and diplomats.

Latin gradually became the language of scholarship beyond the Alps. A German scholar emphatically asserted that the German language was "the noblest, most distinguished, most humane of tongues," but he expressed his view in Latin. German, French, Spanish, and English historians borrowed from the style of the Roman historians to celebrate their own medieval past. Unlike Italian historians, they viewed the medieval period not as a sad interlude between two glorious epochs but as a time when their own political institutions and customs had been established.

In England, Latin became the language of high culture, arguably as important as English until William Shakespeare's time at the end of the sixteenth century. There Machiavelli's *The Prince* was widely read and debated in Latin. When continental scholars went to England, they could discuss common texts with their English counterparts. Sir Thomas More (1478–1535), English lawyer and statesman, reflected the influence of Renaissance humanism, writing poetry in Latin. In his *Utopia* (1516), a satire of contemporary political and social life, More asked readers to consider their own values in the context of their expanding knowledge of other societies, including those of the New World.

In France, Francis I established the Collège de France in 1530, which soon had chairs in Greek, Hebrew, and classical Latin. Northern universities became centers of humanistic study, gradually taking over the role royal and noble households had played in the diffusion of education. But some universities were quite slow to include humanists; only one humanist taught at Cambridge University early in the sixteenth century.

The spread of the cultural values of Renaissance humanism across the Alps into the German states and Northern Europe helped prepare the way for the Reformation. For, like the Renaissance, the Reformation was in some ways the work of humanists moving beyond what they considered the constraints of Church theology. Humanists, who had always been concerned with ethics, attacked not only the failings of some clerics but also some of the Church's teachings, especially its claim to be immune to criticism. They also condemned superstition in the guise of religiosity. Northern Renaissance humanists were the sworn enemies of scholasticism, the medieval system of ecclesiastical inquiry in which Church scholars used reason to prove the truths of Christian doctrine within the context of assumed theological truths. By suggesting that individuals who were not priests could interpret the Bible for themselves, they threatened the monopoly of Church theologians over biblical interpretation.

Erasmus' Humanistic Critique of the Church

An energetic Dutch cleric contributed more than any other person to the growth of Renaissance humanism in Northern Europe. Born to unmarried parents and orphaned in Rotterdam, Desiderius Erasmus (c. 1469–1536) spent seven years in a monastery. Ordained a priest in 1492, he taught at the universities of Cambridge and Louvain, then worked as a tutor in Paris and in Italy. As a young man, Erasmus may have suffered some sort of trauma—perhaps a romantic attachment unreciprocated or inopportunely discovered. Thereafter compulsively obsessed with cleanliness, he was determined to infuse the Church with a new moral purity influenced by the Renaissance.

The patronage of Holy Roman Emperor Charles V and several other statesmen permitted Erasmus to apply the scholarly techniques of humanism to biblical study. Erasmus' *In Praise of Folly* (1509) is a satirical survey of the world as he saw it but also a clear call for a pure Christian morality shorn of the corruption he beheld in the monastic system. Thus, he wrote that priests claimed "that they've properly performed their duty if they reel off perfunctorily their feeble prayers which I'd be greatly surprised if any god could hear or understand." He believed that the scholastics of the Middle Ages had, like the barbarians, overwhelmed the Church with empty, lifeless theology.

Erasmus' attacks on those who believed in the curing power of relics (remains of saints venerated by the faithful) reflected his Renaissance sense of the dignity of the individual. His *Handbook of the Christian Soldier* (1503), which called for a theology that de-emphasized the sacraments, was Erasmus' guide to living a moral life. The little book went through twenty Latin editions and was translated into ten other languages. He wrote at length on how a prince ought to be educated and how children should be raised. The most well-known intellectual figure of his time in Europe, Erasmus greatly expanded the knowledge and appreciation of the classics in Northern Europe. Erasmus and other major Northern Renaissance figures forged a Christian humanism focused on the early Christian past. Following his lead, Northern humanists turned their skills in editing texts in Greek and Latin to the large body of early Christian writings. "All the scholars are Erasmians," a humanist had asserted in 1518, "except for a few skulking monks and petty theologians."

THE ROOTS OF THE REFORMATION

In principle, the pope governed the Church in all of Western Christendom. But in reality, the emergence of the monarchical states of France, England, and the kingdoms of Spain in the late Middle Ages had eroded papal authority. Gradually these rulers assumed more prerogatives over the Church in their states. This expansion of monarchical authority itself provided impetus toward the development of churches that gradually took on a national character as monarchs bargained for authority over religious appointments and worked to bring ecclesiastical property under their fiscal control by imposing taxation.

Portrait of Desiderius Erasmus by Hans Holbein the Younger.

In the Italian and German states and in Switzerland, where many smaller, independent states ruled by princes, urban oligarchies, or even bishops survived, the very complexity of territorial political arrangements served to limit the direct authority of the pope. For in these smaller states, too, the ability of the pope and his appointees to manage their own affairs depended on the cooperation of lay rulers. Furthermore, the very territorial expanse of Western Christendom and daunting problems of transportation and communication made it difficult for the papal bureaucracy to reform blatant financial abuses. That the papacy itself increasingly appeared to condone or even encourage corruption added to the calls for reform.

Yet, although Erasmus and other northern humanists were among those criticizing the Church, they were unwilling to challenge papal authority. The papacy, however, had other, more vociferous critics. First, the monarchs of Europe's strongest states claimed even greater authority in religious affairs. Second, religious movements deemed heretical by the Church rejected papal authority. Some people sought refuge from the turmoil in spiritualism. Others based their idea of religion on personal study of the Bible, turning away from not only papal authority but also the entire formal hierarchy of the Church. Third, within the Church, a reform movement known as conciliarism sought to subject the authority of the popes to councils of cardinals and other Church dignitaries. Fourth, as the Church seemed determined to protect its authority, it also seemed more venal, even corrupt, than ever before. More and more calls echoed for the reform of clerical abuses. By questioning fundamental Church doctrine and the nature of religious faith, the resulting reform movement, culminating in the Reformation, shattered the unity of Western Christendom.

The Great Schism (1378–1417)

The growing reach of monarchical authority undercut the influence of the papacy. The monarchs of France, Spain, and England had repudiated the interference of the pope in temporal affairs and reduced his effective authority within their own states by creating what were, for all intents and purposes, national churches.

In the fourteenth century, the struggle between the king of France and the pope put the authority of the papacy in jeopardy. The French and English kings had imposed taxes on ecclesiastical property. In response, Pope Boniface VIII's bull *Unam Sanctum* (1302) threw down the gauntlet to lay rulers. It asserted "it is absolutely necessary for salvation for everyone to be subject to the Roman pontiff." King Philip IV of France ordered Boniface's arrest, and he died in 1303, shortly after his release from captivity. Philip then arranged the election of a pliant pope, Clement V (pope 1305–1314). In 1309, he installed him in the papal enclave of Avignon, a town on the Rhône River. During the "Avignon Papacy" (1309–1378), the popes remained under the influence of the king of France. At the same time, they continued to build up their bureaucracies and, like the monarchs whose authority they sometimes contested, to extract ever greater revenues from the faithful.

In 1377, Pope Gregory XI (pope 1370–1378) returned to Rome, in the hope that his presence there might calm the political situation in the Italian states. When Gregory XI died a year later, a group of cardinals in Rome, most of whom were French, elected Pope Urban VI (pope 1378–1389), popularly believed to be faithful to the Avignon Papacy. After a Roman mob invaded the proceedings, most of the cardinals fled. Upon their return several months later, a smaller group of thirteen cardinals was vexed by the new pope's denunciation of their wealth and privileges. Furthermore, they now viewed him as temperamentally unstable, unfit to be pope. They elected Clement VII, who claimed to be pope between 1378 and 1394. He returned to set up shop in Avignon, leaving his rival in Rome. The Great Schism (1378–1417) began with two men now claiming authority over the Church.

The two popes and their successors thereafter sought to win the allegiance of rulers. The Avignon popes, like their pre-Schism predecessors, were under the close scrutiny of the king of France, and the Roman pope was caught up in the morass of Italian and Roman politics. France, Castile, Navarre, and Scotland supported the Avignon popes; most of the Italian states, Portugal, the Holy Roman Empire, and England obeyed the

Roman popes. In 1409, Church dignitaries gathered at the Council of Pisa to resolve the conflict and elected a third pope. However, neither of the other two would agree to resign. And, in the meantime, secular rulers forced the popes to make agreements that increased the authority of the former over the Church in their states. The Great Schism enabled lay rulers to construct virtual national churches at the expense of papal power.

Heretical and Spiritual Movements

The chaos of two and then three popes claiming authority over the Church, along with the ruthlessness and greed of the claimants, greatly increased dissatisfaction with the organization of the Church. For many people loyal to the Church, the Great Schism cast disrepute on papal authority itself. From time to time heresies (movements based on beliefs deemed contrary to the teaching of the Church) had denied the authority of the papacy and demanded reform. In the twelfth century, the Waldensians in the Alps and the Albigensians in the south of France had defied the papacy by withdrawing into strictly organized communities that, unlike monasteries and convents, recognized neither Church doctrine nor authority.

An undercurrent of mysticism persisted in Europe, based on a belief in the supremacy of individual piety in the quest for a knowledge of God and eternal salvation. William of Occam (c. 1290–1349), an English monk and another critic of the papacy, rejected scholastic rationalism. Scholasticism had become increasingly linked to the theology of Thomas Aquinas, who had deduced the existence of God from rational proofs that moved from one premise to the next. Occam, in contrast, posited that the gulf between God and man was so great that scholastic proofs of His existence, such as those of Aquinas, were pointless because mankind could not understand God through reason. "Nominalists," as Occam and his followers were known, believed that individual piety should be the cornerstone of religious life. Nominalists rejected papal authority and the hierarchical structure of the Church. Their views reflected and accentuated the turn of more clergy and laymen toward the Scriptures as a guide for the individual's relationship with God, emphasizing the importance of leading a good, simple life. The Great Schism may have increased the yearning for spirituality as well as for the institutional reform of the Church.

The English cleric and scholar John Wyclif (c. 1328–1384) also questioned the pope's authority and claimed that an unworthy pope did not have to be obeyed, views that drew papal censorship. For Wyclif, the Church consisted of the body of those God had chosen to be saved, and no more. Stressing the role of faith in reaching eternal salvation, he insisted that reading the Scriptures formed the basis of faith and the individual's relationship with God. Reflecting tension between faith and an internal conception of religion and Church ritual, Wyclif rejected transubstantiation (the doctrine that holds that during Mass the priest transforms ordinary bread and wine into the body and blood of Christ). This in itself reduced the significance of the Mass, while putting him at odds with Church theology.

Wyclif's de-emphasis of rituals and advocacy of a religion based on faith suggested the significantly reduced importance of the Church as intermediary between man and God. Wyclif, who had powerful English noble and clerical protectors, called for Church reform. But the Peasants' Revolt of 1381 in England, in which wealthy churchmen were targets of popular wrath, gave even Wyclif's powerful protectors pause by raising the specter of future social unrest. An English Church synod condemned Wyclif, but he was allowed to live out his remaining years in a monastery. Some of his English followers, poor folk known as the Lollards, carried on Wyclif's work after his death. They criticized the Church's landed wealth and espoused a simpler religion. Led by gentry known as "Lollard knights," the Lollards rose up in rebellion in 1414, before being crushed.

In Bohemia in Central Europe, Jan Hus (c. 1369–1415), a theologian, had learned of Wyclif's teaching. He, too, loudly criticized the worldliness of some clerics, and called for a return to a more unadorned religion. Rejecting the authority of the papacy and denouncing popes as "anti-Christs," Hus held that ordinary people could reform the Church.

The Challenge of Conciliarism to Papal Authority

The doctrine of conciliarism arose not only in response to the Great Schism, but also to growing demands from many churchmen that the Church must undertake reform. The Council of Constance (1414–1418) was called to resolve the Great Schism and to undertake a reform of the Church. Many of the ecclesiastical dignitaries who attended also wanted to limit and define the authority of the papacy.

There were at least four significant parties to conciliarism: the popes themselves; bishops supporting councils as a way of resolving Church problems; secular rulers, particularly French kings, but also Holy Roman emperors, intervening in the Great Schism; and finally heretics condemned at Constance, who were far more radical than the mainstream conciliarists in their challenge to papal authority.

The Council of Constance first turned its attention to Jan Hus. Holding a safe-conduct pass given him by the king of Bohemia, Hus travelled to the Council of Constance in 1414, but was arrested and put on trial for heresy. Hus refused to recant Wyclif's views, defending his own belief that the faithful, like the priest saying Mass, ought to be able to receive communion, the Church's rite of unity, in the two forms of bread and wine. The council condemned Hus, turning him over to the Holy Roman emperor, who ordered him burned at the stake as a heretic. The Hussites, the only major fifteenth-century dissidents within the Church, fought off several papal armies. They finally won special papal dispensation for the faithful to take communion in both bread and wine; their "Utraquist" ("in both kinds") church lasted until 1620.

The council resolved the ongoing conflicting claims to papal authority by deposing two of the claimants and accepting the resignation of the third. In 1417, the council elected Martin V (pope 1417–1431). But the Great Schism, with its multiple papal claimants, by delaying any serious attempts at reform, had reinforced the insistence of some prelates that councils of Church bishops ought to have more authority than the pope.

In principle convoked by the pope, councils brought together from throughout Europe leading ecclesiastical dignitaries who deliberated on matters of faith, as well as on the organization of the Church. But some councils began to come together in defiance of papal authority. Those holding a "conciliar" view of the Church conceived of it as a corporation of cardinals that could override papal authority. William of Occam had argued a century earlier that, when confronted by a heretical pope, a general council of the Church could stand as the repository of truth and authority. Some reformers wanted to impose a written constitution on the Church, as the papacy moved to reassert its authority. At the Council of Basel, which began in 1431, exponents of unlimited papal authority and their counterparts favoring conciliarist positions both presented their views. A break occurred in 1437, when the pope ordered the council moved to Ferrara, and then to Florence in 1438. At that time and until 1445, some of the participants, mostly conciliarists, continued to meet in Basel, although the pope declared that council schismatic. Fifteen years later, Pope Pius II (pope 1458–1464), who had earlier been active in the conciliar movement, turned against it, declaring it a heresy and reestablishing the absolute authority of the pope.

The assertion by some churchmen that councils had authority over the papacy merged easily with those who called for the reform of blatant abuses within the Church. Some monasteries were mocked as hypocritical institutions no more saintly than the supposedly profane world monks and nuns sought to leave behind. Several new religious orders had been founded at least partially out of impatience if not disgust with ecclesiastical worldliness.

Clerical Abuses and Indulgences

Critics of the papacy attacked with particular energy what they considered ecclesiastical financial and moral abuses. Those critics particularly concerned about the former claimed that the papacy seemed to have become an investment trust run by the priests who administered the papacy's temporal affairs. No clerical financial abuse was more attacked than indulgences. Indulgences were based on the idea of transferable merit. Through granting indulgences, the Church supposedly reduced the time a soul would have to suffer punishment in Purgatory (that halfway house between Hell and Heaven that had emerged in Church belief early in the Middle Ages) for sins committed on earth. The practice of selling indulgences began during the Crusades as a means of raising revenue for churches and hospitals. Those seeking the salvation of their souls did not purchase God's forgiveness (which could only be received in the confessional) but rather cancelled or reduced the temporal punishment (such as the pilgrimages, prayers, or charity) required to atone for their sins. In 1457, the pope had announced that indulgences could be applied to the souls of family members or friends suffering in Purgatory. Some people had the impression that purchasing indulgences rather than real repentence was an immediate entry to Heaven for oneself or one's relatives. "The moment the money tinkles in the collecting box, a soul flies out of Purgatory," went one contemporary ditty. The implication was that wealthy families had a greater chance of opening the doors of Heaven for their loved ones than poor people. One papal critic interpreted all of this to mean that "The Lord desireth not the death of a sinner but rather that he may live and pay." In his *Praise of Folly*, Erasmus wrote, "What should I say of them that hug themselves with their counterfeit pardons; that have measured Purgatory by the hourglass, and can without the least mistake demonstrate its ages, years, months, days, hours, minutes, and seconds, as it were in a mathematical table? And now suppose some Merchant, Soldier, or Judge, parts with some small piece of ill-gotten money. He at once conceives . . . his whole life quite cleansed . . . so bought off that [he] may begin a new score."

Another clerical practice that was much criticized was that of the sale of Church offices (positions). Despite a deluge of indignant criticism, in 1487 the pope put twenty-four posts up for sale. More than ever before, those who participated—and benefited from—this trust were Italian clerics. Most popes appointed Italians as cardinals, many of whom lived in Rome while accumulating great wealth from ecclesiastical sees they rarely if ever visited. One powerful French archbishop entered his cathedral for the first time feet first in his casket at his funeral. Some prominent families looked to the Church to provide lucrative sinecures (offices that generated income but that required little or no work) for their children. Reformers decried the appointment of unqualified bishops who had purchased their offices.

Many priests were resented because they charged exorbitant fees for burial. Resentment also mounted, particularly in the German states, because clerics were immune from civil justice and paid no taxes. It seemed symbolic that Pope Leo X allegedly effused to his brother, "God has given us the papacy—let us enjoy it!" Indulgences and pardons were swapped for gold or services; since about 1300, they had become a papal monopoly. Commenting on Leo's death, one wag remarked "his last moments come, he couldn't even have the [Last] Sacraments. By God, he's sold them!"

The papacy also came under attack for moral abuses. In the diocese of Trent in the early sixteenth century, a fifth of all priests kept concubines. Nepotism, the awarding of posts to relatives or friends, seemed to reign supreme. In the fifteenth century, Paul II was mocked as the "happy father," not revered as the Holy Father. Alexander VI (pope 1492–1503) looked after his own children with the care of any other father. Paul III (pope 1534–1549) made two of his grandsons cardinals. (Their expensive hats were far bigger than the young heads upon which they occasionally sat.)

Finally, the sacrament of penance generated some degree of popular resentment against the clergy. Since 1215, the faithful were required to confess their sins each year to a priest. This sacrament originated in the context of instruction to encourage good behavior—the Ten Commandments gradually replacing the Seven Deadly Sins as the foundation of Christian ethics. But for many people, penance had become the priest's interrogation of the faithful in the confessional, during which the confessor sought out details of misdeeds in order to determine one of the sixteen stated degrees of transgression. Specific confessional questions found in priests' manuals included, "Have you dressed proudly, sung and danced lustily, committed adultery, girl-watched, or exchanged adulterous glances in church or while walking on Sundays?" The contrast between the Church's call for sinners to repent seemed ironic in view of popularly perceived ecclesiastical abuses.

Given a boost by the conciliar movement, calls for reform echoed louder and louder. The representatives of the clergy who had gathered at the Estates-General of France in 1484 criticized simony, the sale of Church offices. In 1510, the Augsburg Diet, an imperial institution of the Holy Roman Empire, refused to grant money to the pope for a war against the Turks unless he first ordered an end to financial abuses. The imperial representative Assembly (Reichstag) had increasingly served as a forum for denunciations against the papacy. In 1511, King Louis XII of France, whose armies had backed up his territorial ambitions in northern Italy, called a council with the goal of reasserting the conciliar doctrine and ordered reforms in the monastic houses of his realm. The Fifth Lateran Council, which met from 1512–1517, urged more education for the clergy, sought to end some monastic financial abuses, and insisted that occupants of religious houses keep their vows of chastity. The council also suggested missions to carry the Church's influence into the Americas. Pope Leo, however, emphatically insisted that he alone could convoke Church councils, and the council itself forbade sermons denouncing the moral state of the Church.

Martin Luther

Martin Luther (1483–1546) was born in the small town of Eisleben in central Germany. He was the second son (of eight children) of a miner whose family had been prosperous peasants for several generations. His

The young Martin Luther by Lucas Cranach.

peasant background could be seen in the coarseness of his language, song, and humor. The pious, determined, stocky Luther went off to a nearby town to attend school. It was there that he may have been punished for speaking German and not Latin. In 1501, he began his studies at the University of Erfurt, where he took courses in philosophy and then began the study of law.

In July 1505, Luther was engulfed in a violent storm as he returned to Erfurt after a visit home. As a bolt of lightning struck not far from where he stood in terror, the young student cried out to the patron saint of travelers, "Help me, Saint Anne, I will become a monk." Returning safely to Erfurt, he gathered his friends together, treated them to a nice meal, and told them, "Today you see me, henceforth, never more." They escorted him to the nearby monastery of the Augustinian monks, which he entered against his father's wishes. Luther prayed, fasted, and, outside the monastery, begged for charity. In 1507, he was ordained a priest and soon became a doctor of theology, administrator of eleven Augustinian monasteries, and dean of the theological seminary in the town of Wittenberg.

Luther had, for some time, been wracked with gnawing doubt concerning his personal unworthiness. Was he not a sinner? He had been saved from the storm, but would he be saved from damnation on Judgment Day? Was there really any connection between good works effected on earth and salvation? Even if he confessed all of the sins on his conscience, were there not sins omitted unintentionally that blotted his soul? If mankind was so corrupted by sin, how could charity, fasting, or constant prayer and self-flagellation in the monastery earn one entry to Heaven? He later recalled, "I tried hard . . . to be contrite, and make a list of my sins. I confessed them again and again. I scrupulously carried out the penances that were allotted to me. And yet my conscience kept telling me: 'You fell short there.' 'You were not sorry enough.' 'You left that sin off your list.' I was trying to cure the doubts and scruples of the conscience with human remedies. . . . The more I tried these remedies, the more troubled and uneasy my conscience grew."

Luther's lonely study of theology in the tower library of the monastery did not resolve his doubts. Like other Augustinians, he had been influenced by the nominalism of the followers of William of Occam. This led Luther closer to his contention that faith, not good works, was the key to salvation. Indeed, the teachings of Saint Augustine himself also suggested to him that each person could be saved by faith alone through the grace of God. Believing man is saved "not by pieces, but in a heap," Luther became obsessed with a phrase from the Bible (Romans I:17), "The just shall live by faith." Such a conclusion broke with the accepted teachings of the Church as defined by medieval scholasticism. But more than faith was troubling Luther. He was also especially troubled by the abuse of the ecclesiastical sale of indulgences.

On October 31, 1517, Luther tacked up on the door of the castle church of Wittenberg "Ninety-five Theses or Disputations on the Power and Efficacy of Indulgences." Other critics before him had denounced the

An allegorical painting of the dream of Frederick the Wise wherein Martin Luther uses an enormous quill to tack his Ninety-five Theses to the door of the castle church at Wittenberg.

sale of indulgences, but Luther attacked the theoretical underpinnings of the papal granting of indulgences out of the "treasury of merits" accumulated by Christ and the saints. "The true treasure of the Church," Luther declared, "is the holy gospel of the glory and the grace of God." He had his theses printed and distributed in the region and invited those who might want to dispute his theses to present themselves to debate with him, as was the custom. In February 1518, Pope Leo X demanded that Luther's monastic superior order him to cease his small crusade. Luther refused, citing his right as a professor of theology to dispute formally the charges now leveled against him. And he found a protector, Frederick III, Elector of Saxony.

In April, as denunciations against Luther poured into Rome, he successfully defended his theses before his Augustinian superiors. Pope Leo was trying to remain on good terms with the Elector Frederick, a strong candidate for election as Holy Roman emperor. Instead of immediately summoning Luther to Rome, he therefore proposed that a papal legate travel to Augsburg to hear Luther out. At their meeting, the legate warned Luther to desist or face the consequences. Luther's friends, suspecting that the pope had authorized his arrest, whisked him away to safety.

Luther sought a negotiated solution. He agreed to write a treatise calling on the German people to honor the Church, and promised neither to preach nor publish anything else if his opponents would also keep silent. At this point Luther did not seek to create a new church, but merely to reform the old one. A papal representative sent to meet with Luther in Leipzig in June 1519 accused him of being a Hussite, that is, of denying the pope's authority. There Luther admitted that he did not believe the pope to be infallible.

Luther crossed his Rubicon, but unlike Caesar moved not toward Rome but away from it. "Farewell, unhappy, hopeless, blasphemous Rome! The wrath of God come upon thee, as you deserve" he wrote a friend, "We have cared for Babylon and she is not healed; let us then leave her. . . ." Luther would not be silenced. "I am hot-blooded by temperament and my pen gets irritated easily," he proclaimed, pouring out vigorous tract after tract, each more adamant than the one before.

Three treatises published in 1520 marked Luther's final break with Rome. Here Luther developed his theology of reform, one that went far beyond the prohibition of indulgences and the sale of ecclesiastical offices. He argued his view that faith alone could bring salvation, that good works follow faith but do not in themselves save the soul. Nor does the absence of good works condemn man to eternal damnation, he claimed. Upon reading one of these tracts, Erasmus, loyal critic of the Church, stated emphatically, "the breech is irreparable."

Developing the theological concept of "freedom of a Christian," Luther's immediate goal was to free German communities from the strictures of religious beliefs and institutions that seemed increasingly foreign to their faith. He called on the princes of the German states to reform the Church in their states. In doing so, he argued that the Scriptures declared the Church itself to be a priestly body that was not subject to the pope's interpretation. Luther acknowledged only two of the seven sacraments, those instituted by Christ, not the papacy: baptism and communion. After first retaining penance, he dropped it, arguing that faith was sufficient to bring about a sinner's reconciliation with God. If this was true, the monastic life no longer seemed to Luther to provide any advantage in the quest for salvation. And he rejected what he called the "unnatural" demands of poverty, chastity, and obedience.

On June 15, 1520, Pope Leo X excommunicated Luther from the Church, accusing him of forty-one heresies, "offensive, erroneous, objectionable to pious ears, misleading to simple minds, and contrary to Catholic teaching." The papal bull called Luther "the wild boar who has invaded the Lord's vineyard." In Wittenberg, a crowd burned papal bulls and documents. Luther defiantly tossed the writ of excommunication into the flames.

Luther's bold challenge to the papacy became a matter of state. Charles V had been elected Holy Roman emperor following his father's death in 1519. He had promised before his election that no one would be excommunicated within the empire without a proper hearing. Through the influence of Frederick of Saxony, Charles summoned Luther to the town of Worms in April 1521 to confront the imperial Diet (assembly).

Before the assembled Diet, Luther was asked if he had written the imposing number of treatises and books placed on the table. Acknowledging them all, Luther told the Diet: "I am bound by the Scriptures I have quoted and my conscience is captive to the Word of God. I cannot and I will not retract anything, since it is neither safe nor right to go against conscience. I cannot do otherwise, here I stand, may God help me. Amen." The Diet condemned Luther's beliefs. Charles V, in agreement with the pope, signed the Edict of Worms in May 1521, placing Luther under the "ban of the empire." This forbade him from preaching and declared him a heretic, thus promising to stamp out his influence. In the meantime, Luther had left Worms. Several men loyal to Frederick of Saxony, Luther's protector, kidnapped him, escorting him to safety. In Wartburg Castle, the reformer took shelter from the storms of controversy, translating, despite moods of depression, Erasmus' critical edition and retranslation of the Bible into German.

By declaring Luther an outlaw and forbidding any changes in religion in the Holy Roman Empire, the Edict of Worms made religious reform an issue of state. But Luther could not have survived the ban of the empire if his influence had not already spread, convincing many that through Luther they had now discovered the true Gospel.

SOCIAL BACKGROUND OF THE REFORMATION IN THE GERMAN STATES

Challenging the ways people in Central Europe had thought about religion for centuries, the movement for reform, spread by preachers, found converts in the German states. During the early 1520s, the proponents of Martin Luther's reform convinced many clergy and lay people to reconsider their religious beliefs and restructure their communities. During this crucial period, clergy and urban people of some means convinced German townspeople to accept reform. Then, in 1525–1526, perhaps encouraged by the quest for religious reform, peasants in the central and southern German states rose up against their lords. These events, roundly condemned by Luther, left no doubt that the Reformation would shake the political foundations of the German states.

Urban Centers of Reform

At first the Reformation was overwhelmingly an urban phenomenon in the German states and then Switzerland. The decentralized political structure of the Holy Roman Empire and traditions of popular participation in urban government aided the movement for reform. There were free cities in the northern German states, such as the still powerful Baltic trading city of Lübeck, leader of the Hanseatic League, and self-governing towns in the southern German states. Some towns were under pressure from princely neighbors who wanted them to contribute to the cost of imperial government. But even towns that had not maintained their independence enjoyed municipal privileges (such as autonomous administration or exemption from certain forms of taxation) that had already been eroded or disappeared in France and Spain as monarchies consolidated and extended their authority. Each German town had its own elite of prosperous burghers. Reformers found these communities fertile ground for Luther's ideas. Complaining of incompetent or lazy priests, some towns had endowed posts for preachers in order to attract vigorous, effective priests, a good many of whom now followed Luther.

German towns had a particularly well-developed sense of civic solidarity that included a sense that all citizens of the town shared a common fate in the material world—vulnerability to bad times, and a certain degree of prosperity in good times—and that salvation itself was something of a group enterprise. Erasmus had asked, "What else is the city but a great monastery?" Many German townspeople, then, tended to see their community as a miniature of Christendom. Luther sought to spark a more personal religion that would make people not only better Christians, but better citizens of their communities as well. In many towns, urban leaders and ordinary people may also have accepted reform because it appeared more promising than unreformed Catholicism for the maintenance of local order.

No simple formula could predict how the Reformation would fare in specific parts of the German states. In some towns in the southern German states, wealthy town leaders such as urban nobles, merchants, and bankers remained staunchly Catholic. These property-owning groups were more conservative by instinct and often had a vested interest in the survival of, for example, stained-glass windows financed by their ancestors. Here, also, the role of personality and the configuration of local social and political life came into play; so did pure chance, including such factors as whether preachers and reform literature arrived, how both were received, and by whom.

The Process of Reform

Social and political factors thus helped shape religious outcomes. While the embrace of the Reformation did not constitute a social revolution, in many cases clergy supporting religious reform were drawn from the middle and lower middle classes, groups with some possibility of social mobility. The "middling sort," in turn, brought reform to the lower classes. This process might be marked by the spontaneous singing of Lutheran hymns by those sitting in Mass, or by some other signs of a turn to reform. While archbishops and bishops in general opposed Luther, the lower clergy, particularly those of recent ordination, became influential converts in their towns. Communities accepted reformers by consensus, as local governments began to bow to the wishes of townspeople.

Thus, a crowd cheered in Basel when a priest carried the Bible instead of the communion host during the feast of Corpus Christi. Priests began to wear simpler clothes instead of rich robes. They attempted to change the liturgy of the Mass, for the first time saying some of it in German. Some began to give the faithful both bread and wine during communion. Some crowds mocked Church rituals in angry ways: ringing cow bells outside churches to disrupt Mass; heckling priests trying to deliver sermons; smashing stained-glass windows, crucifixes, statues, and other images of the saints, and occasionally destroying relics considered sacred. Such largely spontaneous actions bewildered Luther, who remained in most ways a very conservative man.

Luther and his followers denied the special status of the clergy as a group marked off from the rest of the population. In the early days of the Reformation, in some places reformers undertook expeditions to "rescue" nuns from convents. A number of former priests began to take wives, which also first shocked Luther, since this represented the end of clerical celibacy, which the Church had proclaimed in the eleventh century. Luther asserted in 1521, "Good Lord! Will our people at Wittenberg give wives even to monks? They will not push a wife on me!" But by 1525 he changed his mind, and married a former nun. The marriage of clerics further broke down the barrier between the priest and the people, symbolizing the "priesthood of all believers" by eliminating the clerical distinction of celibacy. Nonetheless, Luther limited the task of interpreting the Scriptures to professors of theology.

The Peasants' Revolt

The gap between rich and poor seemed particularly great at the beginning of the sixteenth century. In the southern German states, some burghers worried that law and order would collapse, that the poor might rise up. News of several strange and alarming prophecies circulated. A preacher in Strasbourg reminded magistrates and teachers that the Bible should serve as "a vital, certain, unerring guide against false doctrine, divisions and sects, and how one can survive dangerous times." Some people expressed concern that the people might "turn Swiss," referring to the Swiss towns that lived without lords and were self-governing and independent.

In 1524–1525, peasants rose up against their lords in parts of the central and southern German states (see Map 3.1). They demanded the re-

MAP 3.1 THE PEASANTS' REVOLT, 1525–1526   Sites of peasant uprisings in parts of the central and southern German states. The revolt began in Waldshut and Stühlingen in the southern German states and spread west to the Tyrol and Salzburg in Austria, and north to Thuringia and Saxony.

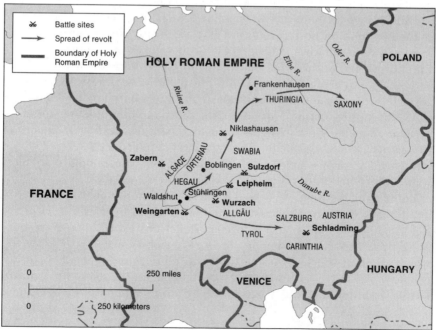

turn of rights (such as to hunt freely and to pasture their animals on the common lands) that the lords had usurped. They also asked for the abolition of serfdom and the tithe, which they declared to be against God's will. Bands of poor people burned castles and monasteries.

The peasants' revolt spread into Austria and Carinthia, and up into Thuringia and Saxony. Pamphlets called for social as well as religious reform. Thomas Münzer (c. 1491–1525), a priest and theologian, merged religious reform with social revolution. He preached against the Church and Luther with equal fury, for he believed that both the Church and Luther had humbled themselves to lay authorities. Münzer led a peasant army in Thuringia, where Luther's reform movement had made many converts.

In the northwestern German states, also in 1525, some towns that had been won over to religious reform rose up against Catholic princes. Swabian peasants promulgated twelve articles against their lords, princes, and bishops, requesting that communities have the right to choose their own pastors. But here, too, the demands of these poor rebels had a social content. They asked for an end to double taxation by both lay and ecclesiastical lords and the "death tax" by which heirs had to give up the deceased's finest horse, cow, or garment. They demanded the end of serfdom, the return of common lands to their use, and free access to forests and streams.

Luther had some sympathy with the plight of the poor. But he rejected the idea that his central theological idea of "Christian freedom," which he believed applied only to the spiritual realm, could be extended into the relationship between lord and peasant. As nobles and churchmen began to accuse him of fomenting insurrection, he denounced the peasants in extravagant language. In *Against the Murdering, Thieving Hordes of Peasants,* he advised the German princes to "brandish their swords. . . . You cannot meet a rebel with reason. Your best answer is to punch him in the face until he has a bloody nose." Catholic and reformed princes put aside their differences to crush the revolt, in which more than 100,000 peasants perished. Münzer was defeated, captured, tortured, and beheaded.

Yet, some of Luther's followers began to see in his teaching a means of resistance against the powerful. Luther asked lords to "act rationally" and "try kindness" when confronted by peasant demands. He asked Christian rulers to "offer the mad peasants an opportunity to come to terms, even though they are unworthy of it." But, when all was said and done, Luther was "opposed to those who rise in insurrection, no matter how just their cause."

THE SPREAD OF THE REFORMATION

Because of the intertwining of religion and politics, what began as a movement for Church reform became entangled in princely rivalries in the

German states. As the breech between Catholic and reformed princes widened, religion became a source of division rather than unity. Although Luther had never intended to bring about a permanent division within Christianity, his followers gradually created a new church in many of the German states. The Reformation then spread beyond the German states.

Divisions within Christendom

The Augsburg Confession, presented by Luther's friends to the Diet that gathered in that city in 1530, became the doctrinal basis of the Lutheran Church. It was implemented by princes and prelates in the reformed states and towns, and in some places by a council, known as a consistory, of ministers and lawyers.

Luther's writing, translated into Latin, then followed trade routes beyond the German states to the west and east. The reformers easily revived the anti-papal Hussite traditions of Bohemia and Moravia and that of the Waldensians in the southwestern Alps. Turkish military victories over Habsburg armies in Hungary left Lutheran missionaries an open field. German merchants carried reform not only to the Baltic states but also north to Scandinavia. In Denmark, King Christian II adopted Lutheranism for his state. In Sweden, the king's conversion and his break with Rome led to a similar reform. When Lutheranism was declared its official religion in 1527, Sweden and its territory of Finland had the first national reformed church.

Some humanists influenced by the Renaissance were attracted by Luther's writing. Erasmus appreciated Luther's call for simple piety and

The Augsburg Confession read before Charles V in 1530.

his denunciation of superstition and corruption within the Church. Furthermore, some humanists, in the tradition of their predecessors who had rediscovered the classics, admired Luther's return to the Scriptures as an original source of knowledge. One of Luther's converts later wrote that his own excitement at the new teaching was so great that he studied the Bible at night with sand in his mouth so that he would not fall asleep. Humanists transformed some monasteries into schools. The first reformed university began in the German town of Marburg in 1527.

But as the gap between reformers and the Church grew larger, Erasmus was caught in the middle. His own criticism of the Church did not go far enough for reformers, but it went too far for churchmen. Erasmus, who had condemned ecclesiastical abuses, remained loyal to Church doctrine. Similarly, Luther and the humanists parted ways by 1525. For the latter, humanistic knowledge was an end in itself; for the reformers, rhetoric was a method for teaching the Scriptures and for arguing in favor of ecclesiastical reform. Many reformers were less committed than humanists to the belief that man is a rational and autonomous being. Luther himself did not share the humanists' Renaissance optimism about mankind. On the contrary, he was not interested in rediscovering mankind, but was preoccupied with an individual's relationship to God, arguing that people depend on grace alone to obtain salvation. Furthermore, Luther opposed attempts by philosophers to intrude in theological questions. Nonetheless, a humanist curriculum continued to influence the training of reform ministers.

Luther's followers gained their first martyrs in 1523, when two former monks were executed in Brussels. German princes requested from the Holy Roman emperor Charles V that a "free general council or at least a national council" consider the growing religious division within the Holy Roman Empire. The Diet of Speyer (1526) proclaimed that each German prince was "to live, govern, and bear himself as he hopes and trusts to answer to God and his imperial majesty." This truce gave reformers time to win even more converts. In 1529, German princes again gathered in Speyer. Some of them prepared a "protest" against the policies of Charles V and the Catholic princes, who had declared themselves against Luther. The followers of Luther became known as "Protestants."

Charles V and the Protestants

Holy Roman Emperor Charles V, the pope's most powerful potential advocate, was a pious man who first denounced Luther with passion. But extensive Habsburg imperial interests kept him fighting a war in Western Europe against King Francis I of France, which prevented him from acting against those who supported Luther. The French king, for his part, was pleased that religion was dividing the German princes, thereby weakening the imperial crown that he had coveted and failed to gain. Charles was away from his German states between 1521 and 1530, for the most part in Italy. These were the crucial years during which the Reformation spread within the Holy Roman Empire; as early as 1524, the first Protestant leagues were formed between states in which reform had won wide appeal.

The Christian crusade against the Turks in Eastern Europe and the Mediterranean also preoccupied Charles and other Catholic princes as well. In 1526, the Turks defeated the king of Hungary at Mohács in Hungary. A subsequent Turkish advance forced Charles to offer concessions to Lutheran princes in exchange for assistance against the Turks. (Luther's hymn "A Mighty Fortress Is Our God" began as a martial song to inspire soldiers against the Ottoman forces.)

For a time, Charles V held out hope for conciliation with the Protestants. In 1531, however, the princes of Hesse, Saxony, and other states and cities that had adopted religious reform formed the Schmalkaldic League. Although first and foremost a defensive alliance, the princes intended that the league would replace the Holy Roman Empire as the source of their political allegiance. Up until this time, Charles had accepted temporary truces, and thus toleration of Protestants. He had suspended the Edict of Worms, until a general council of the Church could be held. When the pope announced that it would be held in the Alpine town of Trent (see p. 127), the stage was set for confrontation with the Protestants. Meanwhile, however, Charles was still preoccupied by hostilities with Francis I of France, who shocked many Christians by allying with the Turks against the Habsburgs. After Charles forced an end to the wars by launching an invasion of France from the Netherlands, he was finally ready to move against Protestants, routing the Schmalkaldic League in battle in 1547, and subsequently forcing reconversion on the people in about thirty German cities. By that time, however, Protestantism had established itself definitively in much of Central Europe.

The Peace of Augsburg

With his attention no longer distracted by war against the Turks and French, Charles tried to bring back more of the German princes and their people into the Catholic fold. He tried without success to impose in Central Europe moderate Catholic reform in order to answer some of the criticism of the reformers. But some of the Catholic princes who had been allied with Charles now left the fold, and three of them took up arms against him in a short war in 1551. The political complexity of the myriad German states mitigated against a general settlement. The Holy Roman emperor gave up the idea of restoring Catholicism in all of the German states.

The Peace of Augsburg of 1555 was a compromise. It was agreed upon by the imperial representative assembly after Charles, worn down by the complexity of imperial politics, refused to participate. It stipulated that the religion of the ruler of each of the empire's states would be the religion of the state (*cuius regio, eius religio*) (see Map 3.2). Although it excluded

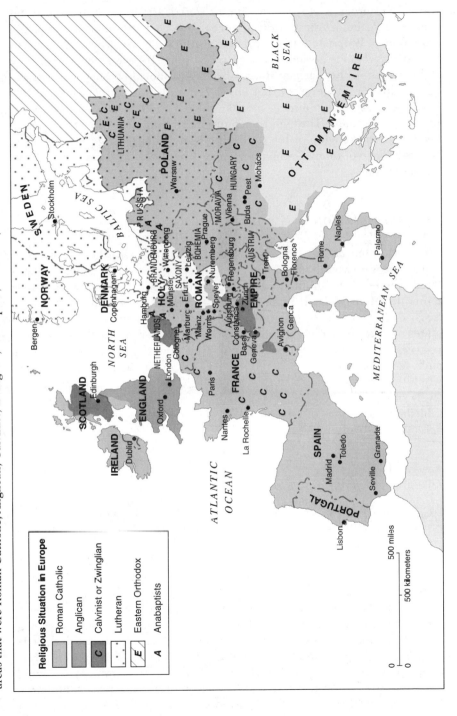

MAP 3.2 THE RELIGIOUS SITUATION IN EUROPE AFTER THE PEACE OF AUGSBURG, 1555   The Peace of Augsburg stipulated that the religion of the ruler of each of the Holy Roman Empire's states would be the religion of the state. The map indicates areas that were Roman Catholic, Anglican, Calvinist, Zwinglian, Anabaptist, Lutheran, and Eastern Orthodox.

Religious Situation in Europe

- Roman Catholic
- Anglican
- C Calvinist or Zwinglian
- Lutheran
- E Eastern Orthodox
- A Anabaptists

500 miles

500 kilometers

BLACK SEA

OTTOMAN EMPIRE

MEDITERRANEAN SEA

NORTH SEA

ATLANTIC OCEAN

BALTIC SEA

SWEDEN
Stockholm

NORWAY

DENMARK
Copenhagen

Bergen

SCOTLAND
Edinburgh

IRELAND
Dublin

ENGLAND
London
Oxford

NETHERLANDS

Hamburg

Cologne
Münster
Marburg
Mainz
Worms

HOLY ROMAN EMPIRE
Erfurt
Leipzig
Wittenberg
SAXONY
BRANDENBURG

PRUSSIA

LITHUANIA

POLAND
Warsaw

Prague
BOHEMIA
Nuremberg
Regensburg
Speyer
Augsburg
Constance
Basel
Zurich
Geneva
Trent
AUSTRIA

MORAVIA
Vienna HUNGARY
Buda Pest
Mohács

FRANCE
Paris
Nantes
La Rochelle
Avignon
Genoa

SPAIN
Madrid
Toledo
Seville
Granada

PORTUGAL
Lisbon

Rome
Bologna
Florence
Naples
Palermo

reformed groups other than Lutherans, Protestants living in states with a Catholic ruler were free to emigrate, as were Catholics in the same situation. The Peace of Augsburg thus recognized that the institutions of the Holy Roman Empire could not provide a solution to what now appeared to be lasting religious divisions in Central Europe. It acknowledged that the Reformation in the German states was an accomplished fact, leaving a religious division in Germany that has lasted until this day. Thus, what had begun as a "squabble among monks" shaped the territorial and political history of Germany. Through the compromise that allowed each prince to determine the religion of his state, the Peace of Augsburg reaffirmed the independence of many German states, or what became known as German particularism.

THE REFORMATION IN SWITZERLAND AND FRANCE

The next stage of the Reformation occurred in Switzerland, a land of rugged peasants, craftsmen, and mercenary soldiers. The sparsely populated (then about a million people) cantons of Switzerland were loosely joined in a federal Diet. In some ways, the thirteen fiercely independent Swiss cantons were closer in organization and in spirit to the Italian city-states than to the German states. Unlike in the German states, where the conversion of a powerful prince could sway an entire state, there were no such territorial rulers in Switzerland. The reformers in Switzerland, then, would be even more closely tied to privileged residents of towns of relatively small size. The Swiss reformers believed that it was imperative to establish the kingdom of God on earth. Their movement would also soon spread to parts of France.

Zwingli and Reform

In Zurich, a town of about 6,000, Huldrych Zwingli (1484–1531) preached salvation through faith alone. Drawing on his strong humanist training, he began preaching from Erasmus' edition of the Greek New Testament. In 1522, several citizens of Zurich publicly munched sausages during Lent in defiance of the Lentan ban on eating meat. Zwingli published two tracts on their behalf in which he insisted that the Scriptures alone should be the basis of religious practice, and that as there was nothing in the Bible about sausages, they could be eaten at any time. This negative scriptural test also led him and his followers to iconoclasm (the stripping of images and altar decorations from churches because nothing about them could be found in the Bible). The Zurich municipal council then embraced reform. It ordered the canton's priests to preach only from the Bible, and two years later forbade the saying of Mass. Zwingli con-

(Left) Woodcut of Huldrych Zwingli. *(Right)* Burning church ornaments and religious statues in Zurich.

vinced the town's magistrates that tithes should be used to aid the poor, whom he believed represented the real image of God.

A doctrinal conflict among reformers helped define the character of the Swiss Reformation. Luther maintained that communion represented the physical presence of Christ. In this he had not diverged far from the Catholic Church, which insisted that through the miracle of transubstantiation (which the pope originally formulated in 1215), the priest transformed bread and wine into the actual body and blood of Christ. But to Luther, who condemned Catholic worship of the Eucharist, the bodily presence of Christ in the Eucharist came from the fact that Christ and God were universally present. Zwingli, by contrast, believed that communion was a *symbol* of Christ's real presence in the Eucharist and that Luther's refusal to abandon this idea demonstrated that he still stood with one foot in Rome. Luther accused Zwingli of reducing Christ's presence to a mere symbol. The "Sacramentarian Controversy" emerged as the first major doctrinal dispute among Protestants. The Augsburg Confession of 1530 sealed the rift by excluding reformers who rejected Lutheranism, including Zwingli and his followers.

Between 1525 and 1530, some German-speaking parts of Switzerland and regions of the southern German states accepted Zwingli's reforms. In 1531, Catholic forces attacked Protestant cantons. Zwingli, the "godly warrior," led the Protestant forces into the Battle of Kappel carrying a sword and a Bible and was killed in the fighting. Both Catholics and Lutherans claimed Zwingli's death to be divine judgment against his religious positions. The peace that followed, however, specified that each canton could choose its own religion, which amounted to a victory for Protestantism.

Radical Reformers

Some Zurich reformers had even more radical changes in mind. Believing that neither Luther nor Zwingli had sufficiently transformed religious morality and communal life, several radical groups, some of whose members were quite poor, formed communities in which they sought to implement "godly living" (see Map 3.3).

Millenarian groups, whose members believed that the end of the world was near, began to spring up. One group of radical reformers who had broken with Zwingli became known as Anabaptists. They rejected the baptism

MAP 3.3 RADICAL RELIGIOUS MOVEMENTS   Areas in which there were Hussites, Utraquists, Anabaptists, and Mennonites.

of infants because no reference to it could be found in the Bible. They believed that only adults could manifest true faith and therefore be worthy of baptism. Starting their own church in 1525, Anabaptists began to rebaptize adults—"anabaptism" means rebaptism in Greek. The Anabaptists also rejected the notion of the Trinity and were therefore sometimes called "Anti-Trinitarians."

The Anabaptists were sectarians, because for them membership was through free will or voluntary self-selection, rather than through territorial organization of churches as was true for Catholics, Lutherans, and Zwinglians. Anabaptists formed communities of believers in Switzerland and southern Germany, seeking isolation—"separation from iniquity," as they put it—from the struggles and temptations of the secular, sinful world. They would not participate in political life and did not believe in having ties with temporal governments. They rejected secular agreements and refused to take civil oaths, pay taxes, hold public office, or serve in the army.

Catholic and Protestant states moved to crush these dissidents who rejected state authority. At the Diet of Speyer in 1529, Charles V made Anabaptism punishable by death, usually by—with intentional irony—drowning, "the third baptism." Many of these groups of radical reformers sought refuge in the mountains of the Tyrol and Moravia, and in Poland. Persecution increased the number of millenarians. Following the Peasants' Revolt of 1525, unsuccessful insurrections in Frankfurt, Cologne, and several other German towns merged social and political goals with opposition to the Catholic Church.

In 1532, a radical group of Anabaptists, millenarians who believed the second coming of Christ was close at hand, took over the town government of Münster by election. The old patrician families left town. The Anabaptists established a council of twelve that expropriated Catholic Church property, then abolished private property and banned the use of money, establishing a system of barter and communally held property.

Their prophet, John of Leyden, convinced the ministers and elders of Münster to allow polygamy (the taking of more than one wife) in the town, ostensibly to solidify the basis of the new theocracy based on endless links of kinship, but perhaps also because there were four times more women than men in the city. John led the way by taking sixteen wives. Under his orders, all books in Münster were burned except the Bible. The Münster Anabaptists then began to kill Catholics and Lutherans. The Anabaptist kingdom of the "new Jerusalem" lasted but sixteen months. Troops sent by Lutheran and Catholic princes alike stormed the town and then tortured to death the leaders, including a number of women, placing their mutilated corpses in an iron cage that still hangs in the church steeple.

Dutch Anabaptists included a group representing the pacifist strand of Anabaptism, which was largely a reaction to the events in Münster. They became known as Mennonites, after their leader, Menno Simons (1492–1559). Some of them emigrated to the Americas in search of religious toleration more than a century later. Likewise, the Unitarian religion has roots in this period, deriving from Anti-Trinitarian views of God as being one, not three.

Jean Calvin and Reform

France, too, provided fertile ground for attacks upon the Catholic Church. In 1520, a Swiss visitor wrote from Paris that "No books are more eagerly bought up than those of Luther. . . . One book shop has sold 1,400 copies. . . . Everywhere people speak highly of Luther. But the chains of the monks are long."

The French monarchy had traditionally maintained a forceful independence from Rome. Pope Leo X had signed the Concordat of Bologna (1516) with King Francis I, giving the king the right to appoint bishops and abbots in France. Initially the Valois ruler was far more preoccupied with his wars against Charles V and the Habsburgs than with the stormy tracts of an obscure German monk. The threat of heresy, however, convinced him in 1521 to order Luther's writings confiscated and burned. Yet, despite the best efforts of the king's expanded bureaucracy, Protestant propaganda arrived in France from Germany through Strasbourg and evangelical attitudes spread during the next several years. In 1534, reformers affixed placards against the Mass in Paris and on the king's bedroom door in his château on the Loire River at Amboise. The "affair of the placards" convinced the king to combat reform in earnest.

Jean Calvin (1509–1564) embodied the second major current of the Reformation. He was born in the small town of Noyon in northern France, where his father worked as a secretary to the local bishop. Calvin's mother

(Left) Jean Calvin. *(Right)* A Calvinist service. Note the austerity of the church.

died when he was about five years old, and his father sent him to Paris to be trained as a priest. He then decided that his son should become a lawyer, because he might earn more money.

Late-Renaissance humanism and particularly the teachings of Erasmus helped stimulate in the pious young Calvin an interest in religious reform during the legal studies that helped to make him a systematic thinker. In 1534, the Catholic hierarchy and the king himself moved to crush this movement. Finding exile in the Swiss town of Basel, Calvin probably still considered himself a follower of Erasmus within the Catholic Church. In Basel, he penned tracts denouncing the papacy and calling on the king of France to end religious persecution.

Throughout his life, Calvin was overwhelmed by anxiety and self-doubt, compounded by his virtual abandonment by his father and forced exile. He was also terror-struck by the power of nature and, in particular, by storms as manifestations of God's power—rather like Luther who made his vow to become a monk in a thunderstorm. Humanity seemed to Calvin to be poised before an abyss, a metaphor he frequently used. He feared that oceans might rise and sweep humankind away. Around him Calvin saw only the absence of order. The world was such that "we cannot be other-wise than constantly anxious and confused."

Like other thinkers of the early sixteenth century, Calvin believed that he lived in a time of extraordinary moral crisis. He assessed the world around him pessimistically: "luxury increases daily, lawless passions are inflamed, and human beings continue in their crimes and profligacy more shameless than ever." It seemed to Calvin that the sense of community that ought to bind people together was dissolving.

Calvin argued that the Catholic Church had made the faithful anxious by emphasizing the necessity of good works in achieving salvation: the anxiety came from never knowing how many good works were enough. This had, Calvin insisted, turned Catholics to seek the intercession of saints. He attacked the sacrament of penance with particular vehemence:

> The souls of those who have been affected with some awareness of God are most cruelly torn by this butchery . . . the sky and sea were on every side, there was no port of anchorage. The more they had crossed over, the greater was the mass ever looming before their eyes, indeed it rose up like high mountains; nor did any hope of escape appear. . . . And at last no other outcome but despair was found.

Calvin rejected the increasingly human-like images given God and Christ over the previous century. Unlike Luther, Calvin emphasized not reconcil-iation with God through faith, but obedience to his will. The reformer sought to provide a doctrine that would reassure the faithful of God's grace and of their own salvation. There was hope in Calvin's thought, faith that the labyrinth—another of his frequent images—of life could be successfully navigated. The imposition of order, based upon the morality dictated by the Bible, would put an end to some of life's haunting uncertainties.

With this in mind, Calvin developed in his *Institutes of the Christian Religion* (begun in 1536, finished 1559) the doctrine of election or pre-destination: "God's eternal decree. . . . For all are not created in equal condition; rather, eternal life is foreordained for some, eternal damnation for others." The belief in predestination called into question the efficacy of good works. If one's fate is predestined and if good works in themselves (as the Catholic Church claimed) did not bring eternal salvation, why lead a righteous life? Calvin believed that good works were signs of having been chosen by God for eternal salvation, though they did not in themselves guarantee Heaven.

Calvinist anxiety over predestination and the question of whether a given individual had been chosen for salvation led to the controversial thesis of the nineteenth-century German sociologist Max Weber that Cal-vinist self-discipline created a "Protestant ethic." Whereas medieval the-ologians had condemned lending money for profit, Calvin, unlike Luther, distinguished between usury and productive loans that would raise capital and increase the well-being of the entire community. Replacing penance as a means of imposing individual discipline, Calvin preached collective, communal discipline in the pursuit of holiness. Validating economic activ-ity, later Calvinists came to view prosperity, along with "sober living," as a sign of election by God.

Late in 1536, Calvin went to the Swiss lakeside city of Geneva, a town of about 13,000 people. With the first successes of the Reformation, word of which had originally been carried there by German merchants, Geneva broke away from the domination of the Catholic House of Savoy. Earlier that year, troops of the Swiss canton of Bern to the northeast, which had embraced Zwinglian reform, occupied the city. Bern established a protec-torate, with Geneva retaining its nominal independence. Citizens elected magistrates and members of two representative councils.

Calvin had become, like Zwingli, convinced that reform must transform not only the individual but society as well. In 1537, he convinced the smaller and most powerful of the two councils to adopt a Confession of Faith, swearing that the people of Geneva "live according to the holy evan-gelical law and the Word of God." Residency in Geneva would be contin-gent on formal adherence to the document. The Mass was banned, and priests were informed that they had to convert to reformed religion or leave the city.

Calvin's plans for Geneva were far-reaching. He hoped to impose Chris-tian discipline, or worldly asceticism, on the city in order to construct a righteous society. His "Ecclesiastical Ordinances" would provide for the organization of religious life in reformed Geneva, but threatened the pow-ers of the councils. Calvin insisted that the Consistory, the judiciary of the reformed church made up of lay elders (called presbyters), would have the right to discipline all citizens and to dispense harsh penalties against those who transgressed Geneva's religious laws. These penalties would include excommunication from the church and exile, imprisonment, and even execution (the councils wanted to reserve such authority for themselves, not the Consistory, however, and the issue would only be resolved a decade later in favor of Calvin). Pastors were to "admonish, exhort, deprecate"; citizens were to "listen to them as to God Himself," and in doing so, lead better lives. Calvin wanted municipal supervisors to monitor the religious behavior of the people, but the councils hesitated to surrender their authority to Calvin—who, like most of the proponents of radical reform, was French—or to assume such a supervisory role. In 1538, the councils asked Calvin to leave Geneva.

In 1540, the majority of citizens of Geneva, believing that the town's ties to Bern limited its sovereignty, elected new magistrates, who executed the leaders of the pro-Bern faction. The councils then invited Calvin to return to oversee reform in Geneva and adopted his "Ecclesiastical Ordinances." Feeling himself called by God to undertake the reform of the city he had called "a place so grossly immoral," Calvin returned. He insisted that "the church cannot stand firm unless a government is constituted as prescribed to us by the Word of God and observed." He created separate, autonomous ecclesiastical institutions that, unlike those of Luther and Zwingli, did not depend on governmental institutions. Although he did not become a citizen of Geneva until many years later, Calvin played a determining role in structuring religious life and simplifying the liturgy in his adopted city.

To John Knox, the Scottish reformer, Geneva seemed "the most perfect school of Christ that ever was on earth since the days of the Apostles." But many citizens of Geneva resisted the close scrutiny of the Consistory. A man named his dog "Calvin" in protest. Always on the alert for the "many ambushes and clandestine intrigues Satan daily directs against us," Calvin forced one man who had publicly criticized him to wear a hair shirt and walk slowly through town, stopping at street corners to pray and acknowledge Calvin's authority. Calvin took it upon himself to decide whether future bridegrooms were free from venereal disease and could marry in Geneva. He determined the punishment of merchants who cheated their clients, and he banned taverns, although cafés were tolerated if no lewd songs were sung or cards played, a Bible was always available, and grace was said before meals. The Consistory imposed penalties for laughing during a sermon, having one's fortune told, or praising the pope.

Calvin's uncompromising nature could be seen in his dispute with the Spanish humanist and physician Michael Servetus, who publicly rejected the concept of the Holy Trinity. The stern reformer warned that if Servetus ever appeared in Geneva, "I will not suffer him to get out alive." He made good on his promise when Servetus foolishly turned up in disguise to hear Calvin preach and was recognized. During his trial in 1553, Servetus at one point so irritated Calvin that the latter blurted out: "May little chickens dig out his eyes a hundred thousand times!" Servetus' death at the stake probably proved to be at least as painful as this. Calvin also cautioned, however, that some pastors were too strict, "pretending zeal . . . terrifying sinners so inhumanely, without any sign of anguish or sympathy, they make God's Word seem insulting and distasteful." Calvin's death in 1564 was brought on by a variety of illnesses that were probably compounded by his chronic state of exhaustion and his fretful anxiety about the possibility of reforming a fallen and sinful world.

Calvinist Conversions

Calvinism proved the most aggressive, expansionist version of the reformed religions. It confronted Catholicism more systematically and over a longer period of time than did Lutheranism. In France, Calvinism made some inroads among all social classes during the 1530s, following the flow of reform literature coming from Switzerland and the German states. People who could not read could nonetheless listen to the Bible being read aloud. Clergy who converted to Calvinism found eager followers, some of whom, distraught by hard times, may have been attracted by Calvinist sermons offering the assurance of the predestination of eternal salvation. In Lyon, a prosperous banking and commercial center, printers were prominent among Calvinists and used their ability to read to convert others.

Henry II, who came to the throne of France in 1547, denounced the "common malady of this contagious pestilence which has infected many noble towns." The Parlement of Paris created a special chamber to hear heresy cases—"the Burning Chamber"—and tried about 500 people. The king, a sadist, attended many of the executions himself. A magistrate from Bordeaux described the courage of the Protestant martyrs:

> Fires were being kindled everywhere . . . the stubborn resolution of those who were carried off to the gallows . . . stupefied many people. Because when they saw innocent, weak women submit to torture so as to bear witness to their faith, facing death calling out only to Christ . . . young virgins heading more joyfully for the gallows than they would have gone to the bridal bed; men exulting upon seeing the dreadful and frightful preparations for and implements of death that were readied for them, and half charred and roasted, they looked down from the stakes with invincible courage and the blows incurred from the hot pincers, bearing a brave mien; and sustaining themselves joyfully between the bayonets of the hangmen, they were like rocks standing against waves of sorrow. In short, they died smiling.

The judicial system could try some heresy cases, but it could not keep up with the rapid pace of conversion, including the conversion of many nobles. By 1560, there were more than 2,000 Protestant, or Huguenot (so named after a leading French reformer in Geneva, Besançon Hugues), congregations in France.

Calvinism became the dominant religion of reform in the Netherlands. There Protestant conversions set the stage for an inevitable clash with the ruling Catholic Habsburg dynasty. Philip II ordered the Spanish Inquisition (which had been set up by the Spanish crown after the expulsion of the Moors and Jews from Spain in 1492 and later extended to the Spanish Empire in the Americas) established in the Dutch Netherlands to root out Protestants. When the Dutch declared independence from Spain in 1581, Calvinism quickly became part of the Dutch national movement during the long war of independence that followed (see Chapter 6).

THE REFORMATION IN ENGLAND

Unlike continental reform, the English Reformation began with a struggle between the king and the Church. But this dispute must be placed in the context of discontentment with ecclesiastical venality and the distant rule of Rome. Lollard influence persisted among the middle and lower classes, which resented the wealth of the high clergy and papal authority. Merchants and travelers returned to England from the continent with Lutheran tracts. John Colet's espousal of a literal interpretation of the Bible placed him close to the thought of Martin Luther. Among Luther's small group of followers at Cambridge University was William Tyndale, who published the first English translation of the New Testament. Burned at the stake as a heretic in 1536, his last words were "Lord, open the eyes of the king of England."

Henry VIII and the Break with Rome

King Henry VIII (ruled 1509–1547), was a religious conservative who published a book (1521) defending the Catholic view of the sacraments against Martin Luther, prompting the pope to grant him the title of "defender of the faith." The Catholic Church in England already enjoyed considerable autonomy, granted by the pope in the fourteenth century, and the king had the authority to appoint bishops.

The issue of royal divorce led to the English break with Rome. Henry's wife, Catherine of Aragon (1485–1536), had given birth five times, but only an extremely frail girl, Mary Tudor, survived. Henry not only urgently desired a male heir for the prestige of the dynasty, he also desired Anne Boleyn (1507–1536), a lady-in-waiting of Irish descent who had long black hair and flashing dark eyes.

Henry had obtained a special papal dispensation to marry Catherine, who was his brother's widow, and now sought the annulment of this same marriage. Obtaining an annulment—which meant, from the point of view of the Church, that the marriage had never taken place—was not uncommon in sixteenth-century Europe and was an escape clause for those of great wealth. Henry justified his efforts by invoking an Old Testament passage that placed the curse of childlessness on any man who married his brother's widow. He furthermore claimed that English ecclesiastical authorities, not the pope, had the authority to grant an annulment. Pope Clement VII (pope 1523–1534), the second Medici pope, was at this time a prisoner of Charles V, the Holy Roman emperor, whose armies had occupied Rome, and who happened to be Catherine of Aragon's nephew. In addition to these political circumstances, the pope opposed the annulment as a matter of conscience. At Henry's insistence, Cardinal Thomas Wolsey (1475– 1530), who had been named at the king's demand as archbishop of Canterbury and hence head of the Church in England, opened a formal church proceeding in London in 1529 to hear the king's case. But Pope Clement ordered the case transferred to Rome, where the English king had no chance of winning.

Furious, Henry blamed Wolsey for this defeat. Stripped of his post, Wolsey died a shattered man in 1530 on the way to his trial for treason and certain execution. The king had named Thomas More to be his lord

(*Left*) Henry VIII. (*Right*) Anne Boleyn.

Sir Thomas More, painting by Hans Holbein the Younger. More, who is here shown as lord chancellor, was later executed for his beliefs.

chancellor in 1529. But More, a lawyer and a humanist man of letters, was a vigorous opponent of the reform movement. Although a layman, each Friday More whipped himself in memory of Christ's suffering at the hands of Roman soldiers.

As a committed Catholic, More balked at Henry's plan to have his marriage to Catherine of Aragon annulled. In 1533, Henry secretly married the pregnant Anne Boleyn. He then convoked Parliament, which dutifully passed a series of acts that cut the ties between the English church and Rome. The Act in Restraint of Appeals (1533) denied the pope's authority. Thomas Cranmer (1489–1556), who succeeded Wolsey as archbishop of Canterbury, showed himself a loyal servant of the throne by mobilizing opinion against Rome and simply declaring Henry's marriage to Catherine, who was sent to a convent, annulled. The Act of Succession in 1534 required all of the king's subjects to take an oath of loyalty to the king as head of the Church of England. Thomas More refused to do so, and Henry ordered his execution. In Henry's eyes, More was a traitor, but he was a martyr and saint to the Catholic Church. When Pope Clement named another cleric languishing in the Tower of London a cardinal, Henry scoffed, "Let the pope send him a [cardinal's] hat when he will, but I will provide that whensoever it cometh, he shall wear it on his shoulders, for his head he shall have none to set it on."

The Act of Supremacy, also passed in 1534, proclaimed the king "supreme head of the Church of England." Another law made possible the execution of anyone who denied the king's authority over the clergy, or who supported "the bishop of Rome or his pretended power." Parliament limited fees that the clergy could assess for burials and forbade bishops from living away from their sees. Reforms brought the clergy under civil law and enhanced the rights and prestige of Parliament. The lack of resistance to Henry's usurpation of ecclesiastical authority reflected the pope's unpopularity, as well as the growing strength of the English monarchy.

After the Break with Rome

Henry's nascent Church of England remained doctrinely conservative in contrast to some of the continental reform churches. Several dozen people were burned at the stake for heresy in the 1530s after Henry broke with Rome, including twenty-five Anabaptists. In 1536, in the Church of England's first doctrinal pronouncement, Ten Articles affirmed the essential tenets of Lutheran reform: salvation by faith alone (although good works were still advised), three sacraments, and rejection of the concept of Purgatory and the cult of saints. However, six more articles promulgated two years later reaffirmed some aspects of orthodox Catholic doctrine, including transubstantiation and clerical celibacy.

Thomas Cromwell (1485–1540), Wolsey's ambitious protégé, oversaw the dissolution of England's 600 monasteries, which was completed in 1538 despite a northern insurrection (the "Pilgrimage of Grace") in defense of the Roman Catholic Church. The members of the clergy dispossessed by the dissolution of the monasteries were pensioned off. Two-thirds of the monasteries were sold within ten years, the largest transfer of land in England since the Norman Conquest of 1066. The appropriation of Church lands doubled royal revenue, allowing the construction of forts along the troublesome border with Scotland and on the Channel coast, as well as paying for new ships of war. Nobles, particularly those living in the more prosperous south, were the chief purchasers of monastic lands. Many turned their acquisitions into pastureland for sheep, or undertook more intensive agricultural production.

A few months after she married Henry, Anne Boleyn gave birth to a daughter, Elizabeth, future Queen of England. But Henry then had Anne tried on charges of adultery with one of his courtiers, claiming that she had coyly dropped her handkerchief in order to attract him. Anne was executed in 1536, but she insisted to the end about Henry that, "a gentler nor a more merciful prince was there never." Next the king married Jane Seymour, who died shortly after giving birth to a son. Another Anne, this one from a small German state, was next in line, as Henry sought allies against Spain and the other Catholic powers. But this Anne did not please Henry—he claimed he had never consummated his marriage to this woman he disparaged as a "Flemish mare," and he divorced her, too. The king ordered the execution of Cromwell, who had the bad judgment in 1540 to boast that if Henry wavered on the path to religious reform, he would take up his sword against him. Catherine Howard became Henry's fifth wife, but in 1542 he ordered her dispatched for "treasonable unchastity." Catherine Parr would have been excused had she felt some trepidation in becoming Henry's sixth wife, but this pious older woman managed to outlive her husband.

THE CATHOLIC REFORMATION

By 1540, the Reformation had carved out large zones of allegiance in Central and Northern Europe, as well as parts of France and most of England. It reached into Scotland, where, following the efforts of the fiery reformer John Knox, the Scottish Parliament accepted Calvinism in 1560 as the national religion. More than 90 percent of Protestants were Lutheran, Calvinist, or Anglicans, the remainder scattered among smaller sects.

The Catholic Church responded to the schism within Christendom by reasserting the pope's authority and strengthening its own organization. The Catholic Reformation (sometimes called the Counter-Reformation) was both a defensive response by the Church to the success of Protestantism and an aggressive attempt to undertake reform within the limits dictated by Catholic theology.

Retreat to Dogmatism

In 1536, Pope Paul III (pope 1534–1549) designated a commission to report on possible reforms in the Church. This commission documented the lack of education of many clergy and scandalous cases of bishops and priests earning benefices from sees and parishes they never visited. At least eighty bishops resided in Rome, most far from their sees.

But the papacy held firm on matters of Catholic Church doctrine. Paul III rejected a last-ditch attempt in 1541 by one of his cardinals and several German bishops to reach agreement on the thorny theological issue of salvation by faith alone. Luther, too, also vehemently refused to accept compromise. The papacy then went on the offensive. The next year, the pope ordered Cardinal Gian Pietro Carafa to establish an Inquisition in Rome to root out Protestantism in Italy. Carafa went so far as to build jail cells in his private residence.

Carafa became Pope Paul IV (pope 1555–1559) despite the veto of Holy Roman Emperor Charles V. He once declared, "If our own father were a heretic, we would gladly carry the wood to burn him!" Recognizing that the break with the reformed denominations was definitive, the new pope retreated into doctrinal orthodoxy and aggressive repression. He formalized pre-publication censorship, establishing a list—the Index—of forbidden books in 1559. Censors ordered other books altered, and refused to authorize the printing of publications they deemed controversial.

As part of the Catholic Reformation's efforts to combat, contain, and eliminate "error" in all forms, Paul IV invented the "ghetto," ordering Jews living in the Papal States to reside in specific neighborhoods, which they could leave only at certain times. In a 1555 bull, he stated that the Jews were guilty of killing Christ, and therefore ought to be slaves. In much of Catholic Europe, Jews had to wear yellow caps to identify themselves, could not own land, and were excluded from most professions.

Ignatius of Loyola and the Jesuits

Ignatius of Loyola (1491–1556), a dashing Basque noble, became one of the leading figures of the Catholic Reformation. While recovering from a grave injury suffered in battle, Loyola read an account of the life of Christ and a book on the lives of saints. He vowed to help rekindle Catholic orthodoxy throughout Europe. Loyola made a pilgrimage to a Spanish monastery, left his sword in a chapel, gave his rich robe to a poor man, put on a sackcloth, and travelled through Spain and Italy.

Gradually Loyola attracted followers. The Inquisition came to suspect him because his claims to help people through "spiritual conversion" seemed dangerously close to heresy. He defended himself ably, however, receiving only a short prison sentence.

Ignatius wanted to establish a new order that could inculcate the same kind of intense religious experience that he had undergone while lying wounded. He travelled to Rome, offered his services to the pope, and organized the Society of Jesus, which was officially approved by the pope in 1540. Under Loyola's military-style leadership, the Jesuits, as the order's members became known, grew rapidly in number and influence as aggressive crusaders for the Catholic Reformation.

The Jesuit order provided a model for Church organization, orthodoxy, and discipline. Jesuits underwent a program of rigorous training and took a special oath of allegiance to the pope. They combined the study of Thomas à Kempis' mystical *Imitation of Christ* (1418) and Ignatius' own intense devotional reflections, examination of conscience, and prayers intended to shape the will of the individual to the service of the Church.

"I can find God whenever I will," became the motto of the charismatic Loyola. When he died in 1556, there were more than a thousand Jesuits. Counselors to kings and princes and educators of the Catholic elite, the Jesuit religious order contributed greatly to the success of the Catholic Reformation in Austria, Bavaria, and the Rhineland. Jesuits also contributed to the Church's reconquest of Poland, where some landowners had converted to Lutheranism. In the service of the Catholic Reformation, Jesuits travelled to North America, Latin America, and Asia. They led "missions," delivering fire-and-brimstone sermons, which were aimed at

The Council of Trent.

rekindling loyalty to the Church. The resourceful German Jesuit Peter Canisius (1521–1597) carried the new Catholic crusade to some of the German states, wrote a triple catechism for different age levels, taught at universities there, and established Jesuit communities.

The Council of Trent

In 1545, at the insistence of Holy Roman Emperor Charles V, Paul III convoked the Council of Trent (1545–1563) to assess the condition of the Catholic Church and to define its doctrines. While such an internal reckoning had seemed inevitable for some time, the papacy had long viewed conciliarism as a potential threat to its authority and invoked every possible reason for delay. Once convened, the Council of Trent, which met off and on for eighteen years, made the split within Western Christendom irreparable. Most of the prelates who came to the Alpine town of Trent believed the central goal of the council was a blanket condemnation of what the Church viewed as heresy, as well as the reaffirmation of theological doctrine. Although the pope himself never went to Trent, the Italian delegates dominated the proceedings, coughing and sneezing during speeches with which they disagreed.

The council rejected point after point of reformed doctrine, declaring these positions "to be anathema." It reaffirmed the authority of the pope and of the bishops, the seven sacraments, and the presence of Christ in the Eucharist. It also unequivocally opposed the marriage of clerics and reaffirmed belief in Purgatory and in the redeeming power of indulgences, although the practice of selling them was abolished.

In 1562, Pope Pius IV (pope 1559–1565), who had fathered three children as a young man before becoming the inquisitor general in Rome, convoked the last session of the Council of Trent. The council ordained the creation of seminaries in each diocese in order to increase the number and quality of priests. The priests were henceforth to keep parish registers listing the births, baptisms, and deaths of the faithful, which in recent times have provided historians with extraordinarily useful demographic information. Some monastic houses undertook reforms. The infusion of better educated clergy in the southern German states and Austria aided the Church's efforts to maintain its influence.

The papacy emerged from the Council of Trent much more centralized, better organized and administered, and more aggressive, like the most powerful European states themselves. Gradually a series of more able popes helped restore the prestige of the papacy within the Church.

Putting Its House in Order

"The best way," one churchman advised, "to fight the heretics is not to deserve their criticisms." Some leaders within the Catholic Church now reasoned that the Church should put its own house in order and seek to reconvert people who had joined the reformed religions. Pius V (pope 1566–1572) declared war on venality, luxury, and ostentation in Rome. But abuses still seemed rampant. In 1569, the Venetian ambassador to France reported that the French "deal in bishoprics and abbeys as merchants trade in pepper and cinnamon." But Pius sent some bishops living in Roman luxury packing to their sees, putting those who refused to leave in prison.

Reformers wanted to bring order and discipline to members of religious orders and the secular clergy. "No wonder the Church is as it is, when the religious live as they do [in monasteries and convents]," Teresa of Avila (1515–1582) exclaimed in response to the demeaning battles between religious houses in Spain, struggles that she tried to end. Some churchmen, however, now rejected monastic life as irrelevant to the activist missionary tasks of the Church, another sign of the influence of Protestant reform. New orders, such as the Capuchins—an offshoot of the Franciscans—and the female order of the Ursulines, worked to bring faith to the poor and the sick. Seeing the success Reformation preachers had with mass-produced pamphlets, the Catholic Church also produced catechisms that spread Church teachings. Thus, catechisms, devotional books (including those by the Jesuits), and lives of the saints circulated widely for popular consumption. Jesuits used drama to renew faith by portraying episodes from Church history and the lives of saints. The Catholic Reformation encouraged other new devotional confraternities (religious brotherhoods of people who heard Mass together), some bringing together laymen of various social classes, begun under the direction of local Catholic elites and clergy. The missionary work of Vincent de Paul (1581–1660) helped restore faith among the poor.

The Reformation had emphasized the religious life of the individual and the development of his or her personal piety through Bible study and personal reflection. The Catholic Reformation, too, now encouraged individual forms of devotion and spirituality. In Spain, where reform had made few inroads, there was a deep spiritual revival, one that extended throughout Spanish society. Nobles, artisans, and peasants joined religious confraternities. A spirit of idealism and contemplative self-reflection merged with the intensely emotional religious devotion and piety that had characterized medieval monasticism in its purest form. Teresa of Avila, later canonized as a saint, believed that in order for spiritual values to survive, "mystical theology," a belief that the individual could have direct access to God through prayer and contemplation, had to be restored, and that monasteries and convents had to be reformed.

CULTURE DURING THE TWO REFORMATIONS

The Reformation began as a religious reaction against established abuses within the Church. But it also reflected profound changes in European society. The Reformation followed the expansion of commerce, the arteries of which became the conduits of reform. Both the Protestant and Catholic Reformations affected art, architecture, print culture, education, popular culture, and family life.

The Baroque Style

The monumentalism, flamboyance, and theatrical religiosity of the baroque style complemented the Catholic Reformation. "Baroque" refers to a style of extravagant and irregularly shaped ornamentation (the term itself comes from Old French for "irregularly shaped pear"). As an architectural, artistic, and decorative style, the baroque triumphed in southern Germany, Austria, Flanders, and other Catholic regions during the first decades of the seventeenth century (but was also popular in Protestant England, where it merged with the classical style).

As in the Renaissance, in Rome the Church remained a major patron of the arts, expressing religious themes through visual representation. Its goal was to impress, indeed to overwhelm, the emotions through awe-inspiring dimensions, opulence, movement and, in painting, lurid color. Baroque style emphasized the metaphysical side of humanity, seeking to express the experience of the soul. Baroque palaces and churches featured exuberant curves and ornate decoration and were cluttered with lustrous marble altars, ornate statues, golden cherubs, and intensely colorful murals and ceiling paintings. The baroque merged easily with neo-classicism—the revival of an architectural design dominated by Greek and Roman forms. The Gesú Church of the Jesuits in Rome is a masterpiece of baroque style. With its vast ceilings and enormous paintings of the ascen-

Bernini's *Ecstasy of Saint Theresa.*

sion of Christ and the assumption of the Virgin Mary, it symbolizes the spirit of the Catholic Reformation. The baroque style used optical illusions such as Gesú's false cupola to achieve the impression that the viewer was reaching for Heaven.

The work of Venetian sculptor Gianlorenzo Bernini (1598–1680) best represents the period of high baroque of the Catholic Reformation. His monumental fountains were spread throughout Rome. He planned the piazza outside the entrance to St. Peter's Basilica and sculpted the magnificent canopy over the high altar of St. Peter's. Bernini sought to communicate the intensity of religious experience. In the altarpiece *The Ecstasy of Saint Theresa* (1645–1652), Bernini depicted the saint's convulsions of joy when an angel stabs her with a spear as beams of sunlight engulf the scene. Bernini wrote, "It pleased the Lord that I should see this angel in [this] way. . . . In his hands I saw a long golden spear and at the end of the iron tip I seemed to see a point of fire. With this he seemed to pierce my heart several times so that it penetrated to my entrails." This highly sexual description stands in marked contrast with the puritanical impulse that had seen Renaissance popes order the painting of fig leaves on nudes.

Print Culture

The printing press helped expand the Reformation without causing it. There was, to be sure, nothing about the rapid increase in print culture that would help the cause of religious reform and not the Roman Catholic Church. But a rapid expansion in the publication of pamphlets, books, and other printed material occurred at a time when reformers were challenging Church doctrine and papal authority. The printing of Luther's works facilitated their rapid diffusion, with perhaps a million copies circulating through the German states by the mid-1520s. In 1521, a papal ambassador wrote that "daily there is a veritable downpour of Lutheran tracts in German and in Latin . . . nothing is sold here except the tracts of Luther." The German reformer called the printing press "God's highest and ultimate gift of grace by which He would have His Gospel carried forward." Luther's Wartburg translation of the Bible went through fifty printings in two years. He wrote 450 treatises and delivered more than 3,000 sermons, in addition to thousands of letters; his collected works fill more than 100 volumes and 60,000 pages. Catechisms became his major instrument of religious education. Luther directed many of his dialogues, poems, and sermons to ordinary Germans, and even to children, adopting popular religious themes and images. Luther's book *A Simple Way to Pray, Written for a Friend* was intended for his barber.

Since about 1480, the diffusion of printing had contributed to the expansion of a lay culture in the German states. Much of what was printed was published in the vernacular, that is, German, as opposed to Latin. Although religious literature was the greatest output of early printing presses, other favored themes of books and pamphlets included nature (which fascinated sixteenth-century people), the discoveries of the explorers, the acquisition of technical skills (such as medical skills from self-help medical handbooks), manuals of self-instruction (such as how to defend yourself in court, or how to make beer and wine), and everyday morality.

Visual, often satirical images such as woodcut illustrations and broad-

Satirical images of the pope as a genie and as a donkey playing the bagpipes.

sheets, directed at those who could not read, probably reached far more people than did printed tracts, however. Luther also published a hymnal containing many hymns that are still sung today. Caricatures and cartoons portrayed the reformer as Hercules, as an evangelical saint doing battle with wretched animals representing the Church, as a new Moses, as a miracle worker (and in one popular legend, as the inventor of bratwurst sausage).

Lay Education and Reading

The Reformation, drawing on printing, also profited from increased lay education in Europe, which engendered a critical spirit among students and scholars. The number of universities rose steadily during the last half of the fifteenth century. More people could read than ever before—although in most places this still amounted to no more than 5 to 10 percent of the population. They could read the Scriptures themselves, as Luther, Calvin, and Zwingli encouraged them to do, and they could read them to other people. Lutherans and Calvinists stressed the importance of education as essential to individual and critical study of the Scriptures, and de-emphasized the clergy's role in religious instruction.

During the Reformation, princes and ecclesiastical leaders intensified their efforts to secure religious conformity by controlling what people read. The "blue library" (so called because they were wrapped in blue paper) helped diffuse orthodoxy through pamphlets deemed acceptable and sold at a low price by itinerant peddlers. Each Western European country had such a "literature of bits and pieces." Didactic stories were meant to

Private devotion: An old woman reading the Bible.

instruct people about religious events, saints, and ideals approved by the Church, and to distance them from the "superstitions" of popular culture. Yet, many people living in England probably still knew far more about Robin Hood than they did about the Bible. A chapbook (a small book of popular literature) published in Augsburg in 1621 told the story of St. George slaying the dragon. The Catholic hierarchy removed the dragon from the story, while Protestants left out Saint George.

Popular Rituals and Festivals

Protestant ministers, like their Catholic counterparts, tried to root out such rituals as placing the wedding ring on every finger of the hand and baptizing a child by dunking her three times for good luck. Songs rife with pagan imagery had survived virtually unchanged since medieval times. Religion and magic remained closely intertwined; the Catholic Church had been unable to eradicate the difference in the popular mind between prayer and good luck charms, for example. Archbishops and papal legates undercut the cult of some popular saints.

Many a village became the site of an elaborate tug-of-war between state and ecclesiastical authorities and ordinary people, with the local priest caught in the middle. The clergy, often previously active participants in festive occasions, moved away from what they considered "profane" amusements.

The Catholic hierarchy also tried to suppress some popular festivals and rein in others, returning them to the control of the clergy by imposing a religious purpose that seemed to have been lost in all the fun. The struggle between regulation and tradition began first in the towns and then spread to the countryside. Dances known as the "twirl" in southern France were banned in 1666 because boys tossed girls into the air "in such an infamous manner that what shame obliges us to hide most of all is uncovered naked to the eyes of those taking part and those passing by."

Ecclesiastical and lay hierarchies, Catholic and Protestant, came to view popular festivity as immoral, or at least licentious. *Combat between Carnival and Lent* (1559), a painting by Pieter Bruegel, the Elder, depicts Carnival as a fat man and Lent as a thin woman. Under the twin assault of absolutism and ecclesiastic hierarchy, Lent won. The prominent role of women and youth in festivity drew special condemnation. The clergy also condemned the role in Carnival and other festivals of the lay confraternities. These pious brotherhoods had had their origins in religious devotion, but they now were often fiercely independent and more like festive clubs. The clergy began a long—and often unsuccessful—struggle for control over these lay confraternities. Carnival was largely eradicated in Protestant countries, but it survived in some Catholic ones, although often much transformed. Moreover, local variations in popular culture waned, and cults such as that of Mary became more popular.

Pieter Bruegel, the Elder's *Combat between Carnival and Lent* (1559).

Social and political elites contrasted the "civility" of their beliefs, conduct, and manners with the "barbarity" or "savagery" of popular beliefs and customs. Didactic literature stressing polite comportment and etiquette became popular among people of wealth, further separating them from those less favored. The Church tried to impose more strict sexual mores on ordinary people, while encouraging gestures of deference toward social superiors.

The Role of Women

With convents and nunneries abolished in Protestant states, reformers nonetheless encouraged women to take a more active role in the religious process of being saved. Protestant women, like men, were encouraged to read the Bible themselves, or, as most could not read, to have it read to them. In the case of Anabaptists, women appear to have made decisions about not baptizing their children; most Anabaptist martyrs were female. More women than men seem to have converted to Calvinism in France, perhaps because their legal position was deteriorating—for example, with regard to their dowries and possessions. Perhaps they were attracted by special catechism classes, or by the fact that in Calvinist services, men and women sang psalms together.

Yet, Protestant reformers, too, believed women were subordinate to men. Although a few women published religious pamphlets in the early

1520s and others undertook devotional writing and publishing later, women could not be ministers nor could they hold offices within the new churches. Calvin himself believed that the subjugation of women to their husbands was crucial for the maintenance of moral order. Protestant denominations provided a domestic vision of women, emphasizing their role in the Christian household. The rights of women to manage their own property and undertake legal transactions in their own name were gradually withdrawn.

The fact that a Protestant minister could now marry, however, reflected a more positive view not only of women but of the family as a foundation of organized religion. One pamphleteer admonished husbands that their wives were "no dish-clouts . . . nor no drudges, but fellow-heirs with them of everlasting life, and so dear to God as the men."

Because they no longer considered marriage a sacrament, Protestants also reluctantly accepted divorce in limited cases. Luther viewed adultery, impotence, and abandonment as reasons for divorce, but he counseled bigamy over divorce in the case of Philip of Hesse, and condemned Henry VIII's effort to divorce Catherine of Aragon. Divorce remained quite rare and occurred only after a long, expensive legal process.

In Catholic areas, women could still rise to positions of importance in convents, or in the new charitable orders. But the Council of Trent reaffirmed the Catholic Church's ideal of female chastity, reinforced by the widespread cult of Mary. The chapbooks of the Catholic Reformation still taught that the female body was a source of sin, and therefore had to be controlled.

Witches came to symbolize superstitious aspects of popular religion. Catholic and Protestant churchmen identified and persecuted witches as part of the campaign to acculturate the masses with "acceptable" beliefs. Witch hunts peaked during the first half of the seventeenth century. In the southwestern states of the Holy Roman Empire alone, more than 300 separate witch trials resulted in the execution of 2,500 people between 1570 and 1630, almost all women (in itself not surprising, as Church authorities and priests were all male).

Theologians and judges sought to demonstrate that accused witches embodied the kingdom of the devil. To some extent, the Catholic Reformation wanted to create the idea of a satanic kingdom of evil on earth with which to juxtapose orthodoxy. "Witches," identified by common reputation, sometimes stood accused of saying Latin prayers backward, or performing "black masses" while standing facing their "congregations," instead of facing the altar, defiantly inverting the kingdom of God. One woman was accused of "consuming" several husbands. Often "witches" were blamed for evil that had befallen villagers: a fire, the unexplained death of a cow, a male suddenly smitten with impotence.

Most of those accused of being witches were rural, poor, and single women who confronted the hostility of other villagers, particularly small town officials and wealthy peasants (it was the opposite in 1692 in Salem, Massachusetts, where a good many of the women accused of witchcraft had just inherited property, and therefore were resented by the community). Some "witches" confessed under pain of torture, such as one woman in southern France, who was "scorched like a pig" and cooked alive, having been accused of spreading an evil powder while committing crimes.

Women were targets for repression because they were transmitters of the collective memory of popular culture. They were genealogists, storytellers, and healers, but almost always without formal education. Women were in many ways the guardians of tradition. But they were also regarded by the Catholic hierarchy as the source of sin. The social exorcisms of women had a social value for those in power, affirming authorities' position and role as interpreters of beliefs and customs deemed appropriate.

After the persecution of witches virtually ended, some lay authorities then turned their attention to outcasts, the socially marginal. In the Austrian Netherlands, a sign "useless to the world" was hung above the head of a beggar. Monarchies increasingly demonstrated their authority in carrying out sentences of royal justice and, therefore, the justice of God. Those found guilty of capital crimes—at least those of the lower classes— were tortured and then executed in public, often before throngs, their mutilated bodies exhibited for some time for all to see.

THE LEGACY OF THE TWO REFORMATIONS

In 1600, considerably more than half of Europe remained primarily Catholic, including Spain, France, and Habsburg Austria, three of the four most powerful states in Europe. The fourth was England, and it was overwhelmingly Protestant. The Dutch Netherlands, at war with its Spanish overlords, was largely Protestant as well. Yet, of all of the European states, the Reformation failed to influence directly only Ireland. It generated a strong missionary impulse among Protestants and Catholics alike. With the gradual opening up of the world to European commerce and colonization, the Jesuits, particularly, ranged far and wide. Some made converts, and a few found martyrdom in Asia and Latin America.

In Central Europe, the complexity of the state system facilitated reform. The Peace of Augsburg of 1555 reinforced German particularism, that is, the persistence of a myriad of small, independent states in Central Europe. In contrast, the larger, centralized, and more powerful states like Spain and France most successfully resisted the reform movement. That France and Spain already were large states with relatively strong monarchies helped the Catholic Church remain the dominant religion there, despite the inroads of reform and subsequent wars of religion in the former. Yet, in both states, the Catholic Church remained subordinate to the monarchy, with both the French and Spanish kings retaining considerable authority over ecclesiastical appointments.

The Protestant reformers accepted a separation of functions within the community, what Luther called the "realm of the spirit" and the "realm of the world." Henceforth, the political institutions of the Protestant states remained relatively secularized. In German states and in Scandinavia, Lutheranism was introduced as a state church, in part because reformers originally needed the protection of princes against Catholic rulers, notably Charles V. In England, Anglicanism also took on the status of a state religion. Both Lutheran and Anglican reforms rigorously subordinated the church to the state, separating the spiritual and temporal realms. Whereas Zwingli had called for the complete fusion of church and state, Calvinism alone provided for the institutional separation of both, although in practice the magistrates of Geneva restricted the church's autonomy. Anabaptist sectarians, in contrast, wanted their communities to have nothing at all to do with the state. All reformers called on their rulers to do God's work on earth, arguing that the papacy and the Catholic monarchs had failed to do so.

The Lutheran and Calvinist states were thus not necessarily any more tolerant of religious dissent than those that remained Catholic. Following the Peace of Augsburg in 1555, German princes used their control of the reformed churches to consolidate their political authority. Lutheranism remained wedded to a patriarchal structure of society, which appealed to property owners at all social levels. Yet, the extent to which the princes succeeded in obtaining religious adherence is, of course, almost impossible to know, despite some attempts to make church attendance mandatory and to punish those who were absent.

Nonetheless, compelling people to attend Sunday services did not guarantee what or even if they believed. One can never know how typical were the thoughts of one girl who related that the sermon she had just sat through was "such a deale of bible babble that I am weary to heare yt and I can then sitt downe in my seat and take a good napp." In one English parish in 1547, it was reported that "when the vicar goeth into the pulpit to read what [he] himself hath written, then the multitude of the parish goeth straight out of the church, home to drink."

Finally, the Peace of Augsburg and the Council of Trent did not end the rivalry between Catholics and Protestants, nor, for that matter, the rivalry between different Protestant denominations. Religious conflict would, to a great extent, help define the first half of the seventeenth century, the age of the wars of religion.

CHAPTER 4

THE WARS OF RELIGION

On May 23, 1618, a crowd of protesters carried a petition to Prague's Hradcany Palace, where representatives of the royal government were gathered. The crowd stormed into the council chamber, engaged Catholic officials in a heated debate, organized an impromptu trial, and hurled two royal delegates from the window. The crowd below roared its approval of this "defenestration" (an elegant term for throwing someone out a window), angered only that neither man was killed by the fall. Catholic partisans construed their good fortune as a miracle, as the rumor spread that guardian angels had swooped down to pluck the falling dignitaries from the air. The Protestants liked to claim that the men had been saved because they fell on large dungheaps in the moat below.

The different reactions to the Defenestration of Prague illustrate how the Reformation left some of Europe, particularly the German states, a veritable patchwork of religious allegiances. Religious affiliation, like ethnicity, frequently did not correspond to the borders of states. The Peace of Augsburg in 1555 ended the fighting between German Protestant and Catholic princes. It stated that the religion of each state would henceforth be that of its ruler. Hundreds of thousands of families left home and crossed frontiers in order to relocate to a state where the prince was of their religious denomination.

By contrast, in France in 1572, the Huguenots (the popular name for the French Protestants) rebelled against Catholic domination. This set off a civil war that led to great instability in France. Moreover, after years of mounting religious and political tension, Dutch Protestants led the revolt against Spanish Catholic authority in 1572, beginning a bitter struggle that lasted until the middle of the next century.

From 1555 until 1618, the German states were for the most part at peace. But religious wars then broke out again with unparalleled intensity. The Thirty Years' War (1618–1648) devastated Central Europe, bringing into the conflict, in one way or another, almost all of the powers of Europe. Armies reached unprecedented size, and fought with a cruelty that

Peter Brueghel the Elder's *The Massacre of the Innocents* (1564).

may also have been unprecedented. The Four Horsemen of the Apocalypse seemed to ride back and forth across Central Europe with impunity.

The wars of religion in France and the Thirty Years' War began because of religious antagonisms, but the dynastic ambitions of French princes lay not far behind the rivalry between Protestants and Catholics. In the Thirty Years' War, the dynastic rivalry between the Bourbons of France and the Habsburgs of Austria—both Catholic dynasties—came to the fore, eventually dominating religious considerations.

The wars of religion resulted in the strengthening of the monarchies of France, Austria, and the smaller German states as well. Kings and princes further extended their administrative, judicial, and fiscal reach over their subjects in the interest of maintaining control over their populations and waging war. In France, particularly, a stronger monarchy emerged out of the trauma of religious struggles and competing claimants to the throne. Germany, in contrast, remained divided into several strong states and many smaller ones. Competing religious allegiances reinforced German particularism, that is, the multiplicity of independent German states and strong regional loyalties.

THE WARS OF RELIGION IN SIXTEENTH-CENTURY FRANCE

Early in the sixteenth century, France was divided by law, customs, languages, and traditions. Under King Francis I (ruled 1515–1547), the Valois monarchy effectively extended its authority. Of Francis I, it was said, "If the king endures bodily fatigues unflinchingly, he finds mental preoccupations more difficult to bear." The French monarch ruled with an authority unequaled in Europe, however much it was still dependent on the good will of nobles, above all in time of war. When the king sought loans to continue a war, a Parisian noble assured him that "we do not wish to dispute or minimize your power; that would be a sacrilege, and we know very well that you are above the law."

When the Reformation reached France in the 1540s and 1550s, Calvinism won many converts. At a time when nobles were resisting the expansion of the king's judicial prerogatives and the proliferation of his officials, religious division precipitated a crisis of the French state and brought civil war.

A Strengthened Monarchy

Francis I and his successors became more insistent on their authority to assess taxes on the towns of the kingdom, many of which had held privileged exemptions granted in exchange for loyalty. Kings had asked for tax levies to help out the monarchy in exceptional circumstances, above all, in time of war. Like his medieval forebears, Francis did not automatically command the allegiance of a large standing army with which he could enforce his will. Raising an army or royal revenue depended on the willingness of the most powerful nobles to answer the king's call. The monarchs

Francis I, painted by Jean Clouet.

had justified such requests with an appeal to the common good in tactful language that also held out the possibility of the use of force. Now the French king wished to tax the towns even when there was no war.

Francis reduced the authority of the Catholic Church in France. The Concordat of Bologna (1516), signed between Francis and Pope Leo X, despite the resistance of the French clergy, established royal control over ecclesiastical appointments. Many more royal officials now represented and enforced the royal will in the provinces than ever before. At the time of the concordat, France had about 1 official of some kind for every 115 square kilometers and 1,000 people; forty years later, there was 1 for every 10 square kilometers and 75 people. Francis confirmed and enhanced Paris' identity as the seat and emerging symbol of royal power. The sale of offices originated in Francis' desire for the allegiance of nobles and for the revenue they could provide the monarchy. His successors would depend increasingly on the sale of offices and titles for raising revenue.

The political and religious crises in the middle decades of the sixteenth century threatened monarchical stability. They pushed the country into a period of chaos brought by the lengthy, savage war of religion during which the four Valois kings who succeeded Francis I proved unable to rule effectively.

Economic Crisis

The end of a period of economic expansion provided a backdrop for the political struggles of the French monarchy. The population of France had risen rapidly between the late fifteenth century and about 1570, reversing the decline in population resulting from plagues and natural disasters. Land under cultivation increased during that time, particularly near the Mediterranean, where landowners planted olive trees on hills and terraces. But by 1570, the increase in cultivable land slowed down in much of France. The European population, which had risen from about 2.5 to 4.1 million during the sixteenth century, outstripped available resources. Prices rose rapidly in France, as in most of Europe, pushed upward relentlessly by population increase. Beginning in the late 1550s, the purchasing power of the wage worker declined dramatically, whereas that of landowners remained stable, fed by high prices. As agricultural income fell, nobles demanded vexing services from peasants, such as repairing roads and paths on their estates. Many wealthy nobles rented out land to tenant farmers, then took the proceeds back to their luxurious urban residences. Nobles of lesser means, however, did not do as well as the owners of great estates, because the rents they drew from their land failed to keep pace with rising prices.

One sign of the growing power of the monarchy was that nobles lost some privileges of local jurisdiction to the royal law courts. Finding nobles unwilling to provide all the funds the king desired, the monarchy, in turn, put the squeeze on peasants, extracting more resources through taxation.

As the price of profitable land soared, peasant families tried to protect their children by subdividing land among male offspring. Many peasants with small parcels of land became sharecroppers at highly disadvantageous terms—working someone else's land for a return of roughly half of what was produced. Both trends worked against increased agricultural efficiency, reducing land yields. Landless laborers were barely able to sustain themselves.

Taxes and tithes (payments owed the Catholic Church) weighed heavily on the poor. Peasants, particularly in the southwest, sporadically revolted against taxes, and against their landlords, during the period 1560–1660. The popular nicknames of some of the groups of rebels reflect their abject poverty and desperation: the "poor wretches," who rose against the nobles in central and southern France in 1594–1595 (they first took the name of the Hunters of Thieves as they battled nobles who had impounded their cattle and horses in time of war), and the "bare feet." Many of the rebels espoused the popular belief that their violence might restore an imagined world of social justice in which wise rulers looked after the needs of their people.

French Calvinists and the Crisis of the French State

Protestantism first found a smattering of French converts during the two decades following Luther's posting of his theses on the church door in Wittenberg in 1517. Followers of John Calvin arriving in France from nearby Geneva attracted converts in the 1540s and 1550s. Henry II (ruled 1547–1559), who succeeded his father Francis I, began a religious repression that created Calvinist martyrs, perhaps further encouraging Protestant dissent. The spread of Calvinism led the king to sign the Treaty of Cateau-Cambrésis in 1559, ending the long struggle between France and Spain. After decades of reckless invasions, Henry II agreed to respect Habsburg primacy in Italy and control over Flanders. King Philip II (ruled 1556–1598) of Spain, in return, promised that Spain would desist in its attempts to weaken the Valois kings. These two most powerful kings in Europe ended their struggle for supremacy not only because their resources were nearly exhausted but because as pious Catholic rulers they viewed with alarm the spread of Calvinism in Western Europe, both within the Netherlands (a rich territory of the Spanish Habsburgs) and within France itself. After signing the treaty, Henry II and Philip II could now turn their attention to combating Protestantism.

Some nobles in France, wary of the extending reach of the Valois monarchy and tired of providing funds for the war against Spain, had resisted the monarchy, which had vigorously embraced the Catholic Reformation. Perhaps as many as 40 percent of French nobles had converted to Calvinism, some of them nobles of relatively modest means squeezed by economic setbacks. The conflict between the monarchy and the nobil-

Catherine de Medici, widow of Henry II, served as regent to Francis II.

ity thus compounded religious divisions in the last half of the sixteenth century.

King Henry II, accidentally killed by an errant lance during a jousting tournament celebrating peace with Spain, was succeeded by his fifteen-year-old son, who became Francis II (ruled 1559–1560). Catherine de Medici (1519–1589), Henry II's talented, manipulative, and domineering widow, served as regent to the first of her three sickly and incapable sons. Catherine was reviled as a "shopkeeper's daughter," as her Florentine ancestors had been merchants, bankers, and money changers, all things incompatible with the French concept of nobility (but not with the Italian one). That she was the daughter of the man to whom Machiavelli had dedicated *The Prince* added to the "legend of the wicked Italian queen" in France.

The throne immediately faced the challenge to its authority of three powerful noble families, each dominating large parts of France. Religious differences sharpened the rivalry between them for influence. The Catholic Guise family, the strongest, concentrated its influence in northern and eastern France. In the southwest the Catholic Montmorency family, one of the oldest and wealthiest in the kingdom, held the allegiance of some of the population there. And the influence of the Huguenot Bourbon family extended throughout the far southwest corner and center of France.

In 1560, Louis, prince of Condé (1530–1569), a member of the Bourbon family, conspired to kidnap Francis II and remove him from the clutches of the House of Guise, who were related to Francis' wife, Mary Stuart, queen of Scotland. The Guise clan, who discovered the plot, killed some of the Bourbon conspirators, which understandably damaged relations between these powerful families. Francis died after a stormy reign of only eighteen months, succeeded by his ten-year-old brother Charles IX (ruled 1560–1574), under the regency of their mother, who remained influential throughout Charles' brief reign.

The rivalry between the Guise, Montmorency, and Bourbon families undermined royal authority. Henry II's lengthy war with Spain had drained the royal coffers, and the economic downturn made it almost impossible to fill them again. Catherine's efforts to bring some of the nobles who had converted to Protestantism to the royal court and to effect a rapprochement between the two denominations failed utterly. Such attempts only infuriated the House of Guise, several of whose members held important positions within the Catholic Church hierarchy. For their part, Philip II of Spain and the Jesuit religious order backed the Guise family. The political crisis of France, then, became increasingly tied to the struggle of the Church with the Huguenots.

Taking advantage of the confusion surrounding the throne, French Calvinists had become bolder in practicing their religion. Religious festivals occasioned brawls between Catholics and Huguenots. Calvinists seized control of Lyon in 1562, forcing the rest of the population to attend services. Where they were a majority, Calvinists desecrated Catholic cemeteries, smashed stained-glass windows and shattered altar rails of churches, mocked Catholic ceremonies, and covered statues of saints with mud. Catholics replied by slaughtering Calvinists, more than once forcing them to wear crowns of thorns, like Christ, to their death. Both sides burned the "heretical" books of the other denomination. The violence of a holy war was accentuated by rumors that the Huguenots indulged in orgies, while Protestants accused Catholics of idolatry and of doing the devil's work.

In 1562, the first full-scale religious war broke out in France. It began when Francis, the duke of Guise (1519–1563), ordered the execution of Huguenots whom he and his men had found worshipping on his land. More than 3,000 people were killed in fighting in Toulouse; the bodies of Protestants were tossed into the river, and their neighborhoods were burned as part of a ritual "purification." Members of the Catholic lay confraternities took oaths to protect France against "heresy" and erected crosses in public places as a sign of religious commitment. Catholics won back control of several major cities.

This first stage of the war, during which a Huguenot assassinated the duke of Guise, ended in 1563. A royal edict granted Huguenots the right to worship in one designated town in each region, as well as in places where Calvinist congregations had already been established. Intensifying the eagerness of the powerful quarreling noble families to impose their will on the monarchy was the fact that young King Charles IX and his two brothers were all childless. There was no clear heir to the throne of France.

In 1567, war between French Protestants and Catholics broke out again. It dragged on to an inconclusive halt three years later in a peace settlement that pleased neither side. In 1572, Catherine and Charles, though Catholics, first agreed to provide military support to the Dutch Protestants rebelling against Spanish authority. The goal was to help weaken France's principal rival. This convinced the duke of Guise even more that Protestants slowly but surely were taking control of France. Pressured by his mother, Charles then renounced aiding the Dutch and agreed to accept instead the guidance of the Catholic House of Guise. With or without the king's knowledge or connivance, the Guise family tried but failed to assassinate the Protestant leader Admiral Gaspard de Coligny (1519–1572), a Montmorency who had converted to Protestantism and whom they blamed for the earlier murder of the Catholic duke of Guise.

The marriage between Charles' sister, Margaret, a Catholic Valois, and Henry of Navarre, a Bourbon Huguenot, which took place on August 18, was to be, in principle, one of religious reconciliation. The negotiations for the wedding had specified that the Huguenots in Paris come unarmed. But the king's Guise advisers, and perhaps his mother as well, convinced him that the only way of preventing a Protestant uprising against the throne was to strike brutally against the Huguenots in Paris. Therefore, early in the morning on August 24, 1572, Catholic assassins hunted down and murdered Huguenot leaders. During what became known as the Saint Bartholomew's Day Massacre, the duke of Guise himself killed Coligny, whose battered corpse was thrown through the window, castrated, and then dragged through the dusty streets of Paris by children. For six days Catholic mobs stormed through the streets, killing more than 2,000 Protestants. The Parlement of Toulouse, one of the twelve judicial courts of medieval origin that combined judicial and administrative functions, made

The Saint Bartholomew's Day Massacre, 1572, in which more than 2,000 Huguenots perished in Paris.

it legal to kill any "heretic." Outside of Paris, another 10,000 Protestants perished. The pope had a special Mass sung in celebration, and Protestants claimed that he danced for joy when he heard the news, rewarding the messenger with a large sum of money. Thousands of Huguenots emigrated or moved to safer places, including fortified towns they still held in the southwest.

Charles IX died in 1574 and was succeeded by his ailing brother, Henry III (ruled 1574–1589). At his coronation, the crown twice slipped from Henry's head, a bad omen in a superstitious age. The new king was a picture of contradictions. He seemed pious, undertook pilgrimages, and hoped to bring about a revival of faith in his kingdom. He also enjoyed dressing up as a woman, while lavishing every attention on the handsome young men he gathered around him, and spent money with abandon.

Along with the bitter religious factionalism that had been exacerbated by the massacre, Henry III also had to confront a worsening fiscal crisis compounded by a series of meager harvests. But when he asked the provincial estates (assemblies dominated by nobles) for more taxes, the king found that his promises of financial reform and of an end to fiscal abuses by royal revenue agents were not enough. The estates deeply resented the influence of Italian financiers at court, the luxurious life of the court itself, and the nobles who had bought royal favor.

The Catholic forces around the king themselves were not united. A group of moderates, known as the *politiques,* pushed for conciliation. Tired of anarchy and bloodshed, they were ready to put politics ahead of religion. The *politiques* therefore sought to win the support of the moderate Huguenots, and thereby to bring religious toleration and peace to France.

In 1576, Henry signed an agreement that liberalized the conditions under which Protestants could practice their religion. Concessions, however, only further infuriated the intransigent Catholics, who became known as the "fanatics" (*dévots*). Angered by these concessions to Huguenots, a nobleman in the northern province of Picardy organized a Catholic League. More extensive than smaller local anti-Protestant organizations that had sprung up in the 1560s, the Catholic League (despite an insincere oath of loyalty taken to the king) posed a threat not only to Huguenots but to the monarchy. It was led by the dashing Henry, duke of Guise (1550–1588), who was subsidized by Philip II of Spain, and vowed to fight until Protestantism was completely driven from France. But another military campaign against Protestants led to nothing more than a restatement of the conditions under which they could worship.

Henry III's reconciliation with the House of Guise did not last long. The death of the last of the king's brothers in 1584 made Henry of Navarre, a Protestant, heir to the throne. This was the Catholics' worst nightmare. The Catholic League threw its full support behind the aged, ambitious Catholic Cardinal de Bourbon, who was next in line after Henry of Navarre.

Henry of Navarre, later King Henry IV.

Henry of Navarre

Henry of Navarre (1553–1610) was born in the town of Pau on the edge of the Pyrenees Mountains, the son of Antoine of Bourbon, patriarch of the powerful Bourbon family. Henry inherited the keen intelligence of his mother, Jeanne d'Albret, and his father's indecisiveness. His mother was a committed Huguenot and raised Henry in that faith. When his father, who was notoriously unfaithful to his wife, sent her back to the southwest in 1562, Henry converted to Catholicism, his father's nominal religion. After his father's death in battle, Henry re-embraced Protestantism. Taken to the royal court as a hostage by Catherine de Medici, he was permitted to have Huguenot tutors. Among his friends at court were the future Henry III and Henry, duke of Guise.

Henry consulted a fortune teller, who predicted that he would one day be king of France. A member of the Parlement of Bordeaux described the precocious boy: "We have here the prince of Béarn . . . a charming youth. At thirteen years of age, he has all the riper qualities of eighteen or nineteen; he is agreeable, polite, obliging and behaves to everyone with an air so easy and engaging that wherever he is there is always a crowd. He mixes in conversation like a wise and prudent man, speaks always to the purpose . . . and never says more nor less than he ought." It was after Henry's wedding in Paris in August 1572 to Margaret, Catherine de Medici's daughter, that the Saint Bartholomew's Day Massacre occurred. Henry then was given the choice of embracing Catholicism or being executed. He chose the former. When the fighting temporarily ended, Henry had more time for his favorite pursuits—hunting and pursuing women.

The Huguenots had every reason to be wary of a young man who seemed to change faiths with the ease of someone ordering dinner not long after lunch. Furthermore, he seemed to have reconciled himself to the Saint Bartholomew's Day Massacre, counted the "fanatic" duke of Guise among his friends, had accompanied the Catholic army, albeit under guard, to the siege of La Rochelle, and had written the pope begging forgiveness for past misdeeds.

But having left Paris and the watchful eye of the Catholic dukes, Henry formally abjured Catholicism and took up residence as royal governor in the southwest, where Protestantism was strong. There he tried to steer a path between militant Catholics and Huguenots, and his endorsement of mutual religious toleration won wide approval. When Henry of Navarre became heir to the throne in 1584, an English diplomat reported optimistically that "all the good Frenchmen begin to cast their eyes upon him, and to try more and more to gain his favor."

The Catholic League rallied its forces, drawing its muscle from the artisans of Paris and other northern towns. In defiance of the king, it forced the Parlement of Paris to withdraw the toleration afforded the Huguenots. The Catholic League's goal was to put the Cardinal de Bourbon on the throne, although the duke of Guise wanted it for himself.

The struggle between the "three Henrys" now began in earnest. Henry (Valois) III first allied with Henry (Bourbon) of Navarre and with the duke of Montmorency against Henry, duke of Guise. The Guise family provocatively accused the king in 1585 of destroying the kingdom through inept rule and called for a rebellion that would bring the duke of Guise to the throne and drive Protestantism from the kingdom.

Henry III then switched partners, joining the duke of Guise against Henry of Navarre. The Treaty of Nemours (1585) between Catherine de Medici and Henry, duke of Guise, abrogated all edicts of religious toleration and turned over a number of towns to the Catholic League. Now the odd man out, Henry of Navarre prepared for a new war. He denounced Spanish meddling and in a quintessentially *politique* statement, promised "to rally around me . . . all true Frenchmen without regard to religion." Although he himself increasingly depended on German and Swiss mercenaries for his army and benefited from the intervention of a German Protestant force, Henry's denunciation of foreign influence was a shrewd piece of political propaganda aimed at moderate Catholics—the *politiques*—and the Catholic clergy. The Catholic League replied with a warning that French Catholics would suffer the fate of martyred English Catholics should Henry win.

In 1587, Henry of Navarre defeated the combined forces of the king and the Catholic League at Coutras, near Bordeaux. Here his defensive position and use of artillery and cavalry proved decisive. But instead of following up his surprising victory by pursuing the Catholic army, Henry hesitated and went back to hunting and making love. As a contemporary put it, "all the advantage of so famous a victory floated away like smoke in the wind."

That year, Queen Elizabeth I of England put to death Mary Stuart, the Catholic queen of Scots and the niece of the duke of Guise (see Chapter 5). Angered by Henry III's inability to prevent the execution of his niece, Guise, at the urging of the king of Spain, marched to Paris in 1588, where he and the Catholic League enjoyed great support. The Spanish king hoped to keep the French king from contemplating any possible assistance to England as the Spanish Armada sailed toward the English Channel. When Henry III sent troops to Paris to oppose Guise, the Parisian population rose in rebellion on May 12, 1588, stretching barricades throughout the city center. The king ordered his troops to withdraw. The "Day of Barricades" marked the victory of a council led by clergymen known as the *Seize,* or Sixteen, the number of neighborhoods in Paris.

For several years, the Sixteen had been energetically supporting the League, while denouncing the king, the Catholic *politiques,* and Huguenots with equal fervor. The hostility of the population of Paris convinced the king to accept Cardinal de Bourbon as his heir, Guise as his lieutenant-general, and to convoke the Estates-General (representatives of the provincial estates, which the monarch could summon in times of great crisis).

Later, in 1588, the delegates to the Estates-General, many of them members of the Catholic League, gathered in the Loire Valley town of Blois. Some of the written grievances (*cahiers des doléances*) submitted set the tone for what followed, that of Paris referring to the king as a "cancer . . . filled with filth and infectious putrefaction" and calling for "all heretics, whatever their quality, condition or estate, [to] be imprisoned and punished by being burned alive." By now, however, the English fleet had defeated Philip II's Armada in the Channel (see Chapter 5), and the nobles found Henry III less intimidated than they had anticipated. When Guise heard a rumor that the king was planning his assassination, he replied, "He does not dare." But Henry's bodyguards cut down Henry, duke of Guise, shortly before Christmas 1588 in the Château of Blois, as Catherine de Medici lay dying in a room underneath the bloody struggle that resulted in Guise's death. The Valois king had the Cardinal de Bourbon and other prominent members of the Catholic League arrested.

Guise's assassination drove the Catholic League to full-fledged revolt. The theologians at the Sorbonne declared that the people were no longer obliged to obey the Valois monarch, who had become a "tyrant." More than 300 towns, most of them in the north, now joined the "Holy Union" against the king. As Catholics prepared to fight Catholics, the—again—

Assassination of Henry, duke of Guise.

Protestant Henry of Navarre appealed for peace: "We have been mad, senseless and furious for four years. Is that not enough?"

Henry III was now forced to make an alliance of convenience with Henry of Navarre against the Catholic League. As their combined armies besieged Paris, a monk assassinated Henry III. The king's Swiss guards, who had not done a terribly good job protecting their king, threw themselves at the feet of Henry of Navarre, telling him, "Sire, you are now our king and master."

The Catholic League, however, had proclaimed Cardinal de Bourbon, whom Henry was holding in custody, to be king. Henry's forces defeated Catholic League armies twice in Normandy, in 1589 and in 1590. His able artillery and fearless cavalry carried the day against an army swollen by Spanish reinforcements. But once again Henry failed to take advantage of the situation his shrewd generalship had made possible. He dawdled before finally laying siege to starving Paris.

The arrival of a Spanish army from Flanders to provision Paris helped win Henry further support from moderate Catholics, who resented Spanish intervention that might prolong the siege. Fatigue began to overcome religious conviction. Henry also played on resentment at the involvement of the pope, too, in French affairs (Henry had been excommunicated in 1585 and, for good measure, a second time six years later). As Henry's army besieged Paris, Spanish troops defeated forces loyal to him in several provinces. Henry captured Chartres in April 1591, more for reasons of the heart—the family connections of one of his lovers—than for strategic reasons. The death of Cardinal de Bourbon led Philip II to proclaim the candidacy of the late Henry II's Spanish granddaughter as heir to the throne, and then to suggest that he might claim it himself. In the meantime, Henry's continued successes on the battlefield and conciliatory proclamations furthered his popularity.

Henry of Navarre, a man of changing colors, had another major surprise up his sleeve. In 1593, Henry astonished friend and foe alike by announcing that he would now abjure Protestantism. This move, however, more reflected his shrewd sense of politics than indecisiveness. Paris, as he put it, was worth a Mass, the price of the capital's obedience. Following his coronation as Henry IV at Chartres the following year, Paris surrendered after very little fighting. Henry's entry into his capital was a carefully orchestrated series of ceremonies that included the "cure" of hundreds of people afflicted with scrofula (a tuberculous condition) by the royal touch, a monarchical tradition in France and England that went back centuries. Henry nodded enthusiastically to the women who came to their windows to catch a glimpse of the first Bourbon king of France.

Catholic League forces gradually dispersed, one town after another pledging its loyalty to Henry, usually in return for payments. Henry's declaration of war on Spain in 1595 helped rally people to the monarchy. The

The entry of Henry IV into Paris, 1594.

pope lifted Henry's excommunication from the Church. Henry invaded Philip's territory of Burgundy, defeating his army. In 1598, the last Catholic League army capitulated. Henry, having secured the frontiers of his kingdom, signed the Treaty of Vervins with Philip II to end the war that neither side could afford to continue.

Restoring Stability to France

Henry IV reasoned that after years of civil war, "France and I both need to catch our breath." But bringing stability to France would be no easy matter. The wars of religion had worsened the plight of the poor. Disastrous harvests and epidemics in the 1590s compounded the misery. The wars of the Catholic League caused great damage and dislocated the economy in many parts of France. That both sides had indiscriminately minted coins compounded inflation.

Henry's emissaries gradually restored order by promising that "the Well-Loved," as he became known, would end injustices. Henry once said that he hoped to live long enough to see "a chicken in every pot." He did slightly reduce the direct tax, of which the peasants bore the brunt. Henry also rooted out some of the corruption in the farming of taxes, whereby government officials allowed ambitious middlemen to collect taxes in exchange for a share. But he shifted even more of the tax burden to the poor by raising indirect taxes.

Gradually Henry succeeded in putting the finances of the monarchy on firmer footing. In 1596, he convinced an Assembly of Notables to approve a supplementary tax. A new imposition (the *paulette*) permitted officeholders, through an annual payment to the throne, to assure that their office would remain in the hands of their heirs. The *paulette* gave the wealthiest nobles of the realm a greater stake in the monarchy. But while increasing royal revenue, it intensified the phenomenon of the venality of office (the purchase of offices and the noble titles that went with them).

Henry could rarely rest at ease. In 1602 and again in 1604, he uncovered plots against him formed by nobles in connivance with the Spanish monarchy. He survived nine assassination attempts and at least twenty-three assorted other plots against him. The first followed his expulsion of the Jesuits, whose pamphleteers had called for his assassination. Small wonder that he carried two loaded pistols in his belt and that some nervous soul tasted his food and drink before he did.

Henry restored monarchical prestige and authority. The "new monarchy," strengthened by Francis I, now stood on more solid ground. Much of Henry's success in achieving the political reconstruction of France can be credited to his arrogant minister of finance, Maximilien de Béthune, the baron and, as of 1604, the duke of Sully (1560–1641). Sully was the son of a prosperous Protestant family whose great wealth had earned ennoblement. His influence, deeply resented by many nobles, was such that he was the only male admitted to the king's bedchamber, where he received the day's instructions.

Sully established budgets and systematic bookkeeping, which helped him eliminate some needless expenses. The monarchy gradually began to pay off some international debts, including those owed to the English crown and the Swiss cantons, whose good will Henry needed to counter Spanish influence in the Alps. These repayments allowed Henry to contrast his honor in the realm of finances with that of the Spanish monarchy, whose periodic declarations of bankruptcy left creditors grasping at air.

In 1598, Henry's Edict of Nantes made Catholicism the official religion of France. But it also granted the nation's 2 million Protestants (in a population of about 18.5 million) freedom of conscience. Huguenots now had the right to worship at home, to hold religious services and establish schools in specified towns—almost all in the southwest and west—and to maintain a number of fortified towns, with garrisons and ministers paid by the state. The Edict of Nantes also established chambers in the provincial parlements, or law courts dominated by nobles, to judge the cases of Protestants (see Map 4.1).

MAP 4.1 WARS OF RELIGION IN FRANCE IN THE SIXTEENTH CENTURY France at the time of the Edict of Nantes, 1598. The map indicates Catholic League provinces, Huguenot provinces, and neutral provinces during the wars of religion, as well as Huguenot and Catholic League towns and battle sites during the wars.

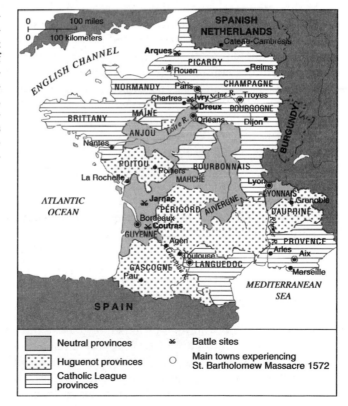

But careful to placate powerful sources of Catholic opposition, a series of secret decrees also promised Paris, Toulouse, and other staunchly Catholic towns that Protestant worship would be forbidden within their walls. The Edict of Nantes thus left the Protestants as something of a separate estate with specified privileges and rights, but still on the margin of French life. "What I have done is for the sake of peace," Henry stated emphatically. The former Catholic Leaguers howled in protest. By registering royal edicts, the parlements gave them the status of law. In this case, they only gradually and grudgingly registered the edict, which provided the Huguenots with more secure status than any other religious minority in Europe.

Many Huguenots, however, who found the Edict of Nantes unduly restrictive, distrusted the king who had abjured their religion on several occasions. Henry's foreign policy, which appeared pro-Protestant, supporting the Dutch rebels against Spain and certain German states against the Catholic Habsburgs, was, in fact, based on dynastic interests. But this support of Protestant rebels and princes made it impossible for Henry to consider further concessions to the Huguenots. Yet, the fact that Sully, a Protestant, rose to become the second most powerful man in France reassured some of them.

At the same time, the Catholic Reformation bore fruit in France. The Church benefited from a revival in organizational zeal and popularity. Henry allowed the Jesuits to return to France in 1604, a sign that religious tensions were ebbing, and he admitted several Italian religious orders.

With various would-be assassins trying to stab him, Henry had to think about an heir. He sought a papal annulment of his marriage to Margaret of Valois, whom he had not seen in eighteen years. While waiting, he prepared to marry one of his mistresses, but she died miscarrying their child. With the blessing of the Church, he then arranged to marry Marie de Medici (1573–1642), a distant relative of Catherine de Medici. This second marriage of convenience brought a sizable dowry that Henry used, in part, to pay off more international debts.

Henry's charismatic and somewhat contradictory personality has always attracted considerable interest. In contrast to the portraits he encouraged depicting him as Hercules or Apollo, or arrayed in a splendid white plume and a warrior's helmet, the king of France was extremely slovenly, sometimes wearing torn or ragged clothes. Henry gave off an odor as powerful as the air of his authority. He became renowned for his physical vigor on the battlefield and in his travels. He gambled large sums, with a notorious lack of success.

Although he knew nothing of music or poetry, and regularly fell asleep at the theater, Henry IV nonetheless was a patron of new architectural projects that added to the beauty of the city of Paris and imprinted his rule upon it. He oversaw the construction of the Great Gallery joining his residence in the Louvre Palace to the Tuileries in Paris. He ordered the construction of four quays facilitating the docking of boats along the Seine. He initiated the splendid Place Dauphine, ringed by buildings of elegant architecture on the west end of the island of Cité, at the point of which his equestrian statue now stands. And he orchestrated the construction of the Place Royale, with pavilions of symmetrical arcades, brick construction, and steeply inclining roofs in the northern architectural style. The new square lay close to the eastern edge of Paris, which was then near many noble residences.

Intelligent and well organized, Henry kept abreast of events throughout his vast kingdom. But he had little sense of protocol, often rushing out of the Louvre by himself as his guards scurried to catch up, once knocking down a messenger as he rushed out a side entrance. His wit was well known: when formally welcomed by a long-winded representative of the town of Amiens, who began "O most benign, greatest and most clement of kings," Henry interjected, "Add as well, the most tired of kings!" When a second spokesman began his official greeting, "Agesilaus, king of Sparta, Sire," Henry cut him short, "I too have heard of that Agesilaus, but he had eaten, and I have not."

Marie de Medici bore the constant burden of her husband's various infidelities and occasional bouts with gonorrhea. Henry produced six illegitimate children by three mistresses, to go with the three born to the queen. His nine offspring made up what he proudly referred to as his "herd." His ease was such that he formally introduced one of his mistresses to his wife, demanding that the latter repeat her curtsy so that she bow a bit lower, and the three dined together in what must have been an uncomfortable meal.

Statemaking

Henry IV laid the foundations for what would become the strongest power in seventeenth-century Europe. His reign was an exercise in early modern European statemaking as he reimposed royal authority throughout the realm. He made the monarchy more powerful by dispensing privilege, favors and, above all, money with a judiciousness that earned loyalty. Provincial governors represented the interests of the monarchy in the face of the privileges and resistance to taxes maintained by the provincial parlements and estates. The difficulties of extracting resources for the state were complicated by the division of the provinces into more peripheral "state provinces" (*pays d'état*) like Languedoc, Burgundy, and Provence, which had been recently added to the realm and retained more of their traditional privileges, and the "election provinces" (*pays d'élection*). In the former, the noble estates assessed and collected taxation; in the latter, royal officials assumed these functions. Henry was suspicious of any representative institutions, which he considered as threatening the exercise of royal authority. He never convoked the Estates-General after having done so in 1593.

Meanwhile, the nobles reaffirmed their own economic and social domination over their provinces. In 1609, Charles Loyseau, a lawyer, published a *Treatise on Orders and Simple Dignities* that portrayed French society as a hierarchy of orders, or three estates: the clergy, the nobility, and, lastly, everyone else. He portrayed the king as the guarantor of this organic society. Henry restored the hierarchy of social orders based upon rank and privilege while imposing his rule. But the boundaries between and within these estates were fairly fluid. A few newcomers even ascended into the highest rank of dukes and peers who stood above even the "nobles of the sword," the oldest and most powerful nobles traditionally called on by the monarchy to provide military support. The "nobles of the robe," while not a coherent or self-conscious group, were men who claimed noble status on the basis of high administrative and judicial office, for example in the parlements. Henry strengthened the social hierarchy by bolstering established institutions, including the parlements, the treasury, and universities, as well as, ultimately, the Catholic Church.

Conciliatory royal language began to disappear when it came to asking for money, however. Royal governors, whose influence had grown during the wars of the Catholic League, strengthened the monarchy at the expense of towns that prided themselves on their ancient privileges, further eroding their fiscal independence.

The royal privy council, some of whose members were chosen, like Sully, from the ranks of lesser nobles known for their competence and dedication, strengthened the effectiveness of state administration and foreign relations. The king personally oversaw this council, excluding troublesome nobles. Henry monitored the activities of his ambassadors and his court, whose 1,500 residents included the purveyors of perfume, of whom he might have made greater use.

Henry also took an intermittent interest in encouraging French manufacturing, particularly of silk and tapestries. To promote internal trade, the king encouraged investment in the construction of several canals linking navigable rivers. He was the first king to take an active interest in supporting a permanent French settlement in the New World, thereby increasing the prospects of French fishermen and trappers following Jacques Cartier's exploration of the St. Lawrence River in 1534. Samuel de Champlain founded the colony of Québec in 1608. This settlement became a base for further explorations by Champlain and those who followed him. Two years later, the first two French Jesuit missionaries arrived in what became known as New France.

On May 14, 1610, Henry set out from the Louvre in a carriage for Sully's residence, accompanied by horsemen and guards. The carriage became ensnared in traffic in central Paris. When some of the guards dashed forward to try to clear the way, a crazed monk named François Ravaillac jumped up to take revenge for the king's protection of Protestants. He stabbed the king three times, as Henry sat listening to a letter being read to him. Henry IV died before the carriage reached the Louvre.

Louis XIII and the Origins of Absolute Rule

Henry's sudden death left Marie de Medici, his widow, as regent for his young son, Louis XIII (ruled 1610–1643), who was eight years old at the time. Neither Philip III of Spain nor James I of England, nor any of the princes of the German states, were in a position to try to intervene in France on behalf of either Huguenots or Catholics. Marie put aside Henry's planned campaign against the Habsburgs and adopted a policy that considered Catholic powers to be friends.

Marie foiled several plots by nobles prepared against her in 1614–1616. The convocation of the Estates-General accentuated the eagerness of noble rivals to gain influence with the young king. One of them, Charles d'Albert, duke of Luynes, an expert falconer and flatterer who shared his passion for training hawks with the young king while using his position to enhance his family's fortune, convinced Louis to impose his own rule. The king ordered the murder of one of his mother's confidants; Louis then exiled his unpopular mother, hoping to restore calm. When a group of nobles took this as occasion to raise the standard of revolt, the king's army defeated them at Ponts-de-Cé near Angers in 1620. The royal army then defeated a revolt by Huguenot nobles in the southwest and west.

Emotionally, the stubborn, ill-tempered, and high-strung boy-king Louis XIII never really grew up. Throughout his life, he demonstrated the psychological burdens of having been regularly whipped as punishment, on his father's orders, on occasions when he was "stubborn or does something bad." His father's murder when he was young also marked him. As his father's body was carried up the stairs of the Louvre, the chubby eight-year-old had shouted, "Ha! If I had been there with my sword, I would have killed [the assassin]." Louis XIII's marriage to an Austrian princess began with a wedding-night fiasco that, whatever happened between the precocious young couple, led to a six-month period in which they did not even share a meal. Finally, things went better. After suffering several miscarriages, the queen produced an heir in 1638, but the royal couple was otherwise unhappy.

Louis XIII was intelligent, though not particularly interested in ideas. He preferred sketching and music, the latter calming him when he fell into a rage. He enjoyed hunting and winning at chess, once hurling the offending pieces at the head of a courtier who had the bad grace to checkmate him.

Louis could be modest and timid, a pious man who attended church every day. But he was invariably willful, ruthless, and cruel, lashing out savagely at his enemies; indeed, no other ruler of France had as many men

Cardinal Richelieu before the Sorbonne, which he founded.

executed as Louis XIII, including a number of nobles convicted of dueling, a practice that the king detested as symbolizing a possible threat to the royal monopoly on force and the possibility that nobles could raise private armies against the throne.

During Louis XIII's reign, Cardinal Armand Jean du Plessis de Richelieu (1585–1642) further centralized royal power, expanding the administrative authority and fiscal reach of the crown, dramatically increasing tax revenues. Richelieu's family, solidly entrenched in the west of France, had long served the monarchy in court, army, and church. Ordained bishop of Luçon, near the Protestant stronghold of La Rochelle, the gaunt, clever Richelieu staked his future on and won the patronage of the queen mother. He perfected the art of political survival during the court struggles of the next few years. Richelieu was a realist. His foreign and domestic policies reflected his *politique* approach to both. Although he was made a cardinal in 1622, he nonetheless always put reasons of state ahead of any consideration of religious principles.

In 1629, Richelieu prepared a long memorandum for his king. "If the King wants to make himself the most powerful monarch and the most highly esteemed prince in the world," he wrote, "he must consider before God, and examine carefully and secretly, with his faithful servants, what is needed in himself, and for the reform of the State. . . . [The Estates and the Parlements] which oppose the welfare of the kingdom by their pretended sovereignty must be humbled and disciplined. Absolute obedience to the King must be enforced upon great and small alike." Richelieu divided France into thirty-two districts (*généralités*), organizing and extending the king's authority. Officials called intendants governed each district, overseen by the king's council and ultimately responsible to the king himself.

In order to enhance the authority of the monarchy and the church, Richelieu turned his attention to the Huguenots. After forcing the surrender of insurgent Protestant forces at La Rochelle in 1628, he ordered the destruction of the Huguenot fortresses in the south and southwest, as well as the châteaux of other nobles whose loyalty he had reason to doubt.

During the Thirty Years' War (1618–1648), Louis XIII, influenced by Richelieu, reversed his mother's pro-Spanish foreign policy, returning to the traditional French position of opposition to the Habsburgs. The dynastic rivalry between the two powers proved greater than the fact that both kings were Catholic. Louis XIII thus surprised and outraged the Spanish king by joining England and the Dutch Republic, both Protestant powers, against the powerful Catholic Austrian Habsburgs during the Thirty Years' War. And in 1635, France declared war against Spain itself.

Richelieu's successes, however, did not stand well with his resentful enemies. His toleration of Huguenot worship drew the wrath of some Catholic nobles, as did continuing costly wars against the Catholic Habsburgs, which included French subsidies to Protestant Sweden. Revolts occurred in Dijon and Aix, both seats of provincial parlements, where local notables resented having to bow to the authority of royal officials.

One of the most conservative Catholic nobles, a royal minister, briefly turned the king against Richelieu. Marie de Medici, returned from brief disgrace, tried to convince her son to dismiss the cagey cardinal. The "Day of Dupes" (November 10, 1630) followed, which amounted to little more than a high-stakes family shouting match between Marie de Medici, Louis XIII, and Richelieu. Marie left thinking she had won the day, but awoke the next morning to find that the king had ordered her exile. The king's own brother led a second plot against Richelieu from 1641 to 1642, backed by the king of Spain.

After decades of religious wars, the assassination of Henry IV, and a fragile, temperamental young monarch around whom plots swirled, the monarchy of France had nonetheless been greatly strengthened. Louis XIII's sometimes decisive and brutal actions enhanced the reputation of the king who was known to many of his subjects as "The Just," whether fitting or not. A hypochondriac whose health was even worse than he feared, Louis XIII died of tuberculosis in 1643 at the age of forty-two. Philippe de Champagne's portrait of the king preserves his sad eyes and premature aging. But the man-child monarch had, with Richelieu, laid the foundations for absolute monarchical rule in France.

THE THIRTY YEARS' WAR (1618–1648)

In Central Europe, religious divisions led to the Thirty Years' War, a brutal conflict between the largely mercenary armies of Catholic and Protestant states that laid waste to the German states. Dynastic rivalries were never far from the stage, bringing the continental Great Powers into the fray.

When the war finally ended, the Treaty of Westphalia (1648) established a territorial and religious settlement that lasted until the French Revolution.

Factionalism in the Holy Roman Empire

The Holy Roman Empire was a loose confederation of approximately 1,000 German autonomous or semi-autonomous states. These states ranged in size from powerful Habsburg Austria to Hamburg, Lübeck, and other free cities in the north, and even smaller territories no more than a few square kilometers in size run by princes or bishops. It would have been almost impossible for a traveler to determine where one state stopped and another began had it not been for the frequent toll stations, which provided much of the revenue for each. The southwest German state of Swabia, for example, was divided between sixty-eight secular and forty ecclesiastical lords and included thirty-two free cities.

Geographic factors further complicated the political life of the German states. A few of the largest states included territories that were not contiguous. The Upper Palatinate lay squeezed between Bohemia and Bavaria; the Lower Palatinate lay far away in the Rhineland. The former was predominantly Lutheran, the latter Calvinist.

Since 1356, when the constitutional law of the Holy Roman Empire had been established, seven electors (four electoral princes and three archbishops) selected each new Holy Roman emperor. The empire's loose federal structure had a chancery to carry out foreign policy and negotiations with the various German princes. But only in confronting the threat of the Turks from the southeast did the German princes mount a consistent and relatively unified foreign policy.

Other institutions of the Holy Roman Empire also reflected the political complexity of Central Europe. An imperial Diet brought princes, nobles, and representatives of the town together when the emperor summoned them. An Imperial Court of Justice ruled on matters of importance to the empire. The Holy Roman Empire, once the most powerful force in Europe, had been weakened by its battles with the papacy in the thirteenth century. Yet, for some states the empire offered a balance between the desire for a figure of authority who could maintain law and order and continued political independence.

The Peace of Augsburg (1555), which ended the war between the Holy Roman Emperor Charles V and the Protestant German states, had stated that, with the exception of ecclesiastical states and the free cities, the religion of the ruler would be the religion of the land (*cuius regio, eius religio*). This formula, however, did not end religious rivalries, or the demands of religious minorities that rulers tolerate their beliefs. The Peace of Augsburg, in fact, reinforced German particularism. It also helped secularize the institutions of the Holy Roman emperor by recognizing the right of the German princes to determine the religion of their states.

The Origins of the Thirty Years' War

Rudolf II (1557–1612), king of Bohemia and Holy Roman emperor (he succeeded his father Maximilian II as Holy Roman emperor in 1576), wanted to launch a religious crusade against Protestantism. With that in mind, he closed Lutheran churches in 1578, reneging on an earlier promise to Bohemian nobles that he would tolerate the religion to which a good many of them had converted. Moreover, Rudolf's brother Archduke Ferdinand II (1578–1637) withdrew the religious toleration his father Maximilian II had granted in Inner Austria.

Rudolf's imperial army, which had been fighting the Turks on and off since 1593, had annexed Transylvania. The emperor moved against Protestants both there and in Hungary. But in 1605, when Rudolf's army undertook a campaign against the Turks in the Balkans, Protestants rebelled in both places. A Protestant army invaded Moravia, which lies east of Bohemia and north of Austria, close to the Habsburg capital of Vienna. In the meantime, Emperor Rudolf, only marginally competent on his best days (he was subject to depression and later to fits of insanity), lived as a recluse in his castle in Prague. His family convinced his brother Matthias (1557–1619) to act on Rudolf's behalf by making peace with the Hungarian and Transylvanian Protestants and with the Turks. This Peace of Vienna (1606) guaranteed religious freedom in Hungary. Matthias was then recognized as head of the Habsburgs and heir to Rudolf.

Rudolf II, Holy Roman emperor, surrounded by six electors. As king of Bohemia, he was the seventh elector.

Most everyone seemed pleased with the peace except poor Rudolf, who concluded that a murderous plague that was ravaging Bohemia was proof that God was displeased with the concessions he had been forced to grant Protestants. He denounced Matthias and Ferdinand for their accommodation with Protestants and with the Turkish "infidels." Matthias allied with the Protestant Hungarian noble Estates and marched against Rudolf, who surrendered. Rudolf ceded Hungary, Austria, and Moravia to Matthias in 1608, and Bohemia to him in 1611. Rudolf was forced to sign a "Letter of Majesty" in 1609 that granted Bohemians the right to choose between Catholicism, Lutheranism, or one of two groups of Hussites (see Chapter 3). Protestant churches, schools, and cemeteries were to be tolerated.

The decline in the effective authority of the Holy Roman emperor, after four centuries of power, contributed to the end of a period of relative peace in the German states. In the last decades of the sixteenth century, these states had become increasingly quarrelsome and militarized. "The dear old Holy Roman Empire," went one song, "How does it stay together?" Rulers of some member states began to undermine imperial political institutions by refusing to accept rulings by the Imperial Supreme Court and even to attend the occasional convocations of the Diet. "Imperial Military Circles," which were inter-state alliances responsible for defense of a number of states within the empire, had become moribund because of religious antagonisms between the member states.

For a time, the Catholic Reformation profited from acrimonious debates and even small wars between Lutherans and Calvinists. But increasingly Protestants put aside their differences, however substantial, in the face of Catholic determination to win back territories lost to Protestantism.

Acts of intolerance heated up religious rivalries. In 1606, in Donauwörth, a south German imperial free city in which Lutherans held the upper hand and Catholics enjoyed toleration, a riot began when Protestants tried to prevent Catholics from holding a procession. The following year, Duke Maximilian of Bavaria sent troops to assure Catholic domination. This angered Calvinist princes in the region, as well as some Lutheran sovereigns. The imperial Diet, convoked two years later, broke up in chaos when Holy Roman Emperor Rudolf II refused to increase Protestant representation in the Diet. The political crisis now spread further when some of the German Catholic states sought Spanish intervention in a dispute over princely succession in the small Catholic territories of Cleves-Jülich, which Henry IV of France threatened to invade. In 1609, Catholic German princes organized a Catholic League, headed by Maximilian of Bavaria. Six Protestant princes then signed a defensive alliance, the Protestant Union, against the Catholic League.

Matthias, who had been elected Holy Roman emperor in 1612, wanted to make the Catholic League an institution of Habsburg will. He also hoped to woo Lutherans from the Protestant Union, which was dominated by the Calvinists. But Matthias' obsession with Habsburg dynastic ambitions, his history of having fought with the Protestant Dutch rebels against Spain, and his opportunistic toleration of Lutheranism cost him the confidence of some Catholic princes. Archduke Ferdinand, ruler of Inner Austria, waited in the wings to lead a Catholic crusade against Protestantism. Ferdinand, who had inherited the throne of Hungary in 1617 and that of Bohemia in 1618, became Holy Roman emperor upon Matthias' death in 1619. Ferdinand was a pious man who had been educated by the Jesuits and whose every decision followed consultation with his confessor, who convinced him that he could save his soul only by launching a war of religion. In the meantime, Protestant resistance in Bohemia mobilized, seeking Protestant assistance from Transylvania and the Palatinate.

Conflict in Bohemia

In Bohemia, Ferdinand, backed by many nobles, imposed significant limitations on Protestant worship. In Prague, Calvinists and Lutherans, including university professors and students and members of literary societies, began to look outside of Bohemia for potential support from Protestant princes. Protestant leaders convoked an assembly of the Estates of Bohemia, citing rights specified by Rudolf's "Letter of Majesty" of 1609, and petitioned Emperor Matthias to order the withdrawal of the repressive dictates. Ferdinand ordered the assembly to disband.

Following the Defenestration of Prague in 1618, Protestant leaders established a provisional government in Bohemia. "This business of Bohemia is likely to put all Christendom in combustion," predicted the English ambassador to the Dutch capital of Amsterdam. It began a destructive war between Catholic and Protestant forces that would last thirty years, lay waste to many of the German states, and finally bring a religious and territorial settlement that would last for two centuries.

Bohemia rose in full revolt against not only the Church but the Habsburg dynasty as well. With almost no assistance from the nobles, the rebels turned to the Protestant Union, promising the Bohemian crown to Frederick, the young Calvinist elector of the Palatinate and the most important Protestant prince in Central Europe. But in their desperate quest for support, the Bohemian Protestants attempted to woo three other rulers with exactly the same promise. In 1619, the Estates offered Frederick the crown. He accepted, saying this was "a divine calling which I must not disobey."

The Protestant cause, like that of the Catholics, became increasingly internationalized and tied to dynastic considerations (see Map 4.2). After his brother died in 1619, the Catholic Archduke Ferdinand received enough votes from electors to become Holy Roman Emperor Ferdinand II. He then learned that Protestant rebels had refused to recognize his authority in Bohemia and had offered his throne to Frederick. Even more deter-

MAP 4.2 THE THIRTY YEARS' WAR, 1618–1648   Protestant and Catholic armies clashed in battles that ranged back and forth across Europe.

mined to drive Protestants from his realm but lacking an army, Ferdinand turned to outside help. The Catholic king of Spain agreed to send troops he could ill afford; the price of his intervention was the promise of the cession of the Rhineland state of the Lower Palatinate to Spain. The Catholic Maximilian I of Bavaria also sent an army, expecting to be rewarded for his trouble with the Upper Palatinate and with Frederick's title of elector in the Holy Roman Empire.

The Expansion of the Conflict

In the meantime, Protestant armies marched on Vienna, the Habsburg capital, and laid siege to it. The Catholic armies lifted this siege in 1619. Had news of this not been so slow to reach Spain, Philip III of Spain might have changed his mind about intervention. But with Spanish armies and monies already on the way, the internationalization of the Bohemian crisis had reached the point of no return. The Dutch could not provide assistance, as they were fighting for independence from Spain. Several of the German Protestant states also declined, fearing Catholic rebellions in their own lands.

During a short-lived truce brought about by the arrival of a seemingly neutral French army in 1620, the Catholic League raised a largely Bavarian army of 30,000 troops. Count Johannes von Tilly (1559–1632) commanded the Catholic forces. The depressed, indecisive count from Flanders managed to subdue Upper Austria and then defeated the main Protestant Union army at the brief but significant Battle of White Mountain, near Prague in November 1620. With the Catholic forces now holding Bohemia, Tilly's army then overran Silesia, Moravia, Austria, and part of the Upper Palatinate. The extent of the Catholic victory expanded the war, increasing the determination of the Catholic League to crush all Protestant resistance and, at the same time, of the Protestant forces to resist at all costs.

Frederick fought on, counting on help from France and other states who had reason to fear an expansion of Habsburg power in Central Europe. He also hoped to convince James I of England that a victory of the Catholic League would threaten Protestantism. But the English king had placed his hopes on the marriage of his son, Charles, to the sister of Philip IV of Spain (who had succeeded Philip III in 1621), an alliance that might bring about a diplomatic settlement to the complicated crisis (see Chapter 6). Again dynastic rivalries outweighed those of religion.

The war went on, with Tilly's army winning a series of small victories and a Spanish victory in 1622 over the Dutch at Jülich in the Rhineland eliminating any possibility of English armed assistance to Frederick through Holland. For the moment, Frederick's only effective force was a plundering mercenary horde in northeastern Germany. Tilly's victory over a Protestant army in 1623 and conquest of most of the Palatinate forced Frederick to abandon his claims to Bohemia's throne after having been king for all of one winter. But encouraged by the renewed possibility of English assistance, after James' plans for the marriage of his son to the Spanish princess fell through, Frederick turned north to Scandinavia for assistance.

The Danish Period

Christian IV (ruled 1588–1648), Protestant king of Denmark, had ambition and money, but not a great deal of sense. Also duke of the northern German state of Holstein, the gambling, hard-drinking Dane wanted to extend his influence and perhaps even territories in the northern German states. Frederick's difficulties seemed to offer the Danish sovereign the opportunity of a lifetime. In 1625, he led his troops into the northern German states, confident that the English and the Dutch, and perhaps the French as well, would rush to follow his leadership against the Habsburgs.

But King James I of England had died, succeeded by Charles I, who was even more beset than his father by opposition to his policies. Moreover, Louis XIII of France, who was besieging Protestants at La Rochelle in France, provided the Danes with only a modest subsidy to aid the fight against the Habsburgs. England and the Netherlands did no more than send some money and a few thousand soldiers to help the Danish king. Christian, essentially left to his own devices, was unaware of the approach of a large imperial army commanded by one of the most intriguing figures of the age of religious wars.

Albert Wallenstein (1583–1634) was a tall, gaunt Bohemian noble who, after marrying a wealthy widow, had risen to even greater fortune as a supplier of armies. Raised a Lutheran, he converted to Catholicism at age twenty and became the most powerful of the Catholic generals. The fact that a convert could rise to such a powerful position again reveals how a religious war evolved into not only a dynastic struggle between the rulers of France, Spain, and Austria, as well as Sweden and Denmark, but also into an unprincipled free-for-all in which mercenary soldiers of fortune played a major part. Wallenstein, an ardent student of astrology, was ambitious, ruthless, and possessed a violent temper. His abhorrence of noise was obsessive, and odd, for a military person. Because he detested the sound of barking or meowing, he sometimes ordered all dogs and cats killed upon arriving in a town, and forbade the townspeople and his soldiers from wearing heavy boots or spurs or anything else that would make noise. He alternated between extreme generosity and horrible cruelty, and was always accompanied by an executioner awaiting his master's command. Wallenstein, entrusted by Ferdinand with raising and commanding as army drawn from myriad nationalities fighting for the Catholic cause, marched north with 30,000 men.

Tilly defeated the Danes in 1626, aided by some of Wallenstein's mercenaries and King Christian's inept generalship. The Catholic army then marched to the Baltic coast and crossed into Denmark, devastating Jutland. But Wallenstein's successes engendered opposition within the Catholic states. Furthermore, his troops devastated the lands of friend and foe alike, extracting money and food, plundering, selling military commands to any buyer, including criminals.

Christian, who had spent much of his personal fortune and bankrupted his kingdom during this ill-fated excursion, signed a peace treaty in 1629 (the Treaty of Lübeck) whereby he withdrew from the war and gave up his claims in northern Germany. The treaty was less draconian than it might have been because the seemingly endless war was wearing heavily on some of the Catholic German states. They feared an expansion of Habsburg power, and some of them did not want to add Protestants to their domains.

The Danish king lost no territory in Denmark (although he did surrender his claims to several northern German bishoprics), but he agreed that he would never again interfere in the affairs of the Holy Roman emperor.

Ferdinand II now implemented measures against Protestants without convoking the imperial Diet. He expelled from Bohemia Calvinist and Lutheran ministers and nobles who refused to convert to Catholicism and ennobled anyone he wanted, including foreigners, as a means of assuring Catholic domination. He confiscated the property of nobles suspected of participating in any phase of the Protestant rebellion. With Frederick's Palatinate electorship now transferred to Maximilian I of Bavaria, the Habsburgs could count on the fact that a majority of the electors were Catholic princes. Captured Habsburg dispatches in 1628 made clear that Ferdinand sought to destroy the freedom of the Protestant Hanseatic cities in the north in the interest of expanding the Habsburg domains. These revelations alarmed Louis XIII of France.

Ferdinand found that it was not easy to impose Catholicism in territories where it had not been practiced for decades. In the Upper Palatinate, the first priests who came to celebrate Mass there were unable to find a chalice. Until the 1640s, half of the parishes in Bohemia were without clergy. Italian priests brought to Upper Austria could not be understood by their parishioners, some of whom rebelled against their authority and were executed on the emperor's command. The Edict of Restitution (1629) allowed Lutherans—but not Calvinists, who were few in number in the German states except in the Palatinate—to practice their religion in certain cities, but ordered them to return all monasteries and convents acquired

Protestant caricature showing two devils vomiting parish priests and Jesuits into Augsburg, which was forcibly converted to Catholicism in 1629.

after 1552, when signatories of the Peace of Augsburg had first gathered. Because the Edict of Restitution also gave rulers the right to enforce the practice of their religion within their territories, the war went on.

The Swedish Interlude

In the meantime, England, the Dutch Republic, the northern German state of Brandenburg, and the Palatinate asked the Lutheran King Gustavus Adolphus (ruled 1611–1632) of Sweden, a kingdom of barely a million inhabitants, to intervene on the Protestant side. The possibility of expanding Swedish territory was more than Gustavus, who had an adventurer's disposition, could resist.

Gustavus, the "Lion of the North," who survived shipwreck at the age of five, had been tutored in the art of war by mercenary soldiers. He also played the flute, composed poetry, and conversed in ten languages. The Dutch ambassador described him as "slender of figure, well set up, with rather a pale complexion, a long-shaped face, fair hair, and a pointed beard which here and there runs into a tawny color." Gustavus retained, as did a disproportionate number of rulers in his century, a violent temper. Once, coming upon two stolen cows outside an officer's tent, he dragged the thief by the ear to the executioner. His courage was legendary; he barely paused as cannonballs exploded nearby and as his horses were shot out from under him or fell through the ice.

Gustavus, influenced by an appreciation of Roman military tactics, formed his battle lines thinner—about six men deep—than those of rival commanders. This allowed battle lines to be more widely spread out; the king personally demonstrated to his men the proper way of firing in such a formation. Gustavus organized his army into brigades of four squadrons with nine cannon to protect them, sending the unit into battle in an arrow-shaped formation. Superior artillery served his cause well, hurling larger shot further and more accurately than that of his enemies.

The dashing young Swedish king subdued Catholic Poland with his army of about 70,000 men. Swedish intervention and the continuing woes of Spain, at war in the Alps, Italy, and the Netherlands, now gave Protestants reason for hope. After defeating a combined Polish and Habsburg army in 1629, Swedish troops occupied Pomerania along the Baltic Sea.

In 1630, sure of a Catholic majority, Emperor Ferdinand convoked the imperial electors to recognize his son as his heir. He also wanted them to support his promise to aid Spain against the Dutch in exchange for Spanish assistance against the Protestant armies. But the electors of Saxony and Brandenburg, both Protestants, refused even to attend the gathering. Catholic electors demanded that the powerful Wallenstein be dismissed; even the king of Spain feared the general's powerful ragtag army. Ferdinand thereby dismissed the one man whose accomplishments and influence might have enabled the Habsburg monarchy to master all of the German states.

King Gustavus Adolphus of Sweden in battle.

Despite a sizable subsidy from the king of France, Gustavus Adolphus enjoyed only the support of several tiny Protestant states. Some Lutheran German states still hoped to receive territorial concessions from the Habsburgs. The Catholic dynasty preferred Lutherans to Calvinists, viewing the latter as more radical reformers. Ferdinand now sent Tilly to stop the invading Swedes. He besieged the Protestant city of Magdeburg in Brandenburg, forcing its surrender in 1631. The subsequent massacre of the population and accompanying pillage had a similar effect as the Defenestration of Prague; the story of the atrocities spread across Europe. Protestant Brandenburg and Saxony now allied with Sweden.

That same year, the combined Protestant forces under Gustavus Adolphus defeated Tilly's imperial Catholic army at Breitenfeld near Leipzig. The Swedish army, swollen by German mercenaries, then marched through the northern German states, easily reversing Habsburg gains over the previous twelve years.

The expansion of Swedish power generated anxiety among both Protestant and Catholic states. Louis XIII now worried about the further expansion of Swedish power, which it had helped finance. In Bavaria, the Swedes defeated Tilly, who was killed in battle (1632). The rout of the Catholic imperial forces seemed complete. Spain, its interests spread too far afield in Europe and the Americas, could not then afford to help. The plague prevented another Catholic army from being raised in Italy; even the pope begged off a request for help by complaining that the eruption of Mount Vesuvius was preventing the collection of taxes. Upon learning that the Swedes had taken yet another city, an imperial official wrote, "We cry 'Help, Help!', but there is nobody there!"

In April 1632, Ferdinand turned once again to Wallenstein to save the Catholic cause, the latter agreeing to raise a new imperial army in return for almost unlimited authority over it. Wallenstein reconquered Silesia and Bohemia. Against him, Gustavus led the largest army (175,000) that had ever been under a single command in Europe. Although reason dictated that the Swedish army should dig in for the winter of 1632, Gustavus took a chance by attacking Wallenstein in the fog at Lützen in Saxony in November. The two sides fought to a bloody draw, but a draw amounted to a Catholic victory. Gustavus fell dead in the battle, facedown in the mud, shot in the arm, back, and head.

Wallenstein's days also were numbered. His new army had accomplished little, and was now living off the land in Central Europe, engendering peasant resistance. Furthermore, Wallenstein, who was ill, demanded command of a Spanish army that had subsequently arrived to help the Catholic forces. In the meantime, it became known that Wallenstein had considered joining Gustavus after the Battle of Breitenfeld in 1631, and that he was offering his services to both France and the German Protestants. Ferdinand dismissed Wallenstein for the final time, and then ordered his murder. In February 1634, an Irish mercenary crept into Wallenstein's room, speared him, wrapped his body in a rug, and hauled it down the stairs for all to see.

With the aid of the remnants of Wallenstein's forces, the Spanish army defeated the combined Swedish and German Protestant army in 1634 in the southern German state of Swabia. The elector of Saxony abandoned the Protestant struggle, making peace in 1635 with Ferdinand. One by

The assassination of Wallenstein, 1634.

one, other Protestant princes also left the war. The Catholic forces now held the upper hand.

The Armies of the Thirty Years' War

The Thirty Years' War was certainly one of the cruelest episodes in the history of warfare. A contemporary described the horror of the seemingly endless brutalities that afflicted Central Europe: "[The soldiers] stretched out a hired man flat on the ground, stuck a wooden wedge in his mouth to keep it open, and emptied a milk bucket full of stinking manure droppings down his throat—they called it a Swedish cocktail. . . . Then they used thumb-screws, which they cleverly made out of their pistols, to torture the peasants. . . . They put one of the captured hayseeds in the bakeoven and lighted a fire in it. . . . I can't say much about the captured wives, hired girls, and daughters because the soldiers did not let me watch their doings. But I do remember hearing pitiful screams in various dark corners."

Several factors may have contributed to the barbarity of soldiers during the Thirty Years' War. Mercenaries and volunteers were usually fighting far from home, knowing they had to live off the land to survive. Strident propaganda against other religions may have contributed to the brutality. In response, Gustavus Adolphus and other leaders, however, imposed harsh penalties, including execution, for atrocities, not wanting to so frighten the local population that ordinary channels of provisioning the army would disappear.

During the Thirty Years' War, at least a million men took arms. The size of the armies was enormous for the time. Even Sweden, where there was no fighting, felt the impact of the death of at least 50,000 soldiers between 1621 and 1632 from battle wounds and, more often, disease. Yet, considering the number of troops engaged in the long war, relatively few soldiers perished in battle, particularly when compared to those who succumbed to illness and to civilians who died at the hands of marauding troops. Armies came and went through the German states, Catholic and Protestant, speaking many languages, taking what they wanted, burning and looting. Marburg was occupied eleven different times. Atrocity followed atrocity.

The armies themselves remained ragtag forces, lacking discipline and accompanied by, in some cases, the families of soldiers. Given the practice of armies living off the land, the safest place was in the train of an army. The presence of large numbers of women (including many prostitutes) and children as camp followers may have contributed to the length of the war, making life in the army seem more normal for soldiers.

Although Gustavus ordered that troops "provide themselves with proper attire instead of their long smocks and peasant attire" so that people would judge them well, the reality was quite the opposite. Soldiers, for the most part, wore what they could find. Some, if they were lucky, had leather clothes, carried rain cloaks against the damp German climate, and wore

Soldiers pillaging a farmhouse during the Thirty Years' War. Note the farmer being tortured over his hearth to reveal where he has hidden money, while other soldiers rape the women and steal the food.

felt hats. Some Habsburg troops sported uniforms of pale gray, at least at the beginning of a campaign. As the months passed, and uniforms disintegrated, soldiers were forced to disrobe the dead, friend and foe alike, or to steal from civilians. At best, soldiers wore symbols indicating their regiment and fought behind banners bearing the colors of the army—thus the expression "show your colors." The Swedes wore a yellow band around their hats. The imperial forces placed red symbols in their hats, plumes, or sashes if they could find them.

Drawn from a bewildering number of nationalities, most armies also lacked a common language. The Habsburg army included Saxons, Bavarians, Westphalians, Austrians; Maximilian's Bavarian army counted Germans, Italians, Poles, Slovenes, Croats, Greeks, Hungarians, Burgundians, French, Czechs, Spaniards, Scots, Irish, and Turks.

Some soldiers may have joined regiments because they were searching for adventure; others joined out of religious conviction. Yet, a multitude of soldiers fought against armies of their own religion. Some states and armies changed sides when a better opportunity arose. Army recruiters gave religion not the slightest thought in their search for soldiers to fill quotas for which they were being handsomely paid. In any case, recruits on both sides were attracted by the strong possibility that they would be better clothed and fed—bread, meat, lots of beer, and occasionally some butter and cheese—than they were at the time they joined up.

The Wars of Religion and Dynastic Struggles (1635–1648)

Between 1635 and 1648, what had begun as a religious war became a dynastic struggle between two Catholic states, France and Habsburg Austria, the former allied with Sweden, the latter with Spain. France declared war on Philip IV of Spain in 1635. Richelieu had planned for the struggle for some time, hoping to force Habsburg armies away from the borders of France. He took as a pretext the Spanish arrest of a French ally, the elector of Trier. Alliances with the Dutch Republic and Sweden had prepared the way, as did reassurances given by neighboring Savoy and Lorraine, and by French protectorates in Alsace.

The French incursions into the Netherlands and the southern German states did not go well. Louis XIII's army found itself short on capable commanders and battle-experienced troops, largely because France was already fighting in Italy, the Pyrenees, the Netherlands, and the northern German states. But France's involvement, like that of Sweden before it, did provide the Protestant states with some breathing room. French forces joined the Swedish army, helping defeat the imperial army in Saxony.

The wars went on. When the pope called for representatives of the Catholic and Protestant states to assemble in Cologne for a peace congress in 1636, no one showed up. Four years later, another combined French and Swedish force defeated the Habsburg army. Maximilian I of Bavaria then sought a separate peace with France. Devastating Spanish defeats in northern France in 1643, as well as in the Netherlands and the Pyrenees, and the outbreak of rebellions inside Spain, left the Austrian Habsburgs with no choice but to make peace.

At the same time, unrest in France, including plots against Richelieu, and the English Civil War, which began in 1642, served to warn other rulers of the dangers that continued instability could bring. The Swedish population was tiring of distant battles that brought home nothing but news of casualties. In the German states, calls for peace echoed in music, plays, marketplace, and song. Lutheran ministers, in particular, began to inveigh against the war from the pulpit. Among the rulers of the great powers, only Louis XIII, hoping to help further diminish his Habsburg rival's power, wanted the war to go on. He helped subsidize an invasion of Hungary by Transylvanian Protestants in 1644. As Swedish and Transylvanian forces prepared to besiege the imperial capital of Vienna, Ferdinand III (ruled 1637–1657), who had succeeded his father, concluded a peace treaty with the prince of Transylvania. The Holy Roman emperor promised to tolerate Protestantism in Hungary. After Habsburg armies suffered further defeats in 1645, Ferdinand realized that he had to make peace and offered an amnesty to princes within the empire who had fought against him.

The preliminaries for a general peace agreement had begun in 1643 and dragged on even as a Franco-Swedish army drove the imperial army out of the Rhineland and Bavaria in 1647. Following another French victory early in 1648, only the outbreak of the Fronde, a rebellion of nobles against the king's authority in France, forced the young Louis XIV to seek peace.

The Treaty of Westphalia (1648)

The Treaty of Westphalia was unlike any previous peace settlement in history, which had invariably been between two or three states, rarely more. Its framers believed that they could restore international stability and diplomatic process in a Europe torn by anarchy by eliminating religious divisions as a cause of conflict. The treaty proved almost as complicated as the Thirty Years' War itself. Two hundred heads of state converged in Westphalia. Thousands of diplomats and other officials shuttled back and forth between two towns. Letters took ten to twelve days to reach the courts of Paris and Vienna, at least twenty to Stockholm, and a month to arrive in Madrid. In the meantime, the French tried to delay any treaty, hoping to force Spain to surrender. In the summer of 1648, the Swedes reoccupied Bohemia, hoping to win a larger indemnity and toleration for the Lutherans. When by the separate Treaty of Münster Spain finally formally recognized the *fait accompli* of Dutch independence, the Spanish Army of Flanders fought against France in a last-ditch effort to help Ferdinand III. In August 1648, a French army defeated a Spanish force a month after the Swedes had captured part of Prague. His back to the wall, Ferdinand signed the peace treaty, finally concluded on October 24, 1648.

The Treaty of Westphalia did not end the war between Spain and France, but it did end the wars of the German states. Sweden absorbed West Pomerania and the bishoprics of Verden and Bremen on the North Sea (see Map 4.3). France, by an agreement signed two years earlier, annexed the frontier towns of Metz, Toul, and Verdun, and parts of Alsace. Maximilian I of Bavaria kept the Upper Palatinate, and therefore the status of elector. Frederick's Protestant son ended up with the Lower, or Rhine Palatinate, and was restored to the status of elector. With this addition of an elector, eight votes would now be necessary to elect the Holy Roman emperor.

With minor exceptions, the territorial settlement reached in Westphalia remained in place until the French Revolution. For the most part, the treaty ended wars of religion in early modern Europe. The Treaty of Westphalia reinforced the strong autonomous traditions of the German states, which emerged from the long nightmare with more independence from the Holy Roman Empire, which was considerably weakened. Member states thereafter could carry out their own foreign policy, though they could not form alliances against the empire. The Habsburg dynasty's dream of forging a centralized empire of states fully obedient to the emperor's will had failed, although the emperor emerged from the wars with more control over most of Austria. Bohemia lost its independence. Bohemian Protestant landowners recovered neither their lands nor their religious freedom.

By the Treaty of Westphalia, German Calvinists gained the same rights as those previously granted to Lutherans. The settlement granted religious

MAP 4.3 EUROPE AFTER THE TREATY OF WESTPHALIA, 1648 The treaty ended the Thirty Years' War.

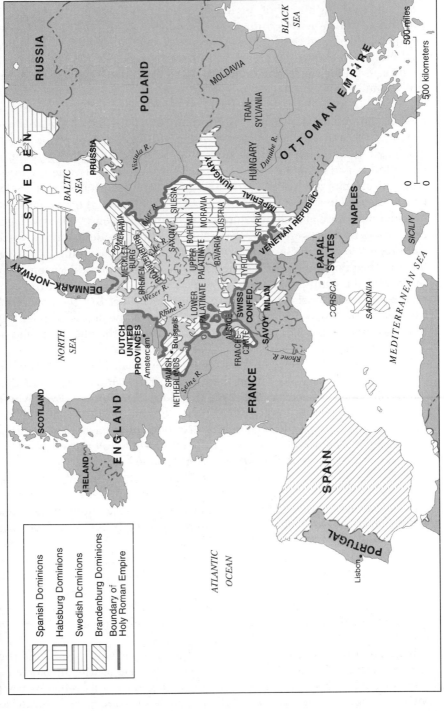

toleration where it had existed in 1624. But it also confirmed the Peace of Augsburg's establishment of territorial churches—Catholic, Lutheran, or Calvinist—still to be determined by the religion of the ruler. Sects were often forbidden, and their followers were persecuted. Generally speaking, Lutheranism remained dominant in the northern half of the Holy Roman Empire, Catholicism in the southern half, with many Calvinists in the Rhineland.

Before his death in battle, Gustavus Adolphus noted "all the wars of Europe are now blended into one." More than 200 states of varying sizes had fought in the war. The devastation brought by thirty years of war is simply incalculable. Catholic Mainz, occupied by the Swedes, lost 25 percent of its buildings and 40 percent of its population. In four years, the predominantly Protestant duchy of Württemberg lost three-quarters of its population while occupied by imperial troops. Almost 90 percent of the farms of Mecklenburg were abandoned during the course of the war. Many villages in Central Europe were now uninhabited. Although devastation varied from region to region, German cities lost a third and the countryside two-fifths of their population during the Thirty Years' War. Central Europe, like the rest of the continent, may have already been suffering from the economic and social crisis that had begun in the 1590s. But the wars contributed to the huge decline of the population of the states of the Holy Roman Empire from 20 to 16 million people during the ghastly period of the wars of religion.

A year before the Treaty of Westphalia, a Swabian family reflected on the Thirty Years' War when one of them wrote in their Bible: "They say that the terrible war is now over. But there is still no sign of peace. Everywhere there is envy, hatred and greed; that's what the war has taught us. . . . We live like animals, eating bark and grass. No one could have imagined that anything like this would happen to us. Many people say there is no God . . . but we still believe that God has not abandoned us."

War was not alone in taking lives: epidemics, the worst of which was the bubonic plague, and other diseases, including influenza and typhus, also took fearsome tolls. This was chiefly so in towns, which were often clogged with starving and therefore more vulnerable refugees from the fighting and marauding. The flight of many peasants from their land reduced agricultural productivity. Relatively little fighting took place in the northwestern German states, so there, at least, less devastation occurred. On the other hand, Mecklenburg and Pomerania, among other states that endured considerable fighting and the coming and going of armies, lost about half of their populations. It would be decades before the German states recovered from the Thirty Years' War.

If much of the religious settlement of the Treaty of Westphalia and the reinforcement of German particularism would prove enduring, dynastic rivalries were hardly at an end. France had emerged from its religious wars with a stronger monarchy; Louis XIII had made his state more centralized

Seventeenth-century Dutch allegory of peasant impoverishment. His home ravished by war and weighed down by the needs of his family, this man wandered the countryside, seeking only to survive.

and powerful. France's rivals, too, would extend their authority within their own states. In the mid-seventeeth century, Europe would enter the era of monarchical absolutism. The most powerful European states, above all Louis XIV's France, would enter a period of aggressive territorial expansion. Dynastic wars would help shape the European experience from the mid-seventeenth century to the French Revolution of 1789.

PART TWO

STATEMAKING

During the last half of the fifteenth century, the balance of economic and political power in Europe began to shift away from the Mediterranean region and the Italian city-states. The discovery and then colonization of the Americas contributed greatly to the development of the Atlantic economy, adding to the strength of Spain and England, transporting their rivalry across the Atlantic Ocean. The surprising English naval victory over the Spanish Armada in 1588 symbolized the subsequent shift in power from Southern to Northern Europe.

In the seventeenth century, when aggressive European monarchs were running roughshod over noble prerogatives and town privileges, England and the Dutch Republic maintained representative government. The English Civil War led to the defeat and execution of the king in 1649, the fall of the monarchy, and in 1688, to the "Glorious Revolution," which affirmed the civil liberties of English people and the rights of Parliament. In the largely Protestant Netherlands, which earned its independence after a protracted struggle against Catholic Spain, the prosperous merchants retained a republican form of government and helped generate the golden age of Dutch culture. In contrast, many European rulers relentlessly extended their power between 1650 and 1750, becoming absolute rulers. In principle, they were above all challenge from within the state itself, affecting the lives of more people than ever before through taxation, military service, and the royal quest for religious orthodoxy.

CHAPTER 5

THE RISE OF THE ATLANTIC ECONOMY: SPAIN AND ENGLAND

Protestant England and Catholic Spain, opposed in religion, commerce, and alliances, drifted toward a war neither could afford. In 1585, England went to war with Spain. In July 1588, after three years of preparation, the Spanish Armada, 130 ships and 30,000 men strong, sailed through the English Channel. King Philip II of Spain had ordered the duke of Medina Sidonia, the king's Captain-General of the Ocean Sea, to meet up with Spanish forces waiting in Flanders for a planned invasion of England. The Armada's commander was an austere aristocrat of great wealth and good sense but with no experience in battle and little idea of how his enormous fleet might meet up with the Spanish army.

On July 30, English watchers on the cliffs above the English Channel first caught sight of the supposedly invincible Spanish fleet. On the night of August 7, the English fleet attacked Philip II's Armada in battles along the English coast. After the Armada anchored near Calais, the English sent ships set on fire against the Armada, which caused the Spanish ships to break their tight tactical formation. With the help of strong winds, the English then pinned the Spanish ships against the shore, and destroyed six Spanish ships in the longest and most intense artillery battle that had yet occurred at sea, much of it at such close range that the sailors could hurl insults at each other. Superior English cannon, shot, and gunners took their toll on the Armada. More than 1,000 Spaniards died during the long battle that day. The captain of one ship that had failed to answer the flagship's call for help was hanged from a yardarm, and his body was hauled from ship to ship to reestablish discipline.

The English ships failed to follow up their advantage, however, letting the fighting Spanish galleons escape. The rough winds of the Channel carried the Spanish ships away from the dangerous Flemish shoals toward the

The English defeat of the Spanish Armada, 1588.

North Sea and a long, northern voyage up to the straits between the Orkney and Shetland Islands, in order to head back to the safety of Spanish ports. More than 30 Spanish ships sank in gales off the western coasts of Scotland and Ireland. When some of the ships of the Armada limped into port in Spain, Medina Sidonia wrote King Philip II, "I am unable to describe to Your Majesty the misfortunes and miseries that have befallen us, because they are the worst that have been known on any voyage; and some of the ships that put into this port have spent the last fourteen days without a single drop of water." Of the 130 ships that had sailed against England, only 60 could now be accounted for. At least a third had been sunk or wrecked, and many others were severely damaged.

Victory over the Spanish Armada accentuated England's rise to international dominance, enormously boosting English self-confidence. With English armies crushing an Irish rebellion in 1595, fears of an effective Irish alliance with Catholic Spain ended. Despite the defeat of the Spanish Armada, however, Philip did not make peace with England, and the war between the two nations dragged on until 1604. The surprising English naval victory over the Spanish Armada symbolized a shift in power from Southern to Northern Europe, although Spain remained militarily stronger until the 1630s.

ECONOMIC EXPANSION

The rise of England and Spain must be seen in the context of the sixteenth-century expansion of the European economy. By 1450, the European population had begun to recover slowly from the Black Death, the murderous plague that had swept the continent a century earlier. In general, the population continued to rise until the mid-seventeenth century, when religious and dynastic wars and new plagues led to such devastation that the period has become known as "the age of crisis." These cataclysms particularly struck Central Europe. But the Mediterranean region, too, suffered population decline.

During the 1600s, the commercial and manufacturing center of Europe shifted from the Mediterranean to Northwestern Europe. By 1700, Venice which alone among the Italian city-states had managed to retain significant trade links with Asia, had become a virtual backwater because it had failed to adapt to the global economy that was expanding across the Atlantic Ocean to the Americas. Spain, then France, England, and (after its long, successful war of independence from Spain) the Dutch United Provinces emerged as powers in the late sixteenth century as they explored new trade routes to Asia.

Spain's preeminence did not survive the end of the seventeenth-century economic crisis, however. Its merchants lacked the flexibility shown by the English and Dutch to adjust to varying demand for colonial products such as pepper and to create new trading opportunities. Furthermore, merchants in Amsterdam and London, not those in the Spanish city of Seville, expanded trade by using innovative commercial techniques. Spanish merchants proved less able than their northern rivals to lower costs of transportation from the New World. In contrast, English textile merchants found new markets in Spain and the Mediterranean for their cloth, which they could produce less expensively.

Increased Agricultural Productivity

Populations cannot grow unless the rural economy can produce enough additional food to feed more people. During the sixteenth century, farmers brought more land into cultivation at the expense of forests and fens (marsh lands) in order to supply a growing population. Moreover, Dutch land reclamation in the Netherlands in the sixteenth and seventeenth centuries provides the most spectacular example of the expansion of farm land; the Dutch reclaimed more than 36,000 acres between 1590 and 1615 alone. Modest agricultural progress was, however, limited to Western Europe. In Russia and Eastern Europe, hundreds of thousands of serfs who were legally bound to the land labored to produce enough grain to feed the masses of population and to generate a surplus that their lords could sell to Western European traders.

Much of the potential for European economic development lay in what at first glance would seem to have been only sleepy villages. Such villages, however, generally lay in regions of relatively advanced agricultural production, permitting not only the survival of peasants but the accumulation of an agricultural surplus for investment. They had access to urban merchants, markets, and trade routes.

Rural industry was an intrinsic part of the expansion of industry. Although at the end of the seventeenth century one textile enterprise in France brought some 1,700 workers together in the same place, woolens and textile manufacturers, in particular, utilized rural cottage (domestic) production, which took advantage of cheap and plentiful rural labor. In the German states, the ravages of the Thirty Years' War further moved textile production into the countryside. Members of poor peasant families spun or wove cloth and linens at home for scant remuneration in an attempt to supplement meager family income. Organizational change within industry remained far more important than technological innovation in the growth of manufacturing. This was also true in the growth of state-sponsored industry—for example, arms production and naval shipbuilding.

Expansion of Trade

More extended trading networks helped develop Europe's economy. English and Dutch ships carrying rye from the Baltic states reached England, the Netherlands, Spain, and Portugal. Population growth generated an expansion of small-scale manufacturing, particularly handicrafts, textiles, and metallurgy in England, Flanders, parts of northern Italy, the southwestern German states, and in some of Spain. Only iron smelting and mining required marshaling a significant amount of capital.

The development of banking and other financial services contributed to the expansion of trade. By the middle of the sixteenth century, financiers and traders commonly accepted bills of exchange in place of gold or silver or other goods. Bills of exchange, which had their origins in medieval Italy, were promissory notes that could be sold to third parties. In this way, they provided credit. At mid-century, an Antwerp financier only slightly exaggerated when he claimed, "One can no more trade without bills of exchange than sail without water." Merchants no longer had to carry gold and silver over long, and in many places, dangerous journeys, nor did they have to identify and assess the approximate value of a variety of coins issued by mints here and there. Thus, an Amsterdam merchant who purchased soap from a counterpart in Marseille could go to an exchanger and pay him the equivalent sum in guilders, the Dutch currency. The exchanger would then send a bill of exchange to a colleague in Marseille, authorizing him to pay the Marseille merchant in his own currency after the actual exchange of goods had taken place.

Bills of exchange contributed to the development of banks, as men dealing in bills and currency began to provide loans, profiting from the interest attached to them. Not until the eighteenth century, however, did banks such as the Bank of Amsterdam and the Bank of England begin to provide capital for business investment. Their principal function was to provide funds for the state.

The money changer's office.

The rapid expansion in international trade increased the role of merchant capitalists, particularly in Northern Europe, in the emerging global economy. The infusion of capital stemmed largely from gold and silver brought by Spanish vessels from the Americas. This capital financed the production of goods, storage, trade, and even credit across Europe and overseas. Moreover, an increased credit supply was generated by investments and loans by bankers and wealthy merchants to states and by joint-stock partnerships, an English innovation (the first major company beginning in 1600). Unlike short-term financial cooperation between investors for a single commercial undertaking, joint-stock companies provided a permanent funding of capital by drawing on the investments of merchants and other investors who purchased shares in the company.

Amsterdam and then London emerged as the banking and trading centers of Europe, although Italian banking houses in Genoa retained their financial role in trading cities like Lyon and Liège. Merchant towns in Castile, Catalonia, Italy, Holland, and England, as well as the Hanseatic cities of northern Germany, each had their own merchant dynasties.

The Global Economy

Trade with the Americas and Asia provided new outlets for European goods, as well as bringing from the New World products such as tomatoes, corn, bell peppers, rum, and spices to those who could afford them. The construction of larger ships, weighing as much as eighty tons, a size that would not be surpassed until the middle of the nineteenth century, facilitated oceangoing trade. From seaports, trade continued along the major rivers—principally the Rhine, which flows from Switzerland to the Baltic Sea; the Danube in Central Europe; the Seine, which links Paris to the English Channel; and the Rhône, which carries boat traffic from Lyon to the Mediterranean. The Scheldt River estuary led from the North Sea to the powerful trading and manufacturing city of Antwerp, which had a population of more than 100,000 people. There, vast quantities of English and Flemish goods were traded for goods from the German and Italian states. Land trade routes also remained important—for example, the route from Marseille to northern France and the Netherlands, that from Valencia on the Mediterranean to Madrid and Toledo in the heart of Castile, and that from Piedmont to the western German states and Holland.

England and the Dutch Netherlands, as well as France, benefited from a new and more complex colonial trading system. In each case, specially chartered East Indian trading companies helped mobilize investment capital and, enjoying monopolies issued to them by each state, set out to make money. When Hugo Grotius published his treatise on the freedom of the seas, he subtitled it *The Right which Belongs to the Dutch to Take Part in the East India Trade* (1609). By the end of the seventeenth century, the Dutch East India Company employed 12,000 people. These companies helped link the dynamism of entrepreneurs eager to make windfall profits and willing to take speculative risks to the political strategies of each state. For, although officially independent of each government, each represented the interests of the state. Yet, only in England did colonial trade play a major role in the development of the national economy, principally because English manufactured goods increasingly found markets in its bustling settlement colony of North America.

Overseas trading remained a risky business; storms, wars, and pirates all posed considerable risks. Appropriately enough, the first English company to receive royal authorization for a monopoly on colonial trade was called the London Merchant Adventurers, which exported wool to Antwerp. Spanish kings, in particular, were notorious for declaring bankruptcy and thus repudiating all debts after borrowing money from wealthy subjects based on the expectation—sometimes in vain—of the arrival of valued colonial goods or bullion.

Price Revolution and Depression

The rise in population and the economic boom of the sixteenth century brought a considerable rise in prices. During this "price revolution," the cost of living badly outdistanced wage increases. Real income thus fell for ordinary people. Those who suffered included small landholders in England, many of whom fell into the ranks of landless laborers; relatively poor nobles in France and Italy, whose tenants had long-term leases; and landless laborers and wage earners in city and country alike.

Those affected adversely by the price revolution were quick to blame rapacious landlords, greedy merchants, hoarders of grain, selfish masters, usurers, and the spirit of acquisition engendered, some people believed, by the Reformation. Basic long-term causes included the infusion of gold and particularly silver brought principally by the Spanish from the New World, currency debasement undertaken by monarchs to help fund their dynastic wars, and the population increase itself, which placed more pressure on scarce resources.

A long depression followed the economic expansion of the sixteenth century. This in itself reflected the relative decline of Mediterranean trade, symbolized by the end of Venetian supremacy in about 1600. The Thirty Years' War (1618–1648) also disrupted trade and manufacturing. International trade fell off dramatically, and manufacturing suffered. Furthermore, Spaniards had begun to exhaust the gold and silver mines of Latin America, disrupting the money supply. But, in all, the leveling off of the population probably compounded the fact that European markets were saturated. Urban growth slowed down, although ports such as Amsterdam, Hamburg, and Liverpool continued to grow with the expansion of the Atlantic trading system. By contrast, many of Europe's old ecclesiastical, administrative, and commercial centers stagnated.

THE RISE OF SPAIN

Sixteenth-century Spain, the most powerful state of its time, was not one kingdom but two: Castile and Aragon. Castile was by far the larger and wealthier; its vast stretch of mountainous land across much of the center of the Iberian Peninsula contained a population of 6 or 7 million, five-sixths of that of Spain as a whole. Aragon, lying in northern Spain, had prospered during the Middle Ages because of its flourishing Mediterranean trade. It became a federation of dominions, including Catalonia and Valencia, and was greatly influenced by Mediterranean peoples and cultures (see Map 5.1). In contrast, Portugal was a poor Atlantic state of mariners lying on the western edge of Iberia. It had a population of about 1 million people (roughly equivalent to that of Aragon) and was merged into the Spanish kingdom during the period 1580–1640. Following the death of the Portuguese king without a male heir, Philip II of Spain had claimed the Portuguese throne by virtue of being the only son of Isabella, daughter of King Manuel I of Portugal.

MAP 5.1 Spain in the Age of Ferdinand and Isabella in the Late Fifteenth Century

Centralization and the Spanish Monarchy

In 1469, Isabella of Castile had married Ferdinand, heir to the throne of Aragon. But even a happy royal marriage could not in itself forge a unified kingdom. Royal policies in Castile, but not in Catalonia, Valencia, or Aragon, were successfully implemented to create a relatively centralized monarchy. In Castile, the crown centralized the system of justice and made the municipalities more subservient. The Castilian dialect gradually emerged as the language of Spain, giving some truth to the old saying that "a language is a dialect with an army."

Ferdinand and Isabella and their successors were known as the Catholic kings because of their devotion to the Church. But like other monarchs, they brought the Church, its privileges, and some of its income from tithes and the sale of indulgences under royal control. While the Reformation shook the foundations of the Church in much of Europe, it barely challenged Spanish religious orthodoxy. The Spanish Inquisition, whose original purpose had been to enforce the conversion of Moors and Jews in the late fifteenth century, served the Catholic Reformation in the late sixteenth century. Its tribunal interrogated and punished those accused of questioning Church doctrine. Housed in Castile, the Inquisition became a respected agent of royal as well as Church authority in some parts of Spain. Elsewhere, above all in Sicily and the Dutch Netherlands, local people considered the Inquisition another aspect of Spanish/Castilian domination and resisted it.

In Castile, Ferdinand and Isabella stripped the Castilian nobles of some of their privileges and power while dispensing titles and positions. In Catalonia and Valencia, on the other hand, nobles resisted any attempts by the monarchy to reduce their privileges (for example, the power of baronial courts), and therefore most of their noble prerogatives were left intact. Nonetheless, because they feared a revolt of the lower classes against them, the Catalan and Valencian nobles did become willing allies with the crown in maintaining social hierarchy and order.

Parliamentary traditions in the Spanish principalities limited the reach of the Castilian monarchy. The rulers of Spain were not able to tamper with Catalonia's traditionally less centralized constitutional traditions, which dated from the late thirteenth and fourteenth centuries, when Catalonia itself had been a Mediterranean power. Thus, the territories of Catalonia and Valencia maintained their political institutions, principally their Cortes (assembly), which continued to limit the authority of the

Ferdinand of Aragon and Isabella of Castile.

monarchy and which had to be consulted in order to achieve compliance with royal edicts. The Spanish monarchy therefore was less a "new monarchy"—at least outside of Castile—than that of France, because particularly strong institutional limits on its effective authority remained.

Disagreements between the monarchy and the Castilian Cortes were frequent during the middle decades of the sixteenth century. The Cortes excluded nobles and had representatives from only the governments of the eighteen most important cities and towns of Castile (forty-four towns had been represented in the Cortes during the Middle Ages). The Castilian Cortes, which maintained the right to approve extraordinary taxes, continued to refuse special taxes to subsidize the monarchy for thirty-five years (1541–1575). Despite the crown's efforts, this battle between monarchy and Cortes over taxes led to an inefficient royal fiscal apparatus. But Philip II, whose reign began (1556) and ended (1598) in royal bankruptcy, had to abide by the Roman law adage that described the medieval customs of his domains: "What touches all must be approved by all."

The Spanish Economy

Spain's colonial empire in the Americas contributed to its expanding economy. Although income drawn from the colonies never accounted for more than about 10 percent of the crown's income, during the first years of the Spanish colonial period Mexican gold helped finance the next wave of conquests. In 1545, Spaniards discovered the rich silver mines of Potosí in Peru, and a year later they uncovered more deposits in Mexico. A new refining process utilizing an amalgam of mercury helped Spain triple the silver resources of Europe at its own profit. Mules carried silver extracted at Potosí on a fifteen-day journey down 12,000 feet and many miles to the port of Arica; then the sea voyage of several months by convoy began. The Spanish empire contributed considerably to the sixteenth-century European trading boom. Spain shipped colonial products and Spanish woolens to France and the Italian city-states. Spanish ships supplied the colonies with wine, oil, European grain, shoes, and clothing.

The Castilian economy developed rapidly. The mountain ranges and central plateaus of Castile were divided between land for agricultural production, areas for raising sheep for the woolens industry, and rocky outcrops. The wool trade formed the basis of the Castilian export economy. The mining of silver, lead, iron, and mercury also developed in sixteenth-century Castile. Agricultural production was closely linked to manufacturing, as were sheep to the production of woolen goods. Nonetheless, 85 percent of the land of Spain could not be plowed because it consisted of mountains or lay on rocky slopes or at high elevations, with no possibility of irrigation.

Spanish royal revenue came from peasant obligations owed on royal domains as well as from taxes on commerce and manufacturing, import and export taxes, levies on sheep owned by nobles, farmers, monasteries, or textile manufacturers as they crossed specific mountain passes, and from the Church as payment for collecting tithes (an ecclesiastical tax of 10 percent of revenue). The crown imposed protectionist measures against foreign goods, banned the export of gold and silver, and attracted Italian and Flemish craftsmen to Spain.

In northern Spain, the rainy Cantabrian coast and mountains and valleys were populated by small farmers and fishermen. To the south, the Castilian provinces of Andalusia and Granada benefited from relatively rich land, producing wheat, olives, and wine. Castilian farmers expanded production by terracing hillsides and planting them in perennials, including grapevines and olive trees. Demand for textiles increased, and farmers planted flax, hemp, and, in Andalusia, mulberry trees. Farm towns built irrigation works and processing facilities such as wine and olive presses, flax-soaking ponds, and grist and fulling mills to turn these crops into market commodities. Wealthier farmers were able to purchase their neighbors' surplus and used their plow animals to transport these goods to the most attractive markets, where they sold them to wholesale merchants. Some of the latter were nobles who collected dues or obligations owed them in wheat, barley, wine, olive oil, cheese, chickens, or other farm products.

Spanish nobles incurred no stigma by engaging in wholesale or international commerce until the eighteenth century. Some of them, like merchants, processed the agricultural surplus and sold it to the rest of Europe. Many nobles capitalized on their revenues from farm products by building facilities to store and process the products—including flour mills, tanneries, and wine cellars, which often doubled as taverns—in the towns where they lived. Several wealthy dukes became shipping magnates. They earned fortunes because they owned the tuna fishing rights on Castile's Mediterranean shore, exporting fish preserved in salt or olive oil all over Europe.

The Expansion of the Spanish Empire

Through marriage and inheritance, Spain's territorial interests reached far and wide. The Spanish throne passed to the Austrian branch of the Habsburg dynasty in 1496, with Ferdinand and Isabella's daughter, Princess Joanna, marrying Philip the Fair, the Habsburg duke of Burgundy, who was the son of Maximilian, the Holy Roman emperor. A year after Isabella's death in 1504, Ferdinand, hoping to produce an heir to the Spanish throne, married a niece of King Louis XII of France. But three years later, their infant son died; royal families, as well as ordinary people, were subject to the harsh demographic realities of the age. In 1516, the Flanders-born son of Joanna and Philip the Fair inherited the throne of Castile and Aragon as Charles I of Spain. In 1519, he became Holy Roman Emperor Charles V (ruled 1519–1558) upon the death of his grandfather, Maximil-

Charles V was the grandson of Ferdinand and Isabella. This portrait is by Titian.

ian I. Along with his Spanish possessions, including Spain's American territories, he also inherited Aragon's Italian possessions. The emperor only briefly resided in Catalonia and rarely visited Castile. But with far-flung dynastic interests, he demanded extraordinary taxes from his Spanish subjects to pay for his wars abroad, including defending the Spanish Italian possessions of Naples, Sicily, and Sardinia against France during the 1520s.

The king's departure from Spain in 1520 was followed by open revolt against royal taxation. The revolt of the *Comuneros* (urban communities) began in Toledo and spread to other towns of northern Castile. Bourgeois and artisans opposed the royal officials Charles had imported from Flanders, but the revolt was also directed against Castilian nobles. After royal forces burned the arsenal and commercial town of Medina del Campo in north-central Castile in August 1520, Charles' regent suddenly switched tactics. He suspended supplementary tax collections and agreed not to appoint any more foreigners to office in Spain. When uprisings continued, Charles' army gradually restored order. One of the leaders of the revolt, the bishop of Zamora, was later tortured and garroted (slowly strangled with a wire) and his body hung from a tower as a warning to those who would challenge royal authority.

With an eye toward his succession, Charles V arranged the marriage of his son, Philip, to the English princess Mary Tudor of England in 1554. Charles formally abdicated as Holy Roman emperor in 1558, dividing the

Habsburg domains between his son Philip and his brother Ferdinand (see Map 5.2). Philip II (ruled 1556–1598) inherited Spain, the Netherlands, the Spanish colonies in the Americas, and parts of Italy. Ferdinand I (ruled 1558–1564), who was elected Holy Roman emperor, inherited the Habsburg ancestral domains, including Austria. This ended the period when one ruler held all Habsburg territories and any remote possibility that a single Catholic monarch would rule all of Europe, but it did not end the cooperation and strong family ties between the two branches of the Habsburg dynasty. Mary Tudor's death in 1558 eliminated the intriguing prospect that England might have become part of the Spanish Empire.

Despite the separation of the Habsburg domains, Philip II inherited the problem of ruling a vast empire. The royal bureaucracy handled the day-to-day operations of the state. Charles V had once asked for a pen and paper in one of the palaces of his various realms and was informed that none could be found. In contrast, his son's reign generated a mountain of paperwork each month. Thus, like its rivals France and England, the Spanish state developed a larger, more centralized bureaucracy, including royal councils, essential to the operations of the empire. The council of state and the council of war offered the king advice on matters of internal and colonial policy. Royal secretaries handled correspondence and busied

MAP 5.2. HABSBURG LANDS AT THE ABDICATION OF CHARLES V, 1558 The division of the Habsburg lands between Philip II (who had already begun to rule Spain in 1556) and Ferdinand I.

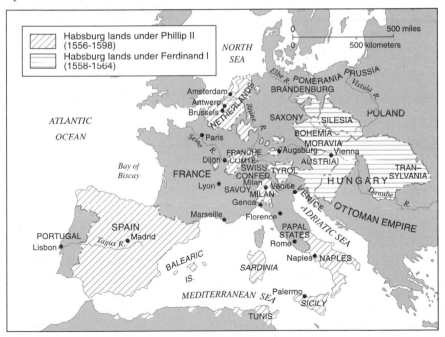

Philip II of Spain.

themselves with the operations of the royal household. Most such officials were commoners, for whom such positions provided financial and social advantages. Many of them were extremely able and devoted to the daunting task of maintaining the Spanish Empire.

The monarchy sent officials, many trained in law, from Spain to represent its interests in America. The growing bureaucracy was such that one judge sent from Spain in 1590 used 50,000 sheets of paper by the time he left thirteen years later. But it could take two years for administrative instructions or correspondence to reach distant officials in Latin America and for their response to arrive in Spain. Another official awaiting instructions put it this way, "If death came from Madrid, we should all live to a very old age."

The Age of Philip II

Spanish power peaked during the reign of Philip II. He chose as his capital the centrally located Castilian town of Madrid, which became a capital city of nobles and bureaucrats, many of whom, in one way or another, lived off the court. The city grew from a town of about 30,000 people in the 1540s to well over 150,000 inhabitants in the 1620s. Madrid survived through a "command economy"; royal commissioners paid government-fixed prices for what they wanted from the capital's hinterland. As Spain's capital grew, it had to be supplied from distant regions by overland transport provided by countless mule trains over mountain ranges and through deep valleys.

Like Francis I of France several decades before him, Philip decided that he needed a permanent royal residence that would provide an elegant symbol of his authority and power. Outside of Madrid, Philip built the magnificent Escorial Palace between 1563 and 1584. Virtually the king's only public appearances after he became crippled by gout were elaborate religious ceremonies at the palace. These were carefully orchestrated to uphold the sanctity of the throne.

Complex rituals of court etiquette affirmed a sense of power, social hierarchy, and order that were supposed to radiate from the Escorial through Spain and to the far reaches of the empire. Once the king had ridden a horse, it could never be ridden again by anyone else except the king. The king received visitors in a room determined by the status of the visitor. The primacy of court ritual and etiquette was such that Philip III (ruled 1598–1621), Philip's son and successor, contracted a fatal fever from a portable coal heater that had been placed too close to him. The duke of Alba, powerful adviser and military commander, recognized the danger, real or imagined, but refrained from moving it, or even saying anything, because the noble in charge of such things was not in the room.

Philip II led a tragic life marred by the premature death of four wives and a number of children. Perhaps because of sadness, he wore only black. The king himself may have contributed to the misfortunes of his offspring.

The Escorial Palace built by Philip II between 1563 and 1584.

In 1568, he ordered Don Carlos, his bad-tempered and irresponsible twenty-three-year-old son by his first marriage, placed under lock and key. Don Carlos seemed unfit to rule; furthermore, detesting his father, he may have even entered into contact with Dutch leaders who had begun to denounce Spanish policies in their land. Don Carlos' death six months later haunted Philip, inevitably generating stories that he had ordered him murdered. The introverted, sometimes indecisive king thereafter lived among the whispers of intrigue and storms of aristocratic rivalries of the noble families and factions.

With Habsburg domination of Italy secured by the 1559 Peace of Cateau-Cambrésis with France, Philip turned his attention to fighting the Turks. The Ottoman Empire had expanded into Europe following the conquest of Constantinople in 1453. Suleiman the Magnificent (ruled 1520–1566) took advantage of the dynastic and religious rivalries of the European states to expand his domain in the Balkans, where the Ottoman cultural heritage endures today, and into the rich plains of Hungary. The Turks also became bolder in their attacks on Spanish ships in the central and western Mediterranean. When the Turks took the Venetian island of Cyprus in 1571, the pope helped initiate the Holy League, an alliance with Venice and Spain. The long naval war against the Ottoman Empire,

The Battle of Lepanto, 1571.

during which Turkish ships raided the coast of Spain, lasted from 1559 to 1577. With southern Spain virtually undefended and with the Moriscos (Moors who had been forced to convert to Christianity) rebelling (1568–1570) against taxes, the Turks might well have captured Grenada. But a Spanish-Austrian Habsburg fleet defeated the sultan's larger navy in the Adriatic at the Battle of Lepanto (1571), a monumental struggle in which more than 200 galleys fought, taking the lives of 15,000 Christians and 30,000 Turks. The Turkish threat in the western Mediterranean ended. Yet, overexpansion had already planted the seeds of Spanish imperial decline.

THE RISE OF ENGLAND

The consolidation and then the extension of the authority of the Tudor monarchy made possible England's emergence as a power late in the sixteenth century. From the reign of Henry VII to that of Elizabeth I, the Tudor monarchs held in check the great landed magnates, putting down rebellions and extending the reach and prestige of royal government. During the same period, the English state expanded its control over Wales and Ireland while holding at bay Scottish threats to the Tudor dynasty.

The House of Tudor

On August 22, 1485, at the Battle of Bosworth Field, King Richard III lost his kingdom for the lack of the proverbial horse, and his life as well. Victorious in the long War of the Roses, Henry VII (ruled 1485–1509) became the first Tudor monarch. In 1487, he crushed a last-ditch uprising by his enemies, the Yorkists. And ten years later, he put down a tax rebellion that began in Cornwall and reached the gates of London. Like Isabella of Castile and Ferdinand of Aragon, the ambitious Henry VII set out to make the Tudor state so powerful that it could resist any challenge from noble factions, the "overmighty subjects," some of whom had been killed at Bosworth Field.

Thomas Wolsey, who was archbishop of York and adviser to the king, brought to the King's Council loyal officials drawn from the ranks of the nobility and high clergy. These men met at Westminster in the Star Chamber, so called because its blue ceiling, like the skies, was spangled with stars. The Star Chamber became one of the highest courts in the land, generating revenue for the crown by assessing fines and other monetary penalties.

Henry strengthened royal authority in England. At the expense of Parliament, which enacted the laws of the land and attempted to restrict monarchical authority, Henry imposed tariffs protecting the cloth and wool industries, decreed acts unifying weights and measures, and put forth edicts punishing vagabondage and begging. He reduced expenses by disbanding his army, while filling royal coffers by selling monopolies (the exclusive right to import and market foodstuffs or commodities). Monopolies were extremely unpopular, however, among the middle and lower classes because they kept the prices of some products artificially high.

The king won the loyalty of most nobles. When selling offices failed, he resorted to the sheer coercive power of the throne. The Star Chamber enforced compliance, exacting fines and sometimes arresting the recalcitrant for real or imagined offenses. Henry obtained from Parliament writs of attainder and forfeiture, by which he could declare anyone guilty of treason, execute them, and seize their property.

Henry VII depended not only upon the personal loyalty of local elites but also on the efficiency and prestige of six or seven hundred unpaid justices of the peace. These unsalaried men, largely drawn from prosperous landed families, dispensed justice, collected taxes, enforced troop levies, and maintained local order. Their judicial authority covered every criminal offense except treason. While maintaining a strong tradition of decentralized government in England, the justices of the peace also strengthened the efficiency and prestige of the monarchy. Gradually, the royal Assize Courts took responsibility for felony cases. Charged with enforcing parliamentary statutes and the orders of the Privy Council, which administered the Tudor state, they also helped extend the state's effective authority.

Henry VIII became king upon his father's death in 1509 and married Catherine of Aragon, who was Ferdinand and Isabella's daughter, as well as his brother's widow. Beneath Henry's proud and impetuous character lay a deep-seated inferiority complex that he tried to overcome with grand deeds. The single-minded Henry dreamed of standing at the head of an empire. The new king spent vast sums fighting against France for more than a decade, beginning in 1512. Cardinal Wolsey, who had been his father's trusted adviser, sought to restrain Henry's ambition. But when the House of Commons refused to provide the king with more funds, Henry simply debased the currency, giving the state more spending power at the cost of higher inflation.

Foreign wars had devastated royal finances. To raise money, the spendthrift monarch heaped more financial obligations on the backs of the poor. Wolsey utilized the cynically named "Amicable Grant," a royal assessment first imposed in 1525 on lay and ecclesiastical revenues. Peasants in southeastern England, sometimes led by local gentry (the rural elite whose status came from its ownership of land and who dominated the House of Commons), rebelled against these new levies. Henry responded to the threat by forcing landowners to loan money to the crown, imprisoning some of the wealthiest, confiscating their estates, selling off property that had belonged to the Roman Catholic Church on unfavorable terms, and further debasing the currency, adding to inflation.

Henry wanted to make his monarchy more efficient. Royal government, including control of the state's finances, passed from the royal household of the king's servants to a small but able bureaucracy of officials and their clerks, who were loyal to both the king and Parliament. He reduced the size of the king's advisory council and formalized its structure. The Privy Council assumed oversight functions and routinized communication with the local justices of the peace. The king appointed new administrative officials and established new revenue courts. At the same time, the general acceptance of the "king's law"—common law—gradually helped generate a sense of national unity.

Henry VIII extended the power of his monarchy by breaking with Rome in the 1530s over his divorce of Catherine of Aragon. He established the Church of England (see Chapter 3), which kept some of the ritual and doctrine of the Catholic Church. Henry became head of the Church of England, dissolving monasteries and confiscating and selling ecclesiastical lands. But while leading the break with Rome, Henry planted the seeds for conflicts between Protestants and Catholics in England.

Fearing the possibility of Welsh or Irish assistance to Holy Roman Emperor Charles V should he attempt to invade England to restore Catholicism, Henry established English domination over Wales and direct rule over Ireland, extending English control on the periphery of the British Isles. Since the late twelfth century, English lords had gradually increased their military colonization of Ireland, pushing back the Gaelic tribes and claiming the finest land by virtue of ancient titles. The English kings delegated authority to English nobles. Yet, effective English authority had remained fragile in Ireland as long as the crown's continental interests took precedence and disorders in Ireland did not compromise English authority. After the English Reformation, the crown selected English Protestants for all posts in Ireland. And after a minor rebellion against royal authority, which was put down with great cruelty, in 1541 Henry proclaimed himself king of Ireland and head of the Irish Church. In exchange for the Gaelic chieftains' recognition of Henry as their king and acceptance of English law, the crown recognized them as Irish lords. Thereafter, however, the costs of administering Ireland increased rapidly, requiring more troops, as the Irish continued to chafe at English rule.

Scotland also proved to be a thorny problem for England. Although in 1503 James IV had married Henry VII's daughter, Margaret Tudor, relations between Scotland and England deteriorated when Henry VIII became king. When James invaded England in 1513 in support of the French, Henry responded by ordering a major military campaign against the Scots. This ended with the wounding or death of more than 10,000 Scots at the battle of Flodden (where James IV was killed). Nonetheless, Catholic Scotland remained an ally of Catholic France. The new Scottish king, James V, first married the daughter of Francis I of France and, after her death, he married a member of the powerful French Catholic family of

Guise. In 1542, an English army again invaded Scotland, defeating the Scots at Solway Moss. Following James V's sudden death a month after the battle, Mary Stuart (James' six-day-old daughter and the granddaughter of Henry VII of England) became queen of the Scots. In 1546, after Henry's war with France dragged to a halt, another English army laid waste to Scotland, sacking the capital and university town of Edinburgh.

Henry VIII died in 1547. On his deathbed, the originator of the English Reformation hedged his bets, leaving money to pay for Catholic Masses to be said for the eternal repose of his soul. The nine-year-old son of Henry and Jane Seymour became King Edward VI (ruled 1547–1553) under the tutelage of his uncle, the duke of Somerset, who governed as Lord Protector. Again, rebellions sparked by economic hardship broke out. While seeking accommodation with Protestant dissenters, the young Edward (who ruled from age nine to fifteen under the influence of advisers) brought theologians from Geneva and Strasbourg to undertake an aggressive campaign on behalf of the Reformed Church of England.

Wars against Catholic Scotland and France continued. The Lord Protector was intent on destroying Catholicism in Scotland. After English troops defeated a French force sent to help the Catholic cause, the young Catholic queen of Scots fled to safety, marrying Francis, the son of Henry II, the king of France.

(*Left*) Lady Jane Grey, queen of England for 9 days. (*Right*) Mary Tudor, later queen of England.

In England, tensions between Protestants and Catholics accentuated anti-Catholicism. Landowners began to resist paying more taxes to finance new wars. Allied with fearful Catholic nobles, the duke of Warwick became the new Lord Protector in 1549, taking the title of duke of Northumberland.

Northumberland quickly betrayed the Catholic lords who had supported him. He tightened the crown's control over the Church of England and undertook a repressive campaign against Catholicism. Northumberland's influence over the sickly young king whetted his desire for power. He plotted for Lady Jane Grey (1537–1554; niece of Henry, she stood third in line to the monarchy) to ascend the throne after she married his son. After Edward's death, Northumberland proclaimed his daughter-in-law queen of England. But most nobles rallied to the cause of Mary Tudor (ruled 1553–1558), the daughter of Henry VIII and Catherine of Aragon. She seemed to them the rightful heir to the throne, despite the fact that she was Catholic.

Mary Tudor succeeded her half-brother and attempted to return England to Catholicism. Mary restored all rituals and doctrines of the Catholic Church, and she acknowledged the primacy of the pope over the Church of England. The queen abrogated Henry VIII's reforms and began to persecute Protestants, some of whom fled to France. "Bloody Mary" embellished the macabre heritage of the Tower of London with the heads of Northumberland, his son, and Lady Jane Grey, who ruled for only nine days. Mary married Philip II, who ascended the Spanish throne in 1556. England joined Spain in its war against France; Calais, the last English outpost in France, was soon lost. Sparked by widespread opposition to her Catholicism, which was popularly identified with England's Catholic rivals, France and Spain, a rebellion broke out against the queen. When Mary died in 1558, few in England grieved.

Elizabeth I (ruled 1558–1603), Anne Boleyn's daughter, became queen at age twenty-five, succeeding Mary, her half-sister. Elizabeth's throne was threatened by religious division, compounded by antagonism with the Catholic powers, France and Spain. Not many people could have expected the young queen to succeed.

Elizabeth was a woman of intelligence, vanity, sporadic fickleness, and an occasional flash of temper. She enjoyed music, dancing, hunting, and the company of men. Tall, with reddish hair and an olive complexion, she was cautious, even suspicious, having been raised in a world of conspiracy. The queen preferred to wait out many pressing problems in the hope that they would go away. Educated in the tradition of Italian humanism, Elizabeth learned French, German, and Italian, as well as Latin, and enjoyed translating texts from these languages into English.

Elizabeth never married. It was not uncommon for women to remain unmarried in early modern Europe—in England, about 10 percent of all women remained single throughout their lives—but it was unusual for a

Queen Elizabeth dancing with Robert Dudley.

monarch to remain single. The question of whether Elizabeth would ever marry preoccupied the other rulers of Europe, as well as her subjects.

In response to a parliamentary petition that she marry and produce a direct heir, Elizabeth responded that she trusted God to ensure that "the realm shall not remain destitute of an heir." As for her, it would be enough that at the end of her life "a marble stone shall declare that a queen, having reigned such a time, lived and died a virgin." Elizabeth had rejected one continental hopeful after another, beginning with the handsome but dull Philip II of Spain, Catholic widower of Mary Tudor. Nor was marriage the outcome of a two-year romance with the handsome Lord Robert Dudley, the death of whose wife in 1560 from a suspicious fall down a flight of stairs understandably fueled rumors for some years.

Elizabeth was an able administrator who chose capable people to serve the crown. She appointed as her principal adviser the clever, loyal Sir William Cecil (Lord Burghley, 1520–1598). A Protestant, Cecil served as royal secretary for nearly as many years as Elizabeth was queen. Nonetheless, in the later years of her reign, bitter battles for influence and power within Elizabeth's inner circle did belie the appearance of relative harmony. In the 1590s, two powerful men battled for power: the ambitious Robert Devereux, the earl of Essex, a soldier who had the ear of the queen, and Robert Cecil, son of William Cecil. From Ireland, where he had failed to crush Irish resistance to English control, the ambitious Essex returned to London without orders to do so in order to destroy his rival. This time, in 1599, Elizabeth forgave him. But two years later, Essex's small private army of followers rose in rebellion; failure led to his execution and that of his most powerful friends.

Religious Settlement and Conflict under Elizabeth I

When Elizabeth took the throne, she was determined to find a means to resolve religious conflict within England, for she recognized that unless the conflict was resolved, it might one day threaten her reign. Elizabeth had been raised a Protestant, but she did not hold particularly strong religious convictions and rarely attended church services. Although she was thought to be favorable to some Catholic rituals, when she first encountered a procession of monks with candles and incense at Westminster Abbey, she cried out, "Away with these torches, we see very well." In the quest for unity, she dismissed many Catholic advisers.

Queen Elizabeth oversaw the religious settlement, which at first aimed to please a wide spectrum of religious beliefs without resorting to heresy hunting or persecution. In 1559, Parliament passed the Act of Uniformity and the Act of Supremacy, which established the lasting foundations of the Church of England, reorganizing it to have Protestant dogma but essentially Catholic structure. The Uniformity Bill imposed the *Book of Common Prayer* (1550) on religious services of the Church of England and required attendance at public worship and imposed fines for not attending services. The bill barely passed the House of Lords (which was primarily composed of Catholics), and probably would not have passed at all had two bishops not been imprisoned in the Tower of London and thus unable to vote. The Act of Supremacy required all officials, clergy, and candidates for university degrees to take an oath acknowledging the queen as "governor" of the English Church. This title replaced that of "head" of the Church and suggested that the queen would not interfere in matters of doctrine.

Thirty-Nine Articles, enacted in 1563, provided an institutional framework for subsequent relations between state and church in England. The landed elite, strengthening its control of Parliament during Elizabeth's reign, generally supported the Church of England. Protestant preachers combed the countryside, seeking to win back people who had converted to Roman Catholicism.

Some English Protestants wanted to carry the anti-Roman reforms further than Elizabeth's religious settlement. They sought to eliminate from the Church of England what some members considered vestiges of elaborate Catholic ceremonies, such as baptismal crosses, altar rails before which Catholics knelt while receiving communion, elaborate priestly garb, and stained-glass windows that they associated with Catholicism.

Puritanism, the English version of Calvinism, first took hold among English exiles on the continent during Queen Mary's reign. It emerged in the late 1550s as a dissident force within the English, or Anglican Church. Puritans could be found in every social stratum, but they were drawn primarily from the middle and lower classes. They drew hostility by insisting on a simplified but more intense religion based on individual conscience, the direct authority of the Holy Scriptures, and a community of belief in which preaching played a preeminent role. Although a few Puritans served as bishops in the Church of England and some fiercely defended Elizabeth's royal supremacy, other Puritans wanted the Church of England to be separate from the English monarchy. The Tudor monarchy, on the other hand, wanted to make the Church serve its secular goals of national glory, prosperity, and public order.

A modest Catholic revival, aided by the arrival of Catholic Jesuit missionaries from the continent, accentuated religious divisions in England. Royal religious policies became more harsh. Dissident Protestants suffered persecution along with Catholics. A Jesuit missionary was tortured to death on the rack in 1581, and six years later the first Puritan was executed for having spoken in Parliament on behalf of free speech in the name of his religion.

Since Elizabeth had no heirs, the Catholic Mary Stuart, niece of Henry VIII, stood next in line for succession to the English throne. After her husband King Francis II of France died in 1560, Mary returned to her native Scotland to assume the power that her mother wielded as regent until her death that same year. The Scottish Reformation had begun in earnest

Mary, queen of Scots.

when the theologian John Knox (*c.* 1505–1572) returned home from Geneva to preach reform. Soon after coming to the throne of England, Elizabeth had made peace with Scotland and France. But Elizabeth and Protestants worried that if Mary became queen of England, she would restore Catholicism to England. When Protestants forced Mary to abdicate the Scottish throne in 1568, she fled to England. There Elizabeth kept her potential rival under virtual house arrest.

In 1569, Catholics in the moors and bogs of the isolated English north rebelled in the hope of putting Mary Stuart on the English throne, precipitating Elizabeth's order for her rival's imprisonment. The Catholic force marched southward, but hastily retreated upon learning that sizable English forces loyal to Elizabeth awaited them. English troops defeated a second Scottish army gathered near the border between the two countries. Elizabeth ordered the execution of over 500 of the rebels. This "Northern Rising" ended in complete failure, and the Catholic Church's hopes for a successful Counter-Reformation in England were finally dashed. Pope Pius V excommunicated Elizabeth in 1570 from the Church to which she did not wish to belong, removing the queen's Catholic subjects from the obligation of obedience to her and encouraging several further plots against her. Two years later, French Catholics undertook the Saint Bartholomew's Day Massacre of Protestants in Paris (see Chapter 4), the horror of which firmed Elizabeth's resolve to resist Mary's claims to the throne at all costs. She then vowed to support the Dutch, most of whom were Protestant, in their rebellion against Catholic Spain. In 1583, she foiled a plot, which involved the Spanish and French embassies, to depose her in favor of Mary Stuart. Four years later, under pressure from Parliament and fearing new Catholic plots against her, Elizabeth ordered Mary Stuart's execution.

Tudor Statemaking

The reach and efficiency of the English state increased under Elizabeth's guidance. Lords and other wealthy gentlemen served on the Privy Council, which consisted of between twelve and eighteen members drawn from the nobility, gentry, and officers in the royal household. It oversaw the lord-lieutenants, a new office that gave noblemen control of local militia. Patronage flowed downward from the monarch. England's queen, like her predecessors, used patronage to foster loyalty to the crown. The most desirable posts were at court, including those in the royal household. Some of these carried life tenures; a few were hereditary. More than 500 men were employed in government departments. The most powerful officials at court, such as the Lord Chancellor, also dispensed patronage by selecting officials and filling local positions in the counties. Closely tied to the satisfaction of the private interests of the landed elite, the office of the Exchequer resembled similar offices created by continental monarchs who did not have to contend with a representative body as powerful as the English Parliament. Although it met during only three of the forty-five years of Elizabeth's reign, Parliament retained an important role in government because the crown needed its assent for new laws and new taxes.

Upon ascending the throne, Elizabeth found the crown's financial situation bleak. Revenues raised through taxation and customs dues were inadequate to finance the war against Spain and the Irish campaigns. The sale of some royal lands, forced loans, the occasional seizure of a Spanish ship laden with silver or gold, and purveyance (the right of agents of the monarchy to buy food at below-market prices) could only be temporary expedients. The collection of "ship money" (a tax on ports, which the crown with dubious logic extended to inland towns as well) was extremely unpopular and generated resistance during the hard times of the 1590s. But by exercising frugality in the expenses of government and increasing taxation, the crown managed to replenish its coffers, another sign of a stronger and more efficient state, despite a decade and a half of expensive warfare against Spain.

The English monarchy in the Elizabethan Age was in some ways relatively more centralized and efficient than that of Spain or France. This was so despite the fact that the French monarchy employed about ten times more officials than did the English crown (taking the difference in population into consideration). In Elizabethan England, unlike in France, churchmen did not serve in the highest offices of the realm. Although English nobles still had retainers, by the 1590s they no longer had full-fledged private armies that could threaten the throne's monopoly on force. This contrasted with the situation in France during the same period, when the Guise and Bourbon families, among others, sent their own armies to fight in the wars of religion. English noble violence was instead channeled into service to the crown, and into dueling.

Foreign wars also served to increase the reach of central government in England. The second half of the sixteenth century brought regular training for the militia, which provided the bulk of troops as needed, along with gentlemen volunteers and cavalrymen still recruited by summons. But in the last eighteen years of Elizabeth's reign, more than 100,000 soldiers were impressed into service for wars on the continent and to maintain English hegemony in Ireland. Lord-lieutenants assumed responsibility for troop levies in the counties. The vast majority who were conscripted as soldiers were the poorest of the poor, unfortunate men who happened to be at the wrong place at the wrong time when the press-gangs turned up to roll them out of taverns or out of church and into the queen's service.

The monarchy imposed English law on northern England, Ireland, and Wales, which Henry VIII had absorbed into England. The emergence of a national market economy that was increasingly tied to London also played an important part in the nationalization of English political institutions. Within England, the sense of belonging to a nationality was certainly more

Queen Elizabeth greeting the Dutch ambassadors.

advanced than anywhere on the continent. With the exception of part of Cornwall in southwestern England (where the Cornish language was spoken by many), the people of England spoke English, however great the variation in dialect and accents. A somewhat Anglicized Welsh gentry had even begun to send their sons to Oxford and Cambridge Universities.

The fact that Britain is an island may have made the English more xenophobic and precociously nationalistic than their continental counterparts. The Venetian ambassador commented in 1555 on the "strange fancies [that] prevail amongst this people, and how much their ideas differ from those of other nations." Indeed, the English seemed "most hostile by their nature to foreigners . . . naturally the enemies of all aliens, but they hate the French and Spaniards most of all." Such sentiments reinforced the strong current of English anti-Catholicism.

Strong traditions of local government and loyalties persisted in England, however, fueled by social differences and the overwhelming influence of wealthy local landed families. The county and parish remained the economic, social, and political universe of most people in England. The state remained an abstraction until the tax collector or the press-gang came to intrude in an individual's life.

Demographic and Economic Expansion

In the last half of the sixteenth century, England emerged as a commercial and manufacturing power. The population of England and Wales—its vassal—grew rapidly, from about 2.5 million in the 1520s to more than 3.5

million in 1580, reaching about 4.5 million in 1610. Reduced mortality rates and increased fertility, the latter probably generated by expanding work opportunities in manufacturing and farming (leading to earlier marriage and more children), help explain this rapid rise in population. While epidemics and plague occasionally took their toll, the people in England still suffered less than did those on the continent. Furthermore, despite the somewhat wrenching effects of the English Reformation, the country had been spared the protracted wars of religion that occurred in France and Central Europe during the same period.

England provides the primary example of the expansion of agricultural production well before the "agricultural revolution" of the eighteenth and nineteenth centuries. A larger population stimulated increased demand for food, as well as for manufactured goods, particularly woolens. English agriculture became more efficient and market oriented through crop specialization than almost anywhere on the continent. Between 1450 and 1650, the yield of grain per acre increased by at least 30 percent. In sharp contrast with farming in Spain, English landowners brought more dense marshes and woodlands into cultivation.

The great estates of the English nobility largely remained intact, and many wealthy landowners aggressively increased the size of their holdings, a precondition for increased productivity. Marriages between the children of landowners also increased the size of landed estates. Primogeniture (the full inheritance of land by the eldest son) helped keep land from being subdivided. Younger sons of independent landowners left behind the family land to find other respectable occupations, often in the church or in urban trades. Larger farms were conducive to more commercialized farming at a time when an expanding population pushed up demand and prices. Some landowners turned a part of their land into pastureland for sheep in order to supply the developing woolens trade.

Some of the great landlords, as well as yeomen (farmers whose holdings and security of land tenure guaranteed their prosperity and status) reorganized their holdings in the interest of efficiency. Open-field farmers selected crops in response to the growing London market. In their quest for greater profits, many landlords put the squeeze on their tenants. Between 1580 and 1620, many landlords raised rents and altered conditions of land tenure in their favor, preferring shorter leases and forcing tenants to pay an "entry fee" before they would agree to rent them land. Landowners evicted those who could not afford their new, more onerous terms. They also pushed tenants toward more productive farming methods, including crop rotation. Many peasants had difficulty competing with their wealthier neighbors. During bad years, the peasants might be forced to sell their land, while wealthy neighbors could survive with relative ease.

Many landowners utilized "enclosure" to expand their holdings. Enclosure included the buying up and hedging of wastelands, the enclosure of one's own land by fences, consolidating arable strips of land and enclosing them, and dividing common lands and pasture areas. The enclosure of common lands, sold by villages to the highest bidders and entailing the end of the common rights of villagers—rich or poor—to use the land, and the removal of tenants in order to consolidate estates, marked a push toward "agrarian individualism." Enclosure in this sense drew considerable resistance, for it left many of the rural poor fenced out of common land on which they had depended for firewood, gleaning, and pasturing. Thomas More's *Utopia* (1516), inspired by news of explorations of the Americas, described an imaginary island where all people lived in peace and harmony and blamed England's economic inequities on enclosure. Riots against enclosure were widespread in the 1590s, a decade in which popular tax rebellions shook France, Spain, Austria, and Ukraine, among other places, and again in the 1620s and 1630s. They were particularly prominent in regions where open fields were being enclosed for pasture or in the fens and forests where drainage and deforestation projects authorized by Parliament eliminated extensive common lands.

England's precocious economic development also drew upon the country's natural resources, including iron, timber and, above all, coal, extracted in far greater quantities than anywhere on the continent. New industrial methods, including furnaces for separating silver from copper ore and for using coal in the making of glass, expanded the production of iron, brass, and pewter in and around Birmingham.

But, above all, textile manufacturing transformed the English economy. Here, too, new industrial methods, such as the stocking knitting frame, increased productivity. Woolens (which accounted for about 80 percent of exports), worsteds (sturdy yarn spun from combed wool fibers), and cloth found eager buyers in England as well as on the continent. Moreover, late in the sixteenth century, as English merchants began making forays across the Atlantic, these textiles were also sold in the New World. Cloth manufacturers undercut production by urban craftsmen by "putting out" work to the villages and farms of the countryside. In such domestic industry, poor rural women and their daughters could do spinning and carding (combing fibers in preparation for spinning) of wool in their homes.

The English textile trade was closely tied to Antwerp, in the Spanish Netherlands, where workers dyed English cloth. Sir Thomas Gresham, a sixteenth-century entrepreneur, became England's representative in the bustling river port. Wining and dining the city's merchants and serving as a royal ambassador, he so enhanced the reputation of English business that English merchants could operate on credit, no small achievement in the sixteenth century. At home, he convinced the government to end special privileges accorded the Hanseatic cities of northern Germany and helped convince the state to authorize lucrative English trading monopolies. Gresham's shrewd sense of finance saved the relatively meager royal coffers from bankruptcy on several occasions through the negotiation of timely loans.

Gresham advised the crown to explore the economic possibilities of the Americas. This led to the first concerted English efforts at colonization. Even more than Spanish colonialism, English overseas ventures were undertaken with commercial profits in mind. When the Spanish, hoping to crush the Dutch rebellion that began against their rule in 1566, closed the Scheldt River, which leads from the North Sea to Antwerp, English merchants responded by seeking new, more distant outlets for trade. From 1577 to 1580, Sir Francis Drake (1540–1596), explorer and privateer who stole treasures brought back by Spanish galleons, sailed around Cape Horn in his search for a passage that would permit commercial ties with Asia. Sir Walter Raleigh (1554–1618; a Renaissance scholar, poet, historian, and explorer) said of Drake, "A single purpose animates all his exploits and the chart of his movements is like a cord laced and knotted round the throat of the Spanish monarchy."

London came to replace Antwerp as Europe's leading center of trade. London's Merchant Adventurers competed with Spanish and Portuguese rivals for spices and other products that fetched increasingly handsome prices at home. They traded textiles and other manufactured goods for slaves, gold, and ivory from the African and Brazilian coasts. West Indian sugar and Virginia tobacco entered the English domestic market in lucrative quantities. English merchants traded in India and Indonesia. In 1600, Queen Elizabeth chartered the East India Company with the goal of competing with Dutch traders. To compete with the Spanish, who already had a colonial empire that stretched several thousand miles from what is now the southern United States to Terra del Fuego at the southern tip of South America, Raleigh sought to establish a colony in Virginia between 1584 and 1587. After a first settlement failed, a settlement colony succeeded in

View of seventeenth-century London, Europe's leading center of trade.

Longeat at Wiltshire, one of the great early Elizabethan manor houses.

Virginia, largely because of the popularity of tobacco, which began to reach England in the first decades of the seventeenth century.

The developing economy produced a marked rise in the number of people working in manufacturing. English towns grew as migrants arrived in sufficient numbers to overcome high mortality rates caused by catastrophic health conditions stemming from poor sanitation. London grew into the largest city in the world, its population rising from about 50,000 in the 1520s to 200,000 in 1600, and jumping its walls to 375,000 in 1650. The next biggest towns in England lagged far behind: Norwich, Newcastle, and Bristol boasted only about 25,000 people each, followed by Exeter and York. On the average, about 6,000 people moved to London each year. Including its developing industrial suburbs, about 8 percent of the population of England lived in London by the mid-seventeenth century.

English Society in the Tudor Period

English society under the Tudors reflected what William Harrison, writing in 1577, called "degrees of people," that is, sharply defined social differences. Contemporaries sometimes simplified English social structure by dividing people into the ranks of "gentlemen," "the middling sort," and "the poor." Ownership of land in the form of estates—inherited or acquired—conferred status, or "gentility," in England. All nobles were gentry, but the vast majority of gentry were not nobles. In order to administer the realm and maintain public order in every corner of the country, the crown required the allegiance and the assistance of the landed elite.

Titles were granted by the crown, originally in exchange for military service, and were inherited by the eldest son. The nobility and gentry had social and political influence and constituted the elite that dominated England for more than the next three centuries. Country manors literally commanded the surrounding countryside. One contemporary exuded, "Nobility is a precious gift, which so glittereth in the eyes of all men that there is no one corporal thing in this world, whereof we make a greater account."

The lord and his family dominated regional economic, social, and political life through ties of kinship and patronage. Ordinary people addressed the nobleman as "your lordship," and the wealthy gentleman as "sir"; poor women curtsied to them as a mark of respect. Village bells were rung in their honor when they passed through. Wealthy landowners mediated in village disputes and provided some charity in exchange for deference. (One man of means chatted with "his people" in the street: "I asked a poor woman how many children she had. She answered 'Six.' 'Here,' I said, 'is a sixpence for them.' 'No, sir,' she said proudly, not realizing the gentleman was offering a gift, 'I will not sell my children.' ")

The Privy Council and Elizabeth's court were remarkably homogeneous from the early 1570s, with few newcomers breaking into the inner circle of like-minded aristocrats. The borders between public and private life within this upper circle of relatives, friends, enemies, and acquaintances were hard to distinguish. The education of gentlemen at Oxford and Cambridge Universities or through private tutoring helped shape common cultural values and social homogeneity among what was increasingly becoming a national elite.

Yeomen stood beneath the gentry on the social ladder, but they could move up if they were able to purchase and maintain large estates. In any case, they possessed, in Harrison's words, "a certain preeminence and more estimation" among the common people. They had political rights and could vote in the parliamentary elections. They improved their houses, bought or built solid furniture, purchased silver and pewter accoutrements, wore nice clothes on Sunday and holidays, and were able to assure the education of their children.

Within the upper reaches of the "middling sort" were men considered "of sufficiency," even if they were not lords or gentlemen. They were believed by virtue of steady income to be worthy of assuming some kind of public responsibility. England's precocious commercial and manufacturing boom in the sixteenth century increased the wealth and status of merchants and manufacturers. Wealthy merchants and artisans served on town councils, perpetuating their influence from generation to generation. Members of these councils led the way in the pageant-like processions during municipal and national celebrations, such as that of

Midsummer Eve, followed by guild members, each wearing the decorative costume of their various trades. Most craftsmen were much better off than the urban and rural poor.

Originally intended to maintain the highest standards in the training of craftsmen and in production, the guilds' influence waned as towns became larger and more complex. Yet, some guilds, particularly in London, held monopolies over specific trades. They could control production and therefore the prices of certain commodities. Since guild regulations and ordinances had to be approved by the civic authorities, disagreements between guilds and municipal governments were frequent.

Lower on the social scale were smallholders, farmers who owned just enough land to get by ("husbandmen"), poor clergymen depending for survival upon small fees rendered for their services, and ordinary craftsmen. The majority of the population owned neither land nor skills, and thus lay at the bottom of the social hierarchy. Most laboring families lived in rented one-room cottages and owned little—if any—furniture. Cottagers, employed as farmhands but also often employed as spinners, weavers, carders, or nailmakers, lived on bread, cheese, lard, soup, beer, and garden greens, occasionally supplemented by harvest-time feasts provided by their employers. Farm servants lived in Spartan accommodations provided by landlords. In London and smaller towns, the urban poor struggled to survive as common laborers, porters, sweepers, and in other menial occupations, living in squalor in whatever pitiful lodgings they could afford, or, for many, living without shelter.

Social divisions in English society were reflected in how people lived, dressed, and even spoke. During the sixteenth century, the rich got richer—and lived that way, dressing and eating differently from those who were poor. Responding to complaints that "a Babylon of confusion" might blur class lines because anyone with money could purchase the most elegant clothing, Parliament had earlier in the century decreed that only dukes, earls, and barons could wear sable cloth woven of gold and embroidered with gold and silver. So could their horses. But no one, not even wealthy merchants—or horses, for that matter—of a lesser rank, even if they could afford to do so, was permitted to wear gold and silver. Gentlemen with land bringing an income of 100 pounds a year could wear velvet in their doublets but not in their gowns and coats. Ben Jonson (1572–1637), author of scurrilous satires on London life, wrote that to become recognized as a gentleman, a man had to go to London, "where at your first appearance 'twere good you turned four or five hundred acres of your best land into two or three trunks of apparel."

Cardinal Wolsey had earlier attempted to moderate the dietary excesses of wealthy people, including the high clergy. Copying sumptuary regulations that could be found throughout Europe since the Middle Ages, he specified the number of separate dinner courses that people of various ranks might consume, with the largest number—nine—reserved for cardinals like himself. But to no avail. A critical commentator wrote toward the end of the century, "Nowadays, if the table be not covered from the one end to the other as thick as a dish can stand by another . . . and to every dish a several sauce appropriate to his kind, it is thought unworthy of the name of dinner." The poor ate no such meals. The condition of life of some artisans, landless cottagers, rural laborers, and unskilled and under-employed workers declined; soaring food and lodging costs sapped their meager earnings. Their lives became even more insecure.

There was, to be sure, some degree of social mobility in Tudor England: new economic opportunities brought greater prosperity to gentry, yeoman, merchants, and manufacturers. By the end of the century, the economic gap between nobles and wealthy gentry landowners had been reduced. Some yeomen achieved gentry status, and merchants and manufacturers made money. The interests and lifestyles of the middling sort gradually moved closer to those of gentlemen and their families as English society became more polarized. And, to be sure, some farm servants were able to save enough money to become husbandmen, or even yeomen; likewise, some apprentices became independent masters within their trades. But social advancement remained relatively rare among the poor, whose num-bers were rapidly expanding along with their impoverishment.

The Quest for Public Order

After almost a century of inflation accentuated by a rising population, har-vest failures in the 1590s brought the period of economic expansion to an abrupt halt in England. Never had there seemed to be so many poor and hungry people on the roads, dressed in rags, sleeping in fields, searching for wild berries or edible roots, and begging, just trying to get by. "They lie in the streets," came a report, "in the dirt as commonly is seen . . . and are permitted to die like dogs or beasts without any mercy or compassion showed them at all." Shakespeare's *Midsummer Night's Dream* refers to contemporary harvest failure and food shortages.

Ordinary people sometimes took matters into their own hands. Food ri-ots spread through much of England, as the poor seized grain and sold it at what they considered a reasonable price. Women usually made up the ma-jority of participants in the food riots because it fell to them to try to make ends meet at the market. Such disturbances increased the resolve of the state to maintain order at all costs. Riots against enclosure also reflected the fact that the poor assumed that they had a right to subsistence and be-lieved there had been better times when elites and ordinary people lived in harmony and the rights of both were respected.

The prosecution of serious crimes increased rapidly during Elizabeth's reign, peaking between 1590 and 1620. Vagrancy, considered a serious of-fense, was the most prevalent of these as people took to the road in search of food. Vagrants were arrested, and placed in stocks for three days, before

Whipping a man arrested for vagrancy and expelling him from town. In view of what's happened to his friend in the upper left corner, he's lucky to have escaped with his life.

being sent home. Untold thousands of poor people did not get that far and died before being arrested, such as the person buried in 1592, "a poor woman which died in a barne at the parsonage whose name we could not learne." Thefts rose rapidly. A contemporary estimated that there were twenty-three different categories of thieves and swindlers, including "hookers," who snatched linen and clothes with a long pole from windows, "priggers of prancers" (horse thieves), and "Abraham men," who "feign themselves to have been mad." But most thieves lacked such colorful names and specializations; they stole what they could in order to survive. Robert Whitehead, a poor man, was typical of those arrested for theft, having stolen a sheep, "beinge a verie poore man and havinge a wiefe and seaven smale children and being most hungery." The theft of goods worth more than twelve shillings could bring the death penalty, but more often offenders were publicly whipped and branded, or perhaps mutilated by having an ear extracted, and perhaps sent to serve as oarsmen in the galley ships. Women were often treated more harshly than men, unless they were pregnant. After 1572, individuals over age fourteen caught begging without a license were to be whipped and also "burned through the grisle of the right ear with a hot iron of the compass of an inch about, manifesting his or her roguish kind of life." Although only about 10 percent of those convicted of capital crimes were actually executed, such punishment was particularly brutal, including hanging by slow strangulation and being slowly crushed to death by weights.

The English upper classes, convinced that most crime went unpunished, became obsessed with maintaining order, a fact reflected in several of Shakespeare's plays, in which ordinary people appear as potential threats to social order. To some people, society stood on the verge of being overwhelmed by lawlessness and sin. At a time when the monarchy was extending its reach, many Elizabethans believed that social order depended on the maintenance of social hierarchy and the securing of obedience to the moral authority of government. Thus, the Tudors formulated a doctrine of obedience to authority, basing their arguments on religious teaching. As early as 1547, one of the first homilies on obedience had instructed that on earth God "hath assigned kings, princes, with other governors under them, all in good and necessary order." Such homilies, which were read in church from the pulpit, warned the English of the consequences of challenging social hierarchy:

> There reigneth all abuse, carnal liberty, enormity, sin and Babylonical confusion. Take away kings, princes, rulers, magistrates, judges, and such estates of God's order, no man shall ride to go by the highway untroubled, no man shall sleep in his own house or bed unkilled, no man shall keep his wife, children or possessions in quietness, all things shall be common; and there needs must follow all mischief and utter destruction both of souls, bodies, goods and commonwealths.

Elizabethan literature and drama constantly returned to the theme of a place for everyone and everyone in his or her place—or moral law based upon the necessity of social order. In Shakespeare's *The History of Troilus and Cressida*, Ulysses proclaims:

> The heavens themselves, the planets, and
>   this centre
> Observe degree, priority, and place,
> Insisture, course, proportion, season, form;
> Office, and custom, in all line of order; . . .
> But when the planets
> In evil mixture to disorder wander,
> What plagues and what portents, what mutiny!
> What raging of the sea, shaking of earth! . . .
> take but degree away, untune that string,
> And hark what discord follows. . . .

Many wealthy English men and women believed that the slightest offense against the monarchy contained the seeds of rebellion; in 1576, a woman was burned at the stake for saying that Elizabeth was "baseborn and not born to the crown." Fear of disturbances and challenges to authority contributed to the development of a sense of national consciousness of England's elite, just as the defeat of Spain's Armada in 1588 led to pride in being both Protestant and English.

In 1598, Parliament passed the first poor law, followed by another in 1601. These laws recognized for the first time the principle that the needy ought to receive some sort of assistance from their communities. Justices of the peace, under the supervision of the clergy, were to oversee the distribution of assistance to the poor in the local communities in which they resided. The poor laws also specified the establishment of poor houses for the incarceration of the poor who could not or would not work (including the aged, sick, and insane).

The poor laws, then, reflected a combination of concern for and fear of the wandering poor. Ministers denounced the poor from the pulpit as sources of disorder, while trumpeting the virtues of sobriety, submission, obedience, and social deference. Orders were sent from London detailing measures to be taken in the interest of social order by the justices of the peace, who only had recourse to troops in dire circumstances. Local elites took a more active role in enforcing ordinances against begging and vagrancy. Landed gentlemen and the merchants and manufacturers of the towns found that they now had more in common than wealth—a fear of the poor.

The Elizabethan Theater

The arts reflected the prosperity of the upper and middle classes in England. Protestant censors were more lax in censoring theatrical performances than had been their Catholic counterparts. In 1576, two professional theaters opened in London, followed by others in a number of provincial towns. Putting aside the repertory of religious allegories and miracle and morality plays that had been staged in royal castles, country manor houses, or entire towns, they staked their survival on their ability to attract audiences that would pay to see the actors perform. The more than 2,000 different plays staged in London between 1580 and 1640 consisted mostly of romances and dramas. During that period, more than 300 playwrights produced enough work to keep 100 acting companies working in London or touring provincial towns.

William Shakespeare (1564–1616) wrote plays that reflected uncertainty, ambivalence, and even disillusionment about contemporary English society. Historians know little about his life, despite the fact that he is perhaps the most revered Western author of all time. He was born in Stratford-on-Avon, where his father made gloves and was able to provide him with a primary school education. Shakespeare moved to London with his young wife to become an actor and in the late 1580s began to write plays. He found first patronage and then unparalleled success, angering rivals, one of whom referred to him as "an upstart crow beautified with our feathers." He became part owner and actor in the Lord Chamberlain's Company of the Globe Theater, which seated 3,000 viewers and hence

(*Left*) William Shakespeare. (*Right*) The Swan Theater, an Elizabethan playhouse that closely resembled Shakespeare's Globe Theater.

was the largest of London's six private theaters. Seats at such private theaters cost at least six times more than the cheapest tickets at the public theaters, which included places for the so-called "penny stinkards" who stood in the uncovered pit below the stage.

Audiences shouted for what they liked and hooted at what they did not. Fights were not infrequent, both inside and outside of the theater. The playwright Christopher Marlowe (1564–1593) died in a brawl in an inn under mysterious circumstances; the actor and playwright Ben Jonson killed another actor in a duel. Because of their rowdy reputations, most London theaters stood outside the city walls. London officials tried to close down the public theaters because they thought that disease spread easily among assembled crowds and because of complaints about profanity and lewdness on stage. Some great landowners found public crowds too socially mixed for their taste and helped revive private theaters.

Elizabethan drama reflected contemporary awareness and disapproval of the machinations of the powerful. In his dramatic, sometimes violent plays, as well as his comedies, Marlowe evoked the Elizabethan elite's unabashed struggle for position and power. Edmund Spenser's complex *Faerie Queen* used the legend of King Arthur to skirt censorship, presenting a thinly veiled criticism of the greed and corruption of contemporary political life. Spenser (1552–1599), a melancholy, frustrated man who never ascended to the heights of influence that he had sought, placed his "kingdom in Fairy land" in uncorrupted Ireland.

Despite the problems of religious division, warfare, and the struggles for influence that were reflected in the drama of the times, England under the

Tudors became a power that would influence the world. Elizabeth died in peace on March 24, 1603, in the forty-fifth year of her reign. She left England a substantially more unified, effectively ruled, and powerful state—despite the social disturbances engendered by harder times—than that she had inherited.

THE DECLINE OF SPAIN

In 1600, the word "decline" was first used to describe the overstretched Spanish Empire. Had the Spain of the Catholic kings fallen from God's favor? Castilians themselves still regarded Spain as a haven of peace and prosperity compared to the rest of Europe, which was wracked by religious wars. Responses from more than 500 towns and villages to a survey that Philip II sent around Castile in 1575 reflected Spanish self-confidence.

The Dutch Revolt

The decline of Spanish power began with the Dutch revolt. In the Netherlands, the Dutch nobles and officials resented higher taxes imposed by the Spanish crown. Above all, many of the Dutch were angered by the Spanish king's attempt to promote the Catholic Reformation by imposing the Inquisition in a land where most people were Calvinists. In the early 1560s, resistance first began against the presence of Spanish border garrisons and then against the unpopular governor.

In 1567, Philip II appointed the arrogant duke of Alba (1507–1582) to restore order in the north with 10,000 Spanish troops. The ruthless Castilian executed prominent Calvinist nobles on the central square of Brussels in the Southern Netherlands, established military courts, imposed heavy new taxes, and virtually destroyed self-government in the Netherlands. But Alba's reign of terror as governor also helped transform the resistance of Dutch nobles and officials, led by William of Orange (1533–1584), into a national revolt.

Alba believed that "Everyone must be made to live in constant fear of the roof breaking down over his head" and warned "I am resolved not to leave a creature alive, but to put them all to the sword." Alba's Council of Troubles, known to the Dutch as the "Council of Blood," executed thousands of people from 1567 to 1573, leading a Catholic bishop to claim later that in six years Alba had hurt the Church more than Luther and Calvin combined.

In 1572, rebellion became full-fledged insurrection. Spanish troops dominated on land, but the Dutch controlled the sea. When a Spanish army undertook a siege of Leiden, southwest of Amsterdam, the people of the town opened the dikes, and Dutch ships sailed over the rushing waters to drive the Spaniards away. But Alba's successor earned victories in the

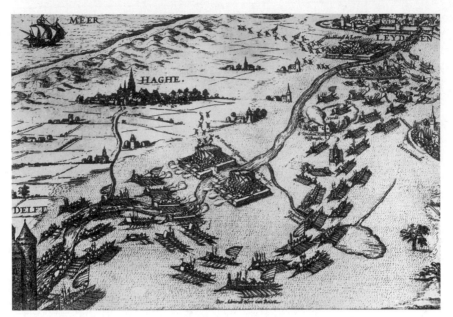

The rescue of Leiden by the Dutch sea beggars, who arrive over the flooded low-lands after the breaching of the dikes.

Southern Netherlands. There Catholic nobles began to have second thoughts about continuing a struggle launched by Dutch Protestants. They detached the southern provinces from the rebellious federation. In 1579, the Dutch provinces formed the Union of Utrecht, and two years later they declared their independence from Spain as the Dutch United Provinces.

For the moment, Spain could supply its armies because Alba's armies had recaptured some of the Southern Netherlands, while Philip maintained peace with England. As the Dutch revolt wore on, however, the problems of fighting a war a thousand miles away plagued the Spanish king. Military contractors or entrepreneurs recruited mercenaries, and Italians, Burgundians, Germans, and Walloons made up much of the Spanish army.

Spanish routes for troops, supplies, and bullion to the Netherlands had to be maintained through a combination of diplomatic charm, cunning, and coercion. As allegiances and the fortunes of war eliminated first the Palatinate, then Alsace and Lorraine as routes through which armies could pass, the Spanish forged the "Spanish Road" as a military corridor (see Map 5.3). It began in Genoa, went overland across the Alps, and then passed through Lombardy and Piedmont, Geneva, Franche-Comté, Lorraine and, finally, the Duchy of Liège, with Spanish agents assuring supplies along the way.

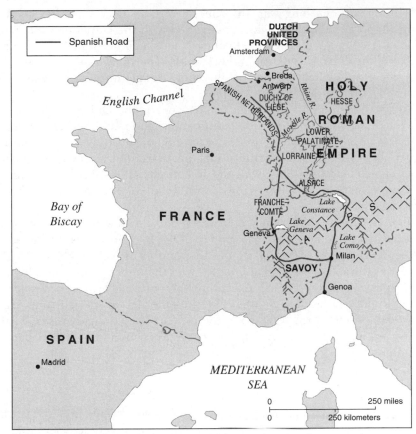

MAP 5.3 THE SPANISH ROAD The route taken by the Spanish armies, supplies, and money from Spain to the Netherlands was long and difficult, as it passed through mountainous terrain and many states.

Spanish officers compounded problems of recruiting and supply, however, by trying to save money. They charged sharpshooters for powder and shot, a dubious strategy at best. Compared to other armies fighting in Europe at the same time, the Spanish army seemed better only in terms of medical attention. The army's guarantee before battle to carry out the written wills made by soldiers seems to have been, on the other hand, a curiously self-defeating approach to inspiring confidence. Mutinies, the largest involving non-Spanish troops, occurred with ever more frequency as troops demanded payment of back wages, better and more regular food, and decent hospital conditions. Soldiers deserted, encouraged and aided by Dutch agents, as well as by those of France, against whom Spain was also warring. By 1577, the Spanish army in the Netherlands, unpaid for months, had dwindled in size from 60,000 to no more than 8,000 men.

Throughout the long war, the superior Dutch fleet kept the Spanish ships in port, while the English navy, allied with the Dutch in 1586, controlled the Channel. When the Spanish fleet sailed north in 1588, the result was the disastrous defeat of the Armada. The ships of "sea beggars," as they were called, fighting under William of Orange (until his assassination in 1584), then harassed Spanish ships.

At the beginning of the seventeenth century, the Dutch gradually fell back behind the protective town fortifications and natural barriers formed by rivers. The war became a series of long Spanish sieges against frontier towns defended by brick fortifications, bastions, and moats—a defensive system that had its origins with the Italian city-states. With the defense having a marked advantage, towns could be conquered only by being starved out.

France withdrew from the war in 1598, and England withdrew six years later. But a truce between Spain and the Dutch, signed in 1609, ended in 1621. In Holland the "war party" led by Maurice of Nassau (1567–1625), who was the son of William of Orange, won the upper hand, appealing for Calvinist religious orthodoxy and calling for a crusade against Catholicism that would also free the Southern Netherlands from Spanish rule. Army officers and merchant traders wanted to keep the struggle against Spain going as long as possible. It dragged on, an expensive drain on the Spanish economy.

Economic Decline

Economic decline—above all that of Castile in the middle decades of the seventeenth century—underlay Spain's fall from a position of European domination. But decline is, of course, relative. Spain remained an important state although its population, which had risen to 8.5 million people between 1541 and 1591, fell by almost a quarter to 6.5 million by the middle of the seventeenth century, as harvest failures, plague, smallpox, and emigration took their toll.

The "price revolution," the sharp rise in the level of inflation during the sixteenth century in Europe, may well have affected Spain less than some parts of Northern Europe, but it still had adverse effects on the Spanish monarchy. Gold and silver from the Americas accelerated inflation, to which royal monetary policies of currency debasement contributed. The monarchy, which had declared bankruptcy in 1557, suspended payments in 1575, and again in 1596, renegotiating loans at more favorable rates. But during the period 1568–1598, Spain had five times the military expenditures of the Dutch, English, and French combined, at least partially because it had to reconstitute the Armada. One of the results of so many expensive wars was that Spain lost its margin of safety when it experienced a series of epidemics, plagues, and harvest failures beginning in 1576 and continuing for most of the last quarter of the century. The economy

The expulsion of the Moriscos from Spain.

slipped into stagnation. To one noble it already seemed that "the ship is sinking."

Forced to take out large loans from foreign bankers at disadvantageous interest rates, the state attempted to find new sources of revenue. To raise funds, the crown imposed a tithe, or assessment of a tenth of the most valuable piece of real estate in each parish, and in 1590 the Castilian Cortes agreed to an extraordinary tax assessed on towns. An excise (sales) tax was imposed on consumption. This undermined the economy by encouraging the middle class to abandon business in favor of the acquisition of perpetual privileges—and thus tax exemptions—as they obtained noble status. The monarchy's massive expulsion of the Moriscos in 1609 (about 300,000 people, a third of the population of Valencia and a fifth of Aragon) proved counterproductive. The king succumbed to pressure from the Catholic Church and from wealthy families eager to seize Moorish land. The region of Valencia lost one-third of its population, including many skilled craftsmen and some of the most able and advanced farmers.

Castile, in particular, suffered a reduction in agricultural output because of twenty-five years of bad weather and crop failure. The rain pattern in Castile, with its annual summer drought, meant that Spanish farmers could not adopt the double-cropping innovations—for example, the summer planting of a nitrogen-fixing forage crop such as alfalfa—that brought agricultural expansion in England and the Netherlands.

Nobles added the lands of indebted peasants to their large estates (*latifundia*), but they showed little interest in increasing the productivity of their land, in contrast to their English counterparts. They turned fields into pastureland or simply left them untended. Royal policies may also have damaged the agricultural economy. In part because royal policies favored sheepherding over farming—because it was easier to collect taxes on sheep than on agricultural produce—many landowners converted marginal land into pasture for sheep and expanded their home textile manufacturing (as occurred in the Netherlands at the same time). But fine woolens manufacturing suffered from foreign textile imports, especially the importing of lighter cloth from France and the Netherlands. Furthermore, the stagnation of the population further reduced demand for Spanish woolens. Despite all those sheep, the production of wool fell by three-quarters in Toledo during the first two-thirds of the seventeenth century, and textile manufacturing completely disappeared from some cities.

At the same time, farmers were hampered by a state-imposed fixed maximum for grain prices, which discouraged ambitious agricultural initiatives. Toward the end of the sixteenth century, Spain had become dependent on imported grain. Its decline in demographic vitality generated less demand for food. This further reduced tax revenue. Many peasants simply abandoned their farms, moving to towns.

"Conquered by you, the New World has conquered you in turn, and has weakened and exhausted your ancient vigor," a Flemish scholar wrote a friend in Spain. The Spanish colonies, too, became something of a financial drain on the crown because of the cost of administering and defending them. The flow of Latin American silver, which had paid less than a quarter of the crown's colonial and military expenses, slowed to a trickle beginning in the 1620s. The colonial market for Spanish goods shrank with a precipitous decline in the Indian population (caused, above all, by disease; see Chapter 1), undermining Spanish commerce and industry. Furthermore, the colonies had also developed their own basic agricultural and artisanal production and relied far less on Spanish goods. The Atlantic ports of northern Castile endured competition in shipbuilding and commerce not only from Seville and Cádiz, but from Spain's own colonies, and above all, from England and the Netherlands.

The monarchy lost its financial autonomy within Spain. The intransigence of the Cortes of Aragon put more pressure on the crown to raise money in Castile. But the Castilian Cortes by 1600 had clearly affirmed its right to supervise state expenditures and was influential in establishing a system of state finance, with the Council of Castile serving as a court of final appeal.

Although the burden of taxes in Castile increased by four times between 1570 and 1670, the Spanish crown proved less efficient in collecting taxes than the monarchs of France and England. More than this, increased taxes on the poor generated more discontent than income. Spain's Italian subjects resisted contributing money for distant wars that did not concern them. Charles V had largely financed his wars through fiscal impositions on the Netherlands, his wealthiest province. But the Dutch revolt, in addition to dramatically raising royal expenses, stopped the flow of money from the Dutch subjects to the crown and thus drastically reduced royal revenue.

During the early years of the seventeenth century, officials, academics, military men, merchants, and clergy flooded the passive Philip III with well-intentioned critiques addressing the question of Spain's decline. Some of these critics (*arbitristas*) offered practical suggestions, such as reducing taxes and digging navigable canals, that they hoped would end Spain's economic malaise.

Other countries, notably France, may have had similar discouraging demographic and economic trends, but their natural resources were greater and their economic structure more solid. Money in Spain that might have gone into economic development often ended up being loaned to the crown at usurious interest, or exchanged for honorific privileges.

There were many families claiming noble titles in Spain, perhaps 10 percent of the population. Although some nobles served as officials and military commanders, others transformed indolence into a high art. One of the king's advisers, for example, was described as having "spent all

The painting *A Soldier's Dream* allegorizes Spanish feelings of morose despair and fatalism as the Spanish Empire begins to crumble.

his life in Madrid in total idleness, almost exclusively shared between eating and sleeping." A doctor gravely urged his aristocratic patients to limit themselves to six courses per meal. The wealthiest aristocrats—the "grandees," a small elite established by Charles V in 1525—spent wildly and ostentatiously, flocking to court to curry favor. They did little besides hunt, gamble, and conspire against their enemies. Many nobles were unwilling to serve as officers in the army. Furthermore, most of the clergy, in a country dotted with monasteries and convents, contributed little to the economy.

Contemporary Spaniards, particularly Castilians, lapsed into a morose acceptance of decline. The novelist Miguel de Cervantes (1547–1616) had fought with the king's armies at the Battle of Lepanto (1571), where he received a wound that permanently crippled his left arm. Several years later, he was captured by Turkish pirates. After five years as a slave, he managed to return to Spain. The first part of *Don Quixote* was published in 1605, the second in 1615. It is more than the tale of a zany noble intent on bringing true chivalry back to Spain, accompanied by his sensible, subservient squire, Sancho Panza. *Don Quixote* is the story of national disillusionment in the face of perceived national decline. Cervantes blamed the nobles, who lamented the end of heroic noble ideals. Among the next generation of great Spanish writers, the dramatist Pedro Calderón de la Barca (1600–1681) tragically portrayed in his plays the floundering Spanish aristocracy struggling to preserve its honor. Nobles and churchmen, the two pillars of Spain, purchased the work of the increasingly gloomy Greek-born artist El Greco (1541–1614). His *The Burial of the Count Orgaz* (1581) shows figures looking up at a vision of celestial glory, while on earth things already did not seem to be going very well.

An Empire Spread Too Thin

Spain's mounting economic problems were exacerbated by the fact that the empire's interests, some of which were defended in costly wars, were spread so widely, not only in Europe, but across the seas. Philip IV (1605–1665), who succeeded to the throne in 1621, was intelligent, strong-willed, lazy, and had a keen interest in the arts. He chose as his chief adviser and the person who handled the affairs of state Gaspar de Guzmán, the duke of Olivares (1587–1645), an Andalusian noble whose family had, like Spain itself, suffered reverses. The short, increasingly obese, and fiery Olivares sketched ambitious plans to shape the rebirth of Spanish might. Confronted with the growing economic strength of the Dutch rebels, as well as that of the English, Olivares sensed that Spain could not remain a power without a marked economic resurgence. "We must devote all our efforts," he had written, "to turning Spaniards into merchants." The Count Duke, as he was called, mastered his master, convincing the lazy king that only hard work and reform could restore the glo-

(*Left*) King Philip IV. (*Right*) The Count Duke Olivares.

ries of the not-so-distant past. He would tutor his king, whose chamber pot he once ceremoniously kissed, in the fine art of monarchy.

The Count Duke espoused the growth of monarchical power and state centralization. His motto "one king, one law, one money" generated resistance, in the latter case because of the by then notorious instability of the Castilian currency. At a time when complaints mounted against the extraordinary excise taxes, Olivares sought to subject all of Spain to the laws and royal administration of Castile. In 1624 he told the king, "The most important thing in Your Majesty's Monarchy is for you to become King of Spain. By this I mean, Sir, that your Majesty should not be content with being king of Portugal, of Aragon, of Valencia and count of Barcelona, but should secretly plan to and work to reduce these kingdoms of which Spain is composed to the style and laws of Castile, with no difference whatsoever. And if Your Majesty achieves this, you will be the most powerful prince in the world."

Olivares wanted to force Dutch capitulation to restore the monarchy's reputation, fearing defeat as dishonorable, anxious that it might begin a chain reaction that would destroy the empire. He persuaded the king to allow the truce with the Dutch to lapse in 1621, thus necessitating massive expenses for land and sea warfare. Olivares concluded from the Dutch surrender of the fortress town of Breda in 1625 that it was God's will that the fight against the Protestant rebels in the north continue. To preserve the "Spanish Road," Olivares sought to bolster Spanish interests in northern Italy and in Austria, the same expensive strategy employed earlier by

Philip II. But France cut the Spanish supply routes in Savoy in 1622 and then in Alsace nine years later. Furthermore, Olivares embroiled Spain in a war in northern Italy when Spanish armies intervened in the hope of preventing the succession of a Frenchman as duke of Mantua, fearing that this might compromise Spanish control of Milan and northern Italy. Intermittent hostilities with France lasted from 1628 to 1631, and made more likely a full-scale conflict between the two powers.

Spain could ill afford such conflicts. In 1628, Dutch pirates captured a Spanish fleet loaded with silver. This enormous loss made it imperative that the crown find new resources with which to wage war. But for the first time, Castile's monarchs could not establish credit with foreign investors to finance Spain's foreign wars. Increased taxation, the floating of short-term loans through bonds, the sale of yet more privileges, and the imposition of new financial obligations on Aragon and the Italian territories all proved inadequate to the task of financing an expensive, distant war. The monarchy was finally able to override the opposition of the towns represented in the Castilian Cortes. But unable to overcome opposition to the centralization of the fiscal apparatus, Philip IV was forced to convoke the Cortes in 1632 to seek another extraordinary tax.

Its interests gravely overextended, Spain's position weakened. English ships began to nip at its imperial interests in the Americas. Dutch ships fought the proud Spanish galleons in the West Indies. Three decades of intermittent warfare with France began in 1635, as the Thirty Years' War (see Chapter 4) became a struggle between competing dynasties. As more and more bullion from the Americas had to be diverted to pay military expenses in the Netherlands and Italy, the monarchy demanded new contributions from Catalonia and Portugal, as Spain had assumed the expensive and ultimately extremely damaging responsibility for protecting Portuguese shipping around the world. Tumultuous tax riots, beneath which lay resentment against Castilian domination, broke out in the Portuguese town of Evora in 1637. The Portuguese upper classes began to resist Spanish authority.

Olivares' decision to demand more taxes from Catalonia proved fateful. Faced with resistance, he ordered the arrest of several Catalan leaders, amid riots in the countryside. Catalan nobles put aside their differences, and a full-scale revolt against Castilian rule began in 1640. Catalan and French forces together defeated the Spanish army. A year later, Andalusian nobles were foiled in a plot to create an independent kingdom there. Nobles in Madrid hatched plots against Olivares. When Portugal proclaimed its independence, there were few Spanish troops there to protest. The vigorous assertion of localism reflected the disillusionment of provincial elites with Castilian power. Philip sent the despondent Olivares into exile in 1643.

However, the illusion of Don Quixote was maintained—that the restoration of traditional aristocratic and ecclesiastical values would restore

Spanish might. Olivares established two court academies intended to train young nobles in the art of government. Heeding the advice of churchmen, he also attempted to ban prostitution and take other such measures in what he considered the interest of traditional morals, censoring the theater and books, prohibiting certain kinds of fancy clothing and long hair. It would not be enough.

By the 1660s, the Cortes was no longer an impediment to monarchical authority in Castile, and thereafter it was convoked only on ceremonial occasions. But, at the same time, the Spanish monarchy may in the long run have been damaged by its inability to reform its financial apparatus. The crown extended its reach and solidified its authority against possible provincial rebellions. Over the long run, Spanish rulers weakened parliamentary traditions. Yet, enhanced centralization was not matched by more efficient tax collection.

Ironically, amid such signs of decline, the last years of Philip IV and the reign of his pathetic successor, Charles II (ruled 1665–1700), sustained a period of considerable cultural accomplishment in the arts and in literature. But this, too, may have been generated by the prevailing mood of introspection. Olivares put dramatists and a small host of other writers to work in the name of glorifying the monarchy and imparting a sense of purpose that he hoped would revive Spain.

King Philip IV added more than 2,000 canvases to what already was a rich royal collection, including many by Italian masters. He covered the palace walls with grandiose paintings of battle scenes. Diego de Velázquez (1599–1660), the court painter, undertook forty portraits of the vain king. Their sharp realism stands as a commentary on the Spanish monarchy's fading glory and disillusionment. Velázquez also commemorated the badly needed—but ultimately fruitless—victory over the Dutch in *The Surrender of Breda* (1634–1635).

In the meantime, the Dutch rebels, aided by increased commercial prosperity, had fought the Spanish armies to a draw. The Treaty of Münster, which was part of the Westphalia settlement of 1648 that ended the Thirty Years' War, officially recognized Dutch independence after a struggle that had lasted three-quarters of a century. The provinces of the Southern Netherlands, that is, modern-day Belgium, which were overwhelmingly Catholic, remained a Habsburg possession. In Catalonia, Barcelona surrendered to royal troops in 1652. Catalan nobles accepted the supremacy of the crown in exchange for an affirmation of social hierarchy and royal protection against ordinary Catalans who resented their privileges. The Aragonese nobles, too, accepted this compromise.

The Spanish monarchy never learned that it could not fight effectively on a variety of fronts. In contrast, the French monarchy, concentrating its efforts in Italy, for the moment realized the wisdom of fighting on one front at a time. Thus, subsequent Spanish victories in the north against French armies were not enough, for when the French turned their atten-

Diego de Velázquez's *Surrender of Breda* (painted 1634–1635).

tion to the Spanish front they easily held their own. The Treaty of the Pyrenees, signed between France and Spain in 1659, established the border between these countries that has lasted, with only a few minor changes, until this day. Spain also gave up Milan to Austria, and Naples and Sicily to the Italian Bourbon dynasty. The Portuguese, aided by the English, turned back several half-hearted invasions by Spanish armies, and in 1668 Spain recognized Portugal's independence. Ten years later, France occupied the Franche Comté, the last major Spanish holding in Northern Europe.

By 1680, when the depression that had lasted almost a century ended, Spain had become a second-rate power. This was because of agricultural and manufacturing decline, to be sure, but, above all, it was because the Spanish crown had overreached.

CONCLUSION

The development of trade across the Atlantic Ocean to the Americas was part of European economic expansion during the sixteenth century. Following the union of the crowns of Castile and Aragon, Spain grew into a great power. Philip II expanded the Spanish Empire, which, in the Americas stretched from what is now the southern United States to the southern tip of Latin America, and in Europe included the Netherlands and several Italian states. The Tudor monarchy in England overcame the country's religious divisions in the wake of the English Reformation to strengthen its authority. In this, it resembled the ruling Valois dynasty of France, another "new monarchy" in that it enhanced its reach, efficiency, and prestige. The burgeoning of English trade, manufacturing, and agriculture in the Elizabethan Age underlay England's relative prosperity, even as social polarization, reflected in the crises of the 1590s, became more apparent.

The surprising English naval defeat of the Spanish Armada in 1588 symbolized not only the rise of England but in some ways anticipated the decline of Spanish power. Spain's rulers had expanded their vast empire and imperial interests beyond the ability of the state to sustain them. When silver from the Americas slowed to a trickle, Spain's own limited natural resources, combined with demographic stagnation that began early in the seventeenth century, undercut Spanish Habsburg power. The inability of the Spanish monarchy to impose fully its authority on Aragon and Catalonia, or to collect taxes efficiently, prevented a revival of Spanish preeminence. The long revolt of the Netherlands ended with recognition of Dutch independence in 1648. That the Dutch Republic and England, two trading nations, had emerged as European powers reflected the shift of economic primacy to Northwestern Europe.

CHAPTER 6

ENGLAND AND THE DUTCH REPUBLIC IN THE SEVENTEENTH CENTURY

England and the Dutch Republic were anomalies in the seventeenth century. At a time when aggressive European monarchs were forging absolute states by overwhelming noble prerogatives, the privileges of towns, and other impediments to an extension of royal authority, these two seafaring, trading nations maintained representative government. It was not always easy, and might well have been otherwise.

The Stuart monarchs' flirtation with absolutism in England brought bitter discord, resistance, and civil war. In the Dutch Republic, which had earned its independence in 1648 after a long war against Spanish absolute rule, the prosperous merchants who dominated the economic and political life of the country brushed aside the absolutist challenge of the House of Orange, which wanted to establish a hereditary monarchy.

In both England and the Netherlands, religious divisions accentuated the struggle between absolutism and constitutionalism. Both the protracted revolt of the largely Protestant Dutch against Catholic Spain and the English Civil War echoed the religious struggles between Catholics and Protestants during the Thirty Years' War (1618–1648) in Central Europe (see Chapter 4). The Dutch had risen up in open rebellion in 1566 in part because the Spanish Habsburgs attempted to impose the Catholic Inquisition on what had become a Protestant country. In England, the attempt of Kings James I and Charles I to return the English Church to elaborate rituals associated by many people with Catholicism pitted the monarchy against Parliament. This constitutional crisis led to the defeat and execution of Charles I in 1649, the fall of the monarchy, and in 1688,

The bustling harbor of Middelburg in the province of Zeeland, southwestern Netherlands, in the early seventeenth century.

to the "Glorious Revolution," which brought King William III and Queen Mary to the throne. Parliament, which historically represented landed interests, succeeded in balancing and constraining royal authority. By virtue of Parliament's victory in the Civil War, England remained a constitutional monarchy. England's new monarchs agreed to a Bill of Rights, which affirmed the civil liberties of English people and the rights of Parliament.

That the two new powers of Northern Europe, England and the Dutch Republic, were largely Protestant has led some historians to associate their success with the "Calvinist ethic" of hard work. Yet, the emergence of England and the Dutch Republic as Great Powers was largely because of their social structure, especially the vitality of the "middling sort" in both nations, the relative unity of the two states, and the location of both rising powers on the Atlantic. Aided by governments quick to realize the benefits to their states of an expansion of international trade, the Dutch Netherlands and England mobilized the resources of its middle classes. England's international commerce rapidly developed. And as Amsterdam emerged as a banking center and first port of call for international trade, the Dutch Republic enjoyed the golden age of its culture.

CONFLICTS IN STUART ENGLAND

Conflicts between the Stuart kings and Parliament, as well as religious conflicts, led to the English Civil War, which helped define the constitutional and political institutions of modern Britain. The monarchy tried to enhance its authority at the expense of Parliament by attempting to impose extralegal taxes without the consent of Parliament. But the English gentry, whose status and influence came from ownership of land, emerged from the period with their parliamentary prerogatives intact. The nature and extent of royal prerogatives were at issue, as well as religious, social, and ideological divisions. These were played out through the English Civil War and its aftermath.

Conflicts between James I and Parliament

King James I (1566–1625) succeeded his cousin Queen Elizabeth to the English throne in 1603. As King James VI of Scotland, he had overcome court factionalism and challenges from dissident Presbyterians. The two countries were joined in a personal union because he ruled both. The first Stuart king of England was lazy, slovenly, and frivolous, particularly enjoying hurling jelly at his courtiers. But there was more to him than that. He was an intelligent and well-read blunderer, once described as "the wisest fool in Christendom." Before coming to the throne, James had sketched out a theory of divine right monarchy. And in a speech to Parliament in 1609 the king had called "The state of MONARCHIE . . . the supremest thing upon earth: for Kings are not only GOD'S Lieutenants upon earth, and sit upon throne, but even by God himselfe they are called Gods." James described Parliament as nothing "but cries, shouts, and confusion." Relations between the monarch and Parliament degenerated rapidly.

The English monarchy was in a precarious financial position. Queen Elizabeth's war debts were at least partially to blame. But the financial weakness of the English crown also resulted from the monarch's growing inability to tax efficiently. (Tax increases helped contribute to the major political crises of the sixteenth century, including the Fronde in France; see Chapter 7.) For the moment, James increased royal revenues by selling the right to monopolies on such essential products as coal and soap. Parliament traditionally had to approve extraordinary expenditures. When the Stuart kings tried to assert the monarchy's authority to raise money in ways many people believed unprecedented and thus unconstitutional, opposition grew in Parliament.

James brought to court like-minded dandies, most of whom proved not only unpopular with Parliament but incompetent and provocative as well. In the last years of his reign, James became increasingly dependent on his young, handsome favorite, George Villiers, the duke of Buckingham (1592–1628). A relative newcomer to court circles, Buckingham convinced the king to sell peerages and titles, offices, monopolies, and other privileges to the highest bidder. Opposition to such attempts to raise money mounted within Parliament.

Although it met sporadically and at the king's pleasure, Parliament transformed itself from something more than a debating society into an institution that saw itself as defending the rights of the English people. The House of Commons, lashing out at the beneficiaries of royal monopolies, impeached on charges of bribery Lord Chancellor Francis Bacon (1561–1626), philosopher of science and once the king's friend. Here, too, there was a principle at stake: the accountability of ministers, if not responsibility, to Parliament.

English foreign policy contributed both to the monarchy's mounting debt and the emerging political crisis. Queen Elizabeth had denied that Parliament had the right to discuss matters of foreign policy unless invited by the monarch to do so. Parliament, however, still insisted on that right. Thus, for example, James favored peace with Spain, but Parliament clamored for war because Bavaria, an ally of Habsburg Spain, had invaded the Protestant Upper Palatinate. And in 1621, asserting its right to influence foreign policy, Parliament refused to provide more funds for the conflict, setting the stage for the greatest constitutional crisis in English history.

Parliament also denounced the monarch's attempt to arrange a marriage between his son, Charles, the heir to the throne, and the daughter of Philip IV of Spain. As dynastic marriages were an essential part of foreign policy, cementing or building alliances, members of Parliament objected to what appeared to be a sudden royal espousal of a foreign policy that seemed pro-Spanish and therefore pro-Catholic. Parliament declared its right to discuss the proposed marriage, and thus foreign affairs. But James defied Parliament by stating that it could not discuss matters of foreign policy, denying that the privileges of Parliament were "your ancient and undoubted birthright and inheritance." Rather he described them as "derived from the grace and permission of our ancestors and us."

James' wedding plans for his son fell through in 1623, however, when the Spanish king refused to allow Charles, who had gone to Madrid with

(*Left*) King James I. (*Right*) The young Charles, heir to the throne and later Charles I.

Buckingham, even to set eyes on his daughter. But two years later, James arranged Charles' marriage to another devout Catholic, Henrietta Maria of France. The secret price of this liaison included the king's promise that he would one day allow English Catholics, who numbered 2 or 3 percent of the population, to practice their religion freely. In a country in which anti-Catholicism had been endemic since the English Reformation of the mid-sixteenth century, James seemed to be taking steps to favor Catholicism.

James was succeeded upon his death by his son, Charles I (ruled 1625–1649). The young king was indecisive and painfully shy, traits compounded by a stammer. Even more than his father, Charles rejected the view that his appointments to ministries and other important offices should represent a wide spectrum of political and religious views. Charles stubbornly refused to oust Buckingham, even as Parliament began impeachment proceedings against the royal favorite.

Religious Divisions

King Charles I once claimed, "People are governed by the pulpit more than the sword in time of peace." In the seventeenth century, no other realm of life so bitterly divided Europeans as religion. In England, religious divisions helped accentuate and define the political crisis. The Established or Anglican Church faced a challenge from the Puritans, a dissident religious group of Calvinists that had emerged during Elizabeth's reign.

It is difficult to define what exactly it meant to be a Puritan in early seventeenth-century England. Many Puritans were more sure of what they were against than what they were for. As Oliver Cromwell, imposing leader of Parliament during the English Civil War, put it, "I can tell you, sir, what I would not have, though I cannot, what I would." Most Puritans were strongly attracted by the Calvinist idea that each individual was predestined by God through His grace to be saved or not to be saved. Puritans emphasized preaching and the individual's personal understanding of the Bible, spiritual devotion, discipline, and sacrifice as the basis of religion. Puritans opposed the role of bishops in the Church of England, in part because they emphasized the personal worth of the individual minister, not the value of an ecclesiastical title. They wanted authority to be taken away from bishops and given to local synods. They de-emphasized the sacraments and wanted worship to be simpler than the contemporary Anglican Church services, which they roundly criticized. Relentlessly hostile to Catholicism, Puritans held that elaborate church accoutrements—such as stained-glass windows and altar rails—smacked of the Roman papacy.

Puritans could be found in all social groups, above all, among the "middling sort"—including merchants, shopkeepers, and artisans—particularly in London, but also among the gentry at one end of the social spectrum and weavers at the other. Puritans did not choose the name by which they came to be known in the late sixteenth century, and which was originally intended as a term of abuse. Considering themselves "the godly," they believed that they represented the true Church of England, and worked for change and moral improvement within it. They remained a minority, probably not more than 10 percent of the population, and perhaps a third of all gentry. As Puritan numbers increased, however, their influence grew. University graduates who had embraced Puritanism formed "a godly preaching ministry" in many parishes, with endowed lectureships providing opportunities for Puritans to preach and win converts.

The Puritans were increasingly hostile to those who espoused a kind of Protestantism known as Arminianism. At first no more than a handful of ecclesiastics with the king's ear, Arminians soon came to wield considerable power. Charles I became an Arminian, and so did Buckingham. English Arminians, like their Dutch counterparts, broke with Calvinists over predestination, which Arminians rejected, but which Puritans accepted, and over the related concept of free will. Arminians accepted free will, while Puritans denied that an individual could achieve salvation through free will.

Puritans and Arminians also clashed over forms of worship. The Arminians accepted rites and rituals that to the Puritans seemed to replicate those of the Catholic Church. Indeed, Charles believed deeply in the traditions and rituals of the High Church, including the ceremonies associated with the Anglican Prayer Book. The Puritans wished to eliminate as much of the ritual as possible. The Arminians emphasized royal authority over the Church of England because they depended on it, and thus at least seemed to be proponents of royal absolutism. Arminians tried to forbid Calvinist preaching on controversial issues. And they emphasized the authority and ceremonial role of bishops, which Puritans opposed with particular vehemence.

The king's aggressive espousal of Arminianism enhanced the influence of William Laud (1573–1645), bishop of London. In 1633, Charles named the Arminian Laud to be the head of the Established Church as Primate of England (archbishop of Canterbury). The pious, hard-working, and stubborn son of a draper, Laud warned Charles that the religious extremes of Catholicism and radical Puritanism both posed threats to the Established Church, that "unless your Majesty look to it, she will be ground to powder." Laud espoused High Church rituals, and because of this, he was viewed with suspicion by the Puritans. Most Puritans also believed that Bishop Laud was secretly working to make Catholicism the established church of England, and therefore feared his influence in government. Under Elizabeth I and James I, Catholics had remained a force in some sectors of English life. Fear of a "popish plot" to restore Catholicism as the religion of the English state existed at all levels of English society. Landowners whose families had purchased ecclesiastical lands during the Reformation now worried that Laud might return them to the Catholic Church. Most people in England identified Catholicism and "popery" with the Spanish Inquisition, the Saint Bartholomew's Day Massacre in France, and the duke of Alba's Council of Blood in the Netherlands (see Chapters 4 and 5). And they viewed with alarm reconversions of some families to Catholicism, including a third of the gentry families of Yorkshire by the first years of the seventeenth century.

Charles I and Parliament Clash

Charles' fiscal policies deepened popular dissatisfaction with his reign. In 1625, the king decreed a forced loan on landowners, demanding that they provide him with subsidies, which he levied without Parliament's consent and which he insisted be paid within three months, an unprecedented short period of time. The next year, he ordered the imprisonment of seventy-six gentlemen, including five extremely prominent knights, who refused to meet the royal demand. Parliament refused to consent to the levies unless Charles met its demands for fiscal reform. The king convoked three Parliaments in four years, but dissolved each when it refused to provide him with funds. Parliament continued to demand that Charles appoint ministers it could trust and began impeachment proceedings against Buckingham. However, Buckingham disappeared as a source of irritation to Parliament when a disgruntled naval officer who had not been paid assassinated him in 1628.

After Buckingham's death, Charles again asked Parliament to provide him with more funds. In response, Parliament promulgated the Petition of Right, which it forced Charles to accept in return for the granting of a tax. This constrained the king to agree that in the future he would not attempt to impose "loans" without Parliament's consent, and that no "gentlemen" who refused to pay up would be arrested—nor would anyone else be imprisoned without a show of just cause. The Petition of Right, which was initially put forward in 1628 by Sir Thomas Wentworth (1593–1641), then an opponent of the crown and one of the men imprisoned for refusing to pay the forced loan, was a significant document in the constitutional evolution of England. It defined the rights of Parliament as inalienable and condemned arbitrary arrest, martial law, and taxes imposed without Parliament's consent.

Angered by the Petition of Right and by Parliament's insistence that his collection of customs duties was a violation of the Petition, Charles ordered Parliament's dissolution in 1629. Members of the Commons, however, physically held in his chair the speaker of the house, whose role was to communicate with the king on behalf of Parliament. They proceeded to declare that anyone who attempted to collect funds not levied with the approval of Parliament should be considered "a capital enemy to the kingdom and commonwealth," as would anyone who sponsored "inno-

Riot in St. Gile's Cathedral, Edinburgh, when the bishop begins to read from the Anglican Book of Common Prayer.

vation of religion," which is what Puritans considered Laud's espousal of elaborate High Church ceremonies. A defiant Parliament then disbanded.

For the next eleven years, Charles ruled without Parliament and tried to raise monies in new and controversial ways. Inflation had increased the royal debt dramatically, as well as greatly increasing the costs of ships and arms for waging war. The monarchy had exhausted its credit. Unlike James, Charles had some scruples about peddling privileges, but none at all about other means of raising funds. He fined gentlemen who did not attend his coronation. Most controversially, Charles ordered that "ship money" (a tax levied on port towns to provide ships for defense in times of emergency) also be imposed on inland towns beginning in 1634. Ship money raised the question of royal prerogatives because the tax seemed an affront to English Common Law and had been imposed without Parliament's consent.

Charles' high-handed royal policies led to a rebellion in Scotland. The king had seized lands from Scottish nobles and, at Laud's instigation, in 1637 he ordered the imposition of the Anglican Book of Common Prayer on the Scottish Presbyterian Church (established as the Scottish national church in the 1560s). The Scots had never been pleased with the union with England that had been weakly forged in 1603 when James VI of Scotland ascended the English throne as James I. They demanded that the prayer book be considered by a general church assembly. In 1638, some Scottish leaders signed the *National Covenant,* attacking the pope and the prayer book and swearing to defend their religion and liberties. Faced with the resolution of Scots to maintain the Presbyterian Church, Charles convoked the church assembly in Scotland, but he also began to prepare for an invasion of Scotland. In the meantime, Scottish nobles and landowners began evicting Anglican bishops and taking over churches, and the Scots rose up in arms.

This was a turning point in the dramatic reign of King Charles I. Desperately needing funds to defeat the Scots, in March 1639 the king demanded that the city of London help pay for the war. After several allocations, insulting in their modesty, London finally consented to lend the crown a large sum, but only on the condition that Charles convene Parliament. Furthermore, London would provide the bulk of the loan only when Charles had proven good faith by permitting Parliament to sit for a sufficient period of time.

Nobles and gentry led resistance to royal policies from the beginning; some were already in touch with the rebellious Scots, who in 1640 captured the northeastern English port of Newcastle without resistance. Running short of cash and facing mutinies in the royal army, in April 1640 the king summoned Parliament for the first time in eleven years. But when it refused to allocate money for the war against Scotland until Charles agreed to consider a list of grievances, the king dissolved this "Short Parliament" after less than two months. Charles I's defiance of Parliament turned political division into a full-fledged constitutional crisis.

THE ENGLISH CIVIL WAR

The political crisis of the Stuart monarchy became a constitutional conflict about how England was to be governed. To the king's opponents, Parliament existed to protect fundamental English liberties that had been established under the Magna Carta in 1215. By this reasoning the king did not have the right to dispense with its counsel and traditional authority to allocate royal finances, nor did he have the right to impose taxes without historical precedent. While Parliament, led by Puritans, was not yet claiming sovereignty, it was clearly asserting its traditional prerogative to balance royal authority.

Defenders of Parliament and local prerogatives were upset at the king's effort to expand his reach. They perceived Laudian religious reforms and the collection of ship money as the work of cynical and power-crazed men perhaps manipulated by the pope. Justices of the peace resented the usurpation of their authority by various decrees of martial law and by royal courts that had impinged on regional courts. Local officials believed that the king's lieutenants were exceeding their traditional authority over military affairs by bypassing established routines of local approval of military levies. Some Londoners felt particularly aggrieved, including those merchants who were not able to export cloth because of royal control over cloth exports through the monopoly of the Merchant Adventurers. The monarchy alienated other Londoners when it allowed some craftsmen to operate outside the structure of the London guilds, tried to regulate construction in London and its growing suburbs, and attempted to force the city to provide sums for the war with Scotland. The sale of the right to collect royal customs generated controversy as well, particularly as the government sold more privileges to pay off those who collected or "farmed" taxes on its behalf.

Many in the country resented the Catholic influences on the king. Charles surrounded himself with confidants, advisers, artists, and musicians whose sense of royal decorum and aesthetic tastes seemed to suggest the influence of continental Catholicism. The queen brought Flemish artists to Court who emphasized the religious themes of the Catholic Reformation, serving to convince critics of royal political policy that a plot was afloat, as a contemporary put it, "to seduce the King himself with Pictures, Antiquities, Images & other vanities brought from *Rome.*"

Those who consistently supported Parliament became known as the supporters of "Country," while those who supported virtually unlimited monarchical prerogatives were identified with "Court." While the terms "Court" and "Country" are something of a simplification and virtually disappeared in the 1640s, they do reflect essential political differences during the political crisis.

Titled nobles, of whom there were about 1,200 in the country, generally supported the king. Gentry formed the core of the political opposition to the king. Nonetheless, the gentry did not make up a monolithic social group, and not all of those in the gentry supported Parliament against the king. During the previous century, many in the gentry had extended their landholdings, and men enriched by commerce or service in the law or army had become part of the gentry through the purchase of land. The roots of confrontation may have come from the struggle of these economically dynamic gentry to obtain political power commensurate with their rising station in English life. And their economic success may have affronted the wealthiest nobles, most of whom supported the king. On the other hand, gentry of modest means may not have experienced either an increase or decline in their holdings and may have been happy with the status quo. Some gentry of lesser means who had fallen upon hard times may have blamed the monarchy for their plight and hence supported Parliament. However, gentry in the economically less advanced north of England may have supported the king as a conservative force for stability.

The English Civil War has been called "the Puritan Revolution" even though its causes extended beyond the question of religion, and Puritans were not alone in resisting the monarchy. There were many Puritans in Parliament, including the body's leader, John Pym (1584–1643). A brilliant speaker and powerful debater, Pym was a zealot, an impetuous and perhaps even paranoid man whose strong convictions were in part defined by an obsession that a "popish plot" existed to restore Catholicism to England. Puritans dominated the ranks of the lesser gentry in the eastern counties, areas that took the side of Parliament during the Civil War. Puri-

(*Left*) John Pym. (*Right*) William Laud, bishop of London and later archbishop of Canterbury.

tan preachers denounced the collection of ship money. Most Puritans believed along with Pym that Laud was trying to restore Catholicism.

As the political crisis grew in the 1630s, the authority of Anglican bishops, their appointment as state officials, and their right to nominate ministers smacked to many of "popery." Charles I echoed the famous statement of his father, James I, "No bishops, no king!," an assertion that would come back to haunt him. Laud expanded the power of ecclesiastical courts, which tried people accused of offenses against the Church of England. This reminded some people of the Spanish Inquisition.

Moving toward Conflict

Having dissolved the "Short Parliament" in May 1640, Charles again convoked a newly elected Parliament the following October. That summer brought religious and social turmoil. Ordinary people smashed altar rails and shattered stained-glass windows. The crown's strengthening of the army with Catholic Irish regiments, commanded by Thomas Wentworth, who was now a supporter and adviser of the king and had been named the earl of Strafford, confirmed to credulous ears that a "popish plot" was in the works. The English army suffered defeat in Scotland, and the war required yet more funds. Led by Pym, Parliament turned its wrath upon Charles' advisers, perpetuating the half-truth that the "eleven years of tyranny" had been the fault of bad advice. It indicted Strafford, who was tried and executed in London before a rejoicing throng. Parliament denounced as illegal the most unpopular royal acts during the previous eleven years (including many of the new taxes introduced by the king) and abolished some of the courts controlled by the monarchy. Parliament proclaimed that it could only dissolve itself, and that in the future the king would have to summon it every three years.

Parliament's session took place at a time when the Irish were rebelling against English rule. Beginning in the summer of 1641, Irish peasants, who were overwhelmingly Catholic, rose up against the English and killed many Protestant landlords. This seemed to many Protestants to confirm their fears of a Catholic conspiracy against English liberties. Furthermore, many believed that the king could not or would not repress the insurgents. The Irish rebellion highlighted crucial questions about the rights of Parliament by making urgent the issue of who controlled the militia.

In November 1641, Parliament passed the Grand Remonstrance. Presenting what Parliament considered a history of royal misdeeds, it denounced "a malignant and pernicious design of subverting the fundamental laws and principles" of English government and called for religious and administrative reforms. Its passage by a narrow margin indicated that Parliament remained divided over how far to carry its opposition to royal policies. Puritans, who narrowly controlled the House of Commons, now wanted to reform both church and state. Wealthy nobles began to form a solid bloc around the cause of the king, fearing that reform might weaken their influence. In November, the high sheriff of Lancashire called upon "gentlemen" to take arms with their tenants and servants on behalf of the king "for the securing of our own lives and estates, which are now ready to be surprised by a heady multitude." In some places, fighting began that month, as both sides fought for control of the militias.

Emboldened by an intransigent Court faction, the king attempted a bold coup against Parliament in January 1642. He personally led several hundred armed soldiers into Parliament and ordered the arrest of Pym and several other leaders. Forewarned, Pym and other leaders had left Commons before Charles arrived, and were protected in London by artisans and craftsmen. All chances of compromise disappeared. Fearing for his safety in London, where people had become more forceful in their support of Parliament and their demands for radical reform, Charles and his family headed north to more friendly country, and his supporters left Parliament. In June, Parliament promulgated "Nineteen Propositions," which denounced confrontational royal policy. In August 1642, Charles responded by mobilizing his forces at Nottingham.

Taking Sides

As civil war spread, Parliament's soldiers came to be known as "Roundheads" for the short, bowl-shaped haircuts many of them wore. The king's "Cavaliers" liked to think of themselves as fighting the good fight for God and king against those who would shatter social harmony by making "subjects princes and princes slaves." But so far as civil wars go, there was relatively little actual fighting. Relatively short "campaign seasons" were interrupted by winter. There were only four major battles, only one very far from London (see Map 6.1). The two sides fought to a draw on October 23, 1642, at Edgehill, near Shakespeare's birthplace of Stratford-on-Avon, south of Birmingham. When a royal military advance on London was turned back, Charles set up headquarters in Oxford, fifty miles northwest of London. In February 1643, the king rejected Parliament's terms for a settlement. When a second royal march on London failed, both sides intensified massive propaganda campaigns to win support. The war became a war of words, among the first in history. More than 22,000 newspapers, newsletters, pamphlets, broadsides, sermons, and speeches were published between 1640 and 1661. At least 2,000 pamphlets were published in 1642, an average of almost 6 a day.

The war nonetheless took its toll. Life in thousands of villages was disrupted, if not by actual fighting and the death of conscripted or volunteer soldiers, then by requisitions, plundering, and general hardship. About 10 percent of the English population was forced to leave home during the war. Many counties—perhaps most—were neutral, as local gentlemen

MAP 6.1 THE ENGLISH CIVIL WAR Major battles during the English Civil War, as well as Cavalier and Roundhead strongholds.

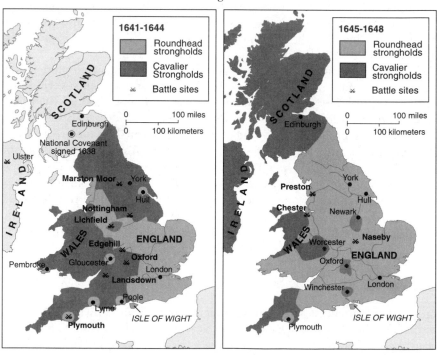

struggled to maintain control and keep their counties free of fighting and devastation.

Each side had to organize the pursuit of the war. In regions of royalist allegiance, the Cavaliers utilized existing administrative hierarchies, above all the justices of the peace. Lacking London's credit institutions, Charles financed the war by selling more titles and received gifts and loans from nobles. But fearful of losing further popular support, the king sought approval for forced levies by calling meetings of freeholders or grand juries.

The Roundheads of Parliament at first had to improvise as they governed territories under their control. Parliament, in keeping with its insistence on local prerogatives and resistance to monarchical centralization, kept civil, fiscal, and military authority relatively decentralized in regions under its control. At first its troops, living off the land, were more ruthless than those of the royalists, though later in the war the situation was reversed. Parliament did not hesitate to impose martial law in some troublesome counties. A regional military structure finally developed, based on associations of counties pledging mutual assistance in the parliamentary cause. Gentlemen organized government as best they could, confiscating the property of some prominent families supporting the king's cause. Parliament raised funds through heavy excise and property taxes.

Patterns of allegiance in the English Civil War were influenced by local economic and social considerations. Parliament drew considerable support from the most economically advanced regions—the south and east—while King Charles I retained the allegiance of most of northern and western England.

For example, Parliament found adherents where commercial agriculture had entailed changes in land use. Cultivation for the urban market had flourished in the aftermath of deforestation, the draining of marshlands, and the privatization of common lands through parliamentary acts of enclosure, some of which the monarchy had opposed. Districts in which cloth manufacturing had developed during the previous hundred years were also particularly likely to support Parliament, perhaps because people were no longer totally dependent on wealthy landowners for work. In the dairying, cattle-grazing, and forested areas of the west, dispersed patterns of settlement had been conducive to small-scale cloth manufacturing, particularly cottage industry. But if in some economically dynamic regions the "middling sort" tended to support Parliament, in others they did not. Here no clear pattern is discernible. Regions of rich but traditional agriculture, such as in the west, often supported the king, perhaps because economic and social hierarchies survived intact.

Villages became sites for religious and political struggle. Festivals served a social function, bringing villagers together to celebrate the holidays of the year. Puritans, however, considered such festivals frivolous, disruptive, ungodly. They associated such events with Catholic festivals, above all the perceived licentiousness of Mardi Gras. Puritans particularly disliked

Roundheads destroying altar railings and paintings of saints.

those festivals called "church ales," which were drinking bouts often over-seen by gentry and even clergy, raising money for the Anglican Church. Puritans believed that village festivals eroded social hierarchy and family life by encouraging all participants to behave as equals in drinking, danc-ing, and sexual freedom. Wanting ordinary people to toe the line, Puritans considered bat and ball games, stoolball, and a game resembling football to be unsightly free-for-alls that defamed the Sabbath. The Puritans spon-sored their own festivals, attempting to replace the merrymaking and pranks of Halloween—the night before All Saints' Day—with less boister-ous gatherings. Support for the king remained strong, however, among villagers in regions where the traditional festive rituals, with the benevo-lent encouragement of wealthy country gentlemen, had survived the Puri-tan assault in the decades before the Civil War.

Oliver Cromwell and the New Model Army

In 1643, Parliament allied with the Scots, many of whom were Presbyteri-ans delighted to participate in what they considered a holy war against the Anglican episcopacy. Pym's sudden death at the end of that year did not lessen Parliament's resolve to force the king to capitulate. A Scottish army crossed into England. In July 1644, Parliament's army combined with the Scots to defeat the Cavaliers at Marston Moor, near York. About 45,000 men fought in this largest battle of the English Civil War. This gave Parlia-ment control of northern England. Scottish participation made an early end to the war unlikely, adding to the determination of the "war party" fac-tion to whom Charles listened.

Oliver Cromwell (1599–1658), who led the Roundheads to victory at

Marston Moor, emerged as the leader of Parliament. Cromwell was born into a gentry family, "by birth a gentleman living neither in considerable height nor yet in obscurity," as he put it. He never lost what well-heeled gentry considered his rough edges. Several years before being elected to Parliament in 1640, he had undergone—perhaps after serious illness—a deep spiritual conversion. Cromwell became convinced that God had chosen him to be one of the elect and that as such he would gain eternal salvation. Strong Puritan views led him into politics, and he believed that his rise to power was God's will. Cromwell combined idealism with the stubbornness of someone who can easily convince himself that he is right all the time.

Combining three existing armies, Parliament formed the New Model Army in 1645. Cromwell, as second in command, instilled strict discipline. Moreover, Roundhead soldiers' morale improved with regular wage payments. Unlike its predecessors, the New Model Army won grudging good will in the counties by paying for supplies and not plundering. (In contrast, the king's army, which was short on funds, began to plunder the countryside.) Although it included a few more commanders of relatively ordinary birth than before, the New Model Army was not unique in the social origins of either its soldiers or officers, but rather in its single-minded discipline and radical purpose.

Cromwell prevailed on Parliament in 1645 to pass a self-denying ordinance, which forced members of Parliament who held military commands to relinquish them. But the ordinance permitted several exceptions to this rule, one of which was for Cromwell. This angered a minority of moderate Parliamentarians, now wary of Cromwell's rising power.

Oliver Cromwell.

Divisions within Parliament

Two political groups emerged in Parliament. "Presbyterians," a majority within Parliament, were moderates both in political and religious matters. Originally a pro-Scottish group that had rallied behind Pym, most (despite the name "Presbyterians") were Puritans. Opposed to the power of bishops, they wanted an established national Calvinist Church in which lay elders selected ministers, and they were against religious toleration. They had agreed to the execution of Archbishop Laud at the beginning of 1645. But they were ready to accept a negotiated settlement with the king.

The Independents were militant Puritans, more radical than the Presbyterians in that they wanted the church to be a loose alliance of congregations that would choose their own ministers. The Independents were less willing to compromise with the king on the issue of parliamentary prerogatives. They favored state toleration of some religious dissent and opposed an established church. More than this, some of them desired more far-reaching political changes that would protect individual rights. Cromwell's rise to leadership reflected the ascendancy of the Independents in Parliament.

Cromwell began to purge Presbyterian commanders within the New Model Army, replacing them with Independents who were loyal to him. Singing psalms as they rushed fearlessly into battle, Cromwell's "Ironsides," as his troops—"base and mean fellows"—were called, maintained an air of invincibility. In June 1645, the New Model Army routed the royalists. Charles surrendered to the Scots a year later, hoping to obtain a less draconian peace than if he capitulated directly to Parliament. But the Scottish army left England, leaving the king in the custody of Parliament in February 1647.

Radicals

As the war dragged on, England fell into virtual anarchy amid growing resentment over the billeting of soldiers, food shortages, and rising prices. The English Civil War unleashed forces that seemed to challenge the foundation of social and political order. During the siege of royalist Oxford, a hungry sentry called down to the besieging forces, "Roundhead, fling me up half a mutton and I will fling thee down a Lord!" At times the Roundheads appeared to hold back as if wary of the consequences of victory. Even some gentry who had taken the side of Parliament feared that a crushing victory might unleash "turbulent spirits, backed by rude and tumultuous mechanic [i.e., ordinary people] persons" and attacks against property by the mob, "that many headed monster."

In such a climate, new religious groups proliferated, some of them radical. Baptists did not believe that children should be baptized, reasoning that only adults were old enough to choose a congregation and hence be baptized. Baptists institutionalized church discussion and debates, which sometimes led to chaotic gatherings. Some Baptists permitted couples to marry by simply making a declaration before the congregation.

"Levellers" were far more radical, demanding major reforms. A group that had begun to form in the mid-1640s, Levellers accepted the sanctity of private property but demanded new laws that would protect the poor as well as the wealthy. Levellers, many of whom had been Baptists, found adherents among small property owners, including many London artisans, as well as great support in the New Model Army, "wherein there is not one lord." Some Levellers may have begun as staunch Puritans before becoming more radical. Royalists and Presbyterians both held that the Levellers wanted "to raise the servant against the master, the tenant against the landlord, the buyer against the seller, the borrower against the lender, the poor against the rich." Henry Denne defended the Levellers against such accusations: "It hath been . . . mine endeavor . . . to give unto every limb and part not only his due proportion but also his due place, and not to set the head where the foot should be, or the foot where the head. I may . . . seem guilty of the crime . . . [of turning] the world upside down, and to set that in the bottom which others make the top of the building, and to set that upon the roof which others lay for a foundation."

Yet, while the Levellers proposed a new English constitution and demanded sweeping political reforms that would greatly broaden the electoral franchise, they still based these rights on property ownership, which they defined as men having "a permanent fixed interest in this kingdom," excluding wage laborers and servants. Women were also prominent in Leveller petition campaigns. They echoed their husbands' demands, although calls for female enfranchisement were extremely rare.

Smaller groups of radicals soon went even further. Unlike the Levellers, the "Diggers," who called themselves the "True Levellers," denied the claims of Parliament to speak for Englishmen, opposed the private ownership of land, and sought the abolition of wage labor. They espoused agrarian reform and even began a brief colony that began to share wasteland with the poor and the landless. Another group, the "Ranters," rejected the idea of Heaven, Hell, and sin, and postulated that the true salvation could be found only in drink and sex.

To some people in mid-seventeenth-century England, the world indeed seemed "turned upside down." Some radicals opposed not only hierarchical authority within the state, but also paternal authority within the family. The assumption that the king ruled his nation as a husband and father directed his wife and children had been prominent in early modern political theory. The expansion in the number of literate people in southern England, in particular, not only exposed more people to the writings of the New Testament but also to radical ideas propagated in pamphlets. Some of these latter demanded education for women and denounced the subjugation of women to their husbands. Conservatives railed against such claims, echoing what seemed to be a growing anxiety about patriarchal order and increasing concern about "unruly women" defying their husbands.

Parliament's Victory

Pressured by the Presbyterians, who feared the radicals of the New Model Army, Parliament ordered the disbanding of part of it without paying the soldiers. The army, however, refused to disband and set up a general council, some of whose members were drawn from the lower officer corps and the rank and file. This reflected Leveller influence within a body that had been previously loyal only to Cromwell.

The New Model Army considered Parliament's attempts to disband it to be part of a plot against the Independents, and a few regiments mutinied and prepared a political platform, the *Agreement of the People,* written by London Levellers. This text anticipated later theorists by claiming that "freeborn Englishmen," not just property owners, were the source of political authority and that "every man that is to live under a government ought first by his own consent to put himself under that government; and . . . that the poorest man in England is not at all bound in a strict sense to that government that he hath not had a voice to put himself under." Cromwell worked to curb the radicals and ruthlessly restored order in the New Model Army, subduing mutinous Leveller regiments and ordering several leaders shot.

The Council of the New Model Army was formed at the end of the Civil War to air grievances and prepare a political platform after Parliament sought to disband the army without paying the soldiers.

Charles I's execution, January 30, 1649.

In November 1647, King Charles escaped the custody of Parliament and fled to the Isle of Wight. At the beginning of the new year, against the opposition of Presbyterians who hoped that some compromise could still be reached with the king, the House of Commons passed a motion that no further addresses should be made to the king. The implication was that Parliament alone should proceed to establish a new government without Charles' participation or consent, probably indicating that Cromwell and many other members of Parliament had already decided that Charles I should be put to death and a republic declared.

In May 1648, a group of Presbyterian moderates joined Cavalier uprisings in southern Wales and southern England. Charles had been secretly negotiating with the Presbyterian Scots, hoping that they now would join an alliance of Anglicans and members of Parliament who had become disillusioned with Cromwell's radicalism. But the New Model Army turned back a Scottish invasion in August. Besieged royalist forces in Wales surrendered after eight weeks. The king was now being held on the Isle of Wight, "more a Prisoner," as an observer put it, "than ever . . . and could not goe to pisse without a guarde nor to Goffe [to play golf]."

Believing itself the virtuous repository of English liberties, a detachment of the New Model Army, under Colonel Pride, surrounded the Parliament house and refused to let Presbyterians—and some Independents as well—enter. "Pride's Purge," which took place without Cromwell's consent or knowledge (although afterward he said that he approved of it), left a "Rump Parliament" of about a fifth of the members sitting.

The Rump Parliament, dominated by Independents, then appointed a High Court to try the king on charges of high treason. Denying the legality of this court, Charles refused to defend himself. Although the decision was taken by a minority of members and was unpopular, the High Court found Charles guilty as charged. Despite international efforts to stay his sentence, Charles I was executed at Whitehall on January 30, 1649, the first monarch to be tried and executed by his own subjects. Charles' beheading had immediate international repercussions; one power after another severed diplomatic relations with England, and the tsar of Russia ended the exclusive trade privileges of English merchants.

The Puritan Republic and Restoration

The Rump Parliament abolished the monarchy and the House of Lords. It established a Puritan republic, the Commonwealth of England, with Cromwell as its leader. It then sought to consolidate power at its borders.

In 1649, Cromwell brutally put down the Irish uprising, which had gone on since 1641, and conquered Ireland. The Act of Settlement in 1652 expropriated for English colonists the land of two-thirds of the Catholic property owners in Ireland and assured the ascendancy of English Protestants in that strife-torn land for the next 300 years. The Scottish Protestants did not fare any better for having supported Charles, however belatedly, as Cromwell from 1650 to 1651 then conquered Scotland. Having defeated both the Irish and the Scots, Cromwell turned his attention to foreign wars. England fought a naval war against the Dutch from 1652 to 1654, and a war with the Spaniards from 1655 to 1659, with an eye toward reducing the power of both these economic rivals.

The Rump Parliament met until 1653. It would not dissolve itself and so Cromwell, torn between his determination to assure a "godly reformation" in England and a mistrust of political assemblies, dissolved it in a military coup. The Long Parliament (if the Rump session is counted) had lasted since 1640. Cromwell now picked 140 men to serve as a new Parliament. This body came to be called the Barebones Parliament, named after one of its members, a certain "Praise-God Barbon," a leather merchant.

England became a military dictatorship. The army council dissolved the Barebones Parliament six months later and proclaimed a Protectorate under a new constitution, the Instrument of Government. Cromwell took the title "Lord Protector." He had not sought but now held almost unlimited power. Thomas Hobbes' description two years after the execution of Charles I of the natural state of mankind as being one of war, "everyone against everyone," seemed to apply to England. What could save England? To Hobbes, England could be saved only by a powerful state, "that great Leviathan . . . to which we owe . . . our peace and defense."

The Puritan republic had turned out to be as oppressive as the monarchy of the Stuart kings. Cromwell imposed taxes without parliamentary approval and purged Parliament when it disagreed with him. When Parliament produced its own constitution, Cromwell sent its members packing in 1655. But he was obliged to recall Parliament the following year to vote money for the war against Spain.

Although Cromwell granted de facto religious freedom to all Puritan sects (including the Presbyterians, Independents, and Baptists), he continued to deny such freedom to both Anglicans and Catholics. He did, however, allow Jews, who had not been allowed in England since 1290, to return in 1655. The Lord Protector proved to be a better military administrator than a civilian one. Dividing the country into twelve districts, he developed a more efficient civil service. But Cromwell lost support as a result of the seemingly endless financial impositions incurred in his war with the Dutch and through having to supply an army of 50,000 men in England. Cromwell also alienated people through his exhortations that people behave in "godly" Puritan ways, as set forth in a code enforced by the army. He began to wear armor under his clothes and took circuitous routes in order to foil assassins who might be stalking him. He still considered himself a humble caretaker of government who would keep order until godly righteousness prevailed.

In 1657, a newly elected Parliament produced another constitution and offered Cromwell the throne of England. He refused, but dissolved Parliament because republicans in it kept discussing the possibility of a new constitution. A year later, Cromwell died, succeeded by his considerably less able son, Richard, the New Protector (1626–1712). Then several military successors stumbled on, backed by remnants of the New Model Army.

Increasingly, however, it seemed to the upper classes that only restoration of the Stuart monarchy could restore order in England. Charles (1630–1685), the heir to the throne of his executed father, lived in exile in Holland. Armed force played a deciding role in a tumultuous time. General George Monck (1608–1670), who commanded the army in Scotland, had shrewdly kept Scottish tax money to pay his soldiers, and thus commanded the only paid, reliable force in England. He was a conservative who had been a royalist officer during the Civil War before developing a personal loyalty to Cromwell once the war had ended. After Parliament tried to assert control over the army, Monck marched with his forces on London and dissolved Parliament. New elections returned an alliance of royalists and Presbyterians, giving Parliament a moderate majority inclined to accept a restoration. When Charles issued a conciliatory proclamation, Parliament invited him to assume the throne of England. Eleven years after the execution of his father, Charles II crossed the Channel in May 1660 and was crowned king on April 23, 1661.

In restoring the monarchy, the new Parliament, on behalf of the upper classes, reacted to the threat of republicanism, popular politics itself, and the profusion of religious sects that seemed to threaten the established order. The command of local militias was wrested from "persons of no degree or quality" and again handed to "the nobility and principal gentry."

A man of considerable ego preoccupied with protecting his throne against future challenges, Charles II also manifested considerable charm, energy, courage, unfailing good humor, and loyalty to those who had remained loyal to him (with the notable exception of the queen, to whom he was anything but faithful). He could also lash out vindictively when he believed himself betrayed. Despite a vague interest in art and science, Charles manifested a lifelong aversion to reading and writing, remaining a man of many words and few letters who allowed himself to be manipulated by his advisers. But he earned the affection of most of his subjects because the return of monarchy seemed also to end the extended period of division and chaos.

The English Civil War had been a victory for parliamentary rule. Yet, in some ways the Restoration turned the clock back before the conflict. The Church of England again became the Established Church; the crown refused other religions official toleration. The Church of England expelled Presbyterian ministers in 1661–1662. Once again the king was chronically short of money and depended on Parliament for funds. Parliament paid off and demobilized the New Model Army, the last reminder of Cromwell's rule.

With the Civil War over and the monarchy restored by a victorious Parliament, the way seemed clear for England to continue to expand its commerce and influence in a climate of social and political peace. Between 1660 and 1688, the tonnage hauled by English ships more than doubled, as the merchant fleet established trade routes to Newfoundland, Virginia, and the Caribbean. In 1664, a small English force seized the Dutch colony of New Amsterdam, which became New York. Although it was retaken by the Dutch, it became part of England again in 1674. England's colonies gradually developed in North America, and settlements took hold on the coasts of India and Africa, where slaves were the principal commodity. Tobacco, calico, furs, sugar, chocolate, and rum began to arrive in England, changing tastes and habits of consumption. London became a booming port, the East India Company a powerful force in shaping royal policy. Lloyd's of London began to insure vessels sailing to the New World in 1688. By 1686, almost half of the English ships were trading with India or America. Exports and imports increased by a third by 1700.

England's foreign policy entered a new, aggressive period in support of English manufacture and commerce. To undermine Dutch commercial competition, Parliament passed a series of Navigation Acts between 1651 and 1673, requiring that all goods brought to England be transported either in English ships or in those belonging to the country of origin. This led to three brief wars with the Dutch, fought in 1652–1654, 1665–1667, and 1672–1674.

THE GLORIOUS REVOLUTION

The struggle for sovereignty between Parliament and the Stuart kings, was manifested in parliamentary opposition to new taxes and fears that Arminianism would lead to the restoration of Catholicism in England. This led to another constitutional crisis and planted the seeds for what became known as the Glorious Revolution of 1688, whereby Parliament would summon a new king to rule England. Moreover, Parliament would also pass the Bill of Rights, which would enshrine the rights of Parliament and of property owners.

Stuart Religious Designs

After the return of the Stuarts to power, religion once again surfaced as a divisive issue in England, threatening to shatter the political unity seemingly achieved with the restoration in 1660. Charles II had returned from France if not with strong Catholic sympathies at least with the conviction that he owed toleration to Catholics who had supported his father. Again a Stuart king's seemingly provocative policies generated determined opposition from Parliament, which again asserted its prerogatives.

Charles favored Catholics among his ministers, and tried to appeal to Dissenters in order to build a coalition against the Church of England. In response, Parliament passed a series of laws against Dissenters between 1661 and 1665 known as the Clarendon Code. The Act of Corporation (1661) required all holders of office in incorporated municipalities to receive communion in the Anglican Church. The Act of Uniformity (1662) stated that all ministers had to use the Anglican Book of Common Prayer. By a further act, Nonconformists had to take an oath that they would not try to alter the established order of church and state in England. Hundreds of Quakers, members of a pacifist group formed in 1649 who refused to pay tithes or take oaths, were incarcerated and died in prison.

In 1670, Charles II signed a secret treaty of alliance with Louis XIV. He promised the king of France that he would declare himself a Catholic when the political circumstances in England were favorable. In return, he received subsidies from the French king. Charles ended restrictions on religious worship and laws that had been directed at Catholics and Dissident Protestant groups as well. The hostile reaction to his actions forced the king to reinstate all restrictive measures. In 1673, Parliament passed the Test Act, which largely superseded the Clarendon Code and excluded non-Anglicans from both military and civil office.

Many people in England still abhorred Catholicism and suspected that there were plots afoot to restore that religion to England. Although Charles II's agreement with Louis XIV remained secret, in 1678 a strange man called Titus Oates loudly claimed the existence of a plot by the

A Quaker meeting. Many Quakers were imprisoned for refusing to take oaths after passage of an act requiring Nonconformists to swear that they would not attempt to alter the Established Church or the state.

Catholic Church against England. Oates claimed that the Jesuits, who were popularly identified with Rome, were preparing to assassinate the king and slaughter all English Protestants. They then would proclaim James, Charles' devout Catholic brother, king (James was heir to the throne, as Charles had no legitimate children, although he had a good many who were illegitimate). Oates had made it all up, as the king knew perfectly well. But he could not speak up because of his own secret promise to Louis XIV of France to restore Catholicism to England. Charles was helpless when parliamentary leaders orchestrated another wave of anti-Catholicism.

In the 1670s, two factions had emerged in Parliament that in some ways echoed the split between "Court" and "Country" before the Civil War. Members of Parliament who supported full prerogatives of the monarchy, some of them trumpeting the theories of divine right monarchy, became known as Tories, corresponding to "Court." Those members of Parliament who were critical of the king's policies and who espoused parliamentary supremacy and religious toleration became known as Whigs (corresponding to Country). Whig leaders orchestrated a plan to exclude James from the royal succession because of his Catholicism. During the ensuing Exclusion Crisis (1678–1681), the Tories defended James as the heir to the throne of England. When in 1679 some members of Parliament tried to make Charles' illegitimate son heir to the throne, Charles dissolved Parliament. In three subsequent parliamentary elections, Whigs profited from the mood of anti-Catholicism to win a majority of seats.

Parliament's passage in 1679 of the Habeas Corpus Act reflected Whig ascendancy. This forced the government to provide a quick trial for those who were arrested. By establishing the legal rights of individuals accused of crimes, it further limited monarchical authority. Habeas Corpus thus was part of the House of Commons' century-long successful struggle for the maintenance of its constitutional role in England's governance.

Charles, however, continued to assert monarchical prerogatives. In 1681, he attempted, like his father before him, to rule without Parliament. His agents worked at the local level to undercut Whig influence by, for example, rewriting town charters to allow his supporters greater local control. In 1683, a number of Whigs were charged with plotting to kill both the king and his brother. Charles had them executed. On his deathbed two years later, Charles II proclaimed his Catholicism.

Thus, in 1685, Charles II's brother assumed the throne as James II (1633–1701). Royal armies put down small insurrections in Scotland and in western England in favor of Charles' illegitimate son and executed him. Naive as he was devout, James forgot the lessons of recent history and began to dismiss advisers who were not Catholics.

In 1687, James made Catholics eligible for office. Dissenters, too, benefited from toleration, because the new king needed them as allies. The king did not denounce Louis XIV when he revoked the Edict of Nantes and thereby ended toleration for the Huguenots (see Chapter 7). This made English Protestants even more anxious. In November 1687, when it became apparent that the queen was pregnant, James boldly predicted the birth of a son and Catholic heir to the throne. For the enemies of the king, the timing of the birth of a son, and the fact that the only witnesses were Catholics, inevitably sparked rumors that the newborn was not really the king's son but a surrogate baby.

In this new dispute over religion, royal prerogative remained the central constitutional issue. James may have entertained visions of implanting monarchical absolutism in England, a tide that approached from the continent. Certainly he sought to restore Catholicism as the state religion. Looking as though he had fallen completely under the influence of the pope and Louis XIV, in April 1688 he issued a declaration of toleration and ordered the Anglican clergy to read it from the pulpit. When seven bishops protested, James put them in prison. The tide was against James, however, as most of the country did not support his actions. When the bishops were tried in court, a jury found them to be not guilty.

William, prince of Orange, the future King William III of England.

The "Protestant Wind"

Mary (1662–1694), one of James' Protestant daughters by a previous marriage, had married the Protestant Dutchman William of Orange (1650–1702). A group of Tories and Whigs now worked together to invite William to restore Protestantism and, from their point of view, the English constitution. William prepared to invade England from Holland. His followers flooded England with propaganda favorable to his cause.

The context of European international politics seemed favorable to William. Louis XIV's revocation of the Edict of Nantes had outraged the Dutch. Furthermore, the Dutch worried that James' successful restoration of Catholicism to England might make the Dutch Republic more vulnerable to Catholic France, as they believed that England was an indispensable partner in helping resist Louis XIV's grand ambitions in Europe. The Dutch hoped that a friendly Protestant monarch on the throne of England might even reduce tensions stemming from the trade rivalry between the Dutch Republic and England.

The Catholic continental monarchs failed to come to the aid of James II. Louis XIV's principal interest remained continental territorial expansion, and his aggressive moves against the German states left him without potential allies against William. Despite declaring war on the Dutch Republic, Louis limited his attacks to verbal bluster and the seizure of several Dutch ships in French ports. Emperor Leopold of Austria, another powerful Catholic monarch who might have been interested in rescuing James, was tied up fighting the Turks in the east. King James II now paid for having devoted too little attention to matters of diplomacy.

Despite all evidence that William was planning an invasion of England, James seemed unable to act. The king did little to prepare military defenses except to appoint Catholic officers in his new regiments and to bring more troops from Ireland. He relied on his navy to protect his throne. Hoping for a last-minute compromise, he promised to summon a "free" Parliament. But it was too late.

In a declaration promulgated early in October 1688, William accused James of arbitrary acts against the nation, Parliament, and the Church of England. Aided by a munificent wind—later dubbed the "Protestant wind"—that blew his ships to the southwestern coast of England while keeping James' loyal fleet away in the Channel or in port, William landed at Torbay with a force of 15,000 men on November 5, 1688. William marched cautiously to London, encouraged by defections from James' cause by gentry and soldiers along the way. Uprisings on William's behalf occurred sooner than expected in several northern towns, further isolating the king. After rejecting a petition from a number of peers and bishops calling for compromise, James was in a state of virtual physical and psychological collapse. At the end of November, he promised to summon Parliament and allow William's supporters to sit. But riots broke out in other towns against his rule and against Catholics. In December, James fled to the coast, anticipating reaching France. After being recognized and mistreated by fishermen, however, he returned to London. Several days later, he left England for exile in France. Parliament, victorious again, declared the throne vacant by abdication and invited William and Mary to occupy a double throne.

The Bill of Rights

This "Glorious Revolution" of 1688, less dramatic than the English Civil War, was arguably of more lasting importance in the constitutional evolution of England. Parliament passed a Bill of Rights in 1689 that put an end to decades of constitutional battles. Accepted by William and Mary, it became a milestone in English history. It was passed at a time when the rights and influence of representative bodies lay in shambles throughout much of the continent as absolute monarchs—above all Louis XIV—consolidated their power (see Chapter 7). The Bill of Rights reaffirmed the rights of Parliament, and guaranteed the rights of property owners to self-government and of the accused to the rule of law. In particular, it reasserted Parliament's financial authority over government by enumerating what a monarch should not do and by reducing royal control over the army. The Bill of Rights stipulated that Protestant dissenters could worship in England as they pleased and that they could establish academies of their own. Anglicanism, however, remained the Established Church of England, and only those who were Anglican could hold office. Catholics faced discrimination. They could not occupy the throne and, like Dissenters, they were excluded from government positions.

The English philosopher John Locke (1632–1704), friend of some of the wealthy landowners who sent James II into exile, was specific about the ways in which the power of monarchs ought to be limited. "The end of government," he wrote, should be "the good of mankind," above all, the protection of the right of property. Thomas Hobbes agreed, writing "The greatest and chief end therefore of men uniting into Commonwealths, and putting themselves under Government is the preservation of their property." But whereas Hobbes, who supported Charles I against Parliament, held that individuals should surrender their rights to the absolute state of unlimited sovereignty in exchange for protection from the "state of nature," Locke argued that the rights of individuals, including the ownership of property, found protection when Parliament's rights limited monarchical prerogatives. Remembering the turmoil of the Thirty Years' War on the continent, Locke also advocated religious toleration and espoused the right of subjects to rise up against tyranny as the English had against Charles I.

The Glorious Revolution also reaffirmed the political domination of the gentry, whose interests Parliament represented above all. The monarchs named nobles to hereditary seats in the House of Lords, but wealthy landowners elected members to the House of Commons. The gentry's economic and social position was more secure than during the inflationary years of the first half of the century. Order and social hierarchy reigned, and the fear of popular disorder ebbed. Benefiting from the consensus of 1688, the elite of wealthy landowners, increasingly more open to newcomers than its continental counterparts, would continue to shape British political life in the eighteenth century.

THE GOLDEN AGE OF THE DUTCH REPUBLIC

The Dutch Republic of the United Provinces (usually known today as the Netherlands, or sometimes simply as Holland, its most populated and prosperous province) was the other European power that defied the pattern of absolute and increasingly centralized rule that characterized seventeenth-century Europe. Spain ruled the Netherlands from 1516, when Charles V, who had inherited the territories of the dukes of Burgundy, became king of Spain. After a long, intermittent war that had begun in 1566 against Spanish rule (see Chapter 5), the Dutch Republic officially became independent in 1648 (see Map 6.2). The United Provinces, a confederation of republics, had been federalist in structure since the Union of Utrecht in 1579, when the provinces and cities of the Dutch Netherlands came together to form a defensive alliance against the advancing Spanish army. The federalist republic, from which William of Orange had

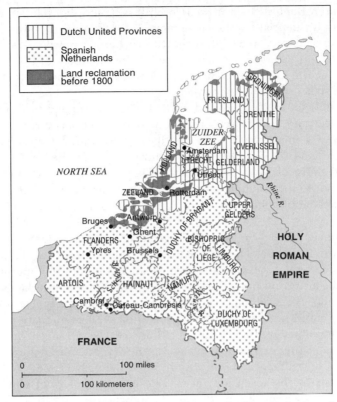

MAP 6.2 THE NETHERLANDS, 1648   At the conclusion of the Thirty Years' War, the Dutch war of independence also ended, with the northern United Provinces becoming the Dutch Republic and the southern provinces remaining under Spain as the Spanish Netherlands.

launched his successful invasion of England, resisted the aspirations of the House of Orange for a centralized government dominated by a hereditary monarchy. Like their English counterparts, most of the Dutch did not want absolute rule, which they identified with the arbitrary acts of the Spanish monarchy.

The Structure of the Dutch State

The States General served as a federal body of delegations from each of the seven provinces of the Dutch Republic. Each held to traditions of autonomy, provincial sovereignty, and religious pluralism. Nobles received automatic representation in the States General. But their economic and political role in the Republic was relatively weak, except in the overwhelmingly agricultural eastern provinces.

The Dutch Republic was in some ways less a republic than an oligarchy of wealthy, influential families who monopolized political power. This political elite remained relatively open to prosperous newcomers. Wealthy merchants and bankers served as regents, the members of the governing oligarchy in the Dutch provinces. They were determined to defend the federalist structure of the Republic.

No republican ideology existed until at least the second half of the seventeenth century. But Dutch citizens enjoyed some basic rights unavailable in the monarchies of the continent. Provincial courts protected the Dutch against both occasional arbitrary acts of the central government and those of town governments. They developed solid fiscal institutions and modern double-entry accounting techniques that generated international confidence, permitting the Republic to raise sizable loans as needed.

The princes of the House of Orange served as stadholders (chief officials) of the Republic. Through patronage, the Orangists also dominated some high federal appointments, naming sons of nobles to important positions in the army and navy. But after the revolt of the Netherlands against Spanish rule, the stadholder had influence, not authority. He was not a ruler, and could not declare war, legislate, or even participate in the important decisions of the Republic. Many of the Orangist stadholders chaffed under the restrictions on their authority, dreaming of establishing a powerful hereditary monarchy. In 1650, William II (1626–1650), stadholder of six of the seven provinces, arrested six leaders of Holland and sent an army to besiege Amsterdam. A compromise reinforced the power of the stadholder. But with William's sudden death two years later, the balance of power swung back to the regents of the provinces, particularly Holland. Any possibility of the Netherlands becoming an absolute state ended. Nonetheless, the House of Orange tried to curry support among the other six provinces against Holland, whose lucrative commercial interests shaped the Republic's foreign policy during the seventeenth century, as it led the resistance against Spain.

Expanding Economy

Despite the war of independence against the Spanish Habsburgs, the Dutch economy developed more rapidly during the first two-thirds of the seventeenth century than did the economies of its competitors, England and France.

In 1609, following the signing of a truce between Spain and the Netherlands, the Amsterdam Public Bank opened its doors, serving as a nexus of Dutch financial operations. The bank's offices were in the town hall, reflecting its conservatism and fiscal solidity. Its principal function was to facilitate Amsterdam's burgeoning foreign trade with other European countries and across the seas by encouraging merchants to make payments in bills drawn on the bank.

The Amsterdam Bourse in the seventeenth century. Merchants had fixed places at
the Stock Exchange where they met to arrange various financial matters.

Amsterdam's banking, credit, and warehousing facilities were soon unmatched in Europe. Although an ordinance in 1581 had included bankers
among those occupations considered disreputable—along with actors,
jugglers, and brothel-keepers—and therefore excluded from receiving
communion in the Dutch Reformed Church, bankers came to be respected by the beginning of the seventeenth century. Thanks to the bankers, investors would now raise capital for frequently risky commercial ventures
with relative ease and invest at the Bourse (Stock Exchange).

Good credit allowed the United Provinces to raise loans by selling nego-
tiable bonds at low interest rates. Bills of exchange became a type of credit;
signed by a merchant, they specified the payment due date. This attracted
foreign merchants to Amsterdam, particularly after mid-century, when
bills of exchange became acceptable as currency.

The United Provinces, small in territory and population, also expanded
its agricultural resources during the first half of the century. Thousands of
workers and horses reclaimed much of the country's most fertile land from
the sea. Increased productivity generated an agricultural surplus that
could be invested in commerce or manufacturing, and a greater food supply sustained a larger population. Commercial livestock raising and capital-intensive farming became lucrative, producing butter and cheese for
ever more distant markets.

Canals and rivers expedited internal trade in the Dutch Republic. These boats along the Spaarne at Haarlem carried goods to the port, where they were loaded for distant trade.

The Dutch Republic's population rose by a third between 1550 and 1650, to almost 2 million people, which made it Europe's most densely populated country after several of the Italian states. More than half the population lived in towns. As Amsterdam became a major international port of trade and London's rival, its population rose from about 50,000 in 1600 to about 150,000 by mid-century.

Early in the seventeenth century, Amsterdam began construction of three large canals, which expanded its area by almost four times. These canals permitted boats to dock outside merchants' warehouses, where they were loaded with goods, which they then carried to the large ships of the port. Handsome tall townhouses had narrow and increasingly ornamented facades, dauntingly steep staircases, and drains and sewers. They were built for the bankers, merchants, and manufacturers of Amsterdam and reached skyward above new tree-lined streets along the canals. The city pushed out from the port along the semi-radial canals that spread out from the sea. Thus, the United Provinces benefited not only from relatively good roads, which expedited internal trade, but also from 500 miles of canals dug during the middle decades of the century.

Dutch traders, specializing in bulk goods carried by specially designed long, flat vessels that could be cheaply built and operated, expanded their range and the variety of goods they bartered. This allowed Dutch merchants to undercut rivals. The Dutch Republic's merchant fleet tripled during the first half of the century. Dutch shipbuilding boomed, aided by wind-powered sawmills. The Dutch Republic's 2,500 ships in the 1630s accounted for about half of Europe's shipping. Amsterdam became the principal supplier of grain and fish in Europe as the Dutch dominated the lucrative Baltic trade. Dutch ships carried wheat and rye from Poland and East Prussia, dropping off what was needed for local consumption and then carrying much that was left to France, Spain, and the Mediterranean. Dutch fishing boats ousted their English competitors from the rich North Sea fishing grounds and from the whaling waters of the Arctic Sea. Dutch ships hauled most of the iron produced in Sweden; until mid-century, they also carried much of the coal extracted from the mines of Newcastle in England. Dutch traders exchanged products in Russia, the West Indies, Brazil, Japan, Southeast Asia, and the West African coast, from which they carried slaves. Herring caught by Dutch fishermen and salted for preservation became available in much of Europe, exchanged for salt, wine, and other commodities.

During the 1620s and 1630s, Dutch merchants extended their reach in the East Indies, where cinnamon, nutmeg, and other valuable spices were produced. In 1602, a group of investors had founded a private trading company, to which the government of the Dutch Republic granted a monopoly for trade in East Asia. The Dutch East India Company proved to be stiff competition for the English company of the same name. Increased

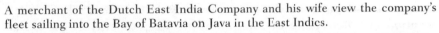

A merchant of the Dutch East India Company and his wife view the company's fleet sailing into the Bay of Batavia on Java in the East Indies.

affluence, in turn, helped the Dutch carry on the war against Spain. When fighting in Central Europe during the Thirty Years' War and a Spanish embargo on Dutch commerce reduced some continental trade, Dutch traders successfully developed trade overseas with India, Ceylon, and Indonesia, establishing a vast network of company settlements.

Dutch Religion and Attitudes

In contrast to England, where religious division led to civil war, the Dutch Republic remained a relative haven of toleration in an era of religious hatred. During the last decades of the sixteenth century, perhaps 60,000 Huguenots fled to the Dutch Republic to escape persecution in France and the Spanish Netherlands. In 1631, about a third of the wealthiest residents of Amsterdam had moved there from the Spanish Netherlands. Published works circulated through the Netherlands defending the rights of religious dissidents, including Mennonites, Lutherans, Quakers fleeing England, and Dutch Collegiants (a dissident Protestant group). By 1672, Amsterdam's Jewish community numbered 7,500 in a city of 200,000 people. Most were immigrants from the German states, and they spoke Yiddish among themselves, as well as German and Dutch. Many other Jewish families had come from Spain. The municipal government rejected a request by Christian merchants that their Jewish competitors be restricted, as in many European cities, to a specific neighborhood, or ghetto. The Amsterdam regents built a thousand dwellings for refugees, and the town of Haarlam established a home for widows and daughters of men who had come to the Republic to flee persecution. Refugees from religious persecution in other countries contributed to the prosperity of the Dutch Republic.

Nonetheless, despite the religious toleration generally accorded in the Dutch Republic, the Dutch Reformed Church, a strict Calvinist confession closely tied to the House of Orange, did persecute and discriminate against some religious groups. Dutch Arminians asked for protection from persecution in a Remonstrance (which gave them their most common name, the Remonstrants). Catholics, most of whom lived in the eastern provinces, also faced Calvinist hostility, although many had fought for Dutch independence. Jews were excluded from most guilds, and gypsies were routinely hounded and persecuted. Over all, however, toleration seemed less divisive to the Dutch than intolerance, and seemed to make economic sense as well.

The Dutch Republic blossomed like the famous tulips that were so popular in Holland (which, in fact, had been originally imported from Turkey). A French visitor reported that Amsterdam was "swollen with people, chock-full of goods, and filled with gold and silver." The Dutch in the middle decades of the seventeenth century reached a level of prosperity

Een dwaes en zijn gelt
zijn haeft gheschenden.

(*Left*) The Dutch Republic's famous tulips. (*Right*) Emanuel de Witte's *The Fish Market* (1672).

unmatched in Europe at the time. Real wages rose in the Republic during the last half of the century while falling elsewhere. Dutch families enjoyed a relatively varied diet, consuming more meat and cheese—as well as, of course, fish—than households elsewhere in Europe. The smell of fruit that had ripened on voyages from Southern Europe and of expensive tobacco filled the air of Amsterdam. Europe's finest market offered a plethora of colonial goods, such as coffee, tea, cocoa, ginger and other spices, dried and pickled herring and other fish, a wide range of grains, finished cloth from Antwerp and Florence, Silesian linens, and English woolens. Dutch manufacturers, with windmills providing power, found lucrative outlets for draperies, worsteds, papers, books, and jewels. At the beginning of the century, Amsterdam had almost 200 breweries and more than 500 taverns.

Although prosperity reached far down the social ladder, the Dutch Republic also had its poor, who lived in the narrow streets away from the Stock Exchange, in poor farmhouses in the eastern flatlands, and in the huts of ethnic Frisian fishermen facing the brutal North Sea waves and wind. The urban poor occasionally rioted and sometimes stole in order to survive. The proliferation of charitable institutions demonstrated Dutch compassion but also their desire to confine vagrants and beggars, as well as a capacity to lash out in brutal repression when patience with the poor grew thin. Beatings, floggings, and branding—and even death—remained common forms of punishment, and gallows stood at the main gates of large cities.

Dike breach at Caevarden. Because so much land had been reclaimed from the sea, many of the Dutch lived in chronic fear of flooding.

Yet, despite prosperity, a sense of precariousness and vulnerability permeated the Republic. The armies of the ambitious king of France camped across the low-lying Southern Netherlands. The Republic had almost no natural resources and was subject to sudden calamities brought by weather. A good part of the Dutch Netherlands would thus have been under water were it not for the famous dikes. These occasionally broke with catastrophic consequences long remembered (a flood in 1421 had claimed over 100,000 lives). A sense that disaster might be looming was reflected by the popularity in the Republic of novels and histories about disasters. This may explain the sense of solidarity and duty that brought people of various classes together against Spanish rule. This also contributed to the relative unity of Dutch culture, which prided itself on being distinct from that of the Southern Netherlands, which was under Flemish and French Catholic influence.

The Dutch Republic remained in some ways sternly Calvinist, however. The Dutch made money to make money, not necessarily to enjoy it. With relative abundance came a sense of guilt that could be resolved only by simplicity of life, although contemporary canvases depicted occasional lavish feasts. Many Calvinists believed the Republic was too successful, too affluent. The Reformed Church cautioned against excess, fearing that the Dutch soul might be compromised by self-indulgence. Churchmen reminded the Dutch that they, like the lands taken from the sea, had to be reclaimed from temptation. Authorities were to be vigilant. An occasional banquet was fine, but excess, identified with the Southern Netherlands or, worse, the French, had to be avoided.

Seventeenth-Century Dutch Culture

Dutch painting in the golden age of the seventeenth century reflected not only the Republic's precocious commercial wealth, but also its toleration and openness to secular styles and subject matter. The Dutch press, too, enjoyed relative freedom; books were printed in the Republic that could not have been printed elsewhere. The first English and French newspapers were both published in 1620 not in London and Paris, respectively, but in Amsterdam. Dutch publishers diffused knowledge of the Scientific Revolution (see Chapter 8). Dutch writers and poets discovered their own language, translated Latin authors, and popularized Dutch accounts of the revolt against Spain.

Dutch painting reflected Dutch society, particularly the wealth and taste of the middle class. Like the artists of the Renaissance, Dutch painters depended on the patronage of people of means, particularly wealthy Amsterdam merchants. Although Delft and several other towns each claimed their own style, the great port dominated the art market. Some shopkeepers and craftsmen were prosperous enough to buy a painting or two, and some well-off peasants did so as well.

Holland's regents, in particular, patronized Dutch painting. In contrast, the princes of Orange patronized French and other foreign artists whose work reflected baroque themes associated with the Catholic Reformation. Dutch nobles purchased few paintings, unlike their counterparts in France and in Southern Europe. When they did buy works of art, they favored the classical religious themes of foreign artists.

The relationship between religion and art in the Dutch Republic contrasted sharply with their relationship in the Southern Netherlands, which remained under Spanish and French influence. The Catholic Reformation had adopted the visual arts as one means by which the Church hoped to resist the Protestant tide. Flanders (the western part of what is now Belgium) became a northern outpost of the Catholic Reformation, encouraging religious themes with emotional appeal. By contrast, in the Dutch Republic ecclesiastical artistic patronage was generally absent, and the Dutch Reformed Church ordered the removal of paintings from its churches.

For the most part, Dutch painters looked to their water-swept country for inspiration. The Dutch school retained much of its cultural unity at least through the first half of the century for several reasons. Until 1650, the Republic remained relatively isolated from outside cultural influences, despite the arrival of refugees and immigrants. Very few Dutch artists and writers had the resources to travel as far as Italy or even France; even

Rembrandt's painting *The Syndics of the Cloth Guild* (1662).

those who earned a comfortable living showed little inclination to go abroad. The group paintings of merchants or regents and municipal governments, which were the most expensive canvases, were usually commissioned by the subjects themselves, as in the case of Rembrandt van Rijn's *Syndics of the Cloth Guild* (1662) and his *The Night Watch* (1642), a theatrically staged masterpiece of a group of city officials in uniform.

Rembrandt (1606–1669) was the son of a miller from Leiden and the grandson of a baker. He was one of the handful of Dutch painters who amassed a fortune, allowing him to marry the daughter of a municipal official. Rembrandt's life was one of brilliant achievement. Certainly few artists, if any, have so successfully portrayed the human emotions of his subjects with his use of color, light, and shadow. Despite his posthumous fame, in his own time the brooding Rembrandt was in some ways a tragic figure, a loner isolated from other painters. He bickered with his patrons and squandered most of what he made on his elegant house in Amsterdam. He lost his investments in the Dutch East India Company. Furthermore, he lost some public favor because he was unwilling to cater to the public's taste. He was nearly ruined financially before rebounding when his baroque portraiture and religious themes found more buyers. Rembrandt increasingly became his own favorite subject, and he thereafter undertook little more than self-portraits, of which there are at least eighty. His self-portraits reveal a thinly disguised sadness.

Dutch painters depicted everyday life. The prolific Jacob van Ruisdael (c. 1628–1682) mastered the visual effects of light on figures, trees, and household objects. Within the Dutch school of the seventeenth century, only Rembrandt (who is sometimes considered to be a baroque painter) often turned to the classical biblical themes that were so predominant in Flemish art, but he did so hoping to capture the Catholic market. Although seascapes and naval scenes proliferated, there were few canvases depicting battles, a favorite subject in absolute states, and those that did exist took their place on the large walls of palaces and châteaux, not in the narrow houses of Amsterdam.

Perhaps more than other early modern Europeans, the Dutch considered the household a place of refuge and safety from the struggles of the outside world, as well as the basis of economic, social, and political order, and therefore worthy of artistic representation. The popularity of household scenes in Dutch painting also reflected the Republic's prosperity. Paintings of families at work, at play, or eating were particularly popular. Jan Steen (1626–1679) portrayed boisterous revelers of different means in *The Fat Kitchen* and *The Thin Kitchen*. Still lifes of platters of food became staples for Dutch artists, as in such paintings as *Still Life with Herring* and *Jug Still Life with Lobster*. The banquet became a favorite subject, with all of its accoutrements, such as oak table and chairs, iron cooking pans, elegant plates and drinking vessels, and its rituals, such as the prayer, the careful carving of the meat, and the rounds of toasts.

The relationship between parents and children emerged as another familiar domestic theme. The Dutch painters also frequently portrayed servants, furniture and other household goods, and domestic pets. Women on Dutch canvases appear more equal to men than they were in reality, however. (A Dutch woman was legally subordinate to her husband's authority, and a cuckolded husband had the right to have his adulterous wife executed. Nonetheless, women could sign contracts, and a good many operated businesses after their husband's death.)

Like Renaissance painters, Dutch artists considered themselves craftsmen and were apprenticed to a master and then became members of a guild. The majority were of modest means. Most painters were harried by creditors, haunted by debts, and sometimes sold their works at reduced prices. Some painters managed only by dealing in the work of other painters, others by holding another job, such as Steen, who operated a brewery and inn in Delft when he was not before his easel. Even in the Dutch Republic, painting proved to be a tough way to earn a living.

THE DECLINE OF THE DUTCH REPUBLIC

The relative decline of Dutch power is perhaps not surprising, given the greater economic resources and population of France and England, its chief rivals. England emerged in the second half of the century as the world's dominant commercial power, although the decline of Dutch trade was not complete until the second or third decade of the eighteenth century.

The Dutch Republic tried to steer a course between England (its greatest commercial rival) and France. But this proved impossible. Three wars against England (1652–1654, 1665–1667, and 1672–1674), fought in defense of Dutch commercial interests, drained Dutch resources. Furthermore, Louis XIV of France had designs on the Dutch. "It is impossible," proclaimed Colbert, "that his Majesty should tolerate any longer the insolence and arrogance of that nation." In 1667, France imposed damaging tariffs on Dutch goods and also forced the Dutch out of the cinnamon-producing island of Ceylon in the Indian Ocean. In Brazil, the Dutch West India Company failed to dislodge the Portuguese, although it did establish small settlements on Africa's west coast. Few Dutch, including missionaries, demonstrated much enthusiasm for these distant places, and the Republic's colonial empire lagged behind those of England and Spain, to be sure, but also behind that of France.

With Spain weakened, Louis XIV coveted the Southern Netherlands, the conquest of which would place the Dutch in direct danger. The Dutch Republic therefore had a vested interest in the survival of the Spanish Netherlands as a buffer against the French threat. Should France be able to open the Scheldt River (closed by the Spanish in 1585 with the goal of breaking the Dutch rebellion) to international trade, Antwerp's return to its former prosperity would certainly be at Amsterdam's expense. In 1672, Louis XIV attacked the Dutch Republic, having signed a secret treaty with King Charles II of England. French armies quickly occupied all of the Republic except for Holland and one other province. But the Dutch successfully defended the Republic by land and sea, defeating the English fleet and pushing back the French army.

Taking advantage of the invasion, William III of Orange (who became King William III of England in 1688) forced the States General to name him stadholder in 1672. He ordered the dikes opened, literally flooding the French into retreat. Royalist mobs murdered the leading official of the Republic, several influential regents of Holland who had dedicated themselves to keeping the stadholders in place, and other leaders of the province of Holland. Supporters of the House of Orange eased into important political positions in that province. The Orangists controlled the Republic's foreign policy until the end of the century, but they still could not impose a monarchy on the provinces. With William's death in 1702, the main Orange dynastic line ended.

After the Glorious Revolution in England in 1688, the United Provinces allied with England and Sweden, fearing that Louis XIV of France might invade the Netherlands again. The alliance helped stave off the French threat in the last decades of the century, but at the same time it dragged the small country into a series of wars with France that lasted until the mid-eighteenth century. Military spending on armies and expensive southern fortifications contributed to the decline of the Dutch Republic as a power. It thereafter assumed a secondary role in European events.

Although the Dutch remained successful traders through the first decades of the eighteenth century, the relative decline of Dutch influence in Europe could be first seen by about 1670 or 1680. Some luxury products, such as linen and Delft porcelain, continued to sell abroad, but Holland's textile industry and shipbuilding failed to keep pace with those of its rivals, above all England. Higher wages in the Republic and a lack of technological innovation were at least partially to blame. Furthermore, some Dutch entrepreneurs invested in the colonies, land, government stocks, or even in English manufacturing, not in Dutch industry. Businessmen reduced investment in agriculture and land reclamation as prices fell.

Spain's golden age of art coincided with its decline as a Great Power. In contrast, Dutch painting languished with decline. Painters began looking abroad for inspiration and, in doing so, lost some of the originality that had catapulted them to prominence. In the 1650s, the Amsterdam regents ignored the influence of the Dutch school when planning the construction and decoration of the new town hall, which combined Italian classicism and the Flemish baroque flamboyance. Some Dutch leaders now took pride in speaking French, believing it the language of good taste. French classicism overwhelmed Dutch literature and poetry. Although the French military invasion of 1672 failed, a cultural invasion succeeded, and Dutch artists came to offer pale imitations of French classical work.

The originality of Dutch political life also waned with relative economic decline. The most powerful merchant families maintained increasingly tight control over the position of regent and other influential posts. A form of municipal corruption ("contracts of correspondence") allowed them to divide up or even purchase lucrative government positions. Spectacular cases of social mobility became rarer. More regents were now landowners, who (though many were nobles living in the republic's cities) had little in common with merchants who had vital interests in government policies. After 1650, no major cultural figures emerged from regent families. There were fewer paintings of attentive and hardworking municipal and provincial officials. Their simple style of life disappeared. And, as if to vindicate Calvinist sermons about excess, so did Dutch power.

Government became more rigid, more distant from the Dutch people, and less tolerant, persecuting religious dissenters and undertaking a witch hunt against homosexuals. The Dutch army became increasingly one of mercenaries, not citizens. The Dutch Republic's loss of vitality and economic primacy was accompanied by its decline in international affairs. At the dawn of the eighteenth century, England and the Netherlands remained the only non-absolutist states among the major European states. While the Dutch languished, England became a Great Power.

CHAPTER 7

THE AGE OF ABSOLUTISM, 1650–1720

In Louis XIV's France, architects and artists were paid to glorify the monarch. In 1662, the king chose the sun as his emblem; he declared himself *Nec pluribus impar*—without equal. To Louis, the sun embodied virtues that he associated with the ideal monarch: firmness, benevolence, and equity. Henceforth, Louis XIV would frequently be depicted as Apollo, the sun god, especially inside and outside the royal château of Versailles.

The rulers of continental Europe, including Louis XIV, relentlessly extended their power between 1650 and 1750. The sovereigns of France, Prussia, Russia, Austria, and Sweden, in particular, became absolute rulers, that is, in principle above all challenge from within the state itself. Rulers extended their dynastic domains and prestige. They made their personal rule absolute, based on loyalty to them as individuals, not to the state as an abstraction. Absolute rulers asserted their supreme right to proclaim laws and levy taxes, appointing more officials to carry out the details of governance and multiplying fiscal demands on their subjects. They ended most of the long-standing municipal privileges, which had survived longer in Western Europe than in Eastern Europe, such as freedom from taxation, or the right to maintain independent courts. The absolute state affected the lives of more people than ever before through taxation, military service, and the royal quest for religious orthodoxy.

Absolute rule thus impinged directly on the lives of subjects, who felt the extended reach of state power through, for example, more efficient tax collection. A Prussian recalled that in school no child would question "that the king could cut off the noses and ears of all his subjects if he wished to do so, and that we owed it to his goodness and his gentle disposition that he had left us in possession of these necessary organs."

Absolutism was, at least in part, an attempt to reassert public order and coercive state authority after almost seventy years of wars that had badly disrupted trade and agricultural production, contributing to social and political chaos. England and Spain had been at war in the last decades of the sixteenth century. Wars of religion had raged through much of Europe on and off for more than a century—above all, the Thirty Years' War (1618–1648). The Dutch war of independence against Spain began in 1572 and did not officially come to an end until 1648. The tumultuous decade of the 1640s was particularly marked by political crises. The wars had led to often dramatic increases in taxes, which multiplied four times in Spain under Philip II, and five times in France between 1609 and the end of the Thirty Years' War in 1648. During the 1640s, the English Civil War led to the execution of King Charles I in 1649 (see Chapter 6). In France, the period of mid-century rebellion known as the Fronde included a noble uprising against the crown and determined, violent peasant resistance against increased taxation. The multiplicity and seemingly interrelated character of these crises engendered considerable anxiety among social elites: "These are days of shaking, and this shaking is universal," a preacher warned the English Parliament.

The illustration for the cover of Thomas Hobbes' *Leviathan* (1651) depicts the absolute state. Note how the ruler's body is made up of the masses over whom he rules.

THEORIES OF ABSOLUTISM

The doctrine of absolutism originated with French jurists at the end of the sixteenth century. Like absolutism itself, this doctrine arose in part as a reaction to the chaos of the sixteenth-century religious wars concluded in the German states with the Peace of Augsburg (1555). This treaty stated that the religion of the ruler would become the religion of the land (*cuius regio, eius religio*).

The emergence of theories of absolutism reflected contemporary attempts to conceptualize the significance of the rise of larger territorial states whose rulers enjoyed more power than their predecessors. France was a prime example of this trend. The legal theorist Jean Bodin (1530–1596) had lived through the wars of religion. "Seeing that nothing upon earth is greater or higher, next unto God, than the majesty of kings and sovereign princes," he wrote in the *Six Books of the Republic* (1576), the "principal point of sovereign majesty and absolute power [was] to consist principally in giving laws unto the subjects in general, without their consent." The ruler became the father, a figure of benevolence. Bodin, who like many other people in France longed for peace and order helped establish the political theory legitimizing French absolute rule.

Almost a century later, the political philosopher Thomas Hobbes (1588–1679) emerged as the thundering theorist of absolutism although he lived in England, the least absolute state in Europe and one of the few nations in which the rule of law was separated from the will of the ruler. Hobbes experienced the turmoil of the English Civil War (see Chapter 6). In *Leviathan* (1651), he argued that absolutism alone could prevent society from lapsing into the "state of nature," a constant "war of every man against every man" that made life "solitary, poor, nasty, brutish, and short." People would only obey, Hobbes insisted, when they were afraid of the consequences of not doing so. Seeking individual security, individuals would enter into a type of contract with their ruler, surrendering their rights in exchange for protection. A ruler's will thus became the almost sacred embodiment of the state. In France, Jacques Bossuet (1627–1704), bishop and tutor to Louis XIV, postulated that kings ruled by "divine right," that is, by virtue of the will of God. Unlike Hobbes' notion of authority based on a social contract, Bossuet held that the ruler's authority stemmed from God alone.

Yet, theorists of absolutism recognized the difference between absolute and arbitrary power. Inherent in their theories was the idea that the absolute ruler was responsible for looking after the needs of his people. As Bossuet wrote: "It is one thing for a government to be absolute, and quite another for it to be arbitrary. It is absolute in that it is not liable to constraint, there being no other power capable of coercing the sovereign, who is in this sense independent of all human authority." But he went on: "it does not follow from this that the government is arbitrary, for besides the fact that all is subject to the judgment of God . . . there are also laws, in states, so that whatever is done contrary to them is null in a legal sense; moreover, there is always an opportunity for redress, either at other times or in other conditions." Thus, according to even the most determined proponents of absolutism, the monarch, whose legitimacy came from God, nonetheless was subject to limits imposed by reason through laws and traditions. Western monarchs recognized at least in theory the necessity of consulting, when the occasion arose, with institutions considered to be representative of interests such as the Church and nobility: parlements, estates, or the Assembly of Notables in France, the Cortes in Spain, and Parliament in non-absolutist England. Theorists thus recognized the difference between absolutism and despotism. Nonetheless, although Bossuet envisioned limits on sovereign authority, he did not sanction armed resistance against that authority, no matter how depraved or evil it might be.

CHARACTERIZING ABSOLUTE RULE

Absolute states were characterized by strong, ambitious dynasties, which through advantageous marriages, inheritance, warfare, and treaties added to their dynastic domains and prestige. They had nobilities that accepted monarchical authority in exchange for a guarantee of their status, ownership of land, and privileges within the state and over the peasantry, whether peasants were legally free, as in Western Europe, or serfs, as in the case of Prussia, Poland, and Russia. Absolute states contained an increasingly centralized and efficient bureaucracy able to extract revenue. And above all, the absolute state was characterized by deployment of a large, standing army capable of maintaining order at home and maintaining or expanding dynastic interests and territories in the context of European power politics.

Although some Western sovereigns were somewhat limited by representative bodies—diets, parlements, estates—absolute monarchies nonetheless created an unprecedented concentration of governing power. Between 1614 and 1788, no king of France convoked the Estates-General, an assembly of representatives from the three estates—clergy, nobility, and commoners—that had been created early in the fourteenth century as an advisory council to the king. The Portuguese assembly of nobles did not meet at all during the eighteenth century.

The absolute states of Central and Eastern Europe—Prussia, Austria, and Russia—shared similar social structures: a strong nobility with ties to rulers who granted concessions and privileges in exchange for cooperation, a subservient peasantry in the process of losing remaining rights to rulers and landlords, including—through progressive enserfment—that of personal freedom, and a relatively weak and politically powerless middle class. Unlike England and the Dutch United Provinces, these states had no representative institutions and few towns of size and importance to stand in the way of absolute rule.

Monarchs and Nobles

Absolute rulers depended on some degree of compliance by nobles. In each absolute state, the relationship between ruler and nobles determined the specific character of absolutism. This delicate balance is reflected in the oath of loyalty sworn to the king of Spain by the Aragonese nobility: "We who are as good as you swear to you who are no better than we to accept you as our king and sovereign lord, provided you observe all our liberties and laws; but if not, not."

Monarchs negotiated compromises with nobles, awarding titles and privileges for obedience, or at least compliance. In some cases, nobles asserted independence vis à vis royal authority. But emphatic assertions of royal authority reduced nobles to the role of junior ruling partners in governance. With some nobles themselves frightened by the social and political turmoil that shook Europe during the first half of the century, they now more willingly served rulers as royal officials and military commanders.

But sovereigns needed to woo nobles to gain their compliance. In exchange for loyalty and in many cases service, rulers confirmed noble privileges and allowed them to continue to dominate state and local government. "Tables of ranks" dividing nobles into distinct grades or ranks were established at the turn of the century by the kings of Sweden, Denmark, Prussia, and Russia, and made it clear that noble privileges were bestowed by monarchs. Louis XIV of France (ruled 1643–1715) asserted the right to monitor the legitimacy of all titles and even to confiscate noble estates. In 1668, he ordered the investigation of "false" nobles holding dubious titles. These measures helped the king maintain the loyalty of nobles,

Dueling Swedish nobles. One of the noble privileges that was confirmed by absolute sovereigns was the right to carry and use swords.

some of whom resented those who held titles they considered suspect. The great noble families thereafter enjoyed an even greater monopoly over the most lucrative and prestigious royal and ecclesiastical posts.

Using the augmented power of the state, rulers also placated nobles by ending a turbulent period of peasant uprisings against taxes, obligations to their lords, and the high price of grain. And they reduced the vagrancy and petty criminality that had increased since the difficult decade of the 1590s. Insurrections occurred less frequently and were savagely repressed by kings.

The gradual centralization of authority in Eastern Europe left nobles with even more autonomy than they had in the West, allowing Russian lords, Polish nobles, and Prussian Junkers the possibility of further increasing their wealth and power through the extension of their estates, which were worked by serfs. Beginning in the late sixteenth century, such seigneurs made fortunes shipping grain to the West, where prices of cereal and food had risen dramatically in response to population growth. Royal decrees in Prussia and Russia and assembly legislation in Poland progressively limited the right of peasants to move from the land they worked, or even to inherit property. Ravaged by hard times, peasant proprietors had to sell their land to nobles. Impoverished and virtually powerless to resist, peasants lost their personal freedom, a process most marked in Russia. Thus, as feudalism gradually disappeared in Western Europe, it became more prevalent in the East as lords dispossessed peasants from their land. In the West, lords increased their power over land; in the East, over both land and persons. The economic crises of the seventeenth century, including the disruptions of the Thirty Years' War and the decline in Western demand for grain imported from the East because of increased production in the West, only made conditions of life harder for serfs.

In the Ottoman Empire, absolutism was even more despotic. All lands were considered the sultan's private imperial possessions. He granted landed estates to those who served him, but because the sultan recognized no rights of property, no hereditary nobility could develop, in sharp contrast to other European states, to challenge his authority. No representative institutions existed. Towns in the overwhelmingly rural empire had neither autonomy nor rights.

Expanding State Structures

Absolute monarchs extended their authority within their territories by expanding the structure of the state. To fill the most prestigious offices, they chose nobles for their influence and wealth more than their competence. But they also began to employ able officials to collect vital information, for example, projected revenues or the anticipated number of soldiers available in times of war.

The Renaissance city-states of Italy had created relatively efficient civil administrations and set up the first permanent diplomatic corps. During the seventeenth century, the apparatus of administration, taxation, and military conscription gradually became part of the structure of the absolute state. The result was that in Europe as a whole, the number of government officials grew about fourfold.

One result of these expanding ranks of officials was the tripling of tax revenues between 1520 and 1670 in France and Spain, and in non-absolutist England as well. To raise money, absolute rulers sold monopolies (which permitted only the holder of the monopoly to produce and sell particular goods) on the production and sale of salt, tobacco, and other commodities, and imposed taxes on the trading towns of their realms. The rulers of France, Spain, and Austria also filled the state coffers by selling hereditary offices. Philip IV of Spain put it this way: "Without reward and punishment no monarchy can be preserved. We have no money, so we have thought it right and necessary to increase the number of honors." James I of England doubled the number of knights during the first four months of his reign. Queen Christina of Sweden doubled the number of noble families in ten years. In addition, as royal power and prestige rose, the monarchs more easily found wealthy families to loan them money, usually in exchange for tax exemptions, titles, or other privileges.

Absolutism and Warfare

The regular collection of taxes and the expansion of sources of revenue increased the capacity of absolute rulers to maintain standing armies, maintain fortifications, and wage war. By the end of the sixteenth century, Philip II of Spain had allocated three-quarters of state expenditures to pay for past wars or to wage new ones. Appropriately enough, the bureau in Prussia that a century later would oversee tax collection itself evolved from the General War Office, making explicit the close connection between the extraction of state revenue and the waging of dynastic wars.

Absolutist statemaking and warfare had direct and indirect consequences for most of the European population. Kings no longer depended on troops provided by nobles or conscripted by military contractors, thereby avoiding the risk that private armies might challenge royal power. Standing armies continued to grow in size during the eighteenth century (see Table 7-1). During the sixteenth century, the peacetime armies of the continental powers had included about 10,000 to 20,000 soldiers; by the 1690s, they reached about 150,000 soldiers. The French army, which stood at about 180,000 men in peacetime, rose to 350,000 soldiers, the largest in Europe, during the War of the Spanish Succession (1701–1714). The Russian army grew from 130,000 in 1731 to 458,000 in 1796. In contrast, England and the Dutch Republic, two non-absolutist states, had relatively small armies and, as sea powers, both depended on their navies.

TABLE 7-1 THE SIZE OF EUROPEAN ARMIES, 1690–1814

	1690	1710	1756/60	1789	1812/14
Britain	70,000	75,000	200,000	40,000*	250,000
France	400,000	350,000	330,000	180,000	600,000
Habsburg Emp.	50,000	100,000	200,000	300,000	250,000
Prussia	30,000	39,000	195,000	190,000	270,000
Spain	na	30,000	na	50,000	na
Sweden	na	110,000	na	na	na
United Prov.	73,000	130,000	40,000*	na	na

*Drop reflects peacetime and non-absolutist character of the state.
na   Figures not available.
Source: Paul Kennedy, *The Rise and Fall of the Great Powers* (New York: Vintage, 1989), p. 99.

As absolute monarchs consolidated their power, the reasons for waging international wars changed. The wars of the previous century had been fought, in principle, over the rivalry between the Catholic and Protestant religions, even if dynastic interests were never far from the surface. Now, although religious rivalries still constituted an important factor in international conflict (as in the case of the long struggle between the Muslim Ottoman Empire and the Catholic Habsburg Empire), "reasons of state" became a prevalent justification for the rulers of France, Prussia, and Russia to make war on their neighbors.

The organization and financing of warfare illuminate the early modern state in action. In some countries, road and bridge improvements were undertaken to enhance the rapid movement of armies. Warfare both encouraged and drew upon the development of credit institutions, further expanding the capacity of the state to raise money to wage war. But as the British and Dutch cases demonstrated, a state did not have to be absolutist in order to marshal sufficient resources to fight sustained wars. English colonial trade generated excise and customs taxes, permitting the expansion of the Royal Navy. The crown's reputation for repayment facilitated raising money through loans at home and abroad. Amsterdam's stature as a great banking center contributed to the ability of the Dutch government to fight extended wars. In contrast, the French monarchy lacked the confidence of wary investors, and despite the sale of privileges, found itself in an increasingly dangerous financial situation. Moreover, the French monarchy often had to pay higher rates of interest than private investors because it was a bad credit risk.

Even in peacetime, military expenditures took up almost half of the budget of any European state. In times of war, the percentage rose to 80 percent, or even more. Inevitably, there came a point even in absolute states when noble and other wealthy families upon which monarchies depended for financial support began to grumble. But as Table 7-1 reveals, huge standing armies characterized absolute states even in peacetime, nowhere more so than in France, the model of absolute rule in Europe. For the first time uniforms, colorful signs of the state's influence, became standard equipment for every soldier.

Absolutism and Religion

Absolute monarchs intruded in matters of faith and self-expression by both aiding established churches and limiting ecclesiastical authority within their states. An alliance with established churches helped monarchs achieve and maintain absolute rule. In particular, the Catholic Church's quest for uniformity of belief and practice went hand in hand with the absolutist monarch's desire to eliminate challenges to his authority. Absolute monarchs lent their authority and prestige to the Catholic Church, the support of which, in turn, seemed to legitimize absolute monarchical power. The Church helped create an image of the king as a sacred figure, benevolent but strict, who must be obeyed because he served God's interests on earth. In turn, absolute monarchs obliged the Church by persecuting religious minorities.

At the same time that they supported established churches, however, absolute rulers also reduced ecclesiastical autonomy in their realms. Although the Catholic Church was a significant economic, social, and political force in the Catholic absolutist states—France, Spain, Austria, and Portugal—it lost authority to their absolute monarchs. The Church owned as much as two-thirds of the land of Portugal, and at least 10 percent in Spain, Austria, and France, as well as half the land of Bavaria and Flanders, in addition to considerable holdings in all of the Italian states. The Church claimed the right to the tithe. But absolute monarchs maintained authority over ecclesiastical appointments, in effect creating national churches to the consternation of the papacy in Rome.

Signs of the victory of absolute rulers over the Catholic Church included shackling or eliminating the Inquisition in France and Spain, closing monasteries and expelling religious orders in France and Austria, assuming control over censorship, reducing ecclesiastical authority over marriage, and establishing the principle of state supervision over education.

In France, the very existence of the French, or Gallican Church, defied papal claims to complete authority over the Church. By the Concordat of Bologna in 1516, the pope had given the kings of France virtual control (subject to confirmation by the pope) over the appointment of bishops and other high ecclesiastical officials in France. It also had allowed the French kings to overrule the judgments of ecclesiastical courts. This irritated French "ultramontane" clergy, who rejected the Gallican Church, recognizing only the authority of the pope "beyond the mountains," that is, beyond the Alps in Rome. The provincial noble parlements, or law courts, by contrast, remained defiantly Gallican. The Gallican Church itself was far more likely to remain loyal to the monarchy that defined its prerogatives.

Yet, Gallicans themselves insisted that the pope and bishops retain spiritual authority, with the king having a monopoly only on temporal power.

The Russian Orthodox Church, independent of the Greek Orthodox Church since the fifteenth century, and the tsarist autocratic state closely supported each other. The Church taught the faithful obedience to the tsar. But in 1716, Peter the Great forced bishops to take an oath that they would not interfere in state affairs. And by the end of the century, the Russian clergy lost the right to be tried in their own courts and became subject to those of the state.

Recognizing no distinction between church and state, the Turkish Ottoman Empire was a theocracy. The sultan's subjects believed his despotic authority was divine. The Muslim religious hierarchy, which included judges, theologians, and teachers, provided officials for the imperial administration. Yet, the supreme religious dignitary occasionally invoked religious law, of which he was the main interpreter, to counter some orders of the sultan, although the latter's political authority remained absolute.

The expansion of the Ottoman Empire had been based upon the concept of the crusading "Holy War" against infidels, or non-Muslims. As the Turks destroyed the Byzantine Empire, capturing Constantinople in 1453, they confiscated many of the resources of the Orthodox Church and other Christian denominations. The Ottoman Turks had enslaved prisoners of war, purchased slaves abroad, or imposed a slave levy upon the Christians of the empire. Many Christian children had been trained as officials or

Janissaries crossing the Drove, a branch of the Danube River.

soldiers and had converted to Islam. The empire also depended on the contributions of non-slave Christians, including skilled Greek sailors who made Turkish galleys feared in the Mediterranean. Some joined the "janissary" infantry, a military corps that assumed police duties in periods of peace.

Yet, the Ottoman Empire tolerated religious diversity. As long as non-Muslims did not resist Turkish authority, they were free to practice their religion and to become officials within the empire. In Albania (where alone conversions seemed to have been forced), Bosnia, and Herzegovina, many people, including some nobles, converted to the Muslim faith. Young Christians captured by Turkish fleets could convert to Islam in order to escape a life chained to benches as galley slaves. In contrast, Muslims captured by Christian powers remained galley slaves, even if they converted.

Monumentalism in Architecture and Art

Absolute monarchs embraced the extravagant emotional appeal of monumental architecture. They designed their capitals to reflect the imperatives of monarchical authority. Madrid, Berlin, St. Petersburg, and Versailles outside of Paris were planned, shaped, and invested with symbols of absolute rule. These cities were laid out according to geometric principles. In contrast to the narrow, winding streets of trading cities that had evolved organically from medieval times, straight, wide boulevards were created in one fell swoop. The boulevards that led from arches of triumph were built in a classic style to celebrate the power of rulers. These boulevards' symmetrical panorama symbolized the organized and far-reaching power of absolutism and the growth of the modern state. Royal armies paraded down the boulevards to squares or royal palaces, on or before which stood imposing statues, and around which were grouped government buildings and noble residences. Barracks housing standing armies also became a prominent feature of the new urban landscape.

Monarchs paid artists and architects to combine baroque elements with a more restrained, balanced classicism, influenced by the early sixteenth-century Roman style of the High Renaissance. This became known as the Louis XIV style. Thus, the facade completing the Louvre palace in Paris, the work of Gianlorenzo Bernini (1598–1680), drew on the architectural style of Roman temples, thereby linking Louis to the glories of Julius Caesar and other victorious generals. In fact, with the Royal Academy laying down the classical rules painters were to follow, myriad sculptures and paintings represented the king during the early part of his reign as a Roman commander (such as François Girardon's 1680 bronze equestrian sculpture). Later on, artists were asked to produce historical representations of Louis' own triumphs. In the gardens of Versailles, the identification of Apollo with the king is made clear both by Jean-Baptiste Tuby's basin sculpture of *Apollo Rising from the Sea* (1668–1671) and

Charles LeBrun's painting of Louis XIV as a Roman commander.

specifically by Girardon's *Apollo Attended by Nereids* (1666– 1672), a marble group in which one of the muses, or sea nymphs, carries a vase that shows Louis crossing the Rhine. Inside the château, Charles LeBrun's ceiling paintings also associate Louis' wars with purposeful *Apollo in His Chariot* (Charles De Lafosse, 1670s), a depiction whose lavish frame suggests the sun looking down on all who walk beneath. Instead of being compared to past heroes, the king himself was setting the standard for glory. Hyacinthe Rigaud's full-length portrait of Louis XIV in 1701 shows a supremely confident and powerful king standing in a regal pose wearing luxurious coronation robes, clutching his staff of authority and looking with condescension at the viewer—his subject.

ABSOLUTISM IN FRANCE

Absolutist France became the most powerful state in Europe. Francis I and Henry IV had extended the effective reach of monarchical authority (see Chapter 4). Louis XIII, aided by his invaluable minister Cardinal Richelieu, had crushed Protestant resistance. Richelieu piled new administrative structures on old ones, using provincial "intendants" (noble royal officials) to centralize and further extend monarchical authority. Richelieu's policies led to the doubling of taxes between 1630 and 1650, sparking four major waves of peasant resistance between 1624 and 1645, including one uprising in the southwest in 1636 in which about 60,000 peasants took arms, some shouting "Long live the king without taxes!" At Louis XIII's death, the stage was set for Louis XIV (ruled 1643–1715) to rule as a divine-right king of an absolute state. But before the young Louis could take control of the government, France would first experience the regency of his mother and the revolt known as the Fronde.

The Fronde: Taming "Overmighty Subjects"

Louis XIV was four years old at the time of his accession to the throne in 1643. His mother, Anne of Austria (1601–1666), served as regent. She depended on Cardinal Jules Mazarin (1602–1661) for advice. Mazarin, a worldly, charming, and witty Italian, always dressed in the finest red silk and was well known for his love of money. A master of intrigue who had served as a papal envoy, rumor had it that he and Anne were secretly married.

During the Regency period, Anne and Mazarin kept French armies in the field, prolonging the Thirty Years' War, which had become a struggle pitting the dynastic interests of France against the Austrian and Spanish Habsburgs (see Chapter 4). Most nobles, with much to lose from civil disturbances, remained loyal to the monarchy. But Mazarin's prolongation of the victorious struggle against Spain generated a political crisis. Peasants, already weighed down by payments in cash, kind, and labor owed to nobles (an increasing number of whom were becoming absentee lords) and suffering the effects of poor harvests, resisted the additional wartime financial burdens imposed by the state.

Resistance to royal authority culminated in a revolt that shook the Bourbon monarchy at mid-century. Between 1648 and 1653, powerful "nobles of the sword" (those nobles who held ancient titles and whose forebears had gathered retainers to fight for the king) tried to regain the influence lost during the reign of Louis XIII. Ordinary people entered the fray, demanding lower taxes because of deteriorating economic conditions. The revolt became known as the Fronde—so named from a slingshot the boys of Paris used to hurl rocks.

Mazarin, whom many nobles considered a "foreign plotter" and an outsider like Anne of Austria, had borrowed money for the state from financiers. He did so against expected revenue from new taxes or the sale of offices. Nobles were willing to suffer extraordinary levies in times of war. But now they complained bitterly that supplementary impositions in peacetime were needless. Furthermore, some of the oldest noble families had claimed for some time that they had been excluded systematically from the highest, most lucrative, and most prestigious offices. In fact, there was some truth in this claim, as the king feared the power of disloyal "overmighty subjects," preferring lesser nobles for military offices and skilled bureaucrats for some civil posts. Several offices had been abolished. Cardinal Richelieu had convinced the king to order the execution of noble plotters on three occasions during his reign. Now nobles of the sword denounced Mazarin, his system of patronage, and his financier friends, some of whom had made fortunes supplying the royal armies.

In 1648, Mazarin attempted to secure the Parlement of Paris' approval for increased taxes. The Parlement of Paris was the chief law court in France and was made up of nobles of the robe, who had purchased their positions from the crown. Wanting to safeguard their privileges and power, they defied the Regency by calling for an assembly of the four sovereign courts of Paris to consider the financial crisis. Meeting without royal permission, the assembly proposed that the courts elect delegates to consider financial reforms in the realm. The provincial parlements joined the protest against what seemed to be unchecked royal authority. Financiers who had earlier purchased titles from the crown now refused to loan the state any more money.

When Mazarin ordered the arrest of some of the defiant members of the parlement in August 1648, barricades went up in Paris and ordinary Parisians rioted in support of the parlement. From inside the Louvre palace, Louis XIV, then a boy of nine, heard the angry shouts of the crowds. At one point the mob burst into Louis' bedroom. Popular discon-

(*Left*) Louis, prince of Condé. (*Right*) Jules Mazarin, the Italian cardinal and royal chancellor.

tent forced the court to flee Paris in January 1649. These events would affect the king's later successful consolidation of his power.

The role of the prince of Condé (Louis de Bourbon; 1621–1686), head of the junior branch of the Bourbon family, was crucial in the Fronde. Condé's great victory in 1643 over the Spanish at the battle of Rocroi in northern France, which ended any possibility of a successful Spanish invasion of the country, earned him the name of "the Great Condé." The king himself called the proud Condé, only half in jest, "the most powerful man in France." But as long as Mazarin had met Condé's demands for money and offices, the latter remained loyal to the young king. In 1648, Condé marched to Paris with his army to defend the king. A temporary settlement was bought by minor and short-lived tax reforms. But major uprisings against taxes, which had doubled in two decades as Richelieu and Mazarin had in turn raised money in order to wage war, broke out in several provinces. Relatively poor nobles, who resented that wealthy commoners were able to purchase titles with the proceeds of tax-farming and various services to the court, led other revolts. Condé himself changed sides in 1649 and supported the *frondeurs*.

Fearing Condé's influence, a Spanish invasion, and further insurrections, Anne and Mazarin found noble allies against Condé and early in 1650 ordered him imprisoned. Condé's arrest further mobilized opposition to Mazarin, whose enemies forced the minister to flee the country early the next year. More revolts broke out in the provinces, notably in Bordeaux, where the parlement joined the rebellion, which gained popular support. A year later, Condé was released from prison at the demand of the Parlement of Paris. In September 1651, at the age of thirteen, Louis XIV declared his majority and right to rule. But he faced an immediate challenge from Condé who, controlling Bordeaux and its region, marched to Paris in 1652 with the goals of reestablishing his own and the other great nobles' political influence and of getting rid of Mazarin (who continued to influence royal policy from his exile in Germany). However, finding insufficient support from the parlement, the municipal government, or ordinary Parisians, Condé fled to Spain. King Louis recalled Mazarin to Paris.

The young Louis XIV restored monarchical authority by ending the nobles' rebellion and putting down peasant resistance against taxation. He tamed the men he called his "overmighty subjects." He exiled ten members of the Parlement of Paris who had been disloyal to the crown and agreed to give amnesty to others if they would submit to royal authority. Louis made clear that henceforth the Parlement of Paris could not meddle in the king's business. To make the point, in 1652 the king summoned the parlement to the Louvre for a formal ceremony that confirmed its humiliation. And in 1673 the king deprived the twelve parlements of their right to issue remonstrances (formal objections to the registration of new royal ordinances, edicts, or declarations, which could be overridden by the king) before they registered an edict. Laying claim to a monopoly on violence, the king also disbanded the private armies of headstrong nobles and tightened royal control over the provincial governors.

Even at the height of the revolt, when the *frondeurs* were demanding that the king abolish the posts of intendants except in frontier regions, most of them would have been hard pressed to describe the kind of government they wanted. They were also divided by personal rivalries. Furthermore, only the king himself could confirm the social ascendancy of the nobles of the sword. Unlike the English Parliament's successful rebellion against the crown in defense of constitutional rule (see Chapter 6), French noble resistance to absolute rule was broken by the French crown's defeat of the *frondeurs*. The king's predecessors, particularly Francis I, had frequently consulted with prominent nobles about important matters. Louis XIV felt no obligation to do so. Yet, the Fronde also demonstrated that the crown had to rule more subtly, even as Louis XIV kept the reins of power for himself.

Mercantilism under Louis XIV

Following Mazarin's death in 1661, Louis XIV, now twenty-two years of age, assumed more personal responsibility for the day-to-day running of the monarchy. The state's firmer financial footing owed much to the cool calculations of Jean-Baptiste Colbert (1619–1683), controller-general of the realm, who directed administration, taxation, and public works. The grandson of a provincial merchant of modest standing, Colbert suffered the hostility of the old noble families. His frosty personality led him to be dubbed "the North." He employed surveyors and mapmakers to assess the economic resources of the provinces. Traditionally, taxes were "farmed" by royal agents who collected the tax for the state and kept part of it for themselves. Whereas formerly only about a quarter of these revenues reached royal coffers, now as much as four-fifths of what was collected poured into the royal treasury. Even though the royal tax on land (the *taille*) had been reduced, state revenues doubled, despite abuses and privileged exemptions (nobles and clergy in France did not pay the *taille*).

Mercantilism provided the financial basis for absolutist France. Mercantilists posited that all resources should be put into the service of the state and that a state's wealth was measured by its ability to import more gold and silver than it exported to other countries. Jealous of English and Dutch prosperity, Colbert became the chief proponent of French mercantilist policies, which emphasized economic self-sufficiency. He founded commercial trading companies to which the king granted monopolies on colonial trade, levied high protective tariffs on Dutch and English imports, and reduced or eliminated—where possible—tolls within France itself. He established the royal Gobelins tapestry manufacture on the edge of Paris and encouraged the textile industry and the manufacture of other goods that could be exported. He improved roads and oversaw the exten-

King Louis XIV visiting the royal Gobelins tapestry manufacture on the edge of Paris.

sion of France's network of canals, including the Languedoc Canal linking the Mediterranean to the Garonne River and thus to the Atlantic Ocean.

Yet, despite the growth of the French merchant fleet and navy, the French East India Company, established by Colbert in 1664, could not effectively compete with its more efficient and adventurous Dutch and English rivals. The monarchy had to bail out the company and later took away its trading monopoly. Trade within France remained hamstrung by a bewildering variety of restrictions and internal tariffs that in some places were not much different from those that characterized the hodgepodge of German states.

While the king was a master of extracting revenue from his subjects, his greatest talent was for emptying the royal coffers with dizzying speed. Louis XIV and his successors plunged the monarchy into an ever-deepening and eventually disastrous financial crisis.

Louis XIV's Absolutism

As Louis XIV grew into manhood, he looked the part of a great king and played it superbly. Handsome, proud, energetic, and decisive, Louis built his regime more on ceremony than on intelligence and sense. His love of gambling, hunting, and women sometimes took precedence over matters of state. But he also supervised the work of the high council of his prominent officials and, though a spendthrift, he closely monitored the accounts of his realm.

The king became a shrewd judge of character, surrounding himself with men of talent. He consciously avoided being dependent on any single person, the way Louis XIII had been on Richelieu, or his mother on Cardinal Mazarin. During a visit to the château of Vaux-le-Vicomte, built by the unpopular minister of finance Nicholas Fouquet, Louis was served with solid gold tableware and viewed pools filled with seawater and large saltwater fish. The king, who was ready to get rid of Fouquet anyway, promptly ordered him arrested and took the magnificent château for himself.

Having affirmed his authority over Paris, Louis dissolved any remaining pretensions of autonomy held by the elites in the major provincial towns. One result of the Fronde was that the monarchy expanded the narrow social base on which state power had previously rested. Louis selected governors, intendants, and bishops who would be loyal to him. The king made mayors into officials of the state who had to purchase their titles in exchange for fidelity to the king. Wealthy merchants and other townsmen now preferred to seek ennoblement rather than try to maintain municipal privileges that seemed increasingly archaic. The presence of royal garrisons, which towns once resisted, not only affirmed the sovereign's authority but were welcomed by local elites as protection against plebeian insurrection. By the early eighteenth century, towns practically begged for garrisons because troops were good for local business.

The development of absolutism affected towns in other ways, bringing intendants and lesser royal officials, lawyers, and clerks to reside there. In 1667, Louis took another important step in affirming his authority by appointing a lieutenant-general of police for Paris. He gave him extensive authority over a wide range of policing activities, ranging from powers of

Louis XIV surrounded by loyal nobles.

arrest to responsibility for street cleaning and fire fighting. And thanks to the lieutenant-general of police, Paris soon had street lighting—thousands of glass-enclosed candles—during the early evening hours.

Louis XIV portrayed himself as God's representative on this planet, charged with maintaining earthly order. He may or may not have said, *L'état, c'est moi* ("I am the state"), but during his long reign the monarch was indeed identified with the state itself. The royal propaganda machine provided ideological legitimacy by cranking out images of the king as a glorious monarch. During the military disasters and hard times of the War of the Spanish Succession (1701–1714), the emphasis shifted toward a view of the king as the father of his people, while hammering home the necessity of obedience. At the same time, royal censors suppressed publications (especially after the Fronde) prohibited imported books, and limited the number of printers.

Louis XIV created the first French ministry of war and shaped it into an effective bureaucracy. The king and his ministers brought the noble-dominated officer corps under royal control, making seniority the determinant of rank and charging wealthy nobles handsome sums for the privilege of commanding their own regiments or companies. The ministry of war ordered the construction of military academies, barracks, and drilling grounds, and fortified key border towns.

Louis XIV described himself as first seigneur of the realm. Nobles still insisted more than ever—though more quietly than at the time of the Fronde—that institutionalized noble privileges were necessary to counter the excesses of absolute authority. In exchange for acknowledgment by the nobles of monarchical legitimacy, the king confirmed their privileges, including titles, ownership of land, and seigneurial rights over peasants. Nobles were almost completely immune from royal taxes (basically paying only indirect taxes) until Louis made them subject to two additional taxes (the *capitation*, a head tax, and the *vingtième*, a tax of 5 percent, usually only on land). They benefited from the economic development the monarchy could encourage, such as by building better roads and networks of canals that were largely underwritten by the state. Greater efficiency in the collection of taxes on wealth, too, benefited nobles, since the taxes (to which the nobles were not subject) provided money for the salaries of various royal officers and for the trips of nobles to Versailles to offer homage to the king, and financed the construction of official buildings.

The king awarded ever more titles, ecclesiastical offices, and government and military positions to those who loyally served him. This was the easiest way for the king to raise money, as well as to enhance loyalty. As one minister put it "as soon as the crown creates an office God creates a fool willing to buy it."

Since the time of Henry IV, offices had effectively become forms of hereditary property. Louis XIV's lavish sale of offices and titles—500 sold with a single edict in 1696—expanded the nobility. Few noble families now could trace their titles back more than several generations. This accentuated differences between the nobles of the sword (some of whom could trace their noble lineage back centuries) and the nobles of the robe (many of whom had purchased their offices). The nobles of the sword dominated court life, but the king did not hesitate to dip into the ranks of commoners to find efficient, loyal officials, exempting them from taxation and providing lucrative posts for their offspring. Louis de Rouvroy, the duke of Saint-Simon, a noble of the sword, denounced the "reign of the vile bourgeoisie," that is, nobles of recent title whom he viewed as upstart newcomers unworthy of prominent posts.

Louis XIV at Versailles

Louis XIV never forgot hearing the howling Parisian mob from his room in the royal palace. Resolving to move his court to Versailles, twelve miles west of Paris, he visited Paris only four times during the seventy-two years of his reign. Realizing that an adequately fed population would be less likely to riot, Louis XIV and his successors worked to assure the sufficient provisioning of the capital.

The Sun King followed Colbert's advice: . . . nothing marks the greatness of princes better than the buildings that compel the people to look

The château of Versailles, built by Louis XIV from 1669 to 1686.

on them with awe, and all posterity judges them by the superb palaces they have build during their lifetime." The staging ground for royal ceremonies was the fabulous château of Versailles (constructed 1669–1686), surrounded by geometrically arranged formal gardens, interspersed by 1,400 fountains supplied by the largest hydraulic pumps in the Western world.

The château, with hundreds of splendidly decorated rooms, was monumental in scale. The royal dining room was so far from the kitchen that the king's food often arrived at his table cold and, during one particularly cold winter, the wine froze before Louis could taste it. The château's corridors were so long that some nobles used them as urinals, instead of continuing the lengthy trek to the water closet.

Louis summoned the greatest nobles of the realm to Versailles to share in his glory. There they could be honored, but none could become too powerful. More than 10,000 nobles, officials, and servants lived in or near the château. Intricately detailed etiquette governed royal ceremonies. They began with the elaborate routine of dressing the king in the morning in the company of the richest and most powerful nobles. As in the king of Spain's palace near Madrid, court rituals at Versailles were orchestrated to inspire a sense of the majesty and power of the monarch, but also to maintain differences in rank and privilege. The ultimate reward for a loyal noble was to be named to a post within the royal household. Louis XIV allowed the nobles to form cabals and conspire, but only against each other.

Nobles attended the expensive theatrical and operatic productions put on at royal expense. These included the works of the great Jean-Baptiste Molière (1622–1673) and Jean Racine (1639–1699), both of whom wrote effusive praise for the king into some of their plays. But for nobles at Versailles there was little else to do except eat, drink, hunt—in the company of the king, if they were favored—gamble, and chase each other's wives and mistresses.

Social struggles mark the plays of Molière. The son of an upholsterer, the playwright started a travelling theatrical company before settling in Paris. The lonely, unhappy Molière poked fun at the pretensions of aristocratic and ecclesiastical society, depicting the private, cruel dramas of upper-class family life. But his popular works also helped reaffirm the boundaries between social classes. He ridiculed the bourgeois, whose wealth could purchase titles but not teach them how to behave as nobles. In *The Bourgeois Gentilhomme* (1670), the parvenu gives himself away with a social gaffe. Molière also detested hypocrisy, which he depicted in *Tartuffe* (1664), a tale of the unfortunate effects of untempered religious enthusiasm on a family. *Tartuffe* brought Molière the wrath of the Church, but he had an even more powerful protector, Louis XIV.

Nobles sustained an aristocratic culture tied to notions of civility, or codes governing how nobles and other people of means ought to behave in public. A guide to manners published about twenty years after Louis XIV

Portrait of the young Jean-Baptiste Molière, playwright.

became king advised: "Formerly . . . it was permitted to spit on the ground before people of rank, and was sufficient to put one's foot on the sputum. Today that is an indecency." The same book had good advice on eating, too: "If everyone is eating from the same dish . . . you should always wipe your spoon when, after using it, you want to take something from another dish, there being people so delicate that they would not wish to eat soup into which you had dipped it after putting it into your mouth."

Louis XIV believed that his court stood as the center and apex of civilization. Indeed, French arts and literature had an enormous influence in Europe, particularly during the first thirty years of his reign. Foreign monarchs, nobles, and writers considered French the language of high culture. In 1700, advertisements placed in London newspapers by private teachers promised that their pupils would soon speak the French spoken at the court of Louis XIV. The château of Versailles encouraged imitation. Philip V of Spain and Frederick the Great of Prussia, among others, ordered similar palaces built. The duke of Saxony rebuilt his capital of Dresden along neo-classical lines. The château also served as a model for noble estates and townhouses built in the classical style.

Louis XIV's Persecution of Religious Minorities

One of the most salient results of the victory of absolute rule in Catholic states was the persecution of religious minorities. Such campaigns in part served to placate the papacy and the Church hierarchy in each Catholic

(*Left*) The symbol of the sun used to glorify the absolute ruler, Louis XIV. (*Right*) This caricature shows Louis XIV, the Sun King, as the exterminator of Protestantism.

state. Louis XIV had little interest in theology, although he was relatively pious, for all his eager attention to his mistresses, several of whom bore him children. But as he grew older, the king brought into his inner circle a number of extremely devout advisers, and into his bedroom a fervently religious mistress.

Reversing the tolerant policies of Henry IV and Louis XIII, in the late 1670s Louis XIV launched a vigorous campaign of persecution against Huguenots, closing most Protestant churches and initiating attempts to force conversions to Catholicism. In 1685, Louis XIV revoked the Edict of Nantes, by which Henry IV in 1598 had extended religious tolerance to Protestants. This pleased the provincial estates in regions where Protestants were a forceful minority and memories of the wars of religion were still fresh. But the economic cost to France was in the long run considerable. Although the king forbade Huguenots from leaving France, many merchants and skilled craftsmen were among the 200,000 Huguenots who nonetheless emigrated during the next forty years. Many went to England, South Africa, Prussia, and to the Dutch United Provinces.

With the motto "one king, one law, one faith," Louis XIV also persecuted Jansenists in his quest for religious orthodoxy. Jansenists were followers of Cornelius Jansen, bishop of Ypres in the Southern Netherlands, who had died in 1638. They could be found in France, the Netherlands, Austria, and several Italian states. Seeking reforms within the Church, Jansenists emphasized the role of faith and divine grace in the pursuit of salvation. Believing mankind to be fallen and hapless, incapable of understanding the will of God, Jansenists came close to accepting a Calvinist doctrine of predestination. Their enemies called them "Calvinists who go to Mass." Calvinists had developed the notion of "vocation," whereby one was to throw oneself into secular life and live as a saint, as if one had the certainty of salvation. Jansenists, in contrast, believed that one should completely withdraw from the world, given the certainty of sin and mankind's ignorance of God's will. Jansenists, who were notoriously ascetic and disapproved of the frivolity of Versailles, criticized the Church for encouraging a lax morality by holding out the possibility of repeated penance, indeed deathbed conversion.

The pope had condemned Jansenism in 1653, perhaps at the insistence of the Jesuits, who were the Jansenists' most determined enemy. Louis XIV continued to tolerate them for several decades. But he began to persecute them in the name of "one faith" in 1709 when, influenced by Jesuit advisers, he ordered the Jansenist community at Port-Royal outside of Paris evicted and its abbey burned to the ground. He convinced Pope Clement XI to issue a papal bull, *Unigenitus* (1713), which condemned Jansenism. The Parlement of Paris, however, refused to register the edict. Louis was still trying to force compliance two years later when he died. The king's attempt to impose religious orthodoxy in France fell short, indicating that absolute rule had its limits.

The Limits of French Absolutism

France, like other countries, was far from being a nation-state in which most people thought of themselves as French, as well as or instead of Norman, Breton, or Provençal. More than half the population did not speak

Protestant allegory representing French Huguenots fleeing religious persecution in France.

French. Inadequate roads isolated mountain regions, in particular, limiting the effective reach of absolute rule.

The absolute monarchy stood at the top of a complex network of patronage based on personal ties that reached into every province and every town. But Louis XIV's intendants still had to take local networks of influence into consideration, using intimidation, cajoling, and negotiating to gain their ends in what was Western Europe's most populous state.

The king played off against one another the jurisdictions and interests of the estates, parlements, and other provincial institutions dominated by the nobles. The provincial estates were assemblies of nobles of the *pays d'état* (regions retaining a degree of fiscal autonomy, including Brittany, Provence, Burgundy, and Languedoc), which claimed to represent each province. The estates oversaw the collection of taxes and tended to details of provincial administration and spending. They met annually amid great pageantry and carefully orchestrated ceremony that, like those at Versailles, reaffirmed social hierarchy. In principle, the estates could refuse to provide the crown with the annual "free grant" (a subsidy provided by each region to the monarch), which was hardly "free," since the king informed the estates of the amount of money he wanted. Louis XIV abolished the custom of allowing the estates to express grievances before voting the amount of their "gift" to the monarchy.

The interests of the nobles also prevailed in the parlements, which were sovereign law courts that registered, publicized, and carried out royal laws. The parlements, most of whose members were nobles, claimed to speak for their province in legal matters, asserting the right to issue binding commands in cases of emergencies. But, unlike the English Parliament, no national representative political institution existed in France.

Louis XIV's successor, Louis XV (ruled 1715–1774) held that "sovereign power resides in my person alone. . . . It is from me that my courts of justice derive their existence and their authority. The plenitude of this authority which they exercise only in my name, remains always with me. I alone possess the legislative power without sharing it with, or depending for it on, anyone. . . . The whole system of public order emanates from me."

But even the king of France was not as omnipotent or omniscient as he would have liked to think. Louis XV, bothered by the traffic in Paris, once complained, "If I were lieutenant-general of police, I would ban two-wheel carriages." Bodin, theorist of absolutism, expressed the view that a ruler would be wise to avoid exercising full power, for example by not interfering with his subjects' property. This ambiguity is perhaps best symbolized by the king's phrase to the estates of a province, "We entreat you but we also command you. . . ."

Even the Bourbons were bound by the so-called fundamental laws of the realm, as well as by those they believed God had established. They therefore were responsible for any crimes they might commit. More than this, an absolute monarch could not stem the tide of change. Louis XIII placed markers around the city of Paris, even beyond the city walls, warning that anyone who built beyond would have his house razed and be slapped with a stiff fine. But Louis XIV had to surrender to spontaneous population growth, finally ordering the walls torn down in 1670.

THE HABSBURG MONARCHY

The eighteenth-century French philosophe Voltaire only somewhat exaggerated when he dismissed the Holy Roman Empire, that cumbersome federal structure of Central European states that once served as a powerful protector of the papacy, as having ceased to be holy, Roman, or an empire. The Holy Roman Empire included almost 300 German states, ranging from Austria to archbishoprics barely extending beyond the walls of towns like Mainz and Trier. Until 1648, seven electors (four princes and three archbishops) picked the Holy Roman emperor, invariably the Habsburg ruler (after 1648, there were eight electors). But in a Europe increasingly dominated by absolute monarchs, the Holy Roman Empire seemed an anomaly.

In principle, the Holy Roman emperor still commanded the allegiance of the states of the empire. These included sizable states such as Bavaria and Saxony, whose rulers oversaw elaborate courts modeled after Versailles, maintained standing armies, and paid for all this by levying taxes on their subjects and customs duties and tolls on merchandise being carried through their territories. The Holy Roman Empire also included many small principalities, duchies, and even towns ruled by bishops. But in reality the empire had increasingly only a shadow existence, despite its mystique as the defender of Catholicism. The Treaty of Westphalia (1648), which concluded the Thirty Years' War, reflected the inability of the Holy Roman Empire to enforce its will, conduct foreign policy, or effectively maintain an army. During the long war, some German princes, with powerful allies outside the empire, had gone their own way. Indeed, the Treaty of Westphalia specifically empowered each member state to carry out its own foreign policy. The imperial Assembly, the Reichstag, thus had virtually no authority to conduct foreign policy with other states. The imperial army was too small and difficult to mobilize to be effective. The imperial court of law was powerless to enforce its decisions, depending entirely on the good will of the individual states.

The strongest state within the Holy Roman Empire, the territories of Habsburg Austria, extended beyond the boundaries of the empire itself. The Habsburgs had ruled Austria without interruption since the thirteenth century. The old Habsburg principle was "Let others wage war. You, happy Austria, marry [to prosper]." Advantageous marriages brought the dynasty the wealthy territories of Burgundy and the Netherlands in the fifteenth century. Charles V, who became Holy Roman emperor in 1519, added Hungary and Bohemia. Counting Spain and its far-flung possessions, he reigned over perhaps a quarter of the population of the European continent, as well as the vast Spanish Empire of the Americas.

When Charles V gave up his power in 1556 and formally abdicated as emperor in 1558, he divided the Habsburg domains into two parts. His brother Ferdinand I inherited the Austrian Habsburg lands (including Austria, Hungary, and Bohemia) and succeeded him as the elected Holy Roman emperor. Charles' son Philip II became king of Spain with his empire including the Netherlands, dependencies in Italy, and colonies in the Americas. The Spanish and Austrian branches of the Habsburgs were henceforth two separate dynasties, although the interests of both as Catholic states, but also as rivals of France, sometimes converged.

The Austrian Habsburg monarchy exercised foreign policy and directed the armed forces, but it had less effective authority within its territories than the kings of France had within their realm. Nobles oversaw the court system and police apparatus. When confronted with threats to their traditional prerogatives, nobles put aside differences, such as those between the great landowners and the lower nobility, and formed a common front to preserve their privileges against monarchical erosion.

Austria was the only power able to exercise its influence equally in both Western and Eastern Europe. The Austrian Habsburgs successfully implemented an effective state administration, expanded educational opportunities for the upper classes, and brought resistant or even rebellious nobles under dynastic control. But timely marriages were no longer enough. Throughout the sixteenth century and during the first half of the seventeenth century, the Habsburgs had been almost constantly preoccupied with politics within and between the German states. During the Thirty Years' War, however, the Habsburgs were unable to expand their domination throughout Central Europe. While still seeking a major role in the German states, the Habsburgs remained vulnerable to French expansionism and to Turkish incursions, forcing the monarchy to confront threats on two fronts.

The Habsburg empire's polyglot structure of territories of different nationalities, including fifteen major languages, was a source of weakness. Leopold I, elected Holy Roman emperor in 1658 (ruled 1658–1705; Louis XIV was the opposing candidate), was simultaneously Holy Roman emperor, duke of Upper and Lower Silesia, count of Tyrol, archduke of Upper and Lower Austria, king of Bohemia, prince of Transylvania, king of Hungary, Slavonia, Dalmatia, and Croatia, and titular ruler of Lombardy, Styria, and Moravia (see Map 7.1). The monarch did not rule through a single administration, but rather in each case through local political institutions. The Hungarian and Croatian provincial diets, or noble estates, impeded Habsburg absolutism. Hungarians also resented German-speaking administrators and tax collectors, as well as the Habsburg armies that

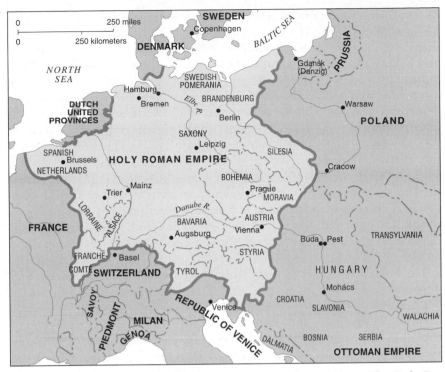

MAP 7.1 THE HOLY ROMAN EMPIRE UNDER LEOPOLD I, 1658 The Holy Roman Empire included a polyglot structure of territories of different nationalities.

helped protect them from the Turks. Some Hungarian Catholic prelates were irritated by the close ties between the ruling dynasty and the Roman papacy. In Bohemia, the scars of the religious conflicts between Catholics and Protestants during the Thirty Years' War healed very slowly. Bohemia, and Moravia as well, remained a center of Protestant intellectual ferment. Furthermore, many Bohemian nobles resented the fact that a decree in 1627 had abolished the principle of an elective monarchy and made the Bohemian crown a hereditary Habsburg possession.

Hungary had been part of the Habsburg domains since the sixteenth century. The Hungarian nobles, proud of their defense of the Habsburg empire against Turkish incursions, seized every opportunity to extract concessions from the Habsburgs. Unlike their Austrian counterparts, most of the Hungarian, or Magyar, nobles had become Protestant during the Reformation. Habsburg persecution of Hungarian Protestants helped spark an insurrection in 1679 against Habsburg rule that spread into Moravia, Slavonia, and Silesia. This led Leopold to promise the Hungarian Estates to restore some landowner privileges that had been suppressed. But dissatisfied Protestants then called for Turkish assistance at a time when the

Turks were preparing to attack Habsburg territories. The Ottoman army besieged Vienna, the Habsburg capital, in 1683. It was saved after two months by the arrival of a combined relief army of Austrians, Germans, and Poles under the command of the crusading Catholic Polish King John Sobieski (ruled 1674–1696). Pope Innocent XI succeeded in convincing Leopold I, who had been trained for the priesthood before becoming emperor and who saw himself as a prince of the Catholic Reformation, to lead a "Holy League" in 1684 against the Turks. In the War of the Holy League (1686–1687), and in subsequent fighting, Habsburg armies recaptured most of Hungary and the eastern province of Transylvania from the Turks, as well as much of Croatia. The Peace of Karlowitz (1699) ratified the Habsburg victory over the Turks and provided for further Turkish concessions to Venice and Poland. Although for the moment Ottoman garrisons remained only eighty miles from Vienna and Turkish galleys still roamed the Mediterranean, the Ottoman threat to Central Europe had passed.

The Habsburg victory over the Turks had also been, for all intents and purposes, over Hungary. In 1687, the Hungarian Estates were forced to declare that the Hungarian throne (the crown of Saint Stephen, named after Hungary's patron saint) would henceforth be a hereditary possession of the Habsburgs and no longer elective. Hungary thereby recognized the sovereignty of the Habsburg dynasty in exchange for a promise that the Hungarian Diet would be convened at regular intervals, Hungary would

Leopold I, the Holy Roman emperor.

Turkish siege of Vienna, 1683.

have its own administration, and Magyar nobles would continue to be exempt from royal taxation. While he consolidated Habsburg authority within the dynasty's domains, however, Leopold failed to impose centralized rule on Hungary. Thus, Hungary's special position within the monarchy revealed the limits of Habsburg absolutism and Austrian power.

The Habsburg monarchy, the least absolute of Europe's absolute states, was less successful than France in maintaining its power. In 1700, Austria's Habsburg dynasty lost its long-standing ties to Spain when that country passed from the Habsburg dynasty to the Bourbon dynasty with the death of the childless Charles II (ruled 1665–1700). France's defeat in the War of the Spanish Succession (1701–1714), fought to determine who would inherit the Spanish Habsburg territories, enabled the Austrian Habsburgs to pick up some of the remaining pieces of the decimated Spanish Empire in Europe. A treaty with the Turks in 1718 added parts of Wallachia, Serbia, and Bosnia to Hungarian territories. However, Austria ceded its preeminence in Central Europe to Prussia during the eighteenth century.

THE RISE OF PRUSSIA

The presence of all the essential components of absolutism explain Prussia's rise as a power: a proud, ambitious dynasty, the Hohenzollern family of Brandenburg; privileged but loyal nobles, or Junkers, whose estates formed the base of the economy and who dominated a downtrodden peasantry devoid of rights; an increasingly centralized and efficient bureaucracy; and, above all, the emergence of a large standing army. Austrian defeats in the Thirty Years' War and vulnerability to French and Turkish challenges left the way open for a rival to emerge among the German states. Bavaria and Saxony were weak claimants for primacy among the German states. Both had relatively weak nobilities, and the rulers of both states had failed to develop either a strong bureaucracy or a strong army. The Catholic clergy undermined the authority of the Bavarian dukes. The attention of Saxony, subject to Swedish influence, was often turned away from German affairs toward the volatile world of Polish politics.

The small north-central German state of Brandenburg-Prussia, stretching across the sandy marshes between the Elbe and Oder Rivers, seemed an unlikely candidate to rival Austria and to grow into a powerful absolute state. In 1618, Brandenburg's ruling Hohenzollern dynasty inherited East Prussia, which lay 100 miles to the east of Brandenburg along the Baltic Sea and was bordered by Poland. It then absorbed several smaller territories in the Rhineland, more than 100 miles to the west (see Map 7.2). Consisting of three diverse, noncontiguous realms, Brandenburg-Prussia lacked not only defensible frontiers but also the developed network of prosperous trading towns of other regions in Germany. During the Thirty Years' War, Swedish and Austrian armies took turns ravaging it. But it

MAP 7.2 THE RISE OF PRUSSIA, 1648–1720   Territories acquired by Brandenburg-Prussia.

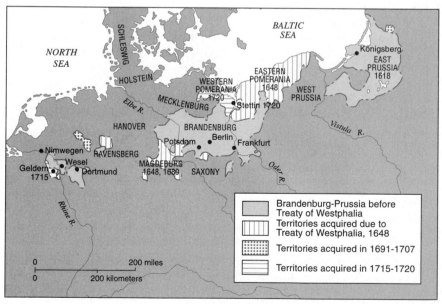

gained territory with the Treaty of Westphalia (1648), which ended the war and permitted Prussia to absorb much of Pomerania, on the Baltic Sea coast.

Prussian nobles accepted Hohenzollern authority as a guarantee of their privileges, the trade-off that underlay statemaking in early modern Europe. Only nobles could own land, evict peasants from their lands, and were free from taxation. But they needed people to work their estates. During the late fifteenth and the sixteenth centuries, the peasants lost their freedom, including their right to free movement and often to inheritance. They became serfs, legally bound to the lord's estate, and could be sold with the land on which they worked. A burgher in a Prussian town in 1614 described serfdom as "this barbaric and Egyptian servitude . . . in our territory serfdom did not exist fifty or a hundred years ago, but lately, it has been brought in on a large scale, with the help of the authorities." The authority of the Hohenzollerns, however, stopped at the gate of the manor: Junkers retained rights of seigneurial justice over their peasants. The bourgeoisie, which included merchants and skilled craftsmen, also stood powerless before the Junkers, in contrast to the middle class in England and the Dutch United Provinces, where they presented an imposing obstacle to the growth of absolutism. Unlike the Prussian nobles, the middle-class burghers could not export grain freely and had to pay tolls, duties, and taxes.

Frederick William (ruled 1640–1688), the "Great Elector" of Brandenburg (so named because the ruler of Brandenburg had the right to cast a ballot in the election of the Holy Roman emperor), initially had neither a standing army nor the resources to raise one. Prussian nobles at first resisted the creation of a standing army, fearful that it might aid the elector in reducing their privileges. In 1653, Frederick William convinced the Junkers to grant him funds with which to build an army in exchange for royal confirmation of their privileges over the peasantry and their right to import goods without paying duties. Furthermore, the king agreed to consult the nobles on matters of foreign policy.

Then Frederick William turned to the business of augmenting state authority in his three fragmented territories. He extracted concessions from each of them, including more taxes and the right to recruit soldiers. With his permanent standing army, Frederick William was able to wage war in alliance with various states and thereby to acquire more territory, as well as recruiting peasants to serve as soldiers and Junkers as officers. The Great Elector established a centralized administrative bureaucracy, arguably the first modern civil service in Europe. The Hohenzollern family owned more than half of East Prussia, which provided considerable state revenue. A state official supervised military affairs and the collection of taxes in each district, pulling in twice as much revenue as extracted by the king of France at the same time. Elected by local nobles, he was responsible to the king, who gradually expanded his duties as a royal representative. The Prussian bureaucracy, which was coordinated by an office with the suitably imposing name of the "General Directory Over Finance, War, and Royal Domains," reached a degree of efficiency unmatched in eighteenth-century Europe. The remaining prerogatives of the towns disappeared in the expanding state. Prussian towns, most of which were small but compelled to pay a disproportionate percentage of taxes, lost their representation in the provincial estates. In 1701, the Great Elector's son Frederick III (ruled 1688–1713) took the title of King Frederick I in Prussia. This claim to royalty through kingship initiated Prussia's claim to European standing as a power.

Frederick William I (ruled 1713–1740), grandson of the Great Elector, succeeded Frederick III as elector of Brandenburg and king in Prussia. As a boy, Frederick William could not count to ten without his tutor's assistance, but upon his succession he continued the centralizing policies of his grandfather and father. Living modestly, he occupied only several rooms of his palace, with the basement serving as the royal treasury. The bad-tempered "Sergeant-King" wore his officer's uniform around the house and turned the royal gardens into a military training ground. He was known for fits of screaming rage, calling everyone in sight "blockhead," sometimes beating officials with a stick, and knocking out the teeth of several judges whose sentences displeased him. Officials known as "fiscals"

King Frederick William I.

went around to make sure that the king's representatives served him well. But the king was astute enough to break with tradition by employing some commoners; finding state service a means of social mobility, many served with uncommon loyalty and efficiency.

A Prussian official described, with some exaggeration, the feature that defined his country's absolutism and the emergence of Brandenburg-Prussia as a power: "What distinguishes the Prussians from other people is that theirs is not a country with an army. They have an army and a country that serves it." Military expenditures accounted for half of Prussia's state budget. King Frederick William I increased the Prussian army from about 39,000 to 80,000 soldiers. He engaged only tall soldiers for his royal guard, those standing more than six feet in height, virtual giants at the time. One of his first royal acts was to abolish the luxury industries in Berlin, the capital of Brandenburg-Prussia, that catered to court and nobles, and to replace them with workshops that made military uniforms. The king ordered all young men in Prussia to register for military service and organized a procedure by which each regiment was assigned a specific canton from which to recruit or conscript soldiers. Prussia established the first system of military reserves in Europe, soldiers who drilled in the summer for two months. This meant that far more men in Prussia experienced military life than in any other country.

THE RUSSIAN AND SWEDISH EMPIRES

Early in the sixteenth century, Muscovy was a relatively small state. It stood vulnerable to invasions by the Mongols, who had conquered what is now Russia in the thirteenth century, the Tartars of Crimea on the edge of the Black Sea, and to the kingdom of Poland-Lithuania, a kingdom and grand duchy joined in a confederation late in the fourteenth century. Gradually, however, the duchy of Muscovy, where Orthodox Christianity had taken hold, emerged as the strongest of the territories of Russia, absorbing Novgorod and other rival states and principalities late in the fifteenth century. Muscovy's ruler Ivan III (ruled 1462–1505) began using the title "lord of all Russia," a title that offended the far more powerful state of Poland-Lithuania. In 1500 and again twelve years later, Ivan brazenly attacked Poland-Lithuania, capturing the fortress town of Smolensk, which guarded the upper Dnieper River.

The Expansion of Muscovy

The rise of Russia as an absolute state and empire began with the further expansion of the state of Muscovy later in the sixteenth century. Tsar Ivan IV (ruled 1533–1584) absorbed parts of the Mongol states to the east, and

Ivan the Terrible watching the beggars of Novgorod being tortured to death.

drove back the Muslim Tartars, conquered the Don and Volga river basins to the south, and unsuccessfully battled Poland-Lithuania for control of the Baltic territory of Livonia. Peasants and hunters expanded the influence of Muscovy into the cold and sparsely populated reaches of Siberia.

Ivan earned his sobriquet "the Terrible." He was raised in a world of violence marked by the bloody feuds of the Muscovite nobles or *boyars,* some of whom poisoned his mother when he was eight years old. Five years later, Ivan ordered a noble ripped apart by fierce dogs; as an adult, he had an archbishop sewn into a bearskin and thrown to hungry wolves. His goals were to assure himself a reliable military force and sufficient revenue. His means was to create a "service state" in which nobles would serve him while receiving protection against peasant insurrections or other nobles. Allying with a group of military retainers, he decimated noble families he viewed as too powerful or slow to obey. Ivan alternated between moods of religious fervor, drunken passion, and stormy brutality. After being defeated in Lithuania in 1564, Ivan became even more paranoid, subjecting his people to an eight-year reign of terror. He killed his own son with a massive blow to his skull and routinely ordered anyone who displeased him tortured to death.

Ivan's death in 1584 led, almost unimaginably, to an even worse period for Muscovy, the "Time of Troubles," a period of intermittent anarchy. Weak successors allowed nobles to regain control of the sprawling country. In 1613, the Assembly of Nobles elected the first Romanov tsar. The next two tsars restored order, regaining some of the lands lost to Poland-Lithuania and Sweden.

For most peasants, life itself was an endless "time of troubles" in the face of state taxation and brutalization at the hands of their lords. Revolts seemed endemic, some led by men who claimed to be the "true" tsar who would restore justice. One of the latter, Stephen Razin, whose symbol was a horsetail, led a huge force of peasants on a march to the cry of "To Moscow against the landlords." The peasant army captured several cities before being decimated in 1670, its leader tortured in Moscow for all to see.

Serfdom emerged as one of the fundamental characteristics of Russian absolutism. In times of dearth or crisis, many peasants traditionally had fled the region of Moscow to settle on the frontierlands of Siberia in the east or on land in Ukraine, an extensive, thinly populated territory standing between Russia, Poland, and a Tartar state on the Crimean peninsula—the word *Ukraine* itself means "border region." The resulting chronic shortage of rural labor, and the need to provide landed estates to loyal nobles, led the state in 1649 officially to establish serfdom, which had become widespread by the end of the sixteenth century. The chronically indebted peasants gave up their freedom in exchange for loans from the crown and from landlords. The Orthodox Church, a major landowner, also contributed to the expansion of serfdom. Thereafter, 90 percent of the peasants were bound to the land, assuring the state and nobles of a relatively immobile labor supply. In exchange for the tsar's support of this system, Russian nobles, like their counterparts in Prussia, pledged their service to the state.

The Romanov dynasty also enjoyed the good will of the Orthodox Church. By the early sixteenth century, the Russian Orthodox Church had become centered in Moscow, which now claimed the title of the third Rome. But after a mid-seventeenth-century schism, the Orthodox Church faced the hostility of the Old Believers, dissidents who claimed authority over the tsars and disliked changes in Church ritual that reformers had implemented. Old Believers participated in violent peasant uprisings until the end of the eighteenth century.

Several neighbors blocked Muscovy's further expansion. The Commonwealth of Poland and Lithuania (which had been formally united in 1569) stood to the west, and Swedish territories were to the north. The northern port of Archangel on the White Sea, its harbor frozen solid much of the year, offered Muscovy its only access to the sea. Through Archangel passed trade with England and Northern Europe. Turks, Cossacks (a warrior people living in southern Russia), and Crimean Tartars were among the southern peoples resisting incorporation into Muscovy and Poland-Lithuania. Polish territories included much of White Russia (Belarus) and Ukraine. The rest of Ukraine was subject to the influence of Poland, Russia, and Cossacks, and was further divided by religion. Most landowners in

Ukraine were Polish Catholics. Most Ukrainian peasants were, like Russians, Orthodox Christians and spoke a language similar to Russian, but were a separate people. Peasant revolts rocked Ukraine in the late 1640s. A Cossack and former officer in the Polish army launched an uprising, driving back the Polish army, before accepting Russian sovereignty in 1654. Under the Treaty of Andrussovo (1667), which concluded a war with Poland, Russia absorbed Ukraine east of the Dnieper River.

The Swedish Empire

In the 1640s and 1650s, Swedish kings added to their dynastic holdings at the expense of Denmark and Norway, Estonia and Lithuania, and West Pomerania and Bremen in northern Germany. Like the Habsburg empire, that of Sweden offered a babel of languages, including Swedish, Finnish, Latvian, Estonian, and German, the language of administration. Sweden was a relatively poor state, but revenues from lucrative copper mines, the sale of Swedish iron and steel, the finest in Europe, and trade with Muscovy and the West generated enough revenue to finance expansion. But

King Charles XII of Sweden crossing the Dvina River in his war against Peter the Great.

expansion also had its costs: Queen Christina (ruled 1632–1654) raised money by selling almost two-thirds of royal lands, with Swedish nobles becoming the main beneficiaries. Swedish peasants, who had their own estate in the Swedish Diet (or assembly), complained of the "unheard-of state of servitude . . . since private persons took hold of the country." Specifically, they demanded, in vain, the return of all alienated lands to the throne. The lower estates did not dare challenge royal prerogatives. They asserted, "We esteem Your Majesty's royal power as the buttress of our liberties, the one being bound up in the other, and both standing or falling together."

Emboldened by his fledgling empire, King Charles XI (ruled 1660–1697) in the 1680s established absolute rule in Sweden. He overcame the resistance of the wealthiest nobles by winning the support of their jealous colleagues of lesser means, as well as that of the estates of burghers, clergy, and peasants, who sought royal protection against the most powerful nobles. His son Charles XII (ruled 1697–1718) became king at the age of fifteen and refused even to take the coronation oath when he came of age in 1700. Symbolically, he snatched the crown and placed it on his own head, and never convoked the estates. Having been instructed only in warfare as a youth, he remained a headstrong military man who acted by impulse, not reflection. Instead of diplomacy, he relied on warfare to achieve Swedish ends. Charles' unwillingness to ally with Prussia or other states against Russia in the long run cost Sweden dearly. Instead of turning Sweden's full military attention toward Denmark, which sought to recapture lost provinces from Sweden, he spent five years campaigning against Russia (see below), a quest that took him into the Ottoman Empire, where he sought assistance against Russia. But during Charles XII's reign, the crown added to its wealth by reclaiming land that had been sold to nobles in the previous decades. Gradually the Swedish monarchy established a bureaucracy and increased state revenue. But when Charles XII was killed in a war in Norway, leaving no heir, the Swedish nobility succeeded in imposing a parliamentary regime based on the prerogatives of the estates and marked by political struggles among the nobility, clergy, burghers, and peasants. In 1772, however, King Gustavus III (ruled 1771–1792) overthrew the parliamentary system, supported by some nobles, and reimposed absolute rule. By then, however, Sweden's empire was a fading memory.

Peter the Great Turns Westward

In Western Europe so little was known about "barbaric" Russia that Louis XIV sent a letter to a tsar who had been dead for twelve years. Peter the Great (ruled 1682–1725) first imposed order on a state torn by bloody uprisings; then he transformed Muscovy into the Russian Empire.

The young Peter the Great, founder of St. Petersburg.

Impressed with the relative efficiency of Western states, Peter forced a number of significant administrative and military reforms on Russia. Whereas Ivan the Terrible and several of his successors had been turned back by Poland and Turkey, Peter aggressively and successfully moved Russian interests toward Europe. Wars brought territorial acquisitions at the expense of Sweden, Poland, and the Turks.

As a boy growing up in the violent world of Russian court politics, Peter learned far more about guns, ballistics, and fortifications than about Russian grammar. Wearing a military uniform, he became tsar at the age of ten after a bloody struggle, which he witnessed firsthand, between the clans of his father's two widows. Seven years later, Peter killed members of his own family whom he perceived to be a threat to his rule.

The tsar, who wore shabby clothes, worn-out shoes, and his hair very long, stood close to seven feet tall and suffered from chronic back problems compounded by frenetic energy. A nervous tic became most apparent when he was anxious or angry, which seemed to be most of the time, as he lashed out with clubs or fists.

When he was twenty-five, Peter visited Western Europe incognito, encouraged to do so by Europeans he had met living in the foreign quarter on the edge of Moscow. Peter undertook his travels dressed as a humble workman. In the West, he shocked statesmen and nobles with his dress and coarse manners, snatching roasts with his hands from fancy buffets. Four months on the Dutch docks taught him ship carpentry. He always preferred the company of artisans and dockworkers to nobles and state officials. In London, the tsar and his entourage virtually destroyed a rented house with wild parties—the tsar loved to dance and drink—leading a bishop to worry aloud that this "furious man had been raised up to so absolute an authority over so great a part of the world."

Peter was not an uncritical admirer of the West. But impressed with the military strength and administrative efficiency of the Western powers, Peter emulated what he considered to be the more "rational" organization of Western monarchies. He borrowed Western technical knowledge, attaching it to the structures of Russian absolutism. He ordered nobles to become educated and told his guards and officials to shave off their beards—which the Old Believers believed distinguished Russians from Westerners. He encouraged the use of individual glasses, bowls, and napkins at meals, and ordered a Western book of etiquette to be translated into Russian. Furthermore, he ordered nobles to build Western-style palaces and to wear Western-style clothes and for women to wear bonnets, petticoats, and skirts. German and, to a lesser extent, French, became the language of court. Purchasing German and Italian paintings and statues, Peter began the royal collection that would later become the world-renowned Hermitage Museum.

Fearing the military superiority of his rivals, Sweden and Poland, Peter now raised the first Russian standing army, gradually replacing Western mercenary soldiers with Russian troops by implementing military conscription in 1705 to complement Cossack cavalrymen. Thereafter, every twenty peasant households had to provide one recruit, most of whom served for life, and to replace the recruit if he were killed. Peter brought Western commanders to train his army and provided soldiers with uniforms and Western flintlock muskets with socket bayonets.

The docks of Amsterdam and London inspired Peter's interest in building first a river navy and eventually an oceangoing fleet. Skilled workers from Prussia and from the Dutch Republic built warships and taught languages and mathematics. The tsar also sent Russian craftsmen abroad to learn new skills. But Russians gradually replaced Western Europeans as designers, builders, and ship commanders. By the end of the century, Russia had a fleet.

Military might, then, also underlay Russian absolutism. Even in peacetime, at least two-thirds of state revenue went to the army and navy. Peter forced nobles to send their sons to new military and engineering schools by decreeing they could not marry unless they did so. In order to pay for his army, the tsar tripled state revenues, imposing a direct tax on each male serf, or "soul." Landlords became responsible for the collection of these new taxes. He established state monopolies on the production and sale of salt, oil, tobacco, rhubarb, and even dice, used for gambling, awarding the profitable right to collect these revenues to his favorite nobles, or to foreigners. Hoping to expand Russian industry and attract gold and silver payments from abroad, Peter oversaw the exploitation of mines and the establishment of a metal industry in the Ural Mountains. But even

absolute authority could not overcome the primitive transportation system, the lack of raw materials and capital, and the absence of a sizable
merchant class.

Western travel and Peter's observers in the absolutist courts of Europe
inspired the reorganization of the civil administration. While remaining an
autocrat, Peter was nonetheless the first tsar to distinguish between his
person as ruler and the state itself. Indeed, he made officials take two
oaths, one to him and one to the state whose power he enhanced.

Peter divided his domains into fifty administrative districts, appointing a
governor for each. He created a Senate, an administrative body charged
with ruling in his absence during wartime and with overseeing state administration in time of peace. He experimented with councils whose members could—if they dared—give him advice. The tsar also put towns under
the direct control of provincial governors, although they retained a measure of self-government. Peter created a cadre of nobles to fill positions in
the bureaucracy. The Table of Ranks (1722) required all male nobles to
enter state service, serving in the army, navy, or bureaucracy, and allowed
commoners who rose through the bureaucracy or military to assume noble
titles. Thus, the nobility became an instrument of the state, instead of, as
in the case of other European absolute states, a social institution that
could impede the ruler's will. Peter also placed the Orthodox Church fully
under state control by first not naming a new patriarch (the head of the
Russian Orthodox Church) upon the death of the incumbent in 1700 and
later simply abolishing the patriarchate.

The tsar's turn toward the West angered the old noble families of
Moscow, traditional Orthodox Church leaders, and Old Believers alike.
Peter executed some nobles who refused his order to provide service to the
state. Old Believers considered the reforms sacrilegious and contrary to
the historical development of Russia. Many churchmen resented that
Peter had subordinated the church to his state. Peter overcame four uprisings and several conspiracies directed against him. When his son announced that he would, on becoming tsar, end the Western reforms and
restore old Russian customs, Peter ordered him tortured to death for opposing his will.

Peter the Great expanded Russian territory (see Map 7.3). He did so, for
the most part, by pushing back the neighbors who had blocked Muscovy's
expansion: Sweden, Poland, and the Ottoman Turks. He added territory
beyond the Ural Mountains along the Caspian Sea, at the expense of the
Turks. Like his successors, Peter dreamed of conquering the Turkish capital of Constantinople, which would give him control over its straits, the
crucial passage between Europe and Asia leading to the Black Sea. A Russian army invaded Moldavia. Peter's new fleet sailed down the Don River,
conquering the Turkish port of Azov on the Sea of Azov, which gives access
to the Black Sea. He later surrendered Azov to the Turks, however, after
his army was subsequently surrounded by a large Turkish force.

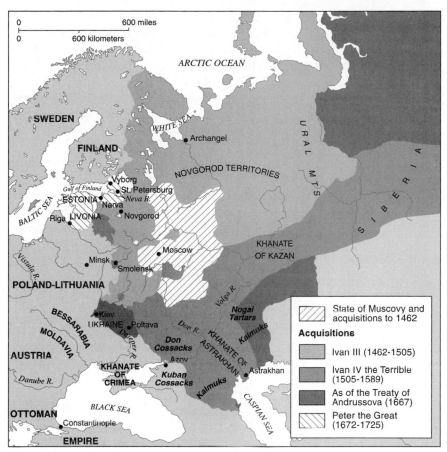

MAP 7.3 THE EXPANSION OF RUSSIA The state of Muscovy was expanded through the acquisitions of Ivan III, Ivan IV (the Terrible), and Peter the Great.

Russia's role in European affairs, however, remained minimal, despite its participation, with Habsburg Austria, Poland, and Venice, in the long series of wars against the Turks in the last decades of the seventeenth century. Russia joined Denmark and Saxony in attacking Sweden in the Great Northern War (1700–1721). The Russian ambassador in Vienna reported that once the news of Peter's victory arrived, "people begin to fear the tsar as formerly they feared Sweden." Peter's goal was to win a "window on the Baltic Sea" at Sweden's expense. The Swedes did turn back the assault of a much larger Russian army at Narva (1700) in Estonia. But after Charles XII passed up the opportunity to pursue the Russian army in order to invade Poland and Saxony, the Russian army conquered the mouth of the Neva River in 1703.

There Peter ordered the construction of a new capital city, where he forced nobles and wealthy merchants to build elegant townhouses. St. Petersburg offered a striking contrast to the chaos of tangled streets and shabby wooden buildings of Moscow, then by far the largest city in Russia. Built on coastal marsh lands, St. Petersburg, from its fortifications to its broad boulevards, reflected architectural ideas borrowed from the West, particularly Amsterdam. State offices, including army and military headquarters, occupied the centrally located islands. Symmetrical facades rose along the Neva's south bank, near the shipyards, admiralty, and fortresses. Geometrically arranged boulevards, squares, and gardens completed the tsar's capital.

Russia supplanted Sweden as the Baltic region's dominant power. In 1709 at the Battle of Poltava, Peter's army first turned back an invading Swedish army in Ukraine, and five years later Russian troops raided Sweden for the first time. After losing its German and Polish territories, Sweden then entered its period of constitutional struggles, marked by attempts by the nobility to reassert economic and social prerogatives lost to the monarchy and allowing Russia to solidify its expansion. The Treaty of Nystadt (1721), after which Peter proclaimed Russia an empire, confirmed Russian primacy in the Baltic region. This settlement added Estonia and Livonia (the southeastern part of modern Finland) to Peter's empire, bringing Russia ever closer into European affairs.

By the time of Peter's death in 1725, Russia's expanse had increased sixfold since the time of Ivan the Terrible. The Russian Empire, thirty times bigger than France, had joined the European state system by virtue of its expanded territorial interests. The accession of Catherine the Great (1729–1796) in 1762 ended a long succession crisis, palace plots, and assassinations. The empress oversaw the next stage of Russian expansion, incorporating Ukraine into the empire.

THE BALANCE OF POWER

During the century beginning about 1650, the concept of a balance of power between states gradually took hold in many of the courts of Europe. Like the evolving European state system itself, the emergence of the concept arose in part out of the decline of religious antagonisms as a dominant cause of warfare. The quest of absolute rulers to add to their dynastic territories and the growing global commercial rivalry between the Great Powers increasingly shaped European warfare.

As a diplomatic concept dating from the time of the Renaissance city-states of fifteenth-century Italy, the balance of power held that Great Powers should be in equilibrium, and that one power should not be allowed to become too powerful. The decline of one power could threaten the balance of power if, as a result, another power considerably enhanced its

Diego de Velázquez's *The Maids of Honor.*

El Greco's *The Burial of the Count Orgaz,* 1586.

Antonio Carnicero's *The Ascension of One of the Montgolfiere Brothers, 1792.*

Abraham van Beyeren's *Still Life with Grapes and Fruit*.

Jan Vermeer's *The Painter and His Model as Klio*, 1660.

Rembrandt's, *The Night Watch*, 1662.

Elizabeth I.

Hyacinthe Rigaud's *Louis XIV*, 1701.

Peter Paul Rubens' *The Disembarkment of Marie de Medici at Marseille*, 1622–1625.

François Boucher's *Madame de Pompadour.*

William Hogarth's *The Marriage Contract*, which pokes fun at the signing of a marriage contract by a wealthy merchant, who is marrying his daughter to the son of a nobleman.

Jean Antoine Watteau's *The Sign of Gersaint*.

strength. Now the main threat to peace ceased to be religious "heresy" but rather French expansionism.

The Origins of International Law

Horrified by the Thirty Years' War, two Northern Europeans systematically analyzed questions of international relations, drawing on the recent history of Europe. They helped lay the foundations for the evolution of modern diplomacy. In 1625, the Dutch jurist Hugo Grotius (1583–1645) sought to establish the foundations of international law by arguing that laws to which nations were subject followed from nature and not from God. Samuel von Pufendorf (1632–1694), a German Protestant who tutored the family of a Swedish diplomat in Copenhagen, found himself under arrest for eight months when he was caught up in the war between Sweden and Denmark. Pufendorf's *Of the Law of Nature and Nations* (1672) postulated legal principles for times of peace—which he argued should be the natural state—and for times of war. He claimed that only a defensive war was justified, pending international arbitration to resolve crises. The problem was, of course, that unless there existed some powerful, impartial body to adjudicate disputes between nations, each side in any conflict invariably claimed that its cause was just. But European power politics swept away such theoretical considerations.

Louis XIV's Dynastic Wars

The connection between absolutism and war, as well as the concept of the balance of power, was particularly clear in the dynastic wars of Louis XIV. Some of the wars of the early modern period were fought to prevent France from becoming dominant, as France's rivals formed alliances to preserve the balance of power. The rulers of Russia, Sweden, and Turkey, like France, were seeking to expand their territories. Habsburg Austria was struggling to retain its territories, but needed help against France, as well as against the Turks, from other powers.

Dynastic interests determined a state's choice of allies. Yet, strong states with large standing armies were quite likely to switch sides, in order to gain the most beneficial terms from new allies. For example, in order to expand its influence in Central Europe, France needed an alliance with either Austria or Prussia. But inevitably such a coalition pushed the other German power into opposition, forcing it to look for allies against France. Usually this partner was England (called Great Britain after 1707), France's rival in North America. Following the conclusion of hostilities that reworked borders, alliances frequently shifted, as rulers anticipated the next opportunity to expand their territories. Nowhere was this process clearer than in the case of Louis XIV's France.

Louis XIV was determined that territorial gain and prestige be the measure of his greatness (see Map 7.4). He sought to expand his kingdom's borders to what he considered to be France's "natural" frontiers, that is, the Pyrenees Mountains to the south and the Rhine River to the east. International conditions seemed conducive to the king's grandiose plans. England had been divided by civil war in the 1640s, and its restored monarch, Charles II, faced mounting political opposition at home. To the north, Sweden confronted a Danish threat to its control of the Baltic Sea. In Central Europe, the Austrian Habsburgs faced opposition from other German princes, as well as from the Turks.

MAP 7.4 EXTENSION OF FRANCE'S FRONTIERS UNDER LOUIS XIV   Louis XIV sought to expand his dynastic territories through wars fought between 1643 and 1715.

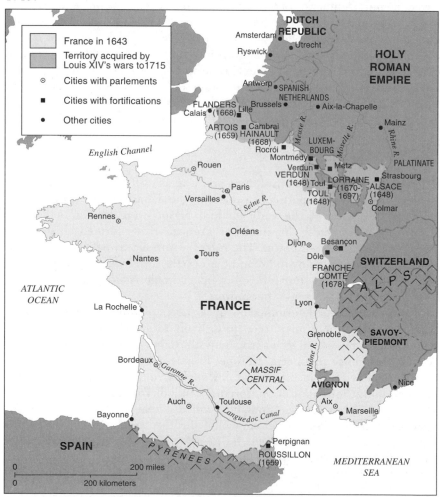

Louis XIV crossing the Rhine before invading the Dutch Republic in 1672.

Louis XIV's "grand strategy" was to contain the two Habsburg powers, Spain and Austria, by initiating a series of wars. Each conflict followed the king's violation of a previous agreement or formal treaty, and was accompanied by the claim that French aggression was "just." Each war was to pay for itself: French armies would force local populations to offer "contributions." The Treaty of the Pyrenees (1659), ending this round of hostilities with Spain, established the frontier between the two nations that exists today.

France again went to war against Spain in 1667. Louis wanted to annex Spain's French-speaking Franche-Comté to the east and the Spanish Netherlands (Belgium) to the north. When French armies invaded the Spanish Netherlands, England, fearful that Flanders and its Channel ports would fall to France, joined the Dutch Republic, Sweden, and Spain to turn back Louis XIV's armies. By the Treaty of Aix-la-Chapelle (Aachen) in 1668, France extended its frontier further north, annexing Lille and part of Flanders. Four years later, Louis XIV invaded the Dutch Republic after assuring English neutrality by making secret payments to King Charles II. The Dutch fended off the French by opening up the dikes to create a barrier of water. After several more years of indecisive fighting and negotiations, France absorbed Franche-Comté, but only tiny parcels of the Southern Netherlands. Still the king of France was not satisfied. He conquered Alsace and Lorraine beyond his eastern frontier by claiming each in turn and then launching an invasion. He annexed Strasbourg and occupied Luxembourg. Despite the opposition of a wary alliance of Habsburg Austria, Spain, Sweden, and Saxony, he ordered the invasion of the Palatinate, intending to secure the Rhine. This initiated the War of the League of Augsburg (1688–1697). England and the Dutch Republic (an alliance in itself solidified by the fact that William III of Orange now was king of

England) and a number of other German states also joined the alliance against France.

After hesitating in the face of massive opposition, in 1692 Louis made a foolish attempt to invade England. Dutch and English ships drove the French fleet onto rocks off the coast of Normandy; the two sea powers then enforced an economic blockade of France. Louis XIV retaliated by turning French privateers loose on his enemies' ships. French defeats as well as rising opposition in the Dutch Republic and England to the cost of the war forced both sides to negotiate. The Treaty of Ryswick of 1697 confirmed French gains in Alsace, but also made clear that the other European powers would ally again if necessary to keep France from further territorial acquisitions in the Southern Netherlands and the German states.

The question of the succession to the throne of Spain soon presented Louis XIV with the greatest temptation of all. Like a compulsive eater confronted by a table of delicious food, it was more than he could resist. The Habsburg King Charles II of Spain had no direct heir. Louis opposed the candidacy of the Habsburg Archduke Charles of Austria (son of Holy Roman Emperor Leopold I), hoping to end the virtual encirclement of France by Habsburg powers. Then Louis XIV, whose wife was the daughter of the late Philip IV of Spain, put forth his own claim to the throne.

When Charles II died in 1700, he left a will expressing his desire that his diminished empire remain intact, and that Louis XIV's grandson, Philip of Anjou, succeed him, but that Philip renounce all claim to the throne of France. However, on ascending the Spanish throne, the Bourbon Philip V (ruled 1700–1746) made clear that he favored the interests of his imposing grandfather. The Austrian Habsburg ruler Leopold I refused to accept Charles II's will as valid and attacked the Italian territories of the Spanish Habsburgs.

Louis XIV refused to rule Philip out of the line of succession to the French throne, so that if Philip's elder brother, the duc de Bourgogne, died without male issue, Philip would then inherit the throne of France and the kingdoms would be joined. The matter became pressing in 1712, after smallpox struck the French royal family, leaving only Bourgogne's youngest son as heir to the French throne. If the future Louis XV had died then, Philip would have become heir to both kingdoms.

The French king's aggressive action drew Great Britain into the wars of the continent. The Dutch Republic again had reason to fear French occupation of the Spanish Netherlands. If the French opened up the Scheldt River to trade, Antwerp would reemerge as a commercial rival to Amsterdam. This vital link to the English Channel had been closed since the Dutch formally received independence from Spain in 1648, thus preventing ships from reaching Antwerp. The Grand Alliance against France also included Austria, Prussia, and Portugal. The War of the Spanish Succession reflected the fact that European wars were gradually taking on a global dimension (see Chapter 6), as the powers fought for markets as well as prestige. As in the War of the League of Augsburg, British and French forces also battled in North America.

France fought with Bavaria and Spain as allies. The English commander, the duke of Marlborough (1650–1722), raised an army of English, Dutch, and mercenary troops. In 1704, at Blenheim in southern Germany, the allied armies, aided by the Habsburg troops of Prince Eugene of Savoy (1663–1736), crushed a combined French and Bavarian force. Louis XIV's armies retreated behind the Rhine. Winning victories in the Spanish Netherlands in 1708 and 1709, the allied armies also drove the French from the Spanish Netherlands and from the Italian peninsula. The English fleet captured Gibraltar (1704), which guards the entrance to the Mediterranean Sea. During the terrible winter of 1709–1710, France suffered military defeat and famine. The great kingdom of Louis XIV seemed on the verge of collapse.

But the French and Spanish armies revived their fortunes. Dynastic changes, too, helped Louis XIV's cause. In 1711, Archduke Charles of Austria became Holy Roman Emperor Charles VI (ruled 1711–1740). Should France and Philip V of Spain be defeated, the British and Dutch now confronted the possibility that Charles might one day become king of Spain, reviving the dynastic union that had made the Habsburgs Europe's strongest power during the first half of the seventeenth century. It was now in the interests of Great Britain and the Dutch Republic to bring the war to an honorable conclusion. Louis XIV, weakened by age and illness and suffering the financial burdens of the war, agreed to negotiate.

Under the 1713 Treaty of Utrecht (confirmed by that of Rastatt in 1714, when Emperor Charles VI accepted peace), Habsburg Austria received the Southern Netherlands as security against future French ambitions and annexed Lombardy and Naples, replacing Spain as the paramount power on the Italian peninsula (see Map 7.5). Philip V was recognized as king of Spain, but renounced all claims to the throne of France. The decline of Spain, which had now lost all of its European possessions beyond the Pyrenees, continued unabated. In North America, France ceded Newfoundland, Nova Scotia, and Hudson Bay to Great Britain.

Louis XIV had reigned so long that on his death in 1715 the throne passed to his great-grandson, young Louis XV, with affairs of state in the hands of a regent. Philip V kept the throne of Spain, but the futures of the monarchies of Spain and France would be separate. Louis XIV was defeated by more than powerful alliances mounted against him. Britain had proved better able to sustain long wars; its more developed commerce and manufactures provided greater tax revenues. The non-absolutist British state collected taxes more efficiently than the absolute monarchy of France, which turned much of the collection process over to tax farmers who kept part of the take. Britain's interests remained overseas, dominated

MAP 7.5 EUROPE IN 1721   Territorial realignments in Europe after the Treaty of Utrecht (1713), the Treaty of Rastatt (1714), and the Treaty of Nystadt (1721).

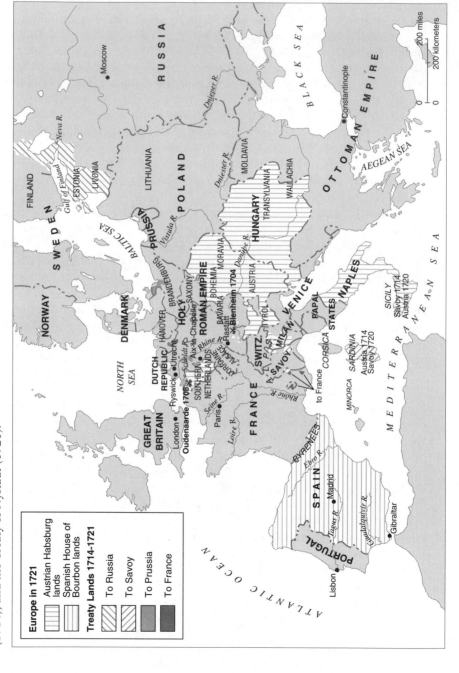

by lucrative commercial concerns, protected by the Royal Navy. France's foreign policy led to more costly wars on the continent.

France had been the preeminent power in Europe at the time of the accession of Louis XIV; this was no longer true at his death. The king's reputation had fallen victim to age and untempered ambition. Perhaps a lingering sense of failure explains why Louis XIV tried to burn his memoirs shortly before his death, although they were rescued from the fire by one of his officials. As he lay dying, Louis confessed with uncharacteristic insight that perhaps he had "loved glory too much."

THE MODERN STATE

As they established absolute rule, the sovereigns of continental Europe constructed the modern state. While extending authority over their subjects and expanding their dynastic territories, they developed state bureaucracies and established large standing armies. They broke noble resistance to absolute rule, confirming their privileges in exchange for loyalty to the throne. This relationship between rulers and nobles thus remained essential to the functioning of most European states in the eighteenth century.

Following a period of relative stability and even moderate economic expansion, the structure of Western European society then began to change as the European economy entered a remarkable period of dynamic growth, particularly during the second half of the eighteenth century. This was the case above all in Britain, where the expansion of capital-intensive agriculture techniques, population growth, and a boom in manufacturing combined to begin the Industrial Revolution. The changing structure of society, in turn, would affect the developing state by encouraging demands for political reform. Beginning in the 1760s and 1770s, the monopoly on political power by oligarchies and absolute rule itself came under challenge. Old scientific assumptions had already been shaken and then fallen as scientists expanded their knowledge of the universe. The scientific methodology, discoveries, and culture of the Scientific Revolution helped create modern science.

PART THREE

NEW CULTURAL AND POLITICAL HORIZONS

During the late seventeenth century and the eighteenth century, Europe entered a period of remarkable intellectual and political ferment. Rejecting the weight of tradition, men and women of science developed the scientific method, a means of understanding based on systematic observation of natural phenomena and experimentation regarding their causes and effects. Their successors, the philosophes, the thinkers and writers of the Enlightenment, believed their role was to bring light and progress to the world through the application of reason to their reflections on the nature of mankind. Influenced by growing religious skepticism and drawing on expanded literacy, the philosophes espoused views of nature, mankind, society, government, and the intrinsic value of freedom that challenged some of the fundamental tenets most Europeans shared.

During this exciting period, Europe also entered a remarkable period of economic and social change. Increased agricultural productivity supported a larger population which, in turn, expanded demand for food and permitted the development of large-scale manufacturing in and around northern English towns.

Changes also came in the realm of political life. The public political sphere was transformed by newly created "public opinion" through the emergence of newspapers and societies, which facilitated political interest and discussion. Reform-minded people in increasing numbers denounced unwarranted privilege and "despotism" and celebrated the British model of constitutional monarchy and the successful rising of the American colonists against British rule. In a time of economic and social change, new cultural and political innovations began to transform Europe.

CHAPTER 8

THE NEW PHILOSOPHY OF SCIENCE

In 1633, ecclesiastical authorities summoned Galileo (1564–1642), born Galileo Galilei, to Rome to face the Inquisition. The stakes were high. In the first year of the new century, the Italian Giordano Bruno (1548–1600), a Dominican friar accused of heresy who loudly proclaimed the virtues of scientific investigation, had been burned along with his books in Rome.

Many Church fathers were now eager to put Galileo on trial. Jesuits vehemently objected to his work on physics, for Galileo espoused an atomistic theory of matter that seemed to challenge the Catholic Church's view that during Communion bread and wine become the body and blood of Christ. The papacy's political situation forced the Church's hand. Protestant armies had recaptured some of the lands in which the Catholic Reformation had appeared victorious. The papacy, its influence weakened by the Protestant Reformation and eclipsed by powerful dynastic rulers, could ill afford another defeat.

Urban VIII, who before his elevation to the pontificate had been Galileo's friend, accused the astronomer only of supporting the views of Copernicus, not of heresy. This would save Galileo from death but might also put the pope in a bad light for having protected the scientist. Although Galileo chose not to die for his principles and agreed to renounce these "errors" as heresies, in 1633 he was still sentenced to a lifetime of house arrest. When guards returned him to his house, however, he cast a glance to the heavens and proclaimed of the earth, "See, it's still moving!"

The origins of modern science date to the seventeenth century, a period so marked by innovative thinking that it has been called the "century of genius." In several different corners of Europe, a few people struggled to understand the workings of the cosmos in a new way. Their own observations of the skies, including those of Galileo, seemed to contradict explanations of the universe that had originated with Aristotle in the fourth

Testeleu's tapestry of the establishment of the French Royal Academy of Science, 1666, and the Foundation of the Observatory, 1667.

century, B.C., and, having acquired the authority of the Church, had been passed down for centuries. Rejecting the weight of tradition, these thinkers developed the scientific method, a means of understanding based on systematic observation of natural phenomena and experimentation regarding their causes and effects. But what we now know as the "Scientific Revolution" owed its impact less to new technology and inventions than to new ways of thinking about the universe.

CHANGING VIEWS OF THE UNIVERSE

The thought of the Greek philosopher Aristotle (384–322 B.C.) dominated European science until the sixteenth century. Trying to understand the universe seemed closely linked to explaining motion. Both problems lay at the heart of the Scientific Revolution. Copernicus, a sixteenth-century Polish astronomer, observed the heavens and concluded that ancient and medieval science could not explain what he saw with his own eyes. His successors, above all Galileo later in the century, made systematic mathematical calculations to explain celestial motion. In doing so, they created scientific methodology, which would also be applied to reach an understanding of the workings of the human body.

Ancient and Medieval Science

Aristotle believed that God placed the earth at or near the center of the universe. He envisioned a hierarchical order of the cosmos comprised of a series of spheres that became progressively purer. Aristotle also believed that terrestrial bodies naturally moved toward the earth, the center of the universe, unless they were propelled in another direction. In this view, impetus imparted motion through contact with an object; when the contact ceased, the object simply stopped moving or fell back to earth. The natural tendency of all matter, then, was toward rest, regarded as a nobler state than motion. Because all motion had to be explained, a "mover" therefore had to be found for every motion.

In the second century, the Greek astronomer Clausius Ptolemy (*c.* 85–165 A.D.) published a massive work that became known as *Almagest* (from the Arabic for "greatest"), which summarized the conclusions of Greek astronomers and presented his own theories and observations. He described instruments such as the quadrant, invented by the Arabs, with which he tried to measure the orbits (which he held to be spherical) of the sun, moon, and planets in the sky. Ptolemy accepted Aristotle's contentions, asserting that the earth was encased by a series of clear spheres—about eighty—revolving around it. The most distant sphere contained the furthest stars, which he believed were fixed points of light. Within those spheres, the moon was closest to the earth; next came the planets Mars, Venus, Jupiter, and Saturn. With minor variations, medieval thinkers still held Ptolemy's views.

Within the context of Christian theology, people of learning in the Middle Ages believed that scientific inquiry should serve theological ends by studying nature and explaining the mysterious ways of God. Church savants never raised the possibility that mankind could, with understanding, alter or even master nature.

Aristotle's belief that the heavens and earth displayed two different kinds of motion—one toward the center of the earth, which seemed the natural state, but also an unnatural violent motion away from it—nicely fit the medieval Church's view that the universe consisted of good and evil. The earth, standing at the center, was heavy, corrupted not only by its weight but by original sin and earthly misdeeds. Angels therefore were placed far off in a weightless existence in Heaven. The goal of human beings was to achieve the lightness of Heaven, God's domain, on the exterior edge of the universe.

The beliefs of the late medieval poet Dante (1265–1321) reflected the prevailing influence of Aristotle's physics and Ptolemy's astronomy. Dante held that the universe comprised ten spheres surrounding the spherical, motionless earth. In his *Inferno*, Dante and the Roman poet Virgil travel to the core of the earth, then climb out to the other side, the Southern Hemisphere, where they find Purgatory. Hell lay at the earth's center, with Heaven the tenth, most distant sphere. Dante and his contemporaries believed that the earth consisted of four elements: earth, water, air, and fire, the first two of which had a natural tendency to fall toward the center of the stationary earth.

Medieval European scholars seemed little interested in astronomy. Yet, to be sure, some medieval thinkers took significant steps toward modern science by embracing the study of natural phenomena and revering the scholar who studied such problems. Medieval scientists made lasting contributions in such fields as optics—inventing eyeglasses—and biology. They classified objects for study and espoused experimentation based on scientific procedures and the use of mathematics to verify theories. But even the contributions of the most brilliant medieval thinkers remained only in the realm of theory.

As the Renaissance drew on the discovery of classical prose and poetry, Italian scholars of the period also turned to classical Greek scientific texts that had been recovered, edited, and printed. The conquest of Greece during the fourteenth century had brought the Arabs into contact with classical learning. Arab scholars, who also made significant original contributions in astronomy, mathematics, and medicine, preserved many ancient Greek and Roman texts, translating them into Arabic. Some of the manuscripts brought by Greek scholars to the West from Constantinople after its conquest by the Turks in 1453 suggested that mathematics could be applied in the quest for knowledge about the universe. Arab scholars had raised troubling questions challenging age-old views of the earth as they observed and even began to measure the heavenly phenomena they beheld. In this way, the texts of Ptolemy became subjects of renewed interest and study.

Ptolemy's view of the cosmos itself reflected the domination of Aristotle's theory of motion. Yet, there had earlier been at least one dissenting voice. Archimedes of Syracuse (c. 287–212 B.C.) had challenged Aristotle's contention that rest was a natural state for all objects and that only the presence of an "active mover" could generate motion. But Ptolemy's view of the cosmos was challenged in the fourteenth century by thinkers at the University of Paris and Oxford University. They observed that falling bodies move at an accelerating speed and that the accompanying presence of a "mover" simply could not be observed. A few scholars also rejected Aristotle's explanation that air itself served as a natural propellant. They observed that an arrow shot from a bow clearly was not continually propelled by air or anything else, but sooner or later simply fell to earth. The gradual development of a theory of motion, based on an understanding of the role of the mass of the moving object, along with the development of mathematics itself, provided the basis for new discoveries in the fields of astronomy and mechanics.

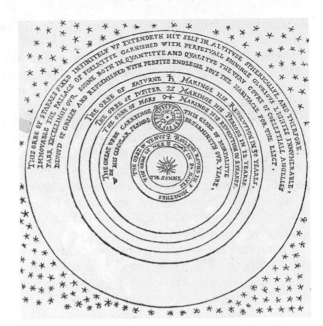

Copernicus's helio-
centric world system.

Copernicus Challenges the Aristotelian View of the Universe

The revolution in scientific thinking moved forward because of a cleric who kept his eyes toward the heavens, but not necessarily in pious contemplation. Nicholas Copernicus (1473–1543) launched the strongest attack yet on the Aristotelian view of the universe. He was born near the Baltic coast in Poland. After the death of his father, Copernicus' uncle (a wealthy bishop) assumed responsibility for his education. From the University of Cracow, Copernicus went to Italy to study medicine and law. After learning Greek, he read medieval scientific and humanist texts. Also trained as a doctor and portrait painter, he devoted his life to observation and discovery.

Copernicus' *Concerning the Revolutions of the Celestial Spheres* was not published until he lay dying in 1543, the same year the work of Archimedes was first translated into Latin. Paradoxically, in view of the intense theological debate it would generate, Copernicus dedicated his study to the pope. Copernicus was troubled by the inability of the Ptolemaic system (itself a refraction of the Aristotelian view of the universe) to account for what his own observations, made with the naked eye, told him: that the planets, the moon, and the stars obviously did not move around the earth at the same speed. Nor did they seem to be in the spherical orbits Ptolemy had assigned them. That Mars seemed to vary in brightness particularly perplexed him. What Copernicus observed, in short, contradicted the fundamental assumptions of the Aristotelian and Ptolemaic universe.

Ptolemy had rejected the idea that the earth might be moving because such a view could not be reconciled with Aristotelian physics. A late medieval thinker, Nicholas of Cusa (1401–1464), a German bishop and theologian who wrote on astronomy, believed the earth might be in motion, but neither he nor anyone else in the period tried to make mathematical calculations that might prove or reject this bold theory. More than this, he had suggested the possibility that the sun stands at the center of the universe and, by implication, that the universe is infinite, and nonhierarchical in nature, unlimited by Aristotelian layers of spheres. The extraordinary Renaissance artist and humanist Leonardo da Vinci, who called wisdom "the daughter of experiment," had also suggested that the earth might move around the sun.

Copernicus concluded that the sun, not the earth, lies at the center of the universe, and that the earth turns on its axis once a day and rotates around the sun once every 365 days. "In the middle of all sits the Sun enthroned," he wrote. "How could we place this luminary in any better position in this most beautiful temple from which to illuminate the whole at once?" Copernicus' postulation was, like his critique of some of Ptolemy's conclusions, not totally original. But his assertions were bold, explicit and, for many, convincing. Furthermore, they suggested that mathematics could verify astronomic theories.

The notion that the earth was but one planet rotating in circular orbit around the sun raised shocking questions about the earth's status. This perplexed and angered Catholic, Protestant, and Jewish theologians by seeming to reduce the standing of mankind. It seemed unbelievable that mere mortals peering into the heavens were themselves moving rapidly through the universe. Martin Luther, himself not given to accepting inherited wisdom without skepticism, said of Copernicus, "This fool wants to turn the whole of astronomy upside down!"

That Copernicus did. Yet, he seemed uninterested in carrying out his own systematic observations and made serious errors in calculations when he did so. He also could not explain why there was no constant wind from the east, which might be expected based on the assumption that the earth moved in that direction around the sun. Copernicus sometimes sought to answer his own doubts by turning to the teachings of the ancients and did not completely abandon the system of celestial spheres postulated by Ptolemy, whom he continued to revere. Copernicus also continued to accept the notion that the spherical universe was finite, and that it perhaps was limited by the stars fixed in the heavens.

The Universal Laws of the Human Body

As scientists began to chart movements in the heavens, some scholars now began to question old assumptions about the human body. They contended that it is subject to the same universal laws that govern celestial and terrestrial motion. The Renaissance had generated interest in human anatomy. Most assumptions about how the body works had been passed down for centuries from the ancient world. Galen (129–c. 210), a Greek contemporary of Ptolemy, was the first person to develop theories about medicine based on scientific experiments. He carried out a number of experiments on apes, assuming that animal and human bodies were essentially the same in the arrangement of bodily organs. Like Aristotle, Galen believed that disease followed from an imbalance in the four bodily humors—blood, phlegm, yellow bile, and black bile. He held that two kinds of blood initiated muscle movement and digestion, respectively: bright red blood, which flowed up and down through the arteries, and dark red blood, which could be found in the veins. Doubting Galen's view of anatomy, Andreas Vesalius (1514–1564) published *On the Fabric of the Human Body* (1543). Arguably the founder of modern biological science, Vesalius rejected old explanations for the circulation of blood and began to dissect and study cadavers—in the Middle Ages, the Church had considered this to be sinful—and was the first to assemble human skeletons.

The English scientist William Harvey (1578–1657) largely solved the riddle of how blood circulates. Like astronomers, he adopted a scientific methodology: "I profess," he wrote, "to learn and teach anatomy not from books but from dissections, not from the tenets of philosophers but from the fabric of nature." Harvey's accomplishment was in the realm of thought and owed virtually nothing to prior inventions. Indeed, he made

(*Left*) Vesalius dissecting a cadaver. (*Right*) A particularly pensive skeleton appears in Vesalius's *Epitome* (1543).

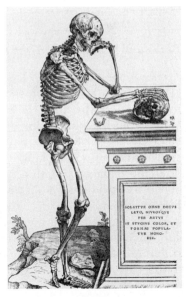

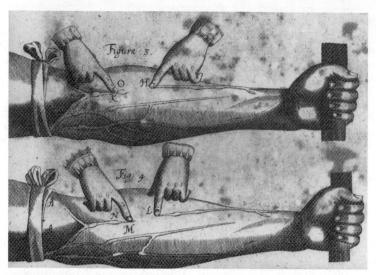

William Harvey demonstrating the circulation of blood.

his discoveries before the invention of the microscope, and he referred only twice in his experiments to a magnifying glass.

Harvey's theory of blood circulation pictured the heart and its valves functioning as a mechanical pump. Yet Harvey, like medieval thinkers, retained a belief that "vital spirits" were to be found in the blood. The long-run consequence of Harvey's work was, as in the case of Vesalius, to undermine further Aristotelian philosophy and medieval science and to help establish a basis for the development of modern biology and medicine in later centuries.

Brahe and Kepler Explore the Heavens

Tycho Brahe (1546–1601), a Danish astronomer, and Johannes Kepler (1571–1630), his German assistant, carried the search for an understanding of the way the universe works to a new stage of scientific knowledge. While studying philosophy at the University of Copenhagen, Brahe became fascinated with the heavens after observing a partial eclipse of the sun. Brahe, an odd-looking nobleman who had lost part of his nose in a duel and replaced it with a construction of silver and gold alloy perched above his handlebar moustache, built an astronomical observatory on a Danish island.

Brahe rejected Copernicus' contention that the earth rotated around the sun. He claimed that if this were true, a cannonball fired from west to east (the direction Copernicus thought the earth moved) would travel farther in that direction, and a weight dropped from a tall tower would strike earth to the west of the tower because of the earth's movement. Brahe came up with a cumbersome, compromise explanation that had the five known planets rotating around the sun, which in turn moved around the stationary earth.

In 1572, Brahe observed a bright exploding star that he called Nova. This and a comet sighted five years later irretrievably compromised the Aristotelian view of the universe as unchanging. Brahe compiled data based upon his own observations, systematically charting what he could see of the planetary orbits, and using mathematics to locate the position of the planets and stars. At the same time, his rejection of the Copernican view that the sun was the center of the universe and the fact that his calculations were often inaccurate remind us that the Scientific Revolution did not develop in a linear fashion. False turns and setbacks were part of the story.

Upon the death of the Danish king, his patron, Brahe had moved to Prague. There he set up an observatory and met Johannes Kepler, who became his assistant in 1600. Kepler was the son of a German mercenary soldier and an herb dealer with an interest in astrology (his mother would later be condemned to be burned at the stake for her dabblings in astrology; Kepler saved her life by undertaking a lengthy legal process). Kepler was a dazzling but strange combination of rigorous astronomer and math-

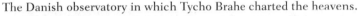

The Danish observatory in which Tycho Brahe charted the heavens.

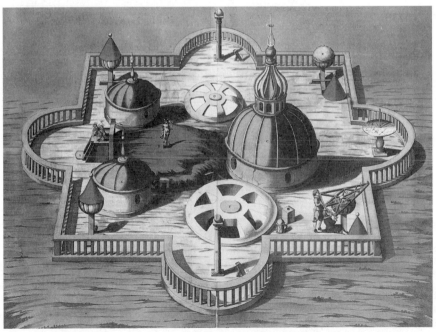

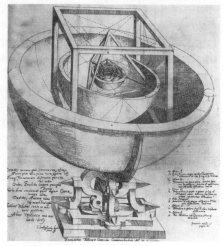

(*Left*) Johannes Kepler. (*Right*) Kepler's depiction of the orbits of the planets.

ematician, religious mystic and astrologer, who took credit for predicting not only a particularly harsh winter, but also peasant uprisings in Germany.

Facing persecution from Lutheran theologians in 1596 because of his Copernican beliefs, Kepler briefly found protection from the Jesuits. But four years later, he was forced to leave a teaching position in Austria because he refused to convert from Lutheranism to Catholicism. Kepler moved to Prague and began to work with Brahe. On his deathbed, Brahe implored Kepler to complete his observation tables by charting movements in the heavens. Holy Roman Emperor Rudolph II, whose interest in science outweighed any concern that Kepler was Protestant, appointed him to succeed Brahe as imperial mathematician.

Kepler shared Copernicus' belief that observers on earth were moving while the sun stood still. After carefully plotting the orbit of Mars, Kepler concluded that the orbits of the planets were "imperfect"—not circular, but rather elliptical. He also concluded that the planets were affected by some sort of force emanating from the sun. William Gilbert (1544–1603), an English scientist, had published a book on the magnet in 1600, the first study written by a university scholar and informed by laboratory experimentation. Gilbert's investigations of magnetic force provided a model for the development of a modern theory of gravitation. Kepler now decided that it was perhaps magnetic force that attracted the earth and sun to each other. He also determined that tides were the result of the magnetic attraction of the earth and the moon.

Based upon his mathematical calculations, Kepler postulated three laws of planetary motion, which he assumed were determined by the power, or specific magnetic attraction, of the sun. Kepler used observation and mathematical calculations to demonstrate that the planets were a separate grouping with different properties from those of the fixed stars, and that Aristotle's crystalline spheres simply did not exist.

Kepler's discoveries, blows to Aristotelian and medieval science, suggested that the hand of the prime mover—God—was not required to govern the movement of the planets. Even more than Copernicus' placing of the sun at the center of the universe, Kepler's conclusions challenged the theological assumptions of the Catholic Church. Kepler, who had been proscribed by his own church, learned in 1619 (three years after Copernicus' work was banned) that some of his writings had been placed on the list of books forbidden to Catholics. Nonetheless, the Scientific Revolution still occurred within the system of Christian belief. Kepler himself sought to glorify God by demonstrating the consistency, harmony, and order of divine creation as expressed in the working of the universe.

Francis Bacon and Scientific Method

From England Sir Francis Bacon (1561–1626), lawyer, statesman and philosopher, launched a frontal assault on ancient and medieval metaphysics and science. Calling himself "a bellringer who is first up to call others to church," Bacon helped detach science from philosophy. Medieval scholasticism had focused, he argued, on abstract problems that were without practical consequences, such as the question of how many angels could stand on the head of a pin. So, too, had Renaissance humanism. Bacon rejected outright all arguments based on the weight of traditional authority, calling for "a total reconstruction of sciences, arts and all human knowledge."

Bacon carried out few experiments and made no discoveries that could have been considered significant by his own standards (he died after catching a bad cold while carrying out an experiment of marginal value: stuffing snow into a dead chicken). But Bacon announced the dawn of a new era in which mankind would gradually begin to understand and then perhaps even overcome its physical environment. Through inductive reasoning, that is, proceeding from observation and experimentation to conclusions or generalizations, the truths of the universe would be revealed by discovery and scientific experiment, not by religion. Bacon's renown—he served for three years as King James I of England's Lord Chancellor (before being dismissed for accepting bribes)—helped create, for the first time, interest in science in England, albeit limited to a small number of people.

"Arts and sciences," Bacon wrote in 1620, "should be like mines, where the noise of new works and further advances is heard on every side." Scientists should divide up the toil by specializing and working in cooperation to "overcome the necessities and miseries of humanity."

(*Left*) Francis Bacon at work. (*Right*) The feisty Galileo at age sixty.

Galileo and Science on Trial

On the Italian peninsula, Galileo emerged as the most dominant figure of the early stage of the Scientific Revolution. The scion of a wealthy family, he studied medicine and mathematics. Like Copernicus, he taught at the University of Padua, the leading center of scientific learning in Europe, at a time when virtually every other university showed little interest in scientific observation. That Padua was under the protection of Venice, which was hostile to the pope, facilitated its university's precocious role in the development of scientific methodology. Scholars in Padua hotly debated Aristotelian explanations of motion, and particularly the question of the relationship between the natural sciences and metaphysics, or the nature of being. The latter debate was especially crucial, because on it hinged the question of whether scientific investigation could be independent of the Catholic Church, which considered revealed religion the only source of knowledge.

New ways of thinking about the heavens, systematic observation, and scientific measurement had played a more significant role in the early stages of the Scientific Revolution than did the development of new technology. The invention of the telescope, however, led to a further advance in the Scientific Revolution. Upon learning in 1609 that a man in Holland had invented a "spy glass," as the first telescope was called, that could magnify objects many times, Galileo constructed one of his own. This enabled him to study stars beyond the view of the naked eye, as well as Jupiter's moons, Saturn's spectacular rings, some of the innumerable stars of the Milky Way, and mountains on the moon. His observation of spots that seemed to move on the surface of the sun led Galileo to conclude that the sun, too, rotated. That sunspots seemed to change also challenged the traditional view of the static nature of the universe.

Galileo undermined Aristotelian notions of motion. He demonstrated that the earth was in perpetual rotation and that balls of varying weights will pick up speed at the same rate as they fall, that their speed is not determined by their mass. From such experiments, he developed a theory of inertia: a body moving at a constant speed in a straight line will continue to move until encountering another force. Galileo thus stood Aristotle on his head. Galileo believed that motion, not rest, was a natural state. He demonstrated that air and clouds move with the earth as it rotates around the sun, while appearing immobile to an observer also moving with the earth. The rooms in his house that he set aside for experimentation served as the first university laboratory.

Unlike other scholars, Galileo did not disdain seeking practical information from craftsmen and artisans. He consulted men who built cannons, and the soldiers who fired them, and people who made compasses, astrolabes, quadrants, and other scientific instruments for navigation. He began to investigate pumps and other means of regulating rivers, as well as planning the construction of stronger military fortresses. Nonetheless, he did not care whether or not his discoveries reached ordinary people. More than this, he claimed that "the mobility of the earth is a proposition far beyond the comprehension of the common people." And he believed that the "all-too-numerous vulgar" ought to be kept in darkness, lest they "become confused, obstinate, and contumacious."

At first, Galileo tried to reconcile his findings and those of Copernicus with early Church texts. But the feisty Galileo's insistence that the universe was mathematical in its very structure and subject to laws of mechanics that could be discovered left him open to attacks by ecclesiastical authorities. In 1610, he wrote Kepler, "here at Padua is the principal professor of theology, whom I have repeatedly and urgently requested to look at the moon and planets through my glass, which he obstinately refused to do. Why are you not here? What shouts of laughter we should have at this glorious folly!" In 1616, the pope condemned Galileo's proposition that the sun is the center of the universe and warned him not to teach it. Undaunted, Galileo published his *Dialogue Concerning Two World Systems—Ptolemaic and Copernican,* in which he taunted Aristotelians by presenting a lengthy dialogue between those espousing the respective systems of Ptolemy and Copernicus. A certain Simplicio took the side of Ptolemy in the dialogues; the character's very name outraged the Church by intimating that a farcical character symbolized the pope. This led to Galileo's condemnation by the Inquisition in 1633. But from house arrest in his villa in the hills above Florence, Galileo continued to observe, experiment, and write, publishing his texts in Holland. When he went blind in 1638, the pope refused to allow him to go into Florence to see a doctor. Despite his blindness, he continued his scientific investigations until his death four years later.

DESCARTES AND NEWTON: COMPETING THEORIES OF SCIENTIFIC KNOWLEDGE

Two brilliant thinkers, one French and the other English, both accepted Galileo's rejection of classical and medieval systems of knowledge. But they offered contrasting theories of scientific knowledge. René Descartes sought to discover the truth through deductive reasoning. Across the English Channel, Isaac Newton followed his countryman Bacon's insistence that the way to knowledge was through scientific experiment. One amazing discovery after another added to the foundations of "the new philosophy" of science. Science played a major part in the quest for demonstrable truth and authority during and following the period of intense social and political turmoil that lasted from the 1590s until the mid-seventeenth century.

Descartes and Deductive Reasoning

The reclusive French philosopher René Descartes (1596–1650) shared Bacon's and Galileo's critiques of ancient and medieval learning. But he offered a different methodology for understanding the universe, espousing deductive reasoning, that is, deducing a conclusion from a set of premises, not from scientific observation.

In 1637, Descartes published *Discourse on Method*. In this deeply personal account, he discussed his rejection of the scientific teaching he had encountered as a young man. Too much of what he had learned had been handed down from tradition without critical commentary. He defiantly "resolved no longer to seek any other science than the knowledge of myself, or of the great book of the world." Bacon had spoken of the necessity of "minds washed clean of opinions." Descartes had read Bacon. But instead of beginning with empirical facts in the quest for general principle, Descartes went much further by attempting to create an entire system of knowledge that began with general principles.

Any person, Descartes claimed, has to begin with a blank slate in order to understand the world through deductive reasoning. "I think, therefore I am" (*Cogito, ergo sum*) was his starting point, the postulation of a self-evident truth and the assertion that the ability to think is the basis of human existence. Then each problem has to be separated, he argued, into "as many parts as may be necessary for its adequate solution," moving from the simplest idea to the most difficult, in the same way as a mathematical proof is formulated. Cartesianism (the philosophy of Descartes and his followers) held that the world could be reduced to two substances: mind and matter, "thinking substance" and "extended substance," the latter defined as an infinite number of particles that fill all space, leaving neither void nor vacuum. Matter could be discovered and described mathematically, as could the laws of motion. Beginning with the certainty of his own existence, Descartes argued that the existence of the material universe and God could be deduced. "Begin with the smallest object, the easiest to understand," he insisted, "and gradually move to a knowledge of those that are the most complex."

This materialist approach to knowledge left little or no room for ancient or medieval learning. As a sign of this break, Descartes published his works in French, identifying Latin with ecclesiastical doctrine and scholasticism. Like Kepler, Descartes viewed God as a benevolent, infinitely powerful clockmaker, who created the universe according to rules that the human mind could discover with proper reasoning. God then stepped back, according to this view, forever absent from the actual workings of what He had created.

Mathematics, Descartes argued, demonstrates "the certainty and self-evidence of its reasonings." It therefore stood as the foundation of all science. Eventually a rule for every phenomenon could be discovered. Like the cosmos, the human body could be understood, its composition deduced.

Descartes thus subordinated experimentation to reason in the quest for truth. One of the stream of savants who went to meet Descartes recalled, "many of them would desire him to shew them his Instruments . . . he would drawe out a little Drawer under his Table, and shew them a paire of Compasses with one of the Legges broken; and then, for his Ruler, he used a sheet of paper folded double."

(*Left*) René Descartes. (*Right*) Sir Isaac Newton.

The Newtonian Synthesis

Sir Isaac Newton (1642–1727) built upon the thought of Kepler, Galileo, and Descartes to effect a bold synthesis of the Scientific Revolution, to which he added his own extraordinary discoveries. Newton's *Principia, The Mathematical Principles of Natural Philosophy* (1687) was the first synthesis of scientific principles. Newton synthesized the empiricism of Galileo and others with the theoretical rigor and logic of Descartes, thereby laying the foundations for modern science, which is based on both theory and experimentation.

Newton conducted some of his experiments while living on his prosperous family's farm. There, sitting under a tree ruminating about celestial motion, Newton observed a falling apple, which led him to recognize that the force that caused objects to fall to earth was related to planetary motion. Newton demonstrated that earthly and celestial motion are subject to laws that could be described by mathematical formulas, the science of mechanics. Going beyond Kepler's three laws of planetary motion, Newton postulated a theory of universal gravitation, the existence of forces of attraction and repulsion operating between objects. Newton concluded that Kepler's laws of planetary motion would be correct if the planets were being pulled toward the sun by a force whose strength was in inverse proportion to their distance from it. The moon, too, seemed to be drawn to the earth in the same way, while the pull that it exerted determined the ocean tides. Every particle of matter, Newton concluded, attracts every other particle with a force proportional to the product of the two masses, and inversely proportional to the square of the distance that separates them.

Newton's remarkable range of accomplishments—the fact that he continued to dabble in alchemy was not one of them—combined drawing on the thought of predecessors with his own brilliant insights and discoveries. He correctly calculated that the average density of the earth is about five and a half times that of water, suggested that electrical messages activate the nervous system, and anticipated some of the ideas that two centuries later would form the basis of thermodynamics and quantum theory. Newton was the first to understand that all colors are composed of a mixture of the primary colors of the spectrum. He explained the phenomenon of the rainbow, calculated sound waves, and invented calculus. In the late 1660s, he also constructed the first reflecting telescope. Newton's first paper on optics, published in 1671, proposed that light could be mathematically described and analyzed. Some scientists still consider it to mark the beginning of theoretical physics.

Unlike his predecessors in the development of science, Newton became wealthy and a hero in his own time. He was knighted by the king, and when he died he was given a state funeral and buried in London's Westminster Abbey. He was elected to Parliament in 1689 representing Cambridge University, where he was professor, and became warden of the

Royal Mint seven years later. However, Newton remained a remote, chaste, humorless figure who published his discoveries with reluctance and initially only when it seemed that rivals might first take the credit for a discovery. He brazenly accused those working on similar problems of copying him, and was ungenerous in acknowledging what he had learned from others. His fame marked the victory of the scientific method, however, over ancient and medieval thought. The eighteenth-century English poet Alexander Pope went so far as to compare Newton's accomplishments with those of God on the first day of creation. Pope penned an "Epitaph Intended for Sir Isaac Newton": "Nature and Nature's laws lay hid in night; God said, Let Newton be! and all was light!"

The Newtonian synthesis of scientific thinking and discovery spread rapidly from England to the continent. Newton's followers clashed with Cartesians, the followers of Descartes. Newton rejected Descartes' materialism, at least partially because it seemed to leave open the possibility that the world was made up totally of matter and that God did not exist, although the French philosopher never made such an assertion. For his part, Newton believed that God had to intervene from time to time to keep the great clock of creation running, lest it run down. That Newton continued to produce manuscripts on theological questions reflected his own belief that there seemed to be no necessary contradiction between science and religious faith.

Like Descartes, Newton insisted on the explanatory power of abstract reasoning. But despite his postulation of theories that could not be demonstrated by scientific method, such as his description of gravity as a force that operates between two objects in space, where possible Newton sought to confirm them experimentally. Until at least 1720, some tension remained between the English scientific groups (who insisted on the necessity of experimentation) and their French and German Cartesian counterparts. Yet, this was a creative tension, based on a common acceptance of the primacy of scientific inquiry.

The Cartesians found an ally in the Spanish-born Dutch philosopher and mathematician Baruch Spinoza (1632–1677), who also believed that thought and matter formed the two categories of reality. While making his living grinding lenses for glasses, he found both a philosopher's introspective isolation—arguing in a Cartesian manner that human understanding advances through inner reflection—and stimulation from the new physics. Expelled from the Jewish community of Amsterdam in 1656 for refusing to participate in religious ceremonies, Spinoza, a proponent of human liberation, called for toleration of all beliefs.

The northern German philosopher and mathematician Gottfried Leibniz (1646–1716) agreed with Descartes and rejected as demeaning to the Creator's divinity Newton's suggestion that God had to intervene from time to time in the operations of the universe. For Leibniz, the universe was, like God, infinite in space and time. The bodies of humans and animals ran like clocks, set in motion, like the universe itself, by God. Leibniz's popularity helped perpetuate the Cartesian challenge to Newton, notably in France. His deductive postulation of the infinite nature of the universe and his Cartesian insistence that God created the universe to run without further divine intervention according to the mathematical laws Newton had discovered became the hallmarks of the "new philosophy."

The Culture of Science

A "culture of science" developed in Western Europe and very gradually spread eastward. By the 1660s, letters, newsletters, and periodicals linked Europeans interested in science. Gradually a "republic of science" took shape, spawning meetings and lectures, visits by travelling scholars, correspondence and book purchases, personal libraries and public experiments. Above all, the formation of learned associations provided a focal point for the exchange of scientific information and vigorous debates over methodology and findings, expanding the ranks of people interested in science. Only several decades after Galileo's condemnation, Louis XIV of France and Charles II of England granted patronage to institutions founded to propagate scientific learning. Attracted by scientific discoveries, rulers realized that science could be put to use in the interest of their states.

The Diffusion of Scientific Method

Like medieval and Renaissance scholars, savants of science travelled widely seeking to exchange ideas and learn from each other, although most scientific exchange still occurred by correspondence. For example, the Czech scholar Comenius (Jan Komensky; 1592–1670), a member of the Protestant Unity of Czech Brethren, left his native Moravia in the wake of religious persecution during the Thirty Years' War. After more than a decade in Poland, he began to visit scholars in many countries. For seven years, he travelled in the German states, Holland, England, Sweden, and Hungary. Publishing hundreds of works, he proposed that one day scientific knowledge should be brought together in a collaborative form.

Learned associations and scientific societies had already begun to appear in a number of cities, including Rome and Paris in the 1620s. In London, a bequest made possible the establishment of Gresham College, which became a center for scientific discussion and research. In Paris, Martin Mersenne (1588–1637), a monk who had translated Galileo into French, stood at the center of a network of vigorous scientific exchange that cut across national boundaries of states. He organized informal gatherings, attended by, among others, Blaise Pascal (1623–1662), a gloomy young physicist and mathematician who originated the science of probability.

Blaise Pascal's calculating machine.

In England, above all, the culture of science became part of public life during the 1640–1660 period, with the vocabulary of science joining the discourse of the English upper classes. Newton's prestige further spurred interest in scientific method. In several London coffeehouses, Newtonians offered "a course of Philosophical Lectures on Mechanics, Hydrostatis, Pneumatics [and] Opticks." Exchanges, debates, and even acrimonious disputes reached an ever wider scholarly audience. An unprecedented number of pamphlets and books on scientific subjects was published in England.

The Royal Society of London for Improving Natural Knowledge was formed in 1662 under the patronage of Charles II. Its diverse membership, which included merchants, naval officers, and craftsmen, reflected the growing interest in science in England. Members included Edmund Halley (1656–1742), an astronomer who catalogued and discovered the actual movement of the stars as well as discovering the comet that bears his name; the philosopher John Locke (1632–1704), founder of British empiricism, who held that laws of society, like those of science, could be discovered; and Christopher Wren (1632–1723), a versatile architect who rebuilt some of London's churches (including St. Paul's Cathedral) in the wake of the fire of 1666, but who was also a mathematician and professor of astronomy.

The Royal Society, to which Newton dedicated *Principia* and of which he served as president, took its motto from one of the letters of the Roman writer Horace: "The words are the words of a master, but we are not forced to swear by them. Instead we are to be borne wherever experiment drives us." The Royal Society's hundred original members doubled in number by 1670, its weekly meetings attracting visiting scholars. One of the latter, who lived in Paris, reported with some astonishment that "no one is in a hurry to speak, nor tries to speak too long, or to tell all that he knows. [The members] never interrupt the speaker and dissension does not rise to the surface, nor even is a tone heard that could displease. One could not find any more civil, respectful or well-organized gathering than this."

The *Philosophical Transactions of the Royal Society* published some of the most important work of members and foreign correspondents, especially in the field of mathematics. A history of the Royal Society published in 1667 boasted that England had become "a Land of Experimental knowledge. And it is a good sign, that Nature will reveal more of its secrets to the English than to others; because it has already furnished them with a Genius so well proportion'd for the receiving, and retaining of its mysteries."

The natural philosopher Margaret Cavendish, the duchess of Newcastle (1623–1673), participated in debates about matter and motion, the vacuum, magnetism, and the components of color and fire. The author of books on natural philosophy, as well as a number of plays and poems, Cavendish also hosted the "Newcastle circle," an informal gathering of distinguished scientists that received Descartes. But she worked in isolation, which she attributed not only to the fact that she was shy, but to her sex. Despite the evidence of her own achievements, she accepted, at least in her early years, the contemporary assumptions that women had smaller and softer brains than men, and thus were somehow unfit for science and

The Newcastle circle hosted by the duke and duchess of Newcastle. Margaret Cavendish, the duchess, is seated on the far right crowned with laurels.

philosophy. Few men of science would have agreed with the assertion in 1673 by one of Descartes' disciples in France that "the mind has no sex." This bold statement reflected his mentor's belief that thought transcended gender differences—and therefore, having sense organs equal to men's, women should be recognized as their equals. But although she was permitted to attend one session, Cavendish and all other women were formally banned from the Royal Society—this would last until 1945—as they were excluded from the English universities.

In 1666, the French Royal Academy of Science held its first formal meeting in Paris. Like the English Royal Society, the French Academy enjoyed the patronage of the king, but its connection to the monarchy, which provided an astronomical observatory, was much closer. Jean-Baptiste Colbert, Louis XIV's minister of finance, sought to steer the Academy toward the study of what he considered useful subjects that might benefit French commerce and industry. Branches of the Academy began in several provincial cities. Unlike members of its English counterpart, adherents spent much time eating and drinking—one of them complained that too much time was wasted at the fancy dinners that preceded scholarly discussion.

With the gradual ebbing of Latin as the language of science, language barriers became a greater obstacle to the diffusion of ideas and research. (Indeed some writers deliberately had used Latin because they believed that knowledge ought to remain the preserve of the educated few.) Galileo had written in Italian to attract a wider audience among the elite, but also to remove science from Latin, the language of religious discourse. Newton wrote *Principia* in Latin, in part because only then could his work be read by most continental scholars. Newton's *Optics,* by contrast, appeared first in English, then in Latin and French translations. Gradually during the eighteenth century, each country's vernacular became the language of its scientists.

By the end of the seventeenth century, Descartes' ideas had overcome Calvinist opposition to find their way into Dutch university curricula. But the further east one went in Europe, the weaker was the impact of the Scientific Revolution. In part because of the success of the Catholic Reformation, which restricted the free flow of scholarly thought, scientific inquiry lagged in Poland, although several printing houses in Gdansk (Danzig) owned by Protestants began publishing scientific works in the second half of the century. Leibniz enjoyed popularity in the Habsburg domains, at least partially because he served several German rulers in a diplomatic capacity, and perhaps also because his contagious optimism and belief that God had preordained harmony found resonance in a kingdom of many peoples. Nonetheless, theological and devotional literature still dominated the shelves of university, monastic, and imperial libraries. The few publications on science remained strongly Aristotelian, and influenced by clerics.

Some savants in the East did become aware of the debates in the West on scientific method. Some Protestant thinkers in Hungary and Silesia, for example, were gradually exposed to the ideas of Bacon and Descartes by travelling scholars from Western Europe, and a few Hungarians and Silesians learned of the new ideas by visiting Dutch universities. Some Bohemian and Polish nobles began to include books on the new science in their private libraries, one of which eventually comprised over 300,000 volumes and 10,000 manuscripts. Theoretical and practical astronomical work spread in the Habsburg lands, carried on in some cases by Jesuits. Mathematics, optics, and problems of atmospheric pressure, too, were the focus of debate. Holy Roman Emperor Ferdinand III studied military geometry, constructing arithmetic toys for his children. But Copernicus and Kepler notwithstanding, early modern Central Europe would be far more remembered for its music than for its science.

Russia's distant isolation from Western culture—the Renaissance had absolutely no influence there—was compounded by the Orthodox Church's antipathy toward the West and hostility to learning outside Byzantine dogma, and therefore its opposition to scientific experimentation. There was, to be sure, acceptance of some practical knowledge from the West, for example relating to the military, mining, or metallurgy, which largely arrived with foreign merchants and adventurous craftsmen. But seventeenth-century Russia had no gifted scientists and no scientific societies. Foreign books began to appear at court only after about 1650. At that point, however, the Orthodox Church, having suffered a schism, launched another campaign against Western ideas, viewing secular knowledge as heresy, and science as the work of the Anti-Christ. But gradually some nobles began to be exposed to ideas from the natural sciences. These were the nobles who were dissatisfied with Church learning and eager to know more, for example, about the geography of their own expanding state. The literate classes in Russia would thereafter in many ways remain divided between those interested in ideas coming from the West and those who rejected them in the name of preserving what they considered Russia's uniqueness as the most dominant Slavic state.

The Uses of Science

The seventeenth-century Scientific Revolution was above all a revolution in thought. Technological inventions that would change the way people lived lay for the most part in the future. But during the second half of the seventeenth century, scientific experimentation led to the practical application of some discoveries. Thanks to Newton, longitude could now be easily established and ocean tides accurately charted. Voyages of discovery, commerce, and conquest to the Americas increased demand for new navigational instruments. Dutch scientists and craftsmen led the way in producing telescopes, microscopes, binoculars, and other scientific instruments.

But gradually, too, physicians, engineers, mariners, instrument makers, opticians, pharmacists and surveyors, many of them self-educated, began to apply the new discoveries to daily life. Robert Hooke (1635–1703), another member of the Royal Society, improved the barometer, which measures atmospheric pressure, and augmented the power of the microscope by adding multiple lenses. This allowed him to study the cellular structure of plants. Biologists began to collect, categorize, dissect, and describe fossils, birds, and exotic fish, adding to contemporary understanding of the richness and complexity of the world around them.

As Francis Bacon had predicted, governments began to tap science in the service of the state. Absolute monarchs on the continent sought out scientists to produce inventions that would give them commercial and military advantages over their rivals. In France, Colbert called on a Dutch scientist to explain his experiments on "the vacuum, force of [gun]powders, steam, wind, and collision." Colbert ordered the collection of statistics on state finance, commerce, and industry, and he commissioned people to make reliable maps of the provinces and colonies. English government officials also began to apply statistics to administrative and social problems.

Tsar Peter the Great (see Chapter 7) was convinced by his trip to the West that Russia would have to borrow from the West. He corresponded with Leibniz, who convinced him that empirical science, along with the creation of a system of education, would bring progress. The tsar wanted to refute the Western view that "we are barbarians who disregard science." Peter's campaign of westernization, which included opening his country to Western scientific ideas, made Russia a Great Power. The sciences that interested Peter were those that were useful in statemaking: mechanics, chemistry, and mathematics aided in building ships and improving artillery. Here, too, science merged with statemaking.

A seventeenth-century apothecary shop used new scientific discoveries.

Although chemistry was not a subject of university study, alchemists pursued knowledge of chemical reactions in their laboratories as depicted here.

Science and Religion

As scientific discoveries led more people to doubt religious authority that was based on faith alone, points of tension not surprisingly continued to emerge between science and religion. This was particularly the case with the Catholic and Orthodox Churches. That there seemed to be a much closer association between Protestant countries and advances in science—given the precocious role of England and, to a lesser extent, the Dutch Netherlands in the emergence of a culture of science—has contributed to the debate over whether Protestantism itself was more conducive to scientific inquiry.

Theological concerns still dominated at most universities, despite the role of the University of Padua, and of the University of Cambridge, where by the 1690s both Newton's theories and those of Descartes were taught. Universities contributed relatively little to the diffusion of the scientific method. During the century as a whole, their enrollments declined as the European population stagnated. In Catholic countries, canon law and in Protestant states civil law predominated in universities, which trained state and Church officials, respectively. The number of German universities more than doubled to about forty during the seventeenth century. The impetus for their creation came from Lutheranism and Calvinism, however, not from an interest in science.

Catholic universities continued to be the most traditional. Following Descartes' death in 1650, the University of Paris, which had about 30,000 students and was the largest university on the continent, forbade a funeral oration. Almost three decades later, the archbishop of Paris declared that "in physics it is forbidden to deviate from the principles of the physics of Aristotle . . . and to attach oneself to the new doctrines of Descartes." The University of Paris continued to exclude the new philosophy until the 1730s. Experimental physics as well as botany and chemistry were absent from university study throughout Europe.

The salient role of Protestants in the diffusion of scientific method reflected differences between the theological stance of the Catholic Church and the more liberal ethos of the Protestant Reformation. Catholic theologians held to dogmas of faith and obedience, leaving little room for innovation or experimentation. Protestant belief that the individual should seek truth and salvation in his or her own religious experience through a personal interpretation of the Bible encouraged skepticism about doctrinal theology. The emphasis on individual discovery seemed to lead naturally to empiricism. In Protestant countries, the Reformation had undermined the institutional monopoly on truth effectively maintained in Catholic countries. While Protestant theologians also could be rigid and unyielding, they had no equivalent to the papal Index of Forbidden Ideas or Books, or the mechanism of the Inquisition. Although the Massachusetts Bay Puritans may have forced religious attendance and sought to control what church members read, the English colonies in general accepted the principle of toleration.

Scientists in Catholic states, confronted by ecclesiastical denunciations or by reports of miracles that seemed to fly in the face of logic, found support in Protestant lands. The Protestant Dutch Republic, fighting a long civil war against Spanish rule, emerged as a center of toleration, where most books could be published. When Descartes learned of the condemnation of Galileo's work, he fled France for Holland, where he published *Discourse on Method.* Francis Bacon had been among the first to associate the Scientific Revolution with the Protestant Reformation. Indeed, many Protestants believed that scientific discovery would lead to a better world, and that the wonders of nature were there to be discovered and to give greater glory to God. Yet, Jesuits in Bohemia protected Kepler, who had faced persecution from Protestant theologians, provided he limited himself to speculation about astronomy and mathematics and avoided what they considered theological questions.

The development of a scientific view of the world in England may be better understood in the context of decades of social, intellectual, and political crisis during the mid-seventeenth century. The cause of Parliament and of Puritanism against Charles I's seeming moves toward absolutism

Astronomers using a telescope at the Royal Observatory of London.

and Catholicism attracted political and religious reformers. Many who considered the Catholic Church an obstacle to scientific inquiry opposed Charles I as they sought a climate of freedom. The reformers' triumph in the English Civil War may have emboldened Newton and other proponents of the new philosophy. Moderate Anglicans, like the Puritans before them, insisted that science could bring progress. They encouraged the creation of the Royal Observatory, founded by Charles II at Greenwich in 1675. Newton and other members of the Royal Society almost unanimously supported the exile of the Catholic King James II to France and the Glorious Revolution of 1688. Censorship was relatively rare in England, where political and ecclesiastical authority were not so centralized.

By way of contrast, state censorship, encouraged by the Catholic Church, had formally begun in France in 1623, five years after the sovereign law court of Toulouse had ordered a defrocked monk burned at the stake for denouncing belief in miracles after studying at the University of Padua. Thereafter, each new manuscript had to be submitted to a royal office for authorization to be published. Six years later, separate offices were established for literature, science, and politics, with ecclesiastics having veto power over books treating religious subjects.

Yet, to be sure, not all churchmen in France adamantly waged a war on science. Some French Jesuits became open-minded in pursuing scientific method. Jansenists, forming a dissident movement within the Church early in the eighteenth century, also favored scientific discovery, discussion, and debate, but faced papal and monarchical opposition (see Chapter 11).

CONSEQUENCES OF THE SCIENTIFIC REVOLUTION

The Scientific Revolution seemed to push theology into the background. The idea that mankind might one day master nature shocked many Church officials, although the earliest exponents of scientific method never doubted God's creation of the universe, but rather sought to understand the laws by which the universe operated. Nonetheless, Descartes' materialism seemed to suggest that mankind could live independently of God. His attempt to deduce the existence of God from the laws of motion brought ecclesiastical wrath. For faith in scientific method had distinct philosophical consequences: "If natural Philosophy, in all its parts, by pursuing this method, shall at length be perfected," Newton reasoned, "the bounds of moral philosophy will also be enlarged." The English poet John Donne had already come to the same conclusion in 1612. "The new philosophy," he wrote prophetically, "calls all in doubt."

The men and women of science espoused the application of scientific method to the study of nature and the universe. But it was a short step to subjecting society, government, and political thought to similar critical scrutiny. The English philosopher John Locke claimed that society was, as much as astronomy, a discipline subject to the rigors of scientific method. Moreover, the Scientific Revolution would ultimately help call absolutism into doubt by influencing the philosophes, the thinkers and writers of the eighteenth-century Enlightenment (see Chapter 10). The philosophes' belief in the intrinsic value of freedom and their assertion that people should be ruled by law, not rulers, would challenge the very foundations of absolutism.

CHAPTER 9

EIGHTEENTH-CENTURY ECONOMIC AND SOCIAL CHANGE

The great English landowners did as they pleased in the eighteenth century. More than one gentleman had an entire village demolished or flooded because it stood in the way of his landscaping plans. Another wrote, "It is a melancholy thing to stand alone in one's own country. I look around, not a single house to be seen but for my own. I am Giant, of Giant's Castle, and have ate up all my neighbors." Fences and servants kept venturesome interlopers far away. Some men of great means gambled fantastic sums on horse races. Sir Robert Walpole's estate guests drank up £1,500 of wine a year, the wages of more than a hundred laborers. English nobles seemed particularly vulnerable to overeating. A certain Parson Woodforde carefully entered in his diary the day of his death, "Very weak this morning, scarce able to put on my clothes and with great difficulty get downstairs with help. Dinner today, roast beef, etc."

At about the same time, a Swiss peasant named Jakob Gujer who was called Kleinjogg (Little Jake) by his friends inherited an indebted small farm and transformed it into something of a model enterprise, where he grew vegetables and new crops and raised cattle. It is said that when the Prince of Württemberg came to see the famous peasant, Kleinjogg told him how flattered he was that a prince should pay a visit to a humble peasant. The prince, teary eyed, replied, "I do not come down to you, I rise up to you, for you are better than I." To which Kleinjogg is alleged to have answered with tactful deference, "We are both good if each of us does what he should. You lords and princes must order us peasants what to do, for you have the time to decide what is best for the state, and it is for we peasants to obey you and work with diligence and loyalty." But there were few peasants with the means and initiative of Kleinjogg on the continent; in England, there were relatively few peasants left at all.

A nobleman and his wife, masters of all they see.

Although in some ways society remained the same as in earlier centuries, economic, social, and political change began to transform parts of Europe during the last half of the eighteenth century. To be sure, these transformations were uneven and regionally specific, above all affecting England and Northwestern Europe, while bypassing most of Central and Eastern Europe. In economically advanced regions, some of the traditional checks on population growth became less imposing. Increased agricultural productivity supported a larger population which, in turn, expanded demand for food. Large-scale manufacturing developed in and around northern English towns, leading to the beginnings of what we know as the "Industrial Revolution."

In a related change, distinctions within the highest social estates or orders were becoming less marked in Western Europe. Moreover, increased wealth generated some fluidity between social groups, contributing, in particular, to the dynamism that made Britain the most powerful state in the world. In France, too, wealth increasingly blurred lines of social class without, however, eliminating them entirely. Distinctions in title no longer necessarily corresponded to patterns of wealth distribution. By contrast, in Central and Eastern Europe social barriers remained much more rigidly defined.

The Social Order

In early modern Europe, social structure was marked by birth into particular estates, or orders, which conferred collective identities and privileges.

Each order was legally defined, with specific functions and rights conferred to it by virtue of being part of the order, not through individual rights. The nobility was a privileged order, with special rights accorded by law, such as exemption from taxation. Noble titles were hereditary, and stemmed in principle from birth (although in reality many families during the century were able to purchase titles). The clergy was also a privileged order, and, like the nobility, was generally exempt from taxation. The "third estate" in France was simply everyone who was neither noble nor a member of the clergy, and included both peasants and townsmen, all of whom were subject to taxation. Within and between these estates, or orders, some degree of social movement was possible, particularly in Western Europe. The extent of social mobility that existed within the "societies of orders" was debated by contemporaries, as it has been subsequently by historians.

Nobles

"In all states of Europe," a noble remarked in 1770 about his estate, "there are a sort of men who assume from their infancy a preeminence independent of their moral character." In most of the continental European states (with the exception of the Dutch Republic and Switzerland), nobles dominated political life during the eighteenth century, although in most of these states they numbered no more than 2 to 3 percent of the population. They accounted for a much larger percentage in Russia, Spain, Poland, and Hungary, which together may have accounted for almost two-thirds of the nobles in Europe. In Spain's northern provinces, more than 10 percent of the male population, and in Poland perhaps even 15 percent (about 1 million men) claimed noble titles. In Hungary, what may have been the first accurate census in European history in 1784 counted more than 400,000 people claiming to be nobles, about 5 percent of the population. In France, by contrast, there were only somewhere between 25,000 and 55,000 noble families, about 125,000 to 300,000 people claiming noble title. In Britain, there were only about 200 nobles, called peers, whose titles and lands were inherited by only their eldest sons and whose younger sons were thus no longer considered nobles.

The vast majority of nobles drew their wealth from land they owned but that other people worked ("I am idle, therefore I am," went a Hungarian saying about Magyar nobles that spoofed the words of the French philosopher Descartes). Social status came from ownership of land. Noble landlords owned between 15 and 40 percent of the land, depending on the country, and an even higher percentage of productive land. In Prussia, only nobles could own land that was exempt from taxes; in Poland, commoners could not own any land at all. In Russia, non-nobles had lost their right to own property to which serfs were legally bound. Austrian nobles held half of the arable land in the Habsburg domains, hiring agents to col-

(*Left*) Hungarian noblemen in the eighteenth century. (*Right*) A satirical French print calling the nobleman a spider and the peasant a fly. The nobleman built his wealth on his ownership of land and the obligations of money, labor, and kind owed to him by the peasant.

lect what peasants owed them. In the Italian states, the nobility's share of the wealth increased even more than that of the Catholic Church.

Many continental nobles retained specific rights, often called seigneurial rights, over the peasantry. Nobles drew income in rent (cash), kind (crops), and dues (often labor) owed them by virtue of their social status and ownership of land. Some dispensed justice in their own courts. Peasants were obligated to pay to have their grain ground in the lord's mill, to bake bread in his oven, and to squeeze grapes in his press. In the 1770s, enlightened thinkers and economists began to argue that such obligations hindered economic development. The burden of seigneurial dues and debts left peasants with little or sometimes nothing left to pay state taxes, church taxes (tithes), or to feed their families.

Nobles proved remarkably adept at maintaining their privileges while adapting to the challenges and possibilities resulting from the growth of the centralized state. Such privileges included being exempt from virtually all taxation, as were nobles in Prussia, Poland, Hungary, and Russia, or exempt from the direct tax on land. Some French nobles paid the direct tax on land (the *taille*), but most did not. In contrast, British nobles did have to pay property taxes and the only special privileges that peers retained were the right to sit in the House of Lords and, if accused of a crime, to be tried there by a jury of their peers. On the continent, however, other noble privileges included the nobles' right to be judged only by their peers in criminal cases, the right to bear a family coat of arms, to wear certain clothing and jewelry, to occupy special church pews near the altar (in some places Mass could not start until the local nobles had taken their accustomed place), to receive communion before anyone else, and to sit in specially reserved sections at concerts and on special benches at university. To affirm the deference of social inferiors, commoners were expected to bow or tip their hats when a noble walked by, gestures upon which nobles increasingly insisted. The right to duel over family "honor" in some states and the right to wear a sword were honorific privileges that served to distinguish nobles from their social inferiors.

There were significant differences in the wealth and status of European nobles, however. The wealthiest, most powerful nobles considered themselves "aristocrats." They were proud possessors of the most ancient titles (in France, they were the nobles of the sword, whose titles originated in military service to the king), and many of them were members of the court nobility, although "aristocrat" was not a legal category. The *grands seigneurs* in France and the *grandees* in Spain were identified by their great wealth and ownership of very large estates. But the wealthiest nobles may have been the great landed magnates of Eastern Europe. Prince Charles Radziwill of Poland was served by 10,000 retainers and a private army of 6,000 soldiers. Another Polish nobleman's property included 25,000 square kilometers of land, territory about four-fifths the size of today's Belgium. A single Russian prince owned 9,000 peasant households.

On the other hand, in every country there were also nobles of modest means who eagerly, even desperately, sought advantageous marriages for their daughters, and state, military, and church posts to provide a living for their sons. Demographic factors put pressure on poorer nobles, because now more noble children survived birth and childhood. Most Sicilian, Polish, and Spanish nobles owned little more than their titles. About 120,000 Polish nobles were landless, many so poor that they were referred to as the "barefoot nobility." The *hobereaux* were the threadbare nobles of France. Spanish *hidalgos* depended on modest state pensions, and some were so poor that it was said that they "ate black bread under the genealogical tree." In Spain, these impoverished nobles retained such privileges as immunity from taxation, the right to display their coat of arms and to be called "Don" (or sir), and freedom from arrest for debt. But they were not permitted to engage in manual work, and hence they had few ways to emerge from poverty. In 1773, the king changed this when he ordered the poorest of the *hidalgos* to take up manual work.

Nobles tried to maintain an aristocratic lifestyle. Those with great wealth were able to live the life of privilege and excess. They generally maintained large châteaux (manor houses) on their rural estates, as well as often owning elegant townhouses with gardens designed to recreate the illusion of a rural manor. Although some nobles had fallen on hard times

The grandiose palace of Blenheim, whose very stones exude a martial feeling.

and wished their fortunes were the equal of their privileges, they still attempted to have an aristocratic lifestyle, often going into debt as a result. Aristocrats viewed themselves as the epitome of integrity, honor, and personal courage, and the embodiment of elite culture.

The British Landed Elite

Although only nobles could sit in the House of Lords, the British ruling elite of great landowners was considerably broader than the aristocracy. Membership in the elite was consistently augmented by wealthy newcomers since the elite was made up of those who had large land holdings, whether or not they were nobles (see below, p. 389). The ownership of landed estates conferred "gentry" status, which a broad range of families claimed. At the time of the Glorious Revolution of 1688, when the rights of Parliament were reaffirmed by the accession of William III to the throne of England, the landed elite numbered about 4,000 gentry families. British landowners became even more prosperous during the eighteenth century, particularly after about 1750, when they raised rents on their estates and amassed fortunes selling agricultural products. The percentage of English land owned by nobles rose from about 15 to 25 percent, a far larger percentage than in either France or the German states.

Because in Britain only the eldest son inherited his father's title and land, younger sons had to find other sources of income. One such source was the Anglican Church's twenty-six bishoprics, the plums of which were reserved for the younger sons of peers and which offered considerable revenue and prestige. Whereas in the previous century, about a quarter of Anglican bishops had been commoners, by 1760 only a few were not the sons of nobles.

The wives of gentlemen oversaw governesses and domestic servants while instructing them in the responsibilities of family, religion, and social status—to behave politely, but confidently. The young had to learn the prevailing social codes. It was considered poor form to show too much emotion, to be too enthusiastic and, above all, to be overly passionate, sensual or, worse, licentious. One did not seek openly to convert the lower classes to better manners and virtue, but rather to set a good example. The writer Horace Walpole (1717–1797) once claimed he attended church only to set a good example for the servants.

Young gentlemen were tutored at home, or they attended secondary schools, such as Westminster and Eton, boarding schools that characterized the shift to out-of-home education throughout Europe. Oxford and Cambridge Universities then beckoned some for a time, though few actually graduated. Scottish universities, in contrast, offered more dynamic thought and research. Young gentlemen were expected to know something about the classics and contemporary poets. Yet, to many if not most wealthy families, academic knowledge seemed superfluous, even suspect. When Edward Gibbon (1737–1794), the historian of ancient Rome, presented one of his books to a duke, the latter exclaimed, "Another damned thick square book! Scribble, scribble, scribble, eh Mister Gibbon?" A wealthy dowager offered her grandnephew and heir a handsome annual stipend if he would "chuse to travel" and thus forsake "one of the Schools of Vice, the Universities," still blamed by some for causing the Civil War. The goal of the "grand tour" of the continent, servants in tow, was to achieve some knowledge of culture and painting. Such trips further enhanced the popularity of the classical style, so called because it followed the rules of Greek and Roman architecture.

Clergy

Although in France and Prussia the clergy was technically the first order or estate, the clergy did not really form a separate corporate entity, but rather reflected the social divisions between rich and poor that characterized European life in general. Most village priests and ministers shared the poverty of their parishioners. The members of the French clergy were likely to be the most literate, Russian Orthodox priests the least.

The lower clergy, drawn from the lower middle class, from artisans, or from the relatively prosperous peasantry, resented the undisguised ambition, greed, and arrogance of the bishops. Wealth and rank, not piety, usually determined such selections, as in the Italian states, where bishops were overwhelmingly drawn from the families of the great landowners. Many bishops did not take their episcopal responsibilities seriously, though few monarchs were as brazen as King Philip V of Spain, who named his eight-year-old son to be archbishop of Toledo. One French cardinal never visited the diocese from which he drew his income. Moreover, in the 1760s at least forty bishops resided in Paris, only one of whom was, in principle, supposed to live there.

Although some parts of Europe, above all, France, had already become "de-christianized," in that religious practice and presumably belief had declined (see Chapter 10), in most places, religion still played an important part in village life. The clergy baptized children and registered their births, married couples, and buried everybody. Priest and minister supervised charitable activities and provided certificates of good behavior for those leaving in search of work elsewhere. Religion offered consolation to many impoverished people: everyone could go to church, even if the poor were restricted as to where they could sit or stand. In general, the quality of the parish clergy seems to have been quite high in the eighteenth century (when compared to the next century), due in part to efforts to improve clerical training. Nonetheless, many parish priests were still caught between the liturgical demands of Catholic Church law and the persistence of popular superstitions shared by all social groups—for example, the duchess of Alba in Spain tried to cure her son's illness by having him ingest powder from the mummified finger of a saint.

The "Middling Sort"

Most of those people who engaged in commerce, trade, and manufacturing were known as the "middling sort" by the English and the "bourgeoisie" by the French, a term whose complexity makes definition difficult. The term "bourgeois" evolved from the medieval sense of "privileged townsmen" (in earlier times they had been exempt from having to pay taxes to territorial rulers; see Chapter 1).

The middle classes ranged from wealthy entrepreneurs, who had developed the economies of trading and manufacturing cities, to struggling retail merchants and innkeepers who made barely enough to hang on to their businesses. Purchasing land and often titles, the wealthiest commoners "lived nobly." They owned about a quarter of the land in France and most of the cantons of Switzerland. *Rentiers* profited from the urban building boom to force their tenants to pay more, and they increased rural rents as well. The middling sort also included merchants of modest means, small manufacturers, physicians, butchers, bakers, candlestick makers, and craftsmen ranging from jewelers and cabinetmakers (who had catered to the wealthy) to shoemakers and tailors (who had more modest clients).

Triumphant merchants at table. Note that one of the merchants and his servants are smoking tobacco, a new fad. Note also the aristocratic wig on the handsome dog on the right.

Great Britain had already become the proverbial "nation of shopkeepers," with one shop for every thirty or forty people.

In Western Europe, above all, the middle decades of the eighteenth century brought an expansion of the liberal professions, particularly in the number of lawyers, who became closely linked to political life in France. Men trained in law took positions in state bureaucracies and law courts. In England and France, some of the best students, or at least the best connected, became barristers; this gave them the right to plead in court, which their subordinates, attorneys (solicitors), could not do. Distinguished medical schools produced few physicians, not yet a profession viewed with great respect. Beneath them were surgeons, some former barbers who had learned to wield a razor-sharp knife with greater consequences. Military surgeons tended to be a cut above the others, their skills honed in the heat of battle. Despite the fact that some universities taught anatomy, surgical techniques were learned on the job.

To some nobles, "bourgeois" was an expression of contempt, seen in the sense of a seventeenth-century play in which a protagonist is jeered by a young nobleman: "Bourgeois is the insult given by these hooligans to anybody they deem slow-witted or out of touch with the court." In the eighteenth century, the term had not lost the sense provided by a seventeenth-century dictionary: "lacking in court grace, not altogether polite, overfamiliar, insufficiently respectful."

Peasants

If nobles stood at the top of the social hierarchy of early modern Europe, peasants lay at the bottom. In 1787, the peripatetic Englishman Arthur Young was travelling in Champagne in northern France when he encountered a peasant woman who looked to be about sixty or seventy years of age. To his astonishment, she gave her age as twenty-eight, a mother of seven children who survived by virtue of "a morsel of land, one cow and a poor little horse." Each year her husband owed one noble 42 pounds of wheat, and another, 168 pounds of oats, 1 chicken, and a cash payment. He also owed taxes to the state. The woman, old before her time, stated simply that the "taxes and seigneurial obligations" were a crushing burden, one that seemed to be getting worse.

Peasants still formed the vast majority of the population on the continent: from about 75 percent (Prussia and France) to more than 90 percent (Russia). Peasants were the source of the surplus wealth that sustained the incomes of crown, nobility, and church.

Peasants stood at the bottom of society, condemned as "a hybrid between animal and human" in the words of a Bavarian official. A Moldavian called peasants "strangers to any discipline, order, economy or cleanliness . . . thoroughly lazy, mendacious . . . people who are accustomed to do the little work that they do only under invectives or blows." Such cruel images were particularly prevalent in regions where lords dominated peasants of another nationality, as in Bohemia, where German landowners drew on the labor of Czech peasants.

The village was the center of the peasant's universe. Villagers viewed outsiders with suspicion; their solidarities helped them pull through as best they could in hard times, through harvest failures, epidemics, and wars. Folk songs celebrated peasant wisdom and wiliness, as humble rural people outfoxed naive and bumbling outsiders, whose wealth could not impart common sense.

All peasants were vulnerable to powerful outsiders in the overlapping and interdependent systems of domination that characterized early modern Europe. The state, nobles, and churchmen extracted taxes, produce, labor, and cash. A peasant song from Auvergne in central France lamented: "The poor peasant, is always tormented/ Paying the salt tax, and cash to the king./ Always at his door, soldiers and sergeant/ Who shout without pause/ 'Bring some money!'" The proportion of peasant revenue in kind or cash that disappeared into the pockets of nobles, officials, and clergy ranged from about 30 percent (France) to 70 percent (Bohemia). Rulers extracted money, commodities, and labor payments, imposing new taxes when their states were at war.

The peasantry was not, however, a homogeneous mass. In Western Europe, where almost all peasants were free, a peasant's status depended upon the amount of land, if any, owned or controlled through leases. In France, Flanders, southwestern Germany, Switzerland, and Sweden, many peasants owned or rented plots of sufficient size and productivity to do well in most years. Swedish peasants owned about a third of the cultivable land in their country. Recognized formally as a fourth estate, the Swedish peasantry maintained a degree of independence perhaps unique in Europe. Charles XII of Sweden bragged that he would rather be the most miserable Swedish peasant than a Russian noble unprotected by law from the whims of the tsar. Rural industry, for example, linens, provided supplementary income for peasant families in parts of France, Switzerland, and a number of German states. In Zurich's hinterland in the 1780s, about a quarter of the population spun or wove at home for the cotton and silk industries.

Many of the landowning peasants were constantly in debt, borrowing against the often empty hope of the next harvest. Sharecroppers worked land owned by landlords in exchange for a third to a half of what was produced. Landless laborers scraped by, if they were lucky, working on rural estates. All over Europe, some peasants took to the road as peddlers. Seasonal migrants left their homes in the Alps, Pyrenees, and other mountain regions each year for construction work in Milan, Lyon, Barcelona, or other large cities, or to work as laborers on the summer grain and fall vineyard harvests.

Serfdom had largely died out in Western Europe. Yet, many free peasants continued to be subject to some kind of seigneurial justice. In France, thousands of manorial courts still existed in 1789, providing lords with additional income by virtue of legal fees and fines assessed on peasants. Most of these courts, presided over by nobles, occupied themselves with minor offenses such as poaching and trespassing, civil suits for debt, and with family matters such as inheritances and guardianships.

In addition to taxes on land (*taille*) and salt (*gabelle*), peasants also owed obligatory labor service (*corvée*), usually work on roads, in France, Denmark, Sweden, Switzerland, Poland, Russia, and some German states. Obligations varied from only a couple of days in parts of France to as much as 200 days per year in Denmark. In Eastern Europe, peasant children were sometimes required to work in the service of the seigneur. Other obligations included the duty to provide the lord's household with a certain amount of food, for example, a chicken or goose on a holiday, or even just a few eggs, or to provide food for the lord's dogs, or to spin or weave cloth for the lord's household. To these were added mandatory payments to the seigneur upon transfer of land held by peasants with hereditary tenure. When a peasant with such tenure died, the lord claimed both money and the best animals the peasant might have owned.

The conditions of peasant life became worse the further east one travelled. Peasants in Russia and Eastern Europe lived in hovels made of earth, clay mixed with straw, branches, twigs, and sometimes caked manure. Floors were of mud and beds of straw. Only peasants of relative wealth could afford wood as building material.

The further east one went, too, the more authority lords enjoyed over peasants. Most peasants east of the Elbe River were serfs, some of whom had to take an oath of loyalty to their seigneur, as during the Middle Ages. There were some free peasants in the Habsburg domains and in Poland, but very few in Russia. The number of people who lost their freedom by becoming serfs had increased in East Prussia and Brandenburg, such that the German term for serfdom had become the same word for slavery.

Gallows stood near some Prussian manor houses, symbolizing the judicial prerogatives nobles held over serfs, including the right to dispense corporal punishment. In Poland, nobles could have their serfs executed (at least until late in the century). Russian lords could sentence their own serfs to killing labor, and even torture them, as long as they did not die immediately from such treatment, or send them into exile in Siberia. In Poland, a noble convicted of murdering a peasant paid only a small fine.

In Russia, proprietary serfs remained personally bound to the land of the nobles and, after Catherine the Great's Charter of 1785, to the nobles themselves. Some serfs owed landowners or, in the case of state serfs, the state, payments in money or in kind; others, somewhat better off, owed only labor—on the average, about three days a week. Lords could sell serfs, or give them away, for example, as part of a dowry, or lose title to them through gambling. Serfs could be sold individually or as a family to another noble, or be exchanged for animals. Lords could refuse permission for their serfs to marry or to choose a certain occupation. A good number of serfs took their chances in setting out to seek their freedom in the vast expanses on the edge or east of the empire. In Russia, as well as in Central and Eastern Europe, a few serfs managed to put together enough money to purchase their freedom.

Flogging a Russian serf.

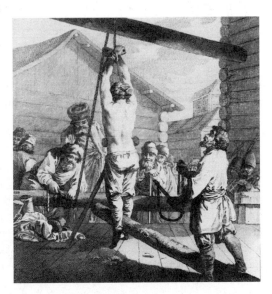

A poll tax on males (called "souls" in Russia), from which only nobles were excluded, added to the dependence of the "bonded people" to the state. Villages were collectively responsible for the payment of taxes. Moreover, all peasants could be conscripted into army service for terms of twenty-five years, a life sentence for most soldiers.

Possibilities for peasant resistance were limited; yet the "weapons of the weak" were not insignificant. These ranged from sullen resentment and foot-dragging to arson, open rebellion, or even full-scale insurrection. All nobles in an idle moment—and there were many—pondered the possibility of a massive uprising of "the dark masses." As the legal and material conditions of the serfs deteriorated, rebellions were endemic in eighteenth-century Russia. During the reign of Catherine the Great, the Cossack Emelian Pugachev appeared on the Siberian frontier claiming to be the pretender, "Tsar Peter III" (the real Peter III had spoken of reforms but had been dethroned and then murdered). He led several million peasants against their lords in 1773–1774. Pugachev's followers included Cossacks, Old Believers (dissidents persecuted by the Orthodox Church and doubly taxed), and the miners of the Ural Mountains, as well as desperate serfs. About 3,000 landowners perished in the Pugachev rebellion before it was crushed. Rebel serfs were hanged by having hooks stuck through their ribs.

In Bohemia during the hungry 1770s, 40,000 royal soldiers were required to put down peasant uprisings. And in the middle of the next decade, about 30,000 Transylvanian peasants rose up after a false rumor spread that those enlisting in the Habsburg army would gain freedom from serfdom. They demanded the abolition of the nobility and burned several hundred manor houses to make their point. The uprising ended with the torture of several of their leaders, parts of whose bodies were nailed to the gates of four towns.

THE BEGINNINGS OF THE INDUSTRIAL REVOLUTION

The Industrial Revolution began in England during the eighteenth century. Its early stages brought, above all, an intensification of forms of production that already existed: small workshops and cottage industry (producing goods at home). Technological innovation played a part, but not as large a one as has sometimes been assumed. Yet, ultimately a new source of inanimate power, the steam engine, would replace animal and human power, and increasingly manufacturing would be characterized by factory production.

The growth in manufacturing itself depended on two interrelated factors: agricultural productivity, then the principal source of wealth, and population growth. The two were so closely linked that it is sometimes difficult to know which followed which. An increase in agricultural productivity permitted the European population to increase during the century. At the same time, greater demand for food encouraged capital-intensive farming, including specialization of cash crops (such as vegetables, fruits, olive oil, wine, and raw silk) and the raising of cattle and poultry. Greater profits from agriculture generated a surplus of funds that could be invested in manufacturing. In turn, a larger population, some of the growth concentrated in and around cities and towns, increased the demand for manufactured goods, and provided a labor supply for town-based and rural industry.

Stagnation and Growth in Agriculture

New agricultural methods, first applied in the middle of the seventeenth century, helped raise farm yields in England, aided by the application of natural and artificial fertilizers. Gradually the practice of leaving part of the land fallow every other or every third year gave way to crop rotation. This helped regenerate the soil. Landowners planted fodder and root crops, such as clover and turnips, instead of periodically leaving land fallow. This provided food for animals as well as for human beings, in addition to enriching the soil by retaining nitrogen. The cultivation of potatoes, brought from the Americas, added badly needed nutrition to the diet of the poor.

By 1750, English agricultural yield had increased to the point that almost 15 percent of what was produced could be exported abroad (although about a third of the population still did not have enough to eat). On average, at the end of the century, an acre of agricultural land yielded perhaps 2.5 times more food in England than in France. Agriculture's contribution to the British gross national product reached a peak of 45 percent in 1770, and then only slowly was overtaken by English manufacturing as it rose in remarkable increments. Increased farm profits provided capital not only for further investment in agriculture but also in manufacturing, although most landowners were more likely to invest in government bonds than in speculative ventures.

One of the impediments to the expansion of agricultural production in England had been the widespread existence of open fields or common lands, which made up about half of the arable land in 1700. Beginning in the sixteenth century, on request from landowners, acts of Parliament permitted the "enclosure" of common land, transforming open fields or land that was communally owned into privately owned, fenced-in fields that could be more intensively and profitably farmed by individual owners (see Chapter 5). Over two centuries, enclosure acts forced perhaps half of English small landholders from the land, swelling the ranks of agricultural laborers. Between 1760 and 1815, 3,600 separate parliamentary acts enclosed more than 7 million acres of land, more than one-fourth of the farmland of England. Small tenant farmers, too, suffered, as many could

Measuring land in preparation for enclosure.

not afford to pay rents that rose rapidly after about 1760. The poorest members of the rural community lost their age-old access to lands on which they had gleaned firewood, gathered nuts and berries, and grazed animals. Before enclosure, it had been said, a "cottager" was a laborer with land; after enclosure, he was a laborer without land. Oliver Goldsmith's *Deserted Village* commented with playful, bitter irony:

> The law locks up both man and woman
> Who steals the goose from off the common,
> But lets the greater felon loose
> Who steals the common from the goose.

Agricultural change came far more slowly on the continent and barely at all in much of the Balkans and Russia. Most producers remained at the subsistence level, farming small plots without an agricultural surplus that they might have used to expand their holdings or improve farming techniques. Primitive farming techniques (wooden plows that barely scratched the surface of rocky terrain) characterized the mountainous and arid land of southern Italy and Sicily, the Dalmatian coast, southern France, much of Spain, and the Balkans. Peasants lacked farm and draft animals and therefore fertilizer, meat, and milk. Markets and transportation networks, too, remained inadequate to the task of agricultural modernization.

In Central and Eastern Europe, an old adage went "there is no land without a lord" because in most places only a noble, the crown, or the Church could own land. Serfdom and the absence of independent peasant proprietors left a formidable obstacle to agricultural development in Prussia, much of the Habsburg lands, and Russia.

On the continent, a bewildering variety of land tenures and agricultural practices under which they were held seemed to set rural poverty in stone.

Most continental farmland remained divided into small strips, and each year more than a third of arable land may have lain fallow (unplanted so that the land could replenish itself), with crops rotated between fields. Traditional peasant agricultural methods also blocked a major expansion of production. "Slash and burn" tillage survived in some parts of Europe where peasants simply burned the stubble on their land once the harvest had been taken in, replenishing soil with ash.

The studied attention many English country gentlemen gave to their lands may be contrasted with the approach of many French and Prussian nobles, content to sit back and live from revenue extracted from peasants. While the state had an interest in increasing farm output to generate additional tax revenue, most royal officials, seigneurs, and churchmen looked first to better ways of extracting peasant surpluses, not to improving yields. Nobles resisted occasional royal attempts to reduce seigneurial obligations, or to change them, such as by commuting labor service to payments in cash or in kind. Furthermore, much of what peasants managed to produce they owed to landlords, the state, and to a lesser extent, the Church. "Why should I build a better house" asked a Bavarian peasant, "so that my seigneur can line his pockets with the requisite fees to be paid?" Serfs had even less interest than other peasants in innovation.

Changes on the continent comparable to those taking place in England were largely confined to Northwestern Europe. In northern France, Flanders, the Dutch Republic, and Schleswig-Holstein (and parts of northern Italy as well as Spanish Catalonia), the land was fertile enough and sufficient capital was available to invest in commercial agriculture. Moreover, these were regions generally farmed by people who owned the lands on which they worked, and who therefore had more incentive to augment production. But even in the less densely populated countryside of Eastern and Southern Europe, more land was brought into cultivation, as in Russia where the population pushed into the steppes of the eastern frontier lands.

Other factors, too, contributed to improvements in Western European agriculture. During the eighteenth century, Europe as a whole experienced warmer, drier weather, particularly in the summers, in stark contrast to the unusually cold and damp seventeenth century. This had a salutary effect on population, agricultural yields, and commerce. Land reclamation projects helped expand the amount of land under cultivation. The Dutch reclaimed more land from the sea through ingenuity and hard work. In Schleswig-Holstein, arable lands increased by almost a quarter by the elimination of fens and heaths. Land reclamation added significantly to the amount of land under cultivation in the Southern Netherlands and as well as in Brandenburg. Even in densely settled France, farmers recovered wastelands for pasture, cereal crops, and vines.

Though not to the same extent as in England, the enclosure of separate strips of land and the sale or consolidation of common lands in Northwestern Europe permitted the development of "agricultural individual-ism," as more land passed to peasant-owners. Beginning in the 1760s, state policies created small farms owned by peasants, helping transform Danish agriculture from the stagnation of serfdom to relative prosperity. Royal decrees abolished serfdom, encouraged enclosure, and forced the commutation of labor obligations to rent payments.

Gradually some techniques that characterized agricultural improve-ments in England reached the continent. Innovative landowners and ten-ant farmers began to rotate crops, replacing the old three-field system so that little or no land lay fallow, growing foliage crops to improve the fertil-ity of fields. As in England, turnips, potatoes, and rice enhanced dietary nutrition. Yet, many peasants remained prisoners of tradition, refusing to plant or eat potatoes (Russian peasants called them "apples of the devil"), despite the fact that they can grow almost anywhere under any conditions. Nonetheless, the cultivation of the sugar beet (from which sugar could be made), the tomato (which some peasants held to be poisonous), and chest-nuts (the "bread of the poor"), also spread in France.

Animal husbandry also benefited from improved techniques. Oxen, mules, and especially horses could pull plows more easily than peasants. More cattle provided manure for fertilizer, and meat and milk for nutri-tion. Sheep-raising developed rapidly, providing both food and wool for manufacturing.

From Bilbao to Warsaw, some landowners formed societies to discuss agriculture and a few began model farms. Such groups included nobles, wealthy bourgeois, clergymen, and an occasional university professor. In France, "physiocrats," economic thinkers who believed that land was the source of all wealth, urged landowners to make their property more profitable and encouraged state policies to free the price of grain. Publica-tions on agriculture increased dramatically.

A few rulers took steps to intervene in the interest of agricultural prog-ress. The elector of Bavaria in 1762 offered farmers an exemption from taxes for ten years in the hope that they would plant foliage crops in their fallow fields. Several German Rhineland princes encouraged the selective breeding of cattle. In 1768, Queen Maria Theresa of Austria ordered the division of common pasture lands in some parts of the Habsburg territo-ries and the establishment of agricultural societies.

Population Growth

The European population rose from about 120 million to about 190 mil-lion people during the eighteenth century (see Table 9-1). Historians have long debated the causes and consequences of this demographic revolu-tion, studying parish registers of births, marriages, and deaths. Europe's birthrate increased, particularly after about 1740, and the number of deaths each year—the mortality rate—declined even more rapidly. These

TABLE 9-1. EUROPEAN POPULATION, 1700–1800 (MILLIONS)

	1700	1750	1800
Great Britain	9.0	10.5	16.5
France	19.0	21.5	28.0
Habsburg Empire	8.0	18.0	28.0
Prussia	2.0	6.0	9.5
Russia	17.5	20.0	37.0
Spain	6.0	9.0	11.0
Sweden	1.5*	1.7	2.3
United Provinces	1.8	1.9	2.0

*Data for Sweden is from Franklin D. Scott, *Sweden: The Nation's History* (Carbondale, Ill.: University of Southern Illinois Press, 1988), p. 260.
Source: Paul Kennedy, *The Rise and Fall of the Great Powers* (New York: Vintage, 1989), p. 99.

changes came first and foremost in densely settled regions of soaring agricultural productivity: England, the Netherlands, Flanders, northern Italy, and northern France (see Map 9.1). This suggests that an increase in agricultural production was the most important factor in explaining why the European population began to rise.

Plagues and epidemics, as well as chronic malnourishment, still intervened periodically to check population growth. Many monarchs ascended the throne because elder siblings had died, as did Frederick II of Prussia, who came to the throne because his two elder brothers had died before their first birthdays. Moreover, poor people were particularly vulnerable to infection, and rates of infant mortality remained high. Epidemics such as influenza, typhus, smallpox, and the plague occasionally ravaged populations. In 1719, 14,000 people in Paris died of smallpox. Malaria epidemics occurred in Spain in 1784–1787, and then again in 1790–1792. Whooping cough alone killed at least 40,000 children in Sweden during a period of fifteen years in the middle of the century, and more than 100,000 people died of bacillary dysentery in Brittany in one year. Epidemics of all kinds devastated the Balkans with murderous regularity. In Moscow, half the population died of disease early in the 1770s. Some states tried to close their frontiers and ports to prevent the arrival of disease, but usually to no avail. Famine, following several successive harvest failures, accentuated disease, particularly for those at opposite ends of the life cycle, infants and the elderly. Hardship turned into calamity. In 1769 alone, as much as 5 percent of the population of France may have died from hunger. Cities and towns remained unhealthy places where more people died than were born.

Yet, life expectancy gradually rose as diseases and epidemics ravaged the population less often and less murderously. In general, people of means lived longer than poor people, with upper-class Genevans living to almost

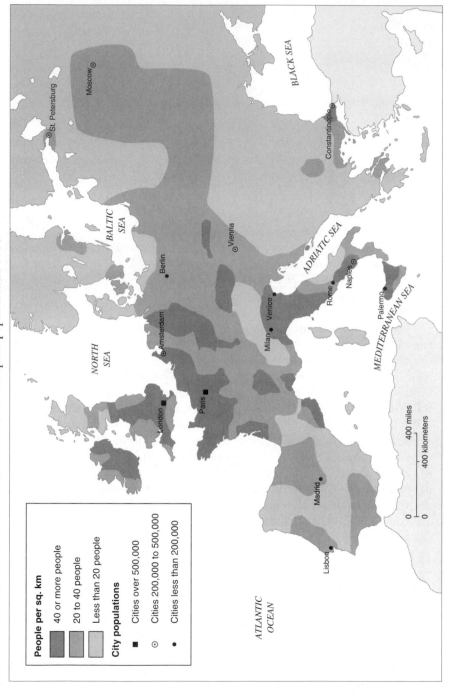

Map 9.1 Population in 1780 Distribution of the European population in 1780.

forty-two years of age early in the century, and to more than age forty-seven at the end of the century. But the average life expectancy for French men and women during the last half of the century still was only twenty-nine, and in Sweden, a country of relative longevity, it stood at about thirty-three years for men and thirty-six for women during the same period. Vaccinations against smallpox gradually proved effective, at least in Western Europe, although mass inoculations were not yet available. Quinine water helped people survive fevers. Scientific and medical societies encouraged towns to supervise waste removal and to take greater care when burying the dead, forbidding inhumations within town walls. The expansion of the cotton industry provided clothing, especially underwear, that was more easily and effectively washed than wool and other materials.

Warfare, which had checked population growth during the seventeenth century, became less devastating. Most of Western Europe was now spared the long, bloody conflicts (such as the Thirty Years' War) that had taken a toll on civilians. Armies became professionalized, and more under the control of stronger dynastic states. Military discipline and supply improved, sparing civilians much of the rapine of earlier centuries. Eastern Europe and the New World offered new sites for battles between the Great Powers.

Economic opportunity, such as the expansion of rural or cottage industry, encouraged couples to marry earlier—in their early twenties in England—and to have more children. There were fewer single women who never married, although the number of spinsters remained unusually high in some places, notably Ireland and Brittany.

The plague ward in a Hamburg hospital. Note the doctor carrying out a painful amputation on a patient. Both are oblivious to surrounding distractions.

Many contemporaries were aware of the rise in population (although some, especially in France, wrongly believed the population was declining by the end of the century). For the English clergyman Thomas Malthus (1766–1834), the rise of the European population was alarming. Malthus predicted in his *Essay on the Principle of Population* (1798) that natural checks on population growth—plague and disease, famine, war, and infant mortality, what he called "nature's auditing with a red pencil"—would become less significant. But he believed that population would "increase beyond the nourishment prepared for it," that is, food supply would grow only arithmetically (2-3-4-5 and so on), whereas population would henceforth multiply exponentially (2-4-8-16-32 . . .). To be sure, the rise in population put more pressure on the land, particularly in France and other places where most land holdings were small and often too subdivided to be profitably farmed. Yet, Malthus did not take into consideration rising agricultural productivity, nor the fact that some people had already begun to limit the size of their families, although it is extremely difficult to measure the diffusion of birth control. We have only hints of this, such as when the British writer James Boswell referred delicately to his sexual encounters "in armor." In France, coitus interruptus is credited with bringing about a small decline in the birthrate after 1770. But birth control was hit or miss, to say the least.

Manufacturing: Guilds and Domestic Industry

The workshop was the basis of manufacturing in eighteenth-century Europe. In some countries, merchants and artisans were organized into corporate guilds by the product they sold; in Russia, by contrast, a decree in 1775 placed them in guilds according to wealth. Guilds were a type of privilege, because rulers awarded them monopolies over the production or sale of certain products, particularly luxury goods. Masters' guilds and journeymens' associations conferred rights and status on craftsmen; they limited and oversaw the training of boys as apprentices, beginning at the age of twelve or thirteen. In France, journeymen perfected their skills while completing the "tour of France," the origin of the modern bicycle race. A craftsman stopped in a number of cities over a period of several years; he was housed in the craft association's "mother house" before returning home with skills acquired from serving many masters, and with hopes of one day becoming a master himself.

It was, however, becoming increasingly difficult for a journeyman to become a master, particularly if he did not have a father or other relative to smooth the way by putting out some money. By the 1770s, Spanish and French skilled trades, in particular, had become glutted. Moreover, Parisian guilds faced competition from outsiders who escaped corporate controls. "Free" or "illegal" workers lived on the outskirts of the city, beyond the customs tax barrier, where a tax on goods brought into town had

William Hogarth's depiction of a weaver's apprentice.

to be paid. Such craftsmen could produce cabinets and other products more cheaply than their Parisian rivals, whose goods were taxed.

Since at least the sixteenth century in England, partially to circumvent the guilds, some merchant-manufacturers had looked to labor in the countryside to produce goods. This shift to domestic industry (also known as proto-industrialization or the putting-out system) contributed to what would eventually become a worldwide revolution in manufacturing. The early stages of the Industrial Revolution showed an increase in domestic industry rather than a shift to new forms of production. New technology would only gradually lead to the mechanization and the standardization of tasks previously done by hand.

Britain's manufacturing base expanded early in the eighteenth century. In 1720, Daniel Defoe (1680–1731) described the Yorkshire countryside as "one continuous village" with a "manufactory or workhouse" attached to each house or farm. Among the houses of the manufacturers "scattered an infinite number of cottages or small dwellings, in which dwell the workmen which are employed, the women and children of whom are always busy carding and spinning." Hand spinning continued throughout the century to be the largest source of female employment. Many families of home spinners, weavers, glove-makers, and shirt-buttoners also worked the land—theirs or someone else's—part time. Rural industry paused at harvest time.

Master clothiers, or merchant-manufacturers, provided domestic workers with raw materials, such as wool or Indian cotton purchased at one of the cloth halls. Home workers carded, spun, or wove with spinning wheels

Carding and spinning at home.

or looms that they either owned or (in most cases) rented. The master clothier later came around again, paying for the goods that had been completed. He would then carry these goods to the next stage in the production process, for example, to a dyer. Low pay rates in the countryside attracted merchant-manufacturers, encouraging the persistence of rural industry. At the end of the century, hand-knitted stockings produced by rural Scottish families still cost less than those knitted on a power loom.

As the cottage industry was organized by household, women had a major, even determining, role in the organization of the household economy, including training young children. There were both male and female "journeymen" wool spinners. One man, later a successful inventor of textile machinery, recalled, "my mother taught me [while too young to weave] to earn my bread by carding and spinning cotton, winding linen or cotton weft for my father and elder brothers at the loom, until I became of sufficient age and strength for my father to put me into a loom."

Inventions

Technological change also contributed to the Industrial Revolution. Between 1660 and 1760, 210 new inventions were patented in England; during the next twenty-nine years, there were 976. Most of the inventors were artisans or yeoman farmers, although inventors at Scottish universities came up with improvements in dyes and bleaching with chlorine.

But inventions at first had very little to do with increased productivity. They were probably less important than the infusion of investment capital into manufacturing and the expansion of the number of workers in the textile industry. Some inventions were only gradually diffused, or their importance was not recognized until later. No invention was of greater long-term significance than the steam engine, invented by James Watt (1736–1819), a Scot who made musical instruments. Watt added a separate condenser to a primitive steam engine, resulting in a more powerful engine, which he patented in 1769. Yet, like its predecessor, Watt's costly invention was first used only to drain mines, making it possible to dig deeper shafts, and its use was only slowly diffused.

Inventions eventually transformed the production of iron. In 1709, Abraham Darby, a foundryman, came up with a process to smelt iron ore into cast iron by using coke instead of charcoal. But this process spread only slowly; in 1775, there were still only thirty-one blast furnaces in Britain. Moreover, charcoal smelting continued to be important, further depleting Britain's forests. In 1784, Henry Cort (1740–1800), an iron-master, invented the "puddling and rolling" process in iron casting. Molten metal in a furnace was raked to remove carbon and other impurities from the iron, producing wrought iron which was far stronger than cast iron. Iron bridges replaced their flimsy predecessors. Iron made new buildings sturdier and basically fire-resistant. Cast-iron railings and gates began to appear on landed estates and in elegant townhouses. Low-cost iron made possible sturdier plows and other farm implements that, in turn, significantly increased the demand for iron. The export of iron increased by nine times in the course of the eighteenth century, helping British foreign trade triple during its last two decades.

Each major invention was the result of the ingenious application of technology already available to production, rather than of brilliant discoveries by genius-inventors. Improvements in the spinning wheel and basic looms accelerated textile production in the seventeenth and first decades

(*Left*) James Watt. (*Right*) The steam engine.

of the eighteenth century. The stocking frame produced lighter and more fashionable cotton and silk stockings that replaced the heavier woolen hose of the upper classes. John Kay (1704–1764) invented the "flying shuttle" (patented in 1733 but not diffused for more than twenty years), which ultimately made it possible to card and weave at a much greater speed, doubling productivity. But Kay's invention, too, has to be seen in the context of traditional manufacturing: its principal effect was to increase the productivity of hand-loom weavers.

Gradually machines powered by water and then by steam eliminated bottlenecks in textile production. In about 1764, James Hargreaves (c. 1720–1778), a carpenter and weaver, invented an apparatus known as the spinning jenny, which wrapped fibers around a spindle. Drawing on medieval technology, Hargreaves multiplied the number of thread spindles a worker could operate from one to eight, and then soon to eighty spindles. In 1769, Richard Arkwright (1732–1792), a former barber turned entrepreneur, patented a mechanized "water frame," which, combining spindles and rollers, became the first spinning mill. The water frame turned out a strong, coarse yarn that transformed the cotton industry and increased production of wool worsteds (combed wool). With the exception of its water-powered rollers, Arkwright built his power spinning machine out of the same materials as the ordinary spinning wheel that had been found in Europe since medieval times. Using the new technology, Arkwright set up large textile mills and earned half a million pounds in just twenty years. He had his portrait painted with his hand touching his famous spinning machine, as the same painter might have formerly depicted a country gentleman standing with his hand touching a fence, his hunting dogs sitting submissively at his feet. The resourceful manufacturer emerged in Britain as someone considered worthy of emulation. A decade later, a farmer combined features of Hargreaves' jenny and Arkwright's water frame to produce a "spinning mule" that could provide sturdier yarn of consistent quality while further increasing the number of spindles a single spinner could operate.

Cottage industry, artisanal workshops, and factory production often coexisted, not only within the same region, but within industries. With the gradual mechanization of spinning, which in some places probably followed a shortage of cheap rural labor, weaving could only keep pace with the rapid expansion of the number of hand-loom weavers. Even a rudimentary power loom, invented in 1784, was too expensive to compete with domestic industry, which continued to be based on the availability of an inexpensive workforce. Mechanization may first even have increased the demand for production of goods that could best be provided by domestic industry. Hand-loom weavers survived well into the middle decades of the nineteenth century.

In any case, the clever inventions that slowly revolutionized the textile industry did not inevitably lead to factory production. Like framework

Richard Arkwright with his famous invention at his fingertips.

knitting, the first spinning jennys and mules were small enough to be adaptable to workshops and even some houses. Manufacturing remained largely based in small workshops, where skilled workers and their apprentices used stronger, more reliable hand-operated machinery or tools. Many small textile entrepreneurs, who had begun as yeoman farmers, rural artisans, or innkeepers, continued to prosper although they owned little more than a single spinning frame.

The factory, however, slowly became the symbol of the new industrial age in England. One of Arkwright's textile mills in the early 1770s had 200 workers, and ten years later it had four times that number. An ironworks employed more than a thousand workers by 1770, a concentration previously seen only in great shipyards. In 1774, James Watt and Matthew Boulton (1728–1809), a toymaker, went into business in Birmingham producing engines and machine parts in the largest factory in the world. It was not a single structure but rather a number of adjacent workshops, employing about 20,000 men, women, and children in the countryside around Birmingham.

The development of the factory at first had little to do with technological imperatives. Manufacturers preferred bringing workers under one roof so that they could more easily supervise them, imposing the discipline of factory work on people used to having their schedule defined by the rise and fall of the sun and the passing of the seasons. When a defective piece of pottery emerged from the kilns, the pottery manufacturer Josiah Wedgwood would storm over and stomp on it with his wooden leg, chiding his workers. "Thou shalt not be idle" was Wedgwood's eleventh command-ment; "Everything gives way to experiment" was his favorite maxim. His goal was to train his workers so thoroughly as "to make such machines of the men as cannot err." Boulton fined workers a part of their wages if they were late. One of his colleagues took deductions from his workers' wages for "being at taverns, alehouses, coffee houses, breakfast, dinner, playing, sleeping, smoking, disputes or anything foreign to my business, or in any way loitering."

By mid-century, factory manufacturing had begun to alter the northern English landscape. "From the Establishment of Manufacturers, we see Hamlets swell into Villages, and Villages into Towns," exclaimed a gentle-man in the 1770s. The locus of English manufacturing shifted from the south and southeast to the north and northwest, around cities like "old smoky Sheffield." Yorkshire, which produced 20 percent of England's wool in 1700, accounted for 60 percent at the dawn of the next century; the production of worsteds, too, concentrated there, leaving areas in south-eastern England. Northern England's industrial centers, then, lay at the heart of the manufacturing revolution that was transforming Britain and had already affected parts of continental Western Europe.

Expanding British Economy

The production of manufactured goods doubled during the last half of the eighteenth century in Britain. Cotton manufacturing led the way; between 1750 and 1770, British cotton exports doubled. The production of iron followed in importance, along with wool and worsteds, linen, silk, copper, paper, cutlery, and the booming building trades. Coal was substituted for wood as fuel.

Despite its relatively small size, Britain's significant economic advan-tages over the nations of the continent help explain why the manufactur-ing revolution first began in Britain. Unlike the German or Italian states, Britain was unified politically. People living in England spoke basically the same language. France and the Italian and German states still had internal tariffs that made trade more costly, whereas in Britain there were no inter-nal tariffs once the union between England and Scotland had been achieved in 1707, creating Great Britain. Moreover, the system of weights and measures in Britain had largely been standardized.

Great Britain was by far the wealthiest nation in the world. Its colonies provided raw materials for manufacturing and markets for goods produced by the mother country. The amount of raw cotton imported from India in-creased by twenty times between 1750 and 1800. English merchants sup-plied slaves snatched from the west coast of Africa for the plantations of the West Indies in exchange for cotton. And, beginning in the 1790s, the United States provided Lancashire manufacturers with cotton picked by southern slaves.

England's precocious banking and credit arrangements facilitated the reinvestment of agricultural and commercial profits in manufacturing. London's financial market could provide information twice a week on what investments were worth in Amsterdam and Paris. London's banks, particularly the giant Bank of England, were profitable and respected. Merchants and manufacturers accepted paper money and bills of exchange with confidence. Gentry invested in overseas trade expeditions and in manufacturing without the reticence of continental landowners. Joint-stock companies, which investors had begun to form in the late seventeenth century, offered limited personal liability, which meant that in the case of a company's financial disaster, each investor would be liable only to the extent of his investment.

Expanded demand for manufactured goods led to a dramatic improvement in Britain's roads, which were already well developed. A new process of road surfacing—macadamization—improved travel on the main routes. Turnpikes were extended and improved; investors formed "turnpike trusts," repairing the highways and turning a profit by charging a toll. In 1700, it took fifty hours to travel from Norwich to London by coach; by 1800, the journey could be achieved in nineteen hours; the daunting trek to the Scottish city of Edinburgh had been reduced to a mere sixty hours of travel.

England's water transportation was also unmatched in Europe, a gift of nature. Rich sources of coal and iron ore lay near water transportation. By 1800, Britain was extracting about 90 percent of the world's coal. That extracted in northeastern England could be transported with relative ease along the coast. No part of England stands more than seventy miles from the sea. Navigable rivers facilitated the transportation of raw materials and manufactured goods; so did canals built in the middle decades of the century, including one ninety miles long linking Manchester to the Mersey River and the Irish Sea.

The state offered British businessmen more assistance than any continental rivals could anticipate from their own governments. The powerful Royal Navy protected the merchant fleet, which tripled during the first three-quarters of the century. Navigation Acts forced foreign merchants to ship export goods to Britain in British ships. Bowing to pressure from woolens producers, the British government in 1700 had imposed protective tariffs on imported silk and calico. Agreements with the Dutch Republic and France in the late 1780s reduced trade tariffs with those states, which helped British exports. Other British state strategies were even more imaginative: a law dating from the late seventeenth century required that all corpses be dressed in woolens for burial, a clever way of helping manufacturers. Furthermore, the political influence of businessmen kept taxes low.

Yet, the British government rarely interfered in operations of the economy in ways that businessmen might have considered intrusive. Adam

Smith (1723–1790), a Scottish professor of moral philosophy at the University of Glasgow, emerged as the first economic theorist of capitalism. In his landmark work, *An Inquiry into the Nature and Causes of the Wealth of Nations* (1776), Smith rejected the prevailing theory of mercantilism and extolled economic liberalism. He also observed that the greater division of labor was increasing productivity. Taking a famous example, he argued that a single worker could probably not make a single common pin in one day, but that ten workers, each repeating the same task, such as straightening the wire, or grinding its point, could make hundreds of pins in a workday. Smith's logic anticipated the age of factory manufacturing.

Expanding Continental Economies

On the continent, too, particularly in the West, manufacturing expanded rapidly in the workshops of large cities and small towns. Moreover, spinning, weaving, and the finishing of artisanal products like knives increased in the countryside. Banks provided more capital and credit to manufacturers and merchants. Despite bewildering differences in, for example, weights and measures, currencies (even within some states), and calendars (Russia's was eleven days behind that of the West), European commerce developed rapidly during the eighteenth century. The development of larger-scale commerce within Europe—for example, the Baltic trade—was very important to the growth of European economies. In addition, trade with the wider world brought new products—Chinese silk and porcelain, Indian cotton, West Indian sugar and rum, East Indian tea, South Seas spices, and much more. In the chancy sweepstakes of colonial trade, traders and their investors could make considerable fortunes, but they could also easily be ruined when a sudden storm or pirate attack destroyed a ship and its cargo.

The great successes—and failures—of colonial trade were those in England and the Dutch Republic, but global trade also contributed to the economies of the Italian and German states, and to those of Spain, Portugal, and France (see Map 9.2). France, too, benefited enormously from a dramatic influx of capital, above all profits from the sugar plantations of Haiti.

Bankers, investors, shipbuilders, wholesale and retail merchants, insurance underwriters, transporters, and notaries profited from the marked increase in international trade. Some of the prosperity trickled down to more ordinary folk as well, particularly in port towns: carpenters who built and repaired ships, dockers who unloaded them, public criers who announced their safe return, haulers who carried their products, and artisans who supplied luxuries for wealthy merchants.

Considerable obstacles remained, however, to further economic development on the continent. Traditional suspicion of paper money, the problems of obtaining credit and raising investment capital, and periodic government debasing of currencies created hurdles for those undertaking

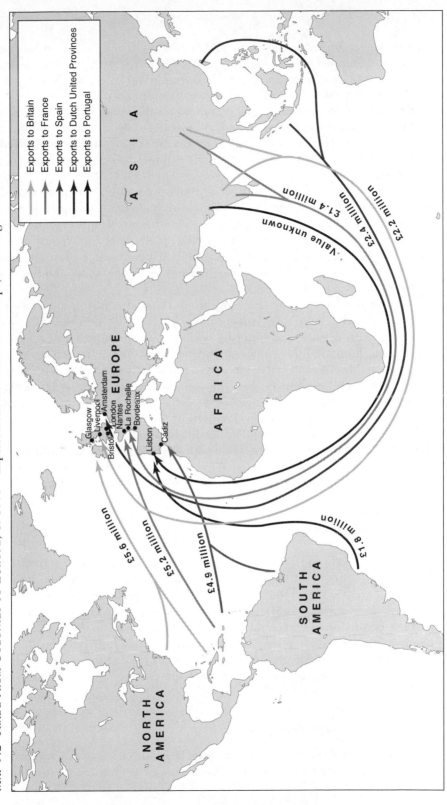

MAP 9.2 TRADE FROM COLONIES TO EUROPE, C. 1775   Exports from the colonies to Europe, including the value of the trade.

Exports to Britain
Exports to France
Exports to Spain
Exports to Dutch United Provinces
Exports to Portugal

£2.4 million
£1.4 million
£3.2 million
Value unknown
£5.6 million
£5.2 million
£4.9 million
£1.8 million

long-distance commerce. London and Amsterdam were alone in having relatively developed banks, credit facilities, relatively low rates of interest, and insurance companies. Even in Western Europe, Britain's South Sea Bubble (see Chapter 11) and the collapse of John Law's bank in France in 1720 scared off investors. Capital remained for the most part in the hands of wealthy families and small groups of associates, who loaned money to states, pushing up the cost of credit. The absence of investment capital led the Prussian and Austrian states to supply capital for some manufacturing enterprises.

France did not lag far behind Britain in the production of manufactured goods, and remained the principal supplier of Spain and its empire. Continental European manufacturing was characterized by small-scale production and cottage industry (taking advantage, particularly in France, of an almost endless supply of laborers). Manufacturing drew upon few technological innovations and very little mechanization. Water, wind, and human and animal motion provided power.

Guild monopolies on the trade and production of certain products, international tariffs and tolls compounded by the vast number of small states in Central Europe, and tariffs within states remained obstacles to more rapid industrial development. Furthermore, as we have seen, relatively few nobles took an active interest in manufacturing, although exceptions were to be found in France, the Austrian Netherlands, and Russia, where they developed coal mines and invested in the iron industry. In the Russian Empire, despite the development of the copper and iron industry of the Ural Mountains, the possibilities for increased manufacturing were limited by monumental distances between population centers and natural resources and an inadequate transportation network that had barely changed since the time of Ivan the Terrible in the sixteenth century.

SOCIAL CHANGES

Economic growth and population increases would ultimately transform Europe into a new industrial world, one in which there would be larger cities and greater social mobility. Urban growth, particularly after 1750, was one of the most visible changes engendered by population growth and the expansion of trade and manufacturing, as well as the continuing centralization of state power. Other changes included the rise of the "middling sort" and the greater vulnerability of the laborer who was displaced by enclosure and forced to move from place to place in search of work.

The Growth of Towns and Cities

Although Europe remained overwhelmingly rural, cities and towns grew faster than the population as a whole, meaning that Europe, particularly

TABLE 9-2. EUROPE'S LARGEST CITIES AT THE END OF THE EIGHTEENTH CENTURY

City	Population	City	Population
London	950,000	St. Petersburg	270,000
Paris	550,000	Vienna	230,000
Naples	430,000	Amsterdam	220,000
Constantinople	300,000	Lisbon	180,000
Moscow	300,000	Berlin	170,000

the West, urbanized. Cities grew as people moved to areas where there was work, or for the poorest of the poor, where they might benefit from charity. New manufacturing centers served as magnets to which those who had no land or prospects were drawn. By the end of the century, Europe had twenty-two cities with more than 100,000 people (see Table 9-2).

The British urban population (any settlement of more than 2,500 people qualified as "urban") grew from slightly less than 20 percent of the population in 1700 to more than 30 percent in 1800, when London's population reached nearly a million people, nearly twice that of Paris. London was the world's largest port, center of banking, finance, insurance, manufacturing, and exports. In the eighteenth century, fully one-fifth of the British population spent part of their lives in London. Early in the century, Norwich, a textile-producing and shoemaking town in East Anglia, was England's second city, with only 30,000 people, followed by Bristol and Exeter, each of which had barely 20,000 inhabitants.

Two-thirds of the residents of London had been born outside of the city and were migrants who had come to the capital in search of opportunity. But many contemporaries believed that wickedness and crime increased almost inevitably with growth and prosperity. *Hell Upon Earth, or the Town in an Uproar* (1729) was subtitled "The Late Horrible Scenes of Forgery, Perjury, Street-Robbery, Murder, Sodomy, and Other Shocking Impieties." It denounced "this great, wicked, unwieldy, over-grown Town, one continued hurry of Vice and Pleasure, where nothing dwells but *Absurdities, Abuses, Accidents, Accusations.*"

London's emerging social geography reflected the paradox that Britain was both an aristocratic and commercial society. Bloomsbury Square and Bedford Square, elite districts in West London, near Westminster, the seat of Parliament, were largely aristocratic creations, as nobles developed some of the land they owned. At the same time, commercial London also expanded rapidly in tune with the British Empire. Near the burgeoning docks of the East End on the River Thames, dilapidated buildings housed the poor.

As England's economic dynamism began to shift northward with increased manufacturing, Liverpool, teeming port on the Irish Sea, "the emporium of the western world," and Manchester, a northern industrial town, grew rapidly. In the 1720s, Daniel Defoe flattered Manchester, already a small center of textile manufacturing, as "the greatest mere village in England" and by 1760, 17,000 people lived there. By 1800, Manchester had become the "metropolis of manufactures," with 75,000 inhabitants and growing industrial suburbs as well.

Paris, Rouen, Lille, Bordeaux, and other French cities, too, continued to grow, although in France only about 10 percent of the population lived in towns of more than 5,000 people in 1789 (compared to 25 percent in England). In the German states, there had been but twenty-four cities with more than 10,000 people in 1500; by 1800, there were sixty of them.

After mid-century, the small towns that were centers of regional trade accounted for most urban growth. Royal officials, courtiers and attendants, tax collectors, lawyers, and soldiers swelled the population of state and regional capitals. In Berlin, which tripled in population, these groups and their families accounted for about 40 percent of the Prussian capital's 140,000 inhabitants in 1783.

In southern Italy, Naples was barely able to support its impoverished population of more than 400,000 people. No other town in southern Italy had 10,000 inhabitants. Other towns languished in stagnation, without sufficient trade, manufacturing, or administrative functions to infuse them with dynamism. In Rome, the clergy constituted about half the population of 160,000 people. The Spanish town of Valladolid housed forty-six monasteries among a population of little more than 20,000 people. Eastern Europe and the Balkans had few cities. By mid-century only three cities within the vast Russian Empire had more than 30,000 inhabitants: Moscow, St. Petersburg, and Kiev, each growing at a relatively rapid pace.

A London coffeehouse.

Elegant shops on Capel Street in Dublin.

People with money and leisure time had more to do in cosmopolitan cities. The largest English towns sported theaters and concert halls, gentlemen's clubs, and scientific societies. In 1740, Parliament limited the number of racetracks to two favored by people of means, stating that betting on horses had "contributed very much to the encouragement of idleness, to the Impoverishment of many of the meaner sort of subjects of this Kingdom." Private clubs thrived. Cafés took their name from the coffee served there, a drink only people of some means could afford. In contrast, cabarets and taverns offered cheap alcoholic drink.

Towns took pride in their development. Some began publishing guides for visitors and directories listing the names of shops. Elegant buildings of brick and stone replaced tottering wood-beamed structures dating from medieval times. Streets were widened, paved, and frequently cleaned. Dublin, Boston, and Calcutta offered smaller versions of English urban society, sporting private clubs and municipal pride.

Wealthy merchants and bankers lived in elegant townhouses near the docks in Hamburg, Nantes, Rouen, and Genoa, bustling port cities of international trade. Expanded trade and urban growth engendered consumerism. As the French language spread throughout the courts and upper classes in Europe, Paris became the European capital of luxury goods. French nobles established standards of conspicuous consumption. The sober frugality of the past disappeared in the quest for luxury. Parisians of means purchased fine wines from Burgundy, champagne from Champagne, and sent servants to the market to buy expensive cheeses and oysters from the Norman coast. Some nobles went broke after borrowing vast sums to provide lavishly for themselves and their families.

A wealthy Dutch family living nobly.

Noble and wealthy bourgeois alike insisted on the personal prerogatives of taste, for example, in decoration and food. It became a compliment to say that someone or something reflected "urbanity." Three-cornered hats, along with wigs, which wealthy commoners as well as nobles increasingly favored, and stockings emerged as recognizable symbols of respectability.

Upper-class men and women became concerned as never before with modesty; "water closets" became more common. Social relations became something of an extension of the fenced-in noble château of the country-side, or the walled townhouse with a private garden. A code of conduct served—with income and private space itself—as a barrier between wealthy and ordinary people.

The eighteenth-century consumer revolution extended to the urban poor, as well. The number of ordinary families able to acquire household utensils and even books and cheap prints increased dramatically. For those with a little money or some credit, the tavern and cabaret provided sociability. For people with neither, there was the street.

Social Movement within the Elite

With the growth of manufacturing, trade, and cities came concomitant social changes, including mobility of the "middling sort." In Paris, wealthy merchants purchased elegant townhouses and mingled with nobles. In Barcelona, members of the trading oligarchy earned the right to carry swords like nobles. The Catalan city's sparkling new town hall and aligned, paved streets reflected bourgeois prosperity and urban pride. The bourgeoisie of the Austrian Netherlands demanded privileges granted by the Habsburg rulers to Belgian nobles.

Bankers and wealthy merchants aspired to social distinction and to live the life of the aristocrat. When possible, they would use their wealth to buy their way into the nobility, or to marry a daughter into it. Although in theory a person was born into an estate and remained there for the rest of his life, noble titles could be purchased in most European states. As the rising cost of warfare (larger armies to equip, train, and send into battle, and expensive fortifications to maintain) and reduced tax revenue during hard economic times weighed heavily on royal coffers, the sale of titles and offices swept more men into the nobility. Wealthy commoners enriched by the expansion of the economy of Western Europe bought titles, thereby acceding to prestigious positions in royal bureaucracies and in the officer corps of the king's standing army. The purchase of noble titles in France (the sale of which began in the fourteenth century), Austria, and Castile provided a relatively easily obtained means of social ascension, without eliminating the distinctions between nobles and commoners. The number of French nobles doubled between 1715 and 1789, and relatively few noble families could trace their origins back more than a couple of generations.

In Britain, on the other hand, it was rare for commoners to move into the nobility. The sale of offices had never been as widespread in England as on the continent, at least not since the Civil War, and the purchase of noble titles was nonexistent. But the crown occasionally elevated spectacularly successful, wealthy commoners into the peerage with hereditary noble titles (baron, viscount, earl, marquess, and duke), which carried with them a seat in the House of Lords. The monarchy rewarded other landed gentlemen with other titles, including knight (a non-hereditary title), baronet (a hereditary title, granted less frequently), both of which carried the title of "sir." Very few people, however, ever rose from trade into a peerage, or even to the upper gentry.

Entry into the British elite, however, was generally more open than into its continental counterparts. Gradual shifts in social structure in English society, beginning in the seventeenth century, contributed to the nation's social stability. The elite consisted of more than the small number of nobles; social status and political influence were based on the ownership of large amounts of land, whether by noble or non-noble. Those who were wealthy enough to purchase estates became part of the landed elite and were considered gentry. Hence, membership in the elite consistently reflected the advent of wealthy newcomers. No legal or cultural barriers in Britain prevented bankers, manufacturers, merchants, and urban professionals from acceding through wealth to social and political predominance as "country gentlemen" through the purchase of landed estates. With national and local influence, these country gentlemen dispensed social and political patronage. Furthermore, though nobles dominated Parliament, that body responded to the needs of all property owners, including merchants and other wealthy commoners.

Daniel Defoe, who wrote *Robinson Crusoe* and other novels for an expanding middle-class readership, claimed that "men are every day starting up from obscurity to wealth." Trade and manufacturing in England were honored occupations. Unlike on the continent, where second and third sons often were automatically relegated by their fathers into Church or military posts, many of these sons marched proudly into business. A Manchester cobbler wrote in 1756:

> See, as the Owners of old Family Estates in your Neighborhood are selling off their patrimonies, how your townsmen are constantly purchasing; and thereby laying the Foundation of a new Race of Gentry! Not adorn'd, its true, with Coats of Arms and a long Parchment Pedigree of useless Members of Society, but deck'd with Virtue and Frugality.

In France, Denmark, and Sweden, tensions between the oldest noble families and those more recently ennobled remained strong. The wealthiest nobles were ever more eager to maintain social distance from poorer nobles and those recently ennobled, whom they viewed as boorish newcomers, *parvenu* commoners little better than merchants. This was, to be sure, hardly a new concern in France; during the seventeenth century, the wealthiest noble families, who could trace their nobility and military service to the king back many generations if not centuries, had resented the rush of wealthy commoners into the nobility through the purchase of noble titles. The number of ennobled commoners in the eighteenth century may not have been significantly greater than that in the previous century, but those who were ennobled were wealthier. By the eighteenth century, few noble families could trace their lineage as nobles of the sword back more than a few generations. But those who could still controlled the most important and lucrative offices in the royal bureaucracy, the Church, and the army (although some of the wealthiest families disdained even such lucrative and prestigious service).

The French army began to phase out the purchase of commissions in the late 1770s, and early in the next decade nobles demanded and received royal assurance that their monopoly over the most significant military titles would be respected by the crown. Directed against *parvenu* nobles, the Ségur Law of 1782 asserted that no one could be appointed to a high post in the army who could not demonstrate at least four generations of nobility on his father's side. A year later, the marquis of Ségur quarreled with a recently ennobled secretary of state and threatened to resign from the royal council: "It is war to the death," he insisted, "between the *robe* [nobles who had purchased their titles] and people like us."

However, barriers between the bourgeois and nobles in many places were starting to break down. Wealthy merchants and manufacturers in many states were permitted to purchase titles. In some states, a small number of nobles entered commerce or manufacturing. The expansion of trade and manufacturing led more continental nobles to seek new sources of wealth. French nobles were the principal owners of mines. Swedish nobles contributed to the modest expansion of manufacturing in their country. In eighteenth-century Spain, little stigma was attached to noble commercial ventures, perhaps because there were so many nobles. Russian nobles were particularly noteworthy for undertaking mining projects. In contrast, in Prussia, Poland, and Hungary most nobles still considered participation in commercial activity (above all, retail commerce) or manufacturing to bring derogation, implying a loss of status and honor. Such derogation also, in principle, existed in France, although such was often not the case in reality.

The Changing Condition of the Poor

For millions of people, only a thin line stood between having enough to eat and hunger or starvation, occasional employment and begging, prostitution and petty theft, and between relatively good health and sudden illness and death. Unskilled workers, including male chimney sweeps and market porters, and female domestic servants, seamstresses, embroiderers, braid weavers, and common day laborers, had no protection against the vicissitudes of the market. Such workers lived in rooming houses in the center of cities, or on the edge of town, where rents were cheaper.

If both partners were young, healthy, and could occasionally find work, marriage increased one's odds of survival. But economic crisis often pulled a couple apart, and one partner might be forced to leave to look for work elsewhere. In one village in central France, the priest reported that "in this place there are twenty-four poor families, who have about fifty children begging for the family bread."

At the century's end, almost 30 percent of the British population depended on some sort of poor relief and more than a million people were classified as "paupers" in England and Wales. Laborers, some of whom had been chased from village common lands by parliamentary acts of enclosure, wandered in search of manufacturing work. Thus, the chronically impoverished were constantly on the move, trying to find work. Yet, residents of a given village or neighborhood were far more likely to benefit from local charity than outsiders, who were feared as thieves or worse. Local officials and residents wanted beggars who were not from their community to move on. For this reason, beggars in Austrian law were referred to as "push people," because authorities always sought to push them away.

In France, in particular, many people survived by smuggling, a way of life made possible by the complexity of customs and tax jurisdictions, which made some commodities, above all, salt, much more expensive in one province than another. Prostitution provided a means for some women to get by, practicing their trade until disease or death ended their careers. In one French village, two sisters, unable to survive as seamstresses, admitted their clients as their blind father sat a few feet away. Such was the degradation that the struggle to survive sometimes entailed.

Meager harvests and bitter winters periodically took terrible tolls of the poor (1709–1710, 1739–1740, 1756–1757, 1766, 1775, and 1781–1788), when indigents in France were found frozen to death in church doorways, barns, or fields in the depth of winter. When a severe food shortage occurred or the police expelled beggars from large cities, country roads swarmed with young children who had been abandoned or told by their parents to make their way as best they could. The elderly, particularly widows, were often the poorest of the poor, unable to move elsewhere, depending on neighbors little better off than themselves.

Unlike peasants, who often could find solidarity and some material support in their villages, or upon occasion, from their lords, the urban poor were even more vulnerable to unrelenting misery. In Paris during the 1770s and 1780s, about one person out of six lived—and died—in a state of absolute impoverishment. However, in good times, market "strongmen," or porters, water-carriers, chimney sweeps and ditchdiggers could get by in "the economy of makeshifts."

The urban and rural poor were perpetually undernourished. Bread remained the basis of the diet of the vast majority of Europeans, consuming well more than half the family income—white bread for people of means; black bread (especially in the East), porridge or gruel made from rye, potatoes, or buckwheat (in Brittany and Russia) for everybody else. Vegetables—peas and beans, and cabbage in Central and Eastern Europe—were prized as occasional additions to soup or porridge. The consumption of meat by poor people was rare, except for heavily salted meat that could be preserved. Yet, the orphanage of Amsterdam, a relatively prosperous city, served meat and fish twice a week and vegetables once a week. But dried peas, beans, porridge, or gruel comprised most meals there. Fish and shellfish were common only at the sea's edge for people of ordinary means (especially because they were not allowed to fish in most rivers and ponds). Water, often not very clean, was the drink of necessity; wine and beer were beyond the budget of most people. Swiss peasants prosperous enough to drink coffee and eat chocolate were the exception in Europe. Yet, ordinary people experienced a modest improvement in housing conditions, diet, and health during the century.

Charitable works, however impressive, fell far short of relieving crushing poverty. In France, where about 40 percent of the population lived in poverty, charity could provide less than 5 percent of what was needed. During the Catholic Reformation of the second half of the sixteenth century, the Church had emphasized the importance of charitable works in the quest for eternal salvation. Most Protestants, too, believed in the importance of good works—after all, Christ had washed a beggar's feet. Parishes and, in Catholic countries, monasteries and convents, regularly provided what relief they could afford to the poor, particularly around Christmas and during Lent. Hospices and other charitable institutions cared for the sick, invalids, and the elderly as best they could. But during hard times, the number of abandoned infants increased dramatically, far beyond the capacity of institutions to care for them. Invariably the numbers of the desperately impoverished far exceeded the charitable resources available.

SOCIAL CONTROL

By the middle of the century, many upper-class Europeans believed that they had entered an age of clamoring crowds and even riots. In the 1770s and 1780s, particularly, the lower orders seemed increasingly less deferential. The poor protested the purchase and removal of grain from their markets at prices they could not afford. They stopped wagons, seized grain, and sold it at what they considered to be the "just price," that which would permit even the poor to buy enough to survive.

Artisanal work stoppages, too, became more widespread. Following a London strike by journeymen tailors protesting cuts in their pay, the British Parliament passed the first Combination Act in 1721. The law established wages and working conditions for tailors and allowed the jailing of striking workers without benefit of a trial. Seeing that many craftsmen and skilled workers were leaving Britain, some for the colonies, Parliament passed legislation forbidding their emigration.

Protecting Property

The British Parliament represented the interests of wealthy landowners, who consolidated their property during the eighteenth century. The property franchise ensured that only wealthy landowners could elect members of the House of Commons. The philosopher John Locke summed up the relationship between government and landed property in early modern England: "The great and chief end . . . of men uniting into commonwealths, and putting themselves under government, is the preservation of their property." Thus, in 1723, Parliament passed without discussion a law that added fifty separate offenses against property for which the death penalty could be imposed, although it rarely was.

Hunting was a badge of living nobly. It was a domesticated, non-lethal—at least for the hunters—version of warfare. The exclusive right to hunt was a vigilantly guarded prerogative of any and all who could claim noble status. But acts against poaching were invoked more often to protect the

A gamekeeper snags a poacher.

property of middle-class and even poor landowners. They were not simply measures taken by the rich against the poor.

Wealthy English landowners set brutal mantraps—including trap-guns —and snares that maimed poachers who snuck onto their property, including the "deer parks" established on land that had once been common land. The felonies listed under the Black Act, among them the blackening of one's face as a form of disguise—hence the law's name—included poaching game or fish, or chopping down trees or gleaning branches blown down in storms. Henry Fielding (1707–1754) called attention to such a felony in his novel *The Adventures of Joseph Andrews:* "Jesu!" said the Squire, "would you commit two persons to bridewell [prison] for a twig?" "Yes," said the Lawyer, "and with great leniency too; for if we had called it a young tree they would have been both hanged."

The concern for protecting property could be seen in legislation affecting marriage. The Marriage Act (1753) forbade clandestine marriages. While its central goal was to extend the uniformity of the law, it specifically sought to protect property against ambitious men who might be tempted to try to elope with the daughters of wealthy property owners. Parliament also passed a law permitting divorce by parliamentary act— which none but the very wealthy and well placed could seek—at least partially because gentlemen wanted to be free to divorce wives who shamed them with adultery or who could not produce heirs to inherit their estates.

Subordination and Social Control

During 1724–1733, the French state initiated the "great confinement" of paupers, beggars, and vagrants in workhouses, where they were to learn menial trades under conditions of strict discipline. The subsequent reorganization and expansion of royal efforts at policing the poor during the 1760s represented a marked increase in the reach of the state into rural life, as well as into cities and towns. Police carried out a policy of selective enforcement, in keeping with a current belief in the efficacy of exemplary punishment.

People of means debated strategies of social control with increasing urgency as economic crises in the 1770s and 1780s widened the gap between rich and poor. Some states established temporary programs of poor relief while enhancing the repressive capacity of the police and of hospitals and other institutions that took in vagrants and beggars. Milan's government began locking up beggars. Since the beginning of the seventeenth century, English parishes or townships provided charity to those wearing the requisite "P" for pauper. In order to keep indigents off the road, some towns established workhouses, where the poor would be forced to work in exchange for subsistence. Such places were notoriously unhealthy: of more than 2,300 children taken into London's workhouses during the 1750–1755 period, only 168 were alive at the end of the period (although some might have been discharged). A 1782 English law replaced workhouses with somewhat more humane "poorhouses." In 1795, the Speenhamland system, so called after the parish in which it was conceived, provided for a sliding scale of assistance, determined by the current price of bread and wage rates. But such programs merely scratched the surface as the problem of poverty entered public discourse to an unprecedented degree.

On the continent, the eighteenth century witnessed a largely successful campaign to limit the number of capital crimes to those that threatened life or the state. In contrast, Britain's Parliament added almost two hundred capital offenses to the law between 1688 and 1810, sixty-three of them between 1760 and 1810. About mid-century, two young men were arrested for poaching. Their wives went to the landlord's estate to beg his merciful intercession. The lord, moved to tears, said that their husbands would be returned to them. True to his word, he sent the two corpses to the wives.

But English juries, in particular, hesitated to convict those accused; only about two hundred criminals were executed each year. Executions—including that of a peer who claimed that his marriage had led him to

A public hanging at Tyburn in London.

murder his steward and who had asked to be hanged in his wedding suit—
drew huge throngs at London's Tyburn. Domestics convicted of stealing
from their masters or mistresses or workmen from their employers could
be executed, but corporal punishment, such as branding or being exhibited in stocks to public contempt, was far more common. Children were
worked and punished as adults, though not all as harshly as the seven-
year-old girl who was hanged in Norwich for stealing a petticoat. England
was relatively underpoliced, particularly when compared to France (Paris
had four times more policemen than London, which was twice its size).

The vocabulary adopted by the French police reflected the tendencies of
authorities everywhere to lump the poor into one of two broad categories—"deserving" and "undeserving." Other less general designations
included the poor, the truly poor, the shameful poor, the disabled poor,
the false poor, the indigent, the miserably poor, the beggar of good faith,
the shameful beggar, the professional beggar, and the wandering beggar.
The false beggar simulated horrifying wounds or injuries with the skill of a
makeup artist and, clutching at the clothes of the wealthy passing by, received a few cents as his benefactors scurried away as rapidly as possible.
These categories reflected the belief that many, if not most, of the poor
were destitute because they were lazy and that stiff punishment would be
enough to end begging.

In small bourgs, villages, and the countryside, people feared bands of
thieves, who by setting a fire could intimidate and rob by virtue of their
number, and who could destroy a harvest or a farm in a matter of minutes.
Brigandage was rampant in southern Italy and in Sicily. In France, some of
the most infamous bands were in the grain-rich Beauce region south of

Paris. There some bandits were known as *chauffeurs* because they held their victims' feet to the fire to force the victims to reveal the hiding place of their valuables, a tactic borrowed from marauding soldiers in the Thirty Years' War. Yet, many poor people considered some bandits heroes, Robin Hoods who stole from the rich and gave to the poor. One of the most notorious bands of thieves was organized by a Breton woman, driven to thievery when she could not support her family by peddling haberdashery at fairs. One of her daughters started her own band. It specialized in burglary and held together for ten years, protected by the people of her village, who greeted the police with stony silence and defiant claims that they could not understand the French language. Band members would tear the tongue from the mouth of a beggar who provided the rural police with incriminating information.

A CENTURY OF CONTRASTS

The eighteenth century was a period of contrasts. Musical performances at court and in châteaux and elegant townhouses took place while peasants and day laborers struggled to survive, toiling in fields they rarely owned, in forests belonging to the state or nobles, or working as dock or market porters, chimney sweeps, or common laborers in town. These con-

The capture of the French bandit-hero Cartouche in the early eighteenth century.

trasts were, to be sure, also geographic. The well-heeled financier, whole-sale merchant, manufacturer, or lawyer of Paris, Amsterdam, Barcelona, Vienna, or Milan lived in a vastly more cosmopolitan world, increasingly shaped by consumerism, than did the small middle classes of Prussia, Poland, Russia, and the Balkans, lands in which towns were few and far between. In the northern Italian states and the Austrian Netherlands, prosperous merchants and manufacturers were blurring the lines between nobles and wealthy commoners.

In many ways a century still dominated politically by nobles, the eigh-teenth century also was a dynamic period of economic and social transfor-mation, beginning with the Industrial Revolution in England, and with the increase in commerce and manufacturing in Northwestern Europe as well. These developments had political consequences during the 1760s and 1770s. The country gentlemen who invariably supported court poli-cies and those who often opposed them began to look and act like political parties. And the domination of political life by an oligarchy of landowners came under challenge from ordinary people without the right to vote. British colonists in North America protested the fact that they were taxed without representation, and then rebelled against British rule.

On the continent, denunciations of unwarranted privilege began to be heard. Calls for reform of the French absolute monarchy came even from one of the ministers of the king, who then tried to abolish guilds and insti-tute free trade. During political crises in the early 1770s, public opinion gradually began to see parlements as blocks against absolute rule and de-fenders of the rights of the "nation," a term that increasingly came into use. Elsewhere on the continent, too, opposition to entrenched privilege became more insistent in some places. At the same time, the thinkers of the Enlightenment (see Chapter 10) espoused freedom as a good in itself and as a motor of progress. Believing in popular sovereignty and rule by law, they opposed the accumulation of too much power by one or a few people. They, too, called for reform. The French Revolution of 1789 would, at least indirectly, be influenced by these ideals of the Enlighten-ment.

CHAPTER 10

ENLIGHTENED THOUGHT
AND THE REPUBLIC
OF LETTERS

"What is the Enlightenment?" wrote the German philosopher Immanuel Kant. His response was *"Dare to know!* Have the courage to make use of your own understanding," as exciting a challenge today as in the eighteenth century. During that period of contagious intellectual energy and enthusiastic quest for knowledge, the philosophes, the thinkers and writers of the Enlightenment, believed their role was to bring light and progress to the world through the application of reason to their reflections on the nature of mankind. Unlike most scientists of the eighteenth century, they wanted their ideas to reach the general reading public. Education therefore loomed large in this view of their mission. Their approach to education was not limited to formal schooling, but instead took in the development of the individual and the continued application of critical thinking throughout one's life.

The Enlightenment began in Paris but extended to much of Western Europe, including the German states, the Dutch Republic, Great Britain, and as far as North America. The philosophes' writings helped confirm French as the language of high culture in eighteenth-century Europe. Indeed, it was reported from Potsdam that at the court of Frederick the Great of Prussia "the language least spoken is German." But French was hardly the only language of philosophic discourse. In Italy, those influenced by the new thinking used the ideas of the philosophes to attack clerical and particularly papal influence in political life. In Britain the philosopher David Hume and Adam Smith, father of economic liberalism, represented the thought of "the Scottish Enlightenment."

The Enlightenment can be roughly divided into three stages. The first covers the first half of the eighteenth century and most directly reflects the influence of the Scientific Revolution; the second, the "high Enlight-

A metal struck to commemorate the death of John Locke. The two figures symbolize tolerance and justice.

enment," begins with the publication of *The Spirit of the Laws* (1748) by Charles-Louis de Montesquieu and ends in 1778 with the death of Voltaire and Jean-Jacques Rousseau; and the third, the late Enlightenment, influenced by Rousseau's work, marks a shift from an emphasis on human reason to a greater preoccupation with the emotions and passions of mankind. This final stage also features new ideas relating the concept of freedom to the working of economies, best represented by the thought of Adam Smith. At this time, too, several monarchs applied the philosophes' principle that rulers work for the good of their subjects. But these experiments in "enlightened absolutism" were most noted for rulers' organizing their states more effectively, further enhancing their authority. This third period saw popular diffusion of the lesser works of would-be philosophes seeking to capitalize on an expanding literary market. These works, too, were influential in undermining respect for the authority of the monarchy of France and thus indirectly contributed to the French Revolution.

ENLIGHTENED IDEAS

The philosophes espoused views of nature, mankind, society, government, and the intrinsic value of freedom that challenged some of the most fundamental tenets Europeans had held for centuries. Slavery, for example, violated their principle of human freedom. The implications of Enlightenment thought were revolutionary, because the philosophes argued that progress had been constrained by social and political institutions that did not reflect humanity's natural goodness and capacity for material and moral improvement. Although many philosophes saw no or little incompatibility between science and religion, they were skeptical of received truths. Thus, they challenged the doctrinal authority of the established churches and launched a crusade for the secularization of political institutions.

It is to the Enlightenment that we trace the origins of the belief that people should be ruled by law, not rulers, that a separation of powers ought to exist within government in order to prevent the accumulation of too much power in one or a few hands, the concept of popular sovereignty, and the assumption that it is the responsibility of rulers to look after the welfare of the people. The consequences of such modern views of sovereignty, political rights, and the organization of states would be seen in the French Revolution and the era of liberalism in the nineteenth century.

Intellectual Influences on Enlightened Thought

Like all intellectual and cultural movements, the Enlightenment did not emerge spontaneously. Creating what David Hume (1711–1776) called "the science of man," the philosophes reflected the influence of the Scientific Revolution, whose proponents had espoused scientific method in the study of nature and the universe. Sir Isaac Newton, the brilliant English scientist and theoretician (see Chapter 8), emphasized that science—reason and experimentation—holds the key to understanding nature, that mankind discovers knowledge, not through religious teaching, but through "observation, analysis, and experiment."

Two thinkers linked the Scientific Revolution and Enlightenment thought: John Locke and Georges-Louis Buffon. Locke (1632–1704) claimed that philosophy was, as much as astronomy, a discipline subject to the rigors of scientific method and critical inquiry. The son of a landowner and a member of the scientific-minded British Royal Society, Locke maintained a strong interest in medicine. After returning from Holland, where he had gone into self-imposed exile during the political crisis swirling around the throne of King James II, Locke remained close to the government of King William and Queen Mary.

Locke believed that the scientific method could be applied to the study of society. In *An Essay Concerning Human Understanding* (1690), Locke postulated that each individual is a *tabula rasa*, or blank slate at birth. Believing that all knowledge is sensory, Locke denied inherited abilities and rejected the idea that humanity is stained by original sin. He anticipated that the discovery of more laws of nature would be the basis of secular laws on which society should be based. He was confident that mankind might thereby be able to improve social conditions.

Locke had asserted the dignity of the individual in contending that every person has the right to life, liberty, and property (though he excluded slaves in the Americas from such innate rights). He argued that monarchies were based on a social contract between rulers and the ruled. People had to relinquish some of their liberty in exchange for security. But, unlike Thomas Hobbes, Locke insisted that mankind's liberty and rights stemmed from the laws of nature. He became a leading proponent of educational reform, freedom of the press, religious toleration, and the separation of political powers.

Locke's interest in the relationship between nature and the social order led him to consider issues of gender. The assumption that the king ruled his nation as a husband and father ruled his wife and children had been prominent in early modern political theory, only briefly challenged by a handful of radicals during the English Civil War of the 1640s. John Locke argued against the contemporary vision of the state in which "all power on earth is either derived from or usurped from the fatherly power." He denied the appropriateness of the analogy between the family and the state as patriarchal institutions. Rejecting the contemporary view that Adam held supremacy over Eve, he viewed marriage, like government, to be organized by social contract. However, Locke went no further than that, and his espousal of equality within marriage remained only an ideal. In everyday life, he believed that women should defer to men. But Locke's precocious analysis of the family as an institution nonetheless helped stimulate intellectual interest in studying the social role of women.

More than any of his contemporaries, Georges-Louis Buffon (1707–1788) linked the Scientific Revolution to the Enlightenment. Buffon, whose initial presentation to the French Royal Academy of Science was a study of probability theory applied to gambling on hopscotch, became the curator of the Royal Gardens. Surrounded by monkeys and badgers in his laboratory, he carried out many experiments, some of which worked, such as his study of the burning effect of the sun through glass, and some of which did not, including his study of the emotional life of birds. Buffon's experiments with cooling metals led him to build a large forge near his home in Burgundy.

The philosophes acknowledged their debt to the late-seventeenth-century proponents of the scientific method. Voltaire saluted Newton, whose funeral he attended in London's Westminster Abbey, for having called on scientists and philosophers "to examine, weigh, calculate, and measure, but never conjecture." Hume insisted that all knowledge came from reason and experience, that is, from critical inquiry and scientific discovery, and that the ability to reason distinguished mankind from other animals. Many philosophes, reflecting the influence of the Scientific Revolution, considered religion, the origins of which they found not in reason but in faith and custom, to be a social phenomenon, like any other to be studied scientifically. Hume blasted away at the idea of religious truths revealed through the Bible. Montesquieu asked, "Is it possible for those who understand nature and have a reasonable idea of God to believe that matter and created things are only 6,000 years old?"

The very universality of their principles led some of the philosophes to suggest that a sense of morality—of what is right and wrong—might vary across cultures, because it emerged from the nature of mankind, but not from religious teaching. Diderot, influenced by Locke, argued that sensory stimulation, or in the case of people who are blind, deprivation, shapes individual moral responses, and that moral principles for a blind man might be somewhat different from those for someone who could see. He described the so-called "savages" of distant Tahiti as forming a rational social order without the benefit of any ecclesiastical doctrine. Hume called for a "science of morals" to serve the interests of Christians, and found a following among Scottish Presbyterian clergy.

The Republic of Ideas

The philosophes' calls for reform were sometimes subtle, sometimes boldly forceful. Yet, they did not lead insurrections. Their pens and pencils were their only weapons as they sought to change the way people thought. They communicated their ideas in letters, unpublished manuscripts, books, pamphlets, brochures, and through writing novels, poetry, drama, literary and art criticism, and political philosophy.

The philosophes glorified the collegiality and interdependence of writers within the "republic of letters," what the men and women of the Enlightenment sometimes called the informal international community of philosophes. By the mid-eighteenth century, Voltaire could claim with some exaggeration that the professional writer stood at the top of the social summit. He, Montesquieu, and Denis Diderot accepted election to the prestigious French Royal Academy, revealing their ambivalence toward the monarchy that they attacked, however subtly, in their work. The most famous of the philosophes gained money as well as prestige, although Voltaire, Montesquieu, and Holbach were among the few who could support themselves by writing.

The philosophes may have shared the fundamental ideas of the Enlightenment, but significant differences existed among them. They came from different social classes, generations, and nations. And they often disagreed, like people in any republic, arguing in person, by letter, and in their published work. They could not agree, for example, whether the ideal state was an enlightened, benevolent monarchy, a monarchy balanced by a parliamentary body representing the nobility, or a kind of direct democracy. Their views on religion also varied. Montesquieu, Voltaire, and Rousseau were deists. Because scientific inquiry seemed to have demonstrated that the persistent intervention of God was unnecessary to keep the world in motion, they viewed God as a watchmaker who set the world in motion according to the laws of nature and then left knowledge and hu-

Voltaire presiding (with his arm raised) over a dinner gathering of philosophes, including Denis Diderot, who is sitting on the far left.

man progress to the discovery and action of mankind. In contrast, Diderot, one of the principal spokesmen of the Enlightenment, became an atheist.

For all the variety and richness of the republic of letters, four philosophes dominated Enlightenment discourse with what were for the time truly startling ideas about society, religion, and politics: Montesquieu, Voltaire, Diderot, and Rousseau. Each is well worth considering separately.

Montesquieu

Montesquieu (born Charles-Louis de Secondat; 1689–1755) inherited a feudal château near Bordeaux and a small income upon the death of his father. He studied law and later inherited from a wealthy relative more property and the title of baron de Montesquieu, as well as the presidency of the noble parlement, or provincial sovereign law court, seated at Bordeaux.

In 1721, after moving to Paris, Montesquieu published the *Persian Letters*. In the form of reports sent home by two Persian visitors to Paris, his work detailed political and social injustices of life in the West. By casting this critique of eighteenth-century France in the form of a travelogue, Montesquieu was able to dodge royal censorship. The work irritated many people, including ecclesiastics who resented its insinuation that the pope was a "magician." As for the king of France, the Persians reported that he "is the most powerful of European potentates. He has no mines of gold like his neighbor, the king of Spain: but he is much wealthier than that prince, because his riches are drawn from a more inexhaustible source, the vanity of his subjects. He has undertaken and carried on great wars, without any other supplies than those derived from the sale of titles of honors." But beneath the satire of the *Persian Letters*, Montesquieu was arguing the point that nature reveals a universal standard of justice that applies for all people in all places at all times, in Islamic Persia as in Christian France.

Montesquieu's ideas reflected the increased contact between Europeans and much of the rest of the world. Merchants, soldiers, missionaries, and colonists had followed the first European explorers to, among other places, the Americas and Asia. Published accounts of travel stirred the imagination of upper-class Europeans who were interested in their societies and in cultures that lay on the fringes or beyond their continent.

In *Persian Letters*, Montesquieu also offered the first critical examination of the institution of slavery by one of the philosophes. He rejected slavery as an extension of despotism, concluding that "slavery is against natural law, by which all men are born free and independent" because "the liberty of each citizen is part of public liberty." He argued that slavery, in contrast, compromised "the general good of men [and] that of particular societies."

The Spirit of the Laws (1748) inaugurated the high Enlightenment. In it, Montesquieu applied the principles of observation, experimentation, and analysis, which lie at the heart of scientific inquiry, to the social and political foundations of states. He described the relationship between climate, religion, and tradition, and the historical evolution of a nation's political life. Laws, he argued, are subject to critical inquiry and historical study because they develop over time. Historians, freeing themselves from the influence of the Church, could now study "general causes, whether moral or physical."

The British political system fascinated Montesquieu, who went to England in 1729 for two years. He was impressed by the historical role of Parliament, a representative body unlike French parlements, or law courts, despite the similarity of their names. The English Parliament seemed an "intermediate power" that had during the Civil War prevented Britain from becoming either a monarchical despotism or a republic, which he identified with chaos. Montesquieu's point was that each political system and legal tradition evolved differently. He feared that the French monarchy was showing signs of becoming despotic because it lacked the separation of powers found in England. Only constitutionalism, he argued, could combine the guarantees for order (offered by monarchy) with those of freedom. Montesquieu believed that noble rights and the maintenance of municipal privileges that had long been eroded by royal absolutism in France could stave off monarchical depotism. Moreover, Montesquieu ar-

(*Left*) Montesquieu. (*Right*) Voltaire.

gued that the sovereignty of the king came not from God, but from the people.

Voltaire

Brilliant, witty, and sarcastic, Voltaire (born François-Marie Arouet; 1694–1778) was the most widely read, cited, and lionized of the philosophes. He was the son of a notary who had enhanced his family's position through a favorable marriage. Voltaire's parents, who wanted him to be a lawyer, sent him to Paris to be educated by the Jesuits. Instead, the brash, ambitious young man made a name for himself as a dramatist and poet—though many of these early works are quite forgettable. Voltaire developed a pen as quick and cutting as a sword. Some of his early works were banned in France; everything he ever wrote was forbidden in Spain. Imprisoned in the Bastille in Paris for having mocked one of the king's relatives, he took the name "de Voltaire" for unknown reasons. He soon ran into more trouble, beaten by servants while a noble he had insulted watched in silent triumph.

Like Montesquieu, Voltaire reflected the Anglophilia of the thinkers of the early and high Enlightenment. He extolled Britain, its commercial empire, relative religious toleration, and freedom of the press. "The English are the only people on earth," he wrote, "who have been able to prescribe limits to the power of kings by resisting them: and who, by a series of struggles, have at last established that wise Government, where the Prince is all powerful to do good, and at the same time is restrained from committing evil."

Unlike the noble Montesquieu, who hoped the parlements would balance the power of the monarchy, as they did in Britain, Voltaire had little faith in them. Voltaire saw them as representing the narrow and selfish interests of the nobility. He believed that the only representative body that might guarantee the natural rights of the king's subjects in France would be the equivalent of the British House of Commons. Whereas Montesquieu looked to the nobility to protect people from monarchical despotism, Voltaire counted on the enlightened monarchs of centralized states to protect their people against nobles' self-interest.

Voltaire claimed that the political organization of each state was at least partially determined by its specific history and circumstances. As science should study the world of nature, so should the philosophe trace the separate development of nations. This line of reasoning convinced him that Montesquieu was wrong to think that the British political system could be successfully transplanted to France.

Voltaire reserved his most scathing attacks for the Church, an institution, like the parlements, that seemed to him to block the development of freedom in his own country. His impassioned cry for a battle against the teaching of the Church—"*Écrasez l'infâme!*" ("Crush the horrible thing!")—became his motto. Of monks, he once said, "They sing, they eat, they digest." The pope and the Parlement of Paris both condemned his polemical *Philosophical Dictionary* (1764). Voltaire believed that there were times when one has to tear down before one can build. His attacks were clever yet devastating; for example, his pithy description of the Chinese as having "an admirable religion free from superstition and the rage to persecute" was read by virtually everyone as suggesting that in France the opposite was true.

Voltaire, a deist, believed that God created the universe and then let it operate according to scientific laws. He espoused a natural religion based upon reason while repudiating the Church itself. "Almost everything that goes beyond the adoration of a supreme being and of submitting one's heart to his eternal order is superstition . . . the fewer superstitions, the less fanaticism; and the less fanaticism, the fewer calamities," he insisted. At least some of what has often been taken for his anti-Semitism was, in fact, part of Voltaire's unrestrained assault on what he considered another variety of religious dogmatism built not upon reason but on faith alone.

Voltaire intended *Candide* (1759) to be an indictment of fanaticism and superstition. In the short tale, the cheerful optimist Candide bumbles from disaster to disaster. Here Voltaire confronts the seeming contradiction between the goodness of God and the evil in the world. He writes about the earthquake that ravaged Lisbon in 1755, killing thousands of people and destroying much of the Portuguese capital. If God is all good and omniscient, why, Voltaire reasoned, would He allow such an event to occur?

But Voltaire nonetheless believed that religion was beneficial because it offered people hope, and therefore made their lives more bearable. It also kept them in line: "If God did not exist, one would have to invent him. I want my attorney, my tailor, my servants, even my wife to believe in God, and I think that I shall then be robbed and cuckholded less often." Voltaire's belief that religion provided a public service by inducing people to act according to moral principles contrasted with that of Diderot, who believed that mankind's essential goodness made organized religion unnecessary.

Voltaire's fame spread when he took up the cause of a man who seemed wrongly accused of murder. In 1761, Jean Calas, a Protestant from Toulouse, stood accused of murdering his own son, who had been found hanging in the family basement. The young Calas had intended to convert to Catholicism. Convicted by the Parlement of Toulouse, the father was tortured to death, though it seemed likely that his son had committed suicide. Voltaire launched a campaign against the parlement. He began his own investigation, attacking what seemed a preposterous conviction followed by barbaric torture. Several years later, the parlement reversed its earlier decision—too late, however, for Jean Calas. But the Calas Affair helped put the philosophes' critique of religious intolerance into the limelight of public opinion. "Shout everywhere, I beg you, for Calas," thundered Voltaire, "and against fanaticism, for it is *l'infâme* that has caused their misery."

Voltaire's energetic interest in the Calas Affair reflected not only his scathing rejection of the notion that "this is the best of all possible worlds" but also his insistence that progress is somehow inevitable without human action. He concludes *Candide* with the famous, though seemingly ambiguous, advice that "one must cultivate one's own garden," as he did at his rural retreat. But Voltaire was counseling anything but a withdrawal into the sanctuary of introspection. He called for each person to follow the path of light and do battle with those institutions that seemed to stand in the way of humanity's potential. The possibility of human action gave Voltaire confidence and hope. In 1764 he predicted, "Everything I see scatters the seeds of a revolution which will definitely come . . . Enlightenment has gradually spread so widely that it will burst into full light at the first right opportunity, and then there will be a fine uproar. Lucky are the young, for they will see great things."

Denis Diderot

Diderot's monumental *Encyclopedia* best reflected the collaborative nature of the Enlightenment, as well as its wide influence. Denis Diderot (1713–1784), the son of an artisan, was something of a jack of intellectual trades, a man of letters who wrote plays, art criticism, history, theology, and philosophy. Like Voltaire educated by the Jesuits, he flirted with the idea of becoming a priest, and for a time supported himself by writing sermons for bishops. Unlike Montesquieu and Voltaire, Diderot underwent a

An illustration of mining in Denis Diderot's *Encyclopedia.*

rugged apprenticeship in the "republic of letters." He penned a porno-graphic novel to earn enough to indulge the fancies of his mistress. But he also argued that through centuries of male domination, women, despite their capacity for reproduction, had come to be considered inferior to men. Diderot claimed that laws that limited the rights of women were counter to nature.

The *Encyclopedia,* on which Diderot worked for twenty-five years, stands as the greatest monument of the Enlightenment. At the heart of the project lay the philosophes' insistence that knowledge was rational, and therefore ordered, following laws of nature. Social and political institu-tions should be submitted to standards of rationality. All things, as Diderot put it, are equally subject to criticism. By elevating mankind to the center of human inquiry, the authors of the *Encyclopedia* sought to achieve Diderot's goal, "to change the general way of thinking," as well as to bring glory to France.

Voltaire had set a goal for the Enlightenment itself: to educate the liter-ate and intellectually curious of the social elite, and perhaps people fur-ther down the social scale. The *Encyclopedia* at least partially fulfilled that goal. Published over a period of more than twenty years beginning in 1751, it consisted of 60,000 articles and 2,885 illustrations in twenty-eight volumes. Subtitled "A Classified Dictionary of the Sciences, Arts and

Trades," this first such compilation in the West was a bold attempt to organize and classify all knowledge gathered from "over the face of the earth."
Its authors insisted that by learning more about the universe, men and
women could improve the world. This marked a departure from the assumption that mankind's ability to penetrate the secrets of the universe
was limited. Montesquieu contributed sections on taste, Rousseau on music, Voltaire on literature, and Buffon on nature. Diderot gave particular
credit to the contributions of everyday artisans by describing how and why
ingeniously simple tools and machines could make tasks easier.

The *Encyclopedia* generated sufficient excitement that advance sales
alone financed its publication. It earned its publishers a handsome profit.
After the first edition, subsequent editions with less expensive paper and
fewer illustrations became available at about a sixth of the original price.
Lawyers, officials, and rentiers (people living from property income) were
more likely to own a copy than merchants or manufacturers, who could afford the volumes but seemed less interested. What began as a luxury product ended up on the shelves of the "middling sort."

The philosophes wanted the *Encyclopedia* to carry the Enlightenment
far beyond the borders of France. Although only about one in ten volumes
traveled beyond the country, its pattern of distribution in the 1770s and
1780s reflected the success of the enterprise (see Map 10.1). To contemporaries, the *Encyclopedia* seemed to embody Kant's bold challenge, "Dare
to know!"

Through Swiss, Dutch, and German booksellers, among others, the
Encyclopedia reached readers in London, Brussels, Turin, Munich, and
St. Petersburg, among other European capitals. The *Encyclopedia*'s pro-
spectus and booksellers' advertisements assured potential buyers that
ownership would proclaim one's standing as a person of knowledge, a
philosophe. In northern Germany and Scandinavia, customers were described as "sovereign princes" and "Swedish seigneurs." A few copies
reached distant African settlements, including the Cape of Good Hope.
Thomas Jefferson helped promote the *Encyclopedia* in America, finding
several subscribers, among them Benjamin Franklin. There was an Italian
edition, despite the opposition of the Church, and a priest was among
those taking orders for it. However, in Spain, Inquisition censorship
frightened booksellers and buyers alike, and in Portugal only a few copies
got by the police.

The *Encyclopedia* did implicitly challenge monarchical authority. It presented ideas that some powerful people did not want in the public domain.
Rousseau and Paul-Henri Holbach (1723–1789) wrote enthusiastically
about representative government and even popular sovereignty, though
only Rousseau came close to espousing a republic.

After initially tolerating the project, French royal censors banned Volume 7 in 1757, after an unsuccessful assassination attempt on Louis XV.
Diderot, whose first serious philosophical work had been burned by the

MAP 10.1 DIFFUSION OF DIDEROT'S *ENCYCLOPEDIA* Subscriptions to Diderot's *Encyclopedia* throughout Europe.

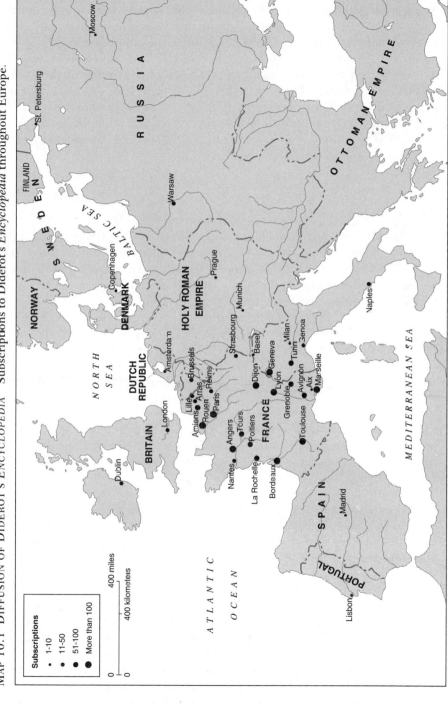

public executioner, was briefly imprisoned before being released on a promise of good behavior. Although the philosophes left their skeptical challenge to the Church implicit, disguising the pope in one satire as a figure in Japanese robes, the pope condemned the volumes in 1759.

In the 1770s, the French state again tolerated the *Encyclopedia*, which it now treated more as a commodity than as an ideological threat to monarchy or Church. The small skirmishes fought over the volumes had more to do with rivalries between publishers, between those privileged with official favor and those without. In this way, Diderot's grand project symbolized the ongoing political struggles within the French monarchy itself.

Jean-Jacques Rousseau

The place of Jean-Jacques Rousseau (1712–1778) in the Enlightenment is far more ambiguous than that of Diderot and his *Encyclopedia*. Rousseau embraced human freedom, but more than any other of the philosophes, Rousseau idealized emotion, instinct, and spontaneity, which he believed to be, with reason, essential parts of human nature.

The son of a Geneva watchmaker, Rousseau, a Protestant, went to Paris as a young man in the hope of becoming a composer. The arrogant, self-righteous Rousseau received an introduction into several aristocratic Parisian salons, informal upper-class gatherings hosted by noble women at which ideas were discussed, where he became friendly with Diderot. In 1749, the Academy of Dijon sponsored an essay contest on the question of whether the progress of science had strengthened or weakened morality. Rousseau's essay concluded that primitive or natural humanity had embodied the essential goodness of mankind; and that in order for humanity to be happy, new social and political institutions would be necessary. Young Rousseau won first prize.

Rousseau remained a contentious loner. By 1762, he had quarreled with the other philosophes. Voltaire mocked his insistence that emotion and passion held sway over pure reason. Exiled by the Parlement of Paris because his writings offended monarchy and Church, he moved back to his native Geneva. After being forced to leave Geneva in the early 1770s following the condemnation of his work, he abandoned his children in an orphanage—as his father had abandoned him—and set off to visit England. The rest of Rousseau's life was marked by increasingly quarrelsome and paranoid behavior. He assumed that when his former friends disagreed with his ideas, they knew that he was right but simply refused to admit it. Gradually he became overwhelmed with thoughts of revenge against those whom he considered to have wronged him. In his *Confessions* (the first volume of which appeared in 1782), he appealed to future generations to see how contemporary thinkers had misinterpreted or misrepresented him.

(Left) Portrait of Jean-Jacques Rousseau. *(Right)* Rousseau and Voltaire in symbolic battle, a clash of ideas and wills.

In his *Discourse on the Arts and Sciences* (1762), Rousseau argued that civilization had corrupted the natural goodness of man, which he called the "fundamental principle" of political thought. The untempered quest for private property had disrupted the harmony that had once characterized mankind in its primitive state by creating a hierarchy of wealth. Rousseau's idealization of relatively primitive, uncomplicated and, he thought, manageable social and political groupings led him to believe that a republic, such as his own Geneva, alone offered its citizens the possibility of freedom. Its size permitted men wealthy enough to enjoy full political rights to participate directly in decision making. However, Rousseau remained suspicious of representative government, believing that people might ultimately vote themselves into slavery by electing unworthy representatives.

As free people in primitive societies joined together for mutual protection, enlightened people could join together for their mutual development in a kind of direct democracy. This view more than likely reflected his support for artisans' guilds and other small, self-governing groups that characterized Old Regime France. In Rousseau's idealized small state, executive authority would be separate from, yet subordinate to, the legislative power. He was, however, vague on how precisely people were to be organized and governed.

The final period of the Enlightenment prefigured nineteenth-century romanticism by giving emotion more free play, as the sensitive individual is awed by nature. Rousseau's *Émile* (1762) became one of the literary sensations of the century. Beginning "Everything is good as it comes from the hands of the Author of nature, but everything degenerates in the hands of man," the novel describes what he considered to be the ideal natural, secular education of the young Émile, who is gradually exposed by his tutor to nature during walks to explore brooks and mills. Rousseau intended such wonders to stimulate Émile's emotions, which were to be developed before his sense of reason, "the one that develops last," Rousseau claims, "and with the greatest difficulty." Émile's primitive virtue must be preserved against the vices of culture, but also developed as an end in itself so that he becomes a developed, autonomous person. Rousseau assigns Sophie, Émile's chosen "well-born" spouse, an education appropriate to what Rousseau considered a woman's lower status in life. Yet, even Rousseau's insistence on the capacity of women for intellectual development surprised many contemporaries, and was ahead of its time.

Voltaire ridiculed Rousseau's espousal of primitiveness as virtue: "I have received, Monsieur, your new book against the human race, and I thank you. No one has employed so much intelligence turning men into beasts. One starts wanting to walk on all fours after reading your book. However, in more than sixty years I have lost the habit." But, in fact, Rousseau clearly believed in social organization, because it seemed to offer mankind the possibility of achieving freedom from revealed religious truths.

In *The Social Contract* (1762), Rousseau tried to resolve the question of how people could join together in society to find protection and justice for person and property, and yet remain free individuals. Locke had described the relationship between a ruler and his people as a contractual one. Hobbes, in contrast, had argued that individuals could find refuge from the brutality of the state of nature only by surrendering their rights to an absolute ruler in exchange for safety. Rousseau imagined a social contract in which the individual surrenders his or her natural rights to the "general will" in order to find order and security. By general will, Rousseau meant the consensus of a community of citizens with equal political rights. Citizens would live in peace because they would be ruled by other citizens, not by dynastic rulers eager to expand their territorial holdings.

Although *The Social Contract* remained largely unknown until after the French Revolution of 1789, it offered an unparalleled critique of contemporary society. Rousseau summed up his thinking with the stirring assertion that "men are born free yet everywhere they are in chains." Whereas Voltaire and other philosophes hoped that rulers would become enlightened, Rousseau insisted that sovereignty comes not from kings or oligarchies, or even from God. Sovereignty comes, he argued persuasively, through the collective search for freedom.

THE DIFFUSION AND EXPANSION OF THE ENLIGHTENMENT

The groundwork for the Enlightenment lay not only in the realm of ideas—those of the Scientific Revolution and Locke—but also in gradual social changes that affected the climate of opinion. These changes, especially but not exclusively found in France, included the declining role of religion in the eighteenth century, at least in some regions, and the emergence of a more broadly based culture.

Religious Enthusiasm and Skepticism

During the first half of the seventeenth century, the Catholic Reformation seems to have engendered a slow but steady religious revival in France, Spain, and the Habsburg domains, where the founding of new religious orders, monasteries, and the popularity of the cults and shrines of local saints reflected religious intensity. Moreover, the established churches still retained formidable authority and prestige.

The development late in the seventeenth century of Pietism among Protestants in the North German states, emphasizing preaching and the study of the Bible, reflected another dimension of both mounting dissatisfaction with established religions and the existence of considerable religious creativity. Disaffected by abstract theological debates and by the Lutheran Church's hierarchical structure, Pietists wanted to reaffirm the Protestant belief in the primacy of the individual conscience. Like English Puritans and French Jansenists, they called for a more austere religion. They wanted a revival of piety and good works, and asked that laymen take an active role in religious life. For Pietists, Bible-reading and small discussion groups replaced the more elaborate, formal services of the Lutherans, helping to expand interest in German language and culture among the upper classes. But by the last quarter of the century, Pietist influence had waned, reflecting not only the diffusion of Enlightenment thought but also the fact that Lutheranism remained the state religion in the northern German states, maintaining a hold on the universities. Likewise the fact that Jansenists were able to win and maintain a wide following in France, despite official proscription, can be taken as evidence of the strength of religious feeling.

In Britain, religious practice seems to have increased among all social classes. The Anglican Church of England was the Established Church, but Britain also had about half a million non-Anglican Protestants, or Dissenters, at the end of the eighteenth century. As many were middle class, some Presbyterians, Congregationalists, Unitarians, Baptists, and Quakers sent their sons to private academies. Yet, Oxford and Cambridge Universities admitted only Anglicans. Moreover, anti-Catholicism was still prevalent in England, where there were about 70,000 Catholics in 1770, most of them in the lower classes.

Although many Baptists, Congregationalists, and Quakers, among other Dissenters, had traditionally been laborers, there was not a particular religion that held the allegiance of ordinary people in England in the eighteenth century until the ministry of John Wesley (1703–1791). An

Anglican trained in theology at Oxford, the intense, brooding Wesley began to believe that his mission was to infuse ordinary people (who seemed ignored by the Established Church) with religious enthusiasm.

Wesley never formally broke with the Anglican Church nor claimed to be setting up a new denomination. Yet, that was the effect of his lifetime of preaching directly to ordinary people on grassy knolls, in open fields, and on highways, and of writing religious tracts directed at ordinary Britons. Wesley, who is said to have given more than 40,000 sermons, attracted about 100,000 followers to Methodism. Stressing personal conversion, Methodism suggested that all people were equal before God's eyes. This offended some upper-class English men and women, not the least because Methodists shouted out their beliefs and sometimes publicly confessed sins that the upper classes thought best left unnamed. A duchess explained that she hated the Methodists, because "it is monstrous to be told that you have a heart as sinful as the common wretches that crawl on the earth. This is highly offensive and insulting and at variance with high rank and good breeding."

Methodist evangelism was both a dynamic and stabilizing force in British society. There was little or nothing politically or socially radical about Wesley, as shown by his unwillingness to break formally with the Established Church. Far from preaching rebellion or revolution, Wesley encouraged work and self-discipline and abstinence from dancing, drinking, and gambling. Popular protest affronted Wesley's sense of respectability.

The Angelican Church, in turn, began to recruit followers among the lower classes. It established associations like the Society for the Promotion of Christian Knowledge and Anglican Sunday schools, which provided poor children with food and catechism. The evangelical Hannah More (1745–1833), the "bishop in petticoats," abandoned the material comforts of upper-class life for the challenges of bringing religion to the poor. In general, although some evangelicals favored improvements in working conditions, most remained politically conservative.

Yet, by the middle of the eighteenth century, in some of Europe religion seemed to play a significantly smaller role in the lives of people of all classes, particularly in regions with expanding economies and relatively high literacy rates. The number of men and women entering the clergy in France declined, as male and female monastic orders lost a third of their members between 1770 and 1790 alone. Fewer wills requested that Masses be said for the deceased or for souls in Purgatory. A Venetian theologian at mid-century claimed that the people of his state had become "de-christianized." Popular dislike of the exemption of the clergy from taxes increased, although the Church offered the monarchy a sizable yearly contribution from its vast wealth. Thus, the philosophes who challenged the role of the established churches in public life were addressing many readers who had lost interest in organized religion.

Expansion of the Cultural Base

The growing influence of the middle class in England and Northwestern Europe also began slowly to transform cultural life, expanding interest in literature, music, and the arts. The number of literary and other associations reflected this change. Lines between the nobility and the wealthy bourgeoisie became less fixed; culture moved from the closed world of court and château into the public domain.

Increasing literacy expanded the size of the potential audience of the philosophes. By the end of the century, somewhere between half and two-thirds of men in England, France, the Netherlands, and the German states could read. A smaller proportion of women—between a third to a half of the female population of these countries—was literate. A far smaller percentage of people could read in Southern Europe, and few people indeed in Eastern Europe and Russia. Opportunities for women, even those from noble families, to obtain more than a minimal education remained quite rare, although several German states began schools for girls. Even Marie-Antoinette, queen of France and one of the wealthiest people in the world, was so poorly educated that she made frequent grammatical and spelling errors.

Publishers, for example in the northern Italian states of Tuscany and Venice, fed the growing appetites of readers eager to know what events were transpiring in their own and other countries. Newspapers published one or two times a week summarized events transpiring in other countries. The number of English periodicals increased sixfold between 1700 and 1780, reflecting an increasing interest in science and natural history. In the German states, the number of books and magazines published grew threefold during the century's last decades. Novels gained in popularity at the expense of books on theology and popular piety. English female novelists gave women an unprecedented public voice in Britain, presenting their heroines as affectionate companions to their husbands and good mothers. Sentimental novels presented syrupy stories of domestic life and tender love. Nevertheless, traditional literature, such as religious tracts, popular almanacs, and folktales, remained the most widely read literature.

The Enlightenment had a direct influence on the growing popularity of history. Reflecting their interest in understanding human experience, the philosophes helped create history as a modern discipline. Since the classical Greeks, there had been relatively little interest in history in Europe. Church fathers, espousing the primacy of theology and viewing the world as little more than a test to prepare Christians for the afterlife, were generally uninterested in history. But suddenly all human experience, including non-Western cultures, emerged as suitable for historical inquiry. Edward Gibbon (1737–1794) was inspired to undertake his *History of the Decline and Fall of the Roman Empire* (published over a period of twelve years beginning in 1776) by visiting the Colosseum of Rome. Natural science, too, developed a following.

There were also more lending libraries than ever before, at least in Western Europe, as well as reading circles or clubs, some organized by resourceful booksellers. In Paris, London, Milan, Berlin, and other large cities, lending libraries rented books for as short a period as an hour. Household libraries became more common. Reading, which heretofore had largely been a group activity in which a literate person read to others—in the same way that storytellers spun their yarns—became more of a private, individual undertaking.

While some of the most significant works of the Enlightenment were virtually unknown outside the republic of letters, others became the best-sellers of the age. Montesquieu's *Spirit of the Laws* went through twenty-two printings—approximately 35,000 copies—in the first eighteen months after publication in 1748. Buffon's thirty-volume study, *The System of Nature* (1749–1804)—despite its bulk—also enjoyed prodigious success. Voltaire's short novel *Candide* was reprinted eight times in 1759, the year of its publication. Abbé Guillaume Raynal's *The Philosophical and Political History of European Colonies and Commerce in the Two Indies* (1770) was reprinted seventy times. Its descriptions of the colonization of the New World, Asia, and Africa, including the development of the slave trade, which he denounced in no uncertain terms, reached an eager market.

Painting

The philosophes sought the same status and freedom for artists as they demanded for writers. They believed that the arts had to be unfettered by censorship in order to thrive, and subject to critical inquiry. Critics helped shape public taste with reviews of paintings, circulated as pamphlets, which generated strong debate and comment.

Some philosophes worked toward a philosophy of art, but they did not espouse a single theory. The distinguished English portrait painter Joshua Reynolds (1723–1792), president of the Royal Academy, believed that classical rules preserved from antiquity had to be followed. But Hume, among other Enlightenment figures, emphasized the aesthetic appreciation of art, rejecting formal rules or standards for art imposed by royal academies or ecclesiastical influence. Diderot, who wrote two mediocre plays, and the German dramatist and critic Gotthold Lessing (1729–1781) called for the theater to portray the lives and passions of ordinary people, instead of only kings and queens, princes and princesses, saints and sinners.

The secularization of culture could be seen in the development of rococo, a new and generally secular decorative style. It evolved from the highly ornamental baroque style that had characterized the art and architecture of the Catholic Reformation, particularly in Austria and Bavaria.

A room in a nobleman's elegant townhouse, furnished in the rococo style.

Closely tied to noble taste, rococo's popularity in France reflected the fact that many nobles now spent more time away from Versailles, in their own country châteaux or, above all, in elegant Parisian townhouses. However spacious, such urban residences afforded them less room than they enjoyed in the countryside. They therefore lavished more attention on decoration.

The rococo style—sometimes called Louis XV style—began in France but also became quite popular in the German and Italian states. Like the baroque, it featured flowing curves, thus suggesting rocks and shells (*rocailles* and *coquilles*), forming its name. Rococo stresses smallness of scale, reducing baroque forms to elegant decorative style, as in gilded molding for theaters or manor bedrooms. It utilized different materials, including wood, metal, stucco, glass, and porcelain, brought for the first time from China during the century and reflecting the West's growing interest in Asia. It combined texture and color with spirited and even erotic subject matter. Elements drawn from nature, such as birds and flowers, replaced religious objects as decorative elements.

Although Greek mythology and religious themes remained popular, eighteenth-century painters found new sources for artistic inspiration.

The French painter Jean Antoine Watteau (1684–1721) influenced the artistic move away from traditional religious subjects laden with didactic meaning toward lighter, even playful, and more secular themes. Adopting a more realistic style than baroque painting, he often depicted elegantly dressed noble subjects at leisure. Breaking away from the system of direct patronage, Watteau sold his paintings through an art dealer. Painters, like François Boucher (1703–1770), who followed him, adopted the rococo style, emphasizing smallness of scale, as well as elegance and frivolity. As the market for painting widened, scenes of nature and everyday life also became popular.

The expanding middle-class art market and the growing secularization of artistic taste was nowhere more apparent than in Britain. William Hogarth (1697–1764) was the most popular artist of the era. Hogarth portrayed everyday life in London with affection and satire. He was as adept at conveying the elegance of London's parks as the depravation of the city's notorious "Gin Lane." He poked fun at the hearty Englishman putting away pounds of roast beef (it seemed somehow fitting that Hogarth himself died after eating a huge steak), the dishonest lawyer, the clergyman looking for a better post while ignoring his pastoral duties, and the laboring poor drowning their sorrows in cheap gin, a plague that led the government to raise the tax on inexpensive liquor.

In France, the Academy of Painting and Sculpture organized the first public art exhibition in Paris in 1737. A description of one such event

Jean Antoine Watteau's *The Gamut of Love.*

William Hogarth's *Gin Lane* (1751) is a deleterious commentary on the impact of alcohol on the poor of eighteenth-century London.

suggests that such public exhibitions facilitated some degree of social mingling.

> Here the odd-job man rubs shoulders with the great noble . . . the fishwife trades her perfumes with those of a lady of quality, making the latter resort to holding her nose to combat the strong odor of cheap brandy drifting her way; the rough artisan, guided only by natural feeling, comes out with a just observation, at which an inept wit nearly bursts out laughing only because of the comical accent in which it was expressed; while an artist hiding in the crowd unravels the meaning of it all and turns it to his profit.

Music

The taste for music also moved beyond the constraints of court, ecclesiastical, and noble patronage. Opera's great popularity in the seventeenth century had been closely tied to ornate opera houses constructed at European courts. The appeal of composers and their music passed from court to court, sometimes transported by aristocratic diplomats. In the early 1750s, Rousseau penned stinging attacks on French opera. Readers understood his strident language as he intended—he was denouncing court and aristocratic taste itself. Specifically, Rousseau compared the Royal Academy of Music's monopoly on French music to a ruthless inquisition that stifled imagination. Rousseau's critique generated a storm of controversy because it seemed to be nothing less than a denunciation of the social and cultural foundations of contemporary French society. In harmony with his philosophical works, Rousseau's operatic compositions extolled the simple, unpretentious life of rural people.

Court composers were considered the equivalent of favored upper servants. When someone asked Franz Joseph Haydn (1732–1809), who worked as *kapellmeister* (orchestra director) for the fabulously wealthy Esterházy family of Hungary, why he had never written any quintets, he replied, "Nobody has ordered any." But by the 1790s, Haydn was conducting his symphonies in public concerts in London. The German composer George Frideric Handel (1685–1759) gratefully accepted the patronage of several English aristocrats and then King George II.

In England, concerts were held at court or in the homes of wealthy families; in Italy, they were sponsored by groups of savants and other educated people who gathered to discuss literature, science, and the arts; and in Switzerland, concerts were sponsored by societies of music lovers. The public concert also emerged in Western Europe, in some German cities, early in the eighteenth century. Gradually public concert halls were built in the capitals of Europe. Handel began to perform his operas and concerts in rented theaters, attracting large crowds.

The short life of Wolfgang Amadeus Mozart (1756–1791) reflected the gradual evolution from dependence on court and aristocratic patronage to the emergence of the public concert. Mozart began playing the harpsichord

(*Left*) George Frideric Handel composing. (*Right*) Franz Joseph Haydn composing at the keyboard.

The young Wolfgang Amadeus Mozart about to perform.

at age three and began composing at five. In 1763, his father took him and his sister on a tour of European courts that would last three years, hoping to make the family fortune. The Mozarts were paid handsomely for their time in Paris and at the court of Versailles, but they were disappointed by the fees they received at the German courts and in London. Mozart returned to Paris in 1778 at his father's insistence that he "get a job or at least make some money." The temperamental Mozart failed to make his way in the social world of Paris: "I would wish for his fortune," a contemporary wrote, "that he had half as much talent and twice as much tact."

Thereafter Mozart often lived in his native Salzburg, where he served as unhappy court musician of the unpleasant archbishop. Mozart wrote church music and light music, including a hunting symphony for strings, two horns, dogs and a rifle, before resigning after quarreling with his patron. Mozart spent money as rapidly as he made it, and was constantly in debt, unable to attract the lavish court, noble, or ecclesiastical patronage he desired. But a list of engagements that he sent his father in 1784 revealed that he had very few evenings free. His schedule included public concerts, which had begun only a year or two earlier. Mozart organized a series of subscription concerts of his own that year, but had only mediocre success, perhaps because his music seemed too innovative and complicated. Opera continued to be the preferred form of music. Unlike Handel, who made a good deal of money during the last ten years of his life, Mozart died a poor man at age thirty-five, buried in an unmarked pauper's grave in Vienna.

A prolific genius, Mozart moved away from the melodious regularity of his predecessors to more varied and freely articulated compositions. The operas *The Marriage of Figaro* (1786) and *Don Giovanni* (1787) demonstrated Mozart's capacity to present characters from many walks of life, revealing not only their shared humanity but their personal moods and expectations. *The Magic Flute* (1791) captures yet again the religious underpinning of contemporary culture, even in the century of rational inquiry. Mozart's last opera expressed his belief in the ability of mankind to develop greater virtue and a capacity for love. He thus expressed the confidence of the philosophes.

The Spread of Enlightened Ideas

Salons, academies, and Masonic lodges helped spread Enlightened thought. Salons, which brought together people of means, noble and bourgeois alike, in private homes for sociability and discussion, were concentrated in Paris above all, but they were also found in Berlin, London, and Vienna, as well as in some smaller provincial towns. The English historian Edward Gibbon claimed that in two weeks in Paris he had "heard more conversation worth remembering than I had done in two or three winters in London." The salons of Paris were organized and hosted mainly by women, who selected topics for discussion and presided over conversations. Women thus became mediators of changing culture. In Warsaw, Princess Sophia Czartoryska's salon played an important role in conveying Western ideas to Polish elites. In London, women hosted similar gather-

An actor reading from a work of Voltaire at the salon of Madame Geoffrin. Note the bust of Voltaire, then in exile.

Franz Anton Mesmer magne-
tizing a distraught patient.

ings, some composed exclusively of women. Sometimes the discussion focused on the place of women in society.

The women of the republic of letters "accustom us to discuss with
charm and clarity the driest and thorniest of subject," commented Diderot
with admiration but also condescension. Madame Geoffrin in Paris hosted
artists on Monday and men of letters on Wednesday. "I well remember seeing all Europe standing three deep around her chair," recalled one of her
visitors. Her husband sat silently at the other end of the table while his
wife put the philosophes through their paces. One night, a regular guest
noted that the place where the silent man usually sat was empty and asked
where he was. "He was my husband," came the laconic reply, "and he's
dead."

Salon guests could discuss the work of the philosophes without fear of
police interference. By the middle of the century, political discussions increasingly captured intellectuals' attention. Not all ideas discussed, of
course, were of equal merit. In the 1780s, a crank German scientist, Franz
Anton Mesmer (1734–1815), proclaimed the healing properties of electromagnetic treatments. "Mesmerism" attracted considerable interest in
the salons of Paris, where discussants debated the nature of the "universal
fluid" Mesmer and his disciples believed linked the human body to the
universe. Ironically, the very success of science opened the way for such
spiritualist healers to step forward, although the French Academy of Sci-

ence vigorously denounced Mesmerism as nothing more than resourceful charlatanism.

In France (and in some Italian cities as well), academies, which were organizations of local people interested in science and philosophy, fulfilled a similar but more formal role to that of the salons. They were not "academies" in the sense of offering an organized curriculum, but rather formal gatherings taking place about every two weeks of people with similar intellectual interests. Meetings consisted of reading minutes and correspondence, debates and lectures. The academies helped spread Enlightenment ideas by gathering a literate, upper-class audience, including some clergymen, eager to discuss the works of the philosophes. Unlike the salons, however, with several exceptions women were not elected to the academies.

The French academies served two masters: the king and the public. They depended on royal intendants, governors, and other state officials for funding and meeting places. The monarchy believed that the academies served the public interest by bringing together savants to consider questions of contemporary importance. Some of them sponsored essay competitions on topics of contemporary interest (for example, an essay on "wisdom") in the arts and sciences—Rousseau was not the least of the winners—which became an important part of intellectual life in eighteenth-century France; during the decade of the 1780s, more than 600 were held. Some of the topics increasingly reflected Enlightenment influence, such as "religious intolerance and the role of magistrates in the defense of liberty."

Many members of the provincial academies by mid-century began to think of themselves both as representing public opinion, serving as informal counselors to the monarchy, and interpreting the sciences and other erudite subjects to a more general audience. The academies contributed to the development in France of a reforming mood. Moreover, some members became increasingly disenchanted with the Church, viewing it as incapable of reforming itself.

Masonic lodges, another medium for the ideas of the philosophes, had begun in Scotland, perhaps as early as the sixteenth century, as stonemasons' guilds. They now brought together freethinkers and others who opposed the influence of the established churches in public life. Masonic lodges proliferated rapidly in Europe during the middle years of the eighteenth century. Members took vows of secrecy, although in fact their meetings, membership lists (which included women), and rituals were widely known. Members held a variety of political opinions, but they shared a general faith in progress, toleration, and a critical spirit about institutionalized religion. In Scotland, clubs, coffeehouses, and taverns also provided the setting for discussion of the new ideas.

There were at the same time several obstacles to the dissemination of Enlightenment ideas. Books and even pamphlets were expensive. Censorship, although erratic and varying greatly from place to place, also discour-

A gathering of a Masonic lodge in Vienna. Masonic rituals included the use of allegorical symbols, blindfolds, and swords.

aged publication. All books and pamphlets published or sold in France, for example, first had to be approved by the censorship office in Paris. Censored books were burned, and those who published material officially considered blasphemous could be, at least in principle, sentenced to death. Far more frequently, officials closed printers' shops. Even the relatively tolerant Dutch Republic banned Diderot's *Philosophic Thoughts* as an attack on religion. In the face of a spate of publications critical of monarchy, aristocracy, and Church, Louis XV promulgated censorship laws in 1757 that were much harsher than those regulating the book trade in England. The French monarchy also controlled what was published through licensing of printers, booksellers, peddlers, and clandestine publishers. Many of the latter were notoriously unscrupulous, living on an excruciatingly thin margin of survival. Some survived by pirating books, eagerly pushing works by whatever authors were popular.

ENLIGHTENED ABSOLUTISM

The philosophes believed that the success of any state depended on the degree of freedom and happiness it was able to assure its people. As David Hume put it, a state is justified by the good that is done in its name. Voltaire and Diderdot, in particular, believed in "enlightened absolutism."

They wanted enlightened monarchs to impose reforms that would benefit their subjects. Leopold II of Tuscany (1747–1792), the most significant reformer of his era, went so far as to declare that "the sovereign, even if hereditary, is only the delegate of his people." Rousseau, however, warned that absolutism and enlightened thinking were incompatible.

Reform of Jurisprudence

Cesare Bonesana, the marquis of Beccaria (1738–1794), had the greatest influence on his era as a reformer influenced by the Enlightenment. A noble from Milan, Beccaria became professor of political philosophy in Habsburg Austria and ended his career advising the state chancellory on such diverse topics as agriculture, mining, and trade. He made his reputation, however, with his ideas on crime and punishment.

In *On Crimes and Punishment* (1764), Beccaria, who had read Montesquieu, Buffon, Diderot, and Rousseau, among other philosophes, applied their analysis to the issues at hand. He argued that the state's task was to protect society while respecting the dignity of all people. This meant that the rights of those accused of crimes, too, had to be protected. Beccaria wanted standard procedures to govern criminal trials, so that rich and poor would stand equal before the law. The Italian philosophe's assumption that the accused was innocent until proven guilty has remained, along with the tradition of English constitutional law and trial by jury, cornerstones of Western judicial systems.

Beccaria argued that the punishment for a given crime should not be linked to the religious concept of sin, but rather rationally determined by an assessment of the damage done to society. He thus rejected the death penalty except in cases when the state itself is threatened by anarchy. Beccaria argued that offenses against religious orthodoxy were not crimes and therefore should go unpunished. Therefore he argued that "It is better to prevent crimes than to punish them." Beccaria's principles reflected the origins of utilitarianism, an influential social theory of the first decades of the nineteenth century.

Beccaria opposed torture to extract confessions or render punishment. He argued that barbarous punishment, instead of protecting society, only encouraged disrespect for the law and hence more awful crimes. For this reason, he also objected to capital punishment, lamenting the enthusiastic crowds attracted to public executions. Leopold II of Tuscany (an admirer of Beccaria), Gustavus III of Sweden, and Frederick the Great of Prussia banned torture—clear examples of the influence of enlightened thought on contemporary rulers. Joseph II of Austria (1741–1790), Leopold's brother, also banned torture and capital punishment, but he substituted many other brutal penalties that he believed would deter crime.

Instruction in an Austrian schoolroom.

Educational Reform

Education in the widest sense was central to the program of the philosophes. The Empress Catherine the Great of Russia (ruled 1762–1796) admired and read Montesquieu and Voltaire, hosted Diderot, and purchased the latter's library for a handsome price. Born a German princess, she was contemptuous of Russian culture and unwilling to speak either Russian or German, preferring French as the language of learning. She seemed to heed the advice she had received from Diderot: "To instruct a nation is to civilize it." Catherine established a school for the daughters of nobles. Without eliminating censorship, she authorized the first private printing presses and encouraged the publication of more books—on an average only a couple dozen titles were published each year until Catherine's reform, when the annual number increased to almost 400.

A few other monarchs implemented educational reforms. But they did so at least partially in order to assure a supply of able civil servants. In 1774, Joseph II established a structured, centralized system of education from primary school to university, which doubled, for example, the number of elementary schools in Bohemia. Textbooks appeared in the Magyar, German, Croatian, Slovak, Ruthenian, and Romanian languages.

Religious Toleration

Although the eighteenth century was a period of relative religious peace, confessional conflicts could still be intense. For example, English Dissenters and particularly Catholics suffered legal discrimination; they were excluded from public offices and some professions. French Protestants had no civil rights; their births, baptisms, and marriages were considered not to have occurred unless registered by a Catholic priest. Huguenots in southern France rose up in defense of their religion in the ill-fated Camisard rebellion of 1702–1705. Protestants suffered discrimination in Hungary and the Catholic Rhineland. In Austria, in 1728 the bishop of Salzburg gave 20,000 Protestants three days to leave their homes, and royal edicts forced Protestants out of Upper Austria and Styria during the next decade.

Europe's 3 million Jews, in particular, suffered intolerance and often persecution across Europe—above all, in Eastern Europe and Russia. Jews could not take titles of nobility, join guilds, or hold municipal office. In many places, they could own land, although in some of the German states they needed special permission to buy houses. They were excluded from agricultural occupations and certain trades in France, Eastern Europe, and Russia. The Habsburg monarchy required Jews to stay inside until noon on Sundays, and in 1745, it suddenly ordered the thousands of Jews living in Prague to leave. In Vienna and Zurich, Jews were confined to ghettos, and in several German towns, they were not allowed inside the city walls. Although the Swedish government allowed Jews to build synagogues beginning in 1782, they could reside only in certain cities, and were forbidden to marry anyone who was not Jewish, to purchase land, or to produce handicrafts.

The Austrian Habsburgs expelling the Jews from Prague.

Because moneylending had been one of the ways Jews survived, Polish, Russian, and Ukrainian Jews faced resentment and hatred from peasants who often owed them money. In Poland the Catholic Church, which condemned usury, often led the way in persecution; rumors that Jews were ritually sacrificing Christian children during Passover found credulous ears. In 1762, Ukrainian peasants killed at least 20,000 Jews in the bloodiest pogrom of the century.

Yet, by about 1750, Western Europe seemed to be entering a more tolerant age. For one thing, intolerance generated periodic rebellions, which took state funds to put down. But a more humanitarian spirit could also be seen. One of Voltaire's disciples in the 1750s achieved great success for his historical novel that denounced religious persecution.

Some of the rulers who undertook what appeared to be religious reforms were inspired less by a Voltarian critique of ecclesiastical authority than by a desire to strengthen their authority. This was the case in the expulsion of the Jesuits from several countries, which highlighted the struggle between the popes and Catholic monarchs. The Jesuits had been closely identified with the papacy since the inception of the order during the Catholic Reformation. They had gained great influence in the Spanish, French, and Portuguese colonies in the Americas, and as tutors to powerful noble families. Furthermore, the order had begun to undertake colonial commercial activity, with mixed results. These factors combined to make Catholic kings perceive the order as a threat to their authority.

In Portugal, King John V's strong-willed minister, Sebastião, the marquis of Pombal (1699–1782), enhanced the monarchy's authority at the expense of the great noble families and the Church. When Jesuits criticized the regime for, among other things, orchestrating anti-Semitism, Pombal accused them of exploiting the indigenous population of Paraguay, where they virtually ran the colonial state, and of planning to extend their influence throughout the world. After Pombal falsely accused the order of planning the king's assassination, the monarch expelled the Jesuits from Portugal in 1759. Ten years later, Pombal ended the Inquisition's status as an independent tribunal, making it a royal court. Other rulers followed suit, including Louis XV of France in 1764. The expulsion of the Jesuits from some of the most powerful Catholic states reflected the diminishing power of the papacy in the face of absolute monarchs determined to retain control over what they considered to be national churches.

In Spain, Charles III (ruled 1759–1788) ordered universities to include instruction in science and philosophy. He also reduced the feared Spanish Inquisition to a series of legal hurdles governing publishing. In 1781, the last person in Spain was executed after having been accused of heretical religious beliefs. Like the kings of Portugal and France, Charles III in 1776 expelled the Jesuits in part because their near-monopoly on education seemed to pose a threat to the monarchy's control over the Church. Leopold II also reduced the authority of the church in Tuscany, ending the

tithe and shackling the Inquisition. Catherine the Great abandoned persecution of Old Believers, a dissident sect within the Orthodox Church, and
granted Jews civil equality. And Louis XVI granted French Protestants
most civil rights in 1787, formalizing the *de facto* toleration accorded
them for some time.

In Britain in 1788, Parliament passed laws reducing restrictions on
Catholics—although they still could not hold public office. Nonetheless,
London crowds shouting "no popery!" then attacked the property of Catholics
during the "Gordon riots." Almost 300 people were killed as the authorities
repressed the disturbances. In 1792, however, the first legal Catholic church
in England since the sixteenth century opened its doors in London.

Protestant states seemed most receptive to the philosophes' call for religious toleration. In the northern German states and Swiss cantons, the
ideals of the philosophes provided support for traditions of religious toleration that had grown out of the sixteenth-century Reformation. The quest
for religious tolerance played an important part in German enlightened
thought. In *Nathan the Wise* (1779), Lessing argued that people of all religions should be citizens. In Catholic Austria, Joseph II's relaxation of censorship permitted a spate of pamphlets and brochures denouncing
ecclesiastical abuses and calling for toleration of Protestants. The king's
Edict of Toleration (1781) extended some toleration to non-Catholics. The
edict included Jews, who were now "free" to bear the burden of a "toleration tax" and to pay an assessment on kosher meat. Joseph also ennobled
several Jews, incurring the wrath of other nobles. Moreover, for the first
time, Protestants could enter the Habsburg civil service.

Frederick the Great

The German states appeared to be the most fertile ground for enlightened
absolutism. German philosophes remained closely tied to the existing order, looking to the individual states and to the church for reforms. They
were less critical of the state than their French counterparts. For Immanuel Kant (1724–1804), the Enlightenment meant the liberation of the
individual intellectually and morally, but not politically or socially. The individual should think critically, but also obey.

Frederick II of Prussia (ruled 1740–1786 and known as Frederick the
Great), wanted to be remembered as an enlightened ruler. He turned his
court into a center of learning for the nobility. Like Catherine the Great,
he considered the only worthwhile learning to be French learning. "Sans
Souci", his rococo château in Potsdam, had French formal gardens and
was considered the height of civility. Frederick, who was a flute-playing
"philosopher-king," made Voltaire (with whom he had begun corresponding when he was still heir to the Prussian throne) the centerpiece of his
palace for two years. Voltaire praised Frederick for having transformed "a
sad Sparta into a brilliant Athens." But he soon became disenchanted with

the cynical, manipulative Prussian king, who coolly invaded the Habsburg territory of Silesia in 1740, in the first year of his reign, demonstrating that the needs of his dynastic state would always take precedence over any issue of justice. Voltaire angered Frederick by lampooning a royal favorite and, when the king ordered his hangman to burn the offending tract publicly, Voltaire took the hint and left Potsdam in 1752.

But Frederick again borrowed Enlightenment discourse in 1770 when he claimed that one of his major tasks was "to make people as happy as is compatible with human nature and the means at my disposal." He once claimed somewhat disingenuously that he was nothing more than the "first servant" of his people as king and said that "I well know that the rich have many advocates, but the poor have only one, and that is I." Frederick freed the serfs of the royal domains and ordered the abolition of particularly vexing ties to noble lands, as well as the lords' right to punish their own serfs physically. Judicial reforms ended some flagrant abuses by magistrates. The Prussian king relaxed censorship and abolished capital punishment, except in the army. Despite once stating that "everyone must be allowed to go to heaven in his own way," he refused to emancipate Prussian Jews, asserting that they "injure the business of Christians and are useless to the state," while continuing to depend on their loans. Nonetheless, the Prussian Code, finally completed and promulgated in 1794, eight years after his death, granted "every inhabitant of the state . . . complete freedom of religion and conscience."

Frederick the Great playing the flute at Sans Souci.

Frederick the Great's "enlightened" reforms were, above all, intended to make the Prussian state more powerful, not more just (see Chapter 11). He made Prussia a more efficient absolutist state. Nobles dominated most of the plum positions as military officers and high officials. Yet, because of the needs of the state, some commoners did in fact rise to important posts, including some army officers, who were subsequently ennobled. Frederick improved the state bureaucracy by introducing an examination system to govern entry. In the courts of justice, where candidates had to pass the most complete examinations, the chances of commoners for success were greatest, and in Berlin only a third of all judges were nobles.

Yet, Prussian law reinforced the distinction between noble and commoner. The Prussian Code divided Prussian society into noble, bourgeois, and common estates. Frederick bolstered the position of Prussian nobles because he was determined to prevent any erosion of their status as the landowning class. He refused to ban serfdom on private estates, and he created institutions that would provide credit to nobles having financial difficulties. Marriages between nobles and commoners were not recognized. Even if nobles fell on hard times, they were not permitted to sell their lands to non-nobles. Furthermore, Frederick refused to promote civilian bureaucrats into the nobility.

Frederick intended his law code to enhance the reach of the state rather than to make his people equal before the law. When he freed the serfs of the royal domains (1763), it was because he needed them in the army. The Prussian monarch's *Essay on the Forms of Government* (1781) offered a recipe for enhancing the efficiency of the absolute state. Frederick's view of the world bound the state and the individual subject together. When their mutual interests could not be reconciled, however, the Prussian state always took precedence. As Voltaire had discovered for himself, Frederick the Great's reign reflected the limitations of enlightened absolutism.

Rural Reform

Several Central European monarchs tried to improve conditions of rural life. Following the disastrous decade of the 1770s, marked by hunger and disease, Austrian Queen Maria Theresa banned the mistreatment of peasants by their lords and tried to limit seigneurial obligations. As she put it, sheep must be well fed if they are to yield more wool and milk. Her son Joseph II abolished serfdom in 1781, converting peasant labor obligations into an annual payment to the lord. By restricting labor obligations, the Habsburg monarchs thus increased the potential for imposing more taxes on peasants. Joseph also ended obligations of personal service to the lord; henceforth a peasant could marry and/or leave the land without the permission of the seigneur. Peasants could also turn to the state for support against an oppressive lord; they could even take the lord to court.

Leopold II, who promulgated a new code of his kingdom's laws in 1786 and established a new and more independent judiciary, ended some restrictions on the grain trade, freeing the price of grain. These moves were popular among merchants and wealthy peasants, but not among poor people, who depended upon bread to survive.

Enlightened Statecraft

Some rulers applied Enlightenment rationality to statecraft. Joseph II announced that he wanted the Habsburg state to follow "uniform principles," which included a reorganization of the imperial bureaucracy. He taxed Church property, abolished some monastic orders, and forced a reorganization of the Church within the Habsburg domains. But a more efficient government administration did not mean more freedom for subjects. None of the so-called "enlightened" rulers gave up any of his or her monarchical prerogatives. Absolute rulers harnessed Enlightenment rationality to state actions in order to strengthen their own power rather than to improve the lives of their subjects.

Thus, "enlightened" reforms had little effect on the lives of most peasants. Enlightened absolutism benefited the Russian state and nobility, but brought virtually no change to the Russian masses. Millions of serfs were now bound even more formally to their lords. Nobles retained arbitrary rights of justice over their serfs, and lords alone could own land. Within the Habsburg domains, peasants, though legally free, remained indebted to their lords. Reasons of state lay behind even these seemingly enlightened reforms. Peasants now owed the state even more taxes and were subject to a longer term of military service. In any case, determined noble resistance undermined Joseph's reforms in Austria, Hungary, and the Southern Netherlands. In Tuscany, aristocrats and state officials sabotaged Leopold's reforms.

Catherine the Great, influenced by Montesquieu's *Spirit of the Laws,* wanted the nobility to serve as an "intermediary body" standing between the crown and its subjects. Catherine hoped that by clarifying their rights, nobles might contribute to the functioning and glory of her state. The Charter of the Nobility of 1785 formalized the relationship between the autocratic state and the nobles, recognizing the nobility of blood as equal to that of service. It confirmed their security of property, the right to hold serfs, and immunity from arrest and confiscation of property by the state. For the first time, nobles could travel abroad without the permission of the emperor. Local elective councils of nobles could henceforth send petitions to the tsar or empress, but the autocracy had no obligation to respond. Catherine herself turned against Enlightenment thought, however, fearing that it might become a tool of those opposed to absolute rule. Diderot's confidence in Catherine ended in disappointment when, to his chagrin, he learned that the empress had imprisoned those with whom she disagreed.

CURRENTS OF THE LATE ENLIGHTENMENT

The end of the "high" or "mature" Enlightenment was symbolized by the deaths of Voltaire and Rousseau in 1778. The late Enlightenment was more complex, sharing several currents. British economists applied the concept of freedom for the first time to the workings of the economy. Meanwhile, on the continent, philosophes turned away from the preoccupation with rationality and the laws of nature. The mark of human freedom was no longer the exercise of reason but the expression of the emotions. Rousseau himself had begun this turn toward what he called "reasoned sentimentality" by stressing the importance of emotional development and fulfillment. In a related development, a number of writers began to "discover" and embrace their own national cultures, seeking their origins in medieval poems and songs. And in France, when there were no more Voltaires or Rousseaus, a generation of would-be philosophes, mediocre writers who attacked the institutional structure of the French monarchy, influenced public opinion.

Calls for the freeing of the economy from state control, the emergence of idealism with its implicit promotion of nationalism through the quest for and emotional embrace of the roots of national culture, the development of the concept of public opinion, and the publication, particularly in France, of scathing attacks on the monarchy all served to undermine the established order (see Chapter 11).

Enlightened Thought and Economic Freedom

The philosophes' quest to discover the laws of nature and society led several of them to try to establish a complementary set of laws that could explain the working of the economy. This search led away from mercantilism, which had formed the basis of seventeenth- and early eighteenth-century economic theory, and to the emergence of classical economic liberalism. Mercantilist theory held that states should protect their economies with restrictions and tariffs that would maintain a favorable balance of trade, with more gold and silver flowing into a nation than going out.

A group of economic thinkers known as physiocrats believed that land, not gold and silver, was the source of all wealth. They wanted to end state interference in agriculture and the commerce of farm products. Writing in the *Encyclopedia,* François Quesnay (1694–1774), a French doctor and economist, called on the monarchy to free the grain trade. Quesnay wanted the end of arbitrary controls on prices, which states sometimes imposed in order to preserve public order. He and his friends insisted that the initially higher prices for goods would encourage production, thereby bringing about lower prices in the long run. The physiocrats encouraged wealthy landowners to put science to work to increase farm yields and enlightened rulers to free the agricultural economy from tolls and internal tariffs. In Britain, where commercial agriculture was already well developed, the physiocrats attracted an interested following. English landowners cheered the physiocrats' exuberant proclamation of the value of land and the sanctity of private property.

However, when the oddly named Anne-Robert Turgot (1727–1781), Louis XVI's controller-general, freed France's grain trade from controls in the early 1770s, disastrous shortages accompanied a series of bad harvests (see Chapter 11). Hoarding contributed to much higher prices; grain riots followed, and the experiment soon ended with the old strictures and controls back in place.

Adam Smith (1723–1790), a Scottish professor of moral philosophy at the University of Glasgow, argued against some of the hallmarks of mercantilism. In the name of freeing the economy from restraints, he opposed guild restrictions and other monopolies as well as trade barriers and other forms of protectionism. Such bold proposals flew in the face of contemporary economic thought, which held closely to regulated monopolies and remained suspicious of free market competition. Merchants looked to the state to provide financial, political, and military protection. The Scottish philosopher's optimistic doctrine came to be known universally by its

Adam Smith admiring his book, *The Wealth of Nations.*

French name, *"laissez-faire,"* or "leave alone." Each person, Smith insisted, should be "free to pursue his own interest his own way." If "left alone," Smith argued, the British economy would thrive naturally, generating foreign and domestic markets. The "invisible hand" of the unfettered economy would over time cause the forces of supply and demand to meet, determining the price of a good and clearing markets. By overcoming that "wretched spirit of monopoly," which made people less energetic, the "virtue of the marketplace" would also enhance social happiness and civic virtue. This was a common theme in the Scottish Enlightenment; Scottish philosophes were particularly concerned with how civic virtue and public morality could be inculcated in a society being slowly transformed by commerce and manufacture.

German Idealism

While in England the late Enlightenment brought an emphasis on economic freedom, on the continent it was marked by subjectivism and a greater emphasis on emotion, a shift already reflected by Rousseau's "reasoned sentimentality." The basic tenet of German idealism was that we perceive and understand the world through the medium of our ideas, and not through the direct application of our senses. The foremost proponent of this school was Immanuel Kant, born an artisan's son in the Prussian town of Königsberg. In his *Critique of Pure Reason* (1781), Kant affirmed that rational inquiry into nature leads to knowledge. In his memorable analogy, reason is like a judge who "compels the witness to answer questions which he himself has formulated." But for Kant, reason alone was not the basis for our knowledge of the world. He argued instead that each person understands the world through concepts that cannot be separated from his or her unique experience. This philosophy undermined faith in rational objectivity and universalism that had characterized the high Enlightenment and invited the subjectivity and relativism of early nineteenth-century romanticism.

In the eighteenth century, writers became interested in discovering the roots of national cultures; Sweden, Denmark, Russia, and Poland all discovered their "national" literatures, written in their own languages. The first Czech national theater opened in Prague in 1737. Lessing proudly wrote in German and called for a national theater. Scottish readers eagerly saluted the discovery by the poet James Macpherson (1736–1796) of the work of an imaginary Gaelic bard of the third century, Ossian. Macpherson's publication in the early 1760s of what he claimed were translations of the poet he called the Gaelic Homer set off a bitter debate, one that contributed, despite Macpherson's falsification, to the emergence of Scottish romanticism. Composers began to borrow from popular culture, especially from folk music not necessarily religious in inspiration. The first Jewish periodicals were published in Königsberg in the century's last decades, and the first Jewish school was established in Berlin in 1778. The emotional search for and enthusiastic identification with national cultures contributed, as in the case of Scotland, to the development of romanticism, and though only very gradually, of nationalism. The latter, in particular, helped undermine the established order in several continental states, notably France. In those states, the established order was based on allegiance to a monarchical dynasty and often to established religion as well, and not to national allegiances.

The Enlightenment and Public Opinion

Public opinion, a concept we take for granted, did not always exist. But it began to take shape in French, English, and several other European languages in the eighteenth century (see Chapter 11). During the 1770s, more people in France discussed the pressing political issues of the day than ever before. Barristers helped establish the concept of public opinion when they sought a wide spectrum of support for the parlements. Louis XV had decided to replace these provincial noble law courts in 1768 with more malleable institutions more directly under royal control. Public opinion forced the king to restore the parlements six years later and brought about an end to Turgot's attempt to rationalize the administration. Public opinion, to which opponents of the monarchy and increasingly the court itself now appealed, provided a forum in which political ideas were increasingly discussed. These ideas were largely shaped by Enlightenment discourse on political sovereignty and the limits of absolute rule.

A number of the treatises published during the late Enlightenment dealt with contemporary political issues, in the tradition of Voltaire's broadsides at the time of the Calas Affair, which had exposed the consequences of intolerance and persecution to public opinion. As the financial crisis of the French monarchy worsened during the 1780s, such publications would help make the question of reform an increasingly national issue.

Forbidden Publications and the Undermining of Authority

Some of the fringe members of the republic of letters, whom Voltaire had dismissed as mere "scribblers," also undermined respect for the monarchy and the royal family. Whereas the milieu of the philosophes earlier in the century had been elegant salons, the would-be philosophes of the last period of the Enlightenment hung around cheap cafés, lived in rooms high above the street, and dodged creditors by frequently changing addresses, while insisting that royal censorship blocked their ascent to better things. Some made a modest living peddling forbidden publications. A few kept afloat by spying for the police. A few others turned to petty crime and others, while claiming common cause with the major philosophes against the unenlightened institutions of France, wrote pornography or slandered prominent people, including the royal family. There had been such publications before the 1770s and 1780s, but never so many of them, and never had they been so widely read.

Banned books nevertheless reached France through the efforts of resourceful shipping agents, transporters, bargemen, dockers, and peddlers, who smuggled books published in Switzerland or the Austrian Netherlands to French booksellers willing to circumvent the controls of the booksellers' guild and the state. In 1783, the crown redoubled its efforts to stem the tide of smuggled books and to still the clandestine presses within France. These houses undercut the legitimate Parisian book trade because they could publish banned books and produce cheaper editions of acceptable works. Moreover, royal officials were concerned about the effects of these smuggled satires on public faith in the monarchy.

Was there any connection between the high-minded philosophes and their "successors," who included the authors of *Venus in the Cloister or the Nun in a Nightgown, Christianity Unveiled,* and *Margot the Campfollower?* In fact, the envious and mediocre descendants of the philosophes continued their predecessors' work by undermining respect for the authority of monarchy, aristocracy, and Church, however much their attacks by character assassination and defamation followed from ambition and financial need more than from adherence to Enlightenment ideals.

Moreover, certain themes of the Enlightenment did find their way into their work. They joined their far more illustrious predecessors in attacking the foundations of the French monarchy. Frustrated authors attacked the privileges, for example, of the printing and booksellers' guild, which they blamed for keeping them on Grub Street. Their identification of censorship with despotism, though self-serving, was nonetheless effective. As they denounced the bureaucratic system of state censorship, they argued that only its abolition could permit the free exchange of ideas. Political events and scandals kept the presses of the literary underground turning, fanning popular hostility to monarchy, Church, and nobility.

LEGACY OF THE ENLIGHTENMENT

The Enlightenment philosophes celebrated reason, while acknowledging the passions, and were suspicious of pure faith. Steeped in respect for science and reason, and confident that humanity would discover the truths of nature, they were optimistic about human potential. The philosophes' belief in progress, which Kant insisted was a sign of modernity, separated them sharply from the Catholic Church. Yet, they were not as naive, uncritical, or foolish as Voltaire's Candide, who thought progress inevitable. The philosophes believed that the combination of thought, study, education, and action would lead to a better future. States, they thought, were not ordained by God, but by mankind and, like other phenomena, should be subject to critical scrutiny.

The philosophes' belief in human dignity led them to oppose all forms of despotism. Most spoke out against religious intolerance, torture, and slavery (although an effective campaign against slavery, launched by the English abolitionists of the Society for the Abolition of the Slave Trade in 1787, stood independent of the Enlightenment). Furthermore, some Enlightenment thinkers and writers recognized that contemporary assertions about the inequality of women contradicted their understanding of nature. Diderot, Montesquieu, and Voltaire favored divorce, but they opposed equal status for women.

Some philosophes had strong reservations about the ability of individuals to develop equally. "As for the rabble," Voltaire once said, "I don't concern myself with it; they will always remain rabble." Those with power and influence first must be enlightened, they reasoned, so that eventually everyone could develop through education. And for all their commitment to freedom and insistence on the fundamental goodness of all people, Hume and the other philosophes still considered women inferior to men, reflecting the prejudices of the times in which they lived.

Rejecting what they considered unnatural hierarchies that fettered progress, the philosophes in their commitment to individual freedom influenced the subsequent history of the Western world. Whereas most people in the eighteenth century still considered the monarchy to be the repository of the public good, the philosophes proclaimed that the public had rights of its own and that freedom was a good in itself. Enlightenment thought helped create a discourse of principled opposition to the foundations of absolutism. If the philosophes themselves were not revolutionary, many of their ideas in the context of eighteenth-century Europe were indeed.

CHAPTER 11

EIGHTEENTH-CENTURY DYNASTIC RIVALRIES AND POLITICS

King George III (ruled 1760–1820) proclaimed that he "gloried in the name of Britain." Indeed during his reign, despite his personal failings, a nationalist cult developed around the British monarchy, significantly after the empire suffered its biggest loss, that of the thirteen American colonies.

The king projected the image of an ordinary family man, surrounded by his homely wife and fifteen children. Less interested in goings-on in Hanover, his family's dynastic home, than his predecessors, he won popular affection in Britain. "This young man," wrote Horace Walpole, "don't stand in one spot with his eyes fixed royally on the ground, and dropping bits of German news; he walks about and speaks to everybody." The king's domesticity also made him a target for the gentle spoofs of caricaturists. His nervousness led him to bombard almost everyone he encountered with questions, ending with "hey, hey?" By the last decade of the century, symptoms of a hereditary disease made George III appear to be quite mad.

Early in his reign, King George III had strong ideas about monarchical prerogatives, even within the context of a constitutional monarchy. Yet, during his reign, not only did British nationalism develop precociously, but the idea developed in and beyond Parliament that a party of parliamentary opposition formed an essential part of the parliamentary system of representation.

The nature of the European state system itself also underwent fundamental change in the eighteenth century as the rivalries between Great Britain, France, Spain, and the Dutch Republic (the United Provinces) broadened to a global scale. Whereas Europe in the period of Louis XIV had been marked by frenetic war-making and the pursuit of alliances against France, Europe's dominant power, the wars fought between the

Great Powers in the middle of the eighteenth century reflected a more even distribution of power. This balance of power was increasingly affected not only by events overseas but also by those in Eastern Europe. There, Russia expanded its empire at the expense of the Ottoman Empire, and Russia, Prussia, and Austria dismembered Poland.

The increasingly global nature of Great Power conflict put strains on the structures of states in Europe. They were forced to reorganize themselves to become more efficient, either by granting more power to representative bodies combined with stronger mechanisms for raising money, as in the case of Great Britain, or through some variant of enlightened despotism, as in Prussia. In Britain, where monarchs could not function without Parliament, the role of the House of Commons expanded and political parties emerged. Newspapers and societies for discussing politics created public opinion, which transformed the political sphere as more people demanded political reform. Patriotism, and by extension, a sense of national identity, emerged in Britain. Allegiance was transferred from the ruler to Parliament, which was seen as representing the interests of all Britons (directly or indirectly).

Reform movements and uprisings alarmed rulers and intrigued intellectuals, who in increasing numbers denounced unwarranted privilege and despotism. Reformers celebrated the British model of constitutional monarchy and the successful rising of the American colonists against British rule. Public opinion on the continent challenged absolute rule; in France, the parlements began to defend the "nation" against monarchical despotism.

The role of lawyers in helping constitute public opinion before which acts of authority were to be judged. One of the lawyers, Target, would help draft the first constitution after the French Revolution.

As contemporaries sought explanations for movements that sought to limit monarchical authority, the Bavarian envoy in Vienna went so far as to claim in 1775 that "the spirit of revolt has become universal." Although the diplomat exaggerated, these movements for reform to some degree influenced and encouraged each other.

THE EIGHTEENTH-CENTURY STATE SYSTEM

Eighteenth-century Europe consisted of states dancing together in temporary partnership until the music changed and old partners were deserted and new ones embraced. The eighteenth-century state system was a pattern of rivalry and alliance in which each state vied for global and dynastic power. Few borders or thrones were secure from challenge by other states and rulers coveting more territory and more power. Rulers sought to expand their power through marriage, inheritance, or warfare. Each state looked out for its own self-interests and forged alliances that would help further those interests. Global and dynastic rivalries led to conflicts and ultimately to wars as states tried to add more territory and other states sought to maintain the balance of power, so that one state did not grow more powerful at the expense of the others. Spain, the Dutch Republic, Sweden, the Holy Roman Empire, and the Ottoman Empire found themselves with far less power than in the seventeenth century, while Britain, Russia, and Prussia continued to expand their power.

The emergence of a global economy increasingly linked to colonial trade engendered rivalries and conflicts between England, France, Spain, and the Dutch Republic, as each battled for commercial and colonial advantage. The wars that resulted were motivated by the hope of economic gain and reflected the primacy of mercantilism, which assumed that there was a finite amount of wealth available in the world, and that the might of any state depended on its success in bringing in more gold than it paid out.

Dynastic rivalries remained a major source of conflict. In England, George I from the German state of Hanover succeeded to the throne in 1714, but his German origins and interests complicated British foreign policy and led to unsuccessful attempts by the Catholic Stuart pretenders to take back the British throne. Meanwhile, on the continent, Frederick the Great of Prussia and Maria Theresa of Austria locked horns in a battle of expansion for the former and survival for the latter. The other Great Powers lined up in alliances on the side of each.

Global Rivalries

As voyages of discovery opened up new horizons to Europeans, the stakes of colonial rivalry between the Great Powers rose. During the seventeenth century, England, the Dutch Republic, France, Spain, and Portugal had gradually expanded their trading routes across the seas. Coffee, tea, molasses, ginger, indigo, calicoes, tobacco, and other colonial products—for the most part luxury goods—fetched high prices. The discovery of gold in Brazil in 1694 and 1719 further whetted the appetites of commercial companies. China also began to fascinate some Europeans. By the end of the seventeenth century, Dutch and French traders began to go there in greater numbers. The land trade routes that stretched through the Middle East and Central Asia still continued to reward the ambition and persistence of merchant-traders, who returned with spices and fine silks. Christian missionaries went out in greater numbers, seeking converts in Asia. Chinese prints, porcelain, gardens, silk, and rugs became popular in Western Europe, particularly during the first half of the century.

In the eighteenth century, the British East India Company carried its trading interests to more distant places, establishing new posts in South India and Bengal. Parliament licensed the company to operate as a military force. British traders exchanged slaves taken from West Africa and textiles and other manufactured goods for colonial products. The British East India Company's ships carried Chinese porcelain, silks, spices, and tea to England in exchange for silver and, increasingly, opium grown in India. An Englishman in the middle of the eighteenth century exclaimed that "the Interests and Commerce of the British Empire are so inseparably united that they may be very well considered as one and the same."

Spain still had the largest empire. It included the largest Caribbean islands, the Philippines in the Pacific, and most of South America except for Brazil, which belonged to Portugal. The Dutch had bases on the coast of South America, West Africa, and South Africa (their colony at the Cape of Good Hope was the only permanent European settlement at the time in Africa), the island of Mauritius in the Indian Ocean, the Indian subcontinent, Indonesia, and Japan.

The British colonies in the New World differed from Spanish colonies and, even more, from French colonies. Many people had migrated to the British colonies seeking economic opportunity, or in the case of Massachusetts Puritans and Maryland Catholics, religious toleration. These settlement colonies also welcomed emigrants from the German states, who hoped to make a living as farmers, artisans, and day laborers. Unlike in the towns and villages they left, men far outnumbered women, although entire families, too, took passage on ships bound for America, where as much as possible they sought to recreate the way of life left behind.

French forts and settlements dotted the North American colony of Nouvelle (New) France, the most important of which was Louisbourg on Cape Breton Island in the Gulf of St. Lawrence. French trappers established posts on the Mississippi River, with the port of New Orleans at its mouth far to the south. The territories claimed by the French, on which they had only scattered military and trading posts, almost tripled in size by mid-century, but by the 1760s the French population of Nouvelle France stood at only about 80,000 people.

Global rivalries led to conflicts between the Great Powers, both on the seas and in the colonies themselves. French and British armies and navies struggled in North America, the West Indies, and India, believing that the gain or loss of Canadian furs, Caribbean spices, or Indian jewels might be a damaging blow to dynastic prosperity and prestige. Spanish colonial rivalry with Britain led to the only war ever fought over an ear. Both Spain and England insisted that their colonies ship goods only on vessels flying their flag. Since 1713 the Spanish had granted the right to Britain to supply its colonies with 4,800 slaves each year; in exchange for this sale, a single English ship each year could call and trade at one Spanish colonial port. Illegal trade, however, continued as before. The Spanish navy sank several English ships, and in 1731 one of its vessels accosted an English frigate suspected of smuggling. A Spanish sword cut off one of the ears of the captain, Jenkins. The incident led to the "War of Jenkins' Ear" in 1939 after a member of Parliament whipped up anti-Spanish sentiment by waving the severed ear in the air during a speech.

The Hanoverians and the Stuarts in Great Britain

In 1702, Queen Anne (1665–1714), Protestant daughter of James II, succeeded her brother-in-law, William III, to the throne of England. Despite eighteen pregnancies and five live births, Anne had no surviving children. The House of Commons had passed the Act of Succession in 1701 to prevent any future restoration of the Catholic Stuart line to the throne. By this act, which broke the strict rules of dynastic succession, the Protestant ruling dynasty of Hanover, related by blood to the English royal family, would become the English royal line upon Anne's death.

In 1707, the Act of Union created the Kingdom of Great Britain, which took the Union Jack as its flag, and linked Scotland to England and Wales. Scotland received seats in the House of Commons, but fewer than its population might have warranted. Parliament's goal in formalizing the existing dynastic union was fear that Scotland might seek to summon Queen Anne's exiled Catholic half-brother (James III) to be king of Scotland, instead of going along with England and Wales' awarding of the throne to the house of Hanover. Ireland, in which English Protestants owned seven-eighths of the land, continued to pay dearly for having supported the Catholic monarch James II after the Glorious Revolution of 1688 had sent him from the throne. Legal restrictions prevented Catholics from being merchants, lawyers, or members of the Irish Parliament, the power of which was strictly limited by the English Privy Council. In England itself, Parliament had not extended the Toleration Act of 1689 to Catholics. British Catholics could not vote, be elected to Parliament, or hold state offices; they also were subject to special taxes, could not possess weapons, be admitted to Oxford or Cambridge Universities, or worship freely, at a time when Protestant Dissenters—that is, Protestants not belonging to the Church of England—were able to rise to respectable positions within the British state.

The Hanoverian George I (1660–1727), a distant cousin of Queen Anne, became king in 1714. He never learned English, brought some of his own advisers from Hanover, was stubborn and obese (many of his subjects referred to their monarch as "King Log"), and may have ordered the murder of his wife's lover in Hanover. All of this was more easily forgiven by wealthy Englishmen than his apparent indifference toward the crown he wore, seemingly demonstrated by the fact that he spent long periods of time in his beloved Hanover.

The Hanoverian dynasty's accession to the throne complicated British foreign policy. The Treaty of Utrecht (1713), the first of two treaties that concluded the War of the Spanish Succession (1701–1714), confirmed Britain's colonial supremacy, adding Newfoundland, Nova Scotia, the Hudson Bay territory, and New Brunswick, as well as Gibraltar and the island of Minorca, and the right to trade in Spanish colonial ports. But George I looked with disfavor on the treaty because it had not furthered the interests of Hanover. Furthermore, many Whigs viewed the compromise treaty as a humiliation for England. It was ratified by the House of Lords only because Queen Anne had created enough new peers to assure passage.

The new Hanoverian dynasty was threatened by remaining support for the Catholic Stuart dynasty. Some conservatives still claimed that James III, the Stuart son of James II, was the legitimate heir to the throne. In 1715, the intransigent supporters (Jacobites) of James III began an uprising in Scotland. Although by the Treaty of Utrecht the king of France had officially renounced support for James, Catholic France still wanted him on the British throne. But troops loyal to George I quickly quelled the rebellion.

George II (1683–1760) became king in 1727. Like his father, he was courageous and had led troops into battle in Germany. But unlike his father, he took the time to learn English (although it remained decidedly his second language). He spoke it with a strong German accent that his subjects mocked ("I hate bainting and boetry!" he once announced). He had a stiff, tedious personality, displaying impatience and a bad temper. On one occasion he bellowed, "I am sick to death of all this foolish stuff, and wish with all my heart that the devil may take all your bishops, ministers, Parliament, and the devil take the whole island—provided I can get out of it and go to Hanover!"

In 1745, the dreamy pretender, Charles Edward Stuart (1720–1788), planned an invasion of England, similar to the one his father had undertaken thirty years earlier. "Bonnie Prince Charlie" landed in Scotland with a small army of enthusiasts, while British troops were engaged on the continent. Adding Scottish clansmen from the Highlands to his force, he then marched southward into England with about 9,000 men. The threat to the

(*Left*) Prince Charles Edward Stuart, "Bonnie Prince Charlie." (*Right*) The Battle of Culloden Moor, 1746, in which hopes for a Stuart restoration were vanquished.

throne was serious enough to give birth to the British anthem "God Save the King," which dates from this time.

But Charles Edward found in England almost no support for his cause. Commercial and manufacturing centers, in particular, rallied against any possibility of a Stuart restoration. The young pretender hesitated a hundred miles from London and then retreated to Scotland. Many highlanders deserted his ranks as English troops ravaged their country. William Augustus (1721– 1765), the duke of Cumberland and third son of George II, overtook and defeated Bonnie Prince Charlie at Culloden Moor near Inverness in April 1746. He earned the nickname of "the butcher" through his ruthless treatment of the defeated rebels. It was the last battle fought on British soil to this day. The pretender hightailed it back to France. The government ordered the execution of two Scottish peers who had thrown their support to the pretender and forbade the wearing of kilts or tartans, symbols of the highlanders. Thereafter, only a handful of Jacobites continued to celebrate Stuart birthdays. They toasted "the king over the water" living in French exile by holding their glasses of spirits over another glass filled with water.

The Prussian-Austrian Dynastic Rivalry in Central Europe

The increased power of Prussia threatened Habsburg interests in Central Europe. Charles VI (ruled 1711–1740), the decent but mediocre Holy Roman emperor, had never recovered from the Habsburg loss of Spain in the War of the Spanish Succession. More than this, he remained obsessed with keeping the remaining Habsburg lands together. As Charles had no son, he spent years during his reign trying to bribe or otherwise convince the other European powers to recognize the integrity of the Habsburg inheritance upon his death. In 1713, he sought to get them to recognize the Pragmatic Sanction, which asserted the indivisibility of the Habsburg domains and recognized the right of female as well as male succession to the monarchy, should Charles have no sons.

When Charles VI died without a male heir, his twenty-three-year-old daughter Maria Theresa (ruled 1740–1780) assumed the Habsburg throne. While Maria Theresa could, as a woman, become empress of Austria, she was barred from becoming Holy Roman empress, thus opening up the question of imperial succession. The young queen had little money, no army, almost no bureaucracy, and bad advisers, and hence was in a poor position to defend her throne against hostile powers. Worse, France and Prussia, despite having pledged to uphold the Pragmatic Sanction, were each preparing to dismember the Habsburg empire.

An immediate threat came from the young Prussian king, Frederick II (ruled 1740–1786). Frederick came to the throne in the same year as Maria Theresa and quickly sought to take advantage of a queen in a world of kings. Confident that the very recent death of the Russian empress would preclude Russian assistance to Austria, Frederick sent his army into Austrian territory.

As a young man, Frederick had little in common with his raging father, Frederick William I (see Chapter 7). The royal son was intelligent, played the flute, enjoyed reading, preferred the French language to his native German, and as a boy expressed little interest in the army. At the age of eighteen, he tried to run off to England to catch a glimpse of his intended

Maria Theresa and her family at the Schönbrunn Palace outside of Vienna. The future Emperor Joseph II stands at her right.

Frederick the Great rides into battle.

English bride. When Frederick's fugue, planned by his best friend—and perhaps his lover—was foiled, the furious king decided to have his son executed. When dissuaded by his officials, Frederick William made the young Frederick watch from a prison cell the decapitation of his friend. Forced by his father to serve in the royal bureaucracy and as an army officer, Frederick became an aggressive absolute monarch.

Frederick, called "the Great" by his subjects, worked twelve hours a day lovingly overseeing minute details of army administration. His own physical courage was legendary—six times in battle horses were killed beneath him. At the same time, he eschewed the extravagant court life of the French Bourbons, allocating a mere 3 percent of state revenue to the court, in contrast to perhaps a third of the budget of the French monarchy.

Frederick the Great's "enlightened" reforms (see Chapter 10) made Prussia a more efficient absolutist state. His intent was to extend the reach of the state rather than to improve the lot of his people. Frederick improved the state bureaucracy by introducing an examination system to govern entry. Through these examinations, talented commoners could be awarded positions in the courts of law; in Berlin, two-thirds of the judges were commoners. Thus, talent as well as birth determined who served the state.

Frederick admired and granted a title of nobility to the rationalist philosopher and theoretician of the absolutist state, Christian Wolff (1679–1754). Wolff contended that the ideal man would follow the dictates of reason and would live to improve the condition of mankind. No one was more suited to this than, he argued, the absolute monarch, whose power, as "first servant of the state," alone could guarantee his subjects' rights and prosperity. In exchange for protection, Wolff argued, like Thomas Hobbes half a century before, the king's subjects would willingly relinquish their freedom. The monarch's absolute, effective rule would replicate the universe as created by God. Frederick saluted Wolff's almost worshipful trust in the state as the source of all rights, taking his ideas to be a blueprint for effective absolutism.

"Old Fritz" strengthened the Prussian economy by establishing state-operated iron- and steelworks, ordering the construction of more canals to haul goods, and encouraging the establishment of workshops in Berlin to produce textiles, glass, clocks, and porcelain. Because he ordered officials to accumulate stocks of grain in good times, Prussia never suffered the desperate periods of dearth that occurred in eighteenth-century France.

With careful budgeting and relative frugality, Frederick the Great managed to pay for his wars. He closely monitored state tax revenues and expenses. He refused to undertake expensive loans, sell noble titles and privileges, or impose ever more crushing levies on the peasantry, policies that were wreaking financial chaos and social havoc in France.

Frederick continued the exemptions of the Junkers (nobles) from many taxes and preserved their domination of the bureaucracy and army. He personally planned educational reforms with an eye to improving the performance of his officials. Nobles oversaw the collection of taxes, and the regional government. Virtually all military officers were nobles. But Frederick also wanted to keep the Junkers in a position of subordination to the crown. Noble army officers could not marry or travel abroad without the king's authority, a constraint that would have been unthinkable in France. Frederick's response to the hint of any disagreement from nobles, officials, officers, or anyone else was "Don't argue!" He tolerated no appeals of royal decisions. In a society with a relatively rigid social structure, aristocratic and military virtues were henceforth inseparable in Prussia, a fact fraught with significance for modern German history.

CONFLICTS BETWEEN THE GREAT POWERS

While the rivalry between Great Britain and France assumed global dimensions, the rise of Prussia and Russia (see Chapter 7) as powers carried European dynastic rivalries and warfare into Central Europe. The War of the Austrian Succession (1740–1748), begun when King Frederick II of Prussia invaded Silesia (a Habsburg territory), revealed the fundamental principle in eighteenth-century power politics: the balance of power. The unchecked success of any one power seeking to expand its territory inevitably brought a combined response from the other powers to maintain a rough balance between the states. The expansion of Prussian power, then, engendered the "Diplomatic Revolution" of 1756, when Austria and France put their long-standing rivalry aside to join forces against Prussia and Britain in the Seven Years' War (1756–1763). The long, costly war between France and Britain was truly global in extent, as both powers battled in North America, the Caribbean, and India. Armies were larger and better drilled than ever before. At the same time, the French and, in particular, the British navy played a greater role in transporting troops and supplies, as well as guarding commercial vessels in the global struggle.

The War of the Austrian Succession

The War of the Austrian Succession reflected naked absolutist aggression. Frederick the Great coveted Silesia (now part of Poland), a Habsburg territory south of Prussia and squeezed between Saxony, Poland, and Austria. With its textile, mining, and metallurgical industries, Silesia was the wealthiest province within the Habsburg domains. In 1740, shortly after succeeding to the throne and without warning, Frederick sent his army into Silesia.

Frederick was the latest in the line of aggressive Prussian kings who identified the interests of the state with a powerful army complemented by a centralized bureaucracy able to raise money through taxes. The Habsburg monarchy embodied, by contrast, the complexity of Central Europe. Austrian Germans dominated the administrative structure of the empire of many different peoples and languages. The multiplicity of privileges (particularly those of Magyar and Croatian nobles), traditions, and cultures undermined the authority, resources, and efficiency of the state. The Habsburg empire also lacked the trading and manufacturing base of Great Britain and the Dutch Republic, foremost among the non-absolutist states, or of France or even Prussia. Mercantilists in Austria hoped that foreign trade would add to the coffers of the state, but the overwhelmingly rural Habsburg lands had little to export, despite the development of manufacturing.

The new empress's troubles were not limited to Silesia. The nobles of Bohemia, the richest province, rebelled against Habsburg rule, offering the throne to the ruler of Bavaria, Austria's rival in southern Germany. Dependent upon the good will of the provincial Diets, no Habsburg monarch could be sure of having either sufficient support from the estates or money with which to raise an effective army.

Now, with Prussian troops occupying Silesia, Maria Theresa travelled to Hungary to ask for the support of the Hungarian Diet, which had agreed to the Pragmatic Sanction in exchange for recognition of Hungary's status as a separate kingdom. Dressed in mourning clothes following the recent death of an infant daughter and clutching one of her sixteen children to her, Maria Theresa convinced the Diet to provide an army of 40,000 men

Aristocratic officers safely above the carnage at the Battle of Fontenoy, 1745.

and cavalry. The Magyar nobles held out their swords to her, shouting their promise to give "life and blood" for her. The gesture could not restore Silesia to the Habsburgs, but it may have saved the Habsburg monarchy. Aided by Hungarian troops, imperial forces put down the Bohemian revolt.

Fearing a disproportionate expansion of Prussian power in Central Europe, other states joined in an alliance against Frederick. Yet, confronted by an alliance of Austria, Russia, Sweden, Denmark, and Saxony, states with a combined population of twenty times its own, Prussia more than held its own, with the help of France as well as Saxony, Spain, and Bavaria, each hoping to help bring about the disintegration of the Habsburg empire. France joined the anti-Austrian coalition because it coveted the Austrian Netherlands, Spain because it wanted to recapture influence in Italy, and the king of Piedmont-Sardinia because he coveted Milan. Frederick, satisfied for the moment with the acquisition of Silesia, withdrew from the war in 1745 after the Peace of Dresden. But Britain was drawn into the conflict by its need to protect the dynastic territory of Hanover from Prussia and France. Indeed, at Dettingen in 1743, King George II became the last British monarch to fight in battle. His horse was spooked and rode off with its frightened royal rider astride. France's army defeated the combined Dutch and British forces in the Battle of Fontenoy in 1745, the bloodiest battle of the century until the French Revolution. Two years later in the United Provinces, with the war going badly, a coup gave William IV of Orange almost monarchical authority as stadholder,

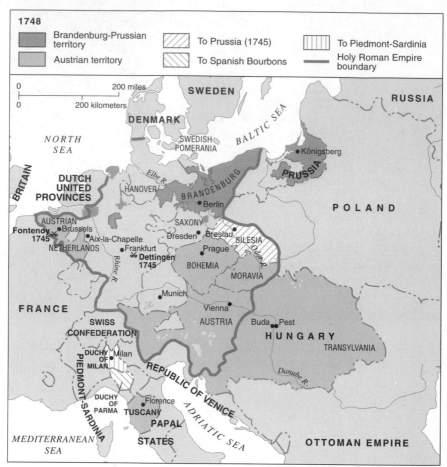

MAP 11.1 THE WAR OF THE AUSTRIAN SUCCESSION, 1740–1748   Major battles and territorial changes at the end of the war.

making the post hereditary. In 1748, the inconclusive Treaty of Aix-la-Chapelle ended the War of the Austrian Succession (see Map 11.1). French forces withdrew from the Austrian Netherlands in return for the English abandoning the fort of Louisbourg on the St. Lawrence River, captured during the fighting. Parma was given to a branch of the Spanish Bourbons, and Piedmont-Sardinia absorbed parts of the Duchy of Milan.

The Seven Years' War

Since the development of absolute states during the seventeenth century, warfare in Europe had been driven by absolutism, specifically the territorial interests of absolute rulers. But previous wars had revealed the limits of absolutism. Wars had dragged to a halt when rulers and states no longer could raise enough money through the sale of offices and titles or by undertaking loans. The Seven Years' War (1756–1763) was remarkable for several reasons. First, it was arguably the first truly global conflict. The commercial interests of France and Britain clashed in North America, the Caribbean, and in India (see Map 11.2). The war intensified the Anglo-French struggle for control of North America. Second, for the first time we can speak of a war not just of kings but self-consciously of nations, at least in the cases of Britain and France. Both states underwent a surge of patriotic enthusiasm, marked, for example, in the case of France by calls for "patriotic gifts" to support the war. In Britain, the sense of being "Britons," as opposed to subjects of the king, developed among all classes, accentuated by an overwhelmingly popular war against Catholic France. In Britain and France, there were calls for the more efficient management of the war, seen as part of pursuing the interests of the country.

Prussia's gains in the War of the Austrian Succession helped engender the Diplomatic Revolution of 1756. This ended more than a century of intermittent warfare between France and the Austrian Habsburgs. Alarmed by the expansion of Prussian power, Austria allied with France, and then Russia, with the goal of recapturing Silesia. The price of France's support would be its future annexation of the Austrian Netherlands (Belgium) and Austrian neutrality in a war between Britain and France (which had effectively already been at war in North America for two years). Frederick the Great now turned to Britain, France's enemy, for an ally. To France and Russia, Britain's sudden and shocking alliance with Prussia seemed a betrayal, even as France reversed its century-old opposition to Habsburg interests. The Great Powers changed partners, then went to war again.

In 1757, Frederick first defeated a large French army and then a Habsburg force. But later a Russian army attacked from the north, occupying Berlin, while more Austrian troops marched on Prussia from the south. Both the French and Russian armies benefited from infantry tactics first implemented by Frederick the Great's army. Prussia's situation seemed desperate, leading the king to compare his state to "a man with many wounds who has lost so much blood that he is on the point of death." But as luck would have it, Peter III became tsar of Russia in 1762, succeeding Empress Elizabeth, Frederick's determined enemy. The new tsar admired the Prussian king and called the Russian troops home. At the cost of perhaps 300,000 soldiers, Prussia had preserved its full independence.

In India, the rivalry took the shape of a struggle between the British and French East India Companies against the background of intrigues and warfare among Indian rulers. In India, where there were only about 5,000 British residents (and 20,000 soldiers), Robert Clive (1725–1774) led an army of British troops and Indian mercenaries into Bengal. There the prince preferred French to British traders and had incarcerated more than

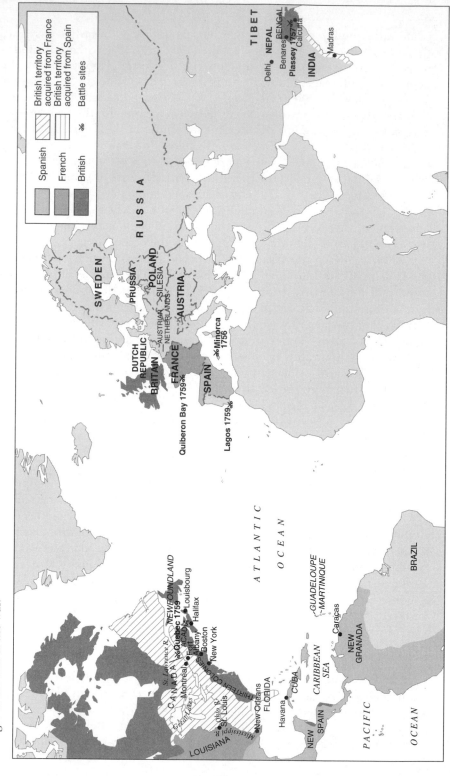

MAP 11.2 THE SEVEN YEARS' WAR, 1756–1763   Areas of conflict, including battle sites, during the Seven Years' War, as well as territorial changes at the end of the war.

a hundred British subjects in a room so small and stuffy that most of them died—the "Black Hole of Calcutta." In 1757, Clive's force defeated the prince's army at Plassey. After putting a pliant puppet on the Bengali throne, Clive continued to use British troops to further his own interests, and that of the British East India Company, defeating several Indian armies. By 1761, the stage was set for British control of most of the Indian subcontinent, with the British navy preventing French traders and soldiers from receiving sufficient supplies.

In what became Canada, there was much more at stake because both powers were fighting for control of a vast territory. In this struggle, France had a decided disadvantage. Even after more than a hundred years as a colony, Nouvelle France had a French population of only about 80,000 people, for the most part clustered in three towns along the St. Lawrence River—Montréal, Québec, and Trois-Rivières—and otherwise scattered over a vast territory. By contrast, the thirteen British colonies already had more than 2 million residents. British incursions into their territory led Indians to ally informally with the French. During what Americans call the French and Indian War (1754–1763), British troops forced over 10,000 French-speaking Acadians (that is, people living in Nova Scotia and New Brunswick) to emigrate. Many of them settled in the French colony of New Orleans, where the word "Cajun" emerged as a corruption of the French "Acadien."

The British navy accentuated its advantage on the seas by seizing 300 French merchant ships and capturing 8,000 sailors even before hostilities formally began. Despite the capture by French troops of several forts in the Great Lakes region, British ships reduced French reinforcements and supplies to a trickle, also defeating a French fleet at Quiberon Bay off the coast of Brittany in 1759.

In 1759, General James Wolfe (1727–1759) led an audacious, successful British attack on the French near Québec, his forces climbing up the cliffs from the St. Lawrence River to surprise their enemy. A year later, the British captured Montréal and then drove the French from the Ohio Valley. In the Caribbean, the British picked off the French islands and their small garrisons one by one.

War left all the combatants exhausted. The British national debt had doubled. The financial crisis of the French monarchy worsened as well, and its capacity to wage war diminished. By the Treaty of Paris of 1763, Austria recognized Prussia's absorption of Silesia in 1740 in exchange for Saxony's retention of independence. The Southern Netherlands, however, would remain an Austrian Habsburg territory. The settlement in North America and the Caribbean was much further-reaching. Canada became British, although France retained fishing rights on the Grand Banks off Newfoundland. But France gave up to Britain all claims to territory east of the Mississippi River, and to Spain territory west of the Mississippi, as well as most of its trading stations in India. It retained the Caribbean islands of Martinique and Guadeloupe, only because English colonists feared com-

General Wolfe's forces scale the heights of the Plains of Abraham in Québec.

petition from sugar produced on those islands if they became British. Spain ceded Florida to Britain (though only, as it turned out, until 1783). Spain also reclaimed the fortress of Havana in Cuba and established control of the enormous Louisiana Territory, which stretched from the almost tropical climate of New Orleans to the freezing plains of central Canada.

Britain then tried to mend fences on the continent, where the balance of power had been preserved. However, Joseph II of Austria wanted to incorporate Bavaria into the Habsburg domains. Austrian troops occupied Bavaria, leading to the brief War of Bavarian Succession (1778–1779). The resistance of Prussia and that of various smaller German states foiled Joseph II's plan. Like Franco-British emnity, Austro-Prussian rivalry continued unabated.

Armies and Their Tactics in the Eighteenth Century

Long after monarchs succeeded in putting an end to private noble armies, warfare remained part of noble culture. Military schools in France, Russia, and several of the German states trained the sons of nobles in the skills of war. In Prussia, Frederick William I believed that any attempt to allow commoners to become officers would be "the first step toward the decline and fall of the army." Noble officers had much more in common with the officers of the enemy than with their own troops, conscripted or impressed from the lower classes. Moreover, the Habsburg state often appointed foreign nobles as officers in its army. Officers captured during a war were treated to a nice glass of wine and a good meal, and then exchanged for their own officers who had fallen into enemy hands. War was fought over territory. In some ways, it seemed like a game of chess played between aristocrats in a manor house parlor. It is said that the French officers at the battle of Fontenoy in 1745 gallantly shouted to their British counterparts, "Fire first, *messieurs les anglais!*"

Recruitment practices differed in the various European states. The Prussian army's military recruitment system was the most comprehensive. Each of its regiments was assigned a district from which to draw recruits, and Prussians were not allowed to serve as mercenaries in other armies. In France, military recruitment was placed directly under the control of the state bureaucracy, which relieved officers of the responsibility for filling a quota of recruits. Villagers now drew lots to see who would be drafted into the reserve force. In Russia, each commune (*mir*) had to provide at least one soldier. Throughout Europe, certain categories of population were exempt from service, including prosperous farmers and the servants of French nobles, Russian merchants, and in many countries, men with families. England was alone among the major powers in not having a standing army, at least partially because in modern times it had not experienced a major foreign invasion. It did not implement mass conscription until World War II.

Yet, mercenaries still sometimes provided the bulk of eighteenth-century European armies, the notable exception being the French army. Military service provided those who joined up with regular meals, shelter, and adventure. The Swiss guards served the French royal family, and their countrymen fought with a variety of armies. The Dutch army included a brigade of Scottish highlanders. However limited the possibilities of social ascension through the army, military service could still provide respectability. Criminals and other men with something unpleasant in their pasts often turned up as soldiers.

Desertion remained widespread, affecting up to 35 percent of an army, despite threats of mutilation for those caught leaving. During the Seven Years' War, about 62,000 soldiers deserted the Habsburg army, 70,000 left the army of France behind, and 80,000 Russians disappeared into the night. Tightly packed formations served to discourage desertions, as they were intended to do, because soldiers were under more constant control. Harsh, even brutal, discipline in camp complemented that in the field. Frederick the Great was not alone in believing that "[the soldier] must be more afraid of his officers than of the dangers to which he is exposed." Although strategies for supplying troops improved during the century, armies rarely moved far from their supply camps. The lack of commitment and unreliability of mercenary and levied troops often helped end fighting.

Military technology had evolved slowly since the invention of gunpowder. The bayonet, a protruding razor-sharp knife first attached to a musket in the previous century, pushed the pikeman, a foot soldier armed with only a spearlike weapon, off the battlefield. The few significant changes in warfare in the seventeenth century included improved flintlock muskets, with cartridges and iron ramrods that permitted riflemen to fire three times per minute, and range increased to 200 meters. Handheld firearms became practical weapons for the first time. Artillery pieces were now also lighter and more mobile, with somewhat greater range. The training of artillery officers, too, improved. Thus, Frederick the Great made exemplary use of artillery to complement infantry during the Seven Years' War.

Soldiers were now far better trained and disciplined than in the previous century; armies were far larger than ever before. Although regular army units in a number of wars were vulnerable to hit and run "guerrilla" attacks by patriots resisting invasion (for example, in the War of the Spanish Succession), the discipline and efficiency of troops in formation won or lost battles. Rifles, inaccurate beyond a short distance, were fired in deadly volleys by rows of soldiers taking turns reloading. Cavalry charges, which generally took place on the flanks with the goal of neutralizing the enemy's cavalry, usually were over quickly.

New tactics had brought great maneuverability in the sixteenth and seventeenth centuries, including linear formations involving coordinated movements that required well-trained and disciplined troops. And in the eighteenth century, even greater troop mobility was achieved by combining line and column formations in a "mixed order." Moreover, the British and Prussian armies were the first to create a light infantry division that could move and engage the enemy more rapidly, often fighting with bayonets, fighting in front of or alongside columns. Yet, defense still dominated in battle, as symbolized by the impregnable fortresses along the northern frontier of France built in the late seventeenth century. Line formation, the basis of contemporary warfare, was more conducive to defense than offense.

Following the unrestrained carnage of the Thirty Years' War (1618–1648), warfare became somewhat more civilized, or at least somewhat more predictable, with fewer civilian casualties. The general acceptance of rules of civility helped reduce the carnage during and after battle. Prisoners of war, even commoners, were kept in relatively decent conditions and were sometimes exchanged for their counterparts. The development of logistical support and professionalized, well-drilled armies meant that soldiers no longer had to "live off the land." The goals of warfare were now generally restrained by traditions of monarchical and aristocratic civility. Once victory was achieved, there seemed no reason to pursue one's enemy to finish him off. Civilians were now generally spared in times of war.

Navies

British statesmen knew that to maintain superiority over France on the seas, their enemy had to be kept busy on the continent, whether by direct military operations or by large subsidies paid to France's enemies among the German states. In the words of the duke of Newcastle, "France will outdo us at sea when they have nothing to fear on land . . . our marine

Siege warfare was still conducted during the eighteenth century. Lines of troops approach and fire on the town.

should protect our alliances on the Continent, and so, by diverting the expense of France, enable us to maintain our superiority at sea." The Royal Navy had begun to grow in size during the second half of the seventeenth century. It ceased to be principally a coastal defense force as it had been under the Tudor monarchs (albeit an able one, as the defeat of the Spanish Armada in the English Channel had demonstrated in 1588; see Chapter 5). As its role in protecting commerce increased, the Royal Navy expanded further, from 105 ships of the line at mid-century to 195 in 1790, while the smaller French navy increased only modestly in size to 81 warships, 9 more than those of the Spanish navy.

Building on earlier improvements in sails and rigging, charts and navigational techniques, the size and quality of ships improved. The British first added copper to hulls, which made their ships more sturdy. Short-barreled cannon of greater caliber proved deadly in close combat. Shipbuilding drew on scientific assistance from experts in mathematics and navigation.

Navies were beset by problems of desertion. Almost one-fourth of the men who joined the British navy between 1776 and 1780, many of whom had been dragged to the docks by press-gangs, deserted. Shipboard disease killed many sailors, despite the use of lemon juice to counter scurvy.

There were few decisive naval confrontations in the eighteenth century. But the British navy did defeat a Spanish fleet in 1718, thereby preventing an invasion of Sicily, and it defeated a French fleet in 1759, making impossible any French plan to assist the rebels against the British monarch. "Do you know what a naval battle is?" asked a French minister. "The fleets manoeuvre, come to grips, fire a few shots, and then each retreats . . . and the sea remains as salty as it was before." Despite the enhanced role of the navies of the Great Powers in defending commercial interests across the seas, such as by guarding merchant and supply ships, it was a century of maritime skirmishes. The cost of full-fledged battles seemed too high; ships were too expensive to build and maintain. Thus, fifteen times more British sailors died of disease between 1774 and 1780 than succumbed to battle wounds.

POLITICAL CHANGE IN GREAT BRITAIN

In England, the Glorious Revolution of 1688 had put an end to fifty years of social and political turmoil. The Bill of Rights of 1689 guaranteed Parliament's right to approve taxation and prohibited the monarch from suspending or dispensing with laws. English monarchs did not consider themselves completely bound by the Bill of Rights, as evidenced by the fact that they maintained standing armies in peacetime in defiance of the 1689 document. But the political struggles of the seventeenth century had demonstrated that the king had to work with Parliament in governing the nation. In turn, the state served as a guarantor of rights of property and patronage. The rights of Parliament and the elective nature of the House of Commons, even if based on an extremely narrow electoral franchise, distinguished British political life from that of its continental rivals. For his part, the English philosopher John Locke had argued that his nation's government should reflect an implicit agreement or contract between the monarchy and the people.

The period of "aristocratic consensus" that followed the Glorious Revolution was not as free from political contention as the term suggests. But it brought major changes in British political life. Thus, beginning in the 1760s, the interests of wealthy property owners were represented in the House of Commons, which gradually became a far more important political forum than the House of Lords, which only represented peers. It also became more difficult for the king to manage the House of Commons. The Whigs reaffirmed the essence of Britain's constitutional monarchy by demonstrating that the king could not rule without Parliament.

Edmund Burke.

Political differences between Tories and Whigs became more consistent. The former were now clearly identified with the prerogatives of the throne, the latter with the rights of Parliament. Whigs believed that the role of Parliament was to defend liberty, property, and the rule of law and thereby preserve the British constitution against possible abuses of power by the throne. In the words of the Irish-born political theoretician Edmund Burke (1729–1797), the British "mixed constitution" (which balanced the institutions of monarchy, the House of Lords, and the House of Commons), stood as an "isthmus between arbitrary power and anarchy." During this period, there emerged a sense that institutionalized opposition within Parliament to government policies was an intrinsic part of a political process in which competing interests were struggling for primacy. Moreover, during the eighteenth century, political life began to spill beyond the narrow confines of the British political elite as ordinary people demanded a voice in political life with increasing insistence. In Britain's North American colonies a similar and in some ways parallel struggle for liberty began, leading to the American War of Independence.

The Growing Powers of Central Government in Britain

During the eighteenth century, Britain, justly famous for its political preoccupation with liberty, saw the powers of central government expand. The increasingly global nature of trade and warfare made greater demands on the state's administrative abilities. The growth, greater centralization, professionalization, and efficiency of military and civilian administration permitted Britain to remain the strongest power on the globe.

Between 1680 and 1780, as the British built and consolidated their empire, their army and navy tripled in size. The power and reach of the Treasury also increased. As the economy grew rapidly, the British state raised taxes and efficiently collected them (the latter in dramatic contrast with the monarchy of France, whose financial plight continued to grow). These included land taxes, as well as excise (taxes on commodities) and customs taxes, which provided an increasing percent of revenue. At the same time, loans to the state greatly raised the national debt. The effective centralization of the British state made it possible for its increasing commercial and manufacturing wealth to be mobilized for the conquest and defense of the empire. The government spent more than three-quarters of its expenditures on the army, navy, or paying back debts from previous wars.

Britain's bureaucracy, though still quite undersized compared to that of France, also grew in size and complexity. A single French province had more officials than the entire government of Britain at the beginning of the century. By the end of the century, this was no longer the case. Limited venality, too, provided Britain with an advantage over its rivals. As the British state increased in size, its officials became more professional (technical expertise became more important), and departments within the bureaucracy became more clearly defined. Posts in the civil service for educated men offered chances for social advancement.

The British government, like its continental rivals, faced the problem of paying off the massive national debt amassed by loans that financed dynastic and trade wars. In 1719, the government had awarded the South Sea Company the right to take over the national debt. The South Sea Company had been founded in 1711 with the backing of a number of Queen Anne's advisers. Two years later, the government had awarded it a monopoly over the slave trade with Latin America and with favorable conditions for European trade. But because of the intermittent fighting with Spain during the War of the Spanish Succession, any profits from such trade seemed in the distant future. Needing a rapid infusion of capital, the directors of the company offered stock for sale on attractive terms. They bribed some potential purchasers and developed ties with high government officials.

With the help of unscrupulous investors, many of whom were holders of part of the national debt who wanted to get their money back, the company converted the debt owed them by the state into company shares. The directors parlayed the price of the stock higher. The scam worked as long as there were more investors whose funds could be used to pay dividends to those who had bought shares earlier. But the profits were all based on the sale of the stock rather than on real commercial gains.

A fever of speculation seized England. Smaller companies started up overnight, most of them insolvent or strangely organized, such as one literally limited to women dressed in calico. One joint-stock company (made

Contemporary lambasting of the South Sea Bubble. "Picture of the very famous Island of Madhead. Situated in Share Sea, and inhabited by a multitude of all kinds of
people, to which is given the general name of Shareholders." (Amsterdam, 1720)

up of shareholders who would divide profits according to the amount of
their investments) had been set up for "a purpose to be announced." The
speculative craze ended with a jolt in 1720. With no gains of any kind
forthcoming, the "South Sea Bubble" burst in September of that year. It
was the first great financial crash (and coincided with the bursting of
smaller speculative "bubbles" in Amsterdam and Paris). Political careers
were ruined in the resulting financial chaos.

The financial scandal hung over political life when Robert Walpole
(1676–1745) became chancellor of the Exchequer in 1721, a post he
would hold for more than twenty years. The son of a landowner of modest
means, the short, ruddy-cheeked Walpole was energetic and ambitious.
And he was determined to restore political confidence. The king quietly
replaced several of his ministers who had been most compromised in the
South Sea Bubble. Parliament passed a law that allowed only companies
chartered by the government to sell stock shares to the public. Walpole
created a sinking fund (intended to "retire" the debt by paying off, or
"sinking," part of it each year) to finance the crown's debts, which helped
restore confidence.

King George II's lack of interest in matters of government made him as
dependent on Walpole as George I had been. Queen Caroline's regard for
Walpole contributed to his ability to weather political storms. He survived

the wrath of some Members of Parliament (MPs) who disliked his unpopular financial reforms, including greater taxes on imports and on salt, and his goal of keeping Britain out of war.

Walpole perfected the system of political patronage, virtually managing the House of Commons. He used the patronage available to him as the effective head of the government to build unwavering support within Parliament and to place MPs loyal to him—"placemen"—in well-paying governmental positions, some of which were veritable sinecures. In return, they voted with the government.

On the local level, landed magnates doled out and received the plums within the administration: the bigger fish became county lord-lieutenants and the smaller fry became justices of the peace. One tombstone epitaph flaunted the obvious in eulogizing a well-connected lady lying therein, "By means of her alliance with the illustrious family of Stanhope, she had the merit to obtain for her husband and children twelve appointments in church and state," not a bad haul.

However, Walpole's support in Parliament eventually began to crumble. His attempt to reform the excise tax by extending it to wine and tobacco failed in 1733 after generating riots. William Pitt (1708–1778) led a coalition of "boy patriots" against Walpole. Specifically, they objected to his inaction against Spain, whose ships were harassing British ships in the

Sir Robert Walpole, standing at the head of the table, directs a cabinet meeting.

Atlantic. After being forced by public outcry to declare war on Spain in 1739—the perfectly trivial War of Jenkins' Ear—Walpole resigned in 1741.

Lesser lights continued Walpole's policies of building a political coalition based upon patronage. The duke of Newcastle (Thomas Pelham-Holles; 1693–1768), whose notorious incoherence led him to be known as "Hubble-Bubble," succeeded Walpole and ably manipulated the patronage of his position. Then Pitt came to power. The "Great Commoner" Pitt was a lonely, unstable man who alternated between feverish excitement and dark depression. He was demagogic, arrogant, and ruthless, commanding respect through fear.

The Role of the House of Commons

The British monarch could declare war or make peace, call or dissolve Parliament, appoint whomever he or she wanted to serve as cabinet minister, officer, bishop, general, or admiral, and the cabinet and government officials carried out the functions of state. But they did this against the backdrop of ongoing practical compromises between Parliament and the monarch.

During the early decades of the eighteenth century, the House of Commons gradually emerged as an epicenter of political life. Unlike the House of Lords, all of whose members were nobles, members of the House of Commons were elected by Britain's narrow electoral franchise based on landed wealth. Although still dominated by "gentle," or landed interests, the number of merchants elected to the Commons increased, for families that had made fortunes in business, whether they were titled nobles, non-titled gentry, or commoners, invested their money in land. Wealthy MPs could easily control blocs of votes in their counties through patronage. In 1776, only 5,700 men in Britain elected half of the members of Commons, most of whose members were routinely re-elected every seven years. In only three boroughs did more than 4,000 men have the right to vote and in several, fewer than 15 men could cast ballots. Thus, one lord confidently assured his son in 1754, "Your seat in the new Parliament is at last absolutely secured and that without opposition or the least necessity of your personal trouble or appearance." Some MPs were returned from "rotten" and "pocket" boroughs. Rotten boroughs ranged from the infamous "Old Sarum," which had no inhabitants but two representatives in Commons, and another that had been under water for centuries, to those with several hundred voters almost as easily managed. Pocket boroughs were in the pocket of the MP because his election was uncontested.

England's growing industrial towns were barely represented in Parliament. Manchester and Birmingham were not represented at all. Many of those in the urban elites no longer accepted the idea that their interests were "virtually represented" by MPs from districts represented in the House of Commons. Furthermore, emerging political discontent reflected alarm that Commons' role as the defender of the constitution against possible tyrannical abuse was being compromised by institutionalized corruption, symbolized by rotten and pocket boroughs.

The Development of Party Politics in the 1760s: Whigs and Tories

Whigs and Tories had governed in reasonable harmony during the Robert Walpole era. But after Walpole, many Whigs came to believe that ministers ought to be acceptable to Parliament as well as to the king. In contrast, Tories traditionally took the view that the prerogatives of king and church had to be maintained at all costs.

After coming to the throne in 1740, George III gave the impression that he intended to rule without Parliament. When George refused to declare war on Spain in 1761 during the Seven Years' War, William Pitt resigned as chief minister. Subsequently, the king appointed his former tutor, the aristocratic, aloof Scotsman John Stuart, the earl of Bute (1713–1792), as secretary of state and then as chief minister of the government. But Bute was an unpopular choice because he was not a member of Parliament, had little political experience and even less influence, and did not want Britain to undertake hostilities against Spain.

The king's appointment of his "dearest friend" seemed to Whigs to violate the unwritten agreement that the king act with Parliament's consent. Determined opposition merely served to strengthen the king's resolve. The press castigated Bute, and crowds in the street howled against him. Rumor insisted that he owed his controversial appointment to having been the lover of the king's mother. On the verge of a nervous breakdown, Bute resigned in 1763.

Bute's appointment raised the question of ministerial responsibility, dividing the House of Commons along ideological lines. George III sought to diminish the decisive role that the parliamentary Whigs had played during the reigns of his grandfather and great-grandfather. He turned against the Whig country gentlemen who no longer could be counted upon to support him on all matters. The king insisted on the monarchy's independence and particularly on his right to choose whomever he wished as minister.

Members of Parliament representing the interests of the "country gentlemen" began to use the term "party," but without the trappings of formal organization that would come late in the next century. Whigs, to be sure, remained loyal to the throne, although George accused them of being otherwise. But, as in the case of the king's appointment of Bute, they insisted on the rights of Parliament. While the issues dividing Tories and Whigs remained in some ways the same as those that had characterized the Walpole period, or even the Civil War, the emerging notion of political parties was perhaps of more lasting significance than the political groupings themselves.

The young King George III
in saner days.

The term "party" had existed since the time of the Glorious Revolution;
it had the sense of a group of people sharing a belief on a specific matter of
political controversy. It had been somewhat synonymous with "faction,"
which since the 1670s had the negative connotation of a cabal of individuals working for their own interests. With the exception of the Jacobite
Tories, however, the differences between Whigs and Tories were vague and
uncertain during the reign of the first two Georges. George III's seeming
determination to create a government above parties helped the old Whigs
revive their party solidarity. The idea developed that a party of parliamentary opposition formed an essential part of the parliamentary system of
representation.

George III insisted that it was his duty to defeat the forces of "faction."
Edmund Burke, for one, rejected the king's efforts to discredit the concept
of "party." In *Thoughts on the Cause of the Present Discontents* (1770), he
defined a party as "a body of men united for promoting by their joint en-
deavors *the national interest* upon some particular principle in which they
are all agreed." He believed that political parties stood as the basis of
representative government and therefore of political order. A newspaper
article in 1770 went even further: "Opposition, in parliament, to the
measures of government, is so far from being in itself an evil, that it has
been often productive of good to the state." By this description, parties
were to be "a regular and desirable feature of politics, not as a cancer on

the body politic which ought to be removed as swiftly as possible." They alone could ensure the preservation "of responsible government," specifically, the notion that ministers ought to be acceptable to Parliament. This concept of a loyal parliamentary opposition did not exist in France or anywhere else on the continent. Nor, for that matter, did it exist in all constituencies within Britain; in many, politics, dominated by family ties and outright patronage, went on as before.

George III could count on about a third of the members of Commons for unconditional support, at least partially because they held court-appointed posts. Unfailing voters for "court" became increasingly known as "Tories," particularly to the Whig opposition. Supporters of the government rejected the term, as they did all labels, but at the same time they lent credence to the concept by cohesively defending a patriarchal society based on monarchy, titled aristocracy, and the Anglican Church.

In 1766, Pitt returned to power for two years. King George depended on the political leadership of the "Great Commoner," but Pitt lost support even among his political friends by accepting a peerage, becoming duke of Chatham. Vigorous debates among Whigs, principally between the imperious Pitt and the duke of Newcastle and his followers, however, did not diminish the emerging notion of "party" most Whigs now accepted. For Whigs, the most significant issue remained the extent to which Parliament could limit the will of the monarch. Although family connections still loomed large, the significance of such an issue carried the party beyond the sense of a vague coalition.

The Rise of British Nationalism

Although king and Parliament were bitterly divided during the crises that led to the English Civil War and the Glorious Revolution, they were thereafter unified in the quest for British commercial and international predominance. During the eighteenth century, a strong sense of nationalism developed in Great Britain. This included pride in the nation's high degree of freedom and reverence for Parliament as the Protestant institution that had turned back the threat of Catholicism and successfully impeded absolute rule.

The fear of Catholicism, endemic in England since the Reformation, fired British nationalism. During the Anglo-French wars, faced with the threat of French invasion, British patriots across the social spectrum embraced the British Isles as the chosen land of God. British patriots never tired of boasting of Britain's prosperity and social stability while denigrating France, the strongest Catholic power. French support of the American rebels and the French Revolution of 1789 would, of course, bring these feelings to a head.

Many increasingly nationalistic Britons firmly believed that their "privileged island" had been chosen by God for a unique imperial destiny.

William Pitt the Elder, in particular, was an empire builder. Believing that the throne's Hanoverian interests were dominating foreign policy, and having made his reputation attacking Walpole's seeming indifference to British interests abroad, Pitt turned his attention to expanding the colonies. "Who will laugh at sugar, now?" thundered the future prime minister in the House of Commons in 1759 to nobles who had scorned colonial trade. Horace Walpole (1717–1797), Robert Walpole's youngest son, who was a novelist as well as the beneficiary of lucrative posts that left him plenty of time to write, was among the few who had some doubts about all of this. "No man ever went to the East Indies with good intentions," the younger Walpole said, adding sarcastically, "it really looks as if we intended to finish the conquest of the world during the next campaign."

The lure of commercial profit thus helped define British nationalism. A financial community of investors in London closely followed not only the vicissitudes of the economy but the ups and downs of British warfare. A good many financiers had, after all, loaned money to their state and therefore eagerly watched what was done with it. Their foreign and colonial trade often depended on naval protection, further linking their interests to the Union Jack. The state itself depended on expanding commercial activity for tax revenue. Economic interest groups and lobbies developed, learning their way around the London financial community and the corridors of government to represent their views on excise and customs taxes. New patriotic societies, some of them drawing ordinary people into the wave of nationalist enthusiasm, sprang up in many places, with mottoes like "For our country."

The generally harmonious relationship between the landed elite and the commercial community was a source of social and political stability in Britain, and of British nationalism. Nobles and gentry benefited from the expansion of state activity, diversifying their investments with loans to the crown. Unlike the continental powers, in Britain all subjects paid taxes. This afforded all social groups the sense of being Britons. At the same time (in contrast to the case in France), improved communications and the development of a national market aided the process of national integration in Britain.

Their commitment to the nation also enabled the British elite, proud of their freedoms and their country's more decentralized form of government, to accept a stronger state apparatus without complaint about infringements on their liberty. Thus, they did not feel the need for constitutional guarantees (based upon equality before the law) against arbitrary tyranny. The stronger state did not diminish the status of British landowners, and in no way infringed on their personal freedoms within civil society. Monarchy and Parliament joined hands in the pursuit of British empire, with the eager support of London's burgeoning financial community. English peers sought to prove, in Burke's words, that "a true natural aristocracy is not a separate interest in the state, or separable from it."

Anglo-Irish, Scottish, and Welsh gentlemen became more integrated into a national British landed elite, with increasing intermarriage a revealing indication of this process. Many Scots, though hardly all, began to see themselves as British, just as fewer English people considered Scots or Welsh to be outsiders who were potentially disloyal to the crown. The British monarchy became increasingly revered and celebrated as a rallying point for the nation.

Although many property-less Britons had reason to fear impressment gangs sweeping up men unlucky enough to be in the wrong place at the wrong time, and many others objected to having to billet troops, many of the king's subjects began to identify with their nation's increasingly professional armed forces. Moreover, the landed elite embraced military service to the nation.

CHALLENGES TO ESTABLISHED AUTHORITY

In the 1760s and 1770s, movements for reform emerged in several countries. In Britain, "liberty" became the watchword of political opposition to the government. In a parallel struggle on the other side of the Atlantic Ocean, the American colonists of Britain's thirteen colonies demanded "no taxation without representation," and then, when rebuffed, the "patriots" rebelled against British rule in the War of American Independence. Some of the reform movements on the European continent sought to reduce the strength of absolute rule, as in Denmark, or wanted to prevent the imposition of stronger centralized authority, as in the resistance of the parlements in France to Louis XV, or by the provincial estates to the Stadholder William V of Orange,in the case of the Dutch Republic. Other movements for reform challenged what seemed to be unwarranted privileges, again most notably in France, where the most significant attempt came from a reforming minister within the state itself. In every Western country, more information about political events in other states was available through newspapers and gazettes, as well as from merchants, other travelers, and diplomats, who exchanged correspondence in an increasingly literate culture. In Britain and parts of Western Europe, political clubs also reflected greater preoccupation with politics. These reform movements, then, influenced each other, however indirectly.

British Radicals

In the 1760s in Britain, ordinary people (called "the swinish multitude" by Edmund Burke) demanded electoral reform, and some even universal manhood suffrage. Reformers asked that constituencies be redrawn so that rapidly growing industrial regions in the north of England be appropriately represented in Parliament, and that London, which was grossly under-represented, elect more Members of Parliament. Moreover, outside the small, formal political arena defined by the right to vote, shouts for freedom swelled among ordinary people.

John Wilkes (1727–1797), the son of a successful London malt distiller, was an MP of modest means and a Protestant Dissenter. Charming, witty, and reckless, Wilkes leapt into the public eye in 1763 with the publication of his newspaper the *North Briton*. Issue number 45 attacked the government—and the king himself directly—for signing the compromise Treaty of Paris with France that year, ending the Seven Years' War. The king ordered "that Devil Wilkes, a trumpet of sedition" arrested for libel. Wilkes announced that he considered his arrest a blow against liberty and the constitution by the unjust, arbitrary power of government, "a question of such importance," as he put it at his trial, "as to determine at once, whether ENGLISH LIBERTY be a reality or a shadow." The court freed Wilkes after a week in jail on the basis of parliamentary immunity. Wilkes triumphantly boasted that his fate was tied to "that of the middling and inferior set of people" in Britain.

Fearing prosecution for pornography, as the government dug up a bawdy old poem he had written (and the House of Commons lifted parliamentary immunity), Wilkes left for France in 1764. He was arrested, tried, and convicted upon his return to Britain in 1768, and then freed after thou-

The supporters of John Wilkes and liberty take to the streets.

sands of people demonstrated on his behalf. Wilkes then stood for election in Middlesex, the county making up most of Metropolitan London north of the Thames and outside of the "City." With the support of many merchants and small manufacturers wealthy enough to be eligible to vote, Wilkes was re-elected to Parliament. Four times he was elected, and four times Parliament refused to seat him because of his previous conviction.

Wilkes claimed that Parliament's action threatened "the first principle of our constitution," the freedom to stand for election. Cloaking himself in a patriot's garb, he became a rallying symbol for the campaign for the rights of the unrepresented in a time of economic hardship, grain riots, and work stoppages.

"Wilkes and Liberty" echoed in speeches, conversation, and song. In 1769, the Society of the Supporters of the Bill of Rights invoked the name of Wilkes as it called for the government to "restore the constitution." The number 45—the libelous issue of the *North Briton*—became a rallying cry. Wilkes' rather misshapen face appeared on posters, handbills, verses, cartoons, tea mugs and dinner plates. He was elected sheriff of London in 1771, and even lord mayor three years later, though he was not allowed to occupy either position.

Reformers now began to demand greater freedom of the press, specifically a redefinition of libel laws (so that the government could be criticized) and the right to publish parliamentary debates. They further demanded that Parliament meet each year and that MPs be required to live in the districts from which they were returned. However, in general, Whigs disassociated themselves from Wilkes, wary of demonstrations for universal manhood suffrage. Few Whigs were willing to go beyond insisting on the principle of ministerial responsibility within the confines of the existing constitution.

Literary and "philosophical" societies, which had sprung up in most large towns, facilitated the emergence in England of political culture even wider than that which had developed during the political crises of the seventeenth century. Now interest in politics was such that some inns and coffeehouses added special reading rooms to accommodate their clientele. By 1760, London printing presses, the number of which had increased from seventy-five in 1724 to about two hundred at the time of Wilkes' first arrest, churned out eighty-nine newspapers, four of which were dailies. Another thirty-five newspapers were published outside London. By 1790, there were fourteen London daily newspapers (Burke wrote for four of them), and the number of provincial papers printed each day had multiplied by four times.

Political pamphlets, handbills, and caricatures inundated the capital and the larger provincial towns. By the 1760s, artists had stopped omitting the names of the targets of their satirical wit. Like its Whig opponents and the extra-parliamentary radicals, the government found itself obliged to utilize newspapers, pamphlets, brochures, and handbills to argue its case before public opinion.

By the 1780s, two relatively well-defined parties contended for power within the context of a constitutional monarchy. But the changes went further than this because some Whigs demanded political reform and, in doing so, carried political life beyond the narrow limits of the British political arena. Ordinary people, unrepresented in Parliament, began to make their voices heard.

American Revolutionaries

During the 1760s, another challenge to the British crown was smoldering far across the Atlantic Ocean in North America. The thirteen American colonies, many times the geographic size of England, had become ever more difficult for the British government to administer. The population of the colonies, which accounted for about 20 percent of British exports and supplied 30 percent of its imports, had grown by tenfold in just seventy years, from about 250,000 in 1700 to more than 2.5 million in 1775, compared to about 6.4 million in England at the same time. Philadelphia had by that time become the second largest city in the British Empire, with 30,000 residents. Those arriving on the shores of the Americas found a land of opportunity. Many were able to purchase land that would have been beyond their means at home. Artisans and even common laborers commanded relatively high wages because of the shortage of labor in the colonies.

Over the decades, the residents of the colonies had developed a sense of living in a separate society. Merchants, a heterogeneous group that stood atop the social hierarchy, lawyers, and wealthy landowners like the Virginians George Washington (1732–1799) and Thomas Jefferson (1743–1826) led the colonists. They resented the continued presence of the British army—sometimes in their very houses through forced billeting—and the attempt of British officers to try to impose on the colonial forces the same standards of discipline that applied in Britain. They believed that they had the right to resist unjust laws in the name of liberty.

For radicals in Britain, "rotten" boroughs symbolized the threat to liberty; for the American colonists, as expressed by John Adams, "liberty can no more exist without virtue and independence than the body can live and move without a soul." Some British Whigs began to identify themselves with the colonists, who took the name Whigs themselves, claiming that corruption was threatening Britain's constitutional balance between monarchy and Parliament. They saw the two movements as parallel struggles.

The quest of George Grenville (1712–1770), who had succeeded Pitt in 1763 as chief minister, for supplementary revenue aggravated the strained relations between the colonists and the mother country. The king's new favorite also ordered massive efforts to stop smuggling. In 1765, Parliament passed the Stamp Act, which forced Americans to purchase stamps for virtually anything printed. A year later, Benjamin Franklin (1706–1790) of

Philadelphia made the colonists' case to the House of Commons. He argued that the act represented the unfair domination of England over another part of the empire. Commons repealed the Stamp Tax, but the government then initiated other taxes. Furthermore, Parliament proclaimed a Declaratory Act in 1766, which asserted its right to tax the colonies as it pleased. A year later, the Townshend Acts levied duties on colonial imports of paper, tea, and other products.

The American colonists' determined protests encouraged British reformers. The colonists' claim that they were being taxed without having the right to representation played nicely into the hands of political radicals in Britain. The shout "Wilkes and Liberty!" began to echo on both sides of the Atlantic. American political pamphlets and brochures found an eager audience among British merchants, manufacturers, artisans, and other people eager for representation in Parliament. Colonists lobbied in Britain to demonstrate that "the cause of America is the common cause of the realm . . . both countries have the same complaint, and therefore claim the same friends."

The British government was at first divided and uncertain in the face of an upsurge of demonstrations at home and agitation in the colonies. In March 1770 in Boston, British soldiers fired on a crowd that was vociferously protesting the quartering of British troops in that city. The "Boston Massacre," which took five lives, outraged colonists. That year, George III appointed Frederick Lord North (1732–1792) first minister. North, an amiable, sensible man who got along well with the king, was skilled at putting together political coalitions and was a brilliant debater in Commons. He sponsored the Tea Act of 1773. North hoped to aid the East India Company by allowing the company to ship a surplus of tea to the colonies, with the British government collecting its tariff only when the tea arrived in American ports. The move would reduce the price of tea but maintain what the colonists viewed as the unacceptable principle that Britain could tax goods imported into the colonies. It would also threaten the interests of American smuggling, a widespread money-making operation.

On December 16, 1773, colonists dressed as Indians forced their way aboard British merchant ships docked in Boston and dumped the cargo of tea into the harbor. Parliament responded to the Boston Tea Party by passing the repressive "Intolerable Acts." These specified that the port of Boston be blocked until the colonists had reimbursed the merchants and government for the tea dumped into the harbor. In September 1774, representatives from the colonies met in the First Continental Congress. By now, Benjamin Franklin was drawing a distinction between "uncorrupted new states," by which he meant the colonies, and "corrupted old ones," one of which seemed to be waging war on liberty. The British sent more troops. In April 1775, in the first open fighting between colonists and British regulars, the colonial militia held its own against British troops searching for weapons at Concord and Lexington, Massachusetts, and

Paul Revere's depiction of the Boston Massacre.

then in the pitched battle at Bunker Hill in Boston, when 1,500 colonists, holding the higher ground, turned back two British attacks until running out of ammunition.

In *Common Sense* (1776), some 100,000 copies of which circulated in the colonies, Thomas Paine (1737–1809) launched a devastating attack on the king. *Common Sense* reflected the influence of the Enlightenment, particularly Rousseau's notion of the "social contract." Furthermore, it reiterated Locke's argument that governments received "their just powers from the consent of the people." All laws, Paine wrote, "are laws of nature." Paine helped convince delegates to the Second Continental Congress to adopt Thomas Jefferson's Declaration of Independence on July 4, 1776. It declared the equality of all people, based on "inalienable rights" and that the authority of government stems from the consent of the governed. It also asserted that when governments violated the "unalienable rights" to "life, liberty, and the pursuit of happiness" of their people, the latter had the right to rebel.

The war now became a fight for independence. The Continental Congress appointed George Washington to command its troops. The British government hoped to recover the colonies at the lowest possible cost; military campaigns were compromised by halfhearted and often inept leadership by the British commanders. The initial British policy, that of isolating and punishing the rebels, quickly failed. There were too few British troops to fight a war over a considerable territory against an increasingly determined foe. Next, the British undertook conventional military operations. But the colonial troops simply scattered. In 1776, Washington's army managed to cross the Hudson River into New Jersey. Washington captured Trenton that December, wintering with his ragtag army in freezing temperatures at Valley Forge, Pennsylvania.

In contrast to British soldiers, each of whom required the transport of a third of a ton of food across the Atlantic each year, the colonial army was virtually self-sufficient and broadly supported by the colonists. Trained in part by an officer in the army of Frederick the Great, it became far more than what a loyalist (someone who supported the British cause) dismissed as "a vagabond Army of Raggamufins, with Paper Pay, bad Cloathes, and worse Spirits." The most significant battles of the war were fought in the classic European style of confrontations, not as engagements between hit-and-run patriots and British regulars. Some of the colonists fought with an almost evangelical fervor that reflected the fact that many of them saw the struggle as one of good against evil. The brutality of the British soldiers in requisitioning goods and maintaining order in the territories they controlled was self-defeating. By the time General Richard Howe (1726–1799), discouraged by the failure of the British government to send promised reinforcements, tried to negotiate with the rebels at the end of 1776, the colonists refused to listen because they had no reason to negotiate.

France signed an alliance with the American rebels in February 1778, agreeing to provide substantial loans in gold. The French monarchy realized that favorable commercial treaties with an independent United States might more than compensate for the loss of all rights to territory east of the Mississippi. Thereafter, the French navy harassed British supply routes. In 1779, Spain joined the war on the American side, hoping to profit from Britain's colonial war by recapturing Gibraltar and Minorca. Seeking to prevent the North American colonies from purchasing Dutch supplies, the British fought the Dutch Republic. Britain also confronted the refusal of Russia, Sweden, Prussia, Portugal, and Denmark to curtail trade with the rebellious Americans.

Great Britain had overextended its capacity to wage war. Its naval advantage, the basis of its strength in modern times, had been eroded. Despite swelling the army to 190,000 men, campaigns on land went badly. On October 19, 1781, Lord Cornwallis surrendered his outnumbered army at Yorktown, Virginia, to a combined force of American and French troops. "Your armies are captured," George III was informed, "the wonted superiority of your navies is annihilated; your dominions are lost." Two years later, Britain officially recognized the independence of the American colonies. News of the struggle of the colonists for freedom from British rule spread throughout much of Europe, reported in newspapers. As pub-

The British surrender at Yorktown, 1781.

lic opinion became surprisingly well informed about events across the Atlantic Ocean, the American victory encouraged movements for reform in other places.

Britain, which had lost its richest colony, did not want to lose any others. In 1774, as the resistance in the thirteen colonies became more determined, Parliament had passed the Quebec Act, in an effort to prevent tensions between the British Anglican conquerors and the Catholic population of Quebec from boiling over. The Test Act, which required all officials to take communion in the Anglican Church, was abolished in Quebec, and the Catholic Church was given the status of an established church by being permitted to levy tithes. The British government also strengthened its control over its other colonies. The India Act (1784) created a board responsible to Parliament to which the East India Company had to report, while establishing the jurisdiction of British courts in cases of fraud or other transgressions. Another parliamentary act in 1791 created more centralized administration in Canada, with a governor-general exercising far more authority than two colonial assemblies elected by restricted suffrage.

The advent to power in 1784 of William Pitt the Younger (1759–1806) restored political stability. The next year, Pitt introduced a wide-ranging bill for political reform. It proposed to reduce the minimum tax required for the electoral franchise and to abolish thirty-six rotten boroughs,

William Pitt the Younger addressing the House of Commons.

awarding their representation to manufacturing regions and cities. Opposition among the country gentlemen, as well as that of the king himself, however, led to the bill's defeat. But Pitt did manage to eliminate useless offices that had become sinecures, introduced more accurate accounting methods into government, facilitated the collection of excise taxes, and encouraged further foreign trade. Despite the personal failings of George III, Britain, which remained the world's premier commercial and manufacturing power, emerged from the relatively turbulent decades with its constitutional monarchy strengthened.

The Parlements and the French Monarchy

Two interrelated struggles in the early 1770s challenged the nature of absolute rule in France. The first was against what seemed unwarranted privileges held by nobles and other corporate groups. The second opposed royal policies and pretensions that seemed to transcend absolute rule and verge on despotism. In a way, this debate somewhat paralleled political issues in Britain. Despite the fact that the British monarchy was not absolute, the insistence of Whigs that Parliament's prerogatives be in no way compromised by royal authority reminded some contemporaries of French noble claims, made through the parlements, that the French monarchy was overstepping its own constitutional limits. Likewise, challenges to the tangle of economic and social privilege in France replicated, even if in a different context, campaigns for political reform by ordinary British subjects unrepresented in Parliament and therefore outside the political arena.

In France, those seeking reforms that would limit royal authority had a much more daunting task because of the absolute nature of monarchical rule. The kings of France nonetheless depended on the support of the parlements. These were law courts made up primarily of nobles and seated in Paris and more than twelve provincial cities. Their principal function was to give royal edicts the force of law by registering them. By refusing to register them, the parlements could impede the functioning of the absolute state. Thus, when the king's edicts had to do with increased or new taxation, political opposition to royal policies sometimes emerged in the parlements.

The increased centralization of the French state had in itself helped create contact between more people and the officials of the king. The concept of a "public" emerged, before which the monarch was in some sense responsible and before which the layers of privilege in French society no longer seemed acceptable. The crises that embroiled the king and the parlements from the 1750s to the 1780s helped shift public opinion toward the view that the parlements represented the rights of the "nation," threatened by a monarchy that seemed to be lapsing from absolute to despotic rule.

The issue of Jansenism set the parlements against royal absolutism by raising the constitutional issue of the right of the monarch to circumscribe their traditional prerogatives. The Jansenists (see Chapter 7) were a dissident group within the Catholic Church. The pope had condemned Jansenism in 1713 with the papal bull *Unigenitus*, which Louis XV supported. But Jansenists found support within some of the parlements, which identified with Jansenist resistance to what seemed to be the absolute monarch's despotic rule. Louis XV's support of the papal bull angered some nobles and magistrates, who were inclined to resist what they considered the papacy's undue interference in French affairs.

The period of conflict between the parlements and the crown really began in 1749. The controller-general attempted to make the *vingtième* tax (a tax applying to both nobles and commoners) permanent, drawing heated opposition from the parlements. And the Church again sought, without success, to force the French clergy to accept *Unigenitus*. Many bishops threatened that sacraments would be refused to laymen who did not have a certificate signed by a priest attesting that the person had made his or her confession to a priest who had accepted the papal bull. Seven years later, the pope tried to defuse the crisis by banning these certificates.

But this concession did not placate the Parlement of Paris. Many of the parlements were manipulated by a handful of Jansenist magistrates and lawyers who managed to convince their colleagues that French acceptance of the papal edict amounted to an abandonment of French sovereignty over the temporal affairs of the Church. The king, refusing to hear the parlements' grievances, made clear that he considered the parlements nothing more than rubber stamps, a means of promulgating his will. When the Jesuit order continued to crusade against Jansenism, the Parlement of Paris responded by ordering Jesuit schools closed in 1761, citing the fact that members of the order took a vow of obedience to the pope.

The successive crises over Jansenism may have weakened the authority of the French monarchy by allowing the Parlement of Paris, and several provincial parliaments as well, to claim they were defending constitutional liberties and the independence of the Gallican (French) Church—since Jansenists saw themselves as part of it—against royal encroachment and against Rome. By weakening the authority of the Catholic Church in France, the crisis over Jansenism also eroded the prestige of the absolute monarchy. Jansenism ceased being a political issue after 1758, when the Parlement of Paris won judicial authority over many ecclesiastical matters. But the self-proclaimed role of lawyers and magistrates as representatives of public opinion and protectors of the sovereign political will of the nation against abuses of powers was an important legacy from the Jansenist crisis.

The layers of economic privilege in France had proliferated with the extension of state power, as each monarch sought revenues with increased desperation. Despite increasing calls for reform, even critics who vociferously challenged monopolies (for example, those of guilds) did not intend to end privileges per se. Rather, many of them wanted a share of the privileges and wanted to eliminate "unjust" monopolies that seemed to benefit others unfairly. Wealthy commoners, enriched by the economic changes, sought the kind of privileges nobles enjoyed, above all exemption from many kinds of taxation. Thus, the issue of taxation would mobilize some of the parlements against the monarchy because it raised the question of the layers of privilege that underlay the French state and of the limits of absolute authority.

In 1771, Chancellor René-Nicolas de Maupeou (1714–1792) provoked the parlements by again attempting to make the *vingtième* tax permanent. Many nobles feared that general tax increases might lead to dangerous peasant uprisings, in which nobles stood to lose the most. Facing mounting resistance, Louis XV effectively abolished the parlements. He then created new, more docile law courts that would not resist royal authority, staffed by magistrates who did not own their offices.

Both sides in the conflict between the parlements and Chancellor Maupeou appealed to public opinion. A declaration of high-ranking nobles stated that the king had abused "the constitution of the government and the rights of the people" by trying to establish "a despotism without bounds, without limits, and consequently without rights." The nobility asserted its "right of assembly," recalling that "the nation, in its assemblies, had charged the parlements with defending its rights." Influenced by the ideas of the Enlightenment, lawyers called for judicial reform, religious toleration, and the end to the abuse of privilege. When the monarchy tried to silence the lawyers, the latter turned courtrooms into forums for political opposition. Lawyers explored notions of sovereignty of the nation and put forward the case of the parlements against the crown.

As the idea of the nation gradually entered political discourse, the possibility emerged that when the interests of the monarchy and the nation clashed, popular allegiance could pass exclusively to the nation. Some degree of popular identification with parlements as defenders of the nation against despotism would not be effaced. The Maupeou "coup" lasted only three and a half years, but it had far-reaching effects on the nature of the opposition to the monarchy. It demonstrated that the parlements were not powerful enough to protect "the nation" against royal despotism, suggesting that only a body such as the Estates-General, which had not been convoked since 1614, could do so.

Louis XV was no stranger to unpopularity. He was held to be lazy and indifferent, as rumor had him obediently following the orders of his favorite mistress and advisers. The Seven Years' War had exhausted the treasury, and the king seemed incapable of restoring public confidence. Furthermore, France had lost Canada and several Caribbean islands to Britain, its hated rival. This loss of prestige, as well as income, increased the number of the king's critics. The structures of absolute rule seemed inadequate to managing the cumbersome French state; inefficient tax collection and the weight of growing expenses left the state coffers inadequately filled.

Louis XV's death in 1774 did not resolve the crisis. Following popular demonstrations and a spate of publications in support of the parlements, the twenty-year-old Louis XVI (ruled 1774–1793) dismissed Maupeou and recalled the parlements. Public opinion seemed to have helped turn back what was popularly conceived to be a despotic assault on the restraints on absolute rule.

Convinced that the financial difficulties of the monarchy stemmed from the stifling effect of privileges on the economy, a new minister, Anne-Robert Turgot, undertook ambitious reforms. His goal was to cut away some of the web of privileges, making the absolute monarchy more efficient. Turgot convinced the young king to issue royal edicts, despite the opposition of the Parlement of Paris. These ended noble and clerical tax exemptions, abolished the guilds, freed the internal commerce of grain (the price of which had been first set free in the 1760s), and exempted peasants from having to work a certain number of days each year repairing roads. Economic liberalization would, he hoped, increase agricultural production and manufacturing, thereby augmenting tax revenue.

But like Louis XV's attempts to override the traditional role of the parlements, Turgot's reforms aroused vociferous opposition. Nobles—with some significant exceptions—rallied against proposed financial reforms intended to extricate the country from its growing financial morass. The parlements, still smoldering over their treatment by Maupeou and Louis XV several years earlier, refused to register—and thereby give the status of law—the reforms of Turgot, who had supported Maupeou. Grain merchants and guilds, among other privileged groups, voiced strident opposition. Ordinary people rose up in protest, blaming the freeing of the grain trade for the higher prices of flour and bread in a period of dearth. Accusations of hoarding abounded. Grain riots, in which women played the leading roles, swept across the country during the spring "flour war" of 1775. The significance of these events was that an increasing number of the king's subjects lost the habit of obedience to him. Lawyers, once again insisting on the difference between absolute and despotic rule, would emerge as leaders as the political crisis of the monarchy accelerated in 1788.

The king dismissed Turgot in 1776, ending the most significant reform effort on the continent. That same year, the American colonists declared their independence from Britain. France allied with the colonial rebels, forcing Louis XVI to borrow ever more money at high interest rates and to sell more offices and titles to those who could afford to pay for them. This helped shift power within the nobility from the embittered "nobles of the sword" to the "nobles of the robe," who had been ennobled through the purchase of office or title. The unreformed French monarchy then slid into an even deeper financial crisis.

Other Movements for Reform

Although the influence of the Enlightenment varied in different places, the philosophes all put forward the claims of freedom against privilege and absolutism. Some rulers, principally those of Prussia, Tuscany, and Austria, introduced reforms inspired by Enlightenment thought, putting into practice reforms that seemed to reflect the "enlightened absolutism" that Voltaire and other philosophes had expected (see Chapter 10).

In other cases, movements for reform came from below. In the Swiss Republic of Geneva, native-born artisans during 1765–1768 exerted pressure for the right to vote, meeting in assemblies and demanding equality with the citizens possessing political rights. But they were rebuffed by wealthy Genevans, who tried to placate them with reductions in their taxes. An uprising in 1782 unseated the ruling oligarchy before the intervention of France, Sardinia, and the Swiss canton of Bern put an end to it.

There were also insurrections. In 1761, an uprising on the Mediterranean island of Corsica in the name of "fatherland and liberty" ended rule by Genoa, a northern Italian port dominated by bankers and merchants, although the French occupied Corsica seven years later. In 1770, Greeks rose up against Turkish domination. They were assisted by Russia, the Turks' enemy, eager to enter the world of Mediterranean politics with

Emelian Pugachev in his cage after he
was apprehended.

the goal of ultimately conquering Constantinople. Empress Catherine the
Great sent soldiers and a small fleet in the hope that Greek success might
encourage other peoples to rise up against Ottoman rule. Turkish troops
crushed the revolt, but the Greek movement for independence, by virtue
of the special place of classical Greece in the development of Western civilization, helped ignite pan-Hellenism. Yet, to be sure, many who supported the cause of Greek independence had reservations about the role of
Russia, a state as despotic as that of the Ottoman Turks.

In the Russian Empire itself, there was a massive rebellion, largely of
Cossacks, in 1773–1774 (see Chapter 9). It was led by Emelian Pugachev,
who promised to respect "liberty," including that of religion. The rebels
killed thousands of landlords before being crushed. And in Bohemia and
Moravia in 1775, peasants rose up against their lords and the state. Although Habsburg troops put down the rebellions, the uprising led Maria
Theresa and her son Joseph II to enact reforms that gradually abolished
feudal dues. Each of these uprisings was a movement for freedom, but
also a return to traditional privileges that seemed imperiled by the centralized absolute state.

In Denmark, where the king had imposed absolute rule in 1660 by suppressing parliament and refusing to consult with the estates, a current of
reform emerged early in the 1770s. In part, it was the inspiration of Johann Struensee (1737–1772), a German doctor, who convinced the ailing
King Christian VII (ruled 1766–1808) to undertake reforms to strengthen
the state economically so that, with Russian support, Swedish Baltic ambitions could be thwarted. The king abolished censorship and the death

penalty for thieves, extended religious toleration, and promised to undertake more agricultural reforms in the interests of creating a free peasantry. But the king's widowed mother and nobles conspired against the reforms. Struensee was tried and convicted of, among other things, living "without religion or morality," and executed in 1772. But after little more than a decade of reaction, the reforms Struensee had encouraged became part of a program for the future, a sign of the times.

In Sweden, the reforms of the 1760s and 1770s were swept away, as in the case of France and Denmark. A virtual coup d'état by King Gustavus III (ruled 1771–1792) imposed absolutism. Thus, while presenting himself as a "patriot king" protecting Swedish peasants from the nobility while reassuring the "intermediary powers," or estates, the king imposed a new constitution in 1772. It reduced the power of the Senate and the Diet. The king's cabinet became the principal arm of Swedish government. Yet, to the secretary of the British embassy in Stockholm, Sweden had not proven ready for liberal reforms. "Liberty," he wrote, "is not a plant of sudden growth; time only can give it vigor. It will not take roots but in a soil congenial to it; and, to be rendered flourishing or lasting, it must be cultivated with care and defended with unremitting attention from the dangers which perpetually surround it."

Political struggles in the Dutch Republic were similar to the struggles between Whigs and the crown in Britain, followed by the emergence of extra-parliamentary demands by ordinary people for political reform. The regents of the Dutch cities, defending the republic's federalism embodied by the Estates-General, which represented the seven provinces, opposed the policies of the bumbling Stadholder William V of Orange (in power 1751–1795). The regents declared war on Britain in 1780 in the hope of weakening their commercial rival. As the war dragged on, they also sought to weaken the monarchical pretensions of William V, who wanted to augment executive authority at the expense of the provinces.

In 1785, in the midst of political crisis, the Dutch Republic had allied with France to counter the Austrian plan to reopen the Scheldt River and restore Antwerp to some of its former commercial glory, which would have undercut Amsterdam's prosperity. The possibility that France might achieve its kings' dream of annexing the Southern Netherlands (Belgium) made the British government anxious, further irritating the pro-British William V.

In the meantime, a radical "Patriot Party," primarily drawn from the middle class and artisans, had begun to demand democratic reforms. Influenced by the success of the American revolutionaries, they demanded more democratic representation in the Estates and the right to have urban militias. These Dutch reformers unseated the stadholder. Prussian King Frederick William II (ruled 1786–1797), whose sister was the stadholder's wife, sent an imposing army in 1787, occupying Amsterdam and putting down the challenge to William V's authority as stadholder. Distracted by mounting political crisis, France backed down against the alliance of

England and Prussia. The balance of power had once again been preserved. Dutch patriot refugees poured into the Austrian Netherlands and France.

The Austrian Netherlands, too, experienced political turmoil. The powerful estate of nobles opposed Joseph II's enlightened reforms, which threatened their privileges, and succeeded in driving out Austrian troops in 1789. There too a movement for democratic reform emerged, calling for the transformation of the Estates into a representative assembly. The Dutch mood seemed to be catching. The prince-bishop of Liège stressed the importance of preventing "the evil schemes of the majority of the Liègois, who would like to become a republic and to join the United Provinces as other provinces . . . the burgomasters and other men of that quality wish to see themselves on chairs of velvet and be received with cannon salutes . . . only troops and fortresses can hold them to obedience." Dutch patriots invaded the Southern Netherlands in October 1789, driving away the Austrians. But a popular movement appealed to the nobles even less than did Austrian rule. Nobles, backed by the clergy and with the tacit support of most peasants, wrested control of the short-lived state from the urban-based reformers. The return of Austrian troops in 1790 occurred without resistance.

FADING POWERS: THE OTTOMAN EMPIRE AND POLAND

The structure of international power in eighteenth-century Europe was not fundamentally changed by the quest for reform during the 1760s and 1770s. But in the new, more competitive European environment of the late eighteenth century, two states that did not have access to the fruits of international trade and that were unwilling to restructure themselves lost their power in Europe. Thus, the Turkish Ottoman Empire entered a period of long decline, and Poland literally disappeared as an independent state, at least until after World War I. The Ottoman Empire, its power overextended and lacking a centralized structure of government, saw its territories in the Balkans and Caucasus eaten away by Austria and Russia. Poland, in contrast, had become a power without becoming an absolute state; weakened by noble domination of the monarchy, it fell prey to its aggressive absolute neighbors: Russia, Prussia, and Austria, which divided up the state in three partitions.

The Decline of Turkish Power in Europe

In contrast to other absolute sovereigns, Turkish sultans ruled indirectly, governing through church or village officials. Indirect rule itself may have hastened the decline of Ottoman absolutism, signs of which were already apparent late in the seventeenth century. The Turkish economy, army, and navy could not keep pace with the Western powers. Turkish cavalrymen, with curved swords and magnificent horses, fell before Western artillery and rifles.

Like the Spanish Empire at its peak, the Ottoman domains were so vast that they defied effective control. Insurrections, including some by the janissaries, challenged the authority of the sultans. Imperial officials, Muslim and Christian alike, became notoriously corrupt. Turkish authority virtually collapsed in mountainous Montenegro and Bosnia, where the Turks battled Habsburg and Venetian forces. The government began to run out of money. Stop-gap measures, such as the debasement of the currency, failed to provide the empire with sufficient revenue.

Incapable sultans, who were unable or unwilling to impose reforms, further weakened the Turkish cause. As boys they lived in virtual isolation in a world of uncertainty among court eunuchs and palace intrigue. No regular pattern of succession had ever been established. Whereas Peter the Great of Russia undertook Western military reforms, the sultans did not. The advice of officials who had been sent to Vienna and Paris to study methods of state went unheeded in Constantinople. There was not a single printing press in the Ottoman capital until well into the eighteenth century. Long wars fought against Persia in the East made it less easy to repress disturbances in the Balkans. In some parts of the empire, a system of land inheritance replaced the old system; new landowners began to force peasants into serfdom. The haphazard and inefficient collection of taxes, often by dishonest tax farmers, engendered peasant resistance. As the system of indirect rule declined in effectiveness, some local Christian and Muslim leaders now commanded their own military forces, virtually independent of the sultan's authority in Constantinople. This was precisely the same phenomenon that the absolute monarchs of France, Prussia, Russia, and Austria had overcome. The long decline of Ottoman power, which began in the last decades of the seventeenth century, during which the empire lost almost all of its European territories, facilitated the rise of Russia.

The Disappearance of Poland

While the Ottoman Empire survived, Poland did not as an independent state (at least until the end of World War I). Poland had been a strong state in the seventeenth century. But during the early decades of the eighteenth century, the kingdom, its population reduced by wars and bubonic plague to only 6 million people, had become increasingly dependent on Russia. Poland's eclipse made possible Russia's gains in Ukraine.

Polish nobles (the *szlachta*) not only maintained their prerogatives, they relegated the king to virtual political impotence. Nobles, who made up 8 percent of the population, elected the king. They considered this period of domination one of "golden liberty," marked by an unworkable political system by which a single vote in the noble assembly (Sejm) would bring about its dissolution (the *liberum* veto). Deputies were forbidden to make speeches in what became known as the "silent Sejm." Furthermore, Poland lacked a standing army and an efficient bureaucracy.

The War of Polish Succession (1733–1735) began when Russia attempted to impose its candidate on the Polish throne over the opposition of the Polish nobles. Because of France's interest in maintaining Sweden, the Ottoman Empire, and Poland as checks against Austrian Habsburg domination of Central Europe, Louis XV proposed a candidate for the throne, his father-in-law, Stanislas Lesczinski, who had reigned as king of Poland from 1704 to 1709 and now had the support of most Polish nobles. But a Russian army forced the election of Augustus III of Saxony (ruled 1733–1763), who was the Austro-Russian candidate.

When the Polish throne again fell vacant in 1763 with the death of the king, Russian influence led the Polish nobles to elect as king the cultured, cosmopolitan Stanislas Poniatowski (ruled 1764–1795), one of the insatiable Russian Empress Catherine the Great's many lovers ("many were called, and many were chosen," as one wag put it). Stanislas was somewhat influenced by Enlightenment thought. Sensing the necessity of reform, he hoped to advance manufacturing in Poland and looked to Britain as a model. He tried to end the *liberum* veto and to curtail the right of seigneurial courts to impose death sentences. He also established a number of schools. Only by such measures, he believed, could Poland escape poverty and backwardness, where killing a peasant was punished only with a fine. Voltaire and Rousseau were among those philosophes who viewed Poland as fertile ground for Enlightenment-based reform of noble prerogatives and ecclesiastical authority, and who concerned themselves with the fate of the "most unhappy realm." But some of the more powerful Polish nobles, who resented Russian influence, now opposed Stanislas and his reforms. They hoped that France or the Ottoman sultan might intervene on their behalf.

Catherine, like the Prussian king, feared that Stanislas' reforms might lead to a stronger, less subservient neighbor. Since 1764, Russia and Prussia had been allies in the attempt to prevent an expansion of French influence in the Baltic, while preventing Poland from reviving its fortunes. Furthermore, Polish nobles had begun to persecute non-Catholics. Catherine, in the interest of the Orthodox Church, demanded that all non-Catholics be granted toleration in Poland. When Polish nobles formed an anti-Russian and anti-Catholic confederation, Catherine sent troops into Poland. Ukrainian peasants took advantage of the chaos to rise up against their Polish lords. When they burned a Turkish town while chasing out Poles, Turkey entered the war against Russia. Catherine annexed Crimea, Wallachia, and several territories along the Black Sea, at Turkish expense.

Alarmed by an expansion of Russian power, Austria and Prussia demanded territorial compensation. Catherine suggested that the three concerned powers might help themselves to parts of beleaguered Poland. The First Partition in 1772 reduced Poland by about a third (see Map 11.3).

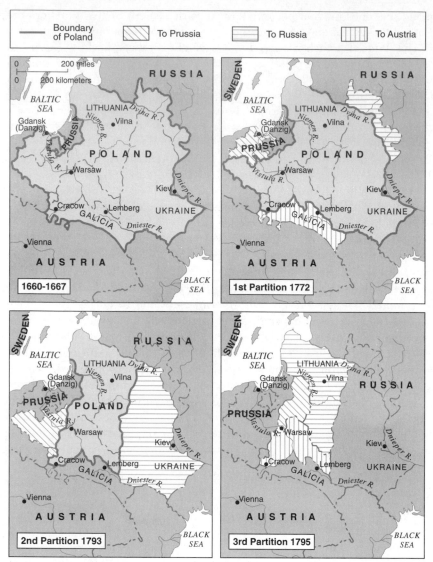

MAP 11.3 THE PARTITIONS OF POLAND   Poland at its greatest extent in
1660–1667, and the loss of territory to Austria, Prussia, and Russia during the
Partitions of 1772, 1793, and 1795.

Maria Theresa of Austria "wept and then took her share," the large
province of Galicia, which lay between Russian Ukraine and the Austrian
empire. Prussia absorbed West Prussia, which had formed a corridor separating East Prussia from the rest of the kingdom. Russia snatched large
chunks of territory of eastern Poland.

Stanislas proclaimed a liberal constitution in 1791 which, establishing a
hereditary monarchy and abolishing the unworkable system of noble veto,
proclaimed that all authority stemmed from the nation. This remarkable

document reflected the influence of the French Revolution. Poland became a constitutional monarchy, with the king naming ministers but with the parliament and Poland's few major towns retaining privileges.

But Poland's days were numbered. When Poles rose up in 1792 against Russian authority in the part of Poland that had been absorbed by Russia twenty years earlier, Russian troops intervened. They were backed by Polish nobles, the grave diggers of Polish independence, who opposed the liberal constitution. Prussia refused to come to Poland's aid, receiving in exchange for looking the other way its own annexation of more Polish territory in the Second Partition in 1793. With the Third Partition in 1795, Prussia and Russia ended Poland's independence for more than a century. The Constitution of 1791, perhaps the most progressive constitution of the century, was torn to shreds. "Poland was but a breakfast," wrote Edmund Burke, "where will they dine?" Russia's new gains drew its interests further into Central Europe, and it now shared a border with the Habsburg monarchy.

CONCLUSION

Some historians have argued that movements against absolutism and against privilege, particularly those against the latter in Great Britain and the successful rebellion of its North American colonies, constituted a general Western "democratic revolution." But, despite the quest for political change in several Western states, calls for universal manhood suffrage were rare, those for the extension of political rights to women even more so (an exception being Geneva in the early 1780s). Even in Britain, after a contentious decade marked by demonstrations for political reform, the most widespread riots of the 1780s were the anti-Catholic Gordon riots. In France, the assault on the Old Order was less an attack on the nobles, per se, than on privilege. The institutions of the Old Regime in continental Europe demonstrated not only resiliency, but also a capacity to undertake reform.

Nonetheless, denunciations in France against privilege, shaped in part by Enlightenment thought (and which echoed in other countries as well, helping spark the rebellion of Britain's thirteen North American colonies), would be revived in the late 1780s. The Seven Years' War and assistance to the Americans had considerably worsened the financial crisis of the French monarchy, as the increasingly global dynastic rivalries and wars placed further strains on European states. France entered a serious political crisis when critics of the monarchy condemned the king of ruling despotically and attacked in the name of freedom the layers of economic and social privilege that seemed to constrain effective government and constrict freedom. Calls for sweeping reform led to the French Revolution of 1789, which proclaimed the principle of the sovereignty of the nation. Once again, the eyes of Europe turned toward France.

PART FOUR

REVOLUTIONARY EUROPE

The French Revolution of 1789 struck the first telling blow in continental Western Europe against monarchical absolutism on behalf of popular sovereignty. Popular involvement pushed the Revolution to the left, while counter-revolution and foreign intervention led to the dramatic centralization of state authority and the Terror.

In 1799, Napoleon Bonaparte helped overthrow the Directory, the last regime of the revolutionary era in France. An admirer of the Enlightenment, Napoleon claimed that he was the heir of the French Revolution. But while Napoleon saw himself as a savior who carried "liberty, equality, and fraternity" abroad, his conquest of much of Europe before his final defeat left a mixed legacy for the future.

Following Napoleon's defeat in 1815 at the Battle of Waterloo, the Congress of Vienna created the Concert of Europe, the international basis of Restoration Europe. The British, Austrian, Prussian, and Russian rulers, restoring legitimate rulers to their states after the fall of Napoleon, hoped to prevent further liberal and nationalist insurrections in Europe. But liberal and national movements could not so easily be swept away. During the subsequent three decades, "liberty" became the watchword for more and more people, particularly among the middle classes, who came to the forefront of economic, political, and cultural life. Liberal movements were in many places closely tied to the emergence of nationalism, the belief in the primacy of nationality as a source of allegiance and sovereignty. Yet, liberal and nationalist movements shattered the Congress of Vienna as democratic and nationalist revolutions began in

France in 1848 and spread into Central Europe, challenging liberal and conservative monarchies alike.

In the meantime, during the first half of the nineteenth century, the Industrial Revolution slowly but surely transformed the way many Europeans lived. Dramatic improvements in transportation, notably the development of the railroad but also road improvements, expanded the market for manufactured and other goods. Rising agricultural production, increasingly commercialized in Western Europe, fed a larger population. Migrants poured into Europe's cities, which grew as never before. Contemporaries, particularly in Western Europe, sensed profound economic, social, political, and cultural changes.

CHAPTER 12

THE FRENCH
REVOLUTION

In 1791, King Louis XVI decided to flee Paris and the French Revolution. A virtual prisoner in the Tuileries Palace by the first months of the year, he had secretly negotiated for possible intervention on his behalf by the Austrian king and other European monarchs. The royal family furtively left the Tuileries Palace late at night on June 20, 1791, disguised as the family and entourage of a Russian baroness riding in a large yellow coach. But in the eastern town of Sainte-Menehould, the postmaster recognized the king, whose image he had seen on a coin. He rode rapidly to Varennes, where the National Guard prevented the king's coach from going on. Three representatives of the National Assembly brought the royal family back to Paris. Near the capital, the crowds became threatening, and National Guardsmen stood by the roadside with their rifles upside down, a sign of contempt or mourning.

The French Revolution mounted the first effective challenge to monarchical absolutism on behalf of popular sovereignty. The creation of a republican government in France and the diffusion of republican ideals in other European countries influenced the evolution of European political life long after the Revolution ended. Issues of the rights of people, the role of the state in society, the values of democratic society, notions of "left" and "right" in political life, the concept of the "nation at arms," the place of religion in modern society and politics, and the question of economic freedom and the sanctity of property came to dominate the political agenda. They occupied the attention of much of France during the revolutionary decade of 1789–1799. The political violence of that decade would also be a legacy for the future.

The revolutionaries sought to make the French state more centralized and efficient, as well as more just. Napoleon Bonaparte, who some historians consider the heir to the Revolution and others its betrayer, continued this process after his ascent to power in 1799.

The arrest of Louis XVI.

Modern nationalism, too, has its roots in the French Revolution. The revolutionaries enthusiastically proclaimed principles they held to be universal. Among these were the sovereignty of the nation and the rights and duties of citizenship. The revolutionaries celebrated the fact that the Revolution had occurred in France. But wars intended to free European peoples from monarchical and noble domination turned into wars of French conquest. The revolutionary wars, pitting France against the other Great Powers, contributed to the emergence or extension of nationalism in other countries as well, ranging from England, where the sense of being British flourished in response to the French threat, to Central and Southern Europe, where some educated Germans and Italians began to espouse nationalism in response to the invading French armies.

THE OLD REGIME IN CRISIS

The French Revolution was not inevitable. Yet, difficult economic conditions in the preceding two decades, combined with the growing popularity of a discourse that stressed freedom in the face of entrenched economic and social privileges, made some sort of change seem possible, perhaps even likely. When a financial crisis occurred in the 1780s and the king was forced to call the Estates-General, the stage was set for the confrontation that would culminate in the French Revolution.

Long-Term Causes of the French Revolution

The increasing prevalence of the language of the Enlightenment, stressing equality before the law and differentiating between absolute and despotic rule, placed the monarchy and its government under the closer scrutiny of public opinion (see Chapter 11). Borrowing Enlightenment discourse, opponents accused Louis XV of acting despotically when he exiled the Parlement of Paris in 1771 and tried to establish new law courts that were likely to be more subservient than the parlements had been. Opponents believed that the king was trying to subvert long-accepted privileges. He was forced to relent and restore the parlements, which maintained their right to register royal edicts.

Enlightenment literature was not in itself revolutionary. But some of its implications would be, as complaints mounted about noble privileges and guild monopolies, as well as arrogant and sometimes corrupt royal officials. In 1774, Controller-General of Finances Anne-Robert Turgot drew up a program to eliminate some monopolies and privileges that fettered the economy (see Chapter 11). However, the decree abolishing the guilds, among other decrees, generated immediate hostility. Two years later, Turgot's experiment ended. But some writers now began to contrast the freedoms Turgot had in mind with the corporate privileges that characterized the economy and society of eighteenth-century France.

The social lines of demarcation between noble and bourgeois had become less fixed over the course of the century; despite increasing opposition from the oldest noble families who believed their ranks were being swamped by newcomers, in the fifteen years before 1789 almost 2,500 families bought their way into the nobility. Yet, many people of means continued to resent noble privileges, above all the noble exemption from most kinds of taxes. Disgruntled bourgeois did not make the French Revolution, but their dissatisfaction helped create a current of demands for reform. The monarchy's worsening financial crisis would accentuate these calls.

France remained a state of overlapping layers of privileges, rights, traditions, and jurisdictions. Nobles and professional groups such as master artisans in guilds and tax farmers (who generally had bought their offices and could pocket some of the taxes they collected) always contested any plan to eliminate privileges.

The sharpest resistance to reform came from the poorer nobility. Among the "nobles of the sword," the oldest noble families whose ancestors had proudly taken arms to serve the king, some had fallen on hard times and clung frantically to any and all privileges as a way of maintaining their status. They resented the fact that the provincial parlements, in particular, had filled up with new nobles who had purchased offices—the so-called "nobles of the robe"—and that power had shifted within the nobility from the oldest noble families to those recently ennobled.

The monarchy depended upon the sale of titles, offices, and economic monopolies for revenue and long-term credit. But by creating more offices—there were more than 50,000 offices in 1789—it risked destroying public confidence and driving down the value of offices and loans already held.

Economic hardship compounded the monarchy's financial problems by decreasing revenue while exacerbating social tensions. High prices, falling wages, and high unemployment darkened the 1770s and 1780s. A series of bad harvests—the worst of which occurred in 1775—made conditions of life even more difficult for poor people. The harvests of 1787 and 1788, which would be key years in the French political drama, were also very poor. Such crises were by no means unusual—indeed, they were cyclical and would continue until the middle of the next century. Meager harvests generated popular resistance to taxation and protests against the high price of grain (and therefore bread), including the seizure of these commodities and their sale at what was considered to be a just, or reasonable, price. A growing population put more pressure on scarce resources.

Many peasants believed that landowners were increasing their hardship. Some historians have argued that a "seigneurial reaction" was underway as smaller agricultural yields diminished noble revenues, while inflation raised the costs of noble life. By this view, noble landowners reacted by hiring estate agents, lawyers, and surveyors to maximize income from their lands, reasserting old rights over common lands, on which many poor peasants depended for pasturing animals and gathering wood for fuel. Landlords raised rents and tried to force sharecropping arrangements on peasants who had previously rented land.

Although the feudal system of the Middle Ages had long since passed, remnants of it remained. Peasants were still vexed by seigneurial dues and cash owed to their lords. Many nobles still held some rights of justice over their peasants, which meant that they could determine guilt and assess penalties for alleged transgressions; seigneurial courts were often used to enforce the landlord's rights over forests, lakes, and streams, and his exclusive rights to hunt and fish on his estate. Hard times made these obligations—such as being assessed higher dues at harvest time than before—seem truly unfair. Forty percent of the *cahiers* (lists of grievances) drawn up in one district before the fateful convocation of the Estates-General noted frustration with the seigneurial regime. The political crisis that led to the French Revolution would provide ordinary people with an opportunity to redress some of these mounting grievances.

The Financial Crisis

The serious financial crisis that confronted the monarchy in the 1780s was the short-term cause of the French Revolution. France had been at war with Britain, as well as with other European powers, off and on for more than a century. The financial support France had provided the rebel colonists in the American War of Independence against Britain had been underwritten by loans arranged by the king's Swiss minister of finance, Jacques Necker (1732–1804). Almost three-fourths of state expenses went to maintaining the army and navy, and to paying off debts accumulated from the War of the Austrian Succession (1740–1748) and the Seven Years' War (1756–1763), as well as from the American Revolution. The monarchy was living beyond its means.

Where were more funds to be found? Nobles had traditionally enjoyed the privilege of being exempt from most, and the clergy from all, taxation. There was a limit to how many taxes could be imposed on peasants, by far the largest social group in France. In short, the financial crisis of the monarchy was closely tied to the very nature of its fiscal system.

The absolute monarchy in France collected taxes far less efficiently than did the British government. In Britain, the Bank of England facilitated the government's borrowing of money at relatively low interest through the national debt. In France, there was no central bank, and the French monarchy depended more than ever on private interests and suffered from a cumbersome assessment of fiscal obligations and inadequate accounting. French public debt already was much higher than Britain's would be a century later, and it continued to rise as the monarchy sought financial expedients. Public confidence rose and fell, as debt charges sometimes absorbed two-thirds of royal revenues. Even when public confidence waned, however, invariably the market for offices and titles bounced back.

The hesitant and naive Louis XVI was still in his twenties when he became king and probably burdened by sexual impotence. He seemed unable to grasp financial details. Louis knew little of his kingdom, venturing beyond the region of Paris and Versailles only once during his reign. He preferred puttering around the palace with the tools of his second favorite hobby, carpentry (hunting, at which he excelled, came first); he particularly enjoyed taking clocks and watches apart and putting them back together.

The unpopularity of Louis' elegant, haughty wife, Marie-Antoinette (1755–1793), accentuated the public's lack of confidence in the throne (whether or not she ever really snarled "Let them eat cake," when told that the people were starving). The daughter of the Austrian queen, Maria Theresa, Marie-Antoinette was married to Louis to strengthen French dynastic ties to Austria. Unhappy in her marriage, Marie-Antoinette lived extravagantly and was embroiled in scandal. Thus, for example, in 1785, she became entangled in a seamy scandal when a cardinal, the former ambassador of France to the Habsburg court in Vienna, gave her a fabulous diamond necklace in the hope of winning favor. The necklace and some of the prelate's money were then deftly stolen by mysterious plotters, a strange scenario that included a prostitute posing as the queen. The "diamond necklace affair," as it was called, increased the public image of the

(*Left*) Louis XVI. (*Right*) Marie-Antoinette.

king as a weak man, a cuckold. The queen's indiscretions and infidelities seemed to undercut the authority of the monarchy itself, and her detractors indelicately dubbed her the "Austrian whore."

In the meantime, Necker continued to float more loans while attempting to sort out the tangled morass of France's financial bureaucracy. But in 1781, some ministers and noble hangers-on convinced the king to dismiss Necker. The following year, Necker produced a naive and —at best—fanciful account of the royal finances that purported to demonstrate that more revenue was coming to the state than was being spent. Necker hoped to reassure French and particularly the foreign creditors who made up his financial network that reform was unnecessary. Bankers, however, did not believe Necker's figures. Some refused to loan the monarchy any more money until the state enacted financial reforms. The new finance minister, Charles-Alexandre de Calonne (1734–1802), demonstrated that Necker's calculations of royal finances were far-fetched. Yet, Calonne spent even more money, purchasing two more châteaux for Louis XVI and putting the royal treasury deeper in debt by borrowing from venal officeholders in order to pay off creditors now gathered at the royal door.

The parlements, or sovereign law courts, were certain to oppose fiscal reform, which they believed would lead to an increase in taxation through a general tax on land. They distrusted Calonne, an old enemy whom they identified with fiscal irresponsibility and governmental arrogance that some believed bordered on despotism.

To sidestep the parlements, Calonne asked the king in February 1787 to convoke an Assembly of Notables consisting of handpicked representatives from each of the three estates: clergy, nobility, and the third estate (everybody else). The crown expected the Assembly to endorse its reform proposals, including new land taxes from which nobles would not be exempt. Believing that the monarchy's policy of borrowing from Peter to pay Paul could not go on, Calonne suggested that France's financial problems were systemic, resulting from a chaotic administrative organization, including the confusing regional differences in tax obligations. The monarchy's practice of selling the lucrative rights to collect, or "farm," taxes worsened the inefficiency. Calonne knew that the crown's contract with the tax farmers would soon have to be renegotiated, and that many short-term loans contracted by the monarchy would soon come due.

Denouncing "the dominance of custom" that had for so long prevented reform and encumbered commerce, Calonne proposed to overhaul the entire financial system. The Assembly of Notables, however, rejected Calonne's proposals for tax reform and refused to countenance the idea that nobles should be assessed land taxes. Moreover, the high clergy of the first estate, some of whom were nobles, also vociferously opposed Calonne's reforms. They, too, feared losing their exemption from taxation. The corporate nature of French society, based upon privilege, was at stake.

Nobles convinced the king to sack Calonne, which he did on April 8, 1788. Louis XVI replaced Calonne with the powerful archbishop of Toulouse, Étienne-Charles de Loménie de Brienne (1727–1794). Like his predecessor, Loménie de Brienne asked the provincial parlements to register—and thus approve—several edicts of financial reform, promising that the government would keep more accurate accounts. But the Parlement of Paris refused to register some of the edicts, including a new land tax and a stamp tax, which evoked the origins of the American Revolution, something Loménie de Brienne had failed to consider.

THE FIRST STAGES OF THE REVOLUTION

Some members of the Assembly of Notables had been willing to accept fiscal reform and to pay more taxes, but only with accompanying institutional reforms that would guarantee their privileges against monarchical despotism. Specifically, they wanted the king to convoke regular assemblies of the Estates-General—made up of representatives of the three estates—which had not been convoked since 1614. They also wanted the monarch to allow the parlements more say in governing France. The king was in a difficult position. He needed to reduce the privileges of the nobles in order to solve the financial crisis, but to do so without their approval would lead to accusations of tyranny. On the other hand, capitulating to the demands of the privileged classes in return for new taxes would compromise his absolute authority and suggest that his word was subject to the approval of the nation, or at least the nobility. The resolution of this dilemma would lead to the events that constituted the first stages of the French Revolution.

Convoking the Estates-General

The "noble revolt" began the French Revolution. In the summer of 1787, the parlements had called on the king to summon the Estates-General to confront the financial crisis. The members of the parlements had expected that the Estates-General would confirm their prerogatives, but they soon found out that they could not control the course of events.

In response to the refusal of the Parlement of Paris to register the land and stamp taxes, in August 1787 Louis XVI exiled its members to Troyes, a town to the southeast of Paris. Nobles and high clergymen protested vigorously. The provincial parlements backed up the Parlement of Paris. The Parlement of Grenoble refused to register the new stamp and land taxes and convoked its provincial Estates (one of the assemblies of nobles which represented the interests of the region) without royal authorization. The "revolt of the nobility" against the monarchy's attempt to force nobles to pay taxes spread. Provincial parlements continued to demand that the Estates-General be convoked. This revolt was not directed against the institution of the monarchy itself, but against what the nobles considered abuses of the rights and privileges of the nation committed by an increasingly despotic crown. In this, the revolt of the nobles recalled the revolt known as the Fronde, vanquished by the young Louis XIV in the mid-seventeenth century (see Chapter 7).

Confronted by mounting opposition, the monarchy sought compromise. Loménie de Brienne agreed to withdraw the new land and stamp taxes in exchange for maintaining the tax on income (the *vingtième* tax), which nobles and other privileged people had first been assessed in the 1750s to pay for the Seven Years' War. He made clear, however, that the crown would be forced to settle its debts in paper money backed by royal decree. Louis recalled the Parlement of Paris from exile in November 1787 and promised to listen to what it had to say. But the king ordered new loan edicts registered without giving the parlement a chance to be heard. When the duke of Orléans, the king's cousin, interjected that such a procedure was illegal, Louis replied, "That is of no importance to me . . . it is legal because I will it." Louis XVI thus seemed to cross the line between absolutism and despotism.

In May 1788, as hostilities between the king's ministries and the Parlement of Paris continued, the king ordered the arrest of two of its most radical members. He then suspended the parlements, establishing new provincial courts to take their place and creating a single plenary court that would register royal edicts. Resistance to the king's acts against the parlements came quickly. The Assembly of the Clergy, which had been summoned to decide on the amount of its annual gift to the crown, protested the abolition of the parlements. Riots in support of the parlements occurred in several towns. In Grenoble, on June 10, 1788, crowds expressed support for their parlement by pelting soldiers with stones and roof tiles.

On August 8, 1788, Louis XVI announced that he would convoke the Estates-General on May 1 of the following year. He hoped that it would avert royal bankruptcy by agreeing to the imposition of the new taxes. Two weeks later, he reappointed Necker as minister of finance, a measure he believed would appease the nobles, investors, and holders of government bonds, who had never objected to his unrestrained borrowing. But the convocation of the Estates-General helped coalesce public opinion against the king. That the nobles forced the crown to convoke the Estates-General became the first act of the French Revolution. Many people believed that the Estates-General, more than the parlements, would represent their interests and check royal despotism.

The question of how voting was to take place when the Estates-General met assumed increasing importance. The issue highlights tensions between conservatives, many of whom were nobles, and reformers, some of whom were bourgeois but whose members also included some liberal nobles. Would each of the three estates—clergy, nobles, and the third estate—have a single vote, which would almost certainly quash any reform since the majority of nobles and clergymen were against reform, or would each member of the estates be entitled to his own vote?

On September 25, 1788, the Parlement of Paris, which had been reinstated amid great celebration, supported the king's insistence that voting within the Estates-General would take place by estate instead of by head. This meant that when the Estates-General met, as in 1614, each of the three estates would have the same number of representatives and be seated separately. Henceforth, the parlements would be seen by many people as defending the prerogatives of their privileged members, losing their claim to defend the nation against the king's despotism.

Popular political writers now began to salute the third estate (which made up 95 percent of the population) as the true representative of liberty and of the nation against royal despotism. Others asked for some sort of representative assembly that would reflect "public opinion." The "patriot party," a coalition of bourgeois and some liberal nobles, began to oppose royal policies, which they contrasted with those of the "nation." "Patriots" denounced the vested interests of the court and the nobles close to it. Political publications began to inundate France, making these debates national political issues. The Society of the Thirty, a group that included liberal nobles from very old families—for example, the Marquis de Lafayette (1757–1834), French hero of the American Revolution—as well as a number of commoner lawyers, met to discuss, debate, and distribute liberal political pamphlets. They proposed that the third estate, which represented everyone not belonging to the first two estates, be entitled to twice as many representatives in the Estates-General as the nobility and clergy. The loose coalition that made up the patriot party increasingly focused its attentions on this issue.

In January 1789, Abbé Emmanuel Joseph Sieyès (1748–1836), an obscure priest, offered the most radical expression of a crucial shift in politi-

(*Left*) The Marquis de Lafayette. (*Right*) The Abbé Sieyès.

cal opinion. "We have three questions to ask and answer," he wrote, "First, What is the Third Estate? Everything. Second, What has it been heretofore in the political order? Nothing. Third, What does it demand? To become something therein." He contrasted the "nation" against royal absolutism and noble prerogative. Sieyès' polemic represented a radical current of opinion that had revolutionary implications. Moved by the question of whether the estates should vote as one, or whether members should vote as individuals, Sieyès demanded a predominant role for the third estate in political life.

The vast majority of the men elected to the Estates-General were residents of cities and towns, two-thirds of whom had some training in the law—indeed, lawyers would dominate the third estate. Two-thirds of those elected to the first estate were parish priests, many of whom were of humble origin and resented the privileges of the bishops and monastic orders. Some of the younger noble representatives elected to the second estate were liberals. They wanted institutional reforms in the organization of the French monarchy that would permit them to check the power of the king, in much the same way as the Parliament in England served as a check on the English crown. Yet, clearly if each estate had but one vote, the reactionary nobles still had a good chance of imposing their will on the third estate, because most people assumed that the clergy (first estate) would, when push came to shove, follow the nobles (second estate). In December 1788, the king agreed to doubling the number of representatives of the third estate, but declined to give all members an individual vote.

The king asked the local electoral assemblies, along with the first two estates, to draw up lists of grievances (*cahiers de doléances*), which the Estates-General would discuss. Thousands of grievances offered the monarchy a wide variety of opinions, ranging from concrete suggestions for reform to the considered opinion that the foul breath of sheep was ruining pasture land in Lorraine. More important, *cahiers* criticized monarchical absolutism and the intransigence of seigneurs, asked for a more consistent and equitable tax structure, and called for the creation of a new national representative body. A few of the *cahiers* denounced as an abuse of royal power the so-called *lettres de cachet,* documents issued in the name of the king that allowed a person to be arrested for any reason and imprisoned indefinitely. They demanded "that no citizen lose his liberty except according to law; that consequently no one be arrested by virtue of special orders, or, if imperative circumstances necessitate such orders, that the prisoner be handed over to the regular courts of justice within forty-eight hours at the latest." But some *cahiers* also reflected continued popular trust and reverence for the king (as the *cahier* of the third estate of one town that wrote "imbued with gratitude prompted by the paternal kindness of the king"), while denouncing the rapacity and bad faith of his advisers and ministers. Unfortunately, the *cahiers* were edited along the way and most never reached the king. Thus, the very process by which the government received the grievances reflected growing disillusionment with the monarchy's response to the crisis.

On May 5, 1789, the nearly 1,000 members of the Estates-General (about 600 of whom represented the third estate) assembled at Versailles. The king greeted the first two estates, but kept the commoners waiting for two hours. When he finished his speech, members of the third estate violated protocol by boldly putting their hats back on, a right reserved for the two privileged orders. When it became apparent that representatives would vote not by head but by estate, the third estate stalled the proceedings for weeks by insisting that all three estates register their delegates together. On June 17, the third estate overwhelmingly approved a motion by Sieyès that declared the third estate to be the "National Assembly" and the true representative of national sovereignty. The third estate now claimed legitimate sovereignty and an authority parallel, if not superior, to that of the king of France.

The first estate now voted to join the third. But on June 20, as rumors circulated that the king might take action against them, representatives of the third estate found that their meeting hall had been locked for "repairs." Led by their president, Jean-Sylvain Bailly (1736–1793), an astronomer, the members of the third estate took the bold step of assembling in a nearby tennis court. There they took an oath "not to separate, and to reassemble wherever circumstances require, until the constitution of the kingdom is established and consolidated upon solid foundations." With principled defiance, the third estate demanded that defined limits be placed on the king's authority.

The king now declared the third estate's deliberations invalid. Yet, on June 23, he announced some substantial reforms, agreeing to convoke periodically the Estates-General, to abolish the *taille* (the tax on land) and the *corvée* (labor tax), to eliminate internal tariffs and tolls that interfered

The Tennis Court Oath, June 20, 1789.

with trade, and to eliminate the *lettres de cachet*. He also agreed that the Estates-General would vote by head, but only on matters that did not concern "the ancient and constitutional rights of the three orders." To the radicalized members of the third estate, the king's concessions were not enough.

Louis XVI dismissed Necker on June 22, but reversed himself after learning that thousands of people in Paris had invaded the courtyard of the Tuileries Palace to demand that Necker, who in December had persuaded the king to double the representatives of the third estate, stay on. After threatening to dissolve the Estates-General by force, on June 27 the king ordered the first two estates to join the third.

Storming of the Bastille

In Paris, ordinary people now began to pay more attention to the ongoing struggle at Versailles. Many now believed that a conspiracy by nobles and hoarders lay behind a shortage of food and high prices. Furthermore, there seemed to be an increase in the number of royal troops around Paris and Versailles. Rumors spread that the National Assembly would be quashed. On July 11, the king once again ordered Necker into exile. The following day, demonstrators carried busts of Necker. Bands of rioters attacked the customs barriers at the gates of Paris, tearing down most of the toll booths. In response to rumors that the king had ordered even more troops to Paris, people began to arm themselves.

On the morning of July 14, 1789, thousands of people—small tradesmen, artisans, and wage earners for the most part—seized weapons stored in the Invalides, a large veterans' hospital. Early that afternoon, the attention of the Paris crowd, now numbering perhaps 80,000 people, turned toward the Bastille, a fortress in the eastern part of the city, where the crowd believed powder and ammunition were stored. For most of the eighteenth century, the Bastille had been a prison, renowned as a symbol of despotism because some prisoners had been sent there by virtue of one of the king's *lettres de cachet,* summarily and without a trial. On that hot summer day, the Bastille's prisoners numbered but seven, a motley crew that included a nobleman imprisoned upon request of his family, a renegade priest, and a demented Irishman, who alternately thought he was Joan of Arc, Saint Louis, and God.

The crowd stormed and captured the Bastille, which was defended by a small garrison. More than 200 of the attackers were killed or wounded. A butcher decapitated the commander of the fortress, and the throng carried his head on a pike in triumph through the streets. The Bastille's fall would be much more significant than it first appeared. Louis XVI responded to

The taking of the Bastille, July 14, 1789.

the news of the fall of the Bastille with "Is it a revolt?" Came the reply, "No, Sire, it is a Revolution." The crowd's uprising probably saved the National Assembly from being dissolved by force. Now unsure of the loyalty of his troops, Louis sent away some of the troops he had summoned to Paris, recognized both the newly elected municipal government, with Bailly serving as mayor of the "Commune of Paris," and a municipal defense force or National Guard (commanded by Lafayette), and capitulated to the popular demand that he recall Necker to office.

On July 17, the king came to Paris to be received by the municipal council at the town hall, accepting and wearing an emblem of three colors, red and blue for the city of Paris, and white for the Bourbons. By doing so, Louis XVI seemed to be recognizing what became the tricolor symbol of the French Revolution.

The Great Fear and the Night of August 4

Now it was the peasants' turn to intervene in the unfolding of revolution. News of the convocation of the Estates-General had brought hope to many rural people that the king would relieve their crushing fiscal burdens. They had expressed their hopes in the grievances they sent with their third estate delegates to Versailles. The past fifteen years had not been good ones for peasants. The cost of renting land rose dramatically in the 1770s and the 1780s, while recent harvest failures brought widespread deprivation and riots against the high price of grain.

Against this background and heightened hopes for reform, news of the Bastille's fall touched off protests in the provinces. Encouraged by the gathering of the Estates-General, between July 19 and August 3 peasants attacked seigneurial châteaux. In some places they burned title deeds specifying obligations owed to lords. These peasant rebellions helped cause a subsequent general panic known as the "Great Fear." Fueled by the rumor of an aristocratic "famine plot" to starve or burn out the people, peasants and townspeople mobilized in many regions of France. To repel the rumored approach of brigands sent to destroy crops, townspeople and peasants formed armed units to defend themselves and save the harvest. In Angoulême in southwestern France, 20,000 people gathered together, anticipating that brigands would soon fall upon them. In towns, new local governments and National Guard units were established to institute reforms and to restore order as the effective authority of the state disintegrated. These events brought to power lawyers, merchants, and other "new men" who had formerly been excluded from political life.

News of peasant violence and the panic engendered by the "famine plot," galvanized members of the National Assembly. Some believed, or half-believed, the rumors that brigands paid by nobles were on the loose in the provinces. A group of liberal representatives from Brittany had formed a "Breton Club" of about 200 men within the patriot party. They came to the conclusion that only radical measures by the Assembly could restore order and give the legislators the time needed to carry through reforms. The Breton Club convinced a very wealthy noble to rise in the Assembly on August 3 and propose the abolition of tax exemptions.

On August 4, in an effort to appease the peasants and to forestall further rural disorders, the National Assembly formally abolished the "feudal regime," including seigneurial rights. This sweeping proclamation was modified in the following week, however, to preserve the sanctity of property rights by providing the nobles with indemnification for their abolished feudal rights. Thus, owners of seigneurial dues attached to land would receive compensation from the peasants (although, in general, such compensation was not forthcoming and was subsequently eliminated). The Assembly abolished personal obligations, which were vestiges of medieval serfdom, without compensation. The members of the National Assembly thus renounced privilege, the fundamental organizing principle of French society during the Old Regime. Other reforms enacted the following week included the guarantee of freedom of worship and the abolition of the sale of offices, seigneurial justice, and even the exclusive right of nobles to hunt. The provinces and cities, too, were required to give up most of their archaic privileges, such as exemption from the hated salt tax granted to the province of Brittany. In these ways, the National Assembly enacted a sweeping agenda that proclaimed the end of the Old Regime.

CONSOLIDATING THE REVOLUTION

In one remarkable session, on the night of August 4, 1789, the National Assembly had swept away much of the Old Regime. The Assembly's decrees destroyed absolutism by redefining the relationship between subject and king. No longer would the king rule by divine right, or buy allegiance by dispensing privileges to favorites. Instead, the king would be constrained by powers spelled out in a constitution. The Assembly then began to create the new regime. It began by promulgating the Declaration of the Rights of Man and Citizen, a remarkable document based on universal principles. It next established a new relationship between church and state, creating a national church, making Catholic Church property "national property," and compelling the clergy to swear allegiance to the nation. The National Assembly then turned to the long process of framing a constitution for the new regime, and is therefore sometimes also known as the Constituent Assembly.

In the meantime, however, Marie-Antoinette and some of the king's most influential advisers balked at accepting any weakening in royal authority. Louis XVI was denounced when he objected to the loss of an absolute veto over legislation. Fearing the influence of nobles at the court, crowds early in October marched to Versailles, returning to Paris with the king and the royal family. Henceforth, while many nobles, among others, fled France for exile and sought the assistance of the monarchs of Europe against the Revolution, the king himself became vulnerable to the tide of Parisian popular radicalism. As nobles and clergy led resistance to the Revolution, the Parisian radical clubs moved further to the left. The days of Louis and of the monarchy itself were numbered.

The Declaration of the Rights of Man and Citizen

As it set out to create a constitutional monarchy, the Assembly promulgated the Declaration of the Rights of Man and Citizen on August 26. This set forth the general principles of the new order and intended to educate citizens about liberty. It would become the preamble to the new constitution that was being formulated by the Assembly. One of the most significant documents in Western political history, the Declaration reflected some of the ideas that Thomas Jefferson had enshrined in the American Declaration of Independence of 1776. Article One proclaims, "Men are born and remain free and equal in rights." The Enlightenment's influence is apparent in the document's concern for individual freedom, civic equality, and the sense of struggle against corporatism, unjust privilege, and absolute rule, a discourse based upon a belief in the primacy of reason. All people were to stand equally before the law. All men were to be"equally eligible to all honors, places, and employments . . . without any other distinction than that created by their virtues and talents."

Proclaiming universal principles, the Declaration clearly placed sovereignty in the nation. The notion of rights stemming from membership in the "nation," as opposed to that in any corporate group or social estate, was a fundamental change. The assertion of equality of opportunity, however, was not intended to eliminate all social distinctions. The preservation of property rights assured that differences due to wealth, education, and talent would remain and be considered natural and legitimate. The Declaration thus helped make wealth, not birth, blood, or legal privilege, the foundation of social and political order in modern France.

The Declaration invoked "universal man," meaning mankind. But at the same time, its authors excluded women from the Declaration and did not espouse or foresee equality of the sexes. The Declaration did not specify to what extent women shared in universal rights, and to what extent women were citizens. Nonetheless, many men and women now began to greet each other as "citizen." Moreover, some calls for women's rights arose from the beginning of the Revolution. One woman wrote that by leaving women without the right to vote or to be educated, the Assembly "destined them to provide the pleasures of the harem."

The Declaration stated that no person could be persecuted for his or her opinions, including those concerning religion. The law itself, before which all men (but not yet women) were to be equal, was to be the work of legally elected and responsible representatives. It was to reflect the notion of the "general will," which would be expressed by national representatives. And the nation itself, not the monarch alone, was to be "the source of all sovereignty." The abolition of feudalism on August 4 and the proclamation of the Declaration of the Rights of Man and Citizen were such monumental achievements that already in 1790 people were referring to the Old Regime as having been that which existed before the representatives of the Estates-General constituted the National Assembly. It remained, however, for Louis XVI to accept the Assembly's work.

"The Baker, the Baker's Wife, and the Baker's Little Boy"

The political crisis was by no means over. The National Assembly's actions challenged the authority of the crown. On one hand, the king's closest advisers, the "court party," rejected any constitutional arrangement that would leave the monarch without the power of absolute veto. Royal authority was at stake. On the other hand, speaking for the patriot party, Sieyès insisted, "If the king's will is capable of equalling that of twenty-five million people . . . it would be a *lettre de cachet* against the general will." The majority of the Assembly, having defeated a motion that an upper chamber like the British House of Lords be created, offered the king on September 11 the power of a "suspending" veto over legislation. Lacking an "absolute" veto, the king henceforth could only delay a measure passed by the Assembly from becoming law for up to four years.

When the king failed to accept these provisions and the decrees of August 4, a flood of pamphlets and newspapers attacked his resistance. The radical journalist Jean-Paul Marat (1743–1793) quickly found a popular following for his new newspaper, *The Friend of the People.* A physician beset by financial woes, Marat was like one of the ambitious, frustrated "scribblers" whom Voltaire, forty years earlier, had scathingly denounced as hacks. He captured with stirring emotion and the colorful, coarse slang of ordinary Parisians the mood of those for whom he wrote. The rhetoric of popular sovereignty, some of it borrowed from the philosopher Jean-Jacques Rousseau, came alive in the outpouring of political pamphlets that undermined popular respect for Louis XVI and, for the first time, even for the institution of monarchy itself.

By October, some "patriots" were demanding that the king reside in Paris, echoing a number of *cahiers*. Like many of the most important events in the French Revolution, the "march to Versailles" began with a seemingly minor event. The officers of the Flanders Regiment, recently ordered to Paris by the king, insulted the newly adopted tricolor emblem at a reception in their honor attended by the king and queen. According to rumor, they shouted "Down with the National Assembly!" As the rumor spread, popular anger turned against the royal family in Versailles.

On October 5, women from the neighborhoods around the Bastille, having found the market insufficiently provisioned, gathered in front of the town hall. From there, some 10,000 people, mostly women, proceeded to

Women of Paris leaving for Versailles.

walk to Versailles, hoping to convince the king to provide them with bread. Some of them occupied the hall of the National Assembly, where they claimed power in the name of popular sovereignty. Later in the day, a large force of National Guardsmen led by Lafayette also arrived at Versailles, hoping to keep order and to convince the king that he should return with them to Paris. Louis cordially greeted the women in the late afternoon, promising them bread. The king met Lafayette's procession shortly before midnight and announced his acceptance of the Assembly's momentous decrees of the night of August 4.

Nonetheless, violence followed at dawn. When people tried to force their way into the château, royal guards shot a man dead, and the crowds retaliated by killing two guards and sticking their heads on pikes. Lafayette announced that the king had accepted the August decrees, but this failed to restore order. The crowd insisted that the royal family join it on the road to Paris. Some of the women sang that they were returning to Paris with "The Baker, the Baker's Wife, and the Baker's Little Boy," reflecting the popular notion that the king was responsible for providing bread for his people. The National Assembly, too, left Versailles for Paris. By putting the king and the Assembly under the pressure of popular political will, the women's march to Versailles changed the course of the French Revolution.

Reforming the Church and Clergy

In Paris, the National Assembly set about creating a constitution that would limit the authority of the king. The Assembly proclaimed Louis "the king of the French," instead of the king of France, a significant change that suggested that he embodied the sovereignty of his people. Alarmed by such changes, the king's brother, the count of Artois, went into exile and was soon followed by more than 20,000 other émigrés, most of whom were nobles, other people of means, and clergymen.

The Assembly turned its attention to reforming the Church. The decrees of August 4–11 had ended the unpopular tithe payments to the Church, and now the Assembly looked to the Church's wealth to help resolve the state's mounting financial crisis. On October 10, Charles-Maurice de Talleyrand (1754–1838), who had been named bishop while still virtually a boy, proposed that Church property become "national property" (*biens nationaux*). After the Assembly narrowly passed Talleyrand's measure on November 2, some 400 million francs in Church property— roughly 10 percent of the nation's land—was offered for sale at auction. The primary beneficiaries of the sale were urban bourgeois and prosperous peasants who could marshal enough cash to buy the fairly large parcels of land put up for sale.

To raise funds immediately, the Assembly issued paper money known as *assignats* that were backed by the value of the Church lands. Although the law required everyone to accept *assignats* in payment of debts, their value fell due to lack of public confidence, and those who used the *assignats* to purchase Church lands or pay debts received a windfall. Even poor peasants were thus able to reduce their debts with inflated currency worth less and less. Among the consequences of the sale of Church land and later lands owned by nobles who had emigrated out of fear of the Revolution was that in some parts of France more land was brought under cultivation by peasants. The resulting clearing of lands that had not been previously cultivated also put increased pressure on the environment as trees and brush were cleared to make room for planting crops and small-scale farming and wine production replaced the raising of sheep in some parts of France. The environmental history of the Revolution, however, largely remains to be written.

The confiscation of the Church's property was not the only change the French Revolution imposed on the clergy and the Catholic Church in France. The Assembly also proceeded to alter dramatically the status of the Church itself. On February 13, 1790, it decreed the abolition of the religious orders, deemed useless and politically suspect by many reformers. Even more significantly, on July 12, the National Assembly passed the Civil Constitution of the French Clergy. The Assembly applied new political principles to the Church, redefining the relationship between the clergy and the state, creating, in effect, a national church. Bishops would retain authority over their districts, but they were to be selected by departmental assemblies made up of parish priests who were now to be elected by the people. The bishops now could only publish pronouncements with the authorization of the government. Ten days later, the king reluctantly accepted these measures affecting the Church.

Priests and bishops could no longer be supported by rents from Church property or by tithes. Rather, the Church was now essentially a department of the state, which henceforth would pay clerical salaries, the expenses of worship, and poor relief. In November 1790, the National Assembly proclaimed that all priests had to swear an oath of loyalty to the Revolution, and thus accept the Civil Constitution of the French Clergy. His authority directly challenged, Pope Pius VI denounced the Declaration of the Rights of Man and Citizen in March, and in April 1791 he condemned the Civil Constitution.

The Civil Constitution of the French Clergy also altered the course of the Revolution, largely because it was widely resisted and contributed directly to the growth of a counter-revolutionary movement. Between one-half and two-thirds of the parish priests refused the oath, and the Assembly prohibited these disloyal, "non-juring" priests from administering the Church sacraments. Nonetheless, many continued to do so with popular support. The issue of the oath split dioceses, parishes, and some households. In some provinces, violence mounted against "non-juring" priests; in others, such as Brittany, refractory priests received popular support and protection. Generally speaking, the clergy of the west of France (particularly Brittany), the north, Alsace, and parts of the south, refused the Civil Constitution; in the rest of France, the clergy evinced at least formal acceptance of the Revolution. Such issues were no small matter, as many Catholics, Louis XVI among them, believed themselves obliged by faith to refuse to take sacraments from the "juring" clergy, that is, those who had taken the oath.

The Reforms of 1791

The most urgent task of the National Assembly was to prepare France's first constitution. The Constitution of 1791 formalized the break with the Old Regime by substituting a constitutional monarchy for absolute rule. Although the king retained the power of only a suspending veto, he would still direct foreign policy and command the army. Acts of war or peace, however, required the Assembly's approval.

But France was far from becoming a republic. In sweeping away the Old Regime, the Revolution had redefined the relationship between the individual and the state by stripping away corporatism and hereditary legal privileges. All citizens were to be equal before the law, the Assembly having in June 1790 abolished titles of hereditary nobility. However, the Assembly carefully distinguished between "active" and "passive" citizens.

The three estates hammering out the next constitution.

Only "active citizens," men paying the equivalent of three days' wages in direct taxes, had the right to vote in indirect elections—they would vote for electors, who were wealthier men, who in turn would select representatives to a new legislature (see Map 12.1). Critics such as Marat and the populist orator Georges-Jacques Danton (1759–1794) denounced the restrictive franchise, claiming that the Assembly had merely replaced the privileged caste of the Old Regime with another by substituting the ownership of property for noble title as the criterion for political rights. Rousseau himself would have been unable to vote.

The National Assembly enacted other important reforms as well. It granted citizenship and civil rights to Protestants and Jews (January 28, 1790). It ended the monopoly of the guilds over the production and distribution of goods by abolishing them, declaring each person "free to do such business as and to exercise such profession, art or trade as he may choose." It subsequently passed the Le Chapelier law on June 14, 1791, prohibiting workmen from joining together to refuse to work for a master. This law was a victory for proponents of free trade. The Assembly also passed laws affecting the family: establishing civil marriage, lowering the age of consent for marriage, establishing divorce proceedings, and specifying that inheritances be divided equally among children.

The National Assembly abolished slavery in France, but not in the colonies. This exception led to a slave rebellion on the Caribbean island of Hispaniola in October 1790 against the French sugar plantation owners, many of whom were nobles. It was led by Toussaint L'Ouverture (1743–1803), himself a former slave who had fought in the French army. The National Convention abolished slavery in the colonies in 1794, hoping that

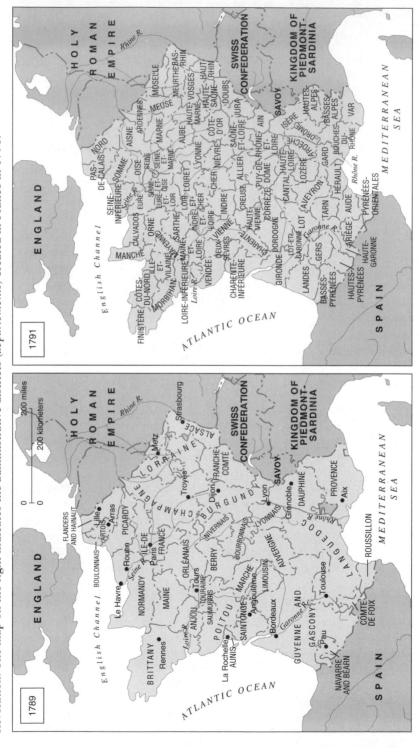

MAP 12.1 FRANCE BEFORE AND AFTER 1789 The map on the left indicates the provinces and provincial capitals in France before the Revolution. The map on the right indicates the administrative districts (*départements*) created in France in 1790.

Olympe de Gouges.

the freed slaves would fight against Britain. Half of Hispaniola—modern-day Haiti—became the first free black state.

In 1791, the call for equal rights for women was first made explicit in France when Olympe de Gouges (1755–1793), the daughter of a butcher, published *The Rights of Women*. "The law," she wrote, "must be the expression of the general will; all female and male citizens must contribute either personally or through their representatives to its formation." Encouraging women to demand their natural rights—and thereby evidencing the influence of the Enlightenment—she called on the Assembly to acknowledge women's rights as mothers of citizens of the nation. She insisted on women's right to education and to control property within marriage and to initiate divorce proceedings. She included an appendix, "a social contract of Man and Woman," defining the nation as "the union of Woman and Man." She suggested that men would remain unfree unless women were granted similar rights: "Enslaved man," she wrote, "has multiplied his strength and needs recourse to yours to break his chains." The concept of "republican motherhood" emerged, stopping short of demanding full political rights for women. Many women saw their role in the near future as supporting their husbands and inculcating their children with republican values. "Women: do you want to be republicans?" went one tract, "Love, obey, and teach the laws that remind your husbands and children to exercise their rights."

Resistance and Revolution

On July 14, 1790, the first anniversary of the fall of the Bastille, an imposing Festival of General Federation took place on the Champ de Mars, a

royal parade ground in Paris, to commemorate the unity of the revolutionary settlement. But, in fact, there was no revolutionary consensus in
France. In the south, nobles had already begun to organize resistance
against the Revolution, and militant Catholics attacked Protestants, who
tended to support the Revolution. By the summer of 1791, as the Assembly promulgated its constitution, open resistance to the Revolution had
broken out in parts of the south and west, and in Alsace in the east.

Such resistance prompted further calls for even more radical changes.
Some of the revolutionaries, who did not accept the distinction between
active and passive citizens, called for more democratic participation in political life. They believed that they were constructing a new nation upon
the ruins of the Old Regime. But from where did this democratic thrust
come? We have seen that the monarchical state had rested on an intertwining network of corporate groups—each with a set of privileges—at virtually every level of society. These included judicial, professional,
administrative, and clerical groups, ranging from provincial estates to artisanal guilds. Participatory and sometimes even democratic procedures
within such bodies (or *corps*), may have contributed to help various participatory and democratic practices that affected the course of the Revolution and pushed France toward a republic.

The first clubs were established by political factions among the deputies
to the National Assembly. Some of the Assembly's most radical members
split off to form the Jacobin Club, so-called because it met in the house of

A patriotic club of women.

(*Left*) The male sans-culotte. (*Right*) The female sans-culotte.

the religious order of the Jacobins. The Cordeliers Club brought together the radicals of Paris, while supporters of the cause of constitutional monarchy gathered at the Club of the Feuillants, whose members had broken with the Jacobins in July 1791. The early success of the Cordeliers and Jacobin Clubs in provincial towns often led monarchists to form royalist clubs. Moreover, some women formed their own political clubs, such as the Club of Knitters, or joined the Fraternal Society of Patriots of Both Sexes. By 1793, there were at least 5,000 clubs in France, struggling to help determine the political course of the Revolution in each region.

During the first years of the Revolution, there was little in France that was not political. The political clubs that had formed among the delegates to the Estates-General, like the Breton Club, were not the only place where political debate occurred. There were also meetings of neighborhood "sections," which had first been defined as electoral districts for the convocation of the Estates-General, and these meetings continued to take place in Paris.

Parisian revolutionaries became increasingly known as sans-culottes. They defined themselves by what they were without—the fancy knee britches or golden pants—or *culottes,* in French—associated with the aristocracy. The sans-culottes were shopkeepers, artisans, and laborers who

(*Left*) Louis XVI dons the Phrygian cap. (*Right*) Planting a liberty tree.

were not opposed to private property, but who stood against unearned property, and especially against those people who seemed to have too much property, or who, living from rents, did not work for a living. They demanded that a maximum price be placed on bread, which alone absorbed more than half of the earnings of the average working family. Sans-culottes were for the Revolution, for "the people," as they put it. They were defined by their political behavior. Even aristocrats could be sans-culottes if they supported the Revolution (which, however, was most unusual). Likewise, laborers or peasants could be called "aristocrats" if they seemed to oppose the Revolution. In a world in which symbols played a crucial political role (for example, the tricolor cockade, patriotic altars for newborns, liberty trees in villages), sans-culottes could be identified by the Phrygian cap—a symbol of freedom drawn from the Roman Republic—red in color, with a tricolor emblem—in contrast to the three-cornered hat that had been worn by urban social elites. The language of the sans-culottes also quickly indicated who they were; they called everyone "citizen," and used the familiar (*"tu"* and never *"vous"*), egalitarian form of address. The political ideal of the sans-culottes was that popular sovereignty had to be practiced every day in direct democracy, in revolutionary clubs and in the sections.

The Flight to Varennes

Fearing the growing violence of the Revolution and counting on the support of the other monarchs of Europe, Louis XVI and his family tried to flee France in June 1791. Apprehended by the National Guard in Varennes after being sighted near the French border, however, the royal family was prevented from continuing their journey into exile and freedom.

The king's attempt to flee turned public sentiment further against him, and strengthened support for a republic. The day after his flight, the Cordeliers Club called for the establishment of a republic, but the majority of the Assembly feared civil war. On July 17, at the Champ de Mars in Paris, people came to sign (or put their "X" on) a petition resting on the "Altar of the Fatherland" that called on the National Assembly to replace the king "by all constitutional means." The National Guard opened fire, killing fifty people. Bailly, the moderate mayor of Paris, and Lafayette, the increasingly disenchanted commander of the National Guard in Paris, declared martial law; Marat and Danton went temporarily into hiding. Even Louis' formal acceptance of the Constitution on September 14 could not stem the popular tide against the monarchy.

WAR AND THE SECOND REVOLUTION

After the king's ill-fated attempt to flee France, the Revolution now entered a new, more radical phase. The king's flight seriously weakened the constitutional monarchists within the Assembly. The leaders of the Parisian population—Georges-Jacques Danton, Jean-Paul Marat, and Maximilien Robespierre—were republican Jacobins who had given up on the idea that a constitutional monarchy could adequately guarantee the liberties of the people. The newly elected National Assembly met on Octo-

(*Left*) Georges-Jacques Danton. (*Right*) Maximilien Robespierre.

ber 1, 1791. Republicans—now identified with the "left" as monarchists were with the "right," due to the location of the seats each group occupied in the Assembly—became a majority in March 1792.

In the meantime, French émigrés at the Austrian and Prussian courts were encouraging foreign intervention to restore Louis XVI to full monarchical authority. The republican followers of Jacques-Pierre Brissot (1754–1793), former radical pamphleteer and police spy as well as a flamboyant orator, called for a war to free Europe from the tyranny of monarchy and nobility. The members of this faction became known as the Girondins because many were from the department, or district, of the Gironde in which the Atlantic port of Bordeaux is located. Under Girondin leadership, the Assembly's proclamations took on a more aggressive tone. Monarchists backed a revolutionary war for other reasons: some, like Lafayette, hoped to restore power to the crown. Others, including the king himself, expected that war would lead to French defeat (because of the desertion of so many noble officers) and to the restoration of the Old Regime. The French declaration of war against Austria in April 1792 led to the Second Revolution in June. The monarchy was overthrown, replaced by a republic. Faced with foreign invasion and full-scale counter-revolution inside France, the Jacobin-dominated revolutionary government lapsed into dictatorship, imposing "the Terror" (during which many suspected counter-revolutionaries were arrested and guillotined).

Reactions to the French Revolution in Europe

The French Revolution had a considerable impact on the rest of Europe even before French armies marched into adjoining states proclaiming the dawning of an era of "liberty, equality, and fraternity." The early work of the National Assembly, particularly the abolition of feudal rights and the establishment of a constitutional monarchy, attracted immediate attention and found considerable favor among educated people in Britain, the Netherlands, and some German and Italian states. Some lawyers and merchants in other lands applauded, for example, measures taken to reduce the independence of the Catholic Church. The promulgation of the principles of national sovereignty and self-determination, however, threatened the monarchies of Europe. The European powers had often gone to war against France over the past century, beginning with Louis XIV's relentless war-making in pursuit of dynastic territorial aggrandizement. The next series of wars against France, however, reflected not dynastic rivalries but rather the threat to the other Great Powers by revolutionary France. The threat posed by the French Revolution brought about a rapprochement between Austria and Prussia, old rivals for domination in Central Europe, as well as a wary alliance between Great Britain and Russia.

The Prussian government's first reaction to the Revolution had been to try to subvert the alliance between France and Austria and then to undermine Austrian authority in the Southern Netherlands (Belgium). In Vienna, the Habsburg Emperor Leopold II was initially preoccupied with demands from the Hungarian nobility for more power, and pressure from the Belgians for independence. In 1789, a rebellion forced Austrian forces out of the Southern Netherlands in December and led to the establishment of a republic that survived only until Austrian troops invaded as winter approached in 1790.

In London, some radical Whigs greeted with enthusiasm the news of the fall of the Bastille and the first steps toward constitutional monarchy in France. But in 1790, the British writer Edmund Burke attacked the Revolution in *Reflections on the Revolution in France*. He contended that the abstract rationalism of the Enlightenment threatened the historic evolution of any nation by undermining its monarchy, its established church, and what he considered the "natural" ruling elite.

The Englishman Thomas Paine (1737–1809) wrote pamphlets denouncing monarchical rule and unwarranted privilege. His pamphlet *The Rights of Man* (1791–1792) defended the Revolution against Burke's relentless attack. Political societies supporting the Revolution sprang up in Britain during the early 1790s, composed mainly of artisans. The French Revolution thus helped revive some interest in political reform in Britain. It also contributed enormously to the development of British nationalism (see Chapter 11). During the revolutionary period, popular respect for the British monarchy and probably also for the nobility seems to have soared, reaffirming social hierarchy (and male domination as well) at a time when to many Britons events in France seemed to demonstrate the consequences of social upheaval. There would be no shortage of volunteers from all classes and religions to fight the French when the nation called for them.

A small group of English women also enthusiastically supported the Revolution. Mary Wollstonecraft (1759–1797), a teacher and writer, greeted the Revolution with optimism, travelling to France to view events first hand. She expressed confidence that the Revolution would lead to a republic that would respect the rights of men and women alike. Angered that the Assembly limited the right to education to men only, she published *Vindication of the Rights of Women* (1792), the first book in Britain demanding that women have the right to vote and hold elected office, as well as demanding greater equality in marriage. The book, damned by most Englishmen as another pernicious work influenced by the French Revolution, was an opening salvo in Britain in the struggle for equality of the sexes.

The rulers of the other European states felt threatened by the proclamation of universal principles embodied in the Declaration of the Rights of Man and Citizen. The Revolution also posed the threat of French expansion, no longer in the interest of dynastic territorial aggrandizement, but on behalf of carrying the revolutionary principles of "liberty, equality, and fraternity" to other lands. Besieged by exiles from France eager to tell tales of terror, the rulers of Prussia, Austria, Naples, and Piedmont undertook the suppression of Jacobin sympathizers in their states. In Britain, the seeming threat of foreign invasion helped forge, principally but not exclusively among the upper classes, a sense of British national identity. Anti-French and anti-Catholic feelings came to the fore as scarcity increased fear of revolution. Pitt the Younger's government lashed out at the development of popular politics in Britain, suspending the freedoms of association, assembly, and the press, as well as in 1794 the writ of *habeas corpus*. "Coercion Acts" facilitated the arrest of those working for parliamentary reform.

Louis XVI's virtual imprisonment in the Tuileries Palace in Paris and the thunderous speeches in the Assembly proclaiming the necessity of "a war of peoples against kings" worried the crowned heads of Europe. On August 27, 1791, King Leopold II of Austria (brother of Marie-Antoinette, who had not seen him in twenty-five years) and King Frederick William II of Prussia promulgated the Declaration of Pilnitz. It expressed their concern about the plight of the French monarchy and stated the common interest of both sovereigns in seeing order restored in France. Despite Robespierre's speeches warning the deputies that the Revolution must first deal with its enemies within France before waging war abroad in the name of "liberty, fraternity, and equality," the Assembly, egged on by General Charles François Dumouriez (1739–1823), who was minister of foreign affairs, in April 1792 declared war on Austria. The stated reason was fear that an Austrian invasion from the Southern Netherlands was imminent. The declaration of war soon seemed a rash move, as the army had been devastated by the desertion of two-thirds of its officers (85 percent of its officers had been nobles before the Revolution) and Prussia soon joined with Austria in fighting the French. The early stages of the war produced many French defeats at the hands of Austrian and Prussian armies.

A Second Revolution

The war greatly influenced the course of the Revolution by sealing the fate of the monarchy and the royal family. As France faced the possibility of foreign invasion by Austria and Prussia, eager to restore Louis XVI to an absolute throne, popular fear that aristocrats and clergymen were betraying the Revolution eventually brought down the monarchy. Early defeats on the northern frontier by Austrian troops and soaring bread prices (in part due to the requisitioning of food for the army) compounded popular anxiety and led to a new revolutionary groundswell, particularly in Paris.

In early April 1792, women from the plebeian districts of Paris marched through the capital demanding the right to bear arms. On June 20, a crowd stormed into the Tuileries Palace and threatened the royal family, shouting, "Tremble, tyrants! Here come the sans-culottes!" Strident calls for the end of the monarchy echoed in clubs and sections. (The sections were administrative districts each of which had assemblies of "active" citizens, many of whom were Jacobins who favored radical action.) On July 11, the Assembly officially proclaimed the *patrie*, or nation, to be "in danger," calling on all citizens to rally against the enemies of liberty within as well as outside of France. The Assembly encouraged the sections to admit the "passive" citizens who had previously been excluded because they had failed to meet tax requirements. Troops from Marseille, among federal volunteers called up to defend the front, sang a new revolutionary song, "The Marseillaise," penned by Rouget de Lisle for the Army of the Rhine. It became the anthem of the Revolution. In the meantime, the Jacobins pressed their attack against the monarchy.

After the Brunswick Manifesto (July 1792), Austria and Prussia warned the French that they would be severely punished if the royal family were harmed. All but one of the forty-eight sections of Paris responded by demanding that the king be immediately deposed. Popular discontent and Jacobin agitation came together in August. A radical committee overthrew the city council and established a revolutionary Commune in Paris on August 9, naming Santerre, a brewer, commander of the National Guard. On August 10, sans-culottes from the Paris sections attacked the Tuileries Palace. The invaders killed 600 of the king's Swiss Guards and servants after they had surrendered. The royal family escaped and found protection in the quarters of the National Assembly. The Assembly immediately proclaimed the monarchy deposed and ordered the royal family's imprisonment.

The popular revolution doomed France's first experiment in constitutional monarchy. The defeat of French armies heightened the mood of anxiety, if not outright panic, in Paris. On September 2, 1792, a Prussian

The September Massacre of 1792 in the abbey of Saint-Germain-des-Prés.

army entered French territory and captured the eastern fortress town of Verdun. The proximity of the allied armies and the fear of betrayal at home led to the imprisonment in Paris of many people suspected of plotting against the Revolution. When a rumor circulated that the prisoners were planning to break out of prison and attack the army from the rear, mobs dragged the prisoners from their cells and killed them. During these September Massacres, more than 1,200 people, including 225 priests, perished at the hands of crowds who constituted themselves judges, juries, and executioners.

But just as Paris seemed vulnerable to foreign invasion, a ragtag army of regular soldiers and sans-culottes stopped the Prussian and Austrian advance with effective artillery barrages on September 20, 1792, near the windmill of Valmy, east of Châlons-sur-Marne. The German poet Goethe, amazed by the victory of such ordinary people over a highly trained professional army, wrote "From this time and place a new epoch is beginning." An officer trained under the Old Regime called the resultant warfare of the revolutionary armies a "hellish tactic," which saw "fifty thousand savage beasts foaming at the mouth like cannibals, hurling themselves at top speed upon soldiers whose courage has been excited by no passion."

The Revolution had been saved by the same people who had first made it. The victory at Valmy helped prepare the way for the proclamation of the First French Republic. Delegates to a new assembly called the National Convention were selected by universal male suffrage in sparsely attended elections dominated by Jacobins (perhaps because the radicals had used scare tactics to keep moderates and royalist sympathizers from voting). The delegates arrived in Paris to draft a republican constitution. Their first act was unanimously to abolish the monarchy and proclaim the republic on September 21, 1792.

In the fall of 1792, not only was the monarchy overthrown and the republic proclaimed, but the revolutionary armies of proud, loyal citizen-soldiers routed the invading foreign armies. Despite the maintenance of strict military discipline, the humblest infantryman now had the same rights as officers: They could be judged by other soldiers, and could no longer be beaten or humiliated as had been the case before the Revolution. Commanders made greater efforts to ensure that their citizen-soldiers were adequately fed and lodged. Yet, conditions often mitigated good intentions. Grain shortages could lead to less available food for troops, and sometimes young soldiers were handed only ancient hunting rifles or even pikes with which to defend themselves. Nonetheless, French forces pushed Prussian troops across the Rhine and entered the city of Mainz on October 21. On November 6, Dumouriez defeated the Austrians at Jémappes, north of Mons in the Austrian Netherlands. The stunned Austrians retreated, and the French revolutionary armies soon occupied all of the Austrian Netherlands (see Map 12.2).

Emboldened by these unexpected military successes, the National Convention on November 19, 1792, promised "fraternity and assistance to all

MAP 12.2 EXPANSION OF REVOLUTIONARY FRANCE, 1792–1799   The map indicates French revolutionary army offensives and foreign anti-revolutionary army offensives. It also shows areas annexed by the French, areas occupied by the French, and dependent republics established by revolutionary France.

peoples who want to recover their liberty." French troops captured Frankfurt and occupied much of the Rhineland. The Convention also declared the outright annexation of the Alpine province of Savoy, belonging to the Kingdom of Sardinia, and the small Mediterranean town of Nice, captured at the end of September. They declared them within the "natural frontiers" of France—a claim that contradicted the principles of popular sovereignty and self-determination contained in the annexation decrees themselves.

In the Austrian Netherlands, the imposition of the new French administrative structure and the creation of Jacobin Clubs failed to win much support, despite the fact that an insurrection against Austrian rule had occurred there in 1791. On December 15, 1792, the Convention abolished all feudal dues and tithes in those territories occupied by French armies.

The governments of both Britain and the Dutch Republic viewed the occupation of the Austrian Netherlands, which lay across the Channel from the former and adjacent to the latter, as a great threat to their interests. When it appeared that both states were considering joining Austria and Prussia in taking action against France, the Convention on February 1, 1793, declared war on Britain and the Dutch Republic. Spain and the Kingdoms of Sardinia and Naples joined this First Coalition against France.

When correspondence between the king and the Austrian government was discovered, the trial of Louis XVI became inevitable. Accused of treason, the king defended himself with grace and dignity. He called on the Convention to look after the needs of his family as he had tried to watch over those of France. But with the words "one cannot reign innocently" ringing in the hall, on January 17, 1793, the Convention condemned the king to death. On the morning of January 21, Louis XVI was guillotined on the Place de la Révolution (as the Place de la Concorde was then called). The huge throng roared its approval as the executioner held up the severed royal head, symbol of the Old Regime, for all to see.

The execution of Louis XVI.

As the Convention and the Paris Commune vied for authority, the French Republic, under continuing attack from beyond its borders, began to split apart. In Paris and the provinces, the Girondins and the Jacobins quarreled bitterly. The Girondins were popularly identified with the economic liberalism that characterized the port cities and with the desire to carry the Revolution aggressively beyond the frontiers of France. Opposed to centralizing power in Paris, they wanted a significant degree of local political control. The deputies of the far left, principally the Jacobins and their followers, sat on the raised side of the Tuileries Hall where the Convention met. They thus became known as "the Mountain," or the *Montagnards*. The political center became known as "the Plain." Backed by the Parisian sans-culottes, the Jacobins insisted on the necessity of centralizing authority in the capital to save the Revolution from internal treason and foreign defeat. The Girondins were moderates in contrast to the Jacobins and believed that the Revolution had gone far enough. The Jacobins accused the Girondins of secretly supporting the monarchy and demanded swift punishment for traitors.

In contrast to eighteenth-century Britain, only a very limited sense of a "loyal" opposition to monarchical policy had developed in Old Regime France. The combination of external and internal threats to the Revolution now made such an evolution virtually impossible. From the point of view of the Jacobins, those who were not for them were against the Revolution. Increasingly all opponents and adversaries were labeled as counterrevolutionaries or conspirators.

The sense of vulnerability and insecurity that greeted the French republic was heightened by reverses in the field. The armies of the First Coalition defeated the French in the Austrian Netherlands in March 1793. Dumouriez then betrayed the Revolution, preparing to march his soldiers to Paris to put Louis XVI's son on the throne as Louis XVII. When his army refused to follow him, Dumouriez fled across the border to join the Austrians and other émigrés. In the meantime, the allies recaptured the left bank of the Rhine.

Counter-Revolution

The Counter-Revolution was aristocratic, clerical, and in some places, popular at the same time. Nobles—including those who had already emigrated—retained considerable prestige, as well as economic influence, in much of western France. Even more, the Counter-Revolution to a great extent had been launched in the name of the Church and occurred in regions where religious practice still seemed strong and where the Civil Constitution of the French Clergy had met considerable resistance (see Map 12.3).

A full-scale insurrection against the Revolution began in March 1793. This revolt in the western part of France became known as the Vendée, after the name of one of the most insurrectionary districts. In August, the

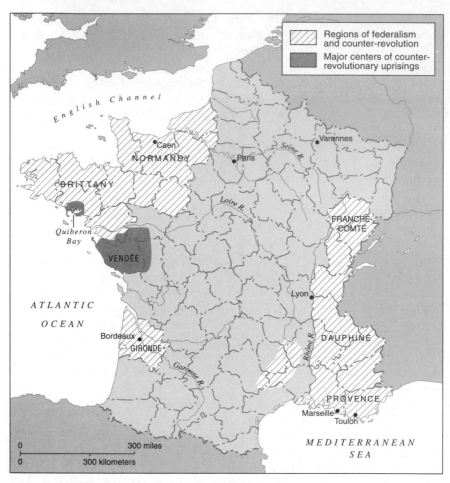

MAP 12.3 THE COUNTER-REVOLUTION   The map indicates areas of federalism and counter-revolutionary activity, including major uprisings.

revolutionary government decreed mass conscription, the *levée en masse*, which initiated the concept of the nation in arms: "Young people will go to battle; married men will forge arms and transport supplies; women will make tents, uniforms, and serve in the hospitals; children will pick rags; old men will have themselves carried to public squares, to inspire the courage of the warriors, and to preach hatred of kings and the unity of the Republic." The unpopularity of military conscription in defense of the republic also generated resistance. Both sides fought with a brutality, including mass executions and systematic pillage, that recalled the Thirty Years' War in Central Europe.

South of the Loire River, the counter-revolutionary forces principally emerged from the relatively isolated bocage, or hedgerow country, where the old noble and clerical elites had been relatively unaffected by the economic changes of the past few decades, specifically the expansion of the market economy. Here peasants had remained relatively isolated from the bourgeoisie of the towns along the Loire River to the north. The latter had benefited economically and politically from the Revolution, buying Church lands and serving in municipal offices, and had a vested interest in the survival of the Revolution. But in Brittany, which had enjoyed a relatively light tax burden during the Old Regime, the revolutionary government was hated for having ended that privilege, thereby increasing taxes. Tenant farmers, bearing the burden of increased taxes, also resented the intrusion of revolutionaries in religious life. Under such conditions, the Counter-Revolution won the allegiance of many people.

The Terror

Facing foreign invasion and civil insurgency, the Jacobins further centralized government authority and implemented a Terror against those considered "enemies" of the Revolution. The Convention set aside the recently promulgated Constitution of 1793 (which was to have replaced the Constitution of 1791). The apparatus of the Terror included special laws reducing the rights of the accused, the establishment of special courts, and the prosecution of those considered disloyal. On March 19, 1793, the Convention passed a law permitting the immediate trial of armed insurgents without a jury. A week later, the Convention established a Committee of Public Safety of nine and then twelve members, which gradually

A revolutionary tribunal during the Terror.

Jacques-Louis David's *The Death of Marat.*

assumed more and more power. The Convention also decreed a special war tax, including a forced levy on wealthy people, and imposed a maximum price on grain. These measures of centralization and government interference in the economy led to an irreversible break between the Jacobins, who believed in state controls, and the Girondins, who believed in economic freedom.

Military requisitions of foodstuffs accentuated hardship. The poor rioted over the high price of grain. More Jacobin Clubs sprang up in the provinces. In Paris, the Society of Revolutionary Republican Women took to the streets to demand laws against hoarding. This group, founded in May 1793, put forward impassioned demands that women be granted citizenship. Another group, called the "enraged" (*enragés*), demanded that bakers be penalized if they charged more than the maximum price for bread.

In June, pushed on by crowds from the radical sections of Paris, the Convention expelled twenty-nine Girondin deputies, accusing them of supporting hoarders, and ordering the arrest of some of them. Among those who left Paris to return home, some began to organize opposition in the provinces against the Jacobins. In Paris, Dumouriez's betrayal of the revolutionary cause added to the tension. Insurgents in Toulon turned over half of the French fleet to the British. In July, Charlotte Corday, a noblewoman, stabbed Marat to death in his bathtub. Tax revenue and foreign trade fell by half. *Assignats,* more of which had rolled off the government presses as the financial crisis continued, plunged further in value.

The Terror represented the appropriation of revolutionary violence from the people by a more centralized apparatus of state power. Its proponents justified it by the external and internal threats to the Revolution. But once established, the Terror also became a means of eliminating all perceived political rivals to Jacobin authority.

Louis Antoine Saint-Just (1767–1794), a precocious, icy young deputy whose mother had once had him incarcerated by *lettre de cachet* in Paris for running off with the family silver, emerged as another central figure of the Terror. After being catapulted to prominence by his denunciation of Louis XVI during the king's trial, he had been largely responsible for drawing up the Constitution of 1793. Now he waged war on royalists, hoarders, and Girondins, all of whom he considered enemies of the Revolution. "Those who make revolutions by halves dig their own grave," he warned.

Maximilien Robespierre (1758–1794), who emerged as the leading figure on the Committee of Public Safety, knew that the Mountain drew its support from the sans-culottes, some of whom were demanding the Terror. But he also believed that the popular movement remained a threat to the orderly transformation of political life in France. Historians have offered widely differing interpretations of Robespierre. These range from the view that he was a popular democrat who saved the essence of the Revolution from counter-revolutionaries to one presenting him as the precursor of twentieth-century totalitarianism.

Robespierre was the son and grandson of lawyers from the northern town of Arras. After the death of his irresponsible, largely absent father, Robespierre depended on scholarships for his schooling. At age eleven, he was chosen to read an address in Latin to the royal family as they passed through Reims. It was raining and the royal family, it was said, without acknowledging the young student, ordered their driver onward. The royal coach splashed Robespierre with mud.

After completing his law degree, Robespierre defended a number of poor clients, including a man unjustly accused of stealing from an abbey. Robespierre discovered that the theft had actually been committed by one of the abbey's own monks. After he was elected to the third estate, Robespierre gradually established a reputation in Paris for his well-organized and thoughtful but colorless speeches. Contemporaries noted the prissiness of the impeccably dressed, slight man with very pale skin and chestnut hair always perfectly powdered. A favorite of the Parisian sans-culottes, the man they called "the Incorruptible" called in 1793 for "a single will" of the nation to save the Revolution.

Insurrections against the Jacobins and the authority of the Convention broke out in Lyon, Marseille, Bordeaux, and Caen, where unlike in the counter-revolutionary west, merchants and others in the urban propertied classes and some of the Girondins played prominent roles in "federalist revolts" against centralized revolutionary authority emanating from Paris. Merchants and lawyers viewed the radicalization of the Revolution as a threat to their own control of political life. Lyon, France's second largest city, fell to republican troops on October 9; bloody reprisals followed, and the city's name was changed to "Liberated City."

The "Law of Suspects" in September deprived those accused of crimes against the nation of most of their remaining rights. The Convention specifically banned clubs and popular societies of women. It did so after

Marie-Antoinette awaits her execution. Sketch by Jacques-Louis David.

listening to a report by a member who contended that women should not be part of political life and that their participation threatened the stability of the family: "Women are disposed by their constitution to an over-excitation which would be deadly in public affairs." Olympe de Gouges was among the Girondins guillotined. Marie-Antoinette, though hardly a feminist, went to the scaffold.

The Jacobins were so intent on destroying the Old Regime and building a new political world that they instituted a new calendar in October 1793. The calendar of twelve months and fifty-two weeks of seven days gave way to a new republican calendar based upon "weeks" or cycles of ten days and "months" taking their names from more secular notions of the changing of the seasons (such as "Germinal"—meaning the budding—and "Ventôse"—windy—and so on). September 22, 1792, the first year of the republic, became, retroactively, day one of "the year I."

Like their more moderate predecessors, the Jacobins put new revolutionary symbols in the service of destroying Old Regime symbolism and maintaining revolutionary enthusiasm. Following the execution of Louis XVI, the revolutionaries chose a female image for liberty and the republic, which was ironic in that they denied political rights to women. They now proudly called the female image "Marianne," the name opponents of the Revolution had derisively dubbed liberty. Unlike lusty and even pornographic images of Marie-Antoinette, the female image of the republic appears gentle, not threatening, and virtuous, representing the abstract virtues of liberty and popular sovereignty, community and nation. Contemporaries contrasted republican virtue with the abuses of power that seemed to have characterized the Old Regime. They did so even as Jacobin representatives of the Revolution abused their power by imposing their will wherever they were resisted in the provinces.

During the "year II" (which began in September 1793), radical revolutionaries undertook an ambitious campaign of "de-christianization," a war on religious institutions and symbols. They closed down churches and removed crosses standing in public places. The campaign failed, unable to overcome centuries of firmly implanted traditions and beliefs, even among many people who supported the Revolution. "De-christianization" also turned many clergy who had accepted the Civil Constitution away from the Revolution, generating further resistance.

In the provinces, "representatives on mission," armed with dictatorial authority in the name of the Convention, tried to maintain order. They worked with local "surveillance committees" and "revolutionary tribunals" of Jacobins. Some of these revolutionary officials sent counter-revolutionaries to the guillotine. "Revolutionary armies" of artisans and day laborers guarded requisitioned provisions for the military and oversaw the melting down of church bells for war use.

Yet, the Terror was never uniformly implemented. The response to the Revolution in the provinces varied widely; so did the abilities and commitment of those sent to represent the Committee of Public Safety. Between

(*Left*) A contemporary seal shows Marianne, the image of the republic. (*Right*) A more aggressive engraving showing "The French people overwhelming the Hydra of Federalism." (August 1793)

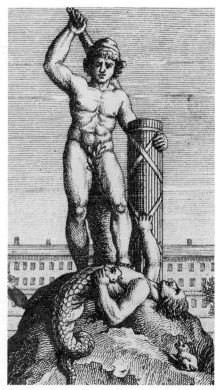

11,000 and 18,000 people perished (a fraction, by comparison, of the deaths that had resulted from the Thirty Years' War, or the American Civil War). About 300,000 royalists, Girondins, or other "enemies of the Revolution" were imprisoned for some period during the Terror. About 15 percent of those killed were nobles or clergy. Thus, nobles and clergy suffered disproportionately in terms of their number in the population as a whole (5 to 8 percent). However, artisans and peasants constituted by far the largest number of those dispatched by the revolutionary tribunals. The majority of these were apprehended near the northern and eastern frontiers that had been invaded by foreign armies or in the counter-revolutionary west where civil war raged. During the winter of 1793–1794, perhaps as many as several thousand prisoners—including priests and nuns—captured from the counter-revolutionary armies of the Vendée were taken out into the swirling waters of the Loire River in boats that had holes bored in them and drowned by virtue of the orders of a cruel revolutionary official.

Some significant French victories on the battlefield undercut the argument that the Terror was necessary because of the immediate external threat to the Republic. A French army defeated the Austrians in the Austrian Netherlands in June. Another French force pushed the foreign armies beyond the Vosges Mountains in the east; a third French army recaptured Savoy. The Spanish royalist army retreated across the Pyrenees.

The Terror struck the *enragés* leaders in March 1794 after they demanded even more economic controls and an intensification of the "dechristianization" campaign. They were brought before the Revolutionary Tribunal, condemned, and guillotined. The Committee of Public Safety then went after Danton and his followers, who believed that the Terror was no longer necessary, and thus had been labeled the "Indulgents." They too were condemned and guillotined. Real and imagined conspiracies provided the justification for the Terror, which now seemed without end. "Who will be next?" was whispered among even those loyal to the most radical members of the Committee of Public Safety. In May, Robespierre survived an assassination attempt.

Besides eliminating his enemies both at home and abroad, Robespierre sought to establish a secularized "Cult of the Supreme Being," which he intended to serve as a "constant reminder of justice" that would bind the people to the new values of republicanism. With the elimination of the *enragés* and the Dantonists, he was able to devote his energies to his Republic of Virtue. Thus, early in June, the republic celebrated the "Festival of Reason." The cathedral of Notre Dame in Paris became a "temple of reason." A popular female opera singer, dressed as Liberty—the image of the republic—wearing a Phrygian cap and holding a pike, bowed down before the flame of reason. The painter Jacques-Louis David constructed huge statues of monsters like Anarchy and Atheism made of pasteboard. After Robespierre set fire to them, a statue of Wisdom rose out of the ashes.

The political use of terror alienated many supporters of the Revolution, especially when more heads rolled in late May and June. The Terror seemed to have taken on a momentum of its own. Saint-Just said, "You must punish not merely traitors, but also the indifferent. . . ."

The Jacobins arrested the Marquis de Condorcet (1743–1794) for alleged counter-revolutionary activity and condemned him to death. Condorcet, an influential philosophe of the late Enlightenment, had been elected to the Assembly in 1791. He believed that all people should have a voice in approving acts of government, albeit indirectly, and that all citizens should be equal before the law. He had campaigned against the death penalty and slavery, and he defended political equality and the rights of women because he considered women fully capable of participating in political life. Condorcet died of apoplexy—or committed suicide—in his cell in the spring of 1794, shortly before he was to be executed. The Revolution seemed to have turned on and destroyed the enlightened reason that had arguably helped bring it about.

THE FINAL STAGES

Growing desire for an end to violence and repression enabled the moderates to regain control of the state. Moderate Jacobins and other members of the Convention, fearing that they might be next in line to be purged, overthrew the Jacobin dictatorship. They established a new government called the Directory, which ended the Terror. Caught between staunch Jacobins on the left and monarchists on the right, the period of the Directory was marked by great political instability, shaped by ongoing wars abroad and economic hardship at home. Although the Directory consolidated some of the gains of the Revolution, it too would be overthrown by conspirators led by the Abbé Sieyès and one of the rising stars of the revolutionary army, General Napoleon Bonaparte.

Thermidor

After the Revolutionary Tribunal was given new powers in June 1794 and used them to send 1,300 people to their deaths over a period of six weeks, the enemies of the Committee of Public Safety in the Convention began to plot against Robespierre and his friends. They were led by fearful fellow Jacobins Joseph Fouché (1758–1820) and Paul Barras (1755–1829), followers of Danton and moderates in the Convention who were afraid that they would be next on Robespierre's list.

Robespierre himself seemed remarkably blind to the plot against him. On July 26, 1794 (the 8th of Thermidor), he haltingly addressed the Convention, calling for one more purge. His voice could barely be heard amidst shouts of "Down with the tyrant!" Unable to respond effectively and anticipating his own martyrdom, Robespierre murmured, "I ask for death." During the night of the 9th of Thermidor, Robespierre, his brother Augustine, and Saint-Just were arrested at the virtually unguarded town hall of Paris. In an attempt to kill himself, Robespierre shattered his own jaw with a shot, a conscious emulation of the classical, stoic death of a hero.

The trial later the same day was as swift and pitiless as those endured by the Terror's other victims. The three Jacobin leaders were guillotined the following morning, followed to the scaffold by more than a hundred of their followers. Lazare Carnot (1753–1823), a talented military engineer and brilliant administrator ("the organizer of victory"), and one of the twelve members of the Committee of Public Safety, survived because the war effort desperately required his administrative talent. In the provinces, particularly in the south, the revenge against the Jacobins by their enemies was swift and brutal. In some southern towns, secret societies organized a "White Terror" (after the color of the Bourbon flag) to lash out against supporters of the Convention.

After dismantling the Paris Commune, the victors of Thermidor—the name taken from the period in the revolutionary calendar in which the Committee of Public Safety was overthrown—set about establishing a new national government. Order was only slowly and incompletely restored in the countryside. The Thermidorians greatly reduced the powers of the Committee of Public Safety on July 31 and then abolished it completely. In November 1794, Jacobin Clubs were ordered shut.

The Directory: Politics and Society

The Thermidorians produced a constitution by creating a two-house legislative assembly and a collective executive of five directors, which provided the name "the Directory" for this period of the Revolution. The two assemblies included the Council of the Ancients (250 members), which discussed and voted on legislation proposed by the second assembly, the Council of Five Hundred. Two-thirds of the members of the new councils were elected from among the members of the existing Convention. In turn, the two councils elected the five directors who formed the collective executive authority, or Directorate. Beginning in 1797, one-third of the members of each council and one of the five directors were to be replaced each year.

People of property benefited from the Thermidorian reaction. The new constitution proclaimed in August limited the vote to a smaller group of men than had voted under the radical republic of 1792–1794, or even in the indirect elections of 1789–1791. But although about 2 million men could vote (out of some 7 million men of voting age), electoral power was further restricted by a system of indirect election that favored the selection of the wealthiest citizens to serve in the assemblies.

The period of the Directory was marked by a decided turn against the asceticism associated with Robespierre's "Republic of Virtue." The *jeunesse dorée,* or gilded youth, drawn from the bourgeoisie and old nobility, set the social and cultural tone of the day. Wearing square collars

The return of high society during the Directory.

and fancy clothes, wealthy young men smashed busts of Marat and shut down theatrical performances favorable to the Jacobins. The red-colored symbols of the sans-culottes—such as the Phyrgian cap—quickly disappeared. Women who could afford to do so wore long flowing white robes of opulence and sensuality, with plunging necklines that would have horrified Robespierre. The familiar (*tu*) form of address, identified with section and club meetings, gave way to the more formal *vous* more characteristic of the Old Regime. Crowds in which women played a prominent part demanded that churches be reopened. Boisterous social events amused the middle class; among them was the macabre "Dance of the Victims," a ball to which only those with a relative who had perished in the Terror could be admitted. Some revelers turned up with their hair cut away from the back of their neck, mimicking the final haircut of those about to be sent to the guillotine.

Under the Directory, the comforts of the wealthy, some of whom had made their fortunes during the Revolution (by buying Church lands or supplying the military), contrasted sharply with the deprivations of the poor. The economy lay in shambles. The winter of 1795 was unusually harsh. The abolition of the Maximum spelled the end of cheap bread, and the price of basic commodities soared. A load of firewood that cost 20 francs in 1790 required 500 francs in 1795. The price of bread rose by thirteen times in Paris during the spring of 1795. Near Paris, people scrambled to eat the carcasses of dead army horses, and in mountainous areas people searched for berries and edible roots while trying to stay warm. The military requisition of food supplies weighed heavily on peasants. The Directory may have ended the Terror, but it did not bring stability to France.

Instability

Nor did the Directory bring peace. France remained at war despite the conclusion of peace agreements with Prussia in April 1795, in which the latter tacitly accepted the French annexation of the left bank of the Rhine, the Austrian Netherlands, and the Dutch United Provinces. But even as these agreements ended hostilities with some of France's enemies, French armies continued to press forward against the Austrian armies in Central Europe and Italy. In the meantime, mass desertion and casualties drastically reduced the size of the French army which, after reaching a million men in the summer of 1794, fell to less than 500,000 a year later.

War compounded the Directory's social and political instability during the terrible year of 1795. That spring, the Directory repressed two small popular demonstrations by crowds demanding a return to controls on the price of bread. Encouraged by the Convention's move to the right, royalists also tried to seize power. The king's son had died in a Paris prison in June 1795, and so the count of Provence, Louis XVI's brother, was now heir to the throne. He denounced the Revolution, making clear that he would never compromise with reforms enacted since 1789. An army of nobles supported by the British landed at Quiberon Bay in Brittany on June

The whiff of grape-shot disperses royalist insurgents, October 5, 1795.

27, but French forces turned back the invaders with ease. On October 5, 1795, royalists attempted an insurrection in Paris, where they found support from the sections in the more prosperous districts. The government called in Napoleon Bonaparte (1769–1821), a young Corsican general, who defeated the insurgents with a "whiff of grapeshot."

Instability continued nonetheless. François-Noël Babeuf (1760– 1797), who was called Gracchus, plotted to overthrow the Directory. Influenced by Rousseau and espousing social egalitarianism and the common ownership of land, Babeuf concluded that a small group of committed revolutionaries could seize power if they were tightly organized and had the support of the poor. Some Marxist historians have considered him an early proponent of socialist thought and twentieth-century revolutionary political tactics. Following Thermidor, Babeuf organized the "Conspiracy of the Equals," finding support among a handful of Parisian artisans and small shopkeepers. But the Directory's police were on their trail. In May 1796, Babeuf and his friends were arrested; they were guillotined a year later after a trial. The Directory took advantage of the discovery of this plot to repress the Jacobins once again.

Caught between the intransigent, dogmatic forces promoted by the followers of Robespierre and the Jacobins on the left and the royalists on the right, and lacking effective and charismatic civilian leaders, the Directory's difficult tightrope act grew more precarious. Its leaders were caught in an atmosphere of intrigue and rumors of coup d'états, fraught with tensions between the directors themselves and the councils.

In 1797, elections returned a good many royalists to the Council of Five Hundred. Fearful that they might press for peace with France's enemies in the hope of obtaining a restoration of the monarchy, the Directory government annulled the election results. The coup d'état of the 18th of Fructidor (September 4, 1797) eliminated two of the directors, including the republican Carnot. In May of the next year, the directors refused to allow recently elected deputies to take their seats on the Council of Five Hundred.

The wily Sieyès (who once replied "I survived" to the question of what he had done during the Revolution) emerged as one of the most influential directors. Sieyès believed France needed a government with stronger executive authority. Because one revolutionary government after another had maintained an aggressive foreign policy, it had gradually become clear to Sieyès that the army would emerge as the arbiter of France's political future.

For all of its failures, the Directory did provide France with its second apprenticeship in representative government. The Constitution of 1795 was an important transition between the political system of the Old Regime, based primarily upon monarchical absolutism and noble privilege, and modern representative government grounded in the sanctity of property. It further preserved the centralized administration of the French state and made efforts to centralize education.

The Directory had rejected cautious British suggestions that a workable peace might be forged without the French having to give up either its Rhineland conquests or the absorption of the Austrian Netherlands. Perhaps fearful that a more bellicose ministry in Britain might replace that of William Pitt the Younger if such a peace were signed, the French fought on.

Under the Directory, France's financial situation deteriorated even further. Inflation was rampant, and the collection of taxes was sporadic at best. *Assignats* were now virtually worthless. Many bourgeois were dissatisfied, having lost money when the Directory cancelled more than half of the national debt in 1797.

Napoleon Bonaparte, the victor over the royalist insurrection, now commanded the Army of Italy, checking in with Paris only when it suited him. His armies overwhelmed the Austrian troops in northern Italy. The fighting ended with the Treaty of Campo Formio (October 17, 1797), which left France in the position of having supplanted Austria as the dominant foreign power in Italy. This victory, and Napoleon's boldly independent diplomatic negotiations in the Italian campaigns, made the general the toast of Paris. The Austrians joined the Prussians in recognizing French hegemony on the left bank of the Rhine and in the Austrian Netherlands. Reorganized in July 1797 as the Cisalpine Republic, much of the north of Italy became a feeble pawn of France.

Despite these victories, years of war had exhausted the French nation and damaged the economy. Peace proved short-lived. In May 1798, Napoleon sailed with an army to Egypt, which had allied with Britain; he hoped to strike ultimately at British interests in India. Fearing that France sought to break apart the Ottoman Empire and extend its interests in an area it had always wanted to dominate, Russia allied with Britain. Austria also joined the alliance, which became the Second Coalition (1799–1802). Austria hoped to undo the Treaty of Campo Formio and to prevent further French expansion in Italy, where French forces had sent the pope into exile and established a Roman Republic.

The combined strength of the Coalition powers for the moment proved too much for the overextended French armies in Italy. In Switzerland, a combined Russian and Austrian army defeated the French. The French unsuccessfully tried to join Irish rebels against British authorities by sending an invasion force that failed to reach Ireland—the logical jumping-off point for an invasion of England. In 1798, British troops crushed a series of Irish rebellions in a bloody struggle in which 30,000 people were killed, and British forces captured one of the French ships sent to aid the insurgents, turning back the rest.

Coalition members began to quarrel over strategy and eventual goals. The tsar withdrew from the Second Coalition in October 1799, as he was irritated with the British for insisting that the Royal Navy had the right to stop and search any vessel on the seas. Nonetheless, after repelling an attack by a Russian and British force, French armies still held the Netherlands and the left bank of the Rhine.

The Eighteenth Brumaire

In the face of endemic instability, Sieyès decided in 1799 to overthrow the Directory in a coup d'état, a move that he had contemplated since his election to the Directorate two years earlier. The go-between was Talleyrand, the foreign minister. The career of the former bishop provides another remarkable example of revolutionary survival; a detractor once claimed that Brie cheese was "the only king to whom he has been loyal." Sieyès contacted Bonaparte, whose successes and attention to the needs of his soldiers seemed to assure their support. Napoleon was summoned back to France, arriving in October. On November 9, 1799 (the 18th Brumaire), Bonaparte (who had been appointed military commander of the Paris region) announced to the hastily convened councils that another Jacobin conspiracy had been uncovered and that a new constitution had to be framed to provide France with a stronger executive authority. The deputies were justly dubious. Some demanded his immediate arrest. Napoleon's response was incoherent and ineffective, but the quick thinking of his brother, Lucien, president of the lower assembly, saved Bonaparte from

A contemporary British caricature of the 18th of Brumaire. "The Corsican Crocodile dissolving the Council of Frogs!!!"

one of his few moments of indecision. Lucien rejected the call for a vote to outlaw Napoleon, and he ordered troops to evict members who opposed him. Those who remained delegated complete power to Sieyès and General Bonaparte.

Many people believed that this latest coup would preserve a moderate republic. Others hoped that Bonaparte would provide an authoritarian government that would end the quarreling factions that dominated the political life of the Directory. A contemporary wrote that "The Revolution of the 18th Brumaire . . . appeared as pure and brilliant rays of sunshine after long and disastrous storms. One can even say that it has begun a new era."

PERSPECTIVES ON THE FRENCH REVOLUTION

The French Revolution, which began in Paris, swept across Europe. In France, it marked a significant break with the past, although, to be sure, important continuities from the Old Regime helped shape the modern world. In other countries, too, the Revolution effected major changes. These included in some places the abolition of feudalism, curtailment of clerical provileges, and a more centralized governmental structure. But while some people welcomed the export of the French Revolution, others did not. To the latter, liberation by the French seemed indistinguishable from conquest. The French presence engendered a patriotic response in some of the German and Italian states, contributing to the emergence of nationalist feeling there.

Like contemporaries viewing the Revolution, historians also have had a variety of different interpretations of it. Many of them still disagree as to the causes, effects, and significance of the Revolution, debating the dramatic events with some of the same passion as those who experienced it first hand.

European Responses to the Revolution

Soldiers in the French revolutionary armies liked to think of themselves as liberating the rest of Europe from feudalism and oppression. During 1793–1794, at least, military successes and political propaganda convinced many if not most soldiers that they carried the cause of freedom on their shoulders along with their backpacks. But, at the same time, French soldiers accepted Thermidor with barely a murmur of regret for the end of the Jacobin period.

In other countries, some people at first viewed the French as liberators who would free them from the domination of nobles and the clutches of kings, nobles, and clergy. But, in fact, the line between a "liberator" and a "conqueror" was quite thin. Enthusiastic shouts for "liberty, fraternity, and equality!," echoed in German, Dutch, and Piedmontese, disappeared in a sea of French muskets, military requisitions, and even vandalism.

The revolutionary wave did bring about sweeping changes in some of the "liberated" territories, and would continue to do so as Napoleon consolidated his authority in France (see Chapter 13). Thus, in Piedmont, French control reduced the influence of the nobility and left a heritage of relative administrative efficiency. The abolition of feudalism in some of the conquered German states, northern Italy, and the Kingdom of Naples increased the number of property owners. The French conquerors proclaimed the rule of law and curtailed some of the influence of the clergy.

But the French faced the realities of almost constant warfare and, increasingly, resistance from the local population. As the wars dragged on and the economic situations of the "republics" grew worse, the benefits brought by the French seemed increasingly less important. Ruined merchants and former officials joined nobles and clerics in opposing rule by France or its puppets. As the Civil Constitution of the French Clergy led to a violent reaction against the Revolution in France, anticlerical measures in the occupied territories had the same effect. The peoples of the Rhineland, the Netherlands, and Flanders bitterly resented the revolutionaries' de-christianization campaign. Increasingly, the French presence bred contempt and hatred. Bavarian, Dutch, Piedmontese, Austrian, and Swiss patriots found willing listeners, while French propagandists heaped abuse on the local populations for their apparent disloyalty. Thus did the French occupation give rise to general opposition and a new wave of national feeling among the conquered. Although Great Britain had not been directly threatened by French invasion, the French Revolution also contributed to the accentuation of British nationalism in the face of a perceived threat by its old Catholic enemy in a new guise.

The French conquests in Europe were themselves an exercise in statemaking, largely unanticipated and unwanted by the local populations. Between 1795 and 1799, the Directory established satellite "sister republics" directly administered by France. The Helvetic Republic (Switzerland), the Batavian Republic (the Netherlands), the Cisalpine Republic (Milan), and the Parthenopean Republic (the Kingdom of Naples) were founded with the goal of shoring up alliances against the other Great Powers. But in the Italian states, only the Cisalpine Republic generated any local enthusiasm for the French invaders, and then only briefly. People "liberated" from the rule of kings and princes found themselves governed by a revolutionary bureaucracy controlled in Paris.

The French found support and hired officials principally from the middle class, which had already provided officials in the old state structure. But the French invasions gradually generated a hatred for the revolutionary invaders and in some places a concomitant nationalist response. This was especially true within the German states, where many writers and other people in the upper classes hoped one day that "Germany,"—300 states, 50 free cities, and almost 1,000 territories of imperial knights of the Holy Roman Empire—would one day be politically unified.

Historians' Views of the Revolution

Until recently, Marxist historians dominated the historiography of the French Revolution. They have described the Revolution as the inevitable result of a bourgeois challenge to the Old Regime. Thus, Marxists interpret the Revolution in terms of the rise of the bourgeoisie and its struggle for social and political influence commensurate with its rising economic power during the expansion of capitalism in the eighteenth century. Marxists use an economic analysis and emphasize that the nobility compromised the authority of the absolute monarchy by refusing to be taxed and that the emboldened bourgeoisie then allied with urban artisans and workers to bring down the absolute monarchy. They then go on to explain the abolition of feudalism by the National Assembly after outbreaks of peasant violence and the replacement of the nobility by the bourgeoisie as the dominant social class in France, reflecting its preeminent role in the country's increasingly capitalist economy.

This traditional Marxist economic interpretation of the French Revolution has been widely criticized. Some historians have noted that differences between aristocrats and bourgeois, and within both social groups, had become considerably blurred during the eighteenth century; that most of the "bourgeois" members of the Estates-General were not drawn from commerce and manufacturing but rather from law, and that, in any case, the upper middle class and nobles by the time of the Revolution shared a common obsession with money, not privilege. Thus, one cannot accurately depict the Revolution as having been simply a victory for the bourgeoisie. Moreover, revisionists have argued that the Revolution did not expedite capitalism but even retarded it, by launching France and Europe into a long series of costly wars.

Views critical of the "bourgeois revolution" thesis have also emphasized that within France the complex nature of local political power, divided among provincial estates and parlements, and among various groups enjoying formal privileges or monopolies and municipalities, served to limit the actual prerogatives of absolute monarchy. Many historians now see the Revolution as affirming the victory of men of property—a rubric that included both nobles and bourgeois—over titled nobles born into status and power.

A related interpretation has seen the Revolution as part of an essentially democratic "Atlantic Revolution" stretching across the Atlantic Ocean. By this view, the American War of Independence was the first manifestation of an essentially political quest for popular sovereignty. It influenced, in turn, the French Revolution and subsequent, related movements for political rights in other European countries, lasting until the Revolutions of

1848, and including movements for independence in Spain's Latin American colonies early in the nineteenth century.

More recently, another revisionist school has argued that a new political culture was already in place in the last decades of the Old Regime. An extreme version of this interpretation sees the French monarchy as a state well on the way to reforming itself through the collaboration of liberal nobles before the Revolution interrupted this process. One related view looks to the 1750s and 1760s for the origins of this new, revolutionary political discourse, or culture, seen in the political and ideological opposition to Louis XV and particularly in the rhetorical violence of the Revolution's first year.

None of these varying interpretations, however, diminishes the significance of the French Revolution in transforming the Western world by providing its first modern democratic experience. This is why its origins and nature continue to generate excitement and debate today more than 200 years after the fall of the Bastille.

CHAPTER 13

NAPOLEON AND EUROPE

The royalist, religious writer François-René de Chateaubriand once called Napoleon, his enemy, "the mightiest breath of life which has ever animated human clay." In a rare moment of introspection, Napoleon once said, "It is said that I am an ambitious man but that is not so; or at least my ambition is so closely bound to my being that they are both one and the same."

Yet, far more than his imposing will, Napoleon's career was shaped by and reflected the breath-taking changes brought by the French Revolution. Statemaking and the emergence of nationalism, accompanied by the increased secularization of political institutions, slowly but surely transformed the European continent. Because Napoleon helped overthrow the Directory (1794–1799) and transformed France into an empire, the question of whether Napoleon was the heir or the undertaker of the French Revolution is an important one.

An admirer of the Enlightenment, Napoleon claimed that he was the true son of the French Revolution. He personally supervised the writing of the new constitution, which made wealth, specifically propertied wealth, the determinant of status. Napoleon's reign was also a watershed in French statemaking: he further centralized the French state and extended its reach, making it more efficient by codifying laws and creating new bureaucratic structures and a new social hierarchy based upon state service.

Napoleon saw himself as a savior who carried "liberty, equality, and fraternity" abroad, freeing the European peoples from sovereigns who oppressed them. From final exile on the distant Atlantic island of Saint Helena, Napoleon claimed to have created European unity. But in the process of "liberating" other nations from the stranglehold of the Old Regime, he also conquered them.

Napoleon's Rise to Power

Napoleon's rise to power would have been unthinkable had it not been for the Revolution. With the emigration of most of the officer corps during the early stages of the Revolution, a generation of talented generals had risen rapidly through the ranks by virtue of their remarkable battlefield accomplishments during the revolutionary wars that had raged across much of Western and Central Europe since 1792. During the Directory, generals became increasingly powerful arbiters in political life. Napoleon manipulated the consuls and ultimately overthrew the Directory.

The Young Bonaparte

Of the strategically important Mediterranean island of Corsica, Jean-Jacques Rousseau in the *Social Contract* (1762) wrote, "I have a presentiment that one day this small island will astonish Europe." The year before, the Corsican patriot Pascale di Paoli (1725–1807) had managed to evict the Genoese from Corsica. But in 1768 the French took Corsica. Carlo Buonaparte, one of Paoli's followers, remained on the island rather than join Paoli in exile in England.

On August 15, 1769, Buonaparte's wife, whose family could trace its noble origins back to fourteenth-century Lombardy, gave birth to a son, Napoleon, named after a cousin who had been killed by the French. It is one of the strange ironies of history that Napoleon would have been

Antoine-Jean Gros' painting of the young Napoleon in *Bonaparte at Arcole* (1796).

British had his father followed Paoli into exile. In 1770, the French government accepted the Buonaparte family as nobles. The island's governor arranged for the young Buonaparte to receive an appointment to the royal military school at Brienne, in Champagne, which Napoleon entered as a boy in 1779. There he was exposed not only to a rigorous program of study but also to the humiliating condescension of the other students. They mocked his strong Corsican accent and his relatively humble economic situation. He fought back. Even in the winter snowball fights, Napoleon showed a remarkable determination to succeed. Unusually bright, he earned appointment to the artillery section of the national military academy in Paris, passing the examinations in a single year.

Napoleon stood five feet two inches, which (despite contemporary and retrospective impressions that he was quite small) was about the average height for a Frenchman of the era. He was barrel-chested, was increasingly corpulent as the years passed, had gray eyes, chestnut-colored hair, and a pale complexion.

Napoleon and the Revolution

With the outbreak of the Revolution, Napoleon returned in September 1789 to Corsica. There he helped organize the National Guard and drew up a petition to the National Assembly in Paris asking that Corsica formally become part of France, with its people enjoying the rights of citizenship. In this way, Napoleon clearly distanced himself from those Corsicans who wanted independence, thus parting ways with his hero Paoli, who had returned from England and joined the island's royalists. Napoleon favored the Revolution for three reasons: he wanted to see a curtailment of the abuses of the Old Regime; he hoped that the Revolution might end his island's status within France as little more than a conquered territory; and he thought the Revolution might provide him with an opportunity for promotion.

Napoleon became a Jacobin. He commanded a volunteer force that on Easter Sunday 1792 fired on rioters supporting the cause of the Catholic Church. When Paoli's victorious forces turned the island over to the English, the Buonapartes were forced to flee. Sent by the Committee of Public Safety to fight federalist and royalist rebels and their British allies in the south, in December 1793 Napoleon planned the successful artillery siege of the port of Toulon, which was held by British forces.

Useful political connections and the lack of direct involvement in the bitter factional struggles in Paris may have saved Napoleon from execution in the Terror or during Thermidor. The result was that Napoleon's star continued to rise, while some of his Jacobin friends went to the guillotine. In the Paris of Thermidor, Napoleon helped put down a royalist uprising on October 6, 1795, with what he called a "whiff of grape-shot." He attracted the attention of—and soon married—Josephine de Beauharnais, the lover of the corrupt Barras, one of the directors, and the widow of a member of the National Assembly who had been guillotined during the Terror. In 1796, the directors made Napoleon commander of the Army of Italy. It now seemed appropriate to eliminate the Italian spelling of his name; Buonaparte became Napoleon Bonaparte. Spectacular successes against the Austrians and their allies in Italy made him the toast of Paris. He later recalled with characteristic modesty that after victory over Austrian forces at the battle of Lodi, which opened the way to Milan, "I realized I was a superior being and conceived the ambition of performing great things, which hitherto had filled my thoughts only as a fantastic dream. I saw the world flee beneath me, as if I were transported in air."

Napoleon was now conducting military and foreign policy virtually on his own. His forceful and virtually independent pursuit of the war and subsequent peace arranged with Austria at Campo Formio (October 18, 1797) gave France control of the Austrian Netherlands, Venetia, and the satellite Cisalpine Republic in northern and central Italy. For the moment, only Great Britain remained as an enemy. Napoleon turned his attention to the Middle East: "The time is not far distant," he said, "when we shall feel that, in order truly to destroy England, we must occupy Egypt. The approaching death of the vast Ottoman Empire obliges us to think in good time of taking steps to preserve our trade in the Levant."

Napoleon then set off on a spectacular voyage to Egypt, part of the Ottoman Empire, which had allied with Britain, Russia, and Austria against France. He was accompanied by 35,000 soldiers and a shipload of scientists, a few of the latter already dreaming of carving a canal through the Isthmus of Suez that would eventually give the French an overwhelming advantage in trade with the Far East. After pausing en route long enough to capture the island of Malta, Napoleon defeated Egyptian forces at the Battle of the Pyramids in July 1798. But the tiny British admiral Horatio Nelson (1758–1805), who was prematurely white-haired, could see

Horatio Nelson on the *Vanguard* after being wounded during the Battle of the Nile.

out of only one eye, had lost an arm, and had few teeth left, trapped and destroyed the French fleet on August 1, 1798, in the Battle of the Nile. Undaunted, and temporarily stranded in Egypt because of the naval defeat, Napoleon set off to conquer Syria, before being forced back by dwindling supplies and disease. After a final victory over the Turks in Egypt, Napoleon returned to France. Austria and Russia, their respective interests threatened by French campaigns in the east, now joined Britain in the Second Coalition against France.

In Paris, Abbé Emmanuel Sieyès plotted to overthrow the Directory. Such a venture now virtually required the participation of one of the powerful, popular young generals whom the incessant warfare had catapulted to prominence. One of them nodded toward Napoleon when approached by Sieyès about undertaking such a plot, "There is your man, he will make your coup d'état better than I." Napoleon helped piece together a political constituency from among the quarreling factions of the Directory. With the coup d'état of the 18th of Brumaire 1799 (November 9, 1799), Sieyès and Napoleon overthrew the Directory.

CONSOLIDATION OF POWER

After the overthrow of the Directory, the conspirators established a new government, the Consulat, which brought political stability to France. It did so by concentrating strong executive authority in the eager hands of Napoleon, who oversaw the drafting of a constitution and made peace with the Catholic Church. Designated "Consul for Life" in 1802, Napoleon crowned himself emperor two years later. In the meantime, he continued to wage wars against Britain, Austria, and Russia, and then Prussia, four rivals driven into coalitions by French expansion. By 1809, although he had failed in his goal of bringing Britain to its knees, a series of remarkable victories confirmed his brilliance as a military strategist and tactician. Napoleon had forged a great empire, the largest in Europe since that of Rome.

Establishment of the Consulat

With the fall of the Directory in 1799, Napoleon Bonaparte, at the age of thirty, joined Sieyès and Roger Ducos to form a new, stronger executive of three consuls, replacing the five directors. When the new constitution was promulgated in December, Bonaparte became first consul, the most powerful man in France. He named men personally loyal to him to fill the other two posts. The Constitution of 1799 gave lip service to universal suffrage, but reflected the authoritarian character Sieyès intended. Indirect election for each political institution reduced the political body of the nation to a small number of notables. A Senate, appointed by the consuls, chose men from a list of 6,000 "notabilities" to serve in a Tribunate. A Council of State, whose members were appointed by the first consul, would propose legislation. The Tribunate would discuss the proposed legislation, and a Legislative Body would vote on the laws but could not debate them. There was more than a little truth to the oft-repeated story that one man who asked what was in the new constitution received the reply, "Napoleon Bonaparte." The constitution was submitted to voters in a plebiscite (voters could vote either yes or no). More than 99 percent of the all-male electorate approved the document. The plebiscite became a fundamental Napoleonic political institution, embodying his principle of "authority from above, confidence from below."

The Consulate provided political stability by institutionalizing strong executive authority. France's districts (*départements*) each received an appointed prefect, whose powers, delegated by the central government in Paris, far surpassed those of the intendants of the Bourbon monarchs. Napoleon's brother Lucien, as minister of interior, helped extend effective executive authority to the most distant corners of the nation, curtailing royalist and Jacobin opposition. Napoleon ruthlessly suppressed the press, reducing the number of newspapers in Paris from seventy-three to thirteen, cowing survivors with threats, or winning their allegiance with bribes.

The Concordat

Napoleon made peace with the Catholic Church, bringing it under state supervision. The Revolution had deeply divided France over the issue of religion, often pitting royalists against anticlerical republicans. Deep hostility remained between priests who had sworn allegiance to the nation during the Revolution—the "juring" clergy—and those who had refused. Napoleon wanted to bring this dispute to an end. Influenced by Enlightenment secularism, he believed the Church should not have an institutional role in the affairs of state. But he was also a cynical pragmatist. "There is only one way to encourage morality," he once said, "and that is to reestablish religion. Society cannot exist without some being richer than others, and this inequality cannot exist without religion. When one man is dying of hunger next door to another who is stuffing himself with food, the poor man simply cannot accept the disparity unless some authority tells him, 'God wishes it so . . . in heaven things will be different.'" An agreement with the Church would also undercut popular support for the monarchist cause by restoring some of the Church's prerogatives, but not any that would threaten the government's authority. Napoleon thus shrewdly sought to detach the Church from the quest for a restoration of the monarchy.

With the death in 1799 of Pope Pius VI (pope 1775–1799), who had refused any accommodation with the Revolution, his more liberal successor, Pius VII (pope 1800–1823), was eager to end a decade of religious turmoil. In 1801, Napoleon signed a Concordat with the papacy that helped solidify some of the changes brought by the Revolution. While declaring Catholicism "the religion of the majority of citizens" in France, it ended the division between juring and non-juring clergy. All of the non-juring clergy were to resign their posts. Some ecclesiastics were angered by what they saw as Pius VII's capitulation to the Revolution. A majority of bishops refused to accept the Concordat and did not resign. The pope would henceforth appoint new bishops, but on the recommendation of the first consul, that is, Napoleon; the state would pay clerical salaries. The Church also abandoned all claims to those ecclesiastical lands that had been sold as "national property" during the first years of the Revolution. The Concordat helped restore ecclesiastical influence in France, reflected by an increase in religious observance and in the number of people entering the clergy. Napoleon also pleased the Church by abandoning the confusing official calendar put in place in 1793, reestablishing Sundays and religious holidays.

The Organic Articles, which Napoleon promulgated without consulting the pope, regulated the Gallican (French) Church's status in France and reduced the pope's authority. The Church would now be subject to virtually the same administrative organization and policing as any other organization; a "minister of religion" would sit with the other ministers in Paris. No papal bull or other pronouncement could be read in France's churches without permission of the government; the clergy would have to read official government decrees from the pulpit. Under Napoleon, the Church gained the freedom of religious practice and improved its position compared to what it had been under the Terror and the Directory, but at the expense of some of its independence. A new catechism required primary students to memorize:

> *Question:* What are the duties of Christians with respect to the princes who govern them, and what are, in particular, our duties toward Napoleon. . . ?

> *Answer:* . . . Love, respect, obedience, fidelity, military service. . . . We also owe him fervent prayers for his safety and for the spiritual and temporal prosperity of the State.

Napoleon granted Protestants and Jews state protection. An article of the Concordat guaranteed freedom of worship for people in both religions (who together made up less than 5 percent of the population, most being Protestant). One set of Organic Articles supervised Calvinists, another

Lutherans. An imperial decree in 1808 organized Judaism into territorial consistories, although rabbis, unlike priests and Protestant ministers, would not be paid by the state.

Napoleon's settlement with the Church alienated some of his cautious supporters on the left, notably the group known as the Ideologues. They resented the return of the Church to officially recognized institutional respectability. After a solemn ceremony at Notre Dame in Paris celebrating the Concordat, one general put it bluntly to Napoleon—"A fine monkish show. It lacked only the presence of the hundred thousand men who gave their lives to end all that."

Napoleon's Leadership

One of his staff would later describe Napoleon as an "ever-restless spirit." He ate rapidly and could work days on end with very little sleep, dictating more than 80,000 letters in his extraordinary career. He seemed to absorb every bit of information that arrived in his office or field headquarters and rapidly mastered subjects related to military or administrative concerns. But he often ignored matters that did not really interest him, such as economics and naval warfare, in which France lagged behind Britain, as the defeat at Trafalgar (1805) would demonstrate.

Napoleon was more than just an optimist. He believed that his wildest dreams of conquest and empire would inevitably become reality. Everyone feared his rages, although he could be surprisingly understanding and generous toward subordinates when he believed they erred. A man of monumental stubbornness, he sometimes succeeded in reconciling others of opposing temperaments and views. He delegated very little meaningful authority, mistrusting even his closest advisers, but he tolerated opposing viewpoints. Napoleon's style of leadership became ever more tyrannical. He made up his own mind, and that mind invariably chose war.

Wars of Conquest and Empire

Napoleon had brought stability to France, but France was still at war with the Second Coalition: Great Britain, Austria, and Russia. In February 1800, when Austria turned down his overtures for peace on the basis of the Treaty of Campo Formio, Napoleon returned to the battlefield, retaking Milan and defeating an Austrian army in June 1800. With the Treaty of Lunéville (February 1801), Austria reaffirmed the conditions of the Treaty of Campo Formio, accepting French gains in Italy, as well as French control over the Southern Netherlands (Belgium).

With Austria defeated and Russia tied up by a war against the Ottoman Empire, the British government signed the Peace of Amiens in March 1802. France kept all of its significant gains on the continent, and Britain returned all the French colonies it had captured. Great Britain gained only the end of hostilities.

In Central Europe, Napoleon was now free to dismember the Holy Roman Empire and to dictate the territorial reorganization of the small German states. France had absorbed the left bank of the Rhine, fulfilling the nationalistic dreams of a France extending to its "natural frontiers." Since this expansion came at the expense of Prussia and Austria, these two powers had to be compensated. By the oddly named Imperial Recess of 1803, the two most powerful German states absorbed a number of small, independent German states, ecclesiastical territories, and most of the free cities. The rulers of Baden, Bavaria, Hesse-Kassel, and Württemberg, the other largest German states, also added to their domains. They were grateful to Napoleon for having made this possible. France's position in Italy also was solidified. Piedmont remained a French possession, with Napoleon naming himself president of the Italian Cisalpine Republic. After imposing a Federal Constitution on the cantons of Switzerland that transformed it into the Helvetic Republic, Napoleon forced a defensive alliance on that strategically important country. By 1802, France was at peace for the first time in a decade. Napoleon had brought his nation to a position of dominance in Europe not seen since the time of Charlemagne a thousand years earlier.

No longer satisfied with the title "first consul," in 1802 Napoleon became "consul for life," a change approved by plebiscite. Napoleon prepared the establishment of a hereditary empire in France. Although thousands of émigrés took advantage of a declared amnesty to return to France, the "discovery" in 1804 of a conspiracy against Napoleon's life by a group of royalists led him to act against the Bourbons and to expedite his plan to become emperor. Napoleon accused Louis de Bourbon-Condé, the duke of Enghien (1772–1804), a member of the Bourbon family who had emigrated to Baden, of involvement in the conspiracy. French troops moved into Baden to arrest him. The duke was hurriedly tried and executed near Paris, despite the lack of any evidence of his involvement in plans to assassinate Napoleon. Public opinion throughout much of Europe was outraged. The German composer Ludwig van Beethoven crossed out the dedication to Napoleon of his symphony *Eroica*, shouting "So he is also nothing more than an ordinary man? Now he will trample on the rights of mankind and indulge only his own ambition; from now on he will make himself superior to all others and become a tyrant!" Before his own execution, one of the royalist conspirators lamented, "We have done more than we hoped to do; we meant to give France a king, and we have given her an Emperor."

The Tribunate, Senate, and the people (through voting in a plebiscite) quickly approved the change from the Consulate to an empire. On December 2, 1804, Napoleon was anointed emperor by Pius VII. Instead of waiting for the pope to crown him, Napoleon snatched the crown from the

Jacques-Louis David's *Emperor Napoleon Crowning the Empress Josephine in the Cathedral of Notre Dame* (1805–1808).

pontiff and placed it on his own head. A new constitution presented a telling contradiction: "The government of the republic is entrusted to an emperor." An unknown officer who had scraped by with little money amid the spendthrift glitter of Thermidor, Bonaparte began to wear a coat of red velvet that would have been fit for Louis XIV.

Napoleon was no more temperamentally suited to live with peace than with defeat. Jealous of Britain's naval and commercial supremacy in the Mediterranean and the Western Hemisphere, he began to goad Britain into a new war. A government-controlled newspaper boasted that France would conquer the road to India.

Haiti, the western side of the island of Hispaniola, had proclaimed its independence from France in 1801 under the leadership of a former slave, Toussaint L'Ouverture. In 1802, Napoleon restored French control of Haiti and reinstituted slavery in the French colonies, in response to pressure from sugar planters. French troops captured Toussaint L'Ouverture and took him to France, where he soon died. Tropical disease killed most of the French troops occupying Haiti, and the British prevented the arrival of reinforcements. The French army surrendered, and in 1804 Haiti again became independent. With his plans to extend France's empire to the Caribbean having come to naught, Napoleon shouted "Damn sugar, damn coffee, damn colonies!"

Seeking to recoup the financial losses France had incurred from war, Napoleon sold the huge Louisiana Territory to the United States in 1803 for 60 million francs (then about 11 million dollars). In retrospect, this was a paltry sum for territory that virtually doubled the size of what was then the United States. Napoleon's hope that its former colony would emerge as a rival to Britain also lay behind the sale.

In July 1805, Russia and Austria joined Britain to form the Third Coalition against Napoleon. The new tsar, Alexander I (ruled 1801–1825), a religious mystic who believed that God wanted him to destroy Napoleon, had succeeded his assassinated father, Paul. Undaunted, Napoleon readied an army and ships of all sizes at the port of Boulogne on the English Channel for an invasion of Britain. In 1805, a French decoy fleet lured Nelson's fleet into pursuit, hoping to inflict a crushing defeat on the Royal Navy. But the hunted became the hunter. When the French fleet sailed from the Spanish Mediterranean part of Cádiz on October 21, 1805, it sighted the Royal Navy. Turning to sail back to port, the French vessels were left vulnerable to attack by two columns of ships that succeeded in breaking the French line. As Nelson lay dying of a wound (which might have been avoided, had he not refused to cover up his medals and epaulets that attracted a French marksman's eye), his fleet earned one of naval history's most decisive victories at Cape Trafalgar, not far from Gibraltar. Any chance for a French invasion of England evaporated. Great Britain controlled the seas.

The French were more successful on the continent. They defeated the Austrians at Ulm in October 1805, capturing 50,000 troops. Napoleon

The Battle of Trafalgar.

finally coaxed the Russians into open battle when the tsar himself, who took command of his army, followed the bad advice of an aide who told him that the combined Russian and Austrian armies could easily defeat the French. At Austerlitz on December 2, 1805, Napoleon tricked his opponents into an attack on his intentionally weakened right flank. He then divided the two armies with a crushing attack at their vulnerable center. When the dust cleared after the battle, the Russians and their Austrian allies had suffered 30,000 casualties, the French fewer than 9,000. Austria asked for peace, giving up the remnants of imperial territories in Italy and Dalmatia. Napoleon's allies, Bavaria, Baden, and Württemberg, once again gained Habsburg territories. Alexander limped back to Russia with his broken armies.

In the wake of Austerlitz, the hesitant King Frederick William III (ruled 1797–1840) of Prussia abandoned his tentative agreement to join the Third Coalition, instead signing an alliance with France. In July 1806, Napoleon abolished the unwieldy Holy Roman Empire and organized the Confederation of the Rhine, composed of sixteen German states, excluding Prussia and Austria (see Map 13.1). Napoleon named himself "Protector" of the Confederation, whose members agreed to accept French garrisons in southern Germany and to support Napoleon if war broke out again. Prussia now joined the Third Coalition.

Wanting to knock Prussia quickly out of the war, Napoleon's armies humiliated Frederick William's army at Jena near Nuremberg on October 14, 1806, and then occupied his capital, Berlin. In February 1807, the French and Russian armies fought to a bloody draw in a Polish snowstorm. Had Austrian and British troops been sent to support the Russians, Napoleon might well have been soundly defeated. But Austria was still reeling from the defeat at Austerlitz, and the English were preoccupied with defending their commercial interests in the Western Hemisphere. Napoleon sent for fresh troops from France and added 30,000 Polish soldiers, some attracted by speculation that the emperor might create an independent Polish state.

After defeating the Russian army at the Battle of Friedland (June 1807), Napoleon met with Tsar Alexander on a raft in the middle of a river. Frederick William, the king of Prussia, paced anxiously on the shore as he awaited the outcome. The news was the worst. By the Treaty of Tilsit (July 1807), Prussia lost territory in western Germany and in Poland, which became, respectively, the Kingdom of Westphalia and the Grand Duchy of Warsaw, the latter annexed by Napoleon's ally, Saxony. Russia suffered only the loss of its Ionian Islands in the Aegean Sea, but was forced to accept the territorial settlements in Western Europe as definitive. In return, the tsar received a promise of French support in Russia's current quarrel with the Ottoman Empire. France thus tacitly agreed to back Russia's long-standing ambitions in Southeastern Europe. Finally, the tsar agreed to close Russian ports to British ships.

With Prussia discouraged and dismembered, Austria defeated and weak-

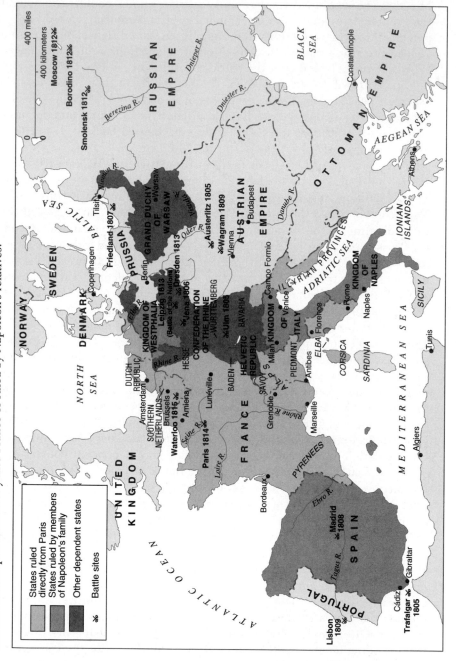

MAP 13.1 THE EMPIRE OF NAPOLEON This map shows the areas conquered by Napoleon, including dependent states and states incorporated directly into France or ruled by Napoleon's relatives.

Alexander I and Napoleon meet on a raft at Tilsit, on the Niemen River, 1807.

ened, Russia neutralized, and Britain once again left alone to challenge France, Napoleon's position in Europe seemed invincible. Two years later, when Austria challenged Napoleon by invading Bavaria in 1809, Napoleon moved rapidly against Vienna, capturing the Habsburg capital. He then crossed to the left bank of the Danube, and after avoiding being pinned against the river by Austrian forces, earned a great victory in July 1809 at Wagram, smashing through the center of the Austrian army. Defeat forced Austria to surrender Illyria to France and other territory to Bavaria, the Grand Duchy of Warsaw, and Russia, which was still technically but uneasily allied to France. Through conquest, the establishment of satellite states, and alliances with smaller powers, Napoleon had constructed a vast empire.

The Corsican Warrior

Napoleon has been considered one of the most brilliant and successful military leaders in modern history. Yet, his talents lay not in originality but in his stunningly innovative adaption of military strategy and tactics developed in the eighteenth century and during the Revolution. Before mass military conscription, warfare had usually involved relatively limited numbers of soldiers. Armies had not moved rapidly nor covered much ground. Since the beginnings of the Thirty Years' War (1618–1648), wars had been fought over dynastic honor, commercial rivalry, and disputed territories (see Chapters 7 and 11). Old Regime armies had consisted largely of mercenaries commanded by nobles. Most battles had been fought in precise, drilled ranks, by two relatively small armies in line formation directly facing each other.

In the eighteenth century, technological and tactical improvements in artillery augmented the value of that arm of warfare. Artillery pieces became lighter and therefore could be moved more easily. Improvements in roads also helped expedite the movement of cannon, as well as troops. Properly positioned artillery, launching more powerful shells, could now play a more decisive role against infantry. The artillery became a more respected part of the army; talented officers, Napoleon not the least of them, found a chance for promotion that they would not have had elsewhere.

Warfare changed when armies were no longer made up of mercenaries but rather of "citizen-soldiers" with greater commitment to a cause. Thus, during the French Revolution committed sans-culottes were first mobilized as citizen-soldiers in the *levée en masse* proclaimed in August 1792. They fought to defend the nation, winning the stunning victory over the Austrian army at Valmy (September 1792). The Revolution inaugurated a period of warfare in Europe in which more soldiers entered battle than ever before. Between 1800 and 1815, perhaps as many as 2 million men served in or allied with Napoleon's armies. Napoleon harnessed French nationalism to win the commitment of his armies.

Bonaparte's genius was his ability to organize, oversee, and assure the supplying of and communication between larger armies than had ever before been effectively assembled, and to move them more rapidly than any-

Citizen-soldiers were conscripted to fight in Napoleon's wars. Here the conscripts of 1807 leave their families to defend the nation.

one before him. "Everything is in the execution," as he put it. He built on the French innovation in 1792–1793 of using combat divisions that combined infantry, cavalry, and artillery, and subdivided his armies into corps, each with its own sense of pride and morale.

Napoleon's ability to select and promote able marshals, and to inspire officer and foot soldier alike, drew the admiration of even his most bitter enemies. He founded a military school in 1803 that produced 4,000 officers by 1815—there were lots of vacancies as the relentless fighting took its toll. As in the administration of the empire, however, Napoleon refused to delegate responsibility for crucial strategic and tactical decisions to his subordinates. In the long run, this would cost him dearly.

The infantry remained the heart of Napoleon's armies and his military planning (there were never more than four artillerymen for every 1,000 foot soldiers). Napoleon perfected the "mixed order" formation developed in the eighteenth century, which combined stretching troops across the field in a thin line about three men deep and bunching them in columns not only for marching but also for attack. Napoleon kept some battalions in columns, others in lines, which allowed battlefield flexibility. When he saw the opportunity, he launched an attack by outflanking his opponent and striking against the enemy's lines of communication. When he confronted an army stretched out before him, skilled marksmen threw the opponent's advance forces into disarray. Napoleon then brilliantly assessed the opposing army's weakest point. The concentration of deadly artillery fire—Napoleon once referred to the twelve-pound cannons as his "beautiful daughters"—prepared the way for the assault of the infantry columns. The speed of his army's movements was such that Napoleon could rapidly attack and defeat part of an enemy army before reinforcements could arrive.

Like a master chess player, Napoleon analyzed all possible moves by his opponents and quickly made decisions. At the same time, he remained flexible, believing that in warfare there are no fixed rules. "There is a moment in every battle in which the least move is decisive and results in superiority, as one drop of water causes overflow." When the corner was turned, instead of stopping to celebrate victory, Napoleon sent his troops, particularly the cavalry, to pursue the enemy. Victory became a rout.

Napoleon's armies, unlike the professional armies of the Old Regime, lived off the land. They requisitioned what they needed. This did not make the French troops very popular, even in those lands officially incorporated into the empire. But it did allow the imperial army to travel far afield, in great numbers, marching up to twenty miles a day. Such speed seemed incredible for the period, particularly in that each infantryman carried with him about sixty pounds of equipment.

Finally, Napoleon enjoyed intense loyalty from his officers and troops, even up to the bitter end. He took to the field with his troops and rewarded good work with promotions and decorations, sometimes given on the field

Charles Meynier's *The Return of Napoleon to the Island of Lobau after the Battle of Essling in 1807*, was intended to show the deeply felt loyalty of Napoleon's soldiers, some of whose wounds are being dressed as they stretch their hands toward the emperor.

of battle. The emperor's own courage was also a source of inspiration to his troops. He had the good fortune to be wounded only twice in his long military career (a slight bayonet cut at the siege of Toulon in 1793 and a wound when he was hit by a spent musket ball at Wagram in 1809). During one battle, the Imperial Guard refused to fight until Napoleon had moved to a safer place. Napoleon personally reviewed his troops before and after major engagements. He treated his soldiers with demonstrable respect and even affection because they seemed willing to die for him. At least 400,000 did just that.

The Napoleonic adventure offered even the most humble soldier a chance for glory. Yet, the risks of death and, above all, injury were considerable (only 2 percent of the casualties at the Battle of Austerlitz were deaths). Disease sometimes killed more soldiers than battlefield wounds. Soldiering was a tough life. In good times, soldiers ate reasonably well—bread, vegetables, even some meat, and drank wine or rum. But after defeat, or when they were far inside inhospitable territory, soldiers were fortunate to find enough to eat. As time went on, it became impossible to supply all troops with the basic necessities.

Medical care remained inadequate, despite the improvements brought by a talented and dedicated doctor, Dominique Jean Larrey. He arranged for the wounded to be cared for while the battle was still raging, rather than afterward when it often was too late. Major surgery—the countless amputations occurring after each major battle—was often fatal. Napoleon remained far more concerned with able-bodied soldiers than with the wounded or sick.

Incessant warfare was the most fundamental characteristic of Napoleon's empire. Military genius or not, the emperor's ability to mobilize France through a combination of appeals to nationalism and utilization of the resources of the centralized state dragged his country and much of Europe into a protracted, damaging series of wars. These stretched across Europe, lasting almost from the very beginning of his empire to final defeat.

THE FOUNDATIONS OF THE FRENCH EMPIRE

The Napoleonic empire was a significant episode in the long story of statemaking in Europe. Continuing the tradition of eighteenth-century monarchs, Napoleon sought to make state administration more efficient and uniform. His aggressive conquests brought centrally controlled, bureaucratic government and the Napoleonic Code to much of the continent. For this reason, it is possible to see him as the embodiment of "enlightened absolutism" awaited by the philosophe Voltaire.

Napoleon created a new social hierarchy based not on blood but on service to the state, particularly in the army and bureaucracy. Beyond French borders, the empire was based on an imperial system in which Napoleon made his relatives and marshals heads of state. Thus, he gave the throne of Westphalia to his brother Jérôme, as earlier he had transformed the Cisalpine Republic in northern Italy into a monarchy ruled by his stepson, Eugène de Beauharnais. He made his brother Louis king of Holland. His brother Joseph became king of Naples and later king of Spain. Everywhere that French armies conquered, Napoleon's daunting will imposed change.

Institutional Foundations: Imperial Centralization

Napoleon's Council of State, made up of his chief ministers, the most prestigious and important administrative body of the empire, oversaw finance, interior affairs, and war. Members advised the emperor and drew up laws and regulations for approval by the Legislative Body. Napoleon attached to the council a corps of young, bright, apprentice bureaucrats, trained to assume important administrative posts in the future. In the provinces, prefects orchestrated imperial administration. The Senate, Legislative Body, and Tribunate lost all but their ceremonial roles, and Napoleon completely eliminated the Tribunate in 1808. Even the members of the Council of State found their influence on the emperor increasingly reduced.

Napoleon established the Bank of France in 1800, which facilitated the state's ability to borrow money. He followed the Directory's policy of abandoning the grossly inflated paper money of the Revolution, which stabilized France's currency. He facilitated the assessment and collection of taxes, ordering a land survey of the entire country upon which direct taxes were to be based. And he expanded the number of indirect taxes collected on salt (which had also been a principal source of revenue for the Old Regime monarchy), tobacco, and liquor, as well as on goods brought into any town of over 5,000 inhabitants.

The empire followed the Revolution, and particularly the Directory, in making higher education the responsibility of the state. In a country in which about half the population was illiterate, Napoleon believed that schools could become a means of creating patriotic and obedient citizens through teaching secular values that would ultimately link education to nationalism. Although a national system of primary school education lay far in the future, the emperor could brag that, sitting in Paris, he knew by looking at his clock what every schoolchild in France was studying at that very moment. In 1802, Napoleon established state secondary schools called *lycées,* thirty-seven of which were operating six years later, for the relatively few boys who went beyond primary school. These schools were intended to educate a new generation of technically trained and loyal military officers. Students read only textbooks approved by the emperor. In 1808, Napoleon created France's first public university system, charging it with "direct[ing] political and moral opinions." Education increasingly became seen as a value in itself, and a means of social ascension.

Legal Foundations: The Napoleonic Code

Napoleon wanted to be known to history as the new Justinian, the Roman lawgiver. The Civil Code of 1804, which became known as the Napoleonic Code several years later, may have been the emperor's most lasting legacy. Many of the *cahiers,* or lists of grievances submitted to Louis XVI on the eve of the Revolution, had asked that French laws be uniform. During the constitutional monarchy, the Convention had begun the process of codifying French laws, but it had been interrupted by the vicissitudes of the Revolution. While the fundamental division in French law had been between the written Roman Law in the south and customary law based upon regional and local traditions in the north, there were hundreds of different legal codes in France. Napoleon ordered the Council of State to seek advice from a battery of lawyers to codify the laws of the land. Napoleon personally participated in the most critical discussions and debates. The Napoleonic Code made the rights of property owners sacrosanct: the majority of the articles concerned private property.

The code, over 2,000 articles long, enshrined the equality of all people before the law and the freedom of religion. It also proclaimed the "freedom of work," reaffirming a 1791 law that forbade associations of workers or employers' associations (the latter were extremely rare). The "freedom" guaranteed in relations between employers and workers left workers legally subordinate to their employers and unable to strike. Furthermore, workers were required to carry small passports that had to be handed over to municipal officials, police, or employers when requested.

The Napoleonic Code reflected Napoleon's traditional attitudes toward the family. He considered the family the most important intermediary between the state and the individual, a means of guaranteeing social order. Rejecting scattered demands during the Revolution for the equality of women, the code reaffirmed the patriarchal nature of the traditional family. It made women and children legally dependent on their husbands or fathers. The code granted men control of family property. A woman could not buy or sell property or begin a business without her husband's permission, and any income she earned would pass to his descendants, not hers. A woman worker's wages, too, went to her husband, and women had no control over their children's savings. As during the First Republic, the state recognized divorce, but it was now more difficult to obtain. More articles in the Napoleonic Code established conditions for the sale of cattle than addressed the legal status of women. In cases of adultery, women risked penalties that were far more severe than those for men. Only adult males could officially witness a legal document. The status of women reflected Napoleon's own views. He had complained: "In France women are considered too highly. They should not be regarded as equal to men. In reality they are nothing more than machines for producing children."

The code also formalized the relationship of children to their parents. As in the Old Regime, parents could put their offspring in jail and retained authority over their children's marriages. The code required equal inheritance by all male children (although at least a quarter of the inheritance was reserved for the eldest child), ending primogeniture (inheritance by the eldest son) in northern France, where it still existed. Yet, siblings often found ways to keep the family property together; one brother could buy out his brothers' shares in an inherited property. The end of primogeniture may also have provided an impetus for French couples to have fewer children in an effort to avoid further division of property.

The Napoleonic Code, despite its obvious inequities, imperfections, and the fact that it was sometimes promulgated by a conquering army, served as the basis for the codification of laws and the reorganization of judicial systems in Switzerland, Piedmont-Sardinia, and the Dutch United Provinces. At the end of his life, Napoleon claimed, "My glory is not to have won forty battles . . . but what nothing will destroy, what will live eternally, is my Civil Code."

Social Foundations of the Empire: The Imperial Hierarchy

Napoleon once wrote, "My motto has always been: a career open to all talents." He considered the end of social distinctions by birth to be one of the most lasting accomplishments of the French Revolution. The empire favored the aspirations of the middle class. The elimination of legal barriers to social ascension left wealth, largely defined by the ownership of property and service to the state (rewarded by grants of property, titles, and pensions), as the main determinant of status. Yet, imposing obstacles to social mobility remained. It took wealth to acquire the background, education, and reputation to take one's place in the imperial hierarchy. But even among bourgeois of more modest means, social ascension was sometimes possible.

The army and the bureaucracy were the two pillars of the empire. Napoleon created a new nobility, an elite of "notables," as they were called, rewarding those who served him well with prestigious titles and lucrative positions. At the pinnacle of the new hierarchy were eighteen marshals appointed in 1804 from the ranks of the Senate, including generals who had earned fortunes waging war. Napoleon began to restore titles abolished by the Revolution: prince in 1804, duke two years later, followed by count, baron, and chevalier. But unlike the titles of the Old Regime, these titles were not hereditary. They did not reflect the ownership of a certain estate or château, but rather service to the state.

Napoleon used titles and awards as pillars of the empire. Jacques-Louis David's the *Oath of the Army after the Distribution of Standards* shows the eagerness of the army to defend Napoleon and the empire.

Between 1808 and 1814, Napoleon created 3,600 titles. Yet, Napoleonic notables totaled only one-seventh of the number of the nobles in France on the eve of the Revolution. Some of the new notables had already become rich through purchase of ecclesiastical and émigré lands sold during the Revolution. More than half of all men granted titles by the emperor had rendered service in the military. The civil service was the second most important avenue to a Napoleonic title, with about six of every ten Napoleonic notables coming from the ranks of the bourgeoisie. Some of those who rose to the top of the imperial hierarchy and received appointment to the Senate were Napoleon's old friends and comrades-in-arms. Thus, promotion in the revolutionary army might ultimately culminate in a position in the imperial hierarchy. The emperor often repeated that "in the backpack of each soldier, there is a marshal's baton." Former royalists who now served the imperial cause could also be promoted within the imperial hierarchy. So too could Italians, Dutch, Germans, and others from conquered lands who found that the French Empire offered them dignified and sometimes even lucrative careers.

In May 1802, Napoleon established the Legion of Honor to reward those who served the nation with distinction. It was, predictably enough, organized along military lines, with commanders, officers, and knights. The Legion of Honor drew some early opposition from the Senate and the Council of State because the very idea seemed to fly in the face of the concepts of liberty and equality. A former Jacobin member of the Council of State complained that the award, a decorated cross that could be displayed prominently on one's coat, was nothing more than a "bauble." To which Napoleon replied, "You may call them baubles, but it is by baubles that mankind is governed." The subjects of territories incorporated into the empire were eligible to receive the Legion of Honor. When Rome became part of Napoleon's vast empire, the following parody on the Legion of Honor appeared on the walls of the Eternal City:

> In fierce old times, they balanced loss
> By hanging thieves upon a cross.
> But our more humane age believes
> In hanging crosses on the thieves.

THE TIDE TURNS AGAINST NAPOLEON

Almost inevitably, French rule generated resistance in countries absorbed into Napoleon's empire through conquest. Napoleon manipulated factional splits in some countries, coopted local elites where he could, brushed aside rulers as he pleased, and tried to establish compliant new regimes, some of which he handed over to his brothers. But ultimately French rule over such an extended empire collapsed. Napoleon's failure to force British submission by strangling its economy with his "Continental System," which aimed to cut off Britain from its continental markets, kept his major enemy in the field, or more appropriately, on the high seas. Spanish resistance against French rule became a full-fledged rebellion (the Peninsular War) that, with British assistance, sapped imperial resources. Moreover, French occupation of some of the German states gave rise to German nationalism, solidifying resistance. Prussian and Austrian military reforms led to stronger opponents in the field. And in a final ill-considered expansion of imperial aggression, Napoleon in 1812 decided to invade Russia. The destruction of his "Grand Army" in the snowdrifts and howling winds of Russia was the beginning of the end.

The Continental System

Knowing that the war was costing the British government huge sums (between 60 and 90 percent of the state's annual revenue), the emperor devised a plan he was sure would force his rival to end the conflict. In November 1806, Napoleon announced his Continental System, which prohibited trade with Britain and which he hoped would strangle the British economy by closing all continental ports to British ships. French merchants and manufacturers, as well as the state, would earn fortunes supplying the captive markets of the continent. Increased hardship might cause popular disturbances in Britain.

British Prime Minister William Pitt the Younger and Napoleon carve up the world.

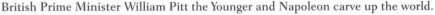

But the blockade of the continental ports was far easier said than done. The continental coastline was vast, the British navy strong (despite the loss of 317 ships between 1803 and 1815), and the merchants and smugglers resourceful. British merchants continued to find American markets for their goods. The banning of British imports did lead to the development of some important innovations in France (for example, the Jacquard loom for silk weaving and the planting of the sugar beet to compensate for the loss of sugar from the West Indies). But France's relative lack of available coal and iron ore, its lack of capital accumulation and investment, and the overwhelming allocation of the nation's material and human resources to war prevented French merchants from taking up the slack left by the absence of British goods in continental markets.

The British government's "Orders in Council" in November and December 1807 demanded that trading ships under all flags purchase a license in a British port. This decision placed Britain at loggerheads with the United States, one of France's principal trading partners. Napoleon retaliated with the Milan Decrees, threatening to seize any ship that had traded with Britain or that had even allowed itself to be searched by British ships. Yet, in 1809, British imports could still be readily found on the continent. The French, suffering a sharp decline in customs revenue, began tolerating violations of the Continental System, even selling special licenses and placing hefty taxes on the importation of British goods to bring in more revenue. The blockade came completely apart in the midst of an economic depression that began in 1811.

Napoleon counted on Britain's deepening crisis with the U.S. government, which opposed the boarding and searching of its vessels by British inspectors, to bring Anglo-American relations to a breaking point. But even the War of 1812 between the British and the United States, which ended with the exhausted British capitulating, could not destroy the British economy. British trade and manufacturing continued to provide the crown with sufficient resources to subsidize continental allies and to defeat Napoleon. French merchants and industrialists began to resent the economic consequences of the blockade, which also seemed to help unify British public opinion against Napoleon and the French at a time when the sense of being British was rapidly taking hold in Britain. The fact that French agents had encouraged an Irish insurrection against British rule in 1798 lingered in the memory of the British upper class. Tory governments, which governed Britain throughout the entire revolutionary and Napoleonic periods, remained committed to defeating Bonaparte (and repressing dissent at home), despite the staggering economic cost of the war.

The Peninsular War

Napoleon's obsession with bringing Britain to its knees led him into the protracted, bloody, and disastrous Peninsular War (1808–1813) in Spain.

In 1807, Napoleon reached an agreement with Charles IV (ruled 1788–1808), the incompetent king of Spain, that permitted French troops to pass through his kingdom to conquer Portugal, Britain's ally. A French army marched on Lisbon, and the Portuguese royal family fled to Brazil. Napoleon started sending more troops to Spain, while a popular insurrection in March 1808 led to the abdication of Charles IV and the succession of his son Ferdinand VII (ruled 1808–1833) to the throne. Believing that the kingdom of Spain was on the verge of falling like an apple into his hands, Napoleon forced Ferdinand to abdicate and summoned his older brother, Joseph Bonaparte (1768–1844), from his wobbly throne in Naples and made him king of Spain.

But Napoleon did not count on the resistance of the Spanish and Portuguese people. Ecclesiastical reforms imposed by Joseph and Napoleon, including ordering a reduction in the number of monastic convents by two-thirds and the abolition of the Inquisition, angered the Church, which remained a powerful force in Spanish life. Napoleon found some allies among the urban middle class, but the Spanish nobility joined their old allies, the clergy, in opposition to the invaders. Local councils organized quick attacks on the French forces, which were easy targets for the small mobile groups of Spanish guerrillas, who attacked and then quickly disap-

Francisco Goya's *The Third of May, 1808,* depicts the execution of citizens of Madrid by French soldiers after the fall of the city during the Peninsular War.

peared into the Spanish landscape. Even after sending fresh troops from Central Europe, victory for Napoleon in Spain seemed ever more distant. British troops led by Arthur Wellesley, later duke of Wellington (1769–1852), arrived to help the Spanish and Portuguese fight the French. By 1810, about 350,000 French troops were tied up in the Iberian Peninsula. Fighting for "church and king," Spaniards sustained what arguably was the first successful guerrilla war in modern Europe. Napoleon's "Spanish ulcer" bled France.

Stirrings of Nationalism in Napoleonic Europe

One of the lasting effects of the Napoleonic period was the quickening of German and, to a lesser extent, Italian national identity. The French revolutionaries had called for a war against the tyrants of Europe. But Napoleon seemed blind to the fact that the exportation of the principles of the French Revolution might encourage resentment and even nationalist feeling against the French in those countries conquered by his armies. Gradually the French discovered that nationalism was a double-edged sword.

In any case, Napoleon's encouragement of nationalist aspirations abroad was little more than a ploy to curry favor in each conquered state in exchange for support against his enemies. Napoleon may indeed have intended that Westphalia, created by the Treaty of Tilsit (1807) out of former Prussian territories and other smaller states that had fought against him, would become a model state. He ended serfdom and gave peasants the right to own land, to move through the kingdom as they pleased, and to send their children to school. But his principal goal was to bolster the Confederation of the Rhine's north flank against possible attacks against his interests.

The subordination of the economic and diplomatic interests of "allied" or "annexed" vassal states to those of France generated understandable resentment. Napoleon considered conquered territories sources for military conscripts and raw materials, or as potential markets for French goods. In Italy, French authorities forbade the importation of textile machinery and imposed disadvantageous tariffs on the local population, fearful of competition with their own industries. With the exception of Jacobin anticlericals, intellectuals, and merchants who stood to profit from the French occupation, most people expressed little enthusiasm for the Napoleonic regime. There was no reason why the people of the Netherlands, where the French occupation had virtually brought the prosperous Dutch trading economy to a standstill, should have welcomed Louis Bonaparte as their sovereign. Poles soon began to doubt Napoleon's promise to reestablish Polish independence; some nobles began to look to the Russian tsar for help, others to the king of Prussia. Yet, among those territories conquered by Napoleon, open insurrections were relatively rare. In the Neapolitan

Republic, where Napoleon had assured his brother Joseph that "all the better people are for you," peasants fighting for church and king overwhelmed the small number of their pro-French countrymen. In the Austrian Tyrol, peasants sang nationalist songs as they fought against the French in 1813.

The impact of the French invasions on nationalism was perhaps clearest in the German states. At first some German intellectuals had praised Napoleon. The philosopher Georg Wilhelm Friedrich Hegel (1770–1831) described the emperor, of whom he caught a glimpse after the Battle of Jena in 1806, as "this world soul . . . dominating the entire world from horseback. . . . It is impossible not to admire him."

But the French invasions carried German nationalism beyond the small ranks of writers and intellectuals. Attacks by German writers against French occupation mounted in 1807. That year, the execution by the French of a Nuremburg bookseller accused of selling anti-French literature prompted Prussia to join the war against Napoleon. Two years later, Napoleon escaped an assassination attempt by a young German student, the son of a Lutheran minister, who shouted "Long Live Germany!" as he was executed.

Gradually German writers discovered, or even invented, the idea of Germany by arguing forcefully that the people of the German states shared a common culture based upon language, tradition, and history. Only in the middle of the eighteenth century had German writers begun to write in their own language; before then, they considered French the language of culture. Like some composers, they began to discover elements of a common culture, drawing on language, literary texts, folk traditions, and other German cultural traditions to express themselves. This emotional quest for cultural and political institutions that would define "Germany" reflected some rejection of the rational tradition of Enlightenment thought identified with France.

German nationalists knew that the multiplicity of states in Central Europe stood in the way of eventual German unification. Hegel, for one, believed that Napoleon had helped the cause of German nationalism by eliminating literally hundreds of tiny states. About 60 percent of the population of the German states passed from one ruler to another during the revolutionary and Napoleonic eras. Still, forty separate German states survived. Among them Baden, Bavaria, and Württemberg, although much smaller and less powerful than Austria and Germany, emerged from the period with their independence and separate traditions for the most part intact.

Even though any possible political unification of Germany seemed distant, if not impossible, German nationalism nonetheless contributed to the determination with which the people of the German states resisted Napoleon. Johann Gottlieb Fichte (1762–1814) called on "the German nation," which he defined as including anyone who spoke German, to discover its spiritual unity. Fichte thundered at a university lecture in February 1813, "This course will be suspended until the close of the [military] campaign, when we will resume it in a free fatherland or reconquer our liberty by death!"

In Spain, people of all classes came to view the French as invaders, not liberators. The constitution proclaimed by the Spanish Cortes in 1812 at Cádiz, which was not under French control, nonetheless reflected the influence of the French Revolution. It proclaimed freedom of the press, established an assembly to be elected by relatively wide suffrage, and abolished the Inquisition. But the constitution, although never implemented because of the eclipse of Spanish liberals in the wake of conservative reaction, was also a self-consciously nationalist document. Some Spaniards, too, were becoming more aware of their own shared linguistic, cultural, and historical traditions, particularly as the French conquerors tried to make their language that of administration.

Military Reforms in Prussia and Austria

Just as the French invasion engendered a nationalist response in some of the Italian and German states, so did the successes of Napoleon's armies lead Prussia and, to a lesser extent, Austria, to enact military reforms. Following the devastating Prussian defeat at Jena in 1806, a minister advised King Frederick William III, "Sire! We must do from above what the French have done from below!" At the instigation of Baron Heinrich Karl vom und zum Stein (1757–1831), a royal decree abolished serfdom and removed class barriers that had served to keep middle-class men from assuming the military rank of officer (it nonetheless also prevented nobles from taking positions considered beneath their status). The Prussian military commander appointed some bourgeois officers and cashiered some of the more inept noble commanders. Stein established a ministry of war, taking away some important decisions from the whims of the king's inner circle and from the monarch himself. The abolition of serfdom improved the loyalty of peasant-soldiers to the state. The elimination of most forms of corporal punishment enhanced troop morale, as did the rewarding of individual soldiers who served well.

Stein also organized a civilian militia, which provided a proud, patriotic reserve of 120,000 part-time soldiers. Napoleon, upon learning of the Prussian reformer's plans, forced the king to dismiss his minister in 1808 (at the time, the Prussians were still bound by the terms of the Treaty of Tilsit, signed the previous year, to limit the size of their army). But henceforth the Prussian army would be much larger and more efficient than the army that Napoleon had previously defeated with ease.

The Empire's Decline and the Russian Invasion

Napoleon now confronted the fact that he still had no legitimate children to inherit his throne. Although he admired his wife Josephine, and may have loved her as well, he was as unfaithful to her during his lengthy absences as she was to him. Napoleon arranged for a bishop in Paris to annul his marriage—the pope having refused to do so—allowing him to remarry with the Church's blessing. Napoleon then considered diplomatically useful spouses. When the tsar would not provide his younger sister, Napoleon arranged a marriage in 1810 with Marie-Louise (1791–1847), the daughter of Austrian Emperor Francis I. She had never even met Napoleon, but that in itself was not as unusual as the fact that the French emperor had his old enemy, the Archduke Charles (brother of Francis I and Napoleon's opponent during the 1809 war with Austria), stand in for him at the wedding ceremony, while he remained in Paris. Napoleon thus entered into a de facto alliance with the Habsburgs, Europe's oldest dynasty. Within a year, Napoleon had a son and heir.

For the first time since Napoleon's remarkable rise to power, dissent also began to be heard openly inside France. Deserters and recalcitrant conscripts dodged authorities in increasing numbers beginning in about 1810. Royalist and Jacobin pamphlets and brochures circulated, despite the censorship of all printed material and theatrical productions. Royalists objected to Napoleon's disdainful treatment of the pope, who excommunicated the emperor after France annexed the Papal States in 1809. Napoleon responded by simply placing Pius VII under house arrest, first near Genoa, and then near Paris in Fontainebleau.

Over the past two years, Napoleon had become increasingly unable to separate options that were feasible or possible from those that were unlikely, or indeed impossible to achieve. One of the emperor's ministers remarked: "It is strange that Napoleon, whose good sense amounted to genius, never discovered the point at which the impossible begins. . . . 'The impossible,' he told me with a smile, 'is the specter of the timid and the refuge of the coward . . . the word is only a confession of impotence' . . . The more I saw of him, the greater was my conviction that he thought only of satisfying his own desires and adding incessantly to his own glory and greatness. The slightest obstacle enraged him . . . death alone could set a limit to his plans and curb his ambition."

Given such megalomania, the emperor's catastrophic decision to invade Russia seems almost inevitable in retrospect. It made almost as little sense as Bonaparte's wild trek into Syria from Egypt fifteen years earlier, though the consequences now would be infinitely greater.

Napoleon's advisers increasingly expressed their doubts about the emperor's endless plans for new conquests. Charles Maurice de Talleyrand, the former bishop who had loyally served as minister for foreign affairs since 1799, had resigned in 1807, after the execution of the duke of Enghien, the member of the Bourbon royal family who had been kidnapped from German exile. Talleyrand now symbolized the "party of peace," which opposed extending the empire past limits that could be effectively administered. In 1809, he began to negotiate secretly with Austria about the possibility of a monarchical restoration in France should Napoleon fall. Members of Napoleon's Council of State began to be increasingly demoralized. Furthermore, as the size of the empire grew, the difficulties of managing it in a period of constant war became even more daunting.

Napoleon's interest in expanding French influence in the eastern Mediterranean and his marriage to a Habsburg princess virtually assured war with Russia. In 1808, he had put the issue succinctly: "Ultimately, the question is always this, who shall have Constantinople?" and thus control access to the Black Sea. For his part, the French emperor was angry that Russia had refused to close its ports to British and neutral vessels carrying English goods. Believing that he could enforce the continental blockade by defeating Russia, Napoleon prepared for war with Russia, forcing vanquished Austria and Prussia to agree to assist him. In the meantime, the tsar signed a peace treaty with the Ottoman Empire, freeing Russia to oppose Napoleon. Alexander I lined up the support of Sweden, whose king was Crown Prince Jean-Baptiste Bernadotte (1763–1844; once one of Napoleon's marshals, he had been elected heir to the Swedish throne in 1810 by the Swedish Estates and would succeed the childless Charles XIII in 1818 as King Charles XIV John). The tsar offered Sweden a free hand in annexing Norway.

In June 1812, Napoleon's "Grand Army," over 600,000 strong, crossed the Niemen River from the Grand Duchy of Warsaw into Russia. Napoleon hoped to lure the Russian armies into battle. The Russians, however, simply retreated, drawing Napoleon ever farther into western Russia in late summer.

The Grand Army may have been the largest army ever raised up to that time, but the quality of Napoleon's army had declined since 1806 through casualties and desertions. Some of his finest troops were tied up dodging guerrilla attacks in Spain. Half of the Grand Army consisted of Prussian, Italian, Austrian, Swiss, or Dutch conscripts. A general complained in 1813, "Some [cavalrymen] had only mounted a horse for the first time in their lives two weeks previously. Most did not know how to handle their horses or their weapons; it was all they could do to hold the reins in one hand and a saber in the other." Officers now were by necessity more hurriedly trained. As the Grand Army was almost constantly at war, there was no chance to rebuild it to Napoleon's satisfaction.

In Russia, disease, heat, and hunger took a far greater toll on Napoleon's army than did the rearguard action of enemy troops. The Grand Army finally reached the city of Smolensk, 200 miles west of Moscow, in the middle of August; there the emperor planned to force the tsar to sign another humiliating peace. The Russian troops continued to retreat deeper into Russia. Napoleon's marshals begged him to stop in Smolensk and wait there. Yet, tempted by the possibility of capturing Moscow, Napoleon pushed on until his army reached Borodino, sixty miles from Moscow. There the two armies fought to a costly draw in the bloodiest battle of the Napoleonic era, with 68,000 killed or wounded, before the Russian army continued its retreat. Napoleon entered Moscow on September 14, 1812. He found it virtually deserted. Fires had broken out, probably set by a few Russian troops left behind for that purpose, and spread quickly through the wooden buildings. Almost three-quarters of the city burned to the ground. There was no enemy left to fight there, nor anywhere else in the region. The tsar and his armies had fled to the east.

Over 1,500 miles from Paris, without sufficient provisions, and with the early signs of the approaching Russian winter already apparent, Napoleon decided to march the Grand Army back to France. The retreat, which began October 19, was a disaster. Russian troops picked off hundreds of the retreating forces, forcing them to take an even longer route to Smolensk, 200 miles away. The Russians were waiting for Napoleon's beleaguered armies at the Berezina River, where they killed thousands of French soldiers. The emperor himself barely escaped capture by the Cossacks. The freezing winter then finished off most of what was left of Napoleon's Grand Army.

The retreat from Moscow was one of the greatest military debacles of any age, and one of the most awful in terms of human suffering and death. A contemporary described some of the French troops: "a mob of tattered ghosts draped in women's cloaks, odd pieces of carpet, or greatcoats burned full of holes, their feet wrapped in all sorts of rags. . . . [We] stared in horror as those skeletons of soldiers went by, their gaunt, gray faces covered with disfiguring beards, without weapons, shameless, marching out of step, with lowered heads, eyes on the ground, in absolute silence. . . ."

The retreat of the Grand Army in Russia, November 1812.

Of the more than 600,000 men who had set out in June from the Grand Duchy of Warsaw, only about 40,000 returned. After racing ahead of the groans of the dying and the frozen corpses, Napoleon issued the famous bulletin sent back to Paris: "The health of the emperor has never been better."

Napoleon arrived at the Tuileries Palace on the night of December 18, 1812. In the wake of a military disaster of such dimensions that press censorship and duplicitous official bulletins (the expression "to lie like a military bulletin" became current) could not gloss over it, the mood of the French people soured.

Undaunted, Napoleon demanded a new levy of 350,000 more troops. This call, coming at a time of great economic hardship, was greeted with massive resentment and resistance. Instead of negotiating a peace that could have left France with the left bank of the Rhine, Napoleon planned new campaigns and further expansion.

The Defeat of Napoleon

Napoleon now faced allies encouraged by his devastating defeat. In February 1813, Russia and Prussia signed an alliance, agreeing to fight Napoleon until the independence of the states of Europe was restored. Napoleon earned two costly victories over Russian and Prussian troops in the spring of 1813, but his casualties were high and opposition to him was growing stronger. Great Britain, still fighting the French in Spain, formally joined the coalition in June. Napoleon rejected Austrian conditions for peace, which included the dissolution of the Confederation of the Rhine, and Austria joined the coalition in August 1813. Napoleon's strategy of winning the temporary allegiance, or at least neutrality, of one of the other four European powers had failed.

In August 1813, Napoleon defeated the allies at Dresden, but then learned that Bavaria had seceded from the Confederation of the Rhine and joined the coalition. In October, his troops outnumbered two to one, Napoleon suffered a major defeat at Leipzig (in the Battle of the Nations) and retreated across the Rhine into France. His armies, ever more filled with reluctant, raw recruits and now lacking adequate supplies, were not the same. Napoleon's military inspiration now seemed less apparent. An insurrection in Holland followed by an allied invasion restored the prince of Orange to authority. Austrian troops defeated a French army in northern Italy. Wellington's English forces drove the French armies from Spain and back across the Pyrenees. Forced to fight on French soil for the first time, Napoleon's discouraged armies were greeted with hostility when they tried to live off the land as they had abroad. Opponents of Napoleon, including some churchmen for whom a Bourbon restoration now seemed a possibility, now spoke more openly in France.

Arthur Wellesley, the duke of Wellington.

Early in 1814, the allies proposed peace (perhaps insincerely, assuming that Napoleon would refuse), if Napoleon would accept France's natural frontiers of the Rhine, the Alps, and the Pyrenees, but Napoleon stalled. An allied army of 200,000 moved into eastern France. In Paris, the Legislative Body approved a document that amounted to a denunciation of the emperor, though it never reached the public. Even Napoleon's normally dutiful older brother Joseph encouraged the members of the Council of State to sign a petition calling for peace. Nonetheless, Napoleon fought on with his 90,000 ill-equipped raw recruits.

Demonstrating that they had learned a key lesson from Napoleon on warfare, the allies were determined not to stop until they had captured Paris. After overcoming stiff French resistance (in February, Napoleon won ten battles in twenty days), the main allied force swept into the French capital in March 1814. Tsar Alexander I of Russia and King Frederick William III of Prussia marched triumphantly into the city. At Fontainebleau, Napoleon's marshals refused to join in his frantic plans for an attack on the allies in Paris and pressured him to abdicate. Talleyrand called the Senate into session; it voted to depose Napoleon. The allies refused to consider Napoleon's abdication in favor of his three-year-old son. Without an army and, perhaps for the first time, without hope, Napoleon tried to kill himself by swallowing poison. That failing, he abdicated on April 6, 1814. The long adventure finally seemed at an end.

MONARCHICAL RESTORATION AND NAPOLEON'S RETURN

The allies sought the restoration of the Bourbon monarchy. In the meantime, Talleyrand had been negotiating with them to obtain the return of the count of Provence to be king of France. The French Senate, too, expressed its wish that Louis XVI's brother return to France as Louis XVIII. By the Treaty of Fontainebleau (April 11, 1814), the allies exiled Napoleon to a Mediterranean island off the coast of Italy. Bonaparte would be emperor of Elba alone. Marie-Louise refused to accompany him, preferring to be duchess of Parma, receiving the title by virtue of being a member of the Austrian royal family. As Napoleon travelled to the Mediterranean to sail to Elba, he heard shouts of "Down with the tyrant!" and "Long live Louis XVIII!" When he saw himself hanged in effigy, he disguised himself in an old blue coat and put on a white Bourbon cockade, later trying to look like an Austrian officer. In the meantime, if in most places the news of the restoration of the monarchy was not greeted with wild outbursts of enthusiasm, there nonetheless seemed to be a palpable sense of relief that the long Napoleonic Wars seemed finally at an end.

The Bourbon Restoration

The count of Provence entered Paris on May 3 as King Louis XVIII (ruled 1814–1815; 1815–1824). With more than a little wishful thinking, he announced that this was the seventeenth year of his reign (counting from the death of the son of Louis XVI, who had died in 1795 in a Paris prison without ever reigning). After the Bourbons were restored to the throne, the allies worked out a surprisingly gracious peace treaty with France, largely thanks to Talleyrand's skilled diplomacy. The Treaty of Paris, signed May 30, 1814, left France with Savoy, and small chunks of land in Germany

Napoleon relegated to the island of Elba after his defeat and abdication.

and the Austrian Netherlands—in other words, the France of November 1, 1792. France could now rejoin the monarchies of Europe.

Despite the opposition of his reactionary brother, the count of Artois, Louis XVIII signed a constitutional "Charter" that granted his people "public liberties," promising that a legislature would be elected, based on a very restricted franchise. This Charter, influenced by the constitution of 1791, distinguished the Restoration monarchy from that of the Old Regime by recognizing the principle of representative government, however much limited to election by a small, wealthy elite. Although the document affirmed monarchical rule by divine right, it confirmed some of the important victories of the Revolution, including equality before the law and freedom of expression and religion, although Catholicism would be the religion of the state. It specified the establishment of a bicameral assembly, which would consent to taxes. Furthermore, the king allowed Napoleon's Code to stand, maintained the centralized reorganization of the state bureaucracy, including the division of the country into "departments," recognized all titles, decorations, and even pensions awarded during previous regimes, and promised that property purchased during the Revolution as "national property" would remain in the hands of the new owners.

A coterie of fanatical nobles and their followers (the Ultra-royalists) convinced the king to enact some measures, however, that were highly unpopular. Many disapproved of the substitution of the white flag of the Bourbon family for the tricolor, the description of the Charter as a "gift" from the king to the French people, the retiring of 14,000 officers at half pay, the restoration of returned émigrés to high positions in the army, and the return to their original owners of national lands that had not been sold.

Napoleon Bonaparte retained the allegiance of a considerable number of Frenchmen, and several attempts to raise local forces to fight the allies occurred. In a good number of towns, crowds attacked customs barriers when the new royalist government reinstituted the collection of indirect taxes. But most of the French were simply exhausted from years of wars and sacrifice, and even Napoleon's most fervent supporters did no more than occasionally shout "Long live the emperor!" and disappear into the night.

The 100 Days

In March 1815, just months after his exile, Napoleon boldly escaped from Elba and landed near Antibes on the French Mediterranean coast. The former emperor knew that he retained considerable popularity in France. Furthermore, so much time had passed and so many dramatic events had occurred since the execution of Louis XVI that one of the monarchy's staunchest supporters claimed, with some exaggeration, "The Bourbons were as unknown in France as the Ptolemies."

Napoleon is acclaimed by the people of Grenoble as he returns from exile.

The word that Napoleon had landed in France and was marching north with a small band of followers stunned everyone. In Grenoble, he won over soldiers, workmen, and peasants by announcing that he had come to save France from the émigrés and uphold the rights won in 1789. Marshal Ney, who had offered his services to the Bourbons, promised to bring Napoleon back to Paris in a cage. But upon seeing Napoleon, Ney fell into his arms. Regiment after regiment went over to Napoleon as he marched north. With Bonaparte nearing Paris, Louis XVIII, his family, and advisers fled for the Austrian Netherlands. Soon Napoleon again paced frenetically through the Tuileries Palace, making plans to raise armies and defend himself against the inevitable allied response, and dreaming of new conquests.

It was not to be. The allies, whose representatives had already gathered in Vienna to create a permanent alliance, declared Napoleon an "outlaw" and quickly raised an enormous army of more than 700,000 troops. Napoleon led an army of 200,000 men into the Austrian Netherlands, engaging Prussian and British forces south of Brussels on June 16, 1815. He forced the Prussians to retreat and ordered one of his generals to pursue them with his army. Napoleon then moved against the British forces commanded by Wellington, his old nemesis. The armies met near the village of Waterloo on June 18, 1815. Wellington had skillfully hidden the extent of his superior infantry behind a ridge. Napoleon watched in horror as a Prussian army arrived to reinforce Wellington. The general sent in pursuit of the Prussians, like all Napoleon's commanders, had been taught to fol-

The Battle of Waterloo, June 18, 1815.

low Napoleon's directives to the letter and not to improvise. He held back, providing no support until it was too late. When the imperial guard broke ranks and retreated, much of the rest of the French army did the same. The defeat was devastating and total.

Napoleon abdicated a second time. The British captured him as he headed toward the Norman coast, hoping to find a way to sail to America. This time the exile would be final. The allies packed Napoleon off to the small island of Saint Helena, in the South Atlantic, 1,000 miles away from any mainland. The closest island of any size was Ascension, a British naval base, some 600 miles distant. Louis XVIII returned to take up the throne of France a second time, 100 days after fleeing Paris.

On Saint Helena, Napoleon's health gradually declined. He died on May 5, 1821, his last words being "France, army, head of the army, Josephine." He died of an ulcer, probably a cancerous one, despite stories that he was poisoned by arsenic.

NAPOLEON'S LEGACY

Napoleon's testament, a masterpiece of political propaganda, tried to create a myth that he saved the Revolution in France. "Every Frenchman could say during my reign,—'I shall be minister, grand officer, duke, count, baron, if I earn it—even king!'" And in some ways, Napoleon was indeed the heir to the French Revolution. He guaranteed the survival of some of its most significant triumphs. Napoleon considered his greatest achievement "that of establishing and consecrating the rule of reason." His Napoleonic Code proclaimed the equality of all people before the law (favoring, however, men over women), personal freedom, and the inviolability of property. Napoleon left the myth, and to some extent the reality, of the "career open to talent," which aided, above all, the middle class, but even peasants in some cases. He consolidated the role of wealth, principally property ownership, as the foundation of the political life of the nation and the measure of one's presumed social value. The result was to increase the number of citizens eligible to participate in political life, however limited by imperial strictures. Furthermore, Napoleon helped turn nationalism into an aggressive secular religion. Bonaparte manipulated this patriotic energy and transformed it into an ideology inculcated by French schools.

Napoleon's reforms, built upon those of the French Revolution, extended into states conquered by his imperial armies. The French imposed constitutions and state control over the appointment of clergy, standardized judicial systems, and abolished ecclesiastical courts. Throughout the empire, Napoleon created new tax structures, standardized weights and measures, ended internal customs barriers, abolished guilds, and established state bureaucracies that were extensions of French rule in the "sister republics" founded by the Directory. In addition to abolishing serfdom in Poland, where the institution was particularly widespread, the French occupation also ended residual peasant seigneurial obligations (such as the requirement to provide labor services to the lord) virtually everywhere, and abolished noble and ecclesiastical courts in northern Italy and the Netherlands. The Napoleonic Code proclaimed freedom of worship, and the French conquest of other European states, including Baden, Bavaria, and the Dutch Republic, helped remove onerous restrictions on Jews. But under pressure from French planters, Napoleon also reestablished slavery in Haiti in 1802, making a mockery of his contention that all men were equal.

Jacques-Louis David's *Bonaparte Leaping the St. Bernard* shows Napoleon crossing the Saint Bernard Pass in the Alps. This painting also shows how Napoleon's myth made him larger than life.

Yet, even Napoleon's success in implementing reforms varied from place to place, depending on existing political structures, the degree of compliance by local elites, and the international situation. In southern Italy, for example, which Napoleon's armies conquered relatively late and where the structures of state authority had always been particularly weak, the French presence had little lasting effect. As the Napoleonic wave subsided, nobles and clerics regained domination over the overwhelmingly rural, impoverished local population.

Napoleon claimed from Saint Helena that he was trying to liberate Europe, but he had actually replaced the old sovereigns with new ones—himself or his brothers. "If I conquered other kingdoms," he admitted, "I did so in order that France would be the beneficiary." Wagons returned from Italy full of art and other treasures, which became the property of Napoleon and his family, his marshals, or the state. French conquests helped awaken nationalist spirit, with the imposition of French administration in the German and Italian states proving especially important for the unification of Germany and Italy later in the nineteenth century. But the effect was, as we have seen, totally unintended and unwanted. Moreover, as the French empire grew in size, it became increasingly difficult to administer effectively.

To the writer Germaine de Staël (1766–1817), the daughter of the Swiss banker Jacques Necker, Louis XVI's minister, Napoleon "regarded a human being as an action or a thing . . . nothing existed but himself. He was an able chess player, and the human race was the opponent to whom he proposed to give checkmate." In the end, his monumental ambition got the best of him. When he could have been satisfied with expanding France's power and place in Europe, he went to war again. About 2 million men served in Napoleon's armies between 1805 and 1814; about 90,000 died in battle and more than three times that number subsequently perished from wounds; over 600,000 were later recorded as prisoners or "disappeared." In all, Napoleon's armies may have suffered as many as 1.5 million casualties. The Napoleonic Wars killed about one in five of all Frenchmen born between 1790 and 1795.

Napoleon's final legacy was his myth. From Saint Helena, Napoleon said, "If I had succeeded, I would have been the greatest man known to history." His career remained the stuff of popular writing throughout Europe for decades. The rise of romanticism helped make the story of Napoleon, the romantic hero, part of the collective memory of Western Europe after his death. Long after Waterloo, peddlers of songs, pamphlets, lithographs and other images glorified Napoleon's life as earlier they had the lives of saints. "I live only for posterity," Napoleon once said. "Death is nothing, but to live defeated and without glory is to die every day." Rumors of his miraculous return to France were persistent long after his death. So powerful was his legend that even the most improbable seemed possible.

CHAPTER 14

CHALLENGES TO RESTORATION EUROPE

At the Congress of Vienna of 1815, representatives of the allies who had defeated Napoleon—Austria, Russia, Prussia, and Great Britain—came together to re-establish peace in Europe. They hoped that by imposing a treaty on France and creating an international mechanism, the Concert of Europe, they could prevent Europe from again being shaken by revolution in France or elsewhere.

Early nineteenth-century Vienna was a perfect setting for a gathering of the representatives of Europe's sovereign powers. The Schönbrunn Palace on the outskirts of the Habsburg capital and Vienna's own elegant baroque buildings still reflected the grandeur of absolutism and traditional court life, despite the fact that years of warfare had virtually bankrupted the Austrian monarchy and left its monuments a bit threadbare.

The Austrian hosts of the Congress, which met between September 1814 and June 1815, revived the aristocratic court life of the pre-revolutionary period. Elaborate dinners, elegant balls, festive fireworks displays, and organized hunts helped relieve boredom. Artists stood ready to paint the portraits of the members of the diplomatic delegations. Aristocratic guests amused themselves by trying to guess which of the hundreds of maids and porters were spying for the Austrians; and by trying to be the first to catch a glimpse of the dashing duke of Wellington, who had defeated Napoleon at Waterloo. The British prime minister and his wife took dancing lessons. The antics of some representatives provided as much comic relief as irritation. A Spanish diplomat put forth the claim that his country should have the right to several small Italian states. The other representatives were so annoyed by this demand that they invited him to go on a ballooning excursion, and sent him off in the general direction of the Alps.

What the English poet George Gordon, Lord Byron (1788–1824), called "that base pageant," the Congress of Vienna provided an opportunity for the informal discussions that had always been an important part of

The Congress of Vienna.

traditional diplomacy. In fact, the Congress met officially but once, to sign the final treaty, which had been negotiated in smaller formal and informal gatherings of the various delegations. And in the wake of the many territorial changes that had occurred during almost twenty-five years of intermittent warfare, the representatives redrew the map of Europe. They established new borders, particularly in Central Europe, putting old rulers back in power in some places, assigning territories to the rule of one power or another.

Between Napoleon's final defeat in 1815 and the Revolutions of 1848, a protracted struggle between the conservative forces of monarchical order and new agents of change took place in Europe. Monarchs and nobles, particularly, were determined to hold the line against political liberals or nationalists who would challenge the existing state system. But liberal and national movements could not so easily be swept away. During the subsequent three decades, "liberty" became the watchword for more and more people, particularly among the middle classes, who protested their exclusion from political life. Liberals demanded political rights for a larger fraction of the male population. They also called for constitutional guarantees of freedom of the press and assembly. Furthermore, most liberals demanded the extension of education to the lower classes as a means of expanding the number of people capable of participating in political life.

Liberal movements were in many places closely tied to the emergence of nationalism (the belief in the primacy of nationality, usually defined by language and cultural traditions) as a source of allegiance and sovereignty. The French Revolution and romanticism (see Chapter 15) helped shape nationalism into a force for change. By espousing the principle that states should correspond to ethnic boundaries, nationalism threatened the territorial settlements effected by the Congress of Vienna. The Habsburg Austrian monarchy, for example, ruled at least fifteen peoples without a state of their own, including Poles and Hungarians, who had once had fully independent states. The German and Italian states, where liberalism became increasingly identified with nationalism, lacked the astonishing cultural, linguistic, and religious diversity of the Habsburg domains, but their fragmentation increased calls by nationalists for political unification. The unification of the German states, too, threatened the settlement of the Congress of Vienna, which restored territories to Prussia, Austria, and many of the lesser states that had long had their own ruling dynasties. Likewise, Italian nationalism threatened Austria's hold on Lombardy and Venetia, as well as the Bourbon dynasty of Naples and Sicily, the Papal States in central Italy, and petty potentates ruling several smaller states.

The next decades were marked by almost constant pressure on the Europe of monarchical restoration. There were liberal and nationalist defeats, but also victories that combined to shatter the settlements made at Vienna. The struggle between liberals and conservatives stretched across much of Europe, revealing an interconnectedness of experience that transcended the particular histories of individual states, despite the unevenness of economic development.

THE POST-NAPOLEONIC SETTLEMENT

Their victory over Napoleon gave the allies the chance to impose a territorial settlement on the continent. Conservative ideology seeking to protect the legitimate sovereigns from liberal and nationalist movements underlay the peace settlements, as did the heritage of eighteenth-century diplomacy.

Revolutionary France had compounded its sins in the eyes of the other Great Powers by becoming too strong and overturning the balance of power. The allied representatives were shrewd enough to realize that they could not turn the clock back to 1789, but they were determined to ensure that France could not again rise to a position of domination in Europe. Thus, even before Napoleon's defeat in 1814, representatives of Prussia, Austria, Russia, and Great Britain had agreed to form a coalition that they hoped would last at least twenty years. The purpose of this "Quadruple Alliance" was to prevent France or any other state or political movement from threatening the legitimate sovereigns of Europe.

The Treaty of Paris

The allies and representatives of the usurped French Bourbon monarchy signed the Treaty of Paris in May 1814. Prince Charles Maurice Talleyrand (1754–1838), who had served Napoleon with flexibility rooted in an uncanny sense of survival, became the intermediary. He exploited tensions between the allies, particularly between Prussia and Austria. In the end, the victorious powers agreed to restore the Bourbons to the throne of France in the person of the count of Provence, brother of the executed Louis XVI. The allies might well have forced the French to sign a draconian treaty. But they were dealing not with the defeated Napoleon but with the restored Bourbon monarch, Louis XVIII, whose throne they wanted to solidify. Stripping France of its imperial gains was one thing. But to leave the country too weak could work against the allies by leaving the king vulnerable to Jacobin challenges from within France.

The allies permitted France to keep lands incorporated before November 1, 1792, including parts of Savoy, Germany, and the Austrian Netherlands, as well as the former papal city of Avignon. France gave up claims to the remainder of the Austrian Netherlands, the Dutch Republic, the German states, the Italian states, and Switzerland. It lost the Caribbean islands of Trinidad, Tobago, Santa Lucia, and part of Santo Domingo to Britain. But despite the enormous cost of the Napoleonic Wars to all powers, the allies would exact no indemnity from the French.

Allied forces occupied France. Extremely difficult territorial issues remained to be resolved in Central and Southern Europe, where Napoleon had disrupted the old structure of states by, for example, breaking apart the Holy Roman Empire in 1806. The Congress of Vienna would establish new European boundaries.

Diplomatic Maneuvering at the Congress of Vienna

The Congress of Vienna was almost entirely the work of diplomats representing Austria, Prussia, Great Britain, and Russia. The rulers and princes of the smaller German states travelled to Vienna in the hope of maintaining their independence and security, a complicated task for those states that had cast their fate with Napoleon. At least at the beginning, defeated France played only the role of a very interested observer (although French was the official language of the conference). But Talleyrand's wily off-stage negotiations gradually brought France to the position of a full-fledged participant in the deliberations. Tsar Alexander I (ruled 1801–1825) of Russia participated personally, but the dominant figures in Vienna were unquestionably the Austrian Chancellor Prince Klemens von Metternich (1773–1859) and, to a lesser extent, British Prime Minister Viscount Robert Castlereagh (1769–1822).

Metternich, born in the German Rhineland, was the son of a noble who had served at the court of the Habsburg monarch. Forced to flee his homeland by the French invasion in 1792, he entered the diplomatic service in Vienna, rising to become the minister of foreign affairs in 1809. Metternich was a handsome and invariably elegantly dressed dandy with immaculately powdered hair who was at home in the social whirl of formal receptions and magnificent balls, as well as in the petty intrigues of high society. Well educated, he could bore people in five languages. But he was also a determined, calculating practitioner of tough-minded diplomacy, unmatched in his ability to understand both the potential consequences of virtually any diplomatic situation and the views and personalities of his colleagues and opponents. He had great faith in his own ability to set and steer the proper course for the continent, whose international affairs he would dominate until 1848. Like the conservatives he represented, Metternich believed that Europe would find peace only if its legitimate sovereigns were unchallenged by the forces of liberalism and nationalism, and if a single state could no longer threaten the international balance of power by becoming too powerful, as France had during the reign of Louis XIV and again during the Revolution and Napoleonic era.

Russian Tsar Alexander I wanted the allies to affirm formally what he considered the religious basis of the European alliance. Deeply religious, the tsar drafted a document that became the basis for the Holy Alliance. It asserted that the relations of the European sovereigns, whom he referred to as "the delegates of Providence," would thereafter be based "upon the sublime truths which the Holy Religion of Our Savior teaches." Emperor Francis I of Austria and Frederick William III of Prussia signed the document, but the British prince regent—the future George IV (ruled 1820–1830)—begged off, claiming that he could not sign the text without the signature of a minister, confirming the constitutional nature of British government. Lord Castlereagh revealed the British attitude toward the Holy Alliance when he called it "a piece of sublime mysticism and nonsense." But the Holy Alliance also reflected Metternich's influence. Prussia, Russia, and Austria promised mutual assistance whenever religion, peace, or justice was threatened. In the moral claims of the Holy Alliance lay justification for the repression by the allies of any liberal and national movements in Europe.

Britain's aloof, cold, and painfully shy Castlereagh, whose single passion was sheep-herding, went to Vienna in the hope of establishing Britain as the arbiter of European affairs. Britain had emerged from the long conflict as Europe's greatest power, with an empire that included one of every five people in the world. Instead of territorial aggrandizement on the continent, the British government sought the elimination of the French threat to its commercial interests as well as security. Castlereagh worked for a declaration to ensure freedom of the seas. Moreover,

Castlereagh and Metternich both viewed the prospect of Russian expansion in Central Europe with anxiety. With France occupied by allied troops and once again ruled by a legitimate sovereign, only Russia seemed in a position to disrupt Europe through unilateral acts, despite the tsar's insistence that he would adhere to an elevated moral position.

The Congress System

The Congress of Vienna drew a map of Europe that lasted for several generations (see Map 14.1). Under Metternich's stern leadership, what became known as the Congress system restored the principle of dynastic legitimacy and the balance of international power in Europe. The balance of power would ensure that no one power would come to dominate the rest, and that when a state gave up territory it would receive other land in compensation. Territory was apportioned to create buffers to France, as well as to prevent Russia from wielding too much power.

For neither the first nor the last time in European history, the future of Poland, which had lost its independence when it was last partitioned by Russia, Prussia, and Austria in 1795, stood at the top of the list of contentious issues. Tsar Alexander I's troops occupied much of Poland, and he wanted to annex all of it to the Russian Empire. Great Britain, France, and Austria, fearing increased Russian and Prussian influence in Central Europe, formed an alliance (proposed by Talleyrand, who was trying to improve France's position in the negotiations) to head off any attack in Central Europe by Russia or Prussia. This forced Alexander and his Prussian supporters to moderate their demands. In May, the Kingdom of Poland was proclaimed. It was to include lands Austria and Prussia had seized during the earlier partitions. But "Congress Poland," as it came to be known, was nothing more than a Russian protectorate, with the tsar himself occupying the Polish throne. Russia also held on to Finland, which it had conquered during the Napoleonic Wars.

To balance Russian gains in the east, Prussia received the northern half of Saxony, which had cast its fate with Napoleon, as well as Posen and the port city of Danzig (Gdansk). The Austrians kept much of Galicia. In the end, both Prussia and Austria gained enough territory to offset Russia's acquisition of most of Poland, although Austrian control of Galicia, Venetia, and part of Dalmatia added to the Habsburg monarchy more non-German-speaking populations, a source of further disharmony.

In comparison with the debates over Poland and Saxony, the resolution of remaining territorial issues seemed easy. Prussia received territories on the left bank of the Rhine in order to discourage French aggression to the east. This left the Prussian Rhineland separated from the eastern Prussian provinces by the states of Hanover and Hesse-Kassel. Prussia also received Swedish Pomerania and parts of Westphalia, but lost its outlet to the North Sea with the return of East Friesland to Hanover. Other buffers

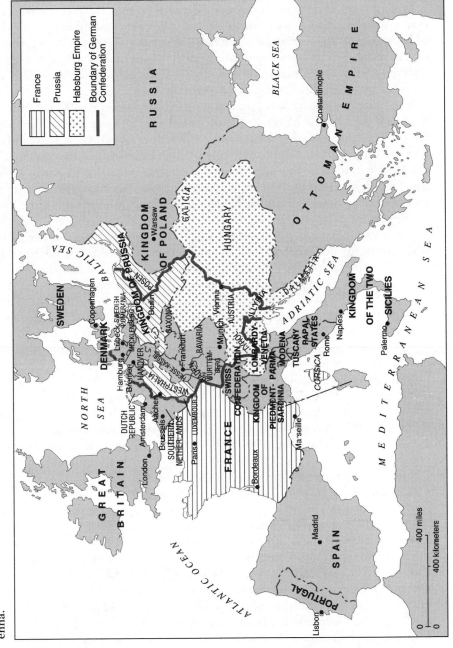

MAP 14.1 EUROPE AFTER THE CONGRESS OF VIENNA, 1815   Changes in boundaries of states after the Congress of Vienna.

against France along its eastern border included Switzerland, reestablished as a neutral confederation of cantons, and the Kingdom of Piedmont-Sardinia (which was enlarged to include Genoa, Nice, and part of Savoy).

Most territorial settlements were made without the slightest consideration of local public opinion. Although the allies emphasized the principle of legitimacy in the territorial settlement, they never hesitated to dispense with a number of smaller legitimate princes whose claims would have interfered with the creation of buffers against France. Thus the republics of Genoa and Venice disappeared from the map.

The Congress placated Britain by awarding the former Austrian Netherlands to the Dutch, leaving a state friendly to Britain as a buffer on France's northern border. The former stadholder of the Dutch Republic became King William I. But Castlereagh's plan to link the Dutch throne to the British monarchy by engineering the marriage of a British princess to the Dutch royal family failed, at least partially because the intended groom became royally drunk in the presence of the intended but most unwilling bride.

Austria was well compensated for the loss of the Austrian Netherlands with Lombardy and Venetia in Italy and Illyria on the coast of Dalmatia. The grand duchies of Parma, Modena, and Tuscany, too, had close family links to Vienna. The Congress also restored the Bourbon dynasty to the throne of the Kingdom of the Two Sicilies (Naples and Sicily). There, Ferdinand I introduced a constitution, but signed an alliance with Austria and promised not to introduce any reforms without the latter's permission. Austrian garrisons and secret police in each Italian state reporting to Metternich helped assure Austrian domination of northern Italy.

Napoleon's remarkable escape from Elba in March 1815 and the dramatic episode of the 100 Days did not change the most important aspects of the Congress's shuffling of European territories. The second Treaty of Paris, signed in November 1815, however, pushed France back from its 1792 borders to those of 1790. Furthermore, the allies now exacted an enormous indemnity of 700 million francs from France. Their armies would occupy France until the debt was settled.

Napoleon's victories in Central Europe had led to the end of the Holy Roman Empire in 1806. On June 9, 1815, the Congress created a German Confederation of thirty-five states loosely joined by a Federal Diet (*Bundestag*) that would meet in Frankfurt. In addition to Prussia and Austria, the Confederation also comprised the so-called middle states of Bavaria, Hanover, Württemberg, the two Hesses, and Baden, each with long traditions of independence, and the independent or "free" cities of Hamburg, Frankfurt, Bremen, and Lübeck. The Confederation did not, however, include the non-German lands of the Austrian Empire. Members of the Confederation pledged to assist each other if any of them were attacked or in any way threatened. But it was unlikely that unanimity could ever be achieved among the member states, or that any state could be compelled to obey a decision made by the Confederation, despite disproportionate Austrian and Prussian preeminence. The Diet merely afforded Metternich a means of bullying the smaller states.

The newly created German Confederation was anything but an affirmation of a move toward German national unification. The German states, large and small, were proud of their traditions of autonomy. By virtue of its Rhineland acquisitions, Prussia emerged as a rival for Austria's leadership of the Confederation and for dominance in Central Europe.

The Concert of Europe

To preserve the settlements enacted at Vienna, the five major European powers, including defeated France, formed a "Concert of Europe." In this extension of the Congress of Vienna, representatives of the powers would meet annually. If necessary, they would join together to put down movements that could threaten the status quo. Metternich's Austria had the most to fear from national claims for independent states. Austria was both a state in the German Confederation and the most important province within its empire of many nationalities. It stretched from the stately elegance of Vienna through the plains of Hungary, to isolated, backward Romanian and Croatian villages. German was the language of the imperial bureaucracy, and of many of the towns, but one could find fifteen major languages within the borders of the empire. The Habsburg monarchy depended on the support of the nobles of the favored nationalities—principally Austrian, Hungarian, and Croat—and the German-speaking middle classes. Metternich exploited the fear that the upper classes of the favored nationalities felt toward any awakening from the lower classes. This kept most Magyar nobles loyal to the Habsburg dynasty, although some desired ultimate independence and resented Metternich's attempt to modernize Hungarian laws and administration.

Tensions remained between the allies. Prussia and particularly Austria still feared that Russia was seeking to expand its influence in the Balkans, especially among peoples of the Orthodox faith. Metternich therefore was willing to use Austrian armies to maintain the status quo, but he sought to avoid any joint Congress military action that might bring Russian armies into Central or Southern Europe. He thus wanted to keep alive the Austrian alliance with Britain against any future French, Prussian, or Russian aggression.

Castlereagh, on the other hand, was somewhat less concerned by Russia's expanded interests in Central Europe. The British prime minister saw the purpose of the Quadruple Alliance as, above all, to contain France. But, unlike Metternich, he had reservations about the appropriateness of the Quadruple Alliance's intervention in the internal affairs of European states. The British participated in the annual gatherings of representatives of the Concert powers, but gradually withdrew from the Congress system.

At Aachen (Aix-la-Chapelle) in 1818, the allies agreed to withdraw their remaining troops from France which, having paid off the indemnity, now joined the Holy Alliance.

RESTORATION EUROPE

The diplomats and monarchs of the Congress of Vienna had worked to restore the state system of Europe. As such, Europe during this period is known as "Restoration Europe." Monarchs and nobles were guided by principles of monarchical legitimacy, with the right to the thrones of Europe determined by hereditary succession, and by close ties to the prerogatives of the established churches. They sought to defend themselves against liberals and nationalists, who espoused organizing states along ethnic or national lines and who demanded reforms in the name of popular sovereignty (with power coming from the popular will rather than from monarchical legitimacy). Conservative principles guided the actions of hereditary monarchs as they sought to put down liberal and nationalist movements that threatened to disrupt their own states as well as the Concert of Europe.

Conservative Ideology

Following the final defeat of Napoleon and the monarchical restoration in France in 1815, conservatives sought to craft a viable political program for the post-revolutionary world that would preserve the monarchies and nobles of Europe against liberal and national movements. The conservative ideology of Restoration Europe drew on several sources. A theory of organic change held Christian monarchies to be, as the French writer Louis de Bonald put it, "the final creation in the development of political society and of religious society. The proof of this lies in the fact that when monarchy and Christianity are both attacked, society returns to savagery." Conservatives insisted that states emerged through gradual growth and that monarchical legitimacy stemmed from royal birthright, confirmed by the sanction of religion. Traditional monarchical institutions of government alone could maintain order. Liberal, republican, and nationalist ideologies suggested that sovereignty lay with the people, and not with a dynastic ruler. Europe's conservative monarchies depended on the support of nobles, and they therefore sought to re-establish the privileges the Revolution and the Napoleonic era had swept away. Conservatives admired the British writer Edmund Burke, who during the French Revolution had argued that monarchical stability and noble privilege were inseparable, the natural pillars of order, along with religion, on which society must stand.

De Bonald and his fellow French writer, Joseph de Maistre (c. 1754–1821), another émigré during the Revolution, espoused the alliance of throne and altar. Both rejected the concept of "natural rights" associated with Enlightenment thought. Holding that all sovereignty stemmed from God, de Maistre believed that the Church stood as the foundation of social order. The king's power could never be limited by his subjects, because that power came only from God. De Maistre blamed the Revolution on the philosophes, particularly Voltaire, who had shaken the faith that underlay the absolutism of hereditary monarchy. Monarchies, he believed, had to reimpose unquestioned obedience through fear. He wrote that "the first servant of the crown should be the executioner."

Romanticism first contributed to the conservative revival. After initially being intrigued by the French Revolution's apparent victory over the strictures of the Old Regime, the early romantic writers had become disillusioned by its violent turn. The English poet Samuel Taylor Coleridge (1772–1834) had been among the first to sing the praises of the Revolution, but he turned against it when French armies began pouring across the frontiers more as conquerors than as liberators.

Many of the early romantic writers were individuals of religious faith who rejected Enlightenment rationalism. "I wept and I believed," wrote the French writer François-René de Chateaubriand (1768–1848), relating his reconversion to Catholicism after the turmoil of the revolutionary and Napoleonic eras. His *The Genius of Christianity* (1802) became one of the most influential works of the period in Europe.

Disillusionment with the French Revolution helped German romantic writers discover in their own nationalism a means of individual fulfillment. Nationalism, too, marked a reaction against Enlightenment tradition. Johann Gottfried von Herder (1744–1803), the son of a Prussian schoolteacher, was one of the impassioned leaders of the *Sturm und Drang* (Storm and Stress) movement, a rebellion by young German writers against Enlightenment thought. Calling for the study and celebration of German literature and history, Herder argued that it was through the enthusiastic identification with the nation that the individual reached his or her highest stage of development. All Germans would be bound together by an awareness of and identity in a common history, culture, and above all, language as part of a *volk,* or living and evolving "national community." Herder thus helped invent the idea of a national culture, which would become crucial to the development of political ideologies espousing a conservative nationalism in the first half of the nineteenth century. Most German romantics glorified the Middle Ages, when kings and nobles, they believed, had undertaken heroic deeds on behalf of a hierarchically organized community of the faithful. Likewise in Britain, the novels of Sir Walter Scott (1771–1832) romanticized the honor, chivalry, and glory in the hierarchical society of medieval Scotland.

Most conservatives saw no difference between reform and revolution, believing that the former would inevitably lead to revolution and radical change. They stood adamantly opposed to political claims based upon any notion of individual freedom, popular sovereignty, or membership in any particular national group. Liberalism seemed to them to be a political philosophy that set no limits on change, and therefore might open a floodgate of demands and concessions to popular sovereignty. Yet, conservatives confronted the problem that their support was limited to a very narrow social and political base in a Europe that was slowly being transformed by the manufacturing revolution.

Restoration of Monarchs, Nobles, and Clergy

Louis XVIII symbolized the return of monarchical legitimacy to France. In the Kingdom of Piedmont-Sardinia, the members of the ruling House of Savoy returned to power wearing powdered wigs, in the style of the eighteenth century. The religious orders also returned in force. In Lombardy-Venetia, consultative assemblies were established in Milan and Venice, but they did little more than assess taxes. With the exception of Baden, in the German states such bodies provided little more than a form of consultation, routinely approving legislation without limiting the power of the sovereign. The governments of the German states that had been occupied by France during the Napoleonic period completely purged the remnants of Napoleonic administration, annulled French-inspired legislation, and imposed strict censorship.

When the French left the Papal States, Pope Pius VII immediately tried to exorcise all traces of the influence of his French captors. Administrative reforms undertaken during the occupation ended; so did street lighting and even vaccinations, identified with the godless French. The clergy reclaimed most public offices. The degree to which French influence in Italy

Louis XVIII, king of the French. Note the perhaps unconscious Napoleonic pose.

was erased may be seen in Tuscany, where the duke ordered the colors of Giotto's portrait of Dante altered, fearing that observers would see in them the French tricolor!

The French Revolution had by no means eliminated noble influence in the states of Europe. Even in Britain, where the lines between landed and business wealth were more blurred than anywhere else, nobles still dominated the House of Commons even after the parliamentary Reform Act of 1832 gave more businessmen the vote. Country gentlemen maintained disproportionate political power, still holding one-sixth of the seats in Commons in 1860. In France, noble émigrés returning from exile enjoyed what has been called "the Indian summer of the aristocracy," as the Bourbon monarchy tried to restore nobles to political primacy. Not all nobles were reactionary, but most were, and an electoral system based on landed wealth gave them a disproportionate advantage. In Spain, nobles were particularly numerous, although many of them were relatively poor. In the Italian states, nobles still held sway in declining or stagnant walled towns like Palermo, Naples, and Rome, as they did in the countryside, until at least 1850. Even in industrializing Milan in Lombardy and Turin in Piedmont, nobles dominated the civic administration.

The farther east one went, the more nobles dominated economic, social, and political life, particularly in states that had been or still were absolute monarchies. Prussian nobles (Junkers) owned 40 percent of the land and maintained their social and political connections to the court. To the Junkers of Brandenberg and Pomerania, entrepreneurs were crass parvenus, outsiders, despite the fortunes they had accumulated, irritating bourgeois who demanded a strong political voice. In Austria, too, 70 percent of those in the top official posts had titles in 1829, and twenty years later the percentage had grown even more. Austrian Chancellor Klemens von Metternich warned his ideological compatriot the Russian Tsar Alexander I about the "intermediate class"—that is, the middle class—which prospered by adopting "all sorts of disguises, uniting and subdividing as occasion offers, helping each other in the hours of danger, and the next day depriving each other of their conquests."

The social composition of the military officer corps remained a telling indicator of the degree to which nobles dominated each state. In Prussia, Junkers retained their stranglehold over the officer corps. The army defiantly brushed aside possible competition from the Landwehr, the civilian reserve force commanded by merchants, teachers, and bureaucrats. In Russia, the officer corps still was a noble stronghold, reinforced by the aristocracy's near monopoly on appointments to military academies and to important posts in the civil service. Nobles also commanded the armies of the Italian states. And in Spain, at least until 1836, young men aspiring to an officer's commission in the army had to provide proof of nobility.

During the revolutionary era, the established churches, particularly the Catholic Church, had suffered at the hands of revolutionaries, who believed that religious authority undermined secular authority. Conservatives (both Catholic and Protestant) insisted that the established churches provided a moral authority that complemented secular authority. Thus, in the German states, Pietism and other revivalist Protestant movements broke with Protestant orthodoxy to teach that mankind was essentially sinful and that it was necessary to maintain strong state sanctions. In Russia, the mystical Tsar Alexander I believed fervently that the Orthodox Church had an important role in keeping his people subservient.

In this atmosphere, Europe witnessed a marked revival in enthusiasm for organized religion. The old religious confraternities returned to France. Pious families of wealth contributed money to rebuild churches, monasteries, and convents destroyed or damaged during the French Revolution. In Britain, the Established (Anglican) Church helped shape the conservative view of the world. Although they rejected the notion of divine-right or absolutist monarchy, most British Conservatives believed the existing social order to be God-given and immutable, represented by the Anglican Church, and strongly opposed Dissenters and, above all, Catholics. In 1818, Parliament passed the Church Building Act, which provided government funding for the construction of more than 200 new churches. Likewise, a largely Lutheran revival of religious enthusiasm occurred in the northern German states.

STIRRINGS OF REVOLT

The allies' commitment to work together to put down liberal and national movements was matched by the determination of each to prevent any stirrings within their own states. The Congress of Vienna resembled the Dutch boy gamely trying to dam the deluge by plugging up the holes in the dike with his fingers. During the first half of the century, virtually every country in Europe experienced a confrontation between the old political order reestablished by the Congress of Vienna and nascent liberalism.

Liberal Movements

Liberals desired change in the old order. They drew on the ideals of the Enlightenment and the French Revolution, especially the right to "liberty" and freedom from the arbitrary exercise of government. Thus, the liberal movements attracted those excluded from participation in political life by their lack of wealth and noble status, or by the absence of representative political institutions. Liberals demanded an expansion of the electoral franchise, freedom of the press, dis-establishment of state churches (that is, the loss of state patronage for the "official" religion), guarantees of religious toleration, and constitutional government. Liberals portrayed themselves as citizens of their century, battling the forces of reaction. "We are the times," boasted one German liberal. Liberalism was perfectly suited to the interests of the expanding economic power of the middle class (see Chapter 15).

Liberal inroads were especially made in Western Europe, where social structures differed significantly from those of the autocracies of Central and Eastern Europe. Britain was a constitutional monarchy in which Parliament included wealthy commoners. It was testimony to the influence of the Napoleonic era that the restored monarchy in France under Louis XVIII granted a Charter to the French people promising essential liberties. Moreover, the French monarchy, as well as those of Piedmont-Sardinia and even the rulers of Metternich's Austria, utilized the bureaucratized state apparatus inherited from Napoleon to repress liberals, instead of restoring the less-centralized ruling structure that had typified Old Regime Europe.

In France and many of the German states, liberal bourgeois formed political organizations that demanded political rights for a wider number of people. Newspapers and political pamphlets deftly sidestepped the heavy hand of censorship to challenge the restored prerogatives of conservative princes and the established churches. In Britain, middle-class spokesmen confronted conservatives and what its enemies referred to as "Old Corruption," a political system based upon the patronage and influence of wealthy landowners. In France, many bourgeois, some enriched by the purchase of Church or noble property during the Revolution, wanted the right to vote. In the German states, the Swiss cantons, and in reactionary Spain, the middle classes clamored for constitutions.

In the German and Italian states and Belgium, liberalism was closely associated with fledgling nationalist movements. Groups of nationalists, including intellectuals, students, and lawyers, called for the creation of independent states based upon nationality. Nationalist demands were anathema to the powers represented at the Congress of Vienna, particularly the leaders of the Russian and Austrian Empires, whose subjects included many different peoples. The creation of new national states would threaten the existence of these empires and also might challenge the hierarchy of social privilege.

Liberal Revolts in Spain, Portugal, and Italy

The first test for the Congress system came in Spain. Upon his return to Madrid in 1814, Ferdinand VII (ruled 1808–1833) declared that he did not recognize the liberal constitution that had been drawn up by the Assembly (Cortes) in 1812. This stillborn document nonetheless became the basis of Spanish liberalism in the nineteenth century and for a time served as a model of a liberal constitution. It provided for a "moderate monarchy" with ministers responsible to the Cortes for the constitutionality of their acts and defined sovereignty as residing "essentially in the [Spanish] Nation," the union of all Spaniards in both hemispheres. It guaranteed the right of property, freedom of the press, and freedom from arbitrary arrest.

King Ferdinand VII may not have been quite the intransigent fanatic that some contemporaries insisted, but he disliked liberals. He repressed Masonic lodges, imposed strict censorship, and welcomed back the Jesuit religious order. Furthermore, he refused to convoke the Cortes, as he had promised upon his return. Ecclesiastics and nobles reclaimed land they had lost during the Napoleonic period. Moreover, the Inquisition, the Catholic Church's institutionalized apparatus to maintain religious orthodoxy, returned to Spain, as the police again began to arrest alleged heretics.

The Spanish monarchy remained inextricably allied with noble and ecclesiastical privilege. The clergy accounted for about 30 percent of adult Spanish males, many living in the monasteries that dotted the countryside. The aristocracy and the Church owned two-thirds of the land, much of it as unproductive as its owners, who collected dues from those tilling the soil. Yet, the vast majority of peasants supported the established order, believing the word of the village priest to be that of God. The small number of nobles and bourgeois who read the country's few newspapers—the majority of the population remaining illiterate—found little except, as one traveler put it, "accounts of miracles wrought by different Virgins, lives of holy friars and sainted nuns, romances of marvelous conversions, libels against Jews, heretics and Freemasons, and histories of apparitions."

The allies were delighted to have a "legitimate" sovereign back on France's southern flank, although Spain had long since ceased to be a European power. Now its empire began to disintegrate. Rebellions against Spanish rule broke out in the Latin American colonies, beginning in Argentina in 1816. Military expeditions, which failed to reconquer the colonies, exacerbated Spain's economic crisis. Simón Bolívar (1783–1830), a fiery Creole aristocrat educated in European Enlightenment ideals who had vowed never to rest until he had freed Latin America from tyrants, skillfully led an army that liberated his native Venezuela in 1821 and defeated Spanish troops in Peru in 1824. Mexico had declared its independence two years earlier. Of the overseas empire that had stretched from North America to the tip of South America in the sixteenth century, Spain retained only the Caribbean islands of Cuba and Puerto Rico, as well as the Philippines in Asia.

Against this background, a revolt broke out in Spain in 1820. Army officers who led the insurrection against Ferdinand were soon joined by merchants and lawyers. The intimidated king agreed to convoke the Cortes and abide by the liberal constitution of 1812. Tsar Alexander of Russia, supported by Prussia, demanded armed allied intervention; so did Louis XVIII, eager to prove himself a reliable ally of reaction. Habsburg Austria adopted a wait-and-see attitude. Great Britain, however, remained

Latin American liberator Simón Bolívar (standing in the center), meeting with his generals.

adamantly opposed to any intervention in Spanish internal affairs, first as a matter of principle, and secondly because of fear that the presence of foreign troops in Spain might jeopardize British commerce or increase French influence there.

Meanwhile, the fires of liberalism broke out in nearby Portugal. Liberal army officers took advantage of the continued absence of King John VI, who had fled to Brazil during the Napoleonic Wars, to rise up against the British-backed regent in August 1820. A provisional National Assembly called for John to return as a constitutional monarch, which he did in 1822.

That same year, army officers and merchants in Naples and Sicily led an uprising against the rule of King Ferdinand I, another monarch who had been restored to his shaky throne by the allies. Some of the revolutionaries were members of a secret society, organized along military lines, known as the "Carbonari." These "charcoal-burners" took their name from their practice of swearing each new member to secrecy by tracing a charcoal mark on his forehead. The Carbonari, originally formed to fight Napoleon's armies, now directed their fervor against the monarch placed on the throne by the Austrians. Another revolt, smaller but also liberal and more consciously nationalistic, broke out in the Kingdom of Piedmont-Sardinia.

Metternich sought to persuade the other Congress powers that intervention was necessary. The Russian, Prussian, and Austrian governments signed an agreement at the Congress of Troppau in Galicia in October 1820. Based on the "principles of the [Holy] Alliance," it proclaimed the right of the signatories to intervene militarily in any country in which political changes were brought about by revolution. Following Castlereagh's suicide in 1822, Britain further distanced itself from the Congress system. Austrian troops quickly put down the uprisings in Naples and Piedmont-Sardinia.

In 1822, the remaining Congress powers reconvened in Verona. Britain's withdrawal cleared the way for military action in Spain, where King Ferdinand VII had been deposed. With the support of Russia, Prussia, and Austria, a French army of 200,000 men took to the field for the first time since Waterloo, but in very different circumstances. It crossed the Pyrenees in 1823 and took Madrid, thereby bolstering the king's campaign against those seeking to limit royal authority. Restored to his throne, the grateful Ferdinand renounced the Constitution of 1812 and ordered the torture and execution of his opponents.

In December 1823, U.S. President James Monroe, fearing that the Concert powers might try to help Spain restore its authority over its former Latin American colonies, issued a proclamation that became one of the bases of subsequent American foreign policy. The Monroe Doctrine stated that "the American continents . . . are henceforth not to be considered as subjects for future colonization by any European powers." Stressing that the political systems of the latter were different from its own, it warned that the United States would "consider any attempt on their part to extend their system to any portion of this hemisphere as dangerous to our peace and safety."

Liberal Stirrings in Germany

In the German states, as in the Italian states, liberals and nationalists were often the same people. Members of student fraternities (the *Burschenschaften*), who had grown up amid the nationalist response to the Napoleonic invasions, sought a united Germany. The members of one fraternity wore gray shirts, carried nationalist flags of black and red stripes with a gold oak branch, and ran around chanting "honor, liberty, and fatherland." Within several years, many of the southern German universities had fraternities, whose members were as much known for their dueling scars as for liberalism. In 1817, a large convocation of student associations celebrated the three hundredth anniversary of Martin Luther's revolt against the papacy. The festivities culminated with the public burning of books, ostensibly to commemorate Luther's burning of the papal bull of excommunication.

The lines between conservatism and liberalism seemed clearly drawn in the German states. Political philosopher Karl von Clausewitz (1780–1831) denounced these commemorations in his pamphlet "On Agitation."

Nationalist German students in 1817 burning books and other objects deemed anti-patriotic.

Clausewitz, who viewed foreign policy as the state's preeminent concern and defined warfare as "an extension of state policy by other means," limited his support for reform within Prussia and the other German states to his desire to have trained civil servants and military officers replace nobles who had been appointed to state positions only because of their titles.

In March 1819, a German student murdered an arch-conservative historian and dramatist commonly believed to be in the pay of the tsar. Metternich persuaded the Austrian Emperor Francis I and Frederick William III of Prussia to impose a series of repressive measures, the Carlsbad Decrees, which the Diet of the German Confederation unanimously accepted. These muzzled the press and dissolved the student fraternities. One decree specified that university instructors should be watched to keep them from "spreading harmful ideas which could subvert public peace and order and undermine the foundations of existing states." Teachers fired in one state were to be blacklisted in other member states. Metternich used the murder to convince Frederick William to renounce any form of "universal representation" in his kingdom. The episode enabled Metternich to clinch his victory over constitutionalism in the German states.

The Greek Revolt

If the Spanish revolt exposed divisions in the Congress system, the Greek revolt against the Ottoman Turks, which followed in 1821, shattered the alliance. Austria and, above all, Russia hoped to extend their influence in the Balkans at the expense of the Ottoman Empire. Russia coveted Constantinople, gateway to Asia and the Black Sea. Britain vehemently opposed Russian acquisition of the Ottoman capital, fearing a potential threat to British control of India and influence in Afghanistan. Austria, threatened by Russian interest in the Balkans, also feared Russian designs on Constantinople. The Greek revolt put the Congress powers in a bind. Much of Christian Europe considered the Turks savage infidels. But at the same time, the Congress powers had to recognize the Ottoman Empire as the historically "legitimate" sovereign of the Greeks, who benefited from certain commercial privileges awarded them by the Turks. Great Power support for the Greeks, then, would represent a renunciation of the status quo, a principle upon which the Congress system had been based.

Building upon a small Greek nationalist movement that had developed at the end of the eighteenth century, Prince Alexander Ypsilantis (1792–1828), a former general in the Russian army and the son of a Greek provincial administrator, founded a secret nationalist organization in 1814, the "Society of Friends." He recruited members among Greeks living abroad, and counted on the tsar's support for a Greek uprising against Turkey, Russia's old enemy. In 1821, he organized a revolt in Turkish Moldavia, hoping that the Romanians would also rebel against Ottoman domination. The Turks were able to crush the initial Greek uprising, since the Romanians did not rebel and the tsar disavowed the rebels. Several weeks later, however, further revolts against the Turks broke out in mainland Greece and on several Aegean islands. The Congress powers, including Russia, immediately condemned the insurrection. Nicholas I, the new Russian tsar, was happy to support a cause that could be used against Turkish interests.

The Greek revolt caught the imagination of writers in Western Europe. Romantic writers now used their literary gifts to challenge the monarchs of Restoration Europe through espousal of national self-consciousness. Members of the Philhellenic movement (scholars and intellectuals who had become passionately interested in classical Greece) now embraced the Greek revolt as a modern crusade for Christianity and independence against what they considered Turkish oppression of the birthplace of Western civilization. The English poets Byron and Percy Bysshe Shelley (1792–1822) took up the cause of Greek independence. Shelley, who called the poet the "unacknowledged legislator of the world," also supported the quest for Irish independence from Britain. He died in a shipwreck off the coast of Italy in 1822. Byron died of fever in Greece two years later.

Eugène Delacroix's *Massacre at Chios*, 1824.

Turkish brutality appalled Western conservatives and liberals alike. In 1822, the Turks massacred the entire Greek population of the island of Chios, after having executed the patriarch of Constantinople in his ecclesiastical robes on Easter Sunday 1821. The French romantic painter Eugène Delacroix (1798–1863) celebrated the Greeks' struggle for national sovereignty in his painting the *Massacre at Chios* (1824). As Greeks continued to hold out against the Turks, the British government also had come to the view that peace could best be maintained by the creation of an autonomous Greek state. In 1827, Britain, France, and Russia signed the Treaty of London, threatening the Turks with military intervention if they did not accept an armistice. When the Turks refused, a combined naval force destroyed the Turkish fleet at Navarino.

Russia, eager to capitalize on the dwindling fortunes of the Turks, declared war on the Ottoman Empire in 1828 and quickly occupied the Balkan territories of Moldavia and Eastern Wallachia. However, long sieges against a Turkish fortress on the Danube and another on the Black Sea coast, and the self-interested disapproval by Britain and France of Russian plans for dismembering the Ottoman Empire, forced Russia to agree to the Treaty of Adrianople (1829). Moldavia and Wallachia became protectorates of Russia, further pushing back Turkey's European territories and expanding Russian influence in the Balkans. In 1832, the Greeks finally won their independence from the Turks, and a Bavarian prince was chosen to be king of Greece (Otto I; ruled 1833–1862).

After the Battle of Navarino in 1827, the allies had actually apologized to the Turkish sultan for sinking his fleet. In doing so, they acknowledged a paradox: the allies of the Concert of Europe had intervened militarily on behalf of a nationalist movement against an established power. The Greek revolt had shattered the Congress system. Like Delacroix's painting, the allied intervention had sanctioned a nationalist insurrection as a noble act.

The Decembrist Revolt in Russia

The sprawling Russian Empire had remained practically immune to change for centuries, despite the flirtations of Peter the Great and Catherine the Great with Western ideas and culture in the seventeenth and eighteenth centuries. At his succession to the throne after the assassination of his autocratic father in 1801, Tsar Alexander I was liberal and idealistic. He initially relaxed the restrictive measures of his father, surrounded himself with advisers who advocated reform, and sought to enact reforming measures. Ruling for the first quarter of the century, Alexander's attempts at reform were concentrated in the first half of his reign.

An enormous social, economic, and legal gulf separated the Russian aristocracy from the millions of destitute serfs bound to the lands of their lords. Most Russian nobles feared that any reform would threaten their prerogatives. Prussia had freed its serfs in the name of military efficiency, but when Alexander gave permission to the nobles to free their own serfs early in his reign in 1803, few chose to do so. Serfdom remained entrenched in the Russian soil.

During the Napoleonic Wars, steps were taken to make the regime more efficient, including proposals for the creation of a council of state and the organization of local governments. Thus, in the first years of the nineteenth century, the Russian state developed a more efficient bureaucracy, with centralized ministries directly responsible to the tsar. The reach of government in the provinces was also strengthened.

After 1815, Alexander became increasingly reactionary. Conservative elements regained power and introduced coercive measures. Universities and schools were closely monitored to root out liberals, and study abroad was now banned. The government established military colonies in which peasant-soldiers were forced to cultivate crops under the command of noble officers. There was heavy and arbitrary censorship of newspapers and books. The police, if anything, became more ruthlessly efficient.

But liberal reform had its supporters in Russia among young nobles who had been educated in Western Europe (before foreign study was prohibited) and influenced by the principles of the Enlightenment, and among some army officers who had lived in France during the allied military oc-

Tsar Nicholas I.

cupation after the fall of Napoleon. By 1820, two loosely linked conspiratorial "unions," as they were called, existed. The educated nobles of the northern section hoped that Russia might evolve toward British constitutionalism. The military officers of the southern section had a more radical goal: to kill the tsar and establish a republic.

Tsar Alexander's sudden death in December 1825 seemed to give the secret society its chance. The tsar had two brothers. Constantine, the eldest, had quietly yielded his succession to the throne in favor of his younger and more reactionary brother Nicholas. The secret society of the Northern Union nonetheless convinced the St. Petersburg garrison to support the succession of the more liberal Constantine. Troops occupied a central square in the capital, shouting the name of their favorite, until Nicholas ordered troops loyal to him to fire. A hastily planned insurrection by the Southern Union was also put down, and the leaders of the Decembrists, as they were subsequently called, were executed.

Nicholas I tightened the grip of the police on education in an attempt to exclude Western ideas from Russia. As a result, the next generation of army officers strongly supported the tsar. Nonetheless, the very repressive nature of Nicholas' reign and, despite censorship, the arrival of liberal ideas from the West encouraged debate and calls for reform from the Russian intelligensia. These trends also encouraged the emergence of a group of reform-minded men within the imperial bureaucracy. Both groups helped expand the perimeters of public opinion within the Russian Empire.

THE BOURBON RESTORATION IN FRANCE AND THE REVOLUTION OF 1830

In a contemporary French lampoon of the return of the Bourbons to the throne, a majestic eagle—the symbol of Napoleon—sweeps out of the Tuileries Palace in Paris as a somewhat plump, unsightly duck waddles in, followed by its ungainly brood. The contrast between the image of Napoleon's bold achievements and the stodgy and pious Restoration was sharp indeed. Former soldiers regaled their families and neighbors with stories of their exploits, real or imagined, during the Napoleonic Wars, showing off bullets from the battles of Austerlitz or Jena. The Bourbons, on the other hand, returned "in the baggage of the allies," as it was said.

Upon the return of the Bourbons to power in May 1814, Louis XVIII promulgated a charter that, in effect, made France a constitutional monarchy. Realizing that he could not ignore liberal opinion, Louis' Charter of 1814 recognized equality before the law and accepted the Napoleonic Civil Code. It established an Assembly consisting of a Chamber of Deputies and a Chamber of Peers. Under the Charter, the king would name members (whose appointment would be for life and hereditary) of the Chamber of Peers, as well as ministers, who would be responsible only to him. Deputies would be elected in a complicated two-stage process. The electoral franchise, however, was extremely narrow, limited to France's 50,000 wealthiest men. Only about a third of that number were eligible to stand for election in a nation of more than 30 million people.

Honoré Daumier's caricature of the less-than-inspiring members of the Chamber of Deputies.

The Charter also guaranteed freedom of the press. It stipulated that the government could levy no taxes without the consent of the Assembly. It reaffirmed the Napoleonic Code's guarantee of the free practice of religion to France's Protestants and Jews. The Catholic Church would still be subject to Napoleon's Concordat with the Church (see Chapter 13). But in other ways, the Church returned to its privileged position, Catholicism again becoming the official state religion. Religious orders, which had left their convents and monasteries during the revolutionary turmoil, now returned to France in force. The observance of Sunday and Church holidays became obligatory. The Church sent a preaching order into most provincial towns to give "missions," several days of intense ceremonies and sermons intended to return the local population to traditional religious values.

The Ultra-Royalists

Many of the noble émigrés and clergymen who returned from foreign exile were eager to exact revenge on those who had served the Revolution and Napoleon (whom they considered "the usurper"), dishonored their religion, and even purchased their land in their absence. During the first several years of the restored Bourbon monarchy, political stability was threatened by Ultra-royalists, or "Ultras," the most fanatical royalist enemies of the Revolution. Following Waterloo, they had launched "the White Terror," so called because of the color of the Bourbon flag, against those who had supported Bonaparte. In Nîmes, Catholics were led by the notorious brigand Trestaillons ("three pieces") who, it was said, cut his victims into that many parts, and his friendly rival, Quatre-Taillons (one more slice). They killed Protestants as Protestants had murdered Catholics in 1793.

In the election for the Chamber of Deputies in August 1815, the Ultras easily defeated the more moderate royalists sponsored by the government. Some of the Ultras even referred contemptuously to Louis XVIII as "King Voltaire" because of his Charter, which they viewed as a compromise with the Revolution. They demanded that the "national property" that had been confiscated and sold during the Revolution be returned to original owners. But so much land had changed hands that such a move might well have brought civil war, the last thing that the monarchy or the allies wanted.

Confronted by the intransigence of the Ultra-dominated chamber, Louis XVIII dissolved it in 1816; new elections produced a somewhat more moderate chamber. Four years later, however, fate seemed to show that the Ultras had been right after all. In 1820, a madman assassinated Charles, the duke of Berry, the king's nephew, the only member of the Bourbon family capable of producing an heir to the throne. France was plunged into mourning. The Ultras cried for revenge, accusing the liberals of being ultimately responsible for the assassination. The king dismissed

King Charles X of France.

the moderate government, restored more stringent censorship, and altered the electoral system to reduce the influence of wealthy bourgeois voters living in towns.

Soon, however, the church bells stopped their mournful cadence and rang out in joy. Incredibly enough, it turned out that the duke's wife had been pregnant at the time of his death. Royalist France celebrated the birth of a male heir, "the miracle baby," as he came to be called, the duke of Bordeaux (later known as the count of Chambord). Confident that God was with them, the Ultras, at least for the moment, retained the upper hand.

Upon Louis XVIII's death in 1824, his brother, the count of Artois, took the throne as Charles X (ruled 1824–1830). The new king was one of those intransigent Old Regime nobles who "had learned nothing and forgotten nothing" during the long revolutionary and Napoleonic eras. The French monarchy seemed to be defying the new century. Charles' coronation ceremony in the Cathedral at Reims could have come right out of the Middle Ages: the newly anointed monarch attempted to cure cripples with the "healing touch of kings."

Many people believed rumors that the pious king was going to allow the Catholic Church to collect the tithe, that is, require them to pay 10 percent of their income to the Church. The Chamber of Deputies passed a law making sacrilege—any crime committed in or against a church—a capital offense. That no one was ever executed for such an offense did not diminish public outrage. Amid rumors that noble land sold during the Revolution was to be returned to its original owners, the government financed the indemnification of those who had lost land by reducing the interest paid to holders of the national debt, most of whom were from the middle class. All this, as well as the government's control of the press, the Church's control over education, and the dissolution of the National Guard, led to dissatisfaction and unrest among liberal elements of the population.

The Revolution of 1830

Liberal opposition to the Restoration monarchy increased during the late 1820s. Some young men, like Julien Sorel, the antihero of Stendhal's novel *The Red and the Black* (1831), maintained a romantic allegiance to Napoleon's memory. Many merchants and manufacturers believed that the Restoration monarchy paid insufficient attention to commerce and industry, listening only to rural nobles. Former Napoleonic soldiers, particularly those officers pensioned off on half pay, looked back on the imperial era as their halcyon days. In 1820–1821, some had joined the Carbonari, a secret society named after its Italian equivalent, and plotted to overthrow the Restoration.

Pressure on the Bourbon monarchy mounted in 1827, amid an economic crisis that had begun with the failure of the harvest the previous year. Elections that year increased liberal strength in the Chamber of Deputies. But in August 1829, Charles X threw caution to the wind, violating the principle of ministerial responsibility (whereby the king's ministers were subject to the approval of the Assembly) and brought in as his premier the reactionary Prince Jules de Polignac (1780–1847), one of only two members of the Chamber of Deputies who had refused an oath of allegiance to the Charter granted by Louis XVIII.

The opposition to the government of Charles X received a boost from a new generation of romantic writers. Wealthy Parisian bourgeois patronized romantic music, particularly the opera, while nobles and churchmen denounced romanticism. In the remarkable preface to his controversial play *Hernani* (1830), the production of which caused a near riot outside the theater, Victor Hugo (1802–1885) clearly set liberalism and romanticism against the established order of the restored monarchy:

> Young people, have courage! However difficult they make our present, the future will be beautiful. Romanticism, so often badly defined, is, on the whole . . . nothing less than *liberalism* in literature. . . . literary liberalism will be no less popular than political liberalism. Liberty in art, liberty in society . . . that is the banner that rallies to it all but a few (and they will see the light) of today's so strong and so patient youth . . . literary liberty is the daughter of political liberty. That is the principle of this century, and it will prevail.

Liberals were convinced—not without reason—that the king planned to undo the constitutional restraints upon his authority. In 1828, they formed an association to refuse to pay taxes in protest of the government's policies. Members of another association, with the cumbersome name of "Heaven Helps Those Who Help Themselves," worked to register all eligible voters. Benjamin Constant (1767–1830), an influential Swiss novelist and political essayist and a member of the French Chamber of Deputies, provided the political program for the liberal forces, demanding that the electoral franchise be extended. He espoused a philosophy of liberalism based on a separation of powers and "a government of laws and not men." In response to Charles' bellicose speech opening the 1830 session of the Chamber, 221 deputies signed an address to the throne that attacked the government in no uncertain terms. When the king dissolved the Chamber and called for new elections, the liberal opposition won a majority in the new Chamber of Deputies.

In the meantime, Charles had sent an army to conquer Algeria, whose ruler was a vassal of the sultan of Turkey. Since 1827, French warships had been blocking the port of Algiers because of disputes over French trading and fishing rights. The king now hoped that a victory would quiet domestic political discontent. But even with the news of the capture of Algiers on July 9, nothing was going well for Charles X. The king and his minister Polignac then settled on a move that they hoped would bring an end to the crisis. It brought revolution instead.

On July 26, 1830, Charles X promulgated five decrees that amounted to nothing less than a coup d'état. These July Ordinances dissolved the newly elected Chamber of Deputies; disfranchised almost three-quarters of those currently eligible to vote, leaving virtually all political power in the hands of the wealthiest property holders; ordered new elections under the newly restricted franchise; and muzzled the press. This was an abandonment of the principles of the Charter of 1814.

When the public learned of the July Ordinances, unemployed workers, students, artisans, and republicans turned out to demonstrate. Not anticipating this reaction, Charles had not ordered enough troops to Paris to disperse the angry crowds. Demonstrations on July 27 led to skirmishes with troops the following day. When someone climbed one of the towers of Notre Dame Cathedral and unfurled the tricolor flag, symbol of the French Revolution, Parisians rose up in revolt, blocking the capital's narrow streets with barricades. Fired upon in the street and pelted by rocks and tiles thrown from rooftops, the king's soldiers became increasingly demoralized.

On July 31, Charles X named Louis-Philippe to be Lieutenant-General of the Realm. Louis-Philippe, a member of the Orléans family, the junior branch of the Bourbon family, had the reputation for being relatively liberal. He had fought with the revolutionary armies and his father (known as Philippe Égalité) in the National Assembly had voted for the execution of Louis XVI. He had visited the United States, expanding his horizons by drinking Kentucky bourbon.

Honoré Daumier's print showing a wealthy banker as a victor in the Revolution of 1830.

When Charles finally realized he could not save his dynasty, he abdicated in favor of his grandson on August 2. But to the horror of Metternich and the crowned heads of Europe, the liberals rejected the Bourbon dynasty and instead offered the throne to the duke of Orléans, who became Louis-Philippe I (ruled 1830–1848), king of the French. This title, rather than king of France, was intended to convey that the king's power came from the people and a greater sense of accommodation with the constitutional heritage of the French Revolution. Louis-Philippe agreed that the tricolor flag would replace the white flag of the Bourbons, and he agreed to a revised version of the Charter of 1814.

Despite its revolutionary origins, the new regime won relatively quick acceptance from the initially hostile other European powers. The Revolution of 1830 marked a victory for French liberals. The new Orleanist regime almost doubled the number of voters, but France was still far from being a republic. Many of those enfranchised by the revised Charter were drawn from the middle class enriched by commercial and industrial development, although land remained the source of most wealth. In addition to being known as the "July Monarchy," the Orleanist reign also came to be known as "the bourgeois monarchy."

The portly Louis-Philippe himself contributed to this image. He rose early and went to bed quite late, reading all diplomatic dispatches and working closely with his ministers. "There's no distance between Philippe and me," went one popular though extremely exaggerated refrain, "he's

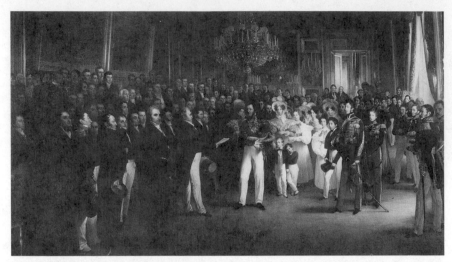

Louis-Philippe receiving black-suited members of the Chamber of Deputies, who present him with the act by which they confer the crown on him.

king-citizen, and I am citizen-king." The first official portrait of the monarch includes not only a throne of modest proportions but a number of dark-suited businessmen being shown in to see the new king.

While the continuing influence of France's nobles should not be underestimated, the Revolution of 1830 marked the end of noble privilege in national politics. Lawyers and men of other professions significantly increased middle-class representation in the legislature. The king catered to the desires of this enlarged bourgeois constituency. The government helped generate economic growth and industrial development by improving roads and implementing other policies that benefited wealthy manufacturers and merchants.

Having achieved political power and doubled the electorate, the Orleanists defiantly slammed the drawbridge shut behind them. Benjamin Constant called Louis-Philippe's constitutional monarchy "our last ark of safety" against revolution. While all citizens were proclaimed equal before the law, only the privileged elite—as defined by wealth, in the tradition of the first French republic and the empire—would have the right to vote. "I strongly support the cause of the new society that the Revolution has made," François Guizot, historian and prime minister, wrote, with "the middle class as its fundamental element." His rallying cry to its supporters was "Enrich yourselves!" The July Monarchy brought another significant change in tune with the close association between liberalism and secularization. Catholicism ceased to be the official religion of the state, although it remained the nominal religion of the vast majority of French men and women. Moreover, a law passed by the Chamber of Deputies in 1833 required each commune to have a school.

The Orleanist regime attracted little enthusiasm except among the

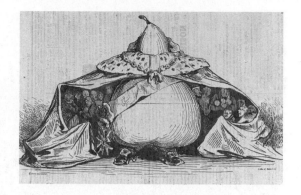

Louis-Philippe's pear-shaped body with his cloak protecting the ministers and deputies deemed responsible for the murders of working-class families in Paris, 1834.

black-coated businessmen and lawyers who tolerated rampant electoral corruption and approved of Louis-Philippe's commitment to social order at all costs. The new monarchy could claim neither the principle of monarchical legitimacy asserted by the Legitimists (supporters of Charles X's Bourbon grandson) or that of popular sovereignty assumed by republicans. The latter, dissatisfied with the limited political change, demanded universal manhood suffrage, claiming to represent the will of the people and the tradition of the Revolution. Legitimists launched several small insurrections in the west against the Orleanists. In Paris, crowds of workers, disappointed by the government's lack of attention to their demands, sacked the archbishop's palace the year after the July Revolution. Silk workers in Lyon rose up in 1831 and 1834. The July Monarchy responded

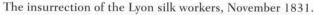

The insurrection of the Lyon silk workers, November 1831.

Napoleon's remains being returned to Paris in 1840.

by sending in government troops and enacting repressive measures. Following the second insurrection by silk workers in Lyon in April 1834 and an uprising by republicans in Paris a month later, the Chamber of Deputies passed a law severely restricting the right to form associations, and the next year it passed another fettering the press. The great caricaturist Honoré Daumier (1808–1879) nonetheless continued indirectly to poke fun at "Robert Macaire," a swindler who represented for the artist and his viewers the corruption of the Orleanist regime.

Besieged by political enemies, Louis-Philippe survived an assassination attempt in 1835; a plot by a secret organization of revolutionaries, the "Society of the Seasons," to overthrow him in 1839; and another attempt to kill him in 1840. Less serious—for the moment—seemed two attempts by Louis Napoleon Bonaparte, Napoleon's nephew, to invade France and rally support. In 1836, he failed to win over the garrison in Strasbourg and was arrested. In 1840, he tried his luck on the other side of the country, landing at Boulogne in a small boat with a few followers, before being arrested and shunted off to jail by a patrol of gendarmes. Put on trial, Louis Napoleon told the peers, "There is no quarrel between you and me." To an extent, he was right. The majority of the peers had grown up during, and some had served, the Napoleonic Empire. Napoleon's legend remained deeply rooted in rural France. The Orleanists themselves tried to cultivate the idea that they were the heirs to the Revolution, facilitating social mobility and expanding the electorate. In 1840, the government brought Napoleon's ashes from Saint Helena to be interred in Paris. Hundreds of thousands of people turned out to pay their tribute to the emperor. The cult of Napoleon, accentuated by the vogue for the literature of romanticism, served only to highlight the shortcomings of the July Monarchy.

LIBERAL ASSAULTS ON THE OLD ORDER

The success of the French Revolution of 1830 directly encouraged liberal and national movements in other countries, further assaults on the Old Order. Metternich pessimistically called the July Revolution "the collapse of the dam in Europe," fearing that it would eventually lead to his nightmare, popular sovereignty. The Revolution of 1830 both reflected and accentuated the rise of liberalism in Europe. Liberal successes followed in Belgium and Switzerland. Moreover, the Belgian revolt of liberals was also a nationalist struggle (in which both French and Dutch speakers participated) against the union with the Dutch Netherlands.

The Revolt in Belgium

The Dutch Netherlands had achieved independence from Spain in the seventeenth century. Catholic Belgium had never been united or autonomous and was divided between Flemish speakers in the north and west and Walloon, or French speakers, in its southern and eastern parts (see

Revolution in Brussels, 1830.

Map 14.2). Brussels, the largest city in Belgium, lies within Flemish Belgium, but much of its population spoke French.

What Belgians called "Dutch arithmetic" left Belgium with fewer seats in the Dutch Estates-General than its population should have warranted and far fewer positions in the bureaucracy. Catholics had to contribute to Protestant state schools and paid higher taxes. In the late 1820s, Belgian liberals allied with Catholics against the Protestant Dutch government. Following petition campaigns demanding that ministers be responsible to the Estates-General and that taxes be reduced, Dutch King William I (1772–1843) granted only more press freedom.

MAP 14.2 THE BIRTH OF BELGIUM, 1831–1839   The boundaries of the Dutch Republic and Belgium, including within Belgium the areas that were Protestant and Catholic, as well as Flemish and Walloon areas. The Grand Duchy of Luxembourg was created in 1831 and united with Holland in the person of the grand duke, who was King William I of the Netherlands.

Following the arrival of news from France of the July Revolution, the Brussels opera presented a production about an insurrection in Naples in 1648 against Spanish rule. Inspired by what they had seen, the audience left the theater to demonstrate against a government newspaper and other symbols of Dutch authority. Workers, suffering unemployment and high prices, put up barricades, and were soon joined by units of bourgeois militia from outside Brussels. The Estates-General called for the separation of Belgium and Holland. But William was determined to crush the rebellion, which had spread to other cities.

The Dutch army could have overwhelmed the hastily organized force of several hundred defending Brussels. But having been reassured by nobles that the elite of Brussels still supported the royal cause and fearing that a full-fledged assault would generate more opposition, a halfhearted attack floundered when young, inexperienced Dutch troops panicked as the ranks of the defenders swelled. After three more days of fighting, the Dutch troops withdrew to the north. The Dutch bombardment of Flemish Antwerp sealed the Dutch defeat, for it led the Flemish of northern Belgium to support the rebels.

In early October, a provisional government declared Belgium an independent state. A Belgian Congress offered the throne to one of Louis-Philippe's sons, but he was forced to decline because Britain would not tolerate such French influence in Belgium. The Congress then offered the throne to a German prince, Leopold of Saxe-Coburg (who was a British subject and the widower of Princess Charlotte of England). Leopold accepted the offer and was crowned King Leopold I (ruled 1831–1865) in July 1831. The European powers had guaranteed Belgium's independence, and when the Dutch invaded Belgium in August 1831, taking Antwerp, French military intervention returned that city to the new nation. Belgium became a constitutional monarchy with a parliament of two houses, elected by 50,000 voters (only one of every thirty males).

Liberalization in Switzerland

Another liberal success came in Switzerland, which the Congress of Vienna had reestablished as a federation of semi-autonomous cantons, dominated by Zurich, Bern, and Lucerne. Because of Switzerland's long tradition of decentralized government, the Great Powers had been willing to tolerate a constitution that allowed relatively extensive political freedoms. But Swiss liberals resented the three most powerful cantons within the federation. Fearful that some cantons might become havens of liberalism, the Congress powers forced the Swiss cantons in 1823 to restrict freedom of the press and curtail the activities of foreign political exiles.

The 1830 revolution in France also inspired intellectuals, shopkeepers, artisans, and landowning peasants in Switzerland who wanted greater constitutional guarantees of freedom, more efficient government, and limits on the political influence of the Protestant and Catholic clergy. In December, the federal Diet declared its willingness to accept constitutional changes, initiating a period of "regeneration." The constitutions of ten cantons were liberalized, guaranteeing freedom of expression and giving all adult men the right to vote, a victory unique at that time. In Zurich, another pathbreaking law required that all children attend school from the age of six to sixteen and allowed schools to waive fees for poor families. Victorious liberals recognized Zurich's administrative and judicial structure, knocked down the walls that stifled the city's growth, undertook urban improvements, and inspired a livelier cultural life.

But Metternich was not far away. Austria pressured the German-speaking Swiss cantons to oppose secularization. During the winter of 1844–1845, when the canton of Lucerne announced that the Jesuit order would again be welcome within its borders, liberals rebelled. Seven Catholic cantons withdrew from the Swiss Confederation, forming a *Sonderbund,* or separate league. In 1847, the other cantons declared war and, in what amounted to little more than a skirmish, defeated the Catholic cantons within a month. In 1848, Switzerland adopted a new liberal constitution, becoming a federal state with universal male suffrage.

NATIONALIST STRUGGLES

Nationalism also gradually emerged as a force for change in Europe. It was closely tied to liberalism in that exponents of both ideologies demanded far-reaching political change that threatened the state system of Central Europe (see Map 14.3). In 1831, Polish nationalists rose up against Russian domination but were crushed. During the 1830s and 1840s, more people living in the German and Italian states began to favor the political unification of their respective peoples. Many German businessmen believed that the creation of a "Germany" would eliminate some trade barriers. Some of them began to acquire positions of political influence in the Rhineland, Prussia's rapidly industrializing western territory.

Intellectuals representing other ethnic groups demanded that national boundaries correspond to linguistic frontiers; during the 1830s, the first scholarly books written in Czech, Hungarian, and Romanian were published. Polish and Serb nationalism, too, had their respective exponents. And, in Ireland, where the upper class was almost entirely English, Daniel O'Connell (1775–1847), barrister turned demagogue, stimulated national awareness among Irish peasants.

The Revolt in Poland

The Congress of Vienna had left most of what had been Poland as a kingdom ("Congress Poland") with its own army, but with the Russian tsar as king of Poland. Tsar Alexander I granted the Poles the liberal Constitu-

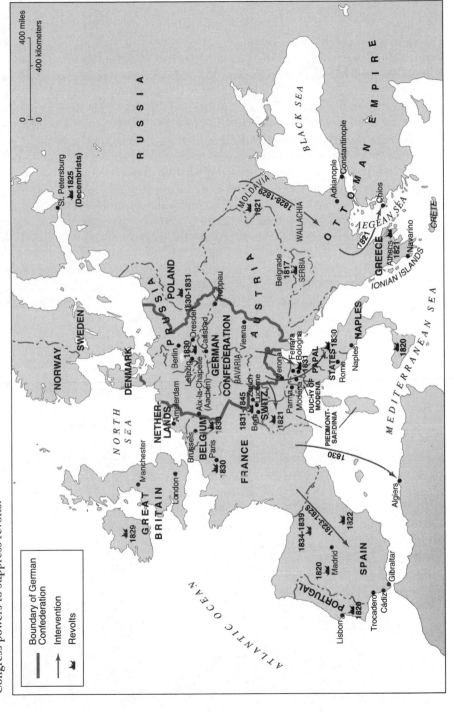

MAP 14.3 LIBERAL REVOLTS Liberal or national uprisings in Congress Europe. Arrows indicate intervention by conservative Congress powers to suppress revolts.

tional Charter of 1818, which provided for a parliament of two houses, a Senate of appointed members drawn from noble families and Catholic bishops, and a lower house (the Sejm) elected by people of means. Neither assembly, however, possessed much autonomy. In 1820, Alexander forbade the Sejm from meeting for five years as punishment for opposing Russian policies, which included imposing disadvantageous customs barriers on grain.

Many Poles hoped that France would send forces to help them expel the Russians. The composer Frederic Chopin (1810–1849) moved to Paris in 1831 from his native Poland. Chopin went to France hoping to make his fortune, and was not really a political refugee. Yet, ardent nationalism infused his music, as he drew upon Polish folk themes and dances in his polonaises, which inspired Polish nationalists. But the newly established monarchy of Louis-Philippe feared intervention in its own affairs by the other powers and, in any case, the issue of Polish independence interested only republicans, not the liberal monarchists who had brought Louis to power.

The Polish uprising of 1830–1831 in some ways replicated that of the Decembrists in Russia in 1825. Tensions between Poles and Russians had mounted after Nicholas I became tsar of Russia and king of Poland. In October 1830, fearing a Polish insurrection, Nicholas ordered the mobilization of the Polish army (commanded by his brother, Grand Duke

An English caricature, "The clemency of the Russian monster," depicting Tsar Nicholas I addressing the Poles, whose 1831 rebellion he has just crushed.

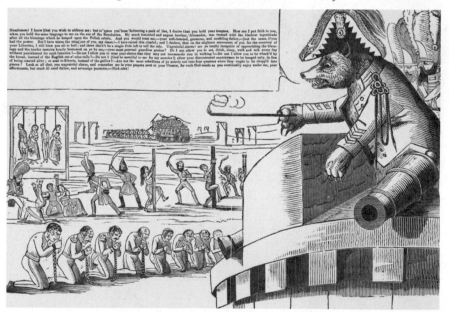

Constantine, governor-general of Poland) and gave orders that young officers under suspicion be arrested. Polish military cadets rose up in Warsaw in November 1830, capturing the arsenal and its stock of rifles. Constantine withdrew the Russian troops from the Polish capital in the hope that its municipal government could restore order. The more radical insurgents, their ranks swelled by artisans, were determined to achieve complete independence.

In January 1831, a large crowd surrounded the Sejm and shouted for independence. The Sejm declared that Tsar Nicholas was no longer king of Poland. A provisional national government formed. The Sejm, however, refused to mobilize peasants in support of the insurrection, fearing that they might demand land reform and attack their lords instead of the Russians. At the end of August 1832, the tsar's troops surrounded Warsaw, where tensions between moderates and radicals erupted into violence, making its defense even more difficult. The rebels awaited assistance from the French and British, but liberals in those countries were not able to convince their governments to intervene. Warsaw fell to Russian troops in the autumn. Poland now lost even its separate status within the Russian Empire, its assembly, and its army. Thousands of Poles fled Russian oppression, including artists and musicians who helped infuse Polish nationalism with romanticism. They enriched the cultural life of Paris and other Western capitals while dreaming of the day that Poland would be free.

Uprisings in Italy and Spain

Unlike the revolutions in France and Belgium and the ill-fated Polish insurrection, popular stirrings in the Italian states, beginning with movements in Bologna and the Duchy of Modena, started as protests against inefficient and corrupt rule. Several of these uprisings had a comic-opera quality to them, as when rebels in Parma literally locked Duchess Marie-Louise out of the city by shutting the gates until an Austrian army arrived in March 1831 to let her back in and restore her to power. Several cities in central Italy that had proclaimed their independence from the Papal States tried to create the "United Provinces of Italy."

Like the Poles, insurgents against Austrian rule in several towns within the Papal States unrealistically counted on help from French armies, some still believing that France had a mission to free the oppressed peoples of Europe. With Austrian troops approaching from the north, an army of volunteers marched toward Rome, defeating the pope's army, which had been weakened by desertion. But by then the Austrians had taken Modena, Parma, and Ferrara. Three weeks after its creation, the United Provinces surrendered to the Papal States. A papal army mopped up resistance, sacking several towns so viciously that Austrian troops had to return to save the local population. The Italian insurrections, compromised by tensions between moderates and radicals, collapsed without really winning popular support.

Giuseppe Mazzini (1805–1872), a lawyer by training and an energetic revolutionary by temperament, emerged as a guiding spirit in the quest for Italian unification under a republic. Influenced by the liberal romanticism of Wordsworth and Byron, Mazzini asserted the need "to redeem the peoples by their consciousness of a special mission entrusted to each of them," that is, to bring peace to Europe by liberating all peoples. Mazzini imputed to the idea of the "nation" an almost mystical religious quality. He was one of the first to suggest that the states of Europe might evolve into a loose federation of democratic states based on the implementation of the principle of nationality.

Mazzini believed that a defeat of Austria would serve as a first step toward creating a federation of European democratic republics. Rejecting the Carbonari's conspiratorial tradition, he was convinced that he could expand his nationalist organization, Young Italy, whose membership was limited to individuals under forty years of age. "Italy in revolution," he bragged, "would be strong enough to defeat three Austrias." Jailed and then expelled from one country after another, he launched several futile insurrections in 1834–1836 and again in 1844. In doing so, he legitimized Italian nationalism abroad, keeping it alive in European international relations.

As conspiracies and insurrections failed and brought repression in their wake, some Italian nationalists began to look to the liberal Kingdom of Piedmont-Sardinia, Italy's strongest state, to effect national unification. But for the moment, the Italian peninsula remained dominated by an outside power, as it had been since the early sixteenth century, and divided into small states that were proud of their independence. The dream of Italian unification remained, for the most part, limited to a small number of middle-class intellectuals.

The quest for Italian unification began to stir romantic artists and composers. The Italian composer Gioacchino Rossini (1792–1868) represented this change. He had been asked by the reactionary Prince Metternich of Austria in 1822 to attend a meeting of the Congress powers in Verona to symbolize international harmony, as assembled representatives of the Great Powers discussed how to crush national movements. But Rossini soon changed his tune and came to espouse Italian nationalism. His allegoric opera *William Tell*, performed in Paris in 1829, told the story of a fourteenth-century Swiss patriot who, refusing to pay homage to Austrian rule, is forced by an official to shoot with bow and arrow an apple off the top of his young son's head, and who eventually kills the Austrian. "This art of music which is based solely on sentiment and ideals," Rossini wrote, "cannot escape the influence of the times we live in, and the sentiment and ideals of the present day are wholly concerned with steam, rapine, and barricades."

Liberals also failed in Spain. In 1830, Ferdinand VII, a widower, married Maria Christina, a liberal Neopolitan princess. Their daughter Isabella became the heir to the Spanish throne. But nobles and churchmen insisted that a woman could not rule Spain. After the king's death in 1833, civil war broke out between liberals, who placed their hopes in the little girl, and conservatives (the Carlists), who supported the cause of the late king's brother, Don Carlos. Maria Christina, ruling as regent, promulgated a constitution in 1834 modeled on the French Charter of 1814. As liberals quarreled among themselves over the kinds of constitutional changes they wanted, however, Maria Christina in 1840 turned to the army to maintain order. In 1843, General Ramón Narváez (1800–1868), an Andalusian squire of violent temper who considered himself a liberal, seized power. He implemented a conservative constitution and made peace with the Catholic Church. Narváez soon abandoned his liberal pretensions, muzzling the press. On his deathbed he boasted, "I have no enemies, I have shot them all." The struggle of liberals against a Spanish general would not be the last in Spain.

German Nationalism in Central Europe

In most German states, conservatives had triumphed after Napoleon's defeat, and liberals seeking economic and political change faced an uphill battle. Constitutions implemented during the Napoleonic period had been gradually withdrawn or weakened by amendment. Electoral assemblies in general were selected by limited franchise and had almost no power. Prussian town councils were forbidden to discuss any political matter that did not directly affect their communities.

However, the wave of liberal and nationalist movements unleashed by the Revolutions of 1830 soon reached Central Europe. Revolts shortly afterward broke out against the rulers of several Rhineland states. Popular disturbances forced the rulers of Hanover and Hesse-Kassel to make political concessions. In Saxony, a liberal constitution was enacted following uprisings in Leipzig and Dresden, and liberals won a constitution in the northern German state of Brunswick as well.

The Polish revolt against Russia in 1831 fueled the imagination of a generation of German university students. The movement culminated in a huge meeting in 1832 of 30,000 people at the ruins of a château near the University of Heidelberg, where speakers saluted popular sovereignty. Police foiled an attempt by students to seize Frankfurt, the meeting place of the Federal Diet of the German Confederation. Metternich berated the rulers of the German states for their permissiveness. The Confederation's Diet responded by passing "Ten Articles," which brought the universities under surveillance, coordinated police repression of liberals in the German states, prohibited public meetings, and stipulated that any state threatened by revolution would be assisted by the others.

Yet, despite a lack of popular support, liberalism in the German states slowly gained momentum among professors, students, and lawyers during what later became known as the *Vormärz* ("Before March") period, that is, the period of ferment preceding the revolution of March 1848. The French Revolution of 1830 influenced the "Young Germans," who sought to develop a culture that they considered appropriate for their era. They included the poet Heinrich Heine (1797–1856), who had rushed to Paris after the fall of the Bourbon dynasty. Heine's *French Conditions* sharply contrasted the mood of apparent intellectual freedom and optimism that radiated from Paris with that of the repression and gloomy resignation liberals faced in the German states. Heine predicted that "the new age will give birth to a new art in enthusiastic harmony with itself."

However, German liberals, like German philosophes of the late Enlightenment, shied away from defying the existing structure of state authority. Instead they looked to individual states to undertake reforms in the common interest. Many German liberals considered the state itself, not the people or any representative institution, to be the source of national sovereignty.

The philosopher Georg Wilhelm Friedrich Hegel (1770–1831) made explicit the close connection between the development of German nationalism and the reverence for a strong state that characterized some German liberal thought. The son of a bureaucrat in Württemberg, Hegel had first expressed attachment to the liberating possibilities of the French Revolution before, like most other German intellectuals, recoiling against French expansionism and the Terror. Yet, Hegel increasingly considered the state to be the embodiment and potential of a nation. Hegel's state, like that of Burke before him, develops through history. Nationalism was his equivalent of a secular religion that had the potential of shaping a new morality. However much Hegel believed that reason offered the path to truth, he, like Burke, turned against the natural law of the philosophes. Hegel's state is overwhelming, even frightening, subsuming individual rights to its power.

In contrast to Britain, which had a long tradition of individual liberty, and France, where the complex heritage of the French Revolution included individual freedom, the German states had no real tradition of political liberty. German liberals remained political outsiders, butting their heads against a particularly pervasive respect for ideological conformity. Thus, many German liberals continued to look to the enlightened state to carry out sensible reforms. Liberalism became closely tied to the pursuit of German unification. Alluding to the state, however, a German liberal in 1842 spoke of it in a way that would have seemed strange in Britain: "We all want [the state] to be great, mighty, powerful, and rational. We all have no other wish than to be absorbed into the state, and to devote our strength to it." England had had a civil war in the seventeenth century and France its revolution in 1789; the German states had no revolutionary tradition. Many German liberals were thus both intrigued and frightened by the French Revolution of 1830.

German particularism—the tradition of many independent states, many of them very small—complicated the liberal movement in Central Europe. Liberals did not constitute a party, lacking a precisely defined program for reform. German liberals remained skeptical about the kind of organized movement undertaken by French liberals in the last years of the Restoration. Rejecting the influence of the Catholic or Protestant churches in their states, they wanted some sort of constitutional, representative government. But like British and French liberals, they believed that only men who owned property ought to vote because the independence of their vote would be assured.

Many German liberals supported liberal economic theory. German merchants and manufacturers began to object to the discouraging complexity of customs tariffs that created a series of costly hurdles along roads and rivers. As German manufacturing developed, particularly in the Rhineland, many businessmen demanded an end to these unnatural impediments faced by neither British nor French rivals. They supported a proposed German Customs Union (Zollverein) which, following its creation in 1834, removed many of these tariff barriers from seventeen states (see Chapter 16). But in Germany, not all liberals were proponents of liberal economic theory, perhaps because of the large number of German states that depended on high tariffs to protect local manufacturing. Thus, some merchants and manufacturers denounced any government interference in business, believing that the proposed tariff union would serve the interests of Prussia, the largest northern German state.

German liberals who espoused free trade made greater headway than those demanding political reform. To liberal nationalists, the Zollverein seemed to offer a basis for the eventual political unification of Germany. It breathed life into the movement for political reform. But those people who hoped that Prussia and the other German states would move toward constitutionalism and a liberal franchise were disappointed. Karl Marx called Prussia a "ship of fools," confidently expecting it to run aground on revolution. Prussian King Frederick William IV (ruled 1840–1861) disappointed liberals when he refused to establish a Diet representing the entire country. When he finally did convoke a United Diet in 1847, it was not popularly elected and was to serve the king only in an advisory capacity.

CRISIS AND COMPROMISE IN GREAT BRITAIN

In Britain, the continued call for political reform, specifically the expansion of the electoral franchise to include more middle-class voters, would be the true test of the ability of the British elite to compromise in the interest of relative social harmony. Popular protests swept parts of England during the 1815–1819 period. At a gathering in London in December 1816, speakers demanded a greatly expanded electoral franchise. Poor

Massacre at St Peters or "BRITONS STRIKE HOME"!!!

The Peterloo Massacre in Manchester, 1819.

harvests in 1818 and 1819 led to grain riots, machine-breaking, and other protests by poor people. On August 16, 1819, a mass meeting was held at St. Peter's Fields in the burgeoning northern industrial town of Manchester. A crowd of some 50,000 men and women gathered to demonstrate for the right to form political organizations and to assemble freely. First, deputized local constables moved in to arrest the main speaker. Then soldiers fired, killing eleven and wounding hundreds of other protesters. The ugly incident entered history as "Peterloo," a shameful victory not over Napoleon at Waterloo but over the country's own defenseless laboring poor. Parliament passed Six Acts that, reviving the repressive legislation of the era of the French Revolution, banned demonstrations, suspended the writ of *habeas corpus,* and placed restrictions on the press.

The late 1820s were bleak years for the English poor, with hunger following unemployment. In the north, police and employers were confronted with increased militancy and class solidarity from artisans and skilled workers demanding high wages. In Ireland, violent resistance broke out against the Church's efforts to collect the tithe. In 1830, a wave of food riots and machine breaking (see Chapter 16) spread through southeastern England.

But there would be no revolution in nineteenth-century Britain, despite the prevalence of social tensions in the world's most industrialized society. The landed elite, which dominated Parliament, supported by manufacturing interests, enacted reforms that defused social and political tensions by bowing to middle-class demands for change. The greatest of these were the Reform Act of 1832 and the repeal of the Corn Laws in 1846. The resolution of these crises contributed to the emergence of a liberal consensus in Victorian Britain that lasted throughout the century.

Religious and Electoral Reform

Parliament approved several major controversial reforms because many British conservatives proved willing to compromise. Many Tories, men of great landed wealth, believed that electoral reform would be a dangerous precedent, perhaps opening up the floodgates of popular protest. But the fear of civil war in largely Catholic Ireland led some Tories to compromise, making possible religious reforms. Despite vociferous opposition from the Established Church, Parliament in 1828 repealed the Test and Corporation Acts, which had forced anyone holding public office to take communion in the Anglican Church.

Catholic Emancipation had become a major political issue, at least partly because it was linked to the problem of Catholic Ireland, where a reform movement had begun and where protests against English domination and outright insurrection seemed endemic. Catholics could not vote or stand for election to the Chamber of Deputies, or serve in the army in Britain (although Irish Catholics had been recruited in great numbers to serve overseas during the Seven Years' War). But more than a decade after Waterloo, anti-Catholicism was less of an essential component to British nationalism. In 1829, Parliament passed the Catholic Emancipation Act, which removed the legal restrictions that had kept Catholics from holding office or serving in Parliament.

In Britain, political liberalism continued to be closely linked to the movement led by some Whigs for electoral reform. Businessmen resented being under-represented in the House of Commons. The electoral system was a patchwork that reflected the interests of local elites and particular communities that had gradually developed in England since the fourteenth century. The industrial north and west sent few men to Parliament because electoral districts had not changed since before the Industrial Revolution. No one represented the industrial centers of Manchester and Birmingham in Parliament, and wealthy merchants in those cities were no longer pacified by assurances that they had indirect, "virtual representation" through members of Parliament who had their interests in mind, or that they could personally contact a peer, who might introduce a bill in the House of Lords. On the other hand, some sparsely populated rural districts still were represented in Parliament. Dunwich, the most notorious of these "rotten boroughs," had been covered over by the sea since the twelfth century. "Pocket boroughs" were electoral districts "in the pocket" of a wealthy landowner routinely returned to Parliament (see Chapter 11). In the first half of the century, only one member of the British House of

British reformers chopping down the tree of corruption.

Commons was of working-class origins, and he was a prosperous manufacturer.

With news of the French Revolution in 1830, the British upper classes rallied together, fearful, as they used to say, that when France sneezed, the rest of Europe might catch a cold. However, amid shows of armed force by constables and troops, organized protest was limited to a wildly enthusiastic rally in the Scottish city of Glasgow to celebrate the news of the French and Belgian revolutions, and urban crowds gathering to hear the popular radical William Cobbett (1763–1835) speak on behalf of the extension of the electoral franchise to all men.

The Reform Bill of 1832

The general election following George IV's death in 1830 reduced the conservative majority in Parliament. A broadly based campaign for electoral reform swept the country; some of the 5,000 petitions that were brought to Parliament attacked in patriotic language the selfishness of the landed elite. The new Whig prime minister, Earl Charles Grey (1764–1845), believed reform inevitable in a country in which only one of every fifteen adult males had the right to vote. He feared that English landed gentlemen might lose control over Commons if electoral reform failed. But Grey knew that any reform bill that passed the House of Commons would never get through the House of Lords as then constituted. In 1831, the Lords rejected a bill sponsored by the government that would have eliminated many "rotten" and "pocket" boroughs. Public meetings protested this defeat, particularly in the unenfranchised cities of the industrial north and lowland Scotland. When the House of Lords rejected a second reform bill in October 1831, demonstrators massed in London, and a riot in Bristol ended in twelve deaths.

By this time, more Tories had come around to Grey's view that only the passage of some sort of electoral reform bill could save Britain from a revolution. The Whigs proposed a third bill, which Commons passed in March 1832, and sent it on to the Lords. As the political crisis mounted, the duke of Wellington, commander of British troops at Waterloo, tried and failed to form a ministry. Grey, who again became prime minister, convinced the new king, William IV (ruled 1830–1837), to threaten to create enough new peers in order to get the reform bill through the House of Lords. Wellington agreed not to oppose its passage, and the bill was passed.

Although all women and most men remained unenfranchised, the Reform Act of 1832 was a turning point in the history of modern Britain. The peers, who did not want to see their ranks contaminated with "instant lords," wanted to avoid any possible alliance between frustrated businessmen and radicals supported by the workers, as had occurred in France in the last years of the Bourbon Restoration. The historian Thomas Macaulay warned the peers to keep in mind the fate of the French nobles during the Revolution: "From those magnificent hotels, those ancient castles, they were driven forth to exile and beggary . . . to cut wood in the back settlements of America, or to teach French in the schoolrooms of London." The landed magnates listened and agreed to a liberal compromise which, by lowering the minimum franchise requirement, almost doubled the size of the electorate. The Reform Act thus greatly contributed to the development of more broadly based political parties.

Only about one of every five adult male citizens was able to vote—the bill specifically excluded women from political rights. Hence, Britain was far from a democracy, despite fears among the wealthy that reform pointed in that direction. The British Parliament now more accurately reflected the country's economic and social evolution during the age of the Industrial Revolution. Fifteen percent of the members of the House of Commons in the early 1840s were businessmen, and 35 percent had some other connection to commerce and industry, such as serving on the board of directors of enterprises. What was gained in France by revolution in 1830 was achieved in Britain through reform in 1832. A larger percentage of men could now vote in Britain than in France, Belgium, the Netherlands, or Spain.

The new electorate, as the Tories had feared, increased Whig strength. Commons passed two reforms in 1833 that would have been inconceivable without the Reform Act. Anti-slavery societies, including many organized by women, launched a nationwide campaign against slavery in the British Dominions. Petitions portrayed slavery as incompatible with British freedom. As a result, Parliament abolished slavery in the British Empire. The second reform measure passed in 1833 prohibited all work by children under nine years of age, limited the workday of children from nine through twelve years to eight hours a day (and a maximum of forty-eight hours a week), and that for "young persons," ages thirteen to eighteen, to twelve hours a day (up to a maximum of sixty-nine hours per week). In 1834, Parliament passed the controversial Poor Law (see Chapter 16), by which able-bodied individuals would no longer receive assistance from parishes, but would be incarcerated in "well-regulated" workhouses. And finally the Municipal Corporations Act of 1835 eliminated the old, often corrupt borough governments, creating elected municipal corporations responsible for administration. These reforms allowed many more Whigs, including Dissenters, to assume positions of responsibility in local government, another blow against the domination of public life by the old aristocratic oligarchy and the Established Church.

The Repeal of the Corn Laws and Chartism

The repeal of the Corn Laws directly affected ordinary people in Britain. Passed by a conservative-dominated Parliament in 1815 and 1828, these laws had imposed a sliding tariff on imported wheat (then known as "corn"). When the price of wheat produced in Britain fell below a certain level, import duties would keep out cheaper foreign grain. Foreign grain could be imported virtually free of import taxes when the price of wheat stood at or above a certain level. The laws protected landowners, but were detrimental to the interests of businessmen who imported or sold imported grain, and, above all, to consumers, who were forced to pay higher prices for bread. The bad harvests of 1839–1841 came when an expanding population had created an increased demand for food, even as parishes were cutting back on their allocations to the poor. The "Great Hunger" in Ireland caused by the potato famine that began in 1845 brought mass starvation and sent waves of impoverished emigrants to the United States. This contributed to pressure for repeal of the Corn Laws.

Exponents of liberal laissez-faire economic policies squared off against the interests of wealthy property owners, Whigs against Tories. British manufacturers and spokesmen for the poor denounced the entrenched, landed, "bread-taxing" and "blood-sucking" oligarchy. Proponents of repeal cited biblical texts denouncing those enriched by the hunger of the poor. In 1839, the Anti-Corn Law League, a powerful pressure group largely made up of businessmen, brought together economic liberals, Whig politicians, and radicals. With strong support among working people, John Bright (1811–1889) argued that the repeal of the Corn Laws

The Irish potato famine of 1846.

would be a major step toward political democracy. The son of a Quaker cotton mill owner, he thundered against aristocratic privilege and its close ties to the Established Church. He warned the aristocracy: "Until now, this country has been ruled by the class of great proprietors of the soil. Everyone must have foreseen that, as trade and manufactures extended, the balance of power would, at some time or other, be thrown into another scale. Well, that time has come. . . . We have been living through a revolution without knowing it."

As with the Reform Act, it took a change of heart by a conservative government to get a repeal bill passed. Prime Minister Robert Peel (1788–1850), the son of a cotton manufacturer and a conservative (of whom someone once said that his smile resembled the gleam of silverplate on a coffin), had seen a number of significant reforms through Parliament. He believed in free trade and had pushed through reductions in and even the elimination of a number of tariffs, including those on imported raw cotton for the textile industry. He was contemptuous of aristocrats "who spend their time eating and drinking, and hunting, shooting, gambling, and horse-racing." The Irish famine helped push him to undertake the dismantling of the Corn Laws. Repeal would be an act of political courage, as he was bound to fall from power, but Peel believed only such a move could forestall a popular insurrection. In June 1846, Parliament repealed the Corn Laws. Repeal reduced duties on wheat and other imported agricultural products, which represented a crushing defeat for landed interests (although some wealthy farmers had already concluded that the future lay

in capital-intensive farming, not in protectionism) and a victory for economic liberalism. Peel fell from office the same day, a victim, his supporters insisted, of angering many conservatives by doing the right thing.

If the repeal of the Corn Laws demonstrated the ability of the British
government and political elite to compromise to avoid greater crises, the
Chartist movement reflected the limits of accommodation with popular
politics. Whereas some French and German workers oiled their guns,
their English counterparts took out their pens. In 1836, William Lovett
(1800–1877), a cabinetmaker, founded the London Workingmen's Association for Benefiting Politically, Socially, and Morally the Useful Classes.
Two years later, Lovett and Francis Place, a London tailor, prepared a
charter that would be signed by millions of people and then delivered to
Parliament. The "Great Charter" called for the democratization of political
life, including universal manhood suffrage, annual elections, equal electoral districts, the secret ballot, and salaries for members of Parliament, so
that ordinary people could serve if elected. The movement remained overwhelmingly peaceful, its members committed to acting as a "moral force"
in British life. In 1839, a small "physical force" group emerged within
the Chartist movement in northern England, particularly among workers
whose livelihoods had been eroded by mechanization. They threatened
strikes and even insurrection if Parliament did not yield. But the group remained small and relatively unimportant in the movement itself.

During the next few years, coinciding with economic hard times, Chartism spread throughout much of industrial Britain. Becoming arguably the
largest working-class political movement in the century, it mobilized not

Photograph of the final Chartist Demonstration at Kensington Common, April 10,
1848.

only skilled and organized craftsmen but also unskilled handloom weavers. Chartism led to a rise in working-class consciousness in Britain (see Chapter 16). In May 1839, Parliament summarily rejected a Chartist petition with almost 1.3 million signatures. Undaunted, the Chartists tried again in 1842 when the National Chartist Association carried a giant scroll with 3.3 million signatures to Westminster. Once again, Parliament rejected the Great Charter.

CONCLUSION

Britain remained a constitutional monarchy with representative government, however narrowly based. Whereas it took the Revolution of 1830 to expand the number of those eligible to vote in France, in Britain middle-class men were gradually and peacefully incorporated into the political arena. Political and economic liberalism triumphed through reform within Britain's reformist tradition. The British upper classes who favored reform still believed that France provided an example of the consequences of letting popular demands get out of control. British workers themselves remained committed to peaceful protest.

In France and Belgium, it took revolutions to bring change: in the former, a liberal monarchy; in the latter, independence. Liberals gained momentum in the German states and in the northern Italian states. In Switzerland, more liberal constitutions and educational reforms were implemented. Nationalists, too, gained strength in Europe. Proponents of German and Italian national unification became more vocal. Cultural and nationalist movements began to develop among Czechs, Serbs, and other peoples within the Habsburg domains. However, the Prussian and Austrian monarchies, to say nothing of the Russian tsar, whose troops had crushed the Polish insurrection in 1831, stood as formidable obstacles to constitutional change and national movements. Nonetheless, the Concert of Europe no longer existed. Political momentum was with those seeking to break down the bastions of traditional Europe.

CHAPTER 15

THE MIDDLE CLASSES IN
THE ERA OF LIBERALISM

After the French Revolution, the Old Regime in Europe, dominated by monarchs and nobles, gave way to the "bourgeois century." The dynamic middle classes came to the forefront of economic, political, and cultural life. They were an extremely diverse social group that ranged from merchants and manufacturers of great wealth to struggling shop-keepers and innkeepers. Rapid population growth, particularly in towns and cities, swelled the number of lawyers, notaries, and other middle-class professionals. The entrepreneur replaced the noble as someone to be revered.

One should not exaggerate either the cohesiveness of the middle class, however, nor the extent of its dominance. Indeed, middle-class influence varied greatly within Europe, reflecting the economies and political structures of the various states. The size and influence of the middle class was far greater in Britain (where prosperity provided entry into the gentry through the purchase of land), France, Belgium, the German states, and the northern Italian states, whose economies and politics were slowly being transformed by the Industrial Revolution, than in Spain, the Habsburg monarchy, or Russia, still dominated by nobles.

The middle classes emphasized individual freedom and the respectability that came from work and prosperity. In liberalism, they found an economic and political theory that echoed the way they viewed the world. At the same time, for all the frugality sometimes ascribed to the nineteenth-century middle class, bourgeois prosperity found expression in the development of a culture of comfort. The middle class viewed the family as the basis of social order. Within the family, in which men and women occupied, at least in theory, separate spheres, religion and education played privileged roles. In addition, the middle-class emphasis on individual freedom was reflected by the romantic movement in literature, painting, and music, celebrating individual fulfillment through subjectivity and emotion.

638

DIVERSITY OF THE MIDDLE CLASSES

The middle class included all people who neither held noble title nor were workers or peasants depending on manual labor for economic survival. The terms "bourgeois" and "burghers" had first emerged in the Middle Ages to refer to residents of towns that enjoyed specific rights (such as immunity from some kinds of taxation), or even independence granted by territorial rulers. By the nineteenth century, the middle classes made up roughly 15 to 20 percent of the total population in Western Europe but a far smaller percentage in Eastern Europe. The middle class expanded in size and diversity amid the ongoing economic transformation of Europe.

The nineteenth-century middle class encompassed a great range of economic situations, occupations, social status, education, and expectations. It can be imagined as a social pyramid, topped by a small group of well-connected banking families, industrial magnates, and the wealthiest wholesale merchants, as well as a few top government ministers and ambassadors. Sons in these families tended to follow their fathers into the same or similar businesses, and could count on a healthy inheritance. For this reason, many of the most successful businesses in France were family firms.

Below this extremely wealthy group came families drawing more modest incomes from smaller businesses, rental properties, professions such as law, and lucrative government posts. There were self-made men within this strata, but in general it required some money, connections, and access to credit to make money. Four out of five Berlin entrepreneurs were the sons of bankers, manufacturers, or merchants, with fathers who could

A bourgeois couple out on a walk in Vienna.

bring them into the business or loan them enough money to get started on their own.

At the bottom of the pyramid stood the "petty bourgeoisie," at whose expense nobles and wealthy bourgeois made cruel jokes. This stratum included shopkeepers of modest means and expectations, wine merchants, minor officials, schoolteachers, café owners, and some master artisans— craftsmen in the luxury trades, such as goldsmiths and silversmiths—who proudly considered themselves middle class. They dreamed of doing better and moving up the social scale; at the same time, they feared that economic disaster might one day drop them into the ranks of laborers.

Variations in Bourgeois Europe

Wealthy merchants and industrialists still hungered for social prestige and, in Britain, for the status of gentility that came from owning lots of land. Successful entrepreneurs were more likely to invest their profits in land, the safest investment, than to reinvest them in their own businesses. Thus, the proportion of land owned by the middle class increased rapidly during the first half of the nineteenth century in Britain, France, and the German and Italian states. As ownership of land (specifically taxes paid on it) remained the basis of electoral enfranchisement in much of Western Europe, the political influence of the middle classes increased as well.

The landed elite remained at the pinnacle of social status in Britain, although its share of the nation's wealth fell from about 20 percent to about 10 percent between 1800 and 1850. English nobles kept pace with businessmen as the value of their property continued to rise, allowing them to charge tenants higher rents. Some English "country gentlemen" still looked down their noses at those they scorned as mere "calico printers," "shopkeepers," and municipal officials of modest means. Yet, sons of wealthy landowners, titled or not, sat alongside the sons of nobles at Oxford and Cambridge Universities. England retained a uniquely narrow definition of nobility. Nonetheless, some peers owed their titles to family fortunes made in commerce or industry during the previous century. Likewise, because in Britain the eldest son still inherited the entire family fortune, some second and third sons left country life to become businessmen, without feeling the sense of humiliation that their counterparts might have felt in France or Prussia. Many noble families were delighted to have their offspring marry the sons and daughters of wealthy businessmen.

The remnants of noble political power, perpetuated by patronage and sometimes outright corruption, drew attacks from reformers who believed that self-satisfied indolence could only be constrained by what James Mill called "the wisdom of the middle class." In Western Europe, whereas many nobles still remained loyal to ruling or deposed dynasties, strong feelings of nationalism first developed within the middle class.

Merchants and lawyers had long since been the most prominent citizens of Belgian towns, as well as towns in the German Rhineland and northern trading cities like Lübeck, Bremen, and Hamburg, whose long traditions of political independence stretched back to the Middle Ages. The bankers and shippers of Amsterdam and other commercial centers still set the social and political style of the trading states. In Milan (Lombardy) and Turin (Piedmont), merchants and manufacturers helped convince municipal authorities, following outbreaks of cholera in the mid-1830s, to improve the water supply, pave streets, and move slaughterhouses and cemeteries to the edge of town.

The dedication of urban elites to their towns, however, was not always constant and could vary from place to place. In the manufacturing city of Barmen in the German Ruhr, families who made fortunes in the yarn trade during the first half of the century moved from respected positions within their churches to prestigious posts on municipal councils. During the first decades of the century, they served as members of boards of trustees and chambers of commerce. They organized charitable activities on behalf of the poor, represented Barmen in the provincial assembly, and presided over associations of like-minded citizens. In Barmen, capitalism and public service seemed inextricably linked. But gradually in the middle decades of the century, the elite's sense of civic responsibility ebbed; their successors were interested in making money, and little else. Unlike the previous generation of successful entrepreneurs, Barmen businessmen began to treat their workers with calculated ruthlessness, and paid considerably less attention to the city in which they lived.

In contrast to the middle classes in the West, the Eastern European and Balkan middle classes were minuscule in size and without political influence. The Russian bourgeoisie, which at the beginning of the century accounted for no more than about 2 percent of the population, included Orthodox priests, state officials, and a few intellectuals, but relatively few men whose entrepreneurial instincts and experience were remotely comparable to those of the Western middle class. The Russian Empire had only three large cities: St. Petersburg, Moscow, and Kiev. The state itself managed some industries and, again in contrast with the West, noble domination of business—and of the universities and top ranks of the bureaucracy, as well—continued throughout the century. Some wealthy merchants, including former peasants and freed serfs, gained ennoblement. The Stroganov family, after whom the beef dish is named, was among these privileged few who were wealthy enough to buy meat, sour cream, and pepper for their favorite dinner.

The Scandinavian state of Sweden, too, had a small middle class. Unlike its Russian counterpart, it enjoyed considerable economic and cultural influence. Some of the so-called "harbor nobility"—prosperous traders—were Germans, Scots, or Jews; the powerful merchant families of the west coast trading port of Gothenburg were linked by their credit connections to an international trading network.

The Entrepreneurial Ideal and Social Mobility

The entrepreneur emerged more and more as the man to be revered and emulated. Commerce appeared as "the great emancipator." To Lord John Russell (1792–1878), a British prime minister and liberal reformer of the early Victorian period, "The best way in which to encourage social happiness and to spread Christianity and advance morality was to let commerce take its own course."

The middle class identified its status with the common good and fate of each nation, even in Great Britain, Prussia, and Austria, where nobles retained great power. The Scottish philosopher and economist James Mill (1773–1836) emerged as the political champion of the middle class, which he called "both the most wise and the most virtuous part of the community." Mill's 1820 *Essay on Government* denounced nobles for invariably selfish attention to their own landed interests. "They grow richer as it were in their sleep, without working, risking, or economizing. What claim have they, on the general principle of social justice, to this accession of riches?" The Spanish middle class—bankers, manufacturers, and merchants in the prosperous port of Barcelona, and lawyers and civil servants in Madrid—were considered "the useful classes," the motors of prosperity. They contrasted their penchant for hard work with noble "idleness." Many middle-class families in England, above all, but also in the Netherlands and some of the German states, were influenced by evangelical Protestantism, which stressed the redeeming nature of hard work. The message was often the same in Catholic France. In 1847, a Parisian newspaper defined what it meant to be bourgeois: "The bourgeoisie is not a class, it is a position; one acquires that position and one loses it. Work, thrift and ability confer it; vice, dissipation, and idleness mean it is lost." The novels of Honoré de Balzac (1799–1850) depict Paris in the 1820s and 1830s as an economic and social jungle in which everything—even one's family—is sacrificed in the pursuit of money.

The notion of "respectability" gradually changed in Europe. In Prussia, still dominated by the landed wealth of the nobility, schoolbooks that had early in the nineteenth century emphasized immutable social hierarchy and the necessity of obedience gradually shifted to discussions of the virtues of hard work, self-discipline, and thrift. Middle-class families viewed the expansion of their fortunes as the best assurance of respectability. Bankruptcy seemed a fate worse than death.

The ideal of the self-made man was born. But, like any myth, it far surpassed the reality. Rapid social ascension remained difficult and fairly rare. There were, to be sure, spectacular success stories. The son of an ironmonger and saddler, the Welshman Robert Owen (1771–1858) began his career as a clerk and then sold cloth. Borrowing £100 in Manchester in 1789 to start up his own textile business, he became part owner of the large and prosperous New Lanark Mills. Robert Peel, a British prime minister, is another case in point. His family had been Lancashire yeomen who also produced textiles. Peel's grandfather sold goods door to door; his son, the prime minister's father, became one of the most successful entrepreneurs in Lancashire. By 1790, he sat in Parliament as Sir Robert Peel, one of England's wealthiest men. The younger Peel went on to enjoy extraordinary social and political prominence.

To be sure, some degree of social mobility was possible from the ranks of relatively prosperous master artisans. Yet, downward mobility also occurred; hard times could cause petty bourgeois to fall into the working class. The possibility of being afflicted by economic crises or personal disasters—the illness or death of a spouse, or one's own illness—haunted many such families.

Rising Professions

The growth of cities swelled the ranks of lawyers, doctors, and notaries. For the most part, however, the aspirations of those in these professions remained higher than their incomes and prestige. Balzac depicts Paris as a jungle in which young professionals "kill each other, like spiders in a jar." Many of them fell short of the income necessary to qualify for the electoral franchise. One French monarchist contended that "it isn't the workers one should fear, rather it is the *déclassés,* doctors without patients, lawyers without briefs, all the misunderstood, the discontented, who, finding no place at the banquet table, try to overturn it." During the July Monarchy (1830–1848), many frustrated lawyers, doctors, and army officers would become republicans, joining forces with workers to demand universal manhood suffrage.

Lawyers had less than sterling reputations even as their numbers increased. In the 1830s and 1840s, the French caricaturist Honoré Daumier depicted lawyers as arrogant, self-satisfied, insensitive men far more interested in extracting fees than serving justice. In Britain "gentlemen practicers" worked hard to improve the image of the lawyer. The "pettifogging attorney" of the eighteenth century gradually was replaced by the "respectable lawyer" of the nineteenth, although the educational system turned out more lawyers than needed. Notaries, too, gained in wealth and status with the growth of cities. They earned—though some of their clients would not choose that particular verb—fees that sometimes amounted to a tenth of the value of a property by registering and storing deeds of title. They also prepared marriage documents, dowries, and wills. Notaries thus remained in most countries the financial equivalent of father-confessors, knowing—or at least guessing—most of the deepest secrets concerning their clients' fortunes.

Daumier depicts a lawyer pleading his case.

The number of doctors, too, rose rapidly in nineteenth-century Western Europe, although they still struggled to be recognized as professionals rather than members of a trade. While some brilliant researchers labored in obscurity, notorious hacks received public plaudits. Among the latter was the decorated French doctor who claimed that he had proved that syphilis was not communicable—thus reassuring clients who paid considerable sums for his soothing words. Less celebrated but by no means less wealthy was a colleague who treated mentally disturbed people by strapping them to wooden planks and drenching them with icy water. Doctors were limited in the treatments at their disposal, which also contributed to their profession's minimal prestige. Popular belief in age-old cures, many based upon superstition, persisted throughout the continent.

In Western Europe, doctors began to form professional associations. The British Medical Society began in 1832 with the goal of encouraging standardized training and scientific research, as well as enhancing professional identity. For the first time in some countries surgeons now needed to have studied medicine in order to take up a scalpel, at least legally. The British Medical Act of 1858 standardized credentials for doctors, but did not require them.

Other professions also gradually commanded respect. In 1820, the Scottish writer Sir Walter Scott, assessing the future of a nephew, said that if the young man seemed fit for the army, he might well make his way there, but, if not, "he cannot follow a better line than that of an accountant. It is highly respectable." Newer professions such as veterinary science and pharmacology were open to sons of artisans and peasants. Clergymen and schoolteachers were also increasingly drawn from the middle classes.

The growth of the state also increased the number of officials and bureaucrats, providing attractive careers for middle-class sons. This was particularly true in France, where state centralization was one of the irreversible legacies of the revolutionary and Napoleonic eras. In addition to local justices of the peace and other unpaid officials who carried out many functions, the British government also employed ever more officials.

MIDDLE-CLASS CULTURE

The many dimensions of the bourgeois experience during the nineteenth century shaped middle-class culture. Those in the middle class believed that the family offered the best guarantee of social order. Within the family, most bourgeois held fast to the idea of separate spheres for men and women. Education and religious practice (however varied) provided a common culture for the middle classes within individual states. Middle-class families sought education and advantageous marriages for their children. Many (and probably most) such families considered religion an important part of their lives. Largely because of the interest of the middle classes, voluntary associations proliferated, including many organized for charitable purposes. At the same time, growing middle-class prosperity generated a quest for comfort that permitted social distinction, reflected in residence, dress, and leisure.

Marriage and Family

An astute choice of a marriage partner could preserve and even enhance family wealth and position through the acquisition of handsome dowries and wealthy daughters- and sons-in-law. Although finding a noble spouse for their daughters still remained a prized ambition for French business magnates, there were fewer noblemen to go around. Moreover, the disasters of what were considered ill-advised or inappropriate marriages ("misalliances"), that is, a union between two people far apart on the social ladder, continued to be a popular theme in novels and the theater.

Love could—and increasingly did—play a role in the choice of mates. Prospective partners were more likely to insist that their views be taken into consideration in the arrangement of marriages. One Parisian woman told her father that she could not marry "someone that I do not love, that I am to marry for reason's sake, in order to give myself a lot in life. . . . How could I hold onto him, if I do not love him and desire him?"

With an eye toward assuring the future of their progeny, some middle-class families, above all in France, began to practice contraception after about 1820, limiting their children to two. The economist Jean-Baptiste Say (1767–1832), for one, encouraged family limitation, warning that "one must increase savings accounts more than increase the number of children." Despite the disapproval of the Catholic Church, coitus interruptus certainly became more common, as well as other rudimentary forms of birth control.

The concepts of childhood and adolescence—that age between childhood and adulthood—developed rapidly within middle-class families. The "children's room" and the "children's hour," when the young came forward to see their parents and sometimes to meet guests, were middle-class concepts and could not generally be found among the lower classes. Moreover, in working-class and peasant households, there was no space for a separate room or quarters for children. Most working-class and peasant children had to begin work as soon as it was physically possible for them to do so. Furthermore, many children who were apprentices did not live with their families, but with their masters.

Because children, too, were an investment—and much more, of course—parents had to prepare them for the time when they would take on family responsibilities. Parents sought to pass on self-discipline and self-reliance to their sons. Germans called it *Bildung,* the training of cultivation and character, the subject of many nineteenth-century novels.

Separate Spheres

To the nineteenth-century middle class, the family was the basis of order, what the English called the "nursery of virtue." Many men considered women "virtuous" when they remained in their domestic sphere, "angels"

A woman's separate sphere was inside the household and included supervising children and servants.

The loneliness of a young, unmarried schoolteacher without prospects.

whose obligation was to provide comfort, happiness, and material order to their families, as well as children. *The Magazine of Domestic Economy,* which began publication in Britain in 1835, intoned: "A woman gives up her worldly possessions in exchange for a determinate station; for protection, for support . . . she gains station . . . she gains protection."

A woman's status remained closely tied to that of her father and her husband. In France, the Napoleonic Code made all men legally equal but left women subordinate to their husband's will. Although a woman could inherit property, this right was circumscribed by her husband's right to manage what the family owned, including that which came as a dowry on the day of marriage. A married woman could not freely spend money she earned. Furthermore, penalties for adulterous women in France and other countries were far more severe than for men. On his accession to the throne, King George IV of Britain tried to prevent his wife, Caroline, from becoming queen by blocking her return to England from Italy under threat of prosecuting her for adultery. But the king was forced to abandon his plan and accept his queen when women (particularly middle-class women) petitioned on her behalf, denouncing the king for espousing a double standard, since his own liaisons were notorious. A contemporary ballad went:

> Attend ye virtuous British wives
> Support your injured Queen,
> Assert her rights; they are your own,
> As plainly may be seen.

Middle-class women cared for their children, planned and oversaw the preparation of meals, supervised the servants, and attended to family social responsibilities. They exercised great influence over the education of their children, supplementing formal school instruction. They also assumed responsibility for providing guidance about religion.

Many contemporary bourgeois insisted that women should work only when dire necessity left them with no alternative. The popular British writer Mrs. Sarah Stickney Ellis (1812–1872) argued that women ought to exert a selfless moral authority within the family. Espousing domesticity as a means of maintaining national stability, she wanted the lines between male and female spheres of influence clearly drawn. "Gentlemen," she wrote, "may employ their hours of business in almost any degrading occupation and, if they have the means of supporting a respectable establishment at home, may be gentlemen still; while, if a lady but touch any article, no matter how delicate, in the way of trade, she loses caste, and ceases to be a lady." Yet, although it was unusual for women to play a role in the operation of large businesses, they stood behind the counter to serve customers in shops and cafés. Widows often continued the family business after their husbands' demise.

In Britain, dissenting voices opposed what many Victorians considered the domestic ideal of women not working. During the first decades of the nineteenth century, British feminists debated the issue of "separate spheres" for women and for men. Middle-class British feminists challenged the legal and political subordination of women.

British feminists participated in the campaigns for the abolition of slavery within the empire and the repeal of the Corn Laws in 1846 (see Chapter 14), which had kept the price of food artificially high. They then began to call for the right to vote. Five years later, Harriet Taylor Mill (1807–1858) published anonymously *The Enfranchisement of Women*. In this essay, she stressed the injustice of considering anyone inferior, and therefore not deserving the right to vote, or other rights, by virtue of gender. Believing her time a period of social and political progress, she espoused the view that men seemed less interested in "violent bodily exercises, noisy merriment and intemperance," and that now "for the first time in the world, men and women are really companions." Eighteen years later, her long-time companion and later husband John Stuart Mill (1806–1873) published *The Subjection of Women* (1869). Mill argued that women, like men, should be able to compete as equals in a society defined by market relations. By the time of John Stuart Mill's long essay, Victorian feminism had emerged as a movement organized by women. Feminists demanded, among other things, that married women be allowed to continue to have control over property they had brought with them into marriage.

Opponents of women's rights identified such feminist movements with the violence of the French Revolution, or with surges of working-class militancy. Despite the fact that many women had been active proponents of British nationalism during the Revolutionary and Napoleonic Wars—such

Caricature of John Stuart Mill's espousal of voting rights for women.

"Mill's Logic, or Franchise for Females"

as by organizing patriotic subscriptions—many upper-class Britons identified feminism with Chartism, the massive petition campaign in the 1840s calling on Parliament to expand the suffrage (see Chapter 14). Yet, even Chartist leaders rejected feminist pleas that their movement include demands for the rights of women. Most middle-class Britons, in a time when the European continent was being shaken by social and political turmoil, took the view that the British family offered shelter from such storms. As Chartism faded into the past, the next generation of middle-class feminists, more "respectable" by virtue of their class in the eyes of even those who did not approve of their movement, undertook new campaigns for more rights for women.

A Culture of Comfort

During the first half of the nineteenth century, the European middle classes gradually shaped a culture based on comfort and a quest for privacy that complemented growing prosperity. Differences in the organization and appearance of the middle-class household reflected social differences. Most bourgeois families were able to employ one or more servants and had apartments of several rooms. These usually occupied the first floors of buildings—but rarely the ground floor, where the concièrge, or building caretaker lived—while less well-off neighbors had to hike further up the stairs. In *Old Goriot* (1834–1835), a novel by Honoré de Balzac, as the retired Goriot gives away more of his fortune to his two spendthrift daughters, he moves up another flight of stairs in the shabby but (barely) respectable rooming house in which he lives.

In bourgeois apartments, kitchens and even dining rooms became separate rooms, as did attached offices for notaries, lawyers, and doctors. A distinct middle-class style of interior design slowly emerged, although there

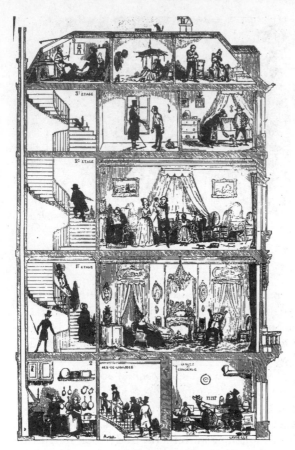

A cross-section of a Parisian apartment building, about 1850. Note that with the exception of the concierge's apartment on the ground floor, the farther you had to walk up the stairs, the less well off you were.

were national and regional variations. The German decorative style, with wallpaper and sparse, austere furnishings and ornamentation, matched the frugality of many burghers.

Increased comfort also indicated social distinction. The accoutrements of the salon were likely to include an armoire or two, a chest of drawers, an elegant table and chairs, Limoges porcelain in France, Wedgwood china in England, crystal glasses, a clock, candelabras, a painting or print or two on the walls, all passed down from one generation to the next. Very wealthy families had much more, some beginning collections of knick-knacks, small statues, and paintings. A Victorian pen manufacturer bought the entire studio collection of the painter J.M.W. Turner to go with his Gainsboroughs. He also possessed a rich collection of musical instruments but, when asked if he wanted to buy a Stradivarius, the finest violin in the world, he replied, "Nay, lad, I shan't buy any more fiddles." Such philistinism, however, was probably unusual. Pianos and other musical instruments became more common in the home and accompanied family singing. Flush toilets with running water would later gradually replace the chamber pots that had caused many unfortunate mishaps when emptied unceremoniously out windows. Countryside secondary residences, retreats from urban life, became considerably more common.

As Europe's large cities grew rapidly during the first half of the century, social segregation developed relentlessly, reinforced by the distribution and cost of public transportation. Within industrial towns, the pollution of smoke and other manufacturing smells also altered residential patterns, driving some middle-class families to new quarters. Paris' western neighborhoods became increasingly reserved for families of means, even if many apartment buildings still counted laborers and seamstresses living on the top floors. The wealthy in London enjoyed wide thoroughfares, vast public gardens, comfortable theaters, and elegant shopping arcades, a jolting contrast to the misery of the proletarian East End. In 1856, a minister compared the West and East Ends of London: "There is little communication or sympathy between the respective classes by which the two ends of London were occupied. They differ in external appearance; in the fashion of their clothes, in their pursuits, in their pleasures, and in their toils; and on the rare occasions when they come into contact, they gape at each other with much the same curiosity and astonishment as would nowadays

The culture of comfort in an elegant Berlin apartment. Note the high ceilings, the paintings on the wall, and the elegant furnishings.

be exhibited by a native of this town at the appearance of an Eskimo in Hyde Park or Regent Street." Public gardens like Copenhagen's Tivoli, Berlin's Tiergarten, and Paris' Champs-Elysées developed at this time and were, for all intents and purposes, domains of the upper classes. Cafés catered to people of means—coffee was expensive—while cabarets, selling cheap drink, attracted a more plebeian clientele.

Expanding readership during the first half of the century encouraged a proliferation of novels, histories, poetry, newspapers, political brochures and pamphlets, and literary reviews, reflecting the diversity of middle-class interests. Balzac's novels were first published in France as install-ments of lengthy serials (particularly as authors were often paid by the word) on the bottom on the front page of newspapers. Charles Dickens (1812–1870), too, first reached his public in monthly installments. *The Pickwick Papers* (1836–1837) attracted 40,000 regular readers. Reading clubs and bookshops, many of the latter lending books, flourished in West-ern Europe.

The old Roman saying that "clothes make the man" rang true of the nineteenth-century bourgeoisie. Middle-class men wore black suits, per-haps enlivened by a cashmere scarf. Middle-class women dressed only somewhat less simply; besides the quality of the material of apparel, it was left to jewelry to suggest family wealth.

Travel for pleasure, previously relatively rare, became common. It also be-came a business. In 1835 in the German Rhineland, a young publisher named Karl Baedeker (1801–1859) published a guide to sites along the Rhine. He soon published similar guides to Paris, several German states, Austria, Belgium, and Holland. In Britain, Thomas Cook (1808–1892) orga-nized his first collective excursion in 1841 when he chartered a special train to transport a group of workers to a temperance meeting. Four years later, he began the first travel agency, building on demand for his services at the time of the Great Exposition of 1851 in London. Craftsmen and their families, too, began to take his tours. Soon Cook was transporting groups across the Channel to Paris, and some as far as the classical ruins of Italy and Greece. Whereas English nobles tended to travel with their families to visit well-heeled continental friends or to stay at a rental château or elegant hotel, preferably near the sea, middle-class families began to view travel as a means of self-improvement. They took in museums and other sights. In London, the National Gallery first opened its doors in 1824; about the same time in Berlin, the middle class came to view the exhibits of the Old Museum.

Education

Secondary education increasingly provided a common cultural back-ground for the middle classes. Prussia's secondary schools (*gymnasien*) were arguably Europe's finest, offering a varied curriculum that included considerable religious instruction. In Britain, the victory of the entrepreneurial ideal was reflected in a gradually changing secondary (high) school curriculum. The English elite had long been exposed to a classical curriculum, as well as to Spartan discipline based upon corporal punishment. Reforms undertaken by Thomas Arnold (1795–1842), headmaster at Rugby School, were intended to spur students on to better performances by stimulating academic competition through examinations and prizes. Arnold's reforms reinvigorated the existing English public [private] secondary schools, and new ones were established.

Many businessmen, however, still believed that experience was the best preparation to carry the family torch. Prosperous French shopkeepers sometimes pulled their children out of school at age eleven or twelve, viewing what they learned there as irrelevant to the family tasks that lay ahead. Some entrepreneurs of family firms preferred to send sons to other companies, sometimes even in other countries, in order to obtain practical experience. In Catholic states, middle-class families sent girls to Church convent schools to learn about drawing, music, and dance.

Although their numbers were still relatively small, more young men went to university in order to prepare for careers in law, medicine, religion, or the civil service. Even in Russia, the number of university students tripled, rising from 1,700 in 1825 to 4,600 in 1848—still precious few in a population of more than 50 million.

Despite the gradual emergence of state systems of education, only a small percentage of people went beyond primary school to secondary education, and far more men than women could do so because of the lack of opportunities for the latter. The educational systems of early nineteenth-century Europe did provide many more people than ever before with basic

Oxford students at mid-century.

reading and writing skills, as the literacy rate in Western Europe moved well above 50 percent. But they also maintained social barriers because relatively few families could afford to send their children to secondary schools (the equivalent of U.S. high schools), which could provide them with more advanced skills needed for better-paying employment. In France in the early 1840s, only two of every thousand people attended a secondary school. Some working-class families still resisted even sending their children to primary school, not only because they could ill afford the modest costs involved, but because they needed their children's wage contributions, however small, to the family income.

Early in the century, the possibility of expanding educational opportunity to the poor divided elite opinion. The British writer Hannah More (1745–1833), for one, believed that poor children should learn how to read so that they could study the Bible, but not to write, because such a skill might make them reject their social subordination. Likewise, Robert Lowe, a British M.P., warned in 1833 that it might be dangerous for society if too many people were educated: they might learn "to despise their lot in life instead of making good servants; instead of teaching them subordination, it would render them fractious; it would enable them to read seditious pamphlets, vicious books, and publications against Christianity; it would render them insolent to their superiors." On the other hand, Thomas Malthus (1766–1834), the English clergyman who predicted that the rise of population would rapidly outdistance the ability of farmers to provide enough food, believed that education would make ordinary people "bear with patience the evils that they suffer," while realizing the "folly and inefficacy of turbulence."

The Reading Lesson, by Jean-François Millet.

Middle-class reformers, however, shared far more optimistic views of education. The National Society campaigned for universal education in Britain. Henry Lord Brougham (1778–1868), a key figure in the passage of parliamentary political reform acts, believed that progress would be served if working men were educated. In 1826, he founded the Society for the Diffusion of Useful Knowledge, which made available to ordinary people cheap pamphlets and other publications of "improvement literature." Brougham and his followers founded a number of schools called Mechanics Institutes, most of them short-lived, which hammered home the entrepreneurial ideal to artisans and skilled workers. But educational reform in Britain proceeded slowly, at least partially because the state provided little direction.

Religion

Religious ideals still played an important part in the middle-class view of the world, though just how much is hard to determine and, in any case, the extent varied from place to place. If disenchantment with organized religion permeated novels in England, France, and the German states, contemporary writing rarely challenged common doctrinal assumptions that closely linked Christianity and morality. Biblical references abounded even in the treatment of secular subjects because they were understood by all literate people. In the German states, as in the Scandinavian countries, the middle classes were more likely to go to church than other social groups. And throughout Europe, women manifested a much higher rate of religious observance than did men.

In Great Britain, religious faith—particularly the non-Anglican Protestant religions—bolstered the self-confidence of middle-class men and women, providing a sense that they were living as they should. Many deplored the materialism that seemed to have lured some of their own away from church. The novels of Jane Austen (1775–1817), the daughter of a clergyman, were highly successful at least partially because she affirmed that character, moral rectitude, and proper conduct, including control of the passions—in short, "respectability"—were not the preserve of wealthy landowners and titled nobles. They could also be found among the men and women of the middle class. Some of her characters were poor relations whose comportment made them as respectable (if not more) than nobles concerned only with wealth and status. In the end, her characters' behavior is the key to respectability. Virtue wins out. Austen's remarkable wit brought forward compelling characters whose struggles to do the right thing engaged contemporary readers.

The English middle class also viewed religion as a way of "moralizing" workers by teaching them self-respect. If in principle, however, religious instruction taught acquiescence to one's inferior social position, it also proved conducive to a view of earthly improvement as well. Sunday

Evening prayer in a Viennese middle-class household.

schools, which had begun to proliferate in the 1780s, helped nourish the nascent English radical movement, one that took root in the middle-class ethic of education, religion, and respectability. By mid-century, more than 2.6 million children attended Sunday schools. Middle-class proponents tended to see them as a source of moral regeneration. But in many respects, Sunday schools were the creation of the working-class communities they predominantly served. They provided the children of workers with educational, social, and recreational opportunities not otherwise available. These schools demonstrated and taught that the middle class did not have a monopoly on "respectability" and its virtues of hard work and discipline.

Secularized education, sponsored by states, only slowly undermined the role of religion in public life. In France, the Chamber of Deputies approved a law in 1833 specifying that each commune was eventually to have a primary school. Private schools operated by the clergy continued to exist, and in many places provided the only schooling. But the existence of a state system, staffed by lay teachers, gradually eroded ecclesiastical control of education, despite the Falloux Law (1850), which allowed the clergy to set up schools and restored clerical supervision of education. Most French liberals and republicans opposed a pronounced role for the Church in public life. Many were staunchly anticlerical, demanding public schools teaching secular values. In the German states, the same battle went on between ecclesiastical and secular authorities and proponents, but the established churches retained greater influence over public education. The clergy still controlled schools in Spain and the Italian states, where in 1847 Piedmont was the first to establish a ministry of public education.

Associational Life and Public Service

Clubs, societies, and other voluntary associations characterized nineteenth-century middle-class life. Some, organized exclusively for leisure activities, manifested an upper-class sense of social distinction, such as the exclusive, expensive clubs of west London and the Anglophile Jockey Club of Paris (founded in 1834). Other more modest clubs included the dueling fraternities of German universities and the sociable "circles" in French towns. Although most such groups excluded women from membership, middle-class women formed their own clubs, principally charitable associations. Outside the home, such activities were among the few public opportunities open to middle-class women.

Charitable activities emerged as an important facet of middle-class life in nineteenth-century Europe. Growing public awareness of the appalling conditions in which hundreds of thousands of workers lived engendered

Charity in the attic. A middle-class woman visits an impoverished family living in an attic apartment without furnishings or comforts. The last thing a poor family would pawn would be their mattress, a symbol of respectability.

impressive charitable efforts among people of means. Charity was more extensively organized in England than anywhere else by middle-class women, often through their churches or clubs. Many of these women came to know and respect the working-class families they assisted. Some families of industrialists took a particularly active role, viewing such works as part of their social and religious responsibilities. In 1860, there were at least 640 charitable organizations in London alone, more than two-thirds of which had been established since the beginning of the century. Moreover, the vast majority of the voluntary hospitals that existed in London at that time had also been founded since 1800.

In the first decades of the century, members of some voluntary associations, above all in England, debated the unsettling social changes engendered by large-scale industrialization. As social distance between the middle class and workers increased and the latter escalated their economic and political demands, middle-class associations joined manufacturers, merchants, and members of the professions in northern English industrial towns in seeking to "moralize" the lower classes by shaping their conduct (for example, by encouraging them to attend church and to drink less). In this way, they sought to undercut radical political movements that drew upon working-class discontent. Some of these associations brought together men and women of different religions and political views. These organizations published newsletters, put on exhibitions, participated in town celebrations, and received deputations from Sunday School Union associations and other groups.

LIBERALISM AND ITS AMBIGUITIES

During the first half of the century, the middle class found a creed that reflected its confidence and economic aspirations. Nineteenth-century liberalism was more than an economic and political theory: it was a way of viewing the world. Liberals—the term became current in the late 1830s— shared a confidence that human progress was inevitable, though gradual. From the Enlightenment, the bourgeoisie inherited a faith in science, which they held to be a motor of progress.

Liberals and the Franchise

Liberals gradually replaced the discourse on the rights of man—which had emerged from the Enlightenment of the eighteenth century and the French Revolution—with that of the legally defined rights of the citizen or subject. They put their faith in political and social rights embodied in constitutions, defined by law, and guaranteed by the state. Middle-class electors, all of whom were male, trusted elected legislative bodies to ensure that their rights as property owners could not be trampled by monarchs and aristocrats.

But liberals wanted the franchise broadened, at least to a certain extent. They denounced electoral systems that were so narrowly constructed that they preserved noble prerogatives and only allowed the wealthiest men the franchise. The electoral system of Restoration France (1815–1830) had left only about 100,000 men eligible to vote in a population of about 25 million; the Prussian three-class franchise excluded the vast majority of the population and awarded the very wealthiest men even more electoral power. But most liberals also opposed universal manhood suffrage (although some, like James Mill, believed that workers, with improved living conditions, would ultimately prove themselves worthy of participation in British political life). Moreover, very few liberals favored extending the franchise to women. All over Europe, as franchise requirements were gradually loosened in response to pressures from the middle class, the percentage of members of representative bodies drawn from the middle class, and particularly from the legal profession, increased rapidly (see Chapter 14).

Liberals and Laissez-Faire

As the guiding philosophy of the middle classes, liberalism was less a clearly defined program than a combination of attitudes, an outlook rather than an agenda. The origins of liberal thought were closely tied to the Enlightenment's uncompromising assertion of individual freedom. The eighteenth-century philosophes had rejected the notion shared by the established churches and absolute monarchs that people were basically evil and had to be kept in line by religious and governmental constraints. Like their enlightened predecessors, classic nineteenth-century liberals believed that humanity could improve itself. But unlike some of the philosophes who had—at least briefly—placed their faith in enlightened absolutism, the first generation of economic liberals believed that non-intervention by the state would bring the greatest degree of prosperity and happiness. Governments were to do little more than protect private property.

Adopting the maxim "that government is best which governs least," liberals therefore sought to place limits on state authority. In particular, they rejected government interference in the operations of the economy. Many liberals opposed protectionism—state-imposed duties on imports. They followed the theories of Adam Smith (1723–1790), who wrote *The Wealth of Nations* (1776). Their motto was "laissez-faire," which meant for them government noninterference in the workings of the economy, the "hidden hand" that engendered change. Smith had argued that the unrestricted functioning of the free economy would ensure the pursuit of private interests. This would, in turn, serve the public interest by creating more wealth. Smith contended that a new social hierarchy would emerge if the economy were allowed to follow its natural course. With their investments augmenting the general good, businessmen would supplant nobles and churchmen as the men to whom ordinary people deferred.

Along with Smith's theories of laissez-faire, utilitarianism formed another cornerstone of the entrepreneurial ideal. Jeremy Bentham (1748–1832) was its most influential exponent. In 1776, he had posited that laws should be judged by their social utility, or whether or not they provided "the greatest good for the greatest number" of people. His famous standard question about any law or government institution was "does it work?" Bentham's utilitarianism reflected the relatively decentralized government of Britain and a pervasive belief among the king's subjects that a government that made few demands and that was efficient was an essential part of the "liberties" of freeborn Britons. "Every law is an evil," Bentham argued, "for every law is an infraction of liberty."

Adam Smith's successors gradually made a science out of speculations about the operations of the economy, insisting that the laws they postulated about the development of capitalism were based on scientific certainty. For inspiration and proof they pointed to the continued economic and social transformation of Britain. Both laissez-faire liberalism and utilitarianism were optimistic, secular doctrines based on the belief that society would continue to improve in the manufacturing age. The theories of Smith and Bentham had a great impact on British businessmen. The social status of an individual increasingly came to be measured in terms of utility.

In 1817, the British economist David Ricardo (1772–1823), the son of a Dutch banker, published his influential *Principles of Political Economy and Taxation*. Ricardo assumed the existence of an "iron law of wages," which held that, if wages were left to the laws of supply and demand, they would fall to near subsistence level. This was certainly more cheering news for manufacturers than for workers. Despite Malthus' apocalyptic prediction that the population of any country would rise far faster than its ability to feed more people, many liberals continued to argue that if manufacturers were permitted to pursue private interests without any obstruction, the interests of everyone would be served.

Elected to Parliament in 1819, Ricardo became a hero to the middle class. Yet, his commentary dampened the optimism of those who thought that increased factory production spurred by mechanization would necessarily benefit everybody. Ricardo reassured liberals by insisting that the absence of government intervention would contribute to economic growth. The "hidden hand" of the economy would allocate resources, with the bulk of entrepreneurial profits going into employers' pockets. Through the Political Economy Club, the *Westminster Review*, first published in 1824, and newspapers, the ideas of Mill and Bentham reached a wide audience. Liberal economists earned academic appointments at the University of

Edinburgh and the University of London (founded in 1828 by religious dissenters). Economic liberalism also found proponents in France.

Middle-class entrepreneurs did not necessarily agree on what economic policies they favored, however. In the 1820s, Tory governments bored the first holes in the wall of protectionism by reducing the duty collected on Baltic timber, which had been kept high to favor Canadian exporters, and by establishing sliding scales for tariffs tied to the price of wheat in England. On the other hand, many French industrialists demanded that the government maintain high tariffs to keep out British manufactured goods and machinery. Merchants living in port cities usually wanted lower trade barriers. Businessmen everywhere demanded improved transportation networks.

Liberals also demanded the "freedom of work," that is, that nothing constrain free agreements between employers and their workers. Many manufacturers concurred, demanding that states keep unions and strikes illegal, despite the decline of wages in many trades. Employers wanted the market to determine wages, because, with the supply of workers far outnumbering demand, remuneration could, as Ricardo predicted, be kept relatively low. And many industrialists opposed state-imposed limits to their authority within the workplace.

Many liberals also believed that a strong state compromised political freedom. British liberals, in particular, held that the French Revolution had culminated in Jacobin state centralization and Napoleonic despotism. Continental liberals remained more "statist," accepting a more active role by government, particularly in the German states, and in Spain, where they relied on a strong state to counteract the influence of nobles and clerics.

State Intervention

Gradually many liberals came to believe that liberty sometimes had to be tempered in a rational way, with the state assuming through the police some authority over individual interests. Middle-class fears of popular insurgency, which they identified with the French Revolution, also could outweigh distrust of a powerful state. During the first half of the century, when property seemed threatened by the economic and political demands of the lower classes, the middle class wanted to hold the line against the "lower orders." Anxious bourgeois were reassured by the greater professionalization of police forces both in France and in Britain, where Home Secretary and future Prime Minister Robert Peel organized the unarmed municipal police, who became known as "bobbies" in his honor. Berlin had only 200 policemen in 1848 to watch over a population of 400,000, which they did with military precision and occasional brutality. In British, German, French, and Italian cities, and in the United States, as well, civilian national guards were established, with membership limited to property owners. Such forces supplemented the police, gendarmerie (national police), and regular army units, and could be called upon to quell local disturbances and protect the propertied classes.

Those calling for more state intervention in economic and social matters did not just have the repression of the lower orders in mind. By about 1830, some Western European liberals became aware of some of the unfortunate social consequences of classical liberalism and pure utilitarianism. They did not object to the wealthy becoming even wealthier, but they did worry that the poor were becoming too poor. The tendency of mechanized production to drive skilled workers' wages downward worried some liberals. Some of Bentham's followers, among others, began to espouse government-sponsored social reform.

Liberals crusaded against slavery (see Chapter 14), which still existed in parts of Africa, Asia, and the United States. During the 1820s and 1830s, ladies' associations distributed campaign literature and organized a boycott of sugar produced by slaves in the West Indies. In 1833, about 100,000 women signed petitions against slavery. Such campaigns reflected the development of Evangelical Christianity (Protestants such as Methodists who aggressively taught the necessity of a personal conversion experience and the authority of the Bible), which had blossomed during the last two decades of the eighteenth century in Britain.

The question of education revealed some of the ambiguities of classic liberalism. Most liberals considered education an essential means of developing the individual. Many poor children attended Sunday schools, charity, or "dame" schools (essentially drop-off centers that charged a fee, allowing working women to leave their children), but government intervention seemed necessary in order to upgrade the education poor children received at these schools. The result of the application of laissez-faire theory, however, was that the state did no more than provide inspectors for schools built by towns or parishes that could afford to do so or that had received random government grants.

Disillusioned by the contrast between liberal ideals of individual self-development and the effects of laissez-faire, the English philosopher John Stuart Mill became a forceful proponent of greater government intervention on behalf of social reform. Mill, who began learning Greek at the age of three at the insistence of his domineering father, James Mill, believed in the capacity of the free individual to develop his or her abilities. "Among the works of man, which human life is rightly employed in perfecting and beautifying," he wrote, "the first in importance surely is man himself." While the younger Mill's *On Liberty* (1859) argued that the individual is the best judge of his or her own interests, and that the individual develops by expressing free choices, it also marked a retreat from pure economic liberalism even in its spirited defense of individual freedom.

John Stuart Mill's espousal of causes such as that of women's rights and union campaigns for economic justice in itself reflected this evolution of liberalism away from laissez-faire principles to a political theory concerned with economic, social, and political justice. Unlike his father, Mill was appalled that relatively few people of means seemed concerned about the awful conditions of working-class life. "I confess I am not charmed," he wrote, "with the ideal of life held out by those who think that the normal state of human beings is struggling to get on; that the trampling, crushing, elbowing, and treading on each other's heels, which form the existing type of social life, are the most desirable lot of human kind, are anything but disagreeable symptoms of the phases of industrial progress." In his *Principles of Political Economy* (1848), the younger Mill called on the state to assist workers by encouraging their cooperative associations. Mill rejected Smith's cheery optimism about the "hidden hand."

ROMANTICISM

The middle classes' emphasis on individual freedom found expression not only in economics and politics but also in literature, art, and music. This emphasis on individual fulfillment makes it even more difficult to define romanticism precisely, as it was a complex and varied movement, an attitude toward art and indeed life itself. Many of the key figures themselves insisted that they best represented the classical heritage.

Romanticism, emphasizing imagination and emotion in personal development, had begun to emerge as a literary, artistic, and musical movement late in the eighteenth century. Romanticism was part of a rebellion against the formality of classicism, such as the emulation of Greek and Roman styles characteristic of eighteenth-century court and aristocratic life, and which had been revived during the French Revolution.

Romantic Literature and Painting

The high Enlightenment of the middle decades of the eighteenth century had emphasized rational inquiry as the means of discovering truth. But in the last stage of Enlightenment thought, Jean-Jacques Rousseau's "reasoned sentimentality" had made emotional development and fulfillment the center of an individual's development. Similarly, German idealism (sometimes called "pre-romanticism") stressed subjectivity. Reflecting this transition away from the rationalism of the Scientific Revolution and early Enlightenment, romanticism as a cultural style celebrated subjectivity. Romantic writers saw the arts as embodying the relationship between nature and spirit in the quest for freedom. In his essay "The Aesthetic Education of Mankind," Friedrich von Schiller (1759–1805) put it this way: "If mankind is ever to solve the problem of politics in practice, he will have to approach it through the problem of the aesthetic, because it is only through Beauty that man makes his way to freedom."

Théodore Géricault's *Portrait of an Officer of the Chasseurs Commanding a Charge* (1812).

In 1798, the English poets Samuel Taylor Coleridge (1772–1834) and William Wordsworth (1770–1850) journeyed to the rugged Lake District in northern England. There they penned a manifesto of the "new poetry" which appeared in the preface to their *Lyrical Ballads*. They called on poets to abandon the formal rules that defined the classical style and instead express their emotional response to nature. Such a contrast may be seen, for example, in the geometrically planned formal gardens of the eighteenth-century English country houses and the more natural, unkempt, overgrown gardens in which nineteenth-century romantic poets sought inspiration. Unlike scientists who might study a mountain objectively in order to discover its geological history and composition, Coleridge and Wordsworth saw mountains as wonders of nature that should best be appreciated emotionally. Moreover, during the romantic era, swooning and fainting came into vogue because they seemed to be honest expressions of emotion.

Like romantic poets, painters sought to convey feeling through the depiction of the helplessness of the individual confronted by the power of nature—gathering storms, surging seas, and immense, dark forests, portrayed with deep, rich colors. In France, Théodore Géricault (1791–1824) reached the public eye with his 1812 *Portrait of an Officer of the Chasseurs Commanding a Charge,* an almost worshipful painting of a Napoleonic officer in the heat of battle. Géricault became obsessed with shipwrecks, a subject that reflected his volatile personality. Géricault sought out real-life survivors of such tragedies in order to paint his powerful *The Raft of the Medusa* (1818–1819), based upon a shipwreck off the African coast of Senegal. Eugène Delacroix (1798–1863), arguably the greatest romantic painter, depicted historic stories as in his *Liberty Leading the People* (1830) in a heroic manner, heightening dramatic, even tragic scenes by portraying movement and intense colors intended to overwhelm the emotions of the viewer.

German romantics like Friedrich von Schiller defined freedom as the unleashing of the senses and passion of the soul. They searched for the "heroic genius" who fulfills himself in spite of constraints placed on him by the state, religion, or societal convention. Johann Wolfgang von Goethe (1749–1832) evoked the impassioned battle raging in the mind of the heroic individual. Goethe's hero in *Faust* (1790) struggles to make his way against a society that fails to understand him.

Like Faust, romantic writers and artists were, at least at the beginning, literary and academic outsiders. Many were loners, without established professional positions, overwhelmed by what they considered the tragedy of their unrequited search for individual fulfillment because less-gifted people did not comprehend their brilliance. Romantics bared the suffering of their souls. The English poet Percy Bysshe Shelley saved his loftiest description for himself in the "Hymn of Apollo":

The young Johann Wolfgang von Goethe communing with the Italian countryside.

I am the eye with which the Universe
Beholds itself and knows itself divine;
All harmony of instrument or verse,
All prophecy, all medicine is mine,
All light of art or nature;—to my song
Victory and praise in its own right belong.

Romantic Music

The romantics also believed that music, like painting, was poetry capable of releasing torrents of emotion in listeners. Whereas romantic literature sought and achieved a sharp break with the rules of classical literature, romantic musical compositions built on the traditions of the eighteenth-century masters, helping the public rediscover them. For example, music that in the nineteenth century would be considered "romantic" was often not dissimilar to earlier "sentimental" music played on flute and harp.

The compositions of Ludwig van Beethoven (1770–1827) form a bridge between the classical and romantic periods, with a foot firmly in each. Beethoven's romanticism is reflected by his perhaps unsurpassed capacity to evoke an emotional response. Beethoven, the son of an alcoholic court musician in the Rhineland town of Bonn, was a homely, isolated, brooding individual. As a young man he earned the patronage of Viennese nobles, winning spirited competitions staged by composers and performers for the entertainment of the nobles.

Before he began to lose his hearing, Beethoven's music followed classical rules of structure and harmony. The German romantic composer Richard Wagner would later say that as Beethoven became increasingly deaf, he was "undisturbed by the bustle of life [hearing only] the harmonies of his soul." Beethoven's audiences struggled to understand his music, which increasingly seemed to defy traditional structures and harmonies. An Austrian monument to Beethoven reflects the duality between classicism and romanticism: it shows the sitting composer wearing an unmistakable bourgeois coat that gives way to a Roman toga.

A critic in 1824 understood Beethoven's close connection to the development of romantic music: "It cannot be denied that he withdraws increasingly within himself. . . . He reveals only his subjective thoughts, and in his composing pays heed to nothing but his own inspiration." Another critic reacted to one of Beethoven's symphonies, "The composer, often bizarre . . . takes the majestic flight of the eagle, then he creeps along rock-strewn paths. After penetrating the soul with a gentle melancholy he immediately lacerates it with a mass of barbarous chords. I seem to see doves put in together with crocodiles!" Beethoven's symphonies and string quartets were widely played in Europe, and his sonatas helped popularize the piano. Whereas only two decades earlier Mozart had struggled to make ends meet, Beethoven enjoyed wealth and fame.

The work of the Viennese-born composer Franz Schubert (1797–1828), whose father was a Moravian peasant, further exemplified romanticism's influence on music. In particular, his compositions, which fused romantic lyric poetry and music, helped make folk songs part of instrumental musical expression. Schubert drew on Hungarian and gypsy airs. Schubert's music was performed in only one public concert in his brief life, which was cut short by typhoid, but his many operas, masses, symphonies, piano sonatas and quartets influenced the subsequent evolution of romantic music.

Although opera remained the most popular form of musical expression, depending on extravagant staging and elaborate, expensive costumes, romantic music grew in popularity during the first half of the nineteenth century. Drawing in part on the great popularity of Beethoven's symphonies, public concerts were attended by a growing number of musically educated listeners. More musicians could now make a living from their performances. During the 1840s in the German states, the conductor (who now no longer played in the orchestra himself) began to stand in front of the musicians, who were grouped in a semicircle around him. The middle classes flocked with unbridled enthusiasm to hear such virtuosos as the Italian violinist Niccolò Paganini (1782–1840). Paganini's performances, the musical effects he produced, and his frenzied appearance suggested to some observers that he was engaging in witchcraft.

Music assumed a greater role in private life. Private concerts in middle-class homes were common: in Vienna during the Carnival season before

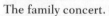

The family concert.

Lent in 1821, chamber groups and small orchestras played at 1,600 private balls. Choral societies provided opportunities for amateur musical performances, largely for the middle class, but also for workers. Nonprofessional orchestras and choruses became more common, some were simply gatherings of friends who enjoyed playing and listening to music. Piano playing became far more common in middle-class homes, often accompanied by a voice recital. More musicians earned money giving children music lessons. In this way, too, the middle class transformed cultural life in modern Europe.

CONCLUSION

During the first half of the nineteenth century, many European states were transformed in significant, lasting ways. Between 1820 and 1850, liberals and nationalists challenged the conservative post-Napoleonic settlement (see Chapter 14). Much of the support for the nationalist groups espousing national unification in the German and Italian states, as well as the massive pressure for an expansion of the electoral franchise in France and Great Britain, came from the middle class, whose diversity and common beliefs and culture we have explored in this chapter.

Of the changes that profoundly transformed the way Europeans lived, none arguably had more important social, political, and cultural consequences than the Industrial Revolution. Having begun in England in the middle decades of the eighteenth century, it accelerated in that country during the first decades of the nineteenth century. Furthermore, it spread to Western Europe in particular, but affected regions in other places as well. Amid the rapid expansion of manufacturing, many workers began, for the first time, to consider themselves a separate class exploited by their employers. The Industrial Revolution and its critics would help shape the modern world.

CHAPTER 16

THE INDUSTRIAL REVOLUTION, 1800–1850

Manufacturing on a small scale had been part of the European experience for centuries. The economy of virtually every region had depended to some extent on the production of clothes, tools, pots, and pans. Most production was carried out by men and women working in small workshops, hammering and shaping household goods, or by country women weaving or knitting clothes.

During the first half of the nineteenth century, the Industrial Revolution slowly but surely transformed the way in which many Europeans lived. In Western Europe, it became easier for entrepreneurs to raise money for investment as banking and credit institutions became more sophisticated. Dramatic improvements in transportation, notably the development of the railroad but also road improvements, expanded markets. Rising agricultural production, increasingly commercialized in Western Europe, fed a larger population. Western Europe underwent a period of rapid urbanization: the number of people living in cities and towns grew more rapidly than did the percentage of people residing in the countryside.

As the population expanded, demand increased for manufactured goods. The percentage of the population involved in industry rose. Mechanized production slowly revolutionized the textile and metallurgical industries, bringing together workers under the same roof. Manufacturers now frequently concentrated workers in large workshops and factories. Workers who had been used to setting their own schedule at home were now summoned to arrive and leave by the bell. Rural industry gradually declined and, in some regions, it had disappeared by the end of the century. Rural producers in much of France, the uplands of Zurich in Switzerland, and Ireland, among others, lost out to more efficient urban, factory-based competitors. Slowly but surely, factory production transformed the way Europeans worked and lived.

A Yorkshire coal miner.

While many contemporaries were amazed and impressed by factory production of goods and watched and rode trains in wonderment and appreciation, others were shocked at what seemed to be the human costs of such
a transformation. Poor migrants flooded into towns and cities, which burgeoned as never before. Conditions of life in the gritty industrial towns of
northern England and Scotland, Lille and Saint-Étienne in France, and
towns in the German Rhineland appalled some visitors. The Industrial
Revolution also threatened artisans, who lost no small degree of protection when guilds were abolished under the influence of the French Revolution. Mechanization, too, undercut their livelihood. And at the same
time, lurid but not inaccurate accounts of the awful conditions of workers
(men, women, and children) in factories and mines began to reach the
public. Calls for state-sponsored reform from state officials and middle-
class moralists echoed far and wide. Moreover, many skilled workers in
Western Europe not only protested harsh conditions of work and life but
began to see themselves as a class with interests defined by shared work
experience. During the 1830s and 1840s (the "hungry forties," at least the
last part of the decade when harvest failure and the potato famine engendered horrific suffering, above all in Ireland, and sent waves of desperate
emigrants to the Americas), workers began to demand social and political
reform. Proclaiming the equality of all people, the dignity of labor, and the
perniciousness of unrestrained capitalism, the first socialists challenged
the existing economic, social, and political order.

PRECONDITIONS FOR TRANSFORMATION

We have come to call the transformation of the European economy the "Industrial Revolution." It began in England and parts of Northwestern Europe during the eighteenth century (see Chapter 9), and during the first half of the nineteenth century it spread through Western Europe. Fundamental changes transformed the way goods were produced. Manual labor was replaced by that of machines. Factory manufacturing accentuated the division of labor, the specialization of manufacturing tasks first described by the British economist Adam Smith in the 1770s. It also increasingly gathered workers who had spun or woven at home or in small shops into the same workplace under the immediate direction of employers or their representatives, ultimately foremen, shop stewards, or managers.

The early histories of the Industrial Revolution tended to emphasize the suddenness of these changes; historians sought to identify the exact period of industrial "take-off" in each country, underlining the role of inventions, mechanization, and factories in the process. This led to an emphasis on "victors" and "laggards," "winners" and "losers" in the quest for large-scale industrialization, a preoccupation that blinded historians to the complexity and richness of the manufacturing revolution.

Recent work, however, has de-emphasized the suddenness of these changes. Despite the importance of inventions such as those that gradually transformed textile manufacturing, first in England and then on the continent, the first Industrial Revolution was largely the intensification of forms of production that already existed. Most industrial work still was organized traditionally, using nonmechanized production. Rural industry and female labor remained essential components of manufacturing. Not until the second third of the nineteenth century, when steam power came to be used in many different industries in Western Europe, did industrial manufacturing leave behind traditional forms of production. Handicraft production remained fundamental to manufacturing, as did domestic industry (such tasks as spinning, weaving, and product finishing done for the most part, but not exclusively, by women in the countryside). Even in England, the cradle of large-scale industrialization, craft production and rural "outwork" (work being farmed out to cheap labor) remained important until the second half of the nineteenth century. In the Paris region in 1870, the average manufacturer still employed only seven people. At mid-century, the majority of British industrial workers were not employed in factories. Moreover, there were twice as many "home workers" as workers employed in German factories.

Regardless of whether goods were produced in homes or factories, by hand or steam power, more goods were certainly being produced in the early nineteenth century. This could not have occurred without increased agricultural productivity, which sustained a dramatically larger population. In turn, an increase in population generated greater consumer demand for manufactured goods. And with the introduction of new modes of transportation, such as trains and steamships, even more goods could be produced and exported to markets that were far beyond the local bounds. The timing and degree of economic change in Europe during the first half of the century may be debated, but its impact on European society and politics over the long run seems undeniable.

Demographic Explosion

The rise in population in Europe that began in the eighteenth century accelerated during the first half of the nineteenth century. It is still debated whether this increase marked the beginning of modern population growth, or if it was part of a traditional cyclical pattern of demographic revival following yet another period of high mortality. Europe's population grew from an estimated 187 million in 1800 to about 266 million in 1850, an increase of 43 percent. Europe was then the most densely populated of the world's continents, with about 18.7 people per square kilometer in 1800 (compared to approximately 14 in Asia and less than 5 in Africa and the United States, respectively), rising to about 26.6 fifty years later. Industrializing Northwestern Europe—Britain, Belgium, and northern France—had the greatest population increases (see Table 16-1). Britain's population tripled during the nineteenth century.

TABLE 16-1. ESTIMATED POPULATIONS OF VARIOUS EUROPEAN COUNTRIES FROM 1800 TO 1850 (IN MILLIONS)

Country	1800	1850
Denmark	0.9	1.6
Norway	0.9	1.5 (1855)
Finland	1.0	1.6
Switzerland	1.8	2.4
Holland	2.2	3.1
Sweden	2.3	3.5
Belgium	3.0	4.3 (1845)
Portugal	3.1	4.2 (1867)
Ireland	5.0	6.6
Great Britain	10.9	20.9
Spain	11.5	15.5 (1857)
Italy	18.1	23.9
Austria-Hungary	23.3	31.3
The German states	24.5	31.7
France	26.9	36.5

Source: Carlo M. Cipolla, *The Fontana Economic History of Europe: Vol. 3, The Industrial Revolution* (London, 1973), p. 29.

Nonetheless, disease and hunger continued to interrupt cycles of growth well into the following century. Cholera tore a deadly path through much of Europe in the early 1830s and reappeared several times until the 1890s. During the Irish potato famine in the late 1840s, between 750,000 and a million people died of hunger in Ireland. Tuberculosis (known to contemporaries as "consumption") still killed off workers, particularly miners and porcelain workers.

Overall, however, the mortality rate fell rapidly in the first half of the century. Vaccination made smallpox, among other diseases, somewhat rarer. Municipal authorities in some places paid more attention to cleanliness, sewage disposal, and the purity of water supply, although the most significant improvements did not come until later in the century. Sand filters and iron pipes helped make water more pure; in 1851, engineers completed the first English reservoir near Manchester, although it would not be put into full use until fifteen years later.

Life expectancy increased in all classes. Individuals surviving their first years could anticipate living longer than their predecessors. Fewer women died young, thus prolonging the period during which they could bear children. Furthermore, wives were less likely to suffer the loss of their partner during this same period, and therefore were more likely to become pregnant. Yet, poor people—above all, urban residents—remained far more vulnerable than people of means to early death because of illness. In Liverpool, working-class life expectancy was only fifteen years, although that fact is somewhat misleading because it includes infant and child mortality—half of all children born to the poorest families died before the age of five. In Eastern and Southern Europe, mortality and birthrates continued to be quite high until late in the century.

Despite the fact that infant mortality rates remained high until the 1880s, the gradual decrease in the death of children created a younger population. The chances of a baby surviving his or her first year of life rose because of rudimentary improvements in sanitation, such as a safer water supply and waste disposal. The practice of "wet-nursing," in which urban families farmed out babies to women in the countryside to nurse them and which traditionally took a heavy toll on infants because of illness and accidents, slowly declined. Among the factors that explain this evolution are the increased availability of fresh milk (with, toward the end of the century, the awareness that it must be sterilized) and a shift in medical and public opinion that emphasized health risks to the newborn from wet-nursing.

The decline in mortality, particularly among infants, preceded and encouraged a fall in the birthrate in Western Europe. With more adults surviving childhood, the subsequent decline in birthrates had much to do with choice. The French birthrate, in particular, gradually fell, then plunged dramatically beginning with the agricultural crisis of 1846–1847. Many farming families had fewer children so that inheritance would not be spread too thin.

Europe also enjoyed nearly a century of relative peace, broken only by the Crimean War (1853–1856), the Franco-Austrian War of 1859, and the wars of Prussia against Denmark (1864), Austria (1866), and France (1870–1871). Wartime population losses could be made up more quickly than before. A Swedish bishop, then, was not wrong to describe the causes of his overwhelmingly rural country's rise in population during the first half of the century as "peace, vaccine, and potatoes."

In some places, population growth in overwhelmingly agricultural regions outstripped that in areas slowly being transformed by manufacturing. This was the case in some of the German states; for example, the population of Pomerania grew faster than that of the industrializing Rhineland town of Düsseldorf. Furthermore, the population of Norway, which had virtually no industry at all besides handicraft production, boomed. In England, by far the most industrialized nation on earth, the rural population also increased by half, rising from 6.6 million in 1801 to 9.9 million in 1851, with the number working the land continuing to rise until the 1850s.

The Expanding Agricultural Base

Agricultural production sustained the rise in population (although more easily in Western than in Eastern or Southern Europe). It also permitted the accumulation of capital, which could be reinvested in commercialized farming or in manufacturing. Capital-intensive production (larger-scale and market-oriented farming) underlay the agricultural revolution. More land gradually came under cultivation as marshes, brambles, bogs, and heaths gave way to the plow. Between 1750 and 1850, 6 million acres—or one-fourth of all the country's cultivable land—were incorporated into larger farms in Britain. In France, migration to the city by peasants from economically marginal rural regions facilitated the consolidation of plots, as the smaller parcels of land they left behind often were bought up by neighbors, who added to their holdings.

Farm yields increased in most of Europe. England produced almost three times more grain in the 1830s than in the previous century. The elimination of more fallow land (land left untilled for a growing season so that the soil could replenish itself) also increased agricultural productivity. Some farmers did well by raising cattle or specializing in vegetables and fruits for the burgeoning urban market. Farmers increased yield by using more intensive agricultural techniques and fertilizers, which, in turn, accentuated demand for sturdier manufactured agricultural tools.

During the first half of the century, continental visitors to England were surprised to find that, in contrast to the world they knew, relatively few small family farms remained. In 1870, about 1,200 families owned a quarter of all of the land in England and Wales. With the ongoing consolidation of plots, the number of rural people dependent on wage labor for survival rose. Farm work in 1831 remained the largest single source of adult male employment in Britain, employing almost a million men. Thus, the English countryside was populated by a relatively small number of "gentlemen" of great wealth who owned most of England, many yeomen (independent landowners and tenant farmers of some means), and a vast proletariat (workers depending upon wage labor) of landless laborers.

On the continent, there was not as much consolidation of land as in England, but there too productivity rose as more land was brought into cultivation and fertilizers became more widely used. French agricultural production rose rapidly after 1815, as northern farmers with fairly large plots began to rotate their crops three times a year. This allowed them to diversify crops and to produce more. In the south, where land was of generally poorer quality and subdivided, many landowners planted vineyards near the Mediterranean coast, although what they produced hardly caused the owners of the great vineyards of Burgundy or the Bordeaux region to lay awake at night worrying.

In Central and parts of Eastern Europe, too, a modest increase in agricultural production occurred with the gradual commercialization of agriculture. In the German states, agricultural productivity rose more than twice as fast as the population between 1816 and 1865, although large-scale capitalist agriculture could be found only in Prussia and Hanover. Prussian agricultural productivity rose during the first half of the century by 60 percent, at least partially because of improved metal plows and other farm implements, as well as because of information disseminated by the 360 agricultural societies that had been formed there by mid-century. Elsewhere, too, the planting of root crops and new crop rotation, the enclosure of common land, and an expansion in arable land enhanced productivity. As in Western Europe, reclamation expanded the amount of land under cultivation; and as in Britain and France, root crops, such as turnips and the potato, added nutrition to the diet of the poor.

In contrast, Russian agriculture had changed little since the sixteenth century. The rich Black Earth region, covering the middle Volga River area and much of Ukraine, still was considerably undeveloped. While grain exports increased during the period, Russian farms could barely feed the empire's huge population in good times and was grossly inadequate in bad times. Serfdom shackled Russian farm productivity, which probably even declined during the first half of the century as landowners imposed harsher conditions on serfs. This made it even more difficult for Russian manufacturing to develop.

Trains and Steamboats

Besides the growth in population and the expansion of the agricultural base, remarkable improvements in transportation—including the development and use of railroads and steamboats—also contributed to the expan-

The opening of the Stockton and Darlington Railway in 1825.

sion of the market for goods and the transformations of the Industrial Revolution. The first railroad train began hauling coal to the northern English port of Stockton in 1820, and the first passenger train began service between Liverpool and Manchester in 1830. (It was macabre testimony to the novelty of the train that the British minister of commerce was run down and killed by a train after stepping out of a carriage.) Gradually embankments, tunnels, and bridges transformed the countryside; railway stations became centers of urban life (see Map 16.1). An industrialist underscored the economic and social consequences of the railroad when he wrote that "the locomotive is the hearse which will carry absolutism and feudalism to the graveyard."

The railroad's development served as a significant catalyst for investment, catching the imagination of the prosperous middle class, which identified the railway with progress that could be seen, heard, and experienced. Private investment completely financed British railways during this period. Whereas earlier investments in businesses had been largely the preserve of patricians, smaller companies undertaking railroad construction attracted middle-class investors. Railway booms accustomed more middle-class people to the benefits, but also to the risks, of investment.

The building and operation of railroads also brought other benefits to the expanding economy as well. Railroad construction provided many jobs, as well as spurring the metallurgical industry, since every line required a good many bridges, countless railway cars, and other materials. Rail transport reduced shipping costs by about two-thirds, dramatically increasing consumption and, in turn, production. Railway construction also brought continental states into the realm of economic decision making; in France, the government and private companies cooperated in building a railway system. In Belgium and Austria, the railway system was state-owned from the beginning (see Map 16.2).

Railroads also provided the means for middle-class families to travel more than ever before simply for the pleasure of visiting family and

MAP 16.1 PRINCIPAL BRITISH RAILWAY LINES, 1851   Railway lines criss-crossed Britain in 1851.

friends. This in turn also led to transformations in the economy and society. In Britain, passenger service accounted for two-thirds of railway profits. Railroad companies were quick to divide their cars into first, second, and third-class service, although at first luxuries were limited to foot-warmers in winter. For people of more modest means, second- or even

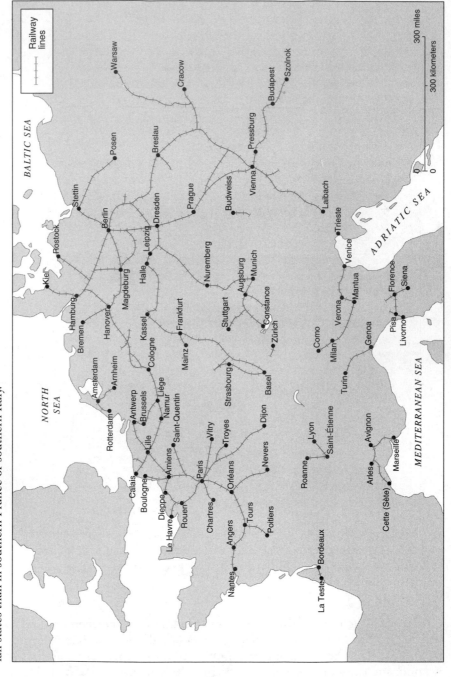

MAP 16.2 PRINCIPAL CONTINENTAL RAILWAY LINES, 1851   More railway lines existed in the north than in the south of Europe, as industrialization proceeded more quickly in northern France, Belgium, the German states, and the northern Italian states than in southern France or southern Italy.

Honoré Daumier's *Third Class Carriage*.

third-class carriages (so-called "penny a mile" travel, with train wagons not sheltered from the elements until the mid-1840s) had to suffice. English seaside resorts attracted middle-class visitors and some craftsmen and their families. Trains ran to German health spas and casinos, whose clientele a century earlier had been limited to princes and noblemen.

There was also good news on oceans and rivers. In 1816, a steamship, combining steam and sail power, sailed from Liverpool to Boston in seventeen days, halving the previous time for the journey. Steamboats, which began to operate on Europe's rivers in the 1820s and 1830s, also revolu-

The Great Western leaving Bristol in 1838 for its maiden voyage to New York. Steam power reduced the trip to nineteen days.

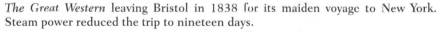

tionized travel and transport. By 1840, the transport of Irish cattle and dairy products to England alone fully engaged eighty steamships. Moreover, a constant procession of steamships travelled the Rhine from Basel, Switzerland, to the Dutch seaport of Rotterdam.

The improvement of roads also contributed greatly to the Industrial Revolution. Here, too, the story of European economic development involved continuity as much as innovation, reminding us that in some significant ways the Industrial Revolution was based upon an innovative expansion of technologies and ways of doing things that were already in place.

A VARIETY OF NATIONAL INDUSTRIAL EXPERIENCES

During this period, the Industrial Revolution affected Western Europe, and particularly Northwestern Europe, more than the countries in Southern or Eastern Europe. Furthermore, within states some regions underwent significant shifts toward a manufacturing economy (Catalonia, but not Castile in Spain; the Ruhr and Rhineland in the German states, but not East Prussia; Piedmont and Lombardy in northern Italy, but not southern Italy and Sicily; see Map 16.3).

Some regions that developed modern industries had the advantage of building on long-standing economic bases (see Table 16-2). Such was the case in Britain, where the Industrial Revolution began. It was also true in Belgium, a small, newly independent (1831) country that emerged with continental Europe's greatest concentration of industry, mechanized production, and large factories. While Belgium's northern neighbor, the once-great trading power of the Netherlands, continued its relative economic

TABLE 16-2. MANUFACTURING CAPACITY THROUGHOUT EUROPE (THOUSANDS OF HORSEPOWER OF STEAM POWER)

Country	1800	1850
Great Britain	620	1,290
The German states	40	260
France	90	270
Austria	20	100
Belgium	40	70
Russia	20	70
Italy	10	20
Spain	10	20
The Netherlands	—	10
Europe	860	2,240

Source: Carlo M. Cipolla, ed. *The Fontana Economic History of Europe: Vol. 4(1), The Emergence of Industrial Societies* (London, 1973), p. 165.

MAP 16.3 THE INDUSTRIAL REVOLUTION IN EUROPE, 1815–1860 Areas of industrial concentration and growth in Britain and on the continent.

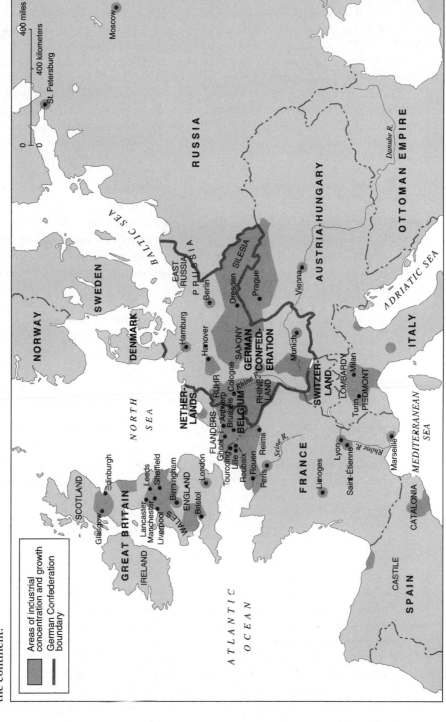

decline, Belgium seemed to offer a blueprint for rapid industrial development. Like the Netherlands, it was densely populated and urbanized, which provided demand for manufactured goods and an available labor supply. Flanders had for centuries been a center of trade and the production of fine textiles. Antwerp, linked to the North Sea by the Scheldt Estuary, remained one of Europe's major ports, generating capital for investment in industry. In 1816, the textile industry of Ghent employed more than 12,000 workers at home and in workshops. Blessed with rich coal deposits, Belgium's railroad construction advanced rapidly, thriving by transporting goods from North Sea ports toward Central Europe. Belgian manufacturing boomed.

In the Vanguard: Britain's Era of Mechanization

Why did the Industrial Revolution begin in England? Britain was well on the way to becoming the "workshop of the world" in the second half of the eighteenth century. Capital-intensive commercialized farming began to transform English agriculture earlier than anywhere else, feeding Britain's growing population. Britain was blessed with coal and iron ore deposits located near water transportation, which made it possible for raw materials to be transported to factories with relative ease. British commercial domination, built in part on its rich colonial trade, provided capital for investment in manufacturing. It also encouraged a precocious banking system, a stock exchange, and the development of credit and insurance. It was far easier to begin a company in Britain than on the continent; after 1840, any number of people could form a company in Britain simply by registering with the government. In contrast, most enterprises on the continent were self-financing, and banks were little more than small clubs of wealthy men who loaned money to the state.

The structure of British society also proved conducive to economic development. By the late eighteenth century, the entrepreneurial ethic had taken hold. There were fewer social barriers between wealthy landowning nobles, prosperous gentry, and eager entrepreneurs. Dissenters (non-Anglican Protestants) were afforded basic toleration; a good number became manufacturers.

The British government encouraged economic expansion in many ways. It adopted a general policy of non-interference in business. However, Parliament protected British manufacturers by enacting tariffs on goods imported in the eighteenth century and, when no foreign economic challenge seemed too strong, by reducing tariffs in the 1820s. Parliament also allocated funds for improving England's transportation network, which helped merchants and manufacturers. Parliamentary acts of enclosure (facilitating the consolidation of arable strips of land and the division of common lands) helped wealthy landowners add to their holdings, augmenting the productivity of their land and permitting the accumulation of investment capital.

English cotton manufacturing, gradually transformed by mechanization, led the Industrial Revolution and carried along other industries in its wake. The popularity of cotton clothing spread rapidly, allowing poor people to be more adequately clothed. Cotton fabric could be more easily cleaned and was less expensive than wool, worsted, and other materials. At the same time, cotton clothing joined silks and linens in the wardrobes of the wealthy.

The cotton manufacturer became the uncrowned king of industrial society in Britain, revered as the epitome of the successful entrepreneur who was enriching himself while embellishing Britain's reputation. Between 1789 and 1850, the amount of raw cotton imported into Britain (much of it picked by plantation slaves in the U.S. south), increased by more than fifty times, rising from about 11 million to 588 million pounds per year. During the same period, British production of cotton textiles increased from 40 million to 2,025 million yards per year. Cotton goods accounted for about half of all British exports through the first half of the century.

In the British textile industry, spinning (the operation by which fibrous materials such as cotton, wool, linen, and silk are turned into thread or yarn) had become gradually mechanized during the last decades of the eighteenth century (see Chapter 9). The advent of power looms and power weaving (the process by which threads are interlaced to make cloth or fabric) removed the last bottleneck to fully mechanized production. The number of power looms in England multiplied rapidly, from 2,400 in 1813 to 55,000 in 1829, 85,000 in 1833, and 224,000 in 1850. At the end of

Power looms in a British cotton factory, 1830.

the Napoleonic Wars, about 100,000 people in Britain worked in factories; by 1830, the number had doubled.

Industrialization in France

France was the world's second leading economy, although the wars during the revolutionary and Napoleonic periods had interrupted economic development. The revolutionary government had eliminated some hurdles for French businessmen by ending the tangle of regional customs barriers and tax differences. But in comparison with Britain, France's coal deposits were less rich and more dispersed and were far from iron ore deposits and from canals. Thus, transportation costs kept up the price of raw materials. Demand was also less in France than in Britain because the French population rose by only 30 percent during the first half of the nineteenth century, compared to that of Britain, where the population had doubled during the same period. Moreover, relatively slow urbanization helped keep down demand for manufactured goods. Yet, many French manufacturers benefited from extremely high protective tariffs, which kept out some lower-cost British goods. French agricultural production developed more slowly than that of Britain; small family farms remained common in much of France. High agricultural tariffs and the continuing existence of considerable common land did not encourage agricultural efficiency.

French banking facilities remained relatively rudimentary compared to those in Britain and the Netherlands. The primary function of the Bank of France, created by Napoleon in 1800, was to loan money to the state. The handful of private banks, which were run out of the deep pockets of wealthy families, preferred to make what appeared to be safer loans to governments. Furthermore, banks—like investors—faced unlimited liability in the event of bankruptcy. Deposit banks were specifically denied the right to invest in private industry, except for investment in companies enjoying state concessions—such as those building the railways. Even normal business transactions were complicated by the fact that more than 90 percent of payments had to be made in specie (gold or silver). Until the late 1850s, the smallest banknote was worth 500 francs (the equivalent of almost a year's earnings for an unskilled worker). Banks thus had considerable difficulty attracting ordinary depositors.

The French state shared investors' suspicions of companies of any size, limiting the number of investment "joint-stock companies" that could be created. Furthermore, many companies were cautious family firms that invested profits in land rather than seeking to expand their businesses. With many peasant families still hiding their money in their mattresses or burying it in their gardens, it was difficult to raise investment capital.

In France, as in England, textile production (primarily of woolens, cotton, and linen) provided the catalyst for industrial development. Between the end of the Napoleonic Wars in 1815 and the beginning of the economic crisis of 1846–1847, industrial production rose steadily. The production of coal tripled, that of pig iron doubled. Nonetheless, twice as many hand looms as power looms were still in operation.

The reputation of French industry, and that of Paris, in particular, still proudly rested on the production of quality items, "articles of Paris" such as gloves, umbrellas, and boots, as well as furniture, the demand for which was accentuated by the consumer revolution in the eighteenth century. During the 1830s and 1840s, workshop production—for example of barrels, pipes, and watches—expanded into many rural areas in response to increased demand, spurred by a modest level of growth in cities and market towns. Labor-intensive rural industry, marked by low capital investment, and often dependent upon countryside labor, remained essential to French economic growth.

French manufacturers benefited from increased state assistance. The July Monarchy (1830–1848) encouraged business interests, sometimes maintaining high tariffs that protected special interests—for example, those of textile manufacturers, who feared outside competition. Taxes on commerce and industry remained extraordinarily low. The government provided a decisive push in the launching of railways in France, purchasing the land and bridges along which the tracks were to pass and guaranteeing a minimum return on investments in railway development. Under Louis-Philippe, bankruptcy laws became less onerous, eliminating the humiliation of incarceration as a penalty. New legislation made it easy for investors to join together to form new companies with people to whom they were not related, or, in some cases, did not even know—hence their name, "anonymous societies." The government also pleased businessmen by crushing popular protest in the early 1830s. Furthermore, strikes, legalized in Britain with the repeal of the Combination Acts in 1824, remained illegal in France until 1864.

Industrialization in the German States

During the first half of the century, German industrialization lagged behind that of Britain and France. The multiplicity of independent states, the labyrinth of tolls and customs barriers, a veritable financial gauntlet through which any wagon or boat carrying merchandise had to pass, and virtual monopolies held by guilds over the production and distribution of certain products undercut manufacturing. Furthermore, the German states remained as a whole overwhelmingly rural, with the percentage of rural population barely declining at all between 1816 and 1872. Furthermore, the harvest failure and subsequent agricultural depression of 1846, compounded by the Revolutions of 1848, temporarily stopped German economic development, like that of France, cold in its tracks.

Yet, beginning in the mid-1830s, textile manufacturing developed in the three most demographically dynamic regions—the Rhineland, Saxony, and

Silesia (see Map 16.3). Berlin emerged as a center of machine production. Coal mining and iron production developed in the Ruhr Basin in western Prussia, which had half of the coal riches of the entire continent. The Prussian state appointed directors to serve on the boards of private companies, brought technical experts from Britain to help develop industries, encouraged technical education, and founded associations for the encouragement of industrialization. In the 1840s, the Bank of Prussia began operation as a joint-stock credit bank, providing investment capital, the lack of which limited industrial development in the other German states.

The German states took a major step toward an expansion of commerce and manufacturing when they formed the Zollverein, a customs union, in 1834 (see Map 16.4). The Zollverein was the brainchild of economist Friedrich List (1789–1846), a tanner's son who became an outspoken proponent of railway building. List argued that the German states had been "robbed of almost all attributes of nationality by earlier divisiveness," and "so desperately needs internal unification of its limbs." Calling a customs

Map 16.4 The Zollverein (German Customs Union), 1834   States and cities within the German Customs Union. Led by Prussia, it was the first attempt by the German states to reduce customs duties and to coordinate economic activity.

union and railway building the "Siamese twins" of economic expansion, List proposed in 1819 the abolition of all tariffs within the German states, although, unlike many other liberal economists, he insisted that protective tariffs be raised to shield German industries from British imports. List, a fiery advocate for the political unification of the German states, believed that only through tariff reform could Germans save themselves from being "debased to be carriers of water and hewers of wood for the Britons . . . treated even worse than the downtrodden Hindu." The Zollverein included four-fifths of the territory of the German states. It contributed modestly to German economic and industrial growth, expanding markets for manufactured goods.

In the Ruhr, young Alfred Krupp (1812–1887) began to manage his late father's small steel manufacturing firm in Essen at the age of fourteen. Krupp travelled through other German states to study manufacturing. Returning to his factory, he served, in his words, as "clerk, letter-writer, cashier, smith, smelter, coke-pounder, [and] night watchman at the converting furnace." In 1832, his firm nearly closed for lack of business. Even after visiting France and England in search of new ideas, business was so bad in 1848 that he melted down the family silver in order to pay his workers. Finally, an order from Russia arrived for machinery to produce knives and forks, followed by another for steel springs and axles for a German railway. Krupp's company produced high-quality machine parts and steel tools. In 1851 at the Crystal Palace in London, he exhibited axles for train coaches and a cannon with a gleaming cast-steel barrel (his newest and ultimately most successful product). Thereafter, Krupp's steelworks became enormously and ominously successful, turning out guns of increasing size and quality.

Sparse Industrialization in Southern and Eastern Europe

Eastern and Southern Europe remained sparsely industrialized, hampered by inadequately developed natural resources. Governments took little interest in encouraging economic growth. And entrepreneurs faced the difficulty of raising investment capital in what were overwhelmingly poor agricultural societies. There were regional exceptions, to be sure: the increasingly mechanized textile production of Piedmont and Lombardy in northern Italy and Catalonia in Spain, and pockets of industrialization in Bohemia and near Vienna.

Industrialization in Spain was slowed by inadequate transportation and laws that discouraged investment. Lacking navigable rivers, Spain also suffered the absence of a railway system until after mid-century. A commercial code in 1829 established the right of the state to impose a veto over any proposed association of investors. Following the continent-wide economic crisis in 1846–1847, the state placed banking under the control of the Cortes and forbade the creation of new companies unless investors could demonstrate that they would serve "public utility."

The social structure of the vast Russian Empire was not conducive to more than gradual economic development. Russia had a relatively tiny middle class—with only about 160,000 merchants out of a population of about 57 million people in 1854. The majority of the population remained bound for life as serfs to land owned by lords or the state. Although some serfs were skilled artisans, their bondage made it difficult for entrepreneurs to recruit a stable labor force since industrial laborers were among the hundreds of thousands of serfs who fled toward the distant eastern reaches of the empire.

Transportation in the Russian Empire was quite poor. Aside from one short line linking St. Petersburg to the Baltic Sea, in the late 1840s the only railway that existed served the iron works of the Urals. The minister of finance from 1823 to 1844, a crucial figure in state economic policy, had opposed the building of railway lines, believing that they would encourage needless travel. Moscow and St. Petersburg were joined by rail only in 1851. Serviceable roads had been built with military considerations in mind, not for commercial or industrial purposes. Rivers were used for transportation, but the boats were not steam-driven and travel was slow. Long-distance trade was thus exceptionally difficult in an empire of vast open spaces. Known coal and iron ore deposits lay thousands of miles from St. Petersburg, Moscow, and Kiev and, because of the poor transportation, could be transported to manufacturing centers only with great difficulty.

Hostility toward industrialization—and toward the West in general—remained entrenched in Russia, in part orchestrated by the Orthodox Church. Despite the development of metal processing, the machine industry, and a textile factory in St. Petersburg, industrialization was so limited in Russia that in the 1860s there still was no generally accepted word in Russian for "factory" or even "worker." Industrial workers remained closely tied to village life. The state undertook only feeble efforts to encourage industrial development. The Council of Manufacturers, created in 1828, included several merchants, industrialists, nobles (characteristic Russian entrepreneurs), professors, and a technical adviser. Trade councils were organized in the largest towns, and several national technical schools were established.

Traditional manufacturing sectors developed slowly in response to population growth. There were even some remarkable success stories. The entrepreneurs of the small town of Ivanovo, northwest of Moscow, were almost all peasants. The most successful of all was a serf who with his master's permission had constructed a textile factory late in the previous century. Adding power looms and lodging his peasant workers—2,600 by 1852—in dormitories, he had created what was by far the largest industrial enterprise in Russia. Another serf had set up a textile workshop in a village near Moscow in 1797 and then, after purchasing his freedom, had moved the operation into Moscow, producing pure calico and other less expensive cloth. He had seventy-four power looms early in the 1850s and became very wealthy.

In Russia, the number of industrial workers (of whom about a fifth were serfs) increased from 201,000 in 1824 to 565,000 in 1860. But at mid-century, there were only 2,000 power looms in the entire country (fifty times fewer than had been counted in Britain sixteen years earlier). Many spinners and weavers labored by hand without the benefit of the new machines in textile production, which remained overwhelmingly a cottage industry. Hundreds of thousands of other workers labored as tailors, shoe-makers, and in other trades essential for urban and rural life, including 300,000 boatmen who pulled barges up the Volga River, a trip of seventy-five days.

IMPACT OF THE INDUSTRIAL REVOLUTION

The Industrial Revolution, to be sure, changed the way people lived. Yet, one should not overestimate either the speed or the extent to which these fundamental changes occurred in the nineteenth century. Even in Eng-land, France, and Prussia, the three most industrialized powers, factory workers comprised between only 2 and 5 percent of the population in 1850. While there were now a handful of giant factories, the average unit of production remained small, the size of a workshop. In many places, in-dustrial workers—particularly miners—were also part-time peasants, who went home to work in the fields part of the year, or even part of the day.

Continuities on the Land

Most rural people in Europe were not landowners. Landless laborers far outnumbered any other category of the rural population, and increased dramatically in nineteenth-century Europe. Agricultural wages were falling, and rural under- and unemployment became chronic. Landlords hired on shorter-term contracts. The abolition of serfdom on the Prussian great estates east of the Elbe River increased the number of rural laborers scrambling to find low-paid farm work. The increase in population put more pressure on the rural poor. Just to survive, many landless peasants were forced to sign disadvantageous leases with their landlords. Yet, even when peasants owned land, they were by no means guaranteed a decent life, because many plots were too small to be profitable, or the land was of poor quality. In Prussia and southern Spain, the number of landless labor-ers soared as owners of small farms were unable to survive and sold off their land.

Rural protest increased in the first two decades of the nineteenth cen-tury. In 1830, a hard year, travelers found people who had died of hunger on the roads, nothing in their stomachs but dandelions. In southern and

Bread riots in England, 1830.

eastern England, many wealthy landowners had begun to use threshing machines, which left many hired hands without work. Grain passed through the rollers of these portable machines and then into a revolving drum. Threshing machines could be set up in any barn or field and operated by one or two horses. Farm workers, whose labor as threshers or "flailers" was no longer needed, began to smash threshing machines in August. Sometimes local artisans supported the protesters, and they sometimes also benefited from the tacit support of smaller landowners who could not afford the machines and were being driven out of business by their wealthier colleagues who could.

Some of the scrawled threats landowners received were signed "Captain Swing" (for example, "revenge for thee is on the wing, from thy determined Captain Swing"). Swing emerged as a mythical figure symbolizing popular justice, created to give the impression that the laborers were numerous and organized enough to force the landowners to renounce—as some did—use of the machines. "Signed on behalf of the whole, Swing," one threat warned, "This is to inform you what you have to undergo gentlemen providing you don't pull down your messhenes and rise the poor mens wages the maried men give tow and six pense a day the singel tow shilings or we will burn down your barns and you in them. This is the last notis." Authorities weighed in to make arrests, exiling some people to Australia, and executing nineteen men. Incidents of machine breaking ended in September 1832. But other incidents occurred between 1839 and 1844 in Wales when poor people attacked tollgates and tollhouses in the "Rebecca riots," which were also named after an imaginary redresser of social wrongs.

A contemporary spoof on machine breaking in Britain, 1830.

Rural poverty weighed even more heavily on the continent. The Prussian political theorist Karl von Clausewitz, travelling in the Rhineland during the brutal winter of 1817, came upon "ruined figures, scarcely resembling men, [prowling] around the fields searching for food among the unharvested and already half rotten potatoes that never grew to maturity." The further east one went in Europe, the more peasants remained fettered by obligations to lord and state. More than a hundred Russian landlords or their stewards were murdered by their peasants and serfs in two decades beginning in 1835. In 1846, peasants in Galicia in Central Europe rose up and slaughtered nobles in a bloodbath.

Russian serfs needed permission to leave their villages. In Silesia, peasant families still owed lords more than a hundred days of labor a year, for which they were to provide a team of animals; they were also obligated to repair roads and to make various payments in kind. Such peasants paid the equivalent of a third of their produce to the lord or to the state in taxes. Even when entrepreneurial landlords began commuting such payments in labor and in kind into cash, some of which they put back into their lands, such reforms did not end subsistence agriculture in parts of Central and most of Eastern Europe.

Conditions of rural life in Eastern Europe may even have worsened since the eighteenth century. Balkan peasants and Russian serfs still lived in wooden huts. People drew warmth from fireplaces during the day and from animals with whom many shared quarters at night. There were few windows because they let in wind and rain, or as in parts of France because farmhouses had been built that way to reduce the tax on doors and windows.

The rural poor of Ireland, Spain, Italy, Russia, and the Balkans ate rye bread, porridge, and vegetables such as potatoes in Northern Europe, cab-

Inside a farm in Brittany, 1844.

bage in Eastern Europe and Russia, and onions and garlic in France. For many people meat was little more than a distant memory of a wedding feast. When they could afford to eat meat at all, poor people were most likely to eat tripe, pigs' ears, or blood-sausage. Most peasants who owned animals could not afford to slaughter them. Fish was relatively rare on peasant plates, unless the peasants lived by the sea, or near a lake or pond in which they were allowed or could get away with fishing (although even the English and Scandinavian poor could afford herring, fished in enormous quantities in the Baltic Sea). Water, however contaminated, remained the drink of necessity for the poor. People in Southern Europe drank poor quality wine; Northern Europeans drank beer when they could, or cider, though both were relatively expensive.

Urbanization

The first half of the nineteenth century brought about a marked urbanization of the European population, as the percentage of people living in towns and cities rose rapidly (see Table 16-3). In 1750, two British cities had more than 50,000 inhabitants (London and Edinburgh); in 1801, there were eight, and by 1851, twenty-nine. London's population rose from about 900,000 in 1800 to 2,363,000 in 1850. At mid-century, half of the population of Britain resided in towns. Paris grew from about 550,000 in 1801 to a million inhabitants in 1846. Everywhere industrial towns grew most rapidly, but commercial and administrative centers, too, gained population.

As urban centers became ever more densely packed, industrial suburbs also developed. The urban periphery offered more available land, proximity to railways, canals, and rivers, and a ready labor supply perched on the edge of the city, where the cost of living was cheaper. Shortly before the

TABLE 16-3. POPULATION OF MAJOR EUROPEAN CITIES

City	1800	1850
London	900,000–1,000,000	2,363,000
Paris	547,000 (1801)	1,053,000 (1851)
Vienna	247,000	444,000
Naples	350,000	415,000 (1871)
St. Petersburg	200,000	485,000
Moscow	200,000	365,000
Berlin	172,000	419,000
Liverpool	77,000	400,000
Birmingham	73,000	250,000
Leeds	53,162	172,023
Manchester	25,000 (1772)	367,000

Revolution of 1830, one of French King Louis-Philippe's ministers warned that the factories and industrial workers of the periphery "will be the cord that wrings our neck one day." Several years later, a member of the Chamber of Deputies warned "the barbarians who now threaten society are not in the Caucasus, nor in the steppes of the [Russian] Tartary; they are in the suburbs of our manufacturing cities." Within cities, the European middle classes withdrew into privileged elite quarters, leaving workers and other poor people in separate, disadvantaged neighborhoods.

The further east one went in Europe, the fewer and smaller the towns. This was true because rural nobles retained control over agricultural exports and over people through serfdom, which tied peasants to the land. Furthermore, there was in general less manufacturing in Eastern Europe, and therefore fewer manufacturing towns and fewer trading ports. Russian cities remained marketing and administrative, not industrial, centers. In Austria, more than four of every five people lived in the countryside; in Sweden, nine of ten. The Russian Empire had only three cities of any size—St. Petersburg, Moscow, and Kiev; parts of Moscow were still indistinguishable from the rural world, dotted with wood or even mud huts inhabited by peasant workers.

French and German urbanization proceeded at a significantly slower pace than that of Britain and Belgium, where half the population at midcentury lived in cities and towns. In 1851, only a quarter of the French population lived in urban areas, which were defined as settlements of at least 2,000 people. Nonetheless, France did have Saint-Étienne, which was a manufacturing center in a region of coal mines, where the population rose from 16,000 in 1801 to 56,000 in 1851.

Hundreds of thousands of migrants, most of whom were poor, swarmed into cities, which had difficulty providing needed services for the mass of people and where living conditions in general were abysmal. Streets may have been better illuminated than ever before, thanks to gas lighting, but working-class districts became much more crowded. Only a fifth of the buildings in Paris were connected to the city's water supply. And even in those, few apartments above the first floor had running water (carriers hauled tubs of water up and down staircases). In 1850, there were 2 million clients at the municipal public baths for a population of slightly over 1 million—in other words, the average Parisian took two baths a year. Crimes against property increased rapidly with urban growth, especially during periods of hardship. Between 1805 and 1848, indictable offenses in England and Wales multiplied by six, although part of this dramatic jump may reflect the result of better policing, and thus reporting, as many towns established police forces for the first time. To the upper classes, rapid urban growth itself seemed threatening during the first half of the century.

Migration and Mobility

As more people died than were born in most large cities, immigration of peasants and unskilled workers (usually young people from regions of marginal agricultural production) accounted in almost every case for urban growth. Thus, only about half of the residents of London and Paris and only about a quarter of those in the even more rapidly growing northern English industrial towns had been born there.

Most migrants moved to town because they knew someone there, usually relatives or friends from home who might be able to help them find a job, and perhaps put them up until they found a job and their own place to live. Within large cities, people tended to live in the same neighborhood as others from their regions, such as the sooty "Little Ireland" in the midst of the largest factories of Manchester in which many of the 35,000 Irish of the city lived in cellars, or the infamous Irish "rookery" of St. Giles in central London. The discrimination faced by the Irish in London was reflected in literature, such as in Elizabeth Gaskell's *North and South* (1855), where the villains are Irish, and in surveys of working-class life, such as the *Condition of the Working Class in England* (1844), in which the Rhineland German Friedrich Engels (1820–1895) described "the southern facile character of the Irishman, his crudity, which places him but little above the savage, in contempt for all humane enjoyments."

Between 1816 and 1850, at least 5 million Europeans booked passage across the seas, particularly during the "hungry 'forties," which struck Central and Eastern Europe, as well as Ireland, particularly hard. One and a half million people of Ireland's population of approximately 8 million left their homeland between 1835 and 1850, particularly during the potato famine in the late 1840s. An Irish migrant to London remembered:

I had a bit o' land, yer honor, in County Limerick. Well, it wasn't just a farrum, nor what ye would call a garden here, but my father lived and died on it—glory be to God!—and brought up me and my sister on it. It was about an acre, and the taties was well known to be good. But the sore times came, and the taties was afflicted, and the wife and me—I have no children—hadn't a bit nor a sup, but wather to live on, and an igg or two. I filt the famine a-comin'. I saw people a-feedin' on the wild green things. . . . The wife and me walked to Dublin . . . and we got to Liverpool. Then sorrow's the taste of worruk could I git, beyant oncete 3 [shillings] for two days of harrud porthering, that broke my back half in two. I was tould, I'd do betther in London, and so Glory be to God! I have—perhaps I have.

Following the Irish, the largest group of emigrants were Germans. After 1820, Norway sent more emigrants to the United States than the number of people remaining in the country in that year. Many more families and individuals began the trek toward a port of departure, such as Bremen or Le Havre, than actually sailed for a new life. Hundreds of thousands of Russian migrants pushed toward the eastern reaches of the empire in the quest for land.

The growth in manufacturing and improvements in transportation expanded the distance people could travel to find work. Seasonal migration took men greater distances to work in towns and cities during the warmer months of the year, while their wives cared for the children and whatever land they might have at home. Before mid-century, seasonal workers may have accounted for as much as a third of the workforce.

INDUSTRIAL WORK AND WORKERS

In 1811–1812, glove makers in Nottingham, England, smashed a thousand stocking-frames that deprived them of work. One of their leaders— perhaps fictitious—was a man called Ned Ludd, a legendary figure. Machine-breaking "Luddites" yearned for a return to the old economic and social order, before mechanization. Two ways of looking at the world clashed: the tradition by which people of means were assumed to help take care of the poor, and the liberal social order that assumed that if landowners could save money by using threshing machines, it was logical to do so.

The English novelist Charles Dickens dubbed the grim, sooty industrial cities of England "Coketown." After completing his novel *Hard Times* (1854), an account of working-class life, Dickens wrote that "one of Fiction's highest uses" is to "interest and affect the general mind in behalf of anything that is clearly wrong—to stimulate and rouse the public soul to a compassionate or indignant feeling that *it must not be.*"

Dickens was not alone in criticizing some of the effects of capitalism. Middle-class socialists and workers themselves began to attack some of the consequences of large-scale industrialization. The growing awareness among some workers that they formed a class apart followed directly from their growing sense that they were particularly vulnerable to the vicissitudes of capitalism.

Gender and Family in the Industrial Age

Not only men found jobs as industrialization proceeded, but women as well were employed in many of the industries, both rural (where their labor had long been predominant in cottage industry) and urban, that were expanding during the industrial age. Female labor remained central to large-scale industrialization. While there were a number of important predominantly male industries, such as iron production, the leather trades, building, and mining, women did work in these industries as well. Thus, in the 1840s, about 6,000 women worked in English mines. The workforce in the textile industry (above all, lacemaking) was to a great extent female. In France, women accounted for 35 percent of the industrial workforce in 1856 and for almost half of textile workers. In Lancashire in northern England, more than a third of all married women worked in textile mills.

Although important social continuities from the preindustrial age remained, wage labor altered family life and the structure of local communities. Wage labor made young women and men less dependent on their parents, enabling many to marry earlier. But marriage still remained to some extent an economic relationship and some couples delayed wedlock until both partners could accumulate the skills or assets to maintain an independent household. A sharp rise in illegitimate births (in Paris, about a third of all births) seems to have been another effect of the rise in employment opportunities and somewhat higher wages affecting unmarried couples in so-called "free unions," or common-law marriages. But illegitimate births also reflected the loneliness and vulnerability of single women arriving in the big city, in many cases no longer influenced by village mores or even forced to marry by their parents.

In Western European nations, domestic service remained the largest category of female occupations at mid-century, employing in Britain 1.3 million women, nearly 40 percent of women workers. Twenty-two percent were employed in the textile industry, which was the second largest employer of women. Working up to eighteen hours a day, servants slept under staircases and in attics, but ate relatively well. They had a higher rate of literacy than did working-class women in general and better prospects of marrying above their social class.

Country women spun and wove wool, linen, and cotton; sewed, embroidered, and knitted stockings by hand; and worked in fields or gardens, while looking after children. On the continent, even in areas of relatively prosperous farming, cottage industry still provided women with work during the winter, allowing country people to maintain the traditional rural family economy well into the nineteenth century. Rural women also continued to work as wet nurses for babies sent to them from the cities. Urban women worked as laundresses, seamstresses, street merchants and peddlers, and some kept boardinghouses. Some middle-class women worked in commerce, some as unpaid clerks in their husbands' shops or as receptionists and secretaries in their spouse's law, medical, or notarial offices.

Although only a relatively small percentage of women's work was organized in factories, a gradual shift to larger textile and clothing workshops and factories occurred in England, above all, as well as in parts of France, Belgium, and several German states. With the expansion in power-loom weaving, many women with experience as cottage laborers found employment in textile mills. Although the place of cottage work remained strong, factories expanded work opportunities during the 1830s and 1840s. Women worked for about half of what their male counterparts earned. As in the preindustrial period, many, if not most, women workers were young (in one French textile town 80 percent of the women workers were less than thirty years of age) and single (including widows and spinsters).

Working-class families were presented with a dilemma: with the growth of factories and the consequent separation of home and work, women had to balance the need for the additional income factory work could provide with that of caring for young children. Many mothers would withdraw from the workforce to care for children for at least a time. But since the family economy also depended on their wages, they generally returned to work as quickly as possible.

Hundreds of thousands of women worked full- or part-time as prostitutes. Prostitution, like other trades, presented a hierarchy of conditions of life and wages, ranging from confident high-class courtesans to poor girls beckoning clients from dark doorways. Some women, including many who were married, were able to earn much more money selling sexual favors than they could earn in textile mills or in domestic service.

To moralists, prostitutes symbolized moral failure and the dangers of modern life. But it was precisely the increase in middle-class male demand for prostitution that helped swell the number of prostitutes in Europe's burgeoning cities. Governments and the middle-class men who dominated them therefore accepted prostitution as a "necessary evil." They sought to police brothels and the comportment of prostitutes in order to keep the profession hidden as much as possible from public view, while trying, by ordering prostitutes to have regular medical checkups, to limit the ravages of venereal disease.

The number of prostitutes in London was so difficult to determine that estimates for the 1840s vary from 7,000 to 80,000. In St. Petersburg, there were over 4,000 registered prostitutes in 1870. In France, many prostitutes were former servants who, after an inopportune pregnancy, now walked the streets or beckoned from doorways, trying to avoid humiliating, obligatory medical inspections because they knew they would be incarcerated if it was demonstrated that they had contracted venereal disease.

Child Labor

Children had always worked in agriculture in such tasks as caring for farm animals, scaring birds away from crops, and gleaning at harvest time. At a very young age, many had also learned to assist in domestic textile production, preparing wool for spinning, and raising silkworms. With industrialization, children came to be employed in factories, where their compact size made them adept at certain tasks, such as mending broken threads, or climbing on machinery to extract something impeding its operations. Teenage girls were considered particularly adept in calico printing. At mid-century, 28 percent of girls between ages ten and fifteen were employed; in Britain during the early 1830s, youths less than twenty-one years of age made up almost a third of the workforce.

As in cottage industry, factory work often employed entire families, with adult males supervising other family members. Children's low wages— about a quarter of what their fathers earned—nonetheless represented a significant contribution to the family economy. One man recalled "being placed, when seven years of age, upon a stool to spread cotton upon a breaker preparatory to spinning," an elder brother turning the wheel to put the machine in motion.

Factory work was often dangerous. An English factory inspector reported that the children working at a punching machine risked losing their fingers. " 'They seldom lose the hand,' said one of the proprietors to me, in explanation, 'it only takes off a finger at the first or second joint. Sheer carelessness—looking about them—sheer carelessness!' " An eight-year-old girl who worked as a "trapper" in the mine pits, opening ventilation doors to let coal wagons pass, related, "I have to trap without a light, and I'm scared. I go at four and sometimes half-past three. . . . Sometimes I sing when I've light but not in the dark. I dare not sing then."

A young girl pulling a coal wagon in the mines.

Some reformers believed that long days of labor instilled discipline, whereas idleness would turn children into sinners and criminals. But British evangelical Protestants, among others, wanted to save them from exhausting and sometimes dangerous work. A British law passed by Parliament in 1833 forced employers to start part-time schools in factories employing children, although in some cases the owners simply designated a worker to be "teacher," whether or not he could read or write very well. The 1833 Factory Act in Britain limited labor by very young children to eight hours (subsequent legislation in 1847 limited older children and women to a ten-hour day). In 1841, France's first child labor law banned factory work for children under eight years of age, limited the workday to eight hours for those eight to thirteen years old and to twelve hours for those thirteen to sixteen years old, and banned child labor at night and on Sundays and holidays. The law, however, was extremely difficult to enforce, and was routinely circumvented by employers and ignored by parents who needed the additional family income. However, the child labor law marked the first time that the French state had intervened in the relations between employers and workers.

Standards of Living of the Laboring Poor

In 1838, a British member of Parliament described a cotton mill:

> [It was] a sight that froze my blood. The place was full of women, young, all of them, some large with child, and obliged to stand twelve hours a day. Their hours are from five in the morning to seven in the evening, two hours of that being for rest, so that they stand twelve hours a day. The heat was excessive in some of the rooms, the stink pestiferous, and in all an atmosphere of cotton flue. I nearly fainted. The young women were all pale, sallow, thin, yet generally fairly grown, all with bare feet—a strange sight to English eyes.

The northern industrial cities of England attracted the attention of horrified observers. An aristocrat in 1843 described Leeds as "the mass of wickedness and mischief . . . this great and terrible wilderness . . . peopled by untutored savages." "The entrance to hell realized!" wrote the general sent to Manchester in 1839 when the government expected disturbances from thousands of unemployed and hungry workers. After seeing Manchester, an American visitor wrote in 1845, "Every day that I live I thank Heaven that I am not a poor man with a family in England." There were, to be sure, people of means in Manchester but Engels believed "that a [middle-class] person may live in it for years, and go in and out daily without coming into contact with a working-people's quarter or even with workers . . . by unconscious, tacit agreement."

The satanic mills of Manchester.

Engels sought and found the grim face of unrestrained capitalism in Manchester:

> At the bottom flows, or rather stagnates, the Irwell, a narrow, coal-black, foul-smelling stream, full of debris and refuse, which it deposits on the shallow right bank. In dry weather, a long string of the most disgusting blackish-green slime pools are left standing on this bank, from the depths of which bubbles of miasmatic gas constantly arise and give forth a stench unendurable even on the bridge forty or fifty feet above the surface of the stream. . . . Above the bridge are tanneries, bonemills, and gasworks, from which all drains and refuse find their way to the Irk, which receives further the contents of all the neighboring sewers and privies . . . here each house is packed close behind its neighbor and a bit of each is visible, all black, smoky, crumbling, ancient, with broken panes and window-frames. The background is furnished by old barrack-like factory buildings. . . . [Beyond] the background embraces the pauper burial ground, the station of the Liverpool and Leeds railway, and, in the rear of this, the Workhouse, the "Poor-Law Bastille" of Manchester, which, like a citadel, looks threateningly down from behind its high walls and parapets on the hilltop, upon the working people's quarter below.

Elizabeth Gaskell's popular novel *Mary Barton* (1848) has the subtitle "A Tale of Manchester Life." The novel was criticized when it was published for being hostile to mill owners, but a magazine recommended the novel to its middle-class readers: "Do they want to know why poor

men . . . learn to hate law and order, Queen, Lords and Commons, coun-
try-party and corn-law league alike—to hate the rich, in short? Then let
them read *Mary Barton*. . . . Do they want to get a detailed insight into the
whole science of starving? . . . Let them read *Mary Barton*."

In 1846, a visitor described the environs of Saint-Étienne in France as
"monotonous and without charm; the countryside is furrowed with railroads. One encounters factories of various kinds almost everywhere, and
especially coal mines with smoking obelisks, forges of coke that give off a
thick, black smoke which can be seen from afar; it paralyses all vegetation
and gives everything a black tint. At night these blast furnaces offer a truly
astonishing spectacle, infernal to all who see the city for the first time."

Many contemporaries believed that the miserable conditions of the laboring poor in much of Europe brought increased social protest. Historians have long debated whether the standard of living for workers increased
or fell as large-scale industrialization transformed society during the first
half of the nineteenth century. The "cheerful" school of historiography has
argued that the Industrial Revolution, at least during the first half of the
century, while increasing employment and lowering the price of some
goods, almost immediately improved the way ordinary people lived. By
contrast, other historians have embraced the view that industrial capitalism was making conditions of life even worse for workers and their families as the number of people depending on their labor for economic
survival increased faster than did job possibilities and wages.

The answer to whether or not living conditions improved depends on
when, where, and who. In general, conditions of life gradually improved
for most European workers, at least partially because the employment of
women and children added to family income. Most salutary changes, however, came only after 1850, when real wages began to rise in Western
Europe.

During the first half of the century, however, the incomes of many artisans, as well as women workers, fell as trades were flooded with the end of
guild restrictions and increasing mechanized production. Women workers,
such as spinners, were often the first to experience unemployment because of the new technology. Some English agricultural laborers and Silesian hand-loom weavers went from a precarious existence to sheer misery.
Hand-loom weavers plunged into incredible poverty as their wages plum-
meted by three-quarters between 1805 and 1833. Wages in many industries
were extremely volatile; boom periods could come and go with numbing
suddenness. Even good years were broken in many industries by "dead seasons" when there was no work. In England, women who had been gradually displaced from farm work and rural spinning could not be absorbed in
factories.

Despite the fact that improved transportation made more goods available to more people, the gap between the rich and the poor increased. In
England, many middle-class heads of household earned three or four

times as much as even a skilled worker. In the late 1820s in Paris, more than three-quarters of people who died left virtually nothing to heirs, because they had nothing to leave in a will which, in any case, they could not afford to have one drawn up by a lawyer.

The poorer a family was, the greater the percentage of its income that still was spent on food, primarily bread. Poor Belgian workers at mid-century spent two-thirds of their income on food. Clothing accounted for the second largest category of expense, followed by housing. All other expenses, including heat, light, tools, supplies, and recreation, had to come out of less than 10 percent of the family income.

Yet, even fairly reliable data on wages and the cost of living leave us without a full appreciation of the vulnerability to hard times of working-class families. Fluctuations in wage levels were part of life. Industrial workers remained susceptible to the effects of economic crisis; furthermore, many manufacturing jobs were interrupted by seasonal layoffs. Most migrants no longer benefited from the kind of community support they had received during hard times in their villages. Recourse to the neighborhood pawn shop was part of the experience of the majority of urban working-class families until at least mid-century.

English workers tended to be better off than most of their continental counterparts, and were more likely to be able to read and write. On the continent, compulsory primary education existed only in Switzerland, beginning in the 1830s. However, within England, a gap existed between the situation of a skilled British worker drawn from the "aristocracy of labor," such as printers, cabinetmakers, and blacksmiths, and dockworkers or agricultural workers, who made their tea from used tea leaves and burnt crusts.

The urban poor probably lived in more miserable housing than their counterparts in the previous century. Buildings in industrial cities, built hurriedly and as cheaply as possible, quickly became dilapidated tenements. A fifth of all Liverpool residents lived in cellars; in St. Petersburg, an inspector found 40 percent of cellar housing flooded when he came around.

Many workers lived amid terrible smells from raw sewage, garbage, industrial pollution such as that caused by sulfurous smoke, and putrid rivers and streams. Warm summers brought outbreaks of serious diseases like typhus and dysentery. In Britain, one of every three people still died of contagious diseases between 1848 and 1872. Despite attempts to improve water supplies and construct sewer systems in several large British cities, the decline in mortality was barely felt in the heart of industrial cities, where tuberculosis and lung diseases were great killers. The causes of death in every city reflected inadequate diet and housing.

The most fortunate of the abandoned were left at the doors of charitable organizations, sometimes with a note such as that found in Rouen in 1831: "It is with the greatest pain that I separate myself from my son, after the great suffering I have gone through to keep him in his present state. . . . I hope to see him again as soon as I can take him back for good." Sadly, this would usually not be the case. Furthermore, foundling homes were overcrowded and notoriously unhealthy. In four towns in one Russian province, more than 90 percent of all of the children taken in by orphanages died within a few years. Human reality lay behind grim statistics.

Poor Relief

Paternalism, the tradition by which employers took some responsibility for helping their workers by providing some supplementary assistance in addition to their salaries, seemed rare in the new factory towns. But some factory owners took pride in paying higher wages, providing decent housing, and insisting that their workers' children attend school. However, such laudable efforts affected the lives of relatively few workers.

Great Britain was the first state to have a national policy of poor relief. Against the background of the French Revolution and economic hardship, justices of the peace met in the village of Speenhamland in 1795 to consider ways of caring for the poor. They agreed to supplement the wages of laborers with funds generated from property taxes ("poor rates"). Doles were based on the price of bread and the number of dependents for whom each head of a poor family had to provide. But the "Speenhamland system" had the drawback of encouraging landowners to pay lower wages, while assuring them of an inexhaustible supply of cheap field hands. It also may have encouraged poor families to have more children, as payments were adjusted to family size.

The Poor Law Amendment Act of 1834 ended the Speenhamland system. It established residential workhouses in which poor people without jobs would be incarcerated. Its rationale was "to make the workhouses as like prisons as possible . . . to establish therein a discipline so severe and repulsive as to make them a terror to the poor." Towns enforced laws

Starving Irish families besiege a workhouse.

against begging in order to force the unemployed poor into workhouses. When families were taken in, husbands were separated from their wives, children from their parents, and all were herded into dormitories. Inmates were forced to work at simple tasks, wearing clothes someone else had worn, eating dreadful food, and chafing under the biting commands of petty tyrants. The stigma of being impoverished was such that one influential official tried to stop the ringing of church bells at pauper funerals. Seven years later, despite organized opposition and although application of the law varied greatly, more than 200,000 people were workhouse inmates in Britain. Still, charitable institutions dispensed more assistance than the workhouses established by the Poor Law of 1834.

The Question of Class Consciousness

During the first half of the nineteenth century, many workers began to consider themselves members of the working class. They began to think of themselves as having interests that were different from those of their employers. They began to have a sense of community based on a belief in the dignity of labor. This class consciousness did not spring up overnight, and it is difficult to fix a certain point in time when it did develop. Moreover, some recent historians have even questioned the entire concept of a unified class consciousness, given the fact that there were great differences in skills, work experience, and productivity among workers in different countries and even among workers in the same country, region, or industrial city, and between male and female workers. They stress the other identities that continued to be important to workers, such as those of family and motherhood, cultural identities (Flemish, Venetian, Welsh), religious adherence, village and neighborhood solidarities, or use of leisure time, most of which had little or nothing to do with a worker's conditions of work or material interests. Nonetheless, it is useful to discuss class consciousness as a way of understanding the perceptions of many workers and the emergence of workers' movements, even if all workers were not conscious of themselves as a class.

Urban artisans were the first workers to begin to express class consciousness, in the sense of identifying themselves as part of a community, sharing the frustrations and goals of other workers. This process occurred very early in the nineteenth century in England, in the 1830s in France, in the 1840s in the German states, and later in other countries.

Large-scale industrialization had deleterious consequences for those in many trades, threatening the control craftsmen had maintained for centuries over their work. Changes in artisanal production were a European-wide phenomenon. Artisans had traditionally organized themselves by trades into guilds, which enabled them to control entry into their trades, as well as controlling the training of apprentices and production. Shoemakers, masons, and tailors, among those in other trades, each had their own craft organizations, some on a national basis, some within a given city. Rival associations within the same trade sometimes engaged in bitter, violent battles. Furthermore, even within trades, despite some trade solidarity (for example, the handing down of "trade secrets" from master to journeyman to apprentice), all artisans did not necessarily share the same interests. Hierarchies of skill and remuneration remained. Even in the Old Regime, however, guild controls could not protect all workers from market forces (for example, from rural cottage production and from workers who avoided corporate controls by working just outside city walls).

As a number of states followed France's lead in 1791 by banning guilds in the name of economic liberalism, the number of artisans expanded rapidly because there were no legal restrictions to entering a given craft. Journeymen tradesmen, having completed their apprenticeships, were more uncertain than ever before that they would become masters and would employ their own journeymen and take on their own apprentices. In Prussia, the number of masters increased by only about half between 1816 and 1849; the number of journeymen and apprentices aspiring to a mastership more than doubled during the same period. Artisans' confraternities and trade associations (some of which governments tolerated, even if they were technically illegal) facilitated the emergence of working-class consciousness (although where they helped to maintain trade exclusiveness, they may have helped delay its emergence).

"De-skilling" reduced the income and status of workers like tailors and skilled seamstresses by taking away opportunities for them to work for piece rates and wages they had once earned. Competition buffeted artisans such as tailors as never before. Merchant-manufacturers, some of them former tailors who had been able to save some money, put work out to master and journeymen tailors, who performed a single task, such as making sleeves in return for less money than if they had tailored an entire suit. In Paris, tailors' incomes plunged during the 1830s and 1840s. Many master tailors were driven out of business or forced by necessity to become subcontractors in their trade. Mechanization also gradually began to undercut tailors. In 1836, a mob burned down a textile factory in Barcelona, denouncing machinery as "the devil's invention." Silesian hand-loom weavers were reduced to desperate poverty by mechanical looms. Movements of social protest and gradual political involvement infused communities of workers with a sense of moral struggle against economic and political forces they could not control.

Continuity with old craft traditions helped shape class consciousness. Workers' views of themselves drew upon the corporate language of the Old Regime that continued to influence workers' culture. This language gave primacy to the idea of work as a value in itself and of the community of workers as a moral entity. Many workers concluded that workers, not entrepreneurs with capital, were the source of wealth and were being exploited. Other workers also began to feel a sense of class consciousness because they suffered unemployment or reduced wages. The likelihood of children of laborers advancing beyond modest or even impoverished origins was remote. Residential patterns and leisure haunts (pubs, cabarets, music halls) contributed to solidarities among such workers.

Workers' Associations and Social Protest

Workers' associations helped shape working-class solidarity and militancy. In Britain, craft-based "friendly societies" had more than a million members in 1815. Almost 10,000 such societies existed in 1803 and more than 32,000 in 1872. Their counterparts were "mutual aid societies" or journeymen's associations in France and in the German states (most of which banned women).

Fledgling trade unions developed in Britain, particularly after Parliament repealed the Combination Acts (1799–1800) in 1824, which had forbidden unions. Members sought to protect wage rates and conditions within their trades. Yet, even in prosperous periods when workers could afford dues, less than 20 percent of workers belonged to such associations during the first half of the century, and the vast majority of these were workers in the more skilled, better-paid trades. Many of these men believed they had little in common with unskilled workers who, in any case, could not afford union dues and who lacked job stability.

Some trade associations, including a minority organized by and for women, provided assistance when a member fell sick (paid out of membership dues) and assured members that they would be spared the indignity of a pauper's grave. They also provided funds to assist workers who refused to agree to conditions imposed by employers or masters. These payments had to be made covertly because strikes remained illegal in most places. Sunday schools, attended by 2 million working-class children in Britain by mid-century, also provided a range of informal social services, such as teaching working-class children to read. They helped inculcate a sense of what the British called "respectability," but they also discouraged militancy.

Artisans led movements of social protest, first in Britain, and then in France and the German states. They had a much higher level of literacy than did unskilled workers—printers were an obvious example, but so were tailors and shoemakers, as well as many seamstresses, who were often self-educated. Literate workers read newspapers and brochures and related the news to those who could not read. The emergence of political movements seeking universal manhood suffrage (or even universal suffrage) and significant social reforms aided the development of a sense of class by emphasizing the language of "liberty, fraternity, and equality," a heritage of the French Revolution.

The period from 1820 to 1850 was arguably the most socially turbulent period in modern British history. Francis Place (1771–1854), a tailor who had been a member of one of the workers' associations sympathetic to the French Revolution, became a leader of the English workers' movement. In part influenced by the industrialist Robert Owen's cooperative philosophy, some workers began cooperative stores, hoping to put aside enough money to finance cooperative villages. Also influenced by Owen, trade unionism made considerable headway between 1829 and 1836. In the latter year, the first national union, composed of spinners, was founded. Some trade union members undertook producers' cooperatives within their trades, but most of these were short-lived.

Skilled workers joined with middle-class radicals to demand political reform. William Cobbett (1763–1835) helped galvanize radical opinion with his journal, the *Political Register.* Artisans and skilled workers led massive demonstrations in 1831 and 1832, which pressured Commons and the House of Lords to pass the Reform Bill of 1832 (see Chapter 14). By expanding the number of those eligible to vote, the Reform Bill temporarily diffused middle-class dissatisfaction. At about the same time, middle-class and working-class support for factory reform, marked by public meetings, petitions, and demonstrations, led to the acts of Parliament in the 1830s limiting work hours for children and then women. The economic depression in Britain that began in the middle of the decade, however, brought hardship, popular disturbances, and more calls for political reform.

Yet, even in Britain, the most industrial nation, major impediments limited working-class militancy. Methodism (see Chapter 10), which won thousands of converts among workers, preached discipline and the acceptance of one's fate on earth, although the total number of adherents probably was not great enough to have made much of a difference. More important, solidarities within specific trades remained stronger than those that cut across trades. Furthermore, unskilled workers lacked the organization and resources of craftsmen.

French and German artisans were arguably more militant than their British counterparts. German craftsmen desperately struggled to try to protect their trades from being flooded by newcomers. Many French workers, now seeing themselves as members of a "confraternity of proletarians," struck against employers during the July Monarchy. They also supported bourgeois republicans in their push for electoral reform, in the hope that a republic would enact reforms on their behalf. Martin Nadaud, a young mason from central France, who, like thousands of people of his region, walked to Paris every March—a journey of several weeks—for eight months' work in the capital, remembered that one day he was astonished when a gentleman stopped him on the street and invited him to a political meeting. Years later, when he had become a solidly respectable member of the Chamber of Deputies, he recounted in his memoirs: "it was the first time that a bourgeois offered me his hand."

THE ORIGINS OF EUROPEAN SOCIALISM

As large-scale industrialization gradually transformed economy and society in Western Europe, the 1830s and 1840s brought lively discussion, heated debate, and startling transformations in thought. The rapid increase in wage labor influenced the emergence of new political forces that, proclaiming the equality of all people, sought dramatic social and political change. One of the most salient results of the growing preoccupation with the condition of workers was the origins of socialism.

Utopian Socialists

Utopian socialists provided an original and far-reaching critique of the changes brought by the Industrial Revolution. Their ideas were in part shaped by their reaction against the social consequences of economic liberalism. The name "utopian" reflected their dreams of creating a perfectly harmonious way of life. But their importance comes not from their sometimes quirky theories, however intriguing they may be, but from the fact that many workers, above all in France, found an explanatory power in the critical reaction of the utopians to liberalism and capitalism. This accentuated their determination to put forward demands for social and political reform.

Socialism as a symbol of hope for the working poor, about 1848.

While most liberals relished the changes being gradually wrought by the Industrial Revolution, utopian socialists agonized over the living conditions of the laboring poor. They doubted the willingness of those enriched by the Industrial Revolution to solve what was often called "the social question," that is, the miserable living conditions of most workers. Rejecting the "egotistic" individualism of the spirit of acquisition, utopian socialists envisioned a gentle world of cooperation. In some ways children of the Enlightenment, utopian socialists were optimistic champions of the power of science and technology to construct new social and political institutions.

Count Henri de Saint-Simon (1760–1825) posited a "religion of humanity," arguing that "Religion should direct society toward the great end of the most rapid amelioration possible of the lot of the poorest class." In 1820, Saint-Simon published a provocative parable. Speaking hypothetically, he asked what the consequences for France would be if all of its dukes and duchesses, princes and princesses, bishops and priests, and other luminaries of altar, throne, and château sank in a terrible shipwreck. As tragic as that event would be, he had to admit that the loss to society would be inconsiderable. However, if France, in a similar tragedy, were to lose all of its most learned men, talented bankers, artisans, and productive farmers, the result, Saint-Simon argued, would be disastrous. The timing of his parable was unfortunate, because soon after its publication in 1820 the heir to the throne of France, the duke of Berry, fell to an assassin's knife (see Chapter 14).

Saint-Simon postulated a hierarchy, or order of status, based not on blood, but on productivity. Believing that history moves through discernible stages, Saint-Simon asserted that mankind could anticipate a future in which science would solve the material problems of humanity in harmony with an era of moral improvement. For this to happen, people of talent must be freed from the fetters of restraint imposed by uncaring, unproductive monarchs, nobles, and priests.

Both contemporary and historical appraisals of Charles Fourier (1772–1837), Saint-Simon's mystical rival, have ranged from sanctifying him as a genius of great insight to ridiculing him as a paranoid crackpot. Born to a commercial family in Besançon, Fourier claimed that at a very early age he discovered that the art of selling was the practice of lying and deception. At his father's insistence, he went off to Lyon as a young man to start a business that quickly failed. Fourier spent the rest of his life preparing a grand scheme for improving the condition of humanity. His cosmology rested upon his conclusion that history moved in great cycles toward a more perfect future. This planet's next stage would be based upon mankind's discovery that the principles of cooperation and harmony would free everyone from the repression of bourgeois individualism. Having determined that there were 810 distinct personality types, Fourier proposed that they be organized into "phalanx" communities made up of 1,620 peo-

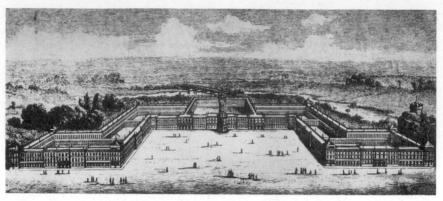

A drawing of a phalanstery contemplated by Charles Fourier.

ple, one man and one woman of each personality type. The phalanx would channel the "passions" of each person in socially productive ways, while individuals would benefit from the opportunity to express their deepest proclivities. In the "phalanstery," the place where the utopians would live, crime would become a distant memory, because criminals' supposed penchant for blood would be safely fulfilled in certain occupations, such as by becoming butchers. With everyone so satisfied, it would not matter that differences in wealth would remain. Fourier sat in his apartment everyday at noon, awaiting the wealthy man who would come, he hoped, to finance the first phalanstery.

While Fourier dreamed and waited, the wealthy British industrialist and philanthropist Robert Owen acted. Believing that education and environment could shape a spirit of cooperation, Owen turned his mill in New Lanark, Scotland, into an experiment in what he called "villages of co-operation." He provided sturdy, clean housing for his workers and established schools for their children. Like Fourier, for whom human progress demanded the emancipation of women, Owen espoused the equality of women, although he also emphasized not political rights but rather the special qualities of motherhood.

No utopian socialist had a greater popular following than Étienne Cabet (1788–1856) in France. Cabet, too, sought to apply the principles of Christianity to the extreme social problems of the day. Cabet's novel *Voyage to Icaria* (1840) became well-known in France. It described an imaginary city of wide streets, clean urinals, and social harmony, a vision of organized economic and social life so attractive that even the bourgeoisie would be converted peacefully to the principles of cooperation and association through education. Cabet's "communist" newspaper had 4,500 subscribers in the early 1840s, and almost certainly reached twenty times that number. Artisans, their livelihoods threatened by the abolition of the guilds and mechanization, were intrigued by Cabet's ideas. A few of them set sail with Cabet for the New World, founding several utopian colonies in Texas and Iowa.

Another group of utopian socialists represented the scientific, or technocratic and even authoritarian tendencies inherent in Saint-Simon's overwhelming respect for science and insistence that the state lead the way toward material progress. One Saint-Simonian, Prosper Enfantin (1796–1864)—called "Father" by his followers—left Paris for Egypt with a small group in search of the Female Messiah; one of the travelling party, Michel Chevalier, came back with the idea of building a canal through the Isthmus of Suez, thus joining the Red Sea and the Mediterranean, a project later achieved by Ferdinand de Lesseps, another Saint-Simonian.

Practical Socialists

Some later utopian socialists carried Saint-Simon's analysis a crucial step further. They relegated the bourgeoisie into the category of nonproducers, because they contributed capital, while workers seemed to them to be the real producers by virtue of their labor. Next, a generation of more practical socialists rose to prominence. In France, a group of Saint-Simonian women in 1832 founded a newspaper, *La Tribune des Femmes,* that vowed only to publish articles by women. Several of its issues proclaimed "with the emancipation of women will come the emancipation of the worker." The women who contributed to the newspaper founded an association to teach poor women, in the belief "that which men have not done it is up to us to do." Although two years later the newspaper ceased publishing, utopian socialist women undertook another newspaper with republican leanings during 1836–1838 which called for political and civil rights for women. It summarized court judgments that seemed unfair to women.

Gender discrimination led Flora Tristan (1801–1844) to socialism. When the French government confiscated her Peruvian father's fortune upon his death and declared Flora to be illegitimate because it refused to recognize her parents' marriage in Spain, Tristan had to take a series of makeshift jobs. She worked for a lithographer and then served as a companion to wealthy women. When she separated from her abusive husband, French law decreed that he receive custody of their children, although she later won custody when he started to abuse them. Tristan campaigned against women's inequality within marriage and before the law. Angered by the fact that women received only half the wages of men, Tristan linked feminism and socialism. She campaigned for female emancipation with impassioned speeches and forceful prose, arguing before largely male audiences that until women were treated equally, the working class would remain disadvantaged. Unlike earlier socialists who imagined utopian communities, Tristan called for a union of workers that would establish throughout France "workers' palaces," where workers could be educated and victims of industrial accidents would be cared for. Tristan's ideas reflected the merging of republican and socialist reformism and the shift away from utopianism in France during the late 1830s.

Louis Blanc (1811–1882) looked to the state for the improvement of the condition of the working class. Governments must, he argued, give scientists a free hand in applying their talents to the betterment of the human condition. The state must also guarantee workers the "right to work," that is, employment in times of distress and a decent wage in the face of unchecked competition. The state would provide credit to workers so that they could form producers' associations within their trades, thereby eliminating the middleman who skimmed off profits that he had not earned. Blanc believed that these workshops would serve as the basis for the reorganization of society along cooperative lines. His book *The Organization of Work* (1839) was well known to many French workers during the July Monarchy. Blanc's socialism was predicated on increasing socialist and working-class influence on government through the establishment of universal suffrage.

In sharp contrast to Blanc, Pierre-Joseph Proudhon (1809–1865) looked not to the state but to its abolition to create a better world. Proudhon, a typesetter, had grown up among landowning peasants in eastern France. He believed that the existence of the state itself was a principal reason why capitalism exploited workers. In 1840, he published a pamphlet that answered the question, "What Is Property?" with the resounding reply, "Theft." Not surprisingly, this provocative work frightened property owners in France, although Proudhon was defining property as unearned profit that came to employers from the labor of their workers,

Proudhon destroying property as seen by a hostile caricaturist.

and not property per se. Proudhon denounced the exploitation of the laboring classes by merchant-manufacturers and factory owners. Suspicious of political movements, which he argued merely substituted one elite for another, Proudhon wanted workers to organize themselves into small, autonomous groups of producers that would govern themselves. By preaching the abolition of the state, Proudhon was arguably the first anarchist.

Karl Marx and the Origins of "Scientific Socialism"

The economic and political theorist Karl Marx (1818–1883) also read the utopian socialists, but although admiring their critique of capitalist society he found them naive and "unscientific." Born in 1818 in the Rhineland, Marx studied philosophy at the University of Berlin. When in 1843 his career as a journalist came to an abrupt halt after his radical newspaper ran afoul of the Prussian government, he went to Paris. There he read the utopian socialists and histories of the French Revolution.

After Marx lambasted the French monarchy in a series of articles, the French police expelled him. He befriended Friedrich Engels, the Rhineland German whose prosperous, conservative family owned a cotton mill in Manchester, England. Marx visited industrial Lancashire, then having the greatest concentration of industry in the world. Marx's observation of evolving capitalist society led him to conclude that capitalism was but a stage in world history, which was marked by stages of class struggle. His theories of revolution were rooted in his attempts to understand the revolutions that he saw around him in Europe.

Marx applied Georg Hegel's concept of dialectical stages of the development of ideas and institutions to the flow of world history. The French Revolution had marked the definitive overthrow of feudal society, represented by the power of the aristocracy and the Church; for Marx, this was a bourgeois revolution. Just as the nobility and the bourgeoisie had battled in the eighteenth century, so the victorious bourgeoisie, who controlled the means of production (capital, raw materials, and equipment needed to produce goods), and the proletariat were in the process of fighting it out in the middle decades of the nineteenth century. English commercial capitalism had brought the bourgeoisie to power, which in turn had facilitated the growth of industrial capitalism. Here, too, by creating a proletariat, capitalists had sown the seeds of their demise. Proletarians would be the "grave diggers" of the bourgeoisie. Inevitably, socialism would replace capitalism when the proletariat would seize power. The end of private property and pure communism would follow.

But that moment, Marx thought, lay in the future, awaiting the further concentration of capitalism and the development of a larger, class-conscious proletariat aware of its historical role. Political exiles living in Paris had carried the works of some of the utopian socialists back to the German states. Marx, in contrast, called his socialism "scientific socialism," because he thought that it *had* to happen, based on the scientific analysis of class struggle.

Marx believed that a revolution by workers would be prepared by the organizational efforts of a group of committed revolutionaries like himself. Gradually winning followers, Marx formed the Communist League. In 1848, he published the *Communist Manifesto,* which ends with the resounding, provocative, "Workers of the world, unite! You have nothing to lose but your chains."

CONCLUSION

Europeans could not help but be impressed with the rapid pace of economic change during the first half of the nineteenth century. Trains truly revolutionized commerce and travel. The population of cities grew even more rapidly than did the population in general. Agricultural productivity increased in Northern Europe with capital-intensive farming. In some places, property-owning peasants gave up rural life, moving to the cities in search of industrial work. More people worked in industry than ever before. More than this, factories now dotted the landscape, although traditional workshop and cottage production, too, continued strong.

Yet, many upper-class contemporaries were worried by what seemed to be teeming, increasingly disorderly cities that were being overwhelmed by new inhabitants. The Industrial Revolution, to be sure, had generated material progress—indeed opulence for some people—but it also seemed to have increased wrenching poverty among laborers. The Revolution of 1830 in France, and liberal and national movements elsewhere in Europe (see Chapter 14), reflected not only middle-class aspirations, but the dissatisfaction of artisans in the face of large-scale manufacturing. Beginning in the 1830s, socialists called for radical political change as the only solution for redressing social inequities. Urban rebellions and full-scale political revolutions suggested that more upheavals and even social revolution might follow. To conservatives, such movements seemed unwanted and unsettling consequences of rapid change. Léon Faucher, French politician and keen observer of economic change, offered a prophetic warning in 1846. Claiming that the middle class now occupied the same position as the nobles had in the previous century, Faucher argued that the middle class could hold its place only by "raising little by little the lower classes." He predicted that if his class failed to serve as "an instrument of progress . . . it will have to contend with another 1789."

CHAPTER 17

THE REVOLUTIONS
OF 1848

The year 1848 was the year of barricades in Europe, the "springtime of the peoples." Few took note when an uprising occurred in January 1848 in Palermo, Sicily, against King Ferdinand II of Naples. But when a revolution drove Louis-Philippe from the throne of France in February, nationalists exiled in London, Brussels, Paris, and Zurich excitedly returned to their native lands, convinced that their time had come. Everything seemed possible.

The establishment of a republic in France, reminding people of the vulnerability of monarchical regimes to revolution, became the catalyst for revolutionary movements in Central Europe. In the face of clumsy attempts by governments to repress opposition by force, barricades and street insurgency forced the rulers of Prussia, Austria, and several other German and Italian states to accept more liberal constitutions when confronted by determined crowds. The existence of the Habsburg monarchy was threatened by insurrections against its rule. People in Lombardy and Venetia in northern Italy, and Czechs, Poles, and South Slavs put forth demands for autonomy. In Austria, liberals demanded political reforms, while some German speakers sought inclusion in a unified Germany. Magyar nobles forcefully asserted demands for Hungarian autonomy. Of the European powers, only Britain (the most economically and politically advanced) and Russia (the most backward) did not experience revolutions. But in Britain, the Chartist petition campaign for the extension of political rights revived in 1848 with news from the continent. In several countries, monarchs capitulated to liberal demands. In Sweden, the king appointed a new, more popular government. Danish nationalists pressured their king to grant a liberal constitution. The Dutch United Provinces received a new constitution in October 1848, and popular pressure forced the expansion of the Belgian electoral franchise.

A common process was present in the revolutions in France, the German states, and in the Habsburg lands: initial mobilizations of liberals, republicans, and nationalists coalesced into movements against existing regimes (see Map 17.1). In each revolution, the hard times of the 1840s, marked by harvest and business failures, had increased popular dissatisfaction with conservative or moderate regimes. Essentially middle-class movements drew on the support of artisans and craftsmen, members of trade organizations who believed that political change would lead to social reforms that would benefit their trades. Following initial victory, ranging from the overthrow of the Orleanist regime in France to political concessions in Austria and Prussia, however, the ensuing struggle to implement change led to a split between moderates and radicals. Then followed the gradual but convincing victory of counter-revolution during the next years.

REVOLUTIONARY MOBILIZATION

The late 1840s were a period of food shortages in Europe. This was a continent-wide crisis that included the tragic Irish potato famine. Unemployment plagued manufacturing towns. Yet, however widespread, economic discontent was not enough in itself to bring about the wave of revolutions that occurred in 1848 (if this was the case, the Irish would certainly have risen up). Rather, hard times provided an impetus to political opponents of existing regimes, which themselves were preoccupied with food riots and other popular protest.

Critics and political opponents included reformers asking for moderate political changes, such as a lessening of restrictions on the press, or, in states with elected assemblies, an expansion in the electoral franchise to allow more people to vote. German nationalists stood ready to push for the unification of the German states. Republicans and socialists demanded more radical reforms, including universal manhood suffrage and social reforms to ameliorate the condition of the laboring poor. Radical reformers also included nationalists within the Austrian Habsburg lands, principally Czechs and Hungarians, who wanted their own independent states. When a spark ignited the fires of protest, moderates and radicals joined forces in revolution. The sudden overthrow of the July Monarchy provided that spark.

The February Revolution in France

In France, the liberal Orleanist monarchy, which had been established by the Revolution of 1830, seemed to have more enemies than friends. It was caught between nobles insisting that the monarchy lacked dynastic legitimacy and republicans demanding a regime based on popular sovereignty. Republicans had begun to campaign for electoral reform in 1840–1841, as the country reeled from a disastrous harvest. France had also suffered international humiliation in 1840 after King Louis-Philippe

MAP 17.1 MAJOR REVOLUTIONS, 1848–1849 The map shows areas of rebellion and centers of revolution during the turbulent period of 1848–1849.

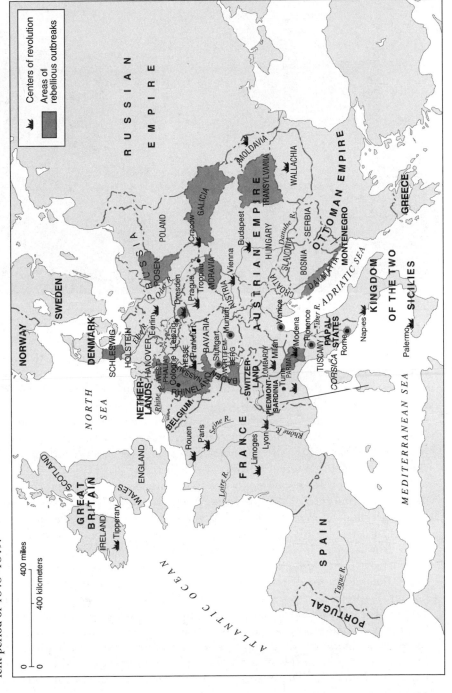

The February Revolution of 1848 in Paris.

seemed to back the Egyptian pasha, Mehemet Ali, who was rebelling against the Turkish ruler. When the other European powers, particularly Britain, opposed the pasha, fearing that his autonomy and recent conquests threatened the stability of the Ottoman Empire, France had to back down to avoid war. It was a blow to French national pride.

Republicans mounted another campaign for electoral reform, organizing banquets to rally public opinion in the midst of another cyclical economic crisis that began with the poor harvest of 1846. Workers demanded the right to vote and state assistance for their trades.

The electoral reform campaign was to culminate in a giant reform banquet on February 22, 1848, in Paris. François Guizot (1787–1874), the king's premier, banned the event. Demonstrators marched through the streets of central Paris, shouting for Guizot's resignation. The next day, large crowds assembled in the pouring rain. The Paris National Guard, drawn from the middle class, refused to disperse the demonstrators by force. Louis-Philippe dismissed Guizot. But that evening, amid continuing boisterous protests, troops panicked and fired on a crowd, killing forty people. The crowds carried the bodies through the streets, and workers (primarily craftsmen) began to construct barricades. After insurgents captured government buildings, King Louis-Philippe abdicated, hoping that the Chamber of Deputies would crown his young grandson, the count of Paris. It was too late. The victorious crowd proclaimed the Second French Republic at the town hall.

The Chamber of Deputies selected a provisional government, headed by nine well-known republicans, a list that reflected a balance between moderate liberals and well-known democrats. A crowd at the town hall pressed for the addition of two well-known socialists supported by the radicals: Louis Blanc and a worker, Alexander Martin, known as Albert. The provisional government immediately proclaimed universal manhood suffrage and abolished slavery in the French colonies.

The revolution spread to the provinces. Enthusiastic crowds planted "liberty trees," intended to commemorate a new era, a ritual borrowed from the French Revolution. Republicans were not the only political group seeking to fill the power vacuum left by the Orleanist regime. "Legitimists" wanted a Bourbon Restoration. Nor could the Orleanists be counted out, for Louis-Philippe had several able sons in exile. Both shades of monarchists could count on the support of local notables (nobles or wealthy bourgeois). Furthermore, Napoleon Bonaparte's nephew, Louis Napoleon (1808–1873), had a coterie of supporters who honored his uncle's memory. At a time when the prominent poet Alphonse de Lamartine (1790–1869) complained that "France is bored," the legend of Napoleon remained strong among many soldiers and former soldiers, peasants, and students. Popular histories of the French Revolution and the empire extolled French nationalism.

Republicans were themselves divided between staunch republicans, who had opposed the Orleanist regime all along, and moderates, who ac-

A priest blessing a liberty tree in the spring of 1848 in Paris.

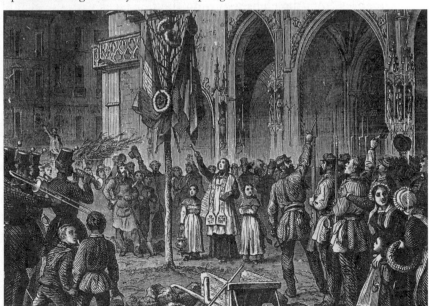

cepted the republic only after its proclamation. Socialists hoped that the republic would be but the first step toward a "democratic and social republic." Louis Blanc and other socialists were committed to the "right to work," as they put it, believing that the government should assume responsibility for providing employment in times of economic crisis, as well as encouraging or even subsidizing workers' associations.

Because of France's revolutionary tradition, the fledgling republic had to reassure the other powers of Europe that the French would not try to export their revolution, as had occurred in the 1790s. The other powers feared that the new regime might publicly support Polish independence or Italian or German nationalism, spurred on by the presence in Paris of political exiles advocating these causes. Some French nationalists called for the annexation of Savoy and Nice (parts of the kingdom of Piedmont-Sardinia), which France had claimed off and on for centuries. Volunteers formed a ragtag army with this acquisition of territory in mind. But Lamartine, the new republic's minister of foreign affairs, assured the European powers that the French had only peaceful intentions.

With elections for a constitutional assembly approaching, political interest was widespread among people previously excluded from political life. In Paris, more than 200 political clubs, mostly republican and republican-socialist, began to meet and almost that many newspapers began publication, joined by others in the provinces. When George Sand (the pen name of Amandine Aurore-Lucie Dudevant; 1804–1876), a writer and activist for women's rights, was locked out of her apartment, she discovered that all three of the neighborhood locksmiths were at club meetings. Representatives from the clubs went into the provinces with the goal of

The national workshops in Paris.

A women's club in 1848 in Paris.

wooing the overwhelmingly rural electorate away from the influence of local notables who favored a monarchy.

The economic crisis immediately cast a shadow over the new regime and widened the gap between moderate republicans and socialists. Unable to secure credit, many businesses closed. Government bonds plunged in value, and the Paris Stock Exchange temporarily shut down. Artisans were left without clients, laborers without work. More than half of the workforce in the capital was unemployed. Younger and more marginal workers were enrolled in an auxiliary paramilitary police force, the Mobile Guard, organized by the provisional government to help maintain order. Short of funds, the provisional government raised direct taxes on an emergency basis by 45 percent.

With unemployment growing and more provincial workers arriving in Paris every day looking for assistance, the provisional government opened "National Workshops," paying unemployed workers to repair roads and level hills. But there was not enough work to go around, and soon after their creation many well-off Parisians began to grumble about the new government having to support unemployed workers. The workers continued to make demands, and the government finally agreed to restrict the workday to a maximum of ten hours in Paris and twelve hours in the provinces. At the request of the socialists, the government also established the "Luxembourg Commission" to study working conditions.

By undermining existing political structures, the 1848 revolution called into question all social institutions, including the existing sexual hierarchy. In Paris, women formed a number of clubs. *La Voix des Femmes (The Women's Voice)* and several other newspapers begun by women called for

Carting away the stones that make up the revolutionary barricades, the conservatives literally and figuratively dismantle the revolution in the spring of 1848.

reforms, including equality of women before the law, the right to divorce, and better working conditions. Petitioners demanded that the republic extend the electoral franchise to women. This groundswell of demands for change frightened the upper classes.

Elections were scheduled for April to select a National Assembly to write a new constitution. The elections, in which an astounding 84 percent of the eligible voters (adult males) cast ballots, brought a conservative majority, including many monarchists, to the National Assembly in Paris. Radical republicans and socialists won only about 100 of 900 seats. The republicans were hurt by the provisional government's imposition of the surtax. Moreover, many peasants, who were voting for the first time in their lives, did not vote for the republican candidates, whom they identified with the tax. Furthermore, many rural people resented the demands of urban workers, including low bread prices and the maintenance of National Workshops. In two industrial cities, Limoges and Rouen, workers, angered by the conservative victory, seized power, at least until troops arrived several days later. Social tensions mounted in Paris and other large cities. France was a republic, but one now in the hands of an assembly dominated by conservatives, many of whom were monarchists. The euphoria of February gave way to the anxiety of the spring.

Revolution in the German States

Unlike the Revolution of 1789, that of 1848 spread rapidly from France into Central Europe. The composer Richard Wagner (1813–1883), a fervent German nationalist, had predicted in 1846: "the new Germany is ready, like a bronze statue that requires only a single blow from a hammer in order to emerge from its mold." Wagner, however, overestimated popular support of German nationalism. While liberals bided their time, young German radicals, few in number, became more restive. During the "hungry forties," in which perhaps 50,000 people died of disease in Prussian Silesia alone, riots against grain merchants and tax collectors occurred in many German states. Craftsmen formed trade associations and mutual aid societies. Although these organizations offered only minimal assistance during times of unemployment and strikes, they provided an apprenticeship in political ideology.

The differences in tactics between German liberals and radicals were clear and significant. Both groups, sometimes sharing newspaper offices, political clubs, and even associations of gymnasts and rifle enthusiasts, demanded an end to all remaining feudal obligations owed by peasants to nobles, the end of political repression, the granting of a constitution, freedom of assembly and the press, and expansion of the electoral franchise. Liberals, however, rejected universal manhood suffrage. Radicals, some of whom were socialists, believed that only revolution could move the German states along the path to a new, more liberal political order, and perhaps to unification.

The news in late February 1848 of revolution in France convinced rulers of the German states to make concessions to liberals. In Bavaria, word of the February Revolution arrived at a time when students had begun protesting the rule of Ludwig I (ruled 1825–1848). As Bavarian demonstrators built barricades and demanded a republic, Ludwig granted freedom of the press and other liberties. When this failed to placate his opponents, the king abdicated in favor of his son. The sovereigns of sev-

German students debate the ongoing Revolution of 1848.

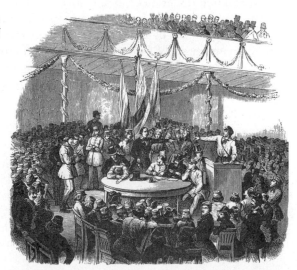

eral smaller states, including Hanover, Württemberg, Saxony, and Baden, also named prominent liberals to ministerial positions. These were the "March governments," formed not out of conviction but rather from fear of revolutionary contagion.

Everyone waited to see what would happen in Prussia and Austria, the two largest and most powerful German states. In the Prussian capital of Berlin, demonstrators agitated for liberal political reforms and in favor of German nationalism. Prussian King Frederick William IV responded by convoking the United Diet, or Parliament. On March 18, he replaced his conservative cabinet with a more liberal one. Addressing a crowd from the balcony of his palace, he promised to end press censorship and grant a constitution. He further stated that the Prussian monarchy would take the lead in pushing for a joint constitution for the German states.

But as troops moved in to disperse the throngs, someone on one side or the other fired shots. Students and workers put up barricades. The next day the army attacked insurgents, killing about 250 people. As in Paris, the shooting of civilians by troops drove the situation out of control. Women were among the casualties. The king sent the troops out of the capital and appealed for calm. Intimidated by the disturbances, he met with representatives of the crowd, authorized the formation of a civic guard, and ordered the release of imprisoned liberals. He paid homage to those killed in the "March Days" and announced that "Prussia is henceforth merged with Germany."

Most of the Berlin insurgents had been journeymen artisans, among whom tailors, cabinetmakers, and shoemakers were prominent, as in the February Revolution in Paris. Although some of them were vaguely nationalist and wanted Prussia to lead the way toward the unification of Germany, most had economic goals. During the "hungry forties," mechanized production had undercut tailors, whose handmade clothes could not compete with mass-produced wear. Cabinetmakers and shoemakers had lost the security afforded by guilds. Now these artisans demanded state protection. Workers in other German states, too, mounted protests, principally in the more industrialized Rhineland. Transport workers who had been put out of work attacked railroads and steamships on the Rhine, forcing temporary government concessions.

As in Paris, clubs and workers' associations began meeting in several German cities in March. A Club of Democratic Women and a congress of workers both demanded equal rights for women. Workers formed the first All-German Society of Labor. The German political theorist and revolutionary Karl Marx hurried back to the Rhineland from Belgium, convinced that revolution was at hand.

Disturbances broke out in the German countryside. In the Black Forest, peasants attacked noble manors. In early March, the rural poor increasingly defied laws forbidding them to use royal and noble forests, and now hunted game and pastured their flocks as they pleased. Some peasants seized and destroyed old documents that had recorded feudal obligations and forced lords to sign formal renunciations of old privileges. Outbreaks of violence occurred even in Brandenburg, where the iron will of the Prussian nobles, the Junkers, had rarely been tested. Several wary German princes formally relinquished long-held rights. Armies, militias, and police hesitated to enforce the laws or obligations that affected the peasantry for fear of sparking a bloody uprising like that in Polish Galicia in 1846. The revolution in the German states had not only quickly shaken Berlin and other capital cities but had reached the countryside as well.

Revolution in Central Europe

To most liberals and nationalists, it seemed unlikely that news of the overthrow of the Orleanists would bring revolution to the multinational Habsburg lands. There were relatively few liberals to trouble the sleep of the feeble-minded Habsburg ruler, Ferdinand (ruled 1835–1848), who could barely sign his name to the reactionary decrees put before him. The emperor decidedly did not share the belief increasingly shared by many literate people that the empire would have to be reorganized in order to become more efficient.

Liberals, most of whom were Austrians seeking political change or Czechs desiring more rights for their people, opposed Habsburg autocracy, not Habsburg rule itself. They wanted constitutional reform, the complete emancipation of the peasantry, and, like Western liberals, freedom of the press and expansion of the electoral franchise.

Although Hungary, over which Ferdinand ruled as king, had an even smaller middle class than Austria, it did have several prominent Hungarian nobles who espoused liberalism and supported constitutional reform. Their chief goal, however, was less political reform within the monarchy than the creation of an independent Hungary. Lajos Kossuth (1802–1894), a lawyer from a lesser noble family, emerged as the leader of Hungarian liberals who had been influenced by British and American constitutional liberalism. Whereas some Magyar leaders believed that Hungary could survive as a nation only within the Austrian monarchy, Kossuth saw Hungary's junior partnership with Austria as an obstacle to liberal reform and to Magyar nationalism. Most nobles were unwilling, however, to support reforms that would inevitably undercut their special privileges. Elsewhere in the Austrian monarchy, small nationalist groups, such as the Polish Democratic Society, Young Italy, and the Italian Carbonari, also demanded national independence from Habsburg rule.

News from Paris encouraged liberals and radicals in the imperial Habsburg capital of Vienna. On March 13, 1848, crowds composed largely of students and artisans demanded reform. Troops opened fire, killing several demonstrators, by now a familiar scenario. Klemens von Metternich, the

Vienna explodes in revolution in 1848.

seventy-five-year-old Austrian premier, was not optimistic: "I am not a prophet and I do not know what will happen, but I am an old physician and can distinguish between temporary and fatal diseases. We now face one of the latter. We'll hold on as long as we can, but I have doubts about the outcome." The Imperial Council advised Ferdinand to sacrifice Metternich. The guiding light and symbol of the post-revolutionary restoration left Vienna in a rented carriage, beginning his voyage to the safety of London amid the spectacle of joyous crowds parading through the streets in triumph. The crown capitulated to protesters' demands and authorized the formation of a National Guard, with a separate battalion (the Academic Legion) for Vienna's students. Workshops, similar to those in Paris, provided many workers with temporary employment.

The emperor then announced several important political concessions, including freedom of the press, a constitution, and the expansion in the narrow electorate for the Diet. But these concessions were not enough to stave off revolts in other parts of the monarchy, notably Bohemia, Hungary, and Milan. Ferdinand hurriedly granted constitutions to Austria, Moravia, and Galicia, adding lower houses to the Diets that were to be elected indirectly by men wealthy enough to pay taxes. When demonstrators protested these requirements, the crown reversed itself, creating a single house of parliament to be elected by universal manhood suffrage in each province. In the elected Assembly, the monarchy's ethnic minorities would outnumber German speakers.

Ferdinand attempted to renege on his promises and ordered the universities closed and abolished the student "Academic Legion" within the National Guard. But again barricades went up in Vienna, and again Ferdinand was forced to relent. Fearing rural rebellions upon which liberals and nationalists might capitalize, the emperor in September decreed the abolition—effective the following year—of all remaining seigneurial obligations. He also abolished the onerous *robot*, the yearly obligation of labor service—sometimes a hundred days working in the fields or on roads—that peasants owed lords. The crown would compensate the lords for their losses. Some landowners had been advocating precisely those reforms that were promulgated in the wake of the March Days, and many had already converted the labor obligation into peasant cash payments.

Meanwhile, the Hungarian nobles proceeded as if the Habsburg monarchy no longer existed. Kossuth, the liberal Hungarian aristocrat, demanded virtually complete Hungarian autonomy. He and his allies proclaimed the "March Laws," under which the delegates to the Hungarian Diet were to be elected by male property holders. The cabinet would be responsible to Hungary's Parliament. The emperor of Austria would remain the king of Hungary, but Hungary would maintain a separate army and conduct its own foreign policy. The Habsburg court, reeling from reverses on all sides, had little choice but to approve the changes. The new Hungarian government immediately proclaimed freedom of the press, established a civilian guard, and affirmed the abolition of the *robot* for peasant landowners, while maintaining it for landless peasants.

Although asserting its own autonomy from the Habsburg empire, the Hungarian Diet virtually ignored that of the other nationalities within the Hungarian domains, including Czechs, Poles, Croats, Slovenes, and Romanians. Croats, the largest of the non-Magyar nationalities in Hungary, were particularly resentful at not having been consulted. A small insurrection of students in Budapest on March 15 first challenged Kossuth's preoccupation with the interests of Hungarian landowners. The narrow electoral franchise, based on property owned and taxes paid, excluded most people of the poorer nationalities from election to the Diet. So did the requirement that each representative speak Hungarian, one of Europe's most difficult languages (though Latin remained the official language of Hungary until 1844).

The problem of national minorities confronting the Magyars became the Habsburg dynasty's hope for holding its empire together. The imperial government began to mobilize the Croats against the Hungarians, with whom the Serbs and Romanians were also angry. In March, the emperor appointed Joseph Jelačić (1801–1859) as the new governor-general for Croatia. Jelačić refused to cooperate with the Hungarians. In retaliation, the Hungarians refused to send troops to help the imperial army battle Italian insurgents. Ferdinand then withdrew the concessions he had made in March to Hungarian autonomy.

Another challenge to the monarchy, again revealing the complexity of Central Europe, came in Bohemia, populated by both Czechs and Germans. In March, Czech nationalists revolted in Prague, the capital of

Bohemia, and demanded that Bohemia, like Hungary, become an autonomous state only loosely tied to the old monarchy. They wanted the Czech language to be made equal to German, which remained the language of the army, the bureaucracy, and commerce. They also wanted to expand the borders of Bohemia eastward into Moravia, where many Czechs lived. At the same time, many Bohemian Germans looked eagerly toward possible unification with the German states to the north. In the meantime, Emperor Ferdinand and his family left Vienna for Innsbruck in May 1848, fearing that revolutionary students and workers might make him, like Louis XVI during the French Revolution, an ill-fated prisoner in his own palace.

Revolution in the Italian States

In the Italian states, March brought insurrections against Austrian rule in Lombardy and Venetia, and against conservative regimes in the other states, notably the Papal States. In Tuscany, the grand duke bowed to reformers by promulgating a constitution. King Charles Albert (ruled 1831–1849) of Piedmont-Sardinia met some liberal demands by creating a bicameral parliament to be selected by a small minority of adult males, easing press censorship, and establishing a civilian guard in Italy's strongest state. The revolutions in the Italian states were animated by different goals: bourgeois liberals called for political reform and Italian unification, radicals wanted a republic, and workers demanded some tangible benefits for themselves.

On March 18, ten thousand people marched to the palace of the Austrian governor-general in Milan carrying a petition calling for liberal reforms echoing those in Paris, Berlin, and Vienna. Barricades went up, and five days (known as the "Five Glorious Days") of bitter street fighting followed. The poorly armed people of the city, whose arsenal included medieval pikes taken from the opera house, drove away the Austrian army of Count Joseph Radetzky (1766–1858). Radetzky would become a major figure in the counter-revolution at age eighty-one (and was energetic enough to have fathered a child only two years before). Radetzky had overcome an unhappy family life and an earlier career setback brought on by his wife's debts. Now in Milan, as insurgents established a provisional republican government, he found his army weakened by the desertion of many Hungarian, Croat, and Slovene soldiers.

Suddenly, much of Italy, particularly the Austrian-controlled north, seemed on the verge of a liberal and national revolution. Other towns in Lombardy rose up against Austrian rule. Venetians forced Habsburg troops to leave their city and declared a republic. In Naples, liberals forced a constitution on King Ferdinand II (ruled 1830–1859), who had also faced a republican insurrection in January in Sicily.

Many Italian nationalists now looked to Charles Albert of Piedmont-Sardinia for leadership in the political unification of Italy. Yet, despite pleas for armed assistance from Lombardy and Venetia, Charles Albert hesitated to send his army against the Habsburg forces. He felt that if the Italian peninsula were to be unified, it should be on his terms, not as a result of rioting commoners and armies swollen by ragtag volunteers. The Piedmontese king feared the specter of popular insurgency in northern Italy. He also worried that if Piedmont launched a war against Austria, the new French republic might take advantage of the situation to invade Savoy and Nice, which French nationalists believed should be annexed to France.

The outpouring of anti-Austrian sentiment in Piedmont and the opinions of his advisers convinced Charles Albert to change his mind. The Piedmontese army, swollen by volunteers from Tuscany, Naples, and Parma, and even the Papal States, marched unopposed through Lombardy, defeating the Austrian army. But instead of crossing the Po River and cutting off Radetzky from supplies in Venetia, Charles Albert decided to consolidate his gains in Lombardy, with an eye toward annexing that territory to Piedmont.

In Lombardy itself, no one seemed able to agree on what should happen next. Wealthy landowners wanted little more than a loose union of Lombardy with Piedmont. Middle-class nationalists hoped to drive the Austrian army from Italy and establish a unified state, perhaps a moderate republic. Radicals, including many Milanese workers, were determined to have a progressive republic that would offer the poor a better life. They were surprised and disappointed when the charismatic nationalist leader Giuseppe Mazzini supported Charles Albert, instead of forcefully arguing in favor of a republic. In a hurried plebiscite, the people of Lombardy approved union with Piedmont.

The other Italian states hesitated. Some rulers mistrusted Charles Albert, fearing that he wanted to expand Piedmont at their expense. Traditional tensions between northern and southern Italy surfaced. Further-

Giuseppe Mazzini dreaming of a unified Italy.

more, the pope helped stymie the movement for Italian unification. Before the revolutions, the new pope, Pius IX (pope 1846–1878), had initiated a few modest reforms in his territories, releasing some liberals jailed by his predecessor. Some nationalists had even begun to think that Italy could be unified around papal authority. But the pope was hardly about to oppose the Catholic Habsburg dynasty on which the papacy had depended for centuries. The pontiff intended to crush republicans within the Papal States who challenged his temporal sovereignty. Pius then tried to recall his army from the north, announcing that he would not support the war against Austria.

Meanwhile, the newly elected French National Assembly unanimously approved a motion calling for the liberation of the Italian states. A French volunteer legion stood ready on the frontier, hoping that its help against Habsburg armies would bring French annexation of Savoy and Nice, as Charles Albert had feared. But facing British opposition and with enough to worry about at home, the new French republic stayed out of the Italian fray. Nonetheless, for the moment the beleaguered Austrian court seemed resigned to losing Lombardy, and willing even to abandon its claim on Venetia, provided that Piedmont would not directly annex either of them.

Benefiting from better troop morale and reinforced by soldiers arriving from Austria, Radetzky believed he could defeat the nationalist armies of the Italian states, which fought with more enthusiasm than experience and lacked effective organization and supplies. One Piedmontese commander complained that the nationalists did "Nothing, except to drown themselves with flowers, dancing, singing, shouting, and calling each other 'sublime,' 'valorous,' and 'invincible.' " Radetzky's army defeated the Piedmontese-led army of Italian nationalists at Custoza near Milan in early August 1848. The people of Milan then scornfully turned against Charles Albert, who slipped out of the city late at night and returned to his capital of Turin. From safer ground, the hesitant king negotiated an armistice with Austria, hoping in vain that he could retain Lombardy for his kingdom of Piedmont-Sardinia.

THE ELUSIVE SEARCH FOR REVOLUTIONARY CONSENSUS

The Revolutions of 1848 generated resistance almost immediately from the political and social forces that had the most to lose from their success. In Prussia, where the revolutionaries included liberals, radicals, and nationalists (and some who were all three), opposition came from the king and nobles. In the Habsburg lands, where nationalism was the most significant factor in the revolution, resistance came from the emperor and his army. In France, where liberals accepted a republic and radicals demanded reforms that would better the lives of workers and peasants, the upper classes generally opposed such changes. The ultimate success of the counter-revolution throughout Europe was aided by the revolutionaries' mixed aims, which were magnified by the anxieties of the moment. The split between liberals and radicals worked to the advantage of those who wanted a return to the way things had been before the spring of 1848.

Crisis in France

In France, where the wave of revolutions had started, the political crisis intensified as the provisional government faced competing demands. France was to be ruled by committees constituted from the Assembly until a new republican constitution could be proclaimed. On May 15, 1848, an attempt by the political clubs of the far left to dissolve the Assembly and declare a "social" republic of the people failed. The new government now began to arrest radical republicans.

With the provisional government rapidly running out of money and credibility, the Assembly voted to halt enrollment in the National Workshops, which were generating considerable opposition from the upper classes. The workers' associations and radical political clubs protested vigorously. On June 23, the Assembly announced that the National Workshops would be closed in three days. Enrolled unmarried men were to be drafted into the army and married workers sent to work in the provinces. When word of the dissolution decree leaked out that morning, Parisian workers rose up in rebellion.

For three days the "June Days" raged in the workers' quarters of central and eastern Paris. General Louis Cavaignac (1802–1857), the minister of war, put down the uprising with brutality, using regular army soldiers, the Mobile Guard, and National Guard units, some of whom arrived from conservative provinces by train and steamboat, two symbols of a new age. In the climate of social tension, fed by false rumors that the insurgents were sawing in half captured Mobile Guardsmen and raping women from the wealthy quarters, between 1,500 and 3,000 insurgents were killed, some summarily executed by National Guardsmen. Afterward, the provisional government deported more than 4,000 workers to Algeria or other colonies, and sent thousands of people to prison.

Karl Marx believed that the June Days were a dress rehearsal for a future proletarian revolution that would pit worker against bourgeois. The short, bloody civil war, however, was more complicated than that. Some younger workers, including artisans, fought alongside unskilled proletarians in the Mobile Guard, which helped put down the uprising. Some radical bourgeois supported the workers. A majority of the insurgents were artisans from working-class quarters; the typical participant was a young journeyman artisan, married, and a member of a trade association.

The Assembly immediately passed legislation to curtail the popular political movements. New laws limited freedom of the press and assembly and closed political clubs, specifically banning women from membership.

Louis Napoleon taking his oath as president of the Second French Republic, which he would then systematically destroy.

The Luxembourg Commission was quickly disbanded. Cavaignac, "the butcher of June," became provisional chief executive of the republic. The government sent new prefects and other officials into the provinces. Many who had begun their administrative careers during the July Monarchy felt only tepid support for the republic they would represent.

Attention now focused on the presidential elections instituted by the new republican constitution that was finally promulgated in November. Louis Napoleon Bonaparte quickly emerged as a leading candidate, largely because of the reputation of his uncle, Napoleon. Although one wag cruelly dubbed him "the hat without the head," it was testimony to the magic of the Napoleonic legend that Louis Napoleon had been elected to the Constitutional Assembly in April 1848, after returning from exile. Many nobles and prosperous bourgeois believed that Louis Napoleon could restore political stability. Marx wrote that because Napoleon's nephew was nothing, that is, unknown, he could appear to be everything. Even those who were against the republic could vote for him because they identified him with the empire. Cavaignac, the other major candidate, was the favorite of those who wanted to combine social order with a very moderate republic. The minister of the interior of the provisional government, Alexandre-Auguste Ledru-Rollin (1807–1874), was the principal candidate of the socialists, while the poet Lamartine, a moderate, also ran, but both were identified with the provisional government and the unpopular 45 centimes tax. Furthermore, outside of Paris many people had never heard of either Ledru-Rollin or Lamartine, while just about everyone had heard of Napoleon. Louis Napoleon also won the support of many people who were for the republic. Like his uncle, he was assumed to have good will toward all people in France and, for that matter, had published a book called *The Extinction of Pauperism* (1844). On December 10, 1848, Louis Napoleon Bonaparte was overwhelmingly elected president of the Second Republic. Some skeptics were already wondering whether he, like his uncle, would serve as the heir to a revolution, or its executioner.

The Frankfurt Parliament

In the German states, liberals and radicals gradually split as conservative forces gathered momentum. Shortly after the February Revolution in Paris, a group of about 50 German liberals, meeting in Heidelberg, invited about 500 like-minded figures to form a preliminary parliament to prepare elections for an assembly that would draft a constitution for a unified Germany. Most liberals among the organizers of the parliament wanted the German states to be united under a constitutional monarchy. Radicals, however, wanted nothing less than a republic based on universal manhood suffrage, and some of them joined a brief insurrection in the Rhineland state of Baden. To conservatives, and to some of the liberals as well, this insurrection raised the specter of "communism," amid rumors that radicals would divide the great estates among landless peasants.

The remainder of the members of the preliminary parliament announced elections for a German Constituent National Assembly, the Frankfurt Parliament. But, distinguishing their liberalism from that of the departed radicals, only male "independent" citizens in the German states would be eligible to vote, with some states using this vague qualification to exclude

The Frankfurt Parliament in 1848.

men who were propertyless. The Diet of the German Confederation accepted the plans for the election of the Frankfurt Parliament.

In May 1848, more than 800 elected delegates of the German Constituent National Assembly filed into Frankfurt's St. Paul's Church, which was decked out in red, black, and gold, the colors of early German nationalist university student organizations. State, municipal, and judicial officials, lawyers, university professors and schoolteachers comprised about two-thirds of the Frankfurt Parliament. Since about a third of the delegates had some legal training, many people began to refer to the gathering as a "parliament of lawyers," whose members debated far into the night. Almost giddy with enthusiasm as news of insurrections came from various corners of the continent, delegates spoke from the church's pulpit, confident that their deliberations would shape the future of the German states. Many were oblivious to the fact that poor acoustics rendered their speeches inaudible to people sitting in the back.

In electing Heinrich von Gagern (1799–1880) president, the delegates chose a man who symbolized the liberal and nationalist idealism of 1848. Gagern, whose father was a prosperous farmer, had fought in the Battle of Waterloo as a boy of sixteen. He had been one of the founders of the nationalist fraternities and a leader of the liberal opposition in his native Hesse. Although not of great intellect, Gagern nonetheless offered an imposing physical presence and carried out his difficult tasks with dignity. He echoed the lofty hopes of nationalists while pushing difficult and insoluble problems into the background, confidently giving the false impression that the unity of the delegates was assured and that German unification lay ahead.

The Frankfurt Parliament operated outside any state structure. It lacked the support of the rulers of Prussia and Austria, and, for that matter, of Bavaria and Württemberg. Without an army, it could not impose its will on any of the German states. Furthermore, considerable division existed over what shape the proposed unified Germany would take. Would it be a centralized state, or only an expansion of the German Confederation? How would sovereignty be defined? Who would have electoral rights?

Amid flowery speeches celebrating German national destiny, the problem of nationality immediately surfaced. Some delegates wanted Austria excluded from a united Germany, leery of the problem posed by non-German speakers within their state. Among these exponents of this "smaller German" (Kleindeutsch) solution, some wanted German unification around Protestant Prussia, fearing the inclusion of Catholic Austria. The more liberal "greater German" (Grossdeutsch) group wanted a unified Germany to include all states and territories within the German Confederation. Some wanted Austria's inclusion to encounter possible Prussian domination, as well as that of northern Protestants.

After months of debate, a compromise solution appeared to be a victory for the "smaller German" plan. On October 27, the Frankfurt Parliament voted that any German state could join the new Germany, but only if it did not bring with it territories having non-German populations. Unless Austria was willing to separate itself from Hungary, it would have to remain outside a united Germany. For the moment, the Austrian government, struggling against resistance to its authority from Hungary and the northern Italian states of Lombardy and Venetia, regarded the Frankfurt Parliament's German nationalism as another threat to its survival.

In the meantime, the United Assembly of Prussia (which had been elected by universal manhood suffrage after the March insurrection in Berlin) gathered in May 1848 to begin to draft a constitution for Prussia. Amid urban and rural unrest, the Assembly provoked the Prussian nobles in October by voting to make the civic guard a permanent institution, which challenged noble control of the army officer corps. It also abolished the Junkers' special hunting privileges and banned the use of all noble titles in anticipation of the abolition of formal class distinctions.

The Junkers, however, were not about to stand by and watch Prussia drift toward a constitutional monarchy or republic. They vowed to defend "God, the King, and the Fatherland," which they identified with their immunity from taxation and other prerogatives. Encouraged by the reaction to the June Days in France, Frederick William dismissed his liberal cabinet, sent troops to Berlin, and then in December dissolved the Assembly. He declared martial law, disbanding the civic guard. Prussian troops crushed opposition in the Rhineland and Silesia.

The Frankfurt Parliament itself put aside its liberalism when it came to the question of Poland, which had lost its independence following the Third Partition of 1795. When a Polish uprising against Prussian rule broke out, a parliamentary delegate rose to denounce Polish nationalism, insisting on "the preponderance of the German race over most Slav races" and calling for "[German] national egotism" and "the right of the stronger." The Frankfurt Parliament voted overwhelmingly in favor of armed Prussian repression of the Polish uprising, also expressing support for the Habsburg monarchy's crushing of the rebellious Czechs.

While counter-revolution gathered momentum in Prussia, the middle-class liberals of the Frankfurt Parliament, powerless to effect German unification on their own, failed to build a base of popular support among workers and peasants. They feared the lower classes perhaps even more than did the Prussian nobles: one member of the Parliament described universal manhood suffrage as "the most dangerous experiment in the world." Thus, the Frankfurt Parliament rejected craftsmen's demands for protection against mechanization and an influx of new practitioners into their trades as being incompatible with economic liberalism. Since the eighteenth century, German guilds had gradually lost their autonomy to the regulatory authority of the states. The influx of apprentices and journeymen into trades had reduced the opportunity for journeymen to become masters. By turning a deaf ear to workers' demands, the Frankfurt

Parliament lost a significant source of popular support. Furthermore, any hope of winning the allegiance of German peasants probably ended when the Parliament proclaimed that peasants must compensate their former lords in exchange for their release from remaining obligations.

Frustrated by the Parliament's moderation and general dawdling, in September several hundred workers charged into St. Paul's and tried to persuade the Parliament to declare itself a national convention of republicans. Austrian, Prussian, and Hessian troops had to rescue the delegates.

After six months of debate, the Frankfurt Parliament proclaimed in December 1848 the Basic Rights of the German People. Influenced by the American Declaration of Independence and the French Declaration of the Rights of Man, it proclaimed the equality of "every German" before the law, freedom of speech, assembly, and of religion, and the end of seigneurial obligations, and the right to private property. Jews gained legal equality. But the document would remain only a theoretical exercise unless a substantial number of states agreed to put it into effect.

The support of Prussia and/or Austria would be necessary to implement the Basic Rights of the German People and to form a united Germany. "To unite Germany without [Prussia and Austria]," would be, as a contemporary put it, "like two people trying to kiss with their backs turned to one another." But Austria's opposition to the Frankfurt Parliament became even stronger. Nationalism was antithetical to the monarchy's existence. The Frankfurt Parliament could do nothing as the Austrian government executed one of its delegates for having led an uprising in Vienna in October 1848. The Habsburgs encouraged other German states to disregard the Parliament and to proceed with their own counter-revolutions. The emperor made it clear that Austria would only consider joining a united Germany if the entire Habsburg monarchy, with its many non-German nationalities, was included. The Parliament had already rejected such a possibility.

In April 1849, the Frankfurt Parliament promulgated a constitution for a united Germany. It proposed the creation of a hereditary "emperor of the Germans" and two houses of Parliament, one representing the individual German states, the other elected by universal manhood suffrage. Austria, Bavaria, and Hanover rejected the proposed constitution.

The only chance for the constitution to succeed was to convince the king of Prussia to become king of a unified Germany. Frederick William had occasionally voiced vague support for German nationalism. The Parliament sent a delegation to Berlin to offer Frederick William the German crown. A Prussian noble shouted: "What, you bring an imperial crown? You are beggars! You have no money, no land, no law, no power, no people, no soldiers! You are bankrupt speculators in cast-off popular sovereignty!" When the head of the delegation asked for a glass of water in the royal palace, he was denied even that. Frederick William refused to accept a "crown from the gutter," a "dog collar" offered "by bakers, and butchers, and reeking with the stench of revolution."

Divided by indecision, lacking popular support, and facing Prussian and Austrian opposition, most of the Frankfurt parliamentarians returned home. The remaining delegates moved to Stuttgart in Württemberg but were dispersed in June by force. The Frankfurt Parliament, which embodied the hopes of German liberals and nationalists, ended in abject failure. Germany would not be unified by liberals.

COUNTER-REVOLUTION

The growing split between liberals and radicals in 1848 helped the cause of counter-revolution. Once middle-class revolutionaries had seized power in Paris or brought about liberal reforms in Berlin and Vienna, they resisted the demands of the lower classes for further change. Most liberals did not want a republican form of government based on universal manhood suffrage, and very few supported significant state intervention on behalf of workers. In France, some of the same men who supported the February Revolution fought against the June insurgents, cheering on the repression that followed. In Frankfurt, lawyers and professors ignored the artisans meeting in the same town. In the Habsburg lands, German liberals rejected the national claims of the Czechs and Hungarians. Each revolution generated its equivalent of the "communist" or "red scare."

Ordinary people were far more interested in concrete reforms than they were in impassioned speeches by Mazzini, for whom a unified Italian republic, not social reform, was the ultimate goal, or by members of the Frankfurt Parliament, who championed German unification. Frederick William and the Junkers were able to capitalize on the estrangement of the Prussian lower classes from the nationalists. When radical uprisings occurred in 1849 in the German states, they found little popular support and the Prussian army was ready.

The high hopes of the revolutionaries of 1848 were thus disappointed by the reality of different aims and a split between liberals and radicals. With the lack of consensus among the revolutionaries, counter-revolution now gained the upper hand in the Habsburg monarchy, the German states, and the Italian states. In the Habsburg monarchy, the initial period of optimism gave way to a grim realization of the complexity of Central Europe. Ethnic conflicts broke out among Hungarians, Croats, and Serbs, as well as between landowners and peasants.

Counter-Revolution in Central Europe

The confusion of competing national claims and rivalries within the monarchy eased the task of counter-revolution within the Austrian empire. If freedom was a central concern of the revolutionaries, it meant different things to different people. Magyar nobles wanted more autonomy for Hungary; Viennese journalists wanted freedom from press censorship;

artisans wanted freedom from the competition of mechanized production; peasants wanted freedom from labor obligations owed to nobles. Czechs demanded freedom from German domination as well as their own national freedom.

German speakers and Czech nationalists in Bohemia had different aims. Despite the opposition of Czechs, who tried to impede the elections, Germans living in Bohemia elected several German speakers to represent them at the Frankfurt Parliament. Czech nationalists, on the other hand, resisted any "Greater German" plan for German unification that would include Bohemia, fearing that this would leave them in an even more subordinate position vis à vis the Bohemian German-speaking population. Other ethnic minorities voiced similar fears.

Czechs hosted a Pan-Slav Congress in Prague in June 1848 to promote the rights of and bolster a union of Slavs within the Habsburg empire and Central Europe. The assembled national groups could agree only on their common dislike for Habsburg policies. Each group had a different plan for the reorganization of the empire, one that would favor its own interests. Finally, the Pan-Slav Congress issued a vague statement in June 1848 that condemned the Germans for having oppressed the Slavic peoples and called for the reorganization of the Austro-Hungarian monarchy into a federation that would take into consideration the rights of each nationality.

While the Pan-Slav Congress, like the Frankfurt Parliament, was discussing lofty national questions, ordinary people were hungry. On June 12, 1848, barricades went up in Prague, manned by artisans and the laboring poor. Prince Alfred Windischgrätz (1787–1862), the imperial governor, ended the insurrection on June 16, bombarding Prague with cannon fire. Meanwhile, in northern Italy, the imperial army defeated the Piedmontese forces, which had moved to assist the revolutions against Austria-Hungary, and Jelačić's Croatian army defeated Hungarian revolutionary forces.

In August, Ferdinand returned to Vienna, welcomed by the middle classes. When Ferdinand began to shut down the workshops (which had been established to provide work for the unemployed), the workers rose up, as they had in Paris, before being crushed by the bourgeois National Guard. Two months later, workers rebelled again. Expected support from Hungary for the revolutionaries did not materialize, once again demonstrating the seeming incompatibility between the goals of workers and students in Vienna and those of national movements for autonomy. Ferdinand left his imperial capital a second time, taking his court to a town in Moravia. The imperial armies under Windischgrätz bombarded Vienna, killing more than 3,000 people. Once again, enthusiastic revolutionaries proved no match for the professional armies of the established powers. The emperor imposed martial law, closed the political clubs, dissolved the National Guard, and reestablished censorship. Arrests, trials, and twenty-

Croatian regiments loyal to the Habsburg emperor attack Viennese revolutionaries, October 1848.

five executions followed. The Habsburg emperor ruled by martial law until the "Patent" of December 31, 1851, officially restored imperial absolutism. The emperor appointed a council of advisers (the *Reichsrat*), but was under no obligation to consult it.

Emperor Ferdinand appointed the noble Prince Felix zu Schwarzenberg (1800–1852) as head of government on November 21, 1848. This ended the period of political uncertainty within Austria that had followed the March insurrection. Schwarzenberg convinced the hapless emperor to abdicate his throne in December 1848 in favor of his eighteen-year-old nephew, Francis Joseph (ruled 1848–1916), who had fled Vienna during the March insurrection and turned up at Radetzky's camp in northern Italy dressed in military uniform. Placing his faith in the army, the new emperor was determined to assure the dynasty's survival and influence in Central Europe and the Italian states.

Prince Schwarzenberg enhanced the effectiveness of the imperial bureaucracy by appointing able commoners to important posts. In order to confront the Hungarian challenge and prevent any further radical uprisings in Vienna, he hoped to win the support of Hungarian moderates, albeit without recognizing the rights of nationalities. Alexander Bach (1813–1893), a lawyer of noble origins, was first appointed to be minister of justice and then of the interior and reformed the Habsburg legal system. At the same time, he implemented a system of carefully coordinated bureaucratic surveillance, spying, and repression—known as the "Bach system"—that helped root out political opposition.

But the Schwarzenberg government still had to deal with the Austrian Parliament. That body, from its exile in the town of Kremsier, had produced a draft for a liberal constitution. The constitution approved the emancipation of the peasantry and sought to establish a decentralized, multinational state, under a constitutional monarchy that would recognize all languages. It would have made ministers responsible to Parliament, which would consist of a lower house elected by universal manhood suffrage and an upper house formed by representatives of the provincial diets. But the liberal Kremsier constitution was never implemented. Schwarzenberg suddenly dissolved the Parliament in March 1849, ordered the arrest of some of the deputies, and imposed a constitution. Although it had liberal aspects, it made virtually no concessions to the non-German nationalities within the Habsburg domains and restored Hungary to its pre-1848 position. Furthermore, Schwarzenberg, with the young emperor's consent, intended to delay putting the constitution into effect until the revolutionary crisis had passed.

In April, the Hungarian Parliament refused to recognize Francis Joseph's ascension to the Habsburg throne and thus his sovereignty over Hungary. In turn, the young emperor refused to recognize Ferdinand's concessions to Hungary. Kossuth tried to rally support in Hungary against Austria. Although the Hungarian army fell back at the approach of a Habsburg army, forcing the provisional government to withdraw to the east, the tables then turned. The Hungarians defeated the imperial forces twice in the spring, taking Budapest and driving the Habsburg army out of Transylvania.

On April 14, 1849, the Hungarian Diet proclaimed Magyar independence and made Kossuth president of the newly formed Hungarian republic. As the monarchy's survival was now defiantly threatened, Francis Joseph called on the Russian tsar for help. Nicholas I responded by sending 140,000 troops into Hungary and Transylvania. Kossuth frantically implored the Frankfurt Parliament for assistance, but that body had no army. The British government disliked the Russian intervention in Central Europe, but it wanted to preserve the Habsburg monarchy as a buffer against French and, above all, Russian interests. Hungarian resistance ended in August as Russian and Austrian forces advanced. Kossuth escaped to Turkey, never to return to Hungary. Austria executed thirteen Hungarian generals for treason, imprisoned thousands of people, and imposed martial law.

In the German states, Prussian King Frederick William's scornful rejection in March 1849 of the "crown from the gutter" was the final blow to German liberals who hoped to unify Germany. Before the Prussian Parliament could approve the constitution proposed by the Frankfurt liberals, the king dissolved it on April 28, 1849, declaring a state of emergency. He then implemented new voting restrictions that greatly favored the conservatives in subsequent parliamentary elections. Henceforth, the wealthiest 3 percent of the Prussian population (paying one-third of all taxes) elected one-third of the representatives; the next wealthiest 10 percent (paying the next third of taxes) elected another third; and the remaining 87 percent of men elected the final third of the Prussian Parliament. Liberal abstentions and popular indifference further assured conservative domination of the new Parliament, which created an upper house of nobles, officials, churchmen, and other members to be selected by the king.

One by one in the other German states, the "March ministries" of 1848 fell from power as rulers abrogated constitutions granted that spring. Even where constitutions remained on the books, the counter-revolution orchestrated by rulers with the help of nobles left parliaments and assemblies with little or no effective power.

As the counter-revolution gained momentum, radicals continued to organize opposition, launching scattered insurrections, all of which failed. After being chased from his duchy in June 1849, the grand duke of Baden returned to oversee the trials of more than a thousand people. Ten thousand people fled Baden, including Karl Marx, many emigrating to the United States. The German Revolution of 1848 was over. On August 23, 1851, the German Confederation annulled the Basic Rights of the German People, the major work of the Frankfurt Parliament.

Prussian-Austrian Rivalry

Prussian King Frederick William IV had grown up with a romantic attachment to the idea of German nationalism, while never losing an iota of his commitment to the interests of the Prussian ruling dynasty. Now that the German revolutionaries had, for all intents and purposes, been swept away by the juggernaut of counter-revolution and their own divisions, he proposed the creation of a "Prussian Union." It would consist of two "unions": the larger would include the states of the defunct German Confederation, as well as non-German Austrian territories; the smaller would be a confederation of all German-speaking lands, including those of Austria. In proposing these clumsy structures, a loose confederation based both on conservative political premises and an expansion of Prussian influence, Frederick William took advantage of the insurrections against Austrian authority in Hungary and northern Italy. Austria, Bavaria, and Württemberg all expressed immediate opposition to the plan. The Habsburg dynasty no more wanted to see an expansion of Prussian influence in Central Europe than it had desired German unification under the liberal auspices of the Frankfurt Parliament. On September 1, 1849, Austria unilaterally proclaimed the revival of the old German Confederation, pressuring member states to withdraw all the concessions to constitutionalism and liberalism they had made in 1848.

As Prussia and Austria both sought to assure the victory of counter-revolution, each seeking a dominant position in Central Europe, relations between the two powers deteriorated to the point that war seemed possible. In September, the prince of Hesse asked the reconstituted German Confederation for assistance when his own people rebelled against the withdrawal of a liberal constitution he had earlier granted. The government of Prussia, however, objected to the involvement of the Confederation in Hesse because Hesse stood between two parts of Prussia. Now Prussia, which had the right to move troops through Hesse, threatened to send an army there if the Diet tried to intervene. But the Russian tsar, who had become wary of a possible expansion of Prussian power in Central Europe, forced Prussia to back down. In October, the German Confederation, with secret Russian backing, sent Bavarian and Hanoverian troops to Hesse, but Prussian forces blocked their way. Once again, the Prussian government backed away from war, agreeing to drop plans for a Prussian Union. The Prussian government signed the so-called "humiliation of Olmütz" (November 29, 1850), in which Prussia agreed to demobilize its army.

The Counter-Revolution in the Italian States

When Habsburg forces were fighting in Hungary, a nationalist "war party" in Piedmont-Sardinia pushed King Charles Albert toward a resumption of hostilities with Austria. The Piedmontese army crossed into Lombardy, but Austrian forces under General Radetzky defeated it at Novara in March 1849. Fearing that Radetzky's strengthened army would invade Piedmont, Charles Albert asked for peace and abdicated in favor of his son, Victor Emmanuel II. The new king signed an armistice with Austria in Milan in August, renouncing Piedmontese claims to Lombardy.

In 1848, revolutionaries even challenged the authority of the pope in the Papal States. In August, workers in Bologna rose up against Pope Pius IX because he had helped the Austrian cause by recalling his army to Rome. But the pope's forces prevailed. The next outbreak of opposition to papal authority came in Rome itself. Fearing an insurrection, Pius named a new, more liberal government, which announced the imposition of a tax on Church property. After one of the government's leaders was assassinated in November 1848, crowds stormed into the streets, calling for a declaration of war against Austria. Pius appointed more liberals to his government and called for parliamentary elections, before fleeing in disguise to Naples, from which he called for the overthrow of the government he had appointed under duress.

In Rome, the new cabinet met many of the workers' demands, setting up charity workshops and ending the grain tax. Like the leaders of the French Revolution of 1789, the new government confiscated Church property, turning some buildings into apartments for poor workers. In elections for a Constitutional Assembly, the radicals won an overwhelming victory. On February 9, 1849, the Assembly proclaimed the Roman Republic. The pope immediately excommunicated some of its officials from the Catholic

Church. The republic, in turn, abolished the Inquisition and proclaimed freedom of the press and the secularization of university education.

Some Italian nationalists now were beginning to think of the Roman Republic as a center around which the peninsula could be unified. Giuseppe Mazzini's arrival in Rome in early March 1849 to join the revolutionary government confirmed the pope's fears in this regard. With the armies of the Habsburgs tied up with struggles in Central Europe, the pontiff had to look elsewhere for a strong army to come to his rescue. Although Piedmont, the strongest Italian state, did not want a Roman Republic, the pope did not solicit Piedmontese assistance, fearing that if its forces came to the rescue, they might never leave.

Beset by severe economic shortages and inflation and discouraged by the news of the Piedmontese defeat at Novara in March, leaders of the Roman Republic now learned that the French were coming to try to restore the pope's temporal power. Louis Napoleon Bonaparte was eager to win the support of French Catholics. He also did not want Austrian influence in Italy to go unchallenged. With the approval of the French National Assembly, an army of 10,000 French troops disembarked near Rome, and then, embarrassingly enough, had to retreat when they were met by fierce resistance. Giuseppe Garibaldi (1807–1882), a more strident—and organized—republican nationalist than Mazzini, arrived with a corps of volunteers from Lombardy to help the besieged republic. As pro-papal forces sent by the king of Naples and the Spanish government approached Rome, the French army began to shell the eternal city in early June. The Assembly capitulated a month later. French troops then occupied Rome, dissolv-

Pope Pius IX puts aside the liberal mask of Christ, revealing his true conservative face.

ing the Roman Assembly and the clubs and reviving press censorship. Three cardinals assumed power, preparing for the pope's return in April 1850 and the brutal repression that followed.

Of all of the governments formed by revolutions and uprisings in the Italian states in 1848, only the Venetian Republic survived. But having defeated the Piedmontese in March, the Austrians now blockaded and bombarded Venice. Morale fell inside the hungry city, and disease spread. The Venetian Republic capitulated on August 22, 1849.

The Italian revolutions were over. The only liberal regime that remained was in Piedmont. Austria retained Lombardy and Venetia. The king of Naples, the grand duke of Tuscany, and the pope were back in power. Italian unification remained a dream of northern middle-class nationalists. The multiplicity of states and lack of strong popular support for unification—reflected by the gap between liberals' and workers' goals—had for the moment proven too powerful.

The Agony of the French Second Republic

In France, where the wave of 1848 revolutions had begun, political reaction was also gaining momentum following the June Days. The election of Louis Napoleon as president in December of that year seemed to guarantee a return to political stability. The economic situation also improved, helped by abundant harvests and the gradual return of business confidence. Most of the wealthiest landowners and businessmen, threatened by the reforming zeal of the radical republicans and universal manhood suffrage, rallied to Louis Napoleon, Bonaparte's nephew, whom they viewed as the savior of property and family. In the meantime, the "prince president" took command of the centralized administrative, judicial, and military apparatus of the state.

Even as better economic times gradually returned, the "democratic-socialists," whose supporters had been primarily drawn from France's largest cities and some smaller market towns, expanded their appeal in the countryside, particularly gaining followers in the south. They won support not only among radical bourgeois and artisans but also among many peasants, for whom the low prices of the long agricultural depression had brought hard times. In some parts of France, the left reversed the pattern in the French Revolution of radical towns and conservative countryside. Taking the name of the far left during the French Revolution, the Montagnards called for specific national reforms such as the establishment of progressive taxation, higher wages, the abolition of the tax on drink, the creation of credit banks for peasants, and free and obligatory primary schools.

Many of the post-revolutionary clubs were reconstituted as electoral organizations before the elections to be held in the spring of 1849. The democratic-socialists effectively used written political propaganda to reach

ordinary people. They also exploited the deep-seated traditions of oral culture in a society in which only somewhat more than half of the people
could read and write; stories, songs, lithographs and engravings also
spread the popularity of radical candidates. In the legislative elections of
May 1849, the left won almost a third of the seats in the National Assembly, harnessing the heritage of the French Revolution in regions in which
it had found enthusiastic support.

Encouraged by the strength of the left in the Chamber of Deputies and
in Paris, Ledru-Rollin, who had been a socialist member of the provisional
government and a candidate in the presidential election, attempted to provoke an insurrection on June 13, 1849. His pretext was the Assembly's
readiness to send a French army to support the pope, which the left
claimed violated the new constitution, because French troops would be
violating the freedom of the Romans. However, intervention in Rome
earned Louis Napoleon the gratitude of conservative Catholics; the uprising discredited the left among the upper classes. But by-elections in the
spring of 1850 reflected the growing popularity of the democratic-socialist
program among ordinary people in Paris and several provinces.

Backed by the "party of order," Louis Napoleon Bonaparte's government
claimed that a massive plot threatened social order. Symbols of the French
Revolution itself, including singing *The Marseillaise*, became illegal. The
government also outlawed red caps and belts, because red was identified
as the color of the left. The police chopped liberty trees down one by one.

Uprooting a liberty tree in Paris.

The government waged war against popular political activity itself, curtailing the freedom of assembly and association. It banned a number of workers' associations, including some that had been granted state funds in 1848 to establish producer and consumer cooperatives. National Guard units in many towns were disbanded if their members were radical republicans or socialists. Politically active mayors were dismissed. Schoolteachers were replaced if they supported the left, and cafés identified with the democratic-socialist cause were closed. Many radical republican and socialist leaders were jailed. These included Jeanne Deroin (1810–1894), a socialist seamstress and feminist, who in 1849 had tried to run for election despite the fact that women were ineligible for election and could not vote. Others were forced into exile or frightened into submission. In March 1850, the Assembly passed the Falloux Law, which allowed the Catholic clergy to open secondary schools and permitted them to serve on education committees. One of the practical consequences was that villages now could turn operation of their schools over to the clergy.

In May 1850, the National Assembly ended universal manhood suffrage by adding a residency requirement that disqualified many workers who travelled from place to place. This reduced the electorate by one-third, eliminating 3 million voters. Many of the disenfranchised lived in the larger cities, where Napoleon and his candidates had not fared well. The repression succeeded in smashing the left in much of France.

But elsewhere, links between economic change and political activity aided the left. In some southern and central regions, the repression drove the left into secret societies, whose members, mostly artisans and peasants, swore an oath of allegiance to defend the "democratic and social Republic." These societies, which started in towns, gradually spread into the surrounding countryside. This occurred particularly where economic growth during the preceding two decades, including cash-crop agriculture and rural handicrafts, had brought more rural artisans and peasants regularly into market towns. Townspeople and rural craftsmen helped bring national politics into many French villages. In contrast, in the north, the agricultural depression augmented tensions between urban workers, who wanted low food prices, and property-owning peasants, who naturally preferred high prices for agricultural products. The precocious politicization of the French Second Republic, through the conduits of voluntary associations and cafés, reflected links between economic growth and political activity.

The constitution limited the presidency to one term of four years. Although Louis Napoleon's term as president was, in principle, nearing an end, he had no intention of stepping aside despite the fact that the Chamber of Deputies had rejected a proposal to allow the president, if reelected, to serve a second term. In the fall of 1851, the government declared a state of martial law in several regions. On December 2, 1851, the anniversary of the battle of Austerlitz and the coronation of Napoleon Bonaparte as emperor, Parisians awoke to read an official poster that announced the dissolution of the National Assembly. The secret societies then undertook the largest national insurrection in nineteenth-century France. A small uprising broke out in eastern Paris and, while troops easily dispersed demonstrations in several other major cities, more than 100,000 people in eighteen *départements* took up arms in defense of the republic. But the ragged forces of artisans and peasants armed with rusty rifles and pitchforks were easily dispersed by troops before they got very far. Military courts tried over 26,000 democratic-socialists, and almost half that many went into exile.

Support for the coup by Louis Napoleon was overwhelming in France as a whole, however. The plebiscite that followed the coup approved the takeover by more than 10 to 1. The Paris Stock Market soared. Louis Napoleon proclaimed a new constitution, which made him chief executive of the republic for ten years. On December 2, 1852, he took the title Napoleon III, emperor of the French.

THE LEGACY OF 1848

The glacial winds of reaction brutally chilled the "springtime of the peoples." The wave of repression dashed the hopes of liberals, republicans, and nationalists throughout Europe. It has often been said, with the advantage of hindsight, that in 1848, at least with reference to the German states, European history reached its turning point and failed to turn.

European states became even stronger after the Revolutions of 1848. The revolutions had succeeded at first because the French, Prussian, and Austrian authorities lacked sufficient military preparedness. All three quickly learned their lessons. With the defeat of the revolutionaries came the end of the era of civic or national guards, which had been demanded by the people of Berlin, Vienna, and Paris. Professional armies enforced the counter-revolution: those of Jelačić, Windischgrätz, and Radetzky re-

The generals who crushed the insurgency within the Habsburg empire: Jelačić, Radetzky, and Windischgrätz.

stored Habsburg authority in Bohemia, Hungary, and northern Italy; the Prussian army crushed the last gasps of revolution in the German states; and the French army put down subsequent resistance to Louis Napoleon's coup d'état. Louis Napoleon's plebiscite reinforced the centralized character of the French state.

Nonetheless, the Revolutions of 1848 marked the first time workers put forward organized demands for political rights. Class antagonisms, already evident in much of Europe during the "hungry forties," would deepen further after the failures of 1848. Radical peasants in southern France helped dispel the myth of the inevitably conservative peasant.

Although the Revolutions of 1848 ultimately failed, they left crucial political legacies. The period was one of political apprenticeship for republicanism in France and nationalism in the German and Italian states. The revolutions were not only separate national phenomena but part of a common process that anticipated the emergence of mass politics. While many of the goals of the revolutionaries centered on middle-class demands for liberal reforms, such as freedom of the press, the Revolutions of 1848 also had a popular quality characterized by demands for universal manhood suffrage, as well as by a few calls for political rights for women. Hundreds of thousands of ordinary people participated, if only somewhat briefly, in political life.

The counter-revolution in Europe scattered a generation of committed republicans and socialists throughout much of the world. Thousands of Frenchmen were exiled to Algeria, while German and Italian political exiles emigrated to the United States. They acquainted many other people with the tenets of republicanism, nationalism, and socialism. The mid-century revolutions influenced the subsequent political evolution of each country that had had a revolution in the spring of 1848.

The failure of the mid-century revolutions was a particularly significant juncture in the history of modern Germany; the hopes of many for its unification along liberal lines—either as a truly constitutional monarchy or a republic—came to naught. But the Revolutions of 1848 accentuated support for German nationalism. A Prussian minister recognized that "The old times are gone and cannot return. To return to the decaying conditions of the past is like scooping water with a sieve." The revolution did produce a Prussian constitution and an elected assembly, however, which the king only slightly modified in 1849–1850 when he again took control.

The Habsburg monarchy, too, survived the liberal and nationalist challenges of 1848. Young Habsburg Emperor Francis Joseph bragged to his mother, "We have thrown the constitution overboard and Austria has now only one master." The Austrian government had adroitly manipulated ethnic tensions, using a Croatian army against a Hungarian uprising. The situation was so complicated that a Hungarian noted that "the King of Hungary declared war on the King of Croatia, and the Emperor of Austria remained neutral, and all three monarchs were the same person." Hungary, in which perhaps as many as 100,000 people were killed during the fighting in 1848–1849, remained within the monarchy as Austria's junior partner. But none of the major reforms undertaken within the monarchy in the wake of the revolution were abolished during the counter-revolution. Peasants were now free from labor obligations previously owed to landowners. Although the progressive Kremsier constitution had been tossed aside, the Austrian constitution of March 1849 did establish a parliament. Yet, the goals of many Hungarians, Czechs, Poles, and other ethnic groups remained unachieved. On the Italian peninsula, Habsburg control of Lombardy and Venetia, the existence of many other separate states, and the indifference of most people to Italian nationalism remained daunting obstacles to Italian unification.

The failure of the Revolutions of 1848 in Central Europe left little doubt that German unification could only be achieved under the auspices of either Prussia or Austria. By revealing the complexity of national tensions and rivalries within the Habsburg monarchy, it now seemed even more unlikely that Austria would have an interest in bringing about German unification, and that instead it would oppose an expansion of Prussian power. Prussia would only be likely to support German unification, however, if it would serve to extend its own power within the German states and in Europe.

German unification under any auspices would potentially entail a drastic change in the European state system, particularly in Central Europe. France and Russia, above all, had reasons not to want to see the emergence of a stronger state in Central Europe. The unification of Italy, too, could alter the balance of power, potentially threatening Austria and perhaps France as well.

Even in failure, the revolutions in the Italian states had only made Italian nationalists more determined to work for national unification. Continued Austrian control of Venetia and Lombardy, and the division of the rest of Italy into a number of small states, including the Papal States, remained serious impediments to Italian unification, despite the eagerness of Piedmontese liberals to unify the peninsula under Piedmont's leadership. Likewise, the defeat of the Hungarian and Bohemian revolutions, as well as the failure of the radical revolution in Vienna that had first challenged Habsburg rule, by no means ended the threat to the Habsburg monarchy.

PART FIVE

THE AGE OF MASS POLITICS

At mid-century, Great Britain, France, and Russia were the three major European powers. However, the unification of Italy and Germany during the 1860s and early 1870s altered the balance of power in Central Europe and dramatically changed international dynamics. Moreover, ethnic minorities in the Dual Monarchy of Austria-Hungary clamored for more rights, setting the stage for further conflict in Europe.

During the century's last three decades, much of Europe entered a period of remarkable economic, social, political, and cultural change. The Second Industrial Revolution, characterized by accelerated mass production, ushered in a period of rapid economic growth, despite the long depression that gripped Europe from 1873 to the mid-1890s. Mass-circulation newspapers—the "penny press"—sporting photos and sensationalistic stories, department stores offering an astonishing variety of goods, bicycles, the emergence of spectator sports, and flashy cabarets symbolized the fin-de-siècle period.

During the second half of the nineteenth century, Europe moved into the age of mass politics. The British Parliament passed a second Reform Bill in 1867, and a third in 1884, giving Britain universal manhood suffrage. France became a republic in the 1870s, and universal manhood suffrage came to Germany, Italy, and Belgium as well, increasing the number of people in the political arena.

Despite a general increase in the quality of life, the difficult conditions of the laboring poor encouraged the creation of mass socialist parties in France, Germany, Italy, Belgium, and most other Western European states. These political parties succeeded in electing representatives to many European parliaments. In Britain, the Labour Party came into existence early in the twentieth century, largely supported by workers. Like the socialist parties of the continent, the more moderate British Labour Party demanded social reform and sent members to Parliament. In Russia, although socialists were forced into exile and the police stalked revolutionary groups, liberal critics of the tsarist autocracy nonetheless grew more bold. The humiliating defeat of Russia by Japan led to the Russian Revolution of 1905. This forced short-lived political reforms and encouraged reformers, some within the bureaucracy, and revolutionaries alike. Moreover, in Russia and in Southern Europe, anarchists vowed to destroy all states.

The rise of aggressive nationalism was one consequence of the advent of mass politics. "Jingoistic" newspapers in every country castigated national rivals and encouraged the "new imperialism" that began in the 1880s. By the outbreak of World War I, the European powers had divided up three-quarters of the world's surface. Imperialism helped sharpen international rivalries. Entangling alliances led the European powers into two heavily armed camps, pitting Germany and Austria-Hungary against Britain, France, and Russia. Ethnic conflicts in the Balkans raised the stakes, particularly fueling the rivalry between Russia and Austria-Hungary, each backed by strongly committed allies.

Amid scientific progress, a boom in manufacturing, and the emergence of mass political parties in Western Europe, many artists and intellectuals worried that Western civilization was moving too rapidly and was almost out of control. Their worries turned out to be fully justified. In the summer of 1914, World War I began.

CHAPTER 18

THE ERA OF NATIONAL UNIFICATION

Born into a family of Piedmontese nobles during the Napoleonic occupation, Camillo di Cavour was educated in a military academy and entered the army, where he became enamored of political radicalism. Upon hearing of the July Revolution of 1830 in France, Cavour ran through his barracks in Genoa with a paper knife, shouting "Long live the Republic! Down with all tyrants!" When he resigned from the army, Cavour came to espouse aristocratic liberalism and became determined to effect the political unification of the Italian peninsula. An idealist of vision and courage, Cavour was also capable of ruthlessness and unscrupulous trickery, all of which would be necessary to form one state from the many that existed on the Italian peninsula at that time.

Small groups of German and Italian nationalists during the first half of the nineteenth century, inspired by the principles of the French Revolution, agitated for the political unification of their respective peoples. Liberals and nationalists in the 1830s and 1840s were often the same people sharing the same goals. Many revolutionaries in 1848 had demanded national unification, notably the lawyers and professors of the Frankfurt Parliament in the German states and the Italian liberals and nationalists opposing Austrian domination of northern Italy. But the outcome of the 1848 revolutions notwithstanding, Germany and Italy were not unified by the popular movements that typified the insurrections and revolutions that in 1848 brought a republic to France, forced constitutional changes in Prussia and Austria, as well as in several other German states, and sparked insurrections against Austrian control of northern Italy.

Italian unification came, not because of the utopian nationalism of Giuseppe Mazzini nor because of the frenzied dashes of Giuseppe Garibaldi and his followers into the south, but rather largely as a result of the expansion of Piedmont-Sardinia, the peninsula's strongest and most liberal state. Italy was unified politically by Camillo di Cavour under the liberal auspices of the Piedmont-Sardinian monarchy, the House of Savoy.

The case of Germany was different. German unification was effected by autocratic Prussia. Prussian King William I and Chancellor Otto von Bismarck achieved unification through shrewd manipulation of both diplomacy and warfare. "Most countries have an army," it was said, "Prussia is an army with a country." The German Empire, like the Prussia that forged it in "blood and iron," was defiantly reactionary.

There was nothing inevitable, however, about the political unification of Italy nor the unification of German-speaking states in Central Europe. Nor was there anything inevitable about the ultimate break-up of the Austro-Hungarian Empire, that polyglot power of Central Europe and part of the Balkans. Without question, however, the emergence of Italy in the 1860s and of Germany in 1871 altered the history of modern Europe. Germany emerged as a Great Power, Italy as a would-be Great Power. And the Austro-Hungarian monarchy increasingly was confronted by demands from its ethnic minorities for their own independence, which remained a factor for instability in its domestic and international politics. The Habsburg monarchy seemed an atavism, out of place in an age of growing nationalism.

THE POLITICAL UNIFICATION OF ITALY

The Austrian statesman Metternich once whimsically remarked that Italy was "a mere geographical expression," an observation that perhaps best captures the basic problem that confronted those who struggled for Italian unification. Since the end of the Roman Empire, Italy had been politically disunited, a cacophony of competing voices. Italy has always had a great diversity of regions and peoples. One contemporary put it this way: "the patriotism of the Italians is like that of the ancient Greeks, and is love of a single town, not of a country; it is the feeling of a tribe, not of a nation. Only by foreign conquest have they ever been united. Leave them to themselves and they split into fragments."

Marked differences in economic development compounded the problem of political fragmentation. Northern Italy has always been considerably more prosperous than the south. The Habsburg monarchy also presented a formidable obstacle to Italian unification, as it retained Venetia and Lombardy, and dominated Parma, Tuscany, and Modena in north-central Italy (the rulers of the latter two states were members of the Austrian royal family). Then there was the pope, whose influence in all Italian states and temporal control over the Papal States around Rome posed another barrier to Italian unification. Furthermore, Italy lacked a tradition of centralized administration. Powerful local elites dispensed patronage, constituting virtual unofficial parallel governments in much of the south and Sicily; they would frustrate any attempt of a centralized state to exercise effective control. Finally, these structural barriers to unification were accompanied by disagreement among elites and nationalists about whether a unified Italy would be governed by a monarchy (constitutional or not), a republic, or even by the pope.

If there were many forces working against Italian unification, some factors promoted this Risorgimento ("Resurgence") of Italy. Nationalist sentiment developed among the liberal aristocracy and the upper middle classes, particularly among northern lawyers and professors. It was fanned by nationalist brochures and newspapers, the memory of the failures of the Revolutions of 1848, and a common hatred of Austria, the latest of the outside powers that had held parts of Italy since the end of the fifteenth century. Although some Italian nationalists could not imagine the separation of church and state, most envisioned a Risorgimento independent of the pope and the Catholic Church.

Leadership for Italian Unification

There seemed to be two possible sources of leadership for Italian unification. First, Victor Emmanuel II (ruled 1849–1878) of the House of Savoy, king of Piedmont-Sardinia (the Kingdom of Sardinia), wanted to unify Italy by gradually extending his control over the peninsula. Piedmont-Sardinia was far and away Italy's most prosperous region, boasting a significant concentration of industrial production, fine sources of water power, and accessible markets. It had inherited from the French revolutionary and Napoleonic eras a relatively efficient bureaucracy modeled after that of its conquering neighbor.

King Victor Emmanuel III, poorly educated and uncouth, loved horses and hunting more than anything else, with the possible exception of his sixteen-year-old mistress, the daughter of a palace guard. But he also had read a book written in the wake of the Revolutions of 1848 that had predicted the unification of Italy under Piedmont-Sardinia with the assistance of the French. In 1852, Victor Emmanuel at least had the good sense to appoint Count Camillo di Cavour (1810–1861) as prime minister.

The Piedmontese Cavour was a pampered child who grew up to be headstrong, somewhat lazy, and bad tempered. His older brother inherited the family title of marquis, and Cavour entered a military academy. Despite several minor misadventures, he did well in mathematics and engineering. Later he would brag that he liked to reduce political problems to graphs on which he had plotted all possible factors and outcomes. As a young man, Cavour came to espouse political radicalism, a view that was unlikely to win him promotion in the army. He resigned his commission as a military engineer, pleading poor eyesight and bad health, the latter at least partially due to a lifelong pattern of eating and drinking too much.

(*Left*) King Victor Emmanuel II of Piedmont-Sardinia. (*Right*) Count Camillo di Cavour.

Cavour read widely in economics and politics and travelled to France and England, both of which impressed him with their prosperity and efficient administration. (Cavour's first language remained French, although his command of Italian improved.) He attributed the well-being of both countries to the same aristocratic liberalism that characterized Piedmont-Sardinia. Back in Turin in 1841, he started an Agricultural Association to encourage rural innovation, making a good deal of money by utilizing crop rotation, land drainage, and mechanized farm machinery. Triumphs in banking and business followed, but none brought the morose Cavour happiness. When he was in his early twenties, he wrote in his diary that he thought of suicide because he believed his life "without purpose, without hope, without desire," copying morbid lines from Shakespeare into his diary. Yet, he found a compelling goal: the unification of the Italian peninsula.

Elected to the Piedmontese Parliament in 1849 in the new constitutional government, named minister of commerce and agriculture in 1850 and prime minister two years later, Cavour orchestrated the unification of Italy around the constitutional monarchy of Piedmont-Sardinia. He initiated the first of a series of loose coalition governments based on the political center, standing between the noble and clerical right and the republican left.

Cavour's policies helped stimulate the Piedmontese economy. He facilitated the availability of credit for businessmen, helped attract foreign capital by lowering tariffs, built railways, and strengthened the army. Reflecting Piedmontese liberal secular values, Cavour made the clergy subject to the same civil codes as everyone else, limited bishops' income, and taxed Church property. Like the liberalism of the French Orleanist monarchy and the early Victorians in Britain, however, Cavour's liberalism stopped well short of republicanism. But he could claim that Piedmont-Sardinia was the rightful leader of Italian liberals and nationalists.

A second, more popular nationalist tradition survived the broken dreams of "the springtime of the peoples" in the Revolutions of 1848. Giuseppe Mazzini remained its spokesman. The Genoese-born Mazzini had as a boy watched Piedmontese patriots leave for exile after an ill-fated revolutionary uprising in 1820–1821. Reflecting his broken dreams and the romantic tradition of his younger years, Mazzini frequently dressed in black (often surrounded by cigar smoke and in the company of his pet canaries), vowing to remain in mourning until Italian unification could be achieved. The failure of conspiratorial uprisings led him to espouse a nationalist movement that had a wider range of support, with the goal of establishing a republic that would implement social reforms. For Mazzini, "patriotism was not a wider form of selfishness, nor ever an end in itself, but should always serve the wider interests of humanity." While he was a determined enemy of monarchism and aristocratic privilege, Mazzini believed that classical liberalism was devoid of moral values and rejected socialism as overly materialistic. He embraced unification as a moral force that would educate and uplift the people of Italy, providing a common faith and purpose that would unlock their great potential and make them worthy of democracy.

Mazzini believed that the unification of Italy had to be the work of the people themselves, and should not be achieved through the expansion of the kingdom of Piedmont-Sardinia. Drawing on the conspiratorial tradition of the Carbonari, Mazzini's secret society, "Young Italy," hoped to mobilize the European masses, beginning in the Italian states, to rise up for nationalism and democracy. He thus supported the goals of other nationalist groups in Europe, including Hungarians, Poles, and Slavs in the hope that "Young Europe," a brotherhood of nations, would eventually come into existence.

Mazzini was undaunted by the failures and repression that followed the Revolution of 1848, including an ill-fated attempt to proclaim the Roman Republic in 1849. However, these debacles discredited him and his movement among the middle classes. Four years later, Cavour tipped off the Austrians that Mazzini was planning an insurrection in Lombardy. King Victor Emmanuel congratulated Austrian Emperor Francis Joseph on the success of the subsequent repression. Yet, Mazzini's effective propaganda kept the Italian question alive in European diplomatic circles while attracting the interest of lawyers and liberal landowners in some of the northern Italian states.

Alliances and Warfare to Further Italian Unification

In the early 1850s, it was still clear that Italian unification was impossible as long as Austria dominated much of northern and central Italy. Having first concentrated on reforms within Piedmont-Sardinia, Cavour now began a series of diplomatic moves that he hoped would bring the support of Great Britain and France. Specifically, he wanted to form an alliance with France against Austria that would further the cause of Italian unification. Austria was not about to withdraw from Lombardy on its own, and Piedmont-Sardinia was too weak to defeat the Habsburg army alone. Cavour initiated commercial agreements with France, as well as with Great Britain, trying to impress both powers with Piedmont-Sardinia's political and economic liberalism.

In March 1854, France and Great Britain joined the Ottoman Empire in fighting against Russia in the Crimean War, which had begun a year earlier. The cagey Cavour worked to make the war serve the interests of Piedmont-Sardinia and Italian unification. In October 1854, while ordering fortresses on the Austrian frontier strengthened, Cavour informed the French and British governments that Piedmont-Sardinia would be willing to join the coalition against Russia in exchange for a role in determining new frontiers in Eastern Europe at the war's end. Knowing that Britain needed more troops for the fight, Cavour sent 15,000 soldiers in January 1855 to Crimea. Mazzini, on the other hand, bitterly opposed intervention as irrelevant to his vision of a united republican Italy. Piedmont-Sardinia signed the Peace of Paris in 1856, which ended the Crimean War, an occasion Cavour used to focus diplomatic attention on the Italian situation.

These successes earned the allegiance of some of the disillusioned followers of Mazzini, who organized a poorly planned, disastrous invasion of the Kingdom of Naples in June 1857. A group of liberal nationalists established the National Society, which supported Cavour, who understood that its moderate nationalist message could undercut support for Mazzini's more radical goals of social reform under a republic. Now, unlike Mazzini, Cavour was eager to ally with imperial France in the interest of working toward Italian unification. Despite a failed assassination attempt against him by an Italian nationalist republican in 1858, French Emperor Napoleon III was eager to extend his country's influence in Italy and hoped to annex Savoy and Nice from Piedmont-Sardinia. He proposed marriage between Victor Emmanuel's fifteen-year-old daughter and his own young cousin, Prince Napoleon Bonaparte. Such an alliance would help cement relations between France and Piedmont-Sardinia, not a happy situation for the Austrians (nor necessarily for the young bride).

Cavour devised an agreement with France against Austria, which was signed in July 1858 at Plombières, a health spa in eastern France. Napoleon III now agreed to support Piedmont-Sardinia in a war against Austria, if such a war "could be justified in the eyes of diplomacy and even more in the eyes of public opinion in France and Europe." Cavour and Napoleon III envisioned an Italy divided into four confederated states: Piedmont-Sardinia as the Kingdom of Upper Italy, which would include Venetia and Lombardy, as well as part of the Papal States and several duchies; a second state in central Italy, with Napoleon III's cousin Prince

Napoleon Bonaparte as king; a third state made up of the remaining papal territories; and the Kingdom of the Two Sicilies as the fourth state. The French emperor could only regard such a situation with glee: three of the four proposed states would require French support to survive, and France would receive Nice and Savoy from Piedmont-Sardinia.

Victor Emmanuel provocatively announced to his parliament in January 1859 that "we are not insensitive to the cry of suffering that rises toward us from so many parts of Italy." That same month, Piedmont-Sardinia and France formalized the Plombières agreement in a treaty. Then the ruling dynasties were united in youthful marriage (the princess had agreed to marry the young Frenchman if "he is not actually repulsive to me"). Russia, Austria's rival in the Balkans, was happy to sit this one out in exchange for French acceptance of a possible revision of the Peace of Paris, which had in 1856 deprived Russia of the right to have a fleet in the Black Sea. In turn, Russia would look the other way if events in Italy altered the settlements enacted by the Congress of Vienna in 1815.

Austria provided an excuse for war, announcing that it would draft men from Venetia and Lombardy into the imperial army. Piedmont-Sardinia, in turn, made it known that it would accept deserters from Austrian conscription, and mobilized troops in March. The Prussian government debated whether it should follow public opinion at home and back Austria, its fellow German state, in the looming conflict. But the British government lobbied so effectively for a peaceful solution that Cavour denounced a "conspiracy of peace" and threatened to resign, suggesting to his friends that he would move to the United States, or perhaps even commit suicide. Napoleon III hesitated, asking Piedmont-Sardinia to demobilize its troops. Austria saved the situation for Cavour by issuing an ultimatum to Piedmont-Sardinia on April 23, 1859, hoping that other German states would support it. With Austria now appearing as the aggressor, Prussia and the other German states felt no obligation to come to its aid. After Piedmont-Sardinia rejected the ultimatum, Austrian troops invaded Piedmont, which brought France into the war. Napoleon III himself led 100,000 troops into northern Italy; many of the troops went by train, the first time that a railway played a major part in warfare.

The French and Piedmontese defeated the Habsburg army at Magenta and Solferino in June 1859, driving the Austrians out of Lombardy (see Map 18.1). But the French feared that a crushing defeat of Austria might yet bring Prussia and other German states into the war against France, with the bulk of the French armies still in northern Italy. Furthermore, Cavour had sparked several nationalist insurrections against the Austrians in Bologna, Tuscany, Modena, and Parma, whose rulers fled, leaving the duchies under Piedmontese control. Further revolts in the Papal States failed; the pope's Swiss mercenaries recaptured Perugia, looting and shooting unarmed civilians. It became apparent to the French, moreover, that if Piedmont-Sardinia were *too* successful, Victor Emmanuel's ex-

MAP 18.1 THE UNIFICATION OF ITALY, 1859–1870   The unification of Italy by Piedmont-Sardinia included territory acquired in 1859, 1860, 1862, and 1866.

panded kingdom might become a rival instead of a grateful, compliant neighbor. Without consulting Cavour, Napoleon III arranged an armistice at Villafranca with Francis Joseph of Austria in July.

Cavour and Victor Emmanuel now believed that France had betrayed them. Austria had lost Lombardy to Piedmont-Sardinia but would retain Venetia. The pope would become the head of an Italian Confederation under the protection of the French. But it was clear to France that the other states of northern and central Italy would inevitably become part of the expanding Italian state. By the Treaty of Turin on March 24, 1860, Napoleon III agreed to Piedmont-Sardinia's annexation of Tuscany, Mod-

Pope Pius IX on the special train given to him by Napoleon III, who protected papal temporal independence.

ena, Parma, and Bologna, in addition to Lombardy. In exchange, Piedmont-Sardinia ceded Savoy and Nice to France. With the exception of Venetia, almost all of northern and central Italy had now been united with the constitutional monarchy of Piedmont-Sardinia.

Garibaldi and the Liberation of Southern Italy

The colorful republican revolutionary Giuseppe Garibaldi (1807–1882) now leapt onto the stage. Born in Nice (and, like Cavour, a French speaker by preference), the charismatic and courageous Garibaldi, a man of simple tastes, had joined Mazzini's Young Italy movement in 1833. After a year in political exile in South America, he fought against the Austrians in Lombardy in 1848 and in Rome in 1849. The war of 1859 provided him with another opportunity to fight the Austrians. Angered that the Treaty of Villafranca had cut short what he considered to be the war for Italian unification, Garibaldi formed an army of volunteers. Cavour tolerated it in the hope of preventing the French from annexing Savoy and Nice. Garibaldi also hoped to drive the Austrians from Venetia and the French from Rome. But his force's ill-prepared attack on Rome failed completely.

On April 4, 1860, a revolt began against Francis II, the Bourbon monarch of the Kingdom of the Two Sicilies (Naples and Sicily), as a protest against the milling tax and the high price of bread. Secretly encouraged by Cavour (who planned to send Piedmont-Sardinia's army later to Rome to rescue the pope and restore "order") and openly urged on by

Giuseppe Garibaldi.

Mazzini, Garibaldi landed in Sicily with an army of 1,000 "Red Shirts" (a "uniform" that made it possible for virtually anyone to join and feel like he belonged to the force). Sicilians welcomed him as a liberator who would help them obtain their independence and rid them of onerous taxes. Garibaldi's followers outfought the larger Neapolitan army, taking Palermo on May 27. This success swelled Garibaldi's ragtag army of nationalists and adventurers. One of his soldiers described Garibaldi after a battle: "The General has ridden through the city on horseback. When the populace sees him, they take fire. There is a magic in his look and in his name. It is only Garibaldi they want."

Garibaldi then announced that he was assuming dictatorial power in Sicily on behalf of King Victor Emmanuel II of Piedmont-Sardinia. In August, Garibaldi's army returned to the Italian peninsula. Aided by an insurrection of craftsmen and day laborers, the Red Shirts took Naples, Italy's largest city, in September. Garibaldi's victories put Piedmont-Sardinia in a difficult situation. If Garibaldi marched against Rome, France might declare war because of the threat to the pope. If Garibaldi moved against Venetia, which seemed inevitable, Austria would almost certainly fight again, perhaps this time with Prussia's support. With a declaration that "the destruction of the pope's temporal power will be one of the most glorious and fruitful facts in all history," Cavour sent Piedmontese troops into the Papal States the same day that Garibaldi's troops took Naples. The ostensible goal was to join Garibaldi, but the real intention of the expedition was to stop the adventurer's dramatic independent operations. The

Garibaldi landing at Marsalla in Sicily around 1860.

combined forces of Piedmontese troops and Garibaldi's colorful army put an end to papal resistance and that of the royal Bourbon family of Naples.

Completion of the Unification of Italy

Plebiscites in October in Naples, Sicily, and the Papal States demonstrated overwhelming support for joining the expanding Italian state of Piedmont-Sardinia. The annexation of these states angered Napoleon III, as Cavour had promised that an international conference would provide arbitration. Now only Venetia—still Austrian—and Rome and its region—the shrinking kingdom of the pope—remained unincorporated into the new Italy.

Victor Emmanuel of Piedmont-Sardinia entered Naples with Garibaldi in triumph in November 1860. He took the title King Victor Emmanuel II of Italy in March 1861. Garibaldi, whose daring exploits had made these events possible, retired to semi-exile to his home on a small island. On June 6, Cavour suddenly died at the age of fifty-one, depriving Italy of his effective decision making and political acumen. Depending on one's point of view, Italy had lost the great hero of the Risorgimento or a scheming Machiavellian—probably something of both.

Two more conflicts completed the political unification of Italy. In 1866, Austria went to war with Prussia after the latter protested Austrian interference in the government of Holstein, a dispute that grew out of the rivalry of the two powers for the leadership of the German states (see below). The Italian army, allied with Prussia, more than held its own in brief fighting in Italy, and then moved into Austrian Venetia. When Prussian forces defeated the Austrians at Sadowa in Bohemia in July, Venetia became part of Italy.

The final piece in the Italian jigsaw puzzle fell into place when French troops left Rome in 1870 at the beginning of the Franco-Prussian War. Italian troops occupied the Eternal City, making it the capital of the new Italian state. The Roman population approved the city's incorporation into Italy by more than 40,000 votes to just 46. On May 13, 1871, the Italian Parliament passed the Law of Papal Guarantees, which reduced the holdings of the pope to the Vatican, barely larger than Saint Peter's Basilica and its adjoining ecclesiastical buildings.

Despite enormous regional differences in economic, social, and cultural development, especially between north and south, Italy had been unified politically. If anything, Cavour's free-trade policies, which further served to concentrate industry in the triangle formed by Milan, Turin, and Genoa by driving out smaller and less efficient manufacturers, accentuated the gap between north and south. Northern large-scale textile production, for example, undercut struggling rural industry in other regions. The south became even more dependent on poor agriculture. The northern and central provinces of the new kingdom included 93 percent of the railways, 88 percent of the roads, 78 percent of the production of silk, and 68 percent of agricultural production.

Cavour's many successors as prime minister—almost one per year— proved considerably less able, perhaps eliminating any hope of creating an effective balance between centralized administration and regional federalism. The great gulf between landowners and the rural proletariat grew wider. To the peasants of the south, northern capitalists and state officials seemed no less oppressive than had been the Bourbon monarchy and its landlords. The new Italian bureaucracy, an extension of that of Piedmont-Sardinia, which had been modeled after that of France, discovered that regional loyalties and parallel local structures of political influence not only persisted but often became further entrenched in response and resistance to the impingement of the centralized state. This was particularly the case in the former Bourbon Kingdom of the Two Sicilies. Several bloody rebellions followed; brigandage and banditry spread throughout much of the south and Sicily. Bandits drew on local resistance to the state and powerful local landowners surrounded by landless laborers, chronic unemployment, and general impoverishment. The savage repression that followed killed more Italians than all the wars of the Risorgimento combined, intensifying suspicion and mistrust of the state.

During the next decades, the limits to Italian unification became increasingly apparent. Significantly, Cavour, the principal architect of Italian unification, had never himself gone farther south than Florence. In 1860, almost 98 percent of the population of Italy spoke dialects in daily

An Italian soldier posing with the corpse of a bandit who has just been killed.

life and not Italian. About that time, schoolteachers sent to Sicily from the north were taken for Englishmen by the local population. In the arts, disillusionment seemed more prevalent than celebration. The French writer Maxime du Camp related that in Naples in 1860 he heard people shout "Long Live Italy!" and then ask what "Italy" meant.

THE UNIFICATION OF GERMANY

In the German states, too, growing nationalist sentiment existed, at least within the middle class. Yet, as in the case of Italy, there were also formidable obstacles to German unification. First, in the wake of the Revolution of 1848, the upper classes were wary of any change that might threaten the status quo. They particularly feared the strong nationalist feeling unleashed by revolution, the extension of which might become, they reasoned, the proclamation of the equality of all citizens. Second, it was still not clear which power, Austria or Prussia, would become the dominant influence in a unified Germany. Some believed in the "small German" solution in which Prussia might effect German unification and exclude Austria. Other German nationalists supported the "big German" ideal, whereby Austria would dominate an expanded German Confederation. Third, in both Prussia and Austria, the 1850s were an extremely repressive period that made it clear to most nationalists that German unification would not come under liberal auspices. The repression following the Revolutions of 1848 had scattered thousands of German democrats and nationalists across Europe and as far as the United States.

Prussia held several trump cards toward achieving German unification: territorial additions in the industrializing Rhineland after the Napoleonic Wars and a relatively strong economic position, which had been bolstered by the Zollverein customs union. Furthermore, Prussia's population was quite homogeneous, almost entirely German-speaking and Protestant. The Prussian royal family, the Hohenzollerns, benefited from the internal stability brought by an effective administrative bureaucracy and were supported by an ambitious and powerful landed nobility, the Junkers, who dominated the officer corps of Prussia's strong army. In sum, Prussia already represented an example of successful statemaking. The expansion of Prussian power therefore seemed to many Prussians to be perfectly natural. Catholic Austria, on the other hand, dominated a multinational population. The Habsburg monarchy had much to lose by the encouragement of national movements that might catch fire among the varied peoples within the imperial boundaries.

All German nationalists, however, did not agree on what political form a unified Germany should take. Most Prussian Junkers had been unrelenting in their opposition to the liberal movements that had championed popular sovereignty during the 1848 revolutions. They rejected the liberalism of Rhineland industrialists who were anxious to enhance their own political power. Many liberals, particularly republicans from the more liberal southern German states, wanted a unified Germany to have a parliamentary government free from the domination by either autocratic, aristocratic Prussia or imperial Austria. Yet, despite Prussia's autocratic and militaristic traditions, some nationalistic republicans still hoped Prussia, not Austria, would lead Germans to unification. To one Protestant republican, "Prussia, with all its repugnant police barbarism, is the only salvation for Germany from Jesuits and reactionaries in politics." Some Prussian Junkers also feared that if the "big German" plan for unification came to be, their influence would be greatly diluted by Austrian strength. Nonetheless, Austria continued to attract the interest of some German nationalists who mistrusted the autocratic, centralized, and military traditions of Prussia. Southern Germans wanted the Habsburg monarchy to champion the cause of the smaller German states, leading to a decentralized federation, not domination by Prussia.

William I, Bismarck, and the Resolution of the Constitutional Crisis

The first step in the unification of Germany was the ascension to power of a monarch equal to the task. In 1858, the pious, conscientious William I (1797–1888) became regent for his brother, the unstable Frederick William IV, who was declared insane. Crowned king following Frederick

William's death in 1861, William made clear from the outset of his reign that, unlike his predecessor, he would look beyond the small group of reactionary Prussian Junkers and bring some more moderate conservatives into his cabinet. Even if Prussia remained an autocracy, William I promised to rule constitutionally, accepting the restraints to which Frederick William IV had agreed in 1849. Political repression became less oppressive. Voters—men of at least moderate wealth—responded by turning out in unprecedented numbers to vote. Liberals won a clear victory in the 1858 elections to the Prussian Parliament, which brought to that assembly a good number of men enriched by Prussia's economic boom in the early 1850s. Liberals who favored German unification now had a public forum in which to be heard. Increasingly, businessmen believed that German unification would be good for them, as many believed that the Zollverein customs union had benefited them in the 1840s.

Italian nationalism and the Austrian war against Piedmont-Sardinia and France in 1859 divided Prussians. Some were torn between dislike for Austria and irritation with French Emperor Napoleon III for helping engineer the outbreak of war. Austria was a member of the loose German Confederation and had the right to expect assistance from fellow members. But Austria was also Prussia's major rival for power within the German states. Prussia remained neutral in the war, but Italy's move toward unification greatly impressed German nationalists. The historian Heinrich von Treischke suggested that Germans follow the Italian example and their "persevering, almost nervous passion which, whether awake or in dreams, can think of only one thing: my country, my country, and always my fatherland." German nationalists who looked to Prussia to forge German unity welcomed Austria's defeat.

In 1858, at the time of the Prussian elections, several "Pan-German" associations formed. The largest and most influential, the National Union (*Nationalverein*), wanted a constitutional and parliamentary German state. The Prussian government remained suspicious of the National Union because many of its members favored the extension of political freedom within the German states. As in the old Frankfurt Parliament, its members were overwhelmingly middle class, including intellectuals, lawyers, officials, and small businessmen, but also several industrialists. They even rebuffed an attempt by workers' organizations to join in 1863. The National Union contributed to the resurgence of political liberalism within Prussia, however, by demanding an effective constitution that would limit the power of the monarchy and Junker prerogatives.

The question of army reform raised the issue of parliamentary control over the budget. The Prussian constitutional crisis that followed became a critical step in the unification of Germany along lines that turned out to be anything but liberal. The Prussian military mobilization in 1859 during the Austrian war against Piedmont and France had revealed serious inadequacies in the Prussian army. The minister of war, the conservative Junker

Albrecht von Roon (1803–1879), proposed reforms of the army, which had last been reformed in 1815. These included reforms that would cost considerable money: expansion of the officer corps, increasing the number of recruits, and an extension of the time of service to three years. Prussian liberals wanted all citizens to serve in the army, but they favored a reduction in the term of military service to two years. They also wanted the National Guard (*Landwehr*) to replace the professional, Junker-dominated army as the foundation of the Prussian military, thus forging a link between the Prussian army and the people.

The Prussian Parliament did not enjoy many prerogatives in autocratic Prussia, but it did have the right to approve new taxes. In response to government pressure, in May 1861 the parliament, despite its liberal majority, passed a provisional bill that gave the army the money it needed until the reform could be considered. Liberal approval of the provisional bill was a fateful event in German history because it provided parliamentary sanction to the virtually unchallenged power of the military in Prussia.

Some leaders among the liberal opposition then formed the German Progressive Party, including some Junkers who supported the constitutional rights of parliament. Emboldened by victory in the 1861 elections, three months later liberals declined to vote for the new military budget when von Roon refused compromise. After William dismissed parliament, new elections returned another liberal majority, which rejected a second army budget. Opposition to the government seemed so strong that the king considered leaving the throne to his more liberal son, Crown Prince Frederick William. The king desperately wanted to end the political crisis created by the army bill by finding a way to overcome the parliamentary opposition. He turned to a strong-willed and intransigently conservative Junker, Count Otto von Bismarck (1815–1898), appointing him prime minister in 1862. Bismarck ended the crisis and then forged the unification of Germany.

(*Left*) Otto von Bismark. (*Right*) William I.

Bismarck was the son of a dull, rather incompetent Junker father and a lively, intelligent mother from a family of middle-class bureaucrats. Rejecting the solemn rural world of the Junkers, Bismarck's mother once related that her single ambition was to have a son "who would penetrate far further into the world of ideas than I, as a woman, have been able to do." In his Berlin school, Bismarck was more noted for dueling scars earned in student fraternities than for academic success. After receiving his law degree, he passed the entrance examination for the Prussian bureaucracy. Bismarck was appointed Prussian representative to the German Confederation in Frankfurt in 1851. He was sent to St. Petersburg as ambassador in 1859, perhaps to mute his noisy denunciations of Austria. Brief stints in London and Paris increased Bismarck's knowledge of European affairs.

As prime minister, Bismarck was convinced that he could create a new German state that would not be too large for Prussia to dominate, nor too democratic for the tradition of the Hohenzollern monarchy. For the next three decades, Bismarck's shrewd manipulation of domestic and international politics dominated relations among the European powers. Bismarck was not as free to pursue policies as he may sometimes have seemed. But dogged determination to maintain personal power probably always remained his first goal. The "iron chancellor" patiently made uncanny assessments of every possible option and then moved with determination to strengthen Prussia's position. Domestic policy occupied just as large a place in Bismarck's plans as did foreign affairs. He wanted to create a modern, bureaucratic state that would be strong and secular. He cleverly used political parties when it suited his purposes, the National Liberals as well as the Conservatives. This type of politics came to be known as *Realpolitik*, the pursuit of a nation's self-interest based on a realistic assessment of the costs and consequences of action. Inherent in *Realpolitik* was an absence of moral or ethical considerations, overrun by Bismarck's unshakable determination to enhance the power of the Prussian monarchy and nobility, and therefore of Germany.

Bismarck evoked contradictory reactions of admiration, respect, and fear among Germans and foreign statesmen alike. He was a very complex man, both a man of iron and one easily moved to tears. He once said of himself: "Faust complains of having two souls in his breast. I have a whole squabbling crowd. It goes on as in a republic." A large man given to excesses of food and drink, he very much looked the part of a Junker, but kept the mien of a senior military officer stuffed into a uniform that was too small. At times outgoing and charming, Bismarck could also lapse into moods of intense, gloomy isolation. He was unforgiving toward those who crossed him. No one could have been surprised to hear him announce that "if I have an enemy in my power, I must destroy him." He once said that he sometimes spent whole nights "hating." Although rejecting the attractions of German intellectual circles, he wrote clearly and elegantly. Driven by an unmitigated desire to serve the Prussian monarchy and unite Germany (someone described him rather grandly as "a veritable Atlas carrying upon his shoulders the destinies of a great nation"), he could also bide his time, always waiting for the most advantageous moment to act, ever willing to choose another strategy when necessary.

Bismarck had been named prime minister to confront the constitutional conflict over the army budget. After first putting parliament in the position of appearing to refuse compromise, Bismarck left no doubt as to the course of action he would take in this crisis and in the future. In September 1862, he linked the ongoing constitutional question to the role of Prussia in German unification. Bismarck could never contain his disdain for parliamentary liberalism: "The position of Prussia in Germany will be determined not by its liberalism but by its power. Bavaria, Württemberg, and Baden may indulge themselves in liberalism but no one will assign to them the role of Prussia; Prussia must concentrate its strength and hold it for the favorable moment, a moment which has already been missed several times, . . . Not through speeches and majority decisions are the great questions of the day decided—that was the great mistake of 1848 and 1849—but through blood and iron." He then announced that the government would operate without constitutional authorization, which it did for four years, using tax money previously voted to finance army reforms.

In June 1863, Bismarck struck against the liberal Progressives by restricting freedom of the press, refusing to confirm the election of Progressive mayors, and banning discussion of political issues in municipal council meetings. The fact that both public opinion and even Crown Prince Frederick William opposed these measures did not dissuade him in the least. Nor did the election of even more liberals to the parliament in October 1863. The Prussian state, with Bismarck holding the reins, simply ignored the constitutional opposition of the liberals. Bismarck's stridently anti-Austrian policy helped split the liberal parliamentary opposition. The army budget crisis was to be a harbinger of the unification of Germany, which would be achieved as a result of three victorious wars, through "blood and iron."

Alliances and Warfare to Establish Prussian Leadership

Russia and France were the two powers that would be most threatened by a unified Germany. The 1863 Polish revolt against Russian domination presented Bismarck with a perfect opportunity to ingratiate himself to the tsar. Whereas the other major powers seemed to side with the Poles, whose insurrection in 1830–1831 had won them great sympathy in Europe, Bismarck immediately voiced support for Russia, going so far as to mobilize troops along the eastern frontier as if ready to spring to the aid of Russian troops. "Hit the Poles so hard that they despair of their life," Bismarck advised. The Prussian government then signed an agreement with

Russia, by which both powers agreed to assist each other in the pursuit of insurgents across their respective frontiers. Austria, which had a sizable Polish population within its borders, found its relations with Russia soured. At the same time, Bismarck headed off an Austrian plan to increase its influence within the German Confederation.

Bismarck's first war was fought against the Danes in 1864 over Schleswig and Holstein, two duchies that were considered Danish territories and included the Baltic port of Kiel. The British prime minister Lord Palmerston (Henry John Temple; 1784–1865) once said that only three men truly understood the problem of Schleswig-Holstein: one was dead, one had gone mad, and the third, Palmerston himself, had forgotten it. The provinces were ruled by the king of Denmark although not incorporated as part of the kingdom of Denmark. Holstein, which was almost entirely German-speaking, also belonged to the German Confederation, and both German and Danish speakers lived in Schleswig. In 1848, the king of Denmark declared the complete union of Schleswig with Denmark, and revolution broke out in both duchies. During the summer, a Prussian army on behalf of the German Confederation intervened in defense of the revolutionary provisional government in Holstein, which seemed determined to join a unified Germany. International opposition (particularly that of Britain and Russia) rallied to the cause of the Danes, who wanted to hold on to the provinces, and who were backed by Sweden. After some fighting, the provisional government was dissolved by the Armistice of Malmö (August 1848).

The London Protocol of 1852 placed Schleswig-Holstein under the authority of the Danish king, but forbade their incorporation into Denmark. In March 1863, however, the Danish king enacted a new constitution that seemed to incorporate Schleswig into his kingdom. German nationalists protested vehemently. Bismarck, capitalizing on the wave of nationalistic support from Prussian conservatives and liberals alike, found an ally in Austria. The latter, also a member of the German Confederation and eager not to be left on the sidelines, prepared to send troops into Holstein to defend the independence of both Holstein and Schleswig.

Prussian coastal battery during the war against Denmark, 1864.

Bismarck issued Denmark an ultimatum in January 1864, demanding that the new constitution for Schleswig be redrawn. The Danish government, assuming that because of its strategic importance, France and Britain would rush to its defense, rejected the ultimatum and found itself at war with Prussia and Austria. To no one's surprise, the Danes were easily beaten, their defeat only forestalled by a hurried attempt by the British to rescue them at a conference in London. The Treaty of Vienna (October 1864) established the joint administration of Schleswig-Holstein by Prussia and Austria—Austria would administer Holstein (which lies between Prussia and Schleswig), and Prussia would administer Schleswig. This awkward arrangement left Prussia with a military corridor and communications line through Austrian-controlled Holstein and use of the port of Kiel.

Bismarck now viewed a military showdown with Austria as inevitable, even desirable. Yet, while preparing for that eventuality by currying the favor of the smaller German states and working to isolate Austria further from the other European powers, he blithely tried—and failed—to tempt Austria into making an agreement that would formally divide their influence in the German states into north-south spheres. Bolstered at home by victory over Denmark, Bismarck was now free to enhance Prussia's diplomatic position in Europe. He persuaded Napoleon III that the French would receive territorial compensation in the Rhineland if they would stay out of an Austro-Prussian war. The French emperor tried to play both sides. Convinced that Austria could defeat Prussia, he signed a secret treaty with the Habsburg monarchy that would give the French Venetia and establish a French protectorate in the Rhineland after an Austrian victory.

Bismarck then drew Italy into a secret alliance, signed in April 1866, by promising it Venetia in the event of a Habsburg defeat. Italy promised Prussia assistance if there was war with Austria, knowing that a Prussian victory would add the last large chunk of the Italian peninsula to Italy.

Hoping to win the support of the other German states, Bismarck sent a plan for reform to the Diet, calling for the establishment of a national parliament to be elected by universal manhood suffrage. That the famous Junker conservative would suggest that manhood suffrage might form a foundation for the creation of a unified German state surprised liberals. While the leaders of the other German states pondered a response, Bismarck moved to instigate war.

Exaggerating reports of Austria's military preparations, Bismarck denounced Austria's "seditious agitation" against Prussia in Schleswig-Holstein. By this he meant Austria's convocation of the Diet of Holstein to reconsider the duchy's status. After Bismarck had secured the temporary alliance with Italy and assured France's neutrality, Prussian troops entered Holstein. Austria allied with some of the smaller states (including Hanover, Saxony, and Hesse-Kassel) of the German Confederation. Prussia left the German Confederation, which then voted (under Austria's leadership) to send troops against the Prussian army.

Within three weeks, Prussian troops had defeated the South German and Hanovarian armies in the Austro-Prussian War (1866). Thanks to the timely arrival of a second force led by the Prussian crown prince and the division of the Austrian forces (half of which were fighting against the Italians), the Prussian army defeated the Austrian forces in the Battle of Sadowa (or Königgrätz) in eastern Bohemia on July 3, 1866; almost 1 million soldiers fought in the battle. Superior military planning as well as the rapid mobilization, deployment, and concentration of troops, talented officers, and more modern weapons—particularly the breech-loading "needle gun," which could be fired from a prone position—brought the Prussian army success.

The North German Confederation

In the aftermath of a victory most people did not expect, Bismarck's first accomplishment was to restrain the Prussian officer corps, many of whom wanted to push on to Vienna. Bismarck, however, realized that he would ultimately need the support of the South German states, some of whom had been allied with Austria, if Germany was to be unified under Prussian auspices. He also did not want to provide France or Russia with an opportunity to enter the conflict. He ended the war as quickly as possible. The Treaty of Prague (August 1866) eliminated Austria as a rival for the domination of the German states. The German Confederation was dissolved. The Habsburg monarchy recognized the North German Confederation (see Map 18.2), a new union of twenty-two states and principalities north of the Main River, with a constitution and a parliament (Reichstag), which Prussia would dominate with William I as president and Bismarck as federal chancellor. Bavaria signed an alliance promising to join Prussia if it were attacked by France, which had been surprised and alarmed by the relatively easy Prussian victory. Austria abandoned all claims to influence in Schleswig-Holstein, which became part of Prussia. By virtue of the annexation of Hanover, Frankfurt, Nassau, and the electorate of Hesse, Prussia ceased to be divided into two separate provinces. The incorporation of the smaller states into Prussia proceeded rapidly, with the centralized government in Berlin quickly establishing channels of administration. Whenever the possibility of sustained opposition to Prussian domination arose, the Berlin government intimidated, bribed, or cajoled the smaller states into compliance.

Bismarck left no doubt that he considered the North German Confederation a provisional solution until Germany could be united under Prussian leadership. In the meantime, the old Zollverein customs union, which included the South German states, was expanded to include an assembly of elected delegates. Bismarck hoped that this economic alliance, however loose, would in the future expedite the political unification of the German states. He received support from Prussian businessmen who would profit

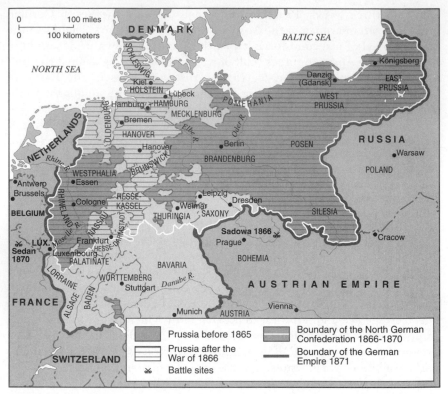

MAP 18.2 THE UNIFICATION OF GERMANY, 1866–1871   The unification of
Germany by Prussia included territory acquired after the Austro-Prussian War
(1866) and the Franco-Prussian War (1870–1871).

from the removal of customs barriers and the centralization of railway networks. As long as unification brought material progress, it did not seem to
matter to them that the traditional class system and restricted political life
that characterized Prussia would form the basis of a united Germany.

Bismarck was the man of the hour, the Prussian state a dynamic force
with which to be reckoned. Bismarck's bitter quarrel with the liberals over
the military budget ended. The Prussian Parliament, elected during the
war, overwhelmingly and retroactively approved the budgets of 1863–
1866. As one parliamentarian who had previously opposed Bismarck on
this issue put it, "The heavenly tribunal of success has cast its decision for
the government."

Some members of the Progressive Party and other liberals still espoused
"a vigilant and loyal opposition" at home. But liberal newspapers willingly
accepted the triumphs of Prussian foreign policy and military might. Bismarck was shrewd enough to realize that German unification would require liberal support, particularly as many of the conservative Junkers
were still wary of any change that might threaten Prussian traditions.

Some liberals were so elated by the prospect of German unification that they left the more hesitant Progressive Party and formed the nationalistic National Liberal Party, which supported Bismarck.

The Franco-Prussian War and German Unification

Prussian victory in the Franco-Prussian War of 1870–1871 completed the unification of the German states (with the exception of Austria). Following Prussia's victory over Austria in 1866, Napoleon III had warned an English diplomat, "I can guarantee peace only as long as Bismarck respects the status quo; if he draws the South German states into the North German Confederation, our guns will go off by themselves." In fact, some of the South German states were moving closer to Prussia through economic and military alliances.

Napoleon III foolishly seized upon the issue of the Hohenzollern candidacy for the vacant Spanish throne as an occasion to go to war against Prussia (which might have left France with Hohenzollern rulers on two sides). Bismarck fanned the embers of the crisis he had hoped would lead to a war he considered inevitable and necessary (see Chapter 19). His

The Prussian Council of War, 1870, including King William I (sitting to the left), Crown Prince Frederick William (standing front left), Chief of the Army General Staff Helmuth von Moltke (sitting in middle), and Chancellor Otto von Bismarck (sitting to the front right).

Prussian troops move to cut a French railway line in the Franco-Prussian War.

carefully planned diplomacy was never more evident. The Russian tsar warmly remembered Prussian support during the Polish rebellion of 1830–1831. The Austrians had not forgiven France for joining Piedmont-Sardinia in the war of 1859. Italy still resented the loss of Savoy and Nice in 1860 to the French. Bismarck played his real trump card with the British, coolly revealing documents proving that the French emperor had in 1866 demanded Belgium and Luxembourg as compensation for Prussia's increased power. This ended any chance of support for the French by the British government, which would never tolerate a potentially hostile power in Belgium, just across the English Channel. France went alone to war against Prussia.

One French army surrendered at Metz at the end of August, and another capitulated at Sedan at the beginning of September. French resistance continued until January 28, 1871, when the French capital, which had been under siege, surrendered.

Bismarck signed a convention with the provisional French government, awaiting the election of a National Assembly in France that could conclude a peace treaty. Bolstered by a surge of nationalist sentiment in the South German states as well as in Prussia, Bismarck demanded the annexation of Alsace and much of Lorraine, where German speakers predominated (although they did not necessarily want to be incorporated into a united Germany). Bismarck made this demand with some misgivings, fearing with reason that a French desire for revenge might poison relations in the foreseeable future. The French had to pay a war indemnity of 5 billion francs, and France also lost a small mining district on its northern frontier.

The German Empire was officially proclaimed in the Hall of Mirrors in the Palace of Versailles on January 18, 1871. King William I became Emperor William I of Germany. Despite grumbling from Bavarian Catholics and several of the rulers of the smaller states, the North German Confederation and its constitution provided the framework for German unification. But this federalism existed in structure only, despite the rich traditions of German particularism. The German Empire took on the autocratic political structure of Prussia, characterized by the influence of Prussian nobles and military officers.

Industrialists and merchants hoped that unification would provide a boost to large-scale industrialization in the new Germany. Hamburg merchants thus grudgingly traded the traditional independence of their city for the economic advantages of operating within a centralized state. Unlike Cavour in Italy, who reached liberal political goals by liberal political means, Bismarck had harnessed economic liberalism to the goals of conservative political nationalism.

William I and Bismarck celebrating the proclamation of the German Empire in the Hall of Mirrors at Versailles.

Unlike their counterparts in Victorian England and France, the German middle class largely remained outside political life in the German Empire, as they had been in Prussia before unification. Germany would be an autocracy based on the alliance of throne and aristocracy, whereas Britain retained its parliamentary government and France became a republic in the 1870s. Many Germans remained indifferent to unification. Others were not enthusiastic, preferring the particularism of their region to the new Germany. Yet, over the long run, Germans came to accept with growing enthusiasm the politically unified state that had been forged by Bismarck's spectacularly successful statemaking. The result was a critical shift in the balance of power in Europe.

National Awakenings in the Habsburg Lands

Nationalism threatened the existence of the Habsburg monarchy, as many ethnic groups pursued competing interests. Whereas Germany and Italy were politically unified when astute leaders mobilized nationalist feeling within the upper classes and successfully carried out an aggressive foreign policy, nationalism would serve to destabilize the Habsburg lands. German and Italian unification altered the balance of power in Central Europe. Unified Germany, not Austria, was now unquestionably the strongest state in Central Europe. Furthermore, the absorption of Lombardy and Venetia into the new Italian state had come at the expense of the Austrian Habsburgs.

Several important factors, however, held the Habsburg lands together. The Habsburg crown itself was a rallying point for many of Emperor Francis Joseph's subjects. The empire's close ties to the Catholic Church encouraged loyalty to the dynasty that had long protected it in the Habsburg lands, where most people were Catholics. Furthermore, the imperial bureaucracy and army not only provided employment opportunities and prestige for German speakers, the largest national group, but also for other ethnic groups as well. Moreover, the very polyglot nature of the empire allowed the emperor and his government to play off nationalities against each other. For example, German speakers in Bohemia, where Czechs formed a majority of the population, and Magyar and Croatian nobles in Hungary remained loyal to the empire. They did so in exchange for the maintenance of their privileges vis à vis ethnic minorities in the territories they dominated.

Diversity and Cohesion in the Habsburg Empire

Far more than the German and Italian-speaking states that came to form two nations, the provinces that formed the Habsburg domains represented extraordinary linguistic, cultural, and historical diversity (see Map 18.3).

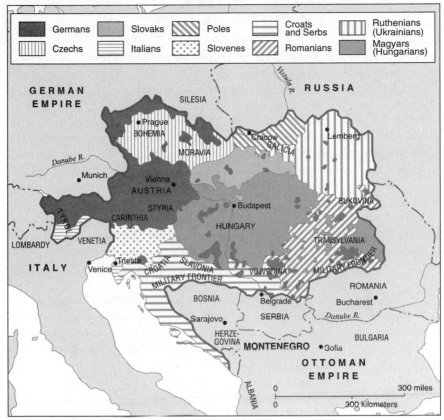

MAP 18.3 NATIONALITIES IN THE HABSBURG EMPIRE The diverse nationalities and lands encompassed by the Habsburg empire during the 1860s and 1870s.

At least twenty nationalities lived within the territorial boundaries of the empire; these included Czechs in Bohemia and Slovaks to their east, Poles in Galicia, Slovenes and Croats in the south, Romanians and Ruthenians in the southeast, and Italians in the Alpine Tyrol, as well as other peoples, including Serbs, Bulgarians, Turks, and Gypsies. But by far the two largest national groups were the Germans (35 percent of the population), living principally in Austria but numerous also in Bohemia, and the Magyars, or Hungarians (23 percent), whose traditional crown lands formed the largest territory in the empire. These lands were divided into five districts: Hungary, Croatia, Transylvania, the Vojvodina, and the Military Frontier. Yet, the Germans and Hungarians were outnumbered by the various Slavic groups, who together accounted for about 45 percent of the empire's population. Czechs comprised 23 percent of Austria's population. In Hungary, Romanians (with 19 percent of the population) formed the next largest group after the Magyars. Inadequate transportation networks accentuated the insular and overwhelmingly rural nature of many ethnic regions—for example, there was no railroad between Vienna and the Croatian capital of Zagreb.

How did this polyglot empire hold together as long as it did among all of the competing ethnic rivalries and demands? The answers tell us something of the process of statemaking from a different point of view, that of the non-national state. First, the tradition of the Habsburg monarchy itself was an important force for cohesion, rooted in centuries of Central European history. Emperor Francis Joseph, who was eighteen when he came to power in 1848, had taken the second part of his name from his enlightened ancestor Joseph II in order to invoke the tradition of the House of Habsburg in those revolutionary times. As one Hungarian statesman put it during the Revolutions of 1848, "It was not the idea of unity that had saved the monarchy, but the idea of the monarchy that saved unity." Francis Joseph, whose long rule was shaped by the fact that he had come to power as his monarchy seemed to be breaking apart, was as devoted to the army as it was to him. The army saved the monarchy and continued to help hold it together.

Second, the Habsburgs depended on the support of the German middle class and of the German-speaking bureaucracy. The most salient cultural traditions (for example, music) of the imperial capital, Vienna, were overwhelmingly German. Viennese liberals celebrated their domination of Austrian political and cultural life during the 1850s and 1860s by building a broad boulevard, the Ringstrasse. The grand artery was built on the traces of the city's fortifications, which Francis Joseph had ordered dismantled in 1857, since they had long since lost all military function except to separate the wealthy center of the city from the proletarian suburbs. The new boulevard also took shape with military motives in mind—troops could be moved rapidly in the event of working-class rebellion. The architecture of central Vienna reflected the taste of the aristocracy and the Catholic Church. In contrast, public buildings (including the university, the opera, and the parliament building) and residences of manufacturers and bankers (constructed in a grand style that copied those of the nobles) that bordered the Ringstrasse reflected the secular cultural tastes of the Viennese upper class.

The empire's largest towns, even outside of Austria, were largely German-speaking; in Prague, Germans outnumbered Czechs by more than three to one. German was the official language of the bureaucracy and the army, and more than half of the officers were native German speakers. German was also the language of the secret police, who kept a careful watch on national movements. To get anywhere, one had to speak German, a fact learned by thousands of non-German migrants to the cities, particularly the capital. The German middle class also benefited from free-trade policies, and profited from the beginnings of industrial concentration in Bohemia.

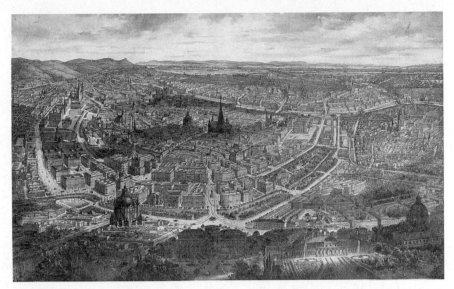

A view of Vienna and its Ringstrasse, 1873.

Third, the monarchy enjoyed the support of Austrian and Hungarian nobles, as well as their Croatian, Polish, and Italian counterparts, landed nobles of ethnic groups with long histories of political sovereignty. The latter
three nobilities depended on the Habsburg monarchy to maintain their
prerogatives vis-à-vis ethnic minorities within their territories and against
the peasants of their own nationality. Thus, the small Croatian nobility
needed the cooperation of Hungarians for the retention of their own privileges in Croatia, and had a long tradition of military service to the Habsburgs. The monarchy therefore depended on the preservation of the status
of the favored nationalities, above all, the Germans and Magyars, from the
challenges of other national minorities within the lands of their domination, such as Slovenes, Slovaks, Ruthenians, Ukrainians, Serbs, and
Czechs.

Fourth, Catholicism, the religion of the majority of the peoples, also was
a force for unity in Austria. In the newly unified Germany, by contrast, the
religious division between the Protestant north and the Catholic south
represented a potential force for disunity.

Repression of Nationalism in the Habsburg Empire

Nationalism among the ethnic minorities in the 1850s and 1860s was still
limited to a relatively small number of intellectuals and people from the
liberal professions who had the literacy and leisure to dream of national
unification. Most nationalists at first aimed at a cultural and linguistic
revival. As a Czech nationalist put it at a meeting of writers in Prague, "If

the ceiling were to fall on us now, that would be the end of the national revival."

If nationalism were recognized as a principle of political organization within the empire, the domination of the German middle classes in Prague would be threatened by the Czechs, who were the major nationality in Bohemia, and the power of the Croatian nobility in Slovenia would be challenged by the Slovene majority there. On the other hand, any talk of nationalism among Polish nobles in Galicia who resented the authority of German bureaucrats quickly ended when they remembered the massacre of Polish nobles by Polish peasants in 1846. The former were grateful for the protection provided by the empire's German-speaking army and the Austrian secret police, although the emancipation of the peasantry from labor obligations in 1848 seemed to have eliminated the threat of widespread insurrection.

The Habsburg monarchy feared that demands for autonomy, or even outright independence, would pull the empire apart. The Habsburg monarch also worried that nationalism, which had frequently been tied to political liberalism, would challenge the empire's authoritarian structure. German and Italian nationalism threatened the empire's territorial integrity by raising the possibility that the Italian and, above all, the German-speaking parts of the empire might prefer inclusion in Italy or Germany, respectively. Furthermore, Hungarians, the second-largest ethnic group within the empire, were demanding political influence commensurate with the size of the Magyar territorial domains.

After the mid-century revolutions, the Habsburg monarchy, like the German states and France, continued an unrelenting repression of liberal and national movements. Beginning with Francis Joseph's accession to the Habsburg throne, the monarchy entered a period of "neo-absolutism," codified in the "Patent" of December 1851. Alexander von Bach (1813–1893) put some of the most potent tools of the state to work, including a hierarchy of officials and police sent out from Vienna into the imperial provinces. The nobles, some of whom resented the abrogation of peasant obligations after 1848, had in general welcomed the restoration of Habsburg authoritarianism. But they also had lost some of their regional privileges and prerogatives to the state. In 1855, Bach signed a Concordat with the Catholic Church, restoring many of its privileges and extending ecclesiastical authority, particularly the right of prelates to judge the clergy and to hear lay cases involving marriage. As in France, the Church made a comeback. The monarchy also eliminated civil marriage and restored the Church's *de facto* control over education. Protestants were not allowed to teach in Catholic schools, and new restrictions limited the right of Jews to acquire property. Corporal punishment was once again legalized.

This centralization and expansion of state power was accompanied by a liberalization of trade within the monarchy, the extension of railway lines, and the imposition of a uniform tax system. But government expenditures far outstripped tax revenue. A contemporary described the Bach system with some accuracy: "The administration was run by a standing army of soldiers, a kneeling one of those praying in church to be acceptable to the government, and a crawling one of informers."

Political Crisis and Foreign Policy Disasters

In the wake of the defeat of Austrian forces in Italy and amid mounting hostility among Germans and non-Germans and the growing unpopularity of neo-absolutism, in August 1859 Francis Joseph dismissed Bach as the head of government. After enlarging the Imperial Advisory Council, Francis Joseph promulgated a new constitution, the October Diploma of 1860. This dismantled much of the Bach system, reestablishing a form of conservative federalism. The provincial assemblies received new authority, placating the nobles. Nonetheless, the October Diploma did not satisfy the Hungarian aristocrats, who lacked the influence and political role enjoyed by German speakers, who had most benefited from the Bach system. German speakers also, however, were unhappy as they lost some power under the new system. One critic assessed this transition harshly: "Absolutism in bankruptcy put on a false constitutional nose in order to extract a few more pennies from the public."

Anton von Schmerling (1805–1893), minister of the interior, drafted the February Patent of 1861, a constitution that established a bicameral parliament in which all the empire's nationalities were to be represented. Yet, the number of non-German representatives, as elected by the diets of the respective crown lands, would not equal those of the Germans, who benefited from electoral restrictions that favored urban elites. Magyars, Croats, and Italians refused to participate in the first election, and Schmerling dissolved the regional parliaments. The February Patent perpetuated the most salient elements of Bach's neo-absolutism, including the German-speaking bureaucracy, police, and spies. It placed virtually no constitutional limitations on the emperor's power, despite the fact that the parliaments were elected by a limited franchise. One political crisis after another marked the mid-1860s, until Francis Joseph finally suspended the constitution in 1865.

The February Patent might well have solved some of the monarchy's problems were it not for continued foreign policy disasters. While Bach's neo-absolutism made many internal enemies, foreign policy failures seriously undermined the monarchy's international position. The Habsburg monarchy's status as a power in European affairs declined as relations with Russia and Prussia deteriorated. In 1863, Schmerling expressed sympathy for the Poles in their struggle against Russia. This pleased the Poles within the Habsburg empire but angered Russia. When his empire went to war with Prussia in 1866, Francis Joseph could not look for support from the tsar, or from the British or French, who were angry that Austria had joined Prussia against Denmark two years earlier.

Prussia's victory over Austria cast doubt on the efficiency of Bach's neo-absolutism and encouraged the other preeminent nationalities—particularly the Magyars, but also the Croats and Poles—to demand a greater share of political power, since the monarchy seemed to be floundering under the domination of German speakers. Humiliated twice in seven years on the field of battle (first by the French and Piedmontese in 1859 and then by the Prussians in 1866), the monarchy's prestige as a Great Power fell almost irretrievably. Many of Francis Joseph's subjects blamed the authoritarian structure of neo-absolutism for the defeat. Liberals called for the implementation of constitutional government, backing their demands by pointing to the inefficient way in which the wars had been fought.

Creation of the Dual Monarchy

The empire's military defeats heightened Magyar demands for more power. Fearing the possible alliance of German liberals with the Magyars, Francis Joseph had visited Budapest, the Hungarian capital, in 1865 and met the Magyar demand for the reincorporation of Transylvania into Hungary. He had already asked Ferencz Deák (1803–1876) to propose a solution that would reconcile Magyar demands with imperial power. Deák, a wealthy Magyar lawyer and noble, believed that Hungary's strength as a nation depended on the continued existence of the Habsburg monarchy. The emperor realized that as long as the Magyars remained dissatisfied and uncooperative, he could not consider a war of revenge against the Prussians.

The Compromise (*Ausgleich*) of 1867 created the Dual Monarchy of Austria-Hungary. The Hungarian Parliament proclaimed Francis Joseph constitutional king of Hungary, as well as emperor of Austria. The bureaucracy in Vienna carried out matters of finance, foreign policy, and defense. But Hungarian now became the language of administration in Hungary, and the Magyar domains henceforth had their own domestic bureaucracy, parliament, and constitution. The halves of the Dual Monarchy would negotiate economic tariffs every ten years. The parliaments of Austria and Hungary elected representatives to the Imperial Assembly, or Delegation.

The *Ausgleich* left intact the domination of German speakers in Austria and Magyars in Hungary. While in principle recognizing the equality of all nationalities, the new constitution nonetheless maintained the disproportionate advantage enjoyed in the empire's parliament by Austria's Germans. The emperor routinely appointed Germans to important ministries, and he could easily circumvent parliamentary opposition by ruling by decree when parliament was not in session, or by refusing to sign any piece of legislation he did not like.

The Hungarian Constitution of 1867 allowed the Magyar nobles to hold sway in the Hungarian Parliament, since the emperor's powers as king of

An image in a Pan-Slav journal published in Vienna.

Hungary were now more limited. Hungarian ministers were not responsible to Francis Joseph, but rather to the Hungarian Parliament's lower house, which was elected by leading property owners, who were Magyars. Hungarians feared that any concession made by the Austrian Germans to any minority, for example the Czechs, might encourage similar demands by minorities in Hungary. The Croats were particularly dissatisfied. The Nationality Law of 1868 gave the peoples of each nationality the right to their own language in schools, church, and in government offices, but did not recognize any separate political identity. The South Slavs also particularly resented the settlement, and growing tensions were reflected by the insistence of one of the architects of the *Ausgleich* that "the Slavs are not fit to govern; they must be ruled." Many Serbs increasingly identified with Russia, which saw itself as the protector of all Slavs.

Conclusion

The *Ausgleich* did somewhat stabilize eastern Central Europe by creating the Dual Monarchy. Francis Joseph retained his dynastic prestige. The Habsburg monarchy remained precariously placed between the newly unified states, powerful Germany to the north and Italy to the south. Russia stood to the east, its self-proclaimed role as the protector of all Slavic peoples a potential threat to Austria-Hungary and ultimately to peace in Europe. The national question in Austria-Hungary remained unresolved; in the oncoming age of militant nationalism, the monarchy's problems would become those of Europe.

In Central Europe, the complexity of ethnicity and the size of ethnic minorities within states represented an imposing barrier to national unity. Yet, virtually every country in Europe contained ethnic minorities who spoke another language than that of its rulers and officials: Bretons, Catalans, and Alsatians in France, among others; and Catalans and Basques in

Spain. Only a minority of people living on the Italian peninsula spoke the Italian language, which had evolved from Tuscan. Some of the dialects within the German states were so different as to be, for all practical purposes, separate languages. The question of nationality and the goal of nationalists to create states in which the borders would be defined as much as possible by ethnicity were further complicated by the fact that some Czech speakers, for example, remained loyal to the Habsburg monarchy, even though German was the language of authority. Many Alsatians who spoke a German dialect considered themselves French.

Dreams of national independence and unification were, however, not easily destroyed. Romania gained its independence largely because of its strategic location at the crossroads of Southeastern Europe between three powers competing for domination in the Balkans: Turkey, Russia, and Austria-Hungary. Russian troops put down a determined Polish rebellion in 1863. Elsewhere in Central and Southern Europe, small groups of Czech, Serb, and Bulgarian intellectuals anticipated national independence. But these groups of intellectuals lacked mass support, especially in Eastern Europe, where the vast majority of the population remained illiterate.

As we have seen, nationalism as a unifying factor in European political life emerged, in the case of Germany and Italy, out of the Revolutions of 1848; however, in the Habsburg lands it was a force that came to challenge the very existence of the empire. In contrast, of Europe's three major powers, all of which had been politically unified for well over a century, Britain and Russia had had no revolution in 1848; France, the third, emerged from the tumultuous period with an authoritarian empire. In the next chapter, we will consider Britain, Russia, and France during the third quarter of the century, a critical and revealing period of change for each.

CHAPTER 19

THE DOMINANT POWERS IN THE AGE OF LIBERALISM: BRITAIN, FRANCE, AND RUSSIA

The Crystal Palace, a vast structure built of glass and iron in London's Hyde Park, housed the Exposition of 1851, the first world's fair. It stood 1,848 feet long, 408 feet across, and 66 feet high, and included a million square feet of glass, 3,300 columns, and 2,300 girders, all of identical size so they could be prefabricated. Gaslight provided illumination, and the first public toilets provided on such a scale offered convenience.

To many British subjects of Queen Victoria, the Great Exposition of 1851 stood for the ascendancy of Christianity, the British constitution, and free trade. It symbolized the social and economic transformation of one of the three most powerful states in Europe during the middle decades of the nineteenth century. Besides Britain, the other dominant powers during the age of liberalism were France, which was more slowly entering the industrial age, and Russia, which remained quite backward despite efforts at reform.

Britain's long tradition of weak executive authority, balanced by parliamentary government, reflected and complemented its liberalism and economic prosperity. France was a strongly centralized empire, but it had a legislature and an emperor dedicated to economic progress and determined to give the state a larger role in making it possible. In contrast, Russia was an autocracy, a police state in which the absolute authority of the tsar was limited only by bureaucratic inefficiency and the impossibility of reaching into every corner of his vast empire. Russian nobles dominated the backward peasant masses, and unlike Britain and France, Russia had

The Crystal Palace, symbol of the new industrial age.

only a tiny middle class, sparse industrialization, and no representative political system.

All three powers undertook significant reforms in the 1850s and 1860s. Economic and social changes seemed to necessitate political reform to keep revolution at bay. Although in 1848 the forces that divided society had led to revolutions in many European nations, they had not done so in Britain, Europe's most liberal nation, nor in Russia, its most autocratic state. In Britain and France, the forces that held society together were strong enough to produce reforms that gave a political voice to a wider segment of society. In Russia, Tsar Alexander II shocked many of his own nobles by emancipating the serfs in 1861. But unlike the political reforms enacted in Britain and France, the tsar's reforms did not significantly alter the autocratic nature of the Russian Empire.

VICTORIAN BRITAIN

In 1840, young Queen Victoria (1819–1901) married the German Prince Albert (1819–1861) of Saxe-Coburg-Gotha. They were happily married, although she described sex as "giving way to the baser passions." Indeed, she warned one of her daughters who was about to be married that a bride was "like a lamb led to the slaughter," and that there would be times when she would simply have to give way to her husband's animal urges and "think of England." Victoria herself bore children only because she thought it part of her duties as queen. She detested pregnancy and never particularly liked infants or children, raising them with little visible affection, as if managing a business from afar.

Albert's tendency to be narrow-minded, socially awkward, and tactless irritated cabinet ministers and other highly placed people. He hovered about the government, dashing off letters and memoranda when the mood struck him, meddling when he could. When Victoria refused to lengthen the time of their honeymoon in order to return to royal duties, Albert summarized his situation: "I am only the husband, not the master, in the house." Although Victoria made clear from the beginning that she would serve as a queen without a king, her devotion to Albert sparked some anti-German feeling in Britain.

Prince Albert organized the Great Exposition of 1851 in London. In his opening prayers, the Anglican archbishop made the connection between Britain's prosperity and the era of peace that had prevailed on the continent since the end of the Napoleonic Wars in 1815. More than this, Great Britain seemed special. The historian Thomas Macaulay wrote in the wake of the Revolutions of 1848 on the continent: "All around us the world is convulsed by the agonies of the great nations. . . . Meanwhile, in our island, the course of government has never been for a day interrupted. We have order in the midst of anarchy."

More than 6 million visitors—most from Britain but a good many from the continent and beyond—could choose among 13,000 exhibits (half from Britain and its colonies), divided into raw materials, machinery, manufactured goods, and fine arts, and ranging from useful household items

Queen Victoria with her family.

to huge guns exhibited by the Prussian industrialist Krupp. These seemed somewhat out of place on an occasion in which many assured themselves that science and industry offered hope for continued peace in Europe.

The Great Exposition celebrated the industrial age, Britain's primacy in manufacturing, and the "working bees of the world's hive." Its catalogue intoned "The progress of the human race . . . we are carrying out the will of the great and blessed God." One of its sponsors boasted that "The history of the world records no event comparable. . . . A great people invited all civilized nations to a festival, to bring into comparison the works of human skill. It was carried out by its own private means [and] was self-supporting."

When Albert died in 1861 at age forty-two of typhoid, Victoria was devastated. She retreated into lonely bereavement and isolation, spending—particularly in the early years of her widowhood—most of her time in a Scottish castle or on the Isle of Wight, ignoring most public duties. Only gradually did Victoria re-emerge to provide a focal point for a nation in the midst of a great transformation during the second half of the century.

Victoria knew virtually nothing about the lives of her subjects and instinctively disapproved of factory reforms and increased opportunity of education for the lower classes (fearing that it would lead them to want to raise their station in life). But the queen remained the personification of the "respectability" that gave her name to an age. This Victorian notion of "respectability"—inculcated by education and contemporary literature—centered on the family and strict rules about public comportment. But it meant different things to families of different strata: three servants to a comfortable middle-class family, a parlor off the kitchen for breakfast for a lower middle-class family, avoiding a pauper's funeral for a lower-class family (since to be buried "on the parish" was widely regarded as the ultimate stigma).

The Victorian Consensus

"Victorian," a term first used in 1851, the year of the Great Exposition, evokes a sense of the contentment and confidence that middle-class Britons enjoyed. A Manchester merchant wrote in his diary in May 1853, "The people of Manchester have never enjoyed it more, nor have I seen clearer evidence of general well-being . . . free trade, peace, and freedom. Oh, happy England! Mayest thou know and deserve thy happiness." For Britain, it was a confident time.

The British middle class forged a consensus in political life. This consensus was formed around the capitalist entrepreneurial ethic, emphasizing self-reliance and faith in progress. In the Victorian entrepreneurial ideal, the individual demonstrated his moral worth through hard work, in contrast to the evils of the old system of aristocratic patronage and parasitic behavior. As Adam Smith, theorist of laissez-faire economics, had put it, landlords "love to reap where they never sowed." Competition would

A contemporary impression of Darwin
looking at human ancestry.

determine those who were fit to rule, not aristocratic monopoly or unearned privilege, nor working-class demands for a greater share in the
prosperity of the nation that middle-class Britons believed their hard work
had created.

In 1859, the belief in the virtues of rugged individualism received a
boost from the publication of *On the Origin of Species* by Charles Darwin
(1809–1882). Darwin, the son of a dominating father, overcame chronic
anxiety, self-doubt, and severe depression to undertake determined, systematic research and analysis on the evolution of living organisms. His
bold book argued that some animal species survived and evolved by virtue
of being better adapted to existing conditions, while others disappeared
because they were less "fit." Although Darwin himself was reluctant to
speculate about the possible economic or social implications of his scientific ideas, it would be a short jump to claim that contemporary society
worked in the same way and that the individual must struggle to get ahead
in order to survive. By implication, Darwin's work seemed to suggest that
the state should stand back and let individuals alone to compete on the
playing field of life. This was more good news for many confident Victorians, but not for churchmen, for Darwin's book challenged the Bible's description of God having created the world in seven days by teaching that
mankind evolved from other animal forms over millions of years. His research and analysis were a damaging blow in the struggle between science
and religion in nineteenth-century Europe.

Samuel Smiles (1812–1904) popularized these beliefs. "What some
men are," the Scotsman insisted, "all without difficulty might be. Employ

the same means, and the same results will follow." Trained as a physician, Smiles had published a biography of George Stephenson, the man who invented the first railway without knowing how to read. In 1859, Smiles published *Self Help,* which sold 20,000 copies in its first year and a quarter of a million copies by 1905. It was translated into Dutch, French, German, Arabic, Turkish, and several Indian languages. Smiles decried state interference in the operations of the economy. Laws, he insisted, could not "make the idle industrious, the thriftless provident, or the drunken sober." Such improvements could only be brought about by "individual action, economy, and self-denial, by better habits rather than by greater rights." Unemployment and low wages could, Smiles reasoned, serve the interests of the poor by forcing them to be thrifty and to save. Smiles' gospel of work nicely complemented laissez-faire economics, a cornerstone of Victorian thought.

Victorian thought and values also strongly reflected the influence of religion, and religious images and references permeated Victorian social and political discourse. Entrepreneurs believed that they were doing God's work by becoming successful and rich. Many Victorians insisted that the pervasive influence of religion more than prosperity explained the apparent social harmony of their age.

Thus, many Britons were surprised and even shocked by the results of a government survey of every church in England and Wales on a Sunday morning in 1851. The goal was to find out how many people went to church, and which denomination they embraced. Out of a population of almost 18 million people, only slightly more than 7.2 million had attended church. Even when the number of people who could not have attended services because they were infirm, sick, or attended religious services on a different day was taken into account, far more than half the population simply had stayed home. The survey also revealed that if everybody in England and Wales had decided to attend church, only 58 percent of the population and only 30 percent of Londoners could be accommodated. Therefore a wave of church-building followed. Between 1841 and 1876, the Anglicans built 1,727 new churches and restored more than 7,000 old ones; among their rivals, Congregationalists and Catholics doubled the number of their churches, and Baptists increased their own by more than five times.

Although there were many exceptions, religious affiliation and class lines usually went hand in hand. The Church of England, closely identified with the British elite, remained a target for liberal reformers. Parliament had repealed the Corporation and Test Acts in 1828, eliminating two significant discriminatory laws that had kept Dissenters (non-Anglican Protestants) who refused to take communion in the Anglican Church from holding office. Parliamentary decrees in 1854 and 1856 allowed non-Anglicans to attend Cambridge and Oxford Universities. Catholics, most of whom were Irish immigrants—in addition to a small number of nobles

The Salvation Army, founded in London in 1880, taking Christianity to the poor.

whose families had converted to Catholicism—still faced popular suspicion, however, reflecting the deep roots of anti-Catholicism in Britain.

Many middle-class Victorians believed that they were doing God's will by becoming enthusiastic reformers. They wanted to make the lower classes more "moral." Congregationalist and Baptist evangelicals (as well as Methodists) won converts among the lower classes, perhaps because leaders of these churches demonstrated far more interest in the conditions of the poor than did the Church of England. Temperance movements proliferated in a wave of concern about lower-class drunkenness—one-third of all arrests were for drunk and disorderly conduct. The Charity Organization Society, founded in 1869, reflected some fears that "indiscriminate charity" would weaken the moral fiber of the poor. It sought to organize charity more systematically, by promoting charitable giving to those who steered clear of drink. And in 1875, the Salvation Army began its work, offering assistance to those who would participate in religious revival services.

The Crimean War

At mid-century, Britain found itself involved in a war that ended the long peace that had lasted almost without interruption since Napoleon's defeat

Map 19.1 The Crimean War, 1853–1856 Russian, British-French-Pied-montese, and Austrian troop movements involved in this war between the Great Powers.

in 1815. Britain entered the Crimean War (1853–1856) in 1854 to support the Turks against Russia, which had invaded the Turkish Danubian principalities of Moldavia and Wallachia (see Map 19.1).

The Russian Empire had for centuries sought control over the Straits of Constantinople, which divide Europe from Asia and could provide the Russian navy with access to the Aegean and Mediterranean Seas. The continued decline of the Ottoman Empire had seemed inevitable since the eighteenth century, and Russia stood poised like a vulture to profit from its once-powerful neighbor's weakness. Egged on by nationalists, Russia presented itself as the protector of Slavic and Orthodox Christian interests in the Balkans, encouraging agitation against the Turks and leading to the Russian occupation of Wallachia and Moldavia.

Britain had opposed expanding Russian interests in the region since the late eighteenth century because the British feared that such expansion threatened the European balance of power. By mid-century, increased British trade with the Ottoman Empire had become another factor in British support for the Turks. With India its most vital colony and with interests in Afghanistan, both of which bordered the Russian Empire,

Britain was ill disposed to the expansion of Russian influence. Furthermore, Austria-Hungary refused to countenance a Russian presence on its doorstep in the Danubian principalities. To Nicholas, this seemed to demonstrate Habsburg ingratitude, since the tsar's army had helped quell revolutionaries threatening the Habsburg empire only four years earlier. Emperor Napoleon III of France, eager for a military victory to solidify support for his regime, also stood ready to stop Russian expansion by supporting Britain.

After Tsar Nicholas I sent troops into Moldavia and Wallachia, the sultan of Turkey declared war on Russia in October 1853. Nicholas' fleet defeated the Turks in the Black Sea, setting fire to the sultan's wooden ships with incendiary shells. But the tsar's confidence that Britain and France would soon quarrel because of conflicting interests proved ill founded. With British public opinion eager for the flag to be shown even after the withdrawal of Russian troops from Moldavia and Wallachia, the British Royal Navy sailed into the Black Sea. Not to be outdone, Napoleon III, too, sent warships.

Britain and France declared war on Russia. Both powers wanted to prevent Turkey from becoming a vassal to the tsar, which might have disrupted the balance of power. British and French forces first moved against the Russian port of Sebastopol on the peninsula of Crimea on the edge of the Black Sea. Invulnerable to sea attack, Sebastopol could only be stormed from land because of recent Russian fortifications. The rusty invading armies fought a war of siege that would have been comic in its mismanagement by aged, inept commanders if it had not cost so many lives. The French army seemed vastly better trained, as well as better fed and supplied than the British. The senior British commander, a veteran of Waterloo forty years earlier, persisted in referring to the Russians as "the French." His personal staff included five of his nephews. Most British officers owed their commissions to the fact that they were aristocrats, not to their competence. One commander spent each night on his private yacht anchored offshore, dining on meals prepared by a French chef while his men shivered in the wind and mud of the Crimean winter.

Far more men died (about 600,000) of disease than in battle, although Alfred Tennyson (1809–1892), Britain's poet laureate, helped make famous the "Charge of the Light Brigade," in which British cavalry rode into "jaws of death." Soldiers sitting in the mud trying to eat ghastly rations and those wounded in battle seemed to face almost equal risks. The first war correspondents sent dispatches by telegraph to eager readers in Britain and France, where interest in the distant siege dramatically increased newspaper circulation.

Into this maelstrom Florence Nightingale (1820–1910) ventured. The daughter of a prosperous family, she had shocked her parents by declaring her intention to become a nurse, an occupation that had a particularly bad reputation as providing a refuge for "disorderly" women. Nightingale vol-

Florence Nightingale.

unteered for service in a Constantinople hospital after hearing of the appalling conditions endured by the wounded and those sick with cholera and dysentery. From Constantinople she bombarded the government with highly detailed information on what was wrong and what was needed. Raising funds through private contributions, she succeeded in improving conditions in the hospital, assuring a sufficient supply of medical equipment and clothing. She had to overcome the conviction of officers that she would "spoil the brutes," that is, the sick and wounded enlisted men, as well as overcoming prejudices against a woman making forceful demands on the government.

As a result of Florence Nightingale's highly publicized work throughout the remainder of her career, nursing emerged as a more respected profession. The British government several years later enacted a series of reforms to improve food and health care for the men in its army.

The Crimean War ground to a halt after Sebastopol finally capitulated in September 1855. The Peace of Paris (March 1856) guaranteed the autonomy of the Danubian principalities (which became independent Romania), Turkey's independence, and the neutrality of the Black Sea. The war left little doubt that Victorian Britain remained Europe's strongest power.

The Liberal Era of Victorian Politics

In Britain, political reform followed compromise, not revolution. Even amid rapid change, a kind of social stabilization occurred, aided by economic growth. Most Victorians of all social classes increasingly felt themselves part of a nation with which they could identify and were not attracted by political extremes. In contrast to their French counterparts active in the Revolutions of 1830 and 1848, English middle-class liberals avoided at all costs prodding workers into street confrontations with authority, fearful of unwittingly unleashing an uncontrollable insurrection. Chartism, the mass petition movement in the 1840s for universal manhood suffrage, faded into the background after its last gasp in 1848. The government arrested suspected radicals, sent 8,000 troops into London, and appointed 150,000 civilian "special constables" while businessmen, anticipating trouble from a Chartist demonstration, hauled out hunting rifles and barricaded their offices. In any case, with the exception of a very small radical component in favor of the use of "physical force," the Chartists were gradualists. The Irish nationalist movement, dormant since a failed insurrection in 1798, reawakened in 1848. But the presence of the British army and the emigration of great numbers of Irish to the United States limited Irish nationalists' efforts in that revolutionary year to one minor uprising.

Benefiting from the 1832 enfranchisement of more middle-class men, the Whigs governed Britain for most of the 1850s and 1860s. Henry John Temple (1784–1865), the Viscount Palmerston, who began his political career as a Conservative, led the Whigs in the early 1850s. The notorious philandering of the shrewd and feisty "Lord Cupid," as he was known to his detractors, stood out in an age of public prudishness. Palmerston outraged Queen Victoria by trying to seduce one of her ladies-in-waiting in Windsor Castle.

In the 1850s, Palmerston held together a coalition of Whigs who were determined to uphold laissez-faire economic policies. Dissenters, Catholics, and liberal Anglicans wanted the Anglican Church to lose its status as the Established Church of England. Gradually these Whigs began to be referred to as the Liberal Party. Their coalition revealed the importance of religious belief but also the growing Liberal refusal to accept the Anglican prerogatives associated with the Conservatives.

Palmerston's bellicose saber-rattling won him personal popularity. Crowds cheered when he ordered the blockade of the Greek port of Piraeus in 1850 to enforce claims against the Greek government by Don Pacifico, a British-born Portuguese Jew whose house an Athens mob had destroyed. Palmerston triumphantly defended himself in the House of Commons, boastfully comparing the might of classical Rome and Victorian Britain.

Palmerston gloried in the unjustified credit he received for Britain's victory in the Crimean War. He then lurched into a short war against China in 1857, after the Chinese government seized a pirate ship that had formerly been registered under the British flag. Considering this a major insult to Britain, but rebuffed by a majority in Commons and opposed by pacifist political radicals outside of Parliament, Palmerston refused to resign and called for a general election. Basing his campaign solely on an appeal to British patriotism, he won the day.

When France and its ally Piedmont-Sardinia coaxed Austria into war in 1859 with the goal of aiding the cause of Italian unification, many in England wanted Britain to jump into the fray on the side of Austria, as old anti-French prejudices poured forth in attacks against Napoleon III. Alfred Tennyson, whose popular poetry reflected Victorian faith in science and religion, dashed off a poem that caught the shrill nationalist mood:

> Be not deaf to the sound that warns
> Be not gull'd by a despot's plea!
> Are figs of thistles, or grapes of thorns?
> How should a despot set men free?
> Form! Form! Riflemen form!
> Ready, be ready to meet the storm!
> Riflemen, riflemen, riflemen form!

For the moment, however, the British government was able to ignore rising popular chauvinism. Later in the century, it would be unable to do so.

William Gladstone (1809–1898) emerged as the leader of the Liberal Party. Gladstone was the son of a wealthy and unscrupulous merchant who had made a fortune in trade with India and the West Indies. The young Gladstone was deeply religious and had seriously considered becoming a clergyman. Gladstone wore his moral vision of the world on his sleeve for all to see, going out into the night to try to convince prostitutes to abandon their trade. He sought to impose his own self-discipline and sense of Victorian Christianity on the nation. During his early years in government, he worked to assure laissez-faire economic policies, campaigning for the abolition of even the very modest income tax.

As chancellor of the Exchequer, Gladstone had waged war against extravagance and waste in government. In contrast to his Conservative rivals, he opposed colonization as being too expensive. Victoria loathed Gladstone, blaming him for almost every domestic and international problem. She resented his *de facto* campaign to reduce the limited role of the monarchy in the constitutional government of Britain. Having supported the repeal of the Corn Laws, he wanted to make the Liberals the party of reform.

Robert Peel had split the Conservatives by supporting the repeal of the Corn Laws in 1846. After Peel's death in 1850, Benjamin Disraeli (1804–1881) became the leader of the Conservatives and Gladstone's great rival. A Jew who had been baptized into the Anglican Church, Disraeli seemed an unlikely leader of a party dominated by rural aristocrats whose social world revolved around vast estates. But he was an energetic, skilled politician and an impressive orator who had the good sense to realize that further Conservative attempts to revive economic protectionism

(*Left*) William Gladstone, Liberal prime minister. (*Right*) Benjamin Disraeli.

were doomed. Unlike Gladstone, Disraeli got along famously with the queen, whom he flattered on every possible occasion. Victoria depended upon Disraeli for advice much as she had on Albert (as Disraeli lay dying, the queen wrote to ask if she might visit the Conservative leader. "It is better not," Disraeli replied, "She'd only ask me to take a message to Albert.").

Working-Class Quiescence

At mid-century, Britain entered a period of relative social harmony. The repeal of the Corn Laws in 1846 convinced many workers that they could place their trust in political reform. Middle-class reformers had broadened their appeal to include the most prosperous segments of the working class. Most British workers seemed to accept the belief that hard work and savings would inevitably be rewarded.

Many British workers, including many union members, joined "friendly societies," or as they were increasingly called, "self-help associations." Membership in such groups rose from less than a million in 1815 to 3 million in 1849 and 4 million in 1872, four times that of unions and twelve times that of cooperative societies. They provided members with minimal assistance in times of unemployment or illness and a decent burial. In some associations, members listened to lecturers speak to them on such virtues as sobriety and thrift. Preaching individual self-help and respectability, such organizations did not offer the socialist vision common among workers in France, Belgium, or the Rhineland.

Like the friendly societies, Britain's "new model unions" also embodied the concept of self-help. Members of these unions first and foremost saw their organizations as representing skilled workers of specific crafts, not the working class as a whole. Most members in Britain lacked the class consciousness more frequently found in comparable organizations in France and parts of Germany. Unions brought together craftsmen and skilled workers (such as carpenters and printers) from the so-called "aristocracy of labor" who could afford high dues. Constituting about 15 percent of the working class, these craftsmen and skilled workers stood apart from the mass of unskilled laborers. Some of them taught in Sunday schools, working men's colleges, reading rooms, and improvement societies.

Even when local unions within a single trade joined to form national organizations, there was no talk of revolution or even of eventually restructuring British economic, social, and political life. For example, the Amalgamated Society of Engineers (machine tenders) vowed to do nothing "illegally or indiscreetly, but on all occasions to perform the greatest amount of benefit for ourselves, without injury to others." Strikers in the 1860s were increasingly willing to accept arbitration boards and to compromise to end strikes and achieve limited goals.

The Reform Bill of 1867

Since 1832, the majority of British subjects had regarded further political reform as virtually inevitable. Workers wanted universal manhood suffrage, and a growing number of middle-class voters, hoping to end disproportionate aristocratic influence in British political life, supported some expansion of the suffrage. Queen Victoria, however, did not, insisting that she "cannot and will not be the queen of a democratic monarchy." John Bright (1811–1889), who represented Manchester in the House of Commons from 1847 to 1857 and was then elected in 1857 from Birmingham, launched several campaigns for electoral reform. In 1866, the National Reform Union, whose membership was overwhelmingly middle class, and the Reform League, which many artisans had joined, allied with Bright's parliamentary radicals. Their goal was household suffrage, that is, the right of the adult male head of each family to have the right to vote.

Gladstone, typically, was convinced that political reform was not only expedient but moral. "You cannot fight against the future," the Liberal leader taunted Conservatives in Parliament, "Time is on our side. The great social forces . . . are against you. They are marshalled on our side." But he wanted to let down the electoral drawbridge only long enough to let in artisans and skilled workers, the "aristocracy of labor."

The issue of extending the suffrage split the Liberals. One of them, Robert Lowe, called reform "a lower form of civilization" and an "Americanization of the constitution." He argued that the utilitarian goal of achieving the greatest happiness for the greatest number could not be achieved through extension of suffrage to workers because workers would all vote as one for radical candidates. He wanted to make unions illegal, and opposed educational reform because he believed workers would be more dangerous if they learned more.

Most Conservatives vigorously opposed any further political reform, fearing that the enfranchisement of more ordinary people would not only add to the ranks of the Liberals but eventually lead to subsequent legislation that might weaken the political influence of wealthy property owners. The Liberal government proposed a bill to reduce the minimum amount of tax one had to pay to be eligible to vote both in the countryside and in towns, where the rate would be set lower. The proposed reform, then, would still exclude ordinary workers and other poor people. The House of Lords rejected the bill because a majority of members opposed any change.

Disraeli, who six years earlier had predicted that "pillage, incendiarism and massacre" would follow universal manhood suffrage in Britain, now believed that electoral reform that maintained some exclusions was not only inevitable but that the Conservative Party could benefit from it. It might bring about a return to the aristocratic leadership and patronage that seemed to have all but disappeared in the Liberal-sponsored free-for-all of laissez-faire. Perhaps influenced by French Emperor Napoleon III's manipulation of universal manhood suffrage, Disraeli took a "leap in the dark," proposing that the vote be given to each head of a household and that the minimum countryside tax requirement be further lowered. Under Conservative auspices, the Reform Bill of 1867 passed, like that of 1832, again doubling the ranks of voters.

Disraeli's Conservatives, however, failed to woo many of the new voters, and their leader resigned. The Liberals won a large majority in Parliament, boosted by support from workers who now could vote. The major goal of the Chartist campaign twenty years earlier had now been reached, giving further impetus to British reform, not revolution.

The Reforming State

The Victorian consensus rested upon a strong belief that the "hidden hand" of the economy would generate economic growth. Many Victorians therefore believed the Poor Law of 1834 was self-defeating because it provided resources to the poor for which they had not worked. But increasingly aware of the devastating poverty of millions of workers, most middle-class Victorians by mid-century had changed their minds about the role of government in society. Edwin Chadwick (1800–1890), a journalist and associate of Jeremy Bentham who had drafted the Poor Law and served as one of the Poor Law Commissioners, compiled a *Report on the Sanitary Condition of the Laboring Population of Great Britain* (1842). It proved to be both a pathbreaking investigation and an impassioned plea for government action after cholera had ravaged poorer urban neighborhoods. Largely thanks to Chadwick's efforts, Parliament passed laws facilitating the inspection of rooming houses.

Thereafter, parliamentary commissions began to call upon "experts" to gather information and assess conditions of British life. The age of statistics had arrived. Regulatory agencies began to spring up. In 1848, Parlia-

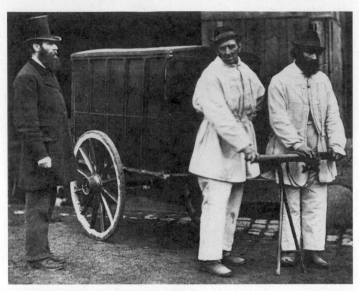

Street disinfectors in London, 1875.

ment passed the first national health act, creating the national Board of Health. In the same year, the city of London named its first health officer.

Gradually, Victorian middle-class liberals came around to the view that social reform was necessary. In part, the acceptance of reform reflected the religious view that one should "do unto others," as well as the prevalent belief in progress. Furthermore, hit-or-miss patronage no longer seemed sufficient to address the very complex problems engendered by industrialization and urbanization. Samuel Smiles may have been an outspoken proponent of the entrepreneurial ideal and of laissez-faire economic policies, but he, too, came to accept the necessity of minimal reforms.

Yet, considerably more than altruism lay behind a shift in middle-class attitudes. An Evangelical reformer put it this way: "The middle classes know that the safety of their lives and property depends upon their having round them a peaceful, happy, and moral population." Manufacturers also knew that demand for their products depended on workers having money to spend. Some nobles, such as those who had supported repeal of the Corn Laws, now also believed that some reforms were in their interest; at a minimum, they reasoned, some timely reforms would limit working-class militancy and spare Britain from the insurrections and revolutions that seemed to plague the continent. In Great Britain, the "age of optimism" became the "age of improvement."

Queen Victoria once asked someone to define "bureaucracy," a term she did not know. "That, Madam," came the reply, "is something that they have in France." Yet, despite the long tradition of English decentralized government, the Victorian state also grew in reach. The administration of the Poor Law itself served to strengthen the role of government in local affairs. Government workhouse inspectors reinforced the acceptance of outside expertise and regulation by civil servants. The municipal councils took over tasks of administering local government from the justices of the peace, who had served in such capacity since the sixteenth century. Municipalities were now responsible for education, as well as for health, housing, roads, and policing. Service in local government, once often nothing more than another honor awarded a landed gentleman, now required a considerable amount of work and the participation of paid officials.

With increased responsibilities, the British civil service became professionalized. In 1854, a parliamentary commission recommended the standardization of requirements for admission to the civil service. With the exception of the Foreign Office, which remained largely an aristocratic preserve, the government administered competitive examinations on which appointment and promotion depended. The queen, like many nobles, worried that commoners would push their way past those whose social background had given them their posts in the first place. But competitive examinations did not democratize entry into the civil service. Applicants who had attended one of the expensive elite public schools (so called because they accepted from all over Britain students whose families could afford them) had a far greater advantage on the examinations than those who had not. Competitive examinations legitimized the existing distribution of power within the social structure.

Chadwick's revelations about public health—or rather, the lack of it—encountered ferocious opposition from those who were against any government intervention in such things as a matter of principle. Some industrialists were unwilling to countenance any possible reduction in their profits. "We prefer to take our chance on cholera and the rest than be bullied into health," groused *The Times*. Yet, by the time Chadwick was driven to resign from the General Board of Health in 1854, the right of the state to intervene in matters of health had been established. Parliamentary acts in the 1860s extended regulations of working conditions in mines and in factories with more than fifty employees and where women and children worked. The Public Health Act of 1866 gave local government more authority to assure a cleaner water supply. In 1871, state inspectors for the first time obtained legal access to workplaces. And a year later, Parliament established health boards in towns and country districts, but local business and political interests often combined to foil the efforts of doctors and other reformers.

Although some of these early reforms bore fruit, their contributions were generally modest. Their significance is that the mid-century Victorians introduced structures facilitating state intervention that would become even more important later. Furthermore, reform leagues, which brought together people specifically concerned about a certain issue, and which urged Parliament to enact reforms, became part of British political life.

The National Education League pressured Victorian governments to undertake more educational reforms. At the time of the Great Exposition, an official report had stated: "Every British child should unquestionably be taught reading, writing and the elements of knowledge." A parliamentary commission determined that only about a quarter of pupils were being educated at an acceptable minimal level. Again, some opponents of educational reform believed that mass education would erode social deference. But the Education Act of 1870 made schooling obligatory for children younger than age thirteen and mandated the formation of elected school boards to build tax-supported schools in areas where there were none. Passed over Anglican opposition, it also placed education in the hands of the state by permitting local education boards to establish schools in districts where neither the Established Church nor its Dissenting rivals had created one. With the help of state grants, the Anglicans had far outdistanced their competitors in building new schools, so that they controlled 90 percent of the elementary schools in England and Wales in 1860. In 1880, the Gladstone government passed an act requiring school attendance for all children between five and ten years old, and specifying conditions under which children younger than fifteen could leave school in order to work.

In the wake of the Conservative defeat following the passage of the Reform Act of 1867, the Liberals enjoyed an overwhelming mandate to enact a number of reforms. At the demand of the vast majority of Irish, in 1874 they ended the favored status of the Protestant Church of Ireland; they ended government subsidies to the Church of England; they ended the purchase of army commissions; they enacted land reform in Ireland; and they recognized the legal existence of trade unions.

Yet, despite presiding over the Victorian age of reform with crusading zeal, Gladstone remained convinced to the end, like many Liberals, that the charitable efforts of individuals were preferable to government action. In one of his last letters, he wrote in 1894, "Of one thing I am and always have been convinced—it is not by the State that man can be regenerated, and the terrible woes of this darkened world effectually dealt with." But in Britain, the role of the state had nonetheless expanded considerably during the middle decades of the century. The era of laissez-faire liberalism ended. Speaking of her father, Gladstone's daughter remembered, "I was accustomed to hear him utter the word 'Government' in a tone that charted it with awe and made it part of my effective religion."

Conservative Revival

Out of government, Disraeli reinvigorated the Conservative Party, establishing a Central Conservative Office to coordinate local party organizations. Like the Liberal Party, which had begun similar national and local organizations, the Conservatives had come a long way from the days when country gentlemen made known what they expected, and a handful of electors deferred to their influence and judgment.

Anticipating mass politics as inevitable and not wanting to be left behind, Disraeli prepared his party for the task of trying to outbid their Liberal rivals for the popular vote. Conservatives began to appeal more systematically to British nationalism, as Disraeli affirmed his support for "maintaining the greatness" of the empire and suggested that the Liberals, because of Gladstone's anti-imperialist views, would weaken Britain. When the Turks and Russians began to quarrel over the Balkans, Disraeli supported the Turks, despite their massacre of thousands of Bulgarians in 1876. Liberal Party leader Gladstone, however, was horrified by the bloodbath and made a political issue of the Balkans. It was easy enough for him to do so: Britain had less to fear from the Ottoman Empire in full decline than from an aggressively expansionist Russia.

When the Conservatives returned to power in 1874, Prime Minister Disraeli pursued what he called "Tory democracy" by pushing his own reform legislation through Parliament. He sought to woo the allegiance of workers from the Liberals by getting Parliament to pass laws that forbade labor by uneducated children in industry and by enacting the Artisans' Dwellings Act, which began a coordinated attack on fetid urban slums. A year later, Parliament legalized picketing by workers and codified existing social legislation.

Yet, as Gladstone never tired of pointing out, the Conservative Party continued to be the party of great landed wealth as it maintained its grip on the English countryside. Because of parliamentary districting, the countryside remained over-represented in Parliament, again to the advantage of landed gentlemen. In 1871, about 1,200 people owned a quarter of the land, and the holdings of 7,000 families amounted to half of England. Landed gentlemen dominated Commons until 1885, the cabinet until 1893, and the aristocratic House of Lords well into the twentieth century. The law of primogeniture helped keep huge estates intact, even if the economic position of some aristocrats suffered during the depression that began in 1873.

The Conservative Party now reflected an important change in modern British political life. The old "country/city" cleavage, although never absolute, between country gentlemen and urban merchants and manufacturers that had characterized politics since the seventeenth century largely ended. The Conservative Party now found new support among some of the wealthiest businessmen, who abandoned the Liberals. Furthermore, many aristocrats were themselves now actively involved in the management of banks and modern industries. The English business elite that had been formed during the first decades of Victoria's reign became as conservative as the aristocrats they emulated. A contemporary in 1879 assessed this evolution when he wrote: "Our territorial nobles, our squires, our rural landlords great and small, have become commercial potentates; our merchant princes have become country gentlemen." Some wealthy businessmen even deserted the Dissenting religions to join the Established Anglican Church. This new Conservative political culture, supported by a faithful minority of nationalist "Tory workers," would be strong enough to survive the economic depression that lasted until the mid-1890s and beyond. The era of mass politics had begun in Britain.

TSARIST RUSSIA

In the mid-nineteenth century, autocratic Russia—an absolutist state based upon an alliance of the tsar and the nobles—presented a particularly sharp contrast with Great Britain—a state with a long tradition of parliamentary rule and commercial and manufacturing prosperity. Since the sixteenth century, the Russian tsars had slowly expanded their empire through the conquest of vast stretches of territories and peoples to the south and west. The Russian Empire was multinational; ethnic Russians formed less than half of the population. Although there had been relatively fewer nationalist stirrings in the Russian Empire than had occurred within the Austro-Hungarian monarchy, ethnic resistance to the empire and to the Orthodox Church, for example from Polish Catholics, increasingly challenged Russian domination.

Since the brief and ill-fated Decembrist uprising of 1825, organized by army officers and students, Russia had seen neither reform nor revolution. Yet, liberal ideas from the West had begun to filter into Russia via intellectuals. Surrounded by and alienated from a society built upon serfdom, which legally bound most peasants to the land, some of them believed revolution inevitable. Serfdom not only was inhumane, it was also economically inefficient. During the Crimean War, the Russian army, largely constituted of illiterate serfs who could barely operate the old guns that they had been given, had acquitted itself poorly. This helped convince the tsar that only through reform and the emancipation of the serfs could Russia compete with the West. Nonetheless, the basic structure of the state remained the same, with no institutional constraints on the tsar's authority.

Russian Backwardness and Stirrings of Reform

The overwhelming majority of Russia's people were impoverished serfs bound to the land. Only about 5 percent of the empire's population lived in towns. In Russia, which had a very small middle class, a small group of intellectuals, some nobles, and some educated commoners demanded reform. In Britain, the movement for political and social reform championed by the middle class had for the most part been pursued through parliamentary means. In contrast, in Russia, because of the daunting reality of Russian backwardness, many intellectuals believed that only revolution could bring change.

A contemporary caricature showing Russian nobles using bundled serfs as poker chips.

Nicholas I (ruled 1825–1855), who had become tsar just after the Decembrist revolt of 1825, was obsessed with keeping Russia sealed from Western ideas, which he blamed for the rebellion of military officers. The Revolutions of 1848 in Western and Central Europe increased the determination of the Russian autocracy to stifle internal dissent. The ministry of education oversaw a policy of tight censorship and repression by the fearsome Third Section, the political police. But the police found it impossible to seal off the colossal empire entirely. More than 2 million foreign books entered Russia just in the 1847–1849 period, most ending up in St. Petersburg and Moscow.

Nineteenth-century Russian intellectuals were unique in Europe. Many were gentry who could survive well enough without a university position or government post. Members of a privileged, educated elite, they could thus afford to write, even if the public opinion they wanted to reach was small indeed. Unlike their counterparts in Western countries, they were not absorbed into the liberal professions. Some of these intellectuals became professional revolutionaries.

During the 1830s and 1840s, some of the gentry were overwhelmed with guilt that they were well off while the masses suffered. Alexander Pushkin (1799–1837), whose mother exiled two serfs to Siberia with a nod of her head after they failed to bow as she passed by, attacked serfdom in his short stories. A few educated commoners joined this group of conscience-stricken gentry, although in all of the empire, there were only 4,000 university students in 1849, about a third of whom were commoners. Steeped in a variety of intellectual currents, the intelligentsia brooded over and debated how Russia might emerge from autocracy and backwardness.

Like the philosophes of Old Regime France, the Russian intelligentsia gathered to discuss ideas that censors considered seditious and dangerous. Trying to avoid censorship and dodging the police, they met in small groups, or "circles" in St. Petersburg and in Moscow, where the atmosphere was somewhat freer than in the tsar's capital. In the 1830s and 1840s, groups of intellectuals and students formed in St. Petersburg to discuss a wide range of historical and philosophical writings from the West.

The intelligentsia also debated the works of Russian writers. P. A. Chaadayev's *Philosophical Letters* had slipped by the censors in 1836. Chaadayev (1794–1856) presented a thinly veiled condemnation of Russia's cultural history. Officials declared him to be mad, and the police hounded him for the rest of his life. His pessimistic piece provoked heated discussion because it suggested that cultural backwardness would keep Russia from joining the ranks of civilized nations.

Chaadayev's *Philosophical Letters* opened the debate between "Westernizers," those Russian intellectuals who, like Tsar Peter the Great in the seventeenth century, looked to the West for a model for progress, and "Slavophiles," who believed that Russia could never be reconciled with Western values. Westernizers like Chaadayev regarded the development of parliamentary institutions and industrialization in Britain, France, and the German states as a model for Russia to emulate. Slavophiles cherished the specificity of Russia's defining institutions: the Orthodox Church, the village commune (the *mir*), and even tsardom itself. They did not want Russia to go forward, as did the Westernizers. Rather, they argued that Russia could avoid the traumas of Western industrial development because it already possessed the basis for a future socialist society in the village. The peasant commune, with a variety of communal buildings (a wind or water mill, a grain supply store, tavern, and a workshop), facilitated survival. Peasants adapted their lives to unbelievably difficult conditions imposed by nature and by powerful outsiders, the state and the lords. The *mir* seemed to provide both a moral vision and revolutionary potential.

Vissarion Belinsky (1811–1848) and Alexander Herzen (1812–1870) forcefully made the case that Russia had to follow the example of the West if it were to emerge from backwardness. Belinsky, the son of a doctor, had been expelled from university for writing an article denouncing serfdom. When the popular writer Nikolai Gogol (1809–1852) refused to criticize the autocracy, Belinsky's circulated *Letter to Gogol* (1847), which helped define the Westernizer position by blasting Gogol's respect for "orthodoxy, autocracy, and nationality," the dominant triad of the Russian Empire: "Advocate of the knout [whip], apostle of ignorance, champion of obscurantism and reactionary mysticism, eulogist of Tartar customs—what are you doing? Look at what is beneath your feet; you are standing at the brink

(*Left*) Vissarion Belinsky. (*Right*) Alexander Herzen.

of an abyss." In Belinsky's view, the inculcation of some Western values and progress would eradicate the superstitions of the past. He argued that in defending Russian political and social institutions, Gogol was betraying all writers by not criticizing evil.

Alexander Herzen, a landowner's son, had vowed following the ill-fated Decembrist revolt to carry on the work of the revolutionary martyrs. Arrested and exiled for participation in a student discussion group, Herzen travelled to France. Returning to Moscow in 1840, he familiarized those in the Moscow Stankevich circle, whose members were for the most part Westernizers, with the French Jacobin and socialist tradition and their belief in the inevitability of progress. Herzen then developed a hybrid version of reform that would combine westernization from below with admiration for the *mir*. In *From the Other Shore* (1855), written in voluntary exile in Paris after the Revolution of 1848, Herzen, like the Slavophiles, expressed confidence that Russia, even while following the lead of the West, would take its own path to socialism. It would thus be able to avoid what he considered the decadence brought by capitalist social relations. Socialism could be easily established in Russia because the village commune already existed as a community of social equals in the face of autocratic and noble exploitation. From London, Herzen implored Russian officials to struggle for peaceful liberal reform. Interestingly enough, both radical reformers and the men of the tsarist state shared a suspicion of Western "bourgeois" political and social life. The Slavophile current of reformism thus had much more in common with the tsarist autocracy than it cared to admit.

A Russian religious procession.

Unlike the Westernizers, the Slavophiles celebrated the religious faith of the Russian masses. Gogol, for one, contended that the Russian people were the most religious anywhere, with village life centering around the Church. The peasant household, which brought together the extended family (parents, children, grandchildren, and sometimes brothers-in-law and their families) under the stern guidance of the patriarch, was itself a place of worship.

Such a view was, however, anathema to Slavophiles who wanted the Orthodox Church to guide Russia's future. Rejecting Western materialism, they believed that an era of social harmony and equality had existed in Russia before Peter the Great transformed the Russian state in the late seventeenth century by importing Western ideals and bureaucracy. "We are a backward people," wrote one young Slavophile, "and therein lies our salvation. We must thank destiny that we have not lived the life of Europe. . . . We do not want its proletariat, its aristocratic system, its principles of state, its imperial power. . . . We believe in the strength of Russia because we believe that we are called to bring into history a new principle . . . and not to repeat the stale old lessons of Europe."

The Emancipation of the Serfs

The emancipation of the serfs in 1861 by Tsar Alexander II (ruled 1855–1881) was the most ambitious attempt at reform in Russia during the nineteenth century. Following the failed Decembrist revolt in 1825 (see Chapter 14), some government officials began to think what for most nobles was the unthinkable—that Russia could develop economically only if serfdom was abolished. The institution of serfdom and its obligations had become more onerous during the first half of the century. Serfdom dictated the organization of taxation, the army, courts, and virtually every other institution of government. Because landowners had a virtually unlimited source of labor, they showed little inclination to try to increase agricultural yields.

After defeat in the Crimean War in 1856, Tsar Alexander II, who was far less intransigent and repressive than his predecessor, Nicholas I, and some of his officials began to believe that his country could not compete with the West if the serfs were not emancipated. The question of serfdom preoccupied public opinion, including not only the intelligentsia, students, and reform-minded bureaucrats, but also some landowners. Russian industrial development and effective agricultural production, he argued, required free wage labor that could be taxed. Serfs only worked halfheartedly; most Russian peasants still tilled their fields with the wasteful three-field system (with one field left fallow each year).

Serf rebellions—more than 1,500 during the first half of the century—shook the empire. Many serfs had joined the army during the Crimean War, believing that they would be freed upon returning home. The flight of thousands of serfs toward the open spaces of the east, as to Crimea in the south, undermined the agricultural economy upon which Russia depended. Now, as rumors spread that the tsar, whom many peasants considered the father of his people, would end Russia's "peculiar institution," peasant rebellions became even more widespread. Alexander told assembled landowners, "You know yourselves that the existing order over souls cannot remain unchanged. It is better to abolish serfdom from above than to wait until serfs begin to liberate themselves from below." Some nobles now believed emancipation inevitable. That Russia could not be considered Europe's most powerful state wounded their nationalist pride. In 1858, a Slavophile noble wrote the tsar that "The abolition of the right to dispose of people like objects or like cattle is as much our liberation as theirs."

On April 5, 1861, Russia became the last European state to abolish serfdom. Alexander II emancipated the 22 million serfs by a proclamation made through the Orthodox Church. For two years the old system would remain essentially in place. But serfs would then receive land through the *mir*, which was administered by male heads of household. Nobles were compensated for their land by the state, and peasants had to repay the state through forty-nine annual redemption payments. The villagers would be collectively responsible for land redemption payments (although the lords' household serfs were freed without land and owed no payments).

Instead of owing labor to the lords, serfs now owed taxes to the state. These would be collected by the communes. Peasants were no longer dependent upon the whims of landlord justice. Henceforth, they could not be beaten, flogged, or even killed with impunity. Peasants, who had

Peasants hailing Tsar Alexander II after the emancipation of the serfs in 1861.

wanted complete and immediate freedom without compensation, were bitterly disappointed by the terms of their freedom. ("We are yours," went an old serf proverb, "but the land is ours.") The allotments of land they received were insufficient for them to grow enough to eat and pay taxes and redemption fees. Furthermore, as the villages were collectively responsible for redemption payments and taxes, former serfs were rather like hostages to their own communities, dependent upon the village fathers for permission to go find work elsewhere.

In tsarist Russia, the serfs were freed practically without bloodshed, while in the United States the slaves found freedom only after one of the most violent struggles—the Civil War (1861–1865)—anywhere in the nineteenth century. Unlike the southern landed elite in the United States, who went to war in defense of slavery, the Russian nobility capitulated without resistance to emancipation. For all of the vast expanse of the Russian Empire, the tsarist state exercised more centralized authority than did the relatively weak central government in the United States. More than this, Americans considered private property more of an absolute right than did even Russian nobles, who wanted, above all, to extract services from peasants. After emancipation, the vast wealth of the Russian nobles could still pay for such services.

Many critics of autocracy now expected further reforms. Alexander rooted out some incompetent ministers and officials and asked the ministry of finance to keep regular budgets. In 1864, Alexander decreed the establishment of district or village assemblies called *zemstvos*. These would elect delegates to regional assemblies. Six years later, the tsar created similar urban institutions called *dumas* (councils), with the authority to assess taxes and to organize public education and public services, such as they were. But the ministry of interior controlled the *zemstvos*, and provincial governors ignored them, treating their members as seditious agitators. Moreover, landowners elected the members of the *zemstvos*, and their votes were given more weight than those of landowning townsmen and peasants.

The emancipation of the serfs necessitated an expanded administrative apparatus, since millions of people were no longer subject to the justice of the lord but rather to that of the state. Village elders helped maintain order. The tsar also introduced regional and lower courts modeled on those of Britain, as well as public trial by jury. In 1864, for the first time a separate judicial branch of government came into existence in Russia, although the tsar could override any court decision. This, too, provided a forum for debate and reformism.

The essential structure of the empire remained the same, however, even after the emancipation of the serfs. The army was no longer made up of loyal, poorly supplied, illiterate, beaten serfs but rather of loyal, poorly supplied, illiterate, beaten free peasants. In the past, few soldiers had been expected to survive the twenty-five-year term of service. This was reflected by the right of their wives to remarry three years after their hus-

A Russian village council.

bands left. With an eye toward reform, the tsar established a Prussian-style general staff, took steps to modernize weapons, and reduced the term of military service to six years, followed by nine years in the reserves and five years in the militia. The goal was to encourage greater dedication among conscripts. Alexander also ordered the elimination of some forms of corporal punishment, including the most brutal—and often fatal—floggings or beatings.

Yet, none of these reforms diminished the arbitrary power of the tsarist state and its Third Section police. Most political cases were gradually removed from the court system and handed over to trial by secret court-martial. Alexander restored the censorship apparatus, which was temporarily weakened in the years before the emancipation, to full strength. The tsar had no intention of creating any kind of national representative institution that would undercut his authority. Nonetheless, the emancipation was followed by the mobilization of peasants, intellectuals, and Poles, three groups demanding further change.

The Expansion of the Russian Empire

The prestige of the Russian Empire in Europe fell after the Crimean defeat. By the Peace of Paris (1856) Russia relinquished Moldavia, Wallachia, and Bessarabia and had to accept the neutrality of the Black Sea, further frustrating imperial designs in Southeastern Europe (see Map 19.2). Following two years of public demonstrations, Poles rose up in 1863, proclaiming a "national government" before being crushed by Russian troops. The brutal repression that followed brought the Poles widespread sympathy in Western Europe, but not independence. In the 1870s, Russia intervened on behalf of its fellow Slavs, the Bulgarians and the Serbs, who had risen up against the Turks. As a Russian army drove toward Constantinople, the Austrian army and British navy readied to prevent the tsar from reaching the Dardanelles Straits. Defeat forced Turkey to sign the Treaty of San Stefano (1878) with Russia. It created a large, independent state of Bulgaria, which Russia would dominate. The mood of Pan-Slavism (a movement aimed at promoting the interests and unity of all Slavs) irritated the other European powers, particularly Britain and Austria-Hungary, which demanded the convocation of an international conference to discuss the matter. The other powers called a conference in Berlin, over which German Chancellor Otto von Bismarck presided. The Congress of Berlin (1878) reduced the size of Bulgaria and recognized Serbia, Montenegro, and Romania (formed by the union of the principalities of Wallachia and Moldavia) as independent states. Russia made some face-saving gains, including a small part of Bessarabia, which allowed it to control the mouth of the Danube River. But Russian Pan-Slavs, in particular, believed themselves aggrieved by Britain and betrayed by Bismarck's Germany.

MAP 19.2 THE EXPANSION OF RUSSIA After territorial losses under the Peace of Paris (1856), Russia turned eastward, expanding through Central Asia toward the Far East and its port at Vladivostok.

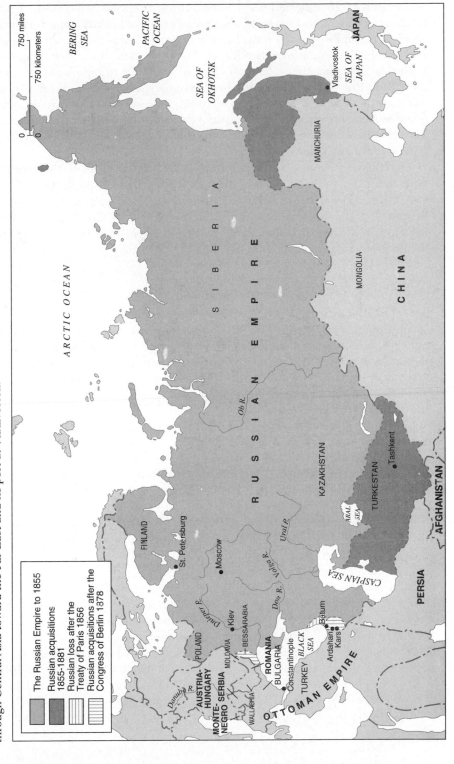

Legend:
- The Russian Empire to 1855
- Russian acquisitions 1855–1881
- Russian loss after the Treaty of Paris 1856
- Russian acquisitions after the Congress of Berlin 1878

Alexander II then turned his attention toward Central Asia and the Middle East. The tsar and many of his officials believed that Russia was destined to expand its empire into the vast regions of Asia that lay to the east and south. Russian armies conquered Turkestan and the other relatively powerless Muslim states in Asia, finally reaching Afghanistan. At this point, the British felt threatened by Russian expansion, which seemed to impinge upon British interests near India. In response, the British army invaded Afghanistan, and in 1881 put a puppet ruler on the throne. In the Far East, Russian forces moved across Siberia, giving its navy access to the Pacific Ocean at Vladivostok.

The Russian Empire now included about one-seventh of the world's land mass. Eastward expansion brought contact and eventually conflict with China. The Chinese emperors were powerless in the face of Russian demands, as they were when confronted by those of Britain. Japan, emerging from centuries of isolation following the Meiji Restoration in 1868, would prove to be a far tougher adversary for Russia.

Nihilists and Populists

The conscience-stricken gentry of the 1830s and 1840s was superseded by revolutionaries in Russia. The latter were drawn from a variety of social backgrounds. They included the sons and daughters of nobles, merchants, peasants, and Orthodox priests. Convinced that one spark might ignite a wave of rebellion, they struck out on their own or in very small groups. They were loners, determined to the point of obsession with what each believed was his or her mission.

Some of the Russian revolutionaries found the old debates between the Westernizers and Slavophiles irrelevant. Some of them became nihilists, who accept no dogmas. The novelist Ivan Turgenev (1818–1883) wrote, "A nihilist is a man who does not bow down before any authority, who does not take any principle on faith." Above all, the nihilists rejected the materialist doctrines of the West, which seemed to have no place for belief in either secular or religious dogmas. But they also disavowed many Russian traditions, and thus repudiated the Slavophiles. Some of them viewed the Orthodox Church as an institution of oppression, whereas others remained fervent believers.

Some nihilists saw in the Russian masses an untapped revolutionary force. Among them were those who believed that the emancipation of the serfs had aided their cause by creating an independent peasantry, which might be more likely to rise up against its oppressors.

Nihilists believed themselves unique because they had freed themselves from constraining dogmas. Like the conscience-stricken gentry before them, they believed in the power of literature to effect change. In 1863, Nikolai Chernyshevsky (1828–1889), a former seminarian, published *What Is to Be Done?* (1863), a novel that had an enormous impact on several generations of intellectuals. Chernyshevsky described committed people of action as "rational egoists" who would form a disciplined vanguard of change. Because nihilists did not feel bound by moral codes, they believed they could take whatever action seemed necessary to achieve their goals. Separated from society, what they called "rational egoism" led them within the context of a ruthless police state to an amoral terrorism. In the 1860s, groups of nihilists turned to violent revolution, plotting the assassination of state officials and the tsar himself. The police infiltrated and drove groups like "Land and Freedom" and "The Organization"—with its central committee called "Hell"—underground, particularly after a student attempted to kill Tsar Alexander II in 1866.

Michael Bakunin (1814–1876) became the most famous anarchist of his or any other time. Anarchists rejected the very existence of the state, thereby quarreling bitterly with socialists, who wanted not to destroy the state but to take it over. A professional revolutionary who complained "Karl Marx is ruining the workers by making theorists out of them," Bakunin left behind his comfortable noble origins. He was a man of enormous energy who slept only a couple of hours a day, eating, drinking, and smoking cigars almost constantly, organizing and plotting between bites, gulps, and puffs. Once calling himself "the devil in the flesh," Bakunin defined the "social question" as "primarily the overthrow of society." That he set out to do. He led the police on a chase from Paris in 1847 to Dresden and other stops in Central Europe in 1848, that year of revolution. Arrested and imprisoned in Russia, he was exiled to Siberia, managed to escape in 1861, reached Japan, and then arrived in London via the United States.

Bakunin believed that "destruction is a creative passion" and that the peasant masses had untapped revolutionary potential. Marx, who reserved

Michael Bakunin, professional anarchist.

a special sarcastic contempt for the anarchists, insisted that peasants, unlike the industrial proletariat, could never be truly revolutionary and seize power because they could not be class conscious. Anarchists, in turn, rejected Marx's belief that a militant working class organized in a centralized party could make a revolution, and feared that Marxists wanted to replace a bourgeois state with a proletarian state, a state all the same.

Unlike revolutionary nihilists and anarchists who dreamed of a spontaneous peasant uprising, Sergei Necheyev (1847–1882) held that a small, tightly organized revolutionary group could seize control of the state. They would begin the peasant revolution that would sweep away autocratic corruption and oppression. "The revolutionary is," Necheyev wrote, "a doomed man. He has no personal interests, no affairs, sentiments, attachments, property, not even a name of his own. Everything in him is absorbed by one exclusive interest, one thought, one passion—the revolution." Fyodor Dostoevsky (1821–1881) based the character of the hero of his novel *The Possessed* (1871–1872) on Necheyev. After murdering one of his colleagues, Necheyev was arrested and sent to prison, where he died. The heyday of nihilism was over, but not that of the Russian revolutionary intelligentsia.

During his anguished life, Necheyev had battled the populists (*narodniki*) within the revolutionary ranks. The populists developed their doctrine in response to nihilism and retained the Slavophiles' faith in the Russian peasantry. They were romantic collectivists who idealized the Russian peasant community. In contrast to Chernyshevsky, who wanted to teach the peasants, the populists wanted to learn from them. In the early 1870s, several thousand young Russians went from St. Petersburg and Moscow into the countryside. These upper-class Russians resembled the conscience-stricken gentry of the 1830s and 1840s. But these populists dressed up like peasants; not only did they want to "go to the people," to learn from the masses, but they also wanted to prepare an insurrection. Claiming that revolution was near, they taught their listeners revolutionary songs. Some of those attracted to direct action worried that the emancipation of the serfs might create a class of conservative peasant proprietors. Time seemed to be running out for Russia to take its own path to socialism before capitalism became entrenched in Russia, as it had in Western Europe.

In 1878, Vera Zasulich (1851–1919), a revolutionary populist, shot and wounded the governor-general of St. Petersburg. Another attack that year, carried out by the "disorganization section" of Land and Freedom, struck down the head of the Third Section police. A wave of largely, but not entirely, unrelated strikes of industrial workers convinced the terrorists that revolution was not far away.

Twice more, Tsar Alexander II escaped assassination attempts. In the hope of placating his enemies without destroying the foundations of the autocracy, Alexander disbanded the Third Section. He dismissed the minister of education, whose restrictive policies on university admission were

The assassination of Tsar Alexander II in 1881.

unpopular, and announced the formation of a new consultative assembly. But in 1881, members of "People's Will" struck, hurling a bomb near Alexander's sleigh. When the tsar foolishly stepped from the sleigh to inspect the damage, another man threw a bomb that killed him. Russian autocracy, however, survived. The assassination did not prove to be the revolutionary spark anticipated by those who carried it out. Millions of the tsar's subjects, among them many who demanded further reform, mourned the ruler who had at least given them freedom.

France's Second Empire

In France, stabilization and identification with the nation followed a period of revolution. After the Revolution of 1848, Louis Napoleon Bonaparte had smashed the democratic-socialist movement, jailed or exiled its leaders, and disbanded or harassed workers' organizations. Louis Napoleon completed his destruction of the Second Republic with his coup d'état of December 2, 1851, proclaiming himself emperor (and taking the name Napoleon III) the following year with the overwhelming support of the upper classes and of peasants in many parts of the country.

During the Second Empire, wealthy businessmen became the equivalent of an imperial aristocracy in France, money standing as the measure of value that blue blood had been in the early modern period. A few owned major newspapers, which provided them with instant influence on public opinion, and had access to the emperor. Some of them lived in Parisian residences and owned country houses that would have made eighteenth-century aristocrats drool with envy. The empress set the tone for Parisian fashion, while critics condemned the "triumphant vulgarity and appalling materialism" of the "imperial festival." Never since the heady days of Thermidor during the French Revolution had people of wealth indulged their appetites for pleasure so openly.

Yet, Napoleon III also set out to pull the nation together. France was the only European power with universal manhood suffrage, however distorted by government pressure. The emperor would promote economic growth as a way of unifying society, encouraging urban rebuilding projects, expanding credit, and constructing more railways so that if all went well not only the rich and middle classes would benefit but also the lower classes. Moreover, in 1859 Napoleon III initiated the "liberal empire," encouraging a series of reforms, including authorizing a liberal trade treaty with Britain in 1860 and permitting the legalization of strikes in 1864.

The Authoritarian Empire

Emperor Napoleon III was a small man with a prominent nose who appeared lethargic. He reminded some people of a sphinx, and one contemporary of "a melancholy parrot." An unimpressed visitor from the United States described the French ruler as "a long-bodied, short-legged man, fiercely mustached, old, wrinkled, with eyes half closed, and such a deep, crafty, scheming expression about them!" Indeed, Bonaparte's hedonistic nephew had consistently demonstrated considerable energy when it came to behind-the-scenes intrigue and the pursuit of women.

Napoleon III ruled with the help of a handful of worldly, trusted cronies who held ministries or who served on the council of state. Ministers were

Emperor Napoleon III deep in thought.

responsible to the emperor, who alone could propose legislation. The empire continued in its authoritarian phase until 1859.

The Bonapartist state clamped down on the remnants of political opposition, maintained press censorship, and sponsored "official" candidates in the elections held every six years for the Legislative Corps, the lower house of the National Assembly. Hand-picked notables made up its upper chamber, the Senate. Napoleon III's men built a Bonapartist party from the remnants of Orleanism, that is, from those conservative bourgeois who had supported the July Monarchy but who now rallied to the empire because it promised to maintain social and political order.

The French state, more than its decentralized British counterpart, could buy political support by dispensing patronage, for example by assuring that a railroad under construction would pass through a certain town. The prefect or subprefect, the most powerful local official, more than the largest landowner, now held the key to patronage. The Second Empire thus further centralized economic and political power in France.

Napoleon III maintained considerable support among peasants, some of whom retained a romantic attachment to stories about Napoleon I. A good many Legitimists—that is, the supporters of the Bourbon royal family and its exiled pretender, the count of Chambord—also came to support the emperor. Like his uncle, Napoleon III had made peace with the Church. The clergy remained grateful that the Falloux Law of 1850 had returned control of education to them, and for the most part continued to be loyal to the regime.

Despite an avalanche of Bonapartist propaganda, most workers still espoused republicanism or democratic-socialism. And as the political repression slackened in the early 1860s, socialist activity increased. In 1862, French workers joined some of their counterparts from the German states as delegates of their trades at the London International Exposition to discuss the situation of labor in their countries. In 1864, several French artisans were among the founders of the first international workers' organization—the First International. Members represented a bewildering variety of experiences and ideologies. Karl Marx emerged as the dominant figure within the International. He was convinced that the unprecedented concentration of capital and wealth meant that the final struggle between the bourgeoisie and the working class was relatively close at hand (calling Darwinism "the basis in natural science for our views"). Yet, it was quickly apparent that his own inflexible beliefs ran counter to the views of the majority of French members, who were anarchists influenced by Proudhon, and to the moderate, reformist inclinations of the more prosperous British workers.

Economic Growth

The rate of French economic growth was such during the Second Empire, particularly during the 1850s, that economic historians sometimes use it

The state's interest in encouraging economic growth was apparent in the International Exhibition of 1867, which was held in Paris. Here the Krupp Works of Prussia is shown exhibiting its finest at the Exhibition. Twenty years later guns like this were used against the French in the Franco-Prussian War.

as an example of an industrial "take-off." French exports doubled between 1853 and 1864. Never before had any state taken such a direct role in stimulating the economy through encouragement and, in the case of the rebuilding of Paris, through investment. Government officials coordinated the efforts of the ministries of agriculture, commerce, and public works, while keeping in close touch with wealthy bankers and industrialists who backed the regime and made fortunes doing so.

Unlike their British rivals, French entrepreneurs had often found it difficult to raise investment capital. Most companies remained family concerns, hesitant to open investment possibilities to outsiders. Napoleon III changed this by expanding credit, providing government guarantees to credit companies and thereby stimulating the economy. The emperor encouraged the creation of state mortgage banks that provided loans to businessmen. In 1852, the Péreire brothers, who were Protestants like many French bankers, created the Crédit Mobilier, an investment bank. Selling shares to raise capital until its collapse in 1867, it provided loans to many businessmen, financing railways, mining, and the Parisian gas companies. Other smaller deposit banks, too, attracted large and medium investors. A mortgage bank (the Crédit Foncier), another one of Napoleon III's pet projects, aided the development of the agricultural sector.

France became a major exporter of capital. French investors financed the construction of Russian, Spanish, and Italian railroads, as well as providing other timely loans to Russia, Spain, Portugal, Austria-Hungary, and Mexico. Ferdinand de Lesseps (1805–1894), an engineer who had served as vice-consul in Egypt during the July Monarchy, raised enough money through loans (half through public subscription) to finance the construction of his brainchild, the Suez Canal. It opened with suitable fanfare on November 17, 1869. Yet, the chief beneficiary of the canal was not France but Britain, the world's leading trader, which had by far the most to gain by considerably reducing the journey to and from India and the rest of Asia. This drain of capital may have limited French economic expansion, at least in comparison with that of Britain.

State encouragement of economic development may be most clearly seen in the French railways. The Bank of France, which had seventy-four branches by 1870, provided financial aid to the companies that for the most part completed the main railway lines that helped stimulate the country's commercial and manufacturing boom. The state guaranteed investors a minimum profit. Between 1851 and 1869, the railway network expanded by five times, reaching almost 10,000 miles of track. French railroads not only helped transform the French economy, they also became one of the largest employers in Europe.

The railway's impact on French agricultural development, too, should not be overlooked. Producers could more easily market their goods; the prices of staples, in turn, fell, aiding consumers. This encouraged farmers to specialize in one or two crops that they could raise most efficiently. Agricultural specialization and greater integration into the market thereafter created conditions for new kinds of agricultural crises, such as those of overproduction, marked by falling prices. The agriculture crisis of 1854–1855 was the last of the harvest failures that had periodically

The opening of the Suez Canal, 1869.

plunged France into economic crisis. Dearth and skyrocketing prices for staples now lay in the past.

Yet, economic "rationalization" drove from the land hundreds of thousands of peasants with small plots of land, as well as sharecroppers. Unable to raise enough produce to take advantage of improved access to urban markets and undercut by falling agricultural prices, many sold their small farms and moved to the cities in search of work.

The railway carried France into a new age of increased consumption that gradually included the lower classes. Because of reduced transportation costs, meat became less of a luxury. People who lived a good distance inland—and who were of some means—found that fish reached them before the ice keeping the fish fresh had melted. The taste for beer spread from the north and east of France. The diet of ordinary people improved, and as a result of improved nutrition, military records revealed that conscripts gradually became taller. Whereas once up to three-fourths of a worker's family budget was devoted to the purchase of bread, the poor, too, now enjoyed a more varied diet, consisting of more vegetables, fruit, lard, and cheese.

Some French large-scale industries achieved a scale of production and concentration comparable to that of their British rivals. The metallurgical industry, in particular, underwent unprecedented growth and concentration. But most French industries remained relatively small in scale, such as those in which luxury goods, including gloves, umbrellas, silk, jewelry, and fine furniture, were produced.

The Rebuilding of Paris

Napoleon III oversaw the rebuilding of Paris. He entrusted the massive project to Baron Georges Haussmann (1809–1891), prefect of the Seine.

Emperor Napoleon III on the left and Baron Georges Haussmann, the rebuilder of Paris or the "Alsatian Attila," depending on how you look at it, on the right.

(*Left*) Garnier's new opera house seems to be rising out of the dust of the construction of the Avenue de l'Opéra during the Second Empire. (*Right*) The completed Avenue de l'Opéra as painted by Camille Pissarro in 1898.

Haussmann, serving as subprefect and then prefect of several departments, had demonstrated an icy demeanor and impressive organizational skills. Although his family had been from Alsace, he had grown up in the capital at a time when migrants from the provinces seemed to overwhelm the city and revolutionary upheaval appeared endemic. Napoleon III showed Haussmann a map of Paris, over which he had sketched a network of boulevards. Together they planned the most massive project of urban renewal since the rebuilding of London following the great fire in the seventeenth century and the rebuilding of Edo (Tokyo) at about the same time following the great conflagration of 1657.

Napoleon III and Haussmann wanted to facilitate the expansion of commerce and industry through the creation of long, wide boulevards, which would be lined by symmetrical apartment buildings. The "great crossing," then the chief intersection of Paris, provided major routes along and perpendicular to the Seine River. The Arch de Triumph became the center of a star-shaped intersection of new boulevards. The Avenue de l'Opéra, begun during the empire, led from the Rue de Rivoli to the new opera.

The new boulevards also cut through some of the most revolutionary neighborhoods, providing troops quick access into the narrow streets in eastern Paris where people had risen up during the June Days in 1848, as well as during the French Revolution, and making it more difficult to erect barricades. In 1877, the impressionist painter Auguste Renoir would lament the transformation of these old Parisian neighborhoods and the new symmetrical "Haussmann" buildings that now lined the boulevards, "cold and lined up like soldiers at review." It seemed an appropriate image to accompany the further consolidation of state power.

Refurbished Paris thus provided a setting for business prosperity and conspicuous consumption. Glittering department stores took shape along several of the long boulevards, showcases to imperial monumentalism.

Paris before Haussmann: Charles Marville's photograph of the Rue Traversine. Notice the drainage ditch down the center of the cobblestone street.

More and more wealthy women sought to differentiate themselves from the middling classes by their attention to high fashion. High-class prostitutes assumed the title of "courtesans." Fancy cafés lined the boulevards. Large structures of iron and glass, in the tradition of the Great Exposition of London of 1851, provided space for Les Halles, the refurbished market of central Paris.

Napoleon III also wanted to make Paris a healthier place. In central Paris, some of the broad boulevards replaced narrow, winding streets, cutting through dirty, unhealthy neighborhoods. Aqueducts were built to provide cleaner water for residents. Four hundred miles of underground sewers improved health conditions in a city that had been ravaged by cholera in 1832 and 1849. The sewers then emptied into the Seine near the suburb of Asnières (uncomfortably close to the participants in and observers of the boat regattas). A British official complimented the emperor when he told him, "May it be said of you that you found Paris stinking and left it sweet."

Although the massive rebuilding provided jobs for many skilled workers and unskilled laborers and did improve living conditions for many, it also forced many thousands of workers and their families to leave the central city for the cheaper rents of the inner suburbs, particularly those to the north and northeast—which were annexed to Paris in 1860—or to the increasingly industrialized suburbs farther out. For the loss of their rental lodgings, they were reimbursed but a single franc, about a third of a day's wages. Property owners then raised rents with impunity. Within a very short walk from Notre Dame Cathedral, more than 14,000 people were displaced from the Ile de la Cité by the construction of a public hospital and the new prefecture of police. Once one of the most crowded neighborhoods in Paris, the Ile de la Cité emerged from the Haussmann era with the smallest population density. The rebuilding of Paris thus increased geographic segregation within the city and exacerbated the differences between the more prosperous west and the relatively impoverished eastern districts.

As an exile, Napoleon III had been impressed by the vast acres of London's Hyde Park. At his instigation, more and larger parks were built in Paris. One of these, the Bois de Boulogne, attracted revelers in search of the countryside—although it was a "planned" countryside that somewhat resembled an English formal garden. Paris, which had only forty-seven acres of parks in 1850, had more than 4,500 acres once Haussmann had completed his work.

The cost of all these projects was enormous and far exceeded original estimates. Speculators made a fortune, tipped off as to where the next demolitions would take place. Financial scandals finally forced Haussmann to resign in 1870.

Science and Realism

New discoveries in the physical sciences enhanced the already soaring prestige of science and the professional stature of its practitioners. These advances contributed to the diffusion of the belief that human progress was inevitable and that it moved in a linear manner. Discoveries in the fields of geology, biology, and medicine helped generate optimism about the future. Anesthesia was discovered in the 1840s, and the French scientist Louis Pasteur (1822–1895) developed germ theory in the 1860s, leading to a virtual revolution in health care.

Louis Pasteur in his laboratory.

The view that the march of science would continue to bring human progress, and that there was an inevitable advance toward this happy state of affairs, became known as positivism. Positivists challenged some of the central tenets of the established churches, particularly those of the Catholic Church, whose theologians held fast to a view of humanity as essentially unchanging and imperfectible. Darwinism, as we have seen, denied the literal biblical description of God creating the world in seven days. Churchmen of many denominations, and many other people who misinterpreted Darwin's theory, were aghast to think that people could have descended from apes.

Auguste Comte (1798–1857) helped diffuse faith in the promise of science in France. Believing that scientific discovery had passed through three stages of development—the theological, the metaphysical, and the positive (or scientific)—Comte concluded that what he called "the science of society" could do the same. Society itself, he reasoned, could be studied in a scientific manner and its development charted. Comte's positivism called for the accumulation of useful knowledge that would help students of society, who came to be called sociologists, to understand the laws of social development.

Influenced by the widening interest in science and the quickening pace of social change, some writers also broke with literary traditions. The escapist popular science fiction fantasies of the French author Jules Verne (1828–1905) reflected contemporary fascination with developing sciences like geography, science, astronomy, and physics, as well as interest in new means of transportation and communication. *Around the World in 80 Days*, first published in 1873, was a best-seller.

Above all, however, realism emerged as the dominant cultural style. Charles Baudelaire (1821–1867) once described himself as the poet of modern life. Best known for his volume of poems *Les Fleurs du Mal* (1857; *The Flowers of Evil*), Baudelaire believed that art had to be the product of an exchange between the individual artist and contemporary society. In this way the artist's own experience, or self-discovery, became critical in the emergence of modern literature. Baudelaire was the consummate dandy and *flâneur*, the observer of modern urban life. Dressed in what modest elegance his small inheritance permitted, the *flâneur* strolled through Paris, observing its revitalized beauty but also gazing at its hideous, even frightening aspects with objective detachment, looking at prostitutes, ragpickers, beggars, and drunks, listening carefully to the varied sounds of the city. The *flâneur* both reacted to and reflected modern urban life. Baudelaire rebelled against bourgeois culture and conventional assumptions about artistic subjects and style. Rejecting the notion that absolute aesthetic values exist, Baudelaire was a crucial figure in the emergence of modern culture in the middle of the century. He observed, reflected upon, and wrote about the transformation of urban society, particularly the leisure of prosperous bourgeois on the sparkling new boule-

Eugène Delacroix's *Liberty Leading the People* (1830). Note the female image of liberty and the presence in the fighting of the top-hatted bourgeois and the heavily armed street urchin, neither of whom actually fought in the Revolution.

J.M.W. Turner's brilliantly colored *Fire at Sea*.

Théodore Géricault's *Raft of the Medusa* (1818–1819). The painting itself became a political issue because the ill-fated ship was commanded by an incompetent loyalist to the Bourbon regime who owed his commission to political favoritism.

John Martin's *The Bard* shows the romantic concept of the poet as at one with nature. Note the wild landscape.

Ernest Meissonier's *The Barricade*.

Jean-François Millet's *The Angelus* (1859).

Édouard Manet's *Déjeuner sur l'herbe* (1863).

Claude Monet's *The Railway Bridge at Argenteuil*. Here the painter juxtaposes images of industry and leisure.

Edvard Munch's *The Scream* (1893) evokes fear and alarm in the viewer.

Pablo Picasso's *The Tragedy* (1903) is from his "blue period" and shows a gloomy obsession with death.

Gustav Klimt's *Judith II* (*Salomé*) (1909).

Jean-François Millet's *The Gleaners* (1857).

vards of Paris. Beyond these symbols of urban modernity stood the popular classes threatening a further democratization of politics and culture.

In the 1850s, the Barbizon painters—so called because they gathered in a village southeast of Paris of that name—emphasized the painting of peasants, harvests, animals, and other symbols of village life. In doing so, they broke sharply with many of the long-accepted styles of painting, including romanticism. Such canvases were accepted for display by the critics and government officials who put on the state-sponsored exhibition (the Salon) on which artists depended in order to attract purchasers. Jean-François Millet (1814–1875) was among the Barbizon painters. He painted peasants at work in such pieces as *The Gleaners* (1857) and *The Angelus* (1859), giving peasants a kind of dignity that repelled many middle-class viewers who thought them unworthy of being painted.

Artistic style evolved far more rapidly than did official views of what constituted good art. Gustave Courbet (1819–1877), the son of a peasant family in eastern France, abandoned the idealization that still characterized painting. "Show me an angel," he scoffed at his critics, "and I will paint one." In 1855, he presented a private showing of his work in Paris; above the entrance was a banner proclaiming his realism. Taking as a compliment the assessment that he was "a democratic painter," he startled viewers by choosing ordinary workers as his subjects, as in his *The Stonebreakers* (1849). Courbet shocked bourgeois opinion with his realism.

Gustave Courbet's *Burial at Ornans* (1849).

Burial at Ornans (1849) portrays a family of some means looking rather unattractive, bored, or even indifferent as the body of a relative is being lowered into a grave in Courbet's home town. *The Bather* (1853) shows a stout naked woman rising from a forest pool. Nudity did not bother many viewers—it was, after all, a staple of classical painting. Rather, viewers were upset by the fact that Courbet portrayed an ordinary-looking woman assuming a classic pose, holding herself up very awkwardly. The artist seemed to be mocking the kind of classical scene painters had been expected to treat with reverence. When Napoleon III saw the exhibited painting, he struck the canvas with a riding-crop. Courbet, a political radical, believed that art should have a social purpose. He exacted some revenge in a later painting by presenting the emperor as a shabby poacher. Like some other artists of his time, Courbet remained torn between the desire for success—he was a specialist in self-promotion—and his determination to pursue his own realist course.

The development of photography during the 1840s may have contributed to the interest in portraying artistic subjects with a vivid sense of immediacy and actuality. The French novelist Émile Zola (1840–1902) shocked many critics with his evocation of working-class life because the subject itself challenged traditional assumptions about literary worthiness, and because of his unabashed realism in depicting ordinary people as he saw them. Zola believed that naturalistic writing was a form of science. He went down into the mine shafts of northern France so that he could offer a realistic depiction of the work there in his novel *Germinal* (1885). He subtitled his twenty-volume series on a French family the "Natural and Social History of a Family under the Second Empire."

French writers were not alone in their discovery of realism and of an increasingly middle-class audience for their work. Russian novels, widely available in translation, took Western capitals by storm. Fyodor Dostoevsky presented disturbingly accurate portraits of troubled individuals whose actions reflected not rationality but aberration, even madness, in such novels as *Crime and Punishment* (1866) and *The Brothers Karamazov* (1879–1880). Sentenced to death by the authorities, he was hauled out of jail early one morning, blindfolded, placed before a firing squad, and then, after a cruelly staged mock execution that understandably shattered his nerves, sent to prison in Siberia. He described his own suffering, but also that of Russian society, in the crucial years following defeat in the Crimean War.

Artists and writers who espoused the new realism sometimes confronted imperial censorship. The historian Ernest Renan (1823–1892) considered himself a proponent of "progressive ideas," above all, a faith in science. "The triumph of science," he wrote, "is in reality the triumph of idealism." The emperor prohibited Renan, named to the prestigious College of France, from giving lectures. Renan then published his controversial, best-selling *Life of Jesus* (1863). It offended the Church by presenting Christ in a historical way, casting some doubt upon his divinity. More than this, Renan argued that the Scriptures had to be studied like any other historical document. Renan lost his academic chair.

The French police hauled the novelist Gustave Flaubert (1821–1880) into court, charging him with obscenity. His novel *Madame Bovary* (1856) describes the affair of a bored bourgeois housewife living in a dreary Norman town. Baudelaire was fined 300 francs (the equivalent of two months'

Gustave Courbet's *The Bather* (1853) in which the subject strikes an awkward pose.

wages for a worker) in 1857 for "obscene and immoral passages or expressions." His *The Flowers of Evil* became even more popular, as his decadence and overt eroticism—he died of syphilis in 1867—angered officials and critics alike. Flaubert and Baudelaire reflected the bohemian underside of bourgeois life. But they, too, depended upon middle-class patronage for their work.

Impressionism

During the Second Empire, a group of French artists developed impressionism, a remarkable artistic movement that lasted until the end of the century. Like the realists of the Barbizon school, impressionist painters rejected traditional religious and historical subjects, and instead painted modern life. In this, they reflected the social and political changes seen in the Second Empire, when more and more French men and women seemed to be turning away from traditional views of religion. The impressionists depicted rural and urban landscapes. They presented scenes from everyday existence, but generally integrated individual figures into landscapes. Like Baudelaire, they freed themselves from the traditional hierarchy of subjects or styles and from formal presentation. Embracing subjectivity, the impressionists preferred direct observation and the study of nature's effects to studio composition and imitation of classic styles. Édouard Manet (1832–1883), another dandy and *flâneur*, aspired to create what a contemporary called an art "born of today." A critic described an "impressionist" painter as "a modernist painter endowed with an uncommon sensibility of the eye [who, by painting] in the bright open air . . . has succeeded in remaking for himself a natural eye, and in seeing naturally and painting simply as he sees." The impressionists painted, in short, what they saw, and how they saw it at first glance. They attempted to capture their initial, fleeting visual sensations, trying to recreate on the canvas nature's wondrous incidents, such as the way sunlight falls on inanimate objects. This distinguished them from the realism of Courbet and his generation. Claude Monet (1840–1926) described what made such painting different: "Try to forget what objects you have before you—a tree, a house, a field, or whatever. Merely think, here is a little square of blue, here an oblong of pink, here a streak of yellow, and paint it just as it looks to you, the exact color and shape, until it gives your own naive impression of the scene before you." The way the impressionists saw what they painted was far more important than what they saw. Turning away from the darker tones of realism, the impressionists increasingly put lighter and brighter colors on large canvases (which previously had been usually reserved for historical themes), applying many small dabs of paint to convey an impression of spontaneity, energy, movement, and change. The subjectivity and artistic style of impressionism challenged basic contemporary assumptions about society and culture.

Although the impressionists did not begin to exhibit their paintings with the self-consciousness of an artistic group until 1874 (and chose not to accept any official name when they did), their movement was shaped by official rejection. In 1863, the jury for the official Salon turned down, among hundreds of paintings, several by Manet. After word of the painters' complaints reached the emperor, he allowed some of the paintings to be shown in other rooms. The "Salon of the Refused" included works by Manet, Auguste Renoir, and Paul Cézanne. Some critics raged against what they saw, but at least the public could now make up its own mind. Manet's *Olympia* (1863) generated a chorus of complaint. The study of a nude shocked public opinion—the outraged Empress Eugénie, not to be outdone by her husband, who had attacked a Courbet canvas with a riding-crop, hit Manet's painting with her fan. Manet's *Déjeuner sur l'herbe* (1863), presented at the same time, drew scathing commentary because it showed a nude female sharing a picnic with well-dressed males. In *Déjeuner,* Manet, even more than the realists, challenged the hierarchy of subjects imposed by classicism. Manet and his younger followers gradually won public support.

Like Baudelaire, Camille Pissarro and his colleagues found the great boulevards of Paris, lined by trees and newspaper kiosks, fitting subjects for their portrayal of modern life. Whatever Napoleon III's ideological intentions, above all, the desire to create a new Rome, his rebuilding of Paris opened up new possibilities for the understanding of modernity. Manet chose provocatively contemporary subjects, including very ordinary people, clients, and café waitresses enjoying themselves. Manet and his younger friend Monet painted the Gare Saint-Lazare, the point of entry each day for thousands of commuters, vacationers, and other visitors. A keen observer of urban life, Manet encountered and painted ragpickers, vagrants, and gypsies in a northern suburb of Paris, where he lived—although he could have afforded to reside in considerably more elegant surroundings—in the 1860s and 1870s.

The early impressionists were thus interested in and influenced by the growing commercialization of leisure in Paris. Edgar Degas (1834–1917) followed wealthy Parisians to theaters, racetracks, cafés, and café-concerts (offering entertainment that included vaudeville acts, poetry readings, comedians, and singers renowned for bawdy, popular lyrics). He observed Parisians from a variety of backgrounds, as they smoked, drank, talked, and sought companionship. Degas frequently chose female entertainers, most of whom were drawn from the popular classes, as his subjects. In the shadows of his ballet paintings lurk wealthy gentlemen awaiting their prey, or, like Napoleon III himself, occupying the loges closest to the stage at the opera, or standing in the shadows of the dressing rooms of the dancers, ready to claim their prizes. Degas, whose banking family had lost its money early in an economic depression, forcing him to sell off some favorite paintings to get by, presented unflattering, dark stereotypes of Parisian speculators in *At the Stock Exchange* (1879).

(*Left*) Edgar Degas' *At the Stock Exchange* (1879). (*Right*) Édouard Manet's *Bar at the Folies-Bergère* (1882).

In Manet's *Bar at the Folies-Bergère* (1882), the barmaid he depicts could be viewed in several ways. She could be merely serving drinks, as countless women did to earn a living. But, more likely than not, she is also arranging a more intimate, paying encounter solicited by the customer in the background. Berthe Morisot (1841–1895), Manet's sister-in-law, portrayed upper-class leisure. She painted her subjects, most of whom were women, in private gardens, in the Bois de Boulogne, boating on the Seine, and at the resorts of the Norman coast, which had been "discovered" by wealthy Parisians. Monet's paintings of the industrializing Parisian suburb of Argenteuil, where he resided, reflected the balance between leisure (seen, for example, in the painting of sailboats on the Seine) and industry (factory smokestacks).

The increasing anonymity of the burgeoning city (by 1891, only about a third of those living in Paris had been born there) was also a frequent impressionist theme. Degas' *L'Absinthe* (1876–1877) shows two disconnected figures in a café, an image of isolation reinforced by the absence of legs holding up the marble table (see p. 883). Such encounters with strangers seemed an intrinsic part of modern life.

The "Liberal Empire"

In 1859, Napoleon III announced his intention to "crown the [imperial] edifice with liberty." He would diffuse opposition by implementing some of the very reforms the opposition desired. Although the large cities—at least those with sizable working classes—remained defiantly opposed to imperial politics and had elected five republicans to the Legislative Corps two years earlier, the emperor had the support of the majority of people. In

1860, the National Assembly received the right to discuss the emperor's annual address—an exercise in sheer boredom, as he was a notoriously poor speaker.

That same year, France and Britain signed a liberal trade agreement lowering tariff barriers between the two nations. In France, the Cobden-Chevalier Treaty was the idea of the emperor himself and an adviser, Michel Chevalier (1806–1879), who had been a Saint-Simonian as a young man. Like the emperor, Chevalier had begun to have doubts about economic protectionism. The Cobden-Chevalier Treaty of 1860 provided a sliding scale on import duties. It helped some French economic interests, such as Bordeaux wine producers.

Having undone protectionism, Napoleon III then promulgated further liberalizing measures. The National Assembly received the right to approve the imperial budget. Press controls were relaxed and the right to strike was established in 1864. The liberalization of imperial political institutions helped increase republican support, which grew considerably during the 1860s. Nonetheless, the socialist First International began to find some support among skilled workers. And opposition to the emperor would again mount several years later.

Foreign policy ultimately revealed Napoleon III's weakness as a ruler, despite the fact that the emperor was widely regarded in Europe as an outstanding man of state, a victor of the Crimean War. In 1859, Napoleon III joined with Count Camillo di Cavour of Piedmont-Sardinia to draw Emperor Francis Joseph of Austria into a war that would enable Piedmont-Sardinia to achieve Italian unification (see Chapter 18) under its direction. In June 1859, the French army defeated the Austrians in northern Italy at Magenta and at Solferino, where the emperor himself commanded the French troops on horseback, if at a safe distance from the actual fighting. France received Lombardy as part of the peace agreement, although in 1861 the emperor gave it up to Piedmont-Sardinia in exchange for Nice and Savoy, both of which France had long coveted. Napoleon III now dreamed of expanding his empire in Africa and Asia. He ordered the expansion of French control of Senegal and sent troops to protect missionaries in Lebanon and distant Indochina, annexing Cochin-China as a colony. At a state dinner in London in 1864, someone voiced the opinion that Napoleon III had been considerably more successful than his famous uncle. Only one of the diners disagreed: the Italian revolutionary Guiseppe Garibaldi cautioned, "We must wait for the end of the story."

An imperial adventure in Mexico, which was in the midst of a civil war, ended in fiasco. The emperor believed that Mexico could become a profitable market for French exports of textiles and wine. Along with Britain and Spain, France in 1861 sent troops to protect French financial interests there. When order was restored, the French troops stayed. In 1864, Napoleon III proclaimed his protégé Austrian Archduke Maximilian (1832–1867), the brother of Habsburg emperor Francis Joseph, to be em-

Édouard Manet's *Execution of Maximilian* (1867).

peror of Mexico. The United States protested that French intervention represented a violation of the Monroe Doctrine (1823), which had declared the Western Hemisphere as off limits to the European powers. The Mexicans, understandably enough, did not want an Austrian emperor. Three years later, Mexican patriots defeated the French forces, who disembarked for France, leaving Napoleon III's hapless protégé to his own devices. Maximilian was executed in June 1867, a blow to Napoleon III's international prestige.

A year earlier, the French emperor had made an error in foreign policy that would come back to haunt him. As Prussia and Austria drew closer to war in 1866, Napoleon III believed that Habsburg Austria would prevail. Bismarck quickly rejected Napoleon III's demand in August 1866 that Prussia compensate France with Rhineland territory. The French emperor then boldly insisted that Prussia go along with a possible French annexation of Belgium and Luxembourg. After an international conference a year later guaranteed Luxembourg's independence, Napoleon III's dreams of territorial compensation from Prussia disappeared. But the cagey Bismarck kept the French emperor's written demand.

In June 1868, the emperor's authorization of a law permitting freedom of assembly helped mobilize opposition among monarchists, republicans, and socialists alike. Napoleon III's advisers wondered aloud if he had not sown the seeds of imperial demise by granting liberal reforms. Early in 1870, strikes spread. That same month, the emperor invited opponents to join the government and to begin drafting a more liberal constitution, one that would make ministers in some way "responsible" to the Legislative Corps. Napoleon III then reverted to a plebiscite, with a craftily worded statement in May 1870 by which those who wanted more extensive changes were forced to abstain, or to vote "yes" as if they approved of the emperor's policies. The plebiscite, in which "yes" overwhelmed "no," thus partially concealed the depth of opposition to imperial policies.

To the end, Napoleon III manifested a bizarre combination of perceptive foresight and bad judgment. When the Spanish throne fell vacant after a military coup deposed Queen Isabella II of Spain in 1868, one of the candidates was Prince Leopold, a Catholic prince of the ruling Prussian dynasty, the Hohenzollerns. Should Leopold become king of Spain, France would find itself with members of the Prussian royal family across both the Rhine and the Pyrenees. Napoleon III threatened war with Prussia if it did not withdraw the Hohenzollern candidacy. He should have left it at that, but he ordered his ambassador to extract a letter from the king of Prussia apologizing to France and promising that Prussia would never revive the candidacy of Prince Leopold.

In July, the French ambassador harangued Prussian King William I in a garden in the spa town of Ems. The king politely dismissed the ambassador and sent Bismarck a telegram stating what had occurred. After learning that the Prussian army was ready to fight, Bismarck embellished the king's telegram (the Ems Dispatch) to make the graceless diplomacy of the French seem positively insulting and the king's response stronger than it had actually been. Prussian public opinion reacted to French demands in the Ems Dispatch with anger. And as for the French, Bismarck's expectation that it would "have the effect of a red cloth upon the Gallic bull" was justified; the incident increased popular support for France's declaration of war on Prussia on July 19. Württemberg, Hesse, Baden, and more hesitantly, Bavaria joined the Prussian side. Bismarck pressured the Austrians, Russians, and Italians to remain neutral. Although the British government had become somewhat alarmed by the rise of Prussian strength, it too would remain neutral as it was outraged with France. Bismarck had produced the French emperor's written offer for French support of Prussia in 1866 in exchange for the latter's acquiescence in France's absorption of Belgium and Luxembourg. For centuries, Britain had opposed a French presence in the Low Countries, and it would not forgive Napoleon III for his suggestion that he would take over these lands. Napoleon III went to war without allies.

The Franco-Prussian War and the Siege of Paris

The Franco-Prussian War was a French debacle. Whereas the French mobilization of troops proceeded slowly and chaotically, the Prussian armies moved quickly into northeastern France from the Palatinate (see Map 19.3). The speed of the Prussian attack and the competence of its generals more than made up for superior French rifles and recently developed ma-

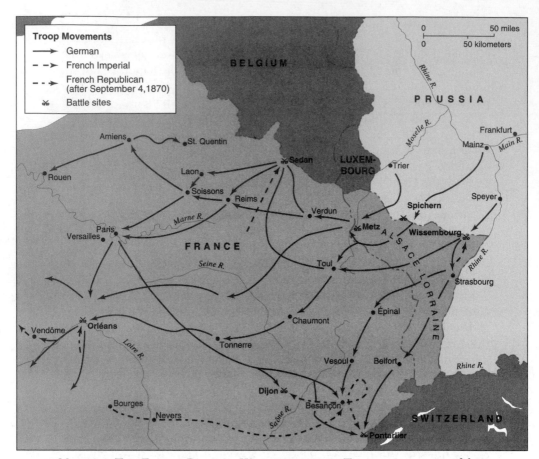

MAP 19.3 THE FRANCO-PRUSSIAN WAR, 1870–1871 Troop movements and battles during the Franco-Prussian War show fighting at Metz and Sedan, as well as Dijon and Orléans, with German troops converging on Paris.

chine guns. In August, Prussian troops cut off the fortress of Metz from the rest of France. When Marshal Marie Edmé de MacMahon (1808–1893) moved north in an attempt to relieve Marshal Achille Bazaine (1811–1888) in Metz, the Prussians cut him off. On August 31, the main French force foolishly retreated to the fortress town of Sedan not far from the Belgian border. Sedan was soon surrounded by Prussians, who captured the emperor, by then so sick that he could barely sit on his horse. In Paris on September 4, crowds proclaimed a republic, and a provisional government was formed. Prussia allowed Napoleon III to leave for exile in Britain.

The Prussian army undertook a siege of Paris. Despite the hurried departure of many people of means who fled to country houses, the population of the capital swelled with soldiers and National Guardsmen. As hunger invaded the capital, dogs and cats disappeared from the streets, finding their way to some of the finest tables. Zoo animals, too, were eaten, including two elephants admired by generations of Parisian children. An attempt to break through the Prussian lines north of the city at the end of October failed miserably. Still, Paris hung on.

In the meantime, Adolphe Thiers (1797–1877), who had served as Orleanist prime minister during the 1830s, had been in touch with Bismarck. He wanted Bismarck's help in facilitating the establishment of a very conservative republic at the war's conclusion, or even restoration of a monarchy. Members of the provisional government began to negotiate with Bismarck in the hope of obtaining an armistice on favorable terms. On January 28, 1871, ten days after the proclamation of the German Empire at Versailles (see Chapter 18), Bismarck and Thiers signed an armistice. France lost Alsace and much of Lorraine to the new German Empire.

Some French leaders protested, demanding that French forces fight on. On February 8, 1871, French voters—though only half of those eligible cast ballots—selected a monarchist-dominated National Assembly. It would be charged with making peace with Prussia and with establishing a new government. Some republican candidates had hurt their own cause by suggesting that the war might be continued. Most people in France wanted peace. The newly elected National Assembly officially elected Thiers to be chief executive of the provisional government.

By signing the Treaty of Frankfurt (May 10, 1871), Thiers' provisional

Jules Favre, peace negotiator, and Adolphe Thiers, provisional head of the government, accede to the loss of Alsace-Lorraine, France's right arm. They drag the weeping female image of France away from the social republic.

government agreed to pay a large indemnity; Prussian troops would occupy Paris and retain garrisons in eastern France until the sum had been paid off. The National Assembly's choice of Versailles, the home of the last Bourbon monarchs, as the temporary capital stirred popular anger and suspicion.

Parisians, who had held out against the Prussians for four months, resented the ease with which the provinces had seemed to capitulate. When the siege ended, wealthy Parisians returned from the safety of the countryside. Landlords insisted that back rents be paid immediately.

The Paris Commune

Early in the morning on March 18, 1871, Thiers sent a small detachment of troops to Montmartre to seize cannon that had belonged to the National Guard during the siege. Women at the market alerted the neighborhood; a crowd surrounded the detachment and put two generals up against the wall and shot them. Thiers had advised the last Orleanist government in February 1848 to move its troops outside of the capital and then besiege the city. Now he ordered his troops, their number increased by prisoners of war released by Bismarck, to surround the capital. A second siege of Paris began, this one a civil war.

During the Prussian siege, socialists had placed bright red posters on the walls of the capital calling for the establishment of the "Paris Commune." Now surrounded by reactionary armies directed by monarchists from Versailles, the Commune set out to defend Paris. The leaders of the Commune were drawn from a variety of political persuasions: Jacobins, socialists inspired by the memory of the French Revolution, and moderate

The beginnings of the Commune, March 18, 1871: the execution of Generals Lecomte and Thomas. (The photo may be a re-enactment.)

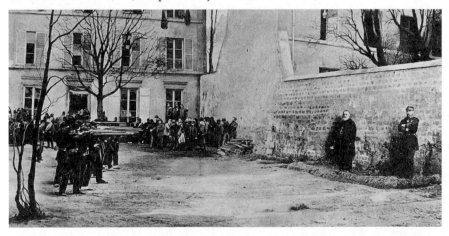

The Champs Elysées in Paris during the Commune.

republicans who wanted Paris to become again the capital of an anticlerical republic. Some Communards had been democratic-socialist activists during the Second Republic; others were followers of the revolutionary Auguste Blanqui (1805–1881), who believed that revolution could be achieved only by a small cell of determined men seizing power. There were also a good many anarchists, followers of Pierre-Joseph Proudhon, the first person to call himself an anarchist, who hoped that independent Paris would serve as a model for a society of producers existing without the tyranny of the state.

Revolutionary clubs sprang up in Paris. With the guns of the provisional government bombarding the capital, the Communards organized Paris' defense and enacted a number of significant social reforms. These included the creation of a Labor Exchange, the abolition of night baking (long a grievance of bakers), the establishment of nurseries for working mothers, and the rights of workers' organizations to receive preference when the municipality contracted work. The Commune recognized women's unions—indeed the role of women in the Commune exceeded that of any previous revolutionary movement in France. Given the severity of the circumstances, it is remarkable how much the Communards accomplished in such a short time.

Much smaller uprisings occurred in Lyon, Marseille, and several other cities. These movements reflected a combination of middle-class dissatisfaction with Bonapartist centralization, republican enthusiasm, and socialist mobilization. But the provinces provided no help to the Paris Commune; rather, conservative regions sent volunteers to fight for the Versailles forces.

On May 21, the troops of Thiers' Versailles government poured into Paris through the western gates, left open for them by monarchist sympathizers. During the "bloody week" that followed, Thiers' army took neighborhood after neighborhood, blasting its way through barricades. Summary executions occurred throughout Paris, particularly after a rumor began that female incendiaries were burning banks and the homes of the wealthy. The Communards retaliated by executing some hostages, including the archbishop of Paris. The last Communard resistance was finally crushed near Père-Lachaise cemetery in one of the most plebeian parts of Paris.

At least 25,000 Parisians died at the hands of the provisional government. "In Paris, everyone was guilty," was the way one magistrate coolly put it. In fact, the death toll may have been much more than that—for example, at the time of the next census, in 1872, the number of shoemakers, a notoriously radical occupation, in Paris had declined by about 12,000. Surely, some of them fled to the provinces, but many undoubtedly were executed, their bodies destroyed in the fires caused by the fighting.

For the left, the Commune seemed to be a glimpse of the future proletarian revolution that would overthrow bourgeois society, although Paris largely remained a city of artisans and skilled workers because small-scale production and craft industries still dominated its economy. To conservatives, the Commune offered a frightening glimpse of plebeian insurrection

Corpses of the Communards executed by the Versailles troops.

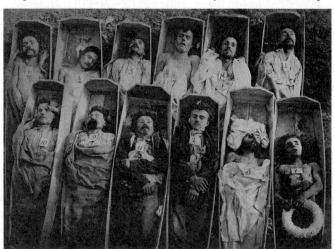

and firmed their resolve to oppose movements for social and political change with armed force. The massacre of the Communards suggested to some people the futility of armed rebellion against modern armies. Many ecclesiastics blamed France's defeat at the hands of Prussia and the Commune itself on religious indifference and anticlericalism. As a form of penance, the Church constructed the basilica of the Sacred Heart on Montmartre, where the Commune had begun.

CONCLUSION

France's conservative provisional government, which became known as the government of "moral order," stood on the line between a constitutional monarchy and a conservative republic. With the passage of the second Reform Bill of 1867, Britain emerged from the tumultuous decades of mid-century with a wider electoral franchise. In the Russian Empire, Tsar Alexander II had tried to effect change from above, but the emancipation of the serfs in 1861 did not change the fundamental institutions of autocracy, based upon a partnership with the nobility.

As reforms changed the balance of political power within the major European states, so too did wars change the balance of power between states. As Russia was humiliated by defeat on its southern doorstep in the Crimean War, Britain's economic strength and great navy left it in a position to dominate international affairs. As both Austria and France were defeated in wars with Prussia, Prussia emerged as the leader of a unified and powerful Germany.

Not only did the last half of the nineteenth century bring about political change, it also brought the beginnings of an era of material progress in Europe (however unequally distributed), above all in Britain, France, and Germany. Remarkable technological advances, increased mass production, and continued urbanization characterized the Second Industrial Revolution, which began about 1870. But as the pace of life seemed to accelerate in a time of material progress, mass culture generated pessimism and anxiety among some artists and writers. Rapid material progress and uncertainty together characterized the remarkable years that brought to a close the nineteenth century and the dawning of the modern world in the first years of the twentieth century.

CHAPTER 20

RAPID INDUSTRIALIZATION AND ITS CHALLENGES, 1870–1914

Jeanne Bouvier was a peasant girl born in 1865 in southeastern France, south of Lyon near the Rhône Valley. In her village, her father earned his living by tilling the fields and as a barrel maker, an occupation closely tied to wine production. But in 1876, a vineyard epidemic began to destroy the vineyards of the Rhône Valley. Her family was forced to sell its land and possessions and travel to find work, pushed along by poverty and unemployment. From age eleven to fourteen, Jeanne worked thirteen hours a day in a silk mill. Four other jobs in various towns and villages in her region followed until Jeanne's mother took her to Paris, where the first job she found lasted only a week. Like so many other single, female migrants to city life, she then worked as a domestic servant until a cousin showed her how to do hat-trimming work. When that trade collapsed because of changes in style and the economic depression, she became a skilled dressmaker in a Parisian workshop, and then developed her own clientele. In this way, Jeanne Bouvier became a Parisian. When she returned home to her native village, Jeanne no longer understood the *patois* her old friends still spoke. She had become an urban woman.

In 1900, the French Catholic writer Charles Péguy expressed the opinion that Europe had changed more in the previous thirty years than it had since the time of Jesus Christ. The period 1870–1914 was indeed one of rapid economic and social change in much of Europe. Despite the long depression that gripped the continent from 1873 until the mid-1890s, these decades brought continued urban growth and the Second Industrial Revolution, marked by startling technological advances and mechanized

844

factory production that transformed the way millions of people worked and lived. Rural areas were changing as well, as agricultural production became more specialized. A smaller percentage of the population worked the land.

Declining mortality rates led to an increase in Europe's population. Longer life expectancy followed better nutrition—a more varied diet with greater caloric consumption—as well as improved sanitation and purer water supplies. Mass education elevated rates of literacy. The middle class expanded in size and complexity; new employment opportunities beckoned in cities.

Living conditions gradually improved for most people. Unions and socialists pressured states to shorten the workday to eight or ten hours. Real wages continued to rise. Many workers now had a little money and time left over for leisure activities. Bicycles, sports, and, early in the new century, movies became part of the lives of millions.

The last years of the nineteenth century—the fin de siècle—would be remembered after World War I as the "Belle Époque,"—the "good old days," a period of material progress and cultural innovation. The ebbing of the long depression in the mid-1890s inaugurated a period of prosperity for more Europeans than ever before.

In 1889, the centenary of the French Revolution, Paris hosted an international exhibition that featured the wrought-iron Eiffel Tower, a symbol of industrial progress (although the tower itself was condemned by many artists and writers as an unsightly "Tower of Babel" that would ruin the skyline). New inventions like the telephone and automobile promised an even better life ahead. But beneath the glittering progress and prosperity lurked cultural pessimism and artistic rebellion, a modernist critique of

(*Left*) The Eiffel Tower. (*Right*) The Palace of Electricity at the Paris Exhibition of 1900.

the idea of progress itself. In 1904, the German sociologist Max Weber wrote that "at some time or another the color changes, the importance of uncritically accepted viewpoints is put in doubt, the path is lost in the twilight." The fin de siècle seemed to be such a time.

THE SECOND INDUSTRIAL REVOLUTION

Technological advances propelled the Second Industrial Revolution of the century's last decades. It swept across much of Northern, Western, and Central Europe, as well as the United States, and some of Southern and Eastern Europe. New manufacturing processes spurred the emergence of the chemical, electrical, and the steel industries. "Big business" took shape as larger companies controlled a greater share of markets.

New Technology and New Industries

The development of steel production led the way in the second burst of industrial creativity. In 1856, the English inventor Henry Bessemer (1813–1898) developed a new method for forging steel from pig iron by forcing air through the molten metal to reduce its carbon content. The result was steel that was barely more expensive to produce than it had been by the old method and that could be turned out in greater quantities (see Table 20-1). Other discoveries over the next twenty years permitted the production of steel of a more consistent quality, lowering its price by two-thirds.

A Bessemer converter.

TABLE 20-1. ANNUAL OUTPUT OF STEEL (IN MILLIONS OF METRIC TONS)

Year	Britain	Germany	France	Russia
1875–1879	0.90	—	0.26	0.08
1880–1884	1.82	0.99	0.46	0.25
1885–1889	2.86	1.65	0.54	0.23
1890–1894	3.19	2.89	0.77	0.54
1895–1899	4.33	5.08	1.26	1.32
1900–1904	5.04	7.71	1.70	2.35
1905–1909	6.09	11.30	2.65	2.63
1910–1913	6.93	16.24	4.09	4.20

Source: Carlo Cipolla, ed., *The Fontana Economic History of Europe,* vol. 3(2) (London: Collins/Fontana Books, 1976), p. 775.

Steel's strength, durability, and flexibility gave it a marked advantage over iron. Steel transformed manufacturing, improving the size, quality, standardization, and precision of machinery. Just three years after Bessemer's discovery, the first British ship constructed of steel slid from drydock into the sea. Larger, sturdier, and faster than their predecessors, steel ships transformed naval warfare, contributing to the Anglo-German naval rivalry that began with the dawn of the new century.

The Electric Revolution

Electricity permitted a stunning variety of innovations that ultimately improved the everyday lives of most Europeans. It made possible the invention of the electromagnetic telegraph, the undersea cable, and the telephone. Yet, electricity still remained little more than a scientific curiosity until Thomas Edison (1847–1931), an American, invented the incandescent lamp in 1879. The invention of electric alternators and transformers and improvements in cable and insulation provided a means by which electric power could be generated and diffused. In 1881, the first electric power stations began operation in England, and during the following decades electricity gradually entered European homes. Yet, although electric street lighting and electric tramways were commonplace by the end of the century, in many parts of Europe electricity remained a luxury identified with elegant hotels, department stores, and fancy neighborhoods, not reaching most households until after World War I.

Electricity accelerated European economic growth and the concentration of industry in the century's last two decades. For all their efficiency, water power, coal, and gas had placed limits on the location of factories. Electric power could be transported with relative ease, which ultimately enabled countries not well-endowed with natural resources to industrialize partially. In Europe, as in the United States, the first results of the electric age were particularly striking in heavy industry and in the construction of public transportation systems. The steel, textile, shoemaking, and construction industries, among others, came to depend upon electric power. Electricity also provided a relatively inexpensive source of power in small workshops. The burgeoning German electrical manufacturing industry helped Germany to challenge Britain for European manufacturing primacy. The company of Werner von Siemens (1816–1892), inventor of the first dynamo (1867), which made possible the production of unlimited amounts of electrical energy, became one of the most successful in Europe.

The sewing machine, invented by the American Isaac Singer (1811–1875), began to be used in the 1850s in industry and homes. The mechanization of the production of ready-made garments rapidly extended consumer markets, setting styles and reducing the price of clothing. But the impact of the sewing machine also demonstrated continuities in industrial work. For the garment industry—attracting Jewish immigrants to Paris and, above all, New York—remained largely tied to home work, as women, and some men, too, worked sewing machines in their apartments and rooms and in cramped sweatshops, turning out ready-made cloaks and dresses. Machines that could do band stitching, make button holes, or embroider led to a further specialization of labor. Singer marketed his machine as a device that would liberate women from tedious work. But the

Women workers working on a sewing machine and sewing by hand.

sewing machine also bound many women to the hectic pace of piecework, and to payments for the machine itself, usually purchased on time-payment plans.

In the 1890s, advertisers began to direct their appeals at the "new woman," the housewife of taste, who had the time to create the model "home" and had some money to spend. By 1900, electrically powered household appliances—refrigerators, fans, and vacuum cleaners—were generally available to those families that could afford to have their houses wired for electricity and could pay for the appliances.

Travel and Communications

In 1885, Karl Benz (1844–1929), a German engineer, invented the internal combustion engine, powered by gasoline, which brought even more dramatic changes in travel. Adding a primitive carburetor, Benz constructed a small automobile. The first automobiles were very expensive, the tires alone costing more than an average worker's annual wages. In 1897, Rudolf Diesel (1858–1913), a German, produced the first successful engine fueled by kerosene or pure oil, which could power larger vehicles capable of carrying heavy loads. By the turn of the century, four-cylinder engines powered automobiles.

Automobile manufacturing quickly became a major catalyst for industrial growth and the implementation of new production methods. Glass manufacturers, producers of steel, aluminum, rubber, and toolmakers were carried along with the automobile's success. The petroleum industry, too, gradually developed, although at the time only the oil reserves in Romania were known and exploited (the first oil refinery in Europe had been built there in 1857). Only slowly did some industrialists and statesmen begin to grasp the economic and strategic significance of oil wealth, particularly after the discovery in 1908 of rich oil fields in Persia.

Automobile manufacturers shifted from the limited production of elite cars, above all, the British Rolls Royce, to less expensive models. Henry Ford (1863–1947), who began his Detroit company in 1903, produced more than 15 million "Model T" Fords, which even his own workers could afford to purchase.

Worried by American competition, particularly in its lucrative export market to Britain, the French car manufacturer Louis Renault (1877–1944) looked for ways to cut production costs. Assembly-line production made it possible for his company to construct cars in segments. Workers mounted components on stationary chassis frames lined up along the factory floor. They used hand files to shape engine parts for expensive cars since interchangeable parts were not yet available. Techniques of scientific management of assembly-line production—"Taylorism," after Frederick W. Taylor (1856–1915), the American engineer who developed them—included careful counting of the number of units assembled by

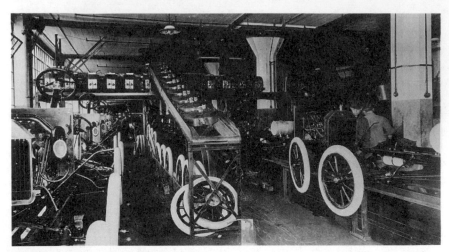

An early automobile assembly line.

each worker in an hour. The assembly line reduced the time it took to produce each car from twelve hours to one and a half hours.

The automobile transformed travel even more than had the railway earlier in the century. Elegant horses and fancy carriages owned by people of
means no longer monopolized travel, although country gentlemen scored
an early triumph, convincing the British Parliament to pass the "Red Flag
Act." Until it was repealed in 1896, the act restricted the speed of motor
vehicles to two miles per hour and required three people carrying red
warning flags to accompany each vehicle, a decided inconvenience. In
1896, the speed limit was raised to fourteen miles per hour.

Car travel necessitated better roads. Early drivers required not only
thick goggles to protect themselves against dust but whips to keep away
startled dogs. Gradually government authorities ordered the paving of
roads, and gas stations began to dot the landscape. In 1900, the Michelin
company in France, one of the first to shift from producing bicycle to automobile tires, first published its guide for travelers, listing garages, hotels,
and restaurants in every town of any size in the country. The number of
cars in Paris tripled between 1906 and 1912. Traffic jams became a way of
urban life. Automobile-taxis and then motorized fire engines superseded
their horse-drawn predecessors.

Whether or not they went by car, more Europeans could now travel for
leisure than ever before. Middle-class vacations became more common.
The travel business boomed. Health spas and resorts, which had developed since mid-century, became even more popular in Western Europe.
Spas claimed that their thermal waters offered healing and sustaining
properties, facilitating the circulation of blood, attacking gout—the en-
cumbering malady of people who were too well fed—or in some other way

restoring to equilibrium the human body victimized by modern life. In 1860, about 20,000 people went to the town of Vichy in central France for its waters; in 1890, 100,000 travelled there.

Mediterranean, North Sea, and Channel resorts offered casinos and beach-front promenades. Claude Monet, among other impressionists, painted Norman ports like Deauville and Étretat, veritable colonies of wealthy Parisians, now an easy train ride from the French capital. English coastal towns attracted middle-class and working-class tourists, oblivious to the cold, rainy climate. The tourist pier and arcade took shape. English nobles, who could afford to flee the British winter, "discovered" Nice and Menton. Upper-class Italians began to frequent their own Riviera. Germans preferred chilly Baltic resorts. Vacationers from many countries discovered the Alps and sent the first postcards back to envious friends. Partially spurred on by tourism, photography emerged as a major visual art, moving from individual poses to mass picture taking. The relatively light Kodak model camera appeared in 1888. Before too long Bretons began to refer to French-speaking tourists as "Kodakers."

As the automobile revolutionized travel, mass transportation transformed residential patterns in large cities. The London underground railway, opened in 1863, made it possible for employees and workers to live

Claude Monet's *Terrace at Sainte-Adresse* (1867) shows middle-class tourists enjoying the sun at a French seaside resort.

farther from their jobs. On July 14, 1900, the first Paris subway—the *métro*—began operation on the right bank of the Seine, and other lines soon followed, connecting the center city with its periphery. Four years later, the first sections of New York City's subway began operation.

The cult of speed next took to the air, after centuries of dreams had brought only balloon ascents and short glider flights. In 1900, a retired German general, Count Ferdinand von Zeppelin (1838–1917), built the first lumbering dirigible airship that bears his name. After years of experimentation with propellers and small engines, Orville and Wilbur Wright, two American bicycle manufacturers, launched the first successful flight in 1903. They then took their air show to England, France, and Germany, where the crown prince of Prussia began to consider the military uses of the airplane. To the young architectural student Le Corbusier, the airplane was "the vanguard of the conquering armies of the New Age."

A revolution in communications also slowly transformed life. The telephone, invented by Alexander Graham Bell (1847–1922) in 1876, reached private homes. Germans made 8 million telephone calls in 1883, 700 million in 1900. Fifteen years after Thomas Edison invented the gramophone in 1876, a number of virtuosos had made their first scratchy recordings. The Italian Guglielmo Marconi (1874–1937) pioneered the first wireless voice communication in the 1890s; by 1913, weekly concerts could be heard on the radio in Brussels. Silent motion pictures, first shown in 1895, became an immediate hit. The first viewers watched brief scenes of modern life, such as a train beginning to move. Entrepreneurs soon offered considerably longer films with plots and action, and silent movies were increasingly accompanied by a piano. By 1908, France had more

Women at work at a telephone switchboard.

than a thousand movie theaters. The Austro-Hungarian army began to experiment with motion pictures, using cameras to study the flight of artillery shells.

Regional Variation

The industrial boom seemed most dramatic in Germany, propelled by advances in iron, coal, steel, textile, and chemical industries. By 1890, both Germany and the United States had moved ahead of Britain in metallurgical production. By the turn of the century, German factories turned out more steel than Britain and France combined. Germany's chemical industry was the most modern in the world, producing fertilizers, sulphuric acid, chlorine, and other products for agriculture and industry.

How can we explain the German industrial boom, which went on even during the long depression? Germany enjoyed the advantage of starting to industrialize after its rivals, thereby being able to employ the most modern equipment in factories specially built to accommodate technological advances. By contrast, some British factories, most of which had been built early in the century (and some even before), seemed to be crumbling.

German banks played a more direct role in German industrialization than did their counterparts in other countries. While providing investment capital, the Dresdner Bank, Deutsche Bank, and other large investment banks themselves acquired large blocks of industrial shares, particularly in heavy industries like coal mining, electricity, and railways. Having entered industry in order to assure proper business management of companies to which they loaned money, they earned big profits and paid high dividends. German banks, then, became industrial entrepreneurs. They also favored the trend of German industry toward cartels, which controlled production and prices and therefore provided security within heavy industries.

German universities were more numerous and of better quality than any others in Europe at the same time, despite their authoritarian structure and their acquiescence in discrimination against Jews, Catholics, and socialists. They emerged as centers of scientific research. By contrast, English employers tended to look down their noses at academic training as a poor substitute for work experience, just as universities in Britain were relatively slow to adopt a more practical curriculum.

German economic growth and the doubling of its foreign trade during the last three decades of the nineteenth century began to make some in Britain anxious, despite the supremacy of the Royal Navy and of London as the world's banking center—Britain accounted for about 45 percent of world investment. In 1896, a British parliamentary commission reported that "the industrial glory of England is departing and England does not know it . . . this result is largely German work." The report exaggerated, but this perception strengthened the government's determination to hold fast to an aggressive colonial policy (see Chapter 22). It also inspired a campaign to establish an empire-wide tariff barrier that would encourage trade within the British Commonwealth, while keeping foreign goods out.

During the late-nineteenth-century depression, British manufactured goods stacked up at the docks as demand declined abroad and prices fell. By the mid-1880s, some of the countries that had purchased British goods were able to meet consumer demand at home with their own production. Shiploads of foreign-made goods in the century's last decades began to undercut British production, which was unprotected by tariff walls. Instead of depending upon British shipping, German, Italian, and French merchants now took advantage of the Suez Canal, opened in 1869, to send their own ships to Asia to make purchases and sell goods directly. English agriculture also suffered, no longer protected by steep protective tariffs since the repeal of the Corn Laws in 1846.

France and Russia lagged behind Britain and Germany, despite their own impressive periods of industrial growth. Both were constrained by dual economies: the combination of a modern manufacturing sector characteristic of the Second Industrial Revolution and traditional handicraft and agricultural production, with strong regional variations within each country.

The Russian economy still was overwhelmingly agricultural. The famine of the 1890s, which killed millions of peasants, demonstrated the fragility and limits of Russian agriculture. Although the empire became an exporter of grain, Russian farms remained relatively unproductive. Absentee ownership of large estates, the many small peasant plots that continued to be farmed at a subsistence level as they had been for centuries, and the existence of village communal lands hindered agricultural development. Furthermore, legal restrictions limited the mobility of peasants, who could not leave their villages unless they had paid off their share of taxes or redemption payments on land gained from the nobles at the time of the emancipation of the serfs in 1861.

Russian industries, despite some impressive growth, lagged well behind their Western European counterparts. They faced the serious physical impediment of sheer distance between resources, manufacturers, and markets. Coal deposits lay far from centers of manufacturing. Many Russians, because of the influence of the Orthodox Church, viewed investment as usurious and therefore dishonest. Subsistence farming and weak banking structures limited the accumulation of sufficient investment capital, which held back manufacturing and the development of the empire's rail network. Russian manufacturers depended on a large infusion of foreign capital; indeed foreign investment, above all, from France, more than doubled during the 1890s. Technology also had to be imported. Russia was confronted by a shortage of technicians and skilled workers as well. Even though nobles and a few former serfs sometimes became manufacturers, the absence of a sizable middle class limited consumer demand for manufactured goods and investment.

Yet, despite these obstacles, Russia's large-scale industries developed

Rural laborers in southern Italy next to their straw huts.

with reasonable speed. Coal extraction doubled, and the production of steel increased fourfold during the last decades of the century. The state focused its attention on heavy metal and fuel production, including oil. In 1914, St. Petersburg had more than 900 large factories, one of the largest concentrations of industry in Europe.

By the turn of the century, railroads at last linked Russia's major cities and facilitated the shipping of grain to the empire's northern ports. The Trans-Siberian railway, inching its way across the vast empire to link Moscow to Vladivostok on the Pacific Ocean, proved an expensive luxury. Moreover, small-scale manufacturing industries flagged, constrained by the fact that the overwhelming majority of people in the empire had almost nothing to spend on consumer products.

Other economies also reflected this duality (see Map 20.1). In France, the production of high-quality handicrafts, centered in Paris, continued to dominate French industry. Moreover, France's economy was still mainly agricultural. Traditional sectors of agriculture and small-scale manufacturing also persisted alongside regionally specific heavy industries in Spain, Austria-Hungary, and Italy. In Spain, the contrast was between the large-scale industries of the Basque country and Catalonia, and the overwhelmingly agricultural economy of the vast Castilian plain and the sleepy capital of Madrid. As in Russia, most of the investment in Spanish industry came from abroad because agriculture generated inadequate surpluses for significant industrial investment. In the Austro-Hungarian monarchy, the dynamism of Bohemia and Moravia contrasted sharply with the small market ways of Austria and the Hungarian plain. In Italy, there was little

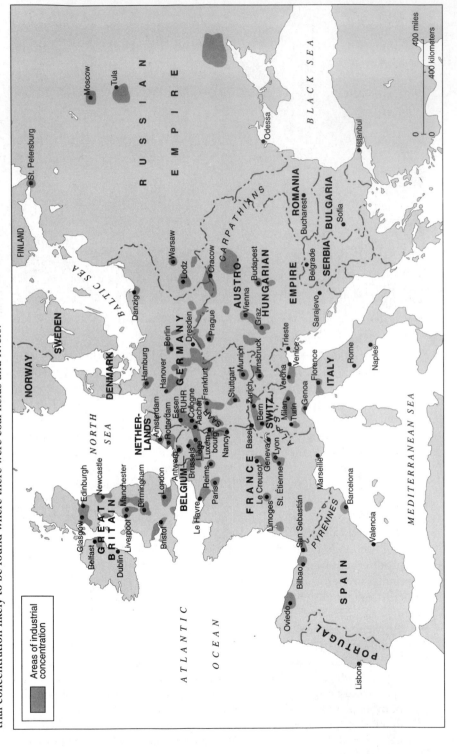

MAP 20.1 AREAS OF INDUSTRIAL CONCENTRATION, 1870–1914   Various regions industrialized more quickly than others, with industrial concentration likely to be found where there were coal fields and rivers.

large-scale industry south of the triangle formed by Milan, Turin, and the port of Genoa, centers of textile production, engineering, and ship building.

In agricultural productivity, too, the European "dual economies" did not keep pace with the burgeoning economies of Britain and Germany. British and, to a lesser extent, German agriculture benefited from capital-intensive strategies. Large, productive farms whose lands were enriched by chemical fertilizers and cultivated with mechanized equipment could also to be found in parts of Belgium and northern France.

A CHANGING POPULATION

During the second half of the nineteenth century, Europe's population continued to change as the continent further industrialized. As mortality rates fell, particularly among children, Europe's population continued to grow rapidly. Most countries urbanized; the number of people living in cities and towns increased even more rapidly than the general population as urban births outnumbered deaths and factory and white-collar employment drew migrants to cities. Increased factory production altered the physical structure of industrial cities: they were characterized by greater social segregation within their limits, and working-class suburbs developed rapidly on the edge of town. As Europeans became ever more geographically mobile, overseas emigration (particularly to the Americas) rose rapidly and did not slow down even with the end of the economic depression in the mid-1890s.

Demographic Boom

Between 1870 and 1914, the population of Europe increased by half, rising from 290 to 435 million (see Table 20-2). By the end of the nineteenth century, one of every four people in the world was a European.

TABLE 20-2. POPULATION GROWTH IN MAJOR STATES BETWEEN 1871 AND 1911 (POPULATION IN MILLIONS)

	c. 1871	c. 1911	% increase
German Empire	41.1	64.9	57.8
France	36.1	39.6	9.7
Austria-Hungary*	35.8	49.5	38.3
Great Britain	31.8	45.4	42.8
Italy	26.8	34.7	29.5
Spain	16.0	19.2	20.0

*Not including Bosnia-Herzegovina.
Source: Colin Dyer, *Population and Society in Twentieth Century France* (New York: Holmes and Meier, 1978), p. 5.

Europe's population grew rapidly because the continent passed from the traditional pattern of high birthrates and high death rates to low rates of both births and deaths. Births outnumbered deaths, despite the fact that fertility rates fell beginning in the 1860s, or even before. In England, dysentery and diarrhea still carried off about 15 of every 100 infants born. But in the 1880s, the infant mortality rate, too, began to fall rapidly, contributing to the rise in population. In France, it declined from about 184 to 159 per 1,000 live births between the early 1880s and the turn of the century. Reasons for this improvement include greater medical knowledge of chest and stomach infections, as well as a general improvement in the standard of living. Poor people could afford to eat more nutritious food and lived in warmer, drier accommodations, although such improvements still lagged behind in large, dirty, industrial cities.

With infant mortality greatly reduced, more couples sought to control the number of births (see Table 20-3). The number of families with more than two or three children fell, despite the fact that couples now tended to marry at a younger age. Although Britain's Queen Victoria had nine children, poor families often had more children than upper-class couples, who seem to have limited births because they wanted to devote more resources to the education and inheritance of each child.

Contraception became more widespread. Coitus interruptus was the most common method, although it was hardly flawless. An upper-middle-class English woman told a friend after she had given birth: "Dear child, you look very pale and must not have another baby for a long time. Henry always withdrew in time, such a noble man!" Rudimentary condoms made of animal intestines were superseded in the 1880s by rubber condoms, although these still were relatively expensive, available mainly in cities, and used primarily for protection against disease rather than for birth control.

French officials and nationalists worried about their country's plunging birthrate. France's slow rate of growth was exceptional and the reasons for it have continued to baffle demographers. Although regions with many practicing Catholics continued to have high rates of birth, the French population grew by only about 15 percent from mid-century until 1914

TABLE 20-3. THE DECLINE IN FAMILY SIZE (NUMBER OF CHILDREN) IN ENGLAND AND WALES

Year	Family Size
1861–1869	6.16
1871	5.94
1876	5.62
1890–1899	4.13
1900–1909	3.30
1910–1914	2.82

Source: E.A. Wrigley, *Population and History* (New York: McGraw-Hill, 1969), p. 197.

(counting the addition of Savoy and Nice in 1860 and the loss of Alsace and much of Lorraine to Germany in 1871). In one part of southwestern France, the birth of a second child—one more mouth to feed—occasioned condolence cards. The division of farmland into small plots may be a partial explanation—another child ultimately meant a further subdivision of land because France did not have primogeniture (inheritance by the eldest son).

Everywhere in Europe, however, births to unmarried couples or to single mothers increased in number. Young female migrants to the city, no longer constrained by living with their parents, were vulnerable to the advances of men promising marriage or promising nothing at all. Unplanned pregnancies followed. A sizable percentage of the population of most countries—about 10 to 15 percent—never married or entered into permanent or long-term relationships. Unmarried women were especially common in Scotland, Ireland, and in Brittany in France, from which more males than females had migrated to urban, industrial regions.

Improvements in municipal sanitation contributed to longer life expectancy. A trip to the doctor was no longer seen as the first step to the undertaker. The French scientist Louis Pasteur's development of the germ theory of disease in the 1860s, which led to the pasteurization of milk, brought about a decline in cases of tuberculosis. Many towns built sewer systems to ensure a cleaner water supply. This reduced some contagious diseases and, as people seemed to become less tolerant of foul smells, some of the more unpleasant odors of urban life. Rat poison killed off millions of disease-carrying rodents. Still, the poor continued to die earlier than people of means, even as the European population rapidly increased.

Teeming Cities

In 1899, an American statistician—the profession itself was another sign of the times—noted that "the concentration of population in cities [is] the most remarkable social phenomenon of the present century." Britain and Germany led the way, but France, Austria, Switzerland, Italy, Sweden, and even Spain and Serbia also had high rates of urban growth. Classic "factory towns" such as Manchester, Saint-Étienne, and Essen grew rapidly in size, but so did the population of other towns, swollen by service workers, factory operatives, and commercial employees.

Rural industry, which had provided spinning, weaving, and finishing work for hundreds of thousands of people, above all, women, on a full- or part-time basis, largely disappeared during the last half of the century. Manufacturing, including home production in the garment industry, now became overwhelmingly concentrated in urban centers. The markets for rural manufactured goods gradually disappeared, as investment capital concentrated in and on the edge of cities. Although farms became larger, mechanized agriculture (which became more prevalent in Western Europe) and falling agricultural prices reduced demand for farm laborers. These changes, as they occurred in parts of France, Switzerland, Italy, and Germany, encouraged temporary and permanent migration. Rural people poured into cities, seeking work in the booming service sector or in industry as employment opportunities in the countryside shrunk. And by the end of the nineteenth century, cities replenished their own populations through natural increase.

Although many working-class families now lived in marginally more spacious lodgings, many densely packed neighborhoods in large cities became ghastly slums. London had its infamous "back to back" row houses, with little or no space between the houses and room for little more between the rows than outdoor toilets, if that, and garbage heaps. For most British workers, a parlor (a family room), a sign of "respectability," remained only a dream. In Glasgow, Scotland, a third of the families lived in one room, as more and more highlanders crowded into tall tenement dwellings.

By 1900, nine European cities had populations of over a million people. London, as it had for over three centuries, dwarfed them all, growing from 1.9 million in 1841 to 4.2 million in 1891. Between one-fifth and one-sixth of the population of Britain lived in London, which was larger than the next seven largest English cities and Edinburgh combined. The sprawling city seemed almost ungovernable, an imposing labyrinth of different jurisdictions with 10,000 people exercising varying degrees of authority. Unlike Paris, which was for the most part administered by the centralized French state, London only had an effective local government after the establishment of the London City Council in 1889.

The largest port in the world, London also remained a center of international banking, finance, and commerce, and the administrative nerve center of the British Empire. Its influence extended across the world, channeling investment capital to innumerable countries within and be-

(*Left*) Tenement housing in Glasgow. (*Right*) Company housing near mines in northern France.

yond the empire. The largest merchant marine fleet in the world shipped woolens and other textiles to China, machine parts and hardware to Russia, toys to New York, settlers to Canada, and soldiers and sailors to India, and it imported Australian wool, Chicago beef, Bordeaux wines, Portuguese port, and Cuban cigars.

London was also a center of small-scale production and finishing in shops usually employing only a few skilled and semiskilled workers each, such as in the clothing industry, furniture making, engineering, and printing. In contrast, its bustling East End docks employed a vast force of "casual labor" depending on seasonal work, that is, semiskilled and unskilled laborers, mostly recent migrants from Ireland and rural England. Two million people lived in London's East End; the homeless slept where they could, in empty or half-collapsed buildings, under bridges and railroad viaducts. To upper-class Londoners, the East End, about which they knew nothing except "from hearsay and report," was a morass of tangled slums "as unexplored as Timbuctoo." Residents of these districts spoke a cockney dialect that was difficult for outsiders to understand, or a thick Irish brogue, or Yiddish. The upper classes viewed "outcast London" with condescension, and some anxiety as well. They feared the pockets of criminality, which centered around underworld pubs, and the seeming possibility of riot and rebellion.

Many social theorists were convinced that the rapid growth of cities bred crime. But, in fact, urban growth in some places seems to have significantly increased only crimes against property. Indeed, crime rates in Glasgow fell during the last half of the century, despite the petty extortion carried out by youth gangs like the Penny Mob, Redskins, and Kelly Boys. Many contemporary observers inveighed against cities as promoting an anonymous, alienated mass of people. Yet, relatives and friends who had the same dialect or accent or religion encouraged others to move to the city and served as conduits for information about jobs and lodgings to share. The resulting "chain" migration created "urban villages" that mitigated against uprooting and lawlessness. Neighborhoods of Irish in Liverpool and London and Italians and Irish in Boston and New York provided solidarities that made the city seem less anonymous to newcomers.

Social segregation within European cities became more pronounced. Elevators carried wealthy occupants of apartment buildings to refurbished dwellings in the upper stories, where poorer people had once lived. Elegant residences lined the boulevards of western Paris, the Ringstrasse of Vienna, and the parks of west London. On the other hand, railway lines and factories, whether in old districts or in new ones on the edge of town, were surrounded by poor-quality, low-rent housing, usually owned by absentee landlords.

Suburbs began to grow rapidly around the edge of Europe's larger cities. Some, particularly on the edge of London, catered to middle-class people who could commute into the city, happy to live in small houses that of-

The margins of urban life on the edge of Paris at the turn of the century.

fered more room than London apartments, and had a garden and proximity to the countryside. These suburbs, unlike most center cities, reflected some degree of planning and improved water and gas supply, among other municipal services.

But European suburbs have been, for the most part, a plebeian phenomenon, quite different from suburbs in the United States. Factories were constructed on the edge of cities so that manufacturers could take advantage of more space, proximity to railways and canals, somewhat lower cost of land and raw materials (avoiding the taxes that were still levied on goods brought into some cities), and the availability of cheap labor. Working-class housing sprung up on the edge of the city, where it was cheaper to live; more and more workers commuted daily into town to work—some still on foot, others by train, tram, subway, and, later, bus.

The Hungarian capital of Budapest reflected not only the social and ethnic complexity of the Austro-Hungarian Empire but also the increased social segregation characteristic of the modern city. This city on the Danube River grew from 280,000 inhabitants in 1867 to almost a million people in 1914, and included many nobles. Rich, middling, and poor people increasingly lived in separate districts; in some parts of town, however, families of means lived on the street side of large rectangular apartments while the poor occupied apartments off dank passageways in the back. The complexity of social differences was such that five forms of salutation were current, depending upon whom one was addressing. These ranged from the ultimate deference of "Gracious Sir," through the only slightly less groveling "Dignified Sir" or "Great Sir," all the way down to the considerably more common "Hey, you!"

With urban growth came civic pride. Municipal governments raised historical monuments, built new hospitals and town halls, sponsored bands, and created beautiful parks complete with ornate bandstands. They prided themselves on an increasingly diverse municipal cultural life, including occasional music festivals and perhaps even a museum. The proliferation of voluntary associations, such as clubs and choral societies, also came to be taken as symbols of urbanity.

Migration and Emigration

European migration was part of a worldwide movement of men and women in what was becoming a global labor force. Migration—both permanent and seasonal—within Europe continued to be significant. France's foreign population was swollen by the arrival of many Italians. Seasonal work took hundreds of thousands of laborers across borders for part of the year as construction and harvest workers. Italian laborers, known as "swallows," spent four weeks a year going to and from Argentina to work the harvests!

Migration to the city did not end the contact between the migrants and their rural origins. In France, many industrial workers still went back to their villages to help with the harvest and many miners were also part-time farmers. In Russia, the peasant-workers of Moscow and St. Petersburg kept one foot in the rural world. They lived on the edge of the cities, dressed like villagers, and were forced by the state to maintain legal ties to their rural commune because they remained responsible for their share of the commune's tax quota. In 1900, peasants made up two-thirds of the population of St. Petersburg, a city of more than 1.4 million people.

Thus, migration was a two-way street, at least when patterns of movement involved relatively short distances. When migrants returned home for visits, they brought with them not only stories about what they had experienced in the cities and towns where they now lived, but different ways of speaking, knowledge of birth control, the habit of reading, a taste for sports, and greater political awareness and interest.

Overseas emigration increased dramatically during the century's last decades, encouraged by the long economic depression. Peasants and laborers, in particular, left Europe in hope of economic opportunity in the United States, Canada, and Latin America. Ireland, Britain, and Germany provided most of the earlier waves of emigrants, although Russia and Eastern Europe also sent an increasing number. Thus, between 1871 and 1914, more than 1.5 million Jews left Russia for the United States, fleeing poverty and periodic anti-Semitic violence in search of freedom and jobs.

With improving economic times in the late 1890s, emigration slowed down from Germany, while remaining high from Ireland and soaring from Italy. During the first decade of the twentieth century, emigration from Europe rose to between 1 and 1.4 million people each year. Most of those packing themselves onto overcrowded steamers went to the United States: Italians and Irish to New York, Boston, and Philadelphia; Russian and Polish Jews to New York's Lower East Side; Germans to Chicago, Milwaukee,

Immigrants from southern Italy arriving in New York City, 1905.

and Philadelphia; Scandinavians to Minneapolis and Seattle (see Table 20-4). Among these millions of people, many left with little more than a few cherished items and great hopes. One Jewish emigrant from a village in Byelorussia (now Belarus) remembered that his family carried empty suitcases as they left home—they did not want the other people they met along the way to know that they owned virtually nothing to carry with them.

Although many families left together for overseas destinations, many married men went alone, hoping either to send for their families when they could afford to do so, or to return themselves after making and saving some money. Single men, too—more than single women—left loved ones

TABLE 20-4. EMIGRATION TO THE UNITED STATES, 1871–1910

Decade	1871–1880	1881–1890	1891–1900	1901–1910
Germany	718,000	1,500,000	505,000	341,000
Ireland	437,000	656,000	388,000	339,000
England/ Scotland/Wales	548,000	807,000	272,000	526,000
Scandinavia	243,000	655,000	372,000	505,000
Italy	56,000	307,000	652,000	2,000,000
Austria-Hungary	73,000	363,000	574,000	2,145,000
Russia/ Baltic states	39,000	213,000	505,000	1,597,000

Source: Leonard Dinnerstein and David M. Reimers, *Ethnic Americans: A History of Immigration and Assimilation* (New York: Harper and Row, 1977), p. 11.

on the docks of European ports, or in farms a distance away. A popular Irish ballad related some of the anguish of leaving one's home,

Oh, farewell to poor old Erin's Isle, I now must leave you
for awhile.
The rent and taxes are so high, I can no longer stay.
From Dublin Quay I sailed away, and landed here but
yesterday.
My shoes and brogues and my shirt are all that's in my kit.
I have just called in to let you know the sights I've seen
before I go.

In new homes, migrants forged new collective identities, a process shaped not only by their own ethnic backgrounds and solidarities but also by conditions in their new homelands. Many never saw their families again. Migrants to the United States from southern Italy were the most likely to return permanently again, with almost two-thirds eventually going back. Only about 20 percent of German emigrants, 15 percent of Irish, and only 5 percent of Jewish migrants went back to their homelands again.

SOCIAL CHANGES

The Second Industrial Revolution engendered further social changes in Europe. Wage labor in factories increasingly defined working-class experience for men and women—from Glasgow to the grim periphery of the Russian capital of St. Petersburg. Although contemporary moralists bemoaned some of the bad effects of the concentration of industrial work in and around cities, arguing that the uprooting of families from villages put them at risk in cities characterized by vice and immorality, conditions of life improved for most Europeans. Most people ate better and lived longer than before. An expansion of white-collar jobs—including positions as clerks, tram ticket collectors, and schoolteachers, among many others—offered some peasants and workers chances for social mobility, particularly in Western Europe. Nonetheless, in many regions—including much of Russia and the Balkans and southern Italy—wrenching poverty remained common, and mobility into the middle class remained exceptional at the turn of the century.

Industrial Workers

Wage laborers, many with prior industrial experience in rural workshops or domestic industry, settled around factories in response to expanding employment opportunities. The German arms manufacturer Krupp employed 72 workers in 1848 and 12,000 in 1873, following Prussia's victories in the Austro-Prussian War (1866) and the Franco-Prussian War (1870–1871). By 1900, more than half of the industrial workers in Britain, Germany, and Belgium were employed in firms with more than 20 workers.

Although artisans, skilled workers, and unskilled workers often found themselves laboring in the same factory, a larger percentage of laborers were now proletarians, that is, workers who were dependent upon their unskilled labor for survival. By the 1880s, most industrial workers came from proletarian families and grew up with few or no illusions about finding a more secure way of earning a living. Working-class families prepared their own offspring for industrial work. But "proletarian" also became a state of mind; class-conscious workers took pride in their work and in their social class. "I was born in the slums of London of working-class parents," a contemporary recalled, "and although I have attained a higher standard of living, I still maintain I am working class."

Yet, enormous differences existed in skill, remuneration, and quality of life among workers. An English skilled worker commented: "The 'old' see that labor-saving machinery is reducing the previously skilled to the level of unskilled labor . . . the 'new' believe that . . . [the] class prejudices that have disintegrated the labor movement in the past must be abolished." But this was not so easily accomplished, despite the tendency of subsequent historians sometimes to romanticize class consciousness and the working-class experience. In Britain, above all, workers who were relatively well off defiantly insisted on their respectability, viewing many kinds of occupations as beneath their dignity. Far more than their continental counterparts, British workers still viewed the upper class with a certain deference.

Nonetheless, one of the effects of "de-skilling" among workers was class consciousness and trade union militancy. Indeed, mechanization eliminated or reduced demand for some trades, skilled or otherwise. Skilled glassworkers in France, for example, were no longer needed when the Siemens furnace, which reduced fuel costs and permitted continuous production, was adapted to the production of bottles in the 1880s. Porcelain painters lost their jobs to unskilled female laborers when factory owners started using decals that could be applied to plates and then baked on. Steam laundries left many washerwomen without clients.

At the same time, however, new professions brought some workers higher status. Engineers, capable of designing, overseeing, and repairing machinery, became fixtures in factories. In the 1880s, some engineers still received training as apprentices, but by the first decades of the twentieth century, many had received university training in their chosen profession. Some, such as graduates of the elite Polytechnic School in Paris, were assured of excellent jobs, but others who had attended lesser technical schools began as manual workers or as railway engineers.

Most female workers were still employed in small workshops or at home, but more women became factory workers. Even in the Habsburg empire, which was much less industrialized than Germany or Britain, about 900,000 women worked in factories, largely in unskilled jobs. Most earned only about half the wages of their male counterparts for, in some cases, the same jobs. Women workers were usually the last hired and the first fired. They also faced the difficulty of raising children while working full-time in factories.

Despite harsh working conditions and relatively low wages, many women saw factory work as bringing an improvement in wages and conditions over agricultural labor, paid or unpaid, cottage industry, or domestic service. A Belfast woman in 1898 remembered her time in a linen mill: "Wonderful times then in the mill. You got a wee drink, got a join [pooled money with others to buy food], done your work and you had your company."

Women's work remained closely tied to their stage of life. Many young, unmarried women became servants upon arrival in the urban world, trying to save enough money for a modest dowry, in the hope of marrying someone of a slightly higher social class. Because upper-class families employed more domestics than ever before, three times more women worked in domestic service in England than in textile factories. By the end of the century, servants accounted for more than half of female workers in Britain.

Some contemporary surveys emphasized the plight of child workers, who constituted 14 percent of the workforce in the British textile industry in 1874. Although most states had long since passed laws limiting the ages of children who could be employed in factories and the hours they could work (see Chapter 16), at the turn of the century many thousands of chil-

Derbyshire pit boys outside of the mines.

dren, including those between the ages of eight and fourteen, were still working part-time. Above age fourteen, children worked as adults.

In Émile Zola's best-selling novel *Germinal* (1885), the thirteenth of his series of twenty novels about a large working-class family, Étienne Lantier goes to work in the mines of northern France. In the shaft, where the temperature rose to ninety-five degrees and air could not circulate, fifteen-year-old Catherine teaches the fully grown Étienne the exhausting and dangerous job of digging coal, filling the coal tub, and pushing and steering it on its tracks up the steep incline with his body. Believing Catherine to be about twelve because she was so small, "he was amazed at the child's strength, a nervous strength with much skill in it. She filled her tub [of coal] quicker than he did, with fast, regular little movements of her shovel, then pitched it to the incline with a long, slow push without any hitch, passing easily under the low rocks. . . . She sweated and panted and her joints cracked, but she never complained, for familiarity had brought apathy, and you would have thought that being doubled up like that was part of the normal course of human suffering."

Industrialization and the Working-Class Family

Contemporary moralists believed that industrial work had an adverse effect on family life. "Social Catholics," concerned with some of the nefarious social effects of factories on workers, blamed the increasing separation of home and work, claiming that moral degradation and promiscuity almost inevitably accompanied the mixing of the sexes in factories. They believed that only moral reforms—more education, marriage, and savings—could save family life. More than a few viewed single working women as by their very nature promiscuous, representing the worse aspects of modern cities, what one called "the blasts of unspeakable exhalations, the pell-mell of fumes, of evil emanations and bad dreams that hover above our darkened cities." Women, they claimed, were being taken away from their reproductive function, and from family life itself.

Although urban-based factory production appeared to loosen community ties that had sustained poor families in the countryside or in small workshops, these same solidarities actually were often reconstituted in cities. Nonetheless, working-class families in cities were much less likely to live with their extended families, that is, with parents and sometimes grandparents and in-laws. More families tended to be broken up early when children sixteen years or younger left villages in search of work in the cities, leaving aged parents on their own at home. Furthermore, long hours in the factory for parents and children alike seemed to erode parental authority. Moralists blamed increasingly homogeneous working-class neighborhoods, where drinking and domestic violence seemed rampant. Women in the city tended to marry earlier, and about a third of urban couples never married at all, either because they did not stay together, could not afford to pay for even the simplest ceremony, or because they just did not want to do so.

Many women of child-bearing age who could afford to do so, or who had no other choice, tended children full time. But once their offspring were old enough to care for themselves, working-class mothers could go back to factory work. Others worked at home, doing piecework and caring for their children at the same time. Many women thus alternated between industrial wage labor and child rearing, sometimes leaving factory work once their children had reached fourteen years of age, old enough to bring home minimal wages themselves.

Prostitution

Many women were forced by economic circumstances into prostitution. In Paris, London, Berlin, and other capital cities, prostitutes numbered in the tens of thousands. Some worked in elegant brothels, under the direction of the "madam," who allowed them only a couple days off per year. Others worked on their own, displaying themselves in doorways, windows, bars, and parks.

Most prostitutes were working-class women—some of whom were married—unable to find industrial work or, in some cases, having been dismissed from their positions as household servants because they were pregnant. Many were young, having had to leave school early to support a younger brother or sister, and were already on their own in the tough world of London's East End, or in rough ports or in shabby seaside resort towns.

Prostitutes began to be perceived more than ever before as a chronic danger to public health. Complaints from the middle class (which was ironic, in that middle-class men constituted a significant part of the clientele for prostitutes) increased. Socialist parties, however, expressed little interest in prostitution as an issue of reform. While blaming capitalism for the low wages or unemployment that forced many women into prostitution, socialists criticized the structure of bourgeois family life and middle-class men for subsidizing the trade.

In 1864, the British Parliament passed the Contagious Diseases Act, which required medical examination of prostitutes. The goal was to stop the spread of venereal disease, particularly syphilis, by hospitalizing prostitutes found to be infected. If a woman refused medical examination, she could be prosecuted for prostitution. The Contagious Diseases Act had the ironic effect of transforming prostitution from a temporary profession for many struggling working-class women to a dead end, permanent job because the law publicly branded them as prostitutes.

Josephine Butler (1828–1906), the devoutly religious wife of a clergyman and president of an association encouraging higher education for women, led a well-organized, determined campaign in Britain and then on the continent against the Contagious Diseases Act. Some opponents of the act objected that the law called only for the inspection of prostitutes, not their clients; others opposed extensive police regulatory authority. Butler espoused the right of women to regulate their own sexuality. Parliament responded by passing a law that banned procuring and brothels. It repealed the acts in 1886 but then forced prostitutes to operate in tolerated "red-light" districts, where they were often subject to violence, as were the prostitutes who constituted almost all of the victims of the still unidentified London killer "Jack the Ripper" in the late 1880s.

In France, where prostitutes had for some time been obliged to submit to medical inspection for venereal disease, state officials also implemented laws to bring them under greater regulatory control. The fear of syphilis contributed to the victory of regulation of prostitution in France, where state and public attitudes toward prostitution were likely to be considered in terms of a hygienic and social problem rather than based on moral and religious imperatives.

Gradually the belief that morality could be legislated ebbed in Europe. Charitable institutions more willingly provided assistance to unwed mothers and their offspring, increasingly considering their sad situations as a social, not a moral, problem.

Improving Standards of Living

Living standards improved for ordinary people in every industrialized country. Standards of living were far higher in Northern Europe than in Southern and Eastern Europe, greater in Britain than in France, with Germany closing the gap with both of its rivals. In Britain, real wages (taking inflation into account), which had increased by a third between 1850 and 1875, rose by almost half during the last three decades of the century; in Germany, they rose by a third during this period. Workers enjoyed higher levels of consumption because the price of food fell, the result of increased agricultural production, better transportation, and the general effect of the economic depression. Working-class families still spent half of their budget on food, but this was almost a quarter less than during the past several centuries. This left more money to spend on clothes, with something left over. Small-town shops were better supplied than ever before, and ready-made clothes sold on market day alongside manufactured household utensils.

More grain and meat, arriving in refrigerated ships, reached Europe from Australia, Canada, the United States, and Argentina. Meat ceased to be a luxury. The average German had consumed almost 60 pounds of meat in 1873 and ate 105 pounds in 1912. Germans consumed on average three times more sugar at the end of the century than thirty years earlier. Even in Russia, ravaged by famine in the 1890s, increases in harvest yield were comparable to those of France and Germany by 1900. Still, workers almost everywhere remained chronically undernourished, reflected in the fact that the average European laborer was several inches shorter than the average middle-class person.

Social Mobility

Gains made by workers seemed paltry when compared to the fortunes being made by industrialists and the adequate salaries received by management personnel. This made "progress" seem galling. These gnawing disparities aided unions and socialist parties in their quest for the allegiance of workers, who walked to and from work while horse-drawn cabs raced by, carrying well-heeled occupants. In the mid-1890s, real wages, which had risen for several decades, entered a period of decline.

Dizzying "rags to riches" tales (especially popular in the United States) suggested that hard work could lead to better conditions of life. Emigrants to the United States often arrived with fantastically high expectations of what life would be like. Their inflated expectations often brought disappointment, as social mobility was extremely limited, particularly for first-generation immigrants. During the last decades of the century, 95 percent of American industrialists came from upper- or middle-class families, and not more than 3 percent were the sons of poor immigrants or farmers. Among immigrants and native-born workers in the United States, the most common form of social advancement was within the working class, not into a higher social group.

The ranks of the middle classes, however, did grow during the Second Industrial Revolution. Nowhere were the economic changes of the late decades of the nineteenth century more evident than in the expansion of lower-middle-class occupations. In Britain, the proportion of the population classified as lower middle class grew from about 7 percent in 1850 to 20 percent in 1900. Clerks working for banks, railroads, utility companies, and insurance companies considered themselves above the working class and therefore "respectable." With the optimism of the age, they

Clerical work toward the end of the nineteenth century.

viewed such employment as a first step to owning their own store. They did not wear work clothes—and thus were described as "white-collar" employees. They did not do manual labor and they made a little more money than did workers. Architects required draftsmen; companies needed accountants and bookkeepers; and the London underground and Paris subway had to have agents. Furthermore, the expansion of governmental functions generated thousands of jobs in every country: tax collectors, postal workers, food and drug inspectors, and recorders of official documents. The number of schoolteachers increased dramatically in every country between the 1870s and 1914—five times more in Italy, thirteen times more in England. Table 20-5 represents the rapid growth in the number of state employees.

Women found jobs as department store clerks, stenographers, and secretaries. There were twelve times as many secretaries in 1901 as there had been two decades earlier; women, who held only 8 percent of post office and government clerical positions in 1861, accounted for more than half in 1911. They now used metal pens that replaced the age-old quill, and then the typewriter, invented in the 1880s. Clerical positions, which required reading and writing, also reflected the gradual expansion of educational opportunity for women. Nursing gradually became a respected profession. Cafés and restaurants employed hundreds of thousands of women.

Despite movement in Western European countries into clerical and other lower-middle-class jobs, however, there were fewer possibilities of movement by workers into the middle class during the depression years of the 1880s than there had been during the middle decades of the century. Manufacturing provided limited opportunities for social advancement for a small number of former serfs in Russia. Some newer professions, including veterinary science and pharmacology, rewarded sons—and, in the cases of teaching and nursing, daughters—of artisans and peasants. But everywhere the gap between craftsmen and semiskilled or unskilled workers remained great.

Low wages and periodic unemployment for industrial workers made saving and the ownership of apartments or houses, both essential components of mobility, extremely difficult to achieve. Craftsmen and skilled workers had a far better chance for social ascension than did unskilled

Table 20-5. Number of Public Servants (Non-Military)

	1881	1901	1911
Great Britain	81,000	153,000	644,000
France	379,000	451,000	699,000
Germany	452,000	907,000	1,159,000

Source: Norman Stone, *Europe Transformed 1878–1919* (Cambridge, MA: Harvard University Press, 1984), p. 130.

workers, but even then those who did move up to middle-class employment were the exceptions. Intergenerational mobility was still relatively rare. The vast majority of marriages in Europe took place between social equals. Working-class women were more likely than men to achieve social mobility, since women could raise themselves by marrying a clerk or railroad station employee. Yet, Charles Booth, middle-class investigator into London poverty, reported that by 1890 London artisans no longer sought clerical positions for their children, believing "that an occupation [in the building trades] that secures nine and a half pence an hour is not to be despised and that a common, dusty coat may after all be better than the formal broadcloth of shop and counting-house."

MASS CULTURE

During the last decades of the nineteenth century, mass culture developed in the countries of Europe, although with considerable country-by-country variation. In every country, states took enormous strides to bring education to more people. In Southern and Eastern Europe, rates of literacy remained behind those in Western and Central Europe, but nonetheless improved significantly. More children went on to secondary school, including, for the first time, some girls. The state's increased role in education in Western Europe contributed to a growing secularization of public life. At the same time, the established churches lost the allegiance of many ordinary Europeans; religious practice declined most precipitously in Catholic France, but also in other countries or regions as well.

The new leisure activities of the Belle Époque themselves reflected the Second Industrial Revolution. Bicycles could be mass produced and by the turn of the century fell within the spending possibilities of many workers. Sports, principally soccer and rugby, bicycle and automobile races (although automobiles were far too expensive for ordinary people), and track and field, attracted participants and spectators and encouraged the formation of clubs. In and around cities and towns, cafés, café-concerts, and taverns attracted throngs of pleasure-seekers, night and day. Finally, department stores reflected and helped shape mass consumer culture, with glossy advertising encouraging shoppers from every social class. In European capitals, department stores displayed in their windows and on their shelves the wonders of mass production as well as fine luxury goods. Consumers far from the spectacle of the stores themselves could order by catalogue.

Mass Education

The percentage of the population able to read and write rose rapidly in Europe as states enacted educational reforms during the last two decades of the century. More men could read than women, and more urban residents than rural people. Jobs in industry increasingly required the ability to read and write. Literacy rates were higher in Western—above all, Northwestern Europe—than in Eastern and Southern Europe. Despite some conservative opposition, the British Parliament passed a law in 1880 requiring that all children attend school up to age ten (to age twelve beginning in 1899). In 1910, Parliament waived school fees. Thereafter, truancy officers made their appearance in working-class neighborhoods, sometimes meeting resistance from parents who preferred the supplementary income from their children's work to more education. State inspectors maintained educational standards, requiring villages to provide better facilities for their schools and accommodations for teachers.

In France, the Ferry Laws (passed 1879–1881, named after Minister of Education and then Premier Jules Ferry) made primary schools free, obligatory, and secular for all children from age three to thirteen. The government coordinated the centralized French school system, although each region was required to operate a teacher-training school. In this way, mass education in European countries increased the number of people among ethnic minorities who could speak and read the dominant language. In Italy, Italian ceased to be a language spoken only by the upper class. In France, more Provençaux, Gascons, Bretons, and other peoples learned French, which was now spoken by the large majority of the population.

The number of secondary students increased rapidly, quadrupling in France between 1875 and 1912, and tripling in Germany during the same period. Even so, with very few exceptions, secondary education remained possible only for families of some means. In England, boarding schools founded in the 1860s and 1870s catered to middle-class students, while the sons of nobles and of other very wealthy landowners attended the nine old "public" schools.

On the continent, literacy also increased, but the numbers still varied from country to country. In France, increased educational opportunity reduced the number of military conscripts who could not read or write from about 40 percent at mid-century to only 6 percent in 1901. In contrast, in Dalmatia, on the Adriatic coast across from Italy, only 1 of every 100 conscripts could read and write in 1870. In 1860, 75 percent of Italian men and almost 90 percent of women could neither read nor write and depended on public letter writers to pen what correspondence they required. But by 1900, 50 percent of the population could read and write; by 1914, 75 percent of all Italians were literate. School attendance in Italy revealed the gap between the more prosperous north and the south, where more than half of the children in many places still did not attend school regularly or at all. In Germany, by the turn of the century less than 1 percent of the population remained illiterate. Even in Russia, literacy rates rose from under 10 percent in the 1860s to about 25 percent by 1910; yet, despite improvements in rural schooling, literacy in the countryside lagged

This French caricature of Jules Ferry sweeping away the nuns represents the secularization of education.

far behind that in the empire's cities. Whereas the older, illiterate generation of Russians mistrusted education ("You can't eat books"), fearing that literacy would erode village religious culture (and perhaps also deference to elders), younger peasants ridiculed their superstitious parents and welcomed self-improvement through education.

Nonetheless, existing educational systems reinforced social distinctions of class and gender. Secondary schools imparted skills and values for social mobility, but they drew very few children from the lower classes. During the 1870s and 1880s, the issue of female education surged to the forefront. But only women whose families were able and willing to pay the required fees received secondary education. Jules Ferry (1832–1893) believed that the extension of educational opportunity to women would solidify French family life. During a five-year period in the 1880s, the number of secondary schools for women in France increased from just 3 to 111. Boarding schools for girls became more common in France, as in Britain. A female German Social Democrat later recalled that the education she had received had been so "that I might one day be able to provide my husband with a proper domestic atmosphere." Many families viewed education as a prerequisite for their daughters' finding suitable employment and marrying well.

The French government in the century's last decades augmented educational opportunity for women by training thousands of female teachers; women were allowed to teach boys, but men were not permitted to teach girls. Both lay teachers and nuns instructed girls in the domestic mission of women, stressing gender differences and promoting deference to their future husbands. Schooling for boys and girls alike emphasized patriotic, secular, and politically conservative themes. Female teachers of girls were to be morally irreproachable and thoroughly secular mother figures within their communities. Textbooks counseled "patient resignation" to one's economic and social condition, with one popular book in 1882 showing a picture of a woman desperately trying to persuade her husband not to go on strike.

Although the number of university students tripled in Europe, higher education remained limited to a tiny proportion of the population drawn from the upper classes. In Prussia, for example, only 1 in 1,000 university students had parents who were workers. In Britain, there were only 13,000 university students in 1913 in a total population of 36 million people, although technical colleges began to attract more students. In Russia, the tsars reversed the European trend during the course of the century, making it more difficult for non-nobles to attend secondary school and university.

The Decline of Organized Religion

In a century of vigorous state secularization, many clergy viewed the period of rapid social change with anxiety. To be sure, the institutional influence of churches on states had declined dramatically in most European states. More than this, in some parts of Europe, the influence of organized religion on society continued to wane. Secular education, espousing nationalist values, accelerated this trend, even though many people in Catholic countries still attended Church schools. Fewer people went to church than earlier in the century. A survey of London's churches at the turn of the century revealed that less than 20 percent of the population regularly attended services, demonstrating a marked decline from the mid-eighteenth century. Charles Bradlaugh, an atheist who propagated his cause among workers, was elected four times to Commons, and each time Parliament refused to seat him because he would not take the MP's oath, which made reference to God. When Bradlaugh finally took his place in 1886, after the Speaker of the House simply ruled that he was entitled to take his seat, the Anglican Church continued to be the "Church of England," but government's role became increasingly independent of ecclesiastical influence.

In some regions of France, many people lived almost completely apart from the Catholic Church. In Marseille, about 50 percent of the people went to church regularly in 1840; in 1901, only 16 percent did so. Reasons for the decline of religious practice remain obscure. In some regions, a high level of religiosity may never have existed. In other regions, however, religious adherence seemed unchanged.

The first Catholic sociologists of religion found a sharp rise in "de-christianized" regions, as demonstrated by rates of couples not having church marriages or not having their children baptized. By the 1890s, the Church considered some parts of France, and most working-class districts of most large cities, to be "missionary" areas, their populations no more attached to the Catholic Church than those of China or the Congo. The loss of Church influence was reflected in the decline in the birthrate, explicable by increased use of birth control. Furthermore, an increasing number of French people called upon the clergy only at the time of baptism, marriage, and death. In Spain, the Basque provinces and much of Castile remained devout, while the southern part of Spain turned its back on the Church. Workers and landless peasants manifested particular indifference to the Church; property owners and women were more apt to go to Mass.

Yet, the decline of religious practice in Europe was neither linear, nor everywhere. A revival of popular religious enthusiasm occurred in some places between 1830 and 1880, particularly among the upper classes. Lithography and printing presses helped rekindle devotion, spreading the news of religious shrines.

Women were more apt to attend church than men (though in part this resulted from the fact that women live longer than men; widows dressed in the black garb of mourning for a year following the demise of their husbands dotted villages in France, Spain, Italy, Portugal, and other Catholic countries). The cult of the Virgin Mary also contributed to the feminization of religion in Catholic countries, perhaps encouraging more young women to enter convents. In France, nuns accounted for almost 60 percent of the clergy.

The growing cult of miracles was part of a revival of popular religion, particularly in France, Italy, and Spain. Near the French central Pyrenees town of Lourdes, Bernadette, a peasant girl later canonized by the Church, had announced in 1859 that the Virgin Mary had appeared to her on the Feast of the Annunciation commemorating Christ's conception. Churchmen and their followers believed that the apparition explained the miraculous cures that seemed to occur at Lourdes, despite the skepticism of scientists and secularizers. Religious pilgrimages by train to sites of miracles became big business. In the first decade of the new century, more than a million people came to Lourdes each year, many hoping to be cured of illness and disease. The popularity of pilgrimages reflected the resiliency of the Catholic Church.

Leisure in the Belle Époque

During the Belle Époque, there was more to do than ever before for those with leisure and money. The French capital set the tone for style in Europe, if not the world. Paris was the European capital of pleasure. Dance halls, cafés, and café-concerts, the latter offering the performances of musicians, singers, poets, comedians, jugglers, acrobats, female wrestlers, and snake charmers, lined the *grands boulevards*, attracting throngs of Parisians and tourists alike. Hundreds of thousands of Parisians went

(*Left*) An Art Nouveau poster advertising Sarah Bernhardt. (*Right*) The actress photographed in a coffin.

to the theater at least once a week. Europeans danced faster; the tango and the turkey trot, both imported from the Americas, offended some observers and were banned in some establishments. German Emperor William II forbade officers from dancing these steps while in uniform and one of his generals killed a Prussian officer in a duel over the issue.

The Parisian hill of Montmartre served as a center of entertainment. It was sprinkled with cafés and café-concerts, several of which advertised themselves with brilliant posters that could now be reproduced in bright colors. Amid the smoke and drink of the "Chat Noir" (Black Cat) and the "Lapin Agile" (Agile Rabbit), poets read their poems and mingled with artists trying to sell their work.

The talented and beautiful actress Sarah Bernhardt (1844– 1923) embodied fin-de-siècle Europe. The daughter of a Dutch immigrant, she became famous for her dramatic expressiveness and ability to communicate tears to an audience through her supremely evocative voice. Bernhardt had learned her trade from the traditions of the popular boulevard theater. Renowned for her dramatic gestures (as a young woman she asked a photographer to take a picture of her in a coffin) and for a variety of sexual liaisons, Sarah Bernhardt's worldwide fame was such that the American circus entrepreneur P.T. Barnum, upon hearing that she risked the amputation of a leg, offered her a fortune if she would allow him to take it on the road and exhibit it with his famous circus.

Sports in Mass Society

Participatory and spectator sports emerged as a prominent feature of mass society during the last decades of the century, a phenomenon linked to modern transportation and to a general increase in leisure time. The first automobile race was held in 1894 in France, from Rouen to Paris and back. Some cars were powered by electricity, others by gasoline or even steam; only fifteen completed the race. Cycling competitions also generated enormous public interest, providing the first heroes of spectator sports. Sporting newspapers catered to riders and fans. Competition between two cycling clubs led to the first Tour de France race in 1903, in which riders covered almost 1,500 miles in nineteen days.

Not only did people watch bicycle races, they also took to riding bicycles themselves, both as a leisure activity and as a source of transportation. The bicycle, in the words of one devotee, represented "the new wheels of the chariot of progress." A simple mechanism, it nonetheless reflected technological innovation and mass production. By the late 1880s, bicycles (which had first been developed twenty years earlier) were lighter, more affordable, and more easily repaired or replaced. The manufacture of bicycles became a major industry, with 375,000 produced in France by 1898, and 3.5 million in 1914.

Both men and women rode bicycles. But some men complained that the clothes women wore while riding bicycles were unfeminine. Female cycling seemed to fly in the face of the middle-class domestic ideal of the "angel of the house" staying home. Moralists worried that the jolts of rough paths and roads might interfere with childbearing, or even lead to debauchery by generating physical pleasure. The president of a feminist congress in 1896, however, toasted the "egalitarian and leveling bicycle." It helped free women from the corset, "a new Bastille to be demolished." It may have also helped change what some people considered the feminine ideal from plumpness to a more svelte line.

Team sports also quickly developed as a leisure activity during the second half of the nineteenth century. The two most popular team sports in Europe, football (known as soccer in the United States) and rugby, both began in England. Rugby, which developed at Cambridge and Oxford Universities in the 1860s, was an upper-class sport. Football had much earlier origins, perhaps going back to when Vikings and Russians used to "kick the Dane's head around"—literally. But football, which also had university origins, evolved into a plebeian sport, like boxing, which was to English workers what rowing, cricket, and golf became to the upper classes. Professional football began in England in 1863; eight years later, there were fifteen clubs playing for the championship. The new century brought the first major brawl between supporters of rival teams: a match between the Catholic Celtics and the Protestant Rangers of Glasgow ended with the stadium burned to the ground. In 1901, 111,000 spectators watched the English Cup Final.

Baron Pierre de Coubertin (1863–1937), a French noble who feared that the youth of his country were becoming soft, organized the first modern Olympic Games, held in Athens in 1896 in homage to their Greek predecessors. Coubertin sought the moral and physical revival of the men of his nation. An Anglophile (at a time when many Europeans thought war between Britain and France inevitable), he revered the image of hard-riding, athletic upper-class Englishmen playing sports at Eton and Cambridge with reckless abandon and then going on to expand the British Empire.

There was more to the rise of sports and the cult of physical vigor than simply games and fun. The development of sports culture also reflected the mood of aggressive nationalism, for example in France, which was still smoldering over being so badly defeated in the Franco-Prussian War of 1870–1871. The popularity of Darwin's theory of the evolution of species led to a growing preoccupation with the comparative characteristics of specific races, or peoples. "Social Darwinists" applied the theory of "survival of the fittest" to international sports competition. Games soon became hotly competitive. Moveover, the development of feminism in Western Europe may have contributed to what has been called a "crisis of masculinity," by which many men took the strengthening of the so-called "weaker sex" as the weakening of men. By this view, growing interest in sports competition was an affirmation of masculinity. Furthermore, the emerging interest in the times it took to run distances may have reflected fascination with scientific management.

The burgeoning interest in sports touched, above all, the young. In Germany, "wandering youth" clubs (*Wandervogel*) became popular, sending young boys out to camp under the stars (girls were then expected to stay at home). In England, Robert Baden-Powell (1857–1941) founded the Boy Scouts. After being rejected for admission to Oxford University and finding his vocation in the army, Baden-Powell in 1908 organized the Boy Scouts in the hope of developing "among boys a power of sympathizing with others, a spirit of self-sacrifice and patriotism, and generally to prepare them to become good citizens." The uniform Baden-Powell had worn in South Africa—a Stetson hat, neckerchief, and khaki shorts—became that of the Boy Scouts, and their motto became "Be prepared."

Interest in sports touched all classes and in fact reflected class differences. The poet Rudyard Kipling, who disliked sports in general, called cricket players (who tended to be from a loftier social class than his own) "fools." Football players, most of whom were from the working class, he dismissed as "oafs." Nobles and other people of great means were no longer the only people able to enjoy sports. While the upper classes had their own sporting associations, which retained a preference for horse racing—"the sport of kings"—working-class biking and gymnastic clubs also began to spring up in the 1880s in Western Europe, particularly as workers won a shorter workweek and workday.

Consumerism and Department Stores

Department stores, which had first opened their wide doors along the *grands boulevards* in Second Empire Paris (1852–1870), accentuated and symbolized consumerism. Glossy catalogues permitted middle-class and even working-class shoppers to make purchases from the comfort of their homes. Many craftsmen feared that mechanized production, which created the products sold in department stores, would drive out craft production.

In London, New York, Chicago and, above all, Paris, department stores transformed the way many families shopped. Stores like the Bon Marché—still a Parisian landmark—attracted prosperous middle-class clients in search of quality ready-made clothes that were less expensive than those stitched by tailors. The stores were, in a sense, monuments to the dynamism of bourgeois culture, displaying and selling products that reflected material progress, celebrating more leisure time and the growing emphasis on consumption. Seeking to increase the volume of sales, they also stocked more inexpensive clothing, while adding umbrellas, tooth-brushes, stationery, and much more. All of this required a remarkable degree of rationality and bureaucratization, with organization into depart-ments overseen by trained managers, which typified the Second Industrial Revolution. The expanding clientele of department stores included the families of shopkeepers, civil servants, and clerks of more modest means, and gradually workers as well. Colorful brochures and posters advanced advertising techniques, as mail-order shopping rapidly developed.

The owners of department stores wanted shopping to become an experi-ence in itself, like a visit to a world's fair—except that one could now buy some of the displayed wonders of human innovation. Architects aimed at monumental and theatrical effects. Department stores were enormous, stately structures topped with cupolas—statues of the gods reclining are part of the decoration of the Bon Marché—with iron columns and an ex-panse of glass giving shoppers a sense of space and light. Shoppers could walk up grand staircases to observe the crowds below. Department stores became tourist sights; dazzled visitors themselves became part of the spec-tacle. Émile Zola went so far as to say that "the department store tends to replace the church. It marches to the religion of the cash desk, of beauty, of coquetry, and fashion. [Women] go there to pass the hours as they used to go to church; an occupation, a place of enthusiasm where they struggle between their passion for clothes and the thrift of their husbands; in the end all the drama of life with the hereafter of beauty."

On an average day in the 1890s, 15,000 to 18,000 people entered the Bon Marché, many more on sale days. An employee of the store described a white sale in 1883, "From eight in the morning the house filled with buy-ers milling about our white displays. As always the store was marvelously adorned, her banisters lined with white calico and flowing with pillow

The bedding department in a Parisian department store.

lace, her columns wrapped with white muslin . . . the sight was fairy-like. . . . And truly the battle heats up, the crowd presses forward, engulfs the doors, masses and crushes about the cashiers, assaults the stairways."

RESPONSES TO A RAPIDLY CHANGING WORLD

Europeans had many reasons to be optimistic at the turn of the century. Since the fall of Napoleon in 1815, Europe had enjoyed a relatively long period of peace broken only by short wars with limited goals, although the bloody but short Franco-Prussian War had spawned lasting hatred. Literacy had risen rapidly, particularly in Western and Northern Europe. Nation-states, increasingly secular in character, commanded the loyalty of their populations. The standard of living had generally risen and, at least in most of Europe, white-collar jobs provided hope of better things for more people. Furthermore, somewhat shorter working hours for employees, including many workers, left more time for leisure activities.

Yet, for all the progress and frivolity of the fin de siècle, rapid industrialization, and with it a rapidly changing world, brought a cultural crisis of previously unparalleled dimensions. Doctors diagnosed more cases of hypochondria, "melancholy," and hysteria, paralyzing nervous disorders that many blamed on the complexities of modern life, which seemed to be overwhelming the nervous system. In particular, neurasthenia seemed to be a sign of the times, with its symptoms of extreme sensitivity to light and noise (two characteristics of urban life), fatigue, worry, and digestive disorders.

Alcoholism was ravaging many countries in Europe. In England, the "habitual soaking" of workers in beer worried reformers. A contemporary investigator claimed that it was not uncommon for some workers to spend a quarter of their earnings on drink. In parts of France, the average person (and thus the figure for adults would be even higher) consumed well more than sixty gallons of wine a year, in addition to beer, brandies, and absinthe, a licorice-tasting drink made from wormwood and that is physiologically addictive. There were almost half a million establishments licensed to serve drink in France at the turn of the century—one for every 54 people, compared to one British "public house" for every 843 inhabitants at about the same time.

French temperance movements were swept aside like tiny dikes by the torrent of drink. Nationalists, worried about the plunging birthrate, joined some doctors and reformers in claiming that France faced "racial degeneration" since its population might cease to reproduce itself because of the ravages of alcoholism. Only by rallying around nationalist values could France, they argued, avoid total collapse. In Britain, the temperance movement began earlier and was far stronger than in France, and much more closely tied to churches. Members of temperance societies had some success convincing people to sign pledges promising not to drink at all.

The use of opium and its derivatives, morphine (the popularity of which increased with its use as an anesthetic), laudanum (a mixture of wine and

Edgar Degas' *L'Absinthe* (1876–1877) shows a woman and her companion and a glass of absinthe. Note how the lack of a table support helps draw the viewer's attention to the glass of absinthe.

opium), and heroin, as well as cocaine and hashish, became common among the artistic avant-garde, well before most people were aware of their devastating effects. These drugs were brought from Turkey, Persia, and India, with coca (from which cocaine is derived) brought from Peru and Bolivia. When Sigmund Freud (1856–1939), the father of psychoanalysis, was invited to the house of the great French neurologist Jean Charcot (1825–1893) in Paris, before the negative effects of drugs were known, he remembered, "I [was] very calm, thanks to a small dose of cocaine." The painter Pablo Picasso (1881–1973) was also for a period a hashish user, which may have influenced his dreamy rose-colored paintings of 1905–1908.

Only in 1908 did the French government ban such drugs, in the wake of a number of drug-related suicides. Less dangerous, exoticism, mysticism, and a fascination with the occult became more popular than ever before, another sign of the rejection of science and the associated preoccupation with the irrational.

"Modernist" culture turned against the century-old acceptance of rationality as one of the dominant values of Western culture. New discoveries in science and theories about the functioning of the universe tore away the old certainties. Social scientists tried to find explanations for the working of society and the inner world of the individual. Intellectuals and artists began to insist on the irrational basis of human nature.

The increasingly rapid pace of modern life worried some intellectuals. At the Paris Exhibition of 1900, which celebrated the dawn of a new century, an uneasy visitor noted, "Life seethes in this immense reservoir of energy . . . a too violent magnificence." In *The Wind in the Willows*, published in 1908 by Kenneth Grahame (1859–1932), the motor car threatens stability. Behind the wheel, Toad, amphibian protagonist, turns into "the terror, the traffic-queller, before whom all must give way or be smitten into nothingness and everlasting night . . . fulfilling his instincts, living his hour, reckless of what might come to him." The airplane, rapidly rising and then swooping dangerously, seemed not only a soaring symbol of scientific advances, but also of the uncertainty that unsettled some fin-de-siècle Europeans. Émile Zola claimed that "modern society is racked without end by a nervous irritability. We are sick and tired of progress, industry, and science."

Artists' Responses to Mass Culture and Mass Production

Progress had a price. Avant-garde writers and artists loathed the culture of what the English aesthete Oscar Wilde called the "profane masses." Mass culture seemed to be eroding the ability of high culture to survive the assault of mass manufacturing and teeming cities.

Sharp reactions against the seeming uniformity of the machine age permeated the arts. The English craftsman and designer William Morris

(1834–1896) voiced reservations about the triumph of industry and the department store. He believed that mass production was in the process of eliminating the aesthetic control craftsmen had maintained over production. Describing "capitalism" as a "defilement" and Victorian England as the "age of shoddy," Morris believed that the machine had become the master of both workers and design, instead of the other way around, and that only a revolutionary transformation of society could save the working class and a revolution in aesthetics could save art and architecture. Morris spearheaded the "arts and crafts movement" in Britain, espousing craft production that would create useful but artistic objects for the general public, thereby elevating taste to a new level.

The great impressionist painter Claude Monet (1840–1926), along with some of his contemporaries, also manifested an uneasy ambivalence toward large-scale industry. In the 1870s, Monet lived in the industrializing Paris suburb of Argenteuil and painted the Seine River with factories in the distance as part of the landscape. But he tired of the hustle and bustle of urban life and moved down the Seine to the village of Giverny. There his garden and its pond and lily pads provided an ideal rural setting for his work. He never painted the railway tracks that ran through his property.

The last ten years of the career of the French impressionist painter and anarchist Camille Pissarro (1830–1903) followed his growing preoccupation with the rapid transformation of city life. Perhaps the preeminent painter of rural life, he later took up urban subjects, painting bridges, riverbanks, and boulevards, crowding myriad forms and figures into his panoramic views. Emphasizing the motion of transportation (his *Place Saint Lazare* is arguably the first serious study of traffic in the history of art), walking, riding, loading, and unloading, he depicted the light, color, nervous movement, and energy of the city and its seemingly uncontrollable throngs. He detested the outsized commercialism of the department stores and called one series of paintings "Social Turpitudes."

Other painters presented urban scenes in a harsh, jarring light that suggested chaos. The German Expressionist painter Ludwig Meidner (1884–1966) argued that painters ought to abandon the gentle, almost rural style that characterized impressionist urban scenes: "A street," he wrote, "is rather a bombardment of hissing rows of windows, of blustering cones of lights between vehicles of all kinds and thousands of leaping globes, human rags, advertising signboards and masses of threatening, formless colors."

Scientists' Advances and Uncertainties

The astonishing advances of nineteenth-century science led one researcher to exclaim that "science strides on victoriously towards a boundless future." But new discoveries revealing nature's complexity began to temper the infectious optimism of the age. During the nineteenth century, scientists concluded that cells form the basis for life, and new knowledge led scientists to a greater awareness of the principles of heredity. Yet, fin-de-siècle scientists discovered that the more they knew about the constitution of the world, the more there was left to know about matter, light, and energy. Mathematicians and especially physicists began to rethink fundamental assumptions about the universe. Radioactivity was discovered in Paris in 1896. Marie Curie (1867–1934), a Polish-born French physicist carrying out research with her husband, Pierre Curie (1859–1906), in 1910 isolated radium, a radioactive element. Marie Curie, who was refused entry to the French Academy of Science because she was a woman, nonetheless earned a reputation as a distinguished scientist. She won two Nobel Prizes. Her English rival, Ernest Rutherford (1871–1937), discovered the alpha and beta rays in radioactive atoms, and posited the disintegration of radioactive atoms, which is the phenomenon of radioactivity. He used this discovery to postulate the structure of the atom, with a positively charged nucleus and negatively charged electrons circling around it.

"Particle theories" in physics cast doubt on contemporary assumptions about the universe. They demonstrated the complexity of motion, light, and matter, which appeared to consist of electrically charged particles. Since the time of the great seventeenth-century English thinker Sir Isaac

(*Left*) An English caricature of Pierre and Marie Curie. (*Right*) Ernest Rutherford, who is holding the apparatus that he used to break up the nucleus of the nitrogen atom.

Newton, scientists had believed that any two objects, whether the sun and the earth, or a coffee cup and a bowl of sugar, acted on each other through gravitational force. There seemed no mechanism for transmitting action but rather only empty space between the two. James Maxwell (1831– 1879), a British scientist, had solved the "action at a distance" problem for the case of electromagnetic forces. His theory of electromagnetic fields postulated that one object creates an electrical field around parti- cles, which in turn exerts forces on electrically charged objects, and that light itself consists of electromagnetic waves. The German scientist Max Planck (1858–1947) discovered that radiant energy is emitted discontinu- ously in discrete units, or quanta. Planck's quantum theory, not finalized until 1925, challenged the fundamental scientific understanding of energy that had survived almost intact since the time of Newton. More than this, it seemed to add an element of chance to the story of the universe, sug- gesting that its operations were not absolutely predictable. Here, too, sci- entists now realized that they knew considerably less about the nature of matter and about the universe than they had thought.

These discoveries were only a beginning. The much more difficult prob- lem of gravity still remained. In Switzerland, German-born Albert Einstein (1879–1955), whose modest position as a patent examiner of other peo- ple's discoveries belied his genius, sought to carry physics beyond New- ton's theory that space and time were absolute quantities. Einstein, who had studied mathematics and physics in Zurich, came up with a brilliant insight that had never occurred to anyone else. Instead of gravity acting at a distance, he theorized that each object produces a field to which other objects respond. In a paper published in 1905, Einstein postulated a spe- cial theory of relativity, arguing that the velocity of light was both constant and independent of the velocities of the source and observer or light. His theory predicted that if a person were to shine a flashlight toward an ob- ject and then follow the light in a rocket, seemingly reducing the gap in speed between the two, the light would in fact be racing away from the moving observer at the same speed as before, with the gap between them increasing, not decreasing.

Einstein also postulated the equivalence of mass and energy in his equa- tion: $E = mc^2$ (energy equals mass multiplied by the square of light). In the mid-twentieth century, this formula would provide the key for the con- trolled release of energy from the atom, the basis of the atomic and hydro- gen bombs. After becoming a professor in Zurich, Prague, and then Berlin, Einstein's search for an exact description of the laws of gravitation led him in 1915 from his relatively simple special theory of relativity to his general principle of relativity, which postulated that the laws of nature operated in exactly the same way for all observers. His theory supplanted traditional theories of gravitation, which saw gravity as a property of objects interact- ing with each other. Rather, Einstein believed that they interacted with space. Yet, Einstein and other scientists remained ill-at-ease with the ele-

Albert Einstein explaining his theories to a stunned audience.

ment of chance suggested by Planck's quantum theory. Trying to explain his conclusion that the universe could not operate in a random way, Einstein later insisted: "God does not play dice." Both Planck's theory, by suggesting any role for chance, and Einstein's staggering achievements themselves left open as many questions for the future as they resolved, not the least of which would be terrifying new applications of the German scientist's famous formula to warfare.

Social Theorists' Analyses of Industrial Society

In the face of rapid social change, intellectuals attempted to understand the structure of contemporary society and the phenomena of social life. They did so by adopting the model of natural science and undertaking objective systematic analysis of observable social data. They gradually developed the science of society, sociology, which asked a fundamental question that in itself revealed social uncertainties: how do societies hold together when confronted by economic and social forces that tend to pull them apart? The question expressed the cultural crisis of the fin de siècle. In 1887, the German Friedrich Tönnies (1855–1936) published a groundbreaking work, *Community and Society (Gemeinschaft und Gesellschaft)*, which sought to synthesize and apply historical experience to understand the unique development of modern Western civilization.

Influenced by Tönnies and fascinated by the emergence of industrial society and the growth of the state, Max Weber (1864–1920), one of the fathers of modern social thought and sociology, sought to create an objective and thus "value-free" science of society that he thought held the key to guiding the future. Trained as a professor of law in Heidelberg, Weber became interested in the relationship between religion and society. He is best known for his *The Protestant Ethic and the Spirit of Capitalism* (1904–1905), which defined the "spirit of capitalism" to be the assumption that whoever works hard in the pursuit of gain fulfills a moral obligation. He identified the origins of capitalism with Calvinist entrepreneurship in the sixteenth and seventeenth centuries. Weber observed the contemporary trend toward larger structures of government and the bureaucratization of state, business, and political structures, which he believed marked the victory of Enlightenment rationalism, as well as increased social stratification. But he worried that in the advancing impersonal age of bureaucracy, state officials would ignore political and social ideals. Weber's modern man seemed to be trapped in what he called "the iron cage of modern life." Theorist of a nervous age, Weber himself had a nervous breakdown before the turn of the century.

Modern life seemed to provide evidence that traditional societies had been uprooted by urbanization and industrialization. Murder in France rose by 30 percent between 1865 and 1890, robberies doubled, and assault and battery increased by four times. Seeking an explanation, the French social theorist Émile Durkheim (1858–1917) came to believe that the rapid, seemingly uncontrollable growth of large cities had destroyed the moral ties that had sustained the individual in traditional society. Durkheim believed that the waning of religious practice had undermined authority and therefore social cohesiveness, and that individuals lost in the faceless urban and industrial world suffered social and moral disintegration, "the state of disorganization, of maniacal agitation," marked by class conflict and social unrest. Durkheim's quantitative study of suicide led him to believe that the stresses and strains of increasingly urban, industrial life were becoming more debilitating. Durkheim's modern individual now faced "alienation" (*anomie* in French) within his society. Some of Durkheim's theories, however, have not been substantiated by recent empirical studies. Yet, Durkheim manifested at least the optimism of the new academic discipline by suggesting that social problems were not mysterious enigmas, but could be solved by studying them in a systematic, scientific manner.

Durkheim was hardly alone in thinking that urban growth, spurred on by the arrival of rural migrants, generated social pathology of which criminality was but one manifestation. In 1895, Gustave Le Bon (1841–1931) published *The Crowd*, in which he worried aloud that modern life submerged the individual in the "crowd." The mob could come alive, Le Bon argued, in violent protest. Riots and strikes, he warned, were becoming part of the political process. To conservatives like Le Bon, crowds threatened traditional elites. He described crowds as lurching erratically, and sometimes dangerously, like drunks—this at a time of growing awareness that alcoholism was ravaging France. This very metaphor was closely tied to elite perceptions of popular politics; in France, many people identified the Parisian Communards of 1871 with "the drunken commoner."

As some contemporaries became uneasy about the rapid pace and tensions of modern life, another sign of the nineteenth-century erosion of faith in science and progress was a growing obsession with "decadence." Some nationalists now worried that their peoples were being undermined by "racial degeneration," which might compromise the natural process of evolution by hereditary debasement. Some scientists claimed that significant racial differences could be identified within specific peoples, and that they accounted for soaring rates of crime, alcoholism, insanity, syphilis, and even popular political action. A degenerate underclass seemed to them to threaten to compromise the vitality of industrializing countries. An Italian anthropologist believed that criminals showed inferior physical and mental development. He described them as being like microbes that pollute society, and held that they could be identified by measuring their skulls.

Freud and the Study of the Irrational

The Viennese doctor Sigmund Freud stressed the power of the irrational, which he placed in the human unconscious. Freud proposed to study the unconscious scientifically, and to develop a therapy for treating disorders rooted in the unconscious.

Freud was born in the small Moravian town of Freiberg (now in the Czech Republic) in the Habsburg monarchy. He was the son of a struggling Jewish wool merchant and his much younger, attractive wife. When Sigmund was three, his father's business affairs went from bad to worse, forcing the family to leave its tranquil, small-town existence for Vienna. The younger Freud never felt comfortable in the imposing imperial capital. But he benefited from the period of liberal ascendancy in Austria, where Jews had received full civil rights in 1867. The Viennese middle class had helped make their city a cultural capital of Europe. To many bourgeois families, art in the 1860s represented an essential expression of middle-class values of rationality, individual freedom, and prosperity. That reassuring atmosphere changed with the stock-market crash in 1873, which began the long economic depression and culminated in the election of an anti-Semite, Karl Lueger ("I decide who is a Jew," Lueger insisted), as mayor of Vienna in 1895.

After beginning his career as a research scientist in anatomy, Freud visited Paris, where he fell under Charcot's influence. From his scientific laboratory, Freud moved to the study of the irrational, or the "unconscious," convinced that it could be studied with the same systematic rigor as human anatomy. In the spring of 1886, Freud opened a small medical office in Vienna, where he treated patients with nervous disorders.

Sigmund Freud and his family.

Freud developed the method of psychoanalysis, a term coined in 1896. It was based on the premises that the mind is orderly and that dreams offer codes that can unlock the unconscious. To Freud, a dream represented "the fulfillment of a [suppressed] wish"; it was the expression of an unconscious conflict. Freud encouraged patients to dream and to "free associate" in order to break down their defense mechanisms (the means by which individuals repress painful memories from childhood or even infancy). Sexuality, specifically the repression of sexual urges, formed the basis of Freud's theory of the unconscious. One of Freud's followers described the role of his mentor's "dream-work": "The mind is like a city which during the day busies itself with the peaceful tasks of legitimate commerce, but at night when all the good burghers sleep soundly in their beds, out come these disreputable creatures of the psychic underworld to disport themselves in a very unseemly fashion; decking themselves out in fantastic costumes, in order that they may not be recognized and apprehended."

Psychoanalysis became both an investigative tool and a form of therapy, in which, very gradually—ranging from several months to many years and at considerable financial cost—the patient could obtain self-awareness and control over his or her symptoms, such as hysteria.

Freud's theories of human development established the irrational as an intrinsic and sometimes even determining part of the human psyche. This in itself generated further anxiety among some critics. They feared that one of the consequences of the Viennese doctor's views might be a further weakening of the moral codes of church and state as individuals turned inward in order to understand themselves. Psychoanalytic theory, which Freud claimed as a new science, emerged, along with Darwin's evolutionary theory and Marx's writings on capitalist development and revolution, as one of the foundations of twentieth-century thought.

Friedrich Nietzsche, philosopher of the irrational.

Nietzsche's Embrace of the Irrational

Friedrich Nietzsche (1844–1900) emerged in this period as the most strident philosophical critic of Enlightenment rationalism. Son of a strict Protestant German minister who died when the boy was young, Nietzsche was raised by his domineering mother. He became a professor of classics in Basel, Switzerland. The tormented Nietzsche, forced by illness to leave the university, moved to the Swiss Alps and thereafter lived by his pen, but with little success. In increasingly bad health, he suffered a mental collapse at the age of forty-five, after sending off telegrams to some of his friends signed "The Crucified." Nietzsche was briefly confined in an asylum toward the end of his life, leading one wag to comment, "At last, the right man in the right place."

Nietzsche hated all religions equally, believing that they had destroyed the individual's capacity for natural development and fulfillment by imposing uniformity. He became an atheist, proclaiming, "God is dead . . . and we have killed him." He claimed strenuously that religion was incapable of providing ethical guidance and that no single morality could be appropriate to all people.

Espousing "philosophy with the hammer," Nietzsche awaited the heroic superman who, as part of a natural nobility of "higher humanity," would rule through the "will to power." While being indirectly influenced by the contentions of Hegel and Darwin that mankind could continue to develop to a higher stage, Nietzsche's thought marked a total rejection of all previous philosophy. His "vital" force, which he believed could be found only in new philosophers like himself, would be morally ambivalent, idealizing power and struggle. The free man, wrote Nietzsche, "is a warrior." Yet for all of his talk about "master races" and "slave races" in a period marked by a growth of racism, he castigated the herd-like instincts of frenetic German nationalists and anti-Semites. After World War I, impassioned German admirers would invoke Nietzsche, seeking a "Germanic religion" freed from the constraints of Christian humanitarianism and from all rationality itself.

The Avant-Garde's Break with Rationalism

In May 1913, the Russian aristocrat Serge Diaghilev's ballet *The Rite of Spring* opened in Paris. For Diaghilev (1872–1929), who organized major art expositions and outraged conventional society by flaunting male lovers, art and life went hand in hand—they imitated each other. Diaghilev sought liberation in erotic ballets, and in life itself. Hitherto, ballet had retained absolute loyalty to classical subjects and presentation, immune to avant-garde challenge. Diaghilev's Russian Ballet Company helped to revitalize ballet. That night in 1913, an uproar began as aesthetes in the audience hissed the men and women of Parisian high society filing into the theater wearing tails and evening gowns. When the curtain went up and the first notes of music were heard, the dancers were jumping up and down, toeing inward in defiance of conventional ballet. The majority of the audience reacted with catcalls, hisses, and then screams of anger. "Listen first, and then whistle!" shouted one enthusiast, drowned out by the din. An elderly countess scoffed that it was the first time that anyone, in this case, the dancers with their provocative performance, had ever made fun of her. The audience was shocked too by the jarring, primitive music of the Russian composer Igor Stravinsky (1882–1971), who

Scene from *The Rite of Spring*, 1913.

completely dispensed with the sentimental music that had invariably accompanied ballet. The avant-garde, however, cheered; art and life had merged.

Rejecting the idea that rationalism should underlie the arts and that objective standards could exist by which to assess literature, painting, and music, the writers, painters, and composers of the avant-garde rebelled against accepted cultural forms, which they believed threatened to render the individual insignificant and powerless. Mass circulation newspapers, the popular theater inevitably playing Gilbert and Sullivan in London or soapy popular operas in Paris, music halls, military band concerts in Hyde Park, and the cinema, which aimed at a mass audience by seeking to entertain by taking the lowest common denominator, were the stuff of popular culture. The avant-garde rejected all of it.

The artists of the avant-garde accepted nothing as absolute, certainly not the traditional forms of cultural expression or morality. Showing Nietzsche's influence, some sought to transcend the limits of reason and moral purpose. Far more than even impressionist painters, the turn of the century avant-garde artists broke with the past. This was, to an extent, a revolt of the young (because of the rise in population, a larger percentage of the population was indeed young)—and self-consciously so. In Austria, the avant-garde called themselves "The Young Ones." They were defiantly "modern," a term they embraced with passion. They paid less attention to their subjects—what, for example, they painted or wrote about—than the response their work would elicit in their audiences. The French playwright Alfred Jarry (1873–1907) staged the play *King Ubu,* a mockery of an authority figure, the story of an avaricious oaf in search of a crown, and willing to kill to get it. The farce ran one tumultuous night in December 1896; it began with one of his characters pretending to hurl human waste at the outraged audience.

By its very nature, the notion of an avant-garde, a term taken from military tactics, implies a small group of people who see themselves in the forefront of artistic expression and achievement. The avant-garde did not write or paint for everybody. In Paris, a group of artists and writers identified themselves as "Bohemians"—gypsy wanderers. This avant-garde of young men gloried in the condition of being outsiders, rebels against the dominant culture in the way that romanticism had been a revolt against the classical tastes of court and château.

Some of them considered their own lives as art itself. They rebelled against the strictures of their own middle-class social origins. They sought to surprise with their spontaneity and creativity, even to offend by creating a scandal. Many of them, including a number who were homosexuals, celebrated their individuality and tried to keep themselves in the public eye. The flamboyant Irish-born poet and dramatist Oscar Wilde (1854–1900), whose witty dialogues greatly improved British comedy, became a symbol of contemporary "decadence." When asked by a customs official if he had anything to declare on arriving in France, Wilde replied, "only my genius." He faced prosecution in 1895 for his sexual orientation, but also on trial, at least implicitly, was his belief in artistic decadence. Wilde, who insisted that "it is personalities, not principles, that move the age," dominated the court proceedings with his performance before he was sentenced to two years' hard labor for "immoral conduct." He died a lonely, premature death in a small Parisian hotel in 1900.

The proponents of cultural modernism believed themselves caught between two forces. They mocked bourgeois "respectability" and mass culture by sporting long hair, strange clothes, and erratic behavior. But, at the same time, they nonetheless sought public acceptance and patronage of their work.

Musical composition reflected the contemporary discovery of the unconscious, and avant-garde composers moved defiantly away from traditional forms, with many abandoning the ordered hierarchical scale, in which certain tones held precedence. Gustav Mahler (1860–1911) sought to release in his audience dreams and fantasies, which he believed could not be distinguished from real life, just as Freud sought to elicit them from the patients on his office couch. The pianist and composer Erik Satie (1866–1925) composed music by the dim light of lampposts as he returned in an alcoholic haze from his favorite cafés and would eat only foods that were white in color. Both Satie and Claude Debussy (1862–1918) set out to free music from all constraints. Satie's compositions with titles like *Three Pieces in the Form of a Pear* explored new relationships between chords that surprised listeners, outraging some while delighting others with their humor. Satie also sought popularity, to the extent that he wanted to write what he called "furniture music," which he hoped would serve as background for daily life. The Austrian composer Arnold Schönberg (1874–1951) began to break the patterns of traditional harmonies to write free atonal music, beginning with his String Quartet No. 2 (1908). He believed atonality realistically and subliminally followed the dictates, instincts, and sometimes suffering of his psyche. "What counts is the capacity to hear oneself, to look deep inside oneself. . . . Inside, where the man of instinct begins, there, fortunately, all theory breaks down." For Schönberg, the self became a refuge from the outside world.

The artists and writers of the avant-garde believed that art could reveal what is hidden in the unsconscious, and thus open up new vistas of experience that could be communicated to viewers and audiences. Albert Jarry held that all meanings that a reader could discover in poetry or prose were equally valid. The poet Guillaume Apollinaire (1880–1918), whose work defied stylistic convention, wrote reviews of books that only existed in his mind. Master of ambiguity, he abandoned direct statement and even punctuation and classical word order to encourage readers to find new meanings in his work. Henri Bergson (1859–1941), the French philosopher of irrationality who challenged prevailing assumptions of materialism and positivism, popularized the idea that each individual and each nation had a creative "dynamic energy" (*élan vital*) waiting for release. One of his contemporaries, affirming the particularly close link between symbolism, which began as a literary movement in the mid-1880s, and music, urged writers to "drop a syllable into a state of pure consciousness and listen for the reverberations."

Post-impressionists painted subjects in ways that even more consciously than impressionism distanced the artist from the subject. Georges Seurat (1859–1891) claimed that painters could evoke emotions through the visual suggestions of discontinuous lines, colors, and tones. Seurat's work was a reaction against impressionism. His paintings intrigued symbolist writers, who believed that symbols would stimulate memory through free association, because they consisted of thousands of dots of color forming figures and landscapes. Seurat's bold style, "pointillism," influenced by the development of photography, left his figures appearing strangely mechanical in appearance and separate from each other. This may suggest the alienation, social division, and isolation—even sadness—of modern urban life. His greatest and still most controversial work, *A Sunday Afternoon on the Island of the Grande Jatte* (1884), may be seen in this way, but it also may be that Seurat sought to portray social cohesion through the social mix of bourgeois and workers enjoying a Sunday afternoon along the Seine, all part of the same colorful matrix of light.

Expressionist painters used daring distortions, curious juxtaposition, and bold, unfamiliar color schemes to express what lay deep inside them and to obtain an emotional response in viewers. They were greatly

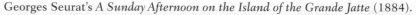

Georges Seurat's *A Sunday Afternoon on the Island of the Grande Jatte* (1884).

Antonio Gaudí's Casa Batlló
in Barcelona.

influenced by the art of primitive societies. The French painter Paul Gauguin (1848–1903) abandoned a comfortable living as a stockbroker for the
uncertainty of a career as a painter. His lengthy stay on the Pacific Ocean
island of Tahiti shaped the primitive appearance of his painting. Edvard
Munch (1863–1944), a Norwegian artist who came to Paris in 1893,
demonstrated Gauguin's influence. His *The Scream* (1893) evokes the
viewer's alarm and fear, because the subject's scream seems to fill the entire canvas. In Munich, which along with Dresden was the center of the
expressionist movement in Germany, the Russian painter Vassily Kandinsky (1866–1944) moved expressionism by 1910 even further away from
surface reality, portraying the inner being in a simplified form with lines,
dots, and intense colors.

Art Nouveau, a sinuous decorative style offering a synthesis between
traditional and modern art, also reflected the anxiety and moodiness of the
fin de siècle. Art Nouveau evinced contemporary fascination with psychia-
try. Charcot, the French neurologist, had opened up the unconscious to
investigation through hypnosis. The dreamlike flowing forms and shapes
of Art Nouveau, then, complemented the growing awareness of the contours and fluidity of the mind and its dreams and fantasies.

Although drawing upon past decorative traditions in furniture, jewelry,
glasswork, and ceramics, Art Nouveau also influenced architecture, seen
in the houses and sweeping entrances to subway stations that Hector
Guimard (1867–1942) designed in Paris, and in the public park, apartment buildings and beginnings of a cathedral undertaken in Barcelona by
Antonio Gaudí (1852–1926).

Leading cultural figures in France identified Art Nouveau's style with the republic, seeing in its highly crafted luxury products something that was very French. At the same time, it could be associated with the conservative republic because the style's rococo origins were rooted in an aristocratic tradition and, perhaps as well, seemed to affirm women's traditional role in household decoration at a time when more feminists were stepping forward to demand equal rights for women.

Vienna became a vital center of avant-garde cultural experimentation. But after first enjoying state sponsorship of their art, the painters and writers of the avant-garde faced rejection in a transformed political climate of intolerance. Some intellectuals and painters embraced aestheticism, which, emphasizing form, beauty, and the artistic side of things over all others, seemed to be a way of surviving in an increasingly irrational, hostile world.

The painter Gustav Klimt (1862–1918), among other Viennese artists, retreated into subjectivism, attaching primary value to individual experience. In 1897, Klimt and his friends adopted the motto "To our era its art, to art its freedom." They wanted, in the words of the Viennese architect Otto Wagner, to "show modern man his true face." Yet, in Vienna—and perhaps there alone—the aestheticism of the avant-garde was not a reaction against the resilient cultural values of the middle class. It was a reaction against political intolerance.

Klimt and the "seccessionists," like their counterparts in Munich who in 1892 announced their "secession" from officially approved art, rebelled against what Klimt considered the unsatisfactory values and haunting dangers of mass society. He sought to stimulate and shock viewers by using, for example, classical images in strange, unprecedented juxtapositions, presenting erotic fantasies and other representations of utopian escape.

Following on the heels of Klimt in Vienna came a disparate but supremely talented group of younger modern painters in Paris. In 1905, they exhibited their work together in Paris. One critic dismissed the show as "touches of crude colorings juxtaposed haphazardly; barbaric and naive games of a child who is playing with the 'box of colors.'" Another critic dubbed them the "fauvists," or wild beasts. The name stuck. The fauvists remained committed to experimentation on canvas in their quest for liberation of both subject and painter. But they also frequently painted landscapes, including some familiar subjects such as coastal resorts, with bright colors and open spaces. One hostile critic in 1905 described a fauvist's brush as having been "dipped in dynamite," affirming the perceived association between artistic and social rebellion in some minds.

Pablo Picasso (1881–1973), a native of southern Spain, is considered by many specialists to be the first painter of the modern movement. Influenced by his homeland, Picasso's work (especially the paintings of his blue period) revealed the gloomy obsession with death that had characterized earlier Spanish painters, notably Goya. As with the other avant-

(*Left*) The young Pablo Picasso in his studio. (*Right*) Picasso's *Les Demoiselles d'Avignon*.

garde artists, Picasso's work drew on his own intense subjectivity. He spent most of his career in Paris, where he admired Jarry's work and lived in the low-life café circles of Montmartre. Because Picasso at first mistrusted art dealers, his work was rarely shown and did not achieve great influence until later.

Picasso's daring *Les Demoiselles d'Avignon* (1907) may mark the beginning of modernist art. Abstract painting is a subjective form of expression. "I paint objects as I think them, not as I see them," Picasso asserted. Above all, abstract art abandoned the artist's system of perspective that had endured since the Renaissance. In Picasso's work, one finds a fragmentation of perception and dismantling of realistic depiction in favor of products of the imagination—sharp, flat, distorted, and highly simplified geometric patterns of solid forms and space divided by sharp angles.

Critics called the Spanish painter's style "cubism" because of his preoccupation with basic shapes, particularly the three-dimensional prism. Picasso considered the prism the fundamental component of reality. The collaboration of Georges Braque (1882–1963) with Picasso helped establish a second, "analytical" phase of cubism with even greater emphasis on geometric shapes, now constructed from inanimate, pasted materials, as seen in Braque's *Newspaper, Bottle, Packet of Tobacco (Le Courrier)* (1914). The cubists became a more cohesive "school" than the fauvists, and relied more on light and shade than color to represent forms.

Futurist artists, most of them Italian, were inspired by technological

The futurist Umberto Boccioni's *Dynamism of a Cyclist* (1913).

change. In 1910, a futurist wrote "All subjects previously used must be swept away in order to express our whirling life of steel, of pride, of fever and of speed." *Dynamism of a Cyclist* (1913) by Umberto Boccioni (1882–1916) depicts the frenetic energy of pedaling without actually showing the cyclist. The poet Filippo Tomasso Marinetti's "Manifesto of Futurism," which was published in the aftermath of Wilbur Wright's triumphant airplane flights in France, proclaimed "We want to sing the love of danger, the habit of energy and rashness. . . . Beauty exists only in struggle. There is no masterpiece that has not an aggressive character. . . . We want to glorify war—the only cure for the modern world." One critic wrote in 1912, "art is moving in a direction of which our fathers would never even have dreamed. We stand before the new pictures as in a dream, and we hear the apocalyptic horsemen in the air."

Artists suffered the shrill denunciations of chauvinists. In France, the nationalist press denounced the cubists, several of whom, like Picasso, were not French, for artistic decadence, specifically for importing "foreign perversions" with the goal of weakening French morale. Insisting on eclecticism and experimentation, some Munich artists affronted German nationalists by insisting that art ought to be international in character and bringing French and Russian artists—including Kandinsky—into their circle. The turn of the avant-garde toward irrationality came at a time when the rational structures that governed domestic political life and international relations seemed to be breaking down amid aggressive nationalism and militarism in Paris, Vienna, Berlin, and other European capitals.

CONCLUSION

Slowly but surely Europe, particularly the West, was becoming an industrialized, increasingly urban society characterized by mass production, factory work, and the separation of work and home. Most Europeans could now read and write, and they lived better and longer than ever before. But at the same time, economic and social inequalities generated union organization, the growth of mass political parties—including a variety of socialist movements—and waves of social protest. Thus, demands for economic, social, and political change characterized the last three decades of the nineteenth century and the beginnings of the twentieth century, engulfing not only the industrialized constitutional monarchies and republics of Western and Southern Europe but also the empires of Central and Eastern Europe.

CHAPTER 21

MASS POLITICS AND NATIONALISM

Red Week began in Italy in June 1914 after police shot two people to death while preventing a crowd leaving an anti-militarist demonstration from marching into downtown Ancona, on the Adriatic coast. Massive protest demonstrations and strikes followed in many cities in Italy. Workers poured into the streets, rioted in several cities, built barricades, and raised the red flag over a number of town halls. The government sent in the army; troops fired on demonstrators. To revolutionary socialists and labor militants proclaiming themselves internationalists, the Liberal government of Premier Giovanni Giolitti (who had dominated Italian politics since 1896) had betrayed Italian workers. In the meantime, the growing nationalist right cheered on the troops, while itself heaping abuse on the government for failing to fulfill Italy's destiny as a Great Power. Two large political movements—one on the left; the other on the right—threatened the Liberal center. Both characterized the age of mass politics that transformed much of Europe between 1880 and 1914, a remarkable period of change. The continent entered a new and dangerous era.

Although British and French nationalism developed during the last decades of the eighteenth century and the first of the nineteenth, most Europeans began to think of themselves as belonging to nation-states during the 1880–1914 period. National consciousness—the construction of an imagined national community—rapidly developed within European states. During those crucial decades, universal manhood suffrage, the prodigious expansion of the popular press, the emergence of organized political parties, and nationalism shaped political life in much of Europe, as contemporaries assessed the economic and social transformation of Europe in the wake of the Second Industrial Revolution.

As liberalism waned in the face of the challenges of rapid economic and social change, socialism, syndicalism, and anarchism emerged from the left side of the political spectrum. At least in principle, socialists, syndical-

Dinnertime in an English workhouse, which provided relief for unemployed workers experiencing the dislocation and social transformation accompanying the Second Industrial Revolution.

ists, and anarchists were resolutely anti-nationalist and internationalist. From the right, partially in response to left-wing challenges, aggressive right-wing nationalism emerged as a dominant political force in twentieth-century life, helping to define the internal politics of and the relations between the European powers.

Nationalism influenced the domestic politics of each of the European powers during the last decades of the nineteenth century. Republican France and parliamentary Britain were as much influenced by nationalism as was imperial Germany. Many of the subjects of the tsar of Russia and of the Habsburg lands were also fanatically loyal to their multinational states (above all, Russians and German-speaking Austrians). Nonetheless, although Tsar Nicholas II and Emperor Francis Joseph commanded great loyalty, nationalism represented not the glue that to a large extent helped shape the political life of the other European powers but rather a potentially destructive force because of the polyglot nature of both empires.

In some states, cultural factors and particularist traditions impeded the development of national consciousness and hindered the development of mass political life. For example, although Italy was a constitutional, parliamentary monarchy, it remained in some ways a "geographical expression." Far less than half the population spoke Italian, and enormous gaps in economic development, transportation networks, literacy, and political participation divided north from south. And like the Habsburg monarchy, the autocratic Russian Empire also consisted of many nationalities. The tsar of Russia, however, drew upon and encouraged a Russian nationalism that was intolerant of the aspirations of other national groups. Thus, he directed campaigns to "Russify" Poles, Ukrainians, Lithuanians, Armenians, and other groups. In these two empires—above all in Russia—autocratic rule and the role of favored nationalities prevented the emergence of mass political life.

FROM LIBERALISM TO NATIONALISM

Mass political parties, encouraged by the gradual implementation of universal male suffrage in many Western countries, mass literacy, and the popular press helped bring Europe into an age in which more people than ever before participated in national political life. More people also probably began to think of themselves as belonging to specific nationalities, an evolution that reflected the enhanced reach of national states. Classroom textbooks, which emphasized national histories, and universal manhood conscription accentuated nationalism. In Western and Central Europe, the expanded dimensions of mass political life itself were based on universal manhood suffrage, large political parties, and noisy electoral campaigns carried to the people with brightly colored posters, catchy slogans, and whistle-stop speeches. Mass political life reflected more than just enhanced national feeling because, after all, the political parties of the left, center, and right often disagreed vehemently on what their nation needed. It also drew on growing social tensions and the lower classes' political dissatisfaction with the limits of liberal reform.

Two significant factors reflected and accentuated the growing influence of the nation-state on citizens and subjects: the enhanced reach of the state, manifested through startling increases in the size of government bureaucracies; and, at the same time, greater secularization. Bureaucracies swelled in size. In 1841, the British government—the least centralized of the major European powers—had employed 40,000 men and 3,000 women; by 1911, 271,000 men and 50,000 women worked for the state. State clerks, not priests and ministers, kept official registers of births, marriages, and deaths. The institutional power of established churches declined within states, as religious practice waned in many countries. Lay teachers, who were public employees and proud representatives of the state, taught respect for and allegiance to the nation-state.

Yet, the new nationalism was increasingly, though not exclusively, anti-democratic in character. Drawing disproportionately on the middle class, it aggressively espoused fanatical loyalty to the nation and support for national aggrandizement at the expense of rival powers while overriding or ignoring the economic and political demands of the underprivileged.

The Waning of the Liberal Era

Liberals had championed the interests of the middle class, basing the right to vote on the ownership of property. Following the largely unsuccessful 1848 revolutions, which had been fought on behalf of universal manhood suffrage and nationalism, liberalism had prevailed in the 1850s and 1860s in Great Britain, Austria, and to some extent, France. Some liberals feared that political democracy would open the gates to socialists and facilitate trade union militancy.

Critics of liberalism believed it inadequate to the tasks of a rapidly changing world. And by the last decades of the century, economic and political liberalism were on the defensive. Conservatives ousted liberals in Belgium in 1870, Italy in 1876, and Austria in 1878. The National Liberal Party of Germany lost more than two-thirds of its seats in the Reichstag at the end of the 1870s. Liberal domination ended in Switzerland. In Spain, real power lay in the greedy hands of powerful local government officials and landowners who rigged elections to the Cortes. In the background, powerful as ever, stood the Catholic Church and the army. Despite constitutional guarantees of political freedom, the liberal era had been but a brief episode in Spain. In 1874, the monarchy was restored just a year after a republic had been established. The new mass socialist parties, and the fears among conservatives that they engendered, helped bring down liberalism.

Whereas liberals had generally wanted to restrict the right to vote to males meeting certain property qualifications, under the impulse of popular pressure electoral franchises were expanded during the last decades of the century. In 1880, France had universal manhood suffrage and was the only major power to have a republican form of government. In the German Empire, Bismarck believed that universal manhood suffrage could be a conservative force and so in 1867 he had put through legislation whereby adult males could vote for members of the Reichstag. The British Parliament approved the secret ballot in 1872, and in 1884 it passed the third Reform Bill, which enfranchised almost all remaining adult males who could not vote, notably farm laborers. Universal male suffrage came to Austria in 1907. The last block to universal manhood suffrage was eliminated in Italy in 1912 when all males, literate or not, received the right to vote. Mass parties gradually replaced old networks of noble patronage. The deflation of land values and agricultural products undercut the economic position of the nobility, although nobles retained considerable power in Germany, the Austro-Hungarian Empire, and Great Britain.

Social and political tensions were exacerbated by the long economic depression starting in 1873. Following a fever of speculation, particularly in Germany, banks failed in the Austrian capital of Vienna. The speed with which the crisis spread to other financial capitals reflected the extent to which improvements in transportation and communication during the middle decades of the nineteenth century further extended the links of an increasingly global economy. Despite intermittent economic revivals, the period of stagnation lasted until the mid-1890s. The British metallurgical and textile industries, which had been at the forefront of the manufacturing revolution, now stood still. Agricultural prices fell virtually everywhere in Europe. Imported grain from the United States and Canada flooded markets, driving prices downward, reducing profits, and therefore limiting subsequent economic investment. Some Marxists crowed that capitalism was on the verge of collapse.

The development of economic cartels dealt a blow to the liberal era of free trade. Cartels are formal agreements by which competitors within the same industry protect profits by sharing markets, regulating output, fixing prices, or taking other measures to limit competition. Cartels permitted a few large companies to dominate production and distribution, enabling heavy industries to protect themselves during periods of falling prices and high unemployment by controlling production and setting prices. In Germany, mining cartels set production goals and kept prices artificially high. In France and Great Britain, informal agreements among industrialists achieved virtually the same results as formalized cartels. Even where there were no cartels, the concentration of business in larger companies continued, in part because in industries such as metallurgy and chemicals, expensive machinery made "start-up" costs prohibitive for smaller firms.

Government expenditures soared in every country, particularly with the cost of aggressive colonial policies and of larger, technologically advanced armies. Germany spent four times as much on its armed forces in 1890 as it had in 1874 (a period of little inflation), while Russian military spending more than doubled. With the depression reducing tax revenues, states therefore looked for new sources of revenue. Some continental states nationalized railways in the 1870s and 1880s; others increased indirect taxes, adding to the burden of people of modest means.

In every industrialized country, tariffs became the focus of impassioned political debate, even in Britain, where economic liberalism remained the prevailing credo. Governments responded to the depression by imposing protective tariffs in the interest of native industries and agriculture: Austria and Russia did so in 1874 and 1875, respectively, and Italy in 1887. In France, the Méline Tariff, supported by industrialists and farmers, went into effect in 1892. The return to protective tariffs aided cartels, protecting them from competition from abroad.

In Germany, the National Liberal Party, backed by big business, abandoned free trade. An alliance between industrialists and agriculturists ("iron and rye") led to protectionist economic policies beginning in 1879, culminating in 1902 with a tariff that imposed a 25 percent duty on heavy industrial and food imports. Moreover, the frantic scramble for colonies that began in Africa in the 1880s contributed to political pressure for protectionist policies supported by nationalists.

The New Nationalism

Although drawing on a wide spectrum of public opinion, the new nationalism was for the most part anti-democratic in nature. During the French Revolution and Napoleonic era, nationalism had been an ideology identified with the political left. Liberals believed that laissez-faire economic policy and parliamentary government combined with an expansion of the right to vote (but not necessarily universal manhood suffrage) would provide a firm base for the establishment of nation-states. The new nationalism, however, differed from the old liberal ideology. Nationalists, convinced that their people were superior to any other, now trumpeted the primacy of the nation over claims of popular sovereignty or belief in human equality. Nationalism became an ideology championed, above all, by right-wing parties that espoused national aggrandizement through increased military strength, territorial expansion, and colonialism (see Chapter 22). "Jingoism" came to define the swaggering self-assurance of nationalists committed to expanding the power of their nation, peopled, they assumed, by the most gifted and deserving race anywhere.

Nationalism merged easily with anti-Semitism and imperialism, both of which were predicated on the assumption that the people of one nation were superior to others, and therefore entitled to dominate "inferior" peoples. Both religious and racial "anti-Semitism" became common. Following the economic crash of 1873, German newspapers whipped up anti-Semitism, denouncing Jewish bankers, industrialists, and rival Jewish publishers. The operatic composer Richard Wagner and his circle of friends were outspokenly anti-Semitic. Wagner believed that the theater (and composers) stood as a center of emotional national culture, and his works reflected strident right-wing German nationalism. Since most Jews retained their cultural traditions and religion and spoke Yiddish as their first language, they were considered outsiders in Vienna, Berlin, Budapest, and other cities to which Jews had migrated fleeing persecution and periodic pogroms in Russia, Russian Ukraine, and Russian Poland. A Jewish industrialist observed in 1911 that "In the youth of every German Jew there comes a painful moment that he never forgets, the moment when he realizes for the first time that he has entered the world as a second-class citizen and that neither his efforts nor his accomplishments will free him from this status. . . . [It is] the harshest thing one man can tell another. . . . 'Your blood, your soul, your sensibility has no place in our community, you are and will remain different, ignoble, alien.'"

The Zionist movement for the establishment of the Jewish homeland in Palestine emerged partially in response to the rising tide of anti-Semitism in Europe. The movement's founder, Theodor Herzl (1860–1904), a gifted journalist and German-speaking Jew from Budapest who had moved to Vienna, gave up all hope for the full assimilation of Jews in a Europe of rising anti-Semitism. In 1897, the first Zionist World Congress took place in Basel.

In an era when for the first time in history most people could read and write, newspapers and other mass publications contributed in no small measure to the cause of nationalists, glorifying deeds done on behalf of the nation and castigating rivals. Nationalist associations and leagues pressured states into greater military spending and more aggressive international diplomacy and action. Lobbies representing interest groups, such as producers of arms and munitions, shipbuilders, industrialists with global trading interests, or military men (in particular, the German and British navies), exerted great influence on policymakers. Gymnastics and rifle clubs, geographic associations, and colonial societies also encouraged aggressive nationalism and imperialism.

At the turn of the century, when the depression had subsided and workers' organizations were able to replenish their ranks, waves of strikes frightened conservatives from Norway and Sweden to Austria and Spain. May Day marches in France and Belgium seemed like dress rehearsals for revolution. There were even rebellions in some rural areas, by far the most serious occurring in Romania, where indebted peasants rose up against the government and suffered the loss of 20,000 dead. Conservatives applauded the use of troops against strikers. The fear of socialism and syndicalism, both resolutely internationalist in claims and appeal, pushed social elites toward the ranks of the nationalist right.

Many middle-class voters remained socially and politically conservative, vulnerable to economic crisis, and apprehensive of organized labor and the mass political parties of the left. In Vienna, middle-class voters supported the anti-Semitic Christian Democratic Party. The German Center Party, the Catholic Party in Belgium, and the Radical Party in France, all socially conservative, directed appeals to middle-class voters.

The lower middle class became an important—perhaps even pivotal—social group in the political evolution of all Western countries. That it had some degree of self-awareness was revealed by the fact that in 1899 the first (and last) World Congress of the Petty Bourgeoisie took place in Brussels. Many Parisian shopkeepers, frustrated by the economic depression, fearful of workers' consumer cooperatives, and losing clients to department stores, swung their support from the Radical Party to right-wing nationalist parties. Many could be convinced by right-wing polemicists that "Jewish capitalists" were responsible for their plight.

Nonetheless, some parties of the left, such as the German Social Democratic Party and the French socialist parties, also found support within the lower middle class. In Britain, where traditions of municipal political autonomy were strong, many retailers and shopkeepers occupied official positions that would have been unthinkable on the continent. Most remained faithful to the Liberal Party, which had first drawn them into national political life following their enfranchisement in 1867.

Social Reform

As large-scale industrialization expanded the number of people working in factories and living in cities, government officials, social reformers, and politicians surveyed the conditions of working-class life, "the problem of problems," as it was called in Britain. While in much of Europe, Karl Marx's gloomy prediction that workers' wages and overall conditions of life would continue to decline had not been borne out. Economic uncertainty and grinding poverty seemed to have engendered a social crisis of unmatched proportions. Descriptions of the dreary slums of blackened industrial cities reached many readers, particularly in Great Britain, France, Belgium, and Germany, through novels and surveys of working-class life.

Many contemporaries believed that state-sponsored social reforms fell short of fulfilling the needs or demands of most workers. The long economic depression that began in 1873 and lasted well into the 1890s added to social and political tensions in almost every country. As the Catholic Church acknowledged the grave social problems that the Second Industrial Revolution seemed to intensify, Christian Socialists believed that the Church ought to win back workers to the faith by attempting to improve their lives. Espousing a different point of view, many feminists contended that social reforms would be inadequate as long as women were without the right to enter universities or vote. Thus, mass political life nurtured radical critiques of capitalist society from socialists and union leaders, among others.

The Trade Union Movement

The trade union movement grew rapidly in Western Europe, above all among skilled workers, most of whom were male. The goals of unions were to raise wages and improve conditions, while increasing the number of unionized workers. By 1914, 3 million workers had joined unions in Britain, 1.5 million in Germany, and 1 million in Italy. The number of white-collar unions also increased, such as those organizing schoolteachers and postal clerks. In 1913, there were more than 400,000 union members in Austria, a country of only 6 million inhabitants. French unions had been tolerated in the guise of friendly associations and mutual aid societies; they proliferated after they were legalized in 1884, reaching 1 million members early in the twentieth century. In 1895, French unions formed the General Confederation of Labor (C.G.T.), with the goal of unifying the trade union movement. The C.G.T., to which about a third of French unions belonged, renounced participation in political life and espoused revolutionary principles. Union membership soared in France, reaching 2.6 million in 1914. Union meeting halls and cafés nurtured class consciousness and organization. May Day demonstrations and festivals, with red flags flying, vigorous political debates, consumer cooperatives, and the kinds of informal contacts provided by factory work and cafés also helped maintain solidarity among workers.

Between 1890 and 1914, strikes increased dramatically, particularly in Western Europe. The organized strike became a social fact of modern life as workers learned to protect their interests. Many local strikes shifted to a national arena and became political issues when unions pressed the state to intervene on their behalf. Thus, workers hoped that they could force government officials to pressure employers to bargain with them. Workers struck when employers seemed most vulnerable; for example, when they had recently received large orders for products. The vast majority of strikes were undertaken by skilled, organized workers in large-scale sectors such as textiles, mining, and metallurgy, whose unions had resources such as strike funds upon which to fall back. Strike movements reflected a more generalized sense of class consciousness among many—but hardly all—workers.

Strikes reflected not only the growth in union membership, but also changes in the organization of industrial work. In addition to low wages and the length of their workday, workers also resented factory foremen. Foremen, representing the company's interests, sought to impose industrial discipline on workers, some of whom had worked on farms or in domestic industry and had more or less controlled their own time. Now they were forbidden to enter and leave the factory as they wished when they had nothing to do, or to talk on the job.

Workers also objected to the implementation of techniques of "scientific management," developed by the American engineer Frederick Taylor. "Taylorism" placed factory workers more directly under the control of factory managers by measuring worker performance, tying pay scales to the number of units produced, which put more pressure on workers. The French car manufacturer Louis Renault implemented some of Taylor's techniques of scientific management. Taylorism wore out workers. Noting that virtually all the factory workers employed by a Philadelphia manufacturer who had become enamored of scientific management were young, a British visitor asked repeatedly where the older workers were. Finally, the owner replied, "Have a cigar, and while we smoke we can visit the cemetery."

Yet, despite the increase in union membership, most European workers did not belong to unions, although they often supported strikes and believed in union goals. The 1875 Trade Union Act ended many limitations on unions in Britain, but by the turn of the century only about 25 percent of British workers were organized. Moreover, the percentage fell to about 10 percent in France and to an even lower percentage in Italy and Russia. Several factors limited the expansion of union membership. Considerable gaps remained between the work experience, salary, organizations, and expectations of skilled and unskilled workers, differences that were most pronounced in Britain. Many workers moved from place to place, following employment opportunities. Those with urban roots were far more easily organized than recently arrived migrants from smaller towns or villages. Differences and tensions between workers of different national groups also served to divide workers, such as between Irish and English workers in London, German and Czech workers in Prague, or Belgian and French workers in northern France.

The union organization of female workers lagged far behind that of men. Women made up 30 percent of the British labor force, but only about 7 percent of union members. Almost all were relegated to relatively unskilled and low-paying jobs and confronted chronic vulnerability to being dismissed. Women also had to take responsibility for their children, something male union members often failed to recognize. Most worked in unskilled jobs, making boxes, knotting fish nets, making buttonholes, doing food-processing work, and many other tasks. Furthermore, many male workers refused to accept women as equals and claimed that they were taking jobs away from men (a French union, which admitted women as members, included the following regulation: "Women may address observations on propositions to the union only in writing and by the intermediation of two male members"). Yet, women workers also struck in the face of tougher working conditions, low wages, and sometimes sexual harassment.

State Social Reform

Confronted with the increased militancy of their workers, some employers sought to maintain worker loyalty through paternalistic policies. Many employers, to be sure, empathized with their workers as they struggled to get by. They encouraged workers to form savings associations by matching whatever small sums the working-class families could put aside for the future. A minority of manufacturers started funds for insurance and pension plans, or provided basic company housing (especially in mining communities).

However, by the 1880s, it was clear that the paternalistic policies of some employers were far from being generalized. Some social reformers, many politicians, and most workers demanded state intervention to protect workers from some of the uncertainties and hardships of their labor.

Imperial Germany, not republican France or parliamentary Britain, first gave workers some protection against personal and family disaster stemming from work-related accidents. Germany's domineering Chancellor Otto von Bismarck sought to outbid the Catholic Center Party and the Social Democrats for working-class support. Determined to preserve his own power and the autocratic structure of the empire, Bismarck carried out domestic policies based upon compromise and conciliation between middle-class political interests and working-class demands. In 1881, he astonished friends and enemies alike in the Reichstag by expressing the view that "a remedy [for the social question] cannot be sought merely in the repression of socialist excesses. There must be at the same time a positive advancement of the welfare of the working classes." He announced that the state would undertake an insurance program, which would incorporate existing voluntary plans. It would compensate workers for injury and illness, as well as provide some retirement funds.

The German chancellor thus placed socialists in the delicate position of either opposing bills that would benefit workers or appearing to compromise their ideologically based refusal to collaborate with the government. The Sickness Insurance Law of 1883 covered all workers for up to thirteen weeks if their income fell below a certain level. Deductions withheld from workers' wages provided most of the funds. A law was passed requiring that all workers be insured against accidents and disability, with half of the funds paid by employers; another law providing pensions for workers who lived until seventy years of age followed the next year. By the turn of the century, many German workers received medical care, small payments when they were ill or injured, and if worse came to worse, a decent burial. By 1913, 14.5 million workers had insurance.

The traditional liberal opposition to state intervention in the working of the economy had begun to change in the middle of the century. Some conservatives, too, believed that some social reform was inevitable, even desirable, if only to prevent socialists from winning the unqualified support of the laboring poor. In Britain, workhouses (legislated by the British Poor Law of 1834) still carried a social stigma, even if conditions had somewhat improved toward the end of the century. Families were separated, and inmates were forced to wear uniforms, attend chapel, participate in group exercises, and sustain periods of silence, all with the goal of attaining proper discipline. A contemporary surveyor of working-class life noted that "aversion to the 'House' is absolutely universal, and almost any amount of suffering and privation will be endured by the people rather than go into it." The vast majority of the inmates of the workhouses were not the able-bodied unemployed, but were children, the infirm, single mothers, the aged, or the insane. But although public opinion had already turned against workhouses, the Poor Law, slightly reformed, remained on the books until 1929.

The first Victorian social reforms were largely limited to establishing minimum health standards, facilitating the education of children, and getting children out of the mines. The Factory Act (1875) reduced the workweek in large factories to fifty-six hours. The Artisans' Dwelling Act (1875) defined unsanitary housing and gave the state the right to order the demolition of slum buildings that fell below a minimum standard. These laws were, however, only very randomly enforced.

By the turn of the century, Conservatives, Liberals, and members of the new Labour Party (founded in 1901 and taking its name in 1906) all ac-

The Townsend Road School, London 1905.

cepted, to varying degrees, the right and the obligation of government to intervene through reform in the lives of the people. The Workmen's Compensation Law (1897) had made employers responsible for bearing the cost of industrial accidents, and another act extended the same protection to agricultural workers. Liberal governments provided lunches to children whose families could not afford to pay for them, and passed the Old Age Pension Act of 1908 (which provided some income for workers over seventy years of age whose incomes fell below ten shillings a week), and banned "sweated" work in tailoring and other trades. As a result of the National Insurance Bill (1911), workers' friendly societies administered insurance payments based on voluntary employee wage deductions, a significant difference between British insurance legislation and that of Germany, reflecting the less centralized structure of the British state. The law's most salutary effect was to provide more workers and their families with direct medical treatment. Yet, a third of the British poor still received no assistance of any kind. Moreover, assistance to unemployed workers in Britain was less well organized and less generous than, for example, that in France.

The British government also put into effect educational reforms. In 1891, Parliament made primary education free and provided government grants to Dissenting and Catholic schools. This effectively served to disestablish the Anglican Church. The Education Act of 1902 brought voluntary schools, as well as schools operated by the school boards, under the control of the local administrative councils, leaving the voluntary schools with the right to select teachers. However, the legislation left Dissenters dissatisfied by granting funds to Anglican and Catholic schools and, by virtue of the strong position of the Established Church, seeming to re-affirm the Anglican monopoly over education.

In France, proponents of "solidarism" believed that employers and workers could put aside their differences in the interest of living harmoniously. But this was easier said than done. The reform legislation of the pre-World War I Third Republic was relatively meager; yet, pushed by Radicals and Socialists, the Chamber of Deputies between 1890 and 1904 passed laws eliminating obligatory special identity papers, or internal passports, for workers (1890), created a system of arbitration for strikes, banned female night work (1892), established employers' legal liability for industrial accidents (1898), reduced the workday to ten hours for women and children (1904), established an obligatory weekly day of rest and a minimum age for industrial workers, affirmed the right of the state to monitor conditions of work and hygiene in factories (although inspection was in many areas nonexistent), established a workmen's compensation law with modest pension benefits, and provided limited medical care for working-class families.

By the last decades of the century, as ecclesiastical influence waned in France, government programs on behalf of poor mothers had largely taken over from private charity, providing some minimal assistance. State involvement reflected fears of depopulation resulting from the country's declining birthrate (a leading politician declared in 1891 that France lost a battalion of soldiers each year by "letting the infants of the poor die"). Assistance to unwed mothers reduced infant mortality, bringing about a sharp decline in the abandonment of babies.

Women's Suffrage

Everywhere in Europe, women remained subordinate to men in legal rights. They were excluded from most universities, could not vote (in contrast, some states in the United States gave women the vote before 1900), and had limited or no control over family financial resources (not until 1907 in France did a married woman have free access to her own salary). Women made very little progress entering the professions because many men feared the advent of the "new woman" who demanded the same access to education and opportunity as men. The term "new woman" came from the title of a lecture given by the Italian feminist Maria Montessori (1870–1952), a doctor and originator of innovative schools that stress the encouragement of creativity in children. Still, the beginnings were difficult. When a female Greek scientist gave her first lecture at the University of Athens, male students disrupted her lecture with shouts of "back to the kitchen!" The Polish-born French scientist Marie Curie, who discovered radium and won two Nobel Prizes, related the isolation and challenges of her studies in Paris in the early 1890s: "It seems that life is not easy for any of us. But what of that? We must have perseverance and above all confidence in ourselves. We must believe that we are gifted for something, and that [our goals], at what ever cost, must be obtained."

Women demanding equal rights faced considerable opposition. Queen Victoria of England called demands by women for equal rights "on which her poor feeble sex is bent . . . a mad, wicked folly . . . forgetting every sense of womanly feeling and propriety." The biologist T.H. Huxley (1825–1895) insisted that women were less intelligent than men, arguing that most women are smaller and physically less strong than men. The claims of such bad science bolstered opposition to the women's movement.

Right-wing political parties opposed women's suffrage on principle. Moderate republicans often claimed that women could not understand political issues; and left-wing socialists in Catholic countries feared that if women had the right to vote, they would support clerical candidates. Socialist parties and unions threw their support to women workers laboring for better wages and conditions. But in France, concern about the plummeting birthrate contributed to swelling opposition to what seemed to many a dangerous "liberation" of women from subordination to their husbands.

The feminist movement (a name that only gradually took hold in Europe and the United States) developed very slowly in Europe and was most active in Britain, where women had gained the right to vote in municipal elections in 1864 and for county and parish councils six years later. In 1889, at the time of the centennial of the French Revolution, the first International Congresses on Women's Rights and Feminine Institutions took place in Paris. By 1900, more than 850 German associations were working for women's rights, including improved educational and employment opportunities and equal wages.

Near the end of the century, British women's groups presented to Parliament a petition with more than a quarter of a million signatures calling for reform. As more occupations, such as jobs in department stores and teaching, opened up to women, the campaign for women's suffrage widened. The International Women's Suffrage Alliance encouraged organizations in a number of countries. A more militant group of feminists undertook a campaign of direct action. Emmeline Pankhurst (1858–1928), who had been elected to the school board in Manchester, founded the Women's Social and Political Union in 1903. Members protested the lack of female suffrage by breaking shop windows on London's fashionable Oxford Street, tossing acid on golf putting greens (the sport identified with aristocratic British males), and bombing the house of Liberal party leader David Lloyd George (1863–1945). Other "suffragettes," as they were called, went on hunger strikes upon being arrested; they were force-fed, or else released and then re-arrested. In 1907, British women gained the right to serve in local government, and three years later Parliament considered a bill that would grant the vote to single women who owned property, but Prime Minister Herbert Asquith (1852–1928) simply let the bill drop. In the most dramatic incident, a suffragette carrying a banner proclaiming

In 1913, the suffragette Emily Davison throws herself before the king's horse at the Derby at Epsom Downs and is killed.

"Votes for Women" hurled herself in front of a horse owned by King George V at the 1913 Derby at Epsom Downs and was killed.

CHALLENGERS TO THE NATION-STATE

Political life within the European states during the 1880–1914 period was shaped by organized challenges from movements that either rejected entirely the economic, social, and political bases of those states or demanded sweeping changes. The Catholic Church (in countries that were Catholic, or at least had many Catholics) had long resisted parliamentary rule based on universal manhood suffrage and felt particularly aggrieved by secularizing policies enacted by states. The Church itself served as an alternative allegiance to the nation-state for Catholics, many of whom supported socially conservative political parties.

Socialist parties, on the left side of the political spectrum, drew largely but not exclusively on industrial workers. Socialists wanted to capture control of the state. Marxist socialists believed that inevitably a working-class revolution would bring down capitalism and that the workers would seize control of the state. Reform socialists, in contrast, believed that electoral victories could lead to a socialist state, and that along the way to ultimate victory socialists could exert pressure on states to improve conditions of life for workers. Anarchists did not want to seize control of the state, but rather to abolish it. Believing that violent acts would provide a spark that would unleash a social revolution, a number of anarchists launched a campaign of terrorism at the turn of the century, carrying out political assassinations. In contrast, trade unionists known as syndicalists (the word comes from the French *syndicats* for trade unions) believed that trade unions would provide not only the means by which workers could take control of the state but also a blueprint of how society would be organized after a successful revolution.

The Catholic Church

In Catholic countries, the Church still provided an alternative allegiance to the nation-state. By promoting the secularization of state and social institutions, however, nationalism reduced the Church's influence. Papal pronouncements seemed to stand steadfastly against social and political change, and particularly against the emergence of the nation-state and parliamentary forms of government, especially in Italy. In a papal encyclical, the *Syllabus of Errors* of 1864, Pope Pius IX condemned as an error the very idea that "the Roman Pontiff can and ought to reconcile himself and come to terms with progress, liberalism and modern civilization." In 1870, the Church proclaimed the doctrine of papal infallibility, which stated that in matters of faith and morals the pope's pronouncements would have to be taken as the absolute truth. The Church backed authoritarian regimes in Spain and Portugal, opposed the newly unified state in Italy, and, at the beginning of the Third Republic, lent tacit support to monarchist movements in France. Yet, forces for change could increasingly be found within the Church. Breaking with his predecessors, Pope Leo XIII (pope 1878–1903) accepted the modern age. His encyclical *Rerum Novarum* (1891) called attention to social injustice, recognizing that many workers were victimized by "the inhumanity of employers and the unbridled greed of competitors."

One of the unintended effects of *Rerum Novarum* was the development of "Christian Socialist" movements in France, Germany, Belgium, and Italy in the 1890s, although the Church generally repudiated them. Christian Socialists hoped to bring employers and workers to Catholic principles. Some clergy and laymen and women organized clubs, vacation colonies, sporting clubs, and charities, and helped workers rent gardens so that they could grow vegetables and fruit. And many Catholics took the pope's encyclical as authorization to participate in national political life. They organized cooperatives, charitable organizations, and even rural banks. Catholic unions tried to counter socialist influence by bringing together workers, employers, and honorary members from local elites. These "mixed" or "yellow" unions drew the unrestrained opposition of most trade unions.

The Socialists

The First International, which had been founded in 1864 in the hopes of strengthening socialist movements within individual countries, was dissolved in 1876 amid internal division, victim of a wave of state repression. Adolphe Thiers, former head of the provisional French government that crushed the Paris Commune, boasted in 1877, "Nobody talks of socialism any more, and rightly so. We are rid of it." Nonetheless, socialism emerged as a major political force in every major European nation. In 1889, at the centennial of the French Revolution in Paris, delegates to a socialist congress founded the Second International. At its congresses, socialists discussed strategies for pushing governments for reform and for coordinating international action (for example, to achieve a shorter workday) and to debate differences over doctrine and strategy in the hope of one day achieving socialist unity.

During the last two decades of the nineteenth century, mass socialist parties developed in the more industrialized, northern countries of Europe—France, Germany, Italy, and Belgium. By the end of the first decade of the twentieth century, every Western European state had working-class representatives in Parliament, some of whom defiantly wore work clothes into debates.

Socialists proclaimed themselves internationalists. Contending that workers in different nations shared a common fate, they believed a revolution would put the working class in power. But socialists remained divided between Marxist revolutionaries, who wanted to organize for the eventual overthrow of capitalism, and reformists willing to participate in the political process, even at the cost of being accused by revolutionary socialists of propping up "bourgeois" regimes by doing so.

The emergence of socialists as contenders for political power reflected economic, social, and political changes in individual countries more than the influence of the Second International. Yet, the debates and divisions that obsessed European socialists revolved around common questions. What should be the relationship between socialism and nationalist movements? Could socialists, proclaiming international solidarity among workers, support demands for Polish independence from the Russian and German Empires, or those by Czechs and other nationalities for independence from the Austro-Hungarian Empire? Czech socialists with national aspirations for their people challenged the domination of the Austrian Social Democrats by German speakers who seemed oblivious to Czech demands. The Polish-born socialist Rosa Luxemburg (1870–1919) found herself in the minority when she opposed demands of many Polish socialists for the independence of their country. Imperialism also divided socialists (see Chapter 22). Should they oppose imperialism in all its forms, or should they hope that the colonial powers might gradually improve the conditions of life of Africans and Asians, who might become adherents to socialism? Finally, amid rising aggressive nationalism, socialists were divided on what response they should take in the event of the outbreak of a European war, with some socialists believing that a declaration of war should be a signal for a mass general strike that could bring the European state system and capitalism to their knees.

For Marx and adherents of his "scientific socialism," emancipation of the workers from capitalism could only be achieved by the conquest of the state through revolution and the subsequent establishment of a socialist society. Revolutionary socialists eschewed reform politics and all compromise with "bourgeois" parties, believing that such actions merely helped prop up the capitalist state.

In France, that country's revolutionary tradition and, above all, the Paris Commune of 1871, encouraged many French socialists to believe that revolution would bring them to power. The Parisian socialist Jules Guesde (1845–1922), rigid, humorless, and doctrinaire (he was known as "the Red Pope" or "the Red Jesuit" by detractors and followers alike), espoused Marxist socialism, which had less influence in France than in Germany. In 1879, Guesde helped found the Federation of the Socialist Workers' Party, which adhered to the Marxist espousal of collectivism. In 1883, Guesde's socialists, irritated that many members were reformists, formed a defiantly Marxist political party, the French Workers' Party, the first modern political party in France. Guesdists tried to subordinate workers' demands for improvements in working conditions to the political goals of their party. Like Kautsky, Guesde viewed electoral campaigns as an opportunity to propagate Marxian socialism, although Guesdists did join the battle for an eight-hour workday and other reforms.

In the Russian Empire, Marxists were "Westernizers," in that they looked to "scientific socialism" as a model for political change in their country (see Chapter 25). Westernizers counted on Russia's emerging industrial proletariat to launch a revolution, but only after Russia had undergone a bourgeois revolution similar to that which they believed had taken place in Paris in 1830, bringing the middle class to political power. In the 1880s, socialists formed reading groups of intellectuals and students—and at least one that was composed of workers—in the imperial capital of St. Petersburg. Exiles began to publish socialist newspapers abroad, smuggling them into Russia.

By contrast, reformism dominated socialist movements in much of Northern Europe. Great Britain's handful of socialists were virtually all intellectuals and reformists. In France and Belgium, reform socialists predominated, although revolutionary socialists maintained some support. German socialists remained reformist.

Reform socialists believed that political participation could win concrete reforms that would improve conditions of life for workers until socialists could take power. Legislation in many countries had brought improvement in conditions of work, however unevenly felt. The extension

The Socialist League at Hammersmith, England, included the craftsman and designer, William Morris, who is standing in the second row with his hand on his chest.

of the franchise also offered hope that progress might come without a revolution that, given the strength of the state, seemed to even some revolutionaries to be increasingly unlikely. Reform socialists were willing to cooperate with non-socialist parties to achieve an extension of the franchise and concluded that socialism could come through the ballot box.

In 1881, H. M. Hyndman (1842–1921), a British speculator in colonial business ventures and former Conservative who had come under the influence of Marx's writing (so much so that he borrowed liberally from his work), founded the small Social Democratic Federation in Britain. It organized marches in London and in the northern industrial cities protesting against economic hardship. In 1884, a group of intellectuals formed the Fabian Society, which took its name from the Roman dictator Fabius, known for his delaying tactics. Committed to gradualism, the Fabians took the tortoise as their emblem. The Fabians were influenced by an American writer, Henry George. The author of the best-selling *Progress and Poverty*, George argued that the great gulf in Britain between rich and poor could be lessened by the imposition of a "single tax" on land, which would force wealthy landowners to pay more taxes. The "single taxers" believed that socialism could be gradually implemented through reform. Fabians started reading groups in London and other major cities, and some were elected to municipal offices, where they worked to improve workers' housing conditions.

Some German socialists, too, believed that the state could be influenced to carry out reforms that would improve the lives of workers and that one day socialists might obtain a parliamentary majority. Most did not accept

Marx's contention that the working class could only take power through revolution.

In 1863, Ferdinand Lassalle (1825–1864), the son of a Prussian merchant, had formed the first independent workers' party in any of the German states. Lassalle only lived a year more—killed in a duel at age thirty-nine by the fiancé of the woman he loved. His socialist party, in principle internationalist in outlook, was small and carried no political weight. In 1875, however, the German Social Democratic Party (S.P.D.), was founded. Despite official proscription in 1878, it slowly grew into a mass political party. At its party congress at Erfurt in 1891, Karl Kautsky (1854–1938), Marx's determined disciple, convinced the S.P.D. to reject reformism and adopt his revolutionary program. Accepting Marx's materialist view of history, which stressed class struggle, Kautsky argued that capitalism's defeat was inevitable. But the S.P.D.'s program also included a list of demands that were decidedly reformist in tone, including proportional representation, political rights for women, and the eight-hour workday for workers. Furthermore, Edward Bernstein (1850–1932), the son of a Berlin plumber who became a railway engineer, rejected in his *Evolutionary Socialism* (1898) the Marxists' insistence that capitalist society was on the verge of final collapse by proving that it was not.

The S.P.D.'s popular vote in the elections for the Reichstag rose from less than 10 percent in 1884 to almost 35 percent in 1912. It earned the support of most workers and many middle-class voters as well. Women, who could join the party following the passage of a national law on associations in 1908 but who still were not permitted to vote, added to the ranks of the S.P.D., which had more than a million members in 1914. Nonetheless, despite the membership of women, the party showed no interest in movements for women's rights, believing that only the end of capitalism could lead to women's equality.

The S.P.D. worked to build cradle-to-grave social institutions that would give members a sense that they belonged to a special culture, establishing consumer cooperatives, choral societies, and cycling clubs. Unlike French socialists, the S.P.D. not only developed a close alliance with the trade union movement but helped create unions.

The S.P.D. became the largest and best-organized socialist party in Europe, publishing more than a hundred newspapers and magazines and holding political meetings and social events. The party's organization and reformism influenced the evolution of similar parties in Belgium, Austria, and Switzerland. The S.P.D. remained, however, caught in the paradox of struggling by electoral means for social and political reform in a society that was fundamentally undemocratic.

In France, the reform socialists were known as "possibilists" because they supported the republic and, in that context, espoused political pressure to win all possible social reforms and believed that socialism would come through the ballot box. They disparaged their revolutionary Guesdist rivals as "impossibilists." Yet, during elections, revolutionary and reform socialists often put their differences behind them, winning control over the municipal governments of several predominantly working-class towns. But the results of "municipal socialism," while subsidizing services for ordinary people, were limited by the strongly centralized French state.

When the reform socialist Alexander Millerand (1859–1943) accepted a cabinet post in 1899, the split between revolutionary and reform socialists was accentuated. To Guesdists, the reform socialists were propping up the bourgeois republic by participating in the government. In 1904, the Socialist International, meeting in Amsterdam, supported Kautsky's proposal that the congress condemn reformism and parliamentarianism.

In 1905, Jean Jaurès (1859–1914), a former philosophy professor whose energy, organizational skills, and stirring oratory swept him to national prominence, achieved the unification of French socialists with the formation of the French Section of the Working-Class International (S.F.I.O.), although the differences between the Guesdists and reformists could not be swept under the rug. The support of some shopkeepers, teachers, and peasants, as well as most workers, helped the socialists become the second largest party in France, gaining in 1914 almost a fifth of the seats in the Chamber of Deputies.

Italian and Spanish socialists had to overcome the entrenched power of local elites, repression (including the jailing in 1887 of the first Italian socialist deputies), and the strong attraction of anarchism, particularly in southern Italy and Sicily. The Italian Socialist Party, founded in 1892, made few inroads in Italy's impoverished south. To many southern workers

The French socialist leader Jean Jaurès delivering a speech beneath a red flag.

and peasants, the party seemed just another obtrusive northern institution, although it did win some support among agricultural workers. By 1912, the revolutionary faction had gained control of the party. The Spanish Socialist Party, founded in 1879, gained a sizable following only in industrial Asturias and the Basque region. The first socialists were not elected to the Spanish Parliament until 1909.

The Anarchists

While socialists were mobilizing in the hope of seizing control of the state, anarchists wanted its abolition, although not all anarchists advocated violence to achieve this end. Anarchism was never more than a minority movement and, hampered by distrust of political organization itself, it had relatively few adherents.

The dramatic increase in the reach of European states in the nineteenth century encouraged the development of anarchism, a philosophy with few roots in earlier periods. In contrast with socialism, anarchism was the very antithesis of a philosophy of political organization because anarchists associated politics itself with a tacit recognition of the state's existence. Socialists had expelled the anarchists from the founding congress of the Second International in 1896 even before the anarchists could storm out in protest.

While many anarchists believed in the violent overthrow of the state, others believed that voluntary mutualism would make the state superfluous. Prince Peter Kropotkin (1842–1921), a Russian geographer, held a vision of a gentle society of equals living in harmony without the strictures

Peter Kropotkin's publication *The Spirit of Revolt.*

of the state. Kropotkin's desire for anarchist communism was rooted not only in his first-hand views of the misery of the Russian masses but also in his own experience living in the Jura Mountains of Switzerland and France in the 1860s, where watchmakers and farmers seemed to coexist in relative prosperity without the benefit, or hindrance, of a state. Kropotkin, like the philosophe Jean-Jacques Rousseau, espoused the primitive as a natural end in itself, believing that each person was born a *tabula rasa,* or blank slate, and then corrupted by society, above all, by the state.

Anarchism gained some adherents in France, the strongest, most centralized state in Europe, but above all in Italy and Spain, two countries in which the national state appeared to many people as a foreign intruder, and in Argentina, a Latin American nation influenced by Spanish and Italian migrants. There was also a smattering of anarchists among recent migrants to the United States in the last decades of the century. In contrast, anarchism found almost no following in Germany, where respect for the state seemed endemic among socialists as well as supporters of the imperial monarchy, and in Great Britain, the least centralized, but also one of the most nationalist states in Western Europe.

A loose organization of anarchists, the International Working-Class Alliance, known as the "Black International" because of the color of the anarchist flag, maintained contacts among anarchists in France, Italy, and the United States. But for the most part, anarchists formed small groups, or struck out on their own. Anti-statist traditions and resistance against local elites and the influence of the Catholic Church aided the recruitment of anarchists in southern Spain and southern Italy. Anarchism also grew in the rugged southern Spanish province of Andalusia, where peasants and rural laborers struggled for higher wages, the abolition of piecework, and the division of landed estates, and where anarchism took on a millenarian character stripped of most of the trappings of organized religion.

Andalusian anarchists told the story of one of their own who, as he lay dying, whispered to one of his religious relatives to summon a priest and a lawyer. Relieved that the anarchist seemed at the last moment to be accepting the conventions of religion by accepting the last rites of the Church and drawing up a will, his relatives sent for both. When they arrived, the anarchist beckoned them to stand on either side of his deathbed. As they leaned forward, one to hear his confession, the other to write down his will, the anarchist proclaimed, "Now, like Christ, I can die between two thieves."

In the 1880s and 1890s, a wave of anarchist assassinations and bombings shook Europe. To violent anarchists, "propaganda by the deed" had a social purpose; claiming to act in the name of the people, perpetrators hoped to spark a revolution. Michael Bakunin's Italian disciple Enrico Maletesta (1853–1932), who had a following in Spain and Argentina as well, expressed the bitter frustration of anarchists who had virtually nothing: "Do you not know that every bit of bread they [the wealthy] eat is taken from your children, every fine present they give to their wives means the poverty, hunger, cold and even perhaps the prostitution of yours?" Bakunin (see Chapter 19) had believed that a single violent act might shock people into a chain-reaction revolution. "A single deed," Kropotkin had once said, "is better propaganda than a thousand pamphlets."

Anarchists killed six heads of states beginning in 1881, when members of People's Will assassinated Tsar Alexander II. Other victims included King Umberto I of Italy, who was killed in 1900 after escaping two other attempts on his life, and President William McKinley of the United States, who was gunned down in 1901. The assassination of the Italian king revealed anarchism's loose international links: his assassin was sent by a group of Italian anarchists living in Paterson, New Jersey.

In 1892–1894, a wave of bombings terrified Paris. Jean Ravachol, an impoverished worker, had thrown one of the bombs. "See this hand," Ravachol told horrified judge and jurors, "it has killed as many bourgeois as it has fingers!" At the same time, he was teaching his landlord's daughter to read. "I shall be avenged," he shouted shortly before the blade of the guillotine severed his head. So widely did Ravachol become known that his name became a verb in the French dictionary: to "*ravacholiser*" is to wipe out one's enemy.

More attacks followed. In March 1893, an unemployed worker unable to feed his family threw a small bomb into the Chamber of Deputies, slightly injuring several members. French President Sadi Carnot (1837–1894) turned down an appeal for mercy for the perpetrator. Next, another worker tossed a bomb into a café near the Saint-Lazare railroad station, killing one man and injuring about twenty other people. "One does not kill an innocent person in striking the first bourgeois one sees," he told the shocked judge. On June 24, 1894, an Italian anarchist assassinated Carnot. The wave of anarchist attacks subsided in France but continued in Spain, where the government tortured and executed militant anarchists. But with the rise of mass socialist parties and unions, anarchism faded into the fringes of popular protest.

The Syndicalists

European trade unions grew in number and size as they began to join workers across trades and attracted some unskilled workers as well as craftsmen and skilled workers. At the turn of the century, syndicalism developed as an ideology that held that union organization could provide a means for workers to gain control of their industries and of the state itself. In this way, free associations of producers would eventually replace the state. Syndicalists rejected participation in political life, refusing to accept the underlying assumption of most socialists that the principal value of trade unions lay in their serving as places of recruitment for socialist party members. Syndicalism, which was centered in France, Spain, and Italy, was sometimes called anarcho-syndicalism, because of its anti-statist thrust.

A retired engineer who proudly wore the prestigious legion of honor awarded by the French state, Georges Sorel (1847–1922) seemed an unlikely candidate to plan any revolution. But Sorel's *Reflections on Violence* (1908) encouraged direct syndicalist action against capitalism and the state, until a "general strike" by workers would bring both to their knees. By the general strike, Sorel meant a series of simultaneous walkouts that would shut down factories and lead to revolution. This hope, or "myth" in the sense of a widely accepted belief capable of motivating action, firmed the resolve of syndicalist workers to demand concessions from their employers.

The French syndicalist Fernand Pelloutier (1867–1901) inspired the establishment of labor exchanges in France beginning with that in Paris in 1887. Labor exchanges gathered information on available jobs and provided small sums of money to assist workers en route to finding a job in another city. By 1895, more than 400,000 French workers had joined labor exchanges through the auspices of their trade unions. The municipal governments of many industrial cities and towns subsidized these labor exchanges, which for many workers provided a model for the organization of a post-revolutionary working-class culture.

The period 1895–1907 is sometimes referred to as "the heroic age of syndicalism" in France because so many strikes spread through so many industries there, as elsewhere in Europe. More than a thousand strikes in France occurred in 1904 alone. The state sometimes intervened with a heavy hand on behalf of employers, and troops fired on and killed demonstrators on several occasions. The most infamous examples were during a peaceful demonstration on behalf of the eight-hour day on May Day, 1891, in the small northern industrial town of Fourmies, and during the "revolt of the South" in 1907, when vineyard owners and vine-tenders protested the state tax on drink.

Italy was a particularly fertile ground for syndicalism. Italian anarchists participated in the waves of strikes and insurrections in Sicily in 1893–1894. Disturbances occurred in Milan in 1898 after workers demanded government control of food prices, the end of taxes on bread, and a further expansion of the suffrage. In fighting that pitted the industrial suburbs against soldiers, nearly 200 workers were killed and hundreds were wounded. When southern Italian and Sicilian agricultural laborers went on strike in 1908, landlords hired private armies, which joined with Italian soldiers to crush them. The number of labor exchanges grew from fourteen in 1900 to seventy-six two years later. Violent disturbances during Red Week shook Ancona and Bologna in June 1914.

Anarcho-syndicalists dominated the labor movement in Barcelona, particularly among dockworkers. In Catalonia's largest city, dockside contacts with Latin American anarchists accentuated anarchist influence; so, too, did the persistence of small-scale industry, the defiance of the wealthiest employers, and police repression orchestrated from Madrid. Waves of strikes took place in Catalonia in 1902, 1906, and 1909, the latter followed by a bloody insurrection ("Tragic Week"). But gradually in Spain, as in France and Italy, revolutionary rhetoric gave way to the pursuit of concrete economic gains.

CHANGES AND CONTINUITIES IN BRITISH POLITICAL LIFE

Queen Victoria's longevity—she ruled Britain and its vast empire from 1837 until 1901—symbolized British social and political stability. She ruled with dignity, also endearing herself to her people on the occasion of her silver jubilee in 1887 by wearing a simple bonnet (albeit one with diamonds) instead of her crown. The Prince of Wales inherited the throne as King Edward VII (ruled 1901–1910). Edward could not have been much more different than his mother, with whom he constantly battled and whom he often embarrassed. He indulged his extravagant tastes in prize horses, good food, fine wines, gambling, and beautiful women.

Prime Ministers William Gladstone and Benjamin Disraeli helped bring mass political life to Britain. British conservatives did not form a mass party before the end of the nineteenth century. As prime minister, Disraeli sought to accommodate conservatives to the era of mass political life. Realizing that his party, which had long been almost exclusively based in the British landed elite and closely tied to the Anglican Church, would have to outbid their Liberal rivals for votes or be condemned to oblivion, he made British nationalism and imperialism part of Conservative Party platforms. He thus expanded the popular appeal of his party. Disraeli created a modern national party organization. Gladstone embarked on whistle-stop "Midlothian" campaigns—so named for one of his first stops that began in

William Gladstone stumping before the election of 1885.

late 1879. His audiences were made up of anyone who wanted to come to the railroad station to hear him. This forced Conservatives to put aside their feelings that such appeals were vulgar, too "American." But Gladstone was no democrat, insisting "I am a thoroughgoing inequalitarian."

In 1885, the Liberal maverick Joseph Chamberlain (1836–1914), a successful manufacturer and radical mayor of Birmingham who wore a monocle in his right eye and an orchid in his buttonhole, carried a Liberal "unauthorized program" to the people. He promised something for almost everybody—including free education and the maintenance of common land and small plots of land for the poor. Chamberlain became a professional politician who helped move British politics away from the leadership of aristocrats for whom political machinations had been a favorite hobby.

The third Reform Act of 1884 added 2 million more voters to the rolls by enfranchising agricultural laborers, among others excluded by the second Reform Act of 1867. With women still excluded from the vote, the only adult males who could not vote were those without a fixed residence, sons living at home with their parents and not paying rent, and domestic servants. The Redistribution Act of 1885 disenfranchised some underpopulated districts while increasing the representation of many urban areas. The establishment of single-member constituencies compensated Conservatives, balancing potential Liberal gains in urban areas.

Irish Home Rule

Despite the reforms achieved by the Liberals, they continued to be faced with the problem of Ireland, which reflected the dilemmas of national identity in late nineteenth-century Europe. In 1868, Gladstone had announced that the most pressing mission of his new government was to "pacify Ireland." In 1869, the Liberal prime minister pushed through both houses of Parliament a bill that disestablished the Protestant Church of Ireland, since Ireland was overwhelmingly Catholic. But to many Irish it seemed that only by owning land could Irish peasants reach any degree of prosperity. The Irish Land Act of 1870 provided tenants with compensation for improvements they had undertaken and protected them from being evicted from property without just cause. But English landlords were not about to turn over lands in Ireland to the peasants who rented from or worked for them. The long depression that began in 1873 drastically reduced the price of agricultural commodities, thus making it more difficult for tenant-farmers to meet their rent payments. In 1879, the Irish Land League, drawing on the remnants of the secret Irish Republican Brotherhood (known in Gaelic as the Fenians) and sworn to win independence, began to pressure Parliament for gradual land reform.

Gladstone's determination to make Ireland his ongoing moral crusade met with opposition within his own Liberal Party, which depended on sup-

Charles Parnell splits the Irish party over Home Rule.

port from Whig landowners in Ireland to maintain a parliamentary majority over Conservatives. Charles Stewart Parnell (1846–1891), a Liberal Irish Protestant, began to build a small parliamentary coalition in favor of Home Rule, which meant the establishment of a separate Irish Parliament, but not outright independence. He managed to get the Irish Catholic Church on the side of Home Rule. Parnell's program, however, fell short of the demands of the Land League, which wanted immediate and sweeping land reform, and the revived Irish Republican Brotherhood, which insisted on complete Irish independence.

During 1879–1882, Irish farmers undertook a "land war" of protest. Irish tenants and laborers began to shun farmers who took over the leases of peasants evicted for nonpayment of rent. A certain Captain Boycott, the agent of a large landowner, was one of the first targets; his name became synonymous with such a strategy. The British government replied with repression, suspending the writ of Habeas Corpus in Ireland in 1881. However, that same year, Gladstone also pushed through a bill (by threatening to dissolve Parliament) protecting any Irish tenant from eviction who could pay one year's back rent. Nonetheless, Irish leaders, who now wanted independence rather than reform, continued to agitate against the British. Parnell was sent to prison for his activities. Moreover, opposition to Home Rule mounted in Parliament among MPs who argued that concessions had encouraged violence. A year later, the British government ordered Parnell's release from prison, in the hope that he would help end disorder in Ireland in exchange for the future passage of a bill to help tenants.

In 1882, Irish republicans hacked to death two British officials who had been walking in Phoenix Park in Dublin after having just arrived in Ireland. The assassinations shocked English public opinion. In response to the Phoenix Park murders, and to more than thirty other deaths in Ireland at the hands of Irish republicans, a Coercion Act facilitated the government repression of the republicans by eliminating some rights of arrested individuals; it led to the arrest and hanging of five of those responsible for the assassinations.

Liberals remained divided over Home Rule. Gladstone, already under Conservative attack because forces sent to relieve General Charles "Chinese" Gordon in the Sudan had arrived too late to save the popular British hero (see Chapter 22), resigned from government in 1885. But he returned to power the next year, convinced that nothing less than Home Rule would bring peace to Ireland, as well as keep Irish voters in the Liberal camp.

In 1886, Gladstone proposed a Home Rule bill intended to establish an Irish Parliament and allow Irish control over most affairs of government but that stopped short of outright independence. The bill did not pass, and Gladstone's government fell as Home Rule divided the Liberal Party. Joseph Chamberlain led the defection of the Liberal Unionists from the Liberal Party over the issue of Home Rule. With the Liberal Unionists, Chamberlain believed that Britain had to hold on to Ireland at all costs. Obsessed with his fear that Britain's power would decline, he believed Irish Home Rule might start a chain reaction that could bring about the collapse of the British Empire.

After the failure of the first Home Rule bill in 1886, the Conservatives formed a government. Moderate bills passed during Conservative governments provided Irish farmers with some relief through land reform but did not end Irish demands for Home Rule or for independence. When in 1892 the elderly Gladstone became prime minister for the fourth and last time, he again proposed Home Rule. However, he had split with Charles Parnell, who had fallen into public disrepute when it was learned in 1889 that the Irish leader had long been a lover of Kitty O'Shea, the wife of an Irish Liberal MP active in the campaign for Home Rule. Captain William O'Shea had filed for divorce, naming Parnell as co-respondent. The scandal had ruined Parnell, taking away his political influence. This tipped the balance against Home Rule, which passed through Commons in 1893, but was tripped up in the House of Lords.

New Contours in British Political Life

The Conservatives again came to power in 1895, and retained the reins of government for ten years. Fearful of having too small a base of support in the age of mass politics, the Conservative Party, long identified with protecting the interests of the landed elite and the Established Church, had greatly expanded its appeal in the 1890s. The agricultural depression and Parliament combined to undermine social hierarchy and privilege in Britain, cutting into English noble fortunes. Some Liberals now joined the Conservative Party. Like their counterparts in France and Germany, the British Conservative Party became more aggressively nationalist, imperialist, and resolutely antisocialist. The Liberal Unionists had allied with the Conservatives over Home Rule. In 1895, their leader Joseph Chamberlain joined the Conservative government as colonial secretary. Gradually the Conservative Party absorbed the extraparliamentary Navy League and the Anti-Socialist Union.

Frustrated by the Conservative government's refusal to initiate parliamentary bills of social reform and by employers' attempts to weaken the unions by hiring non-union labor, British trade unionism entered a more aggressive phase during the depression-ridden last two decades of the century. British trade unions during the middle decades of the century had been largely limited to craftsmen and skilled workers who shared in the prosperity of the booming Victorian economy and could afford union dues. The Trades Union Congress (created in 1868) had provided a forum for organized labor, although during the long depression, the financial resources of unions, limited in the best of circumstances, became even more depleted. During the late 1880s, British unions began to be more militant. This "new unionism" was characterized by the organization of semiskilled workers, including many iron and steel factory workers. It was more militant than the old craft unionism and had limited goals. One union activist contrasted the members of the old craft unions with the semiskilled "new unionists" as they appeared to him in 1890 at a meeting:

> Physically, the 'old' unionists were much bigger than the new. . . . A great number of them looked like respectable city gentlemen; wore very good coats, large watch chains, and high hats and in many cases were of such splendid build and proportions that they presented an aldermanic, not to say a magisterial form and dignity. Amongst the new delegates not a single one wore a tall hat. They looked [like] workmen; they were workmen. They were not such sticklers for formality or court procedure, but were guided more by common sense.

In 1887, for the first time since the last Chartist marches in London in 1848, English workers went into the streets in protest, demonstrating against high rates of unemployment and the high cost of living. On November 13—"Black Monday"—store owners slammed their doors shut amid a "red fear" in central London. The police charged crowds of workers, killing 2 and wounding about 100 protesters.

The first test for these new unions came at the London docks, site of endemic industrial conflict. In 1889, following a victory by gas workers in a London strike that achieved the eight-hour workday, dockworkers struck for a minimum wage. They were led by Ben Tillett (1860–1943). Born in Bristol, Tillett had at the age of seven begun cutting slabs of clay in a brickyard, then ran away with Old Joe Barker's Circus as an acrobat, before joining the merchant marine and then the navy. Finding work as a dockyard laborer, he helped organize thousands of unskilled laborers.

Supporting the unskilled workers, skilled workers marched through central London, a contemporary remembered, "in long scarlet coats, pink stockings and velvet caps, with huge pewter badges at their breasts, like decorated amphibious huntsmen." Australian workers sent funds that helped tide the strikers over. Cardinal Henry Manning (1808–1892), leader of Britain's Catholics, sympathized with the workers' cause and served as a strike mediator. After five weeks, the dock companies capitulated. The strike, which succeeded in obtaining a minimum wage for the dockworkers and the right to overtime pay, encouraged union growth and strike militancy in the following decade. Tillett's new dockworkers' union soon had 30,000 members.

Union organization industry by industry—such as that of the miners', gasworkers', and dockworkers' unions—helped bring together skilled and unskilled workers. But hundreds of thousands of casual laborers, particularly the part-time workers living in London's teeming East End, still were unintegrated into the labor movement. A metalworker described the great gap between skilled and unskilled workers: "Between the artisan and the unskilled worker a gulf is fixed. While the former resents the spirit in which he believes the followers of 'genteel occupations' look down upon him, he in his turn looks down upon the laborer. The artisan creed with regard to laborers is, that the latter are an inferior class, and that they should be made to know and kept in their place." Most casual laborers were uneducated and did not belong to friendly societies. For them the independence of the skilled worker, and the sense of "respectability" that went with it remained only a dream, particularly as wages had not kept up with inflation. While British strikes lacked some of the drama of French work stoppages, strikes in 1897 and 1898 (including Britain's first national walkout, which ended in the workers' defeat) reflected the growing reach of the new unions.

The state went on the offensive against the unions. In 1901, in resolving a railway case in Wales, the House of Lords left unions and their officers legally responsible for losses sustained by companies during strikes. This anti-union Taff Vale decision led to the creation of the Labour Party. The Labour Party had its origins in the small Independent Labour Party, which had been founded in 1893 by MP Keir Hardie (1856–1915). This rough-hewn Scottish miner had outraged the House of Commons by chiding members for sending a congratulatory message to the queen on the birth of a great-grandson instead of a message of condolence to the families of several hundred miners killed in an accident in a mine shaft in Wales. The Labour Party vowed to represent workers in Parliament and specifically to bring about the repeal of the Taff Vale decision.

A split within the Liberal-Unionist-Conservative bloc brought ten years of Conservative government to an end. Some political leaders, including Joseph Chamberlain, supported protective tariffs, believing that they would increase British prosperity by creating a large imperial market.

Chamberlain resigned from the government in 1903 in order to campaign for tariffs and organized a Tariff Reform League. Many Conservatives, including Prime Minister Arthur Balfour (1848–1930), believed that voters preferred traditional free trade policies because they feared protective tariffs would increase food prices. Unable to resolve the split within his party, Balfour resigned in December 1905, and the Liberals swept to a crushing victory in the 1906 elections. Promising to repeal the Taff Vale decision, they garnered many working-class votes, and did well in Wales and Scotland, bastions of Liberal support. The Labour Party, which had managed to win only one seat in 1900, now sent twenty-nine MPs to the House of Commons. True to its word, under the Liberal government, Parliament reversed the Taff Vale decision with the Trade Disputes Act of 1906, which legalized picketing and relieved unions of the legal responsibility for financial losses caused by union members during strikes.

In 1908, Herbert Asquith (1852–1928), a wealthy lawyer and the new head of the Liberal Party, became prime minister. Like the Conservatives, he supported British imperial causes. But dynamic, ambitious, and charismatic Welshman David Lloyd George was the rising star of the Liberals. He had come into the public eye for his criticism of the conduct of the Boer War (see Chapter 22). While crusading against the Conservative Party, which he still considered to represent only the interests of wealthy British landlords, Lloyd George worked to continue the Gladstonian reformist tradition to counter the drift of union members toward the Labour Party. The Liberal government established local boards to set minimum industrial wages. Such a step involved the British government in bargaining between employers and workers to an extent hitherto unseen.

In 1909, Lloyd George (who was chancellor of the Exchequer) proposed a budget that called for increased public benefits to be partially funded by taxes on inheritance and on unearned income and uncultivated land. These "supertaxes" (which were in fact quite small) would fall on the richest families of the nation. About a tenth of the British population garnered half of the national income, 125,000 people owned a third of the country, and twenty-seven lords owned a tenth of England. Lloyd George's proposed budget was popular. He compared the costs of maintaining "a fully-equipped duke" to that of a new "Dreadnought" battleship (see Chapter 23), depicting the aristocratic families as parasitical leeches maintained at public expense.

The Liberal quest for reform, as well as votes, turned on the House of Lords, dominated by Conservatives. In 1909 in the Osborne judgment, the Lords had ruled in favor of a railway worker who had sued his union with the goal of keeping union funds from being used to support Labour candidates for Commons. Like the Taff Vale case, this Osborne judgment struck a damaging blow against the unions. In a climate of social confrontation, the House of Lords vetoed the 1909 budget, exercising a right that it had not used for decades. Asquith called the House of Lord's veto a "break with the constitution and a usurpation of the rights of the Commons." He dissolved Parliament, confident of winning the new elections.

Early in 1910, the Liberals returned to power with the help of Irish nationalists and of Labour, but with a smaller majority than anticipated. Asquith's Parliament Act of 1911 proposed to eliminate the right of the House of Lords to veto any financial bill. Many Britons viewed the passage of such a bill as a final blow to noble privilege. The act also specified that any bill that the Lords did not pass after it had been approved on three occasions by Commons would become law if two years had passed since it had first been introduced in Parliament.

When Asquith threatened to ask King George V (who had succeeded his father as king in May 1910) to create enough new peerages to pass the bill, the House of Lords, despite the opposition of the intransigent "Diehards," approved the Parliament Act in 1911. This was the most significant event in British constitutional history since the electoral franchise had been doubled in 1867. The House of Lords eliminated its own constitutional veto, completing the long revolution in British political life that had begun with the passage of the Reform Act of 1832, which had eliminated most of the disproportionate power of the British nobility. The House of Lords then reversed the Osborne judgment.

A wave of strikes between 1910 and 1912 reflected bitter relations between employers and workers and became national political issues. In 1911, a walkout by seamen, stevedores, bargemen, and ship repairers spread rapidly in London, Manchester, and Liverpool, where troops shot and killed two strikers during riots. The prospect of a food shortage forced the government's hand. Through binding arbitration, the strikers won raises. A national rail strike followed after the railway companies went back on terms of an earlier agreement; it ended in compromise settlements. Next, when the Miners' Federation called the first general coal strike, more than 800,000 men went out, which left another 1.3 million without work. With British industry floundering, the miners gained a minimum wage. But when dockers failed to achieve their strike goals in July 1912, Britain's largest wave of strikes to date ended with the workers' capitulation.

Even Ben Tillett reflected the commitment of almost all British labor leaders and workers to peaceful reform. Denouncing "hare brained chatterers and magpies of Continental revolutionists," he espoused compulsory industrial arbitration as the means of achieving compromise in labor disputes. In any case, collective bargaining had become commonplace in the 1890s, with conciliation and arbitration boards established in many localities. That many strikes ended in defeat may have helped turn British workers further toward parliamentary reformism. Minimal reforms passed by Parliament helped convince many workers that accommodation with the state would ultimately improve their conditions.

Irish Home Rule, still a major political issue, seemed almost inevitable. Irish politicians, peasants, and poets shared the burst of nationalist senti-

William Butler Yeats.

ment characteristic of the first decade of the twentieth century. The Gaelic League popularized Irish music and encouraged people to speak Gaelic, not English. The great poet William Butler Yeats (1865–1939), who helped create a native Irish theater in Dublin, contributed to a literary nationalism that sometimes glossed over class differences among the Irish: "Parnell came down the road and said to a cheering man: 'Ireland will get her freedom, and you shall still break stone.'" Such literature also tended to romanticize the Irish as peasants made virtuous by primitive poverty. In the collection of short stories, *The Dubliners* (1912) by James Joyce (1882–1941), the countryside appears as an idyllic escape from the confusion of Ireland's rapidly growing, impoverished metropolis.

If Irish nationalists would accept nothing less than complete independence from Britain, Irish Protestants living in Ulster, who outnumbered Catholics there by two to one, opposed any measure of Home Rule. To them, Home Rule would be Catholic "Rome Rule." In 1913, Ulster Protestants formed a paramilitary army of volunteers. An Irish Republican Army added men and arms. Century-old wounds split open again, and Ireland seemed on the verge of civil war. In September 1914, Parliament passed a Home Rule bill, despite the intransigent opposition of the Lords. But with Britain—and all the powers of Europe—approaching war, the details were left for the uncertain future. Most Irish Catholics still wanted complete independence, but Ulster Protestants would accept no change at all.

REPUBLICAN FRANCE

In republican France, too, mass politics and fervent nationalism went hand in hand. This emerging nationalism was not that of the French Revolution, when French armies had poured across the frontiers, ostensibly to carry "liberty, fraternity, and equality" to other lands. After the Revolutions of 1830 and 1848, the new regimes had seemed poised, respectively, to bring independence to Belgium and to "liberate" Savoy from Piedmont. Now, following defeat at the hands of Prussia in 1871 and the proclamation of the powerful German Empire, French nationalists became obsessed with recapturing Alsace and Lorraine from Germany. At the same time, French nationalism moved from the political left to the right, in tune with other European nationalisms.

In the meantime, the gradual victory of moderate republicanism in France in the six years after the Commune (see Chapter 19) reflected the fact that most people in France wanted a republic based upon mass political participation. Although a monarchical restoration at first seemed highly likely, the legislative elections of February 1871 gave monarchists a majority in the National Assembly that was to determine France's political future.

Monarchists and Republicans

The Bourbon pretender was the count of Chambord, a lazy man of mediocre intelligence who lived in an Austrian castle and amused himself by playing cards and telling dirty jokes and anti-Semitic stories to his cronies. The Orleanist pretender to the throne was the relatively dashing count of Paris. Yet Chambord seemed to hold the upper hand, for his was the old royal line. But, unlike the count of Paris, he was childless, and his death would bring the end of the direct Bourbon line. A compromise, by which Chambord would become king with the count of Paris as his heir, fell through when the former refused to be king under the tricolor flag, which he identified with the French Revolution.

The close association of monarchism with the Catholic Church led many people to agree with the assessment of the radical republican Léon Gambetta (1838–1882) that "clericalism, there is the enemy." Republicans opposed the political domination of the "notables," the wealthiest men in France. The republic found a groundswell of support from those Gambetta called "the new social strata" (les nouvelles couches), the shopkeepers, café owners, prosperous peasants, craftsmen, and schoolteachers, who often stood for the republic in small towns and villages— the moderate, but adamantly republican lower ranks of the bourgeoisie. The charismatic Gambetta's whistle-stop tours of the provinces reflected the rise of mass politics in France.

Adolphe Thiers, an Orleanist converted to moderate republicanism, resigned under monarchist pressure as provisional head of state in 1873. Prussian troops marched out of France that year after the French government finished paying off the war indemnity, raised by loans and a public subscription. The monarchists, seeing their majority in the National Assembly eroding with each by-election, elected as president Marshal MacMahon, a hero of the Crimean War and the Italian War of 1859, who favored a monarchist restoration. The new government of "moral order," closely tied to the Church, undertook a massive purge of republican mayors, censored newspapers, closed hundreds of cafés, and banned the public celebration of the French Revolution on July 14.

The government of France was a republic with monarchist political institutions. In January 1874, the National Assembly passed the Wallon Amendment by one vote, stating that henceforth "the president of the Republic" would be elected by the Senate and the Chamber of Deputies. The lower house drafted a republican constitution in 1875, but one that seemed so indefinite that the state could easily enough have been converted into a monarchy.

Universal manhood suffrage determined the composition of the Chamber of Deputies. Each district elected a single representative, which gave monarchists an advantage, as local notables would be the most likely beneficiaries from last-minute political negotiations before the second ballot of each election. The Senate would be elected indirectly through a system that was radically tilted to over-represent conservative rural interests. Yet, despite heavy-handed government and ecclesiastical pressure on voters, more than twice as many republicans were elected as monarchists to the Chamber of Deputies in 1876. MacMahon was therefore forced to select a moderate republican, Jules Simon (1814–1896), as premier.

The republican majority in the National Assembly sought to limit the power of the president who was, after all, a monarchist. On May 16, 1877, MacMahon initiated a political crisis by forcing Simon's resignation and naming a monarchist in his place. When the Chamber of Deputies withheld its approval, MacMahon dissolved it and called for new elections. He purged the prefectorial ranks of staunch republicans, and embarked, with the help of the Church, on a bitter campaign to defeat Gambetta and other republicans.

However, France's voters returned republicans again, although with a smaller majority. MacMahon named a republican premier, and resigned in 1879. Henceforth the role of the executive authority would be weak because republicans feared that some Napoleonic character—of which MacMahon was a rather pathetic imitation—might try to impose his rule. With the constitutional privilege of dismissing government cabinets that had lost the confidence of the majority of its members, the Chamber of Deputies would dominate the political life of the Third Republic.

In 1881, the Chamber of Deputies passed a controversial bill giving full amnesty to exiled Communards, a measure unthinkable several years earlier. Towns and villages began to put up statues and busts in honor of the republican tradition.

The Third Republic

The governments of the new republic reflected the center of the political spectrum, that of the "opportunists," so-called because many of them accepted a very conservative republic while preferring something more to the center. Resolved to hold the center against the monarchists and the Church on the right and socialists on the extreme left, the opportunists retained the support of peasant proprietors by implementing high agricultural tariffs.

The opportunist republic guaranteed freedom of the press, legalized public gatherings without prior prefectorial authorization, and gave municipal councils the right to elect their own mayors (with the exception of Paris). The president served as something of a chairman of the board to the Chamber of Deputies. He shook hands with everybody, intrigued pleasantly, and helped form coalitions. Governments came and went, giving an exaggerated image of parliamentary impotence and instability.

The educational reforms of the 1880s had the goal not only of making France more literate but also more republican. Jules Ferry (1832–1893) sponsored laws that made primary education free and obligatory. The state allocated money to build village schools. Although priests and nuns stayed on to teach in what were technically lay schools, the debates ensured the animosity of many prelates and practicing Catholics against the "godless" republic. Catholic institutions of higher learning lost the right to be called universities.

General Boulanger and Captain Dreyfus

As the depression accentuated social and political divisions, during the 1880s the parliamentary center began to melt under pressure from right and left. The threat came from the new nationalist right, obsessed with defeat at the hands of Prussia in 1870 and the subsequent loss of Alsace-Lorraine. Nationalism became a potent political ideology. Following the death of Napoleon III's son in 1879, Bonapartists emerged from obscurity to tout the former emperor's cousin, Prince Napoleon Bonaparte (1822–1891), as a potential savior, and then the latter's conservative son, Prince Victor (1862–1926). Some nationalists began to think that the republic was too weak to ever recapture the lost provinces from Germany. This concern with "revenge" against Germany reflected the passing of nationalism from the liberal left to the right wing in France.

The Boulanger Affair was in some ways the birth certificate of the new right in France, the Dreyfus Affair its baptism. In 1887, French rightists began to place their hopes of overthrowing the republic on the dashing figure of General Georges Boulanger (1837–1891), who had risen rapidly through the ranks to become minister of war. During a bitter strike in the small southern mining town of Decazeville in 1886, the general earned sympathy from workers and soldiers by glibly stating that even as he spoke French soldiers were sharing their rations with French workers. His bellicose noises about recapturing Alsace-Lorraine pleased nationalists while irritating Bismarck. Rightist leaders now were convinced that they had found the man who could overthrow the republic, restore the monarchy, or establish a dictatorship. Flattered by all of the attention, Boulanger decided to run as a candidate for the Chamber of Deputies.

The political movement on behalf of Boulanger, who ran in several districts, was arguably the first mass political campaign in France. Funds provided by a wealthy royalist widow helped inundate France with electoral posters and busts and statues of Boulanger. His supporters now battled their political enemies in the streets, bringing unprecedented violence into an electoral campaign, drawing on rising nationalist anti-Semitism, although there were only about 80,000 Jews in a population of 40 million in France.

Boulanger was elected in by-elections in several *départements* but, because he was in the army, he was ineligible to serve in the Chamber of Deputies. At this point, no one was sure what exactly Boulanger represented, no one probably less than the general himself. If his campaign money came from the right, many of his votes came from the left. The opportunist government sent Boulanger to Clermont-Ferrand in central France in order to remove him from the political limelight of the capital. His followers tried to prevent his train from leaving the station.

A political scandal cast a further shadow on the government, giving another twist to the term "opportunist." A prostitute revealed that the Legion of Honor medal was being peddled to the highest bidder. It turned out that one of the most successful salesmen was Daniel Wilson, the ruthless son-in-law of President Jules Grévy, who had used his political connections to make a killing selling these highly coveted awards. Grévy resigned the presidency. When a deputy asked Georges Clemenceau, the feisty anti-clerical Radical, to suggest someone for whom he could vote as a successor, he replied, "Vote for the stupidest!" In this way Sadi Carnot (1837–1894), grandson of the "organizer of victory" during the French Revolution, became president of France.

All of this added to a feeling among some observers that the Third Republic was at the end of its rope. The government declared General Boulanger retired. Now free to run for the Chamber of Deputies, Boulanger was elected deputy from Paris. To his right-wing followers, it seemed that a perfect occasion for a coup d'état had arrived. In January 1889, triumphant crowds gathered in the street, calling out the general's name while Boulanger sat in a restaurant quietly eating his dinner. But his moment had passed. Two years later, government officials convinced the naive general that they held evidence that could lead to his conviction on charges of state treason. Boulanger caught a train to Belgium and, on the grave of his late mistress, took out his army pistol and blew out his brains.

Having survived Boulanger, the republic received an unexpected boost from its old enemy, the Catholic Church, whose "rallying" to the republic began with an archbishop's toast in 1891 in Tunisia. Henceforth, the moderate republicans could draw on political support from the Catholic right against the socialist parties.

The suicide of General Boulanger.

Another scandal gave the anti-parliamentary right a new focus for opposition. In 1881, a French company had begun to dig the Panama Canal under the direction of Ferdinand de Lesseps, who had overseen the construction of the Suez Canal. This canal proved to be even more difficult to build than the Suez Canal because of difficult terrain and malarial conditions. In order to raise additional funds, company officials bribed government officials and journalists in the hope of gathering sufficient support to get the Chamber of Deputies to approve a loan that would be backed by a national lottery. The Chamber of Deputies obligingly approved the plan, but the financial campaign fell short. When the company went broke in 1889, more than half a million investors lost their money.

In 1892, Édouard Drumont's right-wing newspaper *La Libre Parole* published a series of revelations about the scandal. Six years earlier, Drumont had published a book in which he claimed that Jewish financiers were conspiring to dominate France. Now, the fact that some of the directors of the defunct company had been Jewish helped generate support for the League of Patriots, founded in 1892, a nationalist and anti-Semitic organization of the extreme right. But the next year an indulgent court acquitted all but one of those implicated in the scandal.

The next scandal was such a series of dramatic events that it became known for years simply as "the Affair." It pitted right against left, the army, Church, and monarchists against republicans and, in time, socialists, and family against family. Most people in France seemed to hang on every development.

Alfred Dreyfus (1859–1935) was the son of an old Jewish family from Alsace. His family had been peddlers and then textile manufacturers. They were assimilated Jews, proudly considering themselves French. Following the annexation of Alsace by Germany in 1871, the Dreyfus family moved to Paris. In 1894, evidence surfaced—from an unemptied wastepaper basket in the office of a German military attaché—that someone in the French army had been passing secret information to the Germans about French military operations. Circumstantial evidence pointed to Captain Dreyfus—the writing on a list of documents that had been prepared to be handed over to a German contact resembled that of Dreyfus. Arrested on suspicion of treason but maintaining his innocence, Dreyfus refused the arresting officer's offer of a loaded pistol with which he could kill himself. A hurriedly convened and secret court-martial found him guilty of treason. Dreyfus was stripped of his rank and sent to Devil's Island off the coast of South America. Dreyfus, who had never been allowed to see the evidence used against him, and his family insisted that he had been wrongly convicted. Dreyfus' arrest provided Drumont with the opportunity to renew anti-Semitic attacks on the republic.

Dreyfus had few people on his side. But confidential documents continued to disappear from French army offices. Two years later, a new chief of army intelligence, Lieutenant Colonel Georges Picquart, determined to his own satisfaction that the original list of documents had not been penned by Dreyfus, but by Major Walsin Esterhazy. Picquart, who was an unlikely hero in this case because he made no secret of his anti-Semitism,

(*Left*) Édouard Drumont's anti-Semitic newspaper *La Libre Parole* (*The Free Word*), 1893. (*Right*) Captain Alfred Dreyfus.

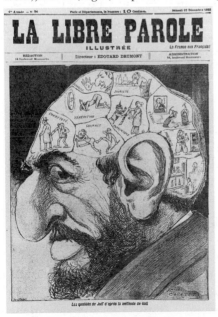

presented his evidence. He assumed that the army would want to work to convict Esterhazy and exonerate Dreyfus. But high-ranking officers who shared Drumont's antirepublican views believed that it was better to have an innocent Jew languishing in increasing depression on Devil's Island than to compromise the army's public image. The army packed Picquart off to a post in Tunisia, and a military court acquitted Esterhazy, despite overwhelming evidence of guilt.

The novelist Émile Zola now took up Dreyfus' case. In January 1898, he wrote an article in a daily newspaper with the bold headline *"J'accuse!"* ("I accuse!"), denouncing the army and the government for covering up the reality of the case. The political right and the Catholic Church hierarchy jumped in on the side of those now known as the "anti-Dreyfusards," seeing the Dreyfus Affair as a conspiracy of Jews and Freemasons to destroy France by undermining the prestige of its army. The newspaper of the Assumptionist Order demanded that all Jews lose their citizenship. Action Française, a right-wing nationalist and monarchist organization led by Charles Maurras (1868–1952), an anti-Semitic novelist, jumped into the fray against Dreyfus, insisting that France's honor was at stake. Although most socialists at first considered the Dreyfus Affair to be a problem for the bourgeois republic, and not their concern, gradually reform socialists began to demand a new trial.

Another officer soon discovered that some new documents had been added to the Dreyfus file. They had been quite badly forged by Lieutenant Colonel Hubert Henry, who hoped they would lead to a new conviction of Dreyfus should the case be reopened. Confronted with the evidence, Henry slit his throat in a military prison. In 1899, the army retried Dreyfus, once again finding him guilty, but this time with "extenuating circumstances." Dreyfus returned, a broken man, to Devil's Island. However, the president of France gave Dreyfus a presidential pardon that year, which allowed him to return to his family, but Dreyfus was not fully exonerated until 1906, when his military rank was restored.

The Radical Republic

Dreyfus' return to France was a republican triumph. It provided the republic with a badly needed period of stability and boosted the Radical Party. The Dreyfus Affair had helped forge a working alliance between moderate republicans, Radicals, and socialists, moving the republic to the left. In 1899, René Waldeck-Rousseau (1846–1904), a moderate republican lawyer, formed a government dominated by Radicals, and accepted socialist support. Alexander Millerand (1859–1943), a reform socialist, became minister of commerce, despite the bitter opposition of many socialists.

The Dreyfus Affair convinced the Radicals that the republic had to purge the army of antirepublican officers. The minister of war began to collect files on right-wing officers and even those who attended Mass.

When news of this project became public, he was forced to resign. The worsening international situation after 1900 expanded the ranks of nationalists to include staunch defenders of the republic, including many officers.

The Radicals, united by anticlericalism, moved to separate church and state against ecclesiastical and conservative opposition. They cited the role of the Jesuit and Assumptionist Orders among the anti-Dreyfusards. In 1902, the Chamber of Deputies, with socialist support, passed legislation exiling religious orders from France. In 1905, church and state were formally separated in France. During the next two years, the state took possession of all ecclesiastical property and assumed responsibility for paying the salaries of priests. Despite papal condemnation and the resistance of some clergy, a *modus vivendi* evolved, with parish councils leasing churches from the state.

The Radical Premier Georges Clemenceau (1841–1929) embodied aggressive French nationalism. The man who later became known as "the "Tiger" had been born into a family of modest noble title; his father was a prominent republican who had been exiled by Napoleon III. The younger Clemenceau began his political career in largely proletarian, artistic Montmartre in Paris. Clemenceau was a wealthy bully and a formidable dueler who hated socialists, unions, and the Catholic Church as much as he did his American ex-wife, whom he had followed by a detective, jailed, and deported. In 1907, he sent troops to crush a determined strike by small property owners and vineyard laborers in the southern town of Narbonne.

In 1911, Premier Joseph Caillaux (1863–1944), unlike Clemenceau, sought accommodation with Germany. The French Socialist Party launched a campaign against militarism and particularly against the extension of the term of military service from two to three years. Anti-militarism remained popular among workers because of the role of troops in the repression of strikes. But the Moroccan confrontation between Germany and France that same year unleashed another wave of nationalism. Besieged by the press for his pacific stand, Caillaux's government fell the following year. Raymond Poincaré (1860–1934), a wealthy lawyer and outspoken nationalist who loved reviewing troops while military bands played, became premier in 1912 and then president in 1913. He eagerly anticipated the chance to win back Alsace and Lorraine and firmed up French support of a Russian role in the Balkans. Poincaré's aggressive nationalism seemed in tune with the times.

Tsarist Russia

Public opinion existed in the Russian Empire, but mass political life did not. Russian liberals believed that the empire could gradually reform itself into a constitutional monarchy. But for the moment, exile was the only safe place from which to criticize the autocracy. Small colonies of political refugees, most of whom were socialists, lived in Geneva, Paris, and London.

Alexander III (ruled 1881–1894), whose father had been assassinated by an anarchist, was in no mood to contemplate any liberalization of Russian imperial institutions. Professors and teachers were brought under stricter state control, and tuition was increased to discourage commoners from going to school. The police received carte blanche to arrest and imprison anyone without reason. But the resulting political trials may have helped the cause of reformers and revolutionaries by serving as tribunals where the autocratic regime was discussed and political issues were brought into the open. What went on in courtrooms helped shape Russian opinion, even when political trials were moved into military courts.

Russification

In the enormous Russian Empire (which had doubled from about 74 million inhabitants in 1861 to about 150 million by 1905), Alexander ordered a vigorous campaign of "Russification," although the Russian people made up only 40 percent of the population. Ukrainians, Poles, and Byelorussians made up the next largest national groups, followed by Lithuanians, Latvians, and Estonians in the Baltic states, Finns, Romanians (in Bessarabia), Crimean Tartars, Armenians, Georgians, and Azeri in the Caucasus, and the Moslem peoples of Central Asia. The tsar banned the use of languages other than Russian in school, and forbade publication in, for example, the Ukrainian language, despite the fact that it was spoken by 25 million people. At the same time, the Russian Orthodox Church launched

A Russian princess in Tartar costume.

campaigns against non-Orthodox religions, which maintained the allegiance of almost a third of the peoples of the empire.

"Russification" firmed the resolve of nationalist groups to persevere in their demands for recognition. The campaign also angered ethnic groups, among them Armenians and Finns, who had been loyal to the tsar. In 1899, the Finnish Assembly was reduced to a "consultative" voice, and Russians replaced Finns in most key administrative positions. In Poland, opposition to Russia grew more daring. The Polish League was founded in 1887 as a conspiratorial organization. The National Democrats were a more moderate nationalist group seeking to keep Polish nationalism alive in Russian Poland, as well as in the German and Austro-Hungarian Empires. Polish socialists hoped eventually to undermine tsardom and create an independent socialist Polish state in which the rights of non-Poles, too, would be recognized.

The Russo-Japanese War (1904–1905)

The Russian Empire, which now reached the Pacific Ocean, began to covet Chinese Manchuria and the peninsula of Korea. The acquisition of Manchuria would permit Russia to construct a more direct rail link to the ice-free Russian port of Vladivostok; that of Korea would protect the new port from possible attack and provide still more ports. In 1894, Japan had goaded China into a war. By the Treaty of Shimonoseki in 1895, the victorious Japanese took the island of Formosa (Taiwan) and gained Chinese recognition of Korea's independence, which placed the peninsula under direct Japanese influence. Japan also acquired the Liaodong (Liaotung) Peninsula (in southern Manchuria), but was forced by Russia, Germany, and France to return it.

Russia viewed the expansion of Japanese interests in the Far East with concern. In 1898, Nicholas II (ruled 1894–1917) signed a treaty with China and obtained a concession to build the Manchurian railway and to construct a port at Port Arthur on the tip of the Liaodong Peninsula, setting up a source of conflict between Japan and Russia. Japan, in turn, signed a treaty in 1902 with the government of Great Britain, Russia's rival for influence in Afghanistan. Britain would remain neutral if Japan and Russia went to war against each other. But Britain would join Japan in any conflict that allied Russia with any other power in a war against Japan.

In February 1904, Japanese torpedo boats launched a surprise attack on the Russian fleet at Port Arthur, destroying a number of ships while the Japanese army drove Russian forces away on land. In March 1905, the Japanese forces defeated the Russians in the bloody battle of Mukden where, for the first time, two armies faced each other across trenches dug for protection. Two months later, the Japanese navy pounced on the Russian fleet, which had spent nine months at sea. The battle of Tsushima ended with nineteen Russian ships sunk, five captured, six forced to neutral ports; only three ships of the fleet reached Vladivostok.

A Russian perspective of Japanese soldiers overrunning Korea at the time of the Russo-Japanese War.

How could the Russian Empire be defeated by a small island nation with no experience fighting a Western power? Only a single-track railway line stretching across thousands of miles supplied the Russian forces. The Russian army was poorly commanded and fighting with outdated artillery and rifles. By the Treaty of Portsmouth (New Hampshire), signed in September 1905 at a conference hastily arranged by President Theodore Roosevelt, Japan took over Russia's lease of the Liaodong Peninsula and Chinese concessions in Manchuria. Russia accepted Japanese influence over Korea. A new world power was born. At the same time, the Russian defeat was a key factor leading to the Revolution of 1905 in Russia.

ITALY

Following the political unification of his country, an Italian politician commented, "We have made Italy: now we must make Italians." The Italian state, despite its centralized character, phalanx of civil servants, police, and large army and navy, seemed irrelevant to many, perhaps even most, of the residents now called Italians. The electoral franchise was small: only about 600,000 men (2.5 percent of the population) were eligible to elect members of the Chamber of Deputies before the expansion of the franchise in 1882, when 2 million voters, or about 10 percent of the population, were enfranchised.

Most Italians remained loyal to their families, towns, regions, and to the Catholic Church (particularly in central and southern Italy), as well as to powerful local leaders or factions. In a country in which almost 70 percent of the population was illiterate in 1871 and 50 percent was still illiterate in 1900, it mattered little that all parts of the peninsula now shared a common written Italian language.

Resistance to the State

Resistance to the state seemed to come naturally. In southern Italy, the Camorra of Naples and the Mafia of Sicily and other criminal organizations with similar codes of honor served as the real basis of authority. Family feuds and vendettas, often accompanied by grisly violence, went on as before. "Italy" was seen as a northern ploy to bilk people out of money through taxes, or to draft their sons into the army, or to undercut what seemed to be the legitimate influence of the local notable, landowner, merchant, or mafioso. To the poor property owners and impoverished laborers trying to scratch out a living, local notables at least could provide what they considered "justice" for the poor. Brigands had traditionally received assistance from the local population, who viewed them as fellow resisters to the state, if not Robin Hoods. Although the state managed to drive bands of brigands out of business in the 1870s, crimes against outsiders remained endemic.

The continued industrialization of Piedmont, Tuscany, and Lombardy, begun in the mid-1890s, made the economic disparities between northern and southern Italy even greater. Northerners dominated Italian politics, as they had Italian unification, treating the people of the south as colonial underlings. Far fewer southerners were eligible to vote than northerners. Mass emigration, principally to the United States and Argentina, could only partially resolve the problems of overpopulation and poverty.

The popes portrayed themselves as Roman prisoners of a godless state. The Church had refused to accept the Law of Papal Guarantees of 1871, which gave it title to the Vatican—Saint Peter's and surrounding ecclesiastical buildings—and the authority to make ecclesiastical appointments within Italy. The popes not only refused to recognize Italy's existence, but banned the faithful from running for elected office or even voting. While some Italian Catholics simply ignored such stern papal warnings, others systematically abstained from casting a ballot. The state paid the salaries of the clergy, but it also confiscated Church property. Secular reforms removed the teaching of theology from the universities, closed convents and monasteries, made priests eligible for military conscription, banned public religious processions, and made civil marriage obligatory. The attitude of the Church hierarchy and prominent laymen to the Italian state was reflected by the headline of one Catholic newspaper after the death of King Victor Emmanuel II: "The King is dead, the Pope is well."

Demonstrations in Milan, 1898.

Centralized Authority

The monarch ruled Italy through a premier and parliament. Italian governments lurched from one political crisis to another in the 1880s, depending on rapidly changing coalitions—a process that became known to critics as *trasformismo*—and on rampant political corruption. King Umberto I (ruled 1878–1900) would leave them alone until his intervention became absolutely imperative. He was lazy, so uneducated that he did not even like to sign his own name if someone was watching, and considered himself above politics. Italy's monarch had more courage—demonstrated in the face of several assassination attempts, including the last, which succeeded—than brains and patience.

The arrogant Francesco Crispi (1819–1901) built longer-lasting political alliances between northern industrialists, who were anticlerical and wanted high tariffs, and southern landowners, who also favored protectionism. Crispi used the army against strikers and demonstrators and used the police to cow opponents daring to organize electoral opposition against him. In 1894, he ordered the disfranchisement of nearly a million voters and banned the Italian Socialist Party. His authoritarian methods angered even the king, who wryly admitted that "Crispi is a pig, but a necessary pig."

In 1901, King Victor Emmanuel III (ruled 1900–1946) signed a decree granting the premier authority over all cabinet posts. Giovanni Giolitti (1842–1928) was a Piedmontese bureaucrat who as premier brought relative stability to Italian political life. Giolitti was a master of *trasformismo*, making party labels essentially meaningless by building a series of effective, though makeshift, coalitions. Armed with new patronage, Giolitti won the loyalty of enough deputies to keep himself in office with negotiations, cajoling, promises of jobs and favors, threats, and outright bribery. With the motto "neither revolution nor reaction," the premier's balancing act depended on votes from the anticlerical Radicals, a progressive party of the north, who supported the increased efficiency of state administration and liked the premier's antisocialism. But Giolitti also depended on southern Catholic moderates, and therefore opposed any land reform that would break up their estates. His government also had to appease the Church by declining to meet the anticlerical demands of the Radicals. To keep the Church relatively happy, he therefore sponsored legislation that turned over education in southern Italy to the clergy. Giolitti also left the Camorra and Mafia alone because they could bring him votes in any region or town they controlled. Before one election, the premier ordered the release of more than a thousand mafiosi from prison in exchange for their votes. But Giolitti also believed that social reforms enacted by his government, supported by the moderate Socialists, could "put Marx up in the attic."

In 1912, parliament passed legislation that more than doubled the number of eligible voters in Italy. Giolitti's social reforms had frightened employers and many other conservative voters, hence the ranks of the anti-parliamentary right swelled, as nationalist candidates rallied public opinion, demanding (in the wake of the Italian invasion of Libya) further aggressive moves in the Mediterranean. With the Socialists angered by the Libyan War and now standing unwilling to be "transformed" into temporary political partners, Giolitti now had to turn to Catholic leaders, who had moved closer to Giolitti and the republic because of fear of the Socialists. (In 1904, the Church had relaxed its antirepublican stand enough to allow practicing Catholics to vote in elections if their participation would help defeat a Socialist candidate.) Giolitti convinced Catholic candidates to support his Liberal candidates if the Liberals agreed to end the campaign against Church schools and for legalized divorce. Angered by Giolitti's promises to the clerical candidates, the left tripled its vote, forcing him from office in March 1914.

The Rise of Italian Nationalism

In a country wrought by political division, aggressive nationalism appeared as one means of bringing Italians together. Crispi had favored a policy of forceful colonization, fearful that Italy would be left out while the other powers snatched up territory (see Chapter 22). He prepared an invasion of the East African state of Abyssinia (now Ethiopia) from the Italian colony of Eritrea in 1896, circumventing parliamentary opposition and refusing to heed the warning of generals that such a move might fail. When the

Abyssinian tribesman Crispi had referred to as "barbarians" crushed the Italian army at Adowa, he resigned. Italian nationalists then began to claim the territory of Trentino in the Austrian Tyrol and the Adriatic port of Trieste as "Unredeemed Italy" *(Italia Irredenta)* and began to dream of conquests in North Africa. In 1911, while Giolitti was premier, Italy launched a war of conquest in Libya, establishing a colony called Tripolitania there (see Chapter 23). But although the war went reasonably well for Italian troops, the right objected to the fact that it seemed mismanaged, and the left did not want the invasion at all. Both left and right moved further away from Giolitti's liberal center, which appeared morally bankrupt to both extremes. The Libyan War thus directly led to the end of Giolitti's political system. In 1914, nationalists defiantly turned their backs on the Liberals and founded a political party, and six right-wing nationalists were elected to the Chamber of Deputies. A nationalist proclaimed that the role of his new party was to teach Italians to respect "international struggle," even if the result was war. "Well, let there be war! And let Nationalism stir up in Italy the will for victory in war!"

Austria-Hungary

The Habsburg monarchy of Austria-Hungary seemed an anomaly in a Europe of vigorous nationalism. The empire encompassed twelve major peoples, some of whom were increasingly determined to have their own independent national states (see Table 21-1). Thus, ethnic loyalties and rivalries reflected nationalist politics in late-nineteenth-century Europe, even if there was by definition no such thing as "Austrian-Hungarian nationalism." The ethnic tensions within the Austro-Hungarian Empire, the second largest European state, were in many ways those of Europe itself.

By the Compromise *(Ausgleich)* of 1867 (see Chapter 18), Hungary and Austria became two separate but equal partners in the Dual Monarchy. But Hungary resented being the junior partner. Although each state had its own constitution, parliament, and administration, Emperor Francis Joseph and his ministers oversaw finance, foreign policy, and war.

Table 21-1. Ethnic Composition of the Austro-Hungarian Empire in 1910 (in millions)

Ethnic Group	Population	Ethnic Group	Population
Germans	12.0	Serbs	2.0
Magyars	10.1	Slovaks	2.0
Czechs	6.6	Slovenes	1.4
Poles	5.0	Italians	0.8
Ukrainians	4.0	Bosnian Muslims	0.6
Romanians	3.2	Others	0.4
Croats	2.9		

Ethnic Tensions in the Dual Monarchy

Whereas most of the crises in France, Germany, Belgium, and Britain centered on the demands of workers and socialists, under the Dual Monarchy ethnic tensions generated political tension stemming principally from Hungarian resentment of Austrian preeminence within the Dual Monarchy and the demands of the subordinate nationalities. Ethnic minorities increasingly resented domination by German speakers and Hungarian speakers, respectively. Half of the population of Hungary consisted of non-Magyar peoples, but all teaching had to be in Magyar (one of Europe's most difficult languages). Croatia, which was technically part of Hungary, sent five representatives to the sixty-member imperial Delegation, while the Slovenes, Serbs, and other minorities were left out. Likewise, Poles held sway over Ukrainians in eastern Galicia.

Bohemia was the empire's most industrialized region with a large, educated Czech middle class. Czech nobles and intellectuals early in the century had worked toward a literary and linguistic revival, compiling and publishing books of Czech grammar and dictionaries. Czech nationalists demanded recognition of the historic Kingdom of Bohemia. But opposition from German speakers in Bohemia, and from Magyars, who feared similar demands from minorities within Hungary, had led Francis Joseph early in the 1870s to refuse such recognition.

Nationalist movements potentially threatened a major reorganization of the Austro-Hungarian Empire, in particular challenging the prerogatives of the Hungarians. Beginning in the 1870s, the Hungarians ignored all demands by the other national groups and relentlessly carried on with a program of Magyarization of everything, ranging from dissolving non-Magyar cultural societies to banning non-Magyar names for villages and streets.

Count Eduard Taaffe (1833–1895) served as prime minister in Austria from 1879 to 1893, balancing off the competing interests of the varied nationalities. While ignoring demands by Slovaks and other smaller national groups for concessions to their languages, Taaffe placated the Czechs, the third largest ethnic group, by declaring their language on an equal footing with German in the state administration in Bohemia and Moravia in 1880. He also encouraged Czech schools and established a university in Prague (1882). But intellectuals within the "Young Czech" movement, which won over many middle-class Czech voters in elections to the Austrian parliament in 1890, wanted national independence. Three years later, Taaffe resigned after the government had to declare martial law when Czechs demonstrated against the withdrawal of an edict, following protests by German speakers, that ordered officials to know both languages.

Hungarian demands put the empire's survival at some risk, leading the emperor at the turn of the century to threaten proclamation of universal suffrage in Hungary and the dissolution of parliament, unless the Magyars gave up their demand that their language be put on an equal footing with

German in the army. Francis Joseph believed that giving in to Hungarian demands would have meant the end of the Dual Monarchy.

Forces of Cohesion

What, then, held the empire together? Francis Joseph, who had become emperor in 1848, lent his own personal prestige and that of the Habsburg dynasty to the empire. The emperor was supposedly above the national rivalries, although, in fact, he was notoriously anti-Hungarian. But his natural caution offered a refreshing contrast to the flamboyant, bellicose William II, emperor of Germany.

The centuries-old support of the Catholic Church for the Habsburg dynasty also undercut nationalist movements among predominantly Catholic nationalities like the Slovaks, Croats and, above all, the Poles. The imposing imperial bureaucracy—more than 3 million civil servants—was also a source of strength for the empire. However, dominated by German speakers, it offered administrative consistency, as well as providing non-German speakers with the possibility of social ascension.

The imperial army retained considerable prestige (though, lacking adequate funds, it had proved more dashing on the parade ground than on the battlefield, as defeats by the French in 1859 and the Prussians in 1866 had demonstrated). German speakers dominated the officer corps, as they did the bureaucracy, holding 70 percent of military positions. Habsburg officers prided themselves on a military esprit de corps (interestingly enough, addressing each other by the familiar *du* form, and not the more formal *sie* that persisted in the German army). Soldiers, drawn from twelve different nationalities, continued to serve loyally in the army, which rarely was forced to intervene in local strikes and popular disturbances, in contrast to the situation in France.

Nationalist Movements

As movements of cultural nationalism grew, they almost inevitably added the goal of national independence. Since the Third Partition in 1795, Poles had been a subject people in the empires of Germany, Austria-Hungary, and Russia, where troops had crushed a Polish insurrection in 1863. Polish nationalism revived during the 1880s, but the relatively favored position of Poles in Austrian Galicia and the dispersion of the Polish people in three empires reduced any immediate Polish threat to the Habsburgs.

The absorption in 1878 of Bosnia and Herzegovina into the empire added a large Serb, as well as Muslim population, at a time when the Pan-Slav movement was growing in Russia and the Balkans. The addition of hundreds of thousands more Serbs increased demands from South Slavs—principally Serbs, Croats, and some Slovenes—that they be allowed to form an integral third part of the monarchy. However, many Serbs wanted to be attached to Serbia, thus forming a "Greater Serbia." Serb nationalism, in particular, gained momentum within Austria-Hungary, not only because of Russian influence, but also because an independent Serbia already existed.

In the southern part of the empire, ethnic tensions greatly added to the potential for international tension (see Chapter 23), particularly after Austria-Hungary formalized the annexation of Bosnia-Herzegovina in 1908. To an extent, the Magyarization campaign in Hungary was a reaction by Hungarians to this growing Pan-Slav movement, combined with Hungarian resentment of junior status in the Dual Monarchy.

Far from Vienna and Budapest within the Habsburg territories, national rivalries were reflected in angry confrontations between German- or Magyar-speaking officials and Serb, Slovene, Romanian, or Czech speakers, among others, trying to register property, births, or deaths. Tomb inscriptions written in Slovene were banned in the Adriatic port city of Trieste, where most of the population spoke Italian.

Beginning in 1912, relations between the aging Habsburg emperor and the Hungarian Parliament deteriorated, just as the Balkan Wars (1912–1913) and rampant South Slav nationalism soured relations between the Austro-Hungarian Empire and Russia. A visitor to the lower house of the Austrian Parliament in March 1914, recalled in amazement: "About a score of men, all decently clad, were seated or standing, each at his little desk. Some made an infernal noise violently opening and shutting the lids of these desks. Others emitted a blaring sound from little toy trumpets; others strummed jew's harps; still others beat snare drums. And at their head, like a bandmaster, stood a gray bearded man of about sixty-five, evidently the leader of this willful faction, directing the whole pandemonium in volume and in tempo. The sum of uproar thus produced was so infernal that it completely drowned the voice of a man who was evidently talking from his seat in another part of the house, for one could see his lips moving, and the veins in his temple swelling. Bedlam let loose! That was the impression on the whole."

THE GERMAN EMPIRE

The newly formed German Empire embodied the rise of aggressive, right-wing nationalism in late nineteenth-century Europe. German national unification had been forged by the expansion of Prussia; the autocratic political institutions of Prussia, which had overwhelmed the Revolution of 1848, became those of the empire. Each of Germany's twenty-five states sent a delegate to a federal council (*Bundesrat*), over which the chancellor presided. That each German state—for example, Bavaria, which had a relatively liberal constitution—retained considerable administrative autonomy, as well as in some cases its own prince, did not alter the authoritarian nature of the German imperial government.

Germany's growing economic power was therefore unaccompanied by an evolution toward effective parliamentary government. The empire had a parliament but the Reichstag had little real authority. Its members, elected by a franchise system that in Prussia grossly over-represented landed interests, could not hold cabinet posts. The chancellor was not responsible to the Reichstag, but rather to the emperor. The Reichstag could not propose legislation. Foreign policy and military affairs remained in the hands of the emperor and the chancellor. The Reichstag's control over the budget could not limit the prerogatives of the throne. The Reichstag was hamstrung by the political institutions of the empire itself.

German political life reflected the close alliance between the throne and the Prussian nobility. Junkers dominated the army and civil service. In exchange for loyalty, they were exempt from most taxation, receiving what amounted to state subsidies for their immense estates. Inevitably, as in England, their economic might declined with the long depression and with the remarkably rapid industrialization of Germany. But Prussian Junkers retained their full measure of political power.

Most middle-class Germans willingly acquiesced to imperial authority and noble influence. The rise of the Social Democrats was, in most cases, enough to keep the German middle class loyal to the empire, even if it meant allying with Prussian nobles. Many German industrialists and other magnates continued to look up to nobles in ways their French counterparts had long since abandoned. Some clicked their heels and tried to look like Junkers—a few dueling in the hope of picking up a stray aristocratic scar—and the emperor awarded some of them with noble titles.

Nationalist versus Internationalist Movements

Chancellor Bismarck hated the Catholic Center and Social Democratic Parties. He doubted their loyalty, because both were to some extent internationalist and antinationalist: German socialists in principle expressed allegiance to socialists in other countries, and many Catholics expressed some degree of loyalty to the pope in Rome. The Catholic Center Party had been founded in 1870 in order to lobby for the rights of Catholics, who made up 35 percent of the German population, most living in Bavaria and the Rhineland. After the Church's assertion of papal infallibility in 1870, Bismarck believed that one day the pope might order in the name of God that German Catholics not obey the government. In 1873, Bismarck launched a state campaign against Catholics (*Kulturkampf*). Priests in Germany henceforth had to complete a secular curriculum in order to be ordained, and the state would now recognize only civil marriage. Subsequent laws permitted the expulsion from Germany of members of the Catholic clergy who refused to abide by discriminatory laws against Catholics. An assassination attempt against Bismarck by a young Catholic in 1874 and papal condemnation of the *Kulturkampf* the following year

A contemporary image of Bismarck pitted against the pope in his campaign against German Catholics.

only hardened the chancellor's resolve. Furthermore, France, intent on regaining Alsace and Lorraine, was overwhelmingly Catholic.

Gradually Bismarck believed that he might in the future need the support of the Catholic Center Party against the Social Democrats. The chancellor quietly abandoned the *Kulturkampf*, although Catholics were still systematically excluded from high civil service positions, as were Jews. The state helped German Protestants purchase bankrupt estates in Prussian Poland so that they would not fall into the hands of Catholics, who made up most of the population there. Alsace and the parts of Lorraine annexed from France, where Catholics formed a solid majority, were administered directly from Berlin instead of being considered a separate state of the Reich.

Bismarck became obsessed with destroying the socialists, who had improved their gains in the elections, although they still held only a couple of seats in the Reichstag. Two attempts to kill Emperor William I in 1878 provided Bismarck with a justification for his war on the socialists, although neither would-be assassin had even the slightest contact with the Socialist Party. The Reichstag obliged Bismarck by passing antisocialist legislation that denied socialists the freedoms of assembly, association, and of the press, and allowed individual German states to force socialist activists to change residence or go into exile. The police arrested socialists (although the S.P.D. members of the Reichstag kept their posts), shut down their newspapers and periodicals, and intimidated workers into quitting trade unions, until the repression finally subsided.

William II and German Nationalism

Following William I's death, Frederick III, a man of foresight and tolerance, reigned for only 100 days, dying of throat cancer. In 1888, William II (ruled 1888–1918) became emperor. A Prussian autocrat who believed that "democratic principles can only create weak and often corrupt pillars of society," William held that "a society is only strong if it recognizes the fact of natural superiorities, in particular that of birth." Referring to himself as "an instrument of God," he boasted, "We Hohenzollerns derive our crowns from Heaven alone and are answerable only to Heaven."

The German emperor compensated for a withered left arm with a love of uniforms and swords. His education had proceeded in a hit-or-miss fashion that mostly missed. William's favorite reading included the pseudo-scientific racist ramblings of the English writer Houston Stewart Chamberlain. He proclaimed his rejection of any art that went "beyond the laws and limits imposed by Myself." Like several of his Hohenzollern ancestors, William considered himself an expert on military affairs but, unlike them, he was not. He was lazy and lacked the patience to concentrate on anything very long at all, talking on at great length superficially about any conceivable subject, rushing to conclusions without reflection. The weak-willed emperor thrived on and encouraged unctuous flattery. His lack of tact—he invariably referred to the diminutive King Victor Emmanuel III of Italy as "that dwarf"—was a common topic of conversation in imperial circles.

Bismarck, as stubborn as the young emperor, lasted two years as William's chancellor. When Bismarck in 1890 sought a pretext to launch another campaign of repression against the Social Democrats, the emperor, wanting to cultivate as much popularity as possible, preferred to win

Emperor William II, third from the left, with the Death's Head Hussars.

mass support by sponsoring more legislation that would improve working conditions. Bismarck balked and tried to keep other advisers away from William. After an unpleasant confrontation in March, Bismarck resigned.

The iron chancellor's less able successors were unable to keep William from impulsively antagonizing Germany's rivals. The emperor's personal foibles, then, became increasingly important as international relations entered a new and dangerous stage. Proving correct Bismarck's assessment that he had "no sense of proportion," the emperor personally contributed to the rise of aggressive German nationalism and the Anglo-German naval rivalry. William zipped around Germany and the North Sea eagerly reviewing troops and christening ships. He enthusiastically supported the expansionist goals of the Pan-German and Naval Leagues. He asserted, "I believe, as it is written in the Bible, that it is my duty to increase [the German heritage] for which one day I shall be called upon to give an account to God. Whoever tries to interfere with my task I shall crush."

The alliance between Conservatives, National Liberals, and the Catholic Center Party provided the German emperor with a conservative base within the Reichstag. The National Liberals wanted a strong, secular state, and mistrusted parliamentary democracy. The German middle class remained considerably more socially conservative—indeed even apolitical—than its counterparts in the rest of Western Europe. No equivalent of the progressive British Liberal Party or the French Radical Party existed in Germany. Liberalism continued to be closely tied to the defense of small-town interests. The German Progressive Party, founded in 1910, earned lower-middle-class support, but it was too small and divided to have much influence. In the meantime, the German Conservatives became increasingly nationalistic and anti-Semitic. Many identified Jews, who had received full legal emancipation with the proclamation of the empire in 1871, with liberalism and socialism. In 1892, the German Conservative Party made anti-Semitism part of its party platform.

An increase of Catholic Center Party working-class votes notwithstanding, the Social Democrats held more seats in the Reichstag in 1912 than any other party. But many Social Democrats, too, seemed engulfed in the mood of nationalism that swept much of Germany, heightened by rivalry with Great Britain and the second Moroccan Affair of 1911, which brought Germany and France close to war (see Chapter 23). Despite the fact that William II continued to view the S.P.D. as a seditious organization and that German socialists may have thought of themselves as internationalists, they nonetheless remained staunchly nationalist in behavior. One socialist reassured the Reichstag in 1907 that the duty of socialists was to ensure that "the German people not be pressed to the wall by any other nation." S.P.D. deputies voted for the prodigious augmentation of funds for naval expansion. Unlike French or Italian socialists, German socialists manifested little anti-militarism, giving every sign that they would support the government in time of war, particularly against Russia.

CONCLUSION

After 1909, the European powers each faced a prolonged political crisis generated by pressure from the left. These crises accentuated shrill nationalist rhetoric as governments rose and fell in France and Italy, among other countries. Ethnic rivalries reduced the Austro-Hungarian Diet to quarreling, turbulent forum for competing views, as monarchical policies became more authoritarian. Strikes shook the Russian Empire, Spain, and Great Britain as well. Aggressive nationalism defined domestic politics. It also helped create the "new European imperialism," which, between the early 1880s and 1914, saw the Europeans greatly increase their domination of the globe. The imperialist powers included Great Britain and France, old rivals for colonies, as well as Germany and Italy, which also sought to extend what each considered its national interests. Imperial rivalries helped solidify international alliances, dividing Europe into two armed camps.

Influenced by Charles Darwin, the idea that the stronger prevail over the weak seemed to undermine the Enlightenment belief that all human beings were created equal. Angry claims that one's own people were superior to any other, combined with the growing wave of nationalism, easily led toward a racism that insisted that one's own people were superior to any other. Amid shrill claims for national superiority, Social Darwinists argued the natural superiority of some races to justify the conquest of the so-called "backward" peoples of Africa and Asia. Shaped in part by aggressive nationalism and growing fears that colonies could partially resolve the crises of the economic depression by providing new sources of raw materials and markets for manufactured goods, beginning in the 1880s the Great Powers began to compete for new colonies in the age of the "new imperialism."

CHAPTER 22

THE AGE OF EUROPEAN IMPERIALISM

In one of the odd twists in the long, bloody history of European imperialism, the vast Congo region in Central Africa was colonized by a monarch acting as a private citizen. When he was heir to the Belgian throne, Leopold II (ruled 1865–1909) had given one of his father's ministers a piece of granite with the inscription "Belgium needs colonies." And so when he was king of Belgium, Leopold organized the Congo Company to explore and develop Central Africa.

In 1879, Leopold sent the British-American journalist Henry Stanley (1841–1904) to the Congo. Stanley emerged with treaties signed with local rulers establishing Leopold's personal claim over the Congo. The Belgian king would now have his "piece of that great African cake."

An international congress of representatives of European states held in Berlin in 1884–1885 to discuss claims to African territory declared the Congo to be the "Congo Free State," with Leopold as its head. This "free state," recognized as the private possession of the Belgian king and as part of his business organization, received the status of a "mandate." The Congress of Berlin established this designation to signify that a European power accepted the "mandate" to govern a territory and to provide, in principle, for the welfare of its "backward people." At the Congress of Berlin, the European powers agreed on ground rules governing the race for colonies. Henceforth no power could simply declare a region its colony unless it exercised effective control over the territory.

Despite Leopold's pledge that each colonial power would "undertake to watch over the preservation of the native races, and the amelioration of the moral and material conditions of their existence," the horrors perpetrated on the people of the Congo at Leopold's orders in his quest for ivory and rubber may have been unmatched in the annals of European imperialism. For the indigenous population, the colonial experience was Hell on earth.

An American missionary reported a macabre way the Belgian soldiers had of trying to reduce the waste of bullets: "each time the corporal goes out to get rubber, cartridges are given to him. He must bring back all not used; and for every one used, he must bring back a right hand . . . in six months, they had used 6,000 cartridges, which means that 6,000 people are killed or mutilated. It means more than 6,000, for the people have told me repeatedly that soldiers killed children with the butt of their guns." Another European employed by the king boasted that he could line up several men in such a way that one bullet could kill them all.

The Belgian Parliament, stung by revelations of brutality uncovered by international investigations, demanded more humane standards. In 1908, it took the Congo away from Leopold and made it a colony of Belgium, a country one-eightieth the size of its colony.

FROM COLONIALISM TO IMPERIALISM

Imperialism is the process by which one state, with superior military strength and more advanced technology, imposes its control over the land, resources, and population of a less developed region. Although the repeated extension of Chinese control over the Vietnamese people of Indochina would fit most definitions of the term, imperialism has above all characterized the relations of the European powers with Africa and Asia. From the 1880s to 1914, the European powers expanded their direct control over much of the globe. Imperialism reflected and contributed to the development of a truly global economy: the manufacturing boom of the Second Industrial Revolution whetted the appetite of merchants seeking new markets and manufacturers seeking new sources of raw materials. The expansion of European empires through what has been called the "new imperialism" generally included the exploitation of African and Asian lands with economic and strategic interests in mind.

Imperialism may be differentiated from colonialism, which from the sixteenth to the middle decades of the nineteenth century had entailed economic exploitation and control over territories through settlement by the colonizing power, as in the case of Britain's relationship with its American colony before the War of American Independence. But as the era of colonialism became that of imperialism, relatively few Europeans settled permanently in Africa or Southeast Asia, both of which had difficult tropical climates, or in China, which was an independent though weak state when compared to its European antagonists.

Europeans had long visited, influenced, learned from, and conquered distant lands. Spain and Portugal began the first sustained European quest for colonies in the fifteenth century with excursions along the West African coast. During the sixteenth century, Spaniards built a vast colonial empire that stretched from what is now the southwestern United States to

Queen Victoria, recently proclaimed empress of India, playing the part in the back-yard of Windsor Castle in England.

the southern tip of Latin America. In the seventeenth century, French traders, missionaries, and soldiers began small settlements in "New France" (present-day Québec). France lost New France to Britain in the 1760s. After the loss of New France, France's modest empire included Algeria (conquered in 1830) and a few Caribbean islands.

During the eighteenth and nineteenth centuries, British merchants sought both raw materials and sizable markets for manufactured goods in Africa, India, and as far as Southeast Asia, China, and Japan. The drive for colonies heightened the rivalry between Britain and France in the era of the American Revolution.

During the nineteenth century, many of the original colonies of Spain and Portugal became independent. Thus, following successful drives for independence early in the nineteenth century, the Spanish Empire in the New World had largely disappeared by 1850. But Spain still held Cuba, Puerto Rico, and the Philippines. After Brazil, many times the size of Portugal, proclaimed its independence in 1822, Portugal was left with only toeholds in Africa, India, and East Asia.

The Dutch had established bases on the coast of West Africa (abandoned in 1872) and small island colonies scattered in the Caribbean, the Indian Ocean, and the Pacific. Dutch traders ended Portuguese control of Java, one of Indonesia's islands, and extended their own influence over the island in 1755. Although the Dutch lost Java to the British in 1811, they reestablished control there in 1816 and then gradually extended their po-

Europeans sitting among warriors and musicians in Borneo in the late nineteenth century.

litical control over the rest of Indonesia, the centerpiece of their colonial empire.

Britain and France had established bases on the west coast of Africa, despite its lack of natural harbors and estuaries. Both powers began to penetrate the giant continent during the nineteenth century—the British from the tip of South Africa, the French from Algeria and the coast of West Africa. In the early 1850s, merchants in the ports of Bordeaux and Marseille had begun to pressure Emperor Napoleon III to help them expand French trading interests in West Africa beyond several coastal bases. In the 1860s, the governor of the French territory of Senegal, who learned the local language and married an African, established a French protectorate over a wider area.

Only Britain still had a large empire by the middle of the nineteenth century. Despite the loss of thirteen of its American colonies (which became the United States of America after the Declaration of Independence of 1776), the British Empire still extended into so many corners of the world that it was commonly said that "the sun never set on the British Empire." Britain's strength partially rested on the pillars of settlement colonies. In search of a more secure future or simply adventure, more than a million people emigrated from the British Isles in the 1850s alone, most of them to Australia, New Zealand, and Canada, as well as to the United States. Australia had become the world's largest exporter of wool by 1851, when the discovery of gold in New South Wales and Victoria brought another wave of immigrants dreaming, like those pouring into California at the same time, of making their fortune. The Australian colonies and New Zealand received the right to maintain their own governments in the 1850s, under the watchful eye of the British Foreign Office, although western Australia remained a convict colony until "transportation" to Australia ceased to be a punishment in England in 1865. Canada achieved Dominion status in 1867 with passage of the British North America Act by the British Parliament. The crown would grant Dominion status to Australia in 1901 and to New Zealand in 1907.

THE "NEW IMPERIALISM" AND THE SCRAMBLE FOR AFRICA

In the early 1880s, the hold of the European powers on the rest of the world was still relatively slight, as Map 22.1 demonstrates. Many leaders could still conclude that the cost of maintaining colonies outweighed the benefits. In 1852, British Prime Minister Benjamin Disraeli, later an outspoken advocate of imperialism, had referred to the colonies as "wretched" and "a millstone round our necks." William Gladstone, Disraeli's great rival, reflected the prevailing liberal view when he pontificated, "The lust and love of territory have been among the greatest curses of mankind."

Distant, underdeveloped lands still seemed remote from urgent European interests. But this changed rapidly. Before the age of imperialism, Shaka, a renowned leader of the Zulus, who had established one of the two dominant African kingdoms in what is now South Africa, prophesied

Trying to establish the frontier between French and German territory in the Congo, 1913.

MAP 22.1 COLONIAL EMPIRES UNTIL 1880 Colonies of Britain, France, Russia, the Netherlands, Spain, Portugal, and the Ottoman Empire.

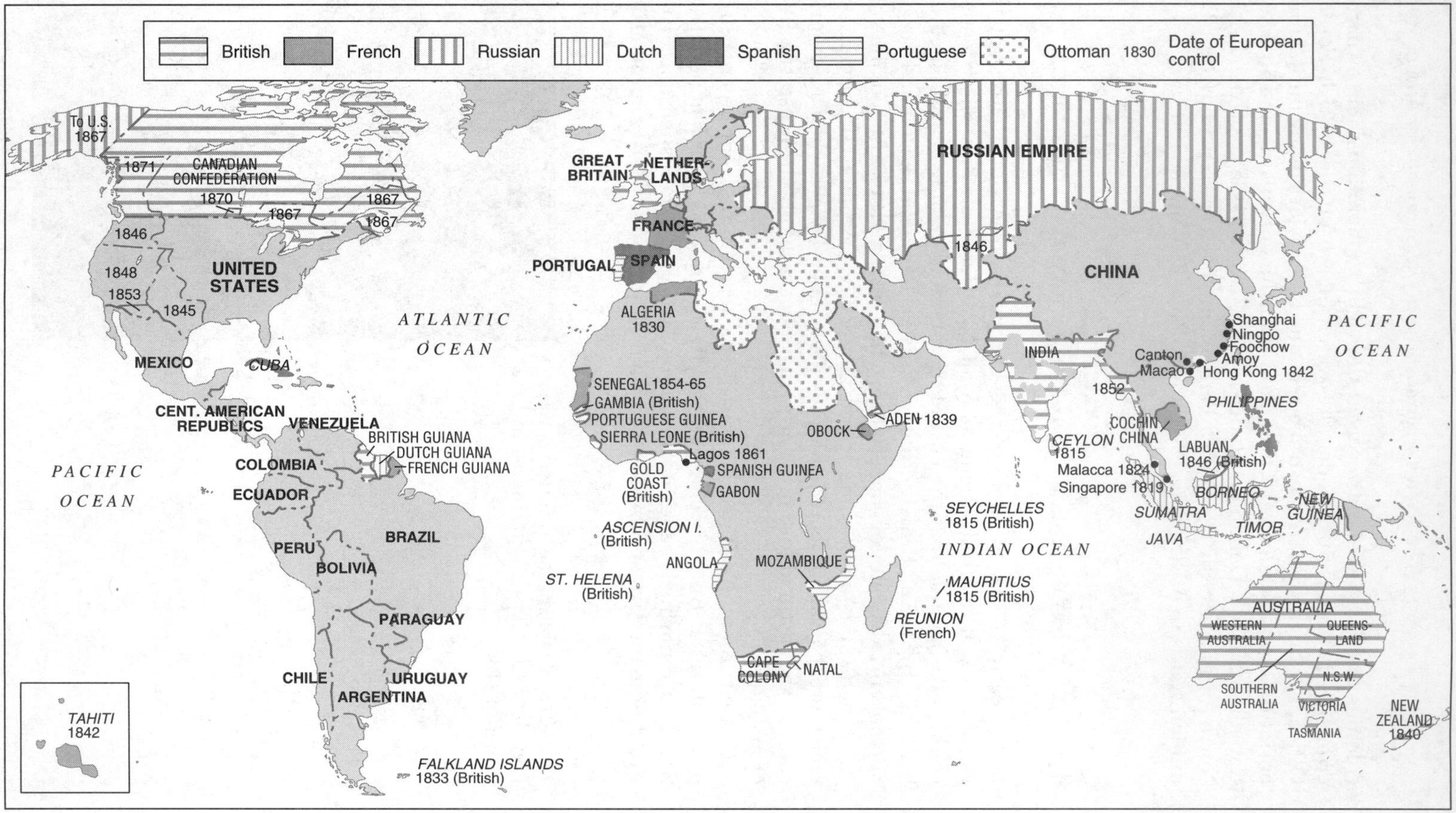

Legend:

- British
- French
- Russian
- Dutch
- Spanish
- Portuguese
- Ottoman 1830
- Date of European control

North America:

To U.S. 1867
CANADIAN CONFEDERATION
1871
1870
1867
1867
1846
1848
1853
1845
UNITED STATES
MEXICO
CUBA
CENT. AMERICAN REPUBLICS

South America:

VENEZUELA
COLOMBIA
ECUADOR
PERU
BOLIVIA
BRAZIL
PARAGUAY
CHILE
ARGENTINA
URUGUAY
BRITISH GUIANA
DUTCH GUIANA
FRENCH GUIANA
FALKLAND ISLANDS 1833 (British)

Europe / Africa:

GREAT BRITAIN
NETHER-LANDS
FRANCE
PORTUGAL
SPAIN
ALGERIA 1830
SENEGAL 1854–65
GAMBIA (British)
PORTUGUESE GUINEA
SIERRA LEONE (British)
GOLD COAST (British)
Lagos 1861
SPANISH GUINEA
GABON
ASCENSION I. (British)
ST. HELENA (British)
ANGOLA
MOZAMBIQUE
CAPE COLONY
NATAL
OBOCK
ADEN 1839

Asia:

RUSSIAN EMPIRE
CHINA
1846
INDIA
Shanghai
Ningpo
Foochow
Amoy
Hong Kong 1842
Canton
Macao
1852
COCHIN CHINA
CEYLON 1815
Malacca 1824
Singapore 1819
LABUAN 1846 (British)
BORNEO
SUMATRA
JAVA
TIMOR
NEW GUINEA
PHILIPPINES

Indian Ocean:

SEYCHELLES 1815 (British)
MAURITIUS 1815 (British)
RÉUNION (French)

Australia / Pacific:

AUSTRALIA
WESTERN AUSTRALIA
SOUTHERN AUSTRALIA
QUEENSLAND
N.S.W.
VICTORIA
TASMANIA
NEW ZEALAND 1840
TAHITI 1842

Oceans:

PACIFIC OCEAN
ATLANTIC OCEAN
INDIAN OCEAN

before his death in 1828 that his people would be conquered by the "swallows," the white men who built mud homes. The prophecy came true.

The rapid spread of a contentious nationalism fueled imperialism. The imperialist powers included Great Britain and France, old colonial powers and rivals, and also newly emerged Germany and Italy. Nations no longer necessarily looked to preserve the balance of power, but rather to extend what each considered to be its national interests. Smaller nations, too, participated in the drive for empire, including the Netherlands as well as Belgium.

A British foreign minister recalled in 1891, "When I left the Foreign Office in 1880, nobody thought about Africa. When I returned to it in 1885, the nations of Europe were almost quarreling with each other as to the various portions of Africa which they should obtain." Another British foreign official would ask incredulously if his country sought to "take possession of every navigable river all over the world, and every avenue of commerce, for fear somebody else should take possession of it?" The colonial race extended even to the North Pole, first reached by the American Robert E. Peary (1856–1920) in 1909.

British and French Imperial Rivalry

A French colonial enthusiast assessed the scramble for Africa that began in the 1880s: "We are witnessing something that has never been seen in history: the veritable partition of an unknown continent by certain European countries. In this partition France is entitled to the largest share." Africa included about a fourth of the world's land area and one-fifth of its population. Explorers plunged almost blindly into the uncharted and unmapped African interior. The source of the Nile River, the lifeline of Egypt, had been located in the Sudan only in 1862; most Western maps still showed blank spots for much of the continent's interior. Europeans discovered the bewildering complexity of a continent that included about 700 different autonomous societies with distinctive political structures.

France's imperial aspirations reveal some of the motives that fueled the new imperialism. After its humiliating defeat by Prussia during the Franco-Prussian War of 1870–1871, the gnawing loss of Alsace-Lorraine hung over France during the next decade and beyond. German Chancellor Otto von Bismarck subtly encouraged the French government to pursue an interest in distant colonies, hoping it would forget about trying to retake Alsace-Lorraine.

At the Congress of Berlin, the French agreed to abandon their claims to Cyprus, while the British gave up claims to Tunisia. The French ambassador to Germany warned his own government in 1881 that if it failed to order bold action in Tunisia, France risked decline as a power, perhaps even "finding itself on a par with Spain." In March 1881, the French government claimed that raiders from Tunisia were harassing their troops in Algeria. French troops invaded Tunisia and crushed Tunisian resistance there. Tunisia became a French protectorate two months later. Between 1895 and 1896, France also seized the island of Madagascar off the coast of East Africa and made it a colony (see Map 22.2).

French merchants and nationalists dreamed of an empire that would stretch across Africa. Railroads had begun to reach across continental Europe in the 1840s and 1850s. They became a symbol of modernity, but

MAP 22.2 IMPERIALISM IN AFRICA BEFORE 1914   British, Spanish, Portuguese, French, Belgian, German, and Italian colonies in Africa and dates of European control.

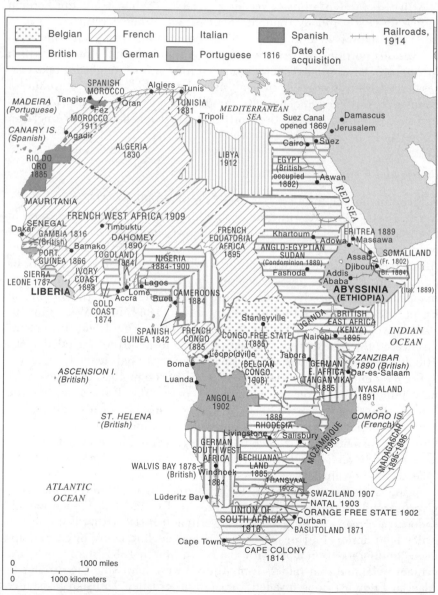

also of conquest, as in the case of the U.S. transcontinental railway. Not surprisingly, then, the railroad captured the imagination of imperialists. Cecil Rhodes (1853–1902), British entrepreneur, colonialist, and multi-millionaire, asserted that rails went farther and cost less than bullets. During the late 1870s, the French Chamber of Deputies subsequently approved a series of expensive, far-fetched plans to build railways across the vast African expanse. In order to extend French interests into the interior, a railway network was mapped out to connect Algeria and Senegal by crossing the Sahara Desert. Much of the money was wasted, because most of the lines were never built, and in any case, could never have generated sufficient revenues to justify their enormous cost. France had little more than a series of forts to show for the expense. Yet, British merchants on the coast of West Africa feared that French advances would lead to the loss of products such as palm oil and potential markets for their own goods in the African interior. The Franco-British rivalry in Africa heated up. Further French advances in western Sudan followed.

British and French rivalries in Egypt, a gateway to the markets and products of the Middle East, dated to the British clash with France during the revolutionary years of the late 1790s. In 1869, a French engineer and entrepreneur, Ferdinand de Lesseps (1805–1894), completed a canal through the Isthmus of Suez, which connects the Red and Mediterranean Seas (see Chapter 19). The canal cut the distance of the steamship voyage from London to Bombay in half by avoiding the treacherous Cape of Good Hope at the southern tip of Africa. The severe financial difficulties of Ismail Pasha, the ruler, or khedive, of Egypt, which was a part of the Ottoman Empire, brought Britain a stroke of incredibly good fortune. In 1875, Britain bailed out the bankrupt Ismail by purchasing a considerable portion of shares in the canal. Under British management the number of ships passing through the canal rose from 486 in 1870 to 3,000 in 1882.

No power had a greater stake in the canal than Britain. The British government traditionally had sought to protect the land and sea routes to India by supporting the Islamic Middle Eastern states—above all, the crumbling Ottoman Empire—against Russian designs. With continuing social and political chaos in Egypt threatening the interests of British bondholders, in 1882 a British fleet shelled the Mediterranean port city of Alexandria. The British then established a protectorate over Egypt, although the country remained nominally part of the Ottoman Empire. The Egyptian khedive henceforth accepted British "advice." Over the next forty years, the British government repeatedly assured the other powers that its protectorate over Egypt would only be temporary. The French, who had loaned the khedive as much money as the British, were particularly aggrieved at the continued British occupation.

Central Africa became the next major focus of European expansion. In 1869, the *New York Herald* hired Henry Stanley to find the missionary and explorer David Livingstone (1813–1873), from whom there had been no word in almost four years. After a trip of fifteen months, he found the mis-

Gunboat diplomacy: The British fleet anchored at Alexandria, Egypt, 1882.

sionary in January 1871 on the shores of Lake Tanganyika and greeted him with that most understated Victorian salutation, "Dr. Livingstone, I presume?" Henry Stanley's subsequent long journey up the Congo River in 1879 to gain treaties for Belgian King Leopold II opened up interior Africa to Great Power rivalry. In 1880, Savorgnan de Brazza (1852–1905), a French naval officer, reached "Stanley Pool," a large lake Stanley had "discovered" in 1877. ("Stanley didn't discover us," one "native" put it reasonably, "we were here all the time.") Brazza returned with a piece of paper signed with an "X" by a king, which Brazza claimed granted France a protectorate over the territory beyond the right bank of the Congo.

Although the French government first showed little interest, French nationalists made ratification of Brazza's "treaty" a major issue. Portugal then declared that it controlled the mouth of the Congo River. The British government demanded trade rights with the region. Leopold of Belgium voiced opposition to any French moves near his Congo territory. Amid continued resentment over British control of Egypt, the French Chamber of Deputies eagerly ratified Brazza's treaty. French colonial activity in West Africa continued unabated.

Germany and Italy Join the Race

Germany was the next power to enter the race for colonies. It did so despite the fact that Bismarck at first viewed colonization as an expensive sideshow that distracted attention from the essential questions of power politics in European diplomacy. He once curtly rejected a German colonial explorer's plea for a more aggressive colonial policy: "Your map of Africa is very nice, but my map of Africa is in Europe. Here is Russia, and here is France, and we are in the middle. That is my map of Africa!"

While encouraging France to burn off some of its nationalist energy in the pursuit of colonies, the chancellor had routinely rejected pleas that Germany intervene in Africa on behalf of merchants, missionaries, and nationalistic adventurers. The Colonial League, formed in 1882, and the Society for German Colonization, a lobby of businessmen and other nationalists formed in 1884, pressured the government to pursue colonies. The German adventurer Karl Peters (1856–1918) sought an outlet for his financial interests and nationalist fervor through his East Africa Company. Peters' chartered company signed commercial agreements, built settlements, and assumed sovereignty over a variety of East African territories. These activities aroused the ire of nationalists in England, exactly what Bismarck had hoped to avoid but, given the sudden intensity of nationalist and colonial fever at home, could not.

Bismarck gradually came to share the imperialist view that colonies might provide new markets for German products. But more than this, he realized that the establishment of colonies would solidify his political support within Germany and might also help defuse social tensions caused by the depression gripping the continent. New markets could create jobs at home or abroad for unemployed German workers. Bismarck concluded that colonies could be administered indirectly at a relatively low cost.

The club car in a train in German East Africa, 1907.

The time also seemed right for the German government to appease its drooling colonial lobby, including merchants. The British foreign office was preoccupied with Islamic fundamentalist rebellions in the Sudan. France, with a new protectorate over Tunisia, was embroiled in debate over colonization in Indochina. In April 1884, Bismarck wired his consul in Capetown, South Africa, ordering him to proclaim that the holdings of a German merchant north of the Orange River—the territorial limit of British colonial authority—would henceforth be the protectorate of German Southwest Africa. Britain acquiesced in exchange for Bismarck's acceptance of the British occupation of Egypt. That summer the German chancellor also decided to establish a protectorate over the Cameroons and Togoland in West Africa.

Bismarck, who played British and French interests off against each other, called the Berlin Conference of 1884–1885 in response to an 1884 agreement signed between Britain and Portugal recognizing mutual interests. The Berlin Conference divided up the territory of the Congo basin between the Congo Free State (Leopold's territory) and France (the French Congo), while declaring the Congo River open to all. French merchants penetrated Dahomey and the Ivory Coast, with French troops reaching the ancient trading town of Timbuktu in 1894.

In 1885, Bismarck agreed to protect Peters' commercial enterprises in Tanganyika, which became German East Africa. Germany also established several coastal trading stations and the colony of Angra Pequena in Southwest Africa, which merchants had portrayed with unerring inaccuracy as a territory of untapped wealth just waiting to be extracted.

The Congress of Berlin, 1878, included Disraeli (standing center left), Bismarck (in the foreground in the middle) and Leopold II of Belgium.

The Germans in Africa. Cartoons originally appearing in the German journal *Jugend* in 1916 show (*left*) an officer arriving to find chaos and (*right*) imposing military order.

To placate Britain, Germany recognized British interests in Kenya and Uganda and the protectorate status of Zanzibar in 1890. In exchange Germany received a small but strategically important island naval station in the North Sea. The German colonial lobby was not happy: "We have exchanged three kingdoms for a bathtub!" moaned Peters. Nonetheless, by 1913, German colonies in Africa, including German East and Southwest Africa, Togoland, and the Cameroons, occupied over one million square miles, five times the size of Germany.

Italy was the last of the major European nations to enter the colonial fray. Its ravenous hunger for empire led Bismarck to note sarcastically that it proceeded "with a big appetite and bad teeth." In 1882, Italy established Assab, a small settlement on the Red Sea, and three years later it occupied Massawa, which in 1889 became the capital of the new Italian colony of Eritrea. Italian merchants began to arrive, hoping to force the adjacent African state of Abyssinia (now Ethiopia) to trade through Eritrea. In 1889, the Abyssinian emperor signed a treaty with Italy which the Italian government took to mean that Abyssinia was now an Italian protectorate. When the French began building a railroad that would link Abyssinia to French Somaliland and the Abyssinians attempted to cancel the treaty, Italian troops launched a war (1894). The result was an Italian disaster. In 1896, a general without adequate maps marched four badly organized columns of Italian troops into battle. Abyssinians, some 70,000 strong, with Russian artillery advisers and French rifles, routed the Italian army in the hills near the coast at Adowa; 6,000 Italian soldiers were killed—many more than in the various wars that had led to Italy's unification—and several thousand were captured. The Italians became the first European army to be defeated in the field by Africans. Under the Treaty of Addis Ababa that same year, Italy was forced to renounce Abyssinia as a protectorate, although it kept the territory of Eritrea on the Red Sea.

Standoff in the Sudan: The Fashoda Affair

In 1898, the Anglo-French rivalry in Africa culminated in the standoff between French and British forces at Fashoda on the Nile in the southern Sudan and almost brought the two powers to war. The French government resented the fact that Egypt served as a base for British initiatives in the hot, dry Sudan.

A fundamentalist Islamic and nationalist revolt led by a former Sudanese slave trader who declared himself to be the Mahdi (the Guided One) in the early 1880s challenged the nominal authority of the khedive of Egypt over Sudan. After the Mahdi and his followers (the Mahdists) began a holy war against Egypt and defeated Egyptian armies led by British officers, the British sent an expedition to the Sudanese capital of Khartoum to evacuate the Egyptian population. It was led by the dashing, eccentric British adventurer General Charles "Chinese" Gordon (1833–1885), so called because he had commanded troops that assisted the Chinese government in putting down the Taiping Rebellion in the 1860s. Besieged for ten months in Khartoum by the Mahdi's forces in 1884, Gordon was killed when the Mahdists stormed the garrison two days before a relief expedition from Britain arrived in January 1885.

Britain lost interest in the Sudan until the French colonial lobby, still smarting from Britain's occupation of Egypt, sought a strategic foothold on the Nile. In January 1895, Britain claimed the Sudan. The French government, in turn, announced that it considered the Sudan open to all colonial powers. The British government responded that it would consider any French activity in the Sudan "an unfriendly act."

Charles "Chinese" Gordon on his camel.

The charge of the dervishes (followers of the Mahdi) at the Battle of Omdurman in the Sudan, 1898.

In 1898, a British force commanded by Lord Horatio Kitchener (1850–1916) set out from Egypt for the Sudan with the Upper Nile outpost of Fashoda as its goal. Kitchener and his army took revenge for Gordon's death, using machine guns to mow down 11,000 Mahdists at the Battle of Omdurman (September 1898), and retaking Khartoum. British troops desecrated the Mahdi's grave, playing soccer with his skull. At Fashoda, they encountered a French expeditionary force, which intended to establish a French colony on the Upper Nile. Kitchener handed his counterpart a mildly worded note of protest against the French presence, and the two commanders clinked drinking glasses, leaving their governments to fight it out diplomatically.

In both Britain and France, nationalists demanded war. But the Dreyfus Affair (see Chapter 21) divided French society; furthermore, as the French foreign minister lamented, "We have nothing but arguments and they have the troops." The Fashoda Affair ended peacefully when France recognized British and Egyptian claims to the Nile basin and Britain recognized French holdings in West Africa. For the moment, there seemed to be enough of Africa to go around. Only Abyssinia and Liberia were independent African states.

The British in South Africa and the Boer War

In South Africa, Britain had to overcome resistance to its presence, first from indigenous peoples and then from Dutch settlers. The British had

Boer commandos cross the Orange River.

taken the Cape of Good Hope at the tip of South Africa from the Dutch in 1795. British settlers moved in, fighting nine separate wars against the Bantu people in the 1850s and 1860s. In 1872, the Cape Colony emerged from under the wing of the British Foreign Office, forming its own government, but remaining within the empire.

Known as the Boers, the Dutch settlers (Afrikaners) in South Africa were a farming people of strict Calvinist belief. The Boers had many grievances against British rule from Capetown. They resented the British abolition of slavery and the fact that the British allowed blacks to move about freely and to own property. In the "Great Trek" from the Cape Colony, which began in 1836 and lasted almost a decade, many Boers began to move inland to carve out states that would be independent of British rule (see Map 22.3). Overcoming Zulu resistance, Boers established the Natal Republic, a strip along South Africa's east coast. When the British intervened in support of the Zulus, the Boers left Natal, which became a British colony in 1843. The Boers crossed the Vaal River in search of new land. Slaughtering Zulus as they went, the Boers founded the Republic of Transvaal (later called the South African Republic) and the Orange Free State, which the British recognized as independent in 1854.

The discovery of diamonds in the late 1860s, first in the Cape Colony and then west of the Orange Free State, attracted a flow of treasure seekers—at least 10,000 people—raising the stakes for control of South Africa. After annexing the Republic of Transvaal against the wishes of the Boers in 1877, the British gradually extended their colonial frontier northward, convinced that more diamonds and gold would be found beyond the Vaal River.

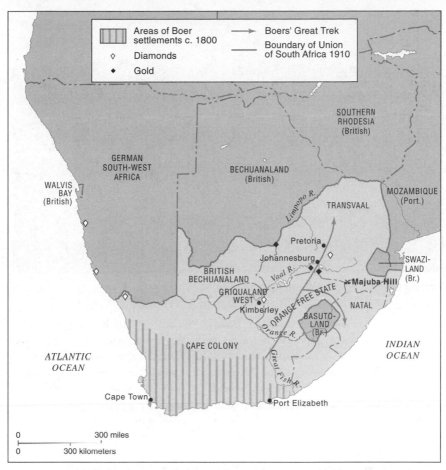

MAP 22.3 SOUTH AFRICA, 1800–1910   The settlement of South Africa by the Boers and English, including the Boers' Great Trek and the 1910 boundaries of the Union of South Africa.

Cecil Rhodes orchestrated British expansion in South Africa, leading to conflict with the Boers, who still bitterly resented annexation into the British Empire. In 1880, the Boers rose up in revolt, their sharpshooters picking off British troops at Majuba Hill a year later. Unwilling to risk further trouble, Gladstone's Liberal government recognized the political independence of the South African Republic. But, at the same time, the British tried to force the Boers to trade through Capetown by denying them access to the sea, reflecting the primacy of commerce in their grand scheme.

The Boers in Transvaal were given a boost by the discovery in the mid-1880s of more gold deposits, which enabled them to buy weapons. Constructing their railway to Port Mozambique on the eastern coast, the Boers offered advantageous shipping rates to Natal and the Orange Free State,

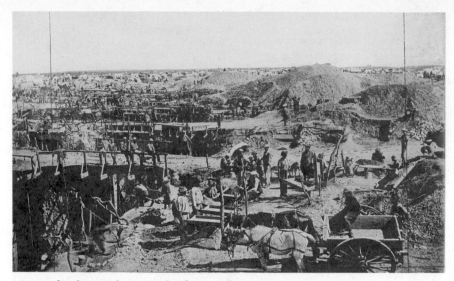

Mining for diamonds in South Africa in the 1870s.

taking business away from British South Africa, and further souring relations between the Boers and Britain. Rhodes then subsidized an uprising
in the Transvaal against the Boers. The British government followed
Rhodes' advice to send a military excursion against the Boers in 1895, but
the Boers fought off the "Jameson Raid" by 500 British cavalry with ease.
The raid discredited Rhodes, but brought the British government even
more directly into the crisis, particularly after Emperor William II of Germany sent Transvaal president Paul Kruger a congratulatory telegram after
the failed Jameson Raid.

In 1899, the British goaded the Boers into a war that lasted three years.
In order to depopulate the farms that supplied the Boer rebels, the British
imprisoned farmers' wives and children in concentration camps in which
thousands died. Some people in Britain criticized these camps, though
there had been few such outcries when the British had killed people of
color during the wars against the peoples of India, Burma, and elsewhere
in Africa. The outnumbered Boers evoked great sympathy in France and
Germany, leaving the British government isolated diplomatically. The war
shocked many people in Britain not only by the extensive, costly military
campaigns it required (almost 400,000 British troops were sent), but also
because of the hostile reaction the British conduct of the war engendered
in other countries. In 1902, the Boers asked for an armistice. Thereafter,
they were forced to take an oath of loyalty to the king of England. In 1906
and 1907, Britain granted the Republic of Transvaal and the Orange Free
State self-government. In 1910, the Boers joined the British Union of
South Africa (which now included the Cape Colony, the Orange Free

State, Transvaal, and Natal, and which was given Dominion status by the British at that time).

The new government immediately proclaimed that it would "permit no equality between colored people and the white inhabitants either in church or state." Apartheid—the unequal separation of whites and blacks by law—was the practical result of the Boer policy of racial domination. It proved to be the most extreme consequence of the "scramble for Africa," which would in the twentieth century leave Africans with daunting challenges.

The European Powers in Asia

The European powers and the United States divided up the entire Pacific region in their quest for raw materials, markets, strategic advantage, and prestige. (Rhodes cosmically announced in the same spirit, "I would annex the planets if I could.") From the populous Indian subcontinent, Britain expanded its interests into and beyond Burma, accentuating a rivalry with Russia for influence in the region. In the meantime, the Dutch extended their authority in Indonesia, while the French turned much of Indochina into their protectorate. By 1900, only Japan, the emerging power in Asia, maintained real independence. Siam (now Thailand) stood as a buffer state between British and French colonial interests, and the Western powers dominated China, forcing trade and territorial concessions on that weakening empire.

India, Southeast Asia, and China

Europe's quest for colonies and domination in Asia had begun even earlier than in Africa. During the Seven Years' War (1756–1763), British troops defeated the French in India. The British East India Company, responsible to the British Parliament, administered India. The Company ruled with the assistance of various Indian princes. The British recognized their local prerogatives in exchange for their obedience and assistance. Britain later expanded east from India into Burma, overcoming Burmese resistance in a war from 1824 to 1826, and then expanded south into Malaya (see Map 22.4).

Using India as a base, British merchants, backed by British naval power, had worked to overcome barriers to trade with East Asia. In the 1830s, British traders had begun to pay for silks, teas, and other Chinese luxury goods with opium grown in India. With opium addiction rampant in southern China, in 1839 the emperor tried to stop trade completely with foreigners. The Royal Navy sent gunboats—hence the origins of the term "gunboat diplomacy"—to Canton (now Guangzhou) to force Chinese

MAP 22.4 INDIA AND THE FAR EAST BEFORE 1914   Areas controlled by the British, French, Dutch, Germans, and Portuguese in Asia.

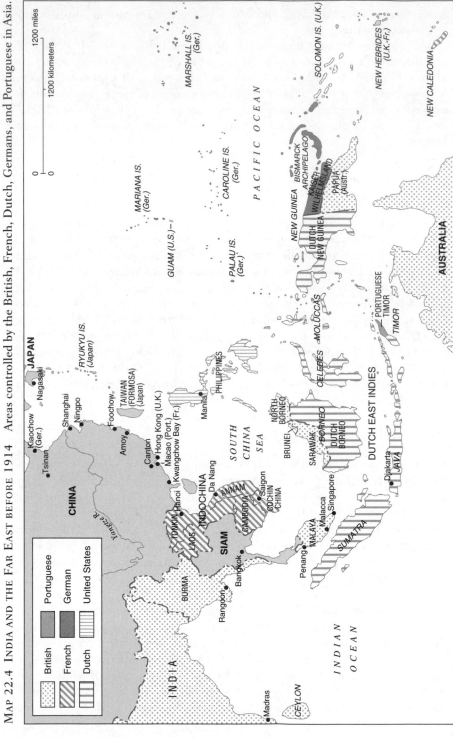

Map legend:

British
French
Dutch
Portuguese
German
United States

Labels on map:

JAPAN
Nagasaki
RYUKYU IS. (Japan)
TAIWAN (FORMOSA) (Japan)
Shanghai
Ningpo
Foochow
Amoy
Canton
Hong Kong (U.K.)
Macao (Port.)
Kwangchow Bay (Fr.)
Kiaochow (Ger.)
Tsinan
CHINA
Yangtze R.
Hanoi
TONKIN
LAOS
INDOCHINA
ANNAM
Da Nang
SIAM
Bangkok
CAMBODIA
Saigon
COCHIN CHINA
BURMA
Rangoon
INDIA
Madras
CEYLON
SOUTH CHINA SEA
PHILIPPINES
Manila
NORTH BORNEO
BRUNEI
SARAWAK
BORNEO
DUTCH BORNEO
DUTCH EAST INDIES
MALAYA
Penang
Malacca
Singapore
SUMATRA
Djakarta
JAVA
CELEBES
MOLUCCAS
PORTUGUESE TIMOR
TIMOR
INDIAN OCEAN
PACIFIC OCEAN
MARIANA IS. (Ger.)
GUAM (U.S.)
MARSHALL IS. (Ger.)
CAROLINE IS. (Ger.)
PALAU IS. (Ger.)
NEW GUINEA
BISMARCK ARCHIPELAGO
KAISER WILHELMSLAND
DUTCH NEW GUINEA
PAPUA (Austr.)
SOLOMON IS. (U.K.)
NEW HEBRIDES (U.K.-Fr.)
NEW CALEDONIA
AUSTRALIA

0   1200 miles
0   1200 kilometers

Chinese smoking opium.

capitulation in the short, one-sided Opium War (1840–1842). By the Treaty of Nanking that followed in 1842, China was forced to establish a number of "treaty ports" open to British trade, including Canton and Shanghai, and granted Britain formal authority "in perpetuity" over Hong Kong. British residents and European visitors received the rights of extraterritoriality, which meant that they were not subject to Chinese law. Britain and France together occupied Canton. In 1858, China opened six more ports to British and French trade.

In 1857, a revolt shook British rule in India, revealing some of the tensions between the colonialists and the colonized. Long-term causes of the mutiny of the Sepoys—Indian troops in the British army—included anger at the British policy of taking direct control over Indian states whose princes died without heirs and the dismissal of an Indian prince whose corruption was well known. The immediate cause was the continued use of animal fat to grease rifle cartridges, an affront to both Hindu and Muslim soldiers. Confronted with British intransigence, the Sepoys rebelled over a wide area, in one place killing 200 British women and children. In retaliation, British authorities hanged rebels and burned a number of villages.

Following the mutiny in 1858, administration of India passed from the East India Company to the British crown, Queen Victoria becoming "Empress of India." British rule became formalized and more direct. Indian princes were guaranteed their lands if they signed agreements accepting British rule. The governor-general of India added the honorific title of "viceroy," as the monarch's personal representative, serving under the secretary of state for India. Lord George Curzon (1859–1925), one of the

(Left) Indian Sepoys using pig-grease cartridges, 1857. *(Right)* Ruins after the Sepoy Mutiny, 1857.

most forceful proponents of British imperialism, was widely praised in Britain for implementing significant changes in India. He strengthened the northwestern frontier defenses against Russia, reduced the cost of government, and took credit for a modest increase in the Indian standard of living.

The British government enacted educational reforms, initiated irrigation projects, reformed the police and judicial systems, and encouraged the cotton industry, which by 1914 became the fourth largest in the world. Frightened by the Sepoy Mutiny, the British government also expedited railway construction in India in order to be able to move troops rapidly. From less than 300 miles of track in 1857, a network of 25,000 miles was established by 1900. By connecting much of the Indian interior with ports, railway development also encouraged production of Indian cotton, opium, rice, oil, jute, indigo, and tea, which could now reach ports by train and then be exported to Britain.

But while some Indian merchants and manufacturers made money from expanded trading opportunities, others lost out. To assure a lucrative market in India, a country of almost 300 million people in 1900, the British at first banned some Indian manufactures that would compete with British goods produced at home, thereby destroying Indian village handicrafts such as textile weaving. Raw Indian cotton was shipped to England to be made into cloth there, and then re-exported to India. British tax collectors increased the indebtedness of peasants in a vast nation beset by rising population, small holdings, and increasing subdivision of land.

Railroads indirectly aided Indians by helping to reduce the ravages of famine. So did the planting of new crops, such as potatoes and corn. Although Indians remained among the most impoverished people on earth, rapid population growth resulted from the greater availability of food. The Indian subcontinent in the twentieth century would become one of the most populous places on earth.

In Indonesia, the Dutch rivaled British interests. The Dutch had maintained a foothold in the jungles of Indonesia since the early seventeenth century, when they fortified their trading posts against marauding sea pirates. Local rulers signed treaties recognizing the Dutch as overlords. The Dutch held the largest islands, Sumatra, Java, and Borneo, dividing New Guinea with Britain. Aggressive Dutch merchants tapped rubber and other natural resources of the region.

France made its first move to colonize Southeast Asia in the late 1850s. French and Spanish forces had bombarded the towns of Da Nang and Saigon (in present-day Vietnam) in joint retaliation for the execution of a Spanish missionary. When the Vietnamese counterattacked, a French admiral annexed three provinces. France attempted unsuccessfully to form a protectorate over northern Annam (the northern part of Vietnam), which became known as Tonkin.

French traders arrived in Indochina in ever-increasing numbers. In the early 1880s, the Emperor of Annam sought Chinese assistance against the French, invoking China's ancient claims to the region. An anti-foreign movement known as the "Black Flags," which included Vietnamese and Chinese brigands, harassed foreigners, aided by Chinese soldiers. In

Lord and Lady Curzon parade in Delhi, 1903.

1883, a French expedition captured the city of Hanoi in Tonkin. Troops sent from Cochin (the southern part of Vietnam) forced the Vietnamese to accept a protectorate that included all of Annam. In 1887, France created the Union of Indochina, which included Tonkin, Annam, Cochin China, and Cambodia, and, in 1893, it unilaterally added Laos to French Indochina.

The colonial race extended to the islands of the South Seas. France claimed Tahiti and New Caledonia. Britain held the Fiji Islands, some of which served as refueling ports, but little else. Germany hoisted its flag over the Marshall Islands and Samoa. Smaller islands were sometimes bartered and traded as trinkets by the European powers in the various agreements signed to settle major disputes over the larger colonies.

Japan and China: Contrasting Experiences

In contrast to other Asian countries, Japan maintained real independence and gradually emerged as a power in Asia. Japan built up its army and navy after being "opened" to Western contact in the 1850s, and by the end of the century had joined the imperialists. The 1868 Meiji Restoration, ending a period of chaos, facilitated a remarkable "Westernization" of economic life there. In Japan, the new centralized state structure encouraged the development of commerce and industry. Military conscription and the implementation of Western technology, assisted by Western technical experts, made it possible for Japan to emerge as a world power at the dawn of the twentieth century. Japan, too, then began to seek colonies in Asia.

In China, the Ching (Qing) dynasty continued to be beset by internal division, as well as by the demands of the imperialist powers, and the government only slowly began to adopt Western technology to its own purposes. In the late 1860s, a few Chinese reformers had begun to favor building railways as a way of modernizing the Chinese state. Yet, conservative opposition to modernization continued within the imperial court. Some Chinese scholars believed that railways damaged "the dragon's vein" across the landscape, threatening the earth's harmony. Imperial officials feared that in case of war China's enemies would quickly seize the rail lines.

With colonial rivalries reaching a fever pitch in the late 1890s, the European powers sought to impose further trade and territorial concessions on China. Military weakness made China an easy target for expansion of European influence. The Sino-Japanese War of 1894–1895 led to an independent Korea and China's loss of the island of Formosa (Taiwan) to Japan. Needing loans to pay off a war indemnity to Japan, China was forced the next year to make further trading concessions and disadvantageous railroad leases to Germany and Russia.

Following the murder of two German missionaries in 1897, the German government forced China in 1898 to grant a ninety-nine-year lease on the north Chinese port of Tsingtao (Qingdao) on Kwangchow (Jiao-zhou) Bay and to grant two concessions to build railways in Shandong Province. German engineers constructed a line from Tsingtao to Tsinan (Jinan). Russia was eager to complete its own line to Vladivostok through Chinese territories, permitting it to open up the Chinese province of Manchuria, rich in soybeans and cotton. Russia seized and fortified Port Arthur (Lüshon) on the pretext of protecting China from Germany and compelled the Chinese government to lease Port Arthur and Dairen (Lüda) for twenty-five years. The Chinese gave France a lease on Canton Bay and recognized its trading "sphere of influence" over several southern provinces.

The U.S. government now claimed to seek what it referred to as "an open door" in China, in accordance with the principle of free trade. The powers agreed not to interfere with any treaty port or with the interests of any other power. China agreed to lease Britain some of the Shandong Peninsula and several ports, and to guarantee a British trade monopoly on the Yangtze River, the entry to much of central China. These forced concessions further weakened the ruling Ching dynasty; China had little more ability than a colony to resist the demands of the European powers.

In northern China, many Chinese resented the foreigners, whom some blamed for floods in 1898 and a drought two years later, events that also were taken to mean that the "mandate of Heaven" of the ruling dynasty was at an end. The "Righteous and Harmonious Fists" was a secret anti-foreign society better known as the Boxers after the training practices of its members. Many of the Boxers believed they were immune to foreign bullets. The targets of their wrath were missionaries who sought to convert the Chinese, railroads that took work away from Chinese transporters, foreign merchants who flooded the Chinese market with cheap textiles, bringing unemployment to the local population, and foreign soldiers, who often mistreated the Chinese.

In 1900, the Boxers attacked Europeans, Americans, and Chinese Christians in Shandong Province, cutting the railway line between Peking (Beijing) and Tientsin (Tianjin). These attacks spread quickly to the imperial capital and other parts of northern China. After the Boxers killed several hundred "foreign devils," British, Russian, German, French, Japanese, and American troops put down the rebellion. Their governments assessed the Chinese government a crushing indemnity of 67.5 million pounds.

The scramble for concessions went on. Russia's competition with Japan for Manchuria in northeastern China led to its shocking defeat in the Russo-Japanese War of 1904–1905. Following its victory, Japan took over and expanded the Manchurian railways. This humiliation and subsequent disadvantageous railway concessions granted to the European powers and Japan intensified Chinese nationalist sentiment, and contributed to the overthrow of the Ching dynasty in 1911.

The United States in Asia

The American imperial venture in the Philippine Islands, an archipelago in the Pacific Ocean, was not all smooth sailing. During the Spanish-American War of 1898, fought largely over the Caribbean island of Cuba, the American admiral George Dewey (1837–1917) sailed into Manila Bay and defeated the Spanish fleet, capturing Manila. The United States had been helped by a Filipino nationalist, Emilio Aguinaldo (1869–1964). But once the peace treaty ending the Spanish-American War was signed, President William McKinley announced that it would be "cowardly and discreditable" to leave the Philippines. In 1899, the Filipinos began to fight the Americans to obtain their independence, but U.S. troops defeated Aguinaldo's guerrilla forces after three years of fighting. American soldiers herded Filipinos into prison camps, torturing and executing some of those they captured. Aguinaldo himself was taken prisoner in 1901 and the insurrection, in which perhaps as many as 200,000 Filipinos died, ended the following year. The Philippines became a territory of the United States.

The U.S. government did not want to be left out of the scramble for Chinese concessions. In 1899, Secretary of State John Hay announced his country's "Open Door Policy" with regard to China, and tried to convince the other powers to leave China open to all trade. Only the British government publicly expressed its agreement with this principle, but the scramble for advantage in China and elsewhere went on.

Map 22.4 demonstrates the remarkable impact of the scramble for colonies in Asia. Only Japan succeeded in keeping its independence, with the government of China virtually helpless in the face of the imperial powers and Siam serving as a buffer state between British and French spheres.

DOMINATION OF INDIGENOUS PEOPLES

The eagerness with which many Europeans embarked on or applauded imperial ventures can be partially explained by their assumptions that non-Western peoples were culturally inferior to them. These were not new views, nor were they the only ones held. During the sixteenth and seventeenth centuries, non-Western peoples—particularly Islamic peoples—had been viewed as enemies by virtue of their religion (as well as because of the threat seemingly posed by the Ottoman Empire). In the nineteenth century, many Westerners viewed Chinese and Africans with disdain.

Nineteenth- and twentieth-century Western academic and literary attempts to understand the special character of dominated or conquered peoples reflected the intellectual and cultural processes of imperialism. The colonial powers, believing themselves racially and culturally superior to the people they had conquered, assumed the right to exploit conquered territories and to decide what was "best" for the colonized. "Orientalism," as this viewpoint was called, began with the assumption that not only were Asian, African, and other colonized peoples different, but they were inferior as well. This was reflected by the Egyptian exhibit at an international exposition in Paris in 1900. An Egyptian visitor was outraged that it seemed "intended to resemble the old aspect of Cairo," the image that the hosts wanted to present, in such a way that "even the paint on the building was made dirty."

The competition for colonies also coincided with the emergence of pseudo-scientific studies that were held to prove the superiority of Western peoples (through, for example, measures of cranium size). Material progress represented by steamboats, railroads, and machine guns was assumed to follow logically from what was considered moral superiority. A French prime minister insisted that "the superior races have rights over the inferior races."

Social Darwinism

In the eighteenth century, the philosophes of the Enlightenment had come to view cultural differences of non-Western peoples with detachment and interest, believing that they could learn from people who seemed in some ways different from themselves. In writing about the "propensity to war, slaughter, and destruction, which has always depopulated the face of the earth," Voltaire had noted that "this rage has taken much less possession of the minds of the people of India and China than of ours." But Social Darwinists in the nineteenth century did not believe that they could learn anything from non-Western peoples. Social Darwinists argued the natural superiority of some races to justify the conquest of the so-called "backward" peoples of Africa and Asia. They applied theories of biological evolution to the history of states, utilizing the principle of "natural selection" developed by Charles Darwin, in which the stronger prevail over the weak. These theories were popularized by another British scientist, Herbert Spencer (1820–1903), who took Darwin one step further by first uttering the chilling phrase "survival of the fittest." Nations, according to this view, must struggle, like species, in order to survive. Success in the international battle for colonies would measure and develop national mettle.

Cultural stereotypes of the peoples of the "mysterious" East or the "dark continent" of Africa held sway. These ranged from "childlike," and therefore in need of being led, to "barbaric," "depraved," "sneaky," and/or "dangerous," and therefore in need of constant surveillance. Curzon called the Indian princes "a set of unruly and ignorant and rather undisciplined school-boys."

Even well-meaning critics of colonial brutality and other reformers assumed the inferiority of those they were trying to help. Late in the nineteenth century, one British woman denounced her government's lack of

The British image of themselves in Africa, from *The Kipling Reader*, 1908: "A young man . . . walking slowly at the head of his flocks, while at his knee ran small naked cupids."

concern for abuses of Africans and wanted the latter to be able to "advance along their own lines." But she also insisted that "racial purity" be preserved. Josephine Butler, a feminist reformer, denounced the prostitution of Indian women, but believed that Indian women stood lower on a scale of human development than did her British "sisters." Yet, at the beginning of the twentieth century, some feminist activists did begin to learn about and respect Indian culture and work closely with Indian women.

Convinced of their cultural superiority, European colonists adopted an aggressive attitude toward non-Western peoples, viewing them as little more than potential obstacles to their goals, peoples whose lives were not equal to those of Westerners. Imperial officials adopted racist ideology to justify colonialism and the brutalization of indigenous peoples. Most colonial businessmen, as well as administrators, paid little attention to the damaging effects of colonialism on the indigenous peoples.

The experience of the Herero people in what had become German Southwest Africa provides perhaps the most egregious example of the consequences of the prevalent European attitude toward non-European peoples. A German official stated the goal of the colonial administration: "Our task is to strip the Herero of his heritage and national characteristics and gradually to submerge him, along with the other natives, into a single colored working class." Germany put down resistance to its domination with particular barbarity. In 1903, the Herero people, losing their land to German cattle raisers and angered by the unwillingness of colonial courts to punish cases of murder and manslaughter against the Herero, rose up in rebellion. The Germans killed about 55,000 men, women, and children, two-thirds of the Herero people, chasing survivors into the desert and sealing waterholes. The German official report stated: "Like a wounded beast the enemy was tracked down from one water-hole to the next until finally he became the victim of his own environment. . . . [This] was to complete what the German army had begun: extermination of the Herero nation."

Social Darwinism had other implications for the home countries. Some prominent Europeans began to believe that the European powers could "export" their more economically marginal or politically troublesome population to the colonies. By this so-called "social imperialism," colonies would help countries easily dispose of their "least fit," such as unemployed or underemployed workers. Social tensions and conflict would be reduced, the challenge of the working class for political power thus defused. Cecil Rhodes put it most baldly: "If you want to avoid civil war, you must become imperialists." The British colonial armies alone absorbed thousands of "surplus" Irish and Scots. By this view, colonies, then, could serve as a social safety valve, just as Lenin believed that capitalists increasingly depended on imperialism to provide outlets for capital.

Similarly, at the turn of the century, the U.S. historian Frederick Jackson Turner held that the expansion of the American frontier westward helped reduce discontent by providing land and opportunity to the surplus population of the East. A French military administrator, Marshal Lyautey, once referred to Algeria and Morocco as the "French Far West." As in the case of the relationship between colonists and Indians in the U.S. West, Europeans viewed the peoples of the distant African and Asian lands as culturally inferior to them. This made it easier for them to justify conquest, domination, and exploitation.

Technological Domination and Indigenous Subversion

Europeans employed technological advances in travel and weaponry in their subjugation of indigenous peoples. Railways aided imperial armies in their conquest and defense of colonial frontiers, although horses, mules, and camels still hauled men and supplies across African deserts and bush country. The steamship, like the train, lessened the time of travel to distant places. In 1825, a steamship first supplemented sailpower. By the end of the century, thanks to the completion of the Suez Canal in 1869, linking the Mediterranean and Red Seas, British bureaucrats, soldiers, merchants, and tourists could reach India in about twenty days. Messages could now travel even faster. The heliograph, which sent messages by means of a movable mirror that reflected sunlight, and then the telegraph speeded up communications and led to better coordination of troop movements.

Advanced military technology invariably overcame open rebellion by indigenous peoples. Power searchlights and observation balloons aided Eu-

Trading ships in Calcutta at the end of the century.

ropean armies. Along the South African frontier, Zulu warriors resisted the British advance in the late 1870s, earning several victories with surprise attacks. But by the 1890s, they were no match for the white outsiders with their guns and cannon. The Gatling, or machine gun, and the single-barreled Maxim gun, which could fire rapidly without being reloaded, proved devastating. A contemporary quip described relations between colonists and the colonized: "Whatever happens we have got the Maxim gun, and they have not." A single gunner or two could fend off a large-scale attack, and British casualties were reduced to almost none. To soldiers colonial battles now seemed "more like hunting than fighting."

The colonial powers tested new, lighter artillery that could be moved quickly and new, more powerful shells. The British developed the "dum-dum" bullet, which exploded upon impact, with the shooting of attacking "natives" in mind. (It took its name from the arsenal in Calcutta where it was developed.) For the most part, there was little to stop the European onslaught other than malaria and yellow fever carried by mosquitoes, and sleeping sickness, carried by the tsetse fly.

Yet, subordinate peoples could express resistance to powerful outsiders in other ways besides risking annihilation in open rebellion. The "weapons of the weak" ranged from riots and individual subversion to foot-dragging and gentle but determined defiance. The latter included pretending not to understand, or sometimes what Chinese called "that secret smile" that suggested not compliance but rather defiance in the guise of deference. Such play-acting in daily life offered only glimpses of the ridicule of Europeans that could be expressed openly in private, or hinted at in theatrical productions, songs, dances, or other public expressions of local folklore. Indigenous peoples used symbols, gestures, double meanings, and images that were easily understood by the subordinate population, but sufficiently disguised from Europeans or ambiguous enough to fall short of being considered "seditious." These were small victories of political dissent, but victories nonetheless.

Imperial Economies

Once they had a foothold, the European powers established "plunder economies" in three ways: they expropriated the land of the indigenous people; they used the soil and subsoil for their own profit; and they exploited the population for labor. In British Ceylon (captured from the Dutch during the Napoleonic Wars), Dutch Java, French Algeria, and German East Africa, indigenous people without deeds or titles to their land lost it to the colonial power. They also lost traditional rights to hunt, graze animals, and gather firewood on land they did not own, a process that had also characterized the early stages of capitalist agriculture in Western Europe.

The European powers imposed commercial controls over natural resources, demands that again reflect the evolution toward the arbitrary, centralized control of the "new imperialism" of the century's last two decades and beyond. Imperial powers routinely blocked long-standing

A Maxim gun and its crew on the northwestern frontier of South Africa, 1898.

trade routes that led to other colonies, preventing commercial exchanges from which their own merchants did not profit. European merchants, protected by high tariffs at home against foreign imports, insisted on maintaining a monopoly on the sale of their manufactured goods in the colonies. Colonialists forced or, in the best circumstances, encouraged local populations to produce for the European market, discouraging or even forbidding the extraction of raw materials or production that would compete with that of the mother country. In Indonesia, for example, the Dutch employed the "culture system," whereby they imposed production quotas on the indigenous population, employed forced labor, and ordered people in West Java to grow coffee when its price rose and to cut down spice-bearing trees and plants when the price of spices fell.

In North Africa, the French government promoted the economic interests of French settlers, giving them the finest Algerian land. The government also ordered land owned collectively by Arabs to be sold as individual plots that only the French could afford to purchase. In Morocco and Tunisia, the French claimed "unexploited" land, such as that belonging to nomad peoples, with French tribunals adjudicating contested cases. Above all, French colonial administrators sought to maintain order and collect taxes, which they did with frequent brutality. One visitor found that "the head tax is above all a very effective agent of civilization," so that in one district "when a village could not or would not pay its taxes in full, the custom was to seize a child and place him in a village named 'Liberty' until the tax was paid." In some regions able to produce for the French market, taxes were collected in kind, or through forced labor.

Portuguese colonists imposed conditions of virtual slavery in their African colonies in the nineteenth century. They kidnapped people from

A German caricature of British imperialism. An Englishman pours whiskey into an African, who is squeezed of all resources, while a missionary reads the Bible and gazes out of the corner of his eye at the money flowing into the cash box.

their colony of Angola, shipped them to the coastal island of Sao Tomé, and forced them to work on the cocoa plantations for a "contract" period of five years, which few workers survived. In Angola, villagers who could not pay their taxes were required to work for the government for 100 days a year. In Southwest Africa, the Germans forced villagers to grow cotton and, if they resisted, to work on plantations, where they died in droves. The use of forced labor on mine and construction sites by colonial merchants and administrators alike was common; in the German Cameroons, it was estimated that 80,000 Africans hauled goods for Germans on a single road in one year.

Colonial Administrations

European notions of the organization of states clashed with the way indigenous people lived. Almost all Africans lacked the European obsession with fixing exact boundaries, one that intensified in the age of nation-states and aggressive nationalism. For most Africans living in tribal societies, European notions of "boundaries" and "borders" seemed strange. Boundaries established by colonial powers left many formerly unified societies arbitrarily separated and sometimes interfered with the movements of migratory peoples.

How the European powers maintained control over colonies varied. Historians have distinguished between "formal" and "informal" imperialism, although the distinction is mainly one of degree, not kind. Britain, above all, took the path of "informal" imperialism by maintaining control through economic and military domination, without taking over political functions. But a "resident," or representative of Britain, retained ultimate authority, which he exercised in international crises. In formal imperialism, the European power assumed "protectorate" status over a territory, or administered the colony directly. The colonial powers viewed colonial administration as a problem to be solved and, for the most part, remained oblivious to the moral consequences of their domination.

The nature of a colonial "protectorate" changed during the scramble for Africa. Originally the establishment of a protectorate meant that a colonial power defended its interests by controlling the foreign relations of a territory, leaving it to each ruler or chieftain to control his people. Thus, for example, British colonial administration remained decentralized, like the home government itself. But gradually the colonial powers extended their authority over the local population through indigenous officials. In 1886, Britain assumed full sovereignty over most of its colonies. Not long after a British politician predicted "nothing but endless expense, trouble and disaster" if his country took over Uganda, Britain declared Uganda a protectorate in 1894, when the East African Company became unable to administer the territory. Indigenous rulers found earlier agreements broken, and were increasingly treated as little more than intermediaries between the imperialists and their own people. Local systems of justice were left intact wherever possible—this, too, cost less money—but whites were subject only to the courts of the colonial power.

The British government wanted colonies to pay for themselves, with chartered commercial companies—which had launched British rule in Nigeria, Uganda, and what became Rhodesia—bearing the bulk of expenses in exchange for the right to extract profit. During the height of the colonial mania in the 1890s, the British still wanted colonialism to come cheap. Even after formally establishing sovereignty over some colonies, the British colonial administration continued to rule indirectly, trying to make the colonies pay for themselves by directing railway development and then private capital toward regions where raw materials could be extracted or markets found.

The fate of the Ashanti kingdom, which dated to the early eighteenth century, in West Africa, illustrates how informal control was transformed into more direct authority. In the early 1860s, British forces skirmished with the Ashanti people on the northern frontier of the Gold Coast, over which Britain had established a protectorate. After defeating the Ashanti in 1873–1874, Britain made the Gold Coast a crown colony, imposing more direct control. In 1891, the British proposed that the Ashanti kingdom itself become their protectorate. The king replied "my kingdom of Ashanti will never commit itself to any such policy; Ashanti must remain independent as of old, at the same time to be friendly with all white men." Five years later, British troops occupied the Ashanti capital and deported the king when he could not come up with a huge sum in gold to buy continued independence. In a bloody sequel, in 1900–1901, British troops crushed an uprising when the Ashanti refused to surrender the golden stool they treasured as the symbol of their people. In 1901, the Ashanti kingdom became a British colony.

African imperial ventures often began with the directors and principal shareholders of trading companies forging out territories from the underbrush and jungle. But gradually the states they represented became involved, and took over the role of protectors and administrators. For example, the Royal Niger Company, with a charter from Parliament conveying administrative powers in 1886, began to develop what became Nigeria. To counter French moves in East Africa, the British government had authorized the Royal Niger Company to launch an expedition through the rain forests to reach the Sudan. When German merchants, newcomers to Africa, began to establish trading posts to the east in the future Cameroons, the British government declared a protectorate over the Niger Delta.

The French government and the Royal Niger Company settled their respective claims through conventions. But when the Royal Niger Company went bankrupt in 1899, the British government took over administration of the territories. This scenario was also common to the colonial experiences of France, the Netherlands, and Germany: merchant companies that had been granted state monopolies established trading interests in a new colony and then ran into financial difficulties, if not bankruptcy, necessitating the intervention of the state itself.

After the government had taken over for the commercial companies, great differences remained from colony to colony as to their status and administration. These ranged from Canada, independent in all but foreign policy, to remote Ascension Island, halfway between Brazil and the west coast of Africa, run "by a captain as if it were a ship" until British interests were directly threatened, at which time formal annexation took place.

Many of Queen Victoria's subjects—200,000 to 300,000 people—served in the colonial administration (including in the army). Given the size of the empire, however, the number was surprisingly small. Near the end of the century, about 6,000 British civil servants governed India's 300 million inhabitants. The British colonial administration provided a career outlet for the sons of aristocrats, who became high-ranking administrators or officers in the navy and army. Eleven of the fourteen viceroys who served in India from 1858 to 1918 were peers by birth.

British officials recruited subordinates selectively from the colonial population, training, for example, upper-class Indians to work in the administration of the subcontinent. In Nigeria, selected tribal chiefs assumed administrative functions. In the first decade of the twentieth century, at least partially in response to the first stirrings of Egyptian nationalism, the British government expanded the participation of Egyptians in running their country. In Malay, the British "resident" was responsible for putting down disturbances that might threaten British control, while the local rulers were placed in paid administrative positions but had authority only in dealing with religious matters.

The British mastered the policy of "divide and rule," carefully playing off ethnic rivalries wherever helpful, favoring and choosing officials from the dominant groups to ensure cooperation. In India, the British effectively manipulated age-old tensions between Hindus, Muslims, and Sikhs to keep the Indian component of its army under control, ruthlessly repressing dissent.

In the colonies, the British lived in isolation from the indigenous population. The upper class tried to replicate the world of the common rooms of Cambridge and Oxford Universities (more than a quarter of all graduates of Oxford's Balliol College at the turn of the century served in the empire) and of gentlemen's clubs in London, served by Indian, African, or Asian waiters. British colonial women served only English recipes to their guests. Architects attempted (with considerable success) to duplicate Victorian architectural styles in far-off lands, so that the British felt closer to home. Many men of the indigenous population who rose to positions of relative responsibility under the British managed to look and sound as much as possible like British gentlemen. But many Victorians maintained disdain for the Westernized Indian; they ridiculed the *babu*, not because he seemed to be rejecting his own culture, but because they thought he could never be good enough to be British.

French colonial rule differed from that of the British in ways that revealed contrasts between the British and French states. French colonial administration reflected the state centralization that had characterized France's development over the past century and more. Military control, more than commercial relations, formed the basis of the French colonial empire. The French colonial administration employed relatively more French officials and relied less on indigenous peoples than did its British rivals.

The ministries of the navy and of commerce administered French colonies until the establishment of the colonial ministry in 1894. The French colonial ministry then took a much greater role in economic decision making, such as the planning of railroads, than its counterpart in the British Empire. The French colonial civilian administration was staffed by bureaucrats, some trained at the Colonial School created in the 1880s. Africans and Vietnamese, among others, worked for the French governor-generals as virtual civil servants. Like their British rivals, French colonial administrators also exploited ethnic and cultural rivalries, using dominant groups to control their enemies.

The French government directly ruled Algeria; Algerians could become French citizens, but with only limited rights. The sultan of Morocco and the bey of Tunisia still ruled their subjects, at least in name, although government and the exercise of justice remained in the hands of the French colonial administration. In Southeast Asia, the French government created the Union of Indochina between 1887 and 1893, which included Cochin, Tonkin, Annam, Cambodia, and Laos under a single governor-general. The French government also centralized the administration of West Africa in 1895 by forming the federation of French West Africa, and in 1910 it established the federation of French Equatorial Africa, made up of its Central African colonies. Governor-generals, based in Dakar and Brazzaville, served as the highest local administrative authority. Military organization remained the basis for the administration of most French colonies.

ASSESSING THE GOALS OF EUROPEAN IMPERIALISM

Someone once summed up the reasons for which the European powers expanded their horizons as "God, gold, and glory," or as the geographer, missionary, and explorer Dr. David Livingstone put it, "Christianity, Commerce, and Civilization." Which, if any, can be singled out as the dominant impulse behind the "new imperialism"? Some British imperialists spoke of "the white man's burden," a phrase unfortunately immortalized by Rudyard Kipling's poem (1899) of the same name: "Take up the White Man's burden/ And reap his old reward:/ The blame of those ye better/ The Hate of those ye guard."

The "Civilizing Mission"

Most colonists insisted that God was on their side. Curzon once gushed that the British Empire was "under Providence, the greatest instrument for good that the world has seen." A South African offered a more realistic perspective when he commented, "When you came here we owned the land and you had the Bible; now we have the Bible and you own the land." The "civilizing" impulse still animated some European missionaries during the age of the "new imperialism." Thousands of Catholic and Protestant missionaries went to Africa, India, and Asia in the name of God to win converts, a mission both religious and cultural. In 1900, about 18,000 Protestant missionaries lived in colonial settlements around the world. Some British officials considered Anglican and Methodist missionaries to be nuisances. Most Dutch, Belgian, and Italian clergy made little pretense of bringing indigenous peoples "civilization," tending primarily to the spiritual needs of their troops and settlers. Yet, in some places, the clergy helped force Europeans to end or at least temper abuses carried out against local populations. Missionary societies may have been the "conscience" of European colonization, and a small conscience was better than none at all.

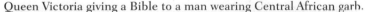

Queen Victoria giving a Bible to a man wearing Central African garb.

For British reformers, the primary goal of the "civilizing mission" in the early part of the century had been to abolish slavery in the British Empire, which was achieved early in the nineteenth century. One aspect of the "civilizing mission" continued to be the attempt of some reformers to limit or to bring to an end abuses of indigenous peoples. In the 1880s, pressure from the British Liberal Party helped end the transport of Chinese laborers to work as indentured workers in South African mines. The British government was embarrassed by the treatment of Indian workers in Natal, which was brought to light by, among others, the young and future Indian leader Mohandas (Mahatma) Gandhi (1869–1948). British officials also protested the brutal labor practices of Portuguese and Belgian entrepreneurs. French religious leaders launched a campaign against the remaining Arab slave trade in Africa, receiving endorsement from Germany and Britain. Britain's claim of holding the high moral ground, however, was open to question. It had declined to press a campaign to reduce or eliminate the sale of arms and liquor to Africans, because both commodities were extremely lucrative to British merchants, as it had refused to stop the sale of Indian opium by British traders in China.

Lord Frederick Lugard (1858–1945), a British colonial official, came up with the term "Dual Mandate" to describe what he considered the "moral" and "material" imperatives of colonial powers. The European powers, he believed, had an obligation to "civilize" native populations and also to "open the door" to the material improvements brought by Western technology. They were establishing "trusteeships." In exchange, the Europeans would extract raw materials and other products. While imperialism would become associated with conservative nationalism in Western Europe, a few socialists in Britain and France believed that the establishment of empire might improve conditions of life for colonial peoples. But, in general, European socialists did not view the question of imperialism as one of their central concerns.

Earlier in the century, the French had seen their "civilizing" mission as the assimilation of colonial peoples into French culture: they would, it was commonly thought, become French. By the end of the century, however, the goal of assimilation had given way to a theory of "association," similar to Lugard's British Dual Mandate. This theory of association held that although colonial peoples were not capable of absorbing French culture, French colonialists would help them develop their economic resources, to the benefit of both. Only in urban settlements in Senegal in West Africa, however, did newborn children automatically become French citizens; in 1914, Senegalese voters elected the first black representative to the Chamber of Deputies.

The Economic Rationale

When missionaries arrived on the shores of Africa or Asia, they usually found that merchants and adventurers were already there looking for gold, ivory, and raw materials. Indeed, Cecil Rhodes once stated that in the business of running colonies "philanthropy is good, but philanthropy at five percent is better." The discovery of new markets seemed absolutely necessary in the 1880s, particularly to British manufacturers, as one continental country after another adopted high protectionist tariffs during the long economic depression that began in 1873. "If you were not such persistent protectionists, you would not find us so keen to annex territories," the British prime minister told France's ambassador to London in 1897. In the rather far-fetched opinion of the brother of Cecil Rhodes, "the Waganda [of Uganda] are clamoring for shoes, stockings and opera glasses and are daily developing fresh wants," which would enrich British manufacturers and merchants peddling the products of the Second Industrial Revolution.

Writing in 1902, the British economist J. A. Hobson (1858–1940) called imperialism "the most powerful factor in the current politics of the western world." He argued that the great powers sought colonies because their economies required outlets for domestically produced manufactured goods and for capital investment. In Hobson's view, businessmen virtually determined British imperial policy; missionaries and soldiers helped them accomplish their goals. Hobson believed that the quest for colonies simply deferred the resolution of the central economic problem at home: underconsumption of industrial goods. He believed that if governments took action to raise wages, and through a gradual and more equitable redistribution of wealth, gave ordinary people the ability to purchase more goods, they could end the problem of domestic underconsumption. This, in his view, would make imperialism unnecessary.

Hobson was not a Marxist, but his views in some ways echoed those of Karl Marx. In *Capital,* Marx, who never used the word imperialism, postulated that the bourgeoisie required "a constantly expanding market for its products." Subsequent Marxists therefore agreed with Hobson's linking of industrial capitalism and imperialism. The Russian revolutionary leader Vladimir Ilyich Ulyanov, better known as Lenin, took Hobson's analysis a step further. He argued that in capitalist nations, bankers and financiers constantly needed new outlets where their capital would earn a greater return than in the nations they now dominated. This incessant expansion of capital brought with it colonial rivalries and conflict. In this final stage of capitalist development, "international trusts" would divide up the globe, he argued.

If Hobson, Rhodes, and Lenin had ever sat at the same dinner table, they would have disagreed about a good many things. But they would have agreed that there was a close connection between the great age of European imperialism and the long economic depression that lasted on the continent from 1873 to the mid-1890s. The quest for colonies took on a somewhat desperate urgency in this period of mounting economic tariffs: there might not be, many thought, enough raw materials and markets to go around.

Merchant traders, like their seventeenth- and eighteenth-century predecessors, counted on finding rich mineral deposits and untapped markets in Africa and Asia. When wildly exaggerated reports of the natural wealth of Africa swept Europe, the competition for colonies increased. In talking to Manchester textile magnates, Henry Stanley described the Congo not in terms of square kilometers but as "square yards of cotton stuff to be exported." Gold and diamond discoveries in South Africa in the 1860s and again in the 1880s unleashed a stampede of prospectors and inspired colonists' dreams. Coastal traders generated further colonial expansion in West Africa. Trade in palm oil, used in large quantities for making soap and glycerin, replaced the slave trade.

Was the hope of economic gain the most significant factor in the frenetic European rush for colonies during the last decades of the nineteenth century? Did the colonial powers actually realize great wealth through their exploration and conquest? In attempting to answer these questions, we must not overlook the enormous human costs to those conquered and colonized.

To be sure, colonies provided some valued products for European markets. Ivory and wild rubber from the Belgian Congo, palm oil from Nigeria, Dahomey, and the Ivory Coast, peanuts from French Senegal, diamonds and gold from South Africa, coffee from British Ceylon, and sugar from Malaya proved to be lucrative commodities. The rubber trade of French Vietnam, Dutch Indonesia, the Congo, and British Malaya expanded rapidly with the popularity of the bicycle and particularly following the invention of the automobile. The British colonies of Nigeria and the Gold Coast produced 4 percent of the world's cocoa in 1905, 24 percent ten years later. The consumption of tea, most of it from China and Ceylon, increased by almost four times between 1840 and 1900.

Colonies provided an inviting market for manufactured goods from the mother country. In the 1890s, about a third of all British exports and about a quarter of all investment went to its colonies, above all India, which principally imported cotton cloth and other textiles, iron, hardware, and shoes from Britain. Yet, British capital investment abroad was still principally directed toward its lost colony, the United States, as well as toward other independent states such as Turkey. British subjects also invested in the settlement colonies, Australia, New Zealand, and Canada, as well as India. The African colonies attracted very little British investment. There was more British trade with Belgium in the 1890s than with all of Africa.

Only a very small percentage of French and German investment was directed into their respective colonies, along with a trickle into the colonies of rivals, because colonial investments were risky. French investment abroad was overwhelmingly directed toward other parts of Europe, particularly Russia. Only about 5 percent of French investment reached its colonies in 1900; in 1914, France bought more goods from its colonies than it sold them in return. Less than 1 percent of German trade was with its colonies. By 1907, German investment in all German colonies fell slightly below the value of investments in a single large bank at home.

Imperial governments, which had to foot the bill for troops, supplies, guns, and administrative and other expenses, therefore became increasingly suspicious of the confident assurances of adventurers that incredible riches lay just a little farther up a barely explored African river or beyond the next oasis. In 1899, a French politician whose ardor for imperialism had waned defined the two stages of colonization as "the joy of conquest," followed inevitably, as after a fine restaurant meal, by "the arrival of the bill." The French colonial lobby, including provincial chambers of commerce in manufacturing cities and ports and geographic societies, had pictured western Sudan as teeming with lucrative commercial opportunities. It turned out that this vast region of desert offered merchants little more than wild rubber, a little gold, some peanuts, and an occasional elephant tusk. Yet, the French government spent vast sums to administer and police an increasingly unwieldy empire.

Even if the economic returns were far less than the colonial lobbies, merchants, and politicians of the European powers had anticipated, the exploitation of natural resources by the imperialists contributed to the economic and political underdevelopment of these regions once they became independent nations in the twentieth century.

The economic interpretation of the imperial race for colonies cannot be discounted, however. Key economic sectors did benefit substantially from raw materials and markets provided by the new colonies, as did individual businessmen. Nonetheless, an economic explanation for colonialism was only one factor, and often a minor one, and difficult to detach from other motives.

Imperialism and Nationalism

The new imperialism was, above all, an extension of the search for security and power on the European continent in a period characterized by aggressive nationalism and bitter international rivalries. Even in the case of Great Britain, the imperialist power with the greatest economic investment in colonies, the international rivalry of the European powers was the strongest impulse for imperialism. Britain expanded its domination into new regions, not only in search of new markets, but simply to keep the French, Germans, or Russians from establishing bases and colonies that might threaten British interests. Britain's definition of its interests in Egypt, the pursuit of which helped launch the landgrab in Africa, had far more to do with fear of competition from its rivals than with economic motives.

Burma, absorbed by Britain after wars in 1824 and 1852 to protect India's eastern frontier against possible colonial rivals, is a case in point.

When France declared its economic interest in Burma in the late 1870s, the British expanded their control over Upper Burma as well, fighting another war with Burma in 1885. After this third war, they packed off the reigning king to India, shipped his throne to a museum in Calcutta, turned his palace into a British club, and annexed Burma to the administration of India. Likewise, the establishment of a British protectorate over Afghanistan in 1880 cannot be explained by economic motives, only by a desire to place a buffer state between India and expanding Russian interests in the region. Britain's goal in what contemporary diplomats called "the great game" between Britain and Russia in the Near East and Asia was to prevent Russian troops from occupying the high range of mountains in and adjacent to Afghanistan. Lord Curzon put the issues at stake for Britain succinctly: "Turkestan, Afghanistan, Transcaspia, Persia—to many these names breathe only a sense of utter remoteness. . . . To me, I confess, they are the pieces on a chessboard upon which is being played out a game for the domination of the world."

The nationalism that surged through all the European powers in the 1880s and 1890s fueled the "new imperialism." In 1876, when Britain opposed Russian moves toward the Turkish capital of Constantinople, a popular British song went: "We don't want to fight, But, by Jingo, if we do, We've got the men, We've got the ships, We've got the money too." The term "jingoism" came into use in English to mean fervent nationalism. Generations of British schoolchildren gawked at maps of the world that displayed colony after colony, however varied the structure and effectiveness of British control, colored red, the map color of Great Britain.

The colonial experience became an important part of British national consciousness. Newspapers, magazines, popular literature, and the publication of soldiers' diaries and letters carried home news from the colonies and made imperialism seem a romantic adventure, a source of titillation.

In 1880, the annual Naval and Military Tournament in London began to present reenactments of colonial skirmishes and battles. One play, *Siege of Delhi*, ended with an Irish officer falling in love and dancing the jig, as the curtain falls on Indians about to be shot out of a cannon. In 1911, an Italian writer's enthusiasm for the feats of his army, which established a colony in Libya through conquest (see Chapter 21), included descriptions of the "lustrous" eyes of the Sicilian horses, who seemed, by their neighing, to be attempting to pronounce the word "Italy." "Let the peace-people croak as they please," a general's daughter exclaims in a contemporary novel about Egypt, "it is war that brings out the truly heroic virtues."

From the drawing rooms of country estates to the wretched pubs of Liverpool and Birmingham, the British howled for revenge for the death of "Chinese" Gordon, killed by the forces of the Mahdi. Few Europeans, at best, wept at the destruction of entire cultures and the death of hundreds of thousands of people at the hands of European armies. "Special artists" and then photographers began to travel with British colonial forces; movie cameras recorded Kitchener's 1899 campaign against the Boers in South Africa. At a time of political opposition in Great Britain to costly colonial commitments, the romanticization of British expeditionary forces helped win support for spending even more.

Voluntary associations pressured the colonial powers to devote more resources to the building of empire. In Great Britain, Germany, and France, geographic societies, associations that met periodically to listen to talks about exploration in Africa and Asia, sponsored voyages that charted unexplored—at least by Europeans—territories.

In Germany and Britain, naval leagues whipped up enthusiasm for imperialism. The Pan-German League (1891) demanded more expenditures for warships. The champion of colonial lobbying groups, the Primrose League in Britain (founded in 1884), had 1.7 million members by 1906, drawn primarily from business, finance, the military, and government, the groups with the greatest stake in imperialism.

To be sure, strident critics of imperialism could be found. In Britain, anti-imperialists were to be found among Liberal or Labour Party intellectuals, some of the latter, in particular, denouncing the Boer War as orchestrated in the interests of British capitalists with investments in South Africa. Anti-imperialist groups included the "Ethical Union," formed in 1896, whose members believed that imperialism marked a setback on the path of human progress. They rejected the "civilizing mission" arguments for imperialism. Like Hobson, who frequently addressed their meetings, they had no illusions about the causes or consequences of imperialism, and disparaged jingoism with passion. They denounced the fact that "imperialists have frightened us . . . into a 'spirited foreign policy,' [with] the bogey of 'Our Trade in Danger,' and the pretense that 'Trade follows the Flag.'" These critics of imperialism wanted moral reason to be applied to international affairs. Future Labour Prime Minister Ramsey MacDonald exclaimed in 1898: "Civilization is not expressed by the reading of the Bible, the drinking of Rum, and the weaving of cotton, for there are other civilizations besides that of the West. . . . English civilization can no more be carried to India by Englishmen and lived up to there by them than they can carry ice in their luggage—we cannot pretend to be a great civilizing agency." But with the end of the Boer War, anti-imperial voices became more faint in Britain, although some critics joined the Congo Reform campaign and other movements seeking to pressure Britain, among other colonial powers, to pay more attention to the welfare of colonized peoples.

In France, anti-imperialists focused on the financial burden of expansion. One member of the Chamber of Deputies complained, "We are being drawn along in an irresistible process, like that of TIME, by the mere force of a colonial expansionism which has got out of control." In the United States at the turn of the century, the American Anti-Imperialist League joined together groups opposing the annexation of the Philippines as a territory. But almost everywhere the strident imperialist roar drowned out dissident voices. It contributed to the aggressive nationalism that fueled the increasingly bitter rivalries between the European Great Powers and further destabilized the continent.

CONCLUSION

In 1500, the European powers controlled about 7 percent of the globe's land; by 1800, they controlled 35 percent; in 1914, they controlled 84 percent. Between 1871 and 1900, the British Empire, which came to include one-quarter of the world's population, expanded to include 66 million people and 4.5 million square miles, the French Empire 3.5 million square miles, and Germany, Belgium, and Italy about 1 million square miles each. Even Spain, despite losing the Philippines and Cuba to the United States in 1898, took new colonies in Morocco and the western Sahara.

Aggressive nationalism shaped the contours of the new European imperialism from the early 1880s to 1914. A British nationalist put it this way: "Today, power and domination rather than freedom and independence are the ideas that appeal to the imagination of the masses—and the national ideal has given way to the imperial." Imperialism sharpened the rivalries of the Great Powers, while solidifying international alliances. Competing colonial interests brought France and Britain to the verge of war after the Fashoda Affair of 1898. Subsequent crises, including the emergence of nationalism among the colonized themselves, assumed even more dramatic dimensions. Infused with the same sense of struggle that seemed to engulf Europe, these crises would defy peaceful resolution. Meanwhile, an enthusiast for imperialism preached a "new Machiavellianism," insisting that national interests outweigh all others.

CHAPTER 23

THE ORIGINS OF
THE GREAT WAR

"The lights are going out all over Europe. They will not be lit again in our lifetime." So spoke Sir Edward Grey, the British foreign secretary, in early August 1914, as the Great War began. His last-minute diplomatic efforts to prevent war having failed, Grey was one of the few to share an apocalyptic vision of a conflict that most people thought would be over by Christmas, if not before. Observers who anticipated that this war would be more destructive than any ever fought were few indeed. International peace conferences, held in The Hague in 1899 and 1907, had considered ways of reducing atrocities in war, but they offered no clue that future wars would be any different from those of the past. Not even Grey could have foreseen the 37.5 million casualties, the downfall of four empires, and shifts in Europe's economic, social, cultural, and political life after the war that made the years before the war seem "the good old days."

The Great War was the first international conflict of great scale since the Napoleonic era. It involved all the Great Powers, with Italy entering the war in 1915, and the United States in 1917. Before the war ended, it would also draw a host of minor powers into the fray. The catastrophic conflagration was set off by a spark—the assassination of Austro-Hungarian Archduke Francis Ferdinand in Sarajevo on June 28, 1914, by a Serb nationalist. In little more than a month, war engulfed the powers of Europe through the decades-old system of entangling alliances that interwove their fates. And while these alliances did not make a general war in Europe inevitable—in fact, the situation in Europe seemed much more precarious in 1905 and 1911 than it did in 1914—most heads of state, diplomats, and military planners expected a major war in their lifetimes. Some were relieved, and others delighted, when it began. Few were surprised.

Entangling alliances, 1906: Britain, France, and Russia on the left; Austria-Hungary and Germany on the right; and childlike Italy trying to choose between them.

ENTANGLING ALLIANCES

Among the national rivalries in Europe, none seemed more irreparable than that between Germany and France. However, none was potentially as dangerous as that between Russia and Austria-Hungary, which, focusing on the Balkans, was accentuated by the presence within the Habsburg empire of South Slav peoples who looked to Russia as the protector of all Slavs. In the meantime, Russia, with its long-standing goal of increasing its influence in the Balkans and perhaps one day holding Constantinople, fanned the flames of Pan-Slavism. Germany and Austria-Hungary became firm allies, their alliance directed, above all, against Russia. In 1882, Italy joined the two Central European powers to form the Triple Alliance. By 1905, growing German and British economic and military rivalry helped drive together France and Britain, the oldest rivals in Europe. Now Russia, France, and Britain were allied in the Triple Entente. Entangling alliances left the Great Powers of Europe divided into two armed camps. Because of these alliances, the outbreak of war between any two rivals threatened to bring all of the powers into the conflict.

Irreconcilable Hatreds

The German Empire, proclaimed at Versailles in the wake of the French defeat in the Franco-Prussian War of 1870–1871, continued to hold Alsace and most of Lorraine after the war indemnity was paid and German occupation troops were withdrawn from the rest of France. The French never reconciled themselves to the loss of two of their wealthiest provinces. Although many Alsatians spoke a German dialect, Alsace had

La germanisation de l'Alsace. Alsacienne apprenant le pas de l'oie. Illustration (1911) de Simplicissimus

An Alsatian woman learning to goose-step. A caricature from the German satirical review *Simplicimus.*

been an integral and strategically important part of France since the seventeenth century. Most people living in the parts of Lorraine absorbed into Germany, including the fortress town of Metz, spoke and considered themselves French. The absorption of Alsace-Lorraine into unified Germany in 1871 alone would have guaranteed animosity between Germany and France.

The growing rivalry between France and Germany over colonial interests added to mutual mistrust. At first, newly unified Germany had no colonies. But Chancellor Otto von Bismarck's successors gradually led Germany into a rivalry with France over colonial interests in the Mediterranean and in North Africa, and with Britain in Africa, Turkey, and the Middle East.

Francis Joseph, the elderly emperor of Austria-Hungary, was a plodding man of integrity who had assumed the throne in 1848 and who had once

The aging Emperor Francis Joseph of the Habsburg monarchy.

told Theodore Roosevelt, the president of the United States, "You see in me the last monarch of the old school." Respected by his people, he remained a largely ceremonial figure identified with the survival of the polyglot Habsburg state in an age of nationalism. Francis Joseph bore a series of family tragedies with dignity: the execution in 1867 of his brother Maximilian in Mexico, where he was briefly emperor, his son's suicide in 1889, and his wife's madness. Throughout his reign, which was even longer than that of Queen Victoria of England, the Habsburg emperor had been determined that the imperial army be strong and that his dynasty maintain international prestige.

Irreconcilable hatreds existed in the Austro-Hungarian Empire, which was made up of a great many different nationalities. The Austrians and the Hungarians, who dominated the other nationalities of their territories, were satisfied, but other peoples were not. Thus, many Slavic peoples, such as Czechs and Slovaks in Central Europe, particularly resented Austrian and Hungarian domination. And Romanians, a Latin people, were especially unhappy with Hungary's vigorous campaign to "Magyarize" public life at the expense of non-Hungarian minorities.

The South Slavs were the most dissatisfied peoples within the Austro-Hungarian monarchy. The southern territories of Austria-Hungary included South Slav peoples, majorities in some regions, who resented subservience to the monarchy, the armies of which depended on soldiers loyal to the emperor no matter what their nationality. These included Slovenes, Croats, and, above all, Serbs (see Map 18.3). Russia's ties to the Slavic peoples of the Balkans, reinforced by similarity of language and, in the case of Serbia, the sharing of the Orthodox religion, challenged Austro-Hungarian influence in that region.

During the mid-nineteenth-century revolutions, the Russian army had bailed out the then youthful Emperor Francis Joseph, invading Hungary in 1849 and defeating its rebellious army. But by the turn of the century, the Russian government was eagerly fanning Pan-Slav fervor in the Balkans, stirring ethnic tension in the southern regions of the Habsburg monarchy. In the mountainous Habsburg Balkan territories of Bosnia and Herzegovina, which included Orthodox Serbs, Muslims, and Catholic Croats, many Serbs were committed to joining Bosnia to Serbia. The threat of Russian-oriented Pan-Slavism made the Habsburgs even more dependent on their alliance with Germany, as they contemplated the possibility of one day being drawn into a war against Russia. The implication of Pan-Slav nationalism, that Slavs sharing a common culture ought also to share a common government, threatened the very existence of the Habsburg monarchy.

For centuries Russia had coveted the strategically crucial Dardanelles and the narrow straits of Constantinople, controlled by the sickly Turkish Ottoman Empire. Russian mastery over the straits that separate Europe and Asia would allow it to control entry to the Black Sea and afford it free

In this Austrian caricature of the Pan Slav Congress of 1867, Czechs approach for their Pan Slav milk.

access to the Mediterranean. British policy in the Balkans had long been predicated on keeping the narrow straits from Russian control. Russia's defeat in the Crimean War (1853–1856) by Britain, France, and Turkey had only temporarily diminished Russian interest in the region. British governments therefore traditionally tried to protect the Turkish Ottoman Empire, above all against Russian encroachment.

The Alliance System

The alliance system of late nineteenth-century Europe, then, hinged on German and French enmity, the competing interests of Austria-Hungary and Russia in the Balkans, and Germany's fear of being attacked from both east and west by Russia and France (see Map 23.1). Great Britain and Italy were more or less free agents: Britain, colonial rival of both Germany and France and opponent of Russian expansion, ultimately came to fear the expanding German navy more than French colonial competition. Italy's support could be purchased by the highest bidder. The foundation of nineteenth-century diplomacy lay in the assumption of each continental power that alliances with other Great Powers would protect it by forcing any nation considering war to face at least two hostile powers. This system, based upon two counterbalancing alliance systems, had helped maintain peace.

MAP 23.1   EUROPE IN 1914   States and contested territories before the outbreak of the Great War.

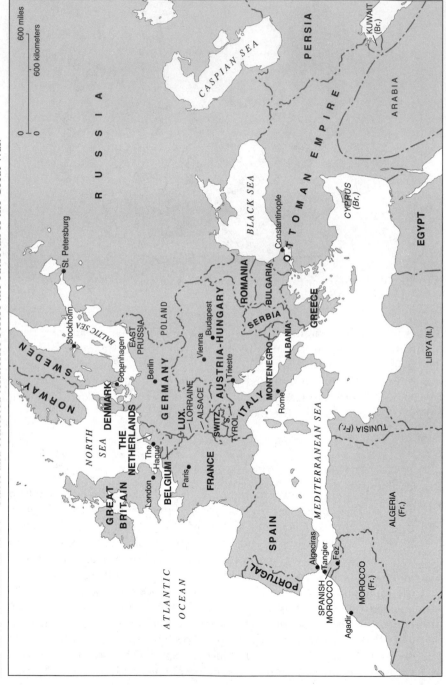

Bismarck captured the urgency the European Great Powers felt about the necessity of alliances, and the delicate nature of the balance of power itself: "All [international] politics reduces itself to this formula: Try to be *à trois* (three) as long as the world is governed by the unstable equilibrium of five Great Powers"—Germany, Austria-Hungary, Russia, Britain, and France.

The diplomats of the powers were the heirs of Metternich, the Austrian leader who dominated international relations in the three decades following Napoleon's defeat in 1815. Many of them were nobles who believed that the Great Powers ought to make decisions in the interest of the smaller ones, and in the interest of peace. Unlike Metternich, they embraced nationalism as a principle, but only when considering the rights of the Great Powers. If they allowed smaller powers some rights, they ascribed the non-European peoples (with the exception of the United States and Japan, the only non-European powers in the world) none at all.

The details and even the existence of most treaties and agreements remained hidden from public scrutiny. Only gradually, during the final diplomatic crisis that immediately led to the war, did the extent to which national destinies were intertwined by alliances become clear to the mass of the population. The cost of secret deals would be high.

Germany and Austria-Hungary against Russia

Germany, united in 1871, first enjoyed good relations with Russia, another autocratic power. In 1873, Bismarck forged the Three Emperor's League, an alliance between his newly unified Germany, Austria-Hungary, and Russia; by the alliance, the three rulers pledged to consult each other in order to maintain the peace "against all disturbances from whatever side they might come." But it was difficult to gloss over tensions between Austro-Hungarian and Russian interests in the Balkans. When Russia sought and found occasions to extend its influence in that region, Austria-Hungary reacted with concern. In 1875, a revolt against Turkish rule had broken out in the Balkan provinces of Bosnia and Herzegovina. Following Russian intervention against Turkey in the Russo-Turkish War (1877–1878), the Congress of Berlin in 1878 divided Bulgaria into two parts, both nominally under the authority of the Ottoman Empire but under Russian influence. The Austro-Hungarian government would henceforth administer Bosnia and Herzegovina, although they would remain within the Turkish Ottoman Empire. But this had the effect of potentially antagonizing Russia, because both territories had populations of Serbs, who as Slavs looked to Russia for leadership. Moreover, in part because Britain and Austria-Hungary feared that Bulgaria might serve Russian interests, the Congress of Berlin recognized the creation of the independent states of Serbia and Romania as buffers against further Russian ambitions in the Balkans.

In 1879, fearing Russian expansionism, Bismarck forged the Dual Alliance, the cornerstone alliance between Germany and Austria-Hungary, predicated on German support for Habsburg opposition to an expansion of Russian interests in the Balkans. Although the details of the alliance remained secret, its general outlines were well known, and became one of the central factors of European diplomacy for the next thirty-five years. When Italy allied with Germany and Austria-Hungary in 1882, the Triple Alliance was formed. Italy was not a Great Power, but wanted to be one. Italian conservatives, who had recently come to power, were more ideologically attracted to the authoritarian powers than to either republican France or parliamentary Britain. Furthermore, Italy sought support against France. The Italian government also wanted support for its aggressive imperial ambitions, which were directed toward the Mediterranean region, particularly North Africa. There France stood in the way, having occupied Tunisia in 1881 before the Italians could get there (see Chapter 22).

Germany's alliance with Austria-Hungary made the Three Emperors' League virtually meaningless. Germany and Austria-Hungary agreed to come to the aid of the other in the event of a Russian attack. Bismarck had intended Germany's alliance with Austria-Hungary to force Russia to seek better relations with Germany. But it had the effect of driving Russia farther away. Moreover, Austria-Hungary's alliance with Germany had the potential to make instability in the Balkans a threat to European peace by putting Russia at odds not only with Austria-Hungary, but with Germany as well.

Germany Encircled: Russia and France Ally

The last thing Bismarck wanted was for his alliance with Austria-Hungary to drive Russia and France together. Such an eventuality might one day leave Germany confronting the necessity of fighting a war on two fronts, Bismarck's nightmare. In 1881, he resurrected the Three Emperors' League, which again allied the tsar of Russia with the emperor of Germany and the ruler of Austria-Hungary. Despite considerable points of tension with the Habsburg monarchy, the Russian government entered this alliance as a hedge against Austro-Hungarian expansion in the Balkans toward the straits of Constantinople. The result was that Bismarck's resourceful diplomacy left Germany allied, in one way or another, with all of its potential enemies except France. As on the eve of the Franco-Prussian War of 1870–1871, France stood without allies.

Yet, several factors seemed to draw Russia and France together, despite the great differences in their political systems. Both France and Russia stood outside the Triple Alliance, which joined the powers of Central Europe with Italy. Russia, too, faced diplomatic isolation, despite the Three Emperors' League, because its Balkan interests clashed with those of Austria-Hungary. Russia hoped that an alliance with France would limit

German support for the ambitions of the Habsburgs in Southeastern Europe. Cultural ties between the Russian aristocracy and France remained strong, as they had been in the eighteenth century; many Russian nobles still preferred to speak French.

Far more important, French investment in Russia increased dramatically in the late 1880s and early 1890s. If the Russian economy and military capability were to be developed, the railway network would have to be improved and expanded. But Russia's relatively small middle class and backward financial structure left it with a chronic lack of capital. French bankers seized the opportunity to provide capital at attractive interest rates for Russian railway and mining development. French investors enthusiastically purchased Russian bonds. By 1914, about one-fourth of all French foreign investment was in Russia. In contrast, Bismarck and his successors made it a policy to discourage and even to forbid German loans to Russia. German private investors, in any case, usually lacked the capital to undertake such loans. At the same time, German and French financial cooperation was extremely limited. French and German capitalists saw each other as bitter rivals.

Franco-Russian ties were further solidified by Tsar Alexander III's visit to Paris during the exposition of 1889, when one of the refurbished bridges across the Seine was named after him. Yet, toasts to Franco-Russian friendship seemed inappropriate to many in France. The French left was outraged by government overtures to the autocratic and often brutal tsarist regime. For their part, Russian Tsar Alexander III and his successor Nicholas II were uncomfortable with close ties to a republic. Still, Nicholas stood while a band played *The Marseillaise*, the anthem of the French Revolution, while greeting a French naval squadron at the Russian Baltic base of Kronstadt.

The Russian government blamed Austria-Hungary for opposing what they considered its natural influence in the Balkans. The Three Emperors' League lapsed. In 1887, Germany and Russia signed a Reinsurance Treaty, by which each pledged to remain neutral if the other went to war, but it did not cover the most likely contingency of all—war between Russia and Austria-Hungary—because Germany was already committed to aid Austria-Hungary if Russian forces attacked. The young, headstrong Kaiser William II dismissed Bismarck as chancellor in 1890. Bismarck's successors failed to maintain sufficiently friendly ties with Russia to prevent the latter's alliance with France.

In 1892, Russia and France signed a military treaty by which each pledged a military response if the other were attacked by Germany or by one or more of its allies. A formal alliance, the details of which remained secret, followed in 1894. It ended Bismarck's isolation of France. The alliance was essentially defensive in nature: the French no more encouraged Russian moves in the direction of the Balkans than the Russians wanted to see France embark on a war of revenge to recapture Alsace-Lorraine from

Germany. But the Dual Alliance, as it was called, countered the Triple Alliance. It defeated the most essential thrust of Bismarck's foreign policy by ending France's diplomatic isolation.

Anglo-German Rivalry

During the 1890s, the possibility of Britain joining the Dual Alliance of France and Russia seemed remote. Whereas Germany and Britain had some competing colonial interests, for example in Africa, hostilities seemed most likely to break out between France and Britain. Their respective interests clashed in West Africa and Indochina, and France was jealous of British influence in Egypt. When a French force encountered a British army unit in 1898 on the upper Nile at Fashoda, war between the two seemed a distinct possibility (see Chapter 22). The French backed down. Furthermore, Afghanistan, lying strategically between British India and Russia, was a particular point of tension between those two powers.

The British government had long made it clear that it sought no alliance with anyone, and that it would stand alone, its empire protected by the great British navy. But the British government's hesitance to seek alliances ended, leading to the signing of the Entente Cordiale ("Friendly Agreement") with France in 1904. Britain did so for several reasons. The hostile reaction from every power in Europe to the Boer War (1899–1902) fought by British troops in South Africa demonstrated that it was one thing to stand in proud isolation from the continent, but another to have no friends at all. Furthermore, Britain's relations with Germany soured markedly. Germany's pointed criticism of Britain's war with the Boers strained relations between the two powers. In 1895, Kaiser William II, in his inimitably clumsy way, had sent a telegram congratulating the President of the Boer Republic of Transvaal in Southern Africa on the Boers' successful stand against a British attacking force. The German kaiser's telegram unleashed a storm of nationalistic fury in both countries. In 1899, British Foreign Secretary Joseph Chamberlain awkwardly responded to German criticism by stating that Britain was waging no more "barbarous" a war than that undertaken by Prussia against France in 1870 (which was not, in any case, true).

Neither Anglo-German cooperation in the suppression of the Boxer Rebellion in China in 1900, nor a joint operation to force Venezuela to pay some of its foreign debts in 1902, significantly improved Anglo-German relations. Gradually the British began to realize the growing extent of German influence in the Turkish Ottoman Empire. British military planners feared that Germany might be able to move troops more quickly overland into the Middle East than the Royal Navy could by ship.

Growing German economic competition with Britain also raised tensions between the two states. But it was the Anglo-German naval rivalry that above all pushed Britain toward a rapprochement with France. Al-

Postcard commemorating Kaiser William II's launching of the *S. S. Imperator*.

though by the 1880s, Germany was a commercial rival with Britain for continental markets, Germany had never been a naval power. But in 1897, the Reichstag allocated funds for the accelerated expansion of the German navy over the next six years. William II's uncontrolled enthusiasm provided no small degree of impetus—the vain kaiser loved putting on his military medals, sword, and polished boots, reviewing his sailors and soldiers, and breaking champagne bottles over the bows of powerful warships. Bismarck once remarked, "The Kaiser is like a balloon. If you don't hold fast to the string, you never know where he'll be off!"

Admiral Alfred von Tirpitz (1849–1930), trusted adviser to the kaiser, made a speech to the Reichstag, wherein he belligerently cited the strength of the British navy as the *raison d'être* for the passage of the bill to build up the German navy. The nationalistic Pan-German League and the Naval League, organizations whose members included powerful commercial and industrial magnates, whipped up popular enthusiasm for the navy and for German colonialism. But the British government viewed the expansion of the German navy with alarm. As the German ambassador to London put it in 1909: "There is scarcely an Englishman of importance who does not see in the German navy . . . and in the tempo of construction, a serious danger to his country." The new German fleet, which was to include some of the biggest, fastest, and wide-ranging warships ever built, would be capable of operating aggressively far from the Baltic ports.

Britain reacted quickly when confronted with the sudden and almost unexpected naval competition. In 1906, Britain launched the most powerful battleship in the world, the Dreadnought. It was faster than any other warship ever built, and whereas its predecessors had four heavy guns, the Dreadnought could carry ten. The following year, Germany began to build comparable ships of war. British naval yards were constructing eight more ships of the Dreadnought class in 1908. But rumors and wild estimates had the Germans turning out even more, leading to a brief panic in 1909 that Germany was about to invade Britain.

British-French Rapprochement

The British government took hesitant steps toward ending its diplomatic isolation by signing a treaty in 1901 with the United States, which permitted the latter to construct the Panama Canal. By undertaking an alliance with Japan in 1902, Britain sought to counter Russian ambitions in East Asia. The Russo-Japanese War of 1904–1905 helped push Britain toward France. The conflict itself followed the development of a rivalry between Russia and Japan in Manchuria, in particular increasing Russian demands for further Chinese economic concessions there. The hostilities began in February 1904 with a surprise Japanese attack on the Russian naval base of Port Arthur (Lüshun). The Russian Baltic fleet, embarking on a disastrous voyage around the world to confront the Japanese navy in the Yellow Sea, sank several British fishing trawlers in the North Sea, somehow mistaking them for Japanese ships. Germany expected that France would immediately support Russia, with whom it was allied. Yet, to most everyone's surprise, French Foreign Minister Théophile Delcassé (1852–1923) helped mediate between Russia and Britain. Russia's defeat by Japan ensured that Russia would be unable to launch a war against Germany's eastern frontier for some time. Furthermore, the defeat of Russia in East Asia confirmed that Britain had far more to fear from Germany than from Russia.

Delcassé was determined to forge a rapprochement with Britain. The Entente Cordiale reached between Britain and France in 1904 had the immediate goal of eliminating points of tension between the two powers. Britain recognized French interests in Morocco in exchange for the French recognition of British control over Egypt; both sides accepted the existence of neutral Siam in Indochina between French Indochina and British-controlled Burma; and they settled a centuries-old dispute over fishing rights off the coast of Newfoundland.

The First Moroccan Crisis

The First Moroccan Crisis (1905) solidified the rapprochement between Britain and France. The British had abandoned their interest in Morocco, which France clearly dominated. But Germany had not, despite the fact that Germany had only modest commercial interests in the North African state. The German chancellor, Bernhard von Bülow (1849–1929), convinced William II to test the recently concluded Anglo-French agreement and perhaps force the British government to leave France to its own devices while casting Germany as defender of Moroccan sovereignty. In March 1905, the German kaiser himself was aboard a German yacht that docked in Tangiers. Seeking to emphasize Morocco's independence from France, William II demanded that Germany receive from Morocco the same commercial benefits as any other trading partner.

The French government reacted with fury, but backed down because it seemed unlikely that Britain would then support it in a war against Germany. Delcassé, who had urged a measured French response to the incident while believing that Britain was on its side, resigned as foreign minister. Anti-German feeling intensified in France. Germany also pulled away from possible conflict, seeing that British support for France had remained firm and that only Austria-Hungary took the German side. The crisis ended with an international conference in the Spanish town of Algeciras in January 1906. Germany recognized the primacy of French interests in Morocco. This left Germany determined that another humiliation must not be suffered. The incident also seemed to confirm the bellicose and bullying nature of German foreign policy to Britain as well as to France. Following the 1905 Moroccan Crisis, French and British generals and admirals began to draw up joint contingency plans for combined warfare against Germany.

The Algeciras Conference, and particularly the policies of Russian Foreign Minister Alexander Izvolsky (1856–1919), also brought Russia and Britain closer together. For Izvolsky, Russian interests were in the Balkans, where they competed with those of Austria-Hungary, not in Asia, where British interests lay. Set on the road to recovery from the disastrous Russo-Japanese War by British loans, Russia was now eager for better relations

"For whom Morocco?" William II of Germany, Marianne (the image of the French Republic), King Edward VII of England, and King Alphonso XIII of Spain chase the sultan of Morocco, 1906.

with Britain. The British government had long viewed Russian economic influence in Persia and Afghanistan as threatening to its interests, in the first case because a strong Russian presence might one day compromise the sea route to East Asia, in the second because Afghanistan served as a buffer between Russia and British India. However, in 1907, the two powers divided Persia into three zones—a Russian zone, a British zone, and a neutral zone—and agreed to respect each other's zone of influence. The Russians accepted British influence in Afghanistan, and both powers agreed to stay out of Tibet. Russia hoped that Britain might support, or at least tolerate, its interests in the Balkans, and its ultimate desire of controlling Constantinople. The elimination of some of the tension between Britain and Russia strengthened the Franco-British Entente.

THE EUROPE OF TWO ARMED CAMPS, 1905–1914

The inclusion of Russia in what was increasingly known as the Triple Entente moved Europe toward a clear division into two camps. Cordial relations, however, continued between Tsar Nicholas II and his cousin, German Kaiser William II. As in centuries past, European royal families had intermarried. The German kaiser was the grandson of Queen Victoria of England—a standing joke in Berlin went that William feared no one except God and his English grandmother. But in the Europe of entangling alliances, blood relations were subordinate to the logic of Great Power interests and alliances.

The German government could find little reassurance in Italy's nominal alliance with Germany and Austria-Hungary. Italian nationalist goals seemed incompatible with its alliance with Austria-Hungary. Italian irredentism (the absorption of adjacent territories with significant Italian populations) could only be fulfilled at the expense of Austria-Hungary, whose territories included the South Tyrol in the Alps and Trieste on the Adriatic coast. Improved relations between Italy and France confronted Germany with the prospect that Austria-Hungary would be its only dependable ally. France had acquiesced to an eventual Italian seizure of Libya in 1911–1912 in exchange for Italian recognition of Morocco's status as a French protectorate.

Should Austria-Hungary cease to be a power or in the worst scenario completely collapse because of national movements from within, Germany might be left alone, encircled by enemies and vulnerable to annihilation. This fear weighed heavily on William, his advisers, and on German public opinion. The German high command prepared for a possible war against both France and Russia, a war that would have to be fought on two fronts. This left the German government in the position of having to support its troubled Habsburg ally unconditionally in the Balkans.

The Balkan Tinderbox and Unrest in the Ottoman Empire

The Balkans increasingly became the key to maintaining peace in Europe (see Map 23.2). In 1897, Russia and Austria-Hungary had agreed informally to respect the status quo in the region. But the development of an intense cultural and political nationalism among the South Slavs living within the boundaries of the Austro-Hungarian Empire, in Serbia, or under Ottoman rule, increasingly challenged the status quo.

Balkan political life remained volatile, suggesting that events there might well quickly move beyond the control of any of the powers. When a

MAP 23.2 THE BALKANS, 1914   The Austro-Hungarian Empire and the Balkan states, including territory acquired in the Balkan Wars of 1912–1913.

bloody revolution led to the assassination of the king and queen of Serbia in 1903, Russia quickly recognized the new king, Peter, hoping that Pan-Slav elements would dominate. Fearing any delay would push Serbia further toward Russia, Austria-Hungary recognized the *fait accompli*. The Serb Parliament voiced its unqualified support for Russian ambitions in East Asia, and its 1904–1905 war against Japan ("Slavic Serbia naturally considers every Russian success as a strengthening of the Slavic cause"). Serbian nationalists began to call for union with Serbs in Macedonia, that volatile southern Balkan territory peopled by Greeks and Bulgarians, as well as Serbs, which belonged to the Ottoman Empire. Such provocative addresses to ethnic minorities within Austria-Hungary worsened tensions, not only between Serbia and Austria-Hungary, but between Russia, seen as the loving protector of Slavic interests, and Austria-Hungary.

Relations between Serbia and Austria-Hungary further deteriorated. When Serbia tried to lessen its economic dependence on Austria-Hungary by signing a commercial treaty with Bulgaria, Vienna responded by forbidding the importation of Serbian livestock. Thus began an economic battle in 1906 that became known to much of Europe as the "Pig War," as the humble pig formed the basis of Serbia's fragile agricultural economy. The Serbs resourcefully found new markets for their sows. The Habsburg government, despite the lack of Hungarian support for economic retaliation, responded in 1908 by announcing construction of a new railroad that would further isolate Serbia economically. Izvolsky worked aggressively to expand Russian influence in the Balkans. Serbian nationalists, for their part, viewed Bosnia and Herzegovina as South Slav states that should, with Russian encouragement, become part of Serbia.

Political instability in Turkey further whetted the appetites of both Russia and Austria-Hungary. The reign of Sultan Abdul-Hamid II (ruled 1876–1909) had been marked by the brutal repression of the non-Islamic peoples of the Ottoman Empire. About 200,000 Armenians were slaughtered in 1894 and 1895 in response to Turkish fears of rising Armenian nationalism. A group of Turkish nationalists influenced by Western political ideas found support in the bureaucracy and army for their slogan "Union and Progress." In July 1908, these "Young Turks," as they were called, who had penetrated the army, revolted and forced the sultan to restore the constitution of 1876. Abdul-Hamid II was deposed in 1909 when he tried to plot a counter-revolution.

The chaos within the Ottoman Empire seemed to promise the realization of the Russian dream of opening the straits of Constantinople to Russian ships, and perhaps only Russian ships. The Austro-Hungarian government faced the possibility that lands still held by the Ottoman Empire might be added to Serbia and Romania. This pushed Russian and Austro-Hungarian relations, which had been, if not improving, at least not becoming any worse, toward a breaking point.

The Bosnian Crisis of 1908

Turkish instability led to the Bosnian Crisis of 1908. In 1878 the Congress of Berlin had authorized Austria-Hungary to occupy Bosnia and Herzegovina, although both territories technically were still part of the Ottoman Empire. Austria-Hungary had done so, at the risk of bringing more Slavs into the empire, not only to solidify its position in the Balkans, but also to prevent Serbia from absorbing them. In October 1908, the Austro-Hungarian government suddenly announced that it was directly annexing Bosnia and Herzegovina in violation of the agreements reached at the Congress of Berlin. The Russian government had been secretly negotiating with Austria-Hungary to accept the Habsburg absorption of Bosnia and Herzegovina in return for Austria-Hungary's support for the opening of the Bosphorus and the Dardanelles Straits to the Russian fleet. Now, in 1908, before the Russian government could even begin marshaling support from the other powers for a revision of the agreements signed at the Congress of Berlin, Austria-Hungary had formally annexed the two territories. The Russians reacted with rage at Austria-Hungary's betrayal of their understanding. Serbia, furious that two territories in which many South Slavs lived were to be incorporated into the Habsburg empire, mobilized its army with Russian support. Austria-Hungary responded in kind. The annexation also considerably strained relations between Austria-Hungary

A street in Sarajevo in 1908 after the annexation of Bosnia-Herzegovina by Austria-Hungary.

and Italy, nominal allies, because of Italian strategic and economic interests on the Adriatic coast.

The resolute opposition to war by Hungarian leaders within the Dual Monarchy, as well as the opposition of the heir to the Habsburg throne, Archduke Francis Ferdinand (1863–1914), helped defuse the crisis. Not only would war be expensive, victory might well add a considerable South Slav population (from Serbia) to Hungarian territories, adding to the potential for instability within the Habsburg lands. Furthermore, despite diplomatic bluster, Russia was not ready to fight, and its ally France was unwilling to go to war over the Balkans, where its own interests were not threatened. Lacking French or British support, the Russian government backed down, forcing Serbia to accept what by now was a *fait accompli* and recognize the annexation.

War had been avoided, but the powers had drawn significant conclusions from the Bosnian Crisis. The German government clearly supported Austrian policy in the Balkans without reservation. Italy remained allied with both Central European powers, but both Berlin and Vienna viewed Italy's commitment to the alliance as uncertain. Italy's economic and colonial rivalry with France became less intense, as Italian business and colonial interests increasingly looked to regions (the Balkans and the eastern Mediterranean) in which the French had no immediate interests. Italy's problematic status as an ally thus firmed up Germany's alliance with Austria-Hungary. German and Austro-Hungarian military commanders met to plan for hostilities with Russia, France, Serbia, and possibly—given its announced interests in Tyrolean Austria and Dalmatia—Italy. Britain and France had discovered that German support for Austria-Hungary was unshakable, even for a potentially dangerous move for which Berlin had received no advance warning. The German government sent a note to the Russian government, demanding that Russia give up support for Serbia and recognize Austria-Hungary's takeover of Bosnia-Herzegovina. The Russian government, viewing itself as a victim of German bullying, now wanted a close relationship with Britain. With German shipyards rapidly producing the most modern and heavily armed fighting ships at a frightening pace, British officials quickly gave up their reservations about the Entente Cordiale with France.

The Bosnian Crisis left deep scars on Russian relations with Austria-Hungary. Russia, in the wake of surprising defeat by Japan, urgently began restoring its army and navy to fighting shape. Serbian relations with Vienna worsened. The Habsburg government presented poorly forged documents to support claims that the Serbian government was trying to stir up the Slav populations within and against the Habsburg empire. In fact, several groups of devoted Serb nationalists, including "The People's Defense" and "The Black Hand," received tacit support from the Serb state, as well as Russian encouragement. The Bosnian Crisis passed, but ethnic tensions and Russian and Habsburg rivalry in the region did not.

The Second Moroccan Crisis

Germany provoked the next international crisis, the Second Moroccan Crisis (1911), which also might have led to war. Germany was reacting to France's establishment of a virtual protectorate in Morocco, which violated the Algeciras agreements of 1906. Using a local rebellion against the new Moroccan sultan as an excuse, a French army marched on Fez, allegedly to protect French settlers. When the French government did not offer to compensate Germany because France had added another protectorate to its empire, the German kaiser sent a small gunboat, the *Panther,* to the port of Agadir. It arrived on July 1, 1911, with demands that Germany receive the entire French Congo as compensation for France's claiming Morocco as a protectorate.

France refused, bolstered by its closer relations with Britain, Russia's increased strength, and a wave of nationalist sentiment at home. David Lloyd George, Liberal British chancellor of the Exchequer and a man usually known for his caution, declared that "the formula of peace at any price is unworthy of a great power." Britain could never accept the possibility of a German port on the coast of North Africa. This response further diminished chances of German-British rapprochement. Even German moderates seemed angered at what appeared to be a British commitment to preventing Germany from finding its "place in the sun."

The Second Moroccan Crisis, like the first, passed without war. William II seemed less willing to follow up bravado with action. The French minister of war's assessment that the army was in no shape to fight forced a moderate French response. On November 4, 1911, Germany agreed to recognize Morocco as a French protectorate in exchange for 100,000 square miles of the French Congo. But the crisis further solidified Europe's antagonistic alliances. Britain and France now formalized the agreement by which each pledged to aid the other in case of an attack by Germany. In April 1912, the British and French admiralties established zones of responsibility for their fleets—the French in the Mediterranean and the British in the English Channel and the North Sea.

The Balkan Wars

The Bosnian Crisis of 1908 had demonstrated that events in the Balkans could carry Europe to war. The Second Moroccan Crisis hardened the increasingly confrontational alliances. Now in 1911, the floundering Turkish Ottoman Empire provided the kindling for another international flare-up. Late in the year, Italy invaded Libya in what became known as the Tripoli War. Italy proclaimed Libya its colony, but the Turks and the Libyan population resisted. The war dragged on until Italy claimed victory in October 1912.

A German image of the
Balkan Wars, 1912. Bul-
garia, Serbia, and Monte-
negro attack Turkey from
behind while the Italians
push from the front.

Taking a cue from the Turkish defeat, Serbia, Bulgaria, Montenegro,
and Greece, who had formed the Balkan League with the intention of
completely freeing the Balkans from Turkish rule, declared war on and defeated Turkey with surprising ease in October 1912. The First Balkan War
lasted less than a month. The successes of the Balkan states worried the
Austro-Hungarian government. Russia and the Austro-Hungarian monarchy seemed on a collision course in the Balkans, where ethnic complexities threatened to carry events beyond the control of diplomacy. Bulgaria,
Greece, and Serbia each annexed territory that had belonged to Turkey,
leaving the former Ottoman Empire with only a small territory on the European side of the straits of Constantinople (see Map 23.2). But the
Balkan League fell apart even before a peace could be signed when Bulgaria, seeking more territory in Macedonia, attacked Serbia and Greece.

But this time Russia and the Habsburgs stayed clear of the brink of war.
New foreign ministers, Sergei Sazonov (1861–1927) of Russia and
Leopold Berchtold (1863–1942) of Austria-Hungary, helped defuse the
crisis. Furthermore, both Francis Joseph and Archduke Francis Ferdinand
opposed war at this time. Austria-Hungary had, in any case, no commitment of any kind to the Turks. Austria-Hungary's goals were to see that no
Balkan state became so strong that it could generate nationalist agitation
within its territories, and to prevent Serbia, Russia's friend, from gaining a
port on the Adriatic. In the interest of peace, Britain and France supported
Austria-Hungary's call for the creation of the independent state of Albania

on the Adriatic, which would prevent Serbia from having its port. The German government now also viewed these issues as sufficiently grave to warrant its unconditional support for Austria-Hungary. The Treaty of London of May 1913 divided up most of the remaining parts of Ottoman holdings in Southeastern Europe among the Balkan states.

The Balkan states remained dissatisfied with the peace settlement. Bulgaria continued to press for more territory, and attacked Serbia. In response, Serbia and Greece, with the assistance of Romania and Turkey, quickly defeated expansionist Bulgaria in 1913 in the Second Balkan War. With the Peace of Bucharest, Serbia received the parts of what had been Turkish Macedonia, which Bulgaria was to have received; Greece gained some more territory on the Aegean coast as well as Crete; Turkey regained Adrianople; and the independent state of Albania came into existence. Serbia emerged from the Balkan Wars larger, stronger, and more confident, but angry that Austria-Hungary had frustrated its quest for an Adriatic port. It also may have emerged with the impression that there were limits to Germany's support for Austria-Hungary, since the German government had appeared to restrain the Habsburg government's aggressive response to Serbia's demand for a port. Defeated Bulgaria became a target for Austro-Hungarian overtures, though it lay within the sphere of Russian influence by virtue of its cultural and linguistic affinities.

South Slav nationalism gained more adherents in the Balkans. After backing down against Austria-Hungary for the second time (the first having been the Bosnian Crisis in 1908), Sazonov irresponsibly placated the Serbs by telling them that their promised land lay inside the frontiers of Hungary. Some Serb political leaders sympathized with the young fanatics of "the People's Will" and "The Black Hand" nationalist organizations. In 1910, a boy who had been taught to shoot a gun by a Serb officer

"The Vortex—Will the powers be drawn in?" This image of the Balkan Wars, 1912–1913, had a ring of prophetic accuracy.

attempted to use it on the Austrian governor of Bosnia; the youth committed suicide after failing, becoming a martyr in Serbia. A few Habsburg personages, possibly including the Archduke Francis Ferdinand, may have been willing to consider the South Slavs as partners in a tripartite empire—the mere suggestion of which infuriated almost all Magyars and most Austrians. But the government of the Dual Monarchy considered the South Slav nationalists to be threats who would ultimately have to be crushed by force. Because of the Balkan situation, the German military command once again turned its attention to readying its army, a reaction to recent Russian measures of military preparedness. But in 1914 Europe seemed far less close to war than it had been in 1905 and 1911, the years of the two Moroccan Crises. When the final crisis came, however, Britain, France, and Russia found themselves fatefully linked, set against the cornerstone alliance of Germany and Austria-Hungary.

BALANCING THE CAUSES OF THE GREAT WAR

The Great War had several causes, with none alone standing as a sufficient cause. To be sure, the entangling alliances of the European Great Powers were undeniably a principal factor in the outbreak of hostilities. Furthermore, aggressive nationalism spilled out of the opposing alliances during this period. Schoolchildren throughout much of Europe were taught that their country was the greatest nation in history, and that their enemies were craven reptiles.

Yet, several other contributing factors are worthy of consideration. Military planners (who were, after all, nationalists themselves) in Germany, Austria-Hungary, France, and, to a lesser extent, Russia, all considered war not only inevitable but desirable. Moreover, as international tensions escalated, political and military leaders felt pressure to mobilize quickly for strategic reasons. For example, German military plans required a lightning attack on France through Belgium, and the great distances troops were required to travel in Russia created an incentive for early—if not premature—mobilization there. Military planners were joined by many political leaders also imbued with Social Darwinist beliefs. Thus, they saw conflict between nations as a natural struggle for survival, which diplomacy could postpone, but not eliminate. To one British writer, "War . . . is the sovereign disinfectant, and its red stream of blood . . . cleans out the stagnant pools and clotted channels of the intellect." In Germany, an official in the chancellory wrote that "Eternal and absolute enmity is fundamentally inherent in relations between peoples; and the hostility that we observe everywhere (is) the essence of the world and the source of life itself." War would be the ultimate test by which the fit—individuals and nations—would be measured. "Give me combat!" rang out from the dueling fraternities in Heidelberg to the gymnastic and shooting clubs of Paris.

Domestic politics, strongly subject to nationalist influence, also played a part in the outbreak of the war, particularly in the case of Austria-Hungary, Germany, and France. In Britain and Russia, domestic politics may have exerted less influence on the decision to go to war than in the case of the other powers, but nationalism played some role. In the case of Germany and Russia, particularly, the personalities of each ruler contributed to the beginning of the conflict.

Military Planning

As alliances cemented the international rivalries of the great powers, military planners prepared for the war most people thought would break out sometime. French Marshal Joseph Joffre (1852–1931), who became chief of staff in 1911, was asked if he thought about war: "Yes," he replied, "I think about it all the time. We shall have a war, I will make it, and I will win it." In 1912, Field Marshal Helmuth von Moltke (1848–1916), Joffre's German counterpart, announced at a military meeting attended by William II that he wanted "war—the sooner the better."

The Russian government was not about to start the war itself, believing that its army needed more time to prepare. But the tsar was ready to go to war when necessary to defend Russia's interests in the Balkans. France also was not eager to initiate a conflict, yet the French army was itching for a chance to redeem itself. Unlike Germany, which had to contemplate fighting a war on two fronts, the French army enjoyed the advantage of being able to focus its full attention on Germany. Joffre's staff drew up plans for a full-scale assault into Alsace-Lorraine, an attack in which *élan*, or patriotic energy, was expected to bring victory: "the French army, returning to its traditions, no longer knows any other law than the offense," an-

Marshal Joseph Joffre dressed in his Sunday military best.

nounced one of Joffre's disciples, "all attacks are to be pushed to the extreme . . . [we need only] to charge the enemy to destroy him." The French
would seize Alsace-Lorraine and then launch a devastating march to
Berlin. The plan envisioned the Russian army attacking Germany from the
east by the sixteenth day of mobilization. The British government, depending on the Royal Navy to defend Britain, had also sketched plans to
send an army to the continent to fight alongside the French forces.

Domestic Politics

Europe's entangling alliances were more important than any other long-
term factor in the origins of the Great War. Patterns of economic investment, principally French in Russia, and German in Austria-Hungary,
solidified these alliances. Yet, the foreign policy of each state was inevitably closely linked to internal political considerations. The complex
nationality problem within the Austro-Hungarian monarchy would condition Habsburg intransigence toward Serbia and opposition to what it considered Russian meddling in the affairs of Southeastern Europe. When
the Austro-Hungarian government saw the opportunity to put an end to
Serbia's provocations of the South Slavs, it would seize it.

British domestic politics had just the opposite effect, pulling Britain
away from war. The Liberals, who had come to power in 1905, had long
opposed entangling international alliances and large military expenditures. The government was beset by a number of pressing political issues:
a revival of labor militancy, the movement for women's suffrage, the refusal of the Conservative-dominated House of Lords to pass the budget,
the subsequent reduction of the Lords' powers by the House of Commons,
and, last but hardly least, the Home Rule Bill for Ireland. While these domestic factors mitigated against Britain's entry into an eventual European
conflict, foreign policy considerations pushed Great Britain in the direction of war.

Yet, in Britain, too, nationalism popularized the expectation that a major
war was inevitable. "Future war novels," published in Britain around the
turn of the century, contributed to the vilification of the enemy against
whom that war would have to be fought. In the 1890s, the ogre-enemy in
these novels had invariably been France. The French were characterized
as untrustworthy and downright sneaky. In one scenario, the French
stealthily construct a tunnel underneath the English Channel while the
unprepared British doze, and then send an invading army through disguised as café waiters, before the heroic English come to their senses and
drive their unscrupulous enemies back to France. But with the Anglo-German naval rivalry, the new enemy in these imaginary future wars became
Germany. The Germans were not depicted as sneaking around. Unlike the
French, they were portrayed as organized and brutal, sending their feared

Dreadnought class warships up and down the eastern coast of England, blasting military and civilian targets indiscriminately, until the British rallied and defeated their new enemy. Similarly, in Germany, one could easily find the stereotype of the bumbling English aristocrat brutalizing the colonial people while sucking the colonies dry of wealth. And in France, one law court felt obliged to rule that it was not defamation to call someone a "Prussian." Such images, carried in the popular press, strengthened the mood of "jingoism" in all the major powers (see Chapter 22).

In France, a revival of nationalist feeling could be felt after the First Moroccan Crisis in 1905, and particularly after the Second Moroccan Crisis in 1911. The popularity of Prime Minister and then President Raymond Poincaré contributed to this patriotic mood. Earlier in the Third Republic, French nationalism had been primarily identified with the anti-parliamentary right; now it affected political moderates who were committed to the republic. Poincaré was among those obsessed with recapturing Alsace and Lorraine from Germany. During his presidency, another huge loan was floated to the Russians, and the Chamber of Deputies passed a controversial bill extending military service from two to three years.

Yet, segments of French society resisted the nationalist revival. Many socialists, above all, opposed France's participation in a war against Germany, hoping that German and French workers would lay down their weapons and refuse to fire on fellow proletarians. They detested strong French ties with tsarist Russia. Anti-militarism ran deep in some of France, not only because the army took sons away from farms, industrial work, and families, but also because of the army's close association with clericalism, and because the French government used the army to break strikes. The government's uncertainty about the popular response to a declaration of war led it to maintain a list of Socialists and other leaders of the left to be arrested in that event.

In Russia, the tsar's immediate circle was divided over the advisability of going to war. Some advisers saw war as a means of rallying the support of an entire people behind the tsar. Yet others remembered Russia's disastrous defeat in the Russo-Japanese War. This in turn contributed to the outbreak of the Revolution of 1905 (see Chapter 25), which brought political reforms—however short-lived. Here, too, it did not seem to be in Russia's interest to push Europe to war.

In Germany, like Austria-Hungary, the influence of domestic politics on foreign policy and particularly on the decision to go to war was considerable. Since unification, the German emperors had sought to discredit and overwhelm the political opposition with noisy military reviews. High civilian officials wore military uniforms even at social events. The emperor and his advisers, as well as most German nationalists, considered their domestic opposition to be made up of devious traitors working against the good of the fatherland.

German Chancellor Theobald von Bethmann-Hollweg (1856–1921) was increasingly overwhelmed by the swing to the right of the German political elite. During the Second Moroccan Crisis of 1911, he complained to the British ambassador that he no longer could listen to Beethoven before going to bed: "How can I play my beloved old music with the air full of modern discords?" For many in Germany domestic politics should only be an extension of foreign policy; former Chancellor von Bülow himself had written in 1890, "Everything must be subordinated to our unity and our position as a European Great Power, and even our internal politics must be tailored to this."

The imperial rivalries of the Great Powers helped make the alliance system more rigid. During the 1880s, the European powers had begun to expand (in the cases of Britain and France) or to begin (Germany and Italy) empires based on the absorption of territories in, first and foremost, Africa, but also Southeast Asia, while demanding concessions from China (see Chapter 22). Imperial ambitions sharpened rivalries between the powers, particularly between Germany and Britain and France. Imperialism also encouraged the aggressive nationalism and militarism manifest in Berlin and Paris at the time of the Moroccan Crises of 1905 and 1911. Nationalists strongly believed that having colonies helped define status as a Great Power: by such reasoning, states had to expand their military forces and be prepared to defend their empires as they would their own borders.

Finally, the personal characteristics of the leaders and diplomats of the Great Powers must be taken into consideration. The elderly Francis Joseph of Austria-Hungary stood apart from the day-to-day operations of government. The Russian Foreign Minister Sazonov had a terrible temper and tended to overreact and exaggerate. Tsar Nicholas II combined stubbornness with indecisiveness and lacked a sharp mind. German Kaiser William II personally antagonized Britain and France with his impulsive bravado; he also annoyed his own advisers with his mood changes, indolence, and occasional withdrawal into sullen depression. Bethmann-Hollweg, who became German chancellor in 1909, stubbornly held the view that Germany's strength must be paramount ("necessity knows no law," he once said). But he brooded and could be indecisive; he was often at the mercy of the kaiser, whom he was supposed to keep from lurching into disasters. Bethmann-Hollweg always looked "a little sad and vaguely overwhelmed." Sir Edward Grey, the British foreign secretary, was often depressed, had a limited first-hand knowledge of the continent, communicated ineffectively, and seemed content to let events shape his policy instead of the other way around. The French ambassador to St. Petersburg, Maurice Paléologue, was a stubborn man, unyielding in his commitment to lock together the interests of Russia and France. In the final crisis, the personalities of key European leaders combined with the entangling alliances and the events themselves to lead Europe to war.

THE FINAL CRISIS

The powers of Europe were poised for conflict, divided into two armed camps by two rival alliances. While the outbreak of war was probably not inevitable—although many nationalists and military planners believed it to be—it was likely. Furthermore, once two powers seemed on the verge of war, the entangling alliances that pitted the Triple Alliance against the Triple Entente seemed likely to bring all of the European powers into the conflict. The crisis that precipitated World War I occurred in the Balkans, when Serb nationalists assassinated the Archduke Francis Ferdinand of Austria. Europe's diplomatic house of cards collapsed and World War I began.

Assassination in Sarajevo

Archduke Francis Ferdinand, sixty years of age, was heir to the Habsburg throne. His first love was his commoner wife, Sophie; his second, hunting—he bragged of having killed 6,000 stags in his lifetime and of having bagged 2,763 seagulls on a single day. The archduke was considered relatively anti-German and, despite being an intolerant person, probably had more sympathy for the problems of the South Slavs than any member of the royal family. For this, the Hungarians disliked him, fearing that when he came to the throne, he might eventually award the South Slavs the same status as the Austrians and Hungarians. Nor did the archduke's relatively understanding view of their position win him points with South Slav nationalists, many of whom would accept nothing less than an expanded independent Slavic state, or what they called Greater Serbia.

On June 28, 1914, Francis Ferdinand and his wife were on an inspection tour of the army in Sarajevo, capital of Bosnia. Serb nationalists, however, were intent on killing them. Gavrilo Princip (1895–1918), who had been expelled from school in Sarajevo two years earlier for participating in anti-Austrian demonstrations, and other youthful members of the Black Hand (one of the Serb nationalist groups) pushed Europe to the brink of war. Princip, who liked to recite a line written by the German philosopher Nietzsche, "Insatiable as the flame, I glow and consume myself," and the other seven assassins took a crash course in the use of firearms. They emboldened themselves in the taverns of the capital of Bosnia-Herzegovina, and then awaited the arrival of the archduke's motorcade. A first bomb exploded under the archduke's car, wounding two Austrian officers. The motorcade continued to the town hall, where a municipal authority stumbled through his speech, and the archduke expressed his indignation at the attempt on his life. When the motorcade departed, the drivers of the cars had not been informed of a change in route chosen to avoid the tangle of narrow streets of central Sarajevo. When the first several vehicles began to turn into a narrow street, the military governor ran ahead, ordering their

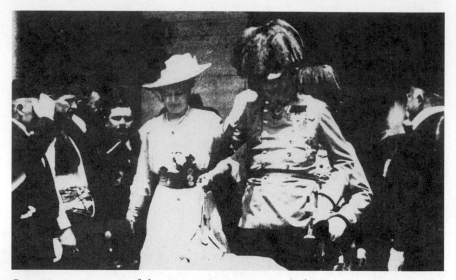

On an inspection tour of the army in Sarajevo, capital of Bosnia, Archduke Francis Ferdinand and his wife bathe in a warm welcome. They were assassinated a few hours later.

drivers to back up. This was Princip's chance, as he happened to be only a few feet from the archduke's car. He opened fire, killing Francis Ferdinand and his wife.

Although the Serbian government had been aware of the Black Hand nationalist organization, and some individual officials had supported it, the Austrian description of the youthful killers as puppets whose strings were pulled in Belgrade was incorrect. Nonetheless, the Serb response to the assassination only seemed to confirm Austria's interpretation: newspapers virtually celebrated the death of the Habsburg heir. In Vienna, even those who had disliked the archduke for having married a commoner now mourned the couple fervently.

The Ultimatum

Within the Habsburg imperial administration, many officials immediately took the view that the chance to crush Serbia had arrived, and that, unlike 1908 and 1912, this time the opportunity would not be missed. The usually indecisive and ineffective Foreign Minister Berchtold, who had opposed war during the Balkan Crisis of 1912, now took a hard line. Although Hungarian leaders had been cautious about foreign entanglements in the past, they, like the government in Vienna, disliked the Serbs and mistrusted the Slavic minorities within their territories. Unlike the Bosnian Crisis of 1908, they now accepted the possibility of war.

Despite its anger and vengeful mood, Vienna delayed its official reaction to the assassination. From Berlin, however, came anything but caution. William II urged retaliation, blaming Serbia for the assassination of Francis Ferdinand, whom he had visited only two weeks earlier. Bethmann-Hollweg doubted that Austria-Hungary could remain a power if it backed down a third time. In Berlin, the German government gave an Austrian official a "blank check" to act with the knowledge of full German support. The German foreign office assured Austria-Hungary that Germany would, if necessary, fight both France and Russia if those two powers intervened once Austria had declared war on Serbia. The German army was prepared to fight a war on two fronts, but expected Britain would remain neutral.

It therefore seemed clear that Germany would maintain its unqualified support for Austria-Hungary at all costs. Bethmann-Hollweg was now determined to stay the course with a numbing fatalism undoubtedly accentuated by the recent death of his wife. He advised his son not to plant his estate with trees that would take a long time to grow, because they would please only the Russians, who by then he expected to have occupied northeastern Germany. He did not want a war, but expected one, and wanted Russia to appear the aggressor.

But for the moment, Austria-Hungary waited. In Vienna, Berchtold convinced the Hungarian leaders to support war against Serbia, promising that no Slavs from territories taken from defeated Serbia would be incorporated into Austria-Hungary. On July 21, Sazonov, encouraged by Paléologue, the French ambassador, warned that "Russia would not be able to permit Austria-Hungary to make any threat against Serbia, or to take any military measures." The Austro-Hungarian government, however, continued to believe that the French and British governments would convince Russia to pull back before the point of war.

On July 23, 1914, almost a month after the assassination, the Austrian ambassador in Belgrade handed a lengthy ultimatum to Serb officials. It denounced what it claimed was Serbian activity aiming to "detach part of the territories of Austria-Hungary from the Monarchy." Austro-Hungarian demands included the elimination of all anti-Habsburg publications, including schoolbooks, the dissolution of all Serb nationalist organizations, a purge of officials and army officers to be named by Austria-Hungary, and a specific response as to the means by which the Serbian government would submit to these demands. The Serbian reply was expected within forty-eight hours. Grey, the British foreign secretary, called the ultimatum "the most formidable document ever presented by one independent state to another."

The Serb government was in a no-win situation. Even the most optimistic Serb could not help but admit that its small army was no match for that of Austria-Hungary. Its options were either to capitulate completely to the ultimatum and suffer a humiliating diplomatic defeat, or, as one official put it, to die fighting. This made Serbia almost totally dependent upon Russian intervention.

The ultimatum sent shockwaves through the capitals of Europe. Upon learning its contents, Sazonov exclaimed "It's the European War!" He blamed Germany for having inspired the Austro-Hungarian response and claimed that the ultimatum was part of a German plan to keep Russia from reaching Constantinople.

Sazonov's first practical concern was to mobilize French support against Austria-Hungary, believing that a united show of strength would force the Central European allies to back down. French President Raymond Poincaré's state visit to St. Petersburg from July 20 to July 23 seemed to indicate that France would stand by Russia, and now Sazonov received quick assurance from the French ambassador of full French support.

On July 25, two days after the Austro-Hungarian ultimatum, the tsar placed the Russian army on alert, a stage that would normally precede mobilization. Such a step was fraught with consequences for the military planners of each power. Mobilization meant preparing an army for war, calling up reserves, declaring martial law in frontier areas, readying the railways for hauling troops and supplies, and accelerating the production of munitions. In these circumstances, the Russian decision to mobilize was therefore tantamount to an act of war. Military planners assumed it would take at least two weeks, perhaps more, for the Russian army to be ready to fight.

General Alfred von Schlieffen (1833–1913), the architect in 1905 of the German (Schlieffen) plan for a two-front war, also had realized that the German armies on the western front would only have about two weeks to defeat the French in a lightning attack before having to confront the Russians in the east. The attack on France would require German forces to violate Belgian neutrality in order to bypass the sturdy defenses in eastern France. Although the Germans still hoped that the British would not fight along with the French, they realized that a German violation of Belgian neutrality might inevitably lead to Britain joining France. But German commanders believed that the war on the continent would be over before the superior British navy could make a difference.

Following the Russian army's mobilization, the British government suggested that the other powers help arrange a peaceful solution. Britain was unwilling to back Russia, a move that at this point might have made both Austria-Hungary and Germany consider backing down. The German government still assumed that the British would remain neutral in a war, even if France and Russia were fighting Germany and Austria-Hungary.

The Russian government continued to believe that its resolute support for Serbia might well be enough to force Austria-Hungary to back down. Austria-Hungary and its ally, Germany, were laboring under the same kind of illusion about Russia. Both believed that a show of unconditional support—the "blank check" by Germany to Austria-Hungary—would force Russia to pull back. Yet, Germany's aggressive support for its ally, combined with the bellicose prodding of the Russian government by the French ambassador, had just the opposite effect.

The Serb government therefore ordered military mobilization on July 25, confident of full Russian support. It then presented a formal reply to the Austro-Hungarian ultimatum. This reply, which reached the Austrian government just before the forty-eight hours had elapsed, seemed surprisingly conciliatory. The Serbs accepted five of the demands without reservation; four others they would accept pending discussion and some further explanation. They rejected only one outright, that the Austro-Hungarian government send representatives to collaborate in the investigation of the Serb "plot" against it.

The Austro-Hungarian government viewed anything less than total compliance as unsatisfactory. It ordered military mobilization against Serbia, but stopped short of declaring war. The British again proposed a meeting of the powers in the hope of avoiding conflict in the Balkans, or at least keeping it limited to the Balkans. Germany rejected such a plan, believing that Britain would not go to war unless it appeared that Germany was intending to conquer and absorb France.

"A Jolly Little War"

Austria-Hungary declared war on Serbia on July 28, 1914, exactly one month after the archduke's assassination. The declaration claimed an unsatisfactory Serbian response to the Austro-Hungarian ultimatum, as well as an attack on Austro-Hungarian troops along the Bosnian frontier, an event that never took place. In a final attempt to avert war, British Foreign Secretary Grey asked if Germany would participate in an attempt to negotiate a settlement to the crisis. Germany accepted, but at the same time did nothing to try to forestall an Austro-Hungarian invasion of Serbia. If anything, Bethmann-Hollweg egged his ally on, recalling the two occasions on which the Habsburg government had backed down, thereby allowing itself to be bullied by Serbia. In St. Petersburg, the Austro-Hungarian declaration of war generated popular support for Serbia. An American diplomat reported tersely, "Whole country, all classes, unanimous for war."

On July 28, Bethmann-Hollweg sent his own telegram to Vienna, expressing anxiety that, in view of various proposals from Britain that the Great Powers mediate the conflict, Germany ran the risk of being blamed for a European war. The telegram also suggested that its ally find a way to make it appear that, if war did come, it would be Russia's fault. And finally he warned that if the Russians did not pull back in their support of Serbia, Austria must stay the course, even if it led to war, or forever renounce its status as a Great Power.

By the time the British cabinet discussed the Serbian crisis on July 24, it was clear that Germany would not, as in 1912, restrain Austria-Hungary. British politicians and the public were principally preoccupied with the

Home Rule crisis—on July 16, British troops had fired on rioters in Dublin—and with vacation plans for the unusually sunny summer. The Royal Navy was placed on alert, so that it could fulfill Britain's obligation to France: to protect the Channel from German warships. The Liberal government was divided over British intervention, at least partially because many Liberals and most Laborites disliked the idea of fighting alongside autocratic Russia. But by July 29, everyone recognized that Britain might well be drawn into the conflict, particularly if Germany marched into Belgium. In Berlin, rumors and then word of Russia's military preparation alarmed Moltke. Should Russia mobilize, Germany would have to move quickly against France.

Bethmann-Hollweg now sent a sealed envelop to the German ambassador in Brussels, which he was to present to the Belgian government when ordered to do so. The envelop contained a demand that German troops be allowed to march through Belgium. But, for the moment, there still seemed to be hope. William II sent a telegram to the tsar, expressing his desire for peace, and assuring him that he was urging Austria-Hungary "to deal honestly and to arrive at a satisfactory understanding with you." He signed it, "your very sincere and devoted friend and cousin, Willy."

Russian ministers and generals had debated since July 28 whether the crisis called for a limited mobilization of a million soldiers on the Polish and Galician frontiers, or a full mobilization. On July 29, word reached St. Petersburg that the Austrians had bombarded Belgrade from the Danube. French Ambassador Paléologue continued to assure Russian officials that France would fight Germany. After twice changing his mind, Nicholas II ordered a full mobilization on July 30 for the following day. The tsar's diary entry for that day read: "After lunch, I received Sazonov. . . . I went for a walk by myself. The weather was hot. . . . I had a delightful bath in the sea." The Russian mobilization put an end to any hope for a negotiated settlement to the crisis. Francis Joseph, also succumbed to his generals' pressure, declaring a general mobilization against Russia and Serbia.

A mood of anxious excitement prevailed in Paris. The army had already taken cautious steps to ready France's frontier defenses, but to avoid any incident with German units, French troops were pulled back several kilometers from the frontier. In France, only the Socialist Party spoke out against the imminent outbreak of the international war that had seemed probable for so long.

In the meantime, the Russian and French ambassadors were hounding British officials, demanding assurance of British military support. The French ambassador even asked rhetorically if the word "honor" were to be stricken from British dictionaries, should Britain not join France and Russia against Germany and Austria-Hungary. Britain, which had for centuries wanted to avoid the presence of a hostile power across the Channel in one of the Low Countries, asked both Germany and France for a guarantee that Belgian neutrality (which had been accepted by Britain,

France, Austria, Prussia, and Russia in 1839) would not be violated. France responded negatively; Germany did not reply, Bethmann-Hollweg having earlier referred to the old guarantee as "a scrap of paper."

In Berlin, even the Social Democratic newspapers now accepted war as inevitable, declaring tsarist Russia the enemy. Moltke pushed for a German attack on France, fearing that should Russian mobilization proceed any further, the Schlieffen Plan for a two-front war might fail. On July 31, Germany warned Russia to suspend mobilization at once. At the same time, the German ambassador demanded that France guarantee its own neutrality in the event of a Russo-German war, and that German troops be allowed to occupy a number of French frontier forts as a show of French good faith. This no French government could accept. When no response was heard from either Russia or France, the German army began mobilization for war on August 1.

The relentless logic of the entangling alliances and military plans propelled Europe to war, as if the Great Powers were being pitched forward on an enormous wave. Grey's frantic attempts to arrange a direct negotiation between Russia and Austria failed. The struggle of socialists in many countries to rally opposition against the war fell far short. On July 31, a rightist assassinated the popular French socialist leader Jean Jaurès. But Jaurès, too, had apparently just come to the conclusion that he should support the war effort against autocratic Germany. The Austrian socialist leader Victor Adler predicted: "Jaurès' murder is just the beginning, war unchains instincts, all forms of madness."

Of the powers, only Italy, bound to the Triple Alliance if its estranged allies were attacked, was not committed by alliance to fight. France ordered mobilization after receiving the impossible German demands. Germany declared war on Russia that same day, August 1. This obliged France, by virtue of its alliance with Russia, to fight Germany. German troops invaded Luxembourg, claiming falsely that a French attack on them was imminent and that they needed to seize the small duchy's railroads to defend themselves. On August 2, the German ambassador in Brussels handed the Belgian government the sealed letter requesting permission to march armies through its territory. The negative reply came the next morning. Britain assured France that the Royal Navy would defend its Channel ports. The next day, August 3, Germany declared war on France, falsely claiming that French planes had attacked Nuremberg. When Moltke's army marched into eastern Belgium shortly thereafter, the British government formally demanded that the German armies withdraw. German troops kept marching toward the massive Belgium fortress at Liège. On August 4, Britain declared war on Germany.

Enthusiastic crowds toasted departing soldiers in Paris with champagne, shouting, "À *Berlin!*" Joyful throngs toasted departing soldiers in Berlin with beer, shouting, "*Nach Paris!*" The German crown prince anticipated "a jolly little war."

PART SIX

CATACLYSM

The Great War began in August 1914. Germany and Austria-Hungary and their smaller allies fought against Great Britain, France, Russia, and their allies. Although most statesmen, military leaders, and ordinary soldiers and civilians believed that the war would be over by Christmas, if not well before, it raged on for more than four years. A military stalemate, featuring trench warfare, particularly in France, took the lives of millions of soldiers. In the war's wake, four empires fell. In 1917, a revolution overthrew the tsar of Russia, and then the Bolsheviks overthrew the provisional government, withdrawing from the world conflict and imposing Communist rule. The German Empire collapsed upon the victory in November 1918 of Britain, France, and their allies (including the United States since 1917). The multinational Austro-Hungarian and Turkish Ottoman Empires, Germany's wartime allies, also collapsed.

The Versailles Peace Treaty, signed by the new German Republic in 1919, carved up the fallen empires, creating successor states in Central Europe—Poland, Czechoslovakia, and Yugoslavia. The treaties signed between the victors and the vanquished left a legacy of nationalist dissatisfaction and hatred in Europe that poisoned international relations during the subsequent two decades. Out of the economic, social, and political turmoil of the 1920s and 1930s emerged authoritarian movements that swept to power in many European countries, beginning with Mussolini's Italian fascists in 1922. In Germany, Hitler's National Socialist Party grew in strength with the advent of the Great Depression in 1929. It drew on extreme right-wing nationalism that viewed the Treaty of Versailles as an unfair humiliation to Germany. In the Soviet Union, Joseph Stalin became head of the Communist Party following Lenin's death in 1924; he purged rivals within the party, launched a campaign of rapid industrialization, forced millions of peasants into collective farms, and ordered the slaughter or imprisonment of those who resisted. Britain and France retained their parliamentary forms of government, despite economic, social, and political tensions.

In the Europe of extremes, the search for political stability after World War I proved illusive. After coming to power in 1933, Hitler rearmed Germany and disdainfully violated the Treaty of Versailles by reoccupying the Rhineland in 1936 and forging a union with Austria. The same year, Hitler and Mussolini supported a right-wing nationalist insurrection in Spain against the Spanish Republic. They sent planes, advisers, and war materiel to aid General Francisco Franco's military forces, which were victorious three years later. After Hitler's initial aggressive moves against Czechoslovakia were unopposed by Britain and France, the German dictator brazenly sent German troops to occupy all of Czechoslovakia in 1938.

Just weeks after shocking the world by signing a non-aggression pact with Stalin's Soviet Union, Hitler began his long planned invasion of Poland, which quickly fell. And after a brief "phony war" of inaction in the west, in the spring of 1940 Hitler invaded France, the Netherlands, and Belgium. Japan's sudden attack on the U.S. military bases at Pearl Harbor, Hawaii, on December 7, 1941, brought the United States into World War II. Seventeen million people were killed in the fighting, and another 20 million civilians perished, including more than 6 million Jews, systematically exterminated by the Nazis during the Holocaust. The war finally ended in 1945, after the defeat of Germany, Italy, and Japan. Europe and the entire world entered a new and potentially even more dangerous period, one in which nuclear arms made the threat of a new war even more horrible.

CHAPTER 24

THE GREAT WAR

In Berlin and Paris during early August 1914, hundreds of thousands of people enthusiastically celebrated the outbreak of the war that many had begun to see as inevitable. On both sides, virtually everyone expected a short, victorious war. Their troops, heading off to the fighting in early August, would be "home before the leaves fall," and then there would be more cheering and celebrations. But the events belied expectations, and the horrors of war, exacerbated by new weapons, quickly replaced the euphoria at its outbreak. The unexpected stalemate that followed shaped not only the course of the war but over the long run helped bring about dangerous political instability in Europe following its conclusion. The war dragged on for more than four years, taking an unprecedented toll of lives. It swept away old empires, created new states, and unleashed some of the demons of the twentieth century.

THE OUTBREAK OF WAR

When war was declared, eager commanders put long-standing military plans into effect. The German general staff counted on a rapid victory against France in the west before the giant Russian army could effectively be brought into action in the east. But anticipating a quick victory, German troops sidestepped French defenses by invading Belgium. However, this violation of Belgian neutrality inevitably brought Britain into the war on the side of France and Russia. Thus, the Great War pitted the Triple Alliance (Germany and Austria-Hungary, minus Italy, which for the moment remained neutral) against the Triple Entente (France, Great Britain, and Russia). These alignments had been shaped by the international tensions of the past decades.

The Schlieffen Plan

Germany's plan for war against France had been established by Count Alfred von Schlieffen, a former chief of the German General Staff. Based on

(*Left*) French soldiers depart for war. (*Right*) British men surge toward a recruiting office.

the assumption that it would take Russia, France's ally, some weeks to pre-pare her armies to fight, the Schlieffen Plan called for the German armies to knock the French out of the war within six weeks. To do this, the German armies would storm around the network of fortifications the French had constructed on their eastern frontier after the Franco-Prussian War of 1870–1871. German troops would march through the flat lands of Belgium and Holland, and turn south once the last soldier on the northern flank had brushed his sleeve against the English Channel. A pincer movement southward would encircle Paris from the northwest, and then turn to trap the French armies struggling in Alsace-Lorraine. It mattered little that the Germans might first have to give ground in Alsace-Lorraine, where the French, as a matter of pride, would surely attack. Schlieffen and his successors all recognized that the plan would probably bring Great Britain into the war because that nation would never accept the violation of Belgian territory and the possible presence of an enemy power just across the Channel. But the Germans believed that the small, volunteer British army posed little threat. Then, once Paris had fallen and the French armies had been put out of action by the wrenching German head-lock, there would still be time to ship enough of the victorious army to the east to defeat the Russians as they rolled slowly toward Germany. This was the solution to Bismarck's nightmare, a simultaneous war on two fronts.

Schlieffen's last words had been "Keep the right wing [of the attacking armies] strong." Yet, his successor, Helmuth von Moltke, reduced the strength of the attacking force by bolstering German defenses in Alsace-Lorraine. Moltke also eliminated the Netherlands from the invasion plan for lack of men; the German army would pass through southern Belgium.

The French high command, which had known the basics of the Schlieffen Plan for years, did not believe the German army could move rapidly through Belgium, in part because the attacking forces would have to overcome the imposing fortress at Liège. The French also knew that the plan called for the incorporation of reserves into the main German army, and doubted they could quickly become an able fighting force. In any case, the French expected a frontal attack between the Meuse River and the hills of the Ardennes in northeastern France.

The French high command had its own plan for war. It, too, envisioned a rapid attack based on the *élan*, or patriotic energy, of the troops. "Plan XVII" would send two French armies into Alsace-Lorraine, as the Germans expected. The French planned another thrust to drive German forces back. With the bulk of the German army tied up by French and British troops in Belgium, and, at worst, northern France, the way to Berlin would be open. But having miscalculated the size of the effective German fighting force, the French also underestimated the speed with which their enemy could mobilize for war and attack.

Opening Hostilities

The Schlieffen Plan dictated the course of the opening hostilities and the stalemate that followed. It was as if Schlieffen's "dead hand automatically pulled the trigger" when the Belgian government on August 2 rejected the German demand that its armies be permitted to march through Belgium. Although the Belgians fought bravely against vastly superior strength, Liège fell on August 16 after a massive bombardment, followed by the fall of Namur. The Germans found easy going elsewhere in Belgium, forcing King Leopold's army to retreat westward to Antwerp. But Moltke deployed seven divisions to prevent the Belgian army from escaping. This weakened the attacking forces that Schlieffen intended to drive as rapidly as possible toward the English Channel.

German armies, supplied by 500 trains that crossed the bridges of the Rhine each day, also defeated the French in battles around Metz. General Alexander von Kluck, commander of the First German army, then turned his troops toward the Belgian town of Mons. He hoped to force the French to surrender before they could bring up more troops from the Paris region. French advances in Alsace, although anticipated by Schlieffen, now convinced the Germans to divert troops to that border region from their primary attacking force attempting to encircle the French capital. Both the French and German high commands considered success in Alsace critical to their strategies and to morale at home.

The British Expeditionary Force arrived to take its place on the French flank on August 20, reaching Mons two days later. One British soldier who went off to war in the summer of 1914 reassured his family, "At least the thing will be over in three weeks." But by August 24, the Allied (Entente

MAP 24.1 THE GERMAN ADVANCE, 1914   The Germans moved quickly into Belgium and France, largely following the Schlieffen Plan of 1905.

Powers) armies were rapidly retreating. At Mons and then Le Cateau, the British army fought its biggest battles since Waterloo in 1815. Its retreat did not yet spell defeat. The Germans, fatigued by the pace of their march, also suffered from Moltke's indecision and inadequate communications. Kluck's army was already spread too thinly across a wide front. Moltke further weakened the attacking force by sending still more troops to defend Alsace. Then, reacting to the news of a preliminary Russian victory on the eastern front, he sent four divisions to the east to confront the surprisingly rapid Russian advance.

Nonetheless, the German armies managed to fight to within thirty-five miles of Paris (see Map 24.1). The French government provisionally withdrew to the safety of Bordeaux on the southeast coast, just as they had

Refugees following a priest out of the battle zone in northern France.

been forced to do during the disastrous Franco-Prussian War. But despite heavy losses, French Marshal Joseph Joffre was able to reinforce his defensive positions around Paris. This was possible because the French had concluded a secret treaty by which Italy agreed to remain neutral if Germany attacked France. Germany, unaware of the treaty, hoped to ally with Italy. The Italian government was playing both sides against each other, assuring its Austro-Hungarian and German treaty partners of its loyalty,

Old combat and new in World War I.

while telling Britain at the same time that Germany and Austria-Hungary were the aggressors. In any case, the Italian commitment to its allies was defensive. Joffre could thus count on troops that otherwise would have been needed in southeastern France to halt a possible Italian invasion.

The French managed to wear down the German offensive. At the dawn of air warfare, a French reconnaissance pilot noticed Kluck's army changing direction as it swept toward a point southeast of Paris, leaving its flank open. The French army rushed every available soldier into action, some arriving at the front in requisitioned Parisian taxis. When the Germans crossed the Marne River on September 5, the French counterattacked. Two German armies retreated, fearing that the French might take advantage of a sizable gap between their forces. It was the end of the Schlieffen Plan, and of the offensive war that the German generals had planned. The British poured through another gap between the German armies, forcing the Germans to retreat forty miles to the Aisne River. There, on September 14, the Germans fortified their position by digging deep defensive trenches. Like the Battle of Valmy in 1792 during the French Revolution, the Battle of the Marne saved France in 1914.

The Germans then tried to outflank the British and French forces— Schlieffen's strategy in the first place. This led to what amounted to a race for the sea, as the Allied armies kept pace, holding much of Picardy and Flanders, before both sides ran out of space. The British and French, too, dug in.

A series of attacks and counterattacks in the fall took frightful tolls, with neither side able to break through. In November 1914, the last open battle of the western front was fought in the mud around Ypres; the British pre-

Paul Nash's *We Are Making a New World,* a tormented painting evoking the pock-marked landscape around Ypres in Flanders.

vented the Germans from reaching the Channel ports in France. By the end of the year, German and French forces had combined casualties of 300,000 killed and 600,000 wounded. The British Seventh Division arrived in France in October with 400 officers and 12,000 soldiers: after eighteen days of fighting around Ypres, it had 44 officers and 2,336 men left. In a special British battalion of football players, originally brought together to play exhibition matches near the front and then sent to fight like everybody else, only 30 of 200 survived. The French writer Charles Péguy (1873–1914), who in 1914 had described his eager anticipation of heroic war, was killed late that same year at the Battle of the Marne.

THE CHANGING NATURE OF WAR

The German and Allied armies stared at each other across a broad front that reached from the English Channel to Switzerland. Two long, thin lines of trenches punctured the dreams of rapid victory based upon a mastery of offensive tactics. Few analysts had considered the possibility of a frozen front that would rarely move more than a few hundred yards in either direction and along which several million soldiers would die.

Besides trench warfare, new weapons dramatically changed the nature of warfare. Before the war finally ended, poison gas, hand grenades, flame-throwers, tanks, the military use of airplanes, and submarines had entered the arsenals of both sides. More than this, a new scale of warfare required an unparalleled, total mobilization of the home front to sustain the war effort.

Trench Warfare

In trench warfare, spades for digging trenches and rows of tangled barbed wire became more important than the rifle and bayonet, weapons of attack. Soldiers on both sides dug about 6,250 miles of trench in France. The front-line trenches were six to eight feet deep and about fifty yards to a mile apart. They were supplemented by support trenches several hundred yards to the rear and linked by communications trenches. Small fortress-like "strong points" held the line together even if part of the system was overrun. Sandbags and rows of barbed wire protected the trenches from attack. As the months passed in sectors where the front lines were immobile, the trenches became more elaborate, offering at least electricity and a certain minimal level of comfort. When there was no fighting, the soldiers confronted boredom. The French theater star Sarah Bernhardt, who had herself lost one leg to amputation (because of several bad falls) was carried on a stretcher near the front so she could entertain soldiers by reciting poetry. Some soldiers read voraciously to pass the time; the British poet Siegfried Sassoon was only half kidding when he remembered, "I didn't want to die, not before I'd finished reading *The Return of*

Trench warfare.

the Native anyway." Since they were below ground, the trenches offered soldiers some protection from rifle or pistol fire, but not from direct artillery hits. The periscope, sticking up from the trench below, provided the only safe way of looking across at the enemy lines without being shot by enemy snipers.

The front-line soldier lived amidst the thunder of barrages and the scream of falling shells. Persistent lice, mice, and enormous starving rats were his constant companions in the stagnant water of the trenches. So, for many, was venereal disease, contracted in the brothels near the front. A British soldier described a night in the trenches in January 1916:

> Lights out. Now the rats and the lice are the masters of the house. You can hear the rats nibbling, running, jumping, rushing from plank to plank, emitting their little squeals behind the dugout's corrugated metal. It's a noisy swarming activity that just won't stop. At any moment I expect one to land on my nose. And then it's the lice and fleas that begin to devour me. Absolutely impossible to get any shut-eye. Toward midnight I begin to doze off. A terrible racket makes me jump. Artillery fire, the cracking of rifle and machine-gun fire. The Boches [Germans] must be attacking. . . . Everything shakes. Our artillery thunders away without pause. . . . I doze off so as to get up at six. The rats and the lice get up too; waking to life is also waking to misery.

The cold and wind tore into the troops, especially in winter. "Before you can have a drink," one soldier wrote home, "you have to chip away the ice. The meat is frozen solid, the potatoes are bonded by ice, and even the hand grenades are welded together in their cases." The German army had been so sure of an easy victory that it had not equipped its men with high lace-up boots or adequate coats. German troops prized the British soldiers' sheepskin coats and removed them from enemy corpses when they had the chance. After battle, the screams of the wounded and dying filled the air, groans in German, French, and English from no-man's-land that grew increasingly faint, but that sometimes lasted for days.

Death was everywhere. A French soldier remembered, "We all had on us the stench of dead bodies. The bread we ate, the stagnant water we drank, everything we touched had a rotten smell." Death numbed. An Austrian soldier, a violinist, wrote: "A certain fierceness arises in you, an absolute indifference to anything the world holds except your duty of fighting. You are eating a crust of bread, and a man is shot dead in the trench next to you. You look calmly at him for a moment, and then go on eating your bread. Why not? There is nothing to be done. In the end you talk of your own death with as little excitement as you would of a luncheon engagement." Hundreds of thousands of soldiers suffered shell shock, psychologically devastated by the battle raging around them, unable to act.

Massive attacks were preceded by an intensive bombardment of enemy positions. Such bombardments, lasting hours and even days, clearly indicated where the next attack could be expected, allowing the enemy to bring up sufficient reserves to prevent a breakthrough. Both sides adopted the use of "creeping barrages," which moved just ahead of the attacking army to soften resistance. But these left huge craters and mangled terrain, which created unanticipated obstacles to the attacking troops, including corpses dislodged by the shells. The attackers then faced the most effec-

No-man's-land, northern France.

tive weapon of trench warfare, the machine gun, which mowed down line after line of advancing soldiers carrying rifles, bayonets, and pistols that they often never had a chance to use.

Piles of the dead filled shell craters left by the first barrages. If attacking Allied troops managed to reach, take, and hold the first line of trenches, they confronted fresh reinforcements as well as an even more solid second line of defense, which the Germans had been able to construct at their leisure. The defensive lines had an elastic quality to them; they could bend, but then snap back against attacking forces that soon outran their cover. Joffre's second offensive in the Champagne in 1915 illustrated this situation well. The French offensive ran right into the second line of defense, took enormous casualties, and then faced a vigorous counterattack. The Germans lost 75,000 killed and wounded, the French 145,000, for not more than a few miles of ravaged land. Still, Joffre ordered another attack. The result was the same.

Soldiers also faced new, frightening perils. German attacks against British positions around Ypres featured a horrifying new weapon, mustard gas, which was carried by the wind and burned out the lungs of the British soldiers. A member of the British medical corps wrote, "I shall never forget the sights I saw by Ypres after the first gas attacks. Men lying all along the side of the road . . . exhausted, gasping, frothing yellow mucus from their mouths, their faces blue and distressed. It was dreadful, and so little could be done for them." The gas mask soon offered imperfect protection, "this pig snout which represented the war's true face," as one combatant put it. Later in the war the flame thrower brought to the front another way to die.

(*Left*) French soldiers wearing gas masks prepare to attack. (*Right*) Victims of a German gas attack lining up at a field hospital.

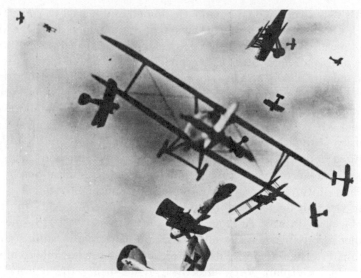

German and British planes in a dogfight high above the trenches.

War in the Air and on the Seas

Airplanes became weapons of combat. In the first month of the war, airplanes were only used for reconnaissance in good weather. But in October 1914, a British plane took off from Antwerp and destroyed a hangar in Düsseldorf with two twenty-pound bombs the pilot dropped over the side. Some pilots kept carrier pigeons in a cage, so that, if they had to ditch their planes, they could scribble their approximate location on a paper and send the information off with the bird. Pilots fired pistols and hurled hand grenades and even bricks at enemy planes and troops below before both sides discovered that machine guns could be mounted and timed to fire between the blades of the plane's propellers.

By the end of 1916, dashing and brave "aces," such as the German Red Baron, Manfred von Richthofen, and later the American Eddie Rickenbacker, chased each other around the skies, cheered on by the trench soldiers. When Richthofen was shot down behind British lines in April 1918, he was buried by his enemies with full military honors. Although the "dogfights" of combat in the skies had a romantic dimension, the airplane soon began to terrorize civilians. Paris and particularly London were bombed several times during the war, as the speed and capacity of the first warplanes increased; the Rhineland German cities suffered heavy bombardments later in the conflict. By the war's end, Germany had produced more than 47,000 aircraft, France more than 51,000, and Britain more than 55,000 planes.

With the European powers fighting a land war unlike any ever seen, and conflict having taken to the skies, the seas remained relatively quiet. There

the British navy retained command; the famed and feared German Dread-
noughts, those enormous battleships that had helped fuel the Anglo-
German naval rivalry before the war, stayed in port. The British navy won
a series of initial encounters as far afield as the coast of Chile, the Falkland Islands near Argentina, and the Indian Ocean. German battleships
trapped in the Mediterranean at the beginning of the war took refuge in
Constantinople and were turned over to the Turks. The German navy took
them back when Turkey entered the war on the side of the Central Powers.
The Austro-Hungarian navy, based in Trieste, was small and its influence
was limited to the Mediterranean. The British public and admiralty, which
possessed the German code book—plucked from the Baltic Sea by Russian sailors—awaited a major confrontation, another Trafalgar. Certain
that the German fleet was going to sail from Wilhelmshaven, the British
Grand Fleet lay in wait. At Dogger Bank on January 24, 1915, one of the
few major naval engagements of the war, the Royal Navy sunk a German
battleship. For the remainder of the war, the British were able to blockade
the principal German ports, effectively neutralizing the kaiser's proud
fleet.

Late in the 1880s, several countries had experimented with underwater
warfare. At the turn of the century, the U.S. Navy was the first to commission a submarine. Although all of the powers had submarines, those of
Germany made the greatest impact in the war. The German navy believed
that its fleet of submarines, which brought another fearful dimension to
warfare, could force Britain to pull out of the war by sinking its warships
and by preventing supplies from reaching the British Isles. In September
1914, a German submarine, or "U-boat," sank three large British armored
cruisers off the coast of Belgium. U-boats, 188 feet long and with a range
of 2,400 miles, could slip in and out of port undetected.

Germany came to depend ever more on unrestricted submarine warfare
against Allied shipping in the North Atlantic, but this later had the catastrophic effect of bringing the United States into the war as an enemy.

Support from the Home Front

For each combatant, the waging of war on such an unprecedented scale
required the full support of the "home front." Sustaining the massive war
effort depended first on mobilizing enough soldiers and food to supply the
front, and then on producing enough guns and shells. It also depended on
maintaining morale at home. With both sides disappointed by the failure
to win a quick victory, popular enthusiasm increasingly fed on a deep hatred of the enemy. German propagandists portrayed the war as a fight for
German culture, besieged by Russian barbarians and the dishonorable
French. A German soldier wrote, "We know full well that we are fighting
for the German idea in the world, that we are defending German feeling
against Asiatic barbarism and Latin indifference." British propagandists

British civilians attack a German-owned store in London, 1914.

depicted the Allies as defending law, liberty, and progress against German violations of national sovereignty and international law. German harshness in dealing with Belgian civilians in the first months of the war convinced the British population more than ever that their cause was just. French propagandists had the easiest case to make: Germany had, after all, invaded France.

Such propaganda mixed elements of truth and myth, a potent concoction. By the end of 1914, tales of Germans impaling children and raping nuns were horrifying the British and French. The German execution in Belgium of the British nurse Edith Cavell, accused of helping British prisoners escape, had a great effect on the home front. Germans shot many civilians in the Belgian town of Dinant and shelled the twelfth-century Cathedral of Reims ("better that a thousand church towers fall than one German soldier should fall as a result of these towers," explained one German historian at the time). These actions foreshadowed a new kind of war—a total war in which civilians were not spared. At the outbreak of hostilities, shops owned by people with German-sounding names were pillaged in Britain and France (in the latter case, many of the victims were French Alsatians for whom the war, at least in part, was supposedly being fought). Not long after the war began, a French teacher insisted, "It is necessary and it is urgent that we eradicate to the last stone and to the last individual this race of vipers that is the Prussian race." Germans held similar beliefs about their enemies, particularly the British, who supposedly used dum-dum bullets that exploded upon impact or who gouged out the eyes of German prisoners.

The outbreak of the war pushed aside bitter political divisions at home.

(*Left*) In the perfect poster, Lord Kitchener summons British males to join the army. (*Right*) A poster showing support from the home front.

In France, competing parties proclaimed a "sacred union," and Jules Guesde, a socialist, became minister of commerce. There was little public criticism of the way the war was being run until later in the conflict when casualties mounted. In Germany, too, socialist opposition to militarism based on class solidarity quickly turned to patriotic support. In Britain, the angry quarrels over strategy among the generals, as well as between them and the cabinet, were well hidden from the public. A volunteer army was raised. This was done with remarkable enthusiasm and speed, aided by an effective recruitment poster sporting the face of Lord Horatio Kitchener, the secretary of war (leading Prime Minister Lord Asquith to observe, "He is not a great man. He is a great poster"). On a single day in September 1914, 33,000 men joined up. By the end of the year, the British had 2 million men in uniform. The volunteer force that German Kaiser William II had called "a comtemptible little army" fought very well. In Russia, only the tsar's will seemed to matter. In Austria-Hungary, the ability of the imperial bureaucracy to supply its multinational army, the prestige of which had helped keep the Habsburg empire together, seemed almost miraculous. Tensions between the empire's nationalities remained beneath the surface, at least in the war's early years.

In Britain, Lloyd George skillfully oversaw the transition from peacetime to wartime industrial production, using the powers specified by the Munitions of War Act of May 1915. The act forbade strikes and provided for the requisition of skilled workers for labor in factories, which were converted to the production of war materiel. Supplying the front with shells alone was a monumental task. The nineteen-day artillery barrage at the third Battle of Ypres in 1917 expended all the shells carried to the front by 321 trains, the output of a year's work for 55,000 armament workers.

The war spurred other changes in daily life at home. As heavy drinking became more widespread, legislation restricted the operating hours of British pubs. Some complained that the war had brought Britain a loosening of morals, frivolous dress and dancing, and an increase in juvenile delinquency. Daylight savings time was introduced for the first time. A successful campaign for voluntary rationing of essential commodities such as sugar allowed the British to avoid mandatory rationing until early 1917, when shortages were generated by hoarding. The government instituted a coupon system, but, in fact, price controls on essential commodities served to ration food.

Suffragette leaders, who had put aside their campaign for women's right to vote, threw their support behind the war. Millicent Garrett Fawcett (1847–1929), a leading British feminist, appealed to the readers of a suffrage magazine: "Women, your country needs you. . . . Let us show ourselves worthy of Citizenship." She announced that she considered pacifism almost the equivalent of treason. Some of the members of the Pankhurst family, committed suffragettes, now spoke at bond-selling rallies, and two members urged supporters to beat up pacifists.

In every belligerent country, women made varied contributions to the war. Nurses in every country served heroically at the front and were acclaimed as heroines. With so many men dead, injured, or still at the front, beginning in 1915 over 1 million British women stepped into jobs from which they had previously been excluded, ranging from skilled and semi-skilled jobs in munitions factories ("Shells made by a wife may save a husband's life" went one public poster in Britain) to positions as tram conductors and gas-meter readers. A visitor to Berlin in March 1916 reported "no men anywhere, women are doing everything."

THE WAR RAGES ON

Early in 1915, the French general staff predicted that its army would break through the German lines. French attacks in the spring in Champagne and then the Artois further north brought little more than enormous casualties on both sides (see Map 24.2). A British assault at Neuve Chapelle on March 10 gained 1,000 yards at a cost of 13,000 casualties. The Allied offensives in 1915 demonstrated that neither side could effect a breakthrough against enemy forces. *Élan* was not enough. In 1916 during the murderous Battle of the Somme, a British captain sought to inspire his men by jumping out of the trench and leading the attack by

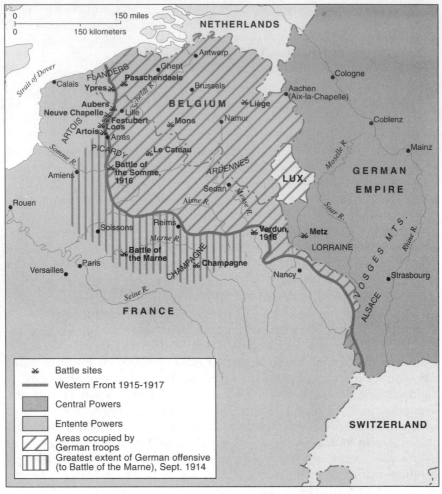

MAP 24.2 THE WESTERN FRONT, 1914–1917   Major battles from 1914–
1917, and location of trenches at the end of 1915 and at the end of 1917.

dribbling a soccer ball across no-man's-land. He was shot dead far from
the goal.

The British lost almost 300,000 men in 1915 alone; the Germans, who
had a much larger army, took at least 610,000 casualties. Both country's
casualties, however daunting, paled alongside those of the French, who
suffered 1,292,000 killed and wounded in 1915. French infantrymen were
not helped by the fact that their uniform pants were, at least in the early
stages of the war, bright red, which could be more easily seen through the
morning mists than the German gray.

Fighting also engulfed the eastern front, where the Russian army fought
both German and Austro-Hungarian forces. In 1915, Italy entered the war

Casualties were heavy on both sides after the Battle of the Somme, 1916.

on the Allied side and Bulgaria entered the war on the side of the Central Powers. The struggle between Britain and Turkey—which was also allied with the Central Powers—carried the war into the Middle East. Japan, coveting several German islands in the Pacific and seeking sanction for its interest in a province of northeastern China, entered the war on the Allied side in 1914. What began as a European war became a world war.

The Eastern Front

Having failed to achieve the anticipated quick victory in the west, German forces now fought on two fronts. In the wide-open spaces of the eastern front, the Russian armies had advanced into Eastern Prussia despite the incompetence of the Russian general staff, intense animosity among commanders, hopelessly archaic equipment, and communications so inadequate that the Germans could easily listen to Russian officers discussing tactics on the telephone. In late summer 1914, the German army drove the Russians back, inflicting casualties of over 250,000 men. The Russians also lost their most able general, who committed suicide in despair. On the more confident German side, sixty-seven-year-old General Paul von Hindenburg (1847–1934), a stolid Prussian who had been called out of retirement, and the determined and organized General Erich Ludendorff (1865–1937), an artisan's son who had convinced the defenders of the Belgian fortress of Liège to surrender after a massive bombardment by pounding on the door with his sword handle, embellished their reputations in these battles.

The Central Powers, with no joint plan of military coordination, found the Russian army an imposing foe. In September 1914, the Russians captured the fortress of Lemberg in Galicia from the Austro-Hungarian armies, and took 100,000 prisoners (see Map 24.3). Many of these were conscripted Slavs, who felt more allegiance to their fellow Slavic Russians than to their German-speaking officers. The Austro-Hungarian army had diverted too many divisions in the punitive invasion of strategically unimportant Serbia.

MAP 24.3 THE EASTERN, ITALIAN, AND BALKAN FRONTS   Russian and Austro-German advances and battles along the eastern front; Austro-Hungarian and Italian armies face off along the Italian front; and Turkish and Allied armies fighting on the Balkan front.

In January 1915, the Habsburg forces launched an offensive against the Russian army in the Carpathian Mountains. Although the offensive looked good on a map, the reality was otherwise. Snow-covered mountains provided an imposing obstacle: supplies had to be moved over ice or freezing marsh; low clouds obscured artillery targets; and soldiers had to warm their rifles over fires before they could use them. When the Russians counterattacked, they found "men already cut to pieces and defenseless. . . . Every day hundreds froze to death; the wounded who could not drag themselves off were bound to die; riding became impossible; and there was no combating the apathy and indifference that gripped the men." The Germans had to send troops to support their ally in the Carpathians, and lost over 350,000 troops. With the stalemate in the west, the Germans wanted to beat the Russians before the latter could defeat the Habsburg army. In May 1915, a massive German attack tore into the Russian army, driving it back almost 100 miles. The Russian retreat, which had been orderly in the beginning, turned into "a mad bacchanalia," with Cossacks abducting female refugees. A million civilians moved eastward with the Russian armies; "while thousands of people trudge along the railway lines they are passed by speeding trains loaded with couches from officers' clubs, and carrying quarter-masters' bird cages." The Russian retreat from the Carpathian Mountains gave the Austro-Hungarian forces some badly needed breathing room.

The Central Powers could not look to Italy for help. Italy had remained neutral at the outbreak of the war but gave in to street demonstrations and entered the war on the Allied side through the secret Treaty of London, signed in April 1915. Britain and France held out as bait territories many

A Russian soldier attempts to stop two deserters from fleeing in Galicia, 1915.

Italian nationalists claimed as part of "Italian Irredenta" ("unredeemed lands"), including the Tyrol in the Alps and Istria along the northern Adriatic coast. Italian nationalism, as well as the desire of powerful Italian businessmen to find new markets in the Balkans, had proved stronger than Italy's pre-war commitment to its former allies. Austria-Hungary now found itself, like Germany, fighting a war on two fronts. The Italians attacked with the port of Trieste as their goal. In the meantime, the German armies reached Brest-Litovsk in August 1915, ending 100 years of Russian control of Poland. One million Russian soldiers were killed or wounded on the front, and another million were captured.

The War in the Middle East, Africa, and the Far East

British military and political leaders were divided between those who believed that victory would have to be won in the west, and others who pushed for a series of dramatic strikes against Germany or its allies on Europe's periphery. The latter included Winston Churchill (1874–1965), the First Lord of the Admiralty, and David Lloyd George, the Liberal politician who headed the wartime Ministry of Munitions. Such victories might also help expand the British Empire, which pleased the colonial lobby at home. This strategy angered the French government, which bitterly opposed any reduction of British support on the western front.

Churchill and Lord Kitchener planned an attack on Germany's ally, Turkey, the perpetual "sick man of Europe." The Ottoman Empire had seen its territory on the European side of the Bosphorus Straits eroded over the past two centuries. In 1908, the "Young Turks," a group of liberal nationalists inspired by the West, including a number of army officers frustrated by imperial inefficiency, had engineered a revolution in Turkey in the name of "order and progress" and established a liberal constitution. Following further territorial losses in the Balkan Wars of 1912–1913, however, the new government did not evolve into a parliamentary regime but rather into a military dictatorship intent on imposing Turkish culture on ethnic minorities. Since entering the war on the side of Germany and Austria-Hungary in November 1914, the Turks closed off the Dardanelles Straits, which separate the Aegean Sea from the Sea of Marmara. This cut off an important route for supplies to Russia through the Black Sea. Turkish forces also tied up Russian troops in the Caucasus Mountains. Now Turkey posed a potential threat to the Suez Canal. The British high command planned an assault on the Dardanelles Straits. If everything went well, a British success might bring an end to the power of the pro-German faction in Constantinople. With Turkey out of the war, Churchill reasoned, the German effort in the Balkans could be undermined, and Bulgaria, which seemed ready to join the Central Powers, would stay out of the conflict.

A well-camouflaged Turkish sniper (center) captured at Gallipoli, 1915.

Following a month-long naval bombardment of Turkish forts, a predominantly British fleet of thirteen battleships entered the Dardanelles Straits in March 1915. After running into a line of mines left along the shore and losing three battleships, the warships retreated. In April, the fleet returned, disembarking five divisions on the beach of Gallipoli (see Map 24.3). The British army hurled itself against the well-defended heights held by the Turks. British troops managed to dig in, and in August launched an assault that failed miserably. After committing more than 400,000 men, half of whom were killed or wounded, the British were fortunate to evacuate their remaining forces in January 1916. Amid harsh criticism of the campaign's humiliating failure, Churchill and Kitchener lost influence. To this day, the Gallipoli Campaign remains controversial. Some historians consider it an imaginative, even brilliant stroke that might have won the war. Others agree with most contemporaries who believed that it was a needless diversion dictated by British colonial interests in the Middle East and for which Australian and New Zealander troops paid a disproportionate price.

Still hoping to knock Turkey out of the war, the Allies tried to coax Bulgaria into the war on their side. But Bulgaria coveted neighboring Serbian Macedonia, and joined the Central Powers in October 1915. A month later, a Franco-British force landed in Salonika, Greece, to try to help Serbia. But within two months, the German, Austro-Hungarian, and Bulgarian armies had crushed the Serbian army. The Germans called Salonika their "largest internment camp," since that campaign tied up an additional

King Peter of Serbia and his general staff retreat across the River Dvina in the winter of 1915.

half million Allied troops in fighting the Bulgarians. The British also fought a desert war against the Turks in Palestine and Mesopotamia.

Smaller British forces were occupied fighting for the German colonies in Africa (see Map 24.4). Togoland fell in August 1914, German Southwest Africa in 1915, and the German Cameroons in 1916. The fighting in German East Africa (Tanganyika) went on for the duration of the war, pitting German troops against British and South African soldiers, and both sides against mosquitoes and disease. In Asia, Japanese forces captured the fortress and port of Tsingtao (Qingdao) from a German garrison, and the undefended German islands of the Marianas, Carolines, and Marshalls in the North Pacific.

The Western Front

With their failure at Gallipoli, the British again focused on the western front. England was so close to this front that officers who had lunch in private railroad cars before leaving Victoria Station could be at the front by dinner. When British miners managed to blow up a previously unconquerable ridge near Messines in western Belgium, Lloyd George was said to have heard the explosion at 10 Downing Street in London. General Douglas Haig (1861–1928) was named commander in chief of the British army in France in December 1915. He agreed with Joffre's plan for a mighty offensive in the vicinity of the Somme River. The assault would have to await the arrival of more British soldiers and spring weather. The

MAP 24.4 THE WORLD WAR The expansion of the war beyond Europe to the German colonies in Africa and the Far East.

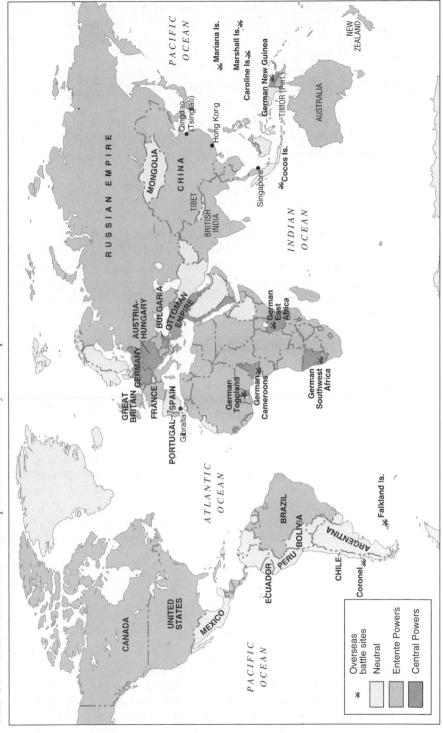

German army, too, had big plans. The new German commander in chief, General Erich von Falkenhayn (1861–1922), planned an assault on the fortresses surrounding Verdun in eastern France. These had been neglected by the French, who had shipped off some artillery pieces to points of attack further west. Falkenhayn had no illusions about breaking through the French lines. But he believed that with a massive attack on Verdun, the Germans could "out-attrition" the French, who, by virtue of a lower birthrate, could not afford to lose as many soldiers as their more populous enemy. Assuming that France would lose five men for every two German soldiers killed, Falkenhayn's goal was "to bleed France white." Realizing that even more German victories on the eastern front would not necessarily knock Russia out of the war, and doubting the ability of Austria-Hungary to hold off both the Russians on their eastern front and Italy in the south, the German command needed to force the French to sue for peace.

After nine days of delay because of bad weather, the German artillery—1,220 pieces strong—began to bombard the French forts stretched around Verdun across a front of eight miles on February 21, 1916 (see Map 24.2). Some of the guns weighed twenty tons; it took nine tractors to move each piece to its place and a crane to load the shells. The French prepared to hold Verdun at all costs. Its loss would be a potentially mortal blow to French morale. In the damp, chilling mists of the hills of the Argonne, hundreds of thousands of men died, killed by shells that rained from the sky, machine guns that seemed never to be stilled, or bayonetted in hand-to-hand fighting within and outside the massive cement forts.

The French army held. General Philippe Pétain (1856–1951), the new commander, became a hero in France. But the cost of this victory came close to fulfilling Falkenhayn's expectations. The French lost 315,000 men killed or wounded; 90,000 died at the appropriately named "Dead Man's Hill" alone. The Germans suffered 281,000 casualties. A French counterattack in the fall recaptured several of the forts the Germans had taken; again the casualties mounted. In all, the French suffered 540,000 casualties and the Germans 430,000 casualties at Verdun. At one of the forts, Douaumont, one can still see plaques put up by proud, grieving relatives after the war, one of which reads, "For my son. Since his eyes closed mine have not ceased to cry."

The Battle of Verdun merely postponed plans for a massive British offensive on the Somme, supported by a similar French thrust. The assault began on July 1 after a week's bombardment. British troops attacked in the sector selected by Joffre, not for strategic or tactical reasons, but because it was where the French and British lines met.

Allied troops climbed out of the trenches at dawn to the whistles of their officers, and moved into no-man's-land. Things could not have gone worse along the eighteen miles of front. Artillery barrages chopped up the terrain over which the attackers had to struggle but left intact most of the German barbed wire, which the British soldiers found was too strong for their

The devastation wrought by the Battle of the Somme did not lead to a clear victory for either side.

wire-cutters. German machine gun emplacements had also survived the barrage. Many British soldiers managed only a few yards before falling with the sixty-six pounds of equipment they were carrying. The Germans moved up reserves to wherever their lines were bending. The British commanders sent wave after wave of infantrymen "over the top" to their death; corpses piled up on top of those who had died seconds, minutes, or hours before. Of 752 men in the First Newfoundland Regiment, all 26 officers and 658 men were killed or wounded within forty minutes. Sixty percent of the 10th Battalion of the West Yorkshires were killed in the initial assault. At the end of the first day of the Battle of the Somme, about 60,000 soldiers of the 110,000 British soldiers had become casualties, including 19,000 killed. (There were more British soldiers killed and wounded in the first three days of the Battle of the Somme than Americans killed in World War I, the Korean War, and the Vietnam War combined, and three times as many killed as had been killed in fifteen years of war against Napoleon.) When the disastrous offensive finally ended in mid-November, Britain had lost 420,000 men killed and wounded. The French lost 200,000 men in what was primarily a British offensive. It cost the Germans 650,000 soldiers to hold on. The maximum German retreat was a few kilometers; in most places, Allied gains were measured in yards. A sign left over one mass grave said, "The Devonshires held this trench, the Devonshires hold it still." The British poet Edmund Blunden, who survived the Battle of the Somme, tried to answer the question of who had won: "By the end of the [first] day both sides had seen, in a sad scrawl of broken earth and murdered men, the answer to the question. No road. No thoroughfare. Neither race had won, nor could win, the War. The War had won, and would go on winning."

Futility and Stalemate

Futility and stalemate also prevailed on the mountainous Austro-Italian front, where in 1916 there were *twelve* different Battles of the Isonzo River. The Italian army considered one of these, the sixth, a great victory because it moved three miles forward. After half a million casualties, the Italians were still only halfway to their objective, the Adriatic port of Trieste.

On the eastern front, General von Hindenburg claimed that there was no way of gauging the number of Russians killed with any accuracy: "All we do know is that, at times, fighting the Russians, we had to remove the piles of enemy bodies from before our trenches, so as to get a clear field of fire against new waves of assault." Even when the Russian general rejected the principle of mass offensive attack, the casualties were staggering. In June 1916, the Russian offensive pushed back the Austrians by combining smaller surprise attacks by specially trained troops, without the preliminary barrages, against carefully chosen targets. But the arrival of more German troops minimized Russian gains. Each side lost a million men in these encounters.

Russian sharpshooters in a trench on the eastern front.

In 1916, the British poet Isaac Rosenberg, who would later die in battle, wrote "Break of Day in the Trenches," one of the most haunting poems to come out of the war.

The darkness crumbles away—
It is the same old druid Time as ever.
Only a live thing leaps my hand—
A queer sardonic rat—
As I pull the parapet's poppy
To stick behind my ear.
Droll rat, they would shoot you if they knew
Your cosmopolitan sympathies.
Now you have touched this English hand
You will do the same to a German—
Soon, no doubt, if it be your pleasure
To cross the sleeping green between.
It seems you inwardly grin as you pass
Strong eyes, fine limbs, haughty athletes
Less chance than you for life,
Bonds to the whims of murder,
Sprawled in the bowels of the earth,
The torn fields of France.
What do you see in our eyes
At the shrieking iron and flame
Hurled through still heavens?
What quaver—what heart aghast?
Poppies whose roots are in men's veins
Drop, and are ever dropping;
But mine in my ear is safe,
Just a little white with the dust.

The winter of 1916–1917 was bleak. There seemed few families on either side who had not lost a relative or friend at the front. On the Allied side, there was some cheer when Romania joined the war in exchange for the promise of some Hungarian territory with a significant Romanian population once the Central Powers had been defeated. But Falkenhayn, removed from the western front in disgrace after Verdun, quickly defeated the Romanians. In Southeastern Europe, the war eroded the resources and morale of Bulgaria and Turkey. Both issued declarations expressing their willingness to discuss terms for peace on December 12, 1916. The following March, Emperor Charles I (ruled 1916–1918) of the Austro-Hungarian Empire, who assumed the throne after Francis Joseph's death in November 1916, sent the Allies a peace proposal, without having consulted Germany. It included a willingness to recognize French claims to Alsace-Lorraine. But talk of a compromise peace was hushed and, in most quarters, deemed unpatriotic.

Unlike the French and British, the Germans realized that victory by breakthrough was extremely unlikely, if not impossible. To the Allies, a compromise peace seemed out of the question given that enemy troops were occupying much of the north of France. The complete withdrawal of German troops required a total victory that would guarantee France's future security. Increasingly criticized for the staggering casualty rate, the French Prime Minister Aristide Briand (1862–1932) replaced Joffre with General Robert Nivelle (1856–1924) as commander in chief of the French forces in 1916. Nivelle, promoted rapidly through the officer corps, had led the troops who had heroically stormed Verdun's Fort Douaumont. He insisted that similar tactics on a much larger scale would bring the long-awaited breakthrough in the west.

In Britain, Lloyd George became prime minister in December 1916. Even after staggering losses on the Somme, he, too, thought military victory possible if the Allies cooperated more closely. The British government thus rejected a peace note sent by Germany on December 12, the aim of which was to force an end to the war by splitting apart Britain and France.

Soldiers and Civilians

In some ways, life in Britain—as in the other countries—seemed to go on as before, which increasingly outraged soldiers returning from the front. The elegantly dressed upper classes dining in the finest restaurants or watching the races at Derby and Ascot contrasted dramatically with the returning trainloads of badly wounded soldiers. A newspaper headline in 1917 gave equal emphasis to its two lead stories: "BATTLE RAGING AT YPRES. GATWICK RACING—LATE WIRE."

Some big businessmen found the war very profitable. Like workers and labor leaders, the men at the front were angered that profiteers amassed fortunes on war supplies: Anglo-Persian Oil, which had lost money in 1914, enjoyed profits of 85 million pounds in 1916, 344 million in 1917, and 1,090 million in 1918. Profits of rubber companies increased fourfold. Women took over many of the jobs of men who left to fight in the war. But women workers, as in the past, received lower wages than their male counterparts, allowing many employers to reduce expenses and increase their profits. In France and Austria, women workers went out on strike in 1917 and 1918 to protest working conditions. Everywhere, shortages and economic hardship made women's tasks of managing the household economy that much more difficult, including standing in line for hours at stores. Crowds of women protested high prices in Italy in 1917.

Censorship, particularly in the first year, prevented the population from knowing about the staggering death toll, or about the various strategic blunders of the generals. "The war, for all its devastating appearances, only seems to be destructive," one Parisian newspaper assured its readers in November 1914, and in July 1915, asserted that "at least [those killed

Women workers in Italy carry shells picked up from an ammunition dump.

by German bayonets] will have died a beautiful death, in noble battle . . . with cold steel, we shall rediscover poetry . . . epic and chivalrous jousting." Other papers emphatically related that "half the German shells are made of cardboard, they don't even burst," and that "Boche corpses smell worse than [those of the] French."

The British poet Robert Graves wrote that "England looked strange to us soldiers. We could not understand the war-madness that ran wild everywhere, looking for a pseudo-military outlet. The civilians talked a foreign language; and it was newspaper language." Newspapers described troops as itching to go over the top, even after the Battle of the Somme. Lord Northcliffe, the press baron named by the government to provide the public with reports of the war, described the trenches, "where health is so good and indigestion hardly ever heard of. The open-air life, the regular and plenteous feeding, the exercise, and the freedom from care and responsibility, keep the soldiers extraordinarily fit and contented." A French newspaper headline in December 1916 read, preposterously enough, "Among the many victims of gas, there is hardly a single death." The poems of Wilfred Owen emphasized the contrast between those who cheered on the war from the home front, and knew little about it, and the soldiers who suffered ("Gas, gas, Quick boys! . . . the blood came gargling from the froth-corrupted lungs"). A French captain wrote to protest newspaper accounts of heroic fighting and glorious death on the battlefield: "How does [the civilian] picture us combatants? Does he really believe we spend our time brandishing great swords with heroic gestures and yelling 'Long live France!' at the top of our lungs? When will these ladies and gentlemen in civilian life spare us their fantasies?"

The men in the trenches forged close bonds to those with whom they served. They bitterly resented senior officers who barked out deadly or-

A captured Canadian soldier (in the middle) and German soldiers help each other through the mud.

ders from the safety of requisitioned châteaux behind the front lines, and they detested government propagandists and censors. On leave, soldiers headed together to music halls, cabarets, and bars, hoping to forget a war they felt uncomfortable trying to describe to civilians who knew so little about it.

More than this, embittered soldiers sometimes felt more sympathy for those in the opposite trenches than for the politicians and generals at home. On Christmas Day, 1914, on the western front in France, German and British soldiers spontaneously declared their own one-day truce, some meeting in no-man's-land to exchange greetings, souvenirs, and even home addresses. A German juggler surfaced to perform, drawing applause from the opposing British trench. In one or two places, soldiers from both sides played soccer. A year later, a British soldier was executed for ignoring orders that such an event was not to recur. There were even occasional informal arrangements between units that had been facing each other across no-man's-land for several months, agreeing not to fire during mealtime, or entertaining each other in verse or song, with the most talented singers in the trenches booming songs from their home regions across the battlefield. But incidents of fraternization became extremely rare as the war dragged on. A British writer later recalled calmly discussing Nietzsche with a German he had captured just minutes after almost killing him. One prevalent rumor in both trenches had an entire regiment of German, French, and British deserters living under no-man's-land in tunnels, coming out only at night to rob corpses and steal food and drink from both sides. They, many soldiers said, were the lucky ones.

What were soldiers to think of the contention of the London *Daily Mirror* in 1916 that the British dead lay on the battlefield looking "more quietly faithful, more simply steadfast than others"? Siegfried Sassoon's "The Hero" attempted to offer a more realistic picture:

"Jack fell as he'd have wished," the Mother said,
And folded up the letter that she'd read.
"The Colonel writes so nicely." Something broke
In the tired voice that quavered to a choke.
She half looked up. "We mothers are so proud
Of our dead soldiers." Then her face was bowed.

Quietly the Brother Officer went out.
He'd told the poor old dear some gallant lies
That she would nourish all her days, no doubt.
For while he coughed and mumbled, her weak eyes
Had shone with gentle triumph, brimmed with joy,
Because he'd been so brave, her glorious boy.

He thought how "Jack," cold-footed, useless swine,
Had panicked down the trench that night the mine
Went up at Wicked Corner; how he'd tried
To get sent home, and how, at last, he died,
Blown to small bits. And no one seemed to care
Except that lonely woman with white hair.

It was impossible to hide the effects of the war. In all combatant countries, women in mourning clothes were an increasingly frequent sight, clutching telegrams that began, "Be proud of X., who has just died like a brave man. . . ." Soldiers who had been badly wounded resented the high-living of the wealthy, who seemed unaffected by the rationing of food and coal. At home, illegitimate births rose rapidly. In Germany, state governments, except for that of Prussia, for the first time allowed "illegitimate" birth certificates and gave unmarried or widowed women the right to call themselves *Frau* (Mrs.) instead of *Fraulein* (Miss).

As casualties mounted and the fighting ground on, opposition to the war emerged in Britain. The most extreme case was that of the Irish Republicans, who opposed Britain in order to gain Ireland's independence. The Germans encouraged Irish Republican preparations for an insurrection in Dublin set for Easter Sunday, 1916. Sir Roger Casement (1864–1916), an Irish nationalist, tried to form an Irish Legion and urged the Germans to send military assistance. But seeing that the Germans had no plans to offer substantial help, he tried to convince the Irish Republicans to call off the insurrection. They went ahead, surrendering after five days of fighting. Casement was among those executed, traitor to the British, hero to many Irish.

Elsewhere in Britain, a relatively small number of pacifists and conscientious objectors protested against the war. Some of them were prosecuted under the Military Services Act and imprisoned. In 1916, when the British abandoned the volunteer army and adopted conscription, pacifists became more vocal in their opposition. In his *No Conscription Leaflet No. 3*, the writer Lytton Strachey (1880–1932) warned, "The Cat kept saying to the Mouse that she was a high-minded person, and if the Mouse would only come a little nearer they could both get the cheese. The Mouse said, Thank you, Pussy, it's not the cheese you want, it's my skin."

In Germany, Clara Zetkin (1857–1933), a militant socialist, went to jail because she refused to stop denouncing the war and tried to mobilize working-class women against a struggle between capitalist states that pitted worker against worker. Rosa Luxemburg, a Polish socialist living in Germany, also went to prison for her efforts to turn more members of her party against the war.

When Dutch socialists initiated a peace conference in Stockholm in December 1917, Britain prohibited British citizens from attending. Siegfried Sassoon, wounded at the front, returned to England and publicly declared, "I believe the War is being deliberately prolonged by those who have the power to end it. I am a soldier, convinced that I am acting on behalf of soldiers." After being incarcerated in a mental asylum, he returned to the front because of his allegiance to friends more than leaders. There he was wounded again.

The French government faced a different set of problems at home than those confronting Britain. The German armies occupied some of France's richest agricultural land and industrial centers of the north and northeast. Refugees from the war zone arrived in Paris and other towns carrying their remaining possessions. But the French home front held together, despite ebbs and flows in morale as the war went on and on. Although there was grumbling about peasants who profited from price rises for commodities, or about skilled workers, exempt from conscription because munitions factories required their skills, and other "shirkers" who escaped service, there were relatively few signs of opposition to the war in France, at least at the start. The government's decision in the war's first month to provide some financial assistance to families with husbands, brothers, and sons in uniform was popular. The French gradually adapted to the war, remaining confident that the Allies would eventually win. With the German army deep inside France, close to Paris, capitulation was unthinkable, as was for most even a negotiated settlement.

The German home front also held together. An American newspaper correspondent in 1916 found the Germans "amazingly solid" against giving in: "They have the habit, as have no other people, of obeying." German morale remained generally strong despite severe shortages, bringing the rationing of food, coal, and other essentials. Even a member of an old Prussian noble family complained, "We are all growing thinner every day and the rounded contours of the German nation have become a legend of the past. We are all gaunt and bony now . . . and our thoughts are chiefly taken up with wondering what our next meal will be, and dreaming of the good things that had once existed." Posters showed an ogre-like British "John Bull," with the caption, "This man is responsible for your hunger."

In 1917 in Germany, signs of war weariness increased, as casualties reached astronomic levels and rumors spread that the campaign of unre-

People in Berlin hunt for food.

stricted submarine warfare against the Allies was failing. Open criticism of officials became more common, despite the repressive structure of what remained an authoritarian state. In July, the Reichstag passed a resolution by a large majority asking the government to repudiate a policy of annexation and commit itself to seeking a peace of reconciliation. But the Reichstag had little influence in what amounted to a military government. In Germany, the kaiser dismissed Chancellor Theobald von Bethmann-Hollweg in 1917, giving Generals Hindenburg and Ludendorff even more power. The Reichstag, in any case, did not attack the political structures of the empire itself, and the military high command now held real power.

Opposition, however, mounted in the streets. Strikes became more common, as the lines outside food shops grew longer. In January 1918, 400,000 Berlin workers went on strike, demanding a democratization of the government and peace without annexation. The Independent Socialist Party, which had been founded in April 1917 by Social Democrats frustrated with their party's continued support of the war, helped mobilize strikers. More Germans began to express opposition to government policies more candidly as leaflets proclaimed, "Down with the kaiser! Down with the government!"

The Final Stages of the War

In 1917, two events of great consequence occurred, each of which appeared to one side to present an opportunity to end the stalemate on the western front. Reacting in part to a German campaign of unrestricted submarine warfare against Allied shipping, the United States entered the war in April on the Allied side. And Russia withdrew from the war after the Bolsheviks seized power in the October Revolution. Meanwhile, the

French armies seemed on the verge of collapse, with widespread mutinies occurring within French divisions in response to a series of catastrophic offensives. And a massive German offensive that began in March 1918 pushed Allied forces back further than they had been since 1914, before grinding to a halt in the face of stiff resistance. The stage was set for the final phase of the war.

The United States Enters the War

In 1916, Woodrow Wilson had been re-elected president of the United States on the platform, "He kept us out of war." The U.S. government had adopted a declaration of neutrality, but American popular sympathy generally lay with the Allies, even though the German government tried to capitalize on American resentment of the British blockade, which entailed searches of American ships. U.S. bankers made profitable loans to both sides, but far more funds went to the Allies than to the Central Powers.

On May 7, 1915, a German submarine sank the British cruise liner *Lusitania* off the coast of Ireland. The ship was, despite U.S. denials, carrying American-made ammunition to the Allies; 128 U.S. citizens were among the almost 1,200 killed. The United States, already outraged by the recent German introduction of mustard gas into combat, protested vigorously, and on September 1 the German government accepted the American demand to abandon the unrestricted submarine warfare. For the next two years, the Germans, wanting to keep the United States neutral, adopted a policy of warning liners before sinking them, providing for the safety of the passengers.

The fact remained that only with submarines could Germany prevent Britain from maintaining total control of the high seas. In 1916, the German fleet left port to challenge the British Royal Navy. The German admiralty hoped to entice part of the main British fleet into a trap by offering a smaller fleet as a target off the Norwegian coast. German submarines lay in wait, with a sizeable surface fleet, which could strike before a rescue force could arrive. The British, who had broken the German code, hoped to have the last laugh when the entire Grand Fleet suddenly appeared. The German and British fleets stumbled into each other off the coast of Denmark, in the battle of Jutland, May 31–June 1, 1916. After a heavy exchange of gunfire, the German ships fled. The British lost fourteen ships and about 6,000 men were killed; eleven German ships were sunk and about 1,500 men were killed. Both sides claimed victory, but British losses were heavier, surprising, and embarrassing (such that one admiral turned to a junior officer and stammered, "Chatfield, there seems to be something wrong with our bloody ships today!").

The continuing success of the British blockade led Germany to announce on February 1, 1917, that its submarines would attack any ship in "war zones." In March 1916, the U.S. government had forcefully protested the sinking of the British ship *Sussex* in the English Channel, with the loss of American lives. Germany agreed to the "*Sussex* pledge," reaffirming the agreement made after the sinking of the *Lusitania* to give up unrestricted submarine warfare. But pressure came from the German high command to turn loose the submarine fleet, now 120 strong, as the only hope for knocking Britain out of the war. This was a calculated risk, because it would surely entail American intervention. Two weeks earlier, the United States had intercepted a coded telegram from the German foreign secretary, Arthur Zimmermann, to his ambassador to Mexico. The "Zimmermann Telegram," which might have been the work of someone within the U.S. or even British government, brazenly offered Mexico German help in taking back the states of Texas, Arizona, and New Mexico if it would go to war against its powerful neighbor. With more Americans killed in submarine attacks, Wilson used the telegram to bolster support for a declaration of war on April 6, 1917. Wilson promised a war that would "make the world safe for democracy." The United States turned its industrial might toward wartime production and drafted and trained an army that reached 4 million, of which half was in France by November 1918. The entry of the United States into the war tipped the balance fatally against Germany.

During 1917, German submarines sank one-fourth of all ships sailing to Britain. They sank 350 British ships in April alone. Half a million tons of shipping were sunk in February, three-quarters of a million in March, and nearly 1 million tons in April. But in the midst of despair, the British admiralty discovered that heavily escorted convoys could get through. Submerged mines at the entrances to the Channel also helped reduce the German U-boat threat. Within a few months, the first American troops reached the continent, along with a steady stream of supplies.

Russia Withdraws from the War

The second remarkable event of 1917 was the Russian Revolution (see Chapter 25). The eastern front had stabilized following the Russian offensive at the end of 1916, leaving the Russian and Austro-Hungarian armies depleted and exhausted. The Russian home front was on the verge of collapse, amid shortages of food far more serious than any faced by the other combatants. As liberals demanded political reforms, soldiers deserted in droves. In February 1917, strikes and bread riots in St. Petersburg spread rapidly. Without troops of sufficient numbers or commitment to keep order, Tsar Nicholas II abdicated on March 15. A provisional government promised the lands of the tsar and the Orthodox Church to the peasantry. In St. Petersburg, a Council (Soviet) of Workers and Soldiers also contended for power in the vacuum left by the sudden disappearance of autocracy. The head of the provisional government, Alexander Kerensky (1881–1970), had no intention of abandoning the war effort, and ordered the commander in chief to launch another offensive on July 1. But "peace, land, and bread" became the motto of the soldiers. Many deserted or refused to obey their officers. Within a matter of weeks, the Germans had easily broken this last Russian offensive; a counterattack pushed the Russians back nearly 100 miles to Galicia.

In the months after the February Revolution of 1917, the well-organized Russian Communist Party, the Bolsheviks, grew in influence in the major cities and in the army. The Bolsheviks aimed to seize power and then take Russia out of the war as quickly as possible. They expected revolutions to break out in other countries as well, beginning with Germany, which had a far larger industrial proletariat than Russia. The German government desperately wanted to force the Russian provisional government to make peace immediately, so that the German high command could turn its full attention to the western front before the American entry into the war could turn the tide. With this in mind, they allowed exiled Bolshevik leader Vladimir Lenin (1870–1924) to return to Russia from neutral Switzerland through Germany and Finland.

On November 6 (October 24 by the Old Russian calendar), the Bolsheviks, who formed a majority within the powerful Petrograd Soviet (St. Petersburg had been renamed Petrograd in 1914), overthrew the provisional government they had helped save. They were supported by "soviets of workers and soldiers" in other cities. In the meantime, the German army, facing virtually no opposition, had captured the fortified town of Riga, and was advancing along the Baltic coast. Now the Germans were happy to comply with Lenin's request for an immediate armistice. In return, the German government wanted the revolutionary government to agree to the independence of Finland, as well as that of Poland, Galicia, Moldavia, and the Baltic states of Estonia, Latvia, and Lithuania. Their goal was to create a series of small buffer states between Germany and Russia that they could dominate. These were strong demands. The Allies were understandably worried that such a peace between Germany and Russia could make it difficult to obtain peace in the west.

The Bolsheviks and German representatives talked into the new year. The French and British governments both rejected Lenin's call for an armistice, fearful of the effect Russia's withdrawal from the war might have on workers and socialists at home, as well as on the war's outcome. French Prime Minister Georges Clemenceau and British Prime Minister Lloyd George denounced the Bolsheviks, but without understanding that relatively few people in Russia wanted the war to continue. In December, the Bolsheviks unilaterally declared the war over and signed an armistice with Germany, although they did not accept the German conditions for a permanent peace. When the revolutionary Russian government did not agree to the German terms for a formal armistice, the German armies marched into the Russian heartland. They reached the Gulf of Finland— only 150 miles from Petrograd—as well as the Crimean peninsula in the south, and advanced far into Ukraine, stopped only by the need to turn full attention to the western front. The Germans then offered a cessation of hostilities in return for virtually all Russian war materiel they could carry with them. They also again demanded the independence of the border states of the Russian Empire, including Finland, Ukraine, Georgia, Lithuania, Latvia, Estonia, and Poland, which they would surely dominate. On March 3, 1918, the Bolshevik government agreed to the terms. The Treaty of Brest-Litovsk officially ended Russian participation in what the Allies called "the Great War for civilization."

Offensives and Mutinies

On the western front, 1917 brought another major Allied offensive. General Nivelle of France convinced his British counterpart in February that the long-awaited knock-out punch was at last possible. A British attack would divert German forces from a French attack along the Aisne River. But the British attack ran headlong into the impenetrable German second line of defense, the "Hindenburg Line." On April 16, Nivelle sent 1.2 million soldiers into battle along the Aisne River in miserable weather. Allied tanks, which had been introduced into battle for the first time in 1916, became stuck in the mud or in shell craters. Ten days later, French losses totaled 34,000 dead, 90,000 wounded, and 20,000 missing. Soldiers sang,

Allied tanks become stuck in the mud.

"If you want to find the old battalion, I know where they are, I know where they are—They're hanging on the old barbed wire. I've seen 'em, I've *seen 'em*, Hanging on the old barbed wire." Robert Graves wrote a poem, "The Dead Fox Hunter," in memory of a friend, a captain, who had been killed:

> We found the little captain at the head;
>   His men lay well aligned,
> We touched his hand—stone cold—and he was dead,
>   And they, all dead behind,
> Had never reached their goal, but they died well;
> They charged in line, and in the same line fell.

Nivelle again promised the increasingly anxious government in Paris that the breakthrough was just around the corner. Like other commanders, he reasoned that such failures occurred because the soldiers lacked sufficient *élan*. The next time, it would work. Without a pause, more troops were sent into the German meat-grinder.

For the first time, soldiers resisted. Some French regiments were heard baaing like sheep led to the slaughterhouse as they marched past their commanding officers. On May 3, mutinies broke out. By the end of May, they had spread to other regiments, even though soldiers who refused to go over the top knew they could be summarily shot. They reasoned that they were going to die anyway. Some soldiers fired their rifles into the air and shouted "Long live peace!" Some regiments elected spokesmen, who declared that they would defend the trenches against German attacks, but would not participate in any more foolish assaults. The mutinies affected half of the French divisions along the western front, and at the beginning of June, only two of twelve divisions holding the line in Champagne had been unaffected. One French commander estimated in June 1917 that he could count on the loyalty of no more than 50 percent of his troops. The loyalty of 35 percent was doubtful, and 15 percent could not be trusted.

Some soldiers were summarily shot where the officers retained the upper hand; 23,000 were court-martialed, 432 sentenced to death, and 55 executed. In all, more than 21,000 French soldiers deserted in 1917. The politicians and some of the generals blamed socialist "agitators" and peace propaganda. General Pétain, the hero of Verdun, knew otherwise, and at least tried to improve the conditions of daily life for the soldiers. The Nivelle offensive ground to a halt.

Despite this, the British commander, Haig, planned another offensive around Ypres, the "fields of Flanders." The goal was to push the Germans back from the coast to Ghent, depriving them of the Belgian railroads they used for supplies. The grim Haig had not bothered to inspect the front himself, nor did he pay attention to the pessimistic reports of his intelligence staff. He also had not reported estimates of German troop strength to the war cabinet in London. The battle began in heavy rain; the preliminary barrage turned the chalky soil into something of the consistency of quicksand. The third Ypres Offensive could claim only one success: the blowing up of the Messines by Welsh miners. In the Battle of Passchendaele ("They died in Hell, they called it Passchendaele"), named after a devastated nearby village, the British gained four miles in exchange for 300,000 dead or wounded. One soldier determined that, in view of such gains, it would take 180 years to get to the Rhine. An officer who rode up for the first time to see the devastated and virtually impassable terrain burst into tears, muttering "My God, did we really send men to fight here, in this?" before being told that it was even worse further up. British prime minister David Lloyd George came to tour the front himself. The offensive ended. Haig kept his command.

The British then launched the first massive tank attack in the history of warfare, on drier ground near Cambrai on November 20, 1917. The tanks rolled over five miles, with few casualties. Like the virtual disappearance of the cavalry, it was a sign of things to come. Yet, the Germans soon recaptured the land they had lost.

Morale plunged during the winter, particularly in Germany and France. A writer was surprised to see a soldier who had lost an arm drunkenly begging on a Parisian boulevard, muttering, "Peace, Peace." Shortages became worse, rationing more vexing. Occasionally in the south of France, sarcastic references were heard to "Paris' war," or to the blond refugees from the embattled northern departments as "the Krauts (*boches*) of the North." The French armaments minister faced shouts of "Down with the War!" when he visited a factory. There were waves of strikes in 1917. More calls for peace were heard, including one for a "peace of understanding" from the German Reichstag.

But Georges Clemenceau, a seasoned veteran of pre-war political battles and former prime minister, rallied the war effort in France after taking office again. He used troops against strikers, as he had before the war. He ordered the arrest of those calling for peace without victory, including his minister of the interior. "Domestic policy?" he shouted, "I wage war! Foreign policy? I wage war! I wage nothing but war!" A cartoon in Britain—unthinkable until 1917—pictured the encounter of two enlisted soldiers at the front. One said, " 'Ow long you up for, Bill?" "Seven years," was the reply. First soldier, "You're lucky—I'm duration."

Compounding this bleak picture for the Allies was a combined Austrian and German offensive in Italy, strengthened by the arrival of German troops from the Russian front. They pushed the Italian army back seventy-five miles in the Battle of Caporetto on the Isonzo River. Despite 200,000 casualties and twice that many desertions, the Italians held along the Piave River, just twenty miles from Venice. The Allies finally moved to coordinate their war efforts. In October 1917, they established a Supreme War Council, which held regular meetings of the prime ministers of France, Britain, and Italy, as well as a representative sent by President Wilson.

Better news for the Allies came from the Middle East. The discovery of oil there prior to the war had dramatically increased the stakes for influence in the region. During the war, the British took advantage of Arab resentment—particularly by Muslim fundamentalists—of the Turks, who had ruled much of the Middle East for centuries, to stir up revolts. The writer and specialist on the Middle East, Colonel T. E. Lawrence (1888–1935), was among the British officers coordinating sudden attacks against the strategically important Turkish railway from the sacred city of Medina to Damascus, among other targets.

In the last decades of the nineteenth century, more Jews in Europe had begun to long for a homeland in Palestine, which was part of the declining Turkish Ottoman Empire, and by 1914, 85,000 Jews had moved there. The British government in principle supported the Zionist movement for a Jewish state, but it also hoped to add to Turkish troubles. On November 2, 1917, the Balfour Declaration, named for the British foreign secretary, Arthur Balfour, expressed British willingness to support the future creation of a "national home" for the Jews, a state in Palestine, once the Turks had been driven out, provided such a state would recognize the rights of the Arab populations who already lived there. This declaration partially contradicted the Sykes-Picot Agreement of 1916, which had secretly divided Syria and other parts of the Middle East into British and French zones of influence. The British government, however, realized that the eventual creation of a Jewish state in Palestine could serve as a buffer between the Suez Canal and Syria, the latter controlled by France. In December 1917, a British force took Jerusalem. The Central Powers' ally Turkey seemed on the verge of collapse.

The German Spring Offensive

In the spring of 1918, the Germans launched their "victory drive," their first major offensive since 1914. But Austria-Hungary showed signs of virtually dissolving, with its major national groups openly calling for independence. Germany had lost its gamble that unrestricted submarine warfare could force Britain out of the war and prevent the United States from making an important contribution to the Allied side. By the spring, 325,000 American soldiers were in Europe. They were commanded by General John Pershing (1860–1948), who had led a "punitive expedition" (which turned out to be a wild-goose chase) against the Mexican bandit Pancho Villa. He had also served in campaigns against Geronimo and against the Sioux in the U.S. west, and had fought in the Philippines and Cuba. Pershing, a tall, tough, stubborn commander who never softened an order with a smile, insisted that his troops remain independent, fearing that French and British generals would lead them to slaughter.

Ludendorff decided on a massive German assault along the Somme, thereby avoiding the mud of Flanders and the hills and forts of eastern

France around Verdun. His forces had been replenished by drafting younger and older men than before. On March 21, 1918, after a relatively brief bombardment of five hours in order to maintain some element of surprise, 1.6 million men attacked the Allied defenses in five separate offensives over a front of forty miles (see Map 24.5). When the weather cleared at noon and British planes could survey the front, the pilots observed that the Germans had succeeded in breaking through the Allied lines. Five days later, some German units had pushed forward forty miles. The Germans now advanced in Flanders, moving forward with relative ease against troops from Portugal, which had recently entered the war on the Allied side. Ludendorff hurled all available reserves into the battle. It looked as though the Germans would take the Channel ports, leading Haig to announce to his British troops that they must fight "with our backs to the wall

MAP 24.5 THE GERMAN OFFENSIVE, 1918   The spring offensive of 1918 in which the Germans attacked the Allies in five separate offenses along the Western front.

and believing in the justice of our cause each of us must fight to the end." Once again, Paris was threatened. The Germans bombarded the French capital with their giant gun, "Big Bertha," which could lob shells each weighing up to a ton twenty-four miles into the air before they fell to earth. Late in May, the offensive pushed the French back to Reims, and then as close to Paris as the Marne in early June. American units engaged in their first sustained action near Château-Thierry in a frantic attempt to stop the German advance, and the French fought the Germans at Compiègne, stopping the German advance short of Paris. In the gloom of the Allied headquarters, French Marshal Ferdinand Foch (1851–1929) assumed command of the combined French, British, and American armies.

Soon the Germans again faced one of the dangers of trench warfare: they had outrun their cover and supplies, and faced fresh Allied reserves. On July 15, another major German offensive was repulsed. Ludendorff's offensive, which he viewed as the last chance to win the war, had failed. The French were not about to negotiate for an armistice. Morale plunged in Germany, which was faced with hundreds of thousands of new casualties and serious food shortages for the first time in the war. In January 1918, 250,000 German workers had defied the government by striking. They did so for economic reasons, however, not to stop the war. Some industrial sabotage occurred here and there. Carefully couched criticism of the war and of Kaiser William II began to appear in the press. The followers of the socialists Rosa Luxemburg and Karl Liebknecht, both imprisoned after the first, brief public demonstration against the war, became bolder. Demonstrations took place in several cities, including Berlin. There were shortages of electricity and gas; food rationing, which had begun in 1915, became more severe. Inflation was rampant, pushed by the circulation of more paper money, as gold and silver were withdrawn to prevent hoarding. Black marketing spread, as people hoarded scarce goods and charged exorbitant, illegal prices for them.

Led by French forces, the Allies counterattacked in July. The British used their tanks with increasing effectiveness to go over craters and barbed wire and to protect the advancing infantry. Coordinated attacks on the German lines began on August 8, 1918, the German army's darkest day, when the British moved forward eight miles along the front north of the Somme. A month later, the Germans had been pushed back to the positions they had held at the start of the spring offensives.

The Allies were now confident that they would win the war, probably in 1919 if all went well. Ludendorff advised the kaiser to press for an armistice before it was too late. With the Allies gaining ground, on October 4 Germany's new chancellor, Prince Max von Baden (1867–1929), a liberal monarchist, asked President Wilson for an armistice based on the American president's call for "peace without victory." The Reichstag passed laws making ministers responsible to it and not to the kaiser. It was a revolution of sorts, but given the circumstances, Kaiser William II could do virtually nothing.

The situation for the Central Powers worsened on the Italian front. His armies in retreat, Austro-Hungarian Emperor Charles I seemed little inclined nor able to continue the war. Desertions from the Habsburg army mounted. Bulgaria left the war, on the verge of total defeat. On November 3, 1918, the Austro-Hungarian Empire withdrew from the war.

The Fourteen Points and Peace

On January 8, 1918, in an address to a joint session of the U.S. Senate and House of Representatives, President Wilson set out a blueprint for permanent peace. His "Fourteen Points" were based upon his understanding of how the Great War had begun, and how future wars could be avoided. The first point called for "open covenants, openly arrived at," in place of the secret treaties whose obligations had pulled Europe into war. Wilson also called for freedom of the seas and freedom of trade, and the impartial settlement of colonial rivalries. Other points included the principle of nonintervention in Russia; the return of full sovereignty to Belgium and Alsace-Lorraine to France; autonomy—without mentioning independence—for the national groups within the Austro-Hungarian Empire; and the independence of Romania, Serbia, Montengro, and Poland. The last of the Fourteen Points called for the establishment of an organization or association of nations to settle other national conflicts as they arose. If the desire of the European peoples to live in states defined by national boundaries had been one—if not the principal—cause of the war, then a peace that recognized these claims would be a lasting one. Or so thought Wilson, and many other people as well.

Germany appeared willing to accept Wilson's Fourteen Points as grounds for an armistice, hoping to circumvent the British and French governments, which clearly would demand unconditional surrender and were not terribly interested in Wilson's idealism. The British, for example, opposed the point calling for freedom of the seas. As Wilson considered what to do with the German proposal for an armistice, a number of U.S. citizens were killed when a U-boat sank a British ship off the Irish coast. An angry Wilson then replied to Prince Max that the German military authorities would have to arrange an armistice with the British and French high command, and not with him. Germany called off unrestricted submarine warfare and tried to convince Wilson that recent changes in the civilian leadership in Berlin amounted to a democratization of the empire. But Foch and Clemenceau demanded unconditional surrender of the German fleet and occupation of the Rhineland by the French.

The collapse of the Central Powers accelerated. Bulgaria signed an armistice in September 1918, and Turkey signed one the next month; the British occupied Damascus and Constantinople. When the Austro-Hungarian Empire followed the Germans in trying to get Wilson to negotiate an armistice based on the Fourteen Points, which trumpeted the sanctity of the nation-state, Czechs in Prague proclaimed an independent Czechoslovakia. Croats and Slovenes announced that they would join the Serbs in the establishment of a South Slav state of Yugoslavia. Hungary, too, proclaimed its independence, as if the Great War had been something forced on it by the Austrians. Facing no opposition, the Italian army finally managed to advance into Habsburg territory. Austria-Hungary signed an armistice on November 3, 1918. In the German Baltic port of Kiel, sailors mutinied. There were major riots in Berlin. An insurrection in Munich led to the declaration of a Bavarian Republic.

On November 7, 1918, an ad hoc German Armistice Commission asked the Allies for an end to hostilities. Two days later, a crowd proclaimed the German Republic in Berlin. William II followed Hindenburg's lead, blaming socialists and Jews for the overthrow of the empire. He then fled across the Dutch border and abdicated. On November 11, 1918, a representative of the provisional German government and General Foch signed an armistice in a railroad car in the middle of the forest near Compiègne, north of Paris. The celebrations in London, Paris, New York, and elsewhere on the Allied side went on for days. The mother of the poet Wilfred Owen received news that he had been killed as the church bells of her village were ringing for victory. A French veteran, tiring of the street festivities in his town, went at dusk to a cemetery. There he came upon a woman crying next to the tomb of her husband. Their small boy was with her, playing with a tricolor flag. Suddenly he cried out, "Papa, we've won!"

THE IMPACT OF THE WAR

There had been nothing like the Great War in history. About 6,000 people had been killed each day for more than 1,500 days. In more than four years of fighting, at least 65 million soldiers were mobilized. Of the 42 million men who served in the Allied armies, 22 million were casualties. The Central Powers mobilized 23 million, and had 15 million casualties. There were approximately 8.5 million men killed and 22 million wounded (of whom an estimated 7 million may have been left permanently disabled). Another 12.6 million died from war-related causes. As Table 24-1 shows,

TABLE 24-1 CASUALTIES DURING WORLD WAR I (IN MILLIONS)

	Mobilized	Casualties	Percentage
Austria-Hungary	7.8	7	90
Russia	12	9.15	76
France	8.4	6	71
Germany	11	7	63
Italy	5.5	2.15	39
Britain	8.9	3	34
United States	4.35	.36	8

Source: James L. Stokesbury, *A Short History of World War I* (New York: Quill, 1981), p. 310.

the Austro-Hungarian, Russian, and French armies suffered proportionally more than the other major combatants, although Serbia had the highest rate of casualties.

But sheer numbers, however daunting, do not tell the whole story. Of the wounded who survived, many were condemned to spend the rest of their lives—shortened lives, in many cases—in veterans' hospitals. Soldiers who had lost limbs or who were mutilated in other ways became a common sight in European cities, towns, and villages after the war. Europe seemed a continent of widows and spinsters; so many men were killed in the prime of life that the birthrate fell markedly after the war. Support for families of the dead soldiers and invalids unable to work strained national budgets. War cemeteries stretched across northern France and Belgium. The carnage was not limited to the European continent: in an outbreak of ethnic hostility and in response to Armenian demands for an independent state, the Turks forced 1.75 million Armenians to leave their homes in Turkey; more than a third of them perished without water in the desert sun on the way to Syria, their bodies consumed by wild animals. Furthermore, about 27 million people died in an influenza epidemic during the last years of and after the war, the most devastating epidemic since the Black Death of the fourteenth century.

The flower of European youth—or much of it—had perished. There were other costs as well. The economic structure of northern France and part of Belgium had been chewed up in the fighting. The German economy, which was devastated by the war, would be further crippled by the terms of the peace treaty (see Chapter 26). The British economy also suffered, though not to the same extent. The Carnegie Endowment for International Peace made a brave attempt to calculate the war's actual cost, and came up with a figure of $338 billion dollars after establishing a rough value for property and even lives lost. It was a truly futile calculation.

No one could begin to measure other dimensions of the war's impact. The psychic damage to the generation of survivors can hardly be measured. "Never such innocence again," observed the British writer Philip Larkin, referring to the period before the war. The post-war period, rampant with hard times and disappointments, caused many people to look back even more on the pre-war period as "the Belle Époque," the good old days.

Wilson was not alone in thinking that the Great War was the war to end all wars. Many people came to believe that such a thing could never happen again. No one, they reasoned, could ever wish such a catastrophe on humanity. The American writer F. Scott Fitzgerald took a friend to a battlefield in the north of France: "See that little stream—we could walk to it in two minutes. It took the British a month to walk to it—a whole empire walking very slowly, dying in front and pushing forward behind. And another empire walked very slowly backward a few inches a day, leaving the dead like a million bloody rags. No European will ever do that again in this generation." He was wrong.

The heroic vocabulary of war that characterized all of Europe in 1914—and the press for the duration of the war—disappeared. As Ernest Hemingway put it in his novel *A Farewell to Arms*, the "abstract words such as glory, honor, courage, or hallow were obscene beside the concrete names of villages, the numbers of roads, the names of rivers, the numbers of regiments and the dates" associated with the deaths of so many people.

For those who had been lucky enough to survive, how much greater the disappointment, disillusionment, and bitterness that would follow. Many soldiers returned home to find skyrocketing prices and unemployment awaiting them. In Britain, parents whose sons had died as foot soldiers in France or Belgium learned that families of aristocratic officers had complained that their sons had been buried alongside ordinary people. One contemporary observer did not mince words: "The World War of 1914–1918 was the greatest moral, spiritual and physical catastrophe in the entire history of the English people—a catastrophe whose consequences, all wholly evil, are still with us." Politicians who had put aside their differences during the war in a common effort for victory—such as the "Sacred Union" in France—reverted to bitter disagreements that were compounded by the dilemmas posed in the peace settlement. The problems of making peace and putting Europe back together again, as well as paying for the war, would not be easily resolved. U.S. participation in the war and, particularly, the Russian Revolution, which we will examine in the next chapter, would each have a profound impact on Europe's future. The Great War could not be relegated to the past. War became the continuing experience of the twentieth century.

CHAPTER 25

REVOLUTIONARY RUSSIA AND THE SOVIET UNION

When Nicholas II (1868–1918) was crowned tsar of Russia upon the death of Alexander III in 1894, he decided to hold a great popular festival on a huge field outside of Moscow, considered the sacred center of the empire. Convinced that it was his duty to uphold the principles of autocracy, Nicholas nonetheless was sensitive to the tsar's traditional role as the Holy Father of all his people and wanted to reaffirm the ties that bound his subjects to him, and he to them. The festival attracted enthusiastic crowds numbering in the hundreds of thousands. It featured rides, fortune telling, and other staples of Russian popular festivals. But in the stampede to get free beer and coronation souvenirs, more than 1,200 people were crushed to death and somewhere between 9,000 and 20,000 were injured. Celebration had turned to tragedy. And during the coronation itself the heavy chain of the Order of Saint Andrew dropped from Nicholas' shoulders to the ground. Many saw these events as bad omens for the tsar's reign, perhaps including the superstitious tsar himself.

Not bad omens, however, but rather the failure to implement meaningful political reform brought down Nicholas II and the Russian autocracy in 1917. First, a revolution shook the Russian state in 1905, leading to reforms but not altering the autocratic nature of the regime. This revolution forced Tsar Nicholas II to grant increased freedom of the press and to create an elected Duma (assembly). These reforms disappeared, for all intents and purposes, when the tsar regained the upper hand, but the Revolution of 1905 demonstrated the vulnerability of even a police state to popular mobilization. In February 1917, the tsar fell. Then, after six months of uncertainty and political division, the Bolshevik (October) Revolution overthrew the provisional government. Russia withdrew from the Great War. The "dictatorship of the proletariat" became that of Vladimir

The ceremonial procession after the coronation of Tsar Nicholas II.

Lenin's Communist Party. Upon Lenin's death in 1924, Joseph Stalin consolidated his personal authority in the Soviet Union, ruthlessly establishing state socialism.

The Russian Revolutions of 1905 and 1917 were not the kinds of revolutions that the Russian populists or anarchists had predicted—massive uprisings of the peasant masses against lords and imperial officials—although peasant rebellion was an essential ingredient in both revolutions. Nor did they correspond to Karl Marx's prediction that a successful bourgeois revolution would be followed by a revolution undertaken by an industrial proletariat. War played a catalytic role in both revolutions: shocking defeat in the Russo-Japanese War (1904–1905) fought in Asia, and the lengthening horror of the Great War that began in 1914.

UNREST, REFORM, AND REVOLUTION

Despite rapid economic change, the Russian Empire at the end of the nineteenth century was as backward as it was enormous. More than a hundred times the size of Great Britain and three times larger than the United States, it was comprised of almost 200 nationalities who spoke 146 languages. The mass of the population was poor: the average per capita income was more than four times higher in Britain, three times higher in Germany, and even 50 percent higher in the Balkan states. In 1900, more than three-quarters of the empire's population over the age of ten was illiterate.

Russia's development during the 1890–1914 period accentuated the differences between its industrializing cities and its backward countryside. The quickening pace of state-sponsored industrialization, aided by foreign investment, though not approaching that of Germany, France, or even Italy, added to the numbers of factory workers. The Russian economy developed rapidly beginning in the mid-1890s. Increases in agricultural production, on which Russian exports largely depended, took place without the evolution of capital-intensive farming that characterized much of Western Europe. Russian agriculture remained bound to small peasant-owned plots and backward techniques (lacking, for the most part, chemical fertilizers, farm machinery, and even enough horses to pull plows). Gradually more land came under cultivation, contributing to an expansion of agricultural production, permitting more exports, even as many Russian peasants without land went hungry and, during the famine of 1891–1892, starved to death.

As Russia industrialized, reformers increased the pressure for reform. Among liberals, populists, and socialists demanding reform, many intellectuals looked to the West for a model of change. Liberal constitutionalists, including some state bureaucrats, hoped that the tsar would grant political reforms; Marxists wanted to work for the overthrow of the regime, counting on the emergence of an organized revolutionary working class, while many populists believed that a massive peasant insurrection would one day sweep the autocracy away. However, the tsarist police made life difficult for revolutionaries, some of whom, including Lenin, were forced to live in exile. When Russian forces fared badly in the Russo-Japanese War, reformers grew more bold amid a wave of strikes. In January 1905, troops fired on demonstrators in St. Petersburg, leading to the Revolution of 1905.

Young workers unloading a barge in St. Petersburg, 1900.

Industrialization and the Movement for Reform

Russian industrialization during the late nineteenth century combined advanced technology imported from Western Europe and large-scale enterprises within the context of a backward society whose peasant masses—85 percent of the population—had been freed from serfdom only several decades earlier in 1861. Although textiles still represented the largest branch of Russian industry, heavy industries, particularly metallurgy, increased productivity, with the output of steel increasing fourfold during the last decades of the century (see Map 25.1).

The Russian working class had grown to about 2.4 million industrial workers by 1914 (compared to over a 100 million peasants), but its labor movement remained small and faced constant police harassment. Although the long economic depression that lasted from 1873 until the mid-1890s had undercut the prosperity of some artisans, the growing number of skilled factory workers supplied the majority of labor militants.

Many Russian industrial workers still worked periodically as agricultural workers. They retained strong ties to their villages, which remained their legal residences. The rural commune carried out functions of local authority, including many fiscal obligations (assuring the payment of taxes), policing (including overseeing the division of communal lands), and rudimentary welfare functions. But one of the key social phenomena of the period was the development of a permanent working class that had broken its ties with the countryside.

The tsarist state knew that Russia had to industrialize in order to remain a power, just as the tsar and his advisers in 1861 had understood that the serfs had to be freed. Russian cities had grown rapidly. During the first fourteen years of the twentieth century, about 4 million peasants had moved to towns to find industrial work, particularly to St. Petersburg, the capital, but also in and around Moscow and other towns. The social and political consequences of these changes could not be controlled, however, within the traditional legal framework of the imperial state.

The more Russia industrialized, the more reformers looked to the West for a successful model. Industrialization swelled the ranks of liberal constitutionalists. Russia had a growing professional middle class because of administrative reforms in the 1860s, expanding education, and industrial development. Some lawyers and bureaucrats, in particular, sought a middle way between state and noble intransigence and revolutionary terrorism.

The Russian army's poor performance in the war against Turkey (1877–1878) proved that military reforms instituted following the Crimean War humiliation (1853–1856) had not been enough. More officials joined those who believed that the tsar had to grant political reforms to complement the gradual modernization of the Russian economy. But the assassination of Alexander II in 1881 had led to a curtailment of the powers of the *zemstvos* (regional assemblies), and the shifting of judicial authority to the police, putting political trials in the hands of military courts.

MAP 25.1 RUSSIAN INDUSTRIALIZATION, 1870–1914   Areas of industrial concentration, including kinds of industry and resources.

Enemies of Autocracy

Growing numbers of liberals, populists, and socialists wanted to bring about change in Russia. Liberal constitutionalism had continued to play a role in the expanding domain of Russian public opinion since the heady days of the 1860s after the emancipation of the serfs. Liberals included a smattering of nobles, leaders of local assemblies (the *zemstvos* and the municipal dumas), and members of professional classes, including economists, *zemstvo* agronomists, physicians, teachers, and students. They demanded an extension of the powers of the *zemstvos,* whose limited authority had been curtailed in 1890, but imagined little more than active consultation between those bodies and the tsar.

Revolutionary groups, however, believed the autocracy incapable of reforming itself. They argued that only revolution could bring reform. The populist Socialist Revolutionaries were the largest radical group, with growing support among peasants, whom they believed were instinctively revolutionary and would one day overthrow the tsar.

A group of Marxists founded the Russian Social Democratic Workers' Party at Minsk in 1898. They were confident that one day, though probably not in their lifetimes, the Russian proletariat would be sufficiently numerous and class conscious to seize power. But this seizure of power could only occur, they believed, after a democratic revolution had successfully overthrown the Russian autocracy. Marxists claimed vindication for their view that peasants had no true revolutionary potential when, despite the terrible suffering and deaths of millions of peasants during the famine and epidemics of 1891–1892, the countryside remained quiescent.

By 1900, the tsar's police had succeeded in disbanding most of the revolutionary groups within the empire by exiling their leaders from Russia, sending them to Siberia, or putting them in prison. Most revolutionaries, whether living in Russia or in exile, shared a belief that their country was far from revolution. A bitter dispute broke out among Russian Marxists. Some believed that revolution in Russia would have to follow the lines Marx had predicted, that is, after further industrialization, a bourgeois revolution would overthrow the tsarist regime, followed, sometime in the future, by a successful proletarian revolution. Lenin, in contrast, held that a highly centralized party organization could bring about a democratic revolution, perhaps in the near future.

Lenin and the Bolsheviks

Lenin was born Vladimir Ilyich Ulyanov in the Volga River town of Simbirsk on April 22, 1870, more than 400 miles east of Moscow. His father served as the director of primary schools for the province and, as a result of loyal service, he obtained nonhereditary membership in the nobility; Lenin's mother, whose family had originally been German, was the daughter of a doctor. His older brother Alexander, who joined the revolutionary group "People's Will," was executed in 1887 after being arrested for participation in a plot to kill Tsar Alexander III. Lenin briefly attended university, but was expelled for participating in a student demonstration. During the next six years, Lenin read widely in history and philosophy, including the works of Marx and Engels. Though returning to receive a degree in law from the University of St. Petersburg, Lenin became a revolutionary committed to the overthrow of the Russian autocracy and world capitalism.

In 1895, Lenin made his first trip abroad. He went to Austria, France, and Switzerland, meeting other Russian political exiles and socialists from other countries. Back in St. Petersburg, Lenin was soon arrested at the end of 1897, charged with organizing and writing articles in a clandestine newspaper *(Iskra,* or *Spark),* and exiled to Siberia. When his term of banishment ended in 1900, he moved to Switzerland.

"I know Russia very little," Lenin admitted. With the exception of a brief return during the Revolution of 1905, he remained in exile until 1917. As a virtually penniless exile, he bore his situation with good humor in what seemed to be a strange, somewhat stodgy land. Lenin had few interests outside of politics and revolution, though he played chess passionately, hunted occasionally, rode a bicycle, and hiked in the mountains. But he viewed most recreational activities—even, at times, simple conversation—as interfering with revolutionary struggle.

There was nothing about Lenin's appearance that would have attracted the attention of tsarist spies or Swiss and French police. An Englishman said that "he looked more like a provincial grocer than a leader." He had piercing gray eyes, and his slightly Asian facial features revealed a glimpse of the eastern heritage of his father's family. The American journalist John Reed described him as: "a short stocky figure with a big head set down on his shoulders, bald and bulging. Little eyes, a snubbish nose, wide generous mouth, and heavy chin, . . . already beginning to bristle with the well-known beard of his past and future. Dressed in shabby clothes, his trousers much too long for him . . . a leader purely by virtue of intellect; colorless, humorless, uncompromising and detached . . . with the power of explaining profound ideas in simple terms, of analyzing a concrete situation."

Lenin combined a powerful ability to theorize with a facility for adapting to changing circumstances. He would later write, "it is not enough to be a revolutionary and an advocate of socialism in general. It is necessary to know at every moment how to find the particular link in the chain which must be grasped with all one's strength in order to keep the whole chain in place and prepare to move on resolutely to the next link." His steely resolve would carry him to cold fury when colleagues or rivals failed to agree with him. "He who does not understand this does not understand anything!" was a typical Lenin rejoinder. A vigorous polemicist, he could be impatient and churlish in speech, cutting and sarcastic with his potent pen.

In 1902, Lenin, who had taken his name as a pseudonym the previous year, published *"What Is to Be Done?"* In this pamphlet, Lenin established what would become the basic tenets of a new revolutionary party. The long tradition of authoritarian rule in Russia helped shape Lenin's view of how tsardom could be overthrown. Lenin believed that Marxist analysis could be applied to a backward nation with a relatively undeveloped working class and a small bourgeoisie. "The one serious organizational principle for workers in our movement must be strictest secrecy," he wrote, "the strictest choice of members and the training of professional revolutionaries." He rejected all compromise with liberals and reform socialists, viewing as self-defeating the struggle of workers for small economic gains, which he viewed as crumbs tossed from the table of the ruling class. Rejecting the common Marxist view that the social experiences of workers would lead the whole working class to revolutionary consciousness, Lenin believed that only a minority of workers would achieve consciousness and that these should join with intellectuals in a party that would direct the masses.

At the second congress of the Russian Social Democratic Workers' Party, held in Brussels and London in 1903, Lenin and his followers became known as the "Bolsheviks," or the "majority" (though much of the time in the years that followed they were not), and their rivals were known as the "Mensheviks," or the "minority." The Mensheviks hoped to become a large party of extreme revolutionary opposition. They believed that a proletarian revolution lay in the future, but that it could not occur until a bourgeois uprising had first succeeded in overthrowing the tsarist state. Mensheviks believed that their historic role was to mobilize support for their party through propaganda, while undertaking timely alliances with liberal groups and rejecting terror. They also objected to the high degree of party centralization on which Lenin insisted.

The Revolution of 1905

Many of the tsar's subjects had blamed government inaction for the murderous famine of 1891–1892, which had captured world attention. Peasants attacked noble property in some districts in 1902, and a wave of industrial strikes followed the next year. Liberals embarked on a campaign to mobilize support for political reform by organizing banquets similar to those employed by French republicans just before the Revolution of 1848. Dissent mounted against forced Russification among the subject nationalities, most notably the Poles and the Finns. Marxist groups were particularly active in Poland—where the issue of Polish nationalism versus internationalism was hotly debated—and in the Jewish Pale—those provinces where Jews were allowed to settle and where they faced endemic anti-Semitism and occasional bloody pogroms.

The Russo-Japanese War (see Chapter 21) revealed the weakness of the Russian army, and therefore of the state itself. Defeats shocked and angered many Russians, increasing calls for liberal reform. A wide-ranging social and political alliance for change extended across classes. Not only were Russian soldiers being killed in a far-off war for reasons that did not concern most of the population, but it soon appeared that the war was being badly fought. After the assassination of his minister of the interior in July 1904 by a Socialist Revolutionary, Tsar Nicholas II appointed a more moderate successor in the hope of calming dissent. He allowed a national congress of *zemstvos* and dumas to be held, which formally asked that its powers be extended and called for the establishment of a national parliament.

Liberal and socialist groups, with the exception of Mensheviks and Bolshevik Social Democrats, began to meet together in the hope of capitalizing on growing dissatisfaction with the tsar's policies. For the first time, liberals and socialists, intellectuals and workers, and Russians and non-Russians came together in common opposition to autocracy. While radicals had helped build a popular base among workers and peasants, reformers within the gentry and professional classes, including some state officials, believed that the tsar could be influenced by a broadly based movement. These groups embraced a loose ideology of liberal reform, although the tsar, his conservative advisers, and the police considered reformers to be no different than terrorists because they threatened the foundations of autocracy.

At the turn of the century, the police had authorized government-controlled labor associations in the hope of undercutting revolutionaries. By encouraging workers to concentrate on their economic grievances and achieve some small victories through negotiation, those in power believed that the structure of autocracy could be left intact. These organizations were supposed to offer meeting places and welfare assistance to workers and occasionally to help resolve disputes with employers without the need for strikes, which remained illegal. But such halfway measures further frustrated workers, while giving them useful organizational experience, reflected in an increasing number of illegal strikes.

In January 1905, a strike by 100,000 factory workers brought St. Petersburg to a standstill. An Orthodox priest led a march of workers to the tsar's Winter Palace, carrying a petition asking for "justice" and political reform. Troops blocked their way. When the marchers locked arms and refused an order to disperse, a commander barked out the order to fire.

Workers on strike outside the Putilov factory in St. Petersburg, January 1905.

Russian troops fire on the workers, Bloody Sunday, January 1905.

More than 300 marchers, including women and children, fell dead and perhaps 1,000 or more were wounded. "Bloody Sunday" helped shatter the myth that the tsar was the Holy Father, the people's friend, enacting evil policies because he was manipulated by selfish nobles and wicked advisers. Social Democrats and Socialist Revolutionaries, the latter particularly influential in the countryside, now encouraged more strikes. The rhetoric of demands for constitutional reform became increasingly revolutionary in tone. Nicholas dismissed his liberal minister of the interior. The tsar's uncle fell to an assassin's bullets. Strikes spread to Poland, Ukraine, and Latvia. In some rural areas of Russia, peasants attacked the homes of their lords. In the southeastern borderlands, Muslim leaders announced the formation of an All-Russian Muslim League. Workers began to organize trade unions in huge numbers and a free press emerged in open defiance of censorship. The experience—brief as it turned out—of having a free press giving voice to new ideas and information as never before had an important and lasting effect on public opinion.

With the bulk of the army fighting the Japanese in Manchuria, the Russian Empire seemed on the verge of collapse. Nicholas appeared to choose the path of reform, appointing Sergei Witte (1849–1915) as his chief minister. Witte was eager to make Russia a modern industrial power, and believed that he could do so if the tsar granted minimal reforms. He persuaded Nicholas to rescind redemption payments to the state for land acquired in the emancipation, to allow Poles and Lithuanians to speak their own languages, to turn political trials back over to the regular courts, and to abolish some of the restrictions on Jews.

Even more important, Nicholas' October Manifesto of 1905 created a national representative assembly, the Duma, to be chosen by universal male suffrage, and promised freedom of the press. Many state officials and most nobles, however, viewed these particular reforms as unacceptable, associating them with the parliamentary regimes of the West.

Some progressive nobles and businessmen were encouraged by the sudden, unexpected turn of events. The liberal Constitutional Democratic Party demanded constitutional government, arguing that the promised reforms left the essential structures of autocracy unchanged. Mensheviks had championed the establishment of St. Petersburg "workers' councils," known as "soviets," neighborhood councils made up of delegates from factories, shops, trade unions, and political parties that helped organize strikes, which became legal in December. The Mensheviks expressed willingness to collaborate with the liberals in order to bring further reforms to workers and peasants.

But a violent uprising in Moscow in December 1905 brought on a vigorous tsarist counter-revolution. Witte ordered the arrest of many of the workers' leaders. The soviets no longer were free to meet. Army units returning from Manchuria crushed nationalist demonstrations in Poland and Georgia and brutally restored order in the Russian and Ukraine countryside. Fanatical Russian nationalists known as the Black Hundreds, perhaps instigated by Orthodox priests, unleashed a wave of violence against Jews (and against German, Russian, and Polish property owners, as well) which lasted more than year. The Black Hundreds were led by small traders and agricultural laborers who feared that economic change would cost them what limited security they had and by police who feared the consequences of political reform. In Odessa, drunken mobs aided by the local police murdered 800 Jews, injured more than 5,000 other people, and left twice that number homeless. The tsar himself intervened to prevent Witte from prosecuting the police, praising the "mass of loyal people"; they had struck out against "troublemakers," who could be conveniently blamed for agitating against autocratic rule.

Against this turbulent backdrop, the Duma had met for the first time in April 1906. The U.S. ambassador described the gathering in the Winter Palace of the members of the Duma: "in every conceivable costume, the peasants in rough clothes and long boots, merchants and tradespeople in frock coats, lawyers in dress suits, priests in long garb and almost equally long hair, and even a Catholic bishop in violet robes." The majority of the Duma members were Kadets (Constitutional Democrats), largely because the Social Democrats and Socialist Revolutionary parties refused to participate in the election. The Kadets wanted to reduce the powers of the tsar.

As the Duma in the wake of agrarian uprisings in early 1906 debated land reform, an issue on which the tsar and most lords refused any compromise, Nicholas decreed the establishment of an upper assembly, the State Council. With members to be drawn from the high clergy, the army, or other loyal institutions, it would counteract the influence of the Duma. The tsar then dismissed Witte and announced that he would promulgate

A member of the Duma greeted
by a barefoot man of the people.

any decree he pleased while the Duma was not in session. When the
Kadets within the Duma petitioned Nicholas to abolish the State Council,
make ministers responsible to the Duma, and turn over some noble estates
to the peasants, he dissolved the Duma.

The Revolution of 1905 had ended in failure, but its memory could not
be so easily effaced. The tsar had been forced to grant a parliament and
the promise of limited civil rights. Many people within the Russian professional class, particularly some bureaucrats and lawyers, remained sympathetic to these reforms after they had been undone by the tsar. These
liberals stood between the autocratic routines of the state and the revolutionaries.

The Revolution of 1905 heightened the divisions among exiled Russian
socialists. Mensheviks contended that compromise with bourgeois reformers would increase socialist support within Russia. Eventually the proletariat would be strong enough to help the bourgeoisie seize power, before
taking its own turn, but not until the number of industrial workers had increased and reached class consciousness. Lenin and the Bolsheviks, on
the other hand, believed that the failed revolution had clearly demonstrated that the Russian proletariat in the large cities was already a revolutionary force, and that the first stage of Marx's promised revolution could
be achieved if workers and peasants joined together.

Nicholas II named Peter Stolypin (1862–1911) as his chief adviser, and
in June 1906 he ordered the dissolution of a second elected Duma even
though it was more conservative than the first. In the meantime, the police and the Black Hundreds systematically beat up and, in some cases,
executed, opponents of the tsar. In an August decree, the tsar established

military field courts that could summarily convict and sentence civilians accused of violent political crimes. This law resulted in nearly 1,000 hangings before it expired six months later. Outraged liberals dubbed the ropes of the gallows used by the field courts "Stolypin's neckties."

After Nicholas changed the rules of election to increase the power of noble votes at the expense of peasants, workers, and non-Russians, a third Duma was elected in 1907 that was more to the tsar's liking. It was dominated by the "Octobrists," who believed that the tsar's promises in his manifesto of October 1905 themselves represented sufficient reform and wanted to stop at that. The repression and Russification campaign went on.

Stolypin undertook some rural reforms beginning in 1906, hoping that they might defuse the political intensity of the agrarian question and reduce agrarian unrest. His goal was to create a class of prosperous farmers while increasing agricultural production by allowing peasants to leave the communes and set up independent farms. He hoped that the enclosure of common lands and a consolidation of holdings would expand peasant plots. As a result, the number of prosperous peasants ("kulaks") increased. Yet, prices for farm products fell, and even peasants with fairly large plots of land still had to struggle to survive. Hundreds of thousands of peasants migrated to Siberia in order to obtain land.

In 1911, Stolypin was assassinated. Although the government claimed the assassin was a Jew, the minister may have been killed with the approval of the tsar at the instigation of noble advisers who considered him too liberal and rejected any agrarian reforms.

A surge of industrial strikes and peasant violence in 1912–1914 reflected mounting popular dissatisfaction with the regime. Liberals, Socialist Revolutionaries, and Menshevik and Bolshevik Social Democrats mobilized support against the regime. Indeed, the growing popularity of Bolsheviks among organized urban workers—revealed in their victories in trade union elections on the eve of the war—reflected their deepening impatience with the path of moderate reform.

WAR AND REVOLUTION

Reformers were still biding their time when Russia went to war again in 1914. But revolutionaries were increasingly active and militant on the eve of the war. However, Lenin was dumbfounded when most socialists in other countries supported their country's mobilization for war. Among Russian socialists, "defensists" (Mensheviks and most Socialist Revolutionaries) argued that Russian workers should defend their country against German attack. "Internationalists" opposed the war, viewing it as a struggle between capitalist powers in which workers were but pawns.

Lenin took the war as a sign that capitalism might be ripe for what he thought was its inevitable fall. The defeat of the Russian autocracy would hasten the process along. "Imperialism is the last stage," he wrote, "in the development of capitalism when it has reached the point of dividing up the whole world, and two gigantic groups have fallen into mortal struggle." He believed that if revolution were to break out in several countries, the fall of Russian autocracy and capitalism could be near, even without a true bourgeois revolution. Even if the Russian working class was less developed than those of Western nations, the corresponding weakness of the Russian bourgeoisie could facilitate a successful revolution, Lenin argued. This revolution would be followed by the establishment of a dictatorship of the proletariat, that is, by a mobilized working class led by its most dedicated elements, the Bolsheviks. The revolution would then spread to other countries, where the working classes would follow the example of the first successful socialist revolution.

Russia at War

The Great War became a catalyst for demands for reform within Russia, first in the management of the war itself, and then in Russian political life. The war had begun with an upsurge of patriotism and political unity, with the tsar blessing icons and the faithful kneeling before him. A Bolshevik noted bitterly that amid shouts of "'God Save the Tsar!,' our class struggle went down the drain." Within a year, however, the war had shattered the "sacred union" that represented a patriotic consensus in 1914. Liberals, relegated to near silence by the repression that had followed the Revolution of 1905, now renewed demands for political reform. Workers agitated for higher wages and better working conditions. By 1917, 15 million men

Tsar Nicholas II, holding an icon, blesses his troops in 1915.

had been drafted into the army, about 12 million of whom were poor, illiterate peasants. It also had proven difficult to transform peasants "who held rifles like rakes" into soldiers. Sent by its high command into battle ill-equipped, losses within the Russian army were staggering, even incalculable.

In the interest of the war effort, the government allowed national organizations to exist that earlier were forbidden. These groups became the organizational base for the liberal opposition. Liberal *zemstvo* representatives established a committee, the Union of *Zemstvos*, to organize relief of the sick and wounded; an organization of municipal governments, the Union of Towns, was also created.

In the spring of 1915, liberal Duma members began to express open dissatisfaction with the way the war was being run. From the outset of hostilities, Russia's relatively backward factories had experienced difficulties in meeting military needs; as a result, the army lacked sufficient rifles and artillery shells. The tsar permitted industrialists to form a War Industries Committee, to which delegations of workers were added, in order to expedite wartime production.

The war gradually transformed Petrograd (St. Petersburg had been renamed after the outbreak of the war to a more Russian-sounding name), accentuating its social polarization. By 1916, most of Petrograd's workers, who made up 35 percent of the population, were producing war matériel, swelling the ranks of metal, textile, and chemical workers. More peasants flocked to the capital, as did some middle-class people seeking jobs and waves of refugees from the war zones of Russian Poland and the Baltic states.

As Russian society strained under the pressures of war, liberals demanded that the Duma be allowed to meet and that Tsar Nicholas dismiss a number of unpopular, reactionary ministers who opposed the creation of any additional councils. With military defeats weighing on him—none more disastrous than that at Tannenberg (August 1914), where 100,000 Russian troops were captured—followed by humiliating retreats, the tsar established a Council for National Defense. He summoned the Duma to meet in July 1915 and replaced four ministers. But the inept Nicholas had also assumed command of the army. Liberals feared this could lead to more military disasters, and would also take him away from Petrograd, leaving imperial decision-making even more subject to the influence of the hated Tsarina Alexandra.

The melancholy, ineffectual tsar remained extremely superstitious. Seventeen was his unlucky number—indeed on January 17, 1895, the day of his first speech as tsar, an elderly noble had dropped a traditional gift of bread and salt, a bad omen, and on October 17, 1905, he had been forced to sign a constitution. But he retained the respect and distant affection of most of the Russian people. Tsarina Alexandra, in contrast, was loathed by her subjects. Born in Germany, the granddaughter of Queen Victoria had been raised in England before marrying Tsar Nicholas in 1894. She had converted from Anglicanism to the Russian Orthodox Church. The illness of their only son, Alexei (1904–1918), a hemophiliac and the heir to the throne, increasingly weighed on the royal couple.

As she became ever more conservative, Alexandra extended her influence over her weak-willed husband. Nicholas dismissed ministers on the whims of the tsarina. ("Lovey, don't dawdle!" she wrote her husband, urging him to fire one.) Many people wrongly believed that Alexandra, "the German," was actively working for the interests of Germany. No German agent could have served Germany as well.

Alexandra's great favorite was Grigori Rasputin (1872–1916), a debauched "holy man." Claiming occult power and ability to heal the hemophiliac tsarevitch (Crown Prince Alexei), Rasputin had moved gradually into the inner circle of court life. On one occasion, he predicted that one of Alexei's spells would shortly subside, and it did. To the consternation of the tsar's ministers, the influence enjoyed by the man the tsarina called "our friend" became a matter of state.

In December 1916, noble conspirators, who feared Rasputin's influence on military operations, put what they thought was enough poison into Rasputin's many drinks to kill a cow. When Rasputin seemed almost unfazed, they shot him repeatedly and smashed his skull in a protracted struggle. The assassins then weighted down his body and threw him into the Neva River.

Tsar Nicholas II and his family: Tsarina Alexandra Fyodorovna, Grand Duchesses (from left) Maria, Tatyana, Olga, and Anastasia, and Crown Prince Alexei.

Tsarina Alexandra with Grigori Rasputin (in the middle).

The Progressive Bloc

In August 1915, some liberal members of the Duma, including Constitutional Democrats, had formed a Progressive Bloc that was committed to working with the tsar in the hope of encouraging reform. A strike at the enormous Putilov munitions factory in Petrograd—the largest factory in Europe with 30,000 workers—added to the tension. When he met in an emergency session with his Council of Ministers, the tsar followed Alexandra's instructions to clutch a religious icon in one hand and, with the other, to comb his hair using Rasputin's comb. Nicholas then dismissed his liberal ministers.

Hard times, including food shortages, eroded the revival of working-class patriotism that had accompanied the beginning stages of the war. The growth of public organizations, which opened up a larger public sphere for discussion and debate, helped mobilize opposition to autocracy. Young, literate, unmarried men were the most organized and politically active workers, despite the fact that government repression had driven trade unions, mutual aid societies, and other formal and informal organizations underground after the outbreak of the war. Cooperative associations formed by workers in order to resist high prices had 50,000 members by the end of 1916. Some workers on the War Industries Committee abandoned hope of reform and pushed for greater working-class militancy. The Bolsheviks again began to build support among industrial workers.

As Nicholas dismissed capable but strong-willed ministers and replaced them with less able and sometimes corrupt but pliant men, liberals remained paralyzed, cowed by tsarist repression amid increased worker militancy. Attacks on the management of the war rang out in the Duma, as well as in the Union of Towns and the Union of the *Zemstvos*. The latter in

December 1916 passed a resolution calling on the Duma to stop cooperating with the tsar and demanded ministerial responsibility. By now, nothing remained of the "sacred union" formed at the beginning of the war.

For the moment, however, the tsar and the liberals needed each other. Outright revolution or violent repression seemed equally dangerous to both. The state needed the continued participation of voluntary committees and agencies of local self-government in order to keep the country from collapsing into shortage-induced anarchy. Liberal-dominated committees and agencies required the centralized apparatus of the state to carry out their work.

Food shortages reached a peak during the harsh winter of 1916–1917 when peasants hoarded their grain. Police repression of strikes helped close the ranks of workers against the government. In Lithuania, nationalists demanded autonomy within the empire. Some nationalist agitation occurred in other Russian borderlands as well. During the second half of 1916, Muslims in Turkestan in Central Asia rose up in arms against Russian rule after the government attempted to move a quarter of a million people to factories near the front. But increasing anger at the continued arrival of Russian settlers in Turkestan also played a role in the unrest. These occurrences did not have any influence on political events within the empire, but they did reveal the complexity of the problem of nationalism in the Russian Empire. Yet, the Petrograd garrison of about 160,000 soldiers still seemed adequate to the task of maintaining order, even though most were raw recruits.

The Progressive Bloc within the Duma gradually became more forceful in demanding change. The Socialist Revolutionary leader Alexander Kerensky (1881–1970), a lawyer, denounced the war in a speech whose daring rhetoric had never been heard in the Duma. This led the tsarina to demand that he be hanged and the Duma dismissed. However, some loyal nobles now urged reforms. But Nicholas replaced members of the Progressive Bloc with uncompromising reactionaries. He and his family withdrew into retreat, leaving the government floundering like a rudderless boat in high seas. Various nobles attempted to convince the tsar that some compromises had to be made, perhaps even the establishment of a ministry responsible to the Duma. Still, Nicholas did nothing.

The February Revolution

The Russian Revolution that began in Petrograd grew out of the massive discontent of hunger and deprivation, amid mounting frustration at tsarist intransigence against reform. Like most large European cities, Petrograd's neighborhoods reflected social segregation. The upper-class (Petrograd counted 138,000 nobles among its 2.5 million residents) and middle-class districts and the palatial buildings of imperial government lay on and near a long street called the Nevsky Prospect. This central artery was lined with

Nevsky Prospect in Petrograd.

banks, hotels, restaurants, cafés, a giant department store, and some offices, including the Singer Sewing Machine Company. The streetcars did not run as far as the muddy streets of the workers' districts, nor in many cases did the city's water mains or electric power lines. Epidemics were still frequent visitors to Petrograd, as to Moscow and other Russian cities, which were characterized by acute overcrowding and inadequate standards of public health and sanitation.

Revolutionary organizations prepared a massive general strike for early January 1917, the anniversary of Bloody Sunday in 1905. During January and February, almost half of the capital's 400,000 workers went out on strike. Three weeks later, demonstrators demanded that a provisional government be appointed with the power to enact major reforms. In the Duma, liberal deputies still hoped for some sign of reform. Food lines stretched longer in Petrograd, Moscow, and other cities in temperatures that reached forty below zero. Demonstrations and bread riots, in which many women and young people participated, became a daily occurrence.

On February 23 (all subsequent dates here refer to the Old Russian calendar, which was thirteen days behind the Western calendar), International Women's Day, more determined demonstrators took to the streets. Workers in the Putilov munitions factory tore up factory rule books and created committees to represent their interests to the company. Female textile workers led the way out of the factories. Almost all of the large factories shut down in one industrial district. Cossack cavalrymen sent to disperse the demonstrators reacted with none of their usual eagerness.

Russian factory workers at a political meeting, 1917.

On February 25, a general strike closed down Petrograd. While Petrograd's Duma debated ways of dealing with severe food shortages, crowds of ordinary people (workers in blue caps women wearing scarves, students wearing green and light blue caps) poured into Petrograd's center. The army had 400,000 troops available within thirty miles of the city, but military attention was focused on the front, not on Petrograd itself. Tsar Nicholas then ordered the commander of the garrison to suppress demonstrations. As street fighting began to spread in the city, some police and troops, in sharp contrast to their actions in the 1905 revolution, hesitated when ordered into the streets to disperse protesters.

On February 26, the police arrested about a hundred Bolsheviks and other militants seeking to turn demonstrations into insurrection. The attitude of soldiers, most of whom were peasants or workers, now became crucial. Many were shocked and disillusioned that they were ordered to fire on insurgents. When a commanding officer tried to restore order by reading a telegram from the tsar, he was shot while trying to flee the barracks. Now thousands of soldiers and some officers went over to the insurgent side. "Do what you think is best," officers told soldiers when mutineers approached the Armored Car Division. Many soldiers loyal to the government received neither orders nor food. Government plans to overwhelm an uprising had not taken into consideration the possible effect of mutinies. Districts began to fall under the loose control of the insurgents; a number of officers and soldiers who continued to resist were summarily executed after being captured.

Miserable conditions of war, the unpopularity of the officers (who addressed the rank and file as masters had spoken to serfs), awful food, and empathy with the demands of the workers for "bread and peace" explain the massive defection of soldiers. Sailors mutinied on ships of the Baltic fleet, killing an admiral. In Petrograd, unrestrained crowds attacked symbols of the autocracy: the law courts, prisons, and the immense fortress of St. Peter and St. Paul. The capture of the arsenal put thousands of rifles and great quantities of ammunition into the hands of workers. "Red Guards," factory militias whose members carried red flags, imprisoned tsarist officials.

Nicholas now ordered the Duma to dissolve. Some of its members, who were drawn from privileged society, obeyed, but the majority simply moved to a new meeting place. They voted to remain in Petrograd—a move not unlike the Tennis Court Oath of the third estate during the first period of the French Revolution, a precedent of which they were keenly aware. The Duma then elected a provisional committee, whose mandate was to restore order. In the meantime, the liberals, who had opposed revolution and tried to walk a tightrope between a desire for reform and their fear of the masses, now were in the position of trying to contain the revolution they had helped set in motion.

The Russian Revolution was unplanned and its outcome uncertain. But the soil was fertile. Experienced in strikes, low-level Socialist Revolutionary, Menshevik, and Bolshevik activists helped impart a sense of direction to the movement. Their goal was not, however, short-term improvement in the food supply and working conditions, but rather the overthrow of the tsarist regime. Amid the turmoil of sudden change effected by groups who did not necessarily agree on what should happen next, the provisional committee began to function as a provisional government, organizing a food supply commission and a military commission to try to bring the soldiers roaming through the city under some control.

On February 27, in response to calls in the streets, the Petrograd Soviet of Workers' and Soldiers' Deputies was created. Members included several hundred workers, some of whom the demonstrators had freed from jail (where they had been placed for their political or trade union activities), as well as many soldiers. They elected officers, discussed ways to defend Petrograd against German military attack, and sent representatives to encourage the formation of soviets in other cities. Menshevik leaders took the lead in the Petrograd Soviet's creation as Bolshevik leaders held back, fearing that a large and effective soviet might make it more difficult for their party to direct worker militancy.

Hoping to overwhelm the rebellion with his presence, the tsar (who had been at his military headquarters when the Revolution broke out) now decided to return to Petrograd from his sea resort, where he had gone to join his family. He spent almost two full days aboard his private train, critical moments in the February Revolution. As his train drew within a hundred miles of the capital, the tsar received an erroneous report that insurgent troops held the next stations and that they would refuse to let his train through. Nicholas then went to the northern military front, hoping to find a loyal army ready to march on Petrograd. In disbelief, he learned that Moscow, too, had fallen to insurgents. His generals, like the liberals who wanted reform but feared revolution, made no effort to save the regime. They believed the tsar's cause lost and that only his abdication could prevent civil war, and perhaps military defeat as well.

Nicholas II abdicated on March 2, 1917, leaving the throne to his brother, Prince Michael. He did so with characteristic calm that appeared to border on indifference—though he scribbled in his diary that day, "All around me—treason and cowardice and deceit." A few hours in revolutionary Petrograd convinced Prince Michael to refuse to succeed his brother. The Soviet placed the tsar and his family under house arrest until the summer, when they were taken by train to a small Siberian town.

The Russian autocracy had fallen in a matter of days, "with a sort of fabulous ease," in the words of a contemporary, with relatively little bloodshed—only about a thousand people had been killed. No legions of faithful peasants had risen up from the land of the black earth to save the "Holy Father."

Russian workers and soldiers guarding a government building, 1917.

The Provisional Government and the Soviet

The provisional government and the Petrograd Soviet were left in the awkward position of serving as dual or parallel governments. The provisional government included Constitutional Democrats, liberals who had demanded that the tsar initiate political reforms. The Petrograd Soviet, in contrast, consisted largely of workers and soldiers who had helped overthrow the tsar. The relationship between the moderate provisional government and the radical Soviet would ultimately define the course of the Russian Revolution itself.

For the moment, the Petrograd Soviet promised to accept the provisional committee's authority "in the measure that it will act in the direction of fulfilling its obligations and struggling decisively with the old government." Several factors explain why the Soviet's Executive Committee ceded power to the provisional government. Some Mensheviks had an ideological reason for not seeking to override the provisional government, seeing it as the expression of the Marxist bourgeois phase of the Revolution. Others, perhaps awed by the mass popular insurrection that appeared to have swept away tsardom, did not seem confident that they could run a government in precarious times (particularly as many of the most influential leaders of the revolutionary parties were still in exile). Furthermore, some leaders of the Soviet feared that radical opposition to the moderate provisional government would bring on an immediate military counter-revolution. For the moment, both the provisional government and the Soviet met in the same palace, with Alexander Kerensky, named minister of justice but also a member of the Soviet, running back and forth between the two bodies, trying to smooth relations between them.

On March 8, the provisional government granted civil liberties, including the right to strike, the amnesty of political prisoners, and the democratization of local government, and announced that it would convene a constituent assembly to establish a constitution. The Petrograd Soviet, now with 3,000 members and an executive committee meeting virtually around the clock, insisted on immediate economic and social reforms. The provisional government and the Soviet quickly became the focus of attention of competing political groups—Liberals, Socialist Revolutionaries, Mensheviks, and Bolsheviks—who wanted to shape Russia's future.

The Army

In the meantime, the army was the last functioning imperial institution. With the war raging on, the Petrograd Soviet instructed soldiers to obey the provisional government's orders, unless they were countermanded by the Soviet. On March 1, the Soviet issued Order Number One, which claimed for the Petrograd Soviet the authority to countermand orders of

A Russian soldier fighting in World War I has attached a red flag to his bayonet.

the provisional government on military matters and called for the election of soldiers' committees in every unit. In fact, such elections had already widely occurred, a remarkable attempt to democratize army life. In some places on the front soldiers had refused to obey officers and, in a few cases, had beat them up or even shot them. The soldiers wanted peace. The danger that the military front might collapse against German pressure seemed quite real. Desertions increased in the first month of the Revolution, though not as rapidly as one might have expected. Even the tempting Bolshevik promise of "land and peace" seemed a distant prospect. As soldiers put it, "What good is land and freedom to me if I'm dead?"

The United States, first, and then Great Britain, France, and Italy quickly gave diplomatic recognition to the provisional government, hoping that the Revolution would not drastically affect the Russian military commitment to hold the eastern front. But in a few places on the front, Russian troops fraternized with astonished German and Austro-Hungarian soldiers.

The Revolution Spreads

News of the Revolution and the abdication of Tsar Nicholas II spread rapidly, despite wartime disruptions of communication and transportation. In Moscow, the imperial regime fell almost overnight. People from seemingly all social classes attacked and disarmed police stations, freed political prisoners, and created provisional governing bodies.

In the distant reaches of the old empire, it sometimes took weeks for "commissars of the revolution" to arrive armed with the dramatic news. In some industrial regions, commissars found that industrial workers had already occupied the factories, demanding that their employers grant them higher wages, an eight-hour day, and worker control over production. But in most places, the situation remained unclear. One Russian's comment reflected this uncertainty: "We feel that we have escaped from a dark cave into bright sunlight. And here we stand, not knowing where to go or what to do."

With Petrograd and much of European Russia caught between war and revolution, some of the minority peoples of the empire began to demand a new, more favorable political status. Their demands were as myriad and complicated as the old Russian Empire itself. Among the nationalities, some nationalists sought only cultural autonomy; others wanted some degree of political freedom within the context of a federal structure; still others demanded outright independence. Such demands soured relations between ethnic groups in regions where tensions had persisted, sometimes for centuries. In the Baltic states of Lithuania, Latvia, and Estonia, nationalist movements grew rapidly, at least partially because of the presence of a sizable minority of ethnic Russians who had benefited from centuries of Russian domination of those nations. In the steppes of Central Asia and in the Northern Caucasus, fighting broke out between Russian settlers and Cossacks (who had begun to settle the regions in large numbers following the emancipation of the serfs in 1861), the Kazakh-Kirghiz, Bashkirs, and other Turkish peoples. Thousands of people perished in these struggles. In regions shared by more than one nationality or religion, disputes were inevitable.

The provisional government's goal was to hold the empire together until a constituent assembly could be elected to establish the political basis of the new state. Its declaration of civil rights for all peoples had made each nationality in principle equal. In some places, representatives of the new regime immediately turned over administrative responsibility to local committees or individuals. But elsewhere, local peoples set up their own institutions of self-rule, which tried to maintain order in the wake of the collapse of imperial institutions. In some places, nationalist movements competed with Socialist Revolutionaries, Mensheviks, and Bolsheviks for allegiance.

The provisional government announced that Poland, which had been an independent state until the Third Partition by Russia, Prussia, and Austria in 1795, would again become independent. But this gesture was meaningless, with German or Austro-Hungarian troops occupying most of Poland. In neighboring Byelorussia (Belarus), like Poland, a battleground, a national committee, led by Socialist Revolutionaries, demanded autonomy, and established a Rada (council).

The situation in Ukraine was particularly complicated. The provisional government feared that if it granted Ukrainian autonomy, other nationalities would demand similar treatment. Shortly after the tsar's abdication, Ukrainian socialists had formed a soviet. On March 4, nationalists and socialists established the Ukrainian Central Council. Centuries-old resentment of Russia, based on cultural and linguistic differences, rose to the surface. As more radical nationalists gathered in Kiev, the Rada summoned a Ukrainian National Congress, which began to draft a statute for autonomy, as Ukrainian soldiers formed their own military units. Serving as a de facto provisional government in Ukraine, the Rada broadened its social and national base by including non-Ukrainian residents. In the meantime, nationalism began to grip Ukrainian peasants, and many of them began to occupy lands owned by Russian or Polish landlords.

In regions with sizable Muslim populations, national movements were divided between religious conservatives, Western-looking liberals, and leftist Socialist Revolutionaries. The First All-Russian Muslim Congress, which began on May 1, reflected these divisions, as conservatives attempted to shout down speakers advocating rights for women. But Westernizers predominated, passing the measure. The congress announced the future formation of a religious administration that would be separate from the state.

In its first days, the provisional government gave top priority to assuring the food supply and insisted that the army curtail its unpopular policy of requisitioning grain. But the provisional government also had to confront two burning issues of even more immediate concern: pressure from the Soviet for economic and social reforms—particularly land reform—and holding the military front. The provisional government authorized the formation of local food supply committees and "land committees" in order to help gather information to formulate a land reform measure for the Constituent Assembly. Liberals wanted land reform, but insisted that it be carried out in a deliberate, legal manner. Peasants, however, wanted action, not committees.

An All-Russian Conference of Soviets began at the end of March in Petrograd. Bringing together representatives of other soviets that had sprung up after the Revolution, this congress transformed the Petrograd Soviet into a national body, establishing a central executive committee dominated by members of the Petrograd Soviet. This, too, increased popular pressure for a radicalization of the Revolution.

A groundswell of opposition to Russia's continued participation in the war, marked by popular demonstrations in Petrograd, gradually drove a wedge between workers and soldiers and the provisional government. Nonetheless, at the All-Russian Conference of Soviets, the Bolsheviks' call for an immediate end to the war was easily defeated. Mensheviks and the Socialist Revolutionaries (who enjoyed a broad base of support among peasants) were willing to continue the war, but on the condition that the provisional government work for peace without annexations.

The issue of the war led to the provisional government's "April Crisis." The minister of foreign affairs, a Kadet leader, added a personal note to an official communication to the Allies that called for "war to decisive vic-

Alexander Kerensky (front center) head of the provisional government, with troops in Petrograd, 1917.

tory," and cited Russia's "historic right" to take Constantinople. Protests by the Petrograd Soviet and demonstrations against the war led to his resignation from the government at the beginning of May.

The April Crisis led to the formation of the first coalition government, which reflected the push to the left. Alexander Kerensky emerged as the government's leading figure. The participation of socialist members of the Petrograd Soviet in this coalition government reinforced its authority by seeming to lend popular legitimacy, making it no longer merely a "bourgeois government."

The provisional government now accepted the Petrograd Soviet's demand that "peace without annexations" be the basis of Russian foreign policy. "Revolutionary defensism" seemed a middle position between those conservatives who wanted the war to continue until "decisive victory" had been reached, and radicals who were most concerned with protecting the Revolution itself. Supporting the provisional government, "revolutionary defensists" wanted "peace without annexations and indemnities," but also demanded that Russian military capacity be fully maintained.

Worsening material conditions radicalized many workers, particularly in trade unions that had sprung up since February. Workers organized factory committees and strikes in May. In the countryside, hundreds of thousands of peasants took news of the February Revolution as a promise of more land. The poorer peasants operated on the simplest principle of all: that those who work the land ought to own it. Many children or grandchildren of former serfs began to occupy the land of the lords for whom they had previously worked, sometimes killing landlords or former imperial officials in the process (although generally peasants did not seem to have expropriated the land of the wealthier peasants in their own communities). The percentage of landless peasants may have fallen by half during the 1917–1920 period. Soviets were also formed in the countryside as civil authority began to disappear. The Orthodox Church could no longer compel obedience. A priest reported: "My parishioners will nowadays only go to meetings of the soviet, and when I remind them about the church, they tell me they have no time."

Lenin's Return

The German government wanted to expedite Lenin's desire to return to Russia from Switzerland, where he had been in exile since 1900. The Bolshevik leader's return might exert further pressure on the provisional government to sue for peace, allowing the German army to concentrate its efforts on the western front. The Germans permitted Lenin to pass through German territory in a sealed railway car to assure that no contact between Russian socialists and the German population could occur. Lenin arrived in Petrograd in early April 1917.

Lenin gradually rallied the Bolshevik Party around his leadership, based on the following propositions: (1) Russian withdrawal from the war, the continuation of which he viewed as a serious obstacle to a Bolshevik victory; (2) no support for the provisional government; (3) a call for revolution in the other countries of Europe; and (4) the seizure of large estates by the peasantry.

In his "April Theses," Lenin argued that wartime chaos had allowed the bourgeois and proletarian revolutions to merge in a dramatically short period of time. The overthrow of the autocracy had suddenly and unexpectedly handed power to a weak bourgeoisie. The bourgeoisie, holding power through the provisional government, could be in turn overthrown by the proletariat, supported by the poorest peasants.

In theory, the soviets embodied Lenin's idea of the revolutionary-democratic dictatorship of the proletariat and the peasantry. Local power would be held by workers, soldiers, and peasants, but under party guidance. Lenin thus called the soviets "the embryo of a provisional revolutionary government," a basis on which a new state could be constructed through the "dictatorship of the proletariat and peasantry."

Aided by the provisional government's division and growing unpopularity, the Bolshevik Party gained a majority of support among the members of the factory committees, workers' militias, Red Guards (factory workers' militias), sailors at the naval base of Kronstadt, and the soldiers within the Petrograd garrison. The failure of the provisional government to provide either peace or land undermined its support among peasants. But it was powerless to resolve industrial disputes or to put an end to land seizures. In the meantime, Menshevik leaders warned that continued Bolshevik radicalism might push conservatives toward launching a coup d'état.

The July Days

Although neither troop morale nor the military situation boded well for a new Russian offensive, in mid-June Kerensky announced an offensive in Galicia. This was to reassure conservatives and moderates that military discipline had been restored, and to convince the Allies that Russia was committed to winning the war.

Pressured by the Petrograd Soviet and by demonstrations, several Kadets who favored a continuation of the war resigned from the provisional government on July 2. The next morning, Bolsheviks rose in insurrection. They had been encouraged by their increasing popularity among workers, the ongoing agrarian revolution, and widespread dissatisfaction with the war. The Bolshevik Central Committee, however, had initially opposed the revolt, fearing that it would be crushed. Nearly 100,000 soldiers who feared being sent to the front joined the chaotic insurrection. Sensing defeat, the Bolshevik Central Committee tried to call off the insurrection the next day. Most troops remained loyal to the provisional government, and the uprising failed.

The "July Days" hardened political lines in Russia. The provisional government ordered the arrest of Bolshevik leaders, and troops closed down party headquarters and the offices of the Bolshevik Party's newspaper, *Pravda* (Truth). Kerensky became prime minister of the second coalition government, depending even more on support from the Kadets. Lenin fled to Finland, certain that the premature insurrection had demonstrated that his party still lacked sufficient unity and support within the soviets.

The provisional government now believed that the Bolsheviks were finished. Kerensky tried to portray Lenin as a German agent, noting that the Bolsheviks in exile had received some German money. Kerensky's government disarmed army regiments it considered disloyal, reinstated the death penalty for disobedience at the front, and staged a state funeral, replete with national and religious symbolism, in honor of soldiers killed at the front.

But the repressive measures undertaken against the Bolsheviks were relatively ineffective because of the disorganization of the judicial apparatus, the rapid turnover of government officials, and the support the Bolsheviks enjoyed in the working-class districts. Many Bolshevik leaders escaped arrest; others were soon released from jail. The repressive measures further discredited the provisional government, which seemed to be using the July Days as an excuse to undertake a counter-revolution.

With Lenin hiding in Finland, several Petrograd Bolsheviks argued that the Bolshevik Party should seek common ground with the moderate socialists. Lenin would have none of that. From exile he tried to convince his party that because of the apparent power vacuum and his party's readiness, the next insurrection would succeed. Doubting the revolutionary potential of the soviets, many of whose members and leaders remained Mensheviks and Socialist Revolutionaries, the Bolsheviks turned to the factory committees to consolidate their support. Months of electing deputies, attending highly politicized meetings, and listening to representatives from the various political parties had provided workers with an intense political education. Bolshevik newspapers and brochures again appeared in factories, denouncing the provisional government and accusing moderate socialists of counter-revolution.

The Kornilov Affair

Disillusioned by Kerensky's indecision, frustrated by the ineffectiveness of the repression against the Bolsheviks, and frightened by peasant land seizures, Russian conservatives, including some military officers and Kadets, began to think in terms of a coup d'état.

General Lavr Kornilov (1870–1918), newly appointed commander in chief of the army, seemed the obvious candidate to overthrow the provisional government. He was a tough, decorated Cossack who had escaped from Hungary after being captured during the Great War and was a favorite of the Kadets. Prelates of the Orthodox Church sent him icons in the hope that the military could restore religious principles to Russia. Making matters worse, the Germans had captured Riga, a major Baltic seaport, and thus posed a direct threat to Petrograd.

In early August, a "Conference of Public Figures," including influential leaders drawn from industry, commerce, banking, and the military, pledged Kornilov their support. A wealthy industrialist predicted that "the bony hand of hunger would grasp by the throat the members of the different committees and soviets" and ultimately defeat the Revolution.

As Russian society became increasingly polarized, Kerensky organized a Moscow State Conference, which he hoped would mobilize support for his second coalition government. Most of the delegates (some of whom were leaders of trade unions, as well as bankers, representatives from the state dumas, military leaders, and professional people) now believed only a military dictatorship could save Russia from the soviets and from having to pull out of the war.

Kerensky wanted Kornilov to form a military government that could restore order, but he believed that the general would remain loyal to him and to the idea of establishing a democratic republic. Kornilov was not nostalgic for the empire per se, but rather for its military style and authority. He probably wanted to seize power and impose a right-wing military regime. A confusing exchange led each leader to misconstrue what the other meant. Kerensky demanded Kornilov's resignation as commander in chief and, when the latter refused, called on the army to remain loyal to the provisional government. On August 27, Kornilov issued an ultimatum to the provisional government declaring that "the heavy sense of the inevitable ruin of the country commands me in this ominous moment to call upon all Russian people to come to the aid of the dying motherland."

Bolsheviks, Mensheviks, and Socialist Revolutionaries formed a committee for struggle against counter-revolution. Workers reinforced security around their factories. Bolsheviks were among those receiving arms at the arsenals in anticipation of a stand against a military coup. But no coup d'état took place, and probably none had been planned. By raising the specter of counter-revolution, however, the Kornilov Affair aided the Bolsheviks, who were able to portray themselves as the only possible saviors of the Revolution.

THE OCTOBER REVOLUTION

Not only the political crisis but also the social crisis added to the instability. The provisional government seemed increasingly powerless. The workers of Petrograd were now organized and armed. At a time when employers were attempting to drive the workers' committees from the factories, striking workers demanded "a minimum living wage," more control over hiring and firing, reduced factory hours, maternity leave for women workers, and called for worker "control" over management. Industrial workers believed that the soviets could bring them practical gains in their struggle for higher wages and generally better working conditions. The provisional government, though dominated by socialists, seemed incapable of solving the worsening economic crisis and unwilling to take Russia out of the war. Only the Bolsheviks promised in their program to turn over to the soviets some degree of political power. The All-Russian Executive Committee of the Soviets approved the Bolshevik demand that a "democratic" republic be declared by a government "of representatives of the revolutionary proletariat and peasantry" from which Kadets would be excluded. The stage was set for the next dramatic stage in the Russian Revolution.

The Bolsheviks Seize Power

Returning to Petrograd in disguise, Lenin on October 10 convinced the Bolshevik Central Committee that a second insurrection could succeed. Kerensky believed a Bolshevik insurrection imminent, but he vastly underestimated the party's influence with the Petrograd workers, the soviets, and within some army units, as desertions had begun to mount rapidly beginning in May. Bolshevik propaganda hammered away at the theme that their party, representing virtuous opposition, was untainted by support for the provisional government. Even if a majority of soldiers or of the population of Petrograd or of Russia did not necessarily favor the Bolsheviks, Lenin's assessment that they would not oppose their seizure of power proved correct. On October 16, the Bolsheviks formed a military revolutionary committee to coordinate the insurrection with factory committees and army regulars.

Late on October 24, 1917, Kerensky shut down Bolshevik newspapers and sent troops to hold the bridges over the Neva River. But the next day, Petrograd residents disarmed military cadets sent to one bridge. About 12,000 young Red Guards launched the insurrection.

Factory committees in Petrograd's industrial districts voted to support the uprising. It was coordinated by Leon Trotsky (Lev Davidovich Bronstein; 1879–1940). Trotsky, the revolutionary son of a wealthy Jewish farmer, had borrowed his alias from one of his prison guards. Bolsheviks repelled an attack by army cadets loyal to the provisional government, the only serious fighting of the Revolution. The regiments upon which Kerensky had counted remained in their barracks, their neutrality striking a blow for the insurrection.

The provisional government simply collapsed before the insurrection. Kerensky left Petrograd the same day in a car borrowed from the U.S. embassy, hoping in vain to rally military support at the front. That night, the battleship *Aurora*, under the control of revolutionaries, lobbed a couple of shells toward the Winter Palace, where the last ministers of the provisional government were holding out. The provisional government surrendered after almost eight months of existence. The Bolsheviks now held power in Petrograd.

The October Revolution had occurred as if in slow motion. There were fewer people killed than in either the February Revolution or the July Days. Life went on in many districts of the city as if nothing unusual was

The Bolsheviks seize the Winter Palace, October 1917.

occurring. Restaurants, casinos, theaters, and the ballet remained open as usual, although banks closed, attendance was down somewhat at the theater, and streetcars were hard to find. The stock market, which had risen in anticipation of a military coup d'état during the Kornilov crisis, now fell. John Reed, an American sympathetic to the Bolshevik takeover, recalled that in Petrograd's fancy quarters "the ladies of the minor bureaucratic set took tea with each other in the afternoon, [each] carrying her little gold or silver or jeweled sugar-box, and half a loaf of bread in her muff, and wishing that the tsar were back, or that the Germans would come, or anything that would solve the servant problem . . . the daughter of a friend of mine came home one afternoon in hysterics because the woman streetcar conductor had called her 'Comrade.' "

Most Mensheviks and many Socialist Revolutionaries walked out of the All-Russian Congress of Soviets to protest the Bolshevik insurrection. On October 26, the remaining members approved the Bolshevik proposal that "all local authority be transferred to the soviets." The Central Committee of the Congress of Soviets, all Bolsheviks except for some leftist Socialist Revolutionaries, now ran the government.

In Moscow, Russia's second city, which was less socially polarized than Petrograd, the insurrection began after the first favorable reports from Petrograd arrived. There, too, the Bolsheviks found support in workers' neighborhoods. After a week of fighting, the forces of the provisional government surrendered.

In the vast reaches of the former Russian Empire, a "revolution by telegraph" took place. The military revolutionary committee kept order in Petrograd, as commissars representing the Bolsheviks went into the provinces (see Map 25.2). In industrial regions, where the Bolsheviks already dominated some soviets, it was easy enough to establish a military revolutionary committee to assume local power. Socialist Revolutionaries believed that they could coexist with the new Bolshevik-dominated government. But the Bolsheviks manipulated ethnic, social, and political tensions, purging the soviets of non-Bolsheviks and pushing aside the local institutions of self-rule that had spontaneously sprung up after the February Revolution, as well as their nominal allies, the Socialist Revolutionaries. In the countryside, the Bolsheviks cultivated support among the poorest peasants.

In Ukraine, the situation remained calm at least partially because the Bolsheviks had early in the Revolution made an agreement with Ukrainian nationalists. In the distant borderlands where ethnic Russians were a minority, however, it was often extremely difficult for the Bolsheviks to take control because of strong anti-Russian national feeling.

The Bolsheviks remained a small minority in Russia at the time of the October Revolution. "We shall not enter into the kingdom of socialism in white gloves on a polished floor," Trotsky had warned shortly before the October Revolution. The revolutionary government, under Lenin's leader-

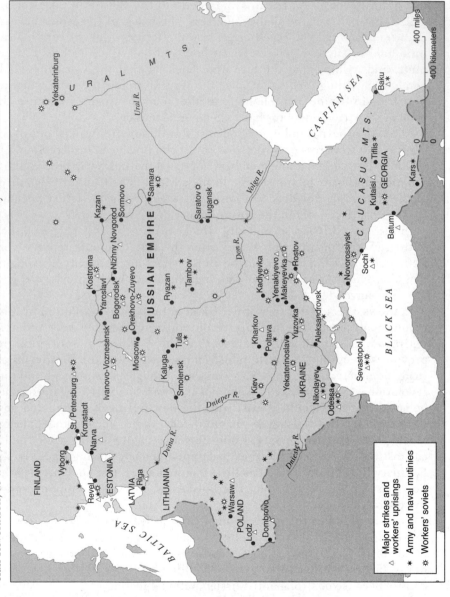

MAP 25.2   THE RUSSIAN REVOLUTION   Sites of strikes, uprisings, army and navy mutinies during the Russian Revolution, as well as the cities in which soviets were established by the revolutionaries.

ship, seized banks, closed down newspapers, banned the Constitutional Democratic Party, and arrested some of its members, as well as arresting a number of Mensheviks. In December, a new centralized police authority, the Cheka (All-Russian Extraordinary Commission), began to root out the Bolsheviks' enemies. Beginning with 120 employees, it rapidly proliferated into a large organization with virtually unlimited power. Arbitrary arrests led the eminent writer Maxim Gorky to ask, "Does not Lenin's government, as did the Romanov government, seize and drag off to prison all those who think differently?"

In elections for the Constituent Assembly, the Bolsheviks were supported only by the left wing of the Socialist Revolutionaries. The Bolsheviks won just 29 percent of the vote, compared with 58 percent for the Socialist Revolutionaries, who maintained their support in the countryside. When the elected deputies arrived early in January 1918, the Bolsheviks forced the assembly to adjourn the next day. It never met again. Red Guards fired on a crowd of protesters.

That month, Lenin proclaimed the "Declaration of the Rights of the Toiling and Exploited People," which stated that the goal of the revolutionary government was "the socialist organization of society and the victory of socialism in all countries." The third All-Russian Congress of Soviets created "The Russian Socialist Soviet Republic," a federation of "Soviet republics." But, as in the Russian Empire, Russia's interests, even under socialism, remained paramount.

The Peace of Brest-Litovsk

After the Bolsheviks took power, Trotsky, the "People's Commissar for Foreign Affairs," offered Germany an immediate armistice. The German government accepted, and an armistice was signed early in December 1917. The Bolsheviks had promised to bring peace, and continued to want an end to the fighting even when it became clear that Lenin's prediction of imminent working-class revolution in Germany and other European states seemed unlikely to be fulfilled. Lenin's priority remained the survival of the Russian Revolution.

Trotsky broke off negotiations for a permanent peace agreement because of draconian German demands, and the Germans resumed the fighting. In mid-February, German troops marched virtually unopposed into Russia, capturing Kiev and much of Ukraine and Crimea, and some of the Caucasus region. On March 3, 1918, the Bolshevik government signed the Treaty of Brest-Litovsk with Germany, giving up a fourth of the surface of what had been imperial European Russia, containing some of its most fertile land and most of its iron and steel production. The Bolsheviks also agreed to German occupation of Estonia, Lithuania, and Latvia and acquiesced to pulling Russian troops out of Ukraine and Finland. Angered by the treaty and demanding rapid attention to the agrarian question, the leftist Socialist Revolutionaries ended their cooperation with the Bolsheviks. The Germans then occupied all of Finland and Ukraine, forcing the latter to sign a separate harsh peace, while setting up puppet regimes in both states.

CIVIL WAR

The Russian Civil War began when Kornilov and other generals raised armies to fight the Bolsheviks (see Map 25.3). The anti-Bolshevik forces became known as the "Whites" because they shared a common hatred of the Bolsheviks, the "Reds." The White armies held Central Asia and Siberia, the Kazan region east of Moscow, and the Caucasus Mountains. A legion of 50,000 Czechoslovak troops, which had surrendered earlier in the war, operated as an anti-Bolshevik force along an extensive stretch of territory into Siberia, holding the crucial Trans-Siberian railway. The White army played upon anti-Semitism by denouncing Trotsky and other Bolshevik leaders because they were Jews. A wave of pogroms spread through Ukraine and parts of Russia. More than 2 million people fled abroad to escape the Russian Revolution and the ensuing Civil War.

Ukraine passed back and forth between Bolshevik and nationalist control in bloody fighting, falling again briefly into the hands of the Germans.

Lenin addressing the troops leaving for the front during the Civil War, 1920. Trotsky is in uniform standing to the right of the podium.

MAP 25.3 THE RUSSIAN CIVIL WAR   Boundaries of areas controlled by the Whites and the Reds during the Russian Civil War, including advances by the White and foreign armies.

A huge peasant army led by the anarchist Makno controlled parts of Ukraine after the Germans had fallen back. In Siberia, General Alexander Kolchak (1874–1920), backed by Britain and France, established a dictatorship, claiming to be the new government of Russia.

Food shortages and even famine spread in the summer of 1918. The Bolsheviks reacted to the crisis by implementing "War Communism." In June, the Bolsheviks established "committees of poor peasants" in order to "carry the class war to the village." The Bolsheviks forcibly requisitioned food and raw materials with brutality, turning poor peasants against wealthier ones, the "kulaks." Peasants from whom grain was being taken sometimes reacted with shock—after all, before the October Revolution the Bolsheviks had loudly proclaimed their support for immediate land reform. Now Communist forces were taking their food. Many peasants resisted. In one village, a hungry crowd stormed the home of the local commissar, beat him to death, and stuffed his mouth full of food ration cards. The Communists then nationalized major industries. War Communism may have saved the Revolution, but it took a terrible toll.

Bolshevik guards moved Nicholas II and his family to Ekaterinburg, a town in the Ural Mountains, as rumors spread that the Czech legion or monarchist generals were planning to rescue them. On July 17—again, the tsar's unlucky number—they were brutally executed on the orders of the local soviet, an act evidently approved by Bolshevik leaders.

The Allies, particularly Britain, supplied the White armies. In August, British, American, and Canadian soldiers landed in the northern port of Murmansk, claiming that such measures were necessary to prevent Russia's northern ports from falling to the Germans. Allied suspicion of the new Bolshevik government strengthened their decision to intervene. British troops attacked Soviet forces, and American troops landed at the icy port of Archangel. Japanese troops established themselves in Siberia, where the Bolsheviks had little effective control, and stayed there until 1922. In Ukraine, a Menshevik-leaning government opposed Bolshevik rule and permitted its territory to be used as a mobilization point for warfare against Russia's revolutionary government.

Allied intervention helped rally popular opinion against the Whites, whose wanton brutality, including routine rape and murder (some victims

The White army executes suspected Bolsheviks during the Civil War.

The Red Army preparing to do battle with the troops of General Denikin in southern Russia, 1919.

were forced to kneel and kiss portraits of the tsar before being killed), exceeded that of the Bolsheviks. Whites filled three freight cars with bodies of Red Guards, sending them along to the Bolsheviks, who were starving, with the wagons labeled "fresh meat, destination Petrograd." In Finland, after a bitter civil war between local Reds and Whites, the "White Terror" took 80,000 victims among those who had supported the Revolution.

Following attempts on the lives of several Bolshevik leaders, including Lenin, the "Red Terror" officially began in September 1918. Government decrees gave the Cheka almost unlimited authority and set up forced labor camps to incarcerate those considered enemies. While many victims were indeed working for the overthrow of the regime, many others were Mensheviks and others were leftist Socialist Revolutionaries. Once this apparatus of terror was in place, there was no guarantee that it would not remain in place once the crisis of the Civil War had passed.

The Red Army defeated the largest White army, 150,000 strong under General Anton Denikin (1872–1947), in Ukraine during the summer of 1919 and turned back a final march on Moscow in October. Kolchak's White army held out until late that year. The next year, the Red Army repelled a Polish invasion of Ukraine and continued on to the outskirts of Warsaw. A final attack launched from Crimea by General Peter Wrangel (1878–1928) in 1920 ended in failure. Victory in the Civil War heightened Bolshevik determination not to tolerate movements for national autonomy. Commissars reestablished Bolshevik authority over the border lands such as Georgia, Ukraine, and Turkestan.

THE SOVIET UNION

The peasant rebellions continued in 1918, unleashed by the February Revolution; they had destroyed the power of the imperial regime in the countryside while breaking the power of the landlords. The Bolsheviks were able to install a centralized state authority to mobilize the countryside against the counter-revolution. This enabled the revolutionary government, backed by a powerful army, to undermine and then destroy the local soviets. Many peasants feared the Whites, and went along with the demands of the Soviet regime, hoping that "peace and land" would follow. The Revolution seemed to offer hope for peasants. But the Bolsheviks controlled the cities and, like the old imperial elites, mistrusted the peasants and their notions of family and village ownership of land, their sense of collective responsibility, and their eagerness to market what they produced. The Civil War reinforced Bolshevik prejudices against peasants, and established a precedent for the use of mass terror to enforce the party's will in rural areas.

A constitution promulgated in July 1918 promised freedom of speech and assembly, the separation of church and state, and required all citizens to work. The "dictatorship of the proletariat" became that of the Bolsheviks. Marxist theory promised the "withering of the state" once socialism had been constructed, and Lenin himself warned against the growing power of the bureaucracy, which he had helped create. But the Soviet state did anything but wither. The "dictatorship of the proletariat" meant, in practice, the growing centralization of state power in the hands of the Bolsheviks at the expense of the local soviets.

The Union of Soviet Socialist Republics, created in 1922, included Russia, Byelorussia (Belarus), Ukraine, and Transcaucasia (Georgia, Armenia, and Azerbaijan, which all became separate republics in 1936), to which Uzbek (Uzbekistan) was added in 1924, Turkmen (Turkestan) in 1925, Tadzhik in 1929, and Kazakh (Kazakhstan) and Kirghiz in 1936 (see Map 25.4). Russian interests prevailed within the party, and thus within the government, and the republics enjoyed virtually no autonomy.

Democratic Centralism

For Lenin, "democratic centralism," which had referred to decisions taken by the Bolshevik Party, was also a goal in itself in the organization of the socialist state. In the summer of 1918, the Bolsheviks took the name of the Communist Party, a name Lenin had favored during the war as a way of more clearly differentiating the more radical Bolsheviks from the Mensheviks, their socialist rivals. Lenin's concept originally called for open and free discussion and debate on policy issues, but once party leaders made a decision all dissent had to end and all party members were to unite around the party line. Major decisions and discipline would thus come

MAP 25.4 THE SOVIET REPUBLICS 1922–1939 Soviet Socialist Republics (SSRs) and their capitals in the Union of Soviet Socialist Republics.

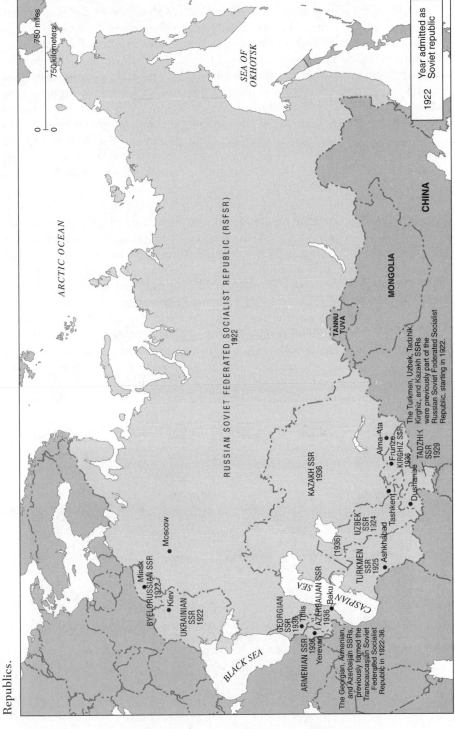

from the top. The structure suffocated the democratic apparatus on the local level, which henceforth received orders that flowed downward and outward from the central party apparatus in the name of the state.

The Communist government did not implement rights of nationalities or tolerate workers' self-management, two of the goals of many people who had helped overthrow the tsarist autocracy. The Left Communists had opposed signing the Treaty of Brest-Litovsk with Germany, arguing that Russia should lead a revolutionary war against the capitalist powers. Furthermore, they denounced the growing centralization of power. In response, Lenin acidly denounced "Left Infantilism and the Petty Bourgeois Spirit" in the summer of 1918, referring to those who criticized the abandonment of the principles of workers' self-management. Now "workers' control" meant state control.

Many industrial workers, who had helped bring the Bolsheviks to power, were not enthusiastic about following the directives of factory managers who had to answer to the state. Workers had taken over about three-fourths of the factories, which continued to operate under the control of factory committees. But in June 1919, the Bolsheviks nationalized most of the large-scale industries. In early 1921, at the end of the Civil War, worker discontent erupted in strikes and demonstrations in some industrial centers. In March, the Red Army crushed a revolt at the Kronstadt naval base, where sailors demanded freely elected soviets. Massive strikes rocked Petrograd after Bolshevik authorities rebuffed demands for better working conditions and more control over their shops and factories. A fundamental tension remained between the state—and therefore the Communist Party—and workers who remained loyal to their trade unions and

Leon Trotsky, leading the way, reviews the Red Band, Red Square, 1921.

wanted to run their plants themselves. Party officials began to push the soviets out of the way as the state turned against the idea of workers' self-management. This angered many workers, the vast majority of whom in Petrograd did not belong to the Communist Party. In 1920, then, two movements of opposition developed within the party: working-class opponents of party control, and Communists who objected to the party's authoritarian nature and the lack of freedom of speech. These opponents wanted to restore the original "democratic" element—free discussion and debate—to the process of decision making. In 1922, someone asked Trotsky, "Do you remember the days when you promised us that the Bolsheviks would respect democratic liberties?" Trotsky replied, "Yes, that was in the old days." That same year, when protests occurred in one region against the confiscation of Orthodox Church treasures, Lenin himself suggested that demonstrators be shot: "The more [of them] we manage to shoot, the better. Right now we have to teach this public a lesson, so that for several decades they won't even dare to think of resisting."

The New Economic Policy

Lenin and the other Bolshevik leaders debated how socialism could be implemented in a vast, backward country of many nationalities. In order to assure effective control over the vast expanse that remained of the former Russian Empire, the new Soviet government had to repair the massive disruption done to a backward economy by the Great War and by the subsequent Civil War. With the economy in near total collapse, Lenin recognized that Communist ideology, which called for the abolition of private ownership, for the moment would have to be sacrificed, and that market incentives would have to be put in place, perhaps for some time.

War Communism had collapsed because of the resistance, active and passive, of peasants and workers. The cities and army had only been fed because the state had been able to requisition or commandeer supplies in the vast countryside. At a time of severe famine—7.5 million people died of starvation and sickness during the famine of 1921 to 1922—the government needed to feed the population and build up a surplus of raw materials and food supplies. After the threat from the White armies had passed, some peasants had violently resisted grain requisitioning. Against this background, in March 1921, Lenin announced a "New Economic Policy" (NEP) which permitted private land ownership and trade of produce at market prices, although the state retained control of heavy industries. Lenin called this a "retreat," a concession to peasant hostility to forced requisitioning. Some merchants whose stores had been nationalized during the Civil War were now allowed to manage them again, and the government permitted small-scale, privately owned manufacturing. Lenin even invited foreign investment in mining and other development projects.

(*Left*) After the collapse of War Communism, a severe famine led to the starvation of millions, including the refugee children pictured here. (*Right*) As a result, Lenin instituted the New Economic Policy in 1921, which permitted free markets such as this one.

The NEP brought economic, but not political concessions. The Bolsheviks further consolidated their hold over most government functions, claiming to be serving the interests of the working class by protecting them against the Western Allies, the middle class, and the kulaks. They declared all other political parties illegal, although Lenin claimed that this ban would be a temporary measure, like the NEP itself. The Bolsheviks imprisoned Socialist Revolutionaries, whose base of support had been in the countryside, and exiled some Mensheviks.

The Rise of Stalin

During the early 1920s, the influence of Joseph Stalin rose within the party. Stalin—an alias taken from the Russian word for "steel"—was born Joseph (Soso) Dzhugashvili (1879–1953) in Georgia, beyond the Caucusus Mountains in the southern reaches of the Russian Empire. His father was a tough cobbler, who may have been killed in a tavern brawl, his mother a religious and doting woman who worked as hard as his father drank. Stalin's early feelings of insecurity would eventually lapse into extreme paranoia.

The young Stalin entered an Orthodox seminary in 1894 in the Georgian capital of Tbilisi. It was perhaps not a coincidence that a good many future revolutionaries in the Russian Empire took their formal education in seminaries. Stalin, like many other seminarians, rebelled against the conservatism of the Orthodox Church. In the seminary Stalin, who spoke Georgian, learned Russian, secretly read Marxist tracts, and joined a radical study circle, for which he was expelled. Arrested in 1902 and exiled to

Siberia the next year, Stalin escaped and returned to Georgia. There he sided with the Bolsheviks against the Mensheviks. The Bolsheviks' hardened secrecy appealed to the young Georgian's acerbic personality. More arrests, jail terms, exile to Siberia, and escapes followed in rapid succession over the next seven years. In 1912, Lenin appointed Stalin to the Bolshevik Central Committee and, after yet another escape from prison, he became editor of *Pravda,* the Bolshevik Party newspaper.

At the time of the February Revolution, Stalin was a prisoner in a desolate part of Siberia, 600 miles from even the Trans-Siberian railway. Stalin managed to return to Petrograd in March and, after the October Revolution, helped Lenin draft the "Declaration of the Rights of the Peoples of Russia," which promised the far-flung peoples of the old Russian Empire self-determination. During the Civil War, he served with Lenin and Trotsky on the military revolutionary council and quarreled with the headstrong Trotsky over military tactics.

Stalin's differences with Trotsky went beyond their old rivalry. Trotsky had surprisingly little gift for the ruthless political in-fighting that was as natural to Stalin as breathing. Trotsky was an intense intellectual and powerful orator. He considered Stalin a "mediocrity." Stalin considered himself a pragmatist who expressed the views of a middle-ranking party official and remained suspicious of "cosmopolitan"—often an anti-Semitic code word for Jewish—intellectuals such as Trotsky. The latter's caustic condemnation of bureaucrats in any guise irritated the old guard and undermined his support among them.

Trotsky espoused "permanent revolution," believing that socialism in the Soviet Union could only be victorious following world revolution and that the capitalist nations of the West were ripe to be overthrown by proletarian revolutions. The Communist International, which had been founded in 1919, aimed to help organize and assist revolutionary Communist parties in other countries. Lenin had believed that workers would overthrow one Western state after another. But this had not happened. The German Revolution of 1919 and the revolutionary government of Béla Kun in Hungary had been crushed by brutal force (see Chapter 26). The International also promised to help colonial people free themselves from imperialist domination. "Colonial slaves of Africa and Asia!," the International proclaimed, "the hour of proletariat dictatorship in Europe will also be the hour of your own liberation."

In May 1922, Lenin suffered a stroke. His increasing incapacity set off a struggle of succession infused with personal as well as ideological rivalries. Stalin was thus well-placed as a potential successor to Lenin, who remained partially paralyzed and could speak only with difficulty. He had demonstrated forceful independence while remaining loyal to the party and a capacity for organization. In April 1922, the Central Committee named Stalin to the powerful, recently created post of general secretary, which allowed him to appoint allies to various important posts and to repress dissent within the party.

The problem of the role of the 180 nationalities in the Soviet Union became ever more pressing. Lenin's support for national self-determination had been principally intended to undermine the provisional government. Furthermore, concerned with the Soviet Union's image in the colonial world, he wanted to give the impression that the various republics enjoyed a degree of sovereignty. Yet, Lenin had believed that national differences posed a threat to "the dictatorship of the proletariat," and would become irrelevant in the new Communist state. Rosa Luxemburg, the Polish socialist, shared this view. She had broken with the majority of Polish socialists, accusing them of heading toward nationalism by demanding the independence of their country.

Stalin, now commissar for nationalities, believed that the various peoples of the old imperial state should simply be incorporated into the existing Russian state. Indeed, during the Civil War, he had returned to his homeland, Georgia, to crush "the hydra of nationalism," despite his earlier insistence that a Communist regime would recognize national self-determination. However, Lenin had rethought the national question during the bloody Civil War, retreating from his earlier stand. No longer having to concern himself with overthrowing the tsarist state but rather with building its socialist successor, he now denounced "dominant nation chauvinism"—that is, Russian—insisting that each major nationality have its own state, which would be incorporated into a union of Soviet peoples. In this way, he hoped—at least in principle—that the various peoples of the Soviet Union would accept socialism without compulsion.

In the meantime, Stalin kept Lenin isolated as much as possible from visitors. In December, a day after suffering another stroke, Lenin dictated his doubts about Stalin: "Comrade Stalin, on becoming general secretary, concentrated boundless power in his hands, and I am not sure whether he will always know how to use this power with sufficient caution." In other writings at the time, Lenin himself warned against the expansion of the bureaucracies of both the Communist Party and the state.

Lenin's death in January 1924 led Stalin to step up his efforts to consolidate his power. Stalin placed his own men on the Central Committee and made Party appointments throughout the Soviet state. He took every occasion to leave the impression that Lenin had handpicked him to be the next Party leader, later doctoring photos so that he appeared to have been constantly at Lenin's side as his chosen favorite. Stringing together quotations from Lenin, Stalin rushed into print his own *The Foundations of Leninism,* which suggested that Stalin was the natural heir to the Marxist theorist.

The Left Opposition to Stalin was led by Trotsky and Gregory Zinoviev (1883–1936), the humorless but scrupulous curly-haired party secretary of Leningrad (Petrograd's name after Lenin's death). They believed that the Soviet Union ought to support even independent—that is, non-Com-

Vladimir Lenin (*left*) with Joseph Stalin (*right*) in a photo doctored by Stalin, who was eager to exaggerate his close association with Lenin.

munist working-class organizations—and criticized Stalin for abandoning Communist internationalism. Stalin, in contrast, argued that the Bolsheviks first had to build "socialism in one country," that is, the Soviet Union. Allying with the "right" of the party between 1925 and 1927, Stalin isolated leaders of the left by assigning their allies to inconsequential posts in distant places.

In 1927, the Left Opposition demanded worker mobilization against bureaucracy. Above all, they wanted accelerated industrialization in the state sector. They considered Lenin's NEP an unnecessary ideological compromise that might inadvertently bring back capitalism. Wealthier peasant proprietors, the Left Opposition argued, could be forced to provide the surplus that would sustain gradual industrialization. If the state, which controlled heavy industries, kept the prices of manufactured goods high, state revenue would increase, permitting further industrial development. In contrast, Nikolai Bukharin (1888–1938), leader of the Right Opposition that formed in 1928, believed that the Bolsheviks needed to maintain the good will of the peasantry. Kulaks had not been the only peasants to expand their holdings during the land seizures of 1917–1918. The Revolution had allowed many others to acquire small plots. Bukharin believed that this should be encouraged (yet, at the same time, he once commented on the two-party political system, "one must be the ruling party and the other must be in jail").

In 1927, the Central Committee voted to expel Trotsky and Zinoviev from the Party and refused to publish Lenin's "Political Testament," which had suggested that Stalin be replaced as general secretary. The Soviet Union entered the long period of the dictatorship of Joseph Stalin.

Five-Year Plans

Stalin believed that socialism could not be fully implemented until the Soviet Union had a stronger industrial base. After defeating the Left Opposition, he openly began to favor their plan of more accelerated industrialization. This would be paid for by extracting more resources from the peasantry. In 1928–1929, he resumed forced requisitioning of "surpluses," and expropriated the land of richer peasants who had been hoarding produce. When this led to growing peasant opposition, he took the next step in 1930: the forced collectivization of agriculture—the elimination of private ownership of land and animals. In doing so, he was prepared to eliminate 1.5 to 2 million kulaks (of the Soviet Union's 28 million peasants). The Five-Year Plan would mark a complete abandonment of Lenin's New Economic Policy, which Stalin believed would have allowed capitalism to be restored.

Within the Communist Party, the Right Opposition, led by Nikolai Bukharin, objected to a policy of renewed requisitioning and immediate collectivization on the grounds that it would greatly undermine peasant support for the regime, ultimately slowing rather than speeding up industrialization. The Right Opposition also disagreed with Stalin's abandonment of the principle of collective leadership. Stalin, with support from other top party leaders, accused Bukharin of trying to surrender to "capitalist elements." He ousted Bukharin from his position as editor of the Communist Party newspaper as well as from the International. By the end of 1930, Stalin had purged the Right Opposition from the party.

In formulating his Five-Year Plan, Stalin sought to take advantage of social tensions in Soviet society. He knew that workers believed that material progress was not coming fast enough and that they blamed peasants and smug bureaucrats. Stalin wanted to inspire workers to storm the "fortress" of remaining inequalities in Soviet society. He used the rhetoric of class struggle as a means of mobilizing effort, trying to turn workers against "bourgeois" managers and kulaks.

The first Five-Year Plan (1928–1933) led to a bloodbath in the countryside. Hundreds of thousands of peasants who refused to turn over their harvests, farm animals, or farms were killed. An officer in the secret police told a foreign journalist: "I am an old Bolshevik. I worked in the underground against the tsar and then I fought in the Civil War. Did I do all that in order that I should now surround villages with machine-guns and order my men to fire indiscriminately into crowds of peasants?" Peasants resisted in many ways, including slaughtering livestock rather than allowing them to be taken by the collective farm. The number of horses fell from 36 million in 1929 to 15 million four years later, cattle from 67 to 34 million during the same period.

Small plots were forcibly consolidated into collective farms. Peasants had to work a certain number of days each year for the collective farm; the

The deportation of prosperous peasants (kulaks) from a Russian village during land collectivization, 1930.

state supplied machinery, seed, and clothing. The free market disappeared, with the state establishing production quotas and setting prices. One of the primary goals of the collectivization of agriculture was to force peasants into industrial labor. Nine million of them became industrial workers during the first Five-Year Plan, during which the Soviet Union's industrial and urban populations doubled.

In March 1930, Stalin signed an article in *Pravda* entitled "Dizzy with Success." He announced that his Five-Year Plan was succeeding beyond even his wildest expectations, and that the time had come for a pause. In fact, forced collectivization had catastrophically reduced Soviet agricultural production. Indeed, Stalin ordered officials to return expropriated animals to their owners. But he viewed this as a lull, not a change in theory. Party officials began to replace elected village officials.

The Five-Year Plan actually ended in 1932 after four years and three months, with 62 percent of the peasants now working for the state in collective farms. The campaign continued, though somewhat less brutally; four years later, the figure was 93 percent. However, peasants were allowed to retain small private plots; the vegetables and fruits that they grew provided almost half of the produce reaching markets but, overall, living conditions declined during the Five-Year Plan, particularly when shortages of fuel and machine parts became severe. Hundreds of thousands of peasants had been killed, and perhaps 2 million had been exiled to Siberia or other distant places under the sentence of hard labor. Another 3 to 6 million people died during the famine of 1932–1933.

The campaign for heavy industrialization proceeded successfully, if the human cost is conveniently forgotten. Despite inaccurate and sometimes misleading Soviet data, the state did meet some ambitious production targets in heavy industry (iron and steel), fuel production (oil and electricity), in new industries (especially chemicals), and in the manufacture of tractors. While the Depression devastated the Western economies, the Soviet economy may have had an annual growth rate of a remarkable 27 percent between 1929 and 1934, although it had the advantage of starting considerably further behind than its rivals. These successes occurred despite inefficiency due to inadequate planning or duplication; chaotic reporting of figures—compounded by the mounting sense of urgency to report successes; and by the replacement of many of the most able technicians because of their social class by dedicated but semi-literate workers suddenly put in charge of complicated machinery or peasants who sometimes mistook mud for oil.

Giant show projects such as the Dnieper Dam and the new industrial city of Magnitogorsk in the Ural Mountains attracted international attention. Foreign visitors found many workers who went to work with great initial enthusiasm. Party officials selected "heroes of labor" to be praised for surpassing their production targets by record amounts. A certain Andrei Stakhanov, a Don Basin miner, was credited in August 1935 with cutting 102 tons of coal during a single shift. A "Stakhanovite" became the idealized Soviet worker, working as fast as he or she could, and ready to step forward to denounce "Troskyite wreckers and saboteurs."

The second Five-Year Plan (1933–1937) relied less on the shrill rhetoric of class warfare, despite ongoing collectivization. Stalin relaxed the ideologically charged "class-war" campaign against "experts" of bourgeois origins, and technocrats again appeared in factories.

In the meantime, Stalin reinforced his dictatorship. Even with most consumer goods still wanting, 4.5 million radios in the Soviet Union broadcast Stalin's speeches in the 1930s. The grandson of a Soviet minister recalled, "Stalin was like a God for us. Somebody told me that Stalin could be the best surgeon. He could perform a brain operation better than anyone else, and I believed it." The dismal poem "There Is a Man in Moscow" reflected such adulation.

> Who is that man who appears to the toilers,
> Spreading happiness and joy all around?
> It is Stalin, I shout, so the whole world will hear,
> It is Stalin, our Leader and Friend.

Soviet Culture

Many artists and writers were enthusiastic about the Revolution, and a spirit of utopianism survived into the early 1920s. The Communists wanted to build a unique culture based upon mass mobilization and commitment that would both reflect and accentuate the collectivization of life in the Soviet Union, helping forge consensus. The culture of utopianism would be defiantly proletarian and egalitarian.

With the determination of the Communists that the Soviet Union rapidly industrialize, the machine and mechanization played major parts in Soviet imagery in the inter-war period. Soviet artists and writers (like Communist leaders) believed that mechanization in the service of capitalists had further enslaved the masses but that technology could be potentially liberating. The state created art schools and provided assistance to struggling artists, hoping to enroll them in the service of the Revolution. In its first years, the Soviet state patronized futurists (see Chapter 21) as revolutionary artists who would provide a novel aesthetic for socialism in the construction of an ideal society. They and other avant-garde artists issued a manifesto in which they promised to "re-examine the theory and practice of Leftist art, to free it from individualist distortions, and develop its Communist aspects." Artists collaborated with designers in producing models for standardized proletarian clothing and household items.

As the Soviet state subsumed most aspects of public life in the name of the proletarian revolution, the initial mini-explosion of cultural forms that had occurred during the first years of the Soviet state gave way to repressive orthodoxy. Rejecting traditional and avant-garde art as bourgeois escapism, Stalin believed that art and literature should assume a social

Soviet workers depicted delivering blow after blow to lazy workers in the lithograph *Fighting Lazy Workers* (1931).

The Soviet state launched an atheist campaign against religion. These children hold letters of the alphabet used to spell out an atheist slogan.

function. "The artist," he said in 1932, "must give first priority to the truthful presentation of life, and if he truly portrays our life, then he cannot but note, cannot but show, that it leads to socialism. This will be socialist art. This will be socialist realism." Stalin preferred monumental murals that could be seen by many people, showing smiling workers toiling for the state. Artists who did not conform stood accused of pandering to "bourgeois values," an increasingly dangerous denunciation. The Union of Communist Youth (Komsomol) sent out members to preach cultural uniformity, disrupting plays considered "bourgeois."

Stalin charmed and deceived many foreign statesmen and visitors, impressing them with the fact that millions of working-class children were now entering school for the first time. Some workers now attended night classes, or even university. Women obtained training and positions in fields from which they previously had been excluded, such as medicine. Soviet guides whisked foreign visitors around on Moscow's new subway to see the Soviet capital's improved housing, water supply, and sewage facilities. Although church and state had been officially separated in 1918, religious life went on as before, at least in the countryside, both in Orthodox regions and in the Islamic republics. Moreover, despite an atheist campaign against the Orthodox Church, Stalin nonetheless discouraged unmarried couples from living together, banned abortion, and forbade homosexuality. Gradually in the 1930s, Stalin's early enthusiasm for equal opportunity for women waned; the state-approved image of the female as mother of committed Soviet children prevailed.

"Darkness at Noon": Stalin's Purges

By 1934, Stalin was no longer content to expel from the party those who did not share his views. In November, he evidently ordered the murder of a trusted associate who ran the Communist Party in Leningrad because he believed the younger man might emerge as a rival. Four days after the murder, Stalin promulgated a state decree that expedited the punishment of those deemed to be "terrorists." Stalin ordered the arrest of Zinoviev, among others, for alleged complicity in the murder; he was sentenced to prison.

As arrests mounted in number, executions replaced sentences of hard labor. The charges became more and more outrageous—accusations of secret plots to overthrow the state, conniving with Trotsky, who had gone into exile in 1929, or with Western European fascists, accusations of "wrecking" Soviet industries, of trying to restore capitalism, or of simply being "bourgeois," or even being the wife of an "enemy of the people."

The first of the great show trials—staged before audiences and cameras—took place in 1936, the last in March 1938, when Bukharin and the remainder of the Right Opposition faced judges who sometimes appeared to be more nervous than they. Those on trial were forced to sign confessions in court, where sympathetic foreign observers sometimes nodded in agreement to absurd accusations. Children—who could be executed at age twelve—were encouraged to denounce their parents for crimes against the state. Estimates of the number of people executed over this period vary from 400,000 (of 4 to 5 million arrested) to 1 million killed (of 7 million arrested). Prison camps, many of them in Siberia, had 600,000 prisoners in 1930, 7 million prisoners in 1937, including elderly women sentenced to camp terms for having said things like "if people prayed they would work better." Stalin's long arm reached far beyond the boundaries of the Soviet Union to force Communist parties in Spain, France, and other nations to purge those who disagreed with his policies. Stalin's agents caught up with Trotsky, who lived outside Mexico City, and stabbed him to death with an ice pick as he sat in a garden in August 1940.

Stalin still feared that nationalism among the many peoples spread across the distant reaches of the Soviet Union might threaten the functioning of the state and thus the centralized party apparatus he controlled. He purged "national deviationists" from the distant Muslim lands of Central Asia, and sometimes applied this label to the Soviet Union's several million Jews. At the same time, Stalin encouraged the training of leaders among each of the peoples of the Soviet Union, publishing tomes of propaganda in each national language. Party leaders in the various republics, however, were subject to particularly close scrutiny from Moscow.

The purge was an economic blow to the Soviet Union, eliminating many engineers and other people with needed technical expertise. Furthermore, at a time when the rise of Hitler to power in Germany was increasing international tensions, the purge weakened the Soviet armed forces. Behind Stalin's move against distinguished military leaders was his paranoid fear that they might one day oppose his conduct of foreign policy. Among the 30,000 to 40,000 officers who perished, all 8 Soviet admirals were executed, as were 75 out of 80 members of the Supreme Military Council.

CONCLUSION

The Russian Revolution, which had begun as a quest for economic and social justice by intellectuals, workers, middle-class and lower-middle-class radicals, and peasants, as well as non-Russian nationalists, led to the dictatorship of the Communist Party. "One of the most striking features of the year 1917," recalled a correspondent, "was the speed with which the masses, after the overthrow of tsarism, created new forms of organization," including soviets of workers and soldiers and factory committees in Petrograd and other cities, military organizations among and between units at the front, and peasant soviets that supplemented township committees and land committees. But once the Bolsheviks seized power on behalf of the working class and poor peasants, they never relinquished it. They destroyed these popular organizations that had embodied the aspirations of millions of people.

Then, under the rule of Joseph Stalin, the Soviet Union's industrial capacity increased dramatically, but at a terrifying human cost. During the first Five-Year Plan and with Stalin's paranoid purges, the Soviet Union took on some of the murderous characteristics of fascist regimes its leaders so bitterly denounced. This was the tragedy of the Russian Revolution.

CHAPTER 26

THE ELUSIVE SEARCH FOR STABILITY IN THE 1920s

In the preface to his novel *The Magic Mountain* (1924), Thomas Mann (1875–1955) wrote that it took place "in the long ago, in the old days, the days of the world before the Great War." Mann's identification of contemporary European civilization with a sanatorium was clear to readers. In that Swiss sanatorium, the tradition of rationality inherited from the Enlightenment (representing democracy to which he was a recent convert) confronted the irrationality of fascism. It was an allegory for the post-war era. Thomas Mann expressed the mood of despair prevalent among European intellectuals: "For us in old Europe, everything has died that was good and unique to us. Our admirable rationality has become madness, our gold is paper, our machines can only shoot and explode, our art is suicide; we are going under, friends."

The Treaty of Versailles, signed in 1919 by a frail new German Republic, and the accompanying treaties signed by the victorious Allies and Germany's wartime partners, did not resolve national rivalries in Europe. Dark clouds of economic malaise, political instability, and international tension descended on Europe in the two decades that followed the war. Although Europe experienced a brief return to relative prosperity and political calm after 1924, the Wall Street Crash of 1929 ended the brief period of hope. The search for what U.S. Senator and future President Warren G. Harding called "normalcy" proved elusive, if not impossible, in the 1920s.

The Great War helped unleash the totalitarian demons of our century, as parties of the political extremes sprang up and threatened parliamentary governments. Nationalist groups, intolerant of those considered outsiders and committed to military territorial expansion, carried their violence into the streets. Many members of these organizations were former sol-

A fascist squad, 1920–1922.

diers who vowed to replace democracies and republics with dictatorships. Moreover, ethnic rivalries within nations, many inflamed by the Treaty of Versailles, intensified social and political conflict in post-war Europe.

THE RESOLUTION OF THE WAR

The Great War swept away the Russian, German, Austro-Hungarian, and Ottoman Empires. The Russian Revolution of 1917 destroyed the tsarist autocracy and took Russia out of the war. Even before the representatives of the victorious Allies (along with those representing a host of smaller states) met in Versailles in 1919 for a peace conference, the German and Austro-Hungarian Empires had collapsed, rocked by revolutions. Amid social and political turmoil, the leaders of the Great Powers set out to reestablish peace in Europe, firmly believing that the Great War had been the "war to end all wars." But the Treaty of Versailles reflected the determination of Great Britain and France to punish Germany for its role in unleashing the conflict. Representatives of the new German Republic were forced to sign a clause essentially accepting full blame for the outbreak of the war, and to agree to pay an enormous sum in war reparations to the Allies.

Despite the idealistic belief of U.S. President Woodrow Wilson that an era of collective security had begun that would prevent future wars of a similar magnitude, the Paris Peace Conference left a legacy of bitterness and hatred that made it even more difficult for the German Republic to find stability because of massive dissatisfaction among nationalists with the terms of the treaty. Furthermore, the individual treaties between the Allies and Germany's wartime partners left several nationalities dissatisfied with the establishment of new states constituted out of the old empires; the newly drawn borders often left them on what they considered the wrong side of frontiers. In fact, the Treaty of Versailles and its accompanying smaller treaties left many significant problems unresolved. Groups of nationalists in Germany, above all, but also nationalists in some other countries, were determined to revise or abrogate the post-war peace settlements.

Revolution in Germany and Hungary

The end of the war brought political crises in Germany and Hungary. In the face of defeat, the German Empire started to come apart at the seams. In late October 1918, German sailors mutinied at two Baltic naval bases, demanding peace and the kaiser's abdication. In southern Germany, socialists proclaimed a Bavarian socialist republic in early November. The new chancellor, Prince Max von Baden, called on William II to abdicate. When the sovereign sought to arrange to keep the throne for his family, the chancellor declared the kaiser to have abdicated. He named Friedrich Ebert (1871–1925), a member of the left-wing Social Democratic Party, the largest party in the pre-war years, to succeed him as chancellor.

The Big Four deciding the future of Europe, 1919. Left to right: Vittorio Orlando of Italy, David Lloyd George of Great Britain, Georges Clemenceau of France, and Woodrow Wilson of the United States.

That same day, a German commission met with Allied representatives to begin drawing up an armistice. On November 9, another Social Democrat, Philip Scheidemann (1865–1939), fearing that radical revolutionaries in Berlin and a few other cities would declare a socialist state, proclaimed the German Republic. That night, William II fled across the border into the Netherlands.

On November 11, 1918, Germany signed the armistice with the Allies, ending the war. Chancellor Ebert named a provisional government, dominated by Social Democrats but with members of the more radical Independent Social Democratic Party also represented.

From its very beginning, the new German Republic was under siege from left and right. Inspired by the success of the Bolshevik Revolution in Russia, workers began to set up "workers' and soldiers' councils" and demanded higher wages and better work conditions, thereby antagonizing their employers. Workers also angered the army by calling for the dismissal of General Paul von Hindenburg and the abolition of the special military schools for officers that for generations had infused them with the elitism identified with Prussian militarism.

The right posed a more serious threat to the fledgling republic, a threat the Treaty of Versailles would strengthen. Germany had virtually no democratic traditions. Royalism and militarism ran deep, particularly in Prussia, the northern German state under whose auspices the unified German Empire had been forged in the 1850s and 1870s. Furthermore, demobilized soldiers, many of whom were anti-republican, had held on to their weapons. Ominously, a veteran wrote that he believed the bloodletting of 1914–1918 was "not the end, but the chord that heralds new power. It is the anvil on which the world will be hammered into new boundaries and new communities. New forms will be filled with blood, and might will be hammered into them with a hard fist. War is a great school, and the new man will be of our cut."

The attitude of the army officer corps would be crucial to the fate of the republic. The head of Germany's Supreme Army Command offered the chancellor the army's support, but on condition that the new government help the army maintain order and fight "Bolshevism." Ebert accepted and, in doing so, made the new republic virtually a prisoner of the army. Some generals had already begun to enlist demobilized soldiers into right-wing paramilitary units known as the "Free Corps."

Within the new government, a rift developed between the Social Democrats and the Independent Social Democrats, the latter demanding immediate assistance for workers. The Independent Social Democrats asked the government to organize a militia loyal to the republic. When Ebert refused, the Independent Socialist Democrats left the governing coalition, weakening the shaky government. The new minister of defense turned over security operations to the army, and continued to encourage the Free Corps. To the left, this seemed like leaving the fox to guard the henhouse.

Karl Liebknecht addresses his supporters in January 1919, shortly before his assassination.

Workers in Berlin mounted huge demonstrations against the security police. In January 1919, police and soldiers put down an uprising by the Sparticists, a group of far left revolutionaries who took their name from the leader of a revolt by Roman slaves in the first century B.C. Military units began to move against the Berlin Sparticists, hunting them down and murdering Karl Liebknecht and the Polish Marxist Rosa Luxemburg, two of their leaders, who had just founded the German Communist Party.

The German Republic's first elections in January 1919 provided a workable center-left coalition of Social Democrats (who held the most seats in the Reichstag), the Center Party, and the German Democratic Party. The members of the Reichstag elected Ebert president, and he in turn appointed Scheidemann to be the first premier of the Weimar Republic. The Reichstag gathered in Weimar, a small, centrally located town, chosen as the new republic's capital to counter the Prussian aristocratic and militaristic traditions identified with the old imperial capital of Berlin.

Following the break-up of the Habsburg monarchy in 1918 at the end of World War I, Hungary also soon became a battleground between the competing ideologies of the post-war period. Demobilized soldiers and former imperial officials were among those stirring up trouble. Hungarian nationalists feared, with reason, that the victorious allies would award disputed territories from pre-war Hungary to rival nationalities. With the collapse of the Austro-Hungarian Empire in the fall of 1918, Count Mihály Károlyi (1875–1955) led an unopposed revolution of liberals and socialists that proclaimed Hungarian independence. Károlyi favored a republic and initiated a program of land reform by turning over his own extensive estate to peasants. The great landowners prepared to defend their vast estates against land-hungry peasants. In March 1919, Béla Kun (1886–c. 1939), a Communist journalist, seized power and tried to impose a Soviet regime. He announced a more extensive land reform, which included the establishment of collective farms, and he proposed the nationalization of large and medium-sized industries. The Romanian army, angered by the Hungarian occupation of Slovakia, invaded Hungary to help overthrow him. Admiral Nicholas Horthy (1868–1957), a former Habsburg naval officer (with not much to do, as Hungary's new borders lacked access to the sea), seized power in 1920. He encouraged attacks against Jews, whose economic role in Hungary was considerable, claiming that they were Bolsheviks, and executed thousands of workers and Communists.

Above all, the specter of revolution frightened Europe's business and political leaders. After the Russian Revolution of 1917, Communist parties sprung up in one country after another. Commenting on the mass strikes of the first two years of peace, a French publisher lamented, "We are reaching the end of our civilization and we are going to be destroyed not by the barbarians without but by those within."

The Treaty of Versailles

In this volatile atmosphere, delegates from twenty-seven nations and the four British Dominions gathered for the Paris Peace Conference in the château of Versailles outside Paris to make the peace that they believed would transform Europe. As they convened in January 1919, the representatives of the "Big Four"—Prime Minister David Lloyd George of Britain, Prime Minister Georges Clemenceau of France, President Woodrow Wilson of the United States, and Premier Vittorio Orlando of Italy—agreed that Germany, the nation they believed responsible for the war, should assume the financial burden of putting Europe back together again.

Beyond this area of agreement, the "Big Four" powers went to Versailles with different demands and expectations. France, which had suffered far greater losses than Britain, Italy, or the United States, demanded a harsh settlement that would eliminate Germany as a potential military threat. The diminutive, elderly Clemenceau, a combative loner nicknamed "the Tiger," realized the dangers of a punitive peace settlement. But he was also mindful that the quest for security against Germany dominated French foreign relations and weighed heavily upon domestic politics. An influential French politician acknowledged a truth that no one wanted to hear and that would only gradually sink in: "France victorious must grow accustomed to being a lesser power than Germany vanquished." Defeated Germany was still potentially a stronger state because of its economic capacity and larger population.

France's victory had been pyrrhic. More than 1.3 million Frenchmen were killed in the Great War, 16.5 percent of all soldiers mobilized. Half of the men between the ages of eighteen and thirty-two in 1914 had died.

A poster advertising a French loan campaign to reconstruct the city of Reims and its cathedral.

France seemed a country of crippled veterans, widows dressed in mourning black, and hundreds of thousands of children left without fathers, for whom pensions would have to be paid. Much of the north and northeast of the country lay in ruins; factories and railways had been destroyed in a region that included 70 percent of the country's coal. With the fighting ended, the state had to borrow money from its wartime allies and from its citizens at high interest rates in order to pay off those who had purchased war bonds.

Wanting to contain Germany in the future, Clemenceau demanded that Germany's military arsenal be drastically reduced and that French troops occupy the fertile Rhineland until Germany had paid its reparations to the Allies. These payments would be based on a rough estimate of damages caused to the victorious powers by the war. Many in France wanted to go further, however, demanding annexation of the left bank of the Rhine, or at least the establishment of an independent state in the Rhineland as a buffer against further German aggression.

The British, represented by the Welsh Liberal David Lloyd George, came to Versailles with more flexible views than the French. Britain had been spared almost all the physical devastation suffered by its cross-Channel allies. Still, the British had suffered horrific loss of life, and had borne more than their share of the war's financial costs. The British government thus supported France's position that Germany had to be contained in the future. At a time when the slogan "Squeeze the German lemon 'til the pip squeaks" was current, one of the British prime minister's campaign slogans had been "Hang the Emperor!" However Lloyd George now concluded that it was in Europe's interest to restore the fledgling German

Republic to reasonable economic strength. In view of the perceived threat posed by the Russian Revolution, he reasoned that Germany could emerge as a force for European stability.

Italian Prime Minister Vittorio Orlando (1860–1952) came to Versailles assuming that his country would receive territories of the former Austro-Hungarian Empire promised by the Allies in 1915, when Italy had entered the war on their side: the port of Trieste; the strategically important Alpine region around Trent (the South Tyrol), which would give Italy a natural boundary; and Istria and Northern Dalmatia on the Adriatic coast (see Map 26.1). President Wilson found acceptable Italian annexation of the first three; all had sizable—though, except in the case of Trieste, not majority—Italian populations. As a result, Italy was able to extend its frontiers to the Brenner Pass and to Trieste. But Wilson staunchly opposed Italian demands for Istria, Northern Dalmatia, and the strategically important Adriatic port of Rijeka (known to its Italian minority as Fiume), which Italy had omitted from its demands in 1915, but now claimed. His reason for doing so was that Italians were only a minority in those territories. Italian nationalists denounced the "mutilated peace" that had not allowed annexation of all of the territories the Italian government had anticipated receiving for its role in the war.

Wilson's position on Italy's territorial demands reflected one of the broad principles this high-minded son of a Presbyterian minister brought with him to Versailles as representative of the United States. Wilson stood for national self-determination, the principle that ethnicity should determine national boundaries. He went to Versailles hoping to "make the world safe for democracy." This was manifest in his Fourteen Points, the blueprint of which Wilson had proclaimed in January 1918, and which he believed would bring lasting world peace. The U.S. president hoped that diplomacy would henceforth be carried out through "open covenants of peace," not secret treaties. Wilson believed that if the victorious powers applied "the principle of justice to all peoples and nationalities. . . whether they be strong or weak," Europe would enter an era of enduring stability.

The U.S. president's main concern at Versailles was with the creation of a League of Nations to arbitrate subsequent international disputes. He was less concerned with specific conditions of peace or forcing a punitive settlement on Germany. In Wilson's opinion, the Great War had been fought largely over the competing claims of national groups, magnified by the commitments of Great Power alliances, and it was not right to separate Rhineland Germans from Germany, as many people in Britain and France desired.

Wilson believed that the outbreak of the Great War had demonstrated that the diplomatic concept of a "balance of power," by which the predominant strength of one power was balanced by alliances between several other powers, was unequal to the task of maintaining peace. Henceforth, Wilson wanted the United States to assume an international role, joining

Territory lost by:
- Germany
- Bulgaria
- Austria-Hungary
- Russia
- Plebiscite areas remaining in country
- Demilitarized zone

MAP 26.1 TERRITORIAL SETTLEMENTS AFTER WORLD WAR I Territories lost by Germany, Austria-Hungary, and Bulgaria as a result of the treaties ending the Great War.

Great Britain, France, Italy, and Japan as permanent members of the League of Nation's Council. By this reasoning, the League would stand for collective security against any power that would threaten the peace.

Yet, as one journalist put it, "the policies of reality and idealism" were at odds at Versailles. Among the leaders of the three victorious powers, Wilson's idealism contrasted with the determined realism of Lloyd George and Clemenceau. All three men read and revised preliminary draft sections of the peace treaty prepared by committees and commissions of experts. As they met and worked together for four months, they wrestled with public pressure, particularly in France, for a harsh peace, which they had to balance against the possibility that a draconian settlement might push defeated Germany, Austria, and Hungary in the direction of the Soviet Union.

During the long sessions at Versailles, Clemenceau and Lloyd George gradually won the day. The Covenant of the League of Nations, which Wilson insisted be added to the treaty, reflected the treaty's nod in the direction of Wilsonian idealism. Wilson had promulgated his Fourteen Points in January 1918, in the midst of the stalemate on the western front. But the last year of the war had brought what appeared to be a decided British, French, and U.S. victory over Germany and its allies. Both Lloyd George and Clemenceau, unlike Wilson, enjoyed the full support of their constituents. French and British realism prevailed in what was called the "victor's peace."

By the "war guilt clause," Article 231 of the treaty, Germany accepted full responsibility for "the loss and damage" caused the Allies "as a consequence of the war imposed upon them by the aggression of Germany and her allies." Many Germans were outraged in April 1919, when they learned the severity of the harsh treaty that had been imposed on Germany. The Allies seemed to be punishing the new democratic German Republic for the acts of the old imperial regime. Premier Scheidemann resigned rather than sign the treaty. The next Social Democratic government signed it a week later, on June 28, 1919, but only after the Allies had threatened to invade Germany. The Treaty of Versailles returned to France Alsace and Lorraine, its two eastern provinces annexed by Germany after the Franco-Prussian War (see Map 26.2). French troops would occupy the parts of Germany that stood on the left, or western, bank of the Rhine, as well as occupying for fifteen years a strategically critical strip of land along its right bank. These territories were to remain permanently demilitarized. France would retain economic control over the rich coal and iron mines of the Saar border region (which would be administered by the League of Nations) for fifteen years, at which time the region's population would express by plebiscite whether it wished to remain German (which would be the result in 1935) or become part of France. Germany also had to cede small pieces of long-contested frontier territory to Belgium (Eupen and Malmédy).

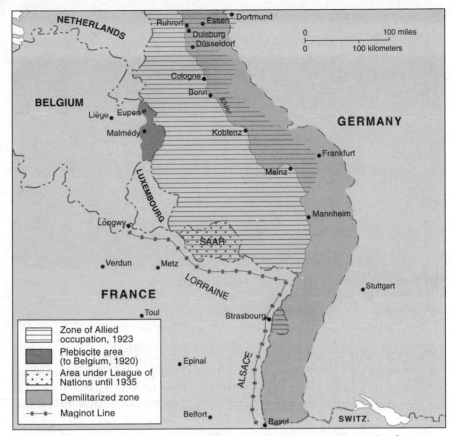

MAP 26.2 AREAS OF FRENCH AND GERMAN DISPUTES, 1920s   Border areas, including the Rhineland and the Saar Basin, which were occupied by Allied troops or part of a demilitarized zone after the Great War.

The German army was to be reduced from millions of wartime troops to the minimal figure of 100,000 volunteer soldiers. The German navy, now blockaded by the British fleet, would be limited to twelve warships, with no submarines, and Germany would be allowed no air force.

Furthermore, Germany was to pay a huge sum—132 billion gold marks, the estimated cost of the war to the victorious Allies—in war reparations (there was a precedent—France had had to pay an indemnity to the German Empire following the French defeat in the Franco-Prussian War of 1870–1871). As part of the reparations agreement in the treaty, the Weimar Republic would be required to turn over to the Allies much of its merchant fleet and part of its fishing fleet and railroad stocks, among other payments. The German Baltic shipyards were to build ships at no

The boxes contain currency that had rapidly lost value because of the out-of-control inflation and that the government is about to sell for gold on the foreign exchange market.

cost to the Allies. Each year, Germany was to give the Allies more than one-fourth of its extracted coal as further compensation.

But how was the new Weimar Republic to raise the remainder of the reparations? Tax revenues were low because the economy was so weak, and powerful German industrialists opposed the implementation of any new taxes on capital or business. The outflow of payments in gold fueled inflation as the government began to sell inflated currency for gold on the foreign exchange market. Government expenses far outweighed income, and prices began to rise far faster than in other countries, destabilizing the new Weimar government.

The reparations issue helped poison international relations in the 1920s. The Allies counted on German payments to help them attack the daunting economic problems of the post-war period. Indeed, the promise of German reparations enabled the British and French governments to accede to conservative demands that taxes not be raised or levies imposed on capital. But, in fact, only a small portion of the reparations were ever paid. Germany received three times as much in loans from the Allies than it paid out. Reparations, then, did not ruin the German economy, but their psychological impact in Germany damaged the very republic the Allies wanted to succeed. That the German parties of the right bitterly resented the burden of reparations compromised the ability of the Weimar Republic to survive.

France wanted the League of Nations to enforce the Treaty of Versailles and to assure German payment of reparations. (Germany was not permitted to join the League of Nations.) But with Lloyd George having successfully led opposition to the formation of a League of Nations army, the League had no way of enforcing its decisions against member—or, for that matter, nonmember—states that chose to ignore its principles or decisions.

After his six-month stay at Versailles, President Wilson returned to the United States to fight for Senate ratification of the treaty, with its provisions for the League. But the elections of November 1918 had given Wilson's Republican opponents control of the Senate. A majority of senators opposed U.S. membership in the League of Nations, fearing that the treaty would commit the nation to entanglements in Europe. Influenced by the large numbers of German, Italian, and Irish American constituents, some senators believed the treaty to be, respectively, too harsh on Germany, insufficiently generous to Italy, and irrelevant to Irish demands for independence from Britain. A mood of isolationism swept the country. The U.S. government refused to participate in the various international organizations set up to enforce the treaty and to air economic and security issues. In November 1919, the U.S. Senate rejected ratification of the Treaty of Versailles.

The absence of both the United States and the Soviet Union from the League doomed it to failure. The new Russian government had not even been invited to Versailles. There were two reasons for this: (1) the Bolsheviks had simply declared an end to the war in 1917 and withdrawn troops from the front; and (2) Great Britain, France, and the United States (distrusting the Bolsheviks, whose leader, Vladimir Lenin, boldly predicted the worldwide victory of communism) had sent troops and military supplies to support the anti-Bolshevik forces in the Civil War in Russia.

The Versailles Settlement left considerable nationalist dissatisfaction among Germany's wartime allies in Central Europe and the Balkans. Even among the victorious powers, the treaty generated some apprehension. It seemed a precarious peace. When Marshal Ferdinand Foch of France read the treaty, he exclaimed, "This isn't a peace, it's a twenty year truce!" He was right.

Settlements in Eastern Europe

A series of individual treaties, each named after a suburb of Paris, officially ended the war between the victorious Allies and the defeated Central Powers. Each treaty sought to recognize the claims of ethnic minorities of each country, in some cases redrawing national boundaries (see Map 26.1). But each also left the defeated country feeling aggrieved, adding to the number of "revisionist" states, that is, those nations that wanted the revision of the Versailles Settlement.

Bulgaria, one of the German wartime allies, lost territory, including its Aegean coast, ceded to Greece by virtue of the Treaty of Neuilly (November 1919), as well as small pieces of land to Romania. Following the Treaty of St. Germain (which specifically forbade Austrian union with Germany), Vienna was reduced to being the oversized capital of a small country; Austria now consisted of even less territory than the old German-speaking parts of the Habsburg domains. By the Treaty of Trianon (June 1920), Hungary lost 70 percent of its territory, as lands with a sizable non-Hungarian population were shifted to other national states. This left more Hungarians living beyond the borders of Hungary than within them.

The Treaty of Sèvres (August 1920), the most severe of the treaties with Germany's wartime allies, dismembered the Turkish Ottoman Empire. Britain, France, Italy, and Greece all coveted—as had the Russian and Habsburg empires in previous centuries—parts of the old Ottoman Empire that had stretched through much of the Middle East. Now the treaty awarded Smyrna, the region around present-day Izmir on the Anatolian peninsula, and Thrace to Greece; the island of Rhodes to Italy; Syria (including Lebanon) to France under mandate from the League of Nations; Iraq and Palestine to Britain, also under mandate from the League of Nations; and Saudi Arabia to Britain as a protectorate (see Map 26.3). Italian troops occupied Turkish territory even as the peace conference was proceeding; Greek forces moved into Smyrna and into Thrace.

In Turkey, the Italian and Greek occupations generated a wave of nationalist sentiment. Mustafa Kemal Pasha (1881–1938)—known as Atatürk—organized armed resistance against the foreign incursions. Turkish forces pushed Greek units out of Smyrna and threatened a neutral zone occupied by British troops. When the British government prepared to intervene, the Greeks were forced to withdraw from the Anatolian peninsula. The Treaty of Lausanne of 1923 left Turkey holding some territory on the European side of the straits, which were declared open to all nations. Italy and Greece had to settle for Turkish islands in the Aegean Sea. The Kurds, an ethnic minority within Turkey and Iraq, were left without an independent state. Atatürk became president of the Republic of Turkey, establishing his capital at Ankara in the interior of the Anatolian peninsula. Seeking to westernize and secularize his country, he promulgated legal codes separating church and state, implemented compulsory education and the Latin alphabet, and prohibited Turks from wearing the *fez* (a traditional brimless hat) on their heads.

NATIONAL AND ETHNIC CHALLENGES

President Wilson's espousal of ethnicity as the chief determinant of national boundaries had unleashed hopes among almost all the Eastern European peoples for independent states based on ethnic identities. The Treaty of Versailles accentuated the role of nationalism as a factor for political instability in Europe after the Great War. At the same time, the failure of the peacemakers at Versailles to address the demands of peoples

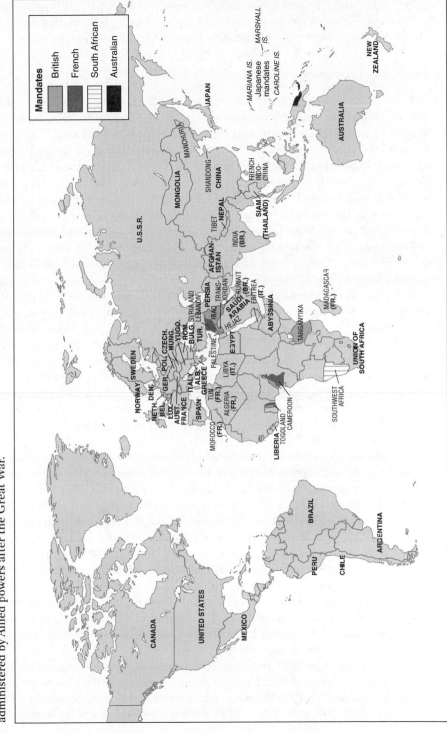

MAP 26.3 MANDATES UNDER THE LEAGUE OF NATIONS German colonies that were made mandates of the League of Nations and administered by Allied powers after the Great War.

colonized by the European powers left a legacy of mistrust, adding fuel to old nationalist movements determined to achieve independence (above all, in Ireland) and helping create new nationalist movements.

The National Question and the Successor States

The Treaty of Versailles created "successor" states out of the ruins of the Austro-Hungarian Empire, as well as out of the territories that had belonged to defeated Germany and the defunct Russian Empire. The creation of these new states by the Treaty of Versailles followed the principle of nationalism—that ethnicity should be the chief determinant of national boundaries—which had helped cause the Great War. The largest of these successor states were Poland and Czechoslovakia in Central Europe, and Yugoslavia in the Balkans. In the north, Finland finally gained its independence after having been for centuries subject to Swedish and, since the beginning of the nineteenth century, to Russian rule. The three Baltic states of Latvia, Estonia, and Lithuania also became independent of Russia (see Map 26.1).

Referring to the new states and redrawn boundaries, Winston Churchill complained "The maps are out of date! The charts don't work any more!" The creation of smaller national states (which Lloyd George referred to as "five-foot-five nations") whose boundaries were largely determined by ethnicity added to the number of independent states in Europe. This number had decreased since 1500 as absolute monarchies had expanded their territories, and with German and Italian unification in the nineteenth century it had further decreased. But after the war, that trend was suddenly reversed. In 1914, there had been fourteen currencies in Europe; in 1919, there were twenty-seven.

Post-war treaties did not create states that satisfied all the nationalities. Poland's extensive territorial claims brought it into conflict with other newly created states, including Lithuania, Czechoslovakia, and the Soviet Union. Religious differences compounded ethnic rivalries. Poland included about 6 million White Russians and Ukrainians who, unlike the Catholic Poles, were largely Orthodox Christians. Life for a Croat or Hungarian in Serb-dominated Yugoslavia seemed not much different than it had been under the Austrian-dominated Habsburg monarchy before the war; it was the same for an Orthodox Ukrainian who now found him- or herself living in the reborn state of Catholic Poland, not the Russian Empire; or a Slovak, who resented the domination of Czechoslovakia by the Czechs as much as he or she had resented the German-speaking bureaucrats of the Habsburg empire before the war.

But the Allies also had the strategic containment of communism in mind when they created these new national states as buffers between the Soviet Union and Western Europe. After the armistice of November 11, 1918, ended the Great War, the Allies permitted German armies to remain inside Russia, Ukraine, and Poland in order to prevent any attempt by the Red Army to carry the Russian Revolution into Central Europe. German troops continued to hold railway lines in the Baltic states in order to thwart any attempted Bolshevik takeover there.

Seeking security against Germany—as well as against the Soviet Union—Czechoslovakia, Romania and Yugoslavia formed the Little Entente by signing alliances in 1920 and 1921. They also sought collective security against Hungary and Bulgaria, both of which demanded revision of the Treaty of Versailles in order to win back territory lost to their new neighbors. Moreover, all three states depended on a series of alliances that each had signed with France. (Poland sometimes worked with these states to achieve mutually beneficial goals but did not formally join the alliance.)

The Allies, it must be said, applied Wilson's idealized formula of one people/one nation unequally when it came to those states that had fought against them in the war. Former German territories now formed the Polish Corridor dividing East Prussia from the rest of Germany. The port city of Danzig (now Gdansk) became a free city under the protection of the League of Nations. Mineral-rich Upper Silesia, claimed by Poland, remained part of Germany after a plebiscite. But in parts of Austria, where German-speaking majorities might have wanted to join Germany, the Allies specifically disallowed plebiscites.

Carved for the most part out of the old Habsburg Balkan domains, Yugoslavia was the most ambitious attempt to resolve the national question through the creation of a multinational state in which the rights of several nationalities would be recognized, at least in the territories they dominated. After complicated negotiations during 1917, the Serb government and a Yugoslav Committee made up of Croat and Slovene émigré leaders had agreed to form a new South Slav state when the war was concluded. They set up a provisional government even before an armistice had been signed. The new parliamentary monarchy would include Serbia, Montenegro, Croatia, Slovenia (which lies between northern Italy and Austria), Bosnia-Herzegovina and the smaller territory of Kosovo, where a majority of the populations had converted to Islam during the centuries of Turkish domination. Yugoslavia also absorbed part of Macedonia, which was populated by Bulgarians and Greeks detached by the Allies from defeated Bulgaria.

From its beginning, Yugoslavia was caught in a conflict between the "Greater Serb" vision of Yugoslavia, in which Serbia would dominate, and a federalist structure in which all nationalities and religions would play equal, or at least proportional, roles. Serbs, who are Orthodox Christians, were the largest ethnic group in Yugoslavia, but they remained a minority (43 percent, with the Catholic Croats accounting for about 23 percent). Belgrade became the capital of Yugoslavia, as it had been of Serbia. Middle-class Serbs held almost all of the key administrative, judicial, and military positions. That concentrations of Serbs lived in Croatia, and Croats in Serbia, complicated the rivalry between the two major peoples of the new state, who spoke essentially the same language, although the Serbs use the Cyrillic alphabet. Other major ethnic groups within Yugoslavia included Hungarians, Romanians, Bulgarians, Greeks, and German-speaking Austrians, as well as gypsies.

The case of Czechoslovakia also illustrates the complexity of the national question. In 1917, a National Council, made up of both Czechs and Slovaks, became a provisional government. The Slovak philosopher Thomas Masaryk (1850–1937), who had spent the war years making contacts in London in the hope of advancing the cause of an independent Czechoslovakia, became the president of the new state in 1918. He was extremely popular among both Czechs and Slovaks. But Czechs and Slovaks together made up only 65 percent of the population of the new country. Three million Germans living in the Sudetenland found themselves included within the borders of Czechoslovakia, as did three-quarters of a million Hungarians. Furthermore, Slovaks complained that promises of administrative and cultural autonomy within the Czechoslovak state were never implemented.

Facing similar economic, social, and political tensions, Poland became a dictatorship. General Joseph Pilsudski (1867–1935), one of the leaders of the Polish independence movement during the last decade of the Russian Empire, led a Polish legion that defended Warsaw in 1920 and drove the Soviet Red Army out of Poland. But the Polish economy lay in ruins. No rail links between Warsaw and other major cities had survived the war; tracks from Germany and Austria simply stopped at the Polish border. Six currencies circulated simultaneously. Inflation was rampant: a dollar was worth 9 Polish zlotys at the end of the war, 2.3 million in 1923! Deep divisions endured between nobles, who owned most of the land and had subverted central authority in virtually every period of Polish history, and the peasants, who demanded land reform. Fifty-nine different political parties existed in the early 1920s. As no party ever enjoyed a parliamentary majority, governments fell on an average of almost two a year. General Pilsudski, who had become chief of state in 1918, refused to stand for election for president in 1922 on the grounds that the constitution did not grant him sufficient executive authority, and resigned. He denounced political parties, criticized the parliamentary regime, and called for a "moral regeneration" of Polish life. In 1926, Pilsudski, backed by wealthy landowners and the army, overthrew Poland's parliamentary government. After saying that he would have to wait to see whether Poland could be governed "without a whip," he imposed his authoritarian rule.

Poland was the first of the Eastern European states to become a dictatorship in the post-war years. In Greece, King Alexander had died in 1920, after being bitten by his pet monkey. Parliament deposed his successor, and Greek political life lurched into an instability accentuated by the arrival of 1.5 million Greeks expelled from Bulgaria and Turkey following an agreement to repatriate populations to their respective home countries. In the small backward Muslim state of Albania on the coast of the Adriatic Sea, moderate reformers battled proponents of the old ways against a backdrop of Italian territorial claims and bullying. Harvard-educated King Zog (Ahmed Zogu; ruled 1928–1939), fearing for his life, fled to Yugoslavia in 1924. The next year, he invaded his own country with an army, assumed the presidency of the Albanian Republic, and set up a dictatorial monarchy in 1928.

In Bulgaria, King Boris III (ruled 1918–1943) was head of the country in name only. Alexander Stamboliski (1879–1923), leader of the Agrarian Union Party, elbowed opponents aside to become premier in 1919. He signed the Treaty of Neuilly, agreeing to try to prevent Macedonian nationalists from using Bulgarian territory to organize attacks inside Greece. Stamboliski assumed dictatorial powers in 1920. Army officers helped engineer a coup d'état in 1923, with the support of the king. Stamboliski fell into the hands of Macedonian nationalists, who cut off his right arm, which had signed the Treaty of Neuilly, then stabbed him sixty times, and decapitated him for good measure. The army killed about 20,000 peasants and workers who wanted reform. It was a sign of the times in the Balkans.

Colonial and National Questions

The peace treaties failed to address the rights—or lack of them—of people living in the colonies of the European powers. Some of these peoples demanded national independence, while others viewed themselves as being stateless. Representatives of ethnic, religious, and national groups—including the Irish, Persians, Jews, Arabs, Indians from the subcontinent, Vietnamese, Armenians, and American blacks—went to Versailles in the hope of attaining recognition of their national rights. Lloyd George denigrated these outsiders as "wild men screaming through the keyholes." The Allies refused to allow Ho Chi Minh (1890–1969), a young Vietnamese, to read a petition that asked that the Rights of Man be applied to the French colonies. Only the representatives of Zionist groups—Jews who wanted the creation of a Jewish national state in Palestine—and their anti-Zionist Jewish rivals ever made it into the conference halls, and then only briefly. Women's groups, too, sent in vain representatives who hoped to be heard at Versailles.

Britain, still the world's largest colonial power, refused to accept President Wilson's plan that the League of Nations or some other international board arbitrate the future of colonies. The British government refused to recognize the right of self-determination. Still, the war had altered the relationship between Britain and its colonies, as well as that between France and its empire. The Dominions (Britain's original "settlement colonies" of

Canada, South Africa, Australia, and New Zealand) had borne a considerable financial and material burden in the Great War. While they were not fully independent, each had a government responsible to its own citizens, and after the war each had its own delegation and signature at the peace conferences and each became a member of the League of Nations. Discussions now began to establish a "British Commonwealth," which was created in 1926 and formalized in 1931. In this union of Britain and the Dominions, each state would be independent and not subordinate to Britain but united by common allegiance to the crown.

The powers created the "mandate system" to deal with Germany's colonies. The latter were placed under the nominal authority of the League of Nations but were actually administered by Allied powers. Through this system, Britain increased the size of its empire by a million square miles, for example, by adding the former German colony of Tanganyika and parts of Togoland and the Cameroons as "mandate" colonies (see Map 26.3).

In Palestine, both Arabs and Jews had reason to be disappointed by the settlement. In 1915, the British government had promised some Arab leaders, in order to encourage Arab resistance against Germany's ally Turkey, that after the war Britain would support an independent Arab state. But a year later, the British and French governments had secretly drawn up plans to divide the Middle East into two spheres of influence. Moreover, in 1917 by the Balfour Declaration (see Chapter 24), Britain had promised to help Jews create a "national home" in Palestine, without necessarily promising to establish a Jewish state. Once the war ended, the promises disappeared in smoke at Versailles. Britain established mandates over Trans-Jordan (which would later become Jordan), as well as over Iraq and Palestine, each of which was ruled by viceroys responsible to the colonial office in London. Britain maintained informal control over Egypt and the Suez Canal even after nominal Egyptian independence in 1922. France established a mandate over Lebanon as well as over Syria.

But the British government could no longer put aside the challenge of the Irish movement for independence. The imposition of military conscription in Ireland in 1918 had angered many Irish, who felt no allegiance to the empire. The Irish Republican Army, which was organized from remnants of the rebel units disbanded after the ill-fated Easter Sunday insurrection against Britain in 1916, gained adherents amid high unemployment, strikes, and sectarian violence between Catholics and Protestants in largely Protestant Ulster (the six counties of northeastern Ireland). In a mood of mounting crisis, British Liberals wanted to begin negotiations as soon as possible with Irish political leaders. Conservatives, in contrast, wanted to crush the Irish Republicans. In the 1918 elections to the House of Commons, Irish voters elected a majority of members of Sinn Fein ("Ourselves Alone" in Gaelic), the Irish Republican political organization. The Sinn Fein members refused to take their seats in Parlia-

Irish republicans behind a barricade in Dublin.

ment and then unilaterally declared a republic. Parliament finally passed the Government of Ireland Act in 1920, dividing Ireland into two districts. The Catholic district in the south—most of the island—was to become a crown colony. Protestant Ulster would remain part of Britain.

Many, if not most, Catholic Irish, however, wanted nothing less than complete independence. The British government kept about 50,000 troops and 10,000 police in Ireland, including the "Black and Tans," a special police force that terrorized the Irish population that supported the Irish Republicans. More than a thousand people were killed in fighting during 1921, half of whom were British policemen or soldiers ambushed by the Irish Republican Army. In January 1922, the British Parliament went a step further, creating the Irish Free State, a Dominion within the British Commonwealth, although many Irish republicans demanded the severance of all formal ties to Britain and the creation of a republic. Ulster, or Northern Ireland, remained within the United Kingdom. Continuing sporadic sectarian violence in Ulster proved that tensions between the Protestant majority and Catholic minority, which did not accept British rule, would not subside.

In colonies that were part of the empires of the European powers, the Great War accentuated nationalist movements for independence. For example, in India, which the British viewed as the key to sustaining the British Empire (it served, for one thing, as a vast reservoir of soldiers for the army), a growing Indian national movement developed. In 1919, Indians held a protest in Amritsar in Punjab against the Rowlatt Acts, which allowed the government to forgo juries in political trials. The British army retaliated by massacring 400 Indian civilians, enraging Indian nationalists, who pointed out the sacrifices Indians had made during the war. Like the Sepoy Mutiny of 1857 (see Chapter 22), the incident exacerbated mutual suspicion and mistrust between Indians and British for decades. Following the war, France also repressed revolutionary nationalist movements in its colonies of Vietnam, Tunisia, Morocco, and the African island of Madagascar, as well as curbing those moderate groups who asked only for the extension of political rights.

Japan, also represented at Versailles, strengthened its position as the only Asian Great Power. Japanese armies were already taking advantage of the turmoil that followed the Bolshevik Revolution to grab land from the old Russian Empire in Asia. Furthermore, Great Britain, France, and Italy had secretly agreed in 1917, in exchange for active Japanese support against the German navy, to back Japanese demands for concessions China had been forced to grant Germany before the war. The Chinese delegation to Versailles in 1919 was unaware of this agreement; nor did it know that its warlord premier had secretly agreed, in return for Japanese loans, to grant Japan a full concession to build railways in the northeast province of Shandong (Shantung). When the Allies publicly agreed to Japanese claims, demonstrations and riots erupted in China. The May 4 (1919) movement in China, named for the day of the first major demonstrations in Beijing against the Treaty of Versailles, accentuated the development of Chinese nationalism.

ECONOMIC AND SOCIAL INSTABILITY

Because of the relief—and for the victors—exhilaration with which many Europeans greeted the end of the Great War, the 1920s has often been described as "the roaring twenties." Europeans thrilled to quests for record speeds or landmark travel by air and automobile. They gathered around radios, lined up to attend movies, watched football games or bicycle races, dressed in more casual clothing styles than ever before, crowded into cabarets and clubs, and danced late into the night.

However, the two decades following the Great War were marked by tremendous economic and social instability. The continent was wracked by inflation and unemployment, factors that exacerbated international tensions and rivalries and poisoned domestic political life in Germany, above all, but also in a number of other states reeling from the impact of the war. In Western Europe, particularly, after the long, bloody war finally ended and with the Russian Revolution fresh in mind, workers (and some womens' groups as well) put forward demands for better conditions of life. Economic and social elites were determined to overcome the challenge to their power launched by organized labor and the political parties of the left. But one of the results of the long ordeal of a war that had necessitated the mobilization of virtually all of the economic resources of the combatant powers was a growing determination among the parties of the political left that states ought to increase the services they provided their citizens. As such, the origins of the welfare state may in part be traced to the immediate post-war period.

Social Turmoil

The staggering economic disruption caused by the war contributed to the international disorder that ensued at its end. The conflict cost more than six times the national debts of all countries in the entire world from the end of the eighteenth century until 1914. Manufacturing and agricultural productivity fell dramatically during the conflict. Only countries far from the battlefields, such as the United States, Canada, India, and Australia, experienced economic growth. But they, too, could not escape high inflation and unemployment when the war ended. European states had borrowed vast sums of money to pay for the war; governments now began to print money to pay it back. This accelerated inflation. Prices were three times higher in 1920 in Britain than before the war, five times higher in Germany, and in an ominous sign of things to come, 14,000 times higher in Austria and 23,000 times higher in Hungary!

Soaring inflation and unemployment destabilized European political life. Workers resented what seemed to be a widening gap between themselves and the wealthy. The British press carried stories about well-placed entrepreneurs who had amassed fortunes selling war materials to the government, living it up while others died for their country and everyone else tightened their belts. The Conservative politician Stanley Baldwin referred to businessmen elected to Parliament in the first post-war election as "hard-faced men who looked as if they had done well out of the war."

Europe's business elite greeted the post-war era with some anxiety. Big businessmen, including French steel magnates and German arms producers, had emerged from the war with huge profits, enhanced by cartel arrangements within their industries that allowed them to monopolize production and set prices. These industrialists enjoyed greater prestige and political influence than ever before. With governments playing the leading role in establishing economic priorities, allocating resources, and recruiting labor during the war, fewer people now embraced the old classic liberal principle of laissez-faire. Some businessmen and state officials, impressed by the degree of wartime cooperation between state, business, and labor, believed these arrangements should be permanent. They hoped that corporate entities could be established in each major industry to coordinate production, ending competition between companies. Sometimes calling themselves "corporatists," and their ideas "corporatism," they believed that such cartel arrangements might well reduce or even eliminate the social and political tensions inherent in capitalist economies by forging an organized alliance of interests, including those of the state, big business, and labor.

For more than a half century, European economic elites had worked to preserve their power against the mounting challenge of organized labor and the political parties of the left. They did so, for example, by trying to maintain the elite character of higher education, pressuring governments to maintain high tariff barriers at the expense of consumers, seeking to limit government intervention in factory conditions, or trying to maintain legislation that restricted the right to strike. Above all, many people of means had wanted to keep their countries from adopting universal manhood suffrage or even democracy. Despite their efforts, however, the role of parliamentary bodies had expanded in every Western country during the last decades before the war, as universal manhood suffrage had come to France, Italy, Belgium, Norway, Sweden, and even imperial Germany.

Women's movements counted among the forces for democratization that gained considerably during the war. Having suspended their suffrage campaigns for the duration of the conflict, women's groups at the end of the war demanded recognition for their wartime contributions—when they had taken the place of conscripts in factories and fields. After the war, women won the right to vote in Germany, Scandinavia, and other countries in Western Europe—excluding Spain, Austria, Portugal, Switzerland—and ultimately in France (where an initial women's suffrage bill had failed in 1922). Women could also vote in the newly created states of Czechoslovakia, Poland, and Hungary. The legal position of women was probably strongest in Britain. Women voted for the first time in the British elections of December 1918, and the first woman was elected to the House of Commons soon after. The Sex Disqualification Act of 1919 opened the way for women to enter professions from which they had previously been excluded. But women who had taken men's jobs during the war gradually lost or abandoned their employment, many returning to domestic service. During the 1920s, the percentage of working women declined for the first time in many decades. Nonetheless, a greater variety of jobs became available to women. During the next two decades, many women found work in textile factories, commerce (including restaurants and hotels), transport, and in new jobs within the service sector (as hairdressers, department store clerks, or telephone operators). For many women, such jobs represented an advance in opportunity and conditions of work, although the harsh realities of economic life in the 1920s and 1930s cast a great shadow over these accomplishments.

Some Britons began to think that their nation, which, unlike its continental rivals, had avoided insurgency and revolution in the nineteenth century, might now be vulnerable to an uprising by dissatisfied workers influenced by the Bolsheviks. In Glasgow, Scotland's largest city, workers demanding a forty-hour workweek raised the Communist red flag on the town hall. But an attempt to call a general strike, organized by the "triple alliance" of railway workers, miners, and dock workers—the three largest unions—fizzled completely on April 15, 1921, "Black Friday" for British workers.

Conservative reaction in France to the Russian Revolution was similar. The French Employers Association printed thousands of posters showing a Bolshevik with a blood-stained knife between his teeth. The "National Block," drawing upon a wave of patriotism following the victory of the blue-clad French soldiers, won the 1919 elections, bringing a strongly nationalist majority to the "horizon blue" Chamber of Deputies. Many French conservatives, who before the war dreamed of a monarchical restoration or the overthrow of the republic by a military man, now supported the republic, as long as it was a conservative republic.

The labor movement gained strength in the immediate post-war period, but it failed to overcome the determined resistance of employers and national governments. In France, the General Confederation of Labor (C.G.T.), which had recruited hundreds of thousands of new members after the war, reached 2 million members in 1920, although the proportion of unionized workers remained small when compared to the proportion in Britain. In Italy, more than 3 million workers joined unions in the first two years of peace. Unions mounted massive campaigns to make the economy more democratic, a goal that was more revolutionary than bread and butter issues like hours, wages, and conditions of work. Strikes spread in all Western countries. In France, a general strike collapsed in May 1920. Union efforts failed to obtain the nationalization of key industries, such as French railroads, or German and British coal mines. Factory councils, which workers hoped would meet with employers to set production targets, wages, and conditions, had within a few years been eliminated in Germany, never got off the ground in France, and were quickly banned in Italy. Rates of unionization fell. "Corporatist" rhetoric gradually disappeared in Germany and France. Everywhere, with the notable exception of the Soviet Union, employers still called the shots.

The Left and the Origins of the Welfare State

The Great War was a devastating experience for the international socialist movement, which had in 1914 split into pro- and anti-war factions. The German Social Democrats and the socialist parties of France, Italy, and Belgium had rallied to the war effort of their respective countries after a few days of internationalist opposition to what they saw as a war between capitalists. The Russian Revolution of 1917, too, divided socialists. The Third Communist International, founded in Moscow in 1919, encouraged the organization of Communist parties in all countries. At the Congress of the French Socialist Party in Tours in December 1920, about a quarter of the delegates opposed joining the International. To the majority of delegates, the unexpected victory of the Bolsheviks in Russia suggested that socialists could come to power through a tightly organized, hierarchical party structure. Those delegates who remained in Tours founded the French Communist Party. Delegates who remained loyal to the French Socialist Party continued to accept reformism and thus loyalty to the republic, as well as to the democratic organization of their party.

In France, Léon Blum (1872–1950) led the Socialist Party. A Jew born into comfortable circumstances in Paris, Blum was an intellectual and literary critic who took a law degree and became a high government civil servant. Like his hero Jean Jaurès, the French socialist leader who had been assassinated in 1914 on the eve of the war, Blum was an idealist for whom socialism followed philosophically from what he considered the humanism of the French Revolution. Blum remained convinced that socialism would be achieved through the electoral process.

For Communists, the economic malaise of the 1920s seemed proof that capitalism's defeat was near. Furthermore, the defeat of most strikes after the war as well as conservative electoral victories in Britain, France, and Germany seemed to Communists to demonstrate that socialist participation in the political process or in conventional trade unions could only be self-defeating.

In two years, the French Communist Party grew as large as the Socialist Party. In 1922, on orders from Moscow, the party purged intellectuals from its membership. The Communist Party attracted many followers in the grim industrial suburbs of Paris, the "red belt" around the capital. Communist-dominated municipalities provided social services, such as unemployment relief funds and adequate light and drinking water for residents living in hastily constructed and insalubrious dwellings. In contrast, the British Communist Party, founded in 1920 and repudiated by the Labour Party, never attracted more than a few thousand followers.

Reformism dominated the parties of the left in post-war Europe. The German Social Democratic Party and the French Socialist Party participated in parliamentary alliances that underlay, respectively, the Weimar Republic and French moderate center-left governments. The British Labour Party, closely allied with the trade unions, emerged as the second largest party in Britain after the war. All three parties of the left depended, to a large extent, on the support of the reformist labor movements in their respective countries. In some ways, unions had become interest groups like any other, bargaining with governments and employers. To this extent, the Communist critics of union reformism may have been correct when they warned that reformism served to integrate workers into the structure of the capitalist state.

The emerging outlines of the welfare state in the 1920s reflected the pressure of the parties of the left and of trade unions. While the Communist parties of Europe espoused, at least in principle, working-class revolution, socialists and most union members demanded that states provide certain minimum protection for workers. Scandinavia, Denmark, Sweden, and Norway evolved into social democracies, implementing pathbreaking social services. The socialist municipal government of Vienna constructed attractive working-class housing on the edge of Vienna. This housing offered communal facilities, such as laundries, bathhouses, and kindergartens, for which residents paid a fee. The fortress-like structure, which provided 64,000 new apartments, reflected the new sense of political power influenced by Viennese workers.

British Prime Minister Lloyd George had promised demobilized soldiers "a country fit for heroes to live in." Although the reality was considerably less grand, the Housing and Town Planning Act of 1919 provided town councils with subsidies to encourage the construction of cheap row houses. This eliminated some slum overcrowding and provided many working-class families with centralized heating and bathrooms. Within old city limits, "council" flats paid for by town councils provided more modest lodgings for some of the poorest workers. In 1920, the British government expanded unemployment insurance coverage to include most industrial workers, and in 1925, Parliament granted pensions to war widows and orphans, major steps in the emergence of the British welfare state. The French Chamber of Deputies in 1930 provided insurance for 10 million workers.

POLITICAL INSTABILITY

The economic crisis that followed the war and the political instability it helped engender were nowhere clearer and ultimately more damaging than in Germany, where the new Weimar Republic sought to steer an even course between threats from the left and the right. Moreover, in Britain and France, states with established parliamentary governments, the subsequent division between left and right was no less bitter, though ultimately it was less bloody.

Germany's Fragile Weimar Republic

The lasting impact of the war on domestic and international politics was most visible in the new German Republic. The newly elected Reichstag adopted the red, gold, and black flag of the ill-fated 1848 Frankfurt Parliament (see Chapter 17). The civil strife in which the Weimar Republic made its start influenced its constitution, approved by the Reichstag in July 1919. The constitution left the German president, who was to be popularly elected, considerable powers. Serving a term of seven years, he could dissolve the Reichstag and call for new elections. Although ministers would be responsible to the Reichstag, the president also retained the power to suspend the constitution in order to restore order, and could rule by decree, leaving the republic vulnerable to the president's power.

Challenges to the republic came from the left and the right. In Bavaria, Kurt Eisner's rebel socialist republic collapsed. Following Eisner's murder by a rightist gunman in February, Bavarian leftists rose up again in Munich to proclaim a Soviet-style republic. When a general strike paralyzed Berlin in early March, members of the Free Corps and regular German soldiers from Prussia gunned down several thousand workers and socialists.

The new republic desperately needed political stability. But many members of several key social groups, including many bureaucrats and university professors who had received their posts under the empire, did not support the republic from the beginning. Several magistrates revealed their views by handing down absurdly light sentences to members of the Free Corps who had been arrested for murder.

Groups of army officers began to plot against the republic during the summer of 1919. Conservative politicians and businessmen attempted a coup d'état, or "putsch," led by Wolfgang Kapp, a former Prussian imperial bureaucrat, with the goal of overthrowing the republic. The Kapp Putsch occurred as the German army was about to be reduced radically in size according to the terms of the Treaty of Versailles. On March 20, 1920, the rebels took over Berlin. The conservative parties proclaimed their support for the new government. In Bavaria, right-wingers forced the resignation of the socialist state government and took over. With the republic on shaky ground, Chancellor Ebert appealed to the workers to defend the republic. They responded by launching a general strike that shut down much of the country. When some Berlin army units began to waver, the putsch collapsed.

But the threat to the republic was not over. The center and center-left parties of the Weimar coalition all suffered substantial losses in subsequent elections, while the conservative parties and radicals gained. When the Social Democrats withdrew from the government, the republic depended on a shaky coalition of Center Party politicians and moderate right-wing parties less committed than the Social Democrats to the republic they now governed. As Germany's economy floundered in ruinous inflation, political instability and violence mounted. In August 1921, two former army officers gunned down the Catholic Center Party leader who had signed the armistice ending the war.

Walter Rathenau (1867–1922), the new foreign minister, was determined to negotiate the reparations issue with British and French officials. He attempted to stop rampant German inflation by delivering goods to the Allies rather than gold as reparations. While a hastily arranged conference at Geneva took place, Rathenau shocked Britain and France by signing a statement of mutual friendship with the Soviet Union, the Rapallo Treaty (April 1922), to counter Western pressure. The Soviet Union received German technical assistance, which it paid for by helping Germany evade some of the military stipulations of the Treaty of Versailles. Subsequently German officers provided technical assistance to the Soviet army. The Soviets, winning diplomatic recognition and German acquiescence to its repudiation of debts contracted under tsarist rule, renounced any future war reparations from Germany. Two months later, right-wing nationalists murdered Rathenau.

The German mark plunged dramatically in value. The Weimar government informed the Allies that it could not meet the schedule of cash reparations payments, but that it would continue payments of coal and other natural resources. With the United States pressuring Britain and France to repay their war debts, the Allies grew all the more determined that Germany pay up. France's new premier, Raymond Poincaré (1860–1934), threatened a military occupation of the Ruhr if Germany failed to meet the reparations schedule. He accused Germany of deliberately withholding payments and trying to force the Allies to make concessions by ruining its own currency.

Britain and France, however, could not agree on a common policy. The French refused a German request for a moratorium so that the mark could be stabilized. The resentful German government, backed by virtually all parties except the Communist Party, called on the miners of the Ruhr region to stop working for the Allies. This seemed to confirm Poincaré's contention that Germany was sabotaging repayment of its war debts.

On January 11, 1923, against the advice of the British government, French and Belgian troops occupied the Ruhr. When the German government began to finance the passive resistance in the Ruhr by simply printing more money with which to pay its miners not to work, inflation in Germany spiraled completely out of control, as Table 26-1 luridly demonstrates.

In 1923, Germans wheeled shopping carts filled with literally trillions of marks down the street in order to pay for a single loaf of bread. Apples went for 300 billion marks a half pound. Employees asked to be paid their wages each morning so that they could shop at noon before merchants posted the afternoon price rises. Spiraling inflation wiped out people with fixed incomes and small savings they had put aside for retirement. Many of

TABLE 26-1. THE MARK AND THE DOLLAR, 1914–1923

Date	Rate: 1 dollar =
July 1914	4.2 marks
January 1919	8.9
July 1919	14.0
January 1920	64.8
July 1920	39.5
January 1921	64.9
July 1921	76.7
January 1922	191.8
July 1922	493.2
January 1923	17,972.0
July 1923	353,412.0
August 1923	4,620,455.0
September 1923	98,860,000.0
October 1923	25,260,208,000.0
November 15, 1923	4,200,000,000,000.0

Source: Gordon Craig, *Germany 1866–1945* (New York: Oxford University Press), p. 450.

A German man sells apples for 30 billion marks per half pound in 1923.

those who believed that they had done their patriotic duty by buying war bonds during the war now blamed the Weimar Republic when those bonds became worthless. No salaries could possibly have kept pace with such runaway inflation. The poor found staples and other goods not only ridiculously expensive but often unavailable at the market as farmers hoarded produce. Nonetheless, those people who were able to pay off bank loans with wildly inflated currency or to invest in property did well. The rich got richer. In such an atmosphere, the German Communist Party attracted workers in great numbers, undercutting the Social Democrats.

In August 1923, Ebert turned to Gustav Stresemann (1878–1929) to form a government. Stresemann, a former monarchist, had been converted (principally by right-wing violence and political murders) to the republic. Governing by decree and supported by the Social Democrats, he convinced the miners to go back to work, and to cease their passive resistance in the Ruhr. France and Belgium ended the occupation after a nine-month period that had been as financially damaging to those nations as ruinous to Germany. German government printing presses stopped cranking out billion-mark notes and issued a new mark, which was equal to a trillion of the old marks. The hyperinflation ended.

Stresemann hoped to meet the Allied demands as much as possible, and in doing so, open the way for Germany's return to respectability as a European power. He hoped that this might clear the way for future Allied concessions, namely on Germany's disputed eastern frontier with the newly independent state of Poland. Stresemann convinced both Britain and France to provide loans to help Germany emerge from the economic crisis.

In 1924, a League of Nations commission, chaired by an American banker, Charles G. Dawes (1865–1951), extended the schedule for payment of German reparations. The Dawes Plan left the Reichsbank partially under the direction of an American commissioner who was to oversee German payments, but it did not lower the amount Germany was expected to pay. Meanwhile, the United States had reduced the debt the Allies owed it by percentages ranging from 30 percent (Britain) to 80 percent (Italy). Still, the Dawes Plan improved relations between the Allies and Germany and, with the revival of the European economy beginning in 1924, the reparations issue receded in importance. The Weimar Republic seemed to find stability as the economy finally began to improve. German industries became more competitive, and unemployment began to decline.

Stresemann's discreet and effective diplomacy, now as foreign minister, paid off. The Treaty of Locarno, signed in 1925 between Great Britain, France, Italy, Belgium, and Germany, signaled Germany's gradual return to international respectability. The following year, Germany became a council member of the League of Nations, in return for agreeing that it would not seek to alter its western boundaries with France and Belgium. The signatories at Locarno pledged to settle all future controversies peacefully. However, the Treaty of Locarno did not address the problem of Germany's eastern borders, which the German government refused to include in the agreement. European leaders and newspapers now began to refer to the "spirit of Locarno," a mood of increasing international cooperation.

Nonetheless, German right-wing parties could never forgive Stresemann for collaborating with the socialists. The opponents of the republic seemed almost more vehement in their denunciations of Weimar when it succeeded than when it failed. Success might generate stability and survival. Even after what appeared to be a diplomatic victory for Weimar, German elections reflected the renewed strength of the right; the old Prussian warrior General von Hindenburg was elected president upon Ebert's death in 1925.

The Established Democracies: Britain and France

Britain and France were, to be sure, not immune from the political tensions of the post-war period. Britain, in particular, remained a class society, despite the intermarriage of aristocratic and industrial families at the top of the social hierarchy. Nowhere in Europe was the concentration of wealth so marked as in Britain. One percent of the population possessed two-thirds of the national wealth, and one-tenth of 1 percent owned a third of the land in England. Education, occupation, dress, accent, the newspapers one read, and leisure all defined and revealed the social class to which one belonged. The distance between the elegant country gentleman or the top-hatted London banker, and the Yorkshire factory worker, the London East End docker with his cloth cap, or the rough-hewn agricultural laborer, remained as great as in the eighteenth century.

Britain's Conservative Party swept to victory in the "khaki" elections (so called because of the color of British army uniforms) held in December 1918 following the armistice. The Labour Party benefited from the decline of the Liberal Party, whose major nineteenth-century issue, free trade, now appealed to relatively few voters. Labour gained the support of most new voters. In 1924, Ramsey MacDonald (1866–1937), a skilled orator who moved in the most elegant social circles, formed the first Labour government. He preached "the inevitability of gradualness," and "the futility of violence."

The fall of MacDonald's Labour government after several months demonstrated the resilience of British Conservatives, as well as a widespread fear of communism. The Conservatives denounced MacDonald after his government became the first to accord official recognition to the Soviet Union. The press fanned the flames of a "red scare," similar to one then sweeping the United States. A newspaper published a letter it claimed had been written by Gregory Zinoviev, the head of the Communist International, detailing for British Communists ways of destabilizing the government. In fact, the letter was a forgery, the work of a Polish anti-Bolshevik. Returned to power, the Conservatives were determined to restore financial stability and to reject working-class demands. The government put Britain back on the gold standard in 1925, which meant that pounds sterling could be exchanged for gold according to a fixed rate of exchange. But this depleted the amount of gold reserves available to back the British currency and led to the pound's overvaluation. British products became more expensive on the international market, particularly when the other European powers stabilized their own currencies at lower rates. British manufacturing, the key to prosperity for more than a century, remained sluggish, its markets increasingly challenged by those of the United States and Japan. The United States had become by far the leading creditor nation. New York City was now the new center of international finance.

In Britain, tensions between industrialists and workers came to the fore in 1926. The mines still employed over a million workers, more than any other industry. After the war, the mining companies had reduced wages and lengthened the workday. A government commission in March 1926 recommended that firms implement safer working conditions, but that the miners accept lower wages. The miners rejected these conclusions with the slogan, "Not a minute on the day, not a penny off the pay." The Trade Union Council launched a general strike of miners in defense of the unions in May 1926. The vast majority of unionized workers in Britain went out in solidarity. The strike enraged the upper and middle classes, inconvenienced by the shutdown of all public transportation. Conservative Winston Churchill castigated the strikers as "the enemy," demanding their "unconditional surrender" as if he were talking about a German bunker in the war. The Labour Party was sympathetic to the plight of the workers,

A barricade during the London General Strike, 1926.

but maintained a safe political distance. Businessmen and students from Oxford and Cambridge Universities drove buses and trucks carrying peo ple in and out of London while troops hauled food. After two weeks, most workers had returned to their jobs (although the miners remained on strike for seven months). The strike was broken. A year later, Parliament passed the Trade Disputes Act, which forbade "sympathy strikes," walk- outs in support of striking workers by those in other industries, and which marked the defeat of labor militancy in Britain.

In France, too, conservatives held the upper hand in political life after the war; with the exception of 1924–1926, they held the reins of govern- ment until 1934. That France had won the Great War suggested to many people that no pressing need existed to implement political reforms. Social elites feared the left. Some increasingly blamed the institutional structure of the republic itself for France's malaise. Political power rested in the Chamber of Deputies; the president, elected by the chamber, had little power.

When the French franc, long considered to be invulnerable to economic shocks, collapsed in value in a financial panic in 1924, the rightist govern- ment went with it. A coalition of Radicals and Socialists, sharing little more than anticlericalism, formed a left-center government. But this al- liance broke apart when the Socialists suggested a sizable tax on capital as a solution to the economic crisis. The government fell in April 1925, suc- ceeded by ministries that came and went with bewildering regularity.

In 1926, the conservative Poincaré returned as premier. He raised taxes on consumption, which the wealthy preferred to levies on capital, because the burden did not fall on them. The franc stabilized, as wealthy Frenchmen brought assets back from abroad and began to buy francs, which then rose rapidly in value. Poincaré became known as the savior of the French currency. But his idea that political consensus existed in France was, like the belief that France was the most powerful country in Europe, only an illusion. Many ordinary French men and women believed that a "wall of money" still held the country hostage and, along with an entrenched bureaucracy, prevented social reform. The Chamber of Deputies increasingly came to be seen as a debating society incapable of responding effectively to domestic and international crises. Political and social tensions, which exceeded those in Britain, encouraged the disillusionment with democracy felt by parties of the political extremes such as the French Communist Party on the one hand, and the fledgling fascist movements intrigued by Mussolini's seizure of power in Italy on the other.

ARTISTS AND INTELLECTUALS IN THE WASTELAND

The effects of the Great War could also be easily seen in European intellectual and artistic life, as writers and painters wrestled with the consequences of a devastating struggle that stood as a great divide between the present and a world that was no more. Thus, a veteran of the trenches described the war's cataclysmic destruction as "a cyclopean dividing wall in time: a thousand miles high and a thousand miles thick, a great barrier laid across our life." Indeed, the resulting cultural uncertainty reflected the economic, social, and political chaos of the period.

The defiant modernism of artists and intellectuals in the wake of the war reflected a revolt against traditional cultural conventions within the arts but also against the strictures of bourgeois society. In Britain, for example, people still read Victorian novels and romantic poetry, but such texts seemed to offer no explanation for what had gone wrong in Europe. Horrified by the war, many artists and writers now rejected the social conventions that had inculcated the values of nationalism and blind obedience. In the wake of the war, the "outsiders" of the Belle Époque had become, at least in the realm of the arts, "insiders." To be sure, most of the experimentation and dramatic changes in artistic expression that followed the war had their origins in the pre-war years, for example the adoption of psychological, subjective themes and approaches to painting and writing. The war had destroyed not only millions of lives but many of the signposts by which artists and writers defined reality. The American writer Gertrude Stein (1874–1946), who bounced back and forth between her artist and writer friends in London and Paris, called the war's survivors "a lost generation." In a 1922 lecture, the French poet Paul Valéry (1871–1945) said "The storm has died away and still we are restless, uneasy, as if the storm were about to break . . . among all these injured things is the mind. The mind has indeed been cruelly wounded. . . . It doubts itself profoundly."

The bleak 1922 poem *The Waste Land,* by American-born poet and critic T.S. Eliot (1888–1965), reflected the impact of the war.

A heap of broken images, where the sun beats,
And the dead tree gives no shelter, the cricket no relief,
And the dry stone no sound of water . . .
Hooded hordes swarming . . .
Falling towers
Jerusalem Athens Alexandria
Vienna London
Unreal

The dadaists, a group of artists who had gathered in Zurich in 1916, were the first to rebel against the absurdity of the slaughter of 1914–1918 by rejecting all artistic convention. They wrote poems that consisted of words gathered from newspapers. They penned and painted nonsense; "dada" is French for babytalk. It was all nonsense, but no more, some argued, than the war itself.

The artists and writers of the post-war generation stressed the primacy of subjectivism. Like soldiers emerging from the ghastly trenches, they looked into themselves in the quest for survival. Their subjectivism unleashed their imaginations, and this defined much of the new art.

The painters Paul Klee (1870–1940) and Max Beckmann (1884–1950), among others, defied viewers with the primitiveness of their vibrant colors and lines. They thumbed their noses at classical rules about painting, and even about what constituted art. The Dutch modernist painter Piet Mon-

A dada poster, 1920.

drian (1872–1944) offered two-dimensional abstractions and straight lines forming grids. Klee's fantasies assumed unexpected shapes and distortions on the canvas; "the artist must distort," he contended, "for therein is nature reborn."

The expressionist movement, too, had its origins before the war. Beckmann rejected the label, but defined the movement when discussing his own work, "What I want to show in my work is the idea which hides itself behind so-called reality. I am seeking the bridge which leads from the visible to the invisible." Expressionist poets rejected linguistic conventions in an attempt to communicate the emotion buried beneath the human exterior. Expressionist playwrights ignored long-established conventions of plot, character, and dialogue in order to represent what they considered to be unseen reality. In his epic *Ulysses* (1922), the Irish writer James Joyce (1882–1941) abandoned long-accepted stylistic constraints to present the chaotic and seemingly unconnected—at least at first glance—"stream of consciousness" dialogue of three characters, through which he revealed all their sensations and feelings. The novel's eroticism led it to be banned in Britain (but not in traditionally prudish Ireland), and in the United States until 1933. Joyce reflected the disillusionment of the 1920s, as he wrestled with the tragedy of so many men dying for abstractions like nationalism. Joyce had spent the war in neutral Switzerland; pacifism is a prevalent theme in *Ulysses* because of the war's searing impact, but also because in his native Ireland British troops were shooting down civilians.

In 1924, a group of nineteen painters and writers, led by the French artist and poet André Breton (1896–1966), published a "Surrealist Manifesto." In it they rejected "traditional humanism" and the respect for reason that seemed to have so manifestly betrayed mankind. The surrealists were obsessed with the crater-pocked landscape of churned-up earth, tree stumps, and the twisted rubble of northern France and Belgium. They sought to shock audiences and viewers by expressing themselves in a spontaneous, deeply personal, but realistic way. Breton's work sometimes defies interpretation because none was intended.

After four years in the trenches, the German surrealist Max Ernst (1891–1976) wrote that he had "died on the first of August 1914 and returned to life on the 11th of November 1918." Ernst joined a circle of dadaists in Cologne. His 1933 painting *Europe after the Rain (I)* depicts with oil and plaster what appears to be a distorted, disfigured, and unsettling aerial relief map of Europe. It suggests the mutilation of the continent, which appears to be slowly swallowing itself.

For his part, the Viennese doctor Sigmund Freud, founding father of psychoanalysis, believed that the war demonstrated the irrational nature of mankind. Freud's scientific analysis of the unconscious, translated into many languages during the 1920s, had begun to influence sociologists, political scientists, and cultural anthropologists. They applied ideas drawn from psychoanalysis in order to try to understand group behavior and social conflict. The war lent a sense of urgency to that enterprise. Freud also

Max Ernst's *Europe after the Rain (I)* (1933).

greatly influenced surrealists such as Breton, who trained as an analyst and drew images and words from his dreams. Some of Freud's early ruminations about the role of the unconscious in art were based on the haunting trauma of seeing shell-shocked soldiers.

THE RISE OF FASCISM

In 1912 in the "Manifesto of Futurism," the work of a small but influential avant-garde futurist movement, which was centered in Italy, had praised "the love of danger, the habit of energy and rashness." "Beauty exists only in struggle," the futurists insisted, seeking to glorify war as "the only cure for the modern world." This embracing of struggle and violence found its first institutionalized form in Italy, where the first fascist state was established.

In Germany, too, a right-wing anti-parliamentary movement—National Socialism, or Nazism—was gaining strength. It was built on nationalist frustrations resulting from defeat in the war. Adolf Hitler's Nazis also drew on widespread economic discontent and fear of socialism and communism. Nazis, like Italian fascists, espoused dictatorial rule. Whereas parliamentary government had been only superficially implanted in Italy, Germany had almost no democratic political traditions at all. Nazism was a mass movement, also like Italian fascism. It would draw on the support of hundreds of thousands of ordinary people in its assault on parliamentary government.

Mussolini and Fascism in Italy

The economic and social tensions of the immediate post-war period desta-bilized Italy's liberal government. The dissatisfaction of Italian nationalists with the Treaty of Versailles, which had awarded Istria and Northern Dal-matia, territories along the Adriatic coast, to the new Yugoslav state, ac-centuated Italy's political crisis. This made Italy, in many ways unified in name only, vulnerable to a growing threat from the right.

Gabriele D'Annunzio (1863–1938), a bombastic, decadent poet, had in 1914 described war as perfect hygiene for the modern world. Having pro-claimed "I am not, and do not wish to be, a mere poet," he now took mat-ters into his own hands. In September 1919, the decorated war veteran who had lost an eye in combat swept into the Adriatic city of Fiume (Ri-jeka). He led a force of 2,000 men, many of whom were demobilized sol-diers like himself. D'Annunzio planted the Italian flag, forcing the Italian government to begin negotiations with the new Yugoslav state, which also claimed the port. Both countries agreed that Fiume would be independent, but that most of Istria and Northern Dalmatia would remain in Yugoslavia, as the Treaty of Versailles had specified. D'Annunzio's little republic lasted sixteen months, until Italian ships lobbed a few shells in the general direc-tion of the city and sent the poet and his small army packing.

Even in failure, D'Annunzio had stolen the thunder of another fervent Italian nationalist, Benito Mussolini (1883–1945). Mussolini was born to a family of modest means in the Romagna region in northern Italy. His fa-ther was a blacksmith, as well as something of a revolutionary who had taught himself to read from socialist tracts and named his son after the Mexican revolutionary, Benito Juarez. The young Mussolini was a bully in school who was quick to raise his fists and pull a knife, once stabbing a girl-friend. He had no close friends—at least after the death of his brother in 1931—and was proud of it ("keep your heart a desert," he once advised).

The young Mussolini read Karl Marx and Friedrich Nietzsche, whose espousal of daring revolt and the "will to power" intrigued him. After a stint in the army, Mussolini proclaimed himself a socialist and anti-mili-tarist and became a political journalist. With other anti-militarists, he took to the streets to denounce Italy's colonial war against Libya (see Chapter 23). Late in 1912, Mussolini became editor of the Italian Socialist Party's newspaper, *Avanti!* At the outbreak of the Great War in 1914, Mussolini led a chorus of socialists demanding that Italy remain neutral.

During the first year of the war, Mussolini's views toward war changed. He wrote that the turmoil of the war might bring about social revolution; "only blood," he wrote, "makes the wheels of history turn." This chilling conclusion demonstrated that the influence of Nietzsche was overwhelm-ing that of Marx in Mussolini's mind. Angered by the opposition his view encountered among socialists, Mussolini began another newspaper that would reflect his views alone.

In October 1914, a small number of syndicalists broke away from the

Socialist Party, demanding that Italy join the war. They took the name "fascists" from the Roman word *fascio,* meaning a bundle of sticks, or, by extension, an association. When Italy entered the war in 1915, Mussolini joined the army. Lightly wounded in 1917, he returned to journalism. As the German and Austro-Hungarian armies suffered major defeats in 1918, Mussolini led the chorus of nationalist demands for a peace settlement favorable to Italian interests. In March 1919, he founded his own fascist organization, which he called the National Fascist Party.

The post-war crisis of Italy's liberal state aided the fascists. The major parties of Italy—the Liberals, the Socialists, and the new Catholic Popular Party—struggled in vain to find consensus. While governments formed and fell in quick succession, severe economic difficulties continued to plague Italy in the immediate aftermath of the armistice. Hundreds of thousands of demobilized troops joined the ranks of the unemployed. Following a brief post-war boom, inflation soared, eroding middle-class savings and undercutting the already low standard of living of workers and landless peasants. Agricultural depression compounded high unemployment.

As in Britain, France, and Germany, Italian workers flocked to organized labor, and waves of strikes spread in 1919 and 1920. Peasant laborers demanded land and formed unions called "red leagues." In the south, thousands of poor families had begun to occupy some of the vast, often uncultivated holdings belonging to large landowners. Banditry became even more prevalent in southern Italy and Sicily.

During these "red years" of 1920–1922, many landowners and businessmen turned against parliamentary government. In Italy more than in any other country, there was considerable interaction and interdependence between urban and rural elites. The Liberal government had alienated the wealthy by proposing a progressive tax on income and a high imposition on war profits, and outraged them by legalizing peasant land seizures. Uniformed squads of fascists intervened on behalf of wealthy landowners and businessmen, attacking syndicalists, Socialists, and Communists. Laborers and sharecroppers fought back against the fascist "black shirts," but had little chance because the landowners supplied these gangs with weapons. The left was divided and hesitant.

In contrast to France, where post-war strikes strengthened the conservative republican government that had been elected in 1919, labor militancy brought down the helpless Italian government. Mussolini, boasting a private army and a sizable claque, or "applause squad," of paid supporters, praised the "bath of blood" that swept parts of Italy. He reveled in rumors of a coup d'état associated with his name, cranking out violent articles denouncing parliamentary government.

In 1921, the Liberals, hoping to find a parliamentary mandate to impose order, offered the fascists qualified support and accepted them as electoral allies. Mussolini and several dozen other fascists were elected to the Italian Parliament. The fascist leader now had an ideal soapbox for his flamboyant oratory, as well as immunity from prosecution. The government of Giovanni Giolitti resigned, succeeded by yet another coalition government.

The fascists were now a powerful political movement with prominent allies, money, newspapers, and hundreds of thousands of members. Fascist thugs had carved out territories in which their word was law. They disrupted local political life, shattering the organization, confidence, and support for the traditional parties. Mussolini, who now took the title of Duce, or "leader," presented himself as a defender of law and order, blaming Socialists and the newly formed Communist Party for the turmoil. Fascists enjoyed the tacit support of many state and police officials, as fascist violence went unpunished. Some prelates within the Church hierarchy began to speak warmly of Mussolini.

For Mussolini, fascism was a theory of violent confrontation, a means of winning and maintaining political power, more than a coherent doctrine of political philosophy. Fascists espoused a strong, virulently nationalist, militarized state with which all Italians must identify: "Everything within the State, Nothing outside the State, Nothing against the State," was how Mussolini put it. Italy would fulfill its "historic destiny."

In October 1922, Mussolini made his move. He pressured the diminutive, indecisive King Victor Emmanuel III (ruled 1900–1946), a shy man who loved to hunt, wear military uniforms, and collect coins, to name him and several other fascists to cabinet posts. The king remained out of Rome for weeks at a time as the crisis built, hoping that it would simply go away. As he planned a coup d'état, Mussolini charmed members of the royal family. He told 40,000 fascists in Naples, "either we are allowed to govern, or we will seize power by marching on Rome." The prime minister asked the king to declare martial law and to use the army to restore order by suppressing the fascists, who had seized control of several towns.

It was typical of the king, who combined indecision and fatalism, that he declared a state of emergency, then changed his mind even as thousands of black-shirted fascists began to surge toward Rome on the night of October 27. Mussolini took a comfortable night train to the capital. When another aged politician refused the king's request to form a government, Victor Emmanuel turned to Mussolini. On October 29, the Duce became prime minister. Fascists celebrated in the streets by beating up political enemies and closing down newspapers.

Despite the fact that his party held a small proportion of the seats in the chamber and could not claim the party allegiance of a single senator, Mussolini convinced both bodies to grant him full powers to rule by decree for a year. Many mainstream politicians endorsed him because the fascists promised to restore social order. They also assumed that Mussolini could not long survive once he was brought into respectable political life.

Mussolini's shrewd management of fascist newspapers and his ability to plant favorable articles in other papers through cajoling and bribery

(*Left*) Mussolini (in back seat) on his way from the train station after being asked to form a government. (*Right*) The Duce and his sovereign, Victor Emmanuel III.

helped win further support. Aided by the intimidating tactics of the fascist militia, the National Fascist Party won enough votes in the 1923 elections to emerge as the majority party, at least with the support of the Catholic Popular Party.

Despite a major political crisis in 1924 that followed his implication in the murder of a Socialist deputy by fascists, Mussolini developed an almost cult-like following. The Duce encouraged the phrase "Mussolini is always right" and managed to convince millions of people that this was indeed the case. He was the first politician of the twentieth century to make use of modern communication techniques. He subsidized several films about his accomplishments; his rambling speeches, voluminous tomes, an autobiography, and several authorized biographies were sold in various glossy editions. By the early 1930s, Italian journalists were required to capitalize He, His, and Him when referring to Mussolini, as they did when mentioning God or Jesus Christ. All Italians at age eighteen had to take an oath to obey Mussolini. Italian press agents worked to enhance his image abroad. In Britain, playwright George Bernard Shaw thought well of the Duce; in Vienna, Sigmund Freud at first praised him; the American poet Ezra Pound remained an admirer. The U.S. ambassador saluted "a fine young revolution" and *Time* magazine put him on its cover eight times.

Not long after Mussolini took power, however, French newspapers began to describe him as a Carnival Caesar. The tag stuck. The Duce strutted about, boasting egregiously, his eyes rolling and his chin jutting out as he piled falsehood upon exaggeration. He insisted that officials and assistants sprint to his desk and ordered photographers to take pictures of him running by troops he was reviewing, fencing, or playing tennis. Mussolini obnoxiously boasted of his sexual energy and prowess. But despite his insistence that he be portrayed as dynamic and hard-working, he was rather lazy and unable to concentrate on any one thing for very long. Mussolini was an actor, the balconies from which he thundered speeches his stage.

Mussolini, who wore so many military decorations that a foreign journalist wrote that he "looked like a circus performer in off hours," planned an army of "eight million bayonets" and an air force that would "blot out the sun." But despite Mussolini's attempt to project an image of fascism that emphasized youthful physical vigor, relatively little military training actually took place in Italy.

The Duce took over the most important operations of the state and was like an orchestra conductor trying to play all of the instruments at once. He warned ministers not to disagree with him because they might divert him "from what I know to be the right path—my own animal instincts are always right." Officials reported only what they thought Mussolini wanted to hear. The consequences in international affairs would be catastrophic, as the gap between Mussolini's assessment of Italy's military strength and reality widened.

Mussolini treated domestic policy as an afterthought, once claiming that "to govern [Italy], you need only two things, policemen, and bands playing in the streets." But in order to placate a potentially powerful source of opposition, Mussolini made peace with the Catholic Church—

Mussolini addressing a crowd at a stadium in Venice.

Italian women mobilize for Mussolini.

fascist squads had smashed Catholic workers' cooperatives along with similar Socialist organizations. In 1929, the Duce signed the Lateran Pacts with the Church, a "Concordat" that left the Vatican an independent papal enclave within Rome. In exchange, the papacy for the first time officially recognized Italy's existence. The Italian dictator returned religious instruction to all schools, and banned freemasonry, swearing in public, all literature that the Church considered obscene, and the sale of contraceptives. Mussolini won Catholic support with his pro-natal campaign (which included a tax on "unjustified celibacy"), vague statements about the importance of the family, measures limiting Protestant publications, and fulminations against women participating in sports. The Duce himself now quickly had his grown children baptized and his marriage recognized by the Church, ten years after his civil marriage to a wife with whom he no longer lived. Pope Pius XI now called Mussolini "the man sent by Providence." Having found favor with the Church hierarchy and enjoying dictatorial power in Italy, Mussolini could turn to implementing an aggressive foreign policy, while dreaming of building another Roman Empire.

Hitler and the Rise of the Nazis in Germany

Like Italian fascism, the rise of the Nazis was closely identified with the rise to power of a charismatic leader, Adolf Hitler (1889–1945). Hitler was born in the small Austrian town of Braunau, on the border with Bavaria. His father had risen to become a customs official of modest means. One teacher recalled "the gaunt, pale-faced youth . . . [Adolf Hitler] had definite talent, though in a narrow field. But he lacked self-discipline, being notoriously cantankerous, willful, arrogant, and bad-tempered. He had obvious difficulty in fitting in at school."

Hitler quit school in 1905. Turned down for admission to the Academy of Graphic Arts in Vienna, he nonetheless moved to the imperial capital where he worked as a paper-hanger and painted and peddled postcards, living in a hostel with little money and few friends. In the 1914 city directory, Hitler had himself listed as "painter and architect."

Hitler was of average height with a large head, dark hair, broad cheekbones, and an unusually high forehead. Wearing baggy clothes and sporting his characteristic trimmed mustache, he was not an impressive-looking man. He had bad teeth and poor eyesight. Hitler was compulsive about daily routines, did not drink coffee or smoke, was a vegetarian, and took only an occasional drink. He enjoyed the company of women—two of whom committed suicide out of love for him—but may, in fact, have been impotent.

At the outbreak of the Great War, Hitler can be seen in a picture of a large crowd cheering the proclamation of war in Munich enthusiastically. He joined the German army and was wounded in the leg in 1916, gased in a British attack just before the end of the war, and decorated on three occasions for bravery. But his superiors found Hitler unfit for promotion to the officer corps, believing that he lacked leadership qualities.

Hitler would later recall "the stupendous impression produced on me by the war—the greatest of all experiences . . . the heroic struggle of our people." He had warned fellow soldiers that "in spite of our big guns victory would be denied" to Germany because of "the invisible foes of the German people," Marxists and Jews. The war accentuated Hitler's fanatical German nationalism.

Several influential German authors had also drawn similar conclusions from the war. In 1918, Oswald Spengler (1880–1936) had published the first volume of *The Decline of the West*. In it, he blamed Germany's defeat on the decay of Western civilization. "We no longer believe," he wrote, "in the power of reason over life. We feel that life rules over reason." He had anticipated that new, powerful leaders would emerge out of the maelstrom of subsequent wars; they would destroy the "impotent democracies." Spengler believed that German culture would survive in its purity, victorious in a biological struggle against its competitors. The result would be "the triumph of the idea of one race over all others." German culture would be embodied in a new state in which the individual would be subsumed in the nation.

In Munich in 1919, Hitler joined the German Workers' Party, a newly formed right-wing nationalist organization. The following year, as Hitler rose to the head of the organization, he renamed it the National Socialist German Workers' Party, or Nazi Party. Impressed by Hitler's single-minded determination, some Nazis now referred to Hitler as the "Führer" or "leader." He was introduced into more elegant social circles, where cash for propaganda and guns could be found.

Some of the first Nazi storm troopers in 1922, with swastikas (symbols of Nazism) on their arms and flag.

Nazis organized a paramilitary organization, the "stormtroopers," known after 1921 as the S.A. (*Stürmabteilungen*), led by the hard-drinking, corpulent Bavarian Ernst Röhm (1887–1934). Like the Free Corps, the S.A. offered comradeship and an outlet for violence to frustrated war veterans. To its members and those of other paramilitary organizations organized in the wake of defeat, Hitler appeared to be a man of action, a survivor of the trenches, one of them, who promised to bring about rearmament and to expand military influence in Germany.

Emboldened by their success at attracting adherents, the Nazis marched out of a beer hall on November 9, 1923, planning to seize power in Munich and then march on Berlin. Troops loyal to the government put an end to the "Beer Hall Putsch." A lenient, anti-republican judge sentenced Hitler to five years in prison. He served only one year and emerged from prison a national figure. Hitler then turned to "legal" tactics, building up the Nazi Party.

In 1925, Hitler published *Mein Kampf* (*My Struggle*), which he had written in his comfortable jail quarters. Here he reiterated the claim, originally that of General Hindenburg, that Germany had been stabbed in the back by Jews and Communists during the war. It was easy to forget that the military front had collapsed before the home front, a convenient collective amnesia. "If, at the beginning and during the war," Hitler wrote, "someone had only subjected about twelve or fifteen thousand of these Hebrew destroyers of the people to poison gas—as was suffered on the battlefield by hundreds of thousands of our best workers from all social classes and all walks of life—then the sacrifice of millions at the front would not have been in vain." He never strayed from the most salient themes of his appeal, believing that people could only absorb a few ideas that must be hammered in over and over again. Germany would rearm, then conquer "living space" at the expense of the "inferior" Slavic peoples to the east and south.

Nazi propagandists portrayed Hitler as an energetic, devoted, and uncompromising leader who could unify Germans of all classes, who stood apart from the weakness, corruption, and compromise the right identified with the Weimar Republic. They pictured him as a God-fearing man (though, in fact, like Mussolini, he was not at all religious) who had overcome opposition to achieve great heights through personal sacrifice. Many Germans now believed that the problem was not that Germany had fought the war, but only that it had not won.

In these early days, the Nazis, like Mussolini's fascists, appealed most to the lower middle class; later they would appeal to the entire spectrum of the German middle class. Many bourgeois families, which had been devastated by the hyperinflation of the early 1920s, stopped supporting the other conservative political parties and the Weimar Republic itself. While renters and debtors paid with inflated currency, pensioners struggled to make ends meet; many small businessmen, shopkeepers, clerks, and craftsmen had to sell or pawn silver or other items of value that had been passed down in their families for generations. They looked to Hitler to protect them from "Bolsheviks" and did not care how he did so.

The Nazis won less than 3 percent of the vote in the 1928 elections. But German political life was moving to the right, led by the powerful National People's Party, most of whose members were increasingly anti-republican but not yet necessarily attracted to the Nazis. They preferred a monarchy

The young Hitler in 1926 during a Nazi parade in Weimar.

Beleaguered Germans look at a poster presenting Hitler as their savior.

or military dictatorship. The death in October 1929 of Stresemann, Germany's able and respected foreign minister, removed a powerful voice of support for the republic and gravely weakened the Weimar coalition in the Reichstag. Socialists, too, were divided. New political coalitions were based far more on makeshift convenience than determined loyalty to the republic. The political center disappeared as support for Weimar crumbled.

The American Wall Street Crash in late October 1929 compounded the social and political instability that had beset Europe since the end of the Great War more than ten years earlier. The economic hardship generated by the Depression swelled the ranks of parties committed to overthrowing parliamentary rule in Germany and other states. As support for the Nazis grew in Germany, Europe entered an even more dangerous period of instability.

CHAPTER 27

THE EUROPE OF DEPRESSION AND DICTATORSHIP

In the two decades following the Great War, one dictator after another ended parliamentary democracy in Europe, imposing totalitarian rule on their states and tolerating no political opposition. They poisoned international relations with nationalist bullying, making grandiose claims on the territories of other states.

In 1922, Benito Mussolini became the first dictator to take power. By the end of 1925, fascist parties demanding the imposition of dictatorships had sprung up in more than forty other nations. Other more traditional right-wing authoritarian movements, too, were on the rise. The army took over in Portugal in 1926, and General Joseph Pilsudski overthrew the Polish Republic the same year (see Chapter 26). All of the Eastern European and Balkan states became dictatorships in the 1920s and 1930s, with the exception of Czechoslovakia. By eliminating all opposition and consolidating power in 1929, Joseph Stalin transformed the Soviet Union into even more of an authoritarian state. In 1933, a right-wing government came to power in Austria, and Adolf Hitler became Nazi chancellor of Germany. The right-wing nationalist revolt against the republic of Spain began in 1936, starting a civil war that ended in 1939 with the victory of General Francisco Franco's right-wing nationalist forces. Britain and France were the only major powers in which parliamentary government was strong enough to resist the authoritarian tide. Yet democracy also survived in the smaller states of Belgium, the Netherlands, Switzerland, Denmark, Sweden, and Norway, despite the existence in each of these states of small fascist movements.

Hitler and Mussolini addressing rallies of their followers.

ECONOMIES IN CRISIS

The global depression that began in October 1929 had significant political consequences in Europe. Economic insecurity and accompanying social unrest undermined parliamentary rule in Germany, Austria, and in other Eastern European countries, and challenged parliamentary rule in France and Belgium. More and more people sought scapegoats who could be blamed for the frustrations of hard times: Jews, socialists, Communists, other nationalities, big business. Under such circumstances, many people could be convinced that parliamentary government itself was to blame and that nationalistic dictatorships were the solution. Amid plunging confidence and general bewilderment, international cooperation became more difficult, particularly as the powers began to blame each other for adopting policies that adversely affected them. Many Germans castigated their wartime enemies for assessing massive, unjust reparations; many British and French citizens blamed Germany for not paying all the reparations; many Americans blamed their own allies, above all, Britain and France, for not paying back loans. The vicious cycle of mistrust grew.

The Great Depression

By 1924, prosperity seemed to have returned to much of post-war Europe, particularly to Britain and France. But beneath the surface, the increasingly interdependent world economy had not recovered from the war. The wartime inflation continued for several years following the armistice. At the same time, the prices of steel and iron declined sharply after the war when demand plunged for tanks, artillery pieces, and munitions. Overproduction and the increasing use of hydroelectricity and oil caused the price of coal to fall rapidly. Slowly some industrial jobs began to disappear.

European agriculture was in a depressed state well before the Crash of 1929. The war had encouraged agricultural overproduction in Europe; more grain, meats, and other food supplies arrived on the continent during the 1914–1918 period from Australia, Argentina, Canada, and the United States, depressing the price of locally produced farm products. Lower farm incomes, like industrial layoffs, in turn reduced demand for manufactured goods.

European states reacted by erecting tariff barriers to try to protect their internal markets for domestic agricultural products. Countries like Bulgaria that depended on agricultural exports saw their foreign markets dry up, or received less for what they sold. With less income, Eastern European and Balkan nations could not repay their wartime debts. Germany's defeat, the dismemberment of the Austro-Hungarian Empire, and the Russian Revolution significantly weakened the region's three largest prewar trading partners.

The contraction of demand and price deflation probably would not have been enough to generate full-fledged economic disaster. But unrestrained financial speculation also eroded the world economy. In Germany, high interest rates had attracted considerable foreign investment since the 1924 economic recovery. Credit was easily available, and companies issued huge amounts of stock shares based upon insufficient real assets. In the United States, a sizable reduction in demand for goods was already apparent by 1927. Wealthy people began to invest in highly speculative stocks.

Wartime loans and post-war debts made the finances of the larger powers more interdependent and helped destabilize the international economy. German reparations also adversely affected the world economy because, ironically, they accentuated the flow of capital into Germany. Following the Dawes Plan, which in 1924 extended the schedule of reparations, Germany borrowed $110 million from U.S. banks in order to meet its reduced reparations payments to the Allies, rather than paying them out of current income through higher taxes. German railroads served as collateral for the loans, which were immediately oversubscribed by ten times in New York. Like bonds and speculative investments, the reparation loans diverted investment away from industry and ignited further foreign lending. Besides loans to pay reparations, other loans also poured into Germany. Most of this debt was short term rather than long term, which made Germany even more vulnerable to a sudden calling in of those loans. In 1928, U.S. banks refused further loans to Germany, investing available funds instead in the Wall Street stock market, further undercutting German banks.

By early 1929, the U.S. economy was in recession. In late October, the New York stock market crashed, ruining many stockbrokers—and sending a few plunging from their Wall Street offices to the street below. Moreover, thousands of large and small investors also were ruined as stocks lost most of their value. American and British investors with assets still tied up in Germany now began to pull their money out as quickly as possible. German gold reserves were depleted, as banks owed far more money to creditors than they had assets. Table 27-1 shows the importance of the U.S.-German financial connection, which contributed to the fact that the Depression began earlier and production fell more in those two countries than in the other major powers.

As unemployment mounted to unprecedented levels, the "roaring twenties" became the "threadbare thirties." As jobs disappeared, families were compelled to spend the savings they had so painstakingly amassed over the previous five years, even as manufacturing and agricultural prices continued to fall because of the dramatic contraction of demand. Manufactured goods piled up on the docks.

Confronted by a catastrophic fall in trade and industrial production, falling prices, and unemployment approaching 20 percent of the workforce, British government officials and economists, as their counterparts in other countries, debated strategies that might revive their floundering economies. There were no easy answers. The economic orthodoxy of the day held that the way out of the crisis was to reduce public expenditures. The inflation of the immediate post-war period, particularly the hyperinflation that ravaged Germany in 1922–1923, frightened statesmen and most economists away from even limited financial or fiscal expansion.

National policy options were further constrained by the interdependence of the international economy, especially under the gold standard. For example, Ramsey MacDonald's British Labour government first reacted to the Wall Street Crash by increasing unemployment benefits and funding more public works, while raising taxes. These expenditures further increased the government deficit, already soaring because of reduced

TABLE 27-1. INDICES OF INDUSTRIAL PRODUCTION (1928=100)

Year	Germany	United States	France	Britain
1925	79.3	93.7	85.0	94.8*
1927	97.2	95.5	86.6	101.2
1929	101.4	107.2	109.4	106.0
1930	83.6	86.5	110.2	97.9
1931				
August	71.9	74.8	99.2	84.6
December	59.4	66.7	87.4	84.7
1932				
January	55.2	64.9	82.7	90.1
August	54.7	53.2	73.2	89.2

*For Great Britain, 1924.
Source: David E. Sumler, *A History of Europe in the Twentieth Century* (Homewood, IL: Dorsey Press, 1973), p. 145.

(Left) The Wall Street Crash, October 1929. *(Right)* An unemployed Briton seeks work, 1930.

tax revenue and the payment of unemployment benefits. But the British government was forced to reduce such benefits in order to be deemed creditworthy by New York and Parisian bankers in the hope of stabilizing the pound and maintaining the gold standard.

The international monetary system collapsed as the world economy plunged into dark depression. With the Depression, those banks and private interests that had loaned money to Germany began to call in debts. Already reeling from agricultural depression in Eastern Europe, the failure of the largest Austrian bank in May 1931 immediately entailed the collapse of several German banks to which it owed money and led to a general financial panic. U.S. President Herbert Hoover (1874–1964) suggested a moratorium on the repayment of all reparations and war debts, hoping that confidence and the end of the cycle of defaults would follow. The other powers accepted the moratorium in August 1931.

As the British economy floundered because of the decline in world trade, European bankers intensified the run on the pound. They exchanged their holdings of British pounds sterling for gold, £2.5 million worth per day during the summer of 1930, dangerously reducing Britain's gold reserves. As investors panicked, sterling quickly lost a third of its value.

In August 1931, MacDonald's government resigned, replaced by a National Government, an inter-party coalition, though MacDonald stayed on as prime minister. Worsening conditions forced the National Government to take Britain off the gold standard in September 1931. This meant that the Bank of England would no longer remit gold in exchange for pounds. This seemed like a step into the economic unknown. Wild fluctuations in the values of other currencies followed. This further discouraged business, and international trade declined even more steeply, but it did permit some domestic recovery. In April 1933, the United States, too, went off the gold standard.

In Britain, the Conservatives' deflationary measures, which sought to reduce expenditures, seemed to British voters to be the only way out of the crisis; in the elections of October 1931, the Tories won an overwhelming majority of seats in Commons. Neville Chamberlain (1869–1940) now became chancellor of the Exchequer. His aloof manner, inveterate dullness, rasping voice, and whiny disposition did little to inspire confidence—one critic suggested that he had been "weaned on a pickle." Chamberlain, who had successfully worked to provide public housing for workers, promised a "doctor's mandate" to extract Britain from the economic crisis. The government imposed higher tariffs, further reducing consumer spending. Many Labourites, calling MacDonald a traitor to his party for going along with deflationary measures because they reduced unemployment benefits, still called for the nationalization of mining, the railways, and other essential industries as beginning steps toward the implementation of a more planned economy. But Labour's campaign ran headlong into traditional Conservative opposition and middle-class fear of socialism, as well as the orthodoxy of deflationary economic policies.

In the depths of the Depression, a fascist movement developed even in Britain, the home of parliamentary democracy. Oswald Mosley (1896–1980), born into a wealthy aristocratic family, had become the youngest member of Parliament in 1918. The vain Mosley, a skilled orator, had left the Conservative Party for a brief fling with Labour (leading the philandering Mosley to proclaim his new motto, "Vote Labour, Sleep Tory"). Attacking "international finance capital" and the Labour Party alike, he formed the British Union of Fascists in 1932 and began to deliver vehement speeches against Jews. An admirer of Mussolini, who provided funds for the British fascist movement, and Hitler, who served as best man at his second wedding, Mosley surrounded himself with black-shirted toughs. However, Mosley attracted more attention than followers (they never numbered more than 20,000). Considerable division existed in Britain as to which policies would best ease the effects of the Depression, but the British people, as throughout history, avoided political extremes.

Across the English Channel, smaller-scale industries, artisans, and family farmers in France at first were sheltered from the Depression because they depended, above all, on local markets. France also had considerable gold reserves, which helped maintain business and consumer confidence and helped keep consumer spending at a relatively high level. The run on the British pound and the German mark, too, at first aided France, as much of the gold exchanged by investors ended up in Paris. But gradually

French prices also fell and unemployment rose, again revealing the interdependence of the world economy. French exports declined with the contraction of the world market, particularly because the franc, which had not plunged like the pound, was now overvalued, making French goods expensive abroad. But most French leaders considered devaluation to be anathema. "Who touches the franc," cautioned one newspaper, "touches France!" The French government, like that of Britain, stuck to classical economic remedies, ignoring demands for active state intervention to stimulate the economy from right-wing corporatists who sought support for cartels and from left-wing socialists who called for the nationalization of crucial industries and higher unemployment benefits.

Gradual European Economic Revival

In the rest of Europe, government leaders debated strategies that they hoped would pull their countries out of the Depression. One after another, the major powers took measures in their own interests. These included establishing high tariffs and devaluing their currencies without prior consultation with other governments. The U.S. and British governments followed contemporary economic orthodoxy. They sharply reduced government spending, cutting unemployment benefits and restricting credit. John Maynard Keynes (1883–1946), a maverick English economist, insisted that recovery would depend upon just the opposite strategy. He recommended an increase in government expenditures, including deficit spending—for example, on public works—to stimulate consumer spending by reducing unemployment. Keynes argued that deflationary measures, such as cutting government spending, reducing unemployment benefits, or encouraging companies to limit production and thus keep prices artificially high, were counterproductive. They could prolong the Depression by reducing the demand for goods. With one-quarter of the labor force out of work early in 1933 and wages falling, there was insufficient demand to generate a manufacturing upswing in Great Britain, the United States, or anywhere else. But Keynes was in a small minority, and most of his writing was still largely unknown.

Only very gradually did the Depression begin to recede, first, as it had begun, in the most industrialized countries. A modest recovery began in Britain in 1932. But it was not due to the dramatic improvement of British international trade upon which the Conservatives had counted. Rather, it followed a slow increase in consumer spending. Keynes had been right. Government decisions in 1934 and 1935 to increase unemployment benefits and restore government salaries to their pre-Depression levels helped. So did the subsidized construction of houses, which pumped money into the economy, restoring consumer confidence. While some inefficient steel and textile manufacturers went under, others consolidated and became more efficient, perhaps benefiting from the imposition of higher tariffs on industrial imports. Real wages slowly rose. The

Reflecting the enormity of class divisions in Britain during the Depression, these working-class boys look in amazement at two Eton students outside a cricket ground.

imposition of quotas on agricultural imports aided farmers. As industry and agriculture gradually returned to prosperity, unemployment began to fall.

The German economy also slowly improved, at least partially because, after Hitler came to power in 1933, rearmament created many jobs, and business confidence slowly returned. In 1930, the Young Plan, named after its American originator, had extended the date to 1988 by which Germany was to have paid all reparations. Then the Lausanne Conference of 1932 simply declared the end of reparations payments. In France, the Depression lingered longer than in any other industrialized power, with the exception of the United States. In 1938, French industrial production still had not reached its 1929 level.

In the United States, where the Depression hit hardest, recovery came even more slowly. Franklin D. Roosevelt (1882–1945), elected president in 1932, implemented his "New Deal." It facilitated loans that saved banks, provided relief for the unemployed through public works programs, and provided assistance to farmers and to businesses. When Keynes learned of Roosevelt's plans, he jumped with glee, "Roosevelt was magnificently right" (he might have said, someone noted, that he was "magnificently left"). Gradually a return of consumer confidence, boosted by the president's low-key "fireside chats" by radio to the American people, improved the economy. But only with the entry of the United States into the Second World War in 1941, with its massive mobilization of economic resources in the production of war materials, did the Depression finally

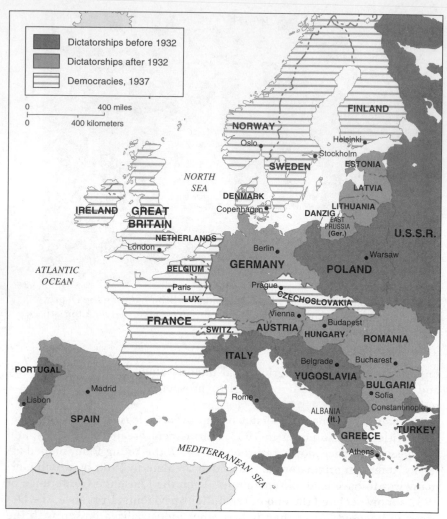

MAP 27.1 DICTATORSHIPS IN EUROPE, 1932–1937   States ruled by dictators before 1932; states that became dictatorships after 1932; remaining democracies in 1937.

end its grip on the United States. It is against this background of the Depression and hard times that the rise of fascism must be seen both in the industrialized countries of Western Europe and in the largely agrarian states of Eastern Europe and the Balkans (see Map 27.1).

FASCIST MOVEMENTS

Anti-communism and anti-Semitism helped give fascism an international character. In 1935, there was even a short-lived attempt to create a fascist international. Mussolini contributed funds to the Belgian, Austrian, and smaller British fascist movements. But the stridently nationalist aspect of fascism in itself worked against such fascist internationalism. Yet, fascist and right-wing authoritarian states found ready allies among similar regimes, as joint German and Italian assistance to the nationalist rebellion during the Spanish Civil War (1936–1939) solidified the alliance between Hitler and Mussolini.

There was no single fascist ideology, and not all of the right-wing authoritarian movements in Europe in the 1920s and 1930s can be qualified as fascist. Francisco Franco imposed a military dictatorship on Spain that was like that of neighboring Portugal; both were predicated upon the influence of traditional elites, the Catholic Church, and the army. Yet, while sharing the anti-Bolshevism of fascist Italy and Nazi Germany, neither the Spanish nor the Portuguese dictatorship shared the expansionist ideology of those states and both were distrustful of the kind of mass movement that helped sweep the Italian fascists and German Nazis to power. The agrarian populist dictatorships of Eastern Europe may also be described as fascist states. They were characterized by aggressive, nationalist mass movements, anti-Semitism, and frenetic opposition to parliamentary rule. They also sought to maintain the social hierarchy within their states by violent means. Unlike the dictatorships in Germany and Italy, however, they had no illusions about expanding their states beyond what each claimed as the "historic" limits of their nationality. Moreover, Stalin's Soviet Union, too, had become a totalitarian dictatorship, like the fascist regimes, but one of the left, based on Communist rhetoric about creating a workers' paradise. Stalin, casting aside the claims of the many non-Russian nationalities, and for that matter, of the workers themselves, tolerated no opposition to or within the Communist Party. Totalitarian states, then, were marked by centralized control of all political functions by a dictator ruling in the name of a single party. They used the police to enforce bans against the freedom of assembly and of the press, and to crush opposition through state-sponsored terror.

The Dynamics of Fascism

Several factors contributed to the rise of the extreme right, with none serving as a sufficient single explanation. If in the nineteenth century the middle class had stood as a bulwark of liberal values in Europe, this was no longer the case in the post-war climate. In Germany, Italy, and Austria, fascists found disproportionate support among the middle class, particularly the lower middle class. By contrast, the British and French middle classes felt many of the same economic frustrations, but only in France did a good number turn to anti-parliamentarian political movements. Even in that case, however, only a minority of people ever believed that things were so bad that anything would have been preferable to the political system they already had.

With the exception of the recovery of 1924–1929, the 1920s and 1930s were decades of economic crisis. When the American stock market crashed in October 1929, small savings accounts and pensions were wiped out. Many middle-class families watched in horror as their modest savings disappeared. They feared union leaders, socialists, and Communists, who demanded an extension of public programs to aid unemployed workers and who espoused social revolution. But middle-class frustrations do not provide a sufficient explanation for the rise of authoritarian movements in Eastern Europe and the Balkans, where the middle classes were extremely small.

Fascist parties, in the largest sense, including the National Socialist German Workers' Party, developed in the 1920s as mass political movements. Yet, unlike those in democratic mass movements—for example, reform socialists—fascists rejected parliamentary rule. There was nothing democratic about fascist organizations: they were hierarchically structured, and aimed at dictatorship, rule by one person. Fascist movements were counter-revolutionary in nature, opposing trade unions, socialists, and Communists with particular vehemence because all three espoused working-class internationalism. The trade unions' success in attracting members immediately after the war and incessant working-class demands for better conditions, backed up by strikes, frightened Europe's social and political elites.

Big business in Italy and Germany, as well as in France, aided the right by turning against parliamentary rule. Wealthy industrialists were key actors in the crisis that brought the Italian fascists and German Nazis to power in their respective states. Yet, at least in the beginning in Germany, many big businessmen were suspicious of Nazism's mass appeal, despite a period of courtship. They preferred more traditional kinds of authoritarian solutions that appealed to their sense of social exclusiveness, such as a monarchy backed by the armed forces in the Prussian tradition. Smaller businessmen were more likely to back the Nazis. In Italy, the link between big business interests and fascism was more direct; in the industrial north, shipowners and iron and mining magnates, among others, provided funds for Mussolini's national movement or to local groups of fascists before the Duce came to power. Fascism was not created in Italy by a handful of wealthy capitalists; rather, big business joined with smaller industrial and commercial concerns, as well as wealthy landowners, to facilitate the rise to power of a leader who promised to impose social and political order and limit the prerogatives of labor.

Fascists and similar right-wing groups blamed parliamentary government itself for the weaknesses and failures of their states in the post-war years. They believed parliamentary regimes to be unstable, chaotic, and soft by their very nature, weakened by factionalism and class divisions. The seeming instability of parliamentary regimes contributed to the attraction of a strong leader, a dictator, who would restore order and embody nationalist aspirations. The irony was, of course, that fascist gangs themselves were largely responsible for creating the political turmoil that ulti-

Hitler at a Nazi rally, 1934.

mately led to the destruction of Central and Eastern Europe's nascent parliamentary governments.

Crowds saluted Mussolini, Hitler, and the dictators of smaller states with almost hysterical frenzy, believing that they embodied the aspirations of their people. They sought to identify themselves with strong leaders committed not only to imposing absolute order at home but also to territorial expansion and nationalistic aggrandizement. Propagandists orchestrated images of Mussolini and Hitler by using new techniques of communication, utilizing the mass press, radio, and even the cinema to monopolize and manipulate their followers.

Fascists most often defined themselves by denouncing who and what they were against. But fascism also had revolutionary elements in that some of its proponents saw themselves as building a new social and political order based upon service to the nation. This idea of creating a new elite also distinguished fascist from authoritarian movements in Spain and Portugal, where nationalists tried to affirm the domination of traditional elites, such as nobles and churchmen, and remained suspicious of mass movements in general. Fascists wanted a more powerful state that would expand its borders through conquest, fulfilling what they considered the "historic destiny" of their national group. Mussolini and Hitler appealed to the masses based on their support for an imagined "national community" that joined all people of the nation, excluding those deemed to be outsiders. But their views and plans directly conflicted with the Versailles Peace Settlement in that they included the intention to undo the agreements signed by the German and Italian governments in 1919. Nonetheless, they now pursued broadly expansionist goals that could only be met by absorbing the territories of other states.

In contrast, socialists and Communists insisted that class tensions and conflicts were endemic in industrial society, and based their political philosophies primarily on the perceived needs of the working class. Fascists, by contrast, viewed economic and social tensions as irrelevant, arguing that it was enough that all people shared a common national identity, and that this national community meant more than did economic disparities between social classes, and would make those divisions obsolete. Mussolini and Hitler covered up the brutal realities of their rule by promising with vague rhetoric that the needs of the "national economic community" would be fulfilled. In the early 1920s, Mussolini had added "international finance capital" to his list of enemies, a holdover from the rhetoric of his days as a socialist before the war, a means of trying to convince workers that he spoke for their interests, too. Like Mussolini, authoritarian dictators Engelbert Dollfuss in Austria and Antonio Salazar in Portugal also added "corporatism" to their list of promises, announcing that associations of employers and workers would be formed within each industry that would be able to increase productivity and thus make class divisions obsolete. Such rhetoric was intended to appeal to employers and workers alike. But fascist states remained capitalistic in nature, with big business accruing great profits and workers lagging far behind.

The factors discussed above—middle-class economic frustration, upper-class fears of socialism, aggressive nationalism, anti-parliamentarianism, and the belief that a dictator could provide order and national fulfillment—were all present in European society before the Great War. But the cataclysmic experience of the war channeled them all in new and frightening directions. The experience of the war itself contributed to the proliferation of aggressive nationalism. The war also had divided Europe into "victors" and "vanquished," countries that accepted the Versailles Settlement and revisionist nations that did not. The latter included Germany, Hungary, and Bulgaria, but also Italy, which had joined the winning side in 1915 but received less at Versailles than Italian nationalists sought. In Germany, right-wing movements attracted demobilized soldiers, who had returned home with habits of military order, marching, weapons, violence, and the camaraderie of the trenches. Paramilitary squads, largely made up of war veterans, destabilized political life. The Free Corps in Germany, the Home Guard in Austria, and the Cross of Fire in France denounced the "decadence" and "softness" of parliamentary regimes.

Aggressive nationalism easily became racism. Germans were not alone in believing spurious literature proclaiming the superiority of their race and the degeneration of other races. In Eastern Europe, dictators identified other nationalities and ethnic groups that could be blamed for practically anything (such as Romanians by Hungarians, anyone else in the case of German nationalists, with Jews in many places becoming the handiest scapegoats of all). The unique character of Hitler's National Socialism stemmed from its ideology of German racial supremacy, which went beyond the assertions of nationalist primacy of other right-wing dictators. From the beginning, Nazism manifested an unparalleled capacity for violence and destruction based upon the assumption that Nazis could assume the authority to determine who could live and who could die. This, too, took Nazi ideology and practice beyond other violent nationalist totalitarian regimes. Yet, anti-Semitism also characterized authoritarian movements in Austria, Poland, Romania, Yugoslavia, France, and Belgium, where Jews could, along with the parties of the left and the unions, be blamed for hard times. Finally, inspired by Hitler, Mussolini also added anti-Semitism to his nationalist ravings in 1938.

Fascism in Mussolini's Italy

By the time of the Depression, Benito Mussolini, who had seized power in 1922, had already transformed Italy into Europe's first fascist state (see Chapter 26). His dictatorship was accompanied not only by blustering promises about Italy becoming a Second Roman Empire, turning the Mediterranean into "our lake," but also providing assurance that fascism, by uniting all Italians in fervent nationalism, would bring both harmony and prosperity. To some foreign visitors, Mussolini's fascism seemed to offer a third way that lay between unchecked capitalism and the contentious challenge of socialism and communism. The Duce became famous abroad as the genius who managed to make Italian trains run on time, although, in fact, such a description applied only to those carrying tourists to the ski resorts in the Italian Alps.

The Italian fascist state's one innovation was to establish the outlines of a "corporative state." The hope was that by creating cartel-like corporations joining all people dependent upon one economic activity or industry, ruinous competition between companies and conflict between bosses and workers could be eliminated in the interest and prosperity of the "national economic community." The Duce created twenty-two corporations, or assemblies, overseen, at least in theory, by a National Council of Corporations, intended to cover every conceivable economic activity. Each corporation was based on a council of employers and employees. But Italian fascist corporatism had very little impact in Italy. Its chief practical consequence, at least until the early 1930s, was to swell the number of state bureaucrats hired to supervise creaky, inefficient, and largely superfluous organizations.

The paradox of Italian corporatism was revealed in Mussolini's rhetoric that there were no social classes in Italy, only Italians. The Duce cheerily proclaimed the end of class struggle and bragged that he had done more for workers than any other leader. But employers and workers were certainly not on an equal footing. Their trade unions destroyed (replaced by fascist trade unions), their conditions of life basically unimproved and strikes now illegal, most workers remained skeptical about Mussolini. The fascist government did limit the workday in 1923, and in 1935 it introduced a five-day workweek. But employers broke contracts with impunity. The conditions of life for sharecroppers and other landless laborers declined during the fascist period.

The Duce wanted to make Italy economically independent. State agencies invested in industries Mussolini considered crucial to the colonial and European wars he was planning. By 1935, no other European state, except Stalin's Soviet Union, controlled such a large portion of industry, with major shares in industries like steelworks and shipbuilding. Despite some successes, including the development of hydroelectricity and automobile manufacturing, Italian industry still depended on raw materials imported from abroad, including copper, rubber, and coal.

Mussolini dubbed his most ambitious agricultural program the "battle for grain." But wheat production was uneconomical in many regions; by converting from labor-intensive crops to wheat, the Duce's pet program merely increased unemployment, while reducing pasture and fruit-growing lands and the number of farm animals. High tariffs on grain imports raised food prices. Land reclamation and irrigation projects also failed. While Mussolini's speeches celebrated "blood and soil," the number of Italian peasant proprietors fell.

The failures of Mussolini's economic policies were compounded by the demands of military spending, which absorbed a full third of Italian income by the mid-1930s. While the state spent heavily on planes and submarines, Italy's per capita income remained about that of Britain and the United States in the early nineteenth century. Illiteracy remained high, particularly in the south, where a fifth of all brides in 1936 could not even sign their names. The economy still depended upon traditional, small-scale agriculture. Under fascism, the gap between the more industrialized north and the poor south continued to grow.

Like Hitler and Stalin, Mussolini sought to eliminate the boundary between private and public life. He wanted the "new Italian woman" to espouse the values of, and serve, the nationalist state. With the fascist motto, "all in the state, nothing outside the state," he viewed the family as an essential component of fascism. "The Nation is served even by keeping the house swept. Civic discipline begins with family discipline," advised the *Decalogue of the Little Italian*. But fascism could never overcome the inevitable tensions between family obligations and what fascists considered national duties. The Duce disliked the fact that women had obtained the right to vote in Great Britain, Germany, and several other countries, and that more Italian women were going to work. In Italy's fascist state, the place of women was to be in the home, obeying their husbands and having babies.

That not all Italians listened to Mussolini's bombastic rhetoric (nor to the Catholic Church) was demonstrated by the continuing fall of the birthrate (from 147.5 births per 1,000 in 1911 to 102.2 in 1936), despite the call of the Duce for more baby soldiers, and despite the state's ban on the sale of birth control devices.

In the south, where peasants particularly resented and resisted the state, the Mafia provided an alternative allegiance, a parallel underworld government. Mussolini failed to destroy the power of the Neapolitan and Sicilian Mafias, even though the number of Mafia-related killings fell dramatically. Even fascist violence could not uproot traditional ways of doing things. But there was a contradiction: Mussolini and the fascists believed they were restoring old values, but the very idea of service to the nation-state was very new—for example, the attempt to create mass fascist organizations of women ranging from after-work recreational clubs to female paramilitary squads.

The Church, too, remained a strong alternative source of influence to fascism. Much of a Catholic revival, which included a rapid rise in the number of priests and nuns, continued to be independent of fascism. The pope lost some of his enthusiasm for Mussolini's fascism, denouncing in the early 1930s "the pagan worship of the state." Few Italians followed fascist cultural policy, such as the Duce's attempts to convince Italians to stop singing in the streets, or his insistence that they dress babies in fascist black shirts. Massive emigration out of Italy continued throughout the 1920s and 1930s. Yet, most Italians still supported Mussolini, if only passively.

Fascist Movements in Eastern Europe

Fascism was a European-wide phenomenon in no way limited to Nazi Germany and Mussolini's Italy. In the overwhelmingly agrarian states of Eastern Europe, parliamentary governments did not survive the instability wrought by the economic dislocation of the 1920s and 1930s. Nor could they survive in the face of the bitter ethnic rivalries within these nations, which included states that already existed at the outbreak of the war (Romania, Bulgaria, and Greece) and newly created states (Poland and Yugoslavia). Not including the new kingdom of Yugoslavia, each of these multinational states had some sort of liberal constitution in the 1920s. Yet, by the end of the 1930s, right-wing dictatorships had overwhelmed political liberalism in each Eastern European nation except Czechoslovakia.

With the exception of Czechoslovakia, which included industrialized Bohemia, all of these countries were poor, heavily agricultural, and had high percentages of illiteracy. When compared with the countries of Western Europe, the countries of Eastern Europe had very small middle classes, except Czech Bohemia, parts of Serbia, and a few major cities, and they had virtually no traditions of parliamentary government.

A daunting variety of conflicting economic interests characterized Eastern Europeans, ranging from those of wealthy Hungarian landowners producing grain to Bosnian mountain dwellers scratching out a meager living from thankless land. After the war, the governments of the Eastern European states implemented ambitious land reform programs that reduced the number and size of the large estates, adding to the ranks of small landholding farmers. But populist agrarian parties, such as the Peasant Party in Poland and the Smallholders in Hungary, hindered the development of stable parliamentary regimes. They were essentially single-interest parties that easily fell under the sway of fascist demagogues playing on anti-urban prejudices. Such agrarian parties vilified Jews as ethnic outsiders, mobilizing resentment against their economic roles as bankers, small businessmen, and shopkeepers. In Bulgaria and, above all, in Hungary and Romania, wealthy landowners, wanting to protect their estates against further land reform and frightened by the rise of small Communist parties, turned toward authoritarian rule.

Poland was the first Eastern European state to become a right-wing dictatorship. General Joseph Pilsudski seized power in 1926, imposing a military dictatorship that survived his death in 1935. The Yugoslav experiment in parliamentary rule ended abruptly in January 1929, when King Alexander (ruled 1921–1934) sent the assembly home from Belgrade and banned all political parties. That year, Croats established the Ustaša (Insurrection) Party, a right-wing nationalist party that demanded an independent Croatia. In 1934, Croatian nationalists assassinated King Alexander. Five years later, Croatia won status as an "autonomous" region with its own assembly, but this did not reduce Serb domination of the multinational state. In Yugoslavia, then, the principal battle was not between partisans of dictatorship and those of parliamentarian government, as in Germany, but between the authoritarian Serb government and right-wing Croat organizations.

In Hungary, Admiral Nicholas Horthy appointed a fascist prime minister in 1932 but repressed the extreme right-wing parties when they threatened to seize power for themselves. Bulgarian political life, too, was marked by assassinations and coups d'état followed by dictatorship in 1935. In Greece, republicans, monarchists, and military officers battled it out. And in 1936, King George II (1890–1947) gave his blessing to the dictatorship of General Ioannis Metaxas (1871–1941) who, in the fascist style, took the title of "leader." In 1938, in Romania King Carol II (1893–1953) established a dictatorship by suspending the constitution. He did so to protect his rule against a challenge from the fascist "Legion of the Archangel Michael" and particularly its murderous shock troops, the "Iron Guard," a fanatically Orthodox religious group with strong anti-Semitic prejudices. Romanian fascists drew upon peasant discontent created by Depression-era agricultural deflation. The king's bloody suppression of the Legion and the Iron Guard only postponed the victory of fascism in Romania (see Chapter 28).

In Eastern Europe, only Czechoslovakia, with a strong liberal tradition and a sizable Czech middle class, managed to achieve political stability as a parliamentary democracy. Despite differences between the country's Czechs and Slovaks, ethnic divisions had not yet necessarily become hatreds. The two largest political parties, the Agrarian Party and the Social Democratic Party, drew members from both peoples. By the late 1930s, it was apparent that the greatest threat to parliamentary rule in Czechoslovakia would come from Nazi Germany, as Hitler seized upon ethnic tensions in the Czech Sudetenland between the German-speaking population and the Czechs. Consequently, even Eastern Europe's most stable country was not immune from destabilizing ethnic rivalries.

Fascism in Austria

In Austria, the undersized, German-speaking remnant of the Habsburg empire, fascism was closely tied to German nationalism and anti-Semitism. Moreover, lying between Germany and Italy, Austria almost inevitably came under the influence of those states. During the 1930s, Mussolini wanted to absorb the Italian-speaking Tyrol, and Hitler wanted Germany to annex all of Austria. The Nazi Party of Austria was eager to help him by destabilizing political life.

The split between left and right was particularly bitter in Austria, where on "Bloody Friday," July 15, 1927, police killed about a hundred striking workers during demonstrations by socialists in Vienna protesting right-wing violence. Yet, in Austria, Vienna had a long tradition of social democracy, rooted in the politically active workers living in public housing on the edge of the city. The contrast between the stately inner city, where some of the old Habsburg nobles still lived, and its "red belt" of working-class housing could not be missed. Much of the tax burden fell on the Viennese bourgeoisie, which was for the most part socially conservative and fervently Catholic and overwhelmingly supported the ruling Christian Social Party. Anti-Semitism had deep roots in Vienna—where the young Hitler had thrived—as well as in provincial Austria. As everywhere, the Depression accentuated existing social and political tensions and violence.

The violent anti-parliamentary groups in neighboring Bavaria served as a point of attraction for the Austrian Nazis. Members of the Austrian right-wing Home Guard wore traditional green woolen coats, lederhosen, and Alpine hats, but carried quite modern machine guns. The socialist Social Democrats formed their own guard units and were considerably less well-armed, but determined to protect their members.

In 1933, Chancellor Engelbert Dollfuss (1892–1934), a diminutive, awkward man who wore traditional Austrian peasant garb because he was proud of his provincial origins, dissolved the Austrian Parliament because it stood in the way of an authoritarian state. In February 1934, after Home Guard raids on workers' organizations and newspapers, the workers of Vienna, led by the Social Democrats, began a general strike. Fighting erupted when Dollfuss unleashed the Home Guard and army against the left. Army units attacked the industrial suburbs with artillery fire, killing several hundred workers during four days of fighting. Police closed down all Social Democratic organizations, and tried and executed some of its leaders. Dollfuss then banned all political parties except the fascist Fatherland Front.

The Popular Front in France against the Far Right

Fascist parties in France had their origins in the anti-republican nationalism of the late nineteenth century. The Great War and the economic and social frustrations of the post-armistice period contributed to the rise of the far right. War veterans were prominent in the Faisceau movement, which was founded in 1919 and which emulated the newly created Italian fascist organization, and in the Cross of Fire, established in 1929. Some French fascist leaders were men of great wealth, including two renowned producers of luxury products, the perfume magnate François Coty and the champagne baron Pierre de Taittinger. The latter's Patriotic Youth movement, founded in 1924, counted more than 100,000 members by the end of the decade.

The rise in immigration to France compounded the xenophobia and racism of the fascists. Beginning in 1935, more people died each year than were born in France, and its population grew only because of the arrival of immigrants—Italians, Poles, Spaniards, and Belgians, in order of number, but also Jews from Eastern Europe. About 7.5 percent of the French population in the late 1930s consisted of immigrants—the highest percentage in Europe. In Britain, by contrast, immigration was much less significant, which may have helped limit the appeal of the nationalistic far-right parties.

French fascists decried the very structure of the Third Republic, which seemed to them an anomaly in a continent of dictators. Political power in France lay not with a strong executive authority but with the Chamber of Deputies. Governments came and went in turn, increasing rightist dissatisfaction. In 1934, a seamy political scandal offered the extreme right an opening for action. The appearance of government complicity in a fraudulent bond-selling scheme engineered by Serge Stavisky (1886–1934), a Ukrainian-born Jew, led to increasingly violent rightist demonstrations against the republic. On February 4, 1934, right-wing groups rioted against the Chamber of Deputies. Communists, too, protested. The rightists charged across the Seine River in Paris toward the Chamber of Deputies before being dispersed, with casualties on both sides. But, unlike the right in Germany, Italy, or Spain, the French right did not have a dominating figure capable of uniting opposition to parliamentary rule. On February 12, millions of French men and women marched in support of the republic. Although the government resigned, the republic was saved, to enjoy what some wags referred to as "another lease on death."

The formation of the Popular Front in France, an alliance between the Radical, Socialist, and Communist parties, must be seen in the context of the clear threat to parliamentary forms of government posed by the right not only in France but throughout Europe. Socialists and Communists had been at odds since the Congress of Tours in 1920. The split became policy when the Communist International of 1927 adopted the tactic of "class against class," which tolerated no concessions to "bourgeois" parties, including the Socialist Party. But in the 1930s, the reality of the threat of the right to France temporarily overcame ideology. Stalin's fear of German rearmament led the Comintern to repudiate the "class versus class" strategy in June 1934. The French Communist Party was now free to join forces with the Socialist and Radical Parties in a Popular Front to defend the republic against fascism. The three parties prepared a compromise program incorporating tax reform, a shorter workweek, increased unemployment benefits, support for the League of Nations and international disarmament, and the dissolution of the fascist leagues.

The Popular Front won a clear victory in the subsequent elections of May 1936, winning 57 percent of the vote. But the Communists, despite having almost doubled their support, refused to participate in the ensuing government. Ideology once again took precedence, on orders from Moscow. Léon Blum (1872–1950) became prime minister of the Popular Front government. That the Socialist leader was a Jew intensified the rage of the extreme right. "Better Hitler than Blum!" echoed in some of the wealthier neighborhoods of Paris.

As unions, encouraged by the Popular Front's pre-election promises, put forward their demands, the largest strike wave in French history broke out across the country. For the first time, workers occupied plants, putting on theatrical productions, mock trials of employers, marching, and singing. The strikes, many by non-unionized workers, took both French labor federations and the Communist Party by surprise. The Communists tried to bring the strikes to a speedy conclusion, fearful that defeat might hurt their influence with workers, or help the Socialists. The Communist Party newspaper *L'Humanité* answered the workers' optimistic slogan "Everything is possible" with the headline "Everything is not possible."

Blum convinced employers and union representatives to sign the "Matignon Agreements," establishing a forty-hour workweek, pay raises, and paid vacations. The strikes gradually ended. But the economy continued to falter, without sufficient support for greater economic reforms, and in the face of intransigent opposition from employers and wealthy families shipping assets out of France. Blum declared a "pause" in his reform program, and cut back social benefits and other state expenditures.

The Popular Front began to unravel. In March 1937, police fired on workers demonstrating against the rightist Cross of Fire group. The Communists denounced the government, which they had helped bring to power but never joined. The government had to devalue the franc several more times because of the flow of gold abroad. Blum asked the Senate to grant him power to rule by decree. When the conservative-dominated Senate refused, he resigned in June. For all intents and purposes, the Popular Front was over. A centrist government lurched on in France as the international situation worsened.

Fascism in Belgium

In Belgium, the fascist party "Rex" (from the Latin for "Christ the King"), led by Léon Degrelle (1906–1994), drew on frustrated white-collar workers and shopkeepers, victims of the Depression, who blamed competition from department stores and socialist consumer cooperatives for their plight. Economic malaise compounded tensions generated by the linguistic division between French-speaking Walloons and the Flemish speakers of Flanders, some of whom demanded Flemish autonomy. Although a wave of strikes in Belgium in 1936, similar to that in France at the same time, frightened the middle class, the Belgian fascists never won more than 12 percent of the vote. The majority of the middle class remained loyal to parliamentary government. Banks and the Socialist and Catholic parties successfully pressured the government for action to assist the lower middle class by increasing credit available to small retailers and extending union rights to white-collar employees. The Catholic Church's condemnation of Rex in 1937 led many of the group's Catholic members to return to moderate Catholic parties.

Similarly, in the Netherlands, the Dutch National Socialist League, which emulated the Nazis, remained far too small to contemplate an overthrow of the government. The movement was condemned by both the Calvinist Reform Church and the Catholic Church and won the support of only 8 percent of Dutch voters in 1937.

NATIONAL SOCIALISM IN GERMANY

In Germany, the Depression helped swell the ranks of not only the Nazi Party but other parties and groups (including powerful army officers and big businessmen) committed to the end of parliamentary government. Political parties, labor unions, and voluntary associations crumbled before the Nazi onslaught. Nazi propaganda espoused the German "national community" that would make all social and political tensions obsolete. Nazi organizations enrolled millions of Germans. The army would loyally serve Hitler, the man some generals had not long before scornfully dismissed as an "Austrian corporal."

The Collapse of the Weimar Republic

The Depression increased opposition to the Weimar Republic, particularly among the middle classes. The Nazis in 1929 were but one of a number of extreme right groups determined to overthrow the republic. The Depression also further eroded the centrist coalition within the Reichstag upon which the republic had depended from the beginning. In March 1930, the last remnants of the Weimar coalition came apart under the pressure of the economic turmoil; the government, led by the Social Democrats, resigned. Thereafter social and political compromise seemed impossible. President von Hindenburg began to rule by decree.

The new elections held in September 1930 confirmed the erosion of the parliamentary center. The Nazis received five times more votes than in the last elections, obtaining 18 percent of the popular vote and winning 107 seats in the Reichstag. The Communist Party, too, gained seats, while the Social Democratic Party lost seats, but remained the largest party with 143 deputies, and the moderate conservative parties also lost representatives. Bolstered by rising numbers of supporters, in 1932 Hitler ran for president against Hindenburg, winning 13.5 million votes to the general's 19 million and the Communist candidate's 4 million. The Nazi Party now had more than 800,000 members.

Traditional conservatives, including a number of important generals, not the least of whom was Hindenburg himself, turned against the republic. Franz von Papen (1879–1969), power broker of the traditional anti-parliamentarian right, became chancellor in June 1932. After elections for the Reichstag were held in November 1932, the Nazis became the largest party in the Reichstag (with 196 seats against 121 held by Social Democrats, 100 by Communists, and 90 by the Catholic Center Party). Between them, the Nazis and their bitter enemies, the Communists, both of whom rejected the Weimar Republic, had won more than half the votes cast. (Nonetheless, support for the Nazis had fallen by 2 million votes, reflecting the fact that some moderate conservatives were repelled by the murders and beatings carried out by Hitler's stormtroopers, the S.A.)

Papen resigned as chancellor in December 1932. His successor, General Kurt von Schleicher (1882–1934), wanted to form a parliamentary majority by wooing some Nazis—but excluding Hitler—and even trade unionists, an improbable idea. When Schleicher's government resigned the next month, Papen sought to bring the Nazis into a coalition government. Hoping to transform Germany from a republic into a military authoritarian regime (perhaps through a monarchical restoration), Papen believed that Hitler could serve his purposes if the Nazis received only three of twelve cabinet posts (including one for Hitler), and that once Hitler and the Nazis had helped assure the end of the Weimar Republic and the establishment of an authoritarian regime, they could be tossed aside. In Italy, Giolitti's Liberals had made the same fatal miscalculation in 1922 in their dealings with Mussolini.

Now joined by members of Hindenburg's family and staff, Papen convinced the old general to appoint Hitler as chancellor, believing that he could control Hitler in his capacity as vice-chancellor. On January 30, 1933, Adolf Hitler formed the seventeenth—and last—Weimar government. "We've boxed Hitler in," was the way Hindenburg memorably put it. "We have hired him," Papen assured his friends.

Many Prussian nobles and generals still mistrusted Hitler. To the former, he seemed a vulgar commoner, a Viennese paper-hanger; to the latter, a mere foot soldier who made boastful claims of military expertise. But the generals had been taught, above all, to obey orders. Furthermore, Hitler's denunciations of Bolshevism appealed to their dislike of Russia, their enemy on the eastern front during the Great War.

Most wealthy businessmen preferred more traditional nationalists like Hindenburg and Papen, and worried about Hitler's unpredictability. Hitler's early denunciations of capitalists and promises to create a new political elite irritated industrialists. The Nazi Party found but one major donor among big businessmen—the Rhineland steel magnate Fritz Thyssen—and a group of industrialists even tried to convince Hindenburg to leave Hitler out of the cabinet. The Nazis boasted that small donors and modest membership fees financed their party. Although some big businessmen shared the Nazis' virulent anti-Semitism, they were uneasy with the foreign condemnation it brought, and concerned that it might one day undercut their markets abroad. A one-day boycott in April 1933 called by the Nazis against Jewish businesses in Germany backfired, failing to attract mass support.

But big business nonetheless contributed to the fall of Weimar. Most Rhineland industrialists were no more in favor of parliamentary government than were Prussian Junkers. Hitler flattered business leaders, telling them that they had "worked their way to the top . . . which again only proves their higher race—they have the right to lead." Big businessmen were not about to oppose Hitler, as he promised public order, which was good for business, even if achieved at gunpoint.

Nazi Totalitarianism

The Nazi state was predicated upon Hitler's willingness—indeed eagerness—to use violence to fortify his power. In this he shared much with the Italian fascist dictator Mussolini and with Joseph Stalin, who made terror an essential part of the bureaucratic apparatus of the Communist Party and who more and more identified the interests of the party with his own rule. In Germany, Hitler's appointment as chancellor sparked a wave of systematic and brutal Nazi attacks on union members, socialists and Communists, Jews, and some Catholics who opposed Nazism.

Mussolini had consolidated his power over the Italian state in about three years. It took Hitler less than three months. During the night of February 27, 1933, someone set the Reichstag building in Berlin on fire, causing considerable damage. The police arrested a deranged, homeless Dutch Communist, charging him with arson. Although the debate on the origins of the Reichstag fire continues, it was probably set by someone working in

Communists under arrest after the Reichstag fire of 1933, which was most likely set by the Nazis themselves.

the Prussian ministry of the interior with the intention of blaming the Communists.

Citing an imaginary Communist plot against the state, Hitler convinced sympathetic members of the Reichstag to vote an emergency decree suspending virtually all individual rights and giving the government authority to maintain order as it saw fit. Hitler suspended the rights of those accused of crimes against the state. Penalties of imprisonment and even death could be imposed without due legal process as police arrested thousands of Communists. Hermann Göring (1893–1946), one of Hitler's long-time disciples and now minister of the interior in Prussia, authorized the creation of an auxiliary police force made up of members of the S.A. and other paramilitary groups.

But the parliamentary elections of March 5, 1933, which Hitler promised would be the last held in Nazi Germany and which took place under enormous Nazi intimidation, did not give Hitler the overwhelming majority he had anticipated—the Nazis emerged with only 44 percent of the vote. Nonetheless, Hitler proceeded as if the vote had been unanimous. On March 23, the cowed Reichstag approved an Enabling Act, which extended the unlimited "emergency" powers of the Nazis and transferred power from the legislative to the executive branch of government. Under terrible pressure, the liberal political parties of the Weimar Republic simply disbanded in late June. On July 14, 1933, Hitler banned all political parties except the Nazi Party. Hundreds of thousands of Germans now stampeded to join the Nazi Party. The party grew from 850,000 to 2.5 million by the end of 1933, adding so many people that the "old fighters"

who had joined early in the 1920s began to grumble that the party was losing its so-called elite character.

The Nazis implemented the apparatus of a totalitarian state. In May
1933, they organized the state-controlled German Labor Front to replace
the unions they had decimated. With labor parties and unions destroyed
and strikes now illegal, workers had no way of opposing decrees that made
them legally subordinate to their employers. Hitler dissolved the state parliaments and took away the remaining autonomy of the individual German
states, appointing Nazis to take over their state governments. A new law
empowered officials to dismiss subordinates whom they considered potentially disloyal to the Nazis, or who could not prove that they were of pure
"Aryan" racial stock (a racism based on the belief that Germans were descended from a superior Caucasian people).

Despite Nazi rhetoric about a racially pure community of Germans,
Hitler was far from envisioning social equality, which he associated with
Socialists and Communists. Still, for some Germans, the Nazi Party, and
particularly the S.S. (*Schutzstaffel*, Security Units that guarded Hitler)
provided a means of social mobility; military trappings conveyed the respectability many people associated with a uniform. Joining the Nazis provided status for young Germans whose economic aspirations had been
blocked and whose contributions to the party would be recognized. Although the Nazis drew support from virtually all of German society (although proportionately less support from workers), the Depression drove
more desperate middle-class Germans into the Nazi fold.

Hitler needed the loyalty of Germany's professional army so that his
power would remain unchallenged and to carry out his foreign policy
ambitions. But many German officers were becoming increasingly wary of
the S.A., which was now almost 3 million strong and which seemed out
of control. Its members openly competed with Nazi officials for local
influence and appointments. Ernst Röhm believed that his S.A. represented the second wave of the Nazi revolution. He announced that henceforth members of his force could not be tried by courts, and were to be
immune from police authority. Foolishly bragging that he would free
Hitler from his "stupid and dangerous" advisers, Röhm complained bitterly, "Adolf is a swine. He will give us all away."

The S.S. and the Gestapo (the Nazi secret police) crushed the S.A. on
June 30, 1934. They executed at least eighty people, including Röhm. The
"night of the long knives" also swept up some noted conservatives and military officers, as Hitler had feared trouble from the old right as well as from
the S.A. Hitler convinced President von Hindenburg that the gory purge
had saved the German Third Reich (or Third Empire) from a plot. Hindenburg concurred, expressing the view that "he who wants to make history
like Hitler must be prepared to let guilty blood flow and not be soft."

Hindenburg's death in August 1934, allowed Hitler to combine the titles
of chancellor and Führer ("leader"), which replaced that of "president," a

Hitler paying homage to Hindenburg shortly before the latter's death.

title that smacked of the republic. The army agreed to take an oath of personal allegiance to the man now considered "the executor of the whole people's will." On August 19, Hitler asked the German people to approve his assumption of both functions in a carefully orchestrated plebiscite. It was approved by 90 percent of those voting. No legal guarantees remained for citizens overheard uttering even a careless word of criticism of the Nazi state.

The Nazi program of "coordination" applied the policy of divide and rule to everyday life. By inserting Nazis into most aspects of civil society, such as organized groups and activities outside the family, the Nazis wanted to prevent any challenge to their monopoly of power. In many towns, the Nazis had already gradually taken over associational life—organizations based, for example, on occupation and universities attended, as well as sports clubs. Almost immediately after Hitler came to power, the Nazis worked to convert schools into mouthpieces for Hitler's state. The Nazis provided new textbooks and gave teachers instructions as to what should be taught, including "racial theory" and "Teutonic prehistory." Pictures of Hitler went up in every classroom and radios were provided so that his speeches could be heard. Physical education and sports became more prominent subjects. Instead of students fearing their teachers, as had often been the case in German schools, now non-Nazi teachers had reason to fear their students; members of the Hitler Youth organization were quick to report to Nazi Party members if a teacher seemed recalcitrant.

While the Nazi Party provided many people with a sense of national commitment, to disdain politics came to be seen as a virtue. An old German proverb says, "He who has choice has torment." In a totalitarian state, people have no choices left. In this way, the Nazis appropriated fears and suspicions of political life held by residents of small towns. Workers' organizations might have provided centers of resistance; many of them had been linked to the Social Democratic Party or the Communist Party.

But these organizations had already been closed. Depoliticized, closely monitored voluntary associations and churches could remain the center of local public life without threatening Nazi domination.

The Nazis brought hundreds of thousands of active Germans into carefully controlled Nazi organizations, the goal of each being to "reach toward Hitler," that is, to share the racist, nationalist goals of the Führer. The Hitler Youth by 1936 included almost half the German boys between ten and fourteen years of age; a League of German Girls also flourished. The Nazis reduced social life to its most basic component, the family (while, however, encouraging children to denounce their parents for being somehow disloyal to the fatherland, and sponsoring "breeding" programs outside the family unit). Vicarious participation in the mass ceremonies and rituals of Nazism also helped augment a sense of national identity.

As head of the German state, Hitler implemented the Nazi "leadership principle," which he defined as a "doctrine of conflict." He applied a strategy of "divide and rule" to the higher echelons of government, such as the three chancellories that replaced the cabinet. He tolerated and even encouraged open, aggressive competition between his most trusted subordinates and between branches of government. Those who enjoyed Hitler's confidence ruthlessly and aggressively carved out personal fiefdoms. Unlike Stalin, who watched over even the most minor details with obsessive care, the Führer provided little supervision to government agencies. Occasionally something would catch Hitler's attention and frenzied activity would follow. But he missed meetings, worked irregular hours, and was often disorganized. Hitler valued personal loyalty far more than efficiency and purposely kept the exact functions of some of his most important officials undefined.

German youths greet Hitler.

The "doctrine of conflict" adversely affected the economic goals Hitler set for the state. The army and the air force quarreled over resources, the S.S. and the police over jurisdiction. The Four-Year Plan launched in 1936 under Göring's direction illustrated the functioning of the Nazi state. Hitler wanted to stimulate economic development, above all in industries necessary for rearmament: steel, iron, and synthetic fuel and rubber. Göring had expanded his own base of strength within the Reich through his contacts with industrialists. But he spent far too much time warring with other branches of government. Furthermore, although government contracts appealed to industrialists, they resisted state intervention in their businesses. The Four-Year Plan failed to achieve its lofty goals.

Hitler realized that sheer terror was not enough to maintain popular support. Although he knew or cared very little about economics, Hitler correctly determined that the rapid rearmament of Germany would help create jobs. Food shortages remained severe until 1936, but public works projects also helped reduce unemployment and inflation. Big industrial concerns prospered, particularly those manufacturing war materials. Hitler bragged that he had wrought an "economic miracle."

More consumer goods, such as radios, reached the consumer market, contributing to a sense of optimism about material conditions of life. The Labor Front organized cut-rate Nazi vacations. Some families of modest means, many of whom had never had the opportunity to travel before, took cruises in the Baltic or even in the Mediterranean Sea. Hitler named this program "Strength Through Joy," perhaps taking the idea from Mussolini, whose fascists inaugurated the "Afterwork" program of recreational trips in Italy in the mid-1920s. However, production of Hitler's planned low-cost "Volkswagen," or "peoples' wagon" was postponed because factories were needed for military production.

Yet, sectors of the German economy remained weak. German industry, particularly the armaments manufacturers, depended on imports of iron ore, copper, oil, rubber, and bauxite. Many Germans found that their share in the "national community" was small. Department stores undercut shopkeepers. And although Hitler liked to identify the German people with what he considered rural virtues—"blood and soil," as he frequently put it—the number of small farms continued to decline, and the income of farmers stagnated. There was no marked return to the soil. Germany continued to urbanize under the Third Reich.

In Nazi ideology, women were inferior to men. The Führer preached that women's place was in the home or in the delivery room. The state offered attractive financial benefits to families with children, and the German birthrate continued to rise, bolstered by an improving economy. Just months after becoming chancellor, Hitler forced women to give up industrial jobs and excluded them from public service and teaching. Certain occupations were classified as "women's work," primarily those involving traditional textile or handicraft production or farmwork. But, despite the slogan "women at home," the reality in Nazi Germany, as in Mussolini's Italy, was increasingly otherwise. The campaign to remove women from paid employment ended in the late 1930s, as women were needed to replace men conscripted into the army. The number of women working in German industry rose by a third between 1933 and 1939.

Some intellectuals and artists jumped on the Nazi bandwagon. Very few members—though the novelist Thomas Mann, who had moved from being an angry conservative to a supporter of the republic by 1922, was one—resigned from the prestigious Prussian Academy of Arts when called upon to pledge allegiance to Hitler. The philosopher Martin Heidegger (1889–1976) saluted the Führer as "guided by the inexorability of that spiritual mission that the destiny of the German people forcibly impresses upon its history." Hitler hauled out the aged Heidegger on formal occasions to claim that Germany's finest scholars had become Nazis. In fact, some of the finest German minds were already contemplating emigration.

The Nazis burned books that espoused ideas of which they disapproved. This policy began in May 1933, when storm troopers coordinated the burning of books by Jews, Communists, socialists, and other disapproved authors. In 1937, posters in the municipal library of Essen actually boasted that in the four years that had elapsed since the book burnings, there had been a "healthy" decline in books borrowed and in the use of the reading room.

Hitler waged war against what he called "decadent" art and its new experimental forms, ordering many works removed from museums. During the Weimar period, Berlin, a city with 40 theaters and 120 newspapers, had become a center of daring and successful experimentation by artists, writers, and composers, as well as scholars. In 1919, the architect Walter Gropius (1883–1969) had begun a school that combined art and applied arts in the town of Weimar. The Bauhaus—Architect's House—set the architectural and decorative style of Weimar, stressing simplicity and beauty, expressing function through form, combining art and craft. By using the most modern materials available in the quest for "total architecture," Gropius hoped to reconcile art and industry. The Bauhaus' modernism and the presence of foreign architects, artists, and designers made it suspect to nationalists. Hitler, the former aspiring artist, detested modernism. He closed the Bauhaus as a symbol of what the Nazis called "cultural Bolshevism."

In 1937, the Nazis in Munich staged an "Exhibition of Degenerate Art," including expressionist and dadaist paintings, among other modernist works. A Great German Art Show opened at the same time, offering samples of officially approved painting. While Stalin's preferred style of "socialist realism" emphasized work, Nazi art celebrated being German. Nazi art glorified the cult of the primitive, offered sentimental portraits of German families tilling the land or at home, blond youths rising before dawn and hiking into the Pomeranian forests, the merging of "blood and soil," and plunging into chilly lakes, or of square-jaw soldiers portrayed as medieval Teutonic knights.

In their attacks upon modernist composers, the Nazis reserved particular vehemence for the works of Jewish composers such as Arnold Schönberg (1874–1951) and Gustav Mahler (1860–1911), while the compositions of the late nineteenth-century anti-Semitic Richard Wagner delighted Hitler. The theater, too, suffered from censorship, as well as from the departure of a number of Germany's leading playwrights. Hitler himself preferred light plays, such as a rustic comedy that earned the Critic's Prize in Berlin in 1934, in which the leading character was a pig. Anti-modernism could be seen in Nazi attacks on the supposed hedonism of the "roaring twenties," associated with a perceived loosening of sexual morals, including homosexuality, neon lights, jazz, and modern dances. Nazis did not do the Charleston.

Joseph Goebbels (1897–1945), Hitler's minister of propaganda who once wrote "Oh, how wonderful it is to be able to hate," permitted movie producers and newspaper editors to exercise self-censorship. They were aware of the costs of making a slip. In Germany, as in all of Western Europe, films—first silent movies and then "talkies"—had become by far the most popular form of entertainment. Like Muzak on elevators invented during the Depression, films provided a temporary escape from hard times. Nazism encouraged the production of a number of virulently anti-Semitic films, above all *The Jew Suess* (1940), the story of an eighteenth-century Jewish financier who betrays a German state and is executed, to the cheers of Nazi audiences.

Hitler commissioned the popular, star-struck film-maker Leni Riefenstahl (1902–   ) to produce *Triumph of the Will*, a remarkable propaganda film that depicts the carefully orchestrated Nuremberg rally of 1934, with its uniforms, banners, and impeccable regimentation as searchlights sweep the stage.

Hitler's New Reich and the Jews

Hitler made anti-Semitism a cornerstone of Nazi ideology and of state policy. In 1935, the Nuremberg Laws, which made the swastika the official symbol of Nazi Germany, deprived Jews (defined by having had at least one Jewish grandparent) of citizenship, declaring them to be "subjects." Jews were forced to wear a yellow Star of David prominently on their clothing when they left their homes. The laws also forbade marriage or sex between non-Jewish Germans and Jews. Signs in restaurants, movie houses, and parks proclaimed that Jews were not allowed. Yet, some Jewish businesses, including banks, continued to operate, if only because Hitler feared the economic consequences if they were closed. Some of these were "Aryanized" (purged of Jewish owners and managers) by the spring of 1938. Shortly thereafter, the German state moved to confiscate the assets of

Jews; it forced families to list the value of what they owned and to turn over their assets to Gentile trustees, who could dispose of these estates as they wanted. A decree expanded the list of professions and occupations from which Jews were to be excluded.

When Hitler came to power, some Jews emigrated immediately, or made plans to do so. With Jews unable to teach in universities after early 1933 or to attend university as of 1937, many distinguished Jewish scholars and artists left for Britain or the United States, including the brilliant physicist Albert Einstein (1879–1955). Other intellectual exiles from Hitler's Germany were not Jewish, among them the poet Stefan George, the writer Thomas Mann, and the painter Max Beckmann. But one had to have some place to go. The borders of Hungary and Yugoslavia were closed to refugees. One by one, countries that had accepted Jewish refugees began refusing to do so. In 1938, the French government greatly tightened restrictions on the admission of refugees, claiming that France was being "saturated" with them. Britain, 80 percent of whose arriving refugees were Jewish, made it harder for Jews to get into Britain or to go to Palestine. Switzerland, which had been known as a haven for political exiles, also that year closed the door on Jews fleeing Germany or Austria. Moreover, the Swiss government suggested that German passport officials stamp "non-Aryan" on passports of Jews so that they could be turned back at the frontier. The German government, in turn, promised not to allow Jews to leave for Switzerland unless they had visas. The Swiss police hunted down refugees living in Switzerland whom they deemed illegal residents, putting them across the German border, or other frontiers.

On the evening of November 9, 1938, following the assassination of a German embassy official in Paris by a Polish Jew whose parents had been deported from Germany, S.S. and other Nazi activists launched planned attacks on specific Jewish businesses and homes throughout Germany.

Nazis posting placards in a Jewish shop window. The notice on the window reads "It is forbidden to buy from this Jewish shop."

They destroyed stores, killed several hundred and beat thousands of Jews. Thirty thousand Jews were imprisoned in camps. The terrifying night became known as *Kristallnacht,* because the sound of shattering glass windows resounded throughout Berlin that night. Few Germans protested.

Hitler's Foreign Policy

As Hitler had never hidden his intention of destroying the Jews, he also had never concealed his goal of shattering the Treaty of Versailles. German foreign policy, then, came to dominate European international affairs. Hitler planned to rearm Germany, and he demanded the return of the Saar, whose rich mines the French held north of their border, and of German parts of Upper Silesia on the border of Poland, the remilitarization of the Rhineland, and the absorption of the Polish or Danzig Corridor, which divided Prussia from East Prussia. But Hitler's long-term goals, which were far greater, were inseparable from his megalomaniacal determination to expand Germany by armed conquest, which he had made clear in *Mein Kampf,* published in 1925.

Hitler's foreign policy was predicated upon his determination that Germany conquer "living space" (*Lebensraum*) in Eastern Europe and his theory that the Aryan race was superior to any other and therefore had the right, indeed the obligation, to assert its will on the "inferior" Slav peoples. On February 3, 1933, a week after becoming chancellor, Hitler told German generals of his plans to rearm Germany and to conquer land for agricultural production and German settlements in Central, Southeastern, and Eastern Europe. The Slavic peoples of the Soviet Union, Poland, and Czechoslovakia would serve the German "master race" as slaves.

Once Hitler came to power, he was less open about his previously stated goals because of Germany's vulnerability to invasion, but these goals did not change. Hitler had to move with particular caution to avoid confrontation with Britain and particularly with France, with whom he considered a war inevitable. For the moment, Poland and Czechoslovakia each had a stronger army than Germany did when Hitler took power. So Hitler had to carry out his foreign policy with patience and resourcefulness. He left in place the foreign minister and much of the old diplomatic corps, although he viewed them as weak and suspected their loyalty. In May 1933, he declared that he had no intention of rearming Germany, assuring the other powers that he wanted only peace. In October, however, Hitler announced that Germany would walk out of the Geneva Disarmament Conference, which had begun the previous year, and that it would leave the League of Nations. Once again, he insisted that Germany wanted only peace and respect and would take only legal steps to "break the chains of Versailles."

Hitler signed a non-aggression agreement with Poland on January 26, 1934. To the surprised generals who knew he intended to wipe Germany's neighbor off the map, he immediately made clear that he had no intention of respecting the agreement. The German-Polish non-aggression pact was a blow to France's plans to maintain Germany's diplomatic isolation by a collective treaty system directed against Hitler. These military alliances with the Eastern European states of Poland, Czechoslovakia, Romania, and Yugoslavia would leave Germany surrounded by potential enemies, albeit relatively small ones, closely tied to France. The Polish dictator Pilsudski did not trust Hitler, but he believed that he might be able to profit from Poland's strategic position between Germany and the Soviet Union and could take advantage of a possible German attack on either Austria or Czechoslovakia to take disputed territories.

Hitler's pact with Poland chilled Russian relations with Germany. It led Stalin to seek security against Hitler. The Soviet Union joined the League of Nations in September 1934; Stalin signed a defense treaty with France in May 1935, and another with Czechoslovakia two weeks later, which bound the Soviets to defend that country in case of a German attack, but only if France fulfilled its treaty obligations.

Hitler and Mussolini

While France scurried to find allies, Germany had none. Hitler had long admired Benito Mussolini. The two dictators had much in common. Both had taken advantage of economic and social crisis to put themselves in a position of unchallenged authority. Both were aggressive nationalists who intended to revise the Treaty of Versailles. Hitler's territorial ambitions in Eastern Europe did not conflict with Mussolini's goal of possible empire-building in the Balkans and North Africa. But because of possible conflicting interests, notably Hitler's long-range intention to annex Austria and Mussolini's claim of the Austrian Tyrol for Italy, both men at first viewed each other with some suspicion. Yet, fascist Italy and Nazi Germany seemed natural allies, sharing France as an enemy. The Duce had pro-

Adolf Hitler and Benito Mussolini, two dictators ready to redraw the map of the world.

claimed in 1933, the year Hitler came to power: "The victory of Hitler is also our victory."

Mussolini had reduced Albania, the small, poor nation across the Adriatic, to a virtual Italian protectorate, although it had almost no Italian population. In the South Tyrol, absorbed under the terms of the post-war settlement, Mussolini ordered a policy of Italianization, forbidding the use of the German and Slovene languages in schools. He also began to transform Somalia, the country at the horn of Africa that Italy had conquered before the war. Burning villages and slaughtering their residents, he turned the country into a military base from which new conquests could be launched. In Libya, Italian forces routinely ordered the use of mustard gas and public hangings to try to solidify their control.

Mussolini worked to increase international tensions wherever possible in the hope of taking advantage of instability. The Duce had signed the Kellogg-Briand Pact in 1928, in which the major powers renounced war as an instrument of national policy, not because he believed in its principles, but because he wanted Britain and France to treat Italy as a Great Power. Meanwhile, Italy funneled secret arms to Germany and trained its pilots in violation of post-war treaties and the policies of the League of Nations, to which Italy belonged. In the Balkans, Italian agents provided financial support to right-wing terrorist groups, including ethnic Hungarians and Croats plotting against the Yugoslav government.

Hitler's plan to absorb Austria required Italian support, or at least neutrality, particularly until Hitler had fully rearmed Germany. But for the moment, Germany was still in no position to antagonize France, whose army could have occupied much of Germany with only minimal resistance. Hitler realized the importance of proceeding cautiously, and not simply sweeping into Austria. But the German dictator took a calculated risk in 1934 when he orchestrated the murder of Austrian Chancellor Dollfuss, who, although he had made himself dictator and waged war on the left, had intended to maintain Austrian independence. Dollfuss had banned the Austrian Nazi Party, which was funded and supplied by German Nazis, and had signed alliances with Italy and Hungary. Austrian Nazis, backed by Hitler, retaliated by assassinating Dollfuss during a badly organized coup attempt. The aloof, steely Kurt Schuschnigg (1897–1977) replaced Dollfuss as leader of an authoritarian government closely tied to the Catholic Church. Schuschnigg, like his predecessor, believed he could maintain right-wing rule in Austria without German help. These dual allegiances—to Austrian independence and to an institutional role for the Catholic Church—separated Austria's authoritarian regime from that in Germany.

Mussolini had sent tanks to the Austro-Italian frontier at the time of the attempted coup. A Nazi takeover of Austria would leave a potentially aggressive power at Italy's northern frontier. But, for the moment, Mussolini was absorbed in preparing for war against the African state of Ethiopia, and it seemed unlikely that he would do more.

Hitler thus correctly assessed that it was unlikely that Britain, France, and Italy would mount an effective, concerted response to blatant German moves to overthrow the Austrian government. Each government limited itself to a protest against German meddling in Austrian internal politics, asserting its interest in Austria's independence. The attempted putsch in Vienna alarmed the British government. But it was convinced that conciliatory moves toward Germany might keep Hitler in line, particularly if, as a good many British conservatives believed, Hitler wanted no more than to be recognized as a power and to be able to defend Germany's borders. Nor was the French government willing to do more than express irritation, as it was confronting a fascist threat in France itself.

In 1935, however, Hitler's foreign policy entered a new and more aggressive phase. He defied the Versailles Treaty in March by announcing that Germany's army would be increased to half a million men and that military service would become compulsory and that the German air force had already been rebuilt, despite the prohibition of the peace agreement. British, French, and Italian representatives met in Stresa, Italy, in April 1935, to discuss and denounce Germany's violation of the Treaty of Versailles—as did the League of Nations itself—and to reaffirm the Treaty of Locarno of 1925, in which the German government had joined Britain, France, and Italy in pledging to resolve future international disputes peacefully. Hitler then made the usual reassuring noises, stating that he would sign bilateral agreements with any of the powers (as opposed to the collective security agreements he had already helped shred), uphold the Treaty of Locarno, and recognize the territorial integrity of Austria.

Great Britain reflected wariness by signing a naval agreement with Germany in June 1935, establishing a ratio of 100:35 between the two navies. This agreement, however, enraged the French government; Britain had not even informed its ally of the hasty negotiations that led to the agreement. France then signed a secret treaty with Italy, the goal of which was to protect Austrian independence.

On October 1935, Mussolini's armies invaded Ethiopia, where Italian forces had suffered humiliating defeat in 1896. Determined to expand Italy's fledgling empire, a quarter of a million Italian women, including the queen, pawned their wedding rings (women who turned in their gold rings received in exchange tin ones blessed by the pope) to help raise money for the war of conquest fought with bombs, machine guns, and poison gas. But Ethiopian Emperor Haile Selassie's army also had some modern weapons, as well as spears. Although the wave of popular enthusiasm Mussolini had anticipated in Italy failed to materialize, the Duce correctly assessed that Britain and France would do little more than denounce the invasion because they still desired Mussolini's support against Hitler. Realizing this, Hitler had encouraged Italy to attack Ethiopia.

Haile Selassie appealed to the League of Nations for help for his country, which had been a member nation since 1923. The League imposed economic sanctions against Italy, but left them weak by excluding oil from the list of products affected and did not try to prevent passage of Italian ships through the Suez Canal on the way to Ethiopia. The British government made it clear that it considered the appeasement of Italy the only way to end the crisis and placed an embargo against the sale of arms to Ethiopia, effectively letting Mussolini have his way. U.S. President Franklin Roosevelt even offered Italy American loans in order to develop the conquered colony.

Italian troops took the Ethiopian capital of Addis Ababa in May 1936. Over half a million Ethiopians were killed in the one-sided fighting. Italy lost only 5,000 soldiers, a number Mussolini decried as so relatively small that it seemed to cheapen his victory. On July 15, the League of Nations formally lifted all sanctions against Italy. The Stresa front—an agreement made by Britain, France, and Italy with the goal of containing Hitler—collapsed as Mussolini defied the League of Nations. The Duce now began referring to himself as the "invincible Duce."

Remilitarization and Rearmament

On March 7, 1936, German troops moved into the Rhineland, which had been declared by the Treaty of Versailles to be a demilitarized zone. Hitler had secretly promised his anxious generals that he would order German forces to pull back if the French army intervened. Whether or not a stiffer, armed British and French response might have stopped Hitler at this point has long been debated.

German ambassadors in the European capitals claimed that the move had been necessitated by the destruction of the Locarno agreements by France's pact with the Soviets. The blustering, lazy Joachim von Ribbentrop (1893–1946), the German ambassador to Britain (who had simply added the aristocratic "von" to his name), attempted without success to browbeat the British into an alliance with Germany. France pushed the British government to react sharply against Hitler's brazen move, but would not act alone. France's unwillingness to act without British support in the crisis was a legacy of its failed occupation of the Rhineland in 1923, when it was forced to act with only Belgian assistance (see Chapter 26). In Germany, Hitler's prestige soared. He had delivered as promised, facing down the powers that had imposed the Treaty of Versailles and destroying the Locarno Treaty.

Hitler now speeded up the pace of German rearmament, particularly of the air force. By 1938, armament production absorbed 52 percent of state expenses and 17 percent of Germany's gross national product. German rearmament forced Britain to modernize its armed forces. Prodded by the Labour Party, British military expenses more than doubled between 1934 and 1937, though this was far less than what Germany spent at the same time (see Table 27-2).

TABLE 27-2. DEFENSE EXPENDITURES OF THE GREAT POWERS, 1930–1938 (IN MILLIONS OF CURRENT DOLLARS)

Year	Japan	Italy	Germany	U.S.S.R.	U.K.	France	U.S.
1930	218	266	162	772	512	498	699
1933	183	351	452	707	333	524	570
1934	292	455	709	3,479	540	707	803
1935	300	966	1,607	5,517	646	867	806
1936	313	1,149	2,332	2,933	892	995	932
1937	940	1,235	3,298	3,446	1,245	890	1,032
1938	1,740	746	7,415	5,429	1,863	919	1,131

Source: Paul Kennedy, *The Rise and Fall of the Great Powers* (New York: Vintage, 1989), p. 296.

Germany had the advantage of rearming with the most up-to-date war materials, while the arsenals of the other powers included old weapons and equipment. Steel had gradually replaced wood in the construction of airplanes. Slotted wings made landings safer by reducing the speed upon approach. Some advanced fighters could now fly up to 400 miles per hour. Bombers with four engines had greatly enhanced range. Aircraft carriers further revolutionized air warfare. There were changes on the ground, too. Both German and French tanks were now much more powerful, protected by thick armor, as well as having radios and carrying heavy guns.

THE SPANISH CIVIL WAR

The German army and air force would try out their new weapons in Spain, which, although neutral in the Great War, became the battlefield of European ideologies during the bloody civil war that lasted from 1936 to 1939. For the first time since the Peninsular War during the Napoleonic era, the world's attention turned to Spain.

Indeed, there was relatively little to distinguish the Spain of 1920 from that of more than a century earlier. The days of empire and glory had long since passed, symbolized by the loss of Cuba and the Philippines to the United States in 1898. With the exception of relatively industrialized Catalonia and the Basque provinces in the northwestern corner of the country, Spain remained an overwhelmingly agricultural society. Coalitions and alliances between the nobility, the Catholic Church, and the army determined political power in Madrid.

Social and Political Instability

The ineffectual King Alfonso XIII (ruled 1886–1931) confronted social and political problems that defied solution. Catalonian and Basque regional separatism challenged the domination by the Spanish government in Madrid. Chronic political and social instability helped push the army into the role of chief arbiter of political life. Labor strife, assassinations, street battles, and police violence became the order of the day in the early 1920s. A humiliating defeat in 1921 of an occupying Spanish army by Moroccans demanding independence weakened the prestige of the government.

In 1923, General Miguel Primo de Rivera (1870–1930) seized power with the support of the army and the king. Four years later, espousing "nation, church and king," Primo set out to "modernize" Spain, ordering the construction of dams, sewers, roads, and prisons. He became a familiar sight in the cafés and bars of Madrid, such tours occasionally being followed by gushing, incoherent bulletins to the Spanish people drafted on his return home. Primo de Rivera antagonized the political left by promulgating a constitution in 1927 that made ministers no longer responsible to the Cortes and upset army officers (so numerous that they made up a sixth of the army) by intervening in promotions. The weak Spanish economy eroded middle-class support for his regime, and Primo de Rivera resigned in 1930.

The following year, Alfonzo XIII abdicated after elections returned an anti-monarchist majority to the Cortes. The army refused to save the monarchy, because most officers now hoped to impose authoritarian rule. The nobles, upon whose support the kings of Spain had for centuries depended, "observed the fall of the monarchy as they might have watched a bad film."

A coalition of republicans and moderate Socialists established the Second Spanish Republic in April 1931. The government of Manuel Azaña

The poverty of Spain in the 1930s: a peasant woman in the fields.

(1880–1940) enacted a series of anticlerical measures, including the formal separation of church and state, imposed new taxes, passed labor reforms, and enacted land reform, including the outright expropriation of some of the largest estates. More strikes, land seizures by peasants, and attacks on churches and convents (movements that in some regions took on the character of a popular revolution) drove more wealthy landowners and churchmen toward the anti-parliamentary right. Although assailed from the right, the Spanish Republic was unable to count on the support of the unions, which wanted more far-reaching social reforms, or of anarchists, who wanted the abolition of the state itself. Azaña fell from power in September 1933.

Thus began the republic's two "black years," marked by increasing social and political violence. The inclusion of the right in a more conservative republican government brought a violent reaction from the left. During the "October Revolution" of 1934, leftists in Madrid, Catalan autonomists, and miners in the northern province of Asturias rose up, quickly setting up local "soviets" throughout their region. They held out for two weeks before being brutally crushed by Moroccan legionnaires commanded by General Francisco Franco (1892–1975).

In 1935, Radicals, Socialists, Communists and some anarchists formed a "Popular Front" in defense of the republic against the right. It barely won a majority in elections held at the beginning of the next year, then quickly fell apart because of ideological differences amid high unemployment and political violence. The Falange, a small paramilitary fascist movement begun in 1933, further destabilized the republic. A paramilitary organization whose members were drawn primarily from the lower middle classes, the Falange emulated the Italian fascist "black shirts" and German Nazis. In response to a wave of violence against republicans, the government declared the Falange illegal and arrested its leader in March 1936.

A military insurrection against the republic began in Morocco on July 17, 1936, quickly followed by garrison uprisings in most of Spain's major cities (see Map 27.2). German and Italian planes then carried the insurgents to the Spanish mainland. Right-wing nationalist rebels overwhelmed loyalist troops and workers in several key cities and soon held the traditionally conservative regions of Castile, Galicia, and Navarre.

The fragility of the loyalist alliance compromised the loyalist defense of the Spanish Republic. In Madrid, Socialist trade unions held the upper hand. In Catalonia and Andalusia, anarchist peasants and workers were a majority; they took the outbreak of the war as a signal to begin a social revolution, expropriating land, occupying factories, and establishing cooperatives. Workers' committees, holding power in some regions, unleashed terror against the upper classes. The Socialists now were in the awkward position of trying to rein in the social revolution for which they had originally called. Communists feared that an attempted social revolution from

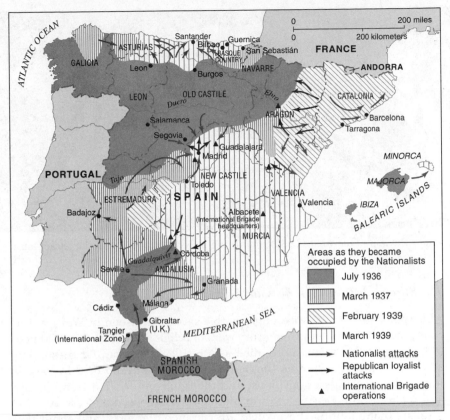

MAP 27.2 THE SPANISH CIVIL WAR, 1936–1939   The growing domination of Spain by the nationalists, as well as arrows showing nationalist and republican loyalist attacks during the Spanish Civil War.

below would compromise the attempt to save the republic and, furthermore, that it might undercut support for their party. The Communist Party grew sixfold in less than a year, adopting the centralized, hierarchical structure upon which Stalin insisted. It purged members who had joined the Workers' Party of Marxist Unification (P.O.U.M.), which supported Trotsky against Stalin. The Communists, determined to destroy their allies on the loyalist side, withheld supplies and ammunition from anarchist and Socialist units.

Whereas the loyalists suffered the consequences of disunity, the nationalists benefited from increasing unity behind General Francisco Franco. Short, portly, and bald, Franco did not look the part of an officer who had risen rapidly through the ranks. Franco blamed freemasons (members of anticlerical Masonic lodges) for Spain's problems as Hitler blamed Jews for those of Germany. Franco considered himself a warrior king struggling against infidels who deserved no quarter.

Pablo Picasso's *Guernica* (1937), mourning a German and Italian air attack on a Basque village.

The Struggle between Loyalists and Nationalists

The Spanish Civil War was fought with a savagery unseen in Western Europe since the seventeenth-century wars of religion. At least 580,000 people, and probably many more, died as a result of the war. Of these, only about a sixth were killed on the battlefield. Ten thousand died in (largely nationalist) air raids on civilians, and thousands more died from disease and malnutrition. During the war, nationalists executed at least 200,000 loyalists (not counting those killed after Franco's victory), and about that same number died at the hands of the republican forces or from disease in prison. Throughout the first two months of the war, in areas controlled by the loyalists, age-old social and political tensions exploded in violence and death. Members of the Falange and nonarchists were taken from their cells in the Madrid prison and shot; in the province of Catalonia alone, more than a thousand clergy and nuns perished. The nationalists made effective propaganda use of loyalist atrocities, real or imaginary, as the pro-nationalist London *Daily Mail* proclaimed "Reds Crucify Nuns." The nationalists organized "fiestas of death" in bull rings, machine-gunning loyalists, including prominent intellectuals, Basque priests, and workers.

The Spanish Civil War polarized Europe because it pitted against each other the political extremes that had emerged in Europe since the Great War. For the political right, religion and social hierarchy were at stake in a pitched battle against socialism, communism, and anarchism. Those supporting the Spanish Republic saw the civil war as a struggle against international fascism. Foreign volunteers, including 20,000 Britons and Irish and many refugees from Nazi Germany, joined the loyalist forces. The volunteers of the Abraham Lincoln Brigade from the United States fought with idealism and determination—but with only occasional effectiveness.

Skeletons of nuns exposed outside a convent in July 1936 by loyalist anticlericals.

However these "International Brigades" were largely responsible for the heroic defense of Madrid that began on November 7, 1936. The writers who fought in the Spanish Civil War, virtually all on the loyalist side, produced some of the most remarkable and surprisingly objective literature about war written in this century, including the American novelist Ernest Hemingway's *For Whom the Bell Tolls* (1940) and the British George Orwell's *Homage to Catalonia* (1938), an account of his service on the loyalist side and of the damaging divisions between the major political factions.

Franco's forces enjoyed a significant military advantage over the loyalists because their forces included the bulk of the armed forces at the outbreak of the civil war. The loyalist army lacked such necessities as field glasses and good maps. Orwell recalled his amazement at being issued an 1896 model German Mauser rifle and at the seemingly insurmountable

The American Abraham Lincoln Brigade arrives in Barcelona to save the Spanish Republic, October 1936.

Francisco Franco at his desk with a photo of Hitler not far away.

difficulties of forging an able fighting force out of a motley crew of illiterate peasants, anarchist workers, shop clerks, and foreign volunteers, many of whom did not speak Spanish and for whom the only word known in common was "comrade."

The republican loyalists counted on receiving arms, munitions, and other supplies from the Western democracies. But the British government wanted to maintain peace at all costs, and many of its prominent political figures admired Franco. In France, Premier Léon Blum's Popular Front government hesitated to take any steps that would widen the Spanish conflict and further polarize his own country. Without tanks, airplanes, and other supplies from the Soviet Union, the Spanish Republic probably would have almost immediately collapsed in the face of the nationalist forces.

German and Italian assistance proved decisive. While Britain, France, and the United States abided by non-intervention agreements, Italy sent 100,000 soldiers to Spain. The loyalists easily defeated the ill-equipped Italian forces, who relied on Michelin tourist maps, in a spring 1937 ground battle. The Italians fared somewhat better in the air, where they faced virtually no opposition, and Mussolini's pilots helped destroy loyalist supply lines. Hitler used the Spanish Civil War as a military training ground, sending planes, guns, munitions, and other supplies through Portugal. German advisers trained nationalist pilots and military personnel. The pilots of the German Condor Legion flew bombing runs against loyalist Spanish forces, as well as against civilians. On April 26, 1937, German and Italian planes bombed and strafed the small town of Guernica, killing more than 100 residents. Within a month, the Spanish-born painter Pablo Picasso had immortalized the martyrdom of Guernica in his large canvas depicting the horrors of modern warfare.

When the nationalists attacked Madrid at the end of August 1937, the Communist militant Dolores Ibarruri, known as "La Pasionaria" (1895–1989), rallied loyalists with her defiant shout, "They shall not pass!" In the north, the nationalists reached the Atlantic Ocean, cutting off the loyalist Basque provinces from France. By October 1937, Franco's forces controlled all of the north coast. The loyalists struggled along an imposing front that stretched from the Mediterranean south of Granada to the Pyrenees. When Franco's army reached the Mediterranean Sea, it isolated Catalonia from remaining loyalist territory; loyalist supplies dwindled. Barcelona fell in January 1939. Britain and France (where the Popular Front had fallen from power) quickly recognized the Franco regime. Republican refugees carried what they could through the mountains and snows of the Pyrenees to France. Those who fled into Portugal, in which the republic had been overthrown in 1926, were returned to Spain by the dictatorship of Antonio Salazar (1889–1970). Despite assurances to Britain and France to the contrary, bloody reprisals against loyalists began immediately.

Franco, now known as "Caudillo," or "leader," established an authoritarian dictatorship based on the support of the army, the Church, and wealthy landowners, three groups that had opposed the republic. But recognizing Spain's weakness, Franco declined to pursue a policy of expan-

Communist leader Dolores Ibarruri, "La Pasionaria," at the siege of Madrid, 1936.

Spanish refugees crossing the Pyrenees to France in 1938.

sion that characterized Italian fascism or German national socialism. Furthermore, like Salazar's Portugal, Franco's dictatorship allowed the Catholic Church an institutional role that would have been unthinkable in Nazi Germany and was less significant in Italy.

THE COMING OF WORLD WAR II

Determined to achieve his territorial goals and willing to go to war if necessary to do so, Hitler in 1936 allied in turn with Italy and Japan. He sent German troops into Austria and then Czechoslovakia, not believing that Great Britain and France would resist, but prepared to go to war if they did so. Finally, Germany and the Soviet Union astonished the world by signing a mutual non-aggression pact, clearing the way for Hitler to launch a murderous attack on Poland. Attempting to avoid war at all costs, Britain and France accepted the occupation of Austria and Czechoslovakia but drew the line at Poland, leading to the confrontation that would begin the Second World War.

The Axis

Joint participation in support of the Spanish nationalists moved Germany and Italy closer together. The Italian dictator no longer dismissed Hitler as a "gramophone that plays only seven tunes" and made it clear that he was willing to sacrifice Austrian independence for a closer relationship with Hitler's Germany. Coming to the conclusion that German military strength could further Italian aims, in October 1936, Mussolini signed a pact with Hitler, forming what the Italian dictator called an "Axis." During Mussolini's visit to Berlin in the fall of 1937, Hitler flattered the Duce, afterward entertaining aides with imitations of Mussolini's strutting speeches. Hitler made clear that Germany's interests lay to the east; Mussolini could have the Mediterranean, and a free hand in Yugoslavia, Albania, and Greece.

The Duce now openly borrowed from Hitler's Nazis in other ways. The Duce ordered his soldiers to goose-step like the Germans, claiming that it was the military stride of ancient Rome. This led to considerable embarrassment to King Victor Emmanuel III, who was too old to attempt it without falling down. Mussolini also ordered his countrymen to stop shaking hands and take up the ancient Roman military salute.

Racial theories had hitherto never played more than a minor part in Mussolini's rise to power or his daily bombast. The Duce, who had a Jewish mistress, had mocked Hitler's "delirium of race," and Mussolini at first enjoyed widespread support among Italian Jews—about one of every three had joined the Fascist Party. But in 1938 Mussolini began a campaign against Italian Jews, who numbered no more than 50,000 in a country of 40 million people. These measures managed only to irritate many Italians in a country in which Jews seemed perfectly well assimilated.

Germany found another authoritarian partner in Japan. Over the last half of the nineteenth century, Japan had made itself an industrial and military power. In need of raw materials such as oil and rubber, the Japanese government sought to create an empire in Southeast Asia. By the late 1930s, the Japanese army had reached a million men, with reserves of twice that strength. The Japanese air force had 2,000 fighters, including the new "Zero" fighter, as fast as any in the world. In 1931, Japan embarked on a piecemeal conquest of Manchuria at the expense of China. Since Japan has virtually no natural resources, its goal was to create a resource base, which would be necessary for fighting the total war that many young Japanese generals eagerly anticipated. A year later, the Japanese government created the client state of Manchukuo, declaring the last emperor of China, Henry Pu-Yi, to be its emperor.

Fearing that the Soviet Union might try to brake its military expansion, Japan late in 1936 also signed a formal friendship treaty with Germany, the "Anti-Comintern" (anti-Communist) Pact, hoping also to discourage possible British and American intervention in Asia. In 1937, Japanese forces began to conquer chunks of northern China in order to establish a buffer zone between Manchukuo and the Soviet Union. This brought conflict with China. Japan then embarked on a major naval expansion program, exceeding both in number and size the limits stipulated by the Washington Naval Conference (1921–1922) to which Japan, among the other powers, had agreed. The United States was entrenched in isolationism and still suffering from the Depression. Angered by Japanese aggression and Japan's alliance with Nazi Germany, Britain and the other Western powers joined the United States in imposing an embargo on the sale of oil and other vital raw materials to Japan.

Aggression and Appeasement

In November 1937, Hitler unveiled to the generals his plans to absorb Austria and Czechoslovakia, perhaps as early as the following year if political unrest in France or a war in the Mediterranean between France and Italy reduced the chances of a French military response (see Map 27.3). Hitler's confidence derived partly from information he had received that Neville Chamberlain, the new Conservative British prime minister, who in a speech had once called Hitler's National Socialism "a great social experiment," might accept Germany's annexation of Austria and the Czech Sudetenland as inevitable and was concerned only that it occur without strife. Chamberlain feared that if Britain went to war against Germany, Hitler's allies Italy and Japan would strike British imperial interests in the Middle and Far East—for example, in Egypt and Burma. Furthermore, he viewed German ambitions toward the German-speaking parts of Austria and Czechoslovakia, as well as toward the Polish Corridor, as in keeping with the principle of nationalism, believing that Germany had been treated too harshly by the Treaty of Versailles.

Convinced that Britain would not act, Hitler bullied Austrian Chancellor Kurt von Schuschnigg to legalize the Austrian Nazi Party. When Schuschnigg announced that a plebiscite on the question of his nation's independence would be held, Hitler ordered German troops into Austria, claiming that German citizens were being mistreated there, and that Austria was plotting with Czechoslovakia against Germany. On March 12, 1938, most of the Austrian population greeted German troops not as conquerors, but as liberators amidst a sea of Nazi flags. Hitler thus effected the unification (*Anschluss*) of Germany and Austria that had been specifically forbidden by the Versailles Peace Settlement. The Nazis ar-

Austrians salute Germany's annexation of Austria, March 1938.

MAP 27.3 GERMAN AND ITALIAN EXPANSION, 1935–1939 Aggression by Germany and Italy against their neighbors.

rested more than 70,000 people and frenzied Viennese crowds beat up Jews. Britain and France sent official protests, but the British government permitted the German Reichsbank to confiscate funds that the Austrian National Bank had deposited in the Bank of England, allowing the Nazis to gain valuable gold and foreign currency reserves.

Czechoslovakia was next on Hitler's list. During the summer of 1938, he orchestrated a campaign against the Czech government, particularly against President Eduard Beneš (1884–1948). At issue was the status of the Sudetenland Germans of Czechoslovakia, but Hitler was also furious that some anti-Nazi Germans had found refuge in Prague. Beneš, with Poland casting a covetous eye on the long-disputed coal-mining region of Teschen, now desperately sought reassurance from France and the Soviet Union, which were obliged by separate treaties to defend Czechoslovakia against attack. But the Soviets refused to act unless joined by France, and France refused to act without the British. In any case, France could really only help its Eastern European allies by attacking Germany itself.

Chamberlain had already decided not to act at all. In April, the British prime minister had warned France that, in case of war with Germany, Britain would not send to the continent military help comparable to that which helped save France and Belgium in 1914. In May, German troops began to mass along the Czechoslovak border. Thus abandoned, the Czech government agreed to a series of German demands regarding the status of the Sudeten Germans.

On September 15, 1938, Chamberlain flew to the Führer's mountain retreat in southern Germany. When Hitler informed him that he would fight a world war in order to unite the Sudeten Germans to their fatherland, Chamberlain agreed to try to convince the French and Czech governments that Germany's absorption of the Sudetenland was the best hope for peace. Hitler promised Chamberlain that this would be the last territorial revision of the Treaty of Versailles that Germany would demand. But

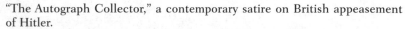

"The Autograph Collector," a contemporary satire on British appeasement of Hitler.

the German dictator continued to orchestrate pressure against the Czech government, encouraging Slovak demands for autonomy, and Polish and Hungarian claims on the Czech borderlands. On September 19, Britain and France virtually ordered the Prague government to cede to Germany territories where the 3 million ethnic Germans formed a majority. Chamberlain returned to Germany to see Hitler again on September 22. He informed the Führer that Czechoslovakia, as well as France, had agreed to the annexation of the Sudetenland, asking only that the new borders of Czechoslovakia be protected by a joint agreement.

Faced with the kind of collective security agreement he loathed, Hitler now threatened that Germany would occupy the Sudetenland by October 1 and would recognize Polish and Hungarian claims on territory ceded to Czechoslovakia in 1918. This would have dismembered Czechoslovakia for all practical purposes. Chamberlain was perplexed. The French government balked, demanding Hitler's original terms as presented to Chamberlain. Hitler then seemed to draw back, offering hope that the crisis might be ended peacefully. He agreed to Chamberlain's proposal that Hitler, Mussolini, Édouard Daladier (1884–1970; the French prime minister), and Chamberlain meet to settle everything once and for all. Back in London, Chamberlain confronted mounting skepticism. The government ordered preliminary measures for civil defense in case of war. Chamberlain tried to rally British public opinion with a speech on September 27: "How horrible, fantastic, incredible it is that we should be digging trenches and trying on gas masks here because of a quarrel in a far-away country between people of whom we know nothing. It seems still more impossible that a quarrel which has already been settled in principle should be the subject of war."

At the multilateral conference at Munich in September 1938, Hitler refused to allow attendance by representatives of the Soviet Union. Czechs were not even allowed to assist at the dismemberment of their own country. Chamberlain and Daladier agreed to immediate German occupation of the Sudetenland (the most industrialized part of the country), Poland's annexation of Teschen, the transfer of parts of Slovakia to Hungary, all in exchange for Hitler's personal guarantee of the redrawn borders of the partitioned nation. Hitler had taken another significant step in the revision of the Treaty of Versailles. Chamberlain stepped off the plane in London announcing to cheering crowds that he had brought his country "peace in our time."

In France, popular opinion did not want another war, and the military expressed apprehension about taking on the refurbished and expanded German armed forces. The French government felt abandoned by Britain, and by neighboring Belgium, which three years earlier had abrogated its 1920 military agreement with France and proclaimed neutrality. France, which had completed a line of bunker-like fortifications—the Maginot Line—to the Belgian frontier and counted on Belgium's ability to defend

Neville Chamberlain promises "peace in our time" after his return from Munich in September 1938.

against a German attack, was now more exposed to a German attack. The French government also feared that Hitler might convince Franco of Spain to join Germany in a war against republican France.

The appeasement—the term would subsequently take on a negative sense—of Hitler at Munich provided the German army with more time to prepare for the conquest of what remained of Czechoslovakia. On March 16, 1939, Hitler shattered the Munich agreements. German troops marched across the Czech border and occupied Prague, establishing the "Protectorate of Bohemia-Moravia." Again, as in the case of Austria, the British government helped Hitler out by allowing the transfer of 6 million pounds of Czech gold deposits from London banks to the German-occupied state. Even more important, Germany strengthened its forces with the addition of the Czech air force and army, and no longer had to maintain strong defenses on its southern border. Even for Chamberlain, this marked the end of illusions.

Hitler's brazen move shocked Mussolini, who complained, "Each time Hitler occupies a country, he sends me a message." In April 1939, Italian troops invaded and annexed Albania, while the Duce expressed confidence that he could force France to give up Corsica and Tunisia. With war on the horizon, British factories began turning out fighter planes as quickly as possible.

Looking east, the euphoric Hitler now demanded that Lithuania relinquish the Baltic port of Memel, which had been given to Lithuania by the Treaty of Versailles. Lithuania did so. He then demanded that Poland relinquish the port of Danzig and international access to the Polish Corridor that had by virtue of the Treaty of Versailles separated East Prussia from the rest of Germany. As always, Hitler offered a concession that would prove empty as soon as it had served its purpose: this time it was support against the Soviet Union's claim to parts of Poland that bordered on Ukraine.

The Polish government, which had been in a state of crisis since Pilsudski's death in 1935, readied its military defenses. The British government, which had refused to consider any alliances with the small states of Central Europe, now hurriedly signed a pact with Poland on April 6, 1939, guaranteeing Polish independence and assistance in case of German aggression. On April 26, Chamberlain told the House of Commons that conscription of men twenty and twenty-one years of age would begin. France (which was committed to Poland by alliance) and Britain then signed pacts with Romania and Greece and offered military support to Turkey. Hitler himself probably hoped that rapid Polish capitulation might present its Western allies with a *fait accompli* that might discourage their military response. Perhaps Poland would be convinced to join in a war against the Soviet Union. But Hitler accepted the strong possibility that war would follow any German move against Poland, even though he knew that the German economy could not reach full capacity for war production until 1943.

Few statesmen in France or Great Britain still harbored any illusions about what was next. British public opinion rapidly turned against appeasement. Winston Churchill (1874–1965), one of the few members of the House of Commons who had been convinced since 1936 that Britain would have to go to war against Hitler, called for an alliance with the Soviet Union against Germany. Chamberlain agreed, but moved slowly, at least partially because he did not trust Stalin. Discussions with Soviet diplomats dragged on, stumbling inevitably on the refusal of either Poland or Romania to accept Soviet troops on their territory, necessary to any effective defense against a German attack. Chamberlain then heard rumors that Stalin and Hitler, bitter enemies, were conducting diplomatic discussions, but laughed them off: "I cannot bring myself to believe that a real alliance between Russia and Germany is possible."

As early as April 3, 1939, Hitler had ordered the German army to prepare for an invasion of Poland on the following September 1. He shored up his alliance with Italy, signing in May 1939 the Pact of Steel, a formal military alliance between the two countries. Mussolini, who called the pact "absolute dynamite," nonetheless thought that he could continue to play off Germany, Britain, and France against each other. He had believed Hitler when he said that he would not begin a war with Poland for several more years. But knowing that doctored statistics could not hide the fact that Italy was unprepared for war, and now tied by a formal alliance to Hitler, the Duce had painted Italy into a corner.

The Unholy Alliance

Stalin himself no longer had doubts about Hitler's ultimate intentions toward the Soviet Union. But the Russian army needed time to prepare for war, Stalin having decimated the officer corps by the purges of the past three years. In the short run, Hitler wished to avoid war with the Soviet Union while he was fighting in Poland; in the longer run, anticipating war with the Western powers, he sought to avoid fighting a war on two fronts. Stalin did not trust the Western Allies to maintain their commitment to resist Hitler and did not think that even a Soviet pact with Britain and France would prevent Hitler from attacking Poland, Russia's old enemy.

In one of the most astonishing diplomatic turnarounds in history, Hitler announced on August 23, 1939, that Germany had signed a non-aggression pact with the Soviet Union, the Molotov-Ribbentrop Pact, named for the two foreign ministers. The man Stalin had called "the bloody assassin of the workers" signed an agreement with the leader Hitler had referred to as "the scum of the earth," a Communist who dominated a state that he planned to conquer. Hitler believed that a German pact with the Soviet Union would smash the will of Britain and France to defend Poland.

Stalin had reasons not to trust Britain or France. After German armies marched into Austria in 1938, the British had rejected a Soviet call for a meeting of the powers to discuss a collective response. Furthermore, the Western Allies had not bothered to consult with the Soviet Union while appeasing Hitler at Munich. Now Hitler assured Stalin that "in the event of a territorial and political rearrangement," the small, independent states of Latvia and Estonia, coveted by Russia, as well as Finland and eastern Poland would be fair game for the Soviet Union. From Stalin's point of view, it was in the Soviet Union's interest to avoid war as long as possible, the assumption being that the imperialist powers, all of them enemies of the Communists, ultimately would destroy each other.

Many—perhaps even most—Germans seemed prepared to follow Hitler into a new war. A popular magazine in April 1939 had cheerfully run the headline, "Gas Masks for German Children Now Ready." Undeterred by Britain's reaffirmation of its commitment to defend Polish independence, or by doubts expressed by some of his confidants, Hitler ordered the German invasion of Poland. It began on September 1, 1939.

CONCLUSION

The collapse of the political center in Europe under the stress of the Treaty of Versailles and the Depression helped create the Europe of dictatorships. German aggression finally brought a response from Great Britain and France, the two powers that remained parliamentary governments. World War II began. In retrospect, given the deterioration of the political climate, the rise of totalitarian governments, and the violence of the interwar period in the Europe of extremes, one can even ask whether the entire period between 1914 (when World War I began) and 1945 (when World War II finally ended after the deaths of millions of people) cannot be viewed as a thirty years' war.

CHAPTER 28

WORLD WAR II

For the second time in just twenty-five years, a conflict began in Europe that would soon become a world war. It would be even more devastating than World War I, wreaking destruction on a global scale. Germany's invasion of Poland in 1939, like its invasion of Belgium twenty-five years before, started a chain reaction that brought all the world powers into the conflict. Japan joined Germany and Italy, and the United States entered the conflict on the side of Great Britain and the free French government exiled in London. Following Hitler's attack on the Soviet Union in June 1941, the Communist state became an ally of Britain and the United States.

The Second World War was the first in which civilian populations became strategic targets and the first in which systematic genocide became part of the war effort. The technology of warfare developed rapidly; existing weapons were perfected and, by the end of the war, new, terrible weapons of mass destruction had taken a terrible toll on human life. When the war ended in 1945, Europe seemed to be entering an even more threatening era. Unlike the end of World War I in 1918, few people dreamed that World War II would be the "war to end all wars."

THE WAR IN EUROPE BEGINS

The war for which Hitler had prepared for so long began with a rapid, brutal German attack on Poland in September. Stalin's Soviet Union, having just signed a non-aggression pact with Nazi Germany, stood by, and then sent an occupying force into eastern Poland. As Nazi troops overran Poland, the latter's Western allies, Great Britain and France, protested, but took no military action. Soviet troops soon invaded Finland, and German forces occupied Denmark and then Norway. Hitler next turned his attention to the west, invading France, the Netherlands, and Belgium, and launching massive bombing attacks against Britain in preparation for an invasion.

German tanks overrun Poland, September 1939.

The German Invasion of Poland

On September 1, 1939, a million German troops, led by an armored division, poured into Poland. Fighters and light bombers thundered overhead, carefully coordinating their attacks to protect the infantry. Britain and France responded two days later by declaring war on Germany, following agreements concluded with the Polish government earlier that year.

Hitler wanted Polish resistance crushed quickly enough that Britain, and possibly France as well, would limit their reaction to a declaration of war. But he was prepared to fight the Western Allies, immediately if necessary, despite the lingering doubts of some of his generals about Germany's preparedness for war on such a massive scale.

Poland had a large and well-trained army of more than 1.5 million soldiers. But it made no difference that the Polish cavalry was the finest in Europe when enemy tanks arrived. The German air force destroyed half of Poland's planes in the first attacks on its bases. Bombers battered Warsaw. Poland's frontier defenses quickly crumbled before the onslaught of motorized columns of the German *Blitzkrieg* ("lightning war"), which were attacking from three directions. The Polish government fled Warsaw for London on September 7, and its capital fell on the 27th.

Following the German invasion of Poland, Soviet armies invaded Poland from the east. They did so with Hitler's blessing, under a secret agreement made between Stalin and Hitler as part of the Molotov-Ribbentrop Non-aggression Pact signed the previous August 23. Poland, which had lost its independence after being partitioned for the third time by its powerful neighbors in 1795, once again was divided up. On Stalin's orders, almost 15,000 Polish officers were executed in the forest of Katyn about 200 miles southwest of Moscow. The Soviet dictator ordered the transfer of Poles in cattle wagons as "special settlers" to the eastern reaches of the Soviet Union.

The "Phony War"

As Hitler had hoped, Britain and France took no military action. Few people seemed willing to "die for Danzig," the Polish port Germany had lost by the Treaty of Versailles. British and French military experts, shocked by the speed of the German victory over Poland, overestimated the strength of Hitler's armies. German submarines and other vessels began to pick off Allied cargo ships in September. But there was no fighting on the ground.

An immediate French and British attack on Germany from the west might have been successful, as long as the Germans were tied up in Poland, where the German army and air force had seriously depleted its supply of munitions. Britain and France had more than twice as many divisions deployed near the German frontier and, for the moment, the German air force had few planes in the west. French troops made one brief, unopposed excursion fourteen miles into Germany, and then retreated. The British Royal Air Force flew over Germany, but dropped only leaflets calling for peace. Both the British and French governments believed that an attack on Germany would fail. They were stunned by Hitler's pact with Stalin; unlike in World War I, it appeared that Germany would only have to fight a war on one front.

Hitler confidently announced to his generals on September 12 that he planned to order an invasion of France in the near future. The German army and air force were readied, while the French army dug in behind the supposedly impregnable fortifications of the Maginot Line, a row of bunkers stretching from Switzerland to the Belgian border (see Map 28.1).

Planned first for November and then for January, the German invasion of Western Europe was finally postponed until the spring of 1940. The winter months that followed the Polish invasion became immediately known as the "phony war." French troops stared into the rain, mist, and fog from their bunkers. Fearing German bombing attacks, the British government issued Londoners gas masks and imposed a nighttime blackout. Italian dictator Benito Mussolini had developed cold feet just before Hitler's invasion of Poland, because he knew that Italy lacked enough coal, oil, iron, and steel to wage a lengthy war. But he now believed a German invasion of France inevitable. Mussolini announced that Italy's status would be one of "non-belligerance," a term he selected to avoid comparisons with the "neutrality" against which he had vociferously campaigned before Italy entered World War I in 1915.

MAP 28.1 THE GERMAN AND ITALIAN ADVANCE, 1939–1942   The opening of
the war included advances by the Germans into Poland, the U.S.S.R., the Scandinavian countries, the Balkans, and North Africa. The Italians sent troops into Albania, and from there into Greece. The British unsuccessfully attempted to take a
stand against the Germans in Norway, and British and French troops were evacuated from the continent at Dunkirk.

The War in the Frozen North

Although the "phony war" continued in the west, fighting began in Northern Europe. The Russian border with Finland, an independent state since
the Russian Revolution, lay only fourteen miles from Leningrad. Stalin demanded that the Finnish government cede strategically important territories to the Soviets. When the Finnish government refused in November
1939, the Red Army invaded. Badly outnumbered Finnish soldiers fought

bravely in subzero temperatures, sometimes on skis, carrying light machine guns against Russian tanks and temporarily holding back the Soviet forces. Finland harbored no illusions about winning the "Winter War," but, like Poland, hoped to be saved by British and French diplomatic or military intervention. France now favored, at least in principle, armed intervention on behalf of Finland. So did Britain's Winston Churchill, the Conservative politician who had angered his party by opposing appeasement of Hitler at Munich. But Finnish resistance soon was broken. Finland suffered 20,000 deaths and 500,000 wounded in the short, bloody war. By the Peace of Moscow, signed March 12, 1940, the Soviet Union annexed about 10 percent of Finnish territory as almost half a million Finns fled.

In April 1940, British ships mined the Norwegian harbor of Narvik, despite the objections of the government of Norway, in an attempt to stop Swedish iron ore from being shipped to Germany. In order to prevent the British from intervening, the Germans first landed in Denmark, which surrendered without a fight (see Map 28.1). Taking the Allies by surprise, German paratroopers landed at Oslo and other Norwegian port cities, followed by reinforcements put ashore by ships. German troops repelled Allied troops who arrived at the end of April with sketchy orders and inadequate weapons. Vidkun Quisling (1887–1945), organizer of a fascist party in the 1930s, became the puppet head of state in Norway, his name entering the dictionary as synonymous with traitor.

Prime Minister Chamberlain had assured the British House of Commons that Germany "had missed the bus" by waiting so long to attack. But Germany's victory in Norway, followed by a lightning occupation of Den-

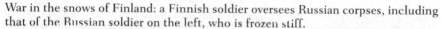

War in the snows of Finland: a Finnish soldier oversees Russian corpses, including that of the Russian soldier on the left, who is frozen stiff.

mark, brought down the Chamberlain government. Churchill, who had sat in the House of Commons off and on since 1900, became prime minister on May 10, 1940, at the age of sixty-five. The outspoken Churchill was an unpopular choice among even some Conservatives, who held an overwhelming majority in Parliament. Many remembered his impulsive and stubborn attachment to far-fetched military operations during the First World War, which had led to the catastrophic defeat of British troops at Gallipoli in 1915. Even one of his trusted advisers said that Churchill had ten new ideas each day, but that nine of them were bad. Still, his resilience, determination, and dedication would make Churchill an extraordinary wartime leader.

The Fall of France

German troops stared across the Rhine River at their French opponents with confidence. The German army could simply sidestep the French Maginot Line, which stopped at the Belgian frontier. Germany enjoyed vast superiority over France in the quality of its tanks and planes (France had only about 500 first-line fighter planes, Germany about 4,000). Furthermore, the German army and air force were already well-practiced, having launched their invasion of Poland.

The French army seemed unequal to the task of holding off a German attack. Soldiers had become demoralized by the winter months in the damp bunkers along the Maginot Line. The plan of the French high command to engage the enemy forces as they moved into the Low Countries was undermined by the Belgian and Dutch governments; both, hoping to remain neutral, had been unwilling to coordinate defense planning with the French army. The French generals lacked confidence in the strength of their forces and—at least some—in the Third Republic itself. French tanks lacked fuel and were dispersed among infantry divisions, instead of concentrated in tank divisions. Teams of horses still pulled French artillery pieces. French communications networks along the front were inadequate. After eight months of "phony war," many people in France were uncertain as to why they might be once again fighting Germany.

Compounding serious military problems, the British and French governments were already sniping at each other. The French resented the fact that their ally had sent a relatively small army to France; the British government seemed willing to defend France down to the last Frenchman. On the other hand, the French had irritated the British by opposing Allied bombing of Germany, fearing that the expected swift reprisals would strike them, not England.

On May 10, 1940, the "phony war" in the west suddenly ended. In a carefully rehearsed attack that astonished the Allies, German gliders landed troops that captured a massive Belgian fortress. Airborne divisions took the airport and central bridges of the Dutch port of Rotterdam; German bombers then destroyed ships, docks, and the heart of the old city, killing 40,000 people. The German assault on France began through the Ardennes on the Belgian border; ten tank divisions pushed seventy miles, brushing aside the lighter French tanks. German planes, controlling the air, swept down on French troops and destroyed half the planes of the British Royal Air Force within three days of the invasion. Mussolini, a portly vulture circling above the wounded French prey, had declared war on France on May 10, but an Italian army managed to advance only about a hundred yards across the border toward Nice.

French commanders then foolishly sent most of their armored reserves into Holland while German tanks, having reached the Meuse River in eastern France, now turned west and began moving toward the Channel. They were vulnerable to an Allied counterattack, but only a minor challenge by a tank column commanded by French General Charles de Gaulle (1890–1970) slowed the German drive to the Channel. The British Expeditionary Force, instead of attacking the exhausted German tank columns, retreated from Belgium into France, heading toward the Channel. German columns reached the Channel on May 21, cutting the Allied forces in half. The Netherlands surrendered on May 15, Belgium on May 28. By now the roads of northern France were choked, not only with retreating British and French troops, but also with Belgian and French refugees fleeing the battle zones, diving into ditches to escape strafing German fighters.

France's defeat was by now only a matter of time. On June 3 and 4, every available English vessel, including fishing trawlers and pleasure craft, evacuated 338,226 British and French troops from Dunkirk, as Al-

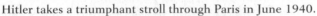

Hitler takes a triumphant stroll through Paris in June 1940.

lied soldiers also escaped the continent from other ports. The German army now wheeled to confront the French troops still uselessly holding the Maginot Line. The French government left Paris for Bordeaux in the southwest, as it had in 1870. The German army occupied the capital on the 14th. With its troops in disarray and with morale completely broken by the loss of more than 100,000 men (compared to 40,000 German dead), the French military command was ready to surrender. But France and Britain had several months earlier agreed that neither ally would ask for an armistice without the approval of the other. The British wanted the French government to move to North Africa and to continue fighting. On June 16, Marshal Philippe Pétain, hero of the Battle of Verdun in 1916, became premier. The next day, he asked Germany for an armistice. On June 22, 1940, the gleeful Hitler accepted the French surrender in the same railway car where Germany had signed a similar document in November 1918. Hitler danced a jig of joy, and then set out to tour Paris.

The Battle of Britain

Britain would fight on. For the moment, it did so alone. Addressing the House of Commons, Churchill declared, "I have nothing to offer but blood, toil, tears, and sweat. We have before us an ordeal . . . many long months of struggle and of suffering. You ask, what is our policy? I will say it is to wage war, by sea, land, and air . . . to wage war against a monstrous tyranny, never surpassed in the dark, lamentable catalogue of human crime."

Hitler now considered whether an invasion of Britain, "Operation Sea Lion," could succeed. Germany held both the French and Belgian Channel ports, a position it had never achieved during World War I. Furthermore, with Ireland having proclaimed its neutrality, Britain no longer had the use of southern Irish ports.

Fearing a German attack, the British government interned German subjects, including some of the 50,000 Jewish refugees from Nazism. In some places, officials took down road signs and place names, and shopkeepers shredded local maps to disorient any German invading army. The German admirals, however, advised Hitler that attacks against British interests in North Africa and the Mediterranean would be the best way of defeating Britain, drawing on Italian and possibly Spanish help.

For Germany to invade Britain, the German air force (the Luftwaffe) had to control the skies. The ensuing Battle of Britain, fought over the Channel and above southern England, lasted four dramatic months, from the last day of July until October 31, 1940, although most of the climactic duels in the sky took place from the second week of August until the end of September. Against the Luftwaffe's 1,200 bombers and 1,000 fighters, the Royal Air Force could counter with only about 900 fighters, not all of which could be put into the air at once. The British used radar, first devel-

(*Left*) Evacuating children from London during the German bombing blitz, 1940.
(*Right*) British Prime Minister Winston Churchill amid the rubble outside of
St. Paul's Cathedral, 1940.

oped in 1935, to detect oncoming German attacks. Recently built British
Spitfires and Hurricanes reached greater speeds than the German Messer-
schmitt fighters and could break through the fighter escorts to get to the
cumbersome German bombers. Frustrated, Hitler ordered the bombing of
key industries and aircraft factories in England even as British bombers
appeared over Berlin in August, demonstrating that Britain was far from
defeated. The German bombing "blitz" of London began on September 7.
Londoners took to the subway stations and underground air-raid shelters
for protection.

Britain lost 650 fighters, but factories were producing replacements and
new pilots were being trained. As German air losses mounted, the Luftwaffe turned to less accurate night bombing to keep the British fighters
out of the air. At the end of September, Hitler was forced to abandon his
plan to invade England. Churchill called the Battle of Britain his country's
"finest hour."

A GLOBAL WAR

World War II rapidly spread to almost all corners of the globe. Total war
absorbed national resources on an unprecedented scale. For the first time,
Britain began military conscription. But civilians, too, had to do their part.
As factories began to turn out weapons, munitions, and wartime materiel,
women entered the industrial workforce in great numbers. The government assumed considerable control over the economy, coordinating pro-

duction, raising taxes, and imposing rationing. Scientists were put to work in the war effort. World War II would require similar efforts from each of the Great Powers.

Hitler counted among his allies Italy, Romania, Hungary, and Bulgaria, as well as Japan, each eager for territorial acquisitions. But Nazi troops had to bail out the Italians in Greece, which Mussolini had ordered attacked in October 1940. After invading Egypt, the Duce soon found his small North African empire reeling from British attacks. In June 1941, Germany launched an air and ground attack on the Soviet Union, shattering the Molotov-Ribbentrop Pact of August 1939. However, like Napoleon more than a century before him, Hitler failed to reckon with determined Russian resistance, as well as with the harsh Russian winter. The largest invading army in history ground to a halt in the frozen snow, having failed to bring the Soviet Union to its knees. Finally, on December 7, 1941, Japanese planes carried out a surprise attack on the U.S. naval and air force base at Pearl Harbor, Hawaii. The raid inflicted great damage on the U.S. Pacific Fleet, and brought the United States into what had become a global conflict fought on an unprecedented scale.

Total War

Britain was the first combatant in World War II to find itself engaged in a total war. As the war expanded, other states confronted similar challenges. German military planners counted on Hitler's confident assertion that the United States would stay out of the war, and that Germany could bring the British to their knees. But the United States, where British resistance won sympathy and admiration, could help Britain in other ways. On December 29, 1940, President Franklin D. Roosevelt announced that the United States would be "the arsenal of democracy," despite its official position of neutrality. Since direct loans might recall for many Americans the defaults by those in debt to the United States after World War I, Congress passed the Lend-Lease Act in March 1941. It authorized the president to lend destroyers, trucks and other equipment, and food to Great Britain, which in exchange would lease naval bases in the Caribbean to the United States.

Unlike Germany, which had been preparing for war virtually since Hitler came to power, Britain had to start almost from scratch. The British government succeeded in rallying the king's subjects to wartime sacrifices. Because very few people had any doubts about the extent of the Nazi threat to Britain itself, including possible invasion, military conscription at the beginning of the war brought less protest than it had in World War I in a nation with a long tradition of resistance to the idea of a standing army. Before the war began, the British armed forces comprised 500,000 people; at the end of the war, 5 million. Women took the places in industry vacated by departing troops, accounting for 80 percent of the increase in the labor force between 1939 and 1943. In 1939, 7,000 women worked in ordnance factories in Britain; in October 1944, there were 260,000.

The British War Cabinet imposed more government control on the economy, and by 1942 it had achieved a high degree of coordination in wartime production. The government imposed higher taxes, implemented rent control, and established rationing (limiting purchases of such English staples as jams and candy), and called for voluntary restraints on wage raises. Pants came without cuffs or zippers; a suspicious gray "utility loaf" replaced white bread. In order to feed a population expanded by the arrival of wartime refugees from France and other countries, British farmers augmented agricultural production by increasing the amount of land under cultivation by a full third.

In October 1940, Churchill established a scientific advisory committee to put some of Britain's most eminent scientists to work designing more powerful and reliable weapons. One of the most significant breakthroughs of the war was not a technological innovation but the solving of the complex puzzle of a secret code. British intelligence officers, aided by mathematicians, deciphered communications between Hitler and his high command during the Battle of Britain. This subsequently allowed the Allies to know many German moves in advance. British intelligence officers then broke the German communications code, facilitating, among other things, the identification of spies. The code breakers by the end of 1943 were reading more than 90,000 messages a month. The British Psychological Warfare Division, with their U.S. counterpart, also put the science of psychology into the service of modern warfare, waging radio and leaflet campaigns in an attempt to weaken the will of the enemy to continue fighting. Germany and Japan countered by employing two Americans ("Axis Sally" and "Tokyo Rose," respectively) to broadcast messages to U.S. troops, trying to convince them that they could never win the war.

Hitler's Allies

Realizing that Germany could not successfully invade Britain, Hitler sought other allies in an attempt to win the war quickly. Seeking to discourage the United States, Japan's rival in the Pacific, from entering the war on the Allied side against Germany and Italy, the two Axis powers signed the Tripartite Pact with Japan in September 1940. By this treaty, Germany and Italy recognized Japan's interests in Asia, while Japan acknowledged those of Germany and Italy in Europe. The treaty specified that each power agreed to cooperate should any one of them be attacked by "a Power at present not involved in the European war or in the Chinese-Japanese conflict." Hitler then tried to convince Francisco Franco, whose victory in the Spanish Civil War Hitler had helped make possible, to join the war of the "Axis" powers against Britain. He envisioned a Spanish seizure of Gibraltar and German use of naval bases in the Spanish Canary Islands. The Spanish dictator pleaded the poverty of his country and, as if to emphasize the point, arrived at the meeting with Hitler hours late on a plodding train. He then made exorbitant demands for future territorial considerations in North Africa. After spending eight hours cajoling Franco, Hitler said "I would prefer to have three or four teeth extracted rather than go through that again." Franco's Spain, however much ideologically in tune with some aspects of Hitler's Germany, would remain neutral.

In Romania, King Carol II was powerless in the face of his greedy neighbors, who were encouraged by Germany. He surrendered to Hungary a part of Transylvania that had been awarded to Romania by the Treaty of Versailles but that included a considerable Hungarian population. Stalin forced Romania to hand over to the Soviet Union Northern Bukovina and Bessarabia, which had once been part of the Russian Empire. Bulgaria, too, helped itself to Romanian territory. As a result, the fascist Iron Guard rebelled and forced King Carol to abdicate in favor of his son Michael in September 1940.

Now convinced it was facing a long war, Germany hurried to secure a supply of raw materials by occupying Romania and its rich oil fields in October 1940. A right-wing general, Ion Antonescu (1882–1946), ran the country with the help of the Iron Guard, which served German interests and unleashed its fury against Romania's Jews and Communists. Both Romania and Hungary formally joined the Axis in November 1940, and Bulgaria in March 1941.

From the beginning, it appeared that Italy's contributions to the German war effort would be minimal at best. Mussolini, who had promised the Italian people new victories, now aimed to take as much territory in North Africa as possible before the British surrender upon which he counted. After having failed to launch air attacks, as Hitler had wanted, on British bases on the Mediterranean island of Malta, Mussolini now invaded Egypt in September 1940, refusing a German offer to supply tanks because he wanted Italy to claim victory on its own. Unable to provide troops with air cover, Italian forces suffered a series of humiliating defeats at the hands of British forces.

Desperate for victory somewhere, on October 28, 1940, the Duce surprised Hitler—as well as his own generals, with whom he rarely consulted—by ordering the Italian army to invade Greece from Albania. Having paid large bribes to Greek generals and officials not to resist invasion, Mussolini anticipated an easy victory. But a Greek patriot army drove the Italians back into Albania, where resistance movements made life difficult for Mussolini's troops. The Italian army took out its frustrations against the Croatian population of Dalmatia on the Adriatic coast. In the meantime, British forces battered the Italian fleet.

General Erwin Rommel, "the Desert Fox," at right in North Africa.

The Italian East African Empire rapidly crumbled in the spring. A British and French force took Addis Ababa, Ethiopia's capital, in April 1941. Italian troops retreated through the North African desert. Hitler sent General Erwin Rommel (1891–1944), commander of a tank division to North Africa, to bail them out. Mussolini vowed to continue the war "until the last Italian is killed."

The German Invasion of Russia

Hitler always intended to invade and defeat the Soviet Union, despite the Molotov-Ribbentrop Non-aggression Pact of August 1939. After occupying eastern Poland following the German invasion of Poland, Soviet troops had occupied the Baltic republics of Estonia, Latvia, and Lithuania during the summer of 1940, claiming that they had been illegitimately detached from Russia after World War I, when they had become independent. German interest in Finland and German moves in Romania now made Soviet Foreign Minister Vyacheslav Molotov (1890–1986) anxious. The Soviets sought reassurance in a new pact, one that Mussolini would sign as well. Molotov went to Berlin. Assured personally by Hitler that Britain lay defeated, Molotov replied, "Then whose bombers are those overhead, and why are we in this bomb shelter?"

Hitler intended "Operation Barbarossa," the invasion of Russia, to be a "quick campaign" of no more than ten weeks' duration. He hoped that Japan would attack Siberia, thereby forcing Stalin to divert troops there.

The German generals held the Russian army in such contempt that they ordered no serious assessment of Russia's existing or potential military strength. If the Finns on skis had been able to hold off Russian divisions with seemingly little more than snowballs, how could German fighters and tanks fail to break through with relative ease? Some of Hitler's generals were not so sure.

The opening of a Balkan front delayed Hitler's invasion of the Soviet Union, planned for May 1941. Britain had sent forces to Greece following the Italian invasion, which made German bases in Yugoslavia even more crucial. An anti-German faction had overthrown the Yugoslav government in March and refused to join the Axis or to allow German troops into the country. Hitler ordered a German invasion of Yugoslavia in April, which then pushed into Greece. As in World War I, Bulgaria cast its fate with Germany, its troops occupying parts of Greek Macedonia and Thrace. The German army forced a British withdrawal from the Greek mainland to the Aegean island of Crete, which soon also fell to the Germans on May 27. By the end of May 1941, Hitler's armies held all of the Balkans.

Hitler could now concentrate on an invasion of the Soviet Union. Stalin, however, failed to heed warnings from Britain and the United States that Russia was Germany's next target. Believing these warnings, including some of his own army's military reports, to be part of a conspiracy to turn him against his German ally, Stalin ordered the execution of some of his intelligence officers.

On June 22, 1941, German planes, tanks, and more than 3 million troops attacked the Soviet Union. When the news came at 4:00 A.M., Stalin was so numb with shock at news of Hitler's betrayal that he did not order resistance for two hours and left it to Molotov to address the Soviet people by radio.

Although the Soviets had many more men, field artillery, tanks, and aircraft than Germany, most of the Soviet weapons were obsolete. Germany, which had rearmed in the 1930s, here enjoyed a considerable advantage. The German military quickly devastated Soviet defenses, communication, and transportation networks. One army pushed toward Leningrad, reaching its suburbs in July and undertaking a siege of the city. But Leningrad held. The battleship *Aurora*, which had served the Bolshevik cause in the Revolution of 1917, was pressed into service, its guns commandeered from a museum. A second German army captured more than a quarter of a million prisoners near Minsk, 250 miles northeast of Warsaw; a third, finding support from anti-Russian Ukrainians, took Kiev on September 24. Hitler rejected his generals' suggestion that the attack on Moscow be given priority. Instead, armored units were transferred to the northern army besieging Leningrad.

The scorched earth tactics of the German troops left Russian towns and villages in ruins, and hundreds of thousands of civilians dead. But despite enormous battlefield casualties, as well as half a million captured prison-

ers dying of hunger and cold in German camps, Russian resistance stiffened. News of Nazi atrocities helped rally virtually the entire population.
German armies bogged down in the face of determined resistance around
Smolensk. With centralized state planning well in place, Soviet state-run
factories were easily converted to wartime production, soon turning out
tanks of equal quality to those of the invader. The United States, still
officially neutral in the conflict, now extended the Lend-Lease policy to
the Soviet Union.

Their drive to victory stalled, despite having captured more than a million square miles of Soviet territory, the German troops, like Napoleon's
armies in 1812, found that a frozen winter, the coldest in a century, followed the chilly Russian fall. "Hitler no more resembles Napoleon than a
kitten resembles a lion," Stalin taunted. Oil for tanks and guns froze. So
did soldiers. The German high command, so certain of a quick victory, had
not bothered to provide them with warm clothing and blankets for temperatures reaching −30 degrees F.

After ordering a halt in the push toward Moscow, Hitler, fearing the
consequences of retreat on German morale, ignored the advice of his generals to pull back and await spring weather. Early in December, a desperate German attack stalled twenty miles from Moscow. The German army
never got closer. During the first year of the Russian campaign, German
casualties reached 1.3 million, or 40 percent of the original invading
force, the greatest losses of any single military operation in history. Hitler
may have conquered Poland, France, Belgium, The Netherlands, and
much of the Balkans, but he had failed to defeat Britain and the Soviet
Union.

Japan's Attack on the United States

Four years of Japanese aggression in Asia brought the resource-poor island
nation to the point of confrontation with the United States. Since invading Manchuria in 1931 and proclaiming it the puppet state of Manchukuo
a year later, Japan had sought to expand its influence and territory in the
Pacific region. Southeast Asian oil was one Japanese target, particularly after the economic boycott imposed by the United States, Great Britain, and
the Netherlands following the Manchurian invasion. The Japanese quest
for rubber, tin, and other raw materials threatened British economic interests in Burma and Malaya, as well as those of the Dutch in Java and of the
United States in the Philippine Islands.

In 1937, Japan joined the Anti-Comintern Pact that Germany and Italy
had signed in November 1936. This further undermined its relations with
the United States. In 1937, the Japanese army invaded China and occupied the main Chinese ports, moves that the American government viewed
with great alarm. The Molotov-Ribbentrop Non-aggression Pact between
the Soviet Union and Germany had voided the Anti-Comintern Pact (since

the Soviet Union was a Communist state). In September 1940, Japan concluded the Tripartite Pact with Germany and Italy. Japanese aggression in Asia continued. In an effort to stop the flow of Allied supplies to Chinese forces over the railway from Hanoi and a long dirt road from Burma, Japan had assumed a "protective" occupation of French Indochina in July 1941. A non-aggression pact with the Soviet Union, signed in April 1941, two months before the German invasion of Russia, bolstered Japanese confidence that it could attack and inflict a stinging defeat on the United States.

On Sunday morning, December 7, 1941, a Japanese force of fighters and dive-bombers surprised the American naval and air force base at Pearl Harbor, Hawaii. Three U.S. battleships were sunk and 5 were severely damaged, 10 other vessels were destroyed or disabled, 188 planes were destroyed and many others were damaged, and 2,403 naval and other military personnel were killed and more than a thousand were wounded. However, 3 aircraft carriers were at sea, and therefore escaped the attack and could still be readied to take on the Japanese fleet in the Pacific Ocean. Vast stocks of oil, too, survived. Japan quickly followed with successful invasions of Malaya, the Philippines, Singapore (where almost 60,000 British soldiers surrendered), and Pacific islands as far distant as the Aleutians near Alaska (see Map 28.2).

Because American intelligence officers had deciphered Japan's coded messages, President Roosevelt had known that Japan was planning to launch a war against the United States. The emperor believed that a rapid Japanese victory would force the Americans to a negotiated settlement. Yet, the attack on Pearl Harbor came as a surprise, in part because U.S. intelligence services were swamped with messages suggesting attacks at other locations. Calling December 7, 1941, "a day that will live in infamy," Roosevelt declared war on Japan.

Hitler, bound by treaty to Japan, then declared war against the United States on December 11, to the surprise and consternation of some of his generals. Hitler believed that public opinion in the United States was against American involvement in another European war. In fact, he knew amazingly little about the United States, viewing it from his strange vantage point as a nation corrupted by racial mixing.

Upon hearing the news of Pearl Harbor, Churchill is reported to have exclaimed, "We have won the war!" The entry of the United States into the war against Germany provided, as in 1917, a crucial material advantage to the Allies. Despite its slow recovery from the Depression, which hit it harder than any other nation, the United States was the largest industrial power in the world, producing more than the next six powers combined. American factories, though privately owned, were quickly converted to military production. Industrial production in the United States doubled by the end of 1943 in response to wartime demand.

MAP 28.2 THE JAPANESE ADVANCE AND ALLIED COUNTEROFFENSIVE, 1941–1945   After launching a surprise attack against the U.S. naval and air force base at Pearl Harbor, Hawaii, the Japanese successfully invaded most of the Southeast Asian countries and many of the Pacific islands.

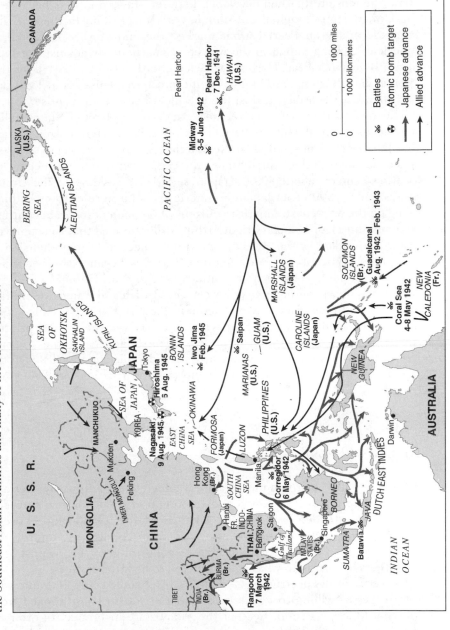

Despite the patronizing attitude of the aristocratic, self-assured, cigar-smoking British prime minister, a warm personal relationship gradually developed between Churchill and Roosevelt. Their rapport helped overcome the tension that had developed between the two powers because of the United States' original unwillingness to join Britain in the war. The Japanese attack on Pearl Harbor marked the end of U.S. isolationism. American citizens rallied to the war effort, particularly against the Japanese. "Remember Pearl Harbor!" struck a chord in the United States that "Remember Belgium" or "France" could not have. This was at least partially because the attack against the U.S. fleet had been a surprise.

The fact that an Asian power had attacked the United States galled Americans, many of whom believed that Asians were inferior. Amid rumors that Japanese citizens and Japanese Americans were preparing to carry out acts of sabotage in the United States, the U.S. government interned in "relocation centers" about 40,000 Japanese citizens residing in the United States and 70,000 of its Japanese Americans, who were citizens by birth living on the west coast. American citizens of German descent, in contrast, were not interned. The playwright Arthur Miller noticed that the men with whom he worked at the Brooklyn Navy Yard had no "comprehension of what Nazism meant—we were fighting Germany because she had allied herself with the Japanese who had attacked us at Pearl Harbor."

The first of several meetings between the British and American military chiefs of staff took place in Washington in January 1942. The Allied commanders decided to give the European theater of war the highest priority. An immediate concentration of attacks against Japanese forces seemed less urgent. In any case, it would take considerable time to dislodge the Japanese from the Southeast Asian countries and Pacific islands they had conquered.

HITLER'S EUROPE

Whether or not each conquered state retained some autonomy, German policies were primarily directed at extracting useful raw materials needed to wage an extended war. The exact nature of the relationship between Germany and each occupied state varied from country to country. Yet, everywhere the Nazis carried out Hitler's policy of genocide against Jews and others belonging to what he considered to be inferior races.

In every country overrun by German troops, people could be found who were eager or willing to collaborate with the Nazis. These ranged from Marshal Philippe Pétain, head of the Vichy state in France, to ordinary people whose political biases or hope for gain or even just survival led them to help the Nazis. Yet, in many countries, resistance movements bravely opposed the rule of the Nazis or their allies. The largest and most successful resistance was in mountainous Yugoslavia, where resisters were able to take on entire German divisions, and, to a lesser extent, in France, where groups of guerilla fighters undertook hit-and-run attacks against the Germans and against the Vichy government. In Germany, resistance to Hitler and the Nazis was extremely limited, notwithstanding a courageous attempt by disenchanted army officers to assassinate Hitler in July 1944. To the end, most Germans remained loyal to the Führer, or at least did not resist.

The Nazi "New European Order"

Hitler sought to exploit the economic resources of the countries his armies had conquered and to assure that no effective opposition could emerge in any of them. Germany annexed the disputed Polish territories it had claimed, including Poznan, Upper Silesia, and the Polish Corridor, because Hitler considered them German in the first place. Direct German administration was extended to Ukraine and Byelorussia (Belarus). Germans who lived in Poland, Lithuania, or those parts of the Soviet Union that were behind German lines were "repatriated" to Germany, or settled in the newly conquered territories (see Map 28.3).

German policies were different in Poland and Russia, whose peoples Hitler considered to be racial inferiors. Following the capture of Warsaw, Hitler had sent five special "action" squadrons to Poland with orders to wipe out the Polish upper class. All over the country businessmen, political leaders, intellectuals, and teachers were executed or sent to concentration camps.

Norway, Denmark, and the Netherlands, deemed by Hitler to be sufficiently "Nordic" or "Aryan" to be "Germanized," were allowed relative autonomy. In Denmark, where the only elections in any country under a Nazi regime took place, the Danish Nazi Party won a paltry 2 percent of the vote.

Hitler left Germany's Central and Southern European "independent" allies with some autonomy, depending on the extent to which they followed his wishes. Admiral Horthy ruled Hungary under increasingly close German supervision, particularly after Hitler learned that he had tried to play both sides by getting in touch with the Allies in 1942. Slovakia, which had been denied independence by the Versailles Settlements, had become autonomous when Germany marched into Czechoslovakia in 1938, splitting the country into two parts. Pro-German nationalist fascists held power in Slovakia. In wartime Romania, Antonescu and his fascist Iron Guard ruled. Hitler divided Yugoslavia into the states of Serbia, Montenegro, and Croatia, allowing Hungary to annex Yugoslav territory awarded by the Versailles Settlements. Placing Serbia under direct German administration, he put Croatia and Montenegro under the rule of an authoritarian leader informally responsible to Mussolini.

MAP 28.3　HITLER'S EUROPE, 1942　Hitler's expansion into the east and west, showing the greatest extent of the German occupation of Europe and major battle sites.

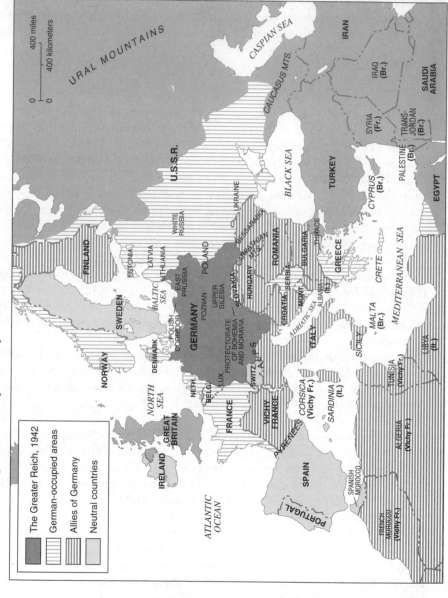

The Greater Reich, 1942
German-occupied areas
Allies of Germany
Neutral countries

URAL MOUNTAINS

CASPIAN SEA

IRAN

IRAQ (Br.)

SAUDI ARABIA

SYRIA (Fr.)

TRANS-JORDAN (Br.)

PALESTINE (Br.)

EGYPT

CYPRUS (Br.)

U.S.S.R.

CAUCASUS MTS.

BLACK SEA

TURKEY

UKRAINE

WHITE RUSSIA

FINLAND

ESTONIA

LATVIA

LITHUANIA

EAST PRUSSIA

POLAND

BESSARABIA

CARPATHIAN MTS.

ROMANIA

SERBIA

BULGARIA

THRACE

GREECE

CRETE

MEDITERRANEAN SEA

SWEDEN

BALTIC SEA

POZNAN

UPPER SILESIA

SLOVAKIA

HUNGARY

CROATIA

MONT.

ALBANIA

ADRIATIC SEA

MALTA (Br.)

SICILY

LIBYA (It.)

POLISH CORRIDOR

GERMANY

PROTECTORATE OF BOHEMIA AND MORAVIA

ALPS

SWITZ.

ITALY

SARDINIA (It.)

TUNISIA (Vichy Fr.)

NORWAY

DENMARK

NETH.

BELG.

LUX.

NORTH SEA

FRANCE

VICHY FRANCE

CORSICA (Vichy Fr.)

ALGERIA (Vichy Fr.)

GREAT BRITAIN

IRELAND

ATLANTIC OCEAN

PYRENEES

SPAIN

PORTUGAL

SPANISH MOROCCO

FRENCH MOROCCO (Vichy Fr.)

400 miles
400 kilometers
0
0

The Germans imposed crushing obligations on conquered lands, including enormous financial indemnities and exchange rates that strongly favored the German currency. Germans operated factories and shipping companies in occupied lands. In France, the Germans first took movable raw materials and equipment useful for war production. As the war went on, German demands became greater; the occupation authorities closely regulated the armament, aircraft, mining, and metal industries. Some French businesses tried to make the best of the situation, working with German firms. Others quietly subverted German demands and expectations for cooperation.

The "Final Solution"

Hitler's obsessive racial theories had become official policy in Nazi Germany before the war (see Chapter 27). For the Nazis, the process of forging the "national community" meant the elimination of groups they considered to be "outsiders." They made a temporary exception of foreign laborers, upon whom the economy depended during the war. In 1939, Hitler had ordered the killing, often by injection, of Germans who were mentally deficient and handicapped. At least 70,000 mentally retarded people perished, including children, before public objections that the victims were German halted this practice in August 1941. In addition, the Nazis sterilized between 320,000 and 350,000 German "outcasts" between 1934 and 1945; these included people determined by Nazi doctors to manifest "hereditary simple-mindedness," alcoholism, homosexuality, chronic depression, schizophrenia, or those who were deemed "work shy." Hitler also mandated experiments to determine how thousands of people could be killed "efficiently" in assembly-line fashion.

In 1939, Hitler told Heinrich Himmler (1900–1945), the leader of the S.S., to plan for the occupation of Poland and the Soviet Union. Himmler, a short, stout man whose glasses gave him the appearance of a schoolteacher, was obsessed with the pagan Germans of pre-history, establishing several spurious academic institutes to investigate his crackpot theories. Himmler welcomed Hitler's order to "eliminate the harmful influence of such alien parts of the population." Hitler announced to the Reichstag on January 30, 1939, that the result of the anticipated war would be "the annihilation of the Jewish race in Europe," the "final solution" to what Hitler considered the problem of the Jews.

Nazi plans to exterminate Jews took shape as German military defeats mounted in Russia, where the massacre of Slavs had already begun. In January 1941, Himmler announced to S.S. leaders a change in policy. Hitler no longer wanted to transform the Slavs into a slave labor force, but rather to destroy at least 30 million of them, so that Germans eventually could occupy their lands. German troops and death squads began mass executions of Russian prisoners and civilians, killing by shooting, starvation,

Jews being massacred in Lithuania, 1942.

or exposure. Before the war ended, at least 3.3 million Soviet prisoners of war—of 5.7 million captured—died or were executed in German prisoner-of-war camps.

In July 1941, the Nazis began to prepare for the Holocaust, the genocide of European Jews. Hermann Göring ordered Reinhard Heydrich (1904–1942), the chief of the secret police, to prepare "with regard to organization, substantive, and financial viewpoints for a total solution of the Jewish question in the German sphere of influence in Europe." A Gestapo directive on July 17, 1941, ordered commanders of prison camps in the east to liquidate "all the Jews." By the end of 1941, a million Jews had been massacred. By the end of the war, 6 million of the Jews transported in cattle cars to the concentration camps in the east would be exterminated. As the European conflict became a world war, Hitler met with Heydrich and other Nazi officials in Wannsee, a Berlin suburb in January 1942. There they drew up even more systematic plans for genocide.

The murders of Jews began, first in mobile vans, using carbon monoxide gas, then in the concentration camp of Auschwitz in Poland, which had been built near the Warsaw ghetto. By 1942, Treblinka, also in Poland, and a number of other camps surrounded by barbed-wire, electrified fences, and watchtowers, had been turned into death camps (see Map 28.4). Gallows stood in an open space near the prisoners' wooden huts. But most victims were exterminated in air-tight gas chambers with Zyklon B gas, chosen because it killed with assembly-line efficiency. Gold from their teeth, eyeglasses, and all other valuables became the property of the Reich.

Inmates of the camps were identified by numbers tattooed on their arms, and wore tattered striped uniforms. Periodically they were ordered to file by an officer, who selected those deemed "unfit" for hard work. He sent them toward a building marked "shower" or "bath," and each was given, in the ultimate cynical gesture, a small piece of soap. A recent, unknowing arrival at Auschwitz inquired of another prisoner as to the whereabouts of his friend. " 'Was he sent to the left side?'. . . 'Yes,' I replied. 'Then you can see him there,' I was told. 'Where?' A hand pointed to the chimney a few hundred yards off, which was sending a column of flame up into the gray sky of Poland. It dissolved into a sinister cloud of smoke." Those people—mostly the young in relatively good health—sent toward the right would continue to live until they dropped dead of fatigue or were subsequently sent to the left side in the next "selection." At Auschwitz, the daily death count reached as high as 15,000 victims.

MAP 28.4 NAZI CONCENTRATION CAMPS   Sites of the concentration camps in Europe.

Germany's allies, Romania, Bulgaria, and the fascist state of Croatia, as well as France, participated in the extermination to varying degrees by carrying out murders themselves (in the case of Croatia and Romania) or condoning and, in the case of Vichy France, assisting in the deportation of French and foreign Jews to Nazi death camps.

Some people protected the Jews. In Amsterdam, a Christian family hid a bourgeois Dutch Jewish family in a secret apartment in their house for several years. In her resolutely cheerful diary, the young Anne Frank described her family's hiding place as "a paradise compared with how other Jews who are not in hiding must be living." It frightened her to think of her friends who had fallen into the clutches of "the cruelest brutes that walk the earth." Several months after her fourteenth birthday, the Germans discovered the Jews hidden in the secret apartment, the girl and her family were deported to Auschwitz and then Bergen-Belsen, where she and most of her family died late in 1944.

Danes saved virtually the entire Jewish population of the country in October 1943. When word came that the German occupying forces were preparing to deport Danish Jews, Danes ferried Jews across the straits to nearby neutral Sweden. Perhaps fearing that mass deportations might spark Danish resistance, in this case German authorities looked the other way. In Croatia, where Italy had established an occupation zone, some Italian army officers protected Jews (and Serbs as well) from Croatian death squads. But when in August 1942, Germany requested that the Italians turn the Croatian Jews over to the Nazis, Mussolini wrote "no objection" across the letter, although he himself had a Jewish mistress.

Dutch Jews on their way to the trains for transport from Amsterdam to a concentration camp.

Mussolini's administrative incapacity, however, may have saved many Italian Jews. Furthermore, as news of more German defeats came, the Italian authorities had little interest in rounding up Italian Jews. They ignored German directives, or could be bribed to look the other way. Some non-Jewish Romans contributed their jewelry to help raise a ransom demanded by the Germans from Jews, under threat of deportation. Others helped Jews hide. But as a whole, European Jews were at the mercy of the Nazis.

Nazi doctors performed barbaric experiments on prisoners. These included measuring the pain a patient could survive when being operated on without anesthesia; how long one could live in subfreezing temperatures; or whether prisoners would allow themselves to be killed if they thought their children might be spared. Gypsies were also Nazi targets, viewed as both "alien" by virtue of not being "Aryan" and "asocial," because they were nomadic, "biological outsiders." During the war, the Nazis killed about 500,000 European gypsies. Communists, socialists, and repeat criminal offenders were also considered "asocial." Many of them perished as well. Himmler persecuted homosexuals ruthlessly, in part because they would not, through procreation, help redress the losses of Germans in World War I: "all things which take place in the sexual sphere," he argued, "are not the private affairs of the individual, but signify the life and death of the nation."

One of the most haunting questions of World War II is at what point the leaders of the Allies and of neutral states actually learned that the Nazis were undertaking the extermination of an entire people. In Germany, persistent rumors of the death camps and other atrocities could be disbelieved because most of the camps themselves were outside the country, in Poland, and elsewhere. Many Germans, in any case, simply did not care ("Who, after all, speaks today of the annihilation of the Armenians [by the Turks in 1915]?," Hitler exclaimed shortly before the outbreak of the war in 1939). Rumors of mass exterminations had begun to reach Britain and the United States in 1942. But even after confirmation provided by four young Jews who escaped from Auschwitz in the summer of 1942, and by information arriving via the Polish underground and diffused by the Polish government in London, it seemed simply too much for leaders of other states to grasp. By the end of that year, however, news of the Holocaust had become widespread.

Many people—including even some leaders of the Jewish communities in Britain, Palestine, and the United States—at first refused to believe "the terrible secret." Pope Pius XII (pope 1939–1958), who had served as the Vatican's representative in Berlin before his election as pope, proclaimed the Vatican's neutrality in the war. By the end of 1942, he knew of the death camps. Yet, despite the efforts of some clergy in a number of countries to help Jews or call attention to what was happening, the Catholic Church limited its protests to occasional reminders of the necessity of "justice and charity" in the world.

The U.S. and British governments had no official reactions to the terrifying news. Some officials expressed disbelief—"wild rumors inspired by Jewish fears"—or believed reports to be exaggerated. Most people did not seem terribly concerned, even when, by the end of the year, there could be no doubt. President Roosevelt certainly knew by the summer of 1942, but rejected the idea of retaliatory bombing of German civilians. He believed that only a sustained military effort could defeat the Nazis. With Hitler's invasion of Russia having gone awry, it looked as though the tide was beginning to turn against Germany. The Allied governments feared that if too much publicity was given to the disappearance of hundreds of thousands of Jews—millions seemed simply too many to believe—it might generate calls to aid them directly. This, they worried, might undercut the united war effort. Hitler's "final solution"—the Holocaust—went on until the very end of the war.

Resistance to the Nazis

Everyone in German-occupied territories knew the potential cost of resistance. In Czechoslovakia, the assassination in 1942 of Heydrich brought savage reprisals, including the destruction of the village of Lidice, where all males were executed, the women were sent to concentration camps, and the children were scattered. When in a Yugoslav town in October 1941 partisans (loyalists) killed ten Germans, the Nazis retaliated by massacring 7,000 men, women, and children.

Resistance movements were most effective where hills and mountains offered protection from German troops, as in central and southern France, Greece, and Yugoslavia. Active and effective resistance was least possible in the flatlands of Holland, western Belgium, Moravia, and northern France, areas in which it was difficult to hide and where there were heavy concentrations of German troops, and many collaborators as well. German military strength made civilian resistance extremely difficult in Poland and in conquered regions of the Soviet Union. Wherever possible, the Allies dropped supplies to resistance groups. But only in Yugoslavia and, to a lesser extent, France, did the resistance movements help bring about Germany's military defeat.

In Yugoslavia, the tenacious Communist Josip Broz (1892–1980), who became known by his code name of Tito, formed the first army of partisans able to engage the Germans effectively in combat situations. Tito had been a "guest worker" in Germany before World War I. He had served in the Austro-Hungarian army during World War I and was badly wounded and captured. Returning in 1920 to newly independent Yugoslavia, Tito became an active trade unionist and in 1923 joined the Yugoslav Communist Party. After spending six years in prison, he went to Moscow to work for the Communist International. Returning again to Yugoslavia, he became general secretary of the Communist Party there. His knowledge of

Josip Broz (Marshal Tito), pictured on the right, Communist head of the Yugoslav Resistance, with his wartime staff in the mountains of Yugoslavia, 1944.

German and Russian made Tito a logical person to represent the Yugoslav Communist Party in negotiations in Germany and the Soviet Union.

Tito's partisans fought courageously against the collaborationist Yugoslav puppet states. The Croatian fascist state, arguably the most vicious of those established in the wake of German conquest, killed 300,000 Serbs and sought to convert survivors by force to Catholicism. The minister of education voiced the opinion that a third of the Serbs should be forced to convert, a third expelled from Croatia, and a third killed. When asked if he did not fear the punishment of God for what he had done, a fascist (Ustaša) guard retorted, "Don't talk to me about that. . . . For my past, present and future deeds I shall burn in hell, but at least I shall burn for Croatia."

Tito insisted on cooperation between Serb and Croat resisters, and maintained contacts with non-Communist groups. Protected by the rugged mountains of Croatia, Tito commanded 20,000 men by 1943. Despite being hounded by German, Italian, Bulgarian, and both Croatian and Serb fascist troops, he managed to carve out entire zones under his control. Late in the war, the British government ended support for a conservative Serb (Chetnik) resistance leader and began to supply Tito's forces with heavy equipment. Yugoslav partisans tied up entire Italian and German divisions. Tito established local Communist committees to serve as governing authorities in each liberated region, and gained support from the Western Allies.

In Western Europe, the Nazis found leaders willing to follow German directives obediently and often enthusiastically. In Belgium, principally in Flanders, the Dutch-speaking part of the country, the German occupation gave the fascist leagues influence they had not had before the war. France, by its armistice with Germany in June 1940, had been divided into an occupied zone and a much smaller southern zone that retained independence through collaboration with the Nazis. The free zone had its capital in the spa town of Vichy in central France. The xenophobia and anti-Semitism of the right-wing politicians and writers of the 1930s came to fruition in Vichy, which gained the support of the fascist leagues and other right-wing groups. Traditional conservatives dissatisfied with the Third Republic for religious and political reasons also lent their support to Vichy.

The elderly Marshal Pétain served as the head of state of the Vichy government, which the United States officially recognized. He remained popular, at least until 1942, because many people in France shared his anti-Marxism and anti-Semitism. He was widely credited with having saved the French state from extinction at the hands of the German invaders.

But, although Vichy may have temporarily saved the French state, Pétain and other collaborators sacrificed the French nation. In the "new order," "Country, Family, Work" replaced "Liberty, Fraternity, Equality" on French coins. Vichy proclaimed a "spiritual revival" against "decadence." Pétain dissolved the Chamber of Deputies and favored the Catholic Church by banning Masonic lodges and divorce. Vichy attempted to impose a new structure of "corporatism" on the French economy and society; these vertical economic structures were intended to eliminate social conflict and replace trade unions, which, as in Germany, were illegal.

Vichy's policies toward Jews revealed the extent of its collaboration with the Nazis. Vichy enacted restrictions on Jews similar to those in force in Germany. Beginning in October 1940, a series of laws forbade Jews from holding jobs in public service, education, or cultural affairs, or in professions such as medicine and law. A law promulgated in July 1941 sought "to eliminate all Jewish influence in the national economy"; the state appointed a trustee who could sell any property or liquidate any business owned by Jews.

These exclusions were only the beginning. French police cooperated with German soldiers after Hitler's May 1941 order to round up 3,600 Polish Jews in France. In December, the Vichy government proclaimed that it would collaborate with the Nazis with "acts, not words." In July 1942, the French police seized 13,000 Jews in Paris, sending them to concentration camps in Germany. Pierre Laval (1883–1945), who became premier of the Vichy government in 1942, insisted that children be sent with their parents to the German death camps. A Parisian woman later recalled, "I saw a train pass. In front, a car containing French police and German soldiers. Then came cattle cars, sealed. The thin arms of children clasped the grating. A hand waved outside like a leaf in a storm. When the train slowed down, voices cried, 'Mama!' And nothing answered except the squeaking of the springs of the train." Vichy France was the only territory in Europe in which local authorities deported Jews without the presence of German occupying forces.

The legacy of French resistance to German occupation and to Vichy France was ultimately more significant than that of collaboration. On June 18, 1940, General Charles de Gaulle, broadcasting from London, called on the French people to resist German rule. The next month, Churchill established an agency in London to provide material assistance to resistance groups.

Churchill grudgingly respected de Gaulle, but also detested him. The same room could not hold the two domineering personalities, a fact compounded by Churchill's bad French. Roosevelt, who considered the towering general "well-nigh intolerable," believed de Gaulle dangerously ambitious, a potential thorn in the Allied side. In December 1941, de Gaulle had surprised the Allies by sending a small force to capture the French islands of St. Pierre and Miquelon off the coast of Newfoundland, which were controlled by Vichy. Seeking to establish the legitimacy of his movement, de Gaulle angered the Allies.

Roosevelt believed that there was nothing to be gained from recognizing de Gaulle's London-based "Free French" movement as the legitimate French government. The U.S. government hoped that Vichy might be convinced to collaborate less openly with Nazi Germany and, above all, to try to keep French North Africa out of German hands. From the American point of view, right-wing French fascist movements might prove even worse than the pro-German Pétain government. The British and U.S. governments worried that recognizing de Gaulle's movement might alienate the mass of the French people. Anti-British Vichy propaganda hammered home that 1,300 French sailors had been killed when the British navy, fearing that they might fall into German hands, had sunk a battleship, a battle cruiser, and several destroyers in July 1940 as they lay in port at Mers el-Kebir in Algeria.

Several resistance movements in France were united only by a hatred of Nazi occupation and Vichy collaboration. Communists, despite not officially turning against Vichy until Germany attacked the Soviet Union in June 1941, formed a well-organized and effective resistance force in France. Jean Moulin, a former departmental prefect during the Third Republic, led de Gaulle's Free French resistance in France. Moulin managed early in May 1943 to unify the resistance groups within the National Council of Resistance. Moulin was betrayed by a collaborator and died under torture in July 1943 without revealing the names of others in the resistance network.

Resistance spread when the Germans stepped up the policy of forcing France to provide workers for factories in Germany. Many of those refus-

The Vichy *milice* (police) raiding a French farmhouse looking for *maquis*.

ing to go to Germany fled into the hills and mountains of France. These resistance bands came to be called the *maquis*, a name for rugged brush in the south of France that could conceal them.

Better armed by airplane drops of guns, the *maquis* grew bolder. On the two occasions they challenged German troops in open conflict, the results were disastrous. But by 1944, the *maquis* controlled several regions of southern France, at least at night, vulnerable only to the arrival of German military columns, diversions that the German army could by then ill afford. General Dwight Eisenhower (1890–1969), commander of Allied forces in the European theater of operations, later said that the resistance in France was the equivalent of fifteen military divisions. The French resistance would enable de Gaulle to emerge from the war with great personal prestige that would contribute to France's rebuilding.

Against Hitler in Germany

The vast majority of Germans remained loyal to their Führer. German morale remained astonishingly high even as the war dragged on and defeats mounted. The German minister of propaganda, Joseph Goebbels (who once said "a lie told over and over again becomes a truth") sought to maintain civilian commitment and confidence in ultimate victory, even as Allied bombers frequently droned overhead and news of horrendous losses on the Russian front became known. Disgruntlement and bitter jokes were common, but they did not threaten the regime. Those who had never approved of Hitler retreated into family life and the daily economic struggle to get by. When wartime deprivation left people grumbling, Germans tended to blame Hitler's subordinates, not the Führer.

Outright resistance to the Nazis or even strikes were virtually impossible because of the certainty of an immediate, savage response. Courts sentenced 15,000 Germans to death for crimes against the state, under an expanded definition of capital crimes, which included listening to B.B.C. radio broadcasts from London. German resistance against Hitler was fragmented and ineffective. Trade union and Communist groups, earlier smashed by the S.S., emerged again as economic conditions worsened in 1942–1943. Some students in Munich and Communists in Berlin bravely distributed anti-Nazi propaganda, but such courageous acts were not widespread.

About a quarter of a million people in Germany were imprisoned or forced to emigrate because of their political opposition and at least 150,000 German Communists were put in concentration camps, and a good many other people were tortured and killed before they got that far. The active connivance of ordinary Germans, who continued to step forward to denounce neighbors for being Jewish or for their political beliefs or statements, aided the S.S. and the Gestapo in rooting out potential sources of opposition. Even humane gestures toward Jews or foreign workers were dangerous. The Nazi terror apparatus, as in any totalitarian state, also operated outside Germany's legal system.

Some young people responded to Nazism by adopting a counter-culture of nonconformity. The members of the Edelweiss Pirates gang of Cologne refused to join the Hitler Youth and brawled with its members. They listened to American music deemed decadent by Hitler, mocked the hiking songs of the Hitler Youth, and scrawled anti-Nazi graffiti on walls. The Nazis arrested some of them, publicly hanging several sixteen-year-old boys. But this dissident subculture represented no more than a mild irritation to the Nazis.

The only serious plot against Hitler came among traditional conservatives within the army. Opposition among officers emerged, not out of a hatred for Nazi ideals or because they did not share Hitler's territorial ambitions, but rather from growing anxiety that Hitler's military decisions would lead to German defeat.

On July 20, 1944, Colonel Klaus von Stauffenberg (1907–1944) carried a bomb in his briefcase to a staff meeting with Hitler near the Russian front. Stauffenberg, who had been badly maimed in battle, was a conservative aristocrat appalled by the systematic Nazi murder of Jews and Soviets and by what he considered Hitler's amateur management of the war. He hoped that Hitler's assassination would allow the army to impose a fascist state similar to that of Italy. He placed the bomb under the table beneath Hitler, who instinctively shoved the briefcase out of his way, moving it to the other side of a heavy table support. The bomb exploded, wounding

Hitler slightly. Those implicated in the plot were quickly arrested and slowly strangled by nooses of piano wire as they writhed on meat hooks. Movie cameras recorded their agonizing death for the later amusement of Hitler, his mistress, and friends. Hitler also ordered the execution of about 5,000 other Germans in positions of authority whose loyalty seemed suspect. A decree of "liability of next of kin" led to the arrest of family members of leading conspirators. Thousands of Germans turned out in several major cities to celebrate their Führer's escape from death. Until the very end, Hitler appeared to hold the allegiance of most Germans.

THE TIDE TURNS

By the end of 1942, the Germans were on the defensive on the high seas, in the Soviet Union, and in North Africa, where Italian forces were routed and German forces pushed back (see Map 28.5). The entry of the United States into the Second World War helped turn the tide against Germany. American war supplies and then armed forces strengthened the Allied cause as they had in World War I. The German war machine was chaotically managed and German resources increasingly inadequate to fighting a war on so many fronts.

Hitler's invasion of Russia turned into a full-fledged military disaster, culminating in crushing, costly defeat and surrender at Stalingrad in February 1943, a turning point in the war. As Hitler's Balkan allies one by one pulled out of the war, the Allies launched an invasion of Italy from North Africa, forcing the king of Italy to agree to a secret armistice and pushing German troops to retreat to the north. On June 6, 1944, Western Allied forces launched a massive invasion of France, landing on the beaches of Normandy, and forcing the German army to pull back, fighting all the way. The Allies first reached the Rhine River in March 1945.

Now confident of victory over Hitler, the Big Three (Churchill, Roosevelt, and Stalin) began to plan for the end of the war. As the Soviet army began to push the Germans back across a broad front in July 1943, it became clear that when the war ended, the Red Army could control large parts of Eastern and Central Europe. This probability brought dissension to the Big Three, particularly as Churchill feared that the Red Army might never leave the Eastern European nations it liberated from German occupation.

Germany on the Defensive

With the majority of German men between the ages of eighteen and fifty in the army, Germany's war machine required new workers. By late 1941, there were already 4 million foreigners working in Germany, including

MAP 28.5 THE DEFEAT OF GERMANY, 1942–1945   Allied advances and Axis withdrawal up to the end of World War II.

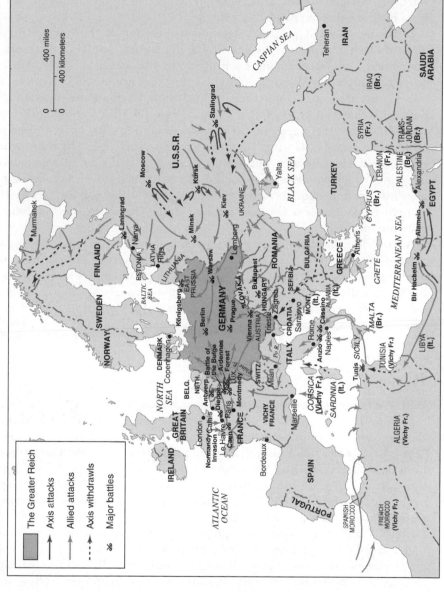

The Greater Reich

↑ Axis attacks

↑ Allied attacks

┄↑ Axis withdrawals

⚔ Major battles

IRAN

Teheran

SAUDI
ARABIA

IRAQ
(Br.)

SYRIA
(Fr.)

CASPIAN SEA

TURKEY

LEBANON
(Fr.)

PALESTINE
(Br.)

TRANS-
JORDAN
(Br.)

Alexandria

EGYPT

CYPRUS
(Br.)

BLACK SEA

Yalta

Stalingrad

Kursk

Moscow

U.S.S.R.

Kiev

UKRAINE

Minsk

Lemberg

Warsaw

Leningrad

Murmansk

Narva

ESTONIA
LATVIA
Riga
LITHUANIA

FINLAND

SWEDEN

NORWAY

BALTIC
SEA

EAST
PRUSSIA

Königsberg

Berlin

GERMANY

Prague

Vienna

AUSTRIA

HUNGARY

Budapest

SLOVAKIA

ROMANIA

BULGARIA

GREECE

Athens

CRETE

MEDITERRANEAN SEA

Bir Hacheim

El Alamein

MALTA
(Br.)

LIBYA
(It.)

TUNISIA
(Vichy Fr.)

Tunis

SICILY

SARDINIA
(It.)

Naples

Anzio

Cassino

Rome

MONT.

ALBANIA
(It.)

SERBIA

Sarajevo

Zagreb

CROATIA

Trieste

ITALY

Milan

Po R.

Rhine

SWITZ.

Battle of
the Bulge

Ardennes
Forest

Lux.

Montmédy

BELG.

NETH.

Antwerp

Dieppe

Calais

Le Havre

Normandy
Invasion

Caen

Paris

VICHY
FRANCE

FRANCE

Marseille

Bordeaux

CORSICA
(Vichy Fr.)

DENMARK

Copenhagen

NORTH
SEA

GREAT
BRITAIN

London

IRELAND

ATLANTIC
OCEAN

SPAIN

PORTUGAL

SPANISH
MOROCCO

FRENCH
MOROCCO
(Vichy Fr.)

ALGERIA
(Vichy Fr.)

0   400 miles
0   400 kilometers

prisoners of war (in violation of international agreements), and in May 1944, almost twice that number, the majority of whom were Soviet citizens. In 1943, more women went to work in factories, despite Hitler's view that German women should only be housekeepers and bearers of Aryan warriors. German industry increasingly depended upon conscript labor from conquered countries.

In the meantime, Germany's day-to-day operation of the war effort remained chaotic, as ministries and military branches, and Hitler's favored henchmen, competed among each other. In the spring of 1942, Hitler named the architect Albert Speer to be minister of armaments production. Speer's organizational competence helped triple German armaments production within two years. But not until 1944 did Hitler grant Speer responsibility for the needs of the air force, Göring's personal preserve. Hitler then awarded Göring "plenipotentiary powers" over the entire war effort. Unlike his enemies, Hitler thus resisted carefully coordinated state planning, which he believed smacked of communism. German war supplies remained inadequate to the enormous goals Hitler had set. Gradually to realists like Speer a German military victory began to seem difficult, even improbable.

As in World War I, German military commanders placed their hopes on closing Allied shipping lanes across the Atlantic, thereby preventing supplies from reaching Britain. Many American ships and crews went down in the icy Atlantic with their crews. But most got through. German U-boats, the hunters, became the hunted. New submarine-detecting devices enabled airplanes and destroyers to sink German submarines with depth-charges.

The War in North Africa

With the failure of the submarine campaign against Allied shipping, Germany now had to depend on its armies' success on land. In North Africa, the German tank division commanded by Rommel, by now known as the "Desert Fox" because of his quick judgment and daring tactical improvisations, had forced British troops back from Libya into Egypt. Victories in the spring of 1942 at Bir Hacheim and Tobruk, where the Germans captured a garrison of 35,000 British troops, put Rommel only sixty miles from Alexandria. However, at the end of August, the British tank force of General Bernard Montgomery (1887–1976) pushed back another Rommel offensive. The arrogant, condescending Montgomery knew his enemy's plan of attack in advance through reports from British intelligence services. The Allied forces, enjoying superior strength and controlling the skies, then attacked Rommel's forces, breaking through the German and Italian defenses at El Alamein (in Egypt) in early November. For the next ten weeks they pursued the German armored division across the desert all the way to Tunisia.

The Allies now faced major strategic decisions. Churchill wanted to strike at what he called the "soft underbelly" of the axis through Italy, the Balkans, and the Danube Basin after driving Hitler's armies from North Africa. This would leave British forces in an excellent position to protect British interests in the Middle East. Stalin, however, continued to insist on a major Allied attack against Germany in the west to force Hitler to divert resources from the Russian campaign. Stalin pointed out that the Red Army had borne the brunt of the war against Hitler, inflicting 90 percent of the losses the German armed forces had suffered in battle since June 1941. Churchill, however, feared that a direct confrontation with the largest concentration of German troops might be disastrous and wanted to postpone a cross-Channel invasion of France as long as possible.

With the Axis reeling in North Africa and British troops now controlling Egypt and Libya, the Allied commanders now decided first to drive all German and Italian troops out of North Africa before contemplating an invasion of France from Britain. They had been sobered by a disastrous cross-Channel raid by Canadian troops against the French port of Dieppe in August 1942 and feared that a massive invasion in France might fail.

In November 1942, the Allies launched "Operation Torch." A British and American force commanded by Eisenhower landed on the coast of French Algeria and Morocco and easily overcame Vichy resistance. To his shock and consternation, de Gaulle now learned that the Allies were negotiating with the Vichy commander in North Africa, Admiral Jean Darlan (1881–1942). Despite Pétain's order that Vichy forces in North Africa continue to oppose the Allied invasion, Darlan ordered his troops to accept a cease-fire after three days of fighting. Hitler used Darlan's capitulation in North Africa as an excuse in November 1942 for Germany to occupy the "free" zone of Vichy France. Little remained of Vichy's illusion of independence. French naval commanders scuttled their own ships to prevent them from being used by the German navy.

The Allies named Darlan as "the head of the French state" in return for his promise that French troops in North Africa would now join the Allies. Darlan's extreme right-wing views and close association with Vichy collaborators soon left him without much British or American support. The Allies then trotted out a general to set up a free French government in North Africa. De Gaulle demanded that Britain and the United States recognize his French Committee of National Liberation as France's legitimate government. But Churchill, an old imperialist, viewed de Gaulle's pressing concerns with maintaining France's empire in the context of the two powers' long-standing imperial rivalry. Churchill feared that if the British government recognized de Gaulle as the head of the French state, it would be committing itself to supporting a new France, the direction of which could hardly then be seen. A French monarchist solved part of the Allied dilemma by assassinating Darlan. The Allies forced de Gaulle to share leadership of Free France with another general, a slap in the face that he neither forgot nor forgave. After the defeat of a vigorous German counter-attack, by the end of May 1943, no German or Italian troops remained in North Africa.

The Allies' strategic bombing campaign, the goal of which was to sap German morale as much as to hamper the production of planes and guns, began to take its toll in 1943. The American poet Randall Jarrell remembered, "In bombers named for girls, we burned/ The cities we had learned about in school." The Royal Air Force could now strike at night with reasonable accuracy, while scrambling German radar, thereby reducing losses. British bombers dumped tons of bombs during night raids over the industrial Ruhr area and major cities. Many American bombers were lost despite fighter escorts because the U.S. Air Force preferred daylight attacks, when pilots could more easily find their targets. The impact of the strategic bombing campaign on German wartime industrial production was far below Allied expectations, however, particularly given the great number of planes and crews lost.

Hitler's Russian Disaster

In the meantime, on the eastern front Hitler's invasion of the Soviet Union turned into a full-fledged military disaster. Defeats in Russia during the last months of 1942 and in 1943 sent the German invaders reeling. Hitler's armies had been forced to retreat from the Moscow region. The Red Army was now receiving better and more plentiful supplies from the Allies through the icy northern port of Murmansk and from Iran in the south. Soviet factories were turning out a steady supply of tanks and trucks equipped to fight in the snow and ice. German tanks faced not only improved Soviet tanks but also handmade incendiary bombs consisting of bottles, gasoline, and cloth fuses that became known as "Molotov cocktails."

Improvements in the organization and discipline of the Red Army also made their mark. Unlike Hitler, Stalin delegated authority to efficient and trusted party members during the war, holding in abeyance the ideological indoctrination and murderous purges that had characterized much of the Soviet Union's post-revolutionary period. The army that Hitler had once mocked was now wearing down German forces.

In the north, Leningrad, first reached by German troops in July 1941, held on against a German siege that lasted 506 days, the longest in modern history, and that killed at least 650,000 Russian civilians. Hitler's printed invitations to celebrate Leningrad's fall could never be sent out. Further defeats in the north made Germany's drive to the Soviet oil fields of the Caucasus Mountains, and the Donets industrial region in the south, all the more critical. In the south, the Red Army slowed the German advance toward Stalingrad, a strategically located industrial city on the Volga River.

During the siege of Leningrad, a couple drags the dead body of their child on a sled down Nevsky Prospect.

The battle of Stalingrad was a great turning point in the European war. The Soviets had begun concentrating a huge force around the city, even as early German successes deluded Hitler into thinking Stalingrad's fall was inevitable. In November 1942, as Soviet troops held off the German assault in house-to-house fighting, Hitler confidently began to transfer some of his exhausted troops to the north. The Soviet army counterattacked on November 19, trapping the weakened German armies as Soviet tanks moved easily across the frozen ground. From Berlin, Hitler ordered his troops to hold out until the last man. By the time German survivors surrendered on February 2, 1943, the German army had lost more than 300,000 soldiers.

Soviet troops then fought their way into Leningrad. In July, in a battle involving more than 9,000 tanks, Soviet troops won another great victory, further depleting the once seemingly invincible German armored divisions. The Soviets were now battering their enemy on three fronts. They recaptured all of the Crimea in the south by May 1943, pushing the Germans back to Ukraine in the summer.

In February 1944, Soviet troops reached what had been the eastern Polish border before the German invasion. On the western front, waves of British and American bombers devastated German cities; over 40,000 people perished in attacks on Hamburg in July 1943, during which more than 9,000 tons of bombs rained down on the port city.

One by one Germany's Balkan allies bailed out. Romanian troops had greatly aided the Nazi campaign in Odessa and the Crimea; Romanian oil and wheat had fueled the German war effort. Now, in March 1944, seeing

(*Left*) Hamburg Germany, after Allied bombing. (*Right*) The devastated Stuttgart after Allied bombing.

the writing on the wall, the Romanian government approached the Allies, hoping to arrange a separate peace. In August, King Michael finally ended Antonescu's military dictatorship, and the new government declared war on Germany. The Red Army soon poured into the country, occupying Bucharest in late August 1944.

Hitler intended Bulgaria to serve as a buffer against a possible Allied invasion from Turkey. Bulgaria enjoyed the most autonomy of any Nazi-held Eastern European state because it provided Germany with badly needed grain, had permitted the establishment of military bases on its territory, and had declared war on Britain and the United States in 1941. Hitler had allowed Bulgaria to annex Thrace from Greece and to take Greek and Yugoslav Macedonia. Now, as Germany's defeat appeared increasingly likely, the Bulgarian government brazenly announced its war against the Allies had ended. But the Soviet Union declared war on Bulgaria on September 5. Following a popular insurrection, the Soviet Union controlled the resulting coalition government, as in the case of Romania. Soviet domination of the Balkan states began to take shape.

The Allied Invasion of Italy

With North Africa and its airfields secure, the Allies decided to invade Sicily as a first step in an invasion of southern Italy. The plunging morale and material conditions of the Italian population, promised an empire by Mussolini but receiving only hardship, contributed to the Allied decision.

In July 1943, Palermo and Messina quickly fell to Allied troops. The fascist Grand Council asked King Victor Emmanuel III to end Mussolini's dictatorship. The king, eager to save his throne and fearing a complete German takeover, dismissed the stunned Mussolini as prime minister and ordered him arrested. The new government, while announcing that Italy would continue to fight alongside of Germany, had begun secret negotiations with the Allies. When Hitler learned this in September, he ordered his troops to occupy Italian airfields.

Churchill remained determined that the Allies should now invade Italy's mainland. At a minimum, such an invasion would tie up considerable numbers of German troops, and probably knock Italy completely out of the war. Romanian oil fields would be within reach of bombers taking off in Italy. The Italian resistance had finally gathered momentum. Socialists, Catholic groups, and, above all, Communists began to print clandestine newspapers and organize scattered attacks against fascists. The United States, still pushing for a full-scale landing in France, reluctantly agreed to the Italian invasion. The German high command hoped to stop the Allied offensive in northern and central Italy, near Florence. In the meantime, the Italian king, fearing that Hitler might order him seized, reassured Germany of Italy's loyal participation in the war as an ally. However, the new Italian government signed an armistice with the Allies on September 3, 1943. Victor Emmanuel naively hoped that Italy could make peace with both Germany and the Allies, and that his monarchy would survive the end of the war.

On the same day as the armistice was signed between Italy and the Allies, British and Canadian troops crossed the Straits of Messina, beginning an invasion of the Italian peninsula. The king and his family fled Rome with the prime minister, leaving a million Italian soldiers with the choice of being interned by the Germans or deserting their units. Most deserted, and 80,000 Allied prisoners of war escaped from camps in Italy.

The Germans slowly retreated behind one river after the next, with both sides taking large losses. The new front settled on a series of fortifications a hundred miles south of Rome, over which stood the old monastery of Monte Cassino. In January 1944, two Allied divisions landed behind the German lines at Anzio. They did so at the instigation of Churchill, who sought the capture of Rome as quickly as possible. Only in the spring, after terrible losses, were Allied troops able to break through the German defenses to free their armies still trapped near Anzio. The Allies took Rome on June 4, 1944. The German armies fell back to establish a new defensive perimeter south of the Po River between Pisa and Florence.

The Allies set up a new government in the south, its members drawn from the resistance groups. In the meantime, on September 12 a daring German commando raid freed Mussolini from a mountaintop prison. In Berlin, Hitler proclaimed the Duce head of the "Italian Social Republic," a puppet regime. Mussolini ordered the execution of the members of the Grand Council who had opposed him and denounced the Italian people for having betrayed him.

The Big Three

Soviet advances against German forces increasingly focused Western attention on the future of Central and Eastern Europe once Hitler's Germany had been defeated. At their Casablanca meeting in January 1943, Churchill and Roosevelt had concerned themselves only with military strategy and not with the future of Europe. With Stalin absent, the British and American governments agreed to put off discussions of the territorial settlements that would follow Germany's defeat. Churchill and Stalin had already informally agreed to Soviet absorption of the Baltic states after the war. They did so despite the opposition of Roosevelt, who argued that Stalin had joined the war against the Nazis only after Hitler had attacked the Soviet Union.

Stalin's insistence that the United States and Britain open another front in the west by invading France in part stemmed from his fear that his allies wanted to see the Red Army slowed in its drive westward. As deliveries of Allied supplies to Russia through Murmansk trickled to a halt, Stalin seemed confirmed in his suspicions.

Meeting at Moscow in October 1943, the British, American, and Soviet foreign ministers reaffirmed an agreement that the Allies would accept nothing less than Germany's unconditional surrender. The Allies also reaffirmed their intention, originally stated in the "Atlantic Charter" of August 1941 signed by Roosevelt and Churchill, that a United Nations organization replace the ineffective, moribund League of Nations. But again they left open the thorny question of the political future of Central and Eastern Europe after the war.

Stalin finally met Churchill and Roosevelt in Teheran in November 1943. Amid heavy meals and clinking glasses, the leaders formulated harsh plans for post-war Germany. Stalin stated that the Soviet Union was not about to contemplate any change in its border with Poland as it existed in June 1941, the result of the Soviet invasion and absorption of much of eastern Poland in 1939. Yet, despite the occasional flurry of map-making, using knives, forks, and matchboxes on the tablecloths, the Big Three left the specifics of the proposed outlines of post-war Europe for the future.

The D-Day Invasion of France

At Teheran, Stalin and Roosevelt convinced Churchill to accept a plan for the invasion of France. General Eisenhower coordinated the "D-Day" landing in France, "Operation Overlord." Born in a small town in Kansas, Eisenhower was a forthright man of integrity. Beneath his sparkling blue eyes, folksy manner, and smile ("He had only to smile at you," Montgomery once said, "and there was nothing you would not do for him") lay shrewdness, cunning, and a remarkable ability for organization. The plan

A modern armada of ships put ashore military supplies following the D-Day invasion, June 1944.

was for 150,000 troops to attack the English Channel beaches of Normandy in western France, followed in the next days and weeks by almost half a million more. About 4 million tons of support materiel would have to be landed as well. Floating caissons and old ships sunk off the coast would provide three makeshift harbors. In the meantime, German commanders believed that the most likely place for an all-out assault was the Pas-de-Calais, the closest French crossing point from England.

The first hours of Operation Overlord would be crucial. The Allies needed to take and protect a beachhead that would allow the bulk of their troops to get ashore quickly. Planes would drop squadrons of parachutists behind German lines. Hitler had assigned General Rommel to organize the German defense against the Allied invasion. His defenders would depend on the rapid arrival of armored units to back up the coastal batteries and infantry units trying to hold their positions against attacking Allied troops.

After a one-day postponement because of a gale, at dawn on the morning of June 6, 1944, Allied troops struggled ashore in shallow water from landing craft and established beachheads on the coast of Normandy. They confronted murderous fire from the cliffs above, taking heavy losses. But the landing succeeded, at least partially because the German air force was outnumbered by 20 to 1, preventing rapid German reinforcement. As more men, tanks, trucks, and materiel came ashore, German troops gradually fell back. By the end of July, despite fierce resistance, the Allies held most of Normandy. After seven weeks, the Allies had landed 1.3 million troops and sustained over 120,000 casualties. The Germans lost half a million men trying to defend Normandy. Hitler allowed Rommel, discovered to have known about the plot against the Führer's life, to escape execution by committing suicide.

Members of the French Resistance sabotaging train tracks before the Normandy invasion.

On August 15, another Allied army landed on the French Mediterranean coast and moved up the Rhône Valley with little opposition. The main Allied army pushed toward Paris. On August 19, an uprising of the resistance movement began in Paris. Because de Gaulle demanded that a French unit be the first to reach the capital, a French force reached Paris on August 22, 1944; de Gaulle himself entered Paris on August 25. Finally in October the British government recognized de Gaulle's administration as that of France.

Churchill and de Gaulle after the liberation of Paris.

German resistance stiffened at the Rhine and the first Allied attempts to cross into Germany failed. Hitler, whose moods varied between wild optimism and resigned depression, had aged rapidly and trembled through recurring bouts with illness. Now, although Germany's collapse seemed imminent, he again seemed confident, telling Speer in November 1944, "I haven't the slightest intention of surrendering. Besides, November has always been my lucky month." In December, Hitler ordered a massive counterattack in the hills and forests of the Ardennes in Belgium and Luxembourg, with the goal of pushing rapidly toward the Belgian river port of Antwerp. At Montmédy, a German S.S. unit massacred captured American soldiers. News of the incident spread rapidly along the front. After retreating forty-five miles, the U.S. army pushed the Germans back in the Battle of the Bulge.

As the Nazi army retreated in northern Italy, the Red Army approached Germany from the east. On every front, Allied troops increasingly found that their enemies turned out to be boys and old men who had been rushed to the front with virtually no training. German cities burned, notably Dresden, which American planes fire-bombed early in 1945. About 50,000 residents of Berlin died in Allied air attacks. The Allies dropped 315 tons of bombs on Germany for every 1 the Luftwaffe had dropped on Britain in 1940. In 1993, almost one World War II bomb a day was still being discovered unexploded in Berlin. The American army crossed the Rhine on March 8 and on April 25, 1945, met up with Soviet troops at the Elbe River just sixty miles south of Berlin.

Hitler, expressing confidence that the Big Three alliance would break

German families fleeing the Red Army.

up, held out hope for Germany's newly developed weapons, in which he had earlier expressed no interest: the deadly V-1 jet-propelled "flying bomb" could strike targets from 3,000 feet at speeds of 470 miles per hour; the terrifying V-2 rocket could fly faster than the speed of sound. Launched from France, the first V-1 struck London on June 12, 1944, doing considerable damage. The first jet- and rocket-propelled fighter planes, the former reaching speeds of 500 miles per hour, arrived in time to join the Battle of the Bulge, but without significant effect.

With defeat ever closer, Hitler accepted, even desired, the total destruction of Germany, considering it better than the shame of surrender: "If the war is lost, the people will be lost also. It is not necessary for us to worry about what the German people will need in order to survive. On the contrary, it is best for us to destroy even these things."

ALLIED VICTORY

Romania and Bulgaria had surrendered in August and September 1944, respectively. With the Red Army in control of much of the Balkans, the question was not if Berlin would be taken, but when, and by whom. Though worried that the Soviets sought a preponderant role in Central Europe, Eisenhower was prepared to allow Stalin the prestige of capturing Berlin. The much greater problem still remained: the future of Germany and Eastern Europe. As the Red Army moved closer to Berlin, the meetings of the Big Three in the waning months of the year proved exceptionally important for the future of Europe. Churchill and Stalin met in Moscow in October 1944 and worked out a rough division of post-war Western and Soviet interests in Central and Eastern Europe. By the time the Big Three came together at Yalta in Crimea in March 1945, German armies were falling back rapidly on every front, and the Red Army was closing in on Berlin.

Victory in Europe

Churchill was determined to work out an informal agreement with the Soviets as to the respective spheres of influence in the Balkans when the war ended. In October 1944, he met with Stalin in Moscow. This time Roosevelt, who suspected Churchill of trying to maintain the British Empire at all costs, did not participate. As Churchill recalled, "I said, 'Let us settle about our affairs in the Balkans. . . . How would it do for you to have ninety percent of the say in Romania, for us to have ninety percent of the say in Greece, and go fifty-fifty about Yugoslavia?' " After adding 75 percent for the Soviet Union in Bulgaria and fifty-fifty for Hungary, the British prime minister pushed the paper across to Stalin. "There was a slight pause. Then he took his blue pencil and made a large tick upon it,

Joseph Stalin, Franklin Roosevelt, Winston Churchill, and Vyacheslav Molotov at the Yalta Conference, 1945.

and passed it back to us. It was all settled in no more time than it takes to sit down."

When the Big Three met in the Soviet Black Sea resort of Yalta in February 1945, the Red Army had drawn within 100 miles of Berlin. The Yalta meeting, then, would be crucial for the future of post-war Europe. Churchill agreed to the post-war division of Germany into British, American, Soviet, and French zones of military occupation. Already in Eastern Europe, Communist Party members were working feverishly to expand Soviet influence. Stalin feared that his wartime Allies might lead a post-war campaign against communism, which had been the case after World War I. He agreed to Roosevelt's demand that the Soviet Union declare war on Japan, which the U.S. president believed would expedite Japan's defeat in Asia. But, in exchange, Stalin asked for and received Allied promises that the Soviet Union would control Outer Mongolia, and the Kurile Islands and the southern half of Sakhalin Island, both north of Japan.

In Poland, the Soviets had established a provisional government dominated by Polish Communists. At Yalta, the other Allies went along with Stalin's insistence that the provisional government (to which would be added representatives from the non-Communist Polish government, which had been functioning in London during the war) would become Poland's new government. Churchill and Roosevelt also went along with Stalin's insistence that the Soviet Union would keep the parts of eastern Poland that had been absorbed by the Soviet invasion in 1939. Poland's western frontier with Germany was to be left to a future conference, one that was never held. The Big Three all agreed that free elections would be held in Eastern Europe.

At Yalta, the Allies agreed that the League of Nations had been doomed in its attempts to keep the peace by the nonparticipation of the United States, because of its isolationism, and of the Soviet Union, which had been excluded by the other powers. They now agreed that the United States and the Soviet Union would be permanent members of the Security Council of the United Nations. Roosevelt wanted to avoid committing the United States to an active role in post-war Europe, while counting on the proposed United Nations to resolve future problems. He also took a dim view of Churchill's commitment to the maintenance of the British Empire, which Roosevelt thought not in keeping with the principle of self-determination.

The war now moved toward an end. The Red Army launched a final attack on Berlin in April 1945. Italian partisans captured Mussolini near the Swiss frontier. They executed him and his mistress, hanging their bodies upside down at a Milan gas station. Himmler, Ribbentrop, and Göring now agreed that Germany must end the war. As Soviet tanks drew near on the night of April 28/29, 1945, Hitler married his long-time mistress, Eva Braun, in the depths of a fortified bunker in central Berlin. Then they committed suicide on April 30 as the rumble of Russian tanks could be heard above. Joseph Goebbels poisoned his six children, shot his wife, and killed himself. Admiral Karl Dönitz, to whom Hitler had delegated authority, surrendered on behalf of Germany to the Allies on May 8, 1945. The Reich that Hitler had once bragged would last for a thousand years lay in ruins twelve years after its creation.

The Defeat of Japan

The German collapse in North Africa, Russia, and Eastern Europe now allowed the Allies to turn their attention more fully to the war in the Pacific.

The corpses of Mussolini, his mistress, and other fascists hanging at a gas station after their execution near Milan in April 1945.

Soldiers from the Red Army hoist the Soviet flag over the German Reichstag in Berlin.

The sheer scope of Japanese military operations, spread from the Aleutian Islands southwest of Alaska to the South Pacific, put Japan on the defensive. Troops and supplies poured into the Pacific from the United States, which had speedily reconstituted its fleet after the Pearl Harbor disaster. Victory in the Battle of the Coral Sea (May 1942), which turned back Japanese ships carrying troops to the southern coast of New Guinea, protected Australia from possible invasion. A month later, the American fleet and torpedo bombers inflicted a major defeat on the Japanese navy at the Battle of Midway, an island almost a thousand miles northeast of Hawaii (see Map 28.2). Four Japanese aircraft carriers were sunk.

In August 1942, an American offensive had begun against Guadalcanal, one of the South Pacific Solomon Islands. Guadalcanal fell on February 8, 1943, the first of the Japanese wartime conquests to be recaptured. American assaults in New Guinea and far north in the Aleutian Islands also succeeded. General MacArthur's forces began driving the Japanese from New Guinea in January 1943, completing the task early in 1944. From then on, the Americans adopted the strategy of driving Japanese forces from one island after another. Some Japanese forces were still tied down in China, and others were scattered on the islands of the Pacific Ocean. Gradually the U.S. navy gained control of the seas, its submarines picking off Japanese supply ships. A Japanese invasion of India, begun from Burma in March 1944, failed in July. With the help of a Chinese attack from the north, British troops recaptured Burma. Hard-earned summer victories brought U.S. troops within 1,400 miles of Tokyo. On October 20,

1944, MacArthur's forces attacked the Philippines, defeating the Japanese fleet and demoralized troops. There, the Japanese first used kamikaze tactics, suicide missions flown by pilots crashing into American ships.

The American capture of the island of Iwo Jima on March 27, 1945, brought U.S. planes to within 700 miles of Japan. On Okinawa, the next stop, piles of bleached human bones could still be seen on the beaches a decade after the war's end. A U.S. marine remembered: "Replacements [got] hit before we even knew their names. They came up confused, frightened, and hopeful, got wounded or killed, and went right back to the rear on the route by which they had come, shocked, bleeding, or stiff." Saipan and Guam provided bases from which American long-range bombers could reach Japan. As the Japanese army reeled back in China, American "superfortress" bombers showered Japanese cities with incendiary bombs that turned wooden buildings into fiery death traps. One attack destroyed 40 percent of Tokyo within three hours. Japan's five largest cities lay in ruins. American forces prepared to invade the southern islands of Japan itself. With the American fleet off Okinawa confronting suicide missions by Japanese pilots who flew their planes into ships, it was clear that such an invasion would cost many lives.

The United States was readying a new weapon of hitherto unimaginable proportions with which it hoped to force an unconditional Japanese surrender. In 1938, a German scientist in Berlin had achieved nuclear fission, splitting the atom and releasing tremendous energy. This meant that if a means could be found to set off a nuclear chain reaction, a bomb of enormous destructive power could be built. During the first years of the war, British and American scientists had worked separately to achieve this powerful nuclear reaction. German scientists, too, were working in the same direction. In the United States, German scientists who had fled the Nazis first discovered that an isotope of uranium could set off the anticipated chain reaction. The United States detonated the first atomic bomb on July 16, 1945, in the New Mexico desert.

Nine days later, President Harry Truman (Roosevelt having died of a cerebral hemorrhage in April) presented Japan with an ultimatum warning that it faced "prompt and utter destruction" if it did not surrender unconditionally. When Japanese resistance continued, an American air force plane dropped an atomic bomb on the Japanese city of Hiroshima on August 6, 1945, engulfing the city in a mushroom cloud of fire, radiation, and horrible death. Two days later, another plane dropped a second atomic bomb that destroyed much of Nagasaki and 80,000 people in a storm of fire. Thousands more would die of radiation sickness in the days, months, and years to follow. The night of the Nagasaki attack, the Japanese emperor called on his cabinet to surrender. On September 2, 1945, Japanese representatives signed documents of unconditional surrender on the aircraft carrier *Missouri*. The Second World War was over. But a new and potentially even more dangerous atomic age had begun.

CONCLUSION

The first Soviet troops arriving at the Nazi death camps discovered night-marish horrors: technology harnessed to the task of genocide, factories of death, piles of corpses, children's shoes, and the lucky survivors, the living dead, barefoot human skeletons fortunate enough to have been liberated before their turn to be exterminated had come. The death camps became perhaps the most awful symbol of the total war that was World War II. About 6 million Jews perished during the war. The Nazis killed about 2.7 million Polish Jews; at the end of the war, only about 40,000 to 50,000 European Jews had survived the Holocaust.

World War II brought mass military mobilization and mass death. Seventeen million people were killed in the fighting and another 20 million civilians perished, half in the Soviet Union; Germany lost more than 6 million people, Japan 2 million, and Britain and France lost about 250,000 and 300,000 respectively. Part of the horror of the period is that we will never really know the full extent of human loss. Millions had been wounded, many crippled for life. Millions of survivors had been carried by luck, good and bad, far from home. Husbands, wives, children, and other relatives were often lost forever. Europe became a continent of "displaced persons," as they were called.

The psychic damage to those who lived through night bombing in shelters, those who spent years waiting for definitive news about missing loved ones, or those who had somehow survived concentration camps, cannot be calculated. Europe seemed haunted by the sad memories of last conversations and letters. Among the hundreds of thousands who emerged with physical or psychological wounds, there were relatively few left to tell the story of Auschwitz or Dachau. One survivor recalled his determination to hold on against all odds "to tell the story, to bear witness; and that to survive, we must force ourselves to save at least the skeleton, the scaffolding, the form of civilization."

After the war, in contrast to the end of World War I, there seemed little optimism that such a total war could not occur again. Two factors, in particular, contributed to this new feeling of angst. First was the rising tension even before the war ended between the Soviet Union and the Western Allies. The second was the development of new techniques and weapons of mass destruction—rockets, the jet plane, and, above all, the atomic bomb, a terrifying weapon for a new age.

The cataclysmic experience of the Second World War weighed heavily on the social, political, and cultural climate of the post-war era. In every country, those who resisted German rule played a major part in the reconstitution of their nations after the war. Politicians, intellectuals, and virtually everyone else would try to come to grips with what had happened to Europe, to assess blame, and to find hope. For the moment, for many, it seemed enough to have survived.

PART SEVEN

EUROPE IN THE
POST-WAR ERA

Following the end of World War II, Europe rebuilt under the growing shadow of the Cold War. The dawn of the nuclear age added to rising tensions between the Western powers (now led by the United States) and the Soviet Union. The Soviet Red Army, which had liberated Eastern Europe from the Nazis, became an occupying force. With Soviet backing, in Poland, Czechoslovakia, Bulgaria, and the other states of Eastern Europe, the Communists pushed other political parties aside, until they held unchallenged authority in each state. They nationalized industries and undertook massive forced collectivization of agriculture. Germany, devastated by total defeat, was divided into a western zone, which became the German Federal Republic, and an eastern zone, which became the Communist German Democratic Republic. Berlin, lying within East Germany, itself remained divided between East and West, and quickly became a particular focus of Cold War rivalry.

Despite the death of Stalin in 1953, several major crises seemed to bring the United States and the Soviet Union dangerously close to open conflict. Soviet intervention in 1956 to crush a revolt against Communist rule in Hungary and in 1968 to clamp down on Communist reformers in Czechoslovakia strained relations between East and West in Europe, even as the Soviet Union and Communist China began to go their own ways in the late 1950s. The Cuban Missile Crisis of 1962 brought the United States and the Soviet Union to the brink of nuclear war.

In the meantime, Western Europe slowly recovered from the ordeal of total war. In Britain, the Labour government laid the foundations for the welfare state. Other Western states, too, increased the number of social services provided by their governments. The sun finally set on the British Empire, as states achieved independence. France, the Netherlands, Belgium, and Portugal also lost their empires, but often after nationalist insurrections and bloody fighting.

France and Italy, restored to parliamentary rule, became considerably more prosperous by the late 1950s. The German Federal Republic also entered a period of great prosperity. In West Germany and France, Socialist parties came to power in the early 1970s and 1980s, respectively. In Greece, Spain, and Portugal, repressive dictatorships gave way to parliamentary regimes. Parties concerned with the environment—the "Greens"—made sizable political inroads in West Germany. But, at the same time, terrorism brought a new, unsettling dimension to political life; terrorist groups included both left-wing and right-wing extremists, groups of nationalists determined to force the creation of new states, and Middle Eastern groups opposed to Israel.

The end of communism in Eastern Europe in 1989 and the subsequent collapse of the Soviet Union were arguably the most significant occurrences of the post-war period. Following his rise to head of state in 1985, Soviet leader Mikhail Gorbachev initiated a bold series of economic and political reforms, hoping to maintain communism by eliminating its authoritarian nature and encouraging greater political participation and economic prosperity. When movements for reform burgeoned in the countries of the Eastern European bloc, beginning in Poland and Hungary, Gorbachev made clear that the Soviet Union would not intervene.

The throngs of East Germans pouring through the Berlin Wall in November 1989 symbolized the fall of communism in Eastern Europe. These dramatic political changes ranged from Czechoslovakia's "velvet revolution" to the violent overthrow of Romanian dictator Ceausescu in December 1989. Germany became a unified state once again. The Soviet Union itself dissolved, as one former Soviet republic after another declared independence. The Cold War, which had largely defined international relations since the end of World War II, ended.

The problems of fostering democracy in the former Soviet Union and its former client states were just beginning, however, as was dramatically revealed in the bloody civil war that broke out in Bosnia in 1992. Despite the long reign of communism in the Soviet Union and Eastern Europe, it may prove easier to have ended communism than it will be to create stable, prosperous parliamentary regimes.

CHAPTER 29

REBUILDING DIVIDED EUROPE

The Second World War ended with little of the optimism that had followed the conclusion of the First World War. Winston Churchill, for one, was pessimistic, "What is Europe now? A rubble heap, a charnel house, a breeding ground of pestilence and hate." Jews who were fortunate enough to have survived the death camps returned to their homes in France, Belgium, the Netherlands, and Germany to find that more than 6 million Jews had been exterminated by the Nazis. Countries that the German armies had occupied or that had been Nazi allies had to deal with collaborators and the challenge of establishing democratic political institutions. In almost every country, the shift from a wartime to a peacetime economy would prove difficult.

More than this, the Red Army's drive into Central Europe in the waning months of the war left Eastern Europe and the Balkans under Soviet domination. In a speech in Missouri in May 1945, Churchill lamented that "an iron curtain is drawn down upon their front. We do not know what is going on behind." Germany was divided into western and eastern zones, the latter a Communist state.

As Europe counted its millions of dead, the hot war gave way to Cold War between West and East. That both the United States and the Soviet Union had at their disposal atomic and nuclear bombs, weapons of unparalleled mass destruction, made enormous the risks of possible conflict. The division of Europe into two camps, Soviet and Western, was formalized by the creation of corresponding military alliances after the war.

In part as a result of the Communist challenge, France, Italy, and the German Federal Republic (West Germany) elected right-center governments strongly influenced by Catholic parties. Moreover, by 1951, the Conservative Party, rejected by voters in 1945, was back in power in Britain. Finally, after the war, movements for independence in the Asian and African colonies of the European powers led to decolonization and further loss of European influence.

Despite the shadow of the Cold War and decolonization, the period between 1950 and 1973 was a period of unprecedented economic and social
growth in Western Europe. The number of people working in manufacturing or the service sector increased dramatically, and the percentage of people working the land fell rapidly. Under the influence of the wartime
experience, economic and social planning played an important part, first
in the recovery of the European economy and then in its rapid expansion.

EUROPE AT THE END OF THE WAR

Putting Europe back together proved a daunting task. By the time World
War II ended (1944 in Europe; 1945 in Asia), at least 37 million people
had been killed as a direct or indirect result of the fighting (about four
times more people than in World War I, which had been the "war to end
all wars"). Although fewer people from France and Great Britain were
killed in the Second World War than the First World War (620,000 and
260,000, respectively), the tolls in Central and Eastern Europe were almost beyond comprehension. In the Soviet Union, deaths due to the war
could only be estimated at between 12 and 20 million people. As a result
of new information from Soviet archives, estimates have since risen to
about 25 million people (and may include several million victims of Joseph
Stalin's purges). Moreover, 1,700 cities and towns and 70,000 villages
were complete destroyed. Over 5 million Germans died in Hitler's war,

Displaced persons in post-war Europe.

more than 20 percent of the Polish population perished (and 90 percent of Poland's Jews), and 10 percent of the population of Yugoslavia was killed.

Damage to property from air raids, ground warfare, and reprisals by re-treating German forces was incalculable. German air raids in the first year of the war devastated sections of London and Coventry in Britain, Leningrad and Kiev in the Soviet Union, and the Dutch port of Rotter-dam. The German army completely leveled Warsaw in retaliation for the 1944 uprising there. In turn, Allied bombing runs left Berlin, Dresden, and the industrial cities of the Rhineland in ruins, as well as severely dam-aging key French industrial and port cities. Bombs that rained from the sky and the bitter land fighting that followed the Allied invasion rendered many houses uninhabitable in the western part of Germany.

The Potsdam Settlement

Decisions taken by the Allies toward the end of the war brought a radical restructuring of the national boundaries of Central and Eastern Europe. The restructuring was largely determined by the Soviet military advance. The Red Army had occupied all of the states of Eastern Europe except Yu-goslavia and Greece. For his part, Churchill had urged that the British and American armies quickly move into Central Europe before the Red Army could get there. But the Western armies held back. In Germany, Soviet troops controlled what became the eastern zone; the British held the in-dustrial Rhineland and Ruhr, as well as much of the north; U.S. and French armies held southern Germany; and the four powers divided Berlin.

In July 1945, Stalin, Churchill, and the new president of the United States, Harry Truman, met in the Berlin suburb of Potsdam to consider the fate of defeated Germany. (Roosevelt had died the previous April.) Rejecting several plans (including one that would have divided Germany into a number of small, deindustrialized states, little more than "tomato patches"), the Allied leaders agreed that Germany should be reunified. The Four Power Allied Control Council (France had joined the Potsdam powers) planned to establish a new, disarmed, and de-Nazified Germany.

The dawn of the nuclear age added drama to the end of the war. The de-velopment of the atomic bomb (and its more lethal successor, the hydro-gen bomb) had its origins in the theories of relativity developed by the brilliant scientist Albert Einstein (see Chapter 20). A series of subsequent scientific discoveries demonstrated that if the nucleus of the atom could be split, a tremendous explosion of energy would result. During World War II, to work on the atomic bomb, the United States had assembled a team of scientists who had escaped from Nazi Germany. Hitler's own scientists were also doing similar work and were close to reaching some of the same conclusions. Soviet scientists were frantically trying to come up with the atomic bomb, but were several crucial years behind American scientists.

Truman, Churchill, and Stalin before the opening of the Potsdam Conference.

In 1945, nuclear theory became reality, and the first atomic bomb was exploded in a desert in the United States.

President Truman learned of the successful atomic bomb test the day before the opening of the Potsdam Conference in July 1945. It seemed clear that the use of the bomb against Japan might hasten the end of the war in the Pacific, and thus negate the usefulness of Russia's agreeing to join the war against Japan. The news of the American atomic bomb made Stalin more hostile toward the United States, which had no intention of sharing its new military secret. The unbelievable devastation wrought by the dropping of atomic bombs on Hiroshima and Nagasaki in Japan on August 6 and 9, 1945, carried Europe and the world into a new and frightening era. Truman, who had gone to Potsdam with idealism inspired by the principles of democracy and nationalism, now confronted grave international problems. This made any hope of an American isolationist retreat to the Western Hemisphere impossible.

The Potsdam Conference was affected by the growing mistrust between the Western Allies and the Soviet Union. Stalin made territorial demands that included not only regions previously considered part of Germany, Russia, Romania, and Czechoslovakia, but also strategically crucial parts of Turkey. The latter would give the Soviet Union virtual control of the Straits of Constantinople—which Russian tsars had sought since the time of Peter the Great. The Soviet Union acquired the three Baltic states (which the Red Army had occupied in 1940) of Latvia, Lithuania, and Estonia, a large chunk of East Prussia, and parts of Finland, Czechoslovakia, and Romania (Bessarabia and some of Bukovina). Poland, which lost much of its eastern territory to the Soviet Union, also gained at Germany's expense (see Map 29.1).

Other territorial adjustments came at the expense of Germany's wartime allies. For example, Yugoslavia acquired a small border region from Italy, and Bulgaria absorbed a territory previously disputed with Romania. As the Allies dictated the new alignments, little attention was paid to the fact

MAP 29.1 POST-WAR TERRITORIAL SETTLEMENTS Territorial changes as of 1947, including British, Russian, French, and American zones in Germany, as well as boundaries of Poland, Bulgaria, Yugoslavia, and the Soviet Union after the war.

that the new borders, as after World War I, left various nationalities dissatisfied. Hungarians living in Transylvania did not want to be left within the redrawn borders of Romania, and Romanians who found themselves inside Hungary were dissatisfied with what they considered punishment for having been forced by the Nazis and their wartime dictators to fight on the side of Germany. Austria, which Hitler had annexed to his Reich in 1938, had its independence and neutrality restored; military occupation by the victorious World War II powers would end in 1955. In Northern Europe, Finland retained its independence, despite sharing a border with the Soviet Union, which accepted Finnish neutrality.

Other issues accentuated the split between the wartime Allies. As after the end of World War I, the allies disagreed on the question of war reparations. The Soviet Union, which had suffered far more than Great Britain and the United States, demanded that Germany be forced to pay for the costs of the war. Specifically, Stalin wanted the equivalent of $20 billion in reparations, as well as German industrial equipment. The Soviet Union eventually received half the amount of money demanded (although in greatly inflated currency), as well as about 25 percent of industrial equipment from the German zones occupied by Britain, France, and the United States. In the meantime, Soviet trains and trucks began to haul German machinery and other industrial materials from the eastern zone back to Russia. By now fully suspicious of Soviet intentions in Eastern Europe, Truman eliminated the Soviet Union from the list of nations eligible for U.S. loans to help with rebuilding their economies.

The Western Allies concurred that the victors should negotiate peace treaties with Germany's former allies (Italy, Hungary, Romania, and Bulgaria), which were to be represented by "recognized democratic governments." But it was soon clear that the governments of the last three nations were anything but democratically elected.

The United Nations and Cold War Alliances

In November 1944, the Dumbarton Oaks Conference in Washington, D.C., planned the United Nations, which would replace the League of Nations. It would serve to protect the freedom and self-determination of member nations. An international conference in San Francisco in 1945 drew up its Charter. The U.N. headquarters was placed in New York, where a secretary general would coordinate its activities. The United Nations would consist of a General Assembly of member nations (fifty-one at the organization's inception), each of which would have one vote, and a Security Council of fifteen members. The United States, Great Britain, the U.S.S.R., France, and the Republic of China (Taiwan) were designated as "permanent members," each with a veto over deliberations, and the other ten seats would be filled on a revolving basis by states chosen by the General Assembly.

The United Nations became a battleground for the Cold War. Yet, it was an arena for verbal battles—words of hostility and denunciation were still better than wars. The United Nations helped the European state system re-emerge after the war. Furthermore, in some cases the United Nations provided necessary mediation in disputes between nations. However limited its powers, the United Nations, unlike the defunct League of Nations, could send peacekeeping forces to various hot spots on the globe, although the accomplishments of these efforts would vary considerably.

Besides founding the United Nations to mediate disputes, the states of Europe also hedged their bets by establishing military alliances, whereby they pledged to come to each others' defense in case any one of them was attacked. Thus, in March 1948, Great Britain, France, Belgium, the Netherlands, and Luxembourg signed the Pact of Brussels. It served as the military component of the subsequent Council of Europe to which most of the nations of Western Europe adhered. The United States joined members of the Pact of Brussels in the North Atlantic Treaty Organization (NATO) in 1949, which subsequently added Italy, Denmark, Norway, Iceland, Portugal, Canada, Greece, and Turkey (see Map 29.2). Directed against the Soviet Union, the treaty bound all of the member countries to defend jointly any of the signatories who were attacked, creating a unified command for a common army and placing NATO's headquarters in Paris. The Cold War also helped shape international economic cooperation among Western states.

The Soviets and their Eastern European allies countered the Western powers in 1955 by signing the Warsaw Pact, which offered its members similar guarantees to those of NATO against attack. It formalized and internationalized the individual pacts of mutual defense that the Soviet Union had signed with its client states during or immediately after World War II, providing a new justification for the stationing of Soviet troops in Poland, Hungary, Czechoslovakia, and East Germany.

Economic and Social Turmoil

After World War II, the European economy lay in ruins. Bombing on both sides had been systematic, destroying with increasing accuracy the industrial structure of Europe. Sunken ships blocked port harbors. Almost all bridges over the major rivers had been destroyed. Only fragments of Europe's transportation and communication networks remained in service, making the distribution of the meager harvests of 1944 difficult. In Britain, gold and silver reserves had sunk dramatically, and the government had been forced to take out large loans, particularly one that helped initiate a long period of virtual British dependence on the United States. Non-military manufacturing had plunged during the war. German bombs had taken their toll. But, most important, the markets for British manufactured goods, which had all but disappeared during the war, could not be quickly reconstituted.

Agricultural production in every war zone fell by about half, leaving millions of people without enough to eat. Inflation was rampant; the value of European currencies plunged. As after World War I, the German mark became virtually worthless. German housewives picked through the rubble of bombed-out buildings looking for objects of value, combing woods for mushrooms and berries for their families to eat. The black market supplied not only luxuries but also necessities.

The European continent had become a world of "displaced persons."

MAP 29.2 EASTERN AND WESTERN BLOCS, 1955   NATO and the Warsaw Pact were the military alliances that defined the post-war world.

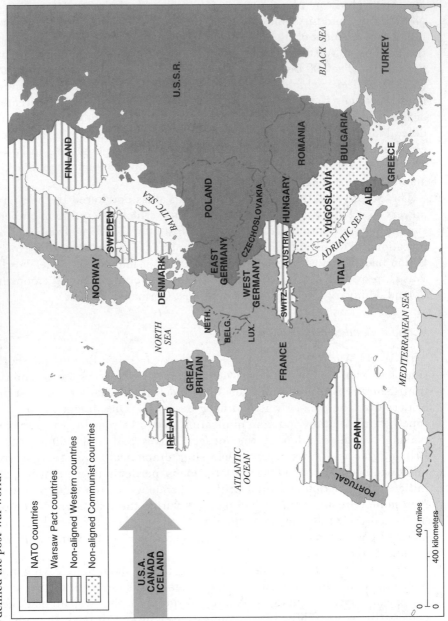

After World War I, the leaders of the victorious powers had redrawn the borders of Poland, Hungary, Yugoslavia, and the other new or redefined Eastern European nations with regard to the location of national majorities and minorities. Now national minorities within newly redefined states were forced into boxcars and moved—displaced—to new locations. In all, there were about 50 million refugees in the immediate post-war period. Furthermore, millions of prisoners of war, such as Germans incarcerated in the Soviet Union, had to be repatriated. Germans living in Lithuania, which in 1940 had been incorporated against its will into the Soviet Union, were sent back to Germany. Ten million Germans who had originally lived in East Prussia (which again became part of Poland) or who had been resettled by the Nazis in German-conquered territories further to the east were returned to Germany. Stalin repopulated East Prussia with about 1 million people hauled from Russia, Byelorussia (Belarus), Ukraine, and even distant Kazakhstan. Germany gave up territory to Poland to compensate that battered nation for land lost to the Soviet Union. Poles whose homeland had become part of the Soviet Union now moved back into Western Poland, which had been part of Germany.

The punishment of those who had collaborated with the Nazis began as soon as the occupied territories were liberated (and, in some cases, had begun during the war itself). In France, resistance forces summarily executed (sometimes after quick trials) about 10,000 accused collaborators— "justice at the cross-roads." Courts sentenced about 2,000 people to death (about 800 were executed) and more than 40,000 to prison. Vichy Prime Minister Pierre Laval was executed. Marshal Philippe Pétain was found guilty of treason, but because of his age and stature as the "hero of Verdun" during the First World War, he was imprisoned on a small island off the western coast of France, where he died in 1951. Women who had slept with German soldiers had their heads shaved and were paraded through their towns in shame.

In countries that had been occupied by Hitler's armies, people struggled to determine degrees of guilt. In Belgium, courts prosecuted 634,000 people for their part in the German occupation—a staggering figure in a country of only 8 million people. Moreover, the disproportionate role of Flemish collaborators further increased the division between Flemish and Walloon (French) speakers. On the other hand, in Austria, where most of the population had seemed to welcome union with Hitler's Germany, only 9,000 people were put on trial and only 35 collaborators were executed. (More than forty years after the end of World War II, it was revealed that Kurt Waldheim, who had served as general secretary of the United Nations and later was elected president of Austria, had known about and may have encouraged atrocities committed against Yugoslavs by the German army in which he proudly served.) In Italy, where reprisals against collaborators at the war's end had been carried out with speed and efficiency (about 15,000 executions), there were few trials of fascists after the war.

A French collaborator whose head has been shaved is paraded through a village near Cherbourg following liberation of the region by Allied troops, 1944.

This was in part because the Italian fascists had been, at least when compared to the Nazis, relatively mild in their treatment of their enemies. Furthermore, millions of people had joined fascist organizations or unions because they felt obliged to, and questions of guilt were ambiguous.

The most dramatic post-war trial occurred in Nuremberg in August 1945 when the Allies put twenty-four high-ranking German officials on trial before an international tribunal. Defendants included Hermann Göring, Alfred Rosenberg, and several generals. The court found twenty-one of the defendants guilty of war crimes, and ten were executed. Göring committed suicide in his cell shortly before he was to be executed. The remainder of those found guilty were imprisoned, including Rudolf Hess, who at the time of his suicide in 1987 was the only inmate in Berlin's Spandau Prison. Less spectacular trials of more minor figures went on in Germany for years.

Many war criminals, however, escaped or were let free after the war. Doctor Josef Mengele, who had carried out brutal experiments on living patients, including children, managed to get to Paraguay. A good many found a warm welcome from right-wing dictatorships. The U.S. government facilitated the escape of a few Nazi war criminals in exchange for information about Communists in Germany and elsewhere in Europe. Other war criminals managed to fade into the chaos of post-war Europe, some with new names and identities. Some did not even bother to change their names, and more than a few eventually served in the West German government. In 1959, Israeli agents kidnapped in South America Adolf

Eichmann, who had participated in the massacre of thousands of Jews, and took him to Israel, where he was tried, convicted, and executed. In the mid-1980s, a French court convicted Klaus Barbie, a Nazi war criminal who had fled after the war, sentencing him to life in prison. The justice meted out to Nazis and collaborators may have been imperfect, and sometimes came quite late, but it was better than no justice at all.

Intellectual Currents in the Post-War Era

Outside of a sense of relief, there seemed little about which to be optimistic at the end of World War II. The British writer George Orwell summed up the general feeling when he wrote, "Since about 1930, the world had given no reason for optimism whatsoever. Nothing in sight except a welter of lies, cruelty, hatred, and ignorance." Unlike the period immediately following World War I, few people believed that another total war was inconceivable. Many writers and artists seemed overwhelmed with pessimism, even hopelessness, in the face of the atomic age and the beginning of the Cold War. Claiming "alienation" from the society they increasingly criticized, many Western intellectuals withdrew into introspection. For some, communism seemed to offer a plan for the harmonious organization of society. Communist parties in Western nations attracted many enthusiastic intellectuals who believed that the Soviet Union offered a successful model to be emulated in their own countries.

French existentialism became an influential cultural current during the first two decades following the war. The French philosopher Jean-Paul Sartre (1905–1980) believed that in the wake of the unparalleled destruction of World War II, the absurdity of life was the most basic discovery one could make. Denying the existence of God, existentialists like Sartre posited that life has no meaning. Their conclusion was that a person could only truly find any fulfillment while living "a suspended death" by becoming aware of his or her freedom to choose and to act. Sartre titled one of his novels *Huis clos (No Exit)*, as he believed there was nothing beyond this life. Sartre's novels glorify the individual spirit seeking freedom, not through Enlightenment rationalism, but rather through the very comprehension of life's irrationality. However, more than this, Sartre believed that violent revolution could free the individual from the human condition by allowing him or her to find truth by redefining reality. To this end, he joined the French Communist Party when the war was over. However, existentialism slowly lost its grip on French intellectual life, at least partially because of growing disillusionment with the Soviet Union among many leftist intellectuals.

The Algerian-born French writer Albert Camus (1913–1960) shared Sartre's view of mankind's tragic situation, but broke with Sartre in 1952 over the latter's enthusiasm for Stalin's Soviet Union. Camus' answer to the dark world of brutality reflected by the war (during which he partici-

A gathering of intellectuals after the war, including Jean-Paul Sartre (seated left), Albert Camus (seated center), Pablo Picasso (standing with his arms folded), and Simone de Beauvoir (to the far right and standing next to some of Picasso's work).

pated in the resistance) and the frustrations of the post-war period was for the individual to search for meaning in life by choosing a path of action—even revolt—against absurdity, irrationality, and tyrannies of all kinds. Camus' rebel acts from a personal sense of responsibility and moral choice that are independent of belief in God or any political system. Confronting the arrival of murderous disease in the Algerian city of Oran, Dr. Rieux, the central figure in Camus' *The Plague* (1947), does not believe in God or absolute standards of morality, but he nonetheless helps people take action to cope with the epidemic.

The "theater of the absurd," which also grew out of intellectuals' reaction to the horrors of the war, was centered in Paris and had a following from 1948 to about 1968. It offered highly unconventional and antirational plays. Like symbolist playwrights before World War I, the Irish-born Samuel Beckett (1906–1989) and other playwrights (who were contemporaries of Sartre and Camus and influenced by existentialism) sought to shock audiences with provocative themes and by stringing together seemingly unrelated events and dialogue in order to demonstrate that existence is without purpose and absurd. They rejected plots, conventional settings, and individual identities. Their clownish, mechanical characters are perpetual exiles alienated in a bizarre, nightmarish world that makes no sense. The lack of causality in these plays is a commentary on life itself. Beckett's *Waiting for Godot* (begun in 1948 but not published in French until 1952 and in English two years later) is the best known of the absur-dist plays. It tells a disconnected tale of two old derelicts, Vladimir and Es-tragon (although they call themselves by childish nicknames). They meet night after night in anticipation of the arrival of a certain Godot (perhaps a diminutive of God), though it is never clear what difference in their lives his arrival would ever make, if any. He never comes, so we never know.

Other intellectuals of the left also reacted to what they perceived as the lack of moral absolutes in a world that had experienced total war. They too were preoccupied by the possibilities of social liberation. Frantz Fanon (1925–1961), a French writer, explored the revolutionary potential of the Third World in *The Wretched of the Earth* (1961). The French anthro-pologist Claude Lévi-Strauss (1908–   ) espoused cultural relativism, moving anthropology away from a Western-centered view of so-called "peripheral" or "underdeveloped" regions with his work on Brazil and Southeast Asia. Lévi-Strauss' interest in how communities behave, too, led away from the emphasis on the individual that characterized both Freud-ianism and existentialism. Change also occurred in the research and writ-ing of history. The French *Annales* (the name of a scholarly journal) school, founded by the medievalist and wartime resistance hero and mar-tyr Marc Bloch (1886–1944), treated political and diplomatic events as mere foam on the waves of history. Instead, these historians espoused a "total history" that would describe and analyze the lives of ordinary people in the context of major economic and social changes of the past.

In contrast to the intellectuals in the West, intellectuals in the Soviet Union itself were stymied by the state. Writers, artists, and film-makers confronted a state apparatus that made the costs of free expression so high that voluntary adherence to state-dictated norms followed. "Socialist real-ism" (art and literature of generally horrendous quality, intended to inspire the population by showing smiling Soviet citizens at work) was the only authorized form of artistic expression; the works of most Western artists were condemned as tools of capitalism. Art was intended to encourage de-votion to and sacrifice for the state. But while he rejected the ideas of Freud and Einstein out of hand, Stalin gave official approval to the crack-pot theories of the geneticist Trofim Lysenko (1898–1976), who insisted that knowledge or beliefs that were experienced by one generation could be genetically inherited. Stalin's particular interest in this theory was that it suggested that party members who learned official orthodoxy and experi-enced conformity in social behavior would pass the same characteristics on to their offspring.

After the war and into the 1950s and 1960s, artistic talent was often channeled into films rather than into the traditional arts. Western Euro-pean film-makers made important contributions to cinema. While most American film producers emphasized light entertainment (such as west-erns and war movies with special effects and love stories), Italy's Federico Fellini (*La Strada*, 1956, and *La Dolce Vita*, 1959) and Sweden's Ingmar Bergman (*The Seventh Seal*, 1956) turned out serious art films (although

Socialist realism *Between Engagements* (1957–1960) by Alexei and Sergei Tkachev.

European audiences, too, flocked to see Hollywood films). French New Wave directors, including Jean-Luc Godard (*Breathless*, 1959) and François Truffaut (*400 Blows*, 1959), rebelled against traditional cinematographic techniques and used innovations such as jump cuts and disruptive editing to create a sense of dislocation and to remind the viewer that he or she was watching a film, not reality. Their experimental films explored human relationships and often portrayed antiheroes. In contrast, the English producer and director Alfred Hitchcock frightened generations of audiences with riveting suspense films like *Psycho* (1960). In France, particularly, some films took their subjects from recent and sometimes painful history, notably Gilles Pontecorvo's *The Battle of Algiers* (1961), which used some actual participants in the Algerian insurrection (see pp. 1319–22), to which the film is highly sympathetic, and Marcel Orphuls' documentary about collaboration and resistance in wartime France, *The Sorrow and the Pity* (1969). In painting, European artists were now considerably less original, at least in comparison with those in the United States.

POLITICAL REALIGNMENTS

Backed by the Soviet Union, Communist governments took power in every Eastern European state in the post-war period. At the same time, Communist parties grew in strength in several Western European states, most notably gaining members among industrial workers in Italy and France. Communists dominated the major trade-union organizations in those countries; they entered post-war governments in Belgium and Denmark. Communist wartime resistance against Nazi Germany helped swell the prestige of Communist parties, even as their close identification with the Soviet Union began to engender suspicion among political elites. France, Italy, and the German Federal Republic had right-center governments in which Catholic parties played a major role, although Communist parties were also strong in France and Italy.

As a response to the growing Communist influence, in March 1947 President Truman announced the "Truman Doctrine," which proclaimed "the policy of the United States to support free people who are resisting attempted subjugation by armed minorities or by outside pressures." While pressuring France and Italy to keep Communists from being named to government posts, the United States undertook a program of massive economic aid to Western Europe. Through the Marshall Plan, named after the American secretary of state who devised it, the United States contributed $9.4 billion over three years toward the rebuilding of the Western Allies' economies. The Marshall Plan was intended to help Western Europe resist communism and to make Europe a powerful trading partner for American industry.

Divided Germany

When the war ended, Germany became the focal point for Cold War tensions. The Soviet-occupied eastern zone became the German Democratic Republic in 1949; the American, British, and French occupation zones became the German Federal Republic. The barbed wire and minefields that divided these zones reflected the ideological division between them.

The Allies oversaw the development of the political institutions of what became the Germany Federal Republic. (Until 1951, when the occupation statute of 1949 was revised, all legislation passed by the Federal Republic had to be approved by the Western Allies.) The constitution of the German Federal Republic stated that parties obtaining a minimum of 5 percent of the popular vote in an election could be represented in the Federal Parliament (the *Bundestag*). This kept small parties, principally those of the extreme right, out of the parliament. (During the Weimar Republic, many small parties had contributed to political instability.) In fact, this federalism was very much in keeping with the long traditions of German particularism: many independent German states had existed until German unification in 1871, and local political and cultural traditions remained strong.

The Allies insisted that the German president's powers be limited in order to avoid the unrestricted executive power that had existed during Weimar when President von Hindenburg had assumed emergency powers, and under Hitler during the Nazi period. The president would be elected by vote of the Federal Parliament for a term of five years. The chancellor, appointed by the president, became the effective head of state. The states of the Federal Republic elected representatives to an upper house (*Bundesrat*). Because the upper house could block legislation, this electoral process, too, strengthened the decentralization of political power in West Germany.

Konrad Adenauer (1876–1967), the Catholic mayor of Cologne, served as chancellor of the German Federal Republic until 1963. His wartime opposition to the Nazis, hostility to the Soviets and to East Germany, and his social conservatism reassured the Allies. The centrist Christian Democratic Union Party, the largest party in the Federal Parliament, with its sister party, the Bavarian Social Union, shaped political life in the Federal Republic. Supported by smaller parties on the right, the Christian Democrats held power from 1949 until 1969, with the Social Democratic Party the chief opposition party. Adenauer forged a close alliance with France intended to serve as a bulwark against Soviet influence.

In the meantime, the Cold War hastened the acceptance by the Western powers of the German Federal Republic in the Western alliance. The Federal Republic became a nonvoting member of the Council of Europe in 1950. Moreover, bolstered by economic recovery and the total discrediting of the extreme political right wing, the German Federal Republic achieved full sovereignty and diplomatic respectability, joining NATO in 1955.

The Soviet-occupied eastern zone of Germany became the German Democratic Republic (G.D.R., then commonly known as East Germany). Walter Ulbricht (1893–1973), who was the solemn son of a Saxon tailor and who had spent the war years in the Soviet Union and returned to Berlin with the Red Army, became secretary of the Communist Party. He remained, for all practical purposes, head of state until his forced retirement in 1971.

The G.D.R. took over the administration of the eastern zone in 1955 from the Soviets, although its government continued to follow Soviet instructions. The Communist Party controlled most facets of intellectual and cultural life. Many writers and artists left for West Germany, although the talented playwright Bertolt Brecht remained.

Eastern Europe under the Soviet Shadow

One by one the states of Eastern Europe fell under the domination of Soviet-backed Communist parties, which benefited in many cases from having led resistance to the Nazis. From the beginning, collaborationist parties and other right-wing groups were excluded from power. The Communists elbowed other parties aside or absorbed them and took control of the police. Coalition governments elected or otherwise constituted at the end of the war disappeared one by one, until the Communists controlled each state. In Hungary in 1947, the Communist Party ousted the other major party, the Smallholders, or Peasant Party. In neighboring Romania, King Michael was forced out in similar circumstances. Bulgarian Communists won a contested victory in a plebiscite that established a "Peoples' Republic," which quickly became a single party state. After the first election in post-war Poland, Communists gradually pushed out the Socialists, who constituted the other major party.

Czechoslovakia had not only been the most industrialized of the Central and Eastern European countries but also the most stable between the wars. Czechoslovakia alone had not become a dictatorship. In the first post-war elections in May 1946, Communists won more than a third of the vote in the elections. Two non-Communists, Eduard Beneš (1884–1948) and Jan Masaryk (1886–1948), served as president and foreign minister respectively in a coalition government. But in 1948, after protesting the Czechoslovak government's overtures to the United States for financial assistance, the Communists seized power, shutting down other political parties. Masaryk died after having jumped—or been pushed—from his office window, and Beneš soon died after resigning from office.

From Moscow, Stalin engineered purges that swept away even loyal party members in the Eastern European nations (half a million alone in Czechoslovakia). Show trials (including those of popular Catholic prelates in Czechoslovakia and Hungary), prison sentences, and some executions followed. Stalin also tightened Moscow's grip on the non-Russian fourteen republics in the Soviet Union, purging "bourgeois nationalists" in several of them. While Stalin promoted economic growth in the Communist states of Eastern Europe, economic policies furthered an economic division of labor whereby some of the satellites produced agricultural products and others manufactured particular goods. The Eastern European

Five-year plans based on the Soviet model were launched in Eastern Europe, heralded as here by this Romanian poster.

CONSTRUIM SOCIALISMUL
fără burghezie si împotriva ei

economies thus favored Soviet interests and gradually channeled the over-whelming proportion of their foreign trade to the Soviet Union. One by one, beginning with Bulgaria and Czechoslovakia in 1949, the states of Eastern Europe launched five-year plans based on the Soviet model, em-phasizing heavy industry and the collectivization of agriculture. The Baltic states, too, became increasingly industrialized.

Stalin's Soviet Union, however, did not dominate all states in Eastern Europe. In Yugoslavia, Communist leader Tito, whose determined resis-tance army had freed his country from German occupation without Soviet military assistance, refused to permit Soviet domination of his multina-tional country. In 1948, Tito took advantage of Stalin's stinging denuncia-tion of his country to break with the Soviet Union. Over the next decades, Yugoslavia received millions of dollars in Western aid. The Yugoslav econ-omy remained "mixed" in the sense that the private sector coexisted with state planning and collectivization.

In Greece, the departure of German troops led to a civil war in the north that pitted Greek Communists against an alliance of forces that sup-ported the monarchy. The Soviet Union held to an agreement made with Churchill in 1944 not to intervene militarily, but it provided the Commu-nists with considerable material assistance. The United States and Britain aided the monarchist forces, which finally prevailed in 1949.

Politics in the West

With Germany, Italy, and Vichy France defeated, political continuity with pre-war governments could be found only in Britain among the major Western European powers. Yet, even in Britain, political change occurred as voters in the first post-war election turned against the Conservatives and brought the Labour Party to power in July 1945. Labour's victory was a repudiation of the Conservative government's pre-war economic policies and inadequate reaction to Hitler's aggressive moves in Central Europe in the late 1930s. Clement Attlee (1883–1967), a hard-working though uninspiring man who lacked defeated leader Churchill's charisma, became prime minister. Attlee was once described as "a sheep dressed in sheep's clothing." Churchill had allegedly disparaged Attlee in remarking, "An empty cab pulled up to 10 Downing Street, and Attlee got out." Nonethe-less, Attlee proved to be an effective leader. In response to a strong pop-ular desire for social reforms, the British Parliament passed bills implementing new social benefits, such as national health insurance, un-employment benefits, retirement pensions, and assistance for widows. It also enacted a series of bills nationalizing the Bank of England, airlines, the railways, roads, canals, buses, London's subway, and the coal and steel industries.

Britain's economic growth was hampered by increasingly obsolete facto-ries and low rates of investment and savings. The British share in inter-

James Ensor's *Entry of Christ into Brussels in 1889*, a precociously modern painting treating surprisingly modern themes. Because the painting was considered radical, it was not publicly exhibited until 1929 (although it had been painted in 1888).

Henri Matisse's *Harmony in Red*, 1908.

Giacomo Balla's *Street Light*, 1909.

Marcel Duchamp's *Nude Descending a Staircase*, 1912.

Wassily Kandinsky's *Painting #200*, 1914.

Ernst Ludwig Kirchner's *Five Women in the Street*, 1913.

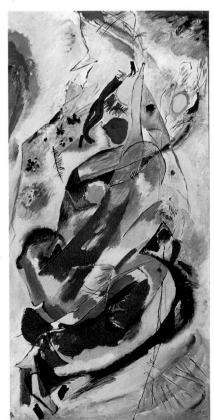

Juan Gris' *Le Petit déjeuner,* 1915.

Paul Klee's *Equilibrist,* 1923.

Joan Miro's *Dutch Interior,* 1928.

Fernand Léger's *Les Constructeurs,* 1950.

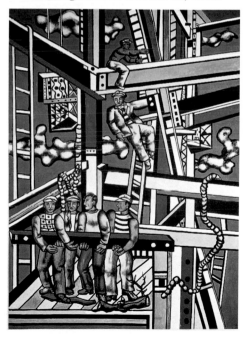

Francis Bacon's *Pope II*, 1951.

Salvador Dalí's *Cruxifixion*, 1954.

Jean Dubuffet's *Virtual Virtue*, 1963.

national trade declined sharply during the next three decades. West Germany and France passed Britain in most economic categories. Conservatives blamed the welfare state and the strength of the unions for Britain's economic decline, arguing that both forced the government and private companies to pay higher wages. Yet, British welfare costs were less than those of France, and British citizens paid proportionally fewer taxes than the Germans or French. Rather, it was the costs of maintaining the British Empire that undercut the government's quest for austerity as it faced enormous trade deficits and debts to the United States. To an extent, the Attlee government had to choose between financing domestic economic recovery and maintaining the British Empire.

Conservatives returned to power in 1951 on a wave of disillusionment with the slowness of the economic recovery. The Tories were committed to undoing the nationalizations and expansion of social services undertaken by Labour after the war. But they found it difficult to privatize such nationalized industries as iron and steel because they had become unprofitable and therefore failed to attract private interest. Privatization (including the sale of most steel and iron companies to private companies) barely scratched the surface. Furthermore, any move against the welfare system of Labour would have been generally unpopular. Labour returned to power in 1964 with the support of the trade unions and in the wake of a juicy scandal (John Profumo, the minister of defense, had been associating with a Russian agent and a prostitute at the same time). But led by the yachtsman Edward Heath, the Conservatives returned to power in 1970.

In some ways France emerged from World War II in better shape than it had from World War I. The war had taken far fewer French lives than had World War I. And although industrial cities and ports had been pounded by bombing raids—German in 1940 and Allied in the last years of the war—the systematic devastation that had taken place in northern and northeastern France during 1914–1918 had not been repeated, in part because the French armies had collapsed so rapidly before German tanks in 1940.

In the eighteen months that followed Charles de Gaulle's triumphant march down the Champs-Elysées to Paris' town hall in August 1944, de Gaulle ruled virtually alone. But his inattention to France's precarious economic situation and the unwillingness of centrists to support tough measures to constrict the money supply (such as by taxing wealth) exacerbated shortages.

In October 1945, the vast majority of French men and women voted against a return to the political institutions of the Third Republic, identified with France's defeat. This referendum was the first election in France in which women could vote. In the subsequent elections for the Constituent Assembly, Communists (whose contributions to the resistance had been invaluable) took the greatest percentage of seats, with the Socialists (led by former Prime Minister Léon Blum, who had been imprisoned during the war by the Vichy government) only a few percentage points behind. The Popular Republican Movement (M.R.P.), a new center-right party, also did well by building on de Gaulle's reputation and the Catholic resistance, and by opposing Communist political influence. Frustrated that the new regime would have a weak executive authority, reflecting Socialist and Communist fears of Caesarism, however, de Gaulle resigned from government in January 1946.

After voters overwhelmingly rejected the Constituent Assembly's proposed constitution, a second Constituent Assembly was elected to write a new constitution. This was approved by a narrow majority of voters in October 1946. Like the Third Republic, the political institutions of the Fourth Republic seemed conducive to governmental instability and immobility. Between 1946 and 1958, France would have twenty-four different governments, most based on left-center coalitions of the M.R.P. (the Catholic democrats), the Socialists, and smaller parties. The president and the prime minister had influence, but little power. While de Gaulle cooled his heels in his village in eastern France, awaiting a call for him to return to power, a new Gaullist party (the Rally of the French People, or R.P.F.) became the opposition party of the right.

In France, the state played a role in the country's economic revival. After the war, the state had assumed control of the airlines, the largest banks, the Renault automobile plants (whose owner had collaborated with the Germans), natural resources (such as gas and coal), and steel and electricity. The brilliant French economist Jean Monnet (1888–1979) headed an Office of Planning, which encouraged and coordinated voluntary plans for modernizing business enterprises and agriculture, drawing on capital and the expertise of government technocrats. Despite mounting inflation and government deficits exacerbated by the unprofitability of newly nationalized industries, the French Gross National Product doubled in ten years and industrial production in 1959 was twice that of 1938.

In Italy, as in France, a new regime had to be constructed after the war. The monarchy's passive capitulation to fascism had discredited King Victor Emmanuel III, who compounded his unpopularity by trying to blame the Italian people for fascism. In June 1946, more than half of those voting repudiated the monarchy (though most southerners voted for it), despite the efforts of the pope to influence the election. Italy became a republic.

In the elections for a Constituent Assembly, women were eligible to vote for the first time, as in France. The new constitution provided for the election of the president by the two houses of parliament, both of which were to be elected by popular vote. The president would have little power, and regional governments would have their own assemblies. Most Italians feared a strongly centralized state, at least partially because it would seem a continuity of fascism, but also because it seemed antithetical to strong regional identities. Furthermore, the Church vigorously opposed the development of a more centralized state, fearful of losing influence.

The new Italy was to be built on values associated with the resistance. But the Italian south had been liberated by the Allies with very little participation by the resistance movement. Therefore, what many Italians referred to as a "cleansing wind from the north," where the resistance had been strong, did not extend into southern Italy and Sicily, both of which largely reverted to strongly antinational domination by powerful landowners, and the Mafia. Furthermore, many fascist officials in the south simply held on to their positions, weakening the prestige of the republic.

The government of Italy remained rooted in the center-right. The Christian Democratic Party, a staunchly anti-Communist centrist force influenced by the Catholic Church and powerful economic interests, dominated post-war political life in Italy, dispensing patronage and bribes. Like its counterparts in West Germany and France, the Italian Christian Democratic Party reflected the accommodation of most Catholics with democracy. The Communist Party became the second-largest political party, claiming the allegiance of as much as a quarter of the population.

In the 1950s, the Italian economy grew rapidly, aided by government noninterventionist policies and with the help of considerable U.S. financial assistance. The gradual rise in the standard of living helped make industrial workers less militant, although most remained dedicated to the Italian Communist Party.

In the 1960s, Italian governments undertook modest social reforms. Moreover, the popular Pope John XXIII (pope 1958–1963) revived the Church's long-dormant social doctrine by calling for social reform. This encouraged the Christian Democrats to form coalitions with the Socialists. Beginning in 1963, control of the government passed from the right-center to the left-center.

The Italian economic miracle in the 1950s. (*Left*) A peasant woman farming next to an autoroute. (*Right*) Assembly-line production in a Fiat factory in Turin, 1955.

Politics in the Soviet Union

In the Soviet Union, Joseph Stalin had emerged from the war with his power within the Communist Party unchallenged and his prestige enormous. Statues, pictures, and other images of Stalin seemed to be everywhere. But weakened by arteriosclerosis, Stalin's paranoia became virtually psychotic as he ordered more purges in the name of the Communist Party. The ruthless Lavrenty Beria (1899–1953), head of the omnipresent secret police, used a gold-plated phone to order arrests. In 1953, Stalin suffered a mild stroke and died. Beria's subsequent arrest, trial, and execution signaled an end to the Stalin period.

After Stalin's death, the Soviet Union entered a period of "collective leadership," a concept that had been abandoned during Stalin's personal dictatorship. Decisions were taken by the fourteen members of the Presidium of the Communist Party, which included Georgi Malenkov (1902–1988), a pragmatist who believed that Stalin's dictatorship had hampered the Soviet economy. Meanwhile, the coarse, rotund Nikita Khrushchev (1894–1971), the son of a miner, was rising within the Communist Party. He was part of the pragmatic, or technocratic, faction, but he was also a successful party organizer. In 1955, Khrushchev, with support within the Soviet bureaucracy, won the upper hand in his struggle with Malenkov for power. While maintaining an emphasis on heavy industry, Khrushchev also concentrated on planning and investing in Soviet agriculture, the sector that he knew best and that had never recovered from the effects of forced collectivization. He understood that the production of consumer goods would have to take a more prominent place in economic planning. The quality of life for most Soviet citizens began to improve gradually, but substantially, although not as fast as that of highly placed Communist Party members, who had automobiles and comfortable country houses.

The Soviet people were largely unaware of the power struggles fought in secrecy within the Kremlin. Like Western Sovietologists, they could only chart the waxing and waning of party leaders' influence by their appearances, ranking, and the omission of their names on official lists, or in the placement of a Soviet leader among the gray heads on the giant reviewing stand in Red Square during the annual May Day military parade.

In February 1956, Khrushchev denounced Stalin's "cult of personality" and his ruthless purges in an unpublished but widely cited speech at the Twentieth Party Congress. Such criticism was unprecedented in the history of the Soviet Union. Furthermore, Khrushchev accepted the fact that different paths to socialism could exist in different countries. Khrushchev allowed the national republics within the Soviet Union more authority over their own affairs. He gave intellectuals and artists in the republics more freedom to develop non-Russian cultural interests. A brief relaxation of censorship permitted the publication of books that offered brutally frank critiques of the Stalin years.

However, democratic centralism—the strict centralization of government and its domination by the Communist Party—continued. The Communist Party's authority over the republics remained for the most part in the hands of ethnic Russians. The thaw in censorship soon ended. Censors banned *Doctor Zhivago* (completed 1956 and translated in 1958) by Boris Pasternak (1890–1960). Published in Italy and winning the Nobel Prize for literature, it offered a nuanced picture of tsarist Russia and therefore implicitly stood as a criticism of the Soviet regime. Soviet artists and film-makers, too, were reined in, although some remained daring and imaginative within the confines of official toleration.

As the Soviet Union's economic difficulties continued and the sixth Five-Year Plan floundered badly, Khrushchev blamed its failure on excessive centralization of planning and administration. His political rivals, however, blamed him. In 1957, Khrushchev overcame a group that challenged his leadership, ousting Malenkov, Molotov, and Bulganin (all of whom were members of the Presidium) from key party positions. In 1961, Khrushchev ordered Stalin's remains to be removed from the Kremlin mausoleum and placed less conspicuously in the Kremlin Wall.

DECOLONIZATION

The Third World had been on the periphery of international politics since the age of the "new imperialism" that began in the 1880s. The Second World War accelerated the independence movements that had developed after World War I. In the colonies in Africa, Asia, and Southeast Asia, the rise of nationalism led to strong pressure for national independence. Thus, beginning in the 1950s, European colonies became central actors in some of the dramas of international politics. The peacemakers at Versailles (particularly President Wilson) in 1919 had espoused nationalism as a principle for the territorial organization of states. But France and Britain, in particular, had been unwilling to grant freedom to their colonies.

Following World War II, most of the colonies of the Western powers achieved independence. Generally, Britain's former colonies achieved it peacefully, while France (particularly in the case of Algeria) and Portugal struggled to retain their colonies even in the face of popular insurgency. The Netherlands and Belgium both resisted nationalist movements briefly before recognizing the independence of their former colonies. Some of the new states then fell into civil war. By 1980, more than half of the 154 members of the United Nations had been admitted to membership since 1956.

The end of the colonial era reflected the relative decline of the European powers in international affairs. Britain and France, in particular, left important traditions of government, culture, and language in Africa, Asia, and the Middle East (for example, the pervasive French influence in

Lebanon). But during the 1960s and 1970s, the United States and the Soviet Union aggressively compteted for the allegiance of these young states.

Decolonization in India and Southeast Asia

India, a densely populated, vastly complex subcontinent of many peoples, languages, cultures, and several major religions, was the largest colony in the world. Great Britain's political domination of the subcontinent dated to the eighteenth century. During the 1920s and 1930s, Indian nationalism developed among an Indian elite, many of whom had been educated in England. When World War II began, the British government asked the Hindu Congress Party, the largest Indian political organization, for its support against the Japanese. When its Hindu leaders, Mohandas Gandhi (1869–1948) and Jawaharlal Nehru (1889–1964), refused to offer unqualified support, the British government ordered them jailed. In 1942, the British government informed them that India would receive full status within the British Commonwealth at the end of the war if India fully cooperated with the British government in the meantime. However, Gandhi and Nehru demanded complete independence for India. Gandhi, in particular, became a symbol of Indian resolution to win independence by peaceful means. When he threatened a massive campaign of nonviolent resistance to British rule, the British government sent him to jail again.

With the British Conservative Party out of government after the war, Labour Prime Minister Clement Attlee announced in 1946 that India would be granted full independence. This led to bitter fighting between

Mohandas Gandhi steps from a third-class train after Indian independence.

Hindus and Muslims. The Muslim League insisted on the creation of a separate Muslim nation, which the Hindu Congress Party rejected outright. Hindus and Muslims battled in much of India. Finally, Britain agreed to form two independent states: India, which would be largely Hindu, and Pakistan, divided between East Pakistan and West Pakistan on either side of India, which would be Muslim. Since millions of Muslims lived in India and many Hindus lived in Pakistan, however, it proved impossible to draw state boundaries so that they exactly corresponded to ethnic and religious differences.

In August 1947, India and Pakistan became fully independent. However, the fighting between Hindus and Muslims continued. Hindus drove thousands of Muslims out of India; many of them starved to death during forced marches to Pakistan. A Hindu extremist assassinated Gandhi in 1948 because he had accepted the establishment of Pakistan.

India became the world's largest democracy (its population reached 900 million by 1990) with many of its daunting problems unsolved: poverty compounded by a phenomenally high birthrate, an insufficient structure of democratic institutions, and bitter religious rivalries. Pakistan, too, faced the challenges of poverty and the lack of a democratic tradition. The awkward division of Pakistan into East and West, separated by Hindu India, ended in 1971 when East Pakistan rebelled against Pakistani authority. After Indian troops intervened against Pakistani forces, Bangladesh became an independent state, one of the poorest nations in the world. Meanwhile, the British government had also granted independence to other British colonies in Asia: the island of Ceylon (Sri Lanka) and Burma (Myanmar) in 1948, Malaysia in 1963, and Singapore in 1965.

In Southeast Asia, the end of Japanese occupation during World War II also left the way open for independence movements. With the economies of the Western European nations still suffering the effects of the war, the costs of resisting independence movements seemed high. Opposition to colonialism came not only from the colonized peoples, but also from intellectuals, students, and political parties of the left at home.

The Japanese occupation had driven the Dutch colonists out of Indonesia. Before the Dutch could return, Sukarno (1901–1970), nationalist leader, proclaimed Indonesian independence. After Indonesian rebels rose up against Dutch rule, negotiations arranged by the United Nations led the Netherlands to grant Indonesian independence in 1949. Eight years later, the Indonesian government expelled Dutch citizens and confiscated their property. Sukarno called his government a "guided democracy," assuming the presidency for life in 1963. As the economy floundered, however, the Indonesian Communist Party grew in size. The Indonesian government maintained neutrality in the Cold War, accepting large sums of money from the Soviet Union and the United States. In 1965, Lieutenant General Suharto (1921–   ) seized power. Undertaking a bloody campaign of terror against Communists, he consolidated his dictatorship.

Britain and the Middle East

The Second World War initiated a period of decline in British influence in the Middle East. Egypt had achieved independence after World War I. But in 1945 the British government still controlled Palestine, which had an Arab majority. Jews, however, considered Palestine their promised land. During the 1920s and 1930s, many Jews had emigrated to Palestine, hoping one day to construct the Jewish state of Israel. In the wake of World War II, they were joined by hundreds of thousands of Jews from Europe who had survived the Holocaust. In 1947, the British government, already facing attacks from militant Jews committed to ending British occupation, asked the United Nations to resolve Palestine's future. In its first major international decision, the U.N. called for the division of Palestine into the Jewish state of Israel and an Arab state, which became Jordan. Backed by the United States, Israel took over much of the British mandate in 1948. Jerusalem, a holy city for Jews, Arabs, and Christians, was to remain temporarily under the control of the United Nations.

When the British left Palestine in 1948, conflict began almost immediately between the Palestinian Arabs and the new state of Israel. The victorious Israeli army expelled large numbers of Arabs from their lands, expanding the borders of their new state. A million Palestinians became refugees without a homeland when they fled to Jordan. The seeds were sown for future conflicts. The Arab states refused to recognize the existence of Israel, which refused to recognize the rights of the Palestinian people. Those Palestinians remaining in Israel were relegated to the status of second-class citizens.

The Suez Canal Crisis

Growing European dependence on oil as a source of energy would make the Middle East increasingly important in international politics. The Suez Canal had been the centerpiece of British interests and defenses in the Middle East since British troops first occupied Egypt in 1882. Although the British withdrawal from India in 1947 had somewhat reduced its strategic importance to Britain, about two-thirds of the oil from the Middle East on which Britain and Western Europe depended was transported through the canal. Egypt had been independent since 1922, but Britain maintained considerable influence there. Furthermore, the canal itself was owned by the British and French governments, as well as by stockholders, primarily British.

In 1952, when Egyptian nationalist sentiment against Britain was running high (in part because the British government refused to allow Egypt to occupy Sudan), a group of young nationalist military officers overthrew Egyptian King Farouk in a bloodless coup. Gamal Abdel Nasser (1918–1970), the head of the new Egyptian government, emerged as one of the most influential figures in rising Pan-Arab nationalism. Nasser established Egyptian neutrality in the tug-of-war between East and West, refusing to sign a treaty with the United States (which had been quick to recognize the new state of Israel in 1948) and castigating Iran and Turkey for their pro-American policies.

As Egyptian nationalism mounted, the Egyptian government (which had renounced the Anglo-Egyptian alliance treaty of 1936) increasingly demanded British withdrawal from the narrow zone along the Suez Canal. In 1954, the Egyptian and British governments signed an agreement (strongly opposed by some British Conservatives) by which British troops would begin a phased withdrawal that would be completed in June 1956. Britain would retain the right to send military forces back should the canal be attacked (presumably by the Soviet Union); the British and Egyptian governments would respect the freedom of navigation through the canal. Many Egyptians (particularly the radical Muslim Brotherhood) opposed this agreement, which seemed to maintain some degree of British control over the Suez Canal. They sought to end once and for all Egypt's semi-colonial status.

Egypt became a pawn in the struggle between the United States and the Soviet Union for influence over non-aligned nations. Gradually, Nasser turned toward the Soviet Union for economic support, resenting Israel's close ties to the United States, and Britain's defensive pact with Turkey and Iraq (the Baghdad Pact, 1955). The Soviet Union sought to increase its influence in the Middle East, capitalizing on considerable dissatisfaction among Arab nationalists with the United States' role in the construction of a Middle East treaty association similar to NATO. The Soviet government signed an agreement with Egypt, promising to exchange arms for Egyptian cotton. Egypt planned to construct the Aswan High Dam on the Upper Nile River, which Nasser believed would help modernize the Egyptian economy. The World Bank had agreed to finance the construction if Britain and the United States would contribute. But the U.S. government was increasingly suspicious of British goals. Indeed, the British government was planning to overthrow Nasser. On July 19, 1956, the United States suddenly withdrew its offer when it seemed that the Egyptian government would accept a sudden offer by the Soviets to finance the dam's construction. On July 26, Nasser announced the nationalization of the Suez Canal, with the assurance, however, that shareholders would be compensated.

The British government, pushed by staunch Conservatives who feared that Nasser would undermine British interests in the Middle East, decided on armed intervention. France, too, wanted Nasser out of power because of French interests in the canal and because Nasser supported the Algerian National Liberation Front, which sought Algerian independence from France. In the meantime, the U.S. government, which opposed military action against Egypt, sought to diffuse the crisis through negotiation.

(*Left*) A Russian cartoon salutes Nasser's seizure of the Suez Canal in July 1956. The banner reads "Shares of the Suez Canal Company Ltd." (*Right*) Sunken ships block the Suez Canal.

The government of Israel was also concerned about emerging ties between Egypt and the Soviet Union; the arrival of Soviet arms in Egypt raised fears of a possible Egyptian invasion. In October, the British government came around to the French view that they should agree to an Israeli invasion of Egypt, which would provide them with an excuse to intervene militarily and occupy the Suez Canal Zone. (The U.S. government was kept unaware of these difficult negotiations.) Israel sent an invasion force into Egypt on October 29. The Egyptian army put up stiff resistance. A Franco-British ultimatum then demanded that Israeli and Egyptian forces withdraw to ten miles from the canal. Indeed, the Israeli government halted the military drive within Egypt toward the canal. An Anglo-French force then landed in Egypt and occupied the Canal Zone after Nasser ordered the scuttling of ships to block the canal. On November 3, the General Assembly of the United Nations called for a cease-fire, and a day later, it authorized a peacekeeping force. On November 6, Britain agreed to accept the cease-fire. Pressure on both Israel and Egypt from the United States, with the support of the Soviet Union (which had reason to be pleased that the world's attention could be diverted from Hungary, where Russian tanks were crushing an anti-Communist revolt; see pp. 1341–43), brought an end to the Suez crisis. British and French troops withdrew. The U.S. government had made clear its unwillingness to support the maintenance of the British and French colonial empires. The Suez Canal crisis had demonstrated that Western powers could no longer impose their will on the Middle East. Thereafter, the process of decolonization proceeded rapidly.

In Britain, Prime Minister Sir Anthony Eden (1897–1977), who had consulted with few British leaders before the Suez crisis, suffered a nervous breakdown and resigned from office in January 1957. Harold Macmillan (1894–1986), who had been a proponent of the Suez action, then undertook what one Conservative leader called the "most spectacular retreat from Suez since the time of Moses." Following the salvaging of the forty ships that Egypt had sunk in the canal, it reopened in April 1957 under Egyptian control. In 1958, British ally King Faisal II was overthrown and assassinated in Iraq. When the island of Cyprus gained its independence in 1960, Britain lost its last base of influence in the Middle East.

French Decolonization

France, too, lost its colonial empire in the post-war era. The French had begun their conquest of North Africa in 1830 and had held much of Southeast Asia since the 1880s. The French left Syria and Lebanon by agreement with the United States and Britain. In Vietnam, Ho Chi Minh (Nguyen Tat Thanh; 1890–1969) had become president of the Democratic Republic of Vietnam after the war. His father was an official under the French who had resigned from his position because of his Vietnamese nationalism. Ho Chi Minh himself worked as a kitchen helper on a French passenger liner before becoming a Communist activist. Founding the Indochinese Communist Party in 1929, he unified three groups of Vietnamese Communists in 1930 around his leadership. After being condemned to death in absentia by the French government, he was saved by the refusal of the British government in Hong Kong to turn him over to French authorities. Nonetheless, the British arrested him in 1931, and he remained in prison in Hong Kong until 1933. During World War II, he led the Vietminh, an organization of Vietnamese nationalists, some of whom were Communists.

Attempting to retain control over some of Indochina, in November 1946, the French army attacked the port of Haiphong, killing 6,000 Vietnamese, and captured Hanoi, the Vietnamese capital. France restored the nominal authority of a playboy emperor. Nonetheless, war between Ho Chi Minh's Vietnamese army, which held most of the countryside, and the French went on. Ho, supported by the Chinese, prophesized "You will kill ten of our men, but we will kill one of yours and you will end up by wearing yourselves out." Early in 1954, the French army suffered a crushing defeat at the hands of the Vietnamese at Dien Bien Phu. Pierre Mendès-France (1907–1982), the new Socialist premier, succeeded in extracting France from war in Vietnam (he would later prove less successful in encouraging the French to drink milk instead of wine, a more hopeless task). At the Geneva Convention that year, France agreed to the division of Vietnam into two states. North Vietnam became a Communist regime led by Ho Chi Minh; South Vietnam became a republic run by a succession of corrupt leaders who carried out U.S. policy in exchange for a free hand.

The end of French colonialism was even more wrenching in North Africa. There were 1.2 million French citizens in Algeria (which was con-

(*Left*) A Vietminh fighter taken prisoner by a French soldier in 1952. (*Right*) A French patrol in Vietnam in 1954.

sidered an integral part of France), 300,000 in Morocco, and 200,000 in Tunisia. These French residents were called *pieds noirs* ("black feet") because of the black boots of the French soldiers. Morocco and Tunisia were French protectorates, although nominally ruled by a sultan and bey, respectively. Algeria, in contrast, was a colony, directly administered by French officials. During the early 1950s, movements for national independence developed in France's North African colonies.

The writer Albert Camus, who was born in Algeria, summed up the difficult choices for some French families who lived there; he said that if given the choice between justice and his mother, he would take his mother. Many of the French living in North Africa had become wealthy; some had successfully developed the land taken from the Arab population over the past century. Others were of modest means, including café owners in Algiers, government functionaries, and farmers with small plots.

In 1954, an Algerian uprising for independence began just four months after the French defeat at Dien Bien Phu. Fearing that the movement might spread to Tunisia and Morocco (where, in fact, some fighting followed), the French government granted virtual independence to both states in 1956, despite protests of French residents and the vigorous opposition of the French officer corps, which believed its honor was at stake.

In Algeria, the struggle between the Algerian National Liberation Front (Front de Libération Nationale or F.L.N.) and the French army intensified in scale. As guerilla actions increased and losses mounted, many people in France began to accept Algerian independence as both inevitable and desirable. In February 1956, French residents in Algiers rioted against the government when French Premier Guy Mollet came to introduce his newly appointed governor of Algeria. In October, the newly crowned king of Morocco met with leaders of the F.L.N., enraging the French right. Mollet, fearing the political consequences of the war, then ordered the kidnapping of Ahmed Ben Bella (1919–   ), a leader of the Algerians, and launched a repression in France of critics of the French Algerian policy. In November, France joined Britain in the ill-fated invasion of Egypt, in part because of French anger at Egyptian support for the Algerian insurrection. As the war dragged on, the left increasingly demanded an end to the war; intellectuals, like Sartre and Camus, denounced the torture of Algerians by the French army.

After humiliating defeats at the hands of the German army in 1940 and by the Vietnamese at Dien Bien Phu in 1954, some French military officers saw the fight in Algeria as a last stand for their honor. The decline in military salaries and living conditions—particularly housing—had followed the decline of the prestige of the French army in France and around the world. Citations for bravery and even the lists of those killed and wounded stopped appearing in government publications. On May 13, 1958, a protest demonstration by French settlers in Algiers turned into a military-led insurrection against the French government. A "Committee of Public Safety" of rightists seized power. There was a distinct possibility of a military coup d'état in France.

Charles de Gaulle, who had been waiting in self-imposed exile for something like this to happen, announced that he was ready to serve France again. Many politicians, fearing a military seizure of power, believed that

French soldiers patrol the Casbah in Algiers in 1959.

de Gaulle alone could prevent chaos. On May 29, President René Coty appointed de Gaulle premier, a move approved by the National Assembly early in June. The general accepted, on the condition that he could rule by emergency decree for six months and could then ask the nation to approve a new constitution. The right, including the army, was delighted with de Gaulle's return to power, thinking that the general would never allow Algerian independence.

The new constitution greatly increased the authority of the president, whose term was set at seven years to end revolving-door ministries. Presidents under the Fifth French Republic would conduct foreign policy, appoint prime ministers, and dissolve parliament. In September 1958, 80 percent of French voters approved the constitution of the French Fifth Republic.

But what about Algeria? De Gaulle went to Algiers and, in a classic speech of noncommittal, told the settlers on June 4, 1958, "I have understood you, I know what you have tried to do here." But he had already decided that the costs of continuing the war in Algeria were too great, too divisive. He removed many of the generals responsible for the coup in Algeria from their posts. For a man whose nationalism underlay his political philosophy, it seemed an astonishing turnaround.

To some officers, de Gaulle's actions seemed an incredible betrayal, a stab in the back by a military man. As the Dreyfus Affair had revealed in the 1890s and the Vichy years had confirmed, a right-wing anti-democratic tradition survived in the officer corps. Many officers now felt betrayed not only by de Gaulle but by much of the population in France. They enjoyed some support among rightist parties, whose followers rioted in Paris in January 1960.

A secret group within the army, the O.A.S. (Secret Army Organization), tried several times to assassinate de Gaulle. Members also planted bombs in Paris in order to terrorize the civilian population. De Gaulle again assumed emergency powers, this time for a year. Given the chance to vote on their future, the Algerians opted for independence; in France, the vote for Algerian independence in July 1961 was 15 million to 5 million. Army officers in Algeria led a new insurrection, which was soon put down. De Gaulle's government foiled a plot by generals to overthrow the Fifth Republic, which began when parachutists briefly seized power in Corsica. The threat seemed so real that loyal air force officers parked planes on the runways of several airports in France to prevent an attempted invasion. Yet, most army units remained loyal to the general. On March 19, 1962, the Algerian War officially ended, with the French people overwhelmingly ratifying the peace terms. In July 1962, Algeria officially became independent.

France maintained its influence in the Third World, at least partially because de Gaulle seemed to have stood up to the United States. Charles de Gaulle believed that France had a special historic mission, and he never doubted for a moment the part he was to play in it. He feared the domina-

Charles de Gaulle with Konrad Adenauer exemplify the French–West German friendship that formed a cornerstone of the new Europe.

tion of Europe and France by Britain and the United States. He insisted that France maintain an independent nuclear capability (the *force de frappe*). Moreover, de Gaulle sought a closer diplomatic relationship with the German Federal Republic. Ending decades of animosity, the close partnership between Germany and France formed the cornerstone of the new Europe.

Throughout his political career, de Gaulle's speeches were full of references to France's "grandeur." Although much of his political support came from the right, the general stated, "De Gaulle is not on the left. Or on the right. Or in the center. De Gaulle is *above*." The general's political style was more that of a monarch than of a president. He often referred to himself in the third person, occasionally using the royal "we." Not long after there had been attempts on his life, one of his aides informed de Gaulle that he ran great risks by plunging into crowds of people during his visits to provincial towns. The general replied, "Get one thing into your head. De Gaulle interests me only as a figure of history."

De Gaulle refused to cooperate with the other Western powers. He never forgot the humiliation of France's exclusion from the Allied conferences at Yalta and Potsdam. In 1966, France left NATO's military command, forcing it to transfer its headquarters from Paris to Brussels. U.S. army and air force bases in France were closed. He angered the U.S. government by refusing to support its policies in Vietnam. He outraged many Canadians by shouting, "Long live Free Québec!" during a state visit in 1967. Although de Gaulle was vehemently anti-Communist, he wanted France to provide leadership as a third force that stood between the Soviet Union and the United States.

Decolonization in Africa

At the end of World War II, only Egypt, Liberia, and Ethiopia had achieved independence in Africa. In the subsequent decades, British rule ended in one African colony after another. In 1957, Ghana became the first British colony in Africa to become independent after the Second World War. Others followed, including Nigeria in 1960, Sierra Leone and Tanganyika in 1961, Uganda in 1962, and Kenya in 1963. Several French colonies became independent in 1960, including the Ivory Coast, Senegal, and Cameroon (see Map 29.3).

The Republic of South Africa left the British Commonwealth in 1961. It continued the system of apartheid, an official policy of racial inequality and segregation, supported by the ultraconservative white Afrikaner population of Dutch origin. In 1965 Rhodesia, which had been a self-governing colony, declared its independence from Britain. It did so, in part, so that its white minority would not have to share power with the black majority population. The British government then led a campaign of international economic sanctions against the white regime. In 1980, Rhodesia was divided into the independent states of Zimbabwe and Zambia, where blacks obtained political rights.

In the Belgian Congo in central West Africa, the Belgian government first tried to placate nationalists with concessions in the late 1950s and then to repress them following rioting in 1959. A year later, the Belgian government suddenly pulled out of its former colony (although the Congo's army retained Belgian officers), declaring the Congo independent in June 1960. Before independence, however, preliminary elections had revealed considerable political division. Civil war began between two nationalist leaders, a bloody conflict complicated by ethnic and tribal loyalties. Soldiers mutinied against their Belgian commanders and began to attack Europeans remaining in the Congo. The Congo's wealthiest province, Katanga, then declared its independence. At the request of the Congo's premier, the United Nations sent troops to restore order. After a year, the civil war ended. Katanga did not end its succession until 1963.

In 1965, Colonel Mobutu Sese Seko (1930–   ) imposed military rule. He nationalized his country's wealthy mines. The old colonial capital of Leopoldville became Kinshasa. Mobuto named Lake Albert after himself and set about amassing enormous personal wealth. In 1971, the country became known as Zaire.

Portugal was another small European state that had had a large appetite for colonies. It struggled to retain its colonies of Angola and Mozambique, which lie on the southwestern and southeastern coasts, respectively, of Africa. A nationalist uprising for independence (led by the Popular Movement for the Liberation of Angola) lasted from 1961 to 1975, when the new Portuguese government, which a year earlier had overthrown the dictatorship that had ruled Portugal for decades, granted independence to

MAP 29.3 DECOLONIZATION   The map shows the movement for decolonization in Africa, Asia, and the Far East, giving the dates at which each of the colonies achieved independence.

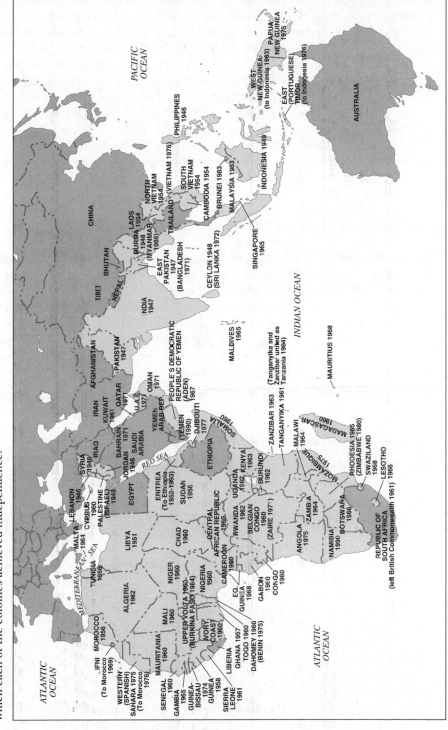

Angola. However, as in the case of the former Belgian Congo, fighting broke out between a Marxist group and an extreme right-wing military faction, the former backed by the Soviet Union, the latter by the United States. The war lasted until 1991, when the Popular Movement, aided by Cuban funds and soldiers, won the war. Nonetheless, the rightists continued to battle the new government. In Mozambique, following independence in 1975 after a long insurrection, warfare between left and right also began. There, too, the far left faction won, while the right, assisted by the South African government, launched a campaign of terror. Ordinary people, the vast majority of them impoverished, suffered untold horrors of famine and slaughter, complicated by increasing tension between Mozambique's leftist government and Zimbabwe.

ECONOMIC AND SOCIAL CHANGES

Amid increased prosperity, Western Europe's population grew rapidly after World War II. Mechanization and commercialization augmented agricultural production. Because of this "Green Revolution," more and more rural people left the land for cities, which grew rapidly. Industries, financial services, and the service sector concentrated in the continent's emerging urban world. At the same time, Western European states assumed more responsibility for the welfare of their citizens than ever before. In the Soviet Union and allied Communist countries of Eastern Europe, despite struggling economies and frequent shortages, states provided essential services.

Economic Recovery and the Welfare State

The Organization for European Economic Cooperation (O.E.E.C.), with seventeen member states (which the United States later joined), helped plan European economic reconstruction after World War II. By 1952, when the Marshall Plan ended, Europe had undergone a remarkable economic recovery to which the Marshall Plan greatly contributed. The GNP (Gross National Product) of the Western nations had increased by 25 percent in three years, and steel production by 70 percent.

Cooperation among the Western states also led to the creation of the European Coal and Steel Community (ECSC; 1952), the inspiration of the French statesman Robert Schuman (1886–1963), by which Western states began to coordinate production in the interest of efficiency. The Treaty of Rome (1957) laid the groundwork for the European Atomic Energy Community and the European Economic Community (EEC, sometimes known as the European Common Market), whose original member nations included France, Italy, the German Federal Republic, Belgium, Luxembourg, and the Netherlands. The European Economic Community gradually eliminated trade barriers between member states in Western Europe, established common customs tariffs, and worked toward equalizing wages and social security arrangements among the member countries.

The role of governments in providing for their people expanded, at least partially an outgrowth of state economic and military planning during World War II. This was true in Western states, in which laissez-faire had long held the upper hand, as well as in Communist states, in which the role of centralized state economic planning was a major part of Communist ideology.

In the post-war period, Western European states greatly expanded subsidized social services for their citizens. The increased role of government during World War II and a general appreciation of the sacrifices ordinary people had made during the long, hard conflict helped encourage greater social services. The welfare state thus partially rose out of the assumption that the monopoly of wealthy people over the economy had contributed to the rise of fascist movements in Europe between the wars.

"Welfare states" would provide cradle-to-grave social services. In 1943, British Conservatives and Liberals had joined the Labour Party in supporting a proposal for establishing a system of national welfare once the war ended. The Labour government increased public services, including medical and hospital care and benefits for the unemployed. Yet, per capita expenses for welfare measures in Britain were lower than every major Western European country except Holland and Italy. The increase in government services added to the size of bureaucracies in most European countries, most notably in France, the Scandinavian nations (above all, Sweden), and the Eastern bloc countries.

In many countries, social legislation provided government assistance to the sick and impoverished. Government insurance programs covered health care costs in Britain, Sweden, Denmark, France, Italy, the Soviet Union, and the other Communist nations. Most countries in the West provided financial assistance to the unemployed; in Communist states, where there was not supposed to be any unemployment, menial jobs were found for almost everyone. In all, states expended four times more funds for social services in 1957 than in 1930, including retirement pensions and health care. Progressive taxation helped raise funds to provide these services. In most European countries, education was made free, or fees were kept at modest rates.

As the standard of living increased, people lived longer, aided by improvements in diet and in health. With a gradual reduction in the workday and higher wages, families had more time and money for leisure.

Economic Growth in the West

There were many signs of economic backwardness in post-war Europe. After World War II, only half of the houses in France had running water, and only a third of those in Austria, Spain, and Italy. Providing decent housing became a goal of governments in most countries. In Germany, one of every six persons was a refugee. Therefore, most countries allocated considerable resources into making available more houses and improving the quality of those that already existed.

The difficult years in the immediate post-war period gave way to a period of strong economic growth that lasted from 1950 to 1973. European economies benefited from the globalization of trade, the availability of a labor supply, and increased state planning (at least in the case of Italy and France). Oil rapidly replaced coal as the principal source of fuel for industrial growth. Natural gas, much of which was imported from the Soviet Union, offered another source of energy.

The concentration of industrial production in large companies characterized the post-war period. Western Europe, slowly following the lead of the United States, entered the world of conglomerates. A single Belgian company controlled from 50 to 80 percent of Belgian bank deposits, 60 percent of insurance business, 40 percent of the iron and steel produced, 30 percent of coal, and 25 percent of Belgian electrical energy. This virtual monopoly did not seem to slow the development of the Belgian economy, which continued to expand rapidly in the 1960s.

Table 29-1 provides comparative rates of industrial productivity for the major nations of Europe, and for Japan and the United States. Great disparities remained between and within European nations. By the end of the 1960s, the German Federal Republic, Switzerland, and Sweden were the most prosperous countries; Ireland, Portugal, Greece, and Spain were the poorest in Western Europe. Romania and Albania were the poorest Communist states. In Table 29–1, Britain's relative decline sticks out.

Factory managers helped manage and modernize production. The number of European "third sector" or "white-collar" workers (as opposed to the

TABLE 29-1. INDEX OF INDUSTRIAL PRODUCTION (1958=100)

	1938	1948	1952	1959	1963	1967
United States	33	73	90	113	133	168
West Germany	53	27	61	107	137	158
France	52	55	70	101	129	155
Italy	43	44	64	112	166	212
Holland	47	53	72	110	141	182
Belgium	64	78	88	104	135	153
Britain	67	74	84	105	119	133
Austria	39	36	65	106	131	151
Spain				102	149	215
Sweden	52	74	81	106	140	176
Japan	58	22	50	120	212	347

Source: Walter Laqueur, *Europe Since Hitler* (New York: Penguin, 1982), p. 194.

"blue-collar" industrial workers) soared. Their incomes and expectations lay somewhere between those of the upper classes and industrial workers. White-collar workers included shop clerks, bank clerks, insurance agents, business assistants, hotel personnel, secretaries, and upper categories of domestic help. They now outnumbered industrial workers in some countries.

Germany and Japan, the two defeated powers, re-emerged as economic giants in the post-war period. The western zones of Germany contained most German natural resources, which contributed to a recovery that surprised even the most optimistic economists. The German Federal Republic had the advantage (one, to be sure, bought at horrific cost during the war) of starting from scratch and building new factories that utilized the most modern equipment. Aided by the implementation in 1948 of a free-market economy and a stable political life, the German Federal Republic reformed the battered Deutschmark, which helped restore confidence and set off a crucial period of growth. Black-marketeering gradually ended as inflation and unemployment were brought under control. West Germany developed a combination of laissez-faire economics and business responsibility for the social welfare of its people, "the social market economy."

An infusion of American aid—$1.5 billion between 1948 and 1952 primarily through the Marshall Plan—facilitated the rebuilding of key industries. The chemical industry developed rapidly. New synthetic products (like plastic), some of which had received impetus from wartime scientific research, engendered a consumer revolution. Industrial production more than doubled between 1948 and 1951, and then again by 1960. As a result of the German economic "miracle," West Germany's GNP tripled between 1950 and 1964. Its industrial production increased by six times from 1948 to 1964, while that of Japan doubled between 1960 and 1966. West Germany's other advantages included a skilled labor force and the fact that, protected by the Western allies, it did not have to spend much for defense. Gradually, as Germans regained self-confidence and prosperity returned, consumer spending fueled the economic resurgence.

The boom of the 1950s and 1960s increased the standard of living for most Europeans, although great gaps between social classes remained. Real wages in Italy in 1954 were more than 50 percent higher than they had been before the war. The resulting rise in the standard of living for Western industrial workers gradually reduced any possibility that workers might be a revolutionary force in Europe. At the same time, the growth in managerial and lower-level white-collar employment decreased the proportional size of the industrial workforce. Trade unions lost some of their influence; union leaders looked increasingly to clerical workers for new members.

The success of the European Economic Community (which helped reduce trade barriers) and nationalizations (notably railroads, coal, and steel) contributed to Europe's economic recovery. The most successful mix seemed to be a combination of state planning, timely nationalizations, and liberal encouragement of private industry. Nationalized railroads aided the process of rebuilding and expansion in West Germany, France, Belgium, and Britain, carrying prodigious amounts of freight and millions of passengers each year. Europe's merchant fleets doubled between the end of the war and 1965. Trucks, however, carried much of Europe's goods to market: there were 2.7 million trucks in 1948, and twice that many nine years later. Moreover, the number of cars on the road increased from 5 million in 1948 to 44 million in 1965.

By the mid-1960s, the government owned almost 30 percent of Italian industry. The French government in 1946 established an office for economic planning. A far cry from the Soviet model of centralized planning, this office did not have the power to force businesses to adopt certain strategies, but it could encourage targets and strategies. The government of the German Federal Republic took a lesser role in economic planning than that of France, but it imposed short-term tariffs and encouraged agricultural modernization. France did not duplicate the West German economic "miracle," but it made considerable progress nonetheless. Smaller nations also thrived. Norway, Denmark, and Sweden all became more prosperous, stable nations thanks largely to the development of fishing, agriculture, and industry.

Travel became an essential part of middle-class and, increasingly, working-class life. The development of a sophisticated network of air travel linked European cities to each other and to other continents. Gradually, particularly with the introduction of the passenger jet in the late 1950s, the airplane replaced the passenger ship for cross-Atlantic travel. The era of the shipboard romance was over.

Telephones facilitated business and family life. By the late 1950s, hardly any large enterprises could afford to be without one. Household phones became more common in the 1960s in most of Western Europe. The telephone's diffusion came slower in France, however, where the minister of communication in 1964 actually referred to the telephone as a "gimmick."

The radio and then television helped shape a mass consumer culture, catapulting entertainers to fame and making household names of politicians who could be heard instead of simply imagined. Although the first television sets could be viewed at the World's Fair in New York City in 1939, it was only in the late 1960s that a majority of Western European households had a television. By the mid-1970s, relatively few were without one. The British Broadcasting System set standards for excellence, but U.S. television, with its diet of westerns, soap operas, situation comedies, and gory police thrillers, left a greater impression on the majority of viewers.

A reaction among many European intellectuals against post-war consumerism, closely identified with the United States, generated anti-Americanism. Lasting until the early 1970s, anti-Americanism accompanied

The television rapidly took its place in many European homes.

hostility to U.S. foreign and nuclear policy during the Cold War, and toward a culture intellectuals criticized as reeking of vulgar materialism. A prominent French sociologist called the American *Reader's Digest* "a pocket-sized stupefier" whose translation into French risked debasing French culture. French governments, too, viewed Americanization as a threat to French culture. There was an economic dimension to this struggle. During the early 1950s, the French government feared the competition that Coca Cola could give the wine industry. Encouraged by the powerful wine lobby, the French government tried—ultimately without success—to keep Coca Cola from the French market as Coke bottles began to sweep across Europe beginning in the late 1940s.

The partial "Americanization" of European consumer culture could readily be seen, however, by the late 1960s. American words and terms crept into European languages (such as *le week-end* and *le snack-bar* in French, leading purists to denigrate such terms as *franglais*). Furthermore, World War II caused only a brief hiatus in the export of Hollywood films to Europe. American film stars became those of the continent. While American films had broad appeal, nonetheless Italian, British, French, and to a lesser extent, Russian, German, and Czech film-makers turned out movies of artistic quality.

The era of television and radio ended the great age of the newspaper. During the first several years after the war, Europeans read more—and arguably better—newspapers than ever before or since. As Europeans increasingly received their news and their entertainment from television and

Delivering Coca Cola in Venice.

radio, however, newspapers merged and many folded. With the exception of the stately, serious dailies like *Le Monde* of Paris, the *Manchester Guardian*, the *Frankfurter Allegemein* in the German Federal Republic, and *La Stampa* of Milan, an increasing number of papers relied upon sensationalism, scandals, and the proclamation of juicy unsubstantiated rumor as truth to attract readers. In the Soviet Union, where the state was the only source of printed news, more than 7 million copies of *Pravda* were printed every day. As in the 1930s, wealthy right-wing interests controlled the majority of newspapers in Western Europe.

Communist Economies

In Communist countries, the housing shortage remained acute into the 1960s. Although in the Soviet Union housing construction tripled between 1953 and 1969, families still had long waits for better apartments. Existing apartments were often horrendously overcrowded, with several families often sharing accommodations.

The planned economies of the Soviet Union and its Eastern allies could count some accomplishments, although adequate attention to the desires of their citizens was not one of them. The Soviet Gross National Product, which had stood at 36 percent of that of the United States in 1957, rose to about 50 percent of that of its great rival in 1962, and edged closer in the subsequent two decades, though not enough to give much credence to Soviet leader Nikita Khrushchev's brazen prediction that the Soviet Union would surpass the West within a decade. Above all, the Soviet economy remained haunted by daunting inefficiency.

Rebuilding the Soviet economy after World War II was a monumental task. The Soviet Union's victory had been decidedly pyrrhic. Those who had managed to flee the war zones returned to devastated cities. Successive years of harvest failure from 1946 to 1947 compounded extreme suffering. The highly centralized planning of the fourth Five-Year Plan, which began in 1945, allowed the Soviets to concentrate on key industries like coal and steel. Soviet planners benefited from the commandeering of industrial capital goods in Germany and Eastern Europe, and from Western assistance after the war. Large-scale industrial production had exceeded pre-war levels by 1950 by a comfortable margin, although such strong results were only modestly reflected in the quality of life of Soviet citizens. Collectivized farms permitted some degree of efficient planning, but they also generated continued peasant resistance.

Once they recovered from being forced to contribute resources to Soviet economic growth and from buying Soviet products at inflated prices, the Communist states of Eastern Europe benefited from Soviet technological assistance. In 1949, the Soviet Union and its Eastern European allies formed the Council of Mutual Economic Assistance (COMECON). This organization sought to coordinate economic planning so that, for example, each country was not trying to build ships, but only the German Democratic Republic and Poland, which had not only the resources but long traditions of shipbuilding. Industrial production rose most rapidly in Eastern Europe in the German Democratic Republic and Czechoslovakia. Bulgaria, Romania, and Yugoslavia, the least industrialized of the Eastern European countries, also developed manufacturing bases. Romania, however, more than any other of the Soviet Union's client states (with the exception of Yugoslavia), managed to retain considerable autonomy in economic matters, although large-scale industry and agricultural collectivization were emphasized as in the other Eastern European states.

The economic development of the German Democratic Republic, however short on freedom, was nonetheless at first impressive. The eastern zone of Germany had had a small industrial base, but it had been pillaged by the Soviet extraction of raw materials and machinery. The collectivization of industrial production proceeded rapidly. By 1952, the state employed three of every four workers. Despite the loss of many skilled workers to the German Federal Republic, East Germany emerged with the strongest economy of the Soviet Union's Eastern bloc; only Hungary boasted a similar standard of living by the 1960s. Steel production and shipbuilding, particularly, expanded rapidly in the 1950s and 1960s, as the German Democratic Republic fulfilled its assigned role in the Soviet government's plan for economic development in the Communist states. Nonetheless, to many East Germans conditions of life seemed more attractive in West Germany than in East Germany. Hundreds of thousands of people voted with their feet and left for West Germany. When Ulbricht announced in 1952 that the government would begin collectivizing farms, about 20,000 farmers immediately fled to West Germany. By 1965, collective farms tilled 85 percent of the land in East Germany.

In Yugoslavia, which Tito had succeeded in making virtually independent of the Soviet Union, workers were permitted more self-administration through workers' councils or committees. In the 1950s, the collectivization of agriculture, which had begun after the war, was abandoned, with farmers retaking their old plots. Yugoslavia's economy, in particular, improved, despite shortages and great inequalities among its six republics.

An Urban World

Europe rapidly urbanized in the decades following World War II. Great Britain, the Netherlands, and the German Federal Republic led the way. In the German industrial Rhineland, it became difficult to tell where one city ended and another began.

Modern architects confronted the challenge of designing large and functional buildings at a reasonable cost. The necessity of housing millions of new urban residents contributed to a uniformity of architectural style. Tall, drab, uniform towers filled with small apartments sprang up in and around major urban centers, providing adequate lodging, but not

The clash of old and new in Europe's changing cities.

much more, in cramped quarters with thin walls. Commuting became a fact of urban life in much of Europe.

In the U.S.S.R. in the early 1960s, the Soviets began to create new suburbs and satellite towns to accommodate the population seeking to live in Moscow, which grew from 2 million in 1926 to more than 5 million in 1959. Leningrad's population increased from 1.7 to 3.3 million during the same period, despite the death of hundreds of thousands of its residents as a result of the German siege during the war.

In France, almost 20 percent of the population now resided in Paris and its surroundings. Of these, only about 3 million lived in the City of Light itself, the rest inhabiting sprawling suburbs. Attempts to create eight "satellite" cities that would decentralize the economy of the Paris region were only moderately successful.

Rapid urban growth, closely tied to the concentration of large-scale industries, posed problems of health and safety. Factories increasingly polluted the air of industrial regions. Nonetheless, projects of urban renewal enhanced the quality of life in cities and towns. Again, Paris provides a good example. Much of its historic center was refurbished, its dilapidated seventeenth-century noble residences were sandblasted clean, and some of them were transformed into fancy apartments and shops catering to visitors. The old market quarter of Les Halles with its historic cast iron pavilions was destroyed by urban planners and developers. West German, Belgian, French, and Dutch cities, among others, sported shining urban centers, with some streets reserved for beleaguered pedestrians tired of dodging onrushing cars and the chaos of honking horns.

Western Europe's burgeoning cities became increasingly clogged with automobiles, which added to factory pollution. The automobile had an enormous impact on work and leisure in Europe, particularly in the West. The construction of new freeways and toll roads could not begin to keep up with the increase of traffic. The traffic jam in Europe began.

The Green Revolution

In the two decades that followed World War II, Western European agriculture was transformed by the "Green Revolution." Large-scale, commercialized agriculture permitted most nations to produce almost all of the food consumed by their populations. Agricultural productivity rose by 30 percent between the end of the war and 1962. In the German Federal Republic, agricultural production increased by two-and-a-half times between 1950 and 1964. In 1950, each farmer in France produced enough food to feed seven people for a year; in 1922, forty people.

There were several reasons for these changes in farming. First, mechanized agriculture was increasingly widespread, particularly use of the tractor. Second, fertilizers augmented farm yields in Northern Europe, while pesticides—a mixed blessing because of the long-term ecological costs—

prevented blight. Advances in types of seeds, animal husbandry (particularly artificial insemination), and irrigation also contributed to greater productivity. Third, the size of many farms increased as smaller and less productive plots were consolidated into larger units. In France, for example, larger and more productive farms were created through sale or through exchanges encouraged by both the government and a Catholic youth organization.

Governments set up programs encouraging the cooperative use of tractors and providing agricultural information to farmers. State-sponsored land reform in Sicily turned over formerly unfarmed large estates to people eager to work the land. Government assistance facilitated reforestation, electrification, irrigation projects, and road building that would have been beyond the means of private initiatives.

The Green Revolution was spread unevenly across Europe. Agriculture became most efficient in the more prosperous northern states of Western Europe: Great Britain, Holland, Belgium, West Germany, Denmark, and northern France. Denmark, France, and other European nations generated agricultural surpluses and became major exporters of food during the 1970s and 1980s.

Fewer farmers fed a much larger population. The continued commercialization of agriculture accentuated the exodus from the land to the rapidly growing cities of Europe. In Italy, the farming population fell from about 40 percent after the war to 24 percent in 1966. In Great Britain, the first European nation in which agriculture was substantially mechanized even before the war, less than 4 percent of the population worked the land by the early 1970s. Before World War I, about half the population of Europe worked in agriculture, a figure that included fishermen and foresters. In 1955, the percentage had fallen to about 24 percent, and it has continued to decline, although it remains higher in Southern Europe. In every country, agriculture's share of the GNP has fallen.

In the Communist countries of Eastern Europe, the collectivization of agriculture proceeded during the 1950s and 1960s. Somewhat greater efficiency (which, to be sure, did not necessarily mean acceptance of the Communist system by landowners whose land had been expropriated by the state) permitted substantial movement of the rural population into cities and factories. In the German Democratic Republic and Bulgaria, 85 percent of the land had been collectivized by the mid-1960s. In Poland at about the same time, more than 85 percent of the land remained in private hands because the Polish Communist leadership feared open popular resistance to massive agricultural collectivization.

Demographic Changes

Following the war, a veritable "baby boom" occurred; Europe's population grew from 264 million in 1940 to 320 million by the early 1970s. The increase in the birthrate after the war more than made up for the loss of hundreds of thousands of emigrants to North America and Latin America, particularly from Italy.

Increases in industrial and agricultural productivity, opening up new jobs, encouraged families to have more children as did government policies that aided families with children. In France, where leaders had openly worried about the low birthrate, special incentives were offered to families that had more than two children. Health improvements (such as the virtual elimination of polio by the end of the 1950s) and an increase in the number of doctors led to further declines in infant mortality. The birthrate increased between 1950 and 1966 in every country in Western Europe, with Switzerland, the Netherlands, the German Federal Republic, and France leading the way. The Soviet Union and Poland, too, saw high annual natural increases. Nonetheless, because of virtually unchecked population growth in India, China, and other Third World nations, Europe's percentage of the world population fell to 16 percent in 1990.

The increase in the birthrate had a far-reaching social and political impact. British, French, and German eighteen-year-olds received the right to vote in the early 1970s, which affected who was elected to office. Moreover, governments had to increase spending dramatically on education to prepare the young for jobs in an economy that was rapidly becoming more complex. Laws obliged parents to send their children to school from the time they were about six until they were fourteen or sixteen years old, depending on the country. Illiteracy became quite uncommon in Europe by the 1960s. University education came within reach of a larger proportion of the population. But despite the tripling of the number of university students in Britain, France, and Italy between 1938 and 1960, there was relatively little democratization of university attendance, which remained the preserve of the upper classes. In 1967, fewer than 10 percent of French university students were the children of workers or peasants. In Great Britain, particularly, but also in the other countries of the West, working-class and farm families could not afford to send their children to university because time away from earning represented too much of an economic hardship.

The plight of the elderly was often lost in the emphasis on youth. As the life expectancy of people increased with improvements in diet and medical advances, there were more old people than ever before and social service budgets began to sag under the weight of an older population.

With the rapid development of the service sector of Western economies, the proliferation of white-collar jobs lifted the expectations, status, and income of hundreds of thousands of families. A more equitable distribution in taxation helped remove some of the tax burden from ordinary people. But enormous economic and social gaps remained between rich and poor, particularly in Britain and France. In 1960, 5 percent of the British population owned about 75 percent of the wealth of Britain.

COLD WAR CRISES

Each international crisis between the Soviet Union and the United States took on great significance because scientists had developed weapons of mass destruction many times more powerful than those that had leveled Hiroshima and Nagasaki. During the 1950s, children in the United States participated in mock air raid drills, putting their heads between their knees to practice bracing for the shock of a nuclear explosion, as if such a position would make the slightest difference in the case of a nuclear attack. The United States and the Soviet Union drew up plans to evacuate American and Soviet leaders into elaborate shelters from which they could order the launching of more missiles and bombs. Plans followed to evacuate civilians from urban centers. Britain and France had nuclear weapons in the late 1950s and early 1960s, respectively. And so did China, although its capacity to employ them seemed uncertain. In the 1970s, Israel, probably India, and perhaps Pakistan as well, gained nuclear capability.

The Cold War focused on a series of crises that, drawing world attention, exacerbated tensions between the United States and the Soviet Union. The Soviet Union claimed that the Western Allies had unilaterally broken the agreements reached at the Potsdam Conference. In July 1948, Soviet troops blocked routes through the German Democratic Republic in order to prevent Allied planes, trucks, and cars from reaching Berlin, thus isolating its western half from supplies. The Allies began an airlift to West

The U.S. airlift to Berlin, 1948–1949.

Chinese children read intently from the works of Chairman Mao.

Berlin; in some periods, planes landed in Berlin every three minutes. After secret negotiations, Stalin backed down, allowing trucks to roll through the German Democratic Republic beginning in May 1949. Berlin remained divided between East and West.

The Cold War came to Asia, as well. Japan's defeat left China divided between the nationalist government of Chiang Kai-shek (1887–1975), which held the south, and the forces of the Communist leader Mao Zedong (1893–1976). In the civil war that followed, Mao's Communist forces gradually pushed the nationalist forces out of China. In full retreat by 1949, Chiang Kai-shek's army occupied the large island of Formosa (Taiwan). There Chiang established a government that claimed to represent all of China. On the mainland, Mao proclaimed the People's Republic of China. The Soviet Union quickly recognized the new, giant Communist state, while the United States recognized the nationalist government of Taiwan as China's legitimate government.

Riots in East Germany in 1953 and what became a full-scale insurrection in Hungary in 1956 revealed mounting dissatisfaction in Eastern Europe against Communist rule. In each case, armed Soviet intervention drew scathing Western denunciations. The arms race between the United States and the Soviet Union heated up. In 1961, the Soviets and the German Democratic Republic tried to stem the tide of East Germans leaving East Berlin for the West by constructing a wall between the zones, making escape an often deadly undertaking. In 1962, U.S.-Soviet relations reached a dangerous nadir when American aerial photographs revealed the presence of Soviet nuclear warheads in Cuba, whose Communist leader was Fidel Castro (1926–   ). The crisis, which brought the two superpowers dangerously close to nuclear war, was diffused when Soviet leader Khrushchev agreed to remove the missiles. U.S. involvement in a protracted struggle between South Vietnam and Communist North Vietnam further strained U.S.–Soviet relations. In the meantime, the Soviet Union and China, once allies, had gone their own ways, as they competed with each other for the allegiance of newly independent Third World states. However, with Leonid Brezhnev (who had helped force out Khrushchev in 1964) in power in the Soviet Union, there seemed little hope in the late 1960s for any significant reduction in Cold War tensions.

The Korean War

After the confrontations between the West and the East in Germany came the first Cold War crisis outside of Europe. China had been divided into Communist and Nationalist states, supported respectively by the Soviet Union and the United States. Similarly, Korea had a Communist "people's republic" in the north, supported by the Soviet Union, and in the south, a republic created under the patronage of the United States.

In June 1950, North Korean troops invaded the southern zone. General Douglas MacArthur took command of the U.S. armies defending South Korea, backed by small forces sent by other members of the United Nations, which had passed a resolution condemning the Communist invasion. For the first time (with the exception of events in Greece), Communist and non-Communist forces engaged in open warfare, a conflict fought with conventional weapons, but with the risk of nuclear bombs lurking in the background.

Although Chinese troops were aiding the northern side, U.S. forces pushed back the Communist forces in 1951. In any case, neither side wanted to see the war expand beyond Korea. A peace settlement left the division between North and South Korea almost the same as before the war, but at the cost of 3 million casualties (including 140,000 U.S. troops killed and wounded).

Because of Chinese participation and Russian support for North Korea, the Korean War heightened Cold War tensions in Europe. To the Allies, the war raised the outside possibility of a Soviet-led invasion of the German Federal Republic. In the United States, the war contributed to a mood of anti-communism that bordered on mass hysteria, carefully orchestrated by Wisconsin Senator Joseph McCarthy. "McCarthyism" entered the dictionary as a term for political name-calling and persecution. In Europe, the Cold War undermined Socialist parties, most of which had been bitter enemies of the Communist parties during the inter-war years, a rivalry that continued in the post-World War II era.

Stirrings in Eastern Europe

Following Stalin's death in 1953, East German workers, whose trade unions were powerless in the face of state control, grumbled loudly about high quotas, low wages, and food shortages. On June 17, 1953, Berlin workers rioted, led by construction workers after production quotas had been again raised without commensurate compensation. East German troops, backed by Soviet tanks, ended the disturbances, and a wave of repression followed. That year alone, more than 330,000 East Germans fled to the West.

The East German Communist government realized that state planning had to provide more consumer goods. Ideology alone could not generate commitment. The Soviet Union sent material assistance to the German Democratic Republic and let it write off most of the war reparations owed from the eastern zone. Despite inadequate housing, an insufficient number of automobiles, and occasional food shortages due to poor planning, more consumer goods gradually became available in the 1960s.

Long rows of drab apartments sprang up near the Brandenburg Gate that divided East and West Berlin. State-sponsored clubs for children provided recreation, as well as ideological inculcation. Through intensive training and programming—and, in some cases, steroids—East Germany began (though not until the late 1960s) to produce athletes of great accomplishment in international sporting events, particularly in swimming and track and field.

Khrushchev's denunciation of Stalin and the "thaw" in foreign and domestic policies had repercussions in Eastern Europe in 1956. In March 1956, the Polish Communist government began to rein in the secret police and amnesty thousands of political prisoners. However, strikes in June led to military repression. In October 1956, Wladislaw Gomulka (1905–1982), a moderate imprisoned during the Stalin era, was selected to head the government by the Polish Politburo. A reformer, Gomulka purged Stalinists, amnestied thousands of political prisoners, and reached accommodation with the Polish Catholic Church. Furthermore, Gomulka halted the collectivization of agriculture in his country. Independent peasants held three-quarters of arable land, a far greater percentage of privately held farms than in any other country in the Eastern bloc. However, Gomulka also reassured the Soviet Union that Poland had no intention of abandoning the Warsaw Pact or turning its back on socialism.

Soviet concessions to Yugoslavia (represented by Khrushchev's Twentieth Party Congress speech) and to Poland encouraged a movement for reform in Hungary, where liberal Communists were already eager to turn their backs on Stalinism. Imre Nagy (c. 1895–1958), a liberal, had risen to become prime minister of Hungary. He had sought to move Hungarian industry away from Stalinist imperatives, including the emphasis on heavy industry (one consequence of which would be to increase production of consumer goods). He also tolerated peasant resistance to the implementation of agricultural collectivization. In 1955, Nagy's policies drew opposition from Communist hard-liners, and he was ousted from office. A profound movement for reform now took root in Hungary. Intellectuals and students held meetings to discuss possible paths to liberalization. A hard-line response from the new prime minister led to a demonstration of 50,000 people on October 23, 1956, at which protesters smashed a statue of Stalin. Police opened fire on a crowd trying to storm a radio station. But Hungarian troops sent to rout the demonstrators refused to fire, in some cases joining those now protesting communism itself. That night, the Hungarian Communist leadership requested Soviet assistance but also named Nagy as prime minister in the hope of ending the demonstrations. Western radio broadcasts into Hungary hinted that outside help might be forthcoming and firmed popular resolve. Nagy named a new coalition government that included liberal Communists. He began to negotiate with the Soviet government, but made clear that he intended to end the one-party system by adding several non-Communists to his government. Furthermore, he called for Hungarian independence from the Warsaw Pact and asked that Soviet troops be withdrawn from his country.

To the Soviet government, Hungary's defection was unthinkable because it might spark similar movements in other Eastern European nations and destabilize the republics of the Soviet Union. On November 4, Nagy announced that Hungary would withdraw from the Warsaw Pact.

Stalin dethroned during the Hungarian uprising of 1956.

While the French, British, and U.S. governments were preoccupied with the Suez Canal crisis, the Soviet government, after first withdrawing its troops beyond the Hungarian border at the end of October, sent soldiers and tanks into Budapest and other major Hungarian cities to crush Hungarian resistance. Nagy, who had been refused asylum by the Yugoslav embassy, was tried and executed, along with about 2,000 other people. More than 200,000 Hungarians fled to Western Europe and the United States. Soviet intervention ended hope that Stalin's death might bring about change in Eastern Europe and end the Cold War. János Kádár (1912–1989) became Hungary's new leader, backed by Soviet military strength. Over the long run, Kádár actually liberalized the Communist regime, while remaining careful not to antagonize unnecessarily the Soviet Union with any ideological justification for his policies. Hungary's "goulash communism" included market-oriented, decentralized reforms, and toleration of some degree of entrepreneurship. The result was a higher standard of living than existed elsewhere in the Communist world.

With their hands full with Hungary, the Soviets were in no position to move aggressively against Poland. In any case, Gomulka was careful to give them no excuse for military action (for example, he never proclaimed a "Polish road to socialism"). He gradually rescinded some of the relatively liberal policies, including toleration of free artistic and political expression, and put workers' councils that had sprung up in 1956 under party control. In the meantime, Poland remained economically dependent on the Soviet Union.

In Yugoslavia, despite its determined independence of the Soviet Union, open political opposition was not tolerated. One of the distinguished founders of post-war Yugoslavia, the Bosnian intellectual Milovan Djilas (1911–1995), was expelled from the party in 1954 for having contended in his book *The New Class: An Analysis of the Communist System* (1961) that privileged party officials had become a ruling caste with little in common with ordinary people.

The liberal agitation in Poland and the Hungarian Revolution in 1956 threatened Khrushchev's authority in the Soviet Union. Stalinists claimed that Khrushchev's attack on Stalin at the Twentieth Congress was to blame for agitation in those countries. Furthermore, Soviet aid to stabilize its Eastern European client states undermined economic development at home. But, at the same time, the failure of the Western powers to intervene on behalf of Hungary (because they feared nuclear war with the Soviet Union) seemed to the Soviets to legitimize the division of Europe into spheres of influence dominated by the United States and the Soviet Union.

Soviet-U.S. Tensions

Khrushchev was responsible for a mild thaw in the Cold War. In 1955, the Soviet leader, who wanted to improve relations with the West, met with

COME UP
AND SEE
ME
SOMETIME

POOCHNIK

U.S.
MISSILE
PROGRAM

SNAFUS

INTER-
SERVICE
RIVALRIES

COMPLACENCY

SALISBURY

DOG DAZE

Russia's second satellite in 1957 carried a dog into space.

U.S. President Dwight Eisenhower (1890–1969) in Geneva, the first of the "summit" meetings between the two Great Powers. At the Twentieth Party Congress, he rejected Stalin's contention that inevitably Communist and capitalist powers would go to war and now claimed that "peaceful co-existence" was possible between the two political worlds. Soviet foreign policy entered a less contentious and somewhat more flexible period. Looking to the Third World for allies, the Soviet leader courted India, Egypt, and Syria, as well as a number of smaller states, winning their friendship with technical and material assistance. Soviet foreign policy was carried out with the aim of detaching countries from the direct influence of the United States.

As Soviet armed intervention in Hungary in 1956 increased mutual suspicion between East and West, rapid advances in Soviet military science further increased tension with the West. In October 1957, the Soviets launched the first space rocket (*Sputnik*), after developing an intercontinental missile. Space exploration became part of the Cold War. The race to the moon, won by the United States when American astronauts landed on the lunar surface in July 1969, reflected the Cold War. Bilateral negotiations between the Soviet Union and the United States to reduce their respective nuclear capabilities failed in 1955 and again in 1958. When Nikita Khrushchev visited the United States in 1959, he provocatively told Vice President Richard Nixon, "We will bury you!"

In May 1960, the Soviets shot down a U-2 American plane taking spy photos from high over the Soviet Union. The Soviets demanded an apology for this violation of Soviet air space and received none. Khrushchev then refused to participate in a Geneva summit meeting (perhaps also because Soviet relations with China were rapidly deteriorating).

In Europe, Berlin lay divided between Soviet and Western zones of occupation. The United States, Britain, and France still refused either to recognize officially the G.D.R.'s existence or to leave West Berlin. In 1958, the hot-tempered Khrushchev threatened to take over the administration of all of Berlin, but backed down in the face of Western intransigence. In the meantime, streams of East Germans—about 2.6 million people between 1950 and 1962—continued to leave for the West, most to the Federal Republic. (Between 1950 and 1964, perhaps 500,000 West Germans moved to the East, some fleeing persecution of Communists in the German Federal Republic, and others simply wanting to be with their families in the East. But this number pales when compared to the number of Germans who moved from East to West.) The exodus included many doctors and other trained specialists vital to East Germany. During the first half of August 1961 alone, more than 47,000 people fled to the West.

On August 17, 1961, Berliners awoke in the morning to find East German workers building a wall to divide the eastern sector from the western. Ground floor windows that permitted escape from East to West were boarded up. Telephone lines leading to West Berlin were cut.

The Berlin Wall became a symbol of the Cold War. American President John F. Kennedy visited Berlin later that summer to view the wall, proclaiming that he, too, was a "Berliner" (not realizing that a *Berliner* was also a popular name for a sweet pastry). Some escape attempts over the

(*Left*) The Berlin Wall goes up in 1961. (*Right*) U.S. President John F. Kennedy addresses Berliners, 1961.

wall or through official checkpoints ended in a hail of bullets and sudden death. Even with a subsequent relaxation of East German controls, which allowed Germans on both sides to visit their relatives, guards checked car trunks and even the bottoms of cars looking for hidden passengers trying to escape. Western tourists climbed stairs strategically placed in West Berlin to view the East German guards staring across from watchtowers and barbed wire on the other side. Still, people tried to escape and many succeeded: they sprinted across no-man's-land, swam across rivers, flew small planes or homemade balloons into West Germany, dug tunnels, and hid in trucks and cars. Some did not make it, and hundreds were killed attempting to escape.

Because of the threat of nuclear war, the Cuban Missile Crisis of 1962 was the world's most dangerous moment since the end of World War II. Cuba, which had been a virtual protectorate of the United States since the Spanish-American War in 1898, became a Communist state in 1959 after Fidel Castro led a guerrilla attack that succeeded in ousting the corrupt American protégé, Fulgencio Batista (1901–1973). Batista's supporters, with the help of the U.S. military, launched an ill-conceived invasion at the "Bay of Pigs" in 1961 that failed miserably. In October 1962, American aerial photographs revealed that Soviet missiles capable of being armed with nuclear warheads were stationed on the island of Cuba. The U.S. government demanded the removal of the missiles and threatened to destroy them if this demand was not met. Some knowledgeable advisers to President John F. Kennedy estimated the chances of the outbreak of a nuclear war at between one-third and one-half, dangerous odds indeed.

(*Left*) Soviet leader Nikita Khrushchev and Cuban leader Fidel Castro meet in Moscow, 1963. (*Right*) U.S. Ambassador to the U.N. Adlai Stevenson reading a statement to Security Council members as an aide points to the location of Soviet missiles in Cuba.

Debates in the United Nations helped buy time while negotiations proceeded. The world breathed a collective sigh of relief as Khrushchev ordered the missiles removed, a Soviet defeat.

In 1963, Khrushchev seemed to be more inclined to negotiate at the disarmament conference in Geneva. In contrast, the U.S. government seemed determined to hold the line against concessions to the Soviets. The Soviet negotiating team at the conference stormed out in anger. Khrushchev banged his shoe on the table for emphasis while denouncing the United States at the United Nations.

Despite the fact that the United States and Soviet Union both signed a 1963 treaty banning nuclear tests, the arms race accelerated. Soviet and American naval vessels and submarines closely monitored each other's movements. Both sides used spies and informers, not only in the "enemy" camp, but in neutral countries as well. The Soviet secret police (K.G.B.) and the American Central Intelligence Agency (C.I.A.) spread their well-financed spy networks worldwide. Periodic spy scandals occurred in the West, most notably in Britain, where several prominent intellectuals turned out to have been spying for the Soviet Union. The growing number of colonies receiving their independence from Britain and France fostered increased competition between the two systems in Africa and Asia.

By the mid-1960s, the rivalry between the United States and the Soviet Union spread to Southeast Asia. In 1964, the United States officially became involved in the civil war in Vietnam. When President Lyndon B. Johnson (1908–1973) announced that an American naval vessel had been attacked off the coast of Vietnam (which in fact never occurred), the American Congress passed the so-called "Tonkin Gulf Resolution" against the North Vietnamese government. The United States committed more and more men and material in support of the South Vietnamese government against the North Vietnamese troops of Ho Chi Minh, and their allies, the Vietcong guerrillas fighting in the south. As in Greece after World War II and in the Korean War, the Soviets backed the Communist forces. The costly American role in the civil war came under increasing opposition at home and in Europe, particularly from university students. The Vietnam War badly divided public opinion in the United States and strained U.S. relations with its allies.

Sino-Soviet Rivalry

The alliance between Mao's China and the Soviet Union, cemented by the Korean War, began to break apart. A common Communist ideology could not gloss over issues of power politics between the two giants. Not only did they share an immense frontier, but certain border regions, above all Mongolia, had long been claimed by both nations. Khrushchev's turn away from Stalinism angered Mao Zedong, the Chinese Communist leader, as did the Soviet leader's overtures for support among Asian political leaders.

A "cult of personality" focused in China on Chairman Mao as that in the Soviet Union had focused on Stalin. In particular, Soviet initiatives to India threatened Chinese relations with the subcontinent. Furthermore, attempts to modernize China's traditional subsistence economy had been heavily influenced by Stalin's five-year plans, which had emphasized heavy industry, while at the same time proceeding with the rapid, ruthless collectivization of all industrial and agricultural production. Moreover, Chinese economic growth would certainly make the Chinese less dependent on Soviet technical advisers.

The Chinese government grew increasingly uneasy about Russia's nuclear capability. Mao believed Stalin's contention that war between capitalism and socialism was inevitable. He resented the unwillingness of the Soviets, who had abandoned that particular tenet of Communist thought, to share their military secrets with their Chinese counterparts. Khrushchev's attempts to relax tensions with the West—and particularly his visit to Washington in 1959—irritated Mao, who used the perceived threat from the West as a means of pushing the Chinese to make more sacrifices to modernize the economy. Numerous Soviet technical advisers in China were sent home. In 1964, Mao accused the Soviet Union of itself being an "imperialist" power because it dominated the smaller states of Eastern Europe.

Chinese and Russian diplomats and advisers now competed as rivals for the ears of Third World leaders. The Chinese Communists received support from an unlikely place. Albania, the small, backward, largely Muslim state squeezed between Yugoslavia and the Adriatic Sea, also broke with the Soviet Union, denying the Soviet claim that Moscow should be the center of communism. The Albanian voice in Europe, Radio Tirana, praised Mao and Chinese socialism while denouncing the Soviet Union for revisionism. However, Albanian Communist leader Enver Hoxha (1908–1985) broke with the Chinese Communist leadership in 1978, criticizing China's improved relations with the United States.

The Brezhnev Era

Soviet economic stagnation and the humiliation of the Cuban Missile Crisis contributed to Khrushchev's sudden fall from power in 1964. Some military leaders had opposed Khrushchev's support of economic planning that emphasized consumer goods over heavy industry. However, despite Khrushchev's cocky assurances that the Soviet Union would within four years produce more meat, milk, and butter than the United States, severe shortages further alienated many Soviet citizens. Old Stalinists surfaced again, resistant to any reform. The army, wary of the Chinese situation, accused Khrushchev of taking too great a risk by establishing missile sites in Cuba. In October 1964, Khrushchev returned to Moscow for a meeting called by his enemies only to find out that he was being retired into honorable obscurity.

Medium-range Soviet strategic missiles taking part in a May Day military parade in Moscow on November 7, 1963, in a Soviet show of strength.

Leonid Brezhnev (1906–1982), who had risen in the Communist Party bureaucracy with Khrushchev's assistance, became general secretary of the Communist Party. Brezhnev, far less impulsive than Khrushchev, returned to Communist orthodoxy. He affirmed the authority and prestige of party bureaucrats and of the K.G.B., but he stopped well short of Stalinism. While building up Soviet military capability, the Soviet leader ordered an increase in the production of consumer goods. Nonetheless, centralized planning and agricultural collectivization remained the basis of the inefficient and technologically backward Soviet economy.

There was little talk of a "thaw" either inside or outside the Soviet Union during the Brezhnev era. Cynicism mounted within the Soviet Union, even among committed Communists who had long awaited the day when the corner would be turned and socialist prosperity would arrive. That day never came.

CONCLUSION

In many ways, the Cold War defined the history of Europe—and of the United States, China, and many other states—for four decades following World War II. The ideological and power struggles between the Soviet Union and the United States greatly affected the political histories of each state. This was also true of the smaller Eastern European states dominated by the Soviet Union. The rivalry between the two Great Powers and their allies strongly influenced the political life and foreign policies of the Western Europe states, as well as those of the emerging states of the Third World. Western colonization receded before movements for national independence.

Europe's place in international affairs declined markedly, although the emerging partnership between France and the German Federal Republic became the cornerstone of Europe in the post-World War II era. Superpower competition between the Soviet Union and the United States made European powers less important in the world. So did the surging economic strength of Japan and the rise of China as a Great Power. Many of the dramas of international politics shifted to the Third World—to the Middle East and Southeast Asia, above all, but also to Africa and Latin America. The decline of Britain as a Great Power was itself symbolic: the sun finally set on the British Empire as its colonies became independent states. At the same time, by the late 1960s, a massive influx of Asians and Africans from desperately overcrowded colonies and then new nations had begun to arrive in Western Europe, where they sought a better life.

CHAPTER **30**

THE EMERGENCE OF CONTEMPORARY EUROPE AND THE COLLAPSE OF COMMUNISM

After almost two decades of growing prosperity and relative political and social calm, domestic political conflict erupted in Europe—above all, in France—and the United States in 1968. The social, political, and cultural revolts centering on that year seemed to pit young people, especially students, against those entrenched in power. Many "baby boomers" born after the war saw their revolt as one of an entire generation against its elders. They blamed them for a world that seemed unresponsive to demands for social justice and change on behalf of the underprivileged and the oppressed. Many felt alienated (a word then much in vogue) from materialistic, industrial, bureaucratic society, and even from the universities where they studied. Feminism, too, was a significant undercurrent during the protests of 1968, but then largely remained a movement of middle-class intellectuals and students.

Demonstrations and protest brought political reaction. The turmoil in France ended amid government repression and a conservative show of force. Demonstrations subsided elsewhere in Western Europe, although they continued to grow in the United States. In Western Europe, conservative or centrist parties dominated the governments of Britain, the German Federal Republic, and Italy for most of the 1970s and 1980s, while the Socialists held power in France between 1981 and 1995. And, in Southern Europe, democratic rule came to Portugal, Spain, and Greece.

1351

Adulation of Mikhail Gorbachev in Stuttgart, West Germany, for his bold moves of reform and liberalization in the Soviet Union.

A period of détente between the United States and the Soviet Union in the 1970s was followed by a chill as a result of Soviet intervention in Afghanistan in 1979. Then in 1989, dramatic change occurred in Eastern Europe. Mikhail Gorbachev, the leader of the Soviet Union, had in the mid-1980s undertaken a dramatic series of reforms liberalizing the economy and political life in the Communist state. His bold moves encouraged further demands for liberal reform, as well as stimulating nationalist movements in the Soviet Union's republics. The impact was soon felt in Eastern Europe. As campaigns for liberalization started up again in Poland and Hungary, it became clear that the Soviet leadership would not intervene to crush reform. Furthermore, Gorbachev made it clear that he viewed reform in Eastern Europe as desirable.

Not only in Poland and Hungary, but also in the other countries of Eastern Europe, movements for reform forced Communist leaders to accommodate the emerging political opposition, overwhelming one Communist regime after another. These revolutions ranged from the "velvet revolution" in Czechoslovakia to the violent overthrow of Nicholae Ceausescu in Romania, until there were no Communist regimes left in Eastern Europe (though in Bulgaria, Romania, and Albania, former Communists retained power). The fall of communism was achieved through a remarkably peaceful process of change in most of Eastern Europe. However, in 1989, Yugoslavia began to break apart in a cacophony of ethnic hatred generated by the very question that the polyglot state's creation after World War I ultimately had failed to resolve: the national question. Civil war raged in Bosnia. Finally, the Soviet Union itself collapsed in 1991. The American official George Kennan's prediction in 1947 that the Soviet system "bears within it the seeds of its own decay" turned out to be correct.

POLITICS IN A CHANGING WESTERN WORLD

During the late 1960s, a loosely connected movement for political and social change swept across university campuses in a number of Western countries. Based largely but not exclusively in the surging generation of baby boomers born after World War II (in the United States, the student age population increased from 16 million in 1960 to 26 million in 1970), the youth revolt challenged long-established hierarchies, party politics, and even consumerism. From Berkeley, California, to Paris, Berlin, and Amsterdam, students protested against American involvement in the Vietnamese civil war, where, despite government claims of a high-minded struggle against communism, the United States seemed to be supporting a corrupt political regime against determined nationalists, albeit Communists. In the United States, particularly, the movements of the sixties were closely tied to the civil rights movement, as students protested against social injustice and racism. In France, student demonstrations, insurgency, and strikes shook the country. Demonstrations also rocked Italy, West Germany, and other Western European countries.

Between 1979 and 1982, liberal or left-wing governments fell in Britain and the German Federal Republic. The economic recession that had begun in 1974 generated considerable dissatisfaction with governments of the left. In each case, succeeding conservative governments cut back on public spending and sharpened anti-Soviet rhetoric. In France, too, a Socialist government elected in 1981 had to reverse its initial policy of expanding government spending and instead begin reducing expenditures.

The Western European states began to turn away from U.S. foreign policy domination. European governments no longer automatically accepted U.S. Cold War rhetoric, which had encouraged the arms race. They reasoned that if the two superpowers went to war, the battlefields (in conventional warfare) or the targets (in case of "limited" nuclear warfare) would be in Europe. Thus, a groundswell of popular opposition emerged in 1983 in the German Federal Republic and Britain, in particular, to NATO's planned deployment of new nuclear missile systems on European soil.

Student Protests Challenge Gaullist France

In the spring of 1968, demonstrations began in Paris against the rigidity of the French university system, which largely remained the preserve of the elite. Intellectual ferment was heightened by the opposition of intellectuals and students to American participation in the war in Vietnam. In France, students rebelled against those in political power, inequality, and

(*Left*) Students battling police in the streets of Paris, May 1968. (*Right*) A counter-demonstration by the well-dressed.

even modern technology, which seemed dehumanizing. Graffiti in the Latin Quarter (where students attended the Sorbonne) proclaimed, "Comrades, the Revolution is daily, it is a *fête* [festival], an explosion."

Early in May 1968, a student radical, Daniel Cohn-Bendit, was expelled from the University of Paris. To protest, students, joined by young faculty members, occupied university buildings at the Sorbonne. After the police entered the university and began arresting students, the demonstrators fanned out and were joined by most of the rest of the student body. Several students were killed and hundreds injured when police attacked hastily improvised barricades.

Unlike in the United States, where most workers found student demands too radical and many supported U.S. participation in the war in Vietnam, many French workers took to the streets in support of the students. A general strike began on May 13 in protest against police brutality. It became the largest wave of French strikes since 1936. Strikers demanded raises, rights of self-management, and better working conditions. Union organizations and the Communist Party, which had considerable influence among industrial workers, had little to do with the movement. The tail seemed to be wagging the dog. If anything, trade union and Communist leaders tried to bring the movement under their control in its first days. Gaullist Prime Minister Georges Pompidou (1911–1974) hurriedly returned from a state visit to Afghanistan to confront the growing crisis.

After assuring himself of the loyalty of French army units stationed in Germany, President Charles de Gaulle dissolved the National Assembly on May 30 and announced that new elections would be held on June 23. Gaullists organized counter-demonstrations in support of the government, capitalizing on the hostility of many middle-class citizens and peasants in traditionally conservative regions to the turmoil in Paris. The strike movement ebbed, in part because the government and many private companies agreed to raise the wages of workers. This left the students standing alone. De Gaulle dismissed Pompidou as prime minister, but his government survived.

While de Gaulle won what amounted to a referendum on his rule, his towering presence seemed increasingly anachronistic. Speeches about national "grandeur" rang hollow as French influence in the world declined. De Gaulle's answer to a general crisis of confidence was to call for more "participation" in the political process, as a way of expressing French "national ambition," which he believed was slipping away. "The French think of nothing but increasing their standard of living," he once complained. "Steak and French fries are fine. A family car is useful. But all that does not add up to national ambition." In 1969, the president announced a national referendum on local administrative reform. This seemed an unlikely issue for de Gaulle, who believed in a strongly centralized state and cared little about regional liberties (he once asked rhetorically how one could rule a country with several hundred different kinds of cheese). De Gaulle lost what turned into a plebiscite on his government. The general curtly announced his retirement from political life, and withdrew for the final time to his village in eastern France.

The contentious year 1968 brought student demonstrations and riots to Italy, as well, and these protests found some support among workers. The University of Rome had been built to accommodate 5,000 students and that year enrolled 60,000 students. Thousands of university graduates were frustrated because they could not find jobs. But, unlike the initial movement in France, the Italian students found no support from workers, and the movement quickly collapsed.

Shifts in Western European Politics after 1968

During the 1970s, a decade of improved relations between the Western powers and the Soviet Union, European domestic politics underwent a shift from the right to centrist governments. This change was most apparent in the German Federal Republic and Britain (where Labour was in power from 1974 to 1979), but also in France, where the Gaullist government was replaced by a centrist government. In Italy, the social upheaval and strikes of 1968 and 1969 generated further political instability, although the Christian Democrats, forming a series of center-left coalition governments, continued to dominate Italian politics.

Following waves of student protest in the German Federal Republic, Social Democrats first bucked the European tide and came to power in 1969. They were helped by an alliance with the centrist Free Democrats, who abandoned their Christian Democrat allies. Willy Brandt (1913–1992), who had fled Nazi Germany and fought with the Norwegian resistance during the Second World War before becoming mayor of Berlin, took office as chancellor. While echoing his predecessors' commitment to NATO, Brandt improved relations with the German Democratic Republic, meeting with East German leaders, and calling for an "opening toward the East." In 1970, Brandt signed a non-aggression pact with the Soviet Union, paving the way for the development of trade between the two states. With an eye toward entering formal relations with Poland, he signed the Treaty of Warsaw, which established the frontier between Poland and East Germany as redrawn after the war. Furthermore, Brandt succeeded in establishing normal relations—at least as much as possible given the circumstances—with East Germany. Brandt thus moved to resolve the remaining diplomatic and territorial disputes in Central and Eastern Europe after World War II, while remaining solidly in the Western bloc.

Brandt's coalition of Social Democrats and Free Democrats drew bitter opposition from the Christian Democratic right and the Christian Social Union, an extremely conservative party based in Bavaria, led by Franz-Joseph Strauss, a controversial rightist who believed that Germans should not suffer any guilt complex for the crimes of the Nazis. Although Brandt's government undertook liberal reforms by increasing welfare payments and aid to education, the left wing of the Social Democratic Party demanded still greater attention to those Germans suffering from the economic slump of the mid-1970s.

Brandt resigned in 1974 following the discovery that one of his aides was a spy for East Germany. Helmut Schmidt (1918–　　), a more conservative Social Democrat, became chancellor. Schmidt weathered subsequent political storms, but drew the wrath of environmentalists and anti-nuclear groups in 1979 when he asked the United States to station medium-range nuclear missiles on West German soil to counter similar Soviet missiles. Economic recession, rising unemployment, and Schmidt's refusal to reduce welfare payments (alienating the Social Democrats' coalition partner, the Free Democrats), led to the return to power in 1982 of the Christian Democrats. They were led by Helmut Kohl (1930–　　), with the support of the Free Democrats and Strauss' Christian Social Union. Kohl cut taxes and reduced government spending. Thus, the Christian Democrats continued to dominate the political life of the German Federal Republic.

In Britain, under the pressure of the oil crisis and following bitter mining strikes, the economic recession helped bring down the Conservative government in 1974. But the subsequent Labour governments of Harold Wilson (1916–1995) and James Callaghan (1912–　　) were buffeted by soaring inflation, exacerbated by a series of major union victories in prolonged strikes during the Callaghan government.

Upper- and middle-class Britons turned against Callaghan, claiming that the unions now held their country hostage. In 1979, Conservative leader

A caricature of the Thatcher years.

Margaret Thatcher (1925–   ), the daughter of a prosperous grocer from the English Midlands, became prime minister. She was the first woman to hold the position (although she vociferously repudiated feminism).

Mrs. Thatcher was committed to ending completely the government's role in industry and to slashing government expenses. The Conservative government eliminated some of the health and education measures Labour had implemented. Mrs. Thatcher, who earned the sobriquet "the Iron Lady," sold off nationalized industries, reduced inheritance and capital taxes, and waged war against the trade unions. Without government subsidies, many factories closed down. By 1983, Britain's 3 million unemployed workers (more than 12 percent of the workforce) received reduced unemployment benefits. Cuts in housing subsidies left hundreds of thousands without adequate places to live.

Mrs. Thatcher retained the support of the upper and middle classes, and even that of a segment of the working-class population—"Tory workers" who proudly displayed pictures of the royal family in their modest residences. Conservatives were thus able to weather the storms of a floundering economy.

In May 1982, the government of Argentina, seeking to reverse a decline in its popularity at home, invaded the Falkland Islands. Although the British occupied the sparsely populated islands, which lie about 300 miles from the coast of Argentina in the Atlantic Ocean, Argentina had claimed them since the nineteenth century. British forces, benefiting from superior military technology, easily recaptured the Falklands. The short war encouraged a burst of patriotism, boosting the prime minister's standing at home. Furthermore, the British economy began to recover in the early 1980s as inflation slowed down.

With the Conservative Party in power, the Labour Party became increasingly divided between radicals and reformers. The creation of the small Social Democratic Party (allied with the Liberal Party) added to the disarray on the left. Mrs. Thatcher and the Conservatives rolled to another impressive victory in the general elections of 1983. However, fearing the revival of the Labour Party, Conservative leaders unseated Mrs. Thatcher in 1990, replacing her with the colorless John Major (1943–   ) as prime minister.

In France, the centrist Valéry Giscard d'Estaing (1926–   ), a technocrat committed to economic modernization, was elected president in 1974. However, both the economic crisis that began in 1973 and financial scandals tarnished Giscard d'Estaing's image. In 1981, the pragmatic Socialist François Mitterrand (1916–1996) was elected president, drawing on a wide spectrum of support.

Undertaking the nationalization of large corporations and more banks and initiating ambitious social reforms, Mitterrand faced determined opposition from the business community. The French franc floundered on the international currency market, as wealthy people began to remove their assets from France. A year after taking office, the Socialist government was forced to devalue the franc and freeze prices and wages. Pressure from the right mounted from the Gaullists and their ambitious leader, Jacques Chirac (1932–   ), the mayor of Paris. The inability of the Socialist government to revive the economy undercut its popularity, as did its anticlerical educational measures.

In the 1986 elections for the Chamber of Deputies, the right triumphed, leading to an awkward period of government known as "cohabitation." This required Mitterrand to select a rightist premier, Chirac, and ministers drawn from the right and center. The new government sold off some nationalized banks and businesses, ended wage and price controls, and sold one television station to private interests. Cohabitation worked fairly well, in part because Mitterrand and Chirac shared similar views on some aspects of foreign policy.

Given a slight majority in the elections for the National Assembly in 1988, Mitterrand appointed Socialist prime ministers, but the right swept into office with the legislative elections of 1993. When his second term ended in 1995, Mitterrand had become the longest serving head of state in France since Napoleon III. Chirac was elected president in 1995. He began his presidency by authorizing the resumption of French nuclear testing in the South Pacific, leading to considerable international opposition, particularly in Australia, New Zealand, and Japan. Facing a high unemployment rate and a growing economic deficit that threatened to undercut the value of the French franc should the European Union initiate a common currency, in November 1995 Prime Minister Alain Juppé announced reductions in health, retirement, and other benefits, sparking strikes that lasted a month, forcing the government to make some concessions.

In Italy, political instability continued to characterize political life. In some ways, Italy remains what Austrian Prince Metternich called it well before national unification in the nineteenth century—a "geographical expression." Despite a general increase in prosperity, inflation and high unemployment left many Italians still dissatisfied with all political parties. A 1970 European survey reported that 72 percent of Italians were "highly" or "completely" dissatisfied with their democracy. Union militancy increased in the face of intransigence from employers and the state.

A seemingly endless series of financial scandals worsened the reputation of Italian politicians, particularly Christian Democrats. A vicious cycle operated: as the Christian Democratic Party lost popular esteem because of what seemed to many to be corrupt practices, it became increasingly obliged to dispense such patronage to obtain votes.

The government of Bettino Craxi (1934–   ) from 1983 to 1986 was the longest and in many ways most stable of the post-war period. Socialists replaced the Communists as Italy's second largest party, forcing the Christian Democrats to accept them as coalition partners in 1986. Craxi himself was convicted of corruption and fled in 1993 into exile in Tunisia; Giulio Andreotti (1919–   ), Christian Democrat prime minister on six different occasions, stood accused not only of corruption, but of authorizing the murder of a journalist who had uncovered evidence of wrongdoing. More than 2,500 Italian politicians and businessmen were arrested for corruption in an eighteen-month period. Campaigns against the Mafia have been periodic (including, most vigorously, following the assassination in 1992 of a public prosecutor who had devoted himself to the difficult legal war against the Mafia). Irritated by what its members considered unnecessary expenditures by taxpayers in northern and central Italy to keep the south afloat, a separatist Northern League emerged in the early 1990s with a stridently anti-government platform, calling even Italian political unity into question. Cynicism and mistrust of politicians has become even more common in Italy, as in other countries.

In every Western country, a new political force began to be felt. "Green" parties, political groups of militant environmentalists angered by the deterioration of the environment, emerged in Western Europe during the 1980s. The "Greens" had a single issue—the environment. In the German Federal Republic, Greens were alarmed by industrial pollution, which was slowly killing their country's forests. Environmental parties stridently opposed nuclear power, even before the Soviet nuclear disaster at Chernobyl in Ukraine in 1986. Their votes proved pivotal in a number of local elections, and they won twenty-seven seats in the German parliamentary elections of 1983. Furthermore, environmentalists protested that virtually uncontrolled tourism was taking a great ecological toll, largely because of the litter and pollution generated by hundreds of thousands of campers,

A nuclear power plant dwarfs a more traditional source of power.

particularly in and around rivers, seas, and oceans. Greens in France and other countries have helped push for agreements that have led to some cleaning up of the Rhine River and Mediterranean beaches.

Finally, in almost all Western states, economic slumps have accentuated complaints that state-subsidized programs are too expensive. In Sweden and Denmark, two welfare states, Social Democratic parties were ousted after decades of rule by conservatives calling for sharp reductions in the tax rates that financed cradle-to-grave social programs. With the recession of the early 1990s reducing tax revenue, Western European governments have tried to reduce social benefits—for example, by reducing unemployment payments.

The Transition to Democracy in Southern Europe

During the 1970s, three Southern European dictatorships underwent a process of democratization: Greece, Portugal, and Spain. Greece, the cradle of democracy, had been controlled by a series of right-wing governments since its civil war of the late 1940s. In 1967, military officers seized power, ruthlessly crushed dissent, imprisoning and even torturing political opponents. The military dictators planned to seize the Mediterranean island of Cyprus, which lies off the coast of Turkey and which both Greece and Turkey had claimed for centuries. Cyprus, which gained independence from Britain in 1960, has a majority of Greeks but also a sizable Turkish minority. Bitter disagreements over the form of a new constitution led to fighting between Greeks and Turks. The Greek Cypriot National Guard overthrew the government of Cyprus. Meanwhile, the Cypriot Turks defeated the Greeks and declared the northeastern, predominantly Turkish part of the island to be independent. Further fighting ended in a cease-fire, and the former government returned to power.

Meanwhile, in Greece, the government of the Greek generals, which had not sent help to the Greek Cypriot insurgents, collapsed, and Greece became a republic. The country's major problems remained a relatively undeveloped, inefficient economy dependent on tourism, and hostile relations with Turkey.

In Portugal, Antonio Salazar, dictator since 1932, died in 1970. His authoritarian successors struggled inefficiently with economic backwardness. Thousands of Portuguese went abroad as seasonal workers each year or emigrated to Western Europe (especially to France) or to the Western Hemisphere. At the same time, the dictatorship was determined to hold on to Portugal's African colonies at all costs. The Portuguese army became entangled in a long, bitter war with nationalist rebels in its African colony of Angola, a conflict that Portugal could neither afford (at the annual cost of half the nation's budget) nor win. In April 1974, a group of liberal army officers overthrew the dictatorship. The Socialist Party emerged victorious in elections the following year and overcame an attempted coup d'état by the Communists. Despite a sometimes bewildering series of governments, the Portuguese transition to democracy occurred without bloodshed.

In Spain, General Francisco Franco survived as dictator long after his friends Hitler and Mussolini had gone to their graves. After World War II, the United Nations had considered imposing sanctions against Spain because of Franco's support of the Axis powers, but U.S. influence prevented this. Franco maintained Spain's authoritarian political structure. His police kept the left at bay, while he undercut the political challenge of other conservative groups—monarchists, Falangists (a fascist group dating to the 1930s), the army, and the Catholic Church (particularly its militant lay organization, Opus Dei). Trade unions and political parties remained illegal. Franco would accept economic modernization, but not if it served as a Trojan horse for secular values, which he vehemently opposed.

In the late 1960s, opposition to Franco's regime mounted in Catalonia and the Basque country, Spain's most industrial regions, each with a strong separatist movement. Franco struck hard against Basque and Catalan separatists; the Catalan language, for example, remained illegal in print. But Franco retained popularity in traditionally religious regions, such as Navarre and his native Galicia.

Franco agreed that Juan Carlos (1938–), the son of the heir to the throne before the civil war, would succeed him as head of state. The general assumed that following his death, Spain would remain an authoritarian country. Within the Spanish government, however, many officials already believed political reform inevitable, even desirable. Socialist and Communist parties existed in fact, although they were illegal. Government censorship itself had become more lax in the 1970s.

In 1975, Franco died after a long illness. Juan Carlos became king, and to the surprise of many people, including Franco's disciples, accepted the transformation of Spain into a constitutional monarchy with a democratic political structure. Spain emerged from authoritarian rule and international isolation. The government foiled several subsequent plots by rightists to overthrow the republic, including the invasion of the Spanish Parliament by gunmen who briefly held members hostage in 1978.

Spectacular economic growth and increasing prosperity helped the centrist Adolfo Suarez (1932–   ) keep a series of governments afloat through skillful political negotiation, even without a parliamentary majority. But Suarez's party lost support because some of its leaders had loyally supported Franco. The charismatic Felipe González and the Socialists swept Suarez aside, winning an overwhelming victory in the 1982 elections and emerging victorious again in 1989.

Catholicism in Modern Europe

Like the nations of Western Europe, the Catholic Church, for centuries a major force in European life, had to respond to pressures for change. It retained considerable influence in much of Europe, particularly Italy, Spain, Portugal, and Ireland. Yet, these countries legalized divorce, despite ecclesiastical opposition. In France, most Catholics depended on the Church only for life's basic rites of passage: baptism, first communion, marriage, and burial, and thus they were known as "four-wheel Catholics," for the carriages identified with each ceremony. There were fewer priests and nuns than ever before, and they were older. Only about 12 percent of French Catholics regularly attend Sunday Mass.

Within the Catholic Church, a strongly liberal current developed in response to some of the social problems of modern life. "Worker-priests" entered factories in the 1950s, trying to win back workers to the Church, while supporting their demands for better working conditions, until the pope condemned the movement. The election in 1978 of the smiling, more liberal Pope John XXIII signaled a new direction, marked by the opening of dialogue with other religions. Pope John presided over a council (Vatican II) that undertook significant changes in Church practices (allowing the Mass to be said in local languages) without altering dogma.

Pope John's successor Paul VI continued the move toward ecumenism, visiting Istanbul and Jerusalem to meet with leaders of the Eastern churches. But several notable theologians who challenged Church doctrine drew the wrath of Rome. In 1978, Paul died, as did his successor, John Paul I, after only two months on the throne of Saint Peter. The puffs of smoke rising from the Vatican chimney then announced the first non-Italian pope since the sixteenth century, the Polish-born Pope John Paul II (Karol Wojtylà; 1920–   ). While remaining extremely conservative on matters of faith and doctrine, the new pope travelled far and wide across the world, calling for social justice while visiting Latin America, Asia, Africa, the Soviet Union, and the United States. He became a symbol of hope for millions of oppressed people. Yet, at the same time, the pope frustrated liberal Catholics who demanded the end of papal interdiction of contraception and who wanted the ordination of women and more active support of the rights of the poor.

The European Community and the European Union

As politics in the countries of Western Europe shifted between left and right, the need for coordination in both economics and politics became apparent to farsighted leaders. To this end, the European Community (EC) was created in 1967, when the European Atomic Energy Community, the European Coal and Steel Community (ECSC), and the European Economic Community (the EEC, or European Common Market) merged their organizations. The original members were Belgium, France, West Germany, Italy, Luxembourg, and the Netherlands (see Map 30.1). The government of Great Britain had first been disinclined to join the European Economic Community, fearing the flooding of its internal market by less expensive agricultural produce. But after British voters overwhelmingly approved their country's application for membership, Britain joined the EC in 1973, after twice having been rejected by virtue of France's veto. Also joining in 1973 were Denmark and Ireland. Moreover, Greece joined in 1981, and Spain and Portugal in 1986. The EC subsidizes farmers (such subsidies accounted for half of its annual budget in 1995) and some favored industries and transfers money from wealthier northern states, notably Germany and France, to poorer members like Greece and Portugal.

The EC eliminated troublesome tariffs, which aided the most efficient producers, who were able to specialize and sell their products easily beyond the borders of their country. But it put less efficient producers at a disadvantage. The Danish dairy industry profited greatly from sales of milk and cheese to other member countries, as did their French counterparts in Normandy; but dairy farmers elsewhere often found that they could not compete with more efficient producers. Vintners producing cheap wine in southern France protested the importation of even cheaper Italian wine by blocking roads at the frontier, and had bitterly opposed the entry of Spain into the EC for the same reason.

Jacques Delors (1925–   ), the French president of the European Community's Executive Commission, led the campaign for a unified Europe unburdened by wrenching national divisions that could undercut the EC's economic clout in the face of Japanese and U.S. economic strength. The EC represents a potential economic union of states with a greater combined population than that of the United States. Eventual political union could make Western Europe a Great Power in itself, with more independence from American influence.

The Treaty of Maastricht was signed in that Dutch city in 1992 by the twelve members of the European Community and most of the seven nations of the European Free Trade Association (Austria, Iceland, Liechten-

ICELAND

FINLAND
1995

NORWAY

SWEDEN
1995

ESTONIA

RUSSIA

LATVIA

NORTH
SEA

DENMARK
1973

BALTIC SEA

LITHUANIA

RUSSIA

IRELAND
1973

BELARUS

GREAT
BRITAIN
1973

NETH.

1990

POLAND

BELG.

GERMANY

ATLANTIC
OCEAN

LUX.

UKRAINE

CZECH
REP.

SLOVAKIA

MOLDOVA

FRANCE

SWITZ.

AUSTRIA
1995

HUNGARY

SLOVENIA

ROMANIA

CROATIA

YUGOSLAVIA

BOSNIA-
HERZEGOVINA

PORTUGAL
1986

SPAIN
1986

ITALY

ADRIATIC SEA

BULGARIA

MACE-
DONIA

ALB.

GREECE
1981

MEDITERRANEAN SEA

EC members, 1970

Subsequent members
(with date joined)

0   400 miles

0   400 kilometers

MAP 30.1 MEMBERS OF THE EUROPEAN COMMUNITY   The original six members of the European Community—France, West Germany, the Netherlands, Belgium, Luxembourg, and Italy—were later joined by Denmark, Great Britain, the Irish Republic, Spain, Portugal, and Greece.

stein, Sweden, Finland, and Switzerland; the seventh member state, Norway, who in the early 1970s had turned down membership in the EC, rejected the treaty). The treaty anticipated the creation of a European Economic Area, providing for the elimination of national barriers to the movement of capital, goods and services, and people between member states. It established greater coordination of government planning from Brussels (the location of EC headquarters) and planned the future use of a common currency (a plan vigorously opposed by British Conservative "Euroskeptics," at least partially out of fear that Germany's strong economy and currency would dominate the other EC members). In 1993, the designation European Union replaced that of European Community, reflecting the hope that ultimately European political unification and a common foreign policy and security might be achieved. Anticipation of a possible common currency spurred government efforts to control national deficits, leading, as in the case of France, to protests and strikes from unions.

Although a growing number of respondents reported to pollsters that they considered themselves to be "European," the European Union engendered not only feelings of ambivalence toward supranational economic and political organizations but also a stridently nationalist response, as in the case of some British Conservatives. Within many countries, strong opposition emerged to what some viewed as the ceding of sovereignty (as well as operational costs) to bureaucrats working for the European Parliament in Brussels, who established strict guidelines for agricultural producers (for example, on procedures for producing cheese). Yet, the inauguration of a single European currency—the "euro"—by 1999 remains possible.

ECONOMIC GROWTH AND LIMITS

Worldwide economic developments accentuated the globalization of the world economy, marked by increasing interdependence of trade and technology. Furthermore, rapid technological developments in communications—above all, the television and the computer—seemed to shrink the scale of the world. The importance of oil to the world economy significantly enhanced the geopolitical importance of the Middle East. However, the Arab oil embargo of 1973 against the Western powers helped generate an international economic recession, one that would have significant political implications in Western countries.

Prosperity and Mass Culture

The fast-paced "American way of life" began to exert a growing attraction on European business and consumers. Television, radio, computers, and billboards promoted material comfort. Some first believed that the quest for material comfort might erode what they considered Western Europe's

A McDonald's restaurant next to a shopping center in a Paris suburb.

moral stature, although they were attracted by the relative affluence of American society. Europeans gradually discovered American "management techniques," using them in both business and government. Thus, French technocrats trained in the Grandes Écoles, the most prestigious schools in France, began to take their place in the 1950s in the highest government circles, espousing efficiency at all costs.

With increased prosperity, American consumerism and popular culture gained even more influence in European societies. By the late 1970s, McDonald's and then Burger Kings had begun to dot European capitals and gradually smaller cities as well, despite becoming far more expensive than their American counterparts. In the 1980s, Euro-Disney (now called Disneyland-Paris), which one French theatrical director called "a cultural Chernobyl" (referring to the nuclear accident in Ukraine in 1986), opened its doors outside of Paris, although for the first several years it lost money.

The rapid rise of international tourism offers another example of economic globalization in the post-World War II era, as well as a result of increased prosperity and more leisure time. In particular, the advent of the "jumbo jet" in the late 1960s increased the number of passengers that could be squeezed into a single plane, reducing the cost of tickets. The era of the "charter flight" began. The French and British governments collaborated on the development of the supersonic Concorde, which, in the late 1970s, began to fly a small number of extremely wealthy passengers from Paris and London to New York and Washington in three hours and fifteen minutes, less than half the time of a regular jet. The railroad equivalent of the Concorde—and a far greater economic success—was the French

"Train of Great Speed" (T.G.V.), which carries passengers at speeds well over 150 miles per hour in comfort. Air travel beyond Europe and rail travel within the continent helped take millions of vacationers each summer to new and exciting places. Tourists from the United States and, in the 1980s and early 1990s, from Japan, arrived in Europe in droves. In 1994, the "Chunnel" opened, linking France and Great Britain by trains running under the English Channel.

Each July and August, millions of Western Europeans began to take to the road, the majority heading toward the sunny beaches of Southern Europe. They were joined by American tourists who found European prices inexpensive in the 1960s and 1970s and horribly expensive by the late 1980s. Crossing international borders became routine, and beginning in 1993 the European Union made most border stops obsolete.

Paid vacations became an expected part of the "good life." Tourism became essential to the economies of the sunny Mediterranean countries, above all, Spain, visited by millions of people each year, but also Italy, France, Portugal, and, until its demise in 1991, Yugoslavia. The Soviet Union (and with the disappearance of the U.S.S.R., Russia) also began to welcome tourists and the Western currency they brought with them. Gradually cars with Hungarian, Czech, and Polish licenses began for the first time to appear with more frequency in Western nations.

Oil and the Global Economy

The Six-Day Arab-Israeli War of 1967 and the 1973 Yom Kippur War both resulted in easy Israeli victories over their Arab rivals. Israel expanded its territory, absorbing Jerusalem, a Holy City for Christians, Jews, and Arabs, and occupying Arab land on the West Bank and in the Gaza Strip. Western support for Israel, particularly that of the United States, was matched by Soviet support for the Arab states and for the stateless Palestinian people. An embargo by the oil-producing Arab states of the Middle East (undertaken by the Organization of Petroleum-Exporting Countries, or OPEC) in 1973 had disastrous consequences for the economies of Western nations, particularly in Europe, which was more dependent on Middle Eastern oil than was the United States.

The Arab oil embargo interrupted the supply of oil from the Middle East. It led to a rapid rise in the price of oil and contributed to the high inflation that undermined Western economies for the rest of the decade. Dependency on oil led states to urge people to consume less gasoline (for example, by encouraging greater use of public transportation and, in the United States, by reducing speed limits). Britain and Norway each began to extract oil in the stormy North Sea. European countries, especially France, had already begun to develop nuclear installations to generate more energy.

The oil embargo contributed to the high rates of unemployment that plagued most Western European states (although they fell in the mid-

1980s), particularly in Spain (20 percent unemployment in the mid-1980s) and France (12 percent in 1995). It also was one of the sources of the economic recession that gripped Western Europe from the mid-1970s to the mid-1980s. High taxes helped European gasoline prices remain approximately three times what they are in the United States.

Changing Contours of Economic Life

Since World War II, the economic transformations in Europe have engendered several major social changes. First, the jobs available to workers have changed radically. The percentage of population working the land has declined sharply, even as peasants began to organize and demand government action on their behalf when their incomes stagnated. Moreover, the proportion of industrial workers, particularly in Western countries, has gradually declined because of remarkable changes in assembly-line production leading to a need for fewer workers; because of the continued growth of service industries, for example in response to increased travel and tourism, and of white-collar work in general; and because of the computer revolution of the 1970s and 1980s, which has accentuated the above changes. Second, in the post-war era, women in every country have entered the workforce in greater numbers than ever before. Third, since the 1970s foreign workers have come to play a greater role than ever before in the economies of Western states.

As the global market increasingly determined agrarian success or failure, beginning in the 1950s Western European peasants started to join organizations to lobby for assistance and favorable tariffs. Peasants blocked traffic in Rome and Paris with tractors and farm animals to protest government policies; in Brittany in the late 1970s, they filled the courtyard of a prefecture with artichokes to protest low prices. Ironically, this phenomenon has come at a time when peasants, because of the rural exodus in Western Europe, have lost most of their political voice.

In Western Europe, more middle-class women have entered the labor force. At the same time, the number of female university students has risen dramatically, and so has the number of women in the professions. Women received legal protection against job discrimination in England in the late 1960s, and in France the government created a Ministry for the Status of Women. In Communist countries, women more easily entered the medical profession, but men dominated the state bureaucracies. Women were most successful in reaching rough equality in the Scandinavian countries, least so in the Mediterranean lands where traditional biases remained more difficult to overcome.

In the decades following World War II, the status of women gradually improved, although unequally across the continent. In Western countries, the important contribution of working women made it difficult to continue to deny half the population the right to vote. Women in France received the vote in 1945. Women probably were more equal in the countries of the Soviet bloc (where there were no free elections) in terms of employment opportunities, although in practice this often meant that they bore the dual burden of wage earning and domestic duties. While women lost some skilled jobs to men returning from service after the war, economic expansion and the creation of ever more white-collar jobs (for example, in travel agencies and department stores) provided new employment possibilities. In the Soviet Union and Sweden, women made up more than half of all employees, and more than a third in every European country.

Beginning in the late 1960s, foreign-born "guest workers" made up an increasing proportion of the workforce in every Western European state. Europe now has an estimated 15 to 18 million foreign workers who hope to share in its prosperity. The ethnic composition of this workforce varies from country to country. For example, many Turks have settled in Germany because of the relative proximity and historically close ties between Turkey and Germany; immigrants from former French colonies in West Africa and especially North Africa, along with Portuguese immigrants, account for a considerable proportion of immigrant workers in France. In Switzerland, foreign workers make up 17 percent of the workforce; in France, they make up about 8 percent of the population. Many of these workers, recruited before the economic recession of the mid-1970s, stayed on in leaner times. While many became permanent residents of the countries where they worked (and some became citizens), they were increasingly joined by hundreds of thousands of illegal workers.

Immigration has become potentially one of the most explosive problems Western European governments now face. When economic recession sharply reduced the number of available jobs, the political tide began to turn against foreign workers. Right-wing political parties (above all, the National Front in France) increasingly adopted anti-immigrant stances; xenophobia (particularly in Germany) generated intolerance and violence against foreign workers, as the welfare budgets of the various states sagged under the additional strain. In Britain, the devastating social effects of economic decline have been particularly felt in Manchester, Liverpool, Sheffield, Leeds, and other northern manufacturing cities of the nineteenth-century Industrial Revolution. Riots by—but also against—immigrants (principally Indians, Pakistanis, and West Indians, many of whose families had migrated to Britain in the 1960s) rocked several industrial cities and East London. While some foreign workers have been assimilated in their countries of residence, many have not and have maintained the customs of their homelands. This has often put the younger generation of foreign workers, born in their countries of residence, in the uncomfortable position of being excluded from the mainstream of life where they reside, and not wishing to return to their parents' country of origin.

THREATS TO PEACE

Post-war Europeans have lived to some extent under the shadow of several considerable threats to peace. First and foremost, the enormous nuclear arsenals of the Soviet Union and the United States, as well as Britain and France among the latter's European allies, made the possibility of any armed conflict between East and West potentially catastrophic. However, the 1970s brought a period of détente between the Soviet Union and the United States, leading to serious negotiations between the two powers to reduce nuclear arms. While the threat of nuclear war seemed remote, terrorism posed an increasing threat in Western Europe, as extremist political groups and Islamic fundamentalist groups launched attacks. Moreover, ethnic and religious conflicts burst out in several countries, including violence between Catholics and Protestants in Northern Ireland, separatist movements in Spain, and the struggle between Serbs and Albanians in the Yugoslav province of Kosovo.

Nuclear Weapons and Tensions between the Superpowers

The phased U.S. withdrawal from Vietnam beginning in 1973 (followed two years later by the victory of the North Vietnamese and their allies, the Vietcong) removed one thorny issue between the two superpowers. Continued tension between the Soviet Union and China (marked by a concentration of Soviet forces along the disputed borders in Manchuria and Siberia) gradually eroded the old U.S. view of communism as a monolithic force, engendering more realistic diplomatic assessments of international politics. Furthermore, the Western powers and the Soviet Union faced daunting economic problems that partially shifted the focus of government to domestic concerns.

In 1972, Soviet leader Brezhnev and U.S. President Richard Nixon had signed an arms reduction agreement known as SALT (Strategic Arms Limitation Talks) I, by which they agreed to maintain parity in nuclear offensive weapons systems. However, as military technology continued to advance rapidly, both sides began to defy the spirit of the agreement by developing new systems. Following Nixon's disgrace and resignation as president in 1974 because of the Watergate Affair (Nixon had approved illegal operations against Democratic headquarters and various other dirty tricks, and then lied about what he knew), the U.S. government sought to link further arms reduction talks to Soviet progress in human rights. In June 1979, President Jimmy Carter stressed support of human rights in his foreign policy. He and Brezhnev signed a new agreement, SALT II, by which the Soviets agreed to limit missile launchers and nuclear warheads and the United States agreed not to develop a new missile. Carter, however, had to withdraw the agreement from consideration by the Senate in January 1980 because of political opposition, primarily from conservatives who feared that SALT II would leave the Soviets with greater nuclear capability than that of the United States.

The period of détente ended with the Soviet invasion of Afghanistan in December 1979 in support of the pro-Soviet government besieged by a variety of rebels, including Islamic fundamentalists. (One of the motives of the Soviet invasion of Afghanistan was to forestall fundamentalist movements in Soviet republics with sizable Muslim populations.) Reacting to the Soviet invasion, the United States limited grain sales to the Soviet Union and boycotted the Olympic Games in Moscow in 1980. Soviet involvement in Afghanistan took a great toll in lives and costs on Soviet society. The Soviet-American chill lasted into the mid-1980s.

Terrorism

During the 1970s and 1980s, in the wake of the failure of the political movements of 1968, small groups on the extreme left and right turned to political terrorism. Violence seemed to them the only means of destabilizing elites in the hope of taking power. Some terrorist groups were militant nationalists seeking independence from what they considered foreign occupying powers. Such groups included factions within the Irish Republican Army committed to ending British rule in Ulster, militant Basque separatists (E.T.A.) seeking independence from Spain, and Kurdish rebels launching periodic attacks in Turkey.

Political terrorists struck most often in Italy. Between 1969 and 1982, they killed at least 1,119 people, the most notorious incident being the bombing of the railroad station of Bologna in 1980 by fascists in which 85 people died. In the early 1970s, left-wing extremists (comprising perhaps as many as a hundred separate groups) launched deadly attacks. Unlike rightist terrorists, who struck out randomly, seeking to create a climate of fear that they hoped would bring a right-wing coup, leftist extremists began to attack prominent political and business leaders. The most well-organized and probably the largest of these guerrilla groups, the Red Brigades, founded in 1970, kidnapped and killed former premier Aldo Moro in 1978. But by the early 1980s, Italian terrorism had ebbed, the campaigns at political destabilization having failed.

In the German Federal Republic, small groups of left-wing terrorists lashed out with bombings, bank robberies, kidnappings, assassinations, and even a plane hijacking. The most notorious of these groups, the Baader-Meinhof gang, had links to terrorist groups in France and other Western countries. Several of their members were captured and imprisoned.

Other extremists also undertook terrorist acts in Europe. Attacks included the massacre of Israelis at the 1972 Olympic Games in Munich and the seizure of a cruise ship in 1985. Terrorists who were thought to be receiving support from the governments of Iran, Iraq, Syria, or Libya

Police discover the body of the Christian Democrat leader Aldo Moro, killed by the Red Brigades in 1978.

staged several attacks in the mid-1980s, particularly in France. In the most deadly attack, a terrorist bomb in 1989 blew up a U.S. passenger jet over Scotland. In 1995, an Algerian Islamic fundamentalist group claimed responsibility for placing on subways and underground trains in Paris several bombs that exploded during rush hour, killing or maiming innocent people.

Islamic fundamentalist groups based in the Middle East have been active recruiting adherents in European states that have large concentrations of Muslims. Thus, the continued rise of Islamic fundamentalism has had repercussions in Europe, most notably in France. Moreover, the case of the Indian writer Salman Rushdie also reflects the reach of fundamentalism: in 1989, Iran's leader Ayatollah Khomeini condemned him to death and placed a price on his head for alleged blasphemy in his novel *The Satantic Verses* (1988). Rushdie was forced into hiding to avoid being killed.

Religious and Ethnic Divisions

Compared to the sixteenth, seventeenth, and eighteenth centuries, religious conflicts have diminished in modern Europe. However, in Northern Ireland, the bitter centuries-old rivalry between Catholics and Protestants generated fighting and terror. Although the Catholic Republic of Ireland had obtained its independence in 1922, Northern Ireland (Ulster) is primarily Protestant (two-thirds of the population) and remains part of Britain. The Irish Republican Army, claiming to represent Ulster Catholics, struck at the British army and Protestants alike. Several weeks of disturbances in 1969 unleashed decades of violence. Secret Protestant paramilitary organizations, claiming that the British army inadequately protected Protestants, struck back against Catholics.

The economic crisis of the 1970s compounded Northern Ireland's problems, making Catholics even more disadvantaged compared to Protestants. The I.R.A., buying guns on the world weapons market with money stolen from banks or contributed by sympathetic Irish Americans, struck not only in Northern Ireland but also periodically in England. In 1988, after the British army gunned down several members of the I.R.A. in Gibraltar, two incidents symbolized the tragedy of Northern Ireland. Protestant gunmen from an Ulster paramilitary force hurled grenades and shot at mourners at a Catholic funeral for I.R.A. members; and at the subsequent funeral for one of the Catholics who had been killed, mourners dragged two British soldiers from their car and murdered them. In 1994, the Irish Republicans agreed to a cease-fire, and for the first time in many years, hope surfaced that a political solution to one of Europe's oldest religious and national conflicts was possible.

In the West, the claims of ethnic minorities, "nations without states," surfaced in several countries. Some German speakers in the Italian Tyrol

The aftermath of the explosion of a bomb planted by the Irish Republican Army in Belfast, Northern Ireland, 1972.

wanted their territory to be included in Austria. Spanish Basque separatists, sometimes hiding in the French Basque country, moved across what they considered an arbitrary frontier to attack Spanish government, army, and police installations. Popular support for the separatists in the Spanish Basque region waned in the 1980s, but the Spanish Socialists who were now in power proved no more successful in resolving such claims of autonomy than had been the Franco regime. In France, small separatist movements existed in Brittany, where leftists planted a harmless bomb or two before government offices; in Alsace, where the few separatists were linked to right-wing German extremists; and in the French south, where there was a smattering of left-wing "Occitan" separatists, as well as a few who dreamed of a monarchist restoration. In Great Britain, Scottish nationalists won 30 percent of the votes in the 1974 elections, but thereafter their total fell off rapidly.

Two world wars and the loss of millions of people did not end problems stemming from unresolved questions and claims based upon nationality. Nowhere was this more dramatically evident and more tragic than in Yugoslavia, where the national question remained a major source of disharmony. Tensions persisted between Serbs and Croats, the country's two largest ethnic groups. They shared a common spoken language (though the Serbs use the Russian Cyrillic alphabet and Croats the Latin alphabet). Yugoslavia's capital, Belgrade, was also that of Serbia. Serbs enjoyed disproportionate influence in the Communist state bureaucracy. Muslims were a majority in Bosnia, but many Serbs and Croats also lived there, and intermarriage was common. Yet, Yugoslavs lived in relative peace during the years of Communist rule.

Regional disparities in economic development and prosperity compounded Yugoslav ethnic divisions. In the north, the republic of Slovenia, which was by far the most ethnically homogeneous of Yugoslavia's republics, enjoyed a standard of living not far below that of her neighbors, Italy and Austria. In the south, the republic of Macedonia remained backward and relatively impoverished. Adjacent to Albania, the territory of Kosovo was largely peopled by ethnic Albanians who were Muslims. Yet, the minority Serbs there and in Serbia viewed Kosovo as sacred Serb soil, because the Ottoman Turks had defeated them there in 1389. The rivalry in Kosovo between the ethnic Albanians and the Serbs who had settled there after World War II (in Kosovo, Serbs and their Montenegran allies accounted for only about 15 percent of the population) turned violent on several occasions in the 1970s and 1980s. At a minimum, ethnic Albanians claimed the right to be the seventh Yugoslav republic.

Other countries in Eastern Europe were not immune to national tensions, despite official ideology holding that such rivalries were irrelevant in Communist societies. Hungarians living in Romania deeply resented their minority status. Many Greeks, left by chance on the Bulgarian side of the frontier after World War II, or in Albania, were unhappy with their lot. In the Soviet Union, ethnic nationalism surfaced in many of the republics, particularly in the Baltic states of Lithuania, Estonia, and Latvia, which the Soviet Union had absorbed during World War II and where a sizable Russian minority now lived. In Ukraine, nationalists kept their movement alive with poetry and literary manuscripts in Ukrainian, passed from hand to hand.

THE FALL OF COMMUNISM

In 1975, the leaders of European states gathered in Helsinki, Finland, to sign the Helsinki Accords, which concluded the first Conference on Security and Cooperation. All European states, with the exception of the small, isolated Communist state of Albania, signed the accords, which recognized as valid the national borders drawn up after World War II. The thirty-five signatories also pledged to respect human rights and to cooperate in economic and scientific matters. To some critics, the Helsinki Accords seemed to recognize Soviet domination of Eastern Europe since the war. To other observers, they were a significant step forward because the heads of Communist states agreed to respect human rights. The accords seemed a healthy pause in the renewed tension between East and West.

Hardly anyone at the time could have anticipated the fact that fourteen years later, communism would collapse in Eastern Europe, nor that in 1991 communism would fall in the Soviet Union, which would disintegrate in turn. As Mikhail Gorbachev undertook reform in the Soviet Union in an attempt to save the Communist state, communism in Eastern Europe collapsed abruptly in 1989 (see Map 30.2). It took ten years in Poland, ten months in Hungary, ten weeks in East Germany, ten days in Czechoslovakia, and ten hours in Romania, almost in inverse proportion to the size and effectiveness of opposition to Communist rule within each Eastern European country. However, the euphoria, arising from the realization that the Cold War had suddenly ended, proved to be brief. New challenges and problems, among them those that had beset Europe for centuries, presented themselves. Decades of Communist rule had prevented the emergence of alternate political organization. Civil society in each country remained seriously undeveloped. The difficulties of changing from planned economies with varying degrees of collectivization to free market economies would prove extremely difficult and disruptive. At the same time, long-simmering ethnic conflicts, above all in Yugoslavia but also in Romania, Hungary, Czechoslovakia, and Bulgaria, have complicated the fall of communism.

Eastern Europe and the Soviet Shadow

Calls for change echoed loudly in Communist Czechoslovakia in 1968. Intellectuals and writers accused the Communist Party leadership of clinging to Stalinism. The party leadership, as well, acknowledged the need for

MAP 30.2 THE FALL OF COMMUNISM IN EASTERN EUROPE AND THE SOVIET UNION, 1989–1991   With the fall of communism came the reunification of Germany and the break-up of the Soviet Union.

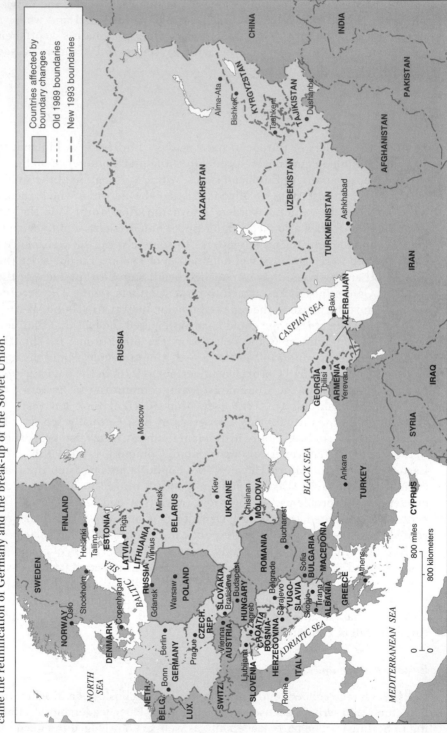

change. In January 1968, party leaders named Alexander Dubček (1921–1992), a liberal Slovak, to be first secretary of the Communist Party, and thus head of state. During the "Prague Spring," Dubček tried to implement "socialism with a human face" by implementing reforms but as he did so he glanced anxiously over his shoulder toward Leonid Brezhnev's Soviet Union. Crucial to these reforms was a democratization of decision making and greater freedom of expression. But, as in the case of Hungary in 1956, the Soviet leadership feared that, despite Dubček's assurances to the contrary, Czechoslovakia might attempt to move away from the Warsaw Pact. On August 21, Soviet tanks and troops moved rapidly across the border, rolling into Prague. They brutally put an end to the Prague Spring.

The Soviet invasion initiated another chill in Soviet-Western relations. Furthermore, the Communist parties of Italy and France criticized the invasion, and a number of intellectuals in those countries abandoned communism. In the mid-1970s, Western Communist leaders, particularly in Spain and Italy, began to call themselves "Eurocommunists." Accepting the fact that the Western nations had taken different paths of historical development than had the Soviet Union, they stressed their own independence, for example by collaborating with Socialists and other left-wing parties. However, Eurocommunism proved unable to slow the decline in membership in and influence of the Communist parties of Western Europe, although the Communist Party of Italy remained strong.

Under the "Brezhnev Doctrine," the Soviet leadership tried to justify the invasion of Czechoslovakia and the possibility of future intervention in any of the satellite states of Eastern Europe. For almost two decades following the Soviet invasion of Czechoslovakia in 1968, the countries of

(*Left*) Communist leaders meet shortly before the Russian invasion of Czechoslovakia. Participants include Walter Ulbricht and Erich Honecker of East Germany (first two on left), and Soviet Communist Party chief Leonid Brezhnev conferring with Premier Alexei Kosygin (first two on the right). (*Right*) Warsaw Pact armies occupy Prague, 1968.

Eastern Europe suffered stifling domination by their Communist parties, backed by the Soviet Union. With the exception of Albania, which remained closed to virtually all foreign contact during the rigid dictatorship of Enver Hoxha, only Yugoslavia retained real independence. (The "Yugoslav experiment" comprised a mixed economy that combined state-owned and private enterprise.)

Opposition to Russian influence and to Communist rule mounted in all of the East European states during the 1980s. The overwhelming economic failures of the Communist regimes grew ever more apparent, particularly in comparison with the standard of living in Western states. Well-developed social services could not compensate for economic inefficiency and massive demoralization.

Only two years after the Soviet invasion of Czechoslovakia, massive unrest led to strikes in Poland. The following years brought increasingly vocal and organized political opposition. Edward Gierek (1913–   ), who became First Secretary of the Polish United Workers' (Communist) Party in 1970, made some political concessions while attempting to stimulate economic growth. However, despite foreign loans and credits, by 1976 Poland again had lapsed into economic stagnation. In 1980, strikes and riots in protest of living conditions spread rapidly in industrial areas, particularly in the vast shipyards of Gdansk. Solidarity, a new, independent, illegal organization of trade unions, gained 10 million members. It was led by Lech Walesa (1943–   ), an electrician from Gdansk. The Catholic Church (whose influence became even greater with the election in 1978 of John Paul II, a Pole, as pope) helped mobilize opposition to the Communist government. In response, the Polish government agreed to tolerate the creation of new unions as long as they did not engage in political activity, and thereby challenge the Communist Party.

In September 1980, the Communist Central Committee responded to the ongoing crisis by forcing Gierek to resign as head of state. Two months later, the government officially recognized Solidarity's existence. However, accommodation between the government and the non-Communist trade unions did not last long, particularly after Solidarity members called openly for free elections. In December 1981, General Wojciech Jaruzelski (1923–   ), the new head of state, imposed martial law and replaced some key Communist Party officials in government with military officers. He suspended Solidarity and put hundreds of leading dissidents under arrest, including Lech Walesa. During this period, a priest active in Solidarity was murdered by the police. Troops brutally crushed strikes that broke out in response to the repression. In 1982, the government declared Solidarity illegal again, although martial law ended a year later. But Poland was stuck in the quicksand of economic stagnation, and the regime's opponents remained organized and active beneath the surface.

East Germany, Bulgaria, and Czechoslovakia were the Eastern European nations that were most loyal to the Soviet Union. The German Democratic Republic's chief, Erich Honecker (1912–1994), who came to power in 1971, proved as intransigent to reform as his predecessor Walter Ulbricht. The Lutheran Church provided a center for some dissidents, organizing weekly "prayers for peace" in Leipzig. A sizable peace group formed in the early 1980s. In Czechoslovakia, the one state in Eastern Europe that had remained a democracy during the inter-war period, the state campaign against dissidents was more intense. Unlike Poland, opposition in Czechoslovakia was limited to students, intellectuals, artists, and clergy. In 1977, about 1,200 writers, philosophers, intellectuals, and musicians signed a protest against government limitation of freedoms in an attempt to force the government to respect the Helsinki human-rights convention it had signed. Despite the fact that this was anything but a revolutionary document (those who signed pledged not to engage in political activity), the members of the "Charter 77" group faced repression, political trials, and harassment, and were prevented from holding good jobs.

Gradual economic liberalization helped make Hungary the most free and the second (after the German Democratic Republic) most prosperous of the Eastern bloc countries. The gradual development of a market economy and a private agricultural sector helped stabilize the Communist regime, while Soviet subsidies aided the Hungarian economy.

In Hungary, which also manifested little economic growth in the 1980s, the Communist leadership tolerated limited organized political opposition. In 1985, Hungary became the first Communist state to declare political pluralism to be an ideal. However, unlike Poland, Hungary had no organized and tested opposition force such as Solidarity.

In sharp contrast, there was no liberalization of any kind in Romania. Nicolae Ceausescu (1918–1989), head of the Communist Party, had brazenly adopted a position of relative independence, or "national communism," with respect to the Soviet Union, criticizing the Soviet invasion of Czechoslovakia, remaining neutral in the Sino-Soviet conflict, and refusing to participate in Warsaw Pact maneuvers. But Romania paid for its attempt to maintain its independence. While the Soviet Union had assigned Bulgaria and Romania the role of concentrating on agricultural production for the Eastern bloc nations, Ceausescu had forged ahead with grandiose plans to generate industrial development. The results were disastrous. Romania became, after Albania, the poorest country in Europe, while caught in the increasingly mad grip of Ceausescu's "cult of personality." The dictator ordered the destruction of 1,500 villages in Transylvania (largely in areas where many Hungarians resided), as well as much of old Bucharest to forge enormous boulevards that would lead to his reviewing stand.

The Gorbachev Era

Soviet leader Leonid Brezhnev reinforced the powers of the oppressive Soviet bureaucracy (with the motto "trust in cadres") and the prestige of the army and the K.G.B. (the secret police). Reflecting the chill in relations with the United States, the Soviet Union, like its rival, poured more money into the manufacture of arms. Brezhnev, whose hands were so shaky in his last years that he had to eat with a spoon at a state dinner, died in 1982.

Brezhnev's successor as general secretary of the Soviet Communist Party (and thus as head of state) was Yuri Andropov (1914–1984), who, despite his long years in the K.G.B., was somewhat more liberal than Brezhnev. Unlike his predecessor, Andropov acknowledged that there was widespread inefficiency and corruption in Soviet economic planning and government. He called for greater popular participation in economic decision making, and purged incompetent party hacks from important positions. But in 1983 Andropov suffered a heart attack, and until his death early the following year could only hope that the mild reforms he had begun would have some effect. Andropov's successor, Konstantine Chernenko (1911–1985), had been a Brezhnev aide and was more in the Brezhnev mold than Andropov. Chernenko was seventy-three and chronically ill when he came to power, however, and both he and the Soviet state treaded water until his death in March 1985.

Mikhail Gorbachev (1931–   ) succeeded Chernenko as general secretary of the Communist Party and head of the Soviet Union in 1985. Born in southern Russia, Gorbachev had worked his way up in the party youth organization and studied law at the University of Moscow. Both his grandfathers had been arrested on false charges during the Stalin era while he was a boy. Gorbachev had become secretary of the Communist Central Committee and assumed responsibility for Soviet agriculture. Less instinctively xenophobic than other Soviet leaders, he was the first Soviet leader since Lenin to have earned a university degree. Charming, flexible, and determined, Gorbachev was a master of Communist Party machinations. When he received a medal at a televised awards ceremony, he was the only member of the Central Committee to say thank you without reading from note cards.

Gorbachev began by exorcizing some remaining ghosts from the Stalinist past, which he believed had destroyed the Communist dream. Like a number of optimistic party officials and intellectuals, Gorbachev believed that the Prague Spring could come to Moscow, but that the Communist Party should continue to dominate political life in the Soviet Union. He embraced a policy of liberation known in Russian as *glasnost* (openness in government combined with a greater degree of free expression). He put some liberals in positions of responsibility and ordered the relaxation of censorship. Artists and writers brought forth new work, including strident criticisms of the Soviet regime. At the same time, more forthright accounts of life in the West appeared on the television news, which served to put the Soviet economy and its living standards in a particularly unflattering light.

Gorbachev increasingly spoke openly about the failure of economic planning without sufficient material incentives for workers. However, he still remained convinced that communism could be rescued by necessary reforms once the inefficiency and brutality of Stalinism had been completely eliminated. Because collective farms had failed, state agricultural planning would have to be scrapped in favor of a free market economy. For the moment, Gorbachev bided his time, although he summarily cashiered some corrupt or incompetent local party officials and launched a full-fledged campaign against alcoholism, which had taken on epidemic proportions in the demoralized Soviet Union.

Gorbachev espoused *perestroika,* a restructuring of the Soviet system in order to make it more efficient and responsive to the needs of Soviet citizens. He had seen Prime Minister Alexei Kosygin's attempt to have the Soviet economy turn out more consumer goods in the mid-1960s overwhelmed by a conservative backlash in the wake of the Prague Spring. Gorbachev insisted that "We need a revolution of the mind." In 1987, he reduced the role state corporations played in the Soviet economy, paving the way for increasing economic privatization. Furthermore, Gorbachev encouraged foreign investment in the Soviet Union. However, decades of economic inefficiency would clearly have to be overcome. Black marketeering remained a way of life for millions of people. Moreover, the enormous costs of social programs weighed heavily on the sagging economy.

In 1988, Gorbachev began to sponsor a series of remarkable political reforms. Dissidents within the Communist Party or even non-Communists could now be elected to the Congress of People's Deputies. He expressed determination to continue the "thaw" with the West that Khrushchev had begun but that had ended during the Brezhnev era, which he ridiculed accurately as the "era of stagnation." In 1985, Gorbachev replaced Andrei Gromyko, a mainstay of the Brezhnev years, as foreign minister with an old friend, Eduard Shevardnadze (1928–   ), a wily Georgian whom he had known since both were officials in the Young Communist League.

Three factors converged in the late 1980s to bring about the fall of communism. First, strongly nationalist movements gained momentum within the Soviet Union, particularly in Lithuania, Latvia, and Estonia, Georgia, Moldavia, Armenia, and Ukraine. These movements, encouraged by the growing vulnerability of the Soviet state to a weak economy, were not placated by the belated granting of greater cultural autonomy. Moreover, in some of the republics, long-festering conflicts between nationalities began to come to the surface, further undermining Soviet authority. In Azerbaijan, Christian Armenians battled Muslim Azerbaijanis, who formed the majority.

Second, in 1989, a forceful democratic opposition to communism emerged, led in Russia by the Nobel Prize winning Russian physicist Andrei Sakharov (who had helped develop the hydrogen bomb). Gorbachev's encouragement of participation in public life (in the hope of benefiting from a groundswell of support for reform) increased the ranks of Soviet citizens demanding reform. For many people, tales of the Gulag became increasingly powerful (exposed by the exiled Russian writer Alexander Solzhenitsyn's *The Gulag Archipelago,* among other books). Moreover, the campaign for human rights, led by Sakharov, discredited the regime, even if the Gulag itself no longer existed. The Helsinki Accords, signed by the Soviet Union as well as by the Western powers, encouraged dissidents because they linked human rights to trade and nuclear limitation. Increasingly, Russian dissidents managed to reach a large audience through the circulation of handwritten, typed, or clandestinely printed manuscripts and through the medium of Western radio broadcasts. The result was a *de facto* alliance within the Soviet Union between reformers and nationalists.

Third, the aggravation of the economic crisis beginning in 1988 increased the number of Soviet citizens convinced that a Communist government could not bring about a meaningful improvement in the quality of their lives. Economic plan followed economic plan, while Gorbachev rejected a rapid transition to a market economy and an immediate transfer of powers to the republics. In short, he vacillated between free market policies and traditional Communist state controls. The result was a further weakening of the economy. Moreover, Soviet subsidies to bolster the economies of Poland and other Eastern European states had taken their toll on the Soviet economy.

As the Soviet economy was collapsing, Gorbachev determined that the Soviet Union could not afford to continue the arms race with the United States. He therefore moved to improve relations with the U.S. government. Gorbachev resumed arms limitation negotiations with the United States, but he refused to sign an agreement because President Ronald Reagan would not include "Star Wars" experiments, however far-fetched, in negotiations. Highly successful visits to Washington (at which a new agreement reducing the number of medium-range missiles was signed) and to New York in 1987 gave the Soviet leader considerable world television exposure, leading to great personal popularity. He charmed Western leaders, notably British Prime Minister Margaret Thatcher, by promising to establish a free-market economy in the Soviet Union. A year later, the Soviet Union began recalling troops from Afghanistan after nine years of fighting against rebels there. For the first time in anyone's memory, government publications admitted the severe economic and social problems that troubled the Soviet Union. The Soviet Union began to allow Soviet Jews to emigrate abroad in greater numbers than ever before (in 1989, almost 70,000 Jews emigrated, most leaving for Israel or the United States). Following an initial attempt to deny its seriousness, the Soviet government was open about the explosion and widespread nuclear contamination that had occurred in Chernobyl in Ukraine in 1986. Gorbachev's push toward accommodation with the West took Western political leaders by surprise.

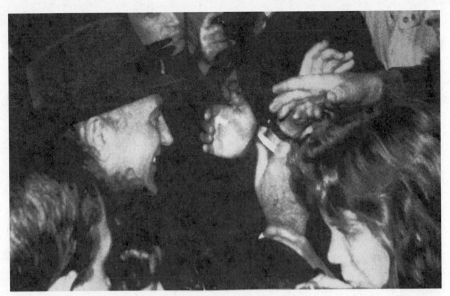

Gorbachev enthusiastically greeted by East Berliners, December 1987. The shout "Gorbi!" ironically became a call for reform.

Meanwhile, in Eastern Europe early in 1989, some reform-minded government officials joined opposition leaders in Poland and Hungary in the belief that economic and political liberalization was urgent. Communist rule slowly floundered under the weight of economic decline and popular dissatisfaction. But in Bulgaria, Czechoslovakia, East Germany, Albania, and Romania, entrenched Communist leaders sought desperately to hold on to power. The East German and Czech governments reverted to force in an attempt to quash popular movements for change. Romania's Ceausescu predictably tried massive repression before being swept aside.

One crucial factor made the outcome of this wave of demands for reform in Eastern Europe in 1989 different from those occurring earlier (in East Germany in 1953, Hungary in 1956, and Czechoslovakia in 1968): the Soviet government no longer was determined to preserve its empire. The shout "Gorbi, Gorbi, Gorbi!" rang out from the ranks of protesters. Even if in Czechoslovakia, East Germany, and Romania, particularly, Communist leaders were determined to overwhelm dissent, Soviet tanks would no longer back them up. Indeed, in a speech to the Council of Europe in Strasbourg in July 1989, Gorbachev made clear that he rejected the Brezhnev doctrine that had brought Soviet intervention in Czechoslovakia in 1968: "Any interference in domestic affairs and any attempts to restrict the sovereignty of states, both friends and allies or any others, are inadmissible." The Soviet leader called events in Eastern Europe "inspiring."

Transition to Parliamentary Government in Poland and Hungary

Poland became the first test case for the new Soviet relationship with its former satellites. The trade union organization Solidarity, which had virtually achieved the status of an unofficial opposition party, now sought legitimacy. The Catholic Church remained a source of organized opposition to communism.

In Hungary, although opposition groups were weaker than their counterparts in Poland, the Hungarian Democratic Forum and several smaller opposition groups began to emerge in 1988 out of café and living-room gatherings of long-time dissidents. Gorbachev's reforms in the Soviet Union greatly encouraged opposition groups. But as the government struggled with the floundering Hungarian economy and resisted implementing a full market economy, reform-minded Communists realized that communism would have to be reformed or it would disappear. In 1988, liberals ousted long-time leader János Kádár and some of his key associates from power and established a new leadership that was intent on reforming Hungary.

In 1989, a combination of economic deterioration (marked by a decline in productivity and rampaging inflation) and organized opposition convinced the Communist leadership in both Poland and Hungary to seek political compromise with opposition leaders. For the Hungarian Communists, a violent insurrection, such as the one that had been crushed by Soviet tanks in 1956, had to be avoided at all costs. Yet, at least in the beginning, opposition groups, with the memory of Soviet intervention still looming large, hesitated to call the legitimacy of the Communist regime into question.

In the summer of 1989, confronted by the intransigence of hard-liners, the Hungarian opposition formed an "Opposition Round Table" and negotiated with the government. Candidates of the Democratic Forum won free elections. Faced with continuing popular mobilization (for example, a massive commemoration of the Hungarian revolution in 1848 against Habsburg rule, which also had been crushed by a Russian army), the Communist leadership decided to try to outbid the Hungarian liberals by initiating reforms. In this way, the government, increasingly dominated by reformers, began to distance itself from the Communist Party. Political opposition forced the Communist Party to acknowledge that it would play no part in Hungary's future. In May, the government ordered the removal of barbed wire that defined the border with Austria. In June, the Communist Party itself admitted that the 1956 trial and execution of reform leaders had been illegal. The former premier Imre Nagy was reburied with national honors. That month, the Communist Party changed its name to the Hungarian Socialist Party. It espoused democratic principles and encouraged the development of opposition parties, as well as accepting a new constitution proclaimed later that year. The transition from communism to multiparty parliamentary rule in Hungary was therefore peaceful, with the Hungarian Democratic Forum leading a subsequent coalition government.

In Poland, the continued pitiful performance of the economy fatally undermined communism. In 1987, the Polish government held a referendum, asking Poles to support price rises. When they were overwhelmingly voted down, the government imposed them anyway. Strikes followed, and demands mounted for the relegalization of Solidarity. A year later, popular frustration with widespread shortages and a grotesquely inflated currency was manifested in more strikes and demonstrations. The government could no longer meet the interest payments on its massive debt to Western banks. In August 1988, the government invited Solidarity to negotiate with it. The opposition agreed to participate in exchange for government recognition of the legal status of Solidarity as the legitimate representative of Poles opposed to Communist rule. Negotiations between Solidarity representatives and the government in 1989 led to the first relatively free elections in Poland since the immediate post-war period (even though 65 percent of the seats in the lower house of parliament would be reserved for Communists). The addition of a senate to the parliament and the creation of the position of president of Poland reflected Solidarity's influence. Still, General Jaruzelski confidently believed he could orchestrate liberalization on his own terms. He badly underestimated the unpopularity of the Communist Party in Poland.

Solidarity's candidates swept to victory. The extent of Communist humiliation was such that candidates supported by Solidarity (with the support of the Catholic Church) won *all* 161 parliamentary seats contested in the elections. Moreover, Communist candidates won only 2 of 35 seats in elections in which they ran unopposed. As a result, the Communists could not put together a government acceptable to Solidarity. When parliament elected Solidarity leader Tadeusz Mazowiecki (1927–   ) as premier, Poland had a non-Communist premier for the first time since Stalin imposed communism in Poland. The Polish Communist Party, pressured by Gorbachev, accepted the *fait accompli*. However, Solidarity leaders, still wary that popular momentum once again could lead to heavy-handed repression, supported the election of Jaruzelski as president.

In 1990, the Communist era ended in Poland when the Polish Communist Party, like its Hungarian counterpart, changed its name and started espousing pluralist politics. In the wake of a split within Solidarity between the followers of Mazowiecki and Walesa (complicated by the candidacy of a wealthy émigré Pole from Canada), Walesa was elected president in December 1990. The Democratic Union, a party formed by Mazowiecki's followers within Solidarity, won the largest number of seats in the lower house and the senate. Economic reforms, aimed at introducing a full-fledged free market economy, were slow to take effect. Poland began a long struggle for economic stability with mounting unemployment and a dramatically increased crime rate.

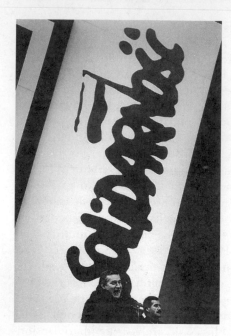

Lech Walesa, leader of the Polish Solidarity movement addresses a crowd at a Chicago rally.

The Collapse of the Berlin Wall and East German Communism

As pressure for change mounted in Poland and Hungary, East Germans fled the G.D.R. in record numbers. Many travelled to the German Federal Republic via Czechoslovakia and then Hungary, whose government in May had torn down the barbed wire stretching across the border with Austria. About 150,000 East Germans reached the West during the first nine months of 1989 alone. Eschewing the reforms undertaken by Gorbachev in the Soviet Union, East German Communist leader Erich Honecker in June 1989 had praised the Chinese army and police for crushing the pro-democracy demonstrations in Beijing. While other Communist governments negotiated with determined reformers, the East German leadership stood firm until it was too late. Honecker retreated into ideological orthodoxy with tired slogans, "Always forward [with socialism], never back!" He demanded that Hungary return fleeing East Germans to their country, as specified in an old treaty between the two Communist states. The Hungarian government refused to do so. East Germans who were returning from Prague on board a train passing through Dresden and Leipzig received permission to emigrate to West Germany. Learning of this, other East Germans frantically tried to climb aboard the train. One and a half million East Germans applied for exit visas. Most of these refugees were young workers and their families, very much like those the first East German Communist leaders had believed would always remain loyal to communism.

When Gorbachev visited East Berlin early in October 1989, demonstrators chanted his name, which had virtually become synonymous with opposition to the East German regime. When demonstrations spread to other major cities, Honecker ordered the police to attack demonstrators, but Egon Krenz, the Politburo member responsible for state security, refused to do so. On October 18, Honecker, old, ill, and ignored, was forced out in favor of Krenz, who was more moderate, but no reformer. In Leipzig, anxious opposition leaders and fearful Communist officials had met and resolved that peace must be maintained at all costs.

On October 23, Soviet foreign minister Eduard Shevardnadze declared that each country in Eastern Europe "has the right to an absolute, absolute freedom of choice." Such words further encouraged demonstrations and meetings in East Germany. On November 4, Krenz announced that East Germans were free to leave for West Germany via Czechoslovakia. A wholesale exodus began. On November 9, Krenz capitulated to the inevitable, announcing a sweeping change in government and promising to initiate legislation that would grant East Germans the right to travel where and when they wanted. Furthermore, he ordered that the Berlin Wall, which had divided East from West Berlin since August 1961, be torn down. Three million East Germans (out of a population of 16 million) poured through, or crossed into West Germany at once-forbidden checkpoints. An East German poet reacted. "I must weep for joy that it hap-

When Egon Krenz announced that East Germans could travel where and when they wanted, people gathered at the Berlin Wall to forge openings with whatever tools they had.

pened so quickly and simply. And I must weep for wrath that it took so abysmally long."

Krenz, however, still hoped that his promise that free elections would follow could keep the Communists in power. But lacking popular support, Krenz's government fell on December 3, succeeded by a series of committees until the elections of March 1990. In the meantime, angry East German citizens demonstrated in front of the offices of the Communist Party and the secret police.

In the elections, conservatives favoring German reunification (led by the equivalent of the West German Christian Democrats) won a surprisingly easy victory over Social Democrats and the remnants of the (now renamed) Communist Party. A number of East German leaders already expressed eagerness for German reunification. Here, again, there would be no Russian opposition (a policy announced by Gorbachev in February 1990, though not without some misgivings) to what had seemed for decades to be unthinkable because of fear in Russia that one day Germany might again threaten the peace. In the meantime, the G.D.R. began selling off state-owned companies. In May, East and West Germany agreed to closer economic cooperation; the West German mark became the currency of both Germanies. In September, Britain, France, and the United States, viewing reunification as inevitable, renounced their rights in Berlin. Unification took effect on October 3, 1990. In December, the first elections in the newly unified Germany returned the Christian Democrats to power, with Helmut Kohl now chancellor of Germany. In this way, German unification was effected with speed, but at great financial cost to the former German Federal Republic, which would for years have to allocate a substantial part of its budget to modernizing the former Communist state and providing public services to new citizens (including unemployment benefits in the wake of the collapse of state-run industries).

The "Velvet Revolution" in Czechoslovakia

In Czechoslovakia, where the Communist leadership resisted the forces for change as vehemently as their counterparts in East Germany, the regime was swept aside in ten days. As the economy weakened and news arrived of the fall of the Berlin Wall, the number of determined dissidents rapidly swelled beyond the ranks of intellectuals who had courageously demonstrated in 1988 on the twentieth anniversary of the Soviet invasion. Czechs and Slovaks alike signed petitions calling for reform. On November 17, 1989, students staged a demonstration in honor of a student executed by the Nazis fifty years earlier. But speakers quickly ignored the program censors had approved and began to call for academic freedom and government respect for human rights. Then, instead of disbanding to outlying squares as promised, the crowd started to march toward the giant St. Wenceslas Square in the center of Prague. A squad of riot police (with or without the authorization of the government) moved into the crowd, throwing canisters of tear gas and beating some students with clubs. Outraged demonstrators, now including workers and employers, protested the police violence.

The next day, a crowd assembled on the spot where police had beaten protesters. Students called for a general strike to begin ten days later. As the demonstrations continued to grow, protesters prepared for a potentially bloody repression. Indeed, the minister of defense announced that the army was "ready to defend the achievements of socialism" amid rumors that troops were being mobilized around Prague.

Yet, without the support of the Soviet Union, the Czechoslovak Communist government took no steps to repress the movement for freedom. On November 19, 1989, the entire Politburo resigned. In a Prague theater, a group of leading dissidents, including students, formed the "Civic Forum," calling on the government to negotiate with them over four demands: the resignation of two Communist officials blamed for the police attack two days earlier, the establishment of a commission to investigate the police attack, the release of political prisoners, and the resignation of Communist leaders responsible for the Soviet invasion in 1968. Civic Forum was led by Václav Havel (1936–   ), a popular playwright (whose plays had been banned by the government but circulated in manuscript) and a veteran of the Charter 77 group. He had been imprisoned several times for dissent, once nearly dying from mistreatment. In 1979, he had chosen to spend time in jail rather than leave Czechoslovakia.

On November 21, the elderly Alexander Dubček, the Slovak reformer who led the Communist Party of Czechoslovakia during the 1968 events and who had called for "socialism with a human face" before being sent packing by the Soviet army, addressed a throng assembled in St. Wenceslas Square. The crowds, however, did not want any kind of socialism. Students went to factories in search of support from workers. Thereafter, crowds poured into the streets almost every day, waving national flags and calling for freedom of speech and the release of political prisoners. Crowds of up to 300,000 heard speeches and calls for the end to communism, and lay wreaths on the spot where a Czech student burned himself to death in 1968 in protest of the Soviet invasion. On November 24, the Communist Central Committee narrowly voted against using the army to put an end to demonstrations. But with the security police in disarray, only ordinary police directing traffic were seen in the streets. In the meantime, in Slovakia, intellectuals formed an organization called "Public Against Violence," the Slovak equivalent of Civic Forum.

The Communist government now had no choice but to negotiate with its opponents who demanded free elections. Yet, unlike Poland and Hungary, where political opposition was well-developed within the constraints of the system, there were virtually no reform-minded Communists within Czechoslovakia, which had one of the most rigid Communist governments

Václav Havel, leader of the Civic Forum and first president elected under free elections in Czechoslovakia after the fall of the Communists in 1989, reads the names of members of Czechoslovakia's first non-Communist government since 1948.

in Eastern Europe. Gorbachev advised the Czechoslovak leaders not to use force. Negotiations between the government and Havel and other representatives of Civic Forum began on November 26. That day, more than half of the top leadership within the party was purged. On November 28, Civic Forum demanded the formation of a new government. A Communist Party official admitted, "We are aware of the fact that we don't have the trust of the people. We simply lost it—this trust. We are aware of it, I say it quite openly." It was quite an understatement.

Confronted by the success of the general strike, the government accepted five non-Communist members on December 3. In December, the Communist-dominated Federal Assembly voted to end the party's domination of political life. On December 10, the first cabinet in Czechoslovakia since 1948 not dominated by Communists was sworn in. The general strike ended, and more than a third of the members of the Communist Party resigned during the first two weeks of December. On December 29, the Federal Assembly unanimously elected Havel president of Czechoslovakia.

As in most places in Eastern Europe, there were very few calls for revenge against the Communist leadership (Romania was a notable exception). Even Havel was surprised by the speed of it all, declaring that "the end of communism took us all by surprise." Sweeping away communism itself had not been the aim of Civic Forum; rather, it seemed possible only to press for the creation of a new government in which non-Communists would play a major role. But a bloodless revolution, what Havel called a "velvet revolution," had succeeded. It was led by writers, actors, and students in tune with the country's inter-war democratic traditions. Free elections in December 1990 gave Civil Forum and its allies a majority of seats. In the spring, the government ended price controls. In June, Soviet troops pulled out of Czechoslovakia. Havel quickly announced that Czechoslovakia "must return to Europe," suggesting that, like Poland, its future lay with the West.

The new government of Czechoslovakia immediately faced not only the problem of creating a viable democracy but also greater tensions between Czechs and Slovaks. Although the two peoples shared seventy years of common political history, much separated them. The Czech part of the state was more urban, Protestant, and industrial than Slovakia, which is more rural and Catholic. (When Pope John Paul II visited the Slovak capital of Bratislava in the spring of 1990, the crowd of 1 million people represented 20 percent of the entire Slovak population.) Many Slovak nationalists called for the creation of an independent Slovakia. On January 1, 1993, the Czech Republic and Slovakia became two separate states. As everywhere in Eastern Europe, their weak economies compounded the problems of creating viable democratic institutions and establishing market economies.

Revolutions in Bulgaria, Romania, and Albania

Communist regimes also fell in Bulgaria, Romania, and Albania, the three Eastern European states without significant movements for reform. In Bulgaria, there had been little organized opposition to the regime from intellectuals or anyone else. Yet, there too, long-suppressed unrest began to emerge in response to pressure for reform in other Eastern European countries. Todor Zhivkov (1911–   ), the First Secretary of the Communist Party of Bulgaria since 1954 and the head of state since 1971, could boast a record of modest economic growth, at least until the late 1970s. He also had orchestrated several cover-ups of the misdeeds of his family members (including the implication of his hard-drinking and gambling son in the death of a television announcer and a sexual assault perpetuated by his grandson). When a Bulgarian airliner crashed at the Sofia airport, killing most passengers, Zhivkov's reputation was tainted when he ordered that his jet leave at once for his Black Sea vacation, flying over the burning jet and its victims. Furthermore, the Bulgarian secret police had achieved international notoriety, being blamed for an attempt to assassinate Pope John Paul II in Rome in 1981, and for a James Bond-like murder of a Bulgarian dissident, killed by the deadly jab of a poison-tipped umbrella in London.

The Bulgarian economy had faltered badly in the late 1980s; Middle Eastern nations owing Bulgaria money could not pay their debts because of falling oil prices. At the same time, Bulgarian exports (principally agricultural produce and light manufactured goods) had difficulty finding markets, particularly as the economic crisis deepened in the Soviet Union. Rural migrants poured into Sofia and other Bulgarian cities in search of work.

As the economy deteriorated, Zhivkov and the Communist leadership sought to displace popular anger in the direction of the country's large and rapidly growing Turkish minority, most of whom live in Central and Eastern Bulgaria. From time to time during the past several decades, the Turks had been the target of discriminatory government measures, including a law in 1984 requiring them to adopt Bulgarian names and forbidding the practice of Islam (the religion of most Turks). Just what the Bulgarian government hoped to achieve by such measures remains unclear (although this was hardly the first time in the often violent history of the region that an ethnic group had been targeted for discrimination in the hope of deflecting public opinion). After launching a harsh campaign against Turkish customs, Zhivkov's government encouraged the ethnic Turks to emigrate to Turkey, which further destabilized the Bulgarian economy. More than 300,000 of them left in three months in 1989. Many, however, soon returned, disappointed that conditions of life in Turkey seemed even worse than in Bulgaria.

As dramatic political changes occurred in the other Eastern European states, the Bulgarian Politburo surprised Zhivkov by suddenly demanding his resignation on November 10, 1989. The ease with which this was accomplished suggests that some party bureaucrats, army officers, and even members of the notorious government security force now believed change to be inevitable. Gorbachev, too, believed that Zhivkov had to go. The new government purged Stalinists, announced the end of the Communist monopoly on political power, and welcomed back the Turks, contributing to a nationalist backlash among many Bulgarians. Zhivkov was tried for misuse of government funds and sentenced to seven years in prison.

In January 1990, the Communist monopoly on political power ended, and the Bulgarian Communist Party changed its name to the Socialist Party. However, in June, the former Communists, capitalizing on resurgent ethnic rivalries and fear of change in the countryside, won a majority of seats in the New National Assembly, which elected Zhelio Zhelev, of the new Union of Democratic Forces, as president. A new constitution followed in October 1991. The Socialist Party and the Union of Democratic Forces remain the two largest parties.

In Romania, the fall of the Ceausescu clan was anything but bloodless. Ceausescu, who had enriched his family (at least thirty of whom held high office), vowed that reform would come to Romania "when pears grow on poplar trees." He awarded himself titles such as "Genius of the Carpathians" and the "Danube of Thought." His wife, Elena, fraudulently claimed to be a brilliant chemist, giving papers prepared by scientists at conferences, and then refusing to answer questions about them. On the occasion of a state visit to Britain, Ceausescu and his wife virtually pillaged a suite at

London's Buckingham Palace, carting away everything of value they could. In order to begin to pay back $10 billion in foreign loans, Ceausescu cut back food imports, increased food exports, rationed electricity, and banned the sale of contraceptives and abortion in the hope of increasing the Romanian population.

Ceausescu's downfall began in 1989 in the Transylvanian town of Timisoara, where opposition by ethnic Hungarians was strong. Ceausescu had ordered the razing of 8,000 largely Hungarian villages and the relocation of their residents. (Thousands of Hungarians had recently left the region for Hungary.) A popular Hungarian pastor loudly denounced the regime and called for democracy. After the Romanian security police broke into the pastor's home and beat him up, people formed a human chain around his home. Crowds rioted, smashing store windows and burning Ceausescu's books and portraits. Romanians joined Hungarians in the protests. Army units refused to fire on demonstrators. The feared security forces (the Securitate, 180,000 strong) stepped in, shooting three army officers for disobeying orders and firing on crowds, killing a number of children.

Discontent spread rapidly. As another cold winter approached Romania amid the usual severe food and fuel shortages, Hungarian and Yugoslav television showed events rapidly transpiring in other Eastern European countries. Demonstrations now spread to various Romanian towns. Ceausescu returned from a trip to Iran in December and called for a massive demonstration of support in Bucharest. Orchestrated cheers from the crowd soon became jeers, drowning out the dictator's pathetic speech blaming riots on Hungarian nationalists. From the safety of his palace, Ceausescu ordered troops to fire on the crowds below. But most units refused to obey and, as a result, the minister of defense was executed on Ceausescu's orders. The hated secret police eagerly fired on the assembled crowds; tanks crushed protesters in a scene hauntingly reminiscent of Beijing earlier that year. After soldiers battled the security forces outside the presidential palace, hundreds of bodies lay in the streets.

Several of the dictator's top officials now decided that Ceausescu's days of iron rule were numbered. Ceausescu and his wife left their stately residence on December 22, 1989, through secret tunnels, and then commandeered a helicopter. They were captured and immediately charged with murder and embezzlement of government funds. On Christmas Day, they were tried by a hastily convoked tribunal (which, in fact, had no legal authority) and condemned to death. They were then taken behind the building and shot, their bloody bodies left lying stiffly in the snow for a worldwide television audience to see while members of the security forces continued their resistance. More than 1,000 Romanians died during the revolution that overthrew Ceausescu.

A number of political parties quickly formed, including the National Salvation Front, which consisted in large part of anti-Ceausescu Commu-

(*Left*) A Romanian prays for countrymen executed on the orders of dictator Nicolae Ceausescu in Timisoara, Romania. (*Right*) A Romanian militiaman watches the execution of Ceausescu and his wife on television.

nists. In the elections of May 1990, the National Salvation Front won an overwhelming victory, drawing votes of peasants and party members. Ion Iliescu (1930–   ), a reformer who had befriended Gorbachev while studying at a technical institute in Moscow, became president of Romania. Former Communists still play a major role, however, in what remains one of Europe's poorest countries. The old Securitate apparatus, essentially intact despite the fall of Ceausescu, in June 1990 aided Romanian miners, many of whom remained loyal to the Communists, in a violent attack on demonstrators (several of whom were killed), who were protesting what they considered the National Salvation Front's neo-communism. Romania tottered in uncertainty.

Communism was swept away even in Albania, which had remained largely isolated from change in Eastern Europe by sealed borders. Ramiz Alia, first secretary of the Communist Party of Labor and president of Albania, confidently asserted in December 1989, "There are people abroad who ask: Will processes like those taking place in Eastern Europe also occur in Albania? We answer firmly and categorically: No, they will not occur in Albania."

In Europe's poorest country, where food shortages had generated sullen anger, news of the fall of Ceausescu in December 1989 emboldened dissidents. Riots occurred in the northern Albanian city of Shkodër. As a crisis mounted, Alia announced greater openness in the selection of government leaders and a larger role for workers in choosing managers. Moreover, agricultural cooperatives for the first time would be allowed to market surplus produce. Alia then announced the right to travel abroad and an abrogation of the long-standing ban on "religious propaganda" and expressed interest in establishing normal diplomatic ties with Washington and Moscow. A group of Albanian intellectuals demanded the end of the Communist monopoly on power. Several thousand Albanians adopted the East

German tactic of entering foreign embassies and legations in the hope of gaining the right to emigrate. Students went on strike. In late 1990, veterans' and youth organizations were declared independent of the Communist Party of Labor. Elections were scheduled for February 1991. Yet, like other Communist leaders, Alia believed that he could maintain control, placating Albanians with minor reforms.

Confronted by demonstrations that began in December 1990, Alia announced that henceforth the Communist Party would cease to be the only approved political party. The Democratic Party quickly constituted itself, and opposition newspapers began to publish, although the Communist Party of Labor retained control of radio and television. In February, a crowd of 100,000 demonstrated in Tirana, pulling down a large statue of former strongman Enver Hoxha. In early March, 20,000 Albanians tried to force their way onto boats departing for Italy. This event, which focused international attention on Albania, produced a Communist backlash, particularly in the countryside, where Hoxha had been a cult figure. In elections that month, the Communists won 68 percent of the vote. Despite this victory, the handwriting was on the wall. In June 1991, the Communist government resigned. For the first time since 1944, a coalition government came to power. Albania, too, entered the post-Communist world with most of its people convinced that economic and political reforms alone could save Albania from grinding poverty and isolation. Elections in 1992 gave the Democratic Party a majority of the seats in the National Assembly, and Alia resigned as Albania's president.

The Collapse of the Soviet Union

As one by one the former Eastern European satellites of the Soviet Union abandoned communism, stirrings of discontent with communism spread to the Soviet Union itself. In March 1990, the Communist government voted to permit non-Communist parties in the Soviet Union and created the office of president. State restrictions on religious practice ended. The Congress of People's Deputies elected Gorbachev president of the Soviet Union, a significant change in that previously the head of the Communist Party was the titular head of state.

Pressure for the break-up of the Soviet Union mounted from the republics. In June 1990, the Russian Republic declared that laws passed by its legislature could override those of the Soviet Union. The other republics followed suit with similar legislation. Gorbachev's attempt to enhance government decentralization fell short of what nationalists in the republics sought. In June, Lithuania unilaterally declared its independence from the Soviet Union; Gorbachev responded by ordering an embargo on Soviet oil and gas shipped to the Baltic state.

Yet, Gorbachev remained fundamentally skeptical of democracy. He still wanted to maintain a role for the Communist Party in the new era, as well as the existence of the Soviet Union itself. In 1990, he appointed several hard-line government officials and ordered a crackdown on nationalist movements in the Baltic states. This led to the dramatic resignation of Shevardnadze, the popular foreign minister.

In Russia, the charismatic, hard-drinking Boris Yeltsin (1931–   ) rose to power as a liberal reformer challenging Gorbachev's authority and the very legitimacy of the Soviet state. Unlike Gorbachev, Yeltsin had no illusions about the survival of communism and harbored grave doubts that the Soviet Union itself would survive. When reactionary Communists attempted to unseat Yeltsin as chairman in the Russian Parliament, he received a show of support from several hundred thousand Moscovites.

As he tried to steer an impossible middle course between the reformers and those committed to maintaining a role for the Communist Party, Gorbachev shifted away from reform, possibly encouraging right-wing officials within the Communist Party, army, and K.G.B., who believed their positions threatened by a reduction in hostility with the United States. The hard-line group had begun putting pressure on Gorbachev in September 1990, when the army undertook mysterious maneuvers around Moscow.

In January 1991, Gorbachev approved an attempt to overthrow the democratically elected government of Lithuania, beginning with an attack on a television installation in the capital of Vilnius. The clumsy plot, which involved army and K.G.B. agents pretending they were a Lithuanian dissident group, failed miserably, costing thirteen lives in the process. A month later, in a referendum deemed by the Soviet government to be illegal, 90 percent of those voting in Lithuania expressed their support for independence, as did 77 percent of those voting in both Estonia and Latvia (the difference explained by the fact that many Russians live in Estonia and Latvia).

In a nationally televised speech in February 1991, Yeltsin called for Gorbachev to resign from office. Gorbachev, in turn, responded by ordering Soviet troops to surround the Kremlin in a show of force against the more liberal Yeltsin.

However, Gorbachev's retrenchment proved short-lived. In April, he abandoned his commitment to preserving the Soviet Union at all costs and accepted the idea of autonomy for the republics. In June 1991, Yeltsin was elected president of the "Russian Federation," another sign of how quickly the Soviet Union was changing. The Communists now had little support in Russia, the largest republic.

It became increasingly clear that Gorbachev was losing control, and that the Soviet Union was vulnerable to a rightist coup. Gorbachev, who had been meeting with Western leaders in London, returned to Moscow and announced a new Communist Party platform, which eliminated Marxism and Leninism in favor of "humane and democratic socialism." He then left for an August vacation in Crimea.

(*Left*) Atop a tank in front of the Russian Parliament building, Boris Yeltsin urges the Russian people to resist the coup d'état of August 1991. (*Right*) Yeltsin seems to be reprimanding Mikhail Gorbachev in the wake of the failed coup d'état.

Intransigent Communists were now firmly convinced that Gorbachev's policies threatened communism and the existence of the Soviet Union. Hard-liners within the Communist Party, army, K.G.B., and some members of Gorbachev's own cabinet (including the minister of defense) placed the Soviet leader under house arrest in his own Crimean residence in what turned out to be a comic-opera attempted coup d'état. The conspirators apparently hoped that they could convince or force Gorbachev to throw his prestige against reform, believing that Gorbachev would agree to declare a state of emergency. Gorbachev agreed to do so, but only if such a move were approved "constitutionally" by the Supreme Soviet. The conspirators then publicly declared the president to be "incapacitated," announcing that the vice president would take charge.

In Moscow, where K.G.B. officials had refused an order of the conspirators to arrest Yeltsin, the Russian leader courageously defied the coup. He stood on a tank outside the Russian Parliament in Moscow and encouraged resistance. The coup fell apart, its leaders having underestimated the strength of both Yeltsin's and Gorbachev's popular support and overestimated their support within the army. Indeed, six years of political debate in the Soviet Union had increased the number of ordinary people committed to reform. Furthermore, the army remained for the most part loyal to Gorbachev. Yeltsin was able to mobilize the Moscow public by calling for resistance and the restoration of Gorbachev as the legitimate Soviet leader. This appeal to constitutionality revealed how much had changed irreversibly in a very short time.

Gorbachev returned to Moscow a hero, and again took a more reformist stance. Yeltsin, as head of the Russian Parliament, used that body to validate a number of decrees he had announced during the crisis. Even as Gorbachev continued to defend the Communist Party before the Supreme Soviet, Yeltsin suspended the Communist Party and its newspaper *Pravda*. These bold moves amounted to the dismantling of communism in Russia. Yeltsin reiterated his commitment to national self-determination.

The failed coup accelerated the collapse of the Soviet Union. Gorbachev appointed new people to key ministries. K.G.B. officials were pensioned off, and television and radio were freed from the constraints of censorship. The Soviet government finally recognized the outright independence of the Baltic republics just months after Gorbachev had insisted on retaining the structure of the Soviet Union.

Gorbachev himself accepted the legitimacy of Yeltsin's decrees. Moreover, at the end of August, the Supreme Soviet voted to put an end to the extraordinary powers previously accorded Gorbachev and to suspend the Communist Party in the entire Soviet Union. Yeltsin quickly moved to initiate a market economy in Russia.

One by one, the republics took steps to leave the Soviet Union. Moldavia, Uzbekistan, and Azerbaijan declared their independence. Other Soviet republics held or planned plebiscites, all of which led to declarations of independence from the Soviet Union. In December 1991, Ukraine declared its independence after 90 percent of the population had voted to leave the Soviet Union. By the end of the year, thirteen of the fifteen Soviet republics had declared their independence. Yeltsin and the presidents of Belarus and Ukraine created the Commonwealth of Independent States, declaring the Soviet Union dissolved. Gorbachev now acknowledged that the Soviet Union no longer existed. Symbolically, Leningrad again assumed its old name of St. Petersburg. On December 25, 1991, Gorbachev resigned, closing one of the most remarkable political eras in modern European history.

The Disintegration of Yugoslavia

In Yugoslavia, Marshal Josip Broz Tito, a Croat, had believed that communism in his country could end ethnic rivalries and Serb domination and had repressed nationalist groups. Following Tito's death in 1980, a collective presidency that rotated every year among eight members governed Yugoslavia.

In the mid-1980s, the Yugoslav government, dominated by Serbs, launched a brutal repression of Albanians living in Kosovo, claiming that Albanian nationalism posed a threat to communism. In April 1987, Slobodan Milošević, the leader of the Serb Communist Party, addressed a throng of 15,000 Serbs and Montenegrans in Kosovo. When the Albanian-dominated police moved in to break up the mass gathering, Milošević made a provocative speech, telling the Serbs and Montenegrans that the land of Kosovo was theirs, and that they should remain at all costs.

Boosted by this public relations success among Serbs, Milošević soon emerged as the dominant figure in Yugoslavia. He turned the Communist Party and state apparatus into instruments serving Serb nationalist interests, preparing to establish a "Greater Serbia" should Yugoslavia break up. Milošević undertook what amounted to a military occupation of Kosovo, ending its administrative autonomy. In 1989, fighting broke out in Kosovo between ethnic Albanians, Serbs, and Montenegrans. Milošević also pushed aside party leaders in several other provinces. Regional Communist Party hierarchies only weakly resisted or completely capitulated under the pressure of Serb nationalism, which was further inflamed by Albanian resistance in Kosovo.

Yugoslavia quickly disintegrated (see Map 30.3). The movement for political reform began in January 1990 in Slovenia, the wealthiest and most

MAP 30.3 THE DISINTEGRATION OF YUGOSLAVIA, 1995   The fall of the Communists in Yugoslavia led to the break-up of the Yugoslav federation and to civil war between Croats, Serbs, and Muslims. This map is in accord with the Dayton Peace Agreement signed in November 1995.

homogeneous of Yugoslavia's six republics. New parties formed in each of the six republics, including in Serbia, where Communist leaders were most opposed to reform. Non-Communists won a majority of the seats in Bosnia-Herzegovina, Croatia, Slovenia, and Macedonia. The Communist Party changed its name to the Socialist Party and won a majority in Milošević's Serbia and in Montenegro, its ally.

In Slovenia and Croatia, calls by nationalists for succession from Yugoslavia grew in strength, although some reformers still wanted the state to survive with a federalist structure. In response, Milošević denounced Croatian nationalists as Ustaša (World War II Croatian fascists). Yet, even within Serbia, Milošević's authority drew increasing criticism from those who wanted reform.

In December 1990, almost 90 percent of Slovenes who voted in a referendum expressed their desire for national independence. In Croatia, the nationalist Franjo Tudjman, a general in the 1950s and 1960s, won a clear electoral victory, accentuating tensions between Croatia and the wider Yugoslav state. Milošević loudly espoused the creation of a Greater Serbia that would include all territories populated by Serbs. Along the Croatian coast of Dalmatia, Serb nationalist groups raided police stations, killing several Croatian policemen, and seizing guns and ammunition.

In May 1991, Serbia prevented the succession of a Croat to the rotating presidency. Attempted intervention by the Yugoslav army in Slovenia was met by strong resistance and was short-lived, since there were very few Serbs in Slovenia. But when Croatia declared its independence from Yugoslavia in June 1991 (as did Slovenia as well), violent conflicts between Croats and Serbs intensified. Serb militias, supported and armed by Yugoslav army units, began occupying large chunks of Croatia that had sizable Serb populations, and within several months they held about 30 percent of Croatian territory. Croats were driven from their villages in an extended series of Serb operations that killed thousands of people. From the heights above, Serbs shelled the walled Croatian city of Dubrovnik on the Adriatic coast, damaging one of Europe's most beautiful cities.

Macedonia declared its independence in September 1991. In Bosnia in March 1992, a majority of Bosnian Muslims and ethnic Croats voted for independence. However, Bosnian Serbs refused to recognize the legality of the plebiscite, and fighting broke out among Serbs and Muslims and their Croat allies. Milošević's surviving Yugoslav state, as well as Serb minorities within each republic, viewed declarations of independence as unacceptable provocations. A bloody civil war broke out in Bosnia-Herzegovina, and in parts of Croatia. Bosnian Serbs carried out "ethnic cleansing" in some regions, which meant that, at a minimum, they forced non-Serbs from their homes and drove them away or imprisoned them. Bosnian Serb militias perpetuated atrocities against Bosnian Muslims, including rapes and mass executions. In the meantime, in predominantly Croat parts of Bosnia, Croats also carried out brutal measures against Muslims. The Muslims occasionally reciprocated against both Serbs and Croats.

(*Left*) A tearful requiem in a Sarajevo cemetery. (*Right*) Croatian civilians take shelter in a ditch while bombs rain down around them.

Milošević, presiding over what remained of Yugoslavia (Serbia and Montenegro), eliminated constitutional guarantees given by the Yugoslav republic to the provinces of Kosovo and Vojvodina. With the support of Serbia, Bosnian Serb forces surrounded the Bosnian capital of Sarajevo, killing residents with mortar and cannon shells lobbed from the heights above or by sniper fire. In response to assistance given the Bosnian Serbs by Milošević's government, the United Nations placed an economic embargo on the rump Yugoslav state. But the NATO alliance stood by and allowed Serbian nationalists to conquer more than 70 percent of Bosnia-Herzegovina. "Europe is dying in Sarajevo," warned a poster in Germany; "The Bosnian crisis has been the major post–Cold-War turning point in Europe, and we missed the turn," sadly noted one French leader. The arrival of blue-helmeted U.N. peacekeepers made little difference. In June 1995, the Bosnian Serbs humiliated the United Nations by taking some of its peacekeepers hostage. Castigation by international opinion had no effect on the Bosnian Serbs, who brushed aside U.N. forces and overran free zones established to provide safe haven to Bosnian Muslims driven from their villages and homes by Serbs. Atrocities against Muslims led to the indictment of Bosnian Serb leader Radovan Karadzić by a U.N. tribunal on crimes against humanity and genocide. Europe's bloodiest conflict since World War II went on, with the United Nations standing by helplessly.

In early August 1995, the Croats now recaptured Krajina, contested territory bordering on Bosnia, which Croatian Serbs had declared to be independent in 1991. Now it was the turn of tens of thousands of Serbs from Krajina to take to the roads as refugees, heading toward Serb strongholds in Bosnia.

Although the threat of nuclear war seems to have been enormously reduced by the end of the Cold War, the Bosnian conflict, fought with conventional weapons, continued to take a terrible toll, created hundreds of thousands of refugees (about half of the population of Bosnia). Croatia entered the conflict with the goal of protecting the U.N.-declared "safe zones" for Bosnian Muslims, but also with an eye toward taking Bosnian territory that it considered Croatian. This moved the region closer to a full-scale Balkan war. That in itself, in the worst scenario, could have serious international repercussions. Germany, a nation with historically antagonistic relations with the Slavs and which during World War II turned loose Croatian fascists on the Serbs, was the first state to recognize the independence of Croatia (as well as Slovenia and Bosnia), and lobbied effectively against the imposition of economic sanctions against Croatia. And although the Russian government has sometimes tried to restrain the Bosnian Serbs, many Russians, as before World War I, still feel a close affinity to their Balkan Slav cousins. As a result of the Dayton Peace Agreement orchestrated in November 1995 by the U.S. government, Bosnia was to remain a single state that included a Bosnian-Croat federation and a Serb republic. This agreement would be supervised by a NATO peacekeeping force, including U.S. troops.

Challenges in the Post-Communist World

The end of communism in the Soviet Union and Eastern Europe has not guaranteed an easy transition to parliamentary, democratic rule. The lack of democratic traditions, economic turmoil, and ethnic rivalries pose daunting challenges. Given the strength of national tensions and conflict in Eastern Europe, a transition to democratic government is not preordained, particularly in Romania, Bulgaria, and Albania. Until the fall of communism, Russia itself had been first a tsarist autocracy and then a Communist dictatorship. Indeed, the history of the inter-war years demonstrates the risks that aggressive nationalism poses to parliamentary government.

Nowhere are the stakes higher for a peaceful transition to democracy than in Russia. The president of Ukraine put it this way: "When there's frost in Russia on Thursday, by Friday there's frost in Kiev." As rivalry between Yeltsin and the Congress of People's Deputies grew in 1992 and early 1993, Yeltsin declared a "special presidential regime" giving him more powers to override opposition to his reform program. Yeltsin insisted that the Russian presidency should have considerable authority, whereas the Congress feared strong presidential prerogatives, with memory still strong of the dictatorship of the Communist Party. In any case, Russian political parties have been slow to develop; parliamentary rule simply could not occur overnight, particularly in view of the continuing economic crisis. A deputy prime minister of Turkmenistan admitted, "We're praying day and night for Yeltsin to stay in power. Any of those who might come after him, all of them have an ax in their hand." National independence can be a fragile thing.

Like the Soviet Union, the Eastern European Communist states were largely atomized societies of one-party rule without a political infrastructures, civic cultures, or adequately developed voluntary associations. Authoritarian states had often made major decisions without considering popular wishes or interests. Only in Poland and Hungary had a non-Communist political leadership gradually emerged in the 1980s. The Polish Solidarity movement and several Hungarian associations provided a basis for the emergence of party politics following the dismantling of one-party rule. Likewise, in 1989, Civic Forum in Czechoslovakia served the same function.

In the first free elections held in Eastern Europe since the late 1940s, two distinct trends were seen. Strongly nationalist right-center parties emerged victorious in eastern Germany, Poland, and Hungary, where the parties of the left, including those formed by former Communists (some of them, to be sure, converted reformers), fared badly. On the other hand, in the Balkan states of Bulgaria and Romania, which had virtually no democratic traditions, former Communist parties (hurriedly renamed and claiming the mantle of reform) came out better than any other parties. They did particularly well in the countryside, where reform movements had been absent and Communist officials had maintained considerable prestige, identified with a modest increase in living standards that had occurred during the decades since the war. In late 1995, the Communist Party emerged as the biggest winner in the legislative elections in Russia. And, six years after the fall of the Berlin Wall, most of the former Eastern European satellites of the Soviet Union—including Bulgaria, Albania, Hungary, Lithuania, and Poland, where Lech Walesa was turned out of office—were now led by former Communists. Many of them benefited from being familiar faces able to draw on old political networks.

However, virtually all of the former Communist states have accepted the necessity of creating modern economic systems based on private enterprise. Yet, in the former Communist countries, where collectivization was a way of life (except in Poland), economic privatization has not been easy. Some former owners of property collectivized by Communist regimes demanded their lands back. Some collectivized farms resisted decollectivization. Throughout Eastern Europe, as well as the former Soviet Union, weak economies and a relatively low standard of living continued to generate political instability. Economic turmoil could potentially bring a return to authoritarian rule. The utilization of free-market "shock therapy," in-

(*Left*) A protest by the homeless against economic misery in Red Square, Moscow. Note the religious image on the tent in the foreground. (*Right*) Well-dressed Russian women seek food in a time of shortage, 1992.

cluding the end of price controls on most consumer goods, brought chaos to Russia and Poland. Economic output in both countries fell drastically. Galloping inflation (up to 20 percent a month in Russia and 40 percent in Ukraine, where economic measures were half-hearted) and widespread unemployment have engendered bitterness. Policy changes have come with numbing speed. Despite the fact that its Western creditors in March 1991 canceled half of the debts owed by Poland, the economic outlook in that country remains bleak. Furthermore, in most of the former Communist countries, the end of authoritarian rule has led to major increases in violent crime, above all, in Russia, where organized crime has burgeoned.

The transition to democratic rule has also been difficult because of ethnic tensions in Eastern Europe. Winston Churchill's comment after the Treaty of Versailles in 1919 still rings true: "Injuries were wrought to the structure of human society which a century will not efface." Extreme economic and political fragility leaves the region dangerously unstable. About 600,000 ethnic Hungarians live in Slovakia, 500,000 in Serbia, and 200,000 in Ukraine. Likewise, there is considerable possibility that conflict between Turks and Bulgarians in Bulgaria and between Hungarians and Romanians in Romania will break out.

In Russia and the other former Soviet republics the potential for violence also remains great because of conflicts between nationalities. Fighting between Azerbaijanis and Armenians in an Armenian enclave of

Nagorno-Karabakh within Azerbaijan may also auger future wars, complicated by long-standing Islamic religious and cultural ties with Turkey, and historical links between Armenia and Russia. In Georgia, too, fighting was widespread between the government of Shevardnadze and supporters of a former dissident elected president in 1991. One observer called the Caucasus "a Yugoslavia that has already begun to happen." Furthermore, Russia's role in such conflicts (particularly in states with sizable Russian minorities) will certainly remain a source of future tension, potentially threatening the honeymoon between Russia and the former republics of the Soviet Union. Russian troops have battled nationalist insurgents in Chechnya (which lies north of Georgia and west of the Caspian Sea). Beginning in 1991, the revolt has taken the lives of thousands of civilians, discrediting Russian President Yeltsin.

The possibility of continued nationalist intolerance and ethnic violence in the former Communist countries is great indeed. It was telling that in Estonia and Romania, no sooner had Communist rule ended than new governments established language tests to determine who was a "real" Estonian or Romanian. Romania continues to discriminate against ethnic Hungarians, as Russians face discrimination in Estonia. Nation-states, which many liberals long assumed were necessary before constitutional rights and equality could be assured, have not always turned out to be liberal and tolerant. In the worst case, "ethnic cleansing" by Bosnian Serbs recalls Nazi (and other) atrocities committed during World War II.

CONCLUSION

As Europe nears the twenty-first century, its influence over the rest of the world has been significantly reduced by the independence of its former colonies. At the same time, despite Germany's economic strength, Japan and the United States boast the two most powerful economies. With the end of the Cold War, U.S. commitment to playing an active role in European affairs may not be assured, despite its role in the brokering of the fragile Bosnian peace settlement in November 1995. However, should the European Union ever become a political reality, its influence in world affairs would be considerable. Yet, the inability of the Western European nations to act effectively in concert in the Bosnian crisis seems to confirm the assessment of a diplomat that "the dream of a unified, decisive Europe which assumes a major world role is not likely to be realized."

While the West breathed a sigh of relief with the collapse of communism, the existence of nuclear weapons in several of the former states of the Soviet Union remains of considerable concern. Kazakhstan's possession of nuclear arms makes events there particularly important. Ukraine's nuclear arsenal and its claim to the remnants of the Soviet Black Sea Fleet docked in Crimea contributed to tension between Russia and Ukraine, by far the two most powerful of the old Soviet republics. In 1992, Ukraine,

Pollution in post-Communist Romania, 1995.

Russia, Belarus, and Kazakhstan all agreed that nuclear weapons stored on their territory would either be destroyed or turned over to Russia within a few years. The problem of preventing the theft and sale of nuclear materials in order to avoid nuclear proliferation, particularly to potentially terrorist states remains one of the most important for the future.

The end of communism has left other problems, as well, though not all have been unique to Russia and Eastern Europe. Among them, the rapid industrialization in East Germany, Romania, and Czechoslovakia under communism left horrendous pollution from coal-burning furnaces and virtually unregulated factories. Acid rain has destroyed forests, killed rivers, and compromised the health of residents. It will take decades and massive financial investment to clean it all up. Moreover, the 1986 Chernobyl disaster clearly demonstrated the vulnerability of the rest of Europe to nuclear fallout.

Suddenly freed from Soviet domination, the newly independent states face the challenge of putting their own foreign relations on a firm footing. For many of the former Soviet republics, relations with Russia are complicated by centuries of animosity, Soviet rule which strongly favored Russian interests, and by the presence of sizable Russian populations and, in some cases, many Russian troops (250,000 were stationed outside of Russia at the time of the break-up of the Soviet Union).

Moreover, freed from Communist rule, some of the Eastern European states have sought to join NATO. The United States and other Western member nations have agreed in principle to enlarging NATO's membership, hoping that the adherence of some of the former Communist states would help consolidate democracy. Russia, however, is wary of the possible expansion of NATO, which, after all, was created with the goal of containing the Soviet Union. Should Poland or Hungary become members of NATO, this would oblige the United States to consider an attack on either country as an attack upon itself, thus providing a formidable obstacle to any resurgence of Russian expansionism. Such a possibility worries Western governments. Furthermore, the inclusion of the former Soviet satellites in NATO could well encourage a revival of aggressive, anti-Western Russian nationalism.

Entrance into the European Union has become a goal of Poland, Hungary, the Czech Republic, and several of the Eastern states. However, the European Union made clear that such expansion in membership would be postponed until after the end of the century. The European Union, with 370 million people, could not afford to subsidize, for example, relatively poor Polish farmers; furthermore, competition from Eastern European agricultural producers could threaten French, Danish, and German farmers. Transfers of money from wealthy Western European member states to Eastern European countries (such as occurs between more prosperous and poorer Western states) might well be financially ruinous. In the meantime, the European Economic Community initially imposed tariffs and quotas to keep out agricultural exports from the fledgling democracies of Eastern Europe.

The opening of Eastern European borders and the elimination of border controls between many Western European states has increased the number of desperate poor people who manage to reach Western Europe from Asia, Africa, and Eastern Europe, seeking a better life in Western states. As social services sag under the additional weight of impoverished and often clandestine newcomers, people in many countries feel themselves overwhelmed by immigrants. Two hundred thousand Albanians crossed the mountains to reach Greece between 1990 and 1993. Between 1980 and 1992, 15 million immigrants arrived in Western Europe, many of them unassimilated in their new countries, residing in virtual ghettos in and on the outskirts of cities. In 1995, an estimated 2.8 million people were living illegally in Western European countries. In response, Western European governments have adopted new laws and strategies in order to reduce the number of immigrants, establishing tougher tests for claims of political asylum and sending plane- and trainloads of illegal immigrants back to their countries. With 7 percent of its population made up of foreigners (60 percent of them non-European), France has turned away from its long-held belief that being born in that country was enough to become a French citizen; it now requires that children born in France to non-French parents must apply for citizenship between ages sixteen and twenty-one. Moreover, the government has made it more difficult for foreigners to acquire French nationality through marriage. Yet, massive migration to Europe will certainly continue. Referring to the smuggling of migrants into his country, the Austrian director of immigration assessed, "There are no distances any longer in this world. There are no islands."

Rising intolerance, racism, and xenophobia have become apparent in both Western and Eastern Europe. In Western Europe, the backlash against immigration has been marked by rising xenophobic opposition orchestrated by extreme right-wing nationalist parties (such as the National Front in France, the Freedom Party in Austria, and the Republican Party in Germany). This has been particularly directed against foreign workers and their families. As attacks against foreigners by Neo-Nazis and skinheads proliferated in Germany, as well as in virtually all other Western European countries, German Chancellor Helmut Kohl warned that "The evil spirits that have come to life again in the Balkans are not unique to that area." The severe recession of the early 1990s, the worst since World War II, has contributed to this explosive situation, amid high unemployment rates (in 1993 over 10 percent in the European Union) and increased discouragement among young people; disproportionately affected by unemployment, they fear that they will not find jobs and that they will be the first generation in the post-war period to do less well economically than their parents.

Neo-Nazis salute in Bavaria.

The new Germany in the new Europe.

Furthermore, in Russia and the Balkans, xenophobia has led to a resurgence of aggressive nationalism. The re-emergence of authoritarian rule, as occurred in every Eastern European country except Czechoslovakia between the two world wars, is very possible. In Russia, the xenophobic Liberal Democratic Party won 8 percent of the vote in 1991 elections; its leader has promised wars of conquest in the name of Russia, insisting that Russia maintain control over the Crimea, now part of Ukraine, and northern Kazakhstan. Rising aggressive nationalism represents one frightening reality that has followed the sudden collapse of centralized authority in regions lacking strong democratic traditions. The end of communism has brought an end to the decades-old struggle between communism and capitalism. But ethnic and religious rivalries, as in centuries past, have by no means been eliminated. It has proven easier to tear down the existing order than to construct a new one.

FURTHER READINGS

GENERAL

Feroz Ahmad, *The Making of Modern Turkey* (1993).

Michael Anderson, *Approaches to the History of the Western Family, 1500–1914* (1980).

Philippe Ariès, *Centuries of Childhood: A Social History of Family Life* (1962).

Philippe Ariès and Georges Duby, eds., *A History of Private Life* (5 vols, 1987–1993).

Geoffrey Barraclough, *The Origins of Modern Germany* (1979).

Geoffrey Best, *War and Society in Revolutionary Europe, 1770–1870* (1982).

Jerome Blum, *The End of the Old Order in Rural Europe* (1978).

Jerome Blum, *Lord and Peasant in Russia from the Ninth to the Nineteenth Century* (1961).

Richard Bonney, *The European Dynastic States 1494–1660* (1991).

John Bossy, *Christianity in the West 1400–1700* (1985).

Fernand Braudel, *Capitalism and Material Life, 1400–1800* (1975).

Fernand Braudel, *The Mediterranean World in the Age of Philip II* (New York, 1992).

Charles Breunig, *The Age of Revolution and Reaction, 1789–1850* (1977).

Robin Briggs, *Early Modern France, 1560–1715* (1977).

Peter Burke, *Popular Culture in Early Modern Europe* (1978).

Raymond Carr, *Spain 1808–1975* (1982).

Owen Chadwick, *The Secularization of the European Mind in the Nineteenth Century* (1976).

S.G. Checkland, *British Public Policy, 1776–1939: An Economic, Social, and Political Perspective* (1985).

Carlo Cipolla, *Before the Industrial Revolution: European Society and Economy, 1000–1700* (1980).

Carlo M. Cipolla, ed., *The Fontana Economic History of Europe* (6 vols, 1976–1977).

Martin Clark, *Modern Italy 1871–1982* (1984).

Eric Cochrane, *Italy, 1530–1630* (1988).

Gordon A. Craig, *Germany, 1866–1945* (1978).

Norman Davies, *A History of Poland: God's Playground* (2 vols, 1981).

David Brion Davis, *The Problem of Slavery in the Age of Revolution, 1770–1823* (1975).

Georges Duby and Michelle Perrot, eds., *A History of Women in the West* (5 vols., 1992–1994).

Christopher Duggan, *A Concise History of Italy* (1994).

Richard Dunn, *The Age of Religious Wars, 1559–1715* (1979).

Elizabeth Eisenstein, *The Printing Revolution in Early Modern Europe* (1993).

Norbert Elias, *The Civilizing Process* (1994).

William Ferguson, *Scotland 1689 to the Present* (1968).

R.F. Foster, *Modern Ireland, 1600–1972* (1988).

Derek Fraser, *The Evolution of the British Welfare State: A History of Social Policy Since the Industrial Revolution* (1973).

François Furet and Jacques Ozouf, *Reading and Writing: Literacy in France from Calvin to Jules Ferry* (1983).

Peter Gay, *The Bourgeois Experience: Victoria to Freud: The Education of the Senses* (1984).

Peter Gay, *The Tender Passion* (1986).

Peter Gay, *The Cultivation of Hatred* (1993).

Felix Gilbert, *The End of the European Era, 1890 to the Present, 4th ed.* (1991).

Robert Gildea, *Barricades and Borders: Europe, 1800–1914* (1987).

J.R. Gillis, *Youth and History: Tradition and Change in European Age Relations, 1770 to the Present* (1981).

Jack Goldstone, *Revolution and Rebellion in the Early Modern World* (1991).

E.J. Hobsbawm, *The Age of Revolution, 1789–1848* (1962).

Paul Hohenberg and Lynn Lees, *The Making of Urban Europe 1000–1950* (1985).

Lynn Hunt, ed., *The New Cultural History* (1989).

Charles Ingrao, *The Habsburg Monarchy 1618–1815* (1994).

Barbara Jelavich, *History of the Balkans* (2 vols., 1983).

Charles and Barbara Jelavich, *The Establishment of Balkan National States, 1804–1920* (1977).

Henry Kamen, *European Society 1500–1700* (London, 1984).

John Keegan, *The Face of Battle* (1976).

John Keegan, *A History of Warfare* (1993).

Tom Kemp, *Industrialization in Nineteenth-Century Europe* (1985).

Paul Kennedy, *The Rise and Fall of the Great Powers* (New York, 1987).

V.G. Kiernan, *European Empires from Conquest to Collapse, 1815–1960* (1982).

H.G. Koenigsberger, *Early Modern Europe, 1500–1789* (1987).

H.G. Koenigsberger, *The Habsburgs and Europe, 1516–1660* (1971).

E.H. Kossman, *The Low Countries, 1780–1940* (1978).

Dominick LaCapra and Steven L. Kaplan, eds., *Modern European Intellectual History: Reappraisals and New Perspectives* (1982).

F.S. Lyons, *Ireland since the Famine* (1971).

C.A. Macartney, *The Habsburg Empire, 1790–1918* (1969).

Roger Magraw, *France, 1815–1914: The Bourgeois Century* (1983).

Mary Jo Maynes, *Schooling in Western Europe: A Social History* (1985).

Peter McPhee, *A Social History of France 1780–1880* (1992).

Alec Reginald Meyers, *Parliaments and Estates in Europe to 1789* (1975).

P.K. O'Brien and C. Keyser, *Economic Growth in Britain and Europe, 1780–1914* (1978).

Geoffrey Parker, *The Cambridge Illustrated History of Warfare* (1995).

Geoffrey Parker, *The Military Revolution: Military Innovation and the Rise of the West, 1500–1800* (1988).

Fritz Ringer, *Education and Society in Modern Europe* (1979).

Colin Russell, *Science and Social Change in Britain and Europe, 1700–1900* (1983).

Peter Sahlins, *Boundaries: The Making of France and Spain in the Pyrenees* (1989).

Joan W. Scott, *Gender and the Politics of History* (1988).

Christopher Seton-Watson, *Italy: From Liberalism to Fascism 1870–1925* (1967).

Hugh Seton-Watson, *The Russian Empire, 1801–1917* (1967).

James Sheehan, *German History, 1770–1866* (1990).

Adrien Shubert, *A Social History of Modern Spain* (1990).

Quentin Skinner, *Foundations of Modern Political Thought* (1978).

Bonnie G. Smith, *Changing Lives: Women in European History since 1700* (1989).

A.J.P. Taylor, *The Struggle for Mastery in Europe, 1848–1918* (1954).

Charles Tilly, *Coercion, Capital, and European States, 990–1990* (1990).

Charles Tilly, *The Contentious French: Four Centuries of Popular Struggle* (1986).

Charles Tilly, Louise Tilly, and Richard Tilly, *The Rebellious Century* (1975).

Mack Walker, *German Home Towns: Community, State, and General Estate, 1648–1871* (1971).

Piotr Wandycz, *The Price of Freedom: A History of East Central Europe from the Middle Ages to the Present* (1992).

Robert K. Webb, *Modern England from the Eighteenth Century to the Present* (1968).

Adna Weber, *The Growth of Cities in the Nineteenth Century* (1963).

Eric R. Wolf, *Europe and the People without History* (1983).

Isser Woloch, ed., *The Ambiguities of Freedom* (1996).

Stuart Woolf, *A History of Italy 1700–1860* (1986).

E.A. Wrigley, *Population and History* (1969).

Theodore Zeldin, *France, 1848–1945* (5 vols, 1978–1981).

CHAPTER 1. MEDIEVAL LEGACIES AND TRANSFORMING DISCOVERIES

Kenneth R. Andrews, *Trade, Plunder and Settlement: Maritime Enterprise and the Genesis of the British Empire, 1480–1630* (1984).

Robert Bartlett, *The Making of Europe: Conquest, Colonization and Cultural Change 950–1350* (1993).

M. W. Beresford, *New Towns of the Middle Ages* (1988).

Marc Bloch, *Feudal Society* (2 vols., 1961).

Brenda Bolton, *The Medieval Reformation* (1983).

John Boswell, *Christianity, Social Tolerance, and Homosexuality: Gay People in Western Europe from the Beginnings of the Church Era to the Fourteenth Century* (1980).

John Boswell, *The Kindness of Strangers: The Abandonment of Children in Western Europe from Late Antiquity to the Renaissance* (1988).

Rosalind B. and Christopher Brooke, *Popular Religion in the Middle Ages* (1984).

Alfred W. Crosby, *Ecological Imperialism: The Biological Expansion of Europe, 900–1900* (1986).

R.O. Crummey, *The Formation of Muscovy 1404–1613* (1987).

Georges Duby, *Rural Economy and Country Life in the Medieval West* (1968).

Edith Ennen, *The Medieval Town* (1979).

Edith Ennen, *The Medieval Woman* (1989).

Wallace K. Ferguson, *Europe in Transition 1300–1520* (1962).

Robert Fossier, *Peasant Life in the Medieval West* (1988).

Charles Gibson, *Spain in America* (1966).

Bernard Hamilton, *Religion in the Medieval West* (1986).

Denys Hay, *Europe: The Emergence of an Idea* (1968).

Denys Hay, *Europe in the Fourteenth and Fifteenth Centuries* (1989).

Norman Housley, *The Later Crusades 1274–1580* (1992).

Emmanuel Leroy Ladurie, *Montaillou: The Promised Land of Error* (1979).

Malcolm David Lambert, *Medieval Heresy: Popular Movements from the Bogomils to Hus* (1976).

Robert S. Lopez, *The Commercial Revolution of the Middle Ages, 950–1300* (1971).

Angus MacKay, *Society, Economy and Religion in Late Medieval Castile* (1987).

Richard Mackenney, *Sixteenth-Century Europe: Expansion and Conflict* (1993).

H.E. Mayer, *The Crusades* (1988).

Michel Mollat, *The Poor in the Middle Ages* (1986).

Michel Mollat and Philippe Wolfe, *Popular Revolution in the Late Middle Ages* (1973).

John H. Mundy, *Europe in the High Middle Ages 1150–1309* (1991)

J.H. Parry, *The Age of Reconnaissance: Discovery, Exploration and Settlement, 1450–1650* (1981).

Fritz Rorig, *The Medieval Town* (1967).

CHAPTER 2. THE RENAISSANCE

Michael Baxandall, *Painting and Experience in Fifteenth-Century Italy* (1972).

Judith Brown, *In the Shadow of Florence* (1982).

Eugene Brucker, *Renaissance Florence* (1983).

Peter Burke, *The Italian Renaissance: Culture and Society in Italy* (1987).

Peter Burke, *Popular Culture in Renaissance Europe, 1450–1620* (1986).

A.G. Dickens, *The Age of Humanism and Reformation: Europe in the Fourteenth to Sixteenth Centuries* (1972).

Carlo Ginzburg, *The Cheese and the Worms: The Cosmos of a Sixteenth-Century Miller* (1982).

Carlo Ginzburg, *Night Battles* (1985).

Richard Goldthwaite, *The Building of Renaissance Florence* (1981).

Anthony Grafton and Lisa Jardine, *From Humanism to the Humanities: Education and the Liberal Arts in Fifteenth and Sixteenth Century Europe* (1986).

J.R. Hale, *Renaissance Europe* (1977).

J.R. Hale, *War and Society in Renaissance Europe, 1450–1620* (1986).

Denys Hay and John Law, *Italy in the Age of the Renaissance, 1380–1530* (1989).

Dale Kent, *The Rise of the Medici* (1979).

Margaret King, *Women in the Renaissance* (1991).

Garrett Mattingly, *Renaissance Diplomacy* (1988).

Lauro Martines, *Power and Imagination: City-States in Renaissance Italy* (1988).

Harry A. Miskimin, *The Economy of Early Renaissance Europe, 1300–1460* (1975).

Harry A. Miskimin, *The Economy of Later Renaissance Europe, 1460–1600* (1977).

J.G.A. Pocock, *The Machiavellian Moment: Florentine Political Thought and the Atlantic Republican Tradition* (1975).

John Stephens, *The Italian Renaissance: The Origins of Intellectual and Artistic Change before the Reformation* (1990).

Hugh Thomas, *The Conquest of Mexico* (1993).

CHAPTER 3. THE TWO REFORMATIONS

Cornelis Augustijn, *Erasmus: His Life, Works, and Influence* (1991).

William J. Bouwsma, *John Calvin: A Sixteenth-Century Portrait* (1987).

Euan Cameron, *The European Reformation* (1991).

Anwar Chejne, *Islam and the West: The Moriscos: A Cultural and Social History* (1983).

William A. Christian, Jr., *Local Religion in Sixteenth-Century Spain* (1981).

P.H. Coles, *The Ottoman Impact on Europe* (1968).

A.G. Dickens, *The English Reformation* (1989).

Ronnie Po-Chia Hsia, ed., *The German People and the Reformation* (1988).

Ronnie Po-Chia Hsia, *Social Discipline in the Reformation: Central Europe, 1550–1750* (1989).

Ronnie Po-Chia Hsia, *Society and Religion in Munster, 1535–1618* (1984).

Lisa Jardine, *Erasmus, Man of Letters* (1993).

David Kirby, *Northern Europe in the Early Modern Period: The Baltic World, 1492–1772* (1990).

Sherrin Marshall, ed., *Women in Reformation and Counter-Reformation Europe: Public and Private Worlds* (1989).

Bernard Moeller, *Imperial Cities and the Reformation* (1982).

Steven E. Ozment, *The Reformation in the Cities: The Appeal of Protestantism to Sixteenth-Century Germany and Switzerland* (1975).

Steven E. Ozment, *When Fathers Ruled: Family Life in Reformation Europe* (1983).

Eugene R. Rice, Jr., and Anthony Grafton, *The Foundations of Early Modern Europe 1460–1559* (1994).

Thomas W. Robisheaux, *Rural Society and the Search for Order in Early Modern Germany* (1989).

Robert W. Scribner, *For the Sake of Simple Folk: Popular Propaganda for the German Reformation* (1984).

Lewis Spitz, *The Protestant Reformation* (1987).

Keith Thomas, *Religion and the Decline of Magic* (1971).

Tessa Watt, *Cheap Print and Popular Piety 1550–1640* (1991).

Merry E. Weisner, *Women and Gender in Early Modern Europe* (1993).

CHAPTER 4. THE WARS OF RELIGION

Natalie Zemon Davis, *The Return of Martin de Guerre* (1983).
Natalie Zemon Davis, *Society and Culture in Early Modern France* (1975).
J.H. Elliott, *Europe Divided, 1559–1598* (1968).
Mark Greengrass, *France in the Age of Henry IV: The Struggle for Stability* (1984).
R.J. Knecht, *Francis I* (1992).
Geoffrey Parker, *Europe in Crisis, 1598–1648* (1979).
Geoffrey Parker, ed., *The Thirty Years' War* (1988).
N.M. Sutherland, *The Massacre of St. Bartholomew and the European Conflict, 1559–1572* (1973).

CHAPTER 5. THE RISE OF THE ATLANTIC ECONOMY:
           SPAIN AND ENGLAND

Ralph Davis, *The Rise of the Atlantic Economies* (1973).
Jan De Vries, *The Economy of Europe in an Age of Crisis, 1600–1750* (1978).
J.H. Elliott, *The Count-Duke of Olivares: The Statesman in an Age of Decline* (1987).
J.H. Elliott, *Imperial Spain, 1469–1714* (1964).
G.R Elton, *England Under the Tutors* (1991).
Felipe Fernández-Armesto, *The Spanish Armada: The Experience of War in 1588* (1989).
John Guy, *Tudor England* (1988).
Henry Kamen, *Spain, 1469–1714: A Society of Conflict* (1991).
John Lynch, *Spain under the Habsburgs, 1516–1700* (2 vols., 1964–1969).
Colin Martin and Geoffrey Parker, *The Spanish Armada* (1988).
Geoffrey Parker, *Philip II* (1978).
Carla Rahn Philips, *Galleons for the King of Spain* (1986).
Peter Pierson, *Philip II of Spain* (1975).
John Salmon, *Society in Crisis: France in the Sixteenth Century* (1975).
Lacey Baldwin Smith, *Elizabeth Tudor* (1975).
Immanuel Wallerstein, *The Modern World System* (1974).
Penry Williams, *The Tudor Regime* (1979).
Joyce Youings, *Sixteenth-Century England* (1984).

CHAPTER 6. ENGLAND AND THE DUTCH REPUBLIC IN THE
           SEVENTEENTH CENTURY

Susan Dwyer Amussen, *An Ordered Society: Gender and Class in Early Modern England* (1988).
Bruce Galloway, *The Union of England and Scotland, 1603–1608* (1986).
Pieter Geyl, *The Revolt of the Netherlands, 1555–1609* (1958).
Christopher Hill, *God's Englishman: Oliver Cromwell and the English Revolution* (1975).
Christopher Hill, *The World Turned Upside Down* (1972).
Derek Hirst, *Authority and Conflict: England, 1603–1658* (1986).
Ronald Hutton, *The British Republic, 1649–1660* (1990).
J.I. Israel, *Dutch Primacy in World Trade, 1585–1740* (1990).
J.R. Jones, *The Revolution of 1688 in England* (1972).

Peter Laslett, *The World We Have Lost: England before the Industrial Age* (1971).
Brian P. Levack, *The Formation of the British State: England, Scotland, and the Union 1603–1707* (1987).
John Morrill, *The Revolt of the Provinces: Conservatism and Revolution in the English Civil War, 1630–1650* (1980).
Geoffrey Parker, *The Army of Flanders and the Spanish Road, 1567–1659* (1972).
J.L. Price, *Culture and Society in the Dutch Republic during the Seventeenth Century* (1974).
Conrad Russell, *The Causes of the English Civil War* (1990).
Simon Schama, *An Embarrassment of Riches: An Interpretation of Dutch Culture in the Golden Age* (1988).
J.A. Sharpe, *Early Modern England: A Social History, 1550–1760* (1990).
Lawrence Stone, *The Causes of the English Revolution, 1629–1642* (1990).
Lawrence Stone, *The Crisis of the Aristocracy, 1558–1641* (1967).
David Underdown, *Fire from Heaven: Life in an English Town in the Seventeenth Century* (1992).
David Underdown, *Revel, Riot, and Rebellion: Popular Politics and Culture in England, 1603–1660* (1985).
Keith Wrightson, *English Society, 1550–1760* (1982).

CHAPTER 7. THE AGE OF ABSOLUTISM, 1650–1720

M.S. Anderson, *Peter the Great* (1978).
Perry Anderson, *Lineages of the Absolutist State* (1974).
William Beik, *Absolutism and Society in Seventeenth-Century France: State Power and Provincial Aristocracy in Languedoc* (1985).
Joseph Bergin, *Cardinal Richelieu: Power and the Pursuit of Wealth* (1985).
J.H. Elliott, *Richelieu and Olivares* (1984).
Richard J. Evans, *The Making of the Habsburg Empire, 1550–1770* (1979).
Pierre Goubert, *Louis XIV and Twenty Million Frenchmen* (1972).
Ragnhild Hatton, *Europe in the Age of Louis XIV* (1979).
Hahil Inalcik, *The Ottoman Empire: The Classical Age, 1300–1600* (1973).
Robert Mandrou, *Introduction to Modern France, 1500–1640* (1975).
Roland Mousnier, *Peasant Uprisings in Seventeenth-Century France, Russia, and China* (1970).
David Parker, *The Making of French Absolutism* (1983)
Theodore Rabb, *The Struggle for Stability in Early Modern Europe* (1975).
Orest Ranum, *The Fronde: A French Revolution* (1993).
Orest Ranum, *Paris in the Age of Absolutism* (1969).
Nicholas Riasanovsky, *The Image of Peter the Great in Russian History and Thought* (1985).

CHAPTER 8. THE NEW PHILOSOPHY OF SCIENCE

Herbert Butterfield, *The Origins of Modern Science, 1300–1800* (1965).
John Fauvel, Raymond Flood, Michael Shortland, and Robin Wilson, eds., *Let Newton Be! A New Perspective on His Life and Works* (1988).
A.R. Hall, *The Revolution in Science, 1500–1750: The Formation of the Modern Scientific Attitude* (1983).

Margaret Jacobs, *The Cultural Meaning of the Scientific Revolution* (1988).

Hugh Kearney, *Science and Change, 1500–1700* (1971).

Alexandre Koyré, *The Formation of the Modern Scientific Attitude* (1983).

T.S. Kuhn, *The Structure of Scientific Revolution* (1989).

Robert K. Merton, *Science, Technology, and Society in Seventeenth-Century England* (1970).

Londa Schiebinger, *The Mind Has No Sex? Women in the Origins of Modern Science* (1990).

R.S. Westfall, *Never at Rest: A Biography of Issac Newton* (1993).

B.H.G. Wormald, *Francis Bacon: History, Politics, and Science, 1561–1626* (1993).

Chapter 9. Eighteenth-Century Economic and Social Change

M.S. Anderson, *Europe in the Eighteenth Century, 1713–1783* (1982).

C.A. Bayly, *Imperial Meridan: The British Empire and the World 1780–1830* (1989).

Maxine Berg, *The Age of Manufacturers, 1700–1820: Industry, Innovation, and Work in Britain* (1985).

Peter Borsay, *The English Urban Renaissance: Culture and Society in the Provincial Town, 1660–1770* (1989).

P.J. Corfield, *The Impact of English Towns 1700-1800* (1982).

Douglas Hay et. al., *Albion's Fatal Tree: Crime and Punishment in Eighteenth-Century England* (1975).

Steven L. Kaplan, *Provisioning Paris: Merchants and Millers in the Grain and Flour Trade during the Eighteenth Century* (1984).

Leonard Krieger, *Kings and Philosophers, 1689–1789* (1970).

Emmanuel LeRoy Ladurie, *The Peasants of Languedoc* (1974).

Paul Langford, *A Polite and Commercial People: England 1727–1783* (1989).

G.E. Mingay, *Land and Society in England 1750–1980* (1994).

J.H. Parry, *Trade and Dominion: The European Overseas Empires in the Eighteenth Century* (1971).

Roy Porter, *English Society in the Eighteenth Century* (1986).

Bernard Semmel, *The Methodist Revolution* (1973).

Marc Raeff, *The Origins of the Russian Intelligentsia: The Eighteenth Century Nobility* (1966).

James C. Riley, *The Seven Years War and the Old Regime in France* (1986).

George Rudé, *Paris and London in the Eighteenth Century* (1971).

Lawrence Stone, *The Family, Sex, and Marriage in England, 1500–1800* (1977).

E.P. Thompson, *Whigs and Hunters: The Origins of the Black Act* (1975).

Isser Woloch, *Eighteenth-Century: Tradition and Progress, 1715–1789* (1982).

Chapter 10. Enlightened Thought and the Republic of Letters

Keith Baker, *Condorcet: From Natural Philosophy to Social Mathematics* (1975).

Keith Baker, *Inventing the French Revolution: Essays in the Political Culture of Eighteenth-Century France* (1990).

Roger Chartier, *The Cultural Origins of the French Revolution* (1991).

Maurice Cranston, *The Noble Savage: Jean-Jacques Rousseau, 1754–1762* (1991).

Maurice Cranston, *Philosophers and Pamphleteers: Political Theorists of the Enlightenment* (1986).

Thomas E. Crow, *Painters and Public Life in Eighteenth-Century Paris* (1985).

Robert Darnton, *The Business of Enlightenment* (1979).

Robert Darnton, *The Great Cat Massacre* (1985).

Robert Darnton, *The Literary Underground of the Old Regime* (1985).

Peter Gay, *The Enlightenment: An Interpretation* (2 vols., 1966–1969).

Peter Gay, *Voltaire's Politics: The Poet as Realist* (1988).

Dena Goodman, *The Republic of Letters: A Cultural History of the French Enlightenment* (1984).

Norman Hampson, *A Cultural History of the Enlightenment* (1969).

J.M. McManners, *Death and Enlightenment: Changing Attitudes to Death among Christians and Unbelievers in Eighteenth-Century France* (1982).

Roy Porter and Mikulás Teich, eds., *The Enlightenment in National Context* (1981).

Franco Venturi, *Italy and the Enlightenment: Studies in a Cosmopolitan Century* (1972).

Chapter 11. Eighteenth-Century Dynastic Rivalries and Politics

Paul Avrich, *Russian Rebels, 1600–1800* (1972).

Bernard Bailyn, *The Ideological Origins of the American Revolution* (1992).

C.B.A. Behrens, *The Ancien Regime* (1967).

C.B.A. Behrens, *Society, Government, and the Enlightenment: The Experiences of Eighteenth-Century France and Prussia* (1985).

David Bell, *Lawyers and Citizens: The Making of a Political Elite in Old Regime France* (1994).

John Brewer, *Party Ideology and Popular Politics at the Accession of George III* (1976).

John Brewer, *The Sinews of Power: War, Money, and the English State, 1688–1783* (1989).

J.C.D. Clark, *English Society 1688–1832* (1985).

Linda Colley, *Britons: Forging the Nation, 1707–1837* (1992).

Linda Colley, *In Defiance of Oligarchy: The Tory Party 1714–60* (1982).

Olwen Hufton, *The Poor of Eighteenth-Century France, 1750–1789* (1974).

Isabel de Madariaga, *Catherine the Great: A Short History* (1990).

Sara Maza, *Private Lives and Public Affairs: The Causes Celèbres of Prerevolutionary France* (1993).

Sara Maza, *Servants and Masters in Eighteenth-Century France: The Uses of Loyalty* (1983).

N. McKendrick, J. Brewer, and J.H. Plumb, *The Birth of a Consumer Society: The Commercialization of Eighteenth-Century England* (1982).

Edmund Morgan, *The Birth of the Republic, 1763–1789* (1977).

Daniel Roche, *The People of Paris* (1987).

Robert M. Schwartz, *Policing the Poor in Eighteenth-Century France* (1988).

Franco Venturi, *The End of the Old Regime in Europe, 1776–1789* (2 vols., 1991).

Ernst Wangermann, *The Austrian Achievement 1700–1800* (1973).

Wayne Ph. te. Brake, *Regents and Rebels: The Revolutionary World of an Eighteenth-Century Dutch City* (1989).

CHAPTER 12. THE FRENCH REVOLUTION

Jean-Paul Bertaud, *The Army of the French Revolution: From Citizen-Soldiers to Instrument of Power* (1988).

T.C.W. Blanning, *The Origins of the French Revolutionary Wars* (1989).

John Bosher, *The French Revolution* (1988).

Richard Cobb, *The Police and the People: French Popular Protest, 1789–1820* (1972).

William Doyle, *Origins of the French Revolution* (1988).

Marianne Elliott, *Partners in Revolution: The United Irishmen and France* (1982).

Alan Forrest, *Conscripts and Deserters: The Army and French Society during the Revolution and Empire* (1989).

Alan Forrest, *The French Revolution and the Poor* (1981).

François Furet, *Interpreting the French Revolution* (1992).

A. Goodwin, *The Friends of Liberty: The English Democratic Movement in the Age of the French Revolution* (1979).

Patrice Higonnet, *Sister Republics: The Origins of French and American Republicanism* (1988).

Lynn Hunt, *The Family Romance of the French Revolution* (1992).

Lynn Hunt, *Politics, Culture, and Class in the French Revolution* (1984).

Peter Jones, *The Peasantry in the French Revolution* (1988).

Georges Lefebvre, *The Coming of the French Revolution* (1989).

Darline Gay Levy, Harriet Branson Applewhite, and Mary Durham Johnson, *Women in Revolutionary Paris 1789–1795* (1979).

Colin Lucas, ed., *The Political Culture of the French Revolution* (1989).

Ted W. Margadant, *Urban Rivalries in the French Revolution* (1992).

Sarah E. Meltzer and Leslie W. Rabine, eds., *Rebel Daughters: Women and the French Revolution* (1989).

Mona Ozouf, *Festivals and the French Revolution* (1988).

R.R. Palmer, *The Age of the Democratic Revolution: A Political History of Europe and America, 1760–1800* (2 vols., 1959–1964).

R.R. Palmer, *Twelve Who Ruled: The Year of the Terror in the French Revolution* (1989).

Ronald Paulson, *Representations of Revolution, 1789–1820* (1983).

Jeremy D. Popkin, *Revolutionary News: The Press in France, 1789–1799* (1990).

Georges Rudé, *The Great Fear of 1789* (1973).

William Sewell, Jr., *A Rhetoric of Bourgeois Revolution: The Abbé Sieyès and What Is the Third Estate?* (1994).

Donald Sutherland, *France, 1789–1815: Revolution and Counter-revolution* (1986).

Timothy Tackett, *Religion, Revolution, and Regional Culture in Eighteenth-Century France: The Ecclesiastical Oath of 1791* (1986).
Charles Tilly, *The Vendée* (1964).
Isser Woloch, *The New Regime: Transformations of the French Civic Order, 1789–1820s* (1994).

CHAPTER 13. NAPOLEON AND EUROPE

Louis Bergeron, *France Under Napoleon* (1981).
J. Christopher Herold, *The Age of Napoleon* (1985).
Georges Lefebvre, *Napoleon* (2 vols., 1969).
Felix Markham, *Napoleon* (1963).
Harold T. Parker, *Three Napoleonic Battles* (1983).
Gunther Rothenberg, *The Art of Warfare in the Age of Napoleon* (1978).
Alan Schom, *One Hundred Days: Napoleon's Road to Waterloo* (1992).
Jakob Walter, *The Diary of a Napoleonic Foot Soldier* (1991).
Stuart Wolfe, *Napoleon's Integration of Europe* (1991).
D.G. Wright, *Napoleon and Europe* (1984).

CHAPTER 14. CHALLENGES TO RESTORATION EUROPE

Michael Brock, *Great Reform Act* (1973).
Clive H. Church, *1830 in Europe: Revolution and Political Change* (1983).
Gordon A. Craig, *The Triumph of Liberalism: Zurich in the Golden Age 1830–1869* (1988).
Eric J. Evans, *Britain before the Reform Act: Politics and Society 1815–1832* (1989).
Norman Gash, *Reaction and Reconstruction in English Politics, 1832–1853* (1965).
André Jardin and André-Jean Tudesq, *Restoration and Reaction, 1815–1848* (1983).
Gareth Stedman Jones, *Languages of Class: Studies in English Working-Class History* (1983).
Clara M. Lovett, *The Democratic Movement in Italy, 1830–1876* (1982).
Steven Marcus, *Engels, Manchester, and the Working Class* (1974).
Harold Nicolson, *The Congress of Vienna: A Study in Allied Unity, 1812–1822* (1946).
David H. Pinkney, *The French Revolution of 1830* (1972).
Nicholas Riasanovsky, *A Parting of the Ways: Government and the Educated Public in Russia, 1801–55* (1976).
John L. Snell, *The Democratic Movement in Germany* (1976).
Alan Spitzer, *The French Generation of 1820* (1987).

CHAPTER 15. THE MIDDLE CLASSES IN THE ERA OF LIBERALISM

Leonore Davidoff and Catherine Hall, *Family Fortunes: Men and Women of the English Middle Class, 1780–1850* (1991).
Friedrich Engels, *The Condition of the Working Class in England* (1993).

Hugh Honour, *Romanticism* (1979).

R.J. Morris, *Class, Sect and Party: The Making of the British Middle Class: Leeds, 1820–50* (1990).

Harold Perkin, *The Origins of Modern English Society 1780–1880* (1972).

Pamela M. Pilbeam, *The Middle Classes in Europe 1789–1914 France, Germany, Italy and Russia* (1990).

Leon Plantinga, *Romantic Music: A History of Musical Style in Nineteenth-Century Europe* (1984).

Barbara Taylor, *Eve and the New Jerusalem: Socialism and Feminism in the Nineteenth Century* (1983).

William Weber, *Music and the Middle Class: The Social Structure of Concert Life in London, Paris and Vienna* (1975).

CHAPTER 16. THE INDUSTRIAL REVOLUTION, 1800–1850

W.L. Blackwell, *The Beginnings of Russian Industrialization, 1800–60* (1968).

Louis Chevalier, *Laboring Classes and Dangerous Classes in Paris during the First Half of the Nineteenth Century* (1973).

G. Kitson Clark, *Churchmen and the Condition of England 1832–1885* (1973).

Michel Foucault, *Madness and Civilization* (1973).

W.O. Henderson, *The Industrialization of Europe 1780–1914* (1970).

Colin Heywood, *Childhood in Nineteenth-Century France: Work, Health, and Education among the Classes Populaires* (1988).

E.J. Hobsbawm and George Rudé, *Captain Swing* (1975).

David J.V. Jones, *Rebecca's Children: A Study of Rural Society, Crime, and Protest* (1989).

David Landes, *The Unbound Prometheus: Technological Change and Industrial Development in Western Europe from 1750 to the Present* (1976).

Lynn Hollen Lees, *Exiles of Erin: Irish Migrants to Victorian London* (1979).

David McLellan, *Karl Marx: His Life and Thought* (1977).

John M. Merriman, *The Margins of City Life: Explorations on the French Urban Frontier, 1815–1851* (1991).

Claire Goldberg Moses, *French Feminism in the Nineteenth Century* (1984).

Roger Price, *A Social History of Nineteenth-Century France* (1987).

John Roach, *History of Secondary Education in England, 1800–1870* (1987).

William Sewell, Jr., *Work and Revolution in France: The Language of Labor from the Old Regime to 1848* (1980).

E.P. Thompson, *The Making of the English Working Class* (1963).

Louise A. Tilly and Joan W. Scott, *Women, Work, and Family* (1987).

Clive Trebilcock, *The Industrialization of the Continental Powers, 1780–1914* (1981).

E.A. Wrigley, *Population and History* (1969).

CHAPTER 17. THE REVOLUTIONS OF 1848

Maurice Agulhon, *The Republican Experiment, 1848–1852* (1983).

Maurice Agulhon, *The Republic in the Village: The People of the Var from the French Revolution to the Second Republic* (1982).

T.J. Clark, *The Absolute Bourgeois: Artists and Politics in France, 1848–1851* (1973).

Istvan Déak, *The Lawful Revolution: Louis Kossuth and the Hungarians, 1848–49* (1979).

Georges Duveau, *1848: The Making of a Revolution* (1967).

Theodore Hamerow, *Restoration, Revolution, and Reaction: Economics and Politics in Germany, 1815–1871* (1958).

Ted W. Margadant, *French Peasants in Revolt: The Insurrection of 1851* (1979).

John M. Merriman, *The Agony of the Republic: The Repression of the Left in Revolutionary France, 1848–1851* (1978).

Peter McPhee, *The Politics of Rural Life: Political Mobilization in the French Countryside, 1845–1852* (1992).

John Saville, *1848: The British State and the Chartist Movement* (1987).

Jonathan Sperber, *The European Revolutions, 1848–1851* (1993).

Jonathan Sperber, *Rhineland Radicals: The Democratic Movement and the Revolution of 1848–49* (1991).

CHAPTER 18. THE ERA OF NATIONAL UNIFICATION

Gordon A. Craig, *The Politics of the Prussian Army, 1640–1945* (1964).

Istvan Déak, *Beyond Nationalism: A Social History of the Habsburg Officer Corps, 1848–1918* (1990).

Lothar Gall, *Bismarck: The White Revolutionary* (2 vols., 1986).

Theodore S. Hamerow, *The Social Foundations of German Unification, 1858–1871* (2 vols, 1969–1972).

Harry Hearder, *Italy in the Age of the Risorgimento* (1982).

Luigi Salvatorelli, *The Risorgimento: Thought and Action* (1970).

Fritz Stern, *Gold and Iron: Bismarck, Bleichröeder, and the Building of the German Empire* (1977).

Denis Mack Smith, *Cavour* (1985).

Denis Mack Smith, *Cavour and Garibaldi 1860: A Study of Political Conflict* (1985).

Denis Mack Smith, *Victor Emmanuel, Cavour, and the Risorgimento* (1971).

CHAPTER 19. THE DOMINANT POWERS IN THE AGE OF LIBERALISM: BRITAIN, FRANCE, AND RUSSIA

Robert Anderson, *Education and Opportunity in Victorian Scotland* (1983).

Derek Beales, *From Castlereagh to Gladstone 1815–1885* (1969).

Asa Briggs, *The Age of Improvement 1783–1867* (1957).

Asa Briggs, *Victorian Cities* (London, 1977).

Asa Briggs, *Victorian People* (London, 1954).

W.L. Burn, *The Age of Equipoise: A Study of the Mid-Victorian Generation* (1964).

G. Kitson Clark, *The Making of Victorian England* (1962).

H.J. Dyos and Michael Wolff, *The Victorian City: Images and Realities* (2 vols., 1983).

Norman Gash, *Aristocracy and People: Britain, 1815–1865* (1979).

Gertrude Himmelfarb, *Darwin and the Darwinian Revolution* (1968).

Gertrude Himmelfarb, *Poverty and Compassion: The Moral Indignation of the Late Victorians* (1991).

E.J. Hobsbawm, *The Age of Capital, 1848–1875* (1976).

Walter Houghton, *The Victorian Frame of Mind* (1957).

Michael Howard, *The Franco-Prussian War: The German Invasion of France, 1870–71* (1981).

Frank E. Huggett, *The Land Question* (1975).

David P. Jordan, *Transforming Paris: The Life and Labors of Baron Haussmann* (1995).

James F. McMillan, *Napoleon III* (1991).

Arthur P. Mendel, *Michael Bakunin: Roots of Apocalypse* (1982).

David H. Pinkney, *Napoleon III and the Rebuilding of Paris* (1972).

Alain Plessis, *The Rise and Fall of the Second Empire, 1852–1871* (1985).

Norman Rich, *The Age of Nationalism and Reform, 1850–1890* (1970).

Bertrand Semmel, *John Stuart Mill and the Pursuit of Virtue* (1984).

Alan Sked, *The Decline and Fall of the Habsburg Empire* (1989).

Peter Stansky, ed., *The Victorian Revolution* (1973).

F.M.L. Thompson, *English Landed Society in the Nineteenth Century* (1963).

Robert Tombs, *The War Against Paris, 1871* (1981).

Frank M. Turner, *The Greek Heritage in Victorian Britain* (1981).

Martha Vicinus, *Suffer and Be Still: Women in the Victorian Age* (1973).

G.M. Young, *Portrait of an Age: Victorian England* (1980).

Theodore Zeldin, *The Political System of Napoleon III* (1971).

Reginald E. Zelnick, *Labor and Society in Tsarist Russia: The Factory Workers of St. Petersburg 1855–1870* (1971).

CHAPTER 20. RAPID INDUSTRIALIZATION AND ITS CHALLENGES, 1870–1914

Elinor Accampo, *Industrialization, Family Life, and Class Relations: Saint Chamond, 1815–1914* (1989).

Steven E. Aschheim, *The Nietzsche Legacy in Germany, 1890–1990* (1992).

François Bedarida, *A Social History of England, 1851–1975* (1980).

Lenard Berlanstein, ed., *Rethinking Labor History* (1993).

Alain Corbin, *Women for Hire: Prostitution and Sexuality in France after 1850* (1990).

David F. Crew, *Town on the Ruhr: A Social History of Bochum, 1860–1914* (1979).

Geoffrey Crossick, ed., *The Lower Middle Class in Britain, 1870–1914* (1977).

Geoffrey Crossick and Heinz-Gerhard Haupt, ed., *Shopkeepers and Master Artisans in Nineteenth-Century Europe* (1984).

Herbert Feis, *Europe: The World's Banker, 1870–1914* (1974).

Daniel Field, *The End of Serfdom: Gentry and Bureaucracy in Russia, 1855–1861* (1975).

Peter Gay, *Freud: A Life for Our Time* (New York, 1988).

Robert Gildea, *Education in Provincial France: A Study of Three Departments* (1983).

Michael P. Hanagan, *The Logic of Solidarity: Artisans and Industrial Workers in Three French Towns, 1870–1914* (1980).

W.O. Henderson, *The Rise of German Industrial Power, 1834–1914* (1976).

Paul M. Hohenberg and Lynn Hollen Lees, *The Making of Urban Europe 1000–1950* (1985).

Temma Kaplan, *The Anarchists of Andalusia, 1868–1903* (1977).

Charles Kindleberger, *Economic Growth in France and Britain, 1851–1950* (1964).

Thomas A. Kselman, *Miracles and Prophecies in Nineteenth-Century France* (1983).

John Lukacs, *Budapest 1900: A Historical Portrait of a City and Its Culture* (1988).

Mary Jo Maynes, *Taking the Hard Road: Life Course in French and German Workers' Autobiographies in the Era of Industrialization* (1995).

Michael B. Miller, *The Bon Marché: Bourgeois Culture and the Department Store, 1869–1920* (1981).

Alan S. Milward and S.B. Saul, *The Development of the Economies of Continental Europe, 1850–1914* (1977).

Leslie Moch, *Moving Europeans: Migration in Western Europe since 1650* (1993).

Michelle Perrot, *Workers on Strike: France, 1871–1890* (1987).

Charles Rearick, *Pleasures of the Belle Epoque* (1985).

Donald Reid, *Paris Sewers and Sewermen: Realities and Representations* (1991).

Carl E. Schorske, *Fin-de-Siècle Vienna: Politics and Culture* (1980).

Joan W. Scott, *The Glassworkers of Carmaux: French Craftsmen and Political Action in a Nineteenth-Century City* (1974).

Jerrold Seigel, *Bohemian Paris: Culture, Politics, and the Boundaries of Bourgeois Life, 1830–1930* (1986).

Roger Shattuck, *The Banquet Years: The Origins of the Avant-Garde in France 1885 to World War I* (1988).

Debora L. Silverman, *Art Nouveau in Fin-de-Siècle France: Politics, Psychology, and Style* (1989).

Bonnie G. Smith, *Ladies of the Leisure Class: The Bourgeoises of Northern France in the Nineteenth Century* (1982).

Gareth Stedman Jones, *Outcast London: A Study in the Relations Between Classes in Victorian Society* (1976).

Mikulás Teich and Roy Porter, eds., *Fin de Siècle and Its Legacy* (1990).

Louise Tilly, *Politics and Class in Milan, 1881–1901* (1992).

Judith R. Walkowitz, *Prostitution and Victorian Society: Women, Class, and the State* (1983).

P.J. Waller, *Town, City, and Nation: England 1850–1914* (1983).

CHAPTER 21. MASS POLITICS AND NATIONALISM

Edward Berenson, *The Trial of Madame Caillaux* (1992).

David Blackbourn and Geoff Eley, *The Peculiarities of German History: Bourgeois Society and Politics in Nineteenth-Century German History* (1984).

Robert Blake, *Disraeli* (1967).

Michael Burns, *Dreyfus: A Family Affair, 1789–1945* (1992).

David Cannadine, *The Decline and Fall of the British Aristocracy* (1990).

Peter Gay, *Freud, Jews, and Other Germans* (1978).

Ruth Gay, *The Jews of Germany: A Historical Portrait* (1992).

Nancy Green, *The Pletzl of Paris: Jewish Immigrant Workers in the Belle Epoque* (1986).

Steven C. Hause with Anne R. Kenney, *Women's Suffrage and Social Politics in the French Third Republic* (1984).

Gertrude Himmelfarb, *The Idea of Poverty* (1984).

Gertrude Himmelfarb, *Poverty and Compassion: The Moral Imagination of the Late Victorians* (1990).

E.H. Hunt, *British Labour History 1815–1914* (1981).

Paula Hyman, *From Dreyfus to Vichy: The Remaking of French Jewry, 1906–1939* (1979).

William Irvine, *The Boulanger Affair Reconsidered: Royalism, Boulangism, and the Origins of the Radical Right in France* (1989).

James Joll, *The Anarchists* (1981).

Tony Judt, *Marxism and the French Left: Studies in Labor and Politics in France, 1830–1981* (1986).

Thomas Laqueur, *Religion and Respectability: Sunday Schools and Working-Class Culture, 1780–1850* (1976).

William C. Lubenow, *Parliamentary Politics and the Home Rule Crisis* (1988).

Michael Marrus, *The Politics of Assimilation* (1971).

J.M Mayeur and Madeleine Rebérioux, *The Third Republic from Its Origins to the Great War, 1871–1914* (1984).

John M. Merriman, *The Red City: Limoges and the French Nineteenth Century* (1991).

P. Pulzer, *The Rise of Political Anti-Semitism in Germany and Austria* (1988).

John P. Rossi, *The Transformation of the British Liberal Party: A Study of the Liberal Opposition 1874–1880* (1978).

Norman Stone, *Europe Transformed, 1878–1919* (1984).

F.M.L. Thompson, *The Rise of Respectable Society 1830–1900* (1986).

Barbara Tuchman, *The Proud Tower: A Portrait of the World before the War, 1890–1914* (1966).

Joan Connelly Ullman, *The Tragic Week: A Study in Anticlericalism in Spain 1875–1912* (1968).

Eugen Weber, *France, fin-de-siècle* (1986).

Eugen Weber, *Peasants into Frenchmen: The Modernization of Rural France, 1870–1914* (1986).

Steven Wilson, *Ideology and Experience: Anti-Semitism in France at the Time of the Dreyfus Affair* (1982).

CHAPTER 22. THE AGE OF EUROPEAN IMPERIALISM

Imran Ali, *The Punjab Under Imperialism* (1988).

W. Baumgart, *Imperialism: The Idea and Reality of British and French Colonial Expansion 1880–1914* (1982).

Raymond Betts, *The False Dawn: European Imperialism in the Nineteenth Century* (1975).

Henri Brunschwig, *French Colonialism, 1871–1914: Myths and Realities* (1966).

Ronald Hyam, *Britain's Imperial Century, 1815–1914: A Study in European Expansion* (1976).

Alan Hodgart, *The Economics of European Imperialism* (1977).

Timothy Mitchell, *Colonizing Egypt* (1988).

Bernard Porter, *The Lion's Share: A Short History of British Imperialism, 1850–1983* (1984).

Ronald Robinson, John Gallagher, with Alice Denny, *Africa and the Victorians* (1981).

Edward Said, *Orientalism* (1979).

W.D. Smith, *European Imperialism in the Nineteenth and Twentieth Centuries* (1982).

CHAPTER 23. THE ORIGINS OF THE GREAT WAR

James Joll, *The Origins of the First World War* (1992).

George F. Kennan, *The Fateful Alliance: France, Russia, and the Coming of the First War* (1992).

Paul Kennedy, *The Rise of Anglo-German Antagonism, 1860–1914* (1980).

Lawrence Lafore, *The Long Fuse* (1965).

Joachim Remak, ed., *The First World War: Causes, Conduct, Consequences* (1971).

CHAPTER 24. THE GREAT WAR

Jean-Jacques Becker, *The Great War and the French People* (1985).

Modris Eksteins, *Rites of Spring: The Great War and the Birth of the Modern Age* (1989).

Paul Fussell, *The Great War and Modern Memory* (1975).

Ross Gregory, *The Origins of American Intervention in the First World War* (1971).

Alister Horne, *The Price of Glory: Verdun, 1916* (1963).

Samuel Hynes, *A War Imagined: The First World War and English Culture* (1990).

Lyn Macdonald, *Somme* (1983).

Arthur Marwick, *The Deluge: British Society and the First World War* (1966).

Arthur Marwick, *Women at War, 1914–1918* (1977).

Kenneth Silver, *Esprit de Corps: Avant Garde Art and the First World War in France* (1990).

James Stokesbury, *A Short History of World War I* (1981).

Norman Stone, *The Eastern Front 1914–1917* (1975).

John W. Wheeler-Bennett, *Brest-Litovsk: The Forgotten Peace* (1971).

John Williams, *The Home Fronts: Britain, France, and Germany 1914–1918* (1972).

J.M. Winter, *The Great War and the British People* (1986).

CHAPTER 25. REVOLUTIONARY RUSSIA AND THE SOVIET UNION

Abraham Ascher, *The Revolution of 1905* (2 vols., 1992).
Paul Avrich, *Kronstadt, 1921* (1991).
Victoria E. Bonnell, *Roots of Rebellion: Workers' Politics and Organizations in St. Petersburg and Moscow, 1900–1914* (1983).
Steven F. Cohen, *Bukharin and the Bolshevik Revolution* (1964).
Robert Conquest, *The Great Terror: A Reassessment* (1990).
Terrence Emmons, *The Formation of Political Parties and the First National Elections in Russia* (1983).
Marc Ferro, *The Bolshevik Revolution: A Social History of the Russian Revolution* (1980).
Orlando Figes, *Peasant Russia, Civil War* (1989).
Sheila Fitzpatrick, *The Russian Revolution 1917–1932* (1982).
Tsuyoshi Hasegawa, *The February Revolution: Petrograd, 1917* (1981).
Geoffrey Hosking, *The First Socialist Society: A History of the Soviet Union from Within* (1993).
John L.H. Keep, *The Russian Revolution: A Study in Mass Mobilization* (1976).
Diane Koenker, *Moscow Workers and the 1917 Russian Revolution* (1982).
Alec Nove, *An Economic History of the U.S.S.R.* (1989).
Richard Pipes, *Russian Under the Bolshevik Regime* (1994).
Alexander Rabinowitch, *The Bolsheviks Come to Power: The Revolution of 1917 in Petrograd* (1978).
William G. Rosenberg, *Liberals in the Russian Revolution: The Constitutional Democratic Party, 1917–1921* (1974).
Teodor Shanin, *The Awkward Class* (1972).
S.A. Smith, *Red Petrograd: Revolution in the Factories, 1917–18* (1983).
Richard Stites, *Revolutionary Dreams: Utopian Vision and Experimental Life in the Russian Revolution* (1988).
Donald W. Treadgold, *Twentieth Century Russia* (1990).
Robert C. Tucker, *Stalin as Revolutionary, 1879–1929* (1973).
Robert C. Tucker, *Stalin in Power: The Revolution from Above, 1928–1941* (1990).
Adam Ulam, *Expansion and Coexistence: The History of Soviet Foreign Policy, 1917–1973* (1974).
Alan Wildman, *The End of the Russian Imperial Army: The Old Army and the Soldiers' Revolt (March-April 1917)* (1980).
Alan Wildman, *The Road to Soviet Power and Peace* (1987).

CHAPTER 26. THE ELUSIVE SEARCH FOR STABILITY IN THE 1920s

Victoria De Grazia, *How Fascism Ruled Women: Italy, 1922–1945* (1992).
Peter Gay, *Weimar Culture: The Outsider as Insider* (1968).
Robert Graves, *Goodbye to All That* (1957).
Robert Graves and Alan Hodge, *The Long Week-End: A Social History of Great Britain, 1918–1939* (1963).
Daniel Guérin, *The Brown Plague: Travels in Late Weimar and Early Nazi Germany* (1994).
Pierre-Jakez Hélias, *The Horse of Pride: Life in a Breton Village* (1978).
William R. Keylor, *The Twentieth Century World* (1992).

Martin Kitchen, *Europe Between the Wars: A Political History* (1988).

MacGregor Knox, *Mussolini Unleashed 1939–1941: Politics and Strategy in Fascist Italy* (1982).

Richard F. Kuisel, *Capitalism and the State in Modern France* (1983).

Gregory M. Luebbert, *Liberalism, Fascism, or Social Democracy: Social Classes and the Political Origins of Regimes in Interwar Europe* (1991).

Charles Maier, *Recasting Bourgeois Europe: Stabilization in France, Germany, and Italy in the Decade after World War I* (1975).

Sally Marks, *The Illusion of Peace: Europe's International Relations, 1918–1933* (1976).

Walter A. McDougall, *France's Rhineland Diplomacy, 1914–1924* (1978).

Detlev J.K. Peukert, *The Weimar Republic* (1989).

Joseph Rothschild, *East Central Europe between the Two World Wars* (1974).

Steven A. Schuker, *The End of French Predominance in Europe: The Financial Crisis of 1924 and the Adoption of the Dawes Plan* (1976).

Alan Sharp, *The Versailles Settlement: Peacemaking in Paris* (1991).

Dan P. Silverman, *Reconstructing Europe After the Great War* (1982).

Denis Mack Smith, *Italy and Its Monarchy* (1989).

Denis Mack Smith, *Mussolini: A Biography* (1983).

Robert Soucy, *Fascism in France: the First Wave, 1924–1933* (1986).

A.J.P. Taylor, *English History, 1914–1945* (1965).

Zerv Sternhell, *The Birth of a Fascist Ideology: From Cultural Rebellion to Political Revolution* (1994).

Mark Trachtenberg, *Reparation and World Politics* (1980).

Piotr Wandycz, *France and Her Eastern Allies, 1919–1925* (1974).

Chapter 27. The Europe of Depression and Dictatorship

William Sheridan Allen, *The Nazi Seizure of Power: The Experience of a Single German Town, 1922–1945* (1984).

Pierre Azéma, *From Munich to the Liberation, 1938–1944* (1985).

George Baer, *Test Case: Italy, Ethiopia and the League of Nations* (1976).

Ivo Banac, *The National Question in Yugoslavia* (1985).

P.M.H. Bell, *The Origins of the Second World War* (1986).

Richard Bessel, ed., *Life in the Third Reich* (1987).

Karl Dietrich Bracher, *The German Dictatorship: The Origins, Structure, and Effects of National Socialism* (1970).

Gerald Brenan, *The Spanish Labyrinth: An Account of the Social and Political Background of the Civil War* (1976).

Alan Bullock, *Hitler: A Study in Tyranny* (1964).

Joel Colton, *Léon Blum: Humanist in Politics* (1987).

Maurice Cowling, *The Impact of Hitler: British Politics and British Policy, 1933–1940* (1977).

Helmut Gruber, *Red Vienna: Experiments in Working-Class Culture 1919–1934* (1991).

H. Stuart Hughes, *Consciousness and Society: The Reorientation of European Social Thought, 1890–1930* (1979).

H. Stuart Hughes, *The Obstructed Path: French Social Thought in the Years of Desperation, 1930–1960* (1968).

Julian Jackson, *The Popular Front in France: Defending Democracy, 1934–1938* (1988).

Ian Kershaw, *The "Hitler Myth": Image and Reality in the Third Reich* (1989).

Charles Kindleberger, *The World in Depression, 1929–1939* (1986).

Detlev J.K. Peukert, *Inside Nazi Germany: Conformity, Opposition, and Racism in Everyday Life* (1987).

Fritz Stern, *The Politics of Cultural Despair: A Study in the Use of the Germanic Ideology* (1974).

Gerald Jackson, *The Spanish Republic and the Civil War, 1931–1939* (1974).

Rudy Koshar, *Social Life, Local Politics, and Nazism: Marburg, 1880–1935* (1986).

David Clay Large, *Between Two Fires: Europe's Path in the 1930s* (1990).

George Orwell, *Homage to Catalonia* (1938).

Anthony Read and David Fisher, *The Deadly Embrace: Hitler, Stalin and the Nazi-Soviet Pact, 1939–1941* (1989).

Joachim Remak, *The Origins of the Second World War* (1979).

David Schoenbaum, *Hitler's Social Revolution: Class and Status in Nazi Germany 1933–1939* (1980).

Robert Soucy, *Fascism in France: The Second Wave, 1933–1939* (1995).

Peter Stansky and William Abrahams, *Journey to the Frontier: Julian Bell and John Cornfield, Their Lives and the 1930s* (1966).

Hugh Thomas, *The Spanish Civil War* (1977).

Christopher Thorne, *The Approach of War, 1938–1939* (1978).

Christopher Thorne, *The Limits of Foreign Policy: The West, the League, and the Far Eastern Crisis of 1931–1933* (1972).

Henry A. Turner, Jr., *German Big Business and the Rise of Hitler* (1985).

Eugen Weber, *France: The Hollow Years* (1995).

Gerhard L. Weinberg, *The Foreign Policy of Hitler's Germany: Diplomatic Revolution in Europe, 1933–1936* (1970).

Gerhard L. Weinberg, *Starting World War II, 1937–1939* (1980).

CHAPTER 28. WORLD WAR II

Omer Bartov, *Hitler's Army: Soldiers, Nazis, and War in the Third Reich* (1992).

Robert Beitzell, *The Uneasy Alliance: America, Britain, and Russia, 1941–1943* (1972).

Marc Bloch, *Strange Defeat* (1968).

Peter Calvocoressi and Guy Wirt, *Total War: Causes and Courses of the Second World War* (1972).

Paul Fussell, *Wartime: Understanding and Behavior in the Second World War* (1989).

Robert Gellately, *The Gestapo and German Society: Enforcing Racial Policy 1933–1945* (1990).

Raul Hilberg, *Perpetrators, Victims, Bystanders: The Jewish Catastrophe, 1933–1945* (1992).

Peter Hoffmann, *The History of the German Resistance, 1933–1945* (1977).

John Keagan, *The Second World War* (1989).

H.R. Kedward, *In Search of the Maquis: Rural Resistance in Southern France, 1942–1944* (1993).

John Keegan, *Six Armies in Normandy* (1982).

Walter Laqueur, *The Terrible Secret: Suppression of the Truth about Hitler's "Final Solution"* (1980).

Michael Marrus, *The Holocaust in History* (London, 1988).

Arthur Marwick, *The Home Front: The British and the Second World War* (1977).

Alan S. Milward, *War, Economy, and Society, 1939–1945* (1977).

Robert O. Paxton, *Vichy France: Old Guard and New Order, 1940–1944* (1972).

Robert O. Paxton and Michael R. Marrus, *Vichy France and the Jews* (1981).

John F. Sweets, *Choices in Vichy France.*

Donald Cameron Watt, *How War Came* (1989).

Gordon Wright, *The Ordeal of Total War, 1939–1945* (1968).

Chapter 29. Rebuilding Divided Europe

Franc Ansprenger, *The Dissolution of Colonial Empires* (1989).

Muriel Evelyn Chamberlain, *Decolonization: The Fall of the European Empires* (1985).

Lynn E. Davis, *The Cold War Begins: Soviet-American Conflict over Eastern Europe* (1974).

A.W. DePorte, *Europe Between the Superpowers* (1979).

Robin Edmonds, *Soviet Foreign Policy: The Brezhnev Years* (1983).

John Lewis Gaddis, *The United States and the Origins of the Cold War, 1941–47* (1992).

Paul Ginsborg, *A History of Contemporary Italy: Society and Politics, 1943–1988* (1990).

Alfred Grosser, *The Western Alliance: European-American Relations since 1945* (1980).

Michael Harrison, *Reluctant Ally: France and Atlantic Security* (1981).

Stanley Hoffmann, *Decline or Renewal? France since the Popular Front: Government and the People, 1936–1986* (1988).

Michael J. Hogan, *The Marshall Plan: America, Britain and the Reconstruction of Western Europe, 1947–1952* (1987).

Alistair Horne, *A Savage War of Peace: Algeria, 1954–1962* (1978).

Tony Judt, *Past Imperfect: French Intellectuals, 1944–1956* (1993).

George F. Kennan, *The Nuclear Delusion: Soviet-American Relations in the Atomic Age* (1983).

Diane Kunz, *The Economic Diplomacy of the Suez Crisis* (1991).

Bruce R. Kuniholm, *The Origins of the Cold War in the Near East: Great Power Conflict and Diplomacy in Iran, Turkey, and Greece* (1994).

Richard Kuisel, *Seducing the French: The Dilemma of Americanization* (1993).

Arthur Marwick, *British Society since 1945* (1982).

Vojtech Mastny, *Helsinki, Human Rights, and European Security* (1986).

Alan S. Milward, *The European Rescue of the Nation-State* (1992).

Alan S. Milward, *The Reconstruction of Western Europe, 1945–1951* (1984).

Kenneth O. Morgan, *Labour in Power, 1945–1951* (1984).

Kenneth O. Morgan, *The People's Peace: British History, 1945–1990* (1991).

Robert A. Pollard, *Economic Security and the Origins of the Cold War* (1985).

Paul Preston, *Franco: A Biography* (1993).

Henry Rousso, *Vichy Syndrome: History and Memory in France since 1944* (1991).

Haig Simonian, *The Privileged Partnership: Franco-German Relations in the European Community, 1969–1984* (1985).

Henry A. Turner, Jr., *Germany from Partition to Reunification* (1992).

CHAPTER 30. THE EMERGENCE OF CONTEMPORARY EUROPE AND THE COLLAPSE OF COMMUNISM

Benedict Anderson, *Imagined Communities: Reflections on the Origins and Spread of Nationalism* (1991).

John Ardagh, *The New French Revolution* (1968).

Paul Arthur and Keith Jeffery, *Northern Ireland since 1968* (1988).

Timothy Garton Ash, *In Europe's Name: Germany and the Divided Continent* (1993).

Timothy Garton Ash, *The Polish Revolution: Solidarity, 1980–1982* (1983).

Ivo Banac, ed., *Eastern Europe in Revolution* (1992).

Corelli Barnett, *The Pride and the Fall: The Dream and Illusion of Britain as a Great Nation* (1987).

P.J. Cain and A.G. Hopkins, *British Imperialism: Crisis and Deconstruction, 1914–1990* (1993).

David Caute, *The Year of Barricades: A Journey through 1968* (1989).

Robert Darnton, *Berlin Journal: 1989–1990* (1991).

Karen Dawisha and Bruce Parrott, *Russia and the New States of Eurasia: The Politics of Upheaval* (1994).

Françoise Gaspard, *A Small City in France* (1995).

Prosser Gifford and William Roger Louis, eds., *Decolonization and African Independence: The Transfers of Power, 1960–1980* (1988).

John D. Hargreaves, *Decolonization in Africa* (1988).

Robert O. Keohane, Joseph S. Nye, and Stanley Hoffmann, *Europe after the Cold War* (1993).

Joseph LaPalombara, *Democracy, Italian Style* (1987).

Walter Laqueur, *The Age of Terrorism* (1987).

Walter Laqueur, *Europe since Hitler* (1983).

Bernard Lewis, *Islam and the West* (1993).

Robert J. Lieber, *Oil and the Middle East: Europe in the Energy Crisis* (1976).

Martin E. Malia, *The Soviet Tragedy: A History of Socialism in Russia, 1917–1991* (1993).

Paul Preston, *The Triumph of Democracy in Spain* (1986).

Peter Riddell, *The Thatcher Era and Its Legacy* (1991).

Joseph Rothschild, *Return to Diversity: A Political History of East Central Europe since World War II* (1993).

Martin J. Sherwin, *A World Destroyed: The Atomic Bomb and the Grand Alliance* (1975).

Anthony Sampson, *The Changing Anatomy of Britain* (1982).

George Weigel, *The Final Revolution: The Breaking of Communist Europe* (1991).

Lawrence Weschler, *Solidarity: Poland in the Season of Its Passion* (1982).

CREDITS

1433

The Raft of the Medusa, Louvre, Paris, Scala/Art Resource, NY; (bottom left) John Martin, *The Bard*, c. 1817, Yale Center for British Art, Paul Mellon Collection; (bottom right) Ernest Meissonier, *The Barricade*, 1848, Louvre, Paris, Giraudon/Art Resource, NY; **p. 3** (top) Jean-François Millet, *The Angelus*, Musée d'Orsay, Scala/Art Resource, NY; (bottom) Édouard Manet, *Déjeuner sur l'herbe*, 1863, Musée d'Orsay, Erich Lessing/ Art Resource, NY; **p. 4** (top left) Claude Monet, *The Railway Bridge at Argenteuil*, Musée d'Orsay, Scala/Art Resource, NY; (center) Edvard Munch, *The Scream*, 1893, © 1994 National Gallery, Oslo, Photograph by J. Lathion; (bottom left) Pablo Picasso, *The Tragedy*, 1903, Chester Dale Collection, © 1995 Board of Trustees, National Gallery of Art, Washington; (right) Gustav Klimt, *Judith II (Salomé)*, 1909, Museum of Modern Art of Ca' Pesaro, Venice, © Cameraphoto Venezia/Art Resource, NY.

Color Section 4: p. 1 (top) James Ensor, *Entry of Christ into Brussels*, 1888, Oil on canvas, 102 ½ X 169 ½" (160 x 430.5 cm), J. Paul Getty Museum, Malibu, California; (bottom) Henri Matisse, *Harmony in Red*, 1908, The Hermitage, St. Petersburg, George Roos/Art Resource, NY; **p. 2** (top left) Giacamo Balla, *Street Light* (Lampada—Studio di luce), dated by the artist 1909, 68 ¾ x 45 ¼" (174.7 x 114.5 cm), The Museum of Modern Art, New York, Hillman Periodicals Fund, Photograph © 1995 The Museum of Modern Art, New York, (top right) Marcel Duchamp, *Nude Descending a Staircase, No.2*, Philadelphia Museum of Art, Louis & Walter Arensberg Collection; (bottom left) Ernst Ludwig Kirchner, *Five Women in the Street*, 1913, Museum Ludwig, Köln, courtesy Rheinsiches Bildarchiv, Köln; (bottom right) Vassily Kandinsky, *Painting Number 200*, 1914, oil on canvas, 64 x 31 ½" (162.5 x 80 cm), The Museum of Modern Art, New York, Mrs. Simon Guggenheim Fund, Photograph © 1995 The Museum of Modern Art, New York, **p. 3** (top left) Juan Gris, *Le petit déjeuner*, 1915, Musée National d'Art Moderne, Centre Georges Pompidou; (top right) Paul Klee, *Equilibrist*, 1923, Paul-Klee Stiftung, Kunstmuseum Bern; (bottom left) Joan Miró, *Dutch Interior, I*, 1928, oil on canvas, 36 ⅛ x 28 ¾" (91.8 x 73 cm), The Museum of Modern Art, New York, Mrs. Simon Guggenheim Fund, Photograph © 1995 The Museum of Modern Art, New York; (bottom right) Fernand Léger, *Les constructeurs*, 1950, Musée National Fernand Léger, Biot France, Bridgeman/Art Resource, NY; **p. 4** (top left) Francis Bacon, *Pope II*, 1951, Städtische Kunsthalle, Mannheim; (top right) Salvador Dalí, *Cruxifixion*, 1954, oil on canvas, 48 ¾ x 76½", The Metropolitan Museum of Art, gift of the Chester Dale Collection, 1955; (bottom) Jean Dubuffet, *Virtual Virtue*, 1963, private collection.

Chapter 1: p. 4 (left) Staatliche Museen Preussischer Kulturbesitz ; (right) Ampliaciones y Reproducciones MAS, Barcelona; **p. 8** Pieter Dan, *Historie van Barbaryen*, Amsterdam, 1684, Special Collections, New York Public Library, Astor, Lenox, and Tilden Foundations; **p. 9** Bibliothèque de l'École des Beaux Arts, Giraudon/Art Resource, NY; **p.10** Hans Sebald Beham, *Saturn*, 16th century, Warder Collection; **p.12** Jerusalem Triptych, Polish school, 16th century, National Museum, Warsaw; **p.13** Miniature from *Heures de Charles d'Angoulême*, late 15th century, Ms. Latin 1173 f.4, © cliché Bibliothèque Nationale de France, Paris; **p. 14** Bibliothèque de l'Arsenal; **p. 16** Hans Wertinger, 1530, Germanisches Nationalmuseum, Nürnberg; **p. 19** From a painting by Bruegel, Metropolitan Museum, New York; **p. 24** Gerini Niccolo' di Pietro, *Storie di S. Matteo* (Banchieri), Scala/Art Resource, NY; **p. 25** Crispin de Passe, woman spinning from *Deliciarum Libeleus*, Hulton Deutsch Collection Ltd; **p. 34** MEPC Print Collection, Miriam and Ira D. Wallach Division of Art, Prints & Photographs, New York Public Library, Astor, Lenox, and Tilden Foundations; **p. 39** Kobe Museum, Japan; **p. 42** Illustration from Lienzo de Tlaxcala, *Antiguedades Mexicanas* (1892), Tozzer Library, Harvard University.

Chapter 2: p. 48 Ghilandaio Domenico, 1485, Sessetti Chapel, Santa Trinita, Scala/Art Resource, NY; **p. 50** Hamburger Kunsthalle, Photograph by Elke Walford; **p. 52** Giovanni Maria Butteri, *The Return from the Palio*, National Gallery of Ireland; **p. 57** Pianta della Catena, *Firenze*, 1490, Scala/Art Resource, NY; **p. 58** Giorgio Vasari, *The Signory Discuss the War against Pisa*, Palazzo Vecchio, Florence, Soprintendenza alle Gallerie, Florence; **p. 59** Giorgio Vasari, *Lorenzo de Medici*, Uffizi Palace, Alinari/Art Resource, NY; **p. 61** (left) Petrarch, Alinari/Art Resource, NY; (right) Ambrosius Holbein, *Aushängeschild eines Schulmeister*, Oeffentliche Kunstsammlung, Basel, Kunstmuseum, Inv. 311; **p. 65** (left) Leonardo da Vinci, *Foetus in the womb*, Her Majesty Queen Elizabeth II/Royal Collection Enterprises

Ltd; (right) Leonardo da Vinci, *Divine proportion*, Alinari /Art Resource, NY; **p. 67** Pitti Palace, Alinari/Art Resource, NY; **p. 69** Raphael, *Leo X and His Cardinals*, Uffizi, Florence, Alinari/ Art Resource, NY; **p. 70** Andrea Mantegna, fresco, Palazzo Ducale, Mantua (Sadea-Sansoni) Alinari/Art Resource, NY; **p. 74** (left) Masaccio, *The Expulsion of Adam and Eve from Eden*, Brancacci Chapel, Florence; (right) Masaccio, *The Trinity*, Santa Maria Novella, Florence, Alinari / Art Resource, NY; **p. 75** Andrea Mantegna, *The Dead Christ*, Brera, Milan, Alinari/Art Resource, NY; **p. 76** Donatello, *The Feast of Herod*, Baptismal Font, Alinari/Art Resource, NY; **p. 77** Leonardo da Vinci, *The Last Supper*, Sta. Maria delle Grazie, Alinari/Art Resource, NY; **p. 78** Michelangelo, detail of *The Last Judgement*, Vatican Palace, Sistine Chapel, Alinari/Art Resource, NY; **p. 83** Unknown artist, *The Burning of Savonarola*, Museo S. Marco, Alinari/Art Resource, NY; **p. 85** Bust of Niccolò Machiavelli from Palazzo Vecchio, Florence, Scala.

Chapter 3: p. 88 Woodcuts from the series *Passional Christi und Antichrist*, Wittenberg, 1521; **p. 90** Albrecht Dürer, *Four Horsemen of the Apocalypse*, Trustees of the British Museum, London; **p. 93** Hans Holbein, *Erasmus*, Louvre, Lauros/Giraudon; **p. 100** Lucas Cranach, *Portrait of Martin Luther as a Young Man*, National Museum, Nuremberg, Scala/Art Resource, NY; **p. 101** Unknown artist, *Dream of Frederick the Wise*, Collection of Dr. Fritz Schleifenbaum, Huttental-Weidenau, Marburg, Foto Marburg/Art Resource, NY; **p. 108** The Augsburg Confession, 1530, Kunstsammlungen der Veste, Coberg; **p. 113** (left) Zwingli, Bettmann Archive; (right) Illustration from *Chronique de Stumpffen* by Johan Stumf, Zurich, 1548; **p. 116** (left) Jean Calvin from Bibliothèque Publique et Universitaire, Genève, Photograph by François Martin; (right) Unknown artist, *Calvinist Service*, 1564, Bibliothèque Publique et Universitaire, Genève, Photograph by François Martin; **p. 122** (left) After Holbein, *Portrait of Henry VIII*, By courtesy of the National Portrait Gallery, London; (right) Unknown artist, *Anne Boleyn*, Musée Condé, Chantilly, Lauros-Giraudon/Art Resource, NY; **p. 123** Hans Holbein, *Sir Thomas More*, © The Frick Collection, New York; **p. 127** Council of Trent, Jahurhundert Wien, Haus-, Hof-, und Staatsarchiv; **p. 130** Gian Lorenzo Bernini, *Ecstasy of St. Theresa*, Alinari/Art Resource, NY; **p. 131** Caricatures of the Pope, 1545, The British Library; **p. 132** Gerald Dou, *Old Woman Reading the Bible*, © Rijksmuseum-Stichting, Amsterdam; **p. 134** Pieter Bruegel the Elder, *Battle between Carnival and Lent*, Kunsthistorisches Museum, Vienna, FotoMarburg/Art Resource, NY.

Chapter 4: p. 139 Pieter Bruegel the Elder, *Massacre of the Innocents*, Kunsthistorisches Museum, Vienna, Photograph by Erich Lessing/ Art Resource, NY; **p. 140** Jean Clouet, Portrait of Francis I, Uffizi Palace, Florence, Alinari/Art Resource, NY; **p. 143** Unknown artist, *Portrait of Catherine de Medici*, Palazzo Riccardi, Alinari/Art Resource; **p. 145** François Dubois d'Amiens, *St. Bartholomew's Day Massacre*, Collection Musée Cantonal des Beaux-Arts, Lausanne, Switzerland; **p. 147** Unknown artist, *Portrait of Henry IV*, Louvre, Paris, Photographie Bulloz; **p. 150** Assassination of the duke of Guise, © cliché Bibliothèque Nationale de France, Paris; **p. 151** *Henry IV Enters Paris*, © cliché Bibliothèque Nationale de France, Paris; **p. 158** Cardinal Richelieu, Warder Collection; **p. 161** Georg Hoefnagel, *Portrait of Rudolf II*, Kunsthistorisches Museum, Vienna; **p. 167** Catholics enter Augsburg, Fotomas Index; **p. 169** Jan Martsen de Jonge, *Gustavus Adolphus in Battle*, Königliches Schloß, Kungl, Husgerlidekammaren, The Royal Collection, Stockholm; **p. 170** Wallenstein assassinated, Fotomas Index; **p. 172** Jacques Callot, *Les Grandes Misères de la Guerre*, 1633, Fotomas Index; **p. 177** Adriaen Pietersz van de Venne, *Allegory of Poverty*, Allen Memorial Art Museum, Oberlin College, Ohio, Mrs. F. F. Prentiss Fund, 1960, © Allen Memorial Art Museum.

Chapter 5: p. 182 Courtesy of the New York Public Library Prints Division, Astor, Lenox, and Tilden Foundations; **p. 185** Jan van Hemessen, *Die Berufung des Matthäus*, Bayer, Staatsgemäldesammlungen; **p. 189** Felipe Bigarny, *Ferdinand the Catholic and Isabella the Catholic*, painted wood, Capilla Real, Granada Cathedral, Francesc Catalá Roca, Scala/Art Resource, NY; **p. 192** Titian, *Charles V*, Alte Pinakothek, Giraudon/Art Resource, NY; **p. 194** Titian, *Philip II*, Galleria Corsini, Alinari/Art Resource, NY; **p. 195** Ampliaciones y reproducciones MAS, Barcelona; **p. 196** Paolo Veronese, *The Battle of Lepanto*, Accademia, Venice, Photograph by Erich Lessing/Art Resource, NY; **p. 200** (left) Master John, *Lady Jane Grey* (# 4451), By courtesy of the National Portrait Gallery, London; (right) Antonio Moro, *La Reina*

Doña Maria de Inglaterra, Segunda Mujer de Felippe II, 1554, Museo del Prado, Art Resource, NY; **p. 202** Marcus Gheerhaerts the Younger, *Queen Elizabeth Dancing with Robert Dudley, Earl of Leicester,* Viscount del Isle, VC, KG, from his collection at Penhurst Place, Kent, Bridgeman/Art Resource, NY; **p. 206** Follower of François Clouet, miniature of *Mary Queen of Scots,* Victoria & Albert Museum, London, Bridgeman/Art Resource, NY; **p. 207** Artist unknown, *Elizabeth I Greeting the Dutch Ambassadors,* Staatliche Museen, Kassel; **p. 210** Anthony van den Wyngaerde, *Panorama of London,* 1543, Guildhall Library; **p. 211** Jan Siberechts, *A View of Longleat in Wiltshire,* Bridgeman/Art Resource, NY; **p. 215** Fotomas Index; **p. 218** (left) Facsimile of the First Folio edition of 1623, Warder Collection; (right) The Swan Theatre, c. 1596. Warder Collection; **p. 220** Franz Hogenberg, *Engravings of Scenes from The History of the Netherlands, France and Germany,* Cologne, 1620s, Miriam and Ira D. Wallach Division of Art, Prints and Photographs, New York Public Library, Astor, Lenox, and Tilden Foundations; **p. 223** Vicente Carducho, *Expulsion of the "Moriscos" from Spain,* 1609, Prado, Madrid; **p. 225** Antonio Pereda, *Sueño del Caballero (The Soldier's Dream),* 1640, Accademia de Bellas Artes de San Fernando, Madrid, Art Resource, NY; **p. 227** (left) Velásquez, *Felipe IV,* Museo del Prado, Ampilaciones y Reproducciones MAS; (right) Velásquez, *Gaspar de Guzmán, Duque de Olivares,* Museo del Prado, Ampilaciones y Reproducciones MAS; **p. 230** Velásquez, *Surrender at Breda,* Museo del Prado, Ampilaciones y Reproducciones MAS.

Chapter 6: p. 233 A. van der Venne, *Harbour at Middelburg,* © Rijksmuseum-Stichting, Amsterdam; **p. 235** (left) James I, By permission of the Trustees of the National Maritime Museum, London; (right) Daniel Mytens, *Charles I when Prince of Wales,* © Her Majesty Queen Elizabeth II/Royal Collection Enterprises, Ltd.; **p. 239** From John Vicar's *Sight of the Transactions of These Latter Years,* etching by Wencelaus Hollar, British Library; **p. 242** (left) John Pym (# 1425), By courtesy of the National Portrait Gallery, London; (right) After A. Van Dyck, *William Laud* (# 171), By courtesy of the National Portrait Gallery, London; **p. 246** From John Vicar's *Sight of the Transactions of These Latter Years,* etching by Wencelaus Hollar, British Library; **p. 247** Sir Peter Lely, *Oliver Cromwell,* Galleria Palatina, Florence, Photo supplied by British Information Services; **p. 250** The New Model Army, Warder Collection; **p. 251** Execution of Charles I, Engraving by Sebastian Furck, Hulton Deutsch Collection Ltd; **p. 256** Quaker meeting, Engraving by Van Heemsterk the Younger, Trustees of the British Museum, London; **p. 258** Adriaen Key, *William the Silent,* Mauritshuis (Royal Picture Gallery), The Hague, The Netherlands; **p. 263** J. Berckheyde, *The Amsterdam Bourse,* 1668, Amsterdams Historisch Museum; **p. 264** Gerrit Berckheyde, *The Waag and Crane on the Spaarne at Haarlem,* © Rijksmuseum-Stichting, Amsterdam; **p. 265** A. Cuyp, *A Senior Merchant of the Dutch East India Company and His Wife,* © Rijksmuseum-Stichting, Amsterdam; **p. 267** (left) Engraving of tulips by Claes Jansz from *Sinnepoppen,* Amsterdam, 1614, By permission of the Houghton Library, Harvard University; (right) Emanuel de Witte, *The Fish Market,* © Rijksmuseum-Stichting, Amsterdam; **p. 268** Romeyn de Hooghe, *The Dike-break at Coevorden,* Engraving, Bodleian Library, Oxford; **p. 270** Rembrandt, *Syndics of the Cloth Guild,* © Rijksmuseum-Stichting, Amsterdam.

Chapter 7: p. 275 Title page from T. Hobbes, *Leviathan,* 1651, New York Public Library Rare Book Division, Astor, Lenox, and Tilden Foundations; **p. 278** Diederich Porath from the folio *Palaestra Suecena,* Stockholm, 1693, Warder Collection; **p. 283** Janissaries cross the Drave, from *History of Soliman II,* Reproduced by kind permission of the Trustees of the Chester Beatty Library, Dublin, Photograph from Rex Roberts Studios; **p. 285** Charles Le Brun, Ceiling of the Hall of Mirrors, Versailles Museum, Giraudon/Art Resource, NY; **p. 287** (left) Rousselet, *Le Prince de Condé, Empereur des Turcs,* from *Courses de Testes et de Bagues faites par le Roy,* 1670, Gift of Mrs. Herbert L. Stern, Courtesy of the Art Institute of Chicago; (right) Philippe de Champagne, *Portrait of Mazarin,* Chantilly, Photographie Bulloz; **p. 290** Gobelins after Le Brun, Louis XIV visiting the Gobelins Factory, Versailles, © R.M.N.; **p. 291** J. B. Martin, The City and the Château of Versailles. . . Château—and Trianon, Giraudon/Art Resource, NY; **p. 293** French school, 17th Century, The Château of Versailles, Photographie Bulloz; **p. 295** C. Coypel, *Portrait of Molière,* Photographie Bulloz; **p. 296** (left) French figurative plaque of the Sun, Cabinet des Médailles, © cliché Bibliothèque Nationale de France, Paris; (right) Louis XIV as the Exterminator of Protestantism, Departement des Imprimés, © cliché Bibliothèque Nationale de France, Paris; **p. 297** J. Luyken,

© Rijksmuseum-Stichting, Amsterdam; **p. 302** G. Lauch, Engraving of Leopold I, Trustees of the British Museum; **p. 303** Pierre-Denis Martin, *The Siege of Vienna*, 1683, Alte Pinakothek, Bayerische Staatsgemäldesammlungen; **p. 306** Frederick William I, Warder Collection; **p. 308** Mathieu Merian the Younger, Engraving of Ivan the Terrible in Novgorod, © cliché Bibliothèque Nationale de France, Paris; **p. 310** T. H. Wedekind, *Charles XII*, Armémuseum, Stockholm, Photograph by Bo Michaëlsson; **p. 312** Peter the Great, Versailles, Lauros-Giraudon/Art Resource, NY; **p. 319** Adam Frans Van der Meulen, *Rhine Passage*, 1672, Louvre, Paris, Alinari/Art Resource, NY.

Chapter 8: p. 328 Tapestry of Testelin after a cartoon by Le Brun, *Establishment of the Academy of Science*, Musée de Versailles, Giraudon/Art Resource, NY; **p. 331** Copernican heliocentricism, Warder Collection; **p. 333** (left) Jan Stephan van Calcar, title page from Vesalius' *De humani corporis fabricia*, 1543, Kupferstichkabinett, Basel; (right) Skeleton from Vesalius, *Epitome*, Kupferstichkabinett, Basel; **p. 334** Circulation of the blood, *De motu cordis*, 1628, British Library; **p. 335** The Science Museum/Science and Society Picture Library; **p. 336** (left) Kepler, Warder Collection; (right) J. Kepler, *Prodromus Dissertationum*, Tubingen, 1596, Rare Book Collection, New York Public Library, Astor, Lenox, and Tilden Foundations; **p. 338** (left) Francis Bacon, Trustees of the British Museum; (right) Galileo, Dr. G. B. Pineider, Florence; **p. 341** (left) Unknown artist, *Portrait of Descartes*, Photographie Bulloz; (right) Sir Isaac Newton (# 2881), By courtesy of the National Portrait Gallery, London; **p. 345** Pascal's calculating machine, Warder Collection; **p. 346** Frontispiece to *Nature's Pictures Drawn by Fancies Pencil*, 1656, By permission of the Houghton Library, Harvard University; **p. 349** 17th Century French apothecary shop, © cliché Bibliothèque Nationale de France, Paris; **p. 350** *The Alchemist*, engraving after a painting by Teniers, Bettmann Archive; **p. 352** Royal Observatory, London, The Science Museum/Science and Society Picture Library.

Chapter 9: p. 355 Thomas Gainsborough, *Mr. & Mrs. Andrews*, National Gallery, London; **p. 357** (left) Alain M. Mallet, *Description de l'universe*, Paris, 1683, Rare Book Collection, New York Public Library, Astor, Lenox, and Tilden Foundations; (right) Nobleman as spider, Warder Collection; **p. 359** Blenheim Palace, Edwin Smith/Warder Collection; **p. 362** William Hogarth, *Lord George Graham*, By permission of the Trustees of the National Maritime Museum, London; **p. 365** Flogging a serf, Bettmann Archive; **p. 368** John G. Maxwell, *Measuring Land for Enclosure*, 1748, County Records Office, Bedford, Jewell-Harrison; **p. 373** Engraving showing conditions in Hamburg hospital, Germanisches Nationalmuseum, Nürnberg; **p. 375** William Hogarth, *The Weaver's Apprentice*, Trustees of the British Museum; **p. 376** Fotomas Index; **p. 377** (left) C. Wagstaff after Sir W. Beechey, James Watt, Warder Collection; (right) Watt's steam engine, Ironbridge Gorge Museum (Elton Collection); **p. 379** John Raphael Smith, after Joseph Wright of Derby, *Sir Richard Arkwright*, 1801, Derby Museum and Art Gallery **p. 386** London cafe, Trustees of the British Museum; **p. 387** James Malton, *Shops by Essex Bridge, Capel Street, Dublin* (detail), *c.* 1790, Victoria & Albert Museum/Art Resource, NY; **p. 388** Cornelius Holsteyn, *Reynier Pauw & His Wife Adriana & Their Children* (detail), Courtesy Christies, London; **p. 394** *Preserve Us from Gamekeepers*, French engraving, Trustees of the British Museum; **p. 396** William Hogarth, *The Idle 'Prentice Executed by Tyburn*, engraving, 1747, Trustees of the British Museum; **p. 397** Roger-Viollet.

Chapter 10: p. 400 John Locke: commemorative medal, Trustees of the British Museum; **p. 404** The *philosophes*, Bibliothèque Nationale, Paris; **p. 406** (left) Montesquieu, Photographie Bulloz; (right) J.A. Houdon, portrait bust of Voltaire, Louvre, Paris, Alinari/Art Resource, NY; **p. 409** Illustration from Diderot's *Encyclopedia*, Warder Collection; **p. 413** (left) Q. de la Tour, *Jean Jacques Rousseau*, Photographie Bulloz; (right) Rousseau and Voltaire fighting, Bibliothèque Nationale, Paris; **p. 419** Oval Salon, Hôtel de Soubise, Paris, Giraudon/Art Resource, NY; **p. 420** Jean-Antoine Watteau, *La Gamme d'Amour*, National Gallery, London; **p. 421** William Hogarth, *Gin Lane*, 1751, Trustees of the British Museum; **p. 422** (left) Philippe Mercier, *Portrait of Handel*, private collection, Photograph courtesy Thames & Hudson, Ltd; (right) Haydn, Warder Collection; **p. 423** The young Mozart performing, Schönbrunn, Bildarchiv, Österreichisches Nationalbibliothek; **p. 424** *Une soirée chez Madame Geoffrin*, Château Malmaison, Lauros-Giraudon/Art Resource, NY; **p. 425**

Mesmer, Photo collection of UCLA Bio-Medical Library, History Division; **p. 427** Freemasons, Museen der Stadt Wien; **p. 429** Austrian classroom, Historischen Museums der Stadt Wien, Photograph by Rudolf Stepanek; **p. 430** Expulsion of the Jews from Prague, 1745, Warder Collection; **p. 433** *Frederick the Great Playing Flute at Sans Souci,* Foto Marburg/Art Resource, NY; **p. 437** Adam Smith, Bettmann Archive.

Chapter 11: p. 443 *The Lawyers,* © cliché Bibliothèque Nationale de France, Paris; **p. 448** (left) Louis Gabriel Blanchet, *Prince Charles Edward Stuart,* 1738, By courtesy of the National Portrait Gallery, London; (right) The Battle of Culloden Moor, Courtesy of the Director, National Army Museum, London; **p. 449** Marten van Meytens II, *Maria Theresa and Her Family,* 1750, Kunsthistoriches Museum, Wien; **p. 450** Frederick the Great, Warder Collection; **p. 453** Pierre Lenfant, *La Bataille de Fontenoy, 11 mai 1745,* Versailles Museum, Giraudon/Art Resource; **p. 458** The Capture of Quebec, 1759, Engraved after a drawing by Smyth, Wolfe's Aide-de-Camp, Hulton Deutsch Collection Ltd; **p. 461** Siege warfare, Courtesy of the Director, National Army Museum, London; **p. 463** Edmund Burke, The Mansell Collection; **p. 465** *Picture of the Very Famous Island of Madhead,* Amsterdam, 1720, Warder Collection; **p. 466** Joseph Coopy, *Robert Walpole and His Cabinet,* Trustees of the British Museum; **p. 469** Benjamin West, *George III,* 1779, © Her Majesty Queen Elizabeth II, Royal Collection Enterprises Ltd.; **p. 473** Wilkes Riots, *c.* 1768, Stock Montage, Chicago; **p. 477** Paul Revere, from *The Boston Gazette,* March 12, 1770, Courtesy of The New-York Historical Society, NYC; **p. 479** Louis Nicolas Blarenberghe, *The Siege of Yorktown* (detail), Versailles Museum, Giraudon/Art Resource, NY; **p. 480** Karl Anton Hickel, *House of Commons,* (# 745), By courtesy of the National Portrait Gallery, London; **p. 485** Pugachev, Warder Collection.

Chapter 12: p. 496 Musée Carnavalet, Photographie Bulloz; **p. 500** (left) Duplessis, *Louis XVI,* Musée Carnavalet, Photographie Bulloz; (right) Marie-Elisabeth-Louise Vigée-Lebrun, *Marie-Antoinette,* Versailles Museum, Photographie Bulloz; **p 504** (left) *Lafayette,* Musée Carnavalet, Photographie Bulloz; (right) Jacques-Louis David, *Abbé Sieyès,* Photographie Bulloz; **p. 506** *Tennis Court Oath,* After David, Bibliothèque Nationale; **p. 507** *The Taking of the Bastille,* Versailles Museum; Giraudon/Art Resource, NY; **p. 512** *Women of Paris March to Versailles,* © cliché Bibliothèque Nationale de France, Paris; **p. 515** *The Three Orders Hammering Out the New Constitution,* Trustees of the British Museum; **p. 517** *Olympe de Gouges,* Musée Carnavalet, Photo Andreani, © Photothèque des Musées de la ville de Paris by SPADEM; **p. 518** Pierre Etienne Lesueur, *Patriotic Women's Club,* Musée Carnavalet, Photo Ladet/Toumazet, © Photothèque des Musées de la Ville de Paris by SPADEM; **p. 519** © cliché Bibliothèque Nationale de France, Paris; **p. 520** (left) Louis XVI with bonnet rouge, Cabinet des Estampes, © cliché Bibliothèque Nationale de France, Paris; (right) *Planting a Liberty Tree,* Musée Carnavalet, © Photothèque des Musées de la ville de Paris by SPADEM; **p. 521** (left) Danton, Musée Carnavalet, Photographie Bulloz; (right) Robespierre, Musée Carnavalet, Photographie Bulloz; **p. 525** *The Massacres of September,* Photographie Bulloz; **p. 528** Execution of Louis XVI, © cliché Bibliothèque Nationale de France, Paris; **p. 531** Hulton Deutsch Collection Ltd; **p. 532** Jacques-Louis David, *Death of Marat,* Photographie Bulloz; **p. 534** Jacques-Louis David, *Marie Antoinette on Her Way to Her Execution,* Bibliothèque Nationale, Photographie Giraudon/Art Resource, NY; **p. 535** (left) Seal of the Republic, Archives Nationales, Paris; (right) The French people overwhelming the hydra of federalism, August 1793, Musée Carnavalet, Photo Briant, © Photothèque des Musées de la ville de Paris by SPADEM; **p. 539** Debucourt, *The Cafe Frascati,* © cliché Bibliothèque Nationale de France, Paris; **p. 540** Bonaparte and the insurrection, Bibliothèque Nationale, Paris; **p. 543** The Corsican Crocodile dissolving the Council of Frogs!!!, Literature BMC.9427, The Trustees of the British Museum.

Chapter 13: p. 549 Jean-Antoine Gros, *Bonaparte at Arcole,* 1796, Louvre, Photographie Giraudon/Art Resource, NY; **p. 551** Nelson at Battle of the Nile, By permission of the Trustees of the National Maritime Museum, London; **p. 557** Jacques-Louis David, *Emperor Napoleon Crowning the Empress Josephine in the Cathedral of Notre Dame,* Louvre, Giraudon/Art Resource, NY; **p. 558** Turner, "The death of Lord Nelson at *The Battle of Trafalgar,*" 1805, Tate Gallery; **p. 561** Alexander I and Napoleon, Mansell Collection; **p. 562** Louis-Léopold Boilly, *Le départ des conscrits en 1807 devant la porte Saint-Denis,* Musée Carnavalet, Giraudon/Art Resource, NY; **p. 564** Charles Meynier, *Napoleon on the Island of*

Lobau, Versailles Museum, © Photo R.M.N.; **p. 568** Jacques-Louis David, *Oath of the Army after the Distribution of the Standards*, Versailles Museum, Alinari/Art Resource, NY; **p. 570** Gillray cartoon, *The Plumb-pudding in danger*, 1805, Print collection, The New York Public Library, Astor, Lenox, and Tilden Foundations; **p. 572** Francisco José de Goya y Lucientes, *May 3 1808: The Execution of the Defenders of Madrid*, 1814, Museo del Prado, Alinari/ Art Resource, NY; **p. 578** Faber Du Faur, *The Last Remnants of the Grand Army en Route to Smolensk*, Bavarian Army Museum, Munich; **p. 580** Francisco José de Goya y Lucientes, *Portrait of Wellington*, National Gallery, London; **p. 581** Napoleon on Elba, *The Sorrows of Boney*, Trustees of the British Museum; **p. 583** *Acclamation of People of Grenoble at the Return of Napoleon*, © cliché Bibliothèque Nationale de France, Paris; **p. 584** A. A. Alken, *Calvary Charge at Waterloo*, Courtesy of the Director, National Army Museum, London; **p. 585** Jacques-Louis David, *Bonaparte Leaping St. Bernard*, Versailles Museum, Photographie Bulloz.

Chapter 14: p. 588 Congress of Vienna, Engraving by L. Lutz, *c.* 1815, Historisches Museen der Stadt Wien; **p. 598** J. B. Isabey, *Louis XVIII*, Louvre, Paris, Warder Collection; **p. 603** Simon Bolivar and his generals, Bettmann Archive; **p. 605** Ludwig Burger, Wartburg Festival, Staatsbibliothek, Berlin, Bildarchiv Preussischer Kulturbesitz; **p. 607** Eugène Delacroix, *Massacre at Chios*, Louvre, Paris, Giraudon/Art Resource, NY; **p. 609** Tsar Nicholas I, Bettmann Archive; **p. 610** Honoré Daumier, Chambre des Deputés *(Le Ventre Législatif)*, Art Resource, NY; **p. 612** François Gérard, *Charles X in Sacred Costume*, Versailles Museum, Roger-Viollet; **p. 615** Honoré Daumier, *Le Banquier*, Le Charivari, 16 October 1835, The Benjamin A. and Julia M. Trustman Collection, Brandeis University Libraries; **p. 616** François-Joseph Heim, *The King Receiving at the Palais-Royal the Deputies of 1830, Who Present the Act by Which They Confer the Crown on Him*, Versailles Museum, Photographie Bulloz; **p. 617** (top) Honoré Daumier, *Pot de vin, arrestations arbitraires, mitraillades, transnoninades, elle couvre tout de son manteau*, Le Charivari, 1834, Gift of Mr. & Mrs. Howard P. Vincent (Mary Wilson Smith, Class of 1926) 1988, Mount Holyoke College Art Museum; (bottom) Insurrection in Lyon, Roger-Viollet; **p. 618** Napoleon's funeral cortege, Roger-Viollet; **p. 619** Gustave Wappers, *Scene of the Revolution September 1830*, Place de l'Hôtel de Ville, Brussels, Musées Royaux des Beaux-Arts, Brussels, © A.C.L., Brussels; **p. 624** Nicholas I as a bear, Fotomas Index; **p. 630** T. Tegg, *The Battle of Peterloo*, Trustees of the British Museum; **p. 632** English caricature on electoral reform, Trustees of the British Museum; **p. 635** The potato famine in Ireland, Mansell Collection; **p. 636** The Great Chartist Meeting on Kensington Common, 10 April 1848, Photo from Royal Archives by W. E. Kilburn, © Her Majesty Queen Elizabeth II/Royal Collection Enterprises Ltd.

Chapter 15: p. 639 Carl Schindler, *Der Wachposten*, Österreichische Galerie, Wien; **p. 644** Honoré Daumier, *The Speech for the Defense*, private collection; **p. 646** V. N. Marstrand, *The Waagepetersen Family*, Statens Museum fur Kunst, Copenhagen; **p. 647** Richard Redgrave, *The Governess*, 1845, Victoria & Albert Museum/Art Resource, NY; **p. 649** "Mill's Logic, or Franchise for Females," *Punch*, 30 March 1867, Warder Collection; **p. 650** Edmund Texier, *Tableau de Paris*, Paris, 1852, Warder Collection; **p. 651** E. Gärtner, *Living Room of the Master Smith, E.F.A. Hauschild, in Stralauer Strasse, Berlin*, Stiftung Stadtmuseum, Berlin; **p. 653** Roger Fenton, Oxford students, 1856, Sammlung Dietmar Siegert; **p. 654** Jean-François Millet, *The Reading Lesson*, *c.* 1860, Francis Welch Fund, Courtesy Museum of Fine Arts, Boston; **p. 656** Peter Fendi, *Evening Prayer*, 1839, Graphische Sammlung Albertina; **p. 657** Karl Girardet, *La charité dans un grenier*, Archives nationale, C.R.D.P. de Paris; **p. 664** Théodore Géricault, *Portrait of an Officer of the Chasseurs Commanding a Charge*, 1812, Louvre, Giraudon/Art Resource, NY; **p. 665** J. H. W. Tischbein, *Goethe in the Country*, Städelsches Kunstinstitut, Frankfurt am Main, Kavaler/Art Resource, NY; **p. 667** Sebastian Gutzwiller, *Basler Family Concert*, 1849, Photo by Martin Bühler for Oeffentliche Kunstsammlung, Basel.

Chapter 16: p. 670 Yorkshire coal miner, British Library; **p. 676** Opening of the Stockton and Darlington Railway, Warder Collection; **p. 679** (top) Honoré Daumier, *The Third-Class Carriage*, *c.* 1862, Metropolitan Museum of Art, New York, Bequest of Mrs. H.O. Havemeyer, 1929, The H.O. Havemeyer Collection; (bottom) *The Great Western*, Collection David Artis; **p. 683** British cotton factory, The Manchester Public Libraries; **p. 690** Bread riot, From "Looking Glass," 1830, British Library; **p. 691** Captain Swing, Fotomas Index; **p. 692** Farmhouse in Brittany, 1844, Bibliothèque Nationale, Paris; **p. 698** Girl pulling coal

NY; **p. 839** Caricature on the cession of Alsace-Lorraine, Photographie Bulloz; **p. 840** Execution during Paris Commune, Bibliothèque Nationale, Paris; **p. 841** Champs Elysées in Paris during the Commune, Photoworld/FPG; **p. 842** Musée Carnavalet, © Photothèque des Musées de la Ville de Paris by SPADEM/ARS, NY.

Chapter 20: p. 845 (left) Eiffel Tower at Paris Exposition of 1900, Bibliothèque Historique de la Ville de Paris, photo by Gerard Leyris; (right) Palace of Electricity at the Paris Exhibition of 1900, Collection George Sirot, Paris; **p. 846** A Bessemer converter, Bettmann Archive; **p. 848** "The Stroke of Midnight," © cliché Bibliothèque Nationale de France, Paris; **p. 850** Automobile assembly line, © 1914 Ford Motor Co.; **p. 851** Claude Monet, *Terrace at Sainte-Adresse*, 1867, The Metropolitan Museum of Art, Purchased with special contributions and purchase funds given or bequeathed by friends of the Museum, 1967 (67.241); **p. 852** Telephone switchboard, Photoworld/FGP; **p. 855** Rural laborers in southern Italy, Hulton Deutsch Collection Ltd; **p. 860** (left) High Street, Glasgow, The Mansell Collection; (right) Company housing near the Mines of Bruay, 1889, © cliché Bibliothèque Nationale, Paris; **p. 862** E. Atget, *Cité Trebert, Porte de Choisy*, 1913, © cliché Bibliothèque Nationale de France, Paris; **p. 864** Lewis W. Hine, *Immigrants on Ellis Island*, 1905, Museum of the City of New York; **p. 867** Pit boys, Warder Collection; **p. 871** Clerks in Cadbury's General Office, 1912, Photo courtesy Cadbury Ltd; **p. 875** Caricature by Gill of Jules Ferry from *l'Eclipse*, Roger-Viollet; **p. 878** (left) A. Mucha, theater poster for *La Dame aux Camelias*, Bibliothèque de l'Arsenal, Giraudon/Art Resource, NY; (right) Sarah Bernhardt photographed in a coffin, Bettmann Archive; **p. 882** Parisian department store, Roger-Viollet; **p. 883** Edgar Degas, *L'Absinthe*, 1877, Musee d'Orsay, Paris, Giraudon/Art Resource, NY; **p. 886** (left) The Curies, English Caricature Lithograph,1904; (right) Ernest Rutherford, Cambridge University Library, Rutherford Collection, courtesy AIP Emilio Segrè Visual Archives; **p. 888** Albert Einstein, The Hebrew University of Jerusalem; **p. 891** Freud and family, Freud Museum/London; **p. 892** Nietzsche, Goethe and Schiller Archives, Nationalen Forschungsu. Gedenkstätten in Weimar; **p. 893** *The Rite of Spring*, 1913, Warder Collection; **p. 896** Georges Seurat, *A Sunday Afternoon on the Island of the Grande Jatte*, 1884, © The Art Institute of Chicago, Helen Birch Bartlett Memorial Collection; **p. 897** Antoni Gaudí i Cornet, *Casa Batlló*, 1905-07, Ampliaciones y Reproducciones MAS, Barcelona; **p. 899** (left) Pablo Picasso, © cliché Réunion des Musées Nationales, Paris; (right) Pablo Picasso, *Les Demoiselles d'Avignon*, 1907, Museum of Modern Art, Lillie P. Bliss Bequest, © 1996 Museum of Modern Art, NY/ARS, NY; **p. 900** Umberto Boccioni, *Dynamism of a Cyclist*, 1913, Collection of Gianni Mattisti, Milan, Bridgeman/Art Resource, NY/ARS, NY.

Chapter 21: p. 903 Dinnertime in an English workhouse, Warder Collection; **p. 913** The Townsend Road School, 1905, Hulton Deutsch Collection Ltd; **p. 916** Emily Davison's death at the Derby, 1913, Mansell Collection; **p. 920** Socialist League at Hammersmith, © The Board of the Trustees of the Victoria & Albert Museum, London/Art Resource, NY; **p. 922** Jean Jaurès, Warder Collection; **p. 923** Peter Kropotkin's *The Spirit of Revolt*, Houghton Library, Harvard University; **p. 927** William Gladstone, Warder Collection; **p. 929** Broadside on Home Rule, E.T. Archive; **p. 935** William Butler Yeats, © Anna MacBride White; **p. 940** Suicide of Boulanger, from *Le Petit Journal*, 10 October 1891, © cliché Bibliothèque Nationale de France, Paris; **p. 941** (left) Emile Courtet, "The Qualities of the Jew after Gall's Method," *La Libre Parole Illustrée*, 23 December 1893, The Jewish Museum, NY; (right) Alfred Dreyfus, Roger-Viollet; **p. 944** Dmitri Ivanovich Yermakov, *Princess Lasarev in Tatar costume*, Tbilisi, *c.* 1890, Moscow State Historical Museum; **p. 946** Russian caricature of the Russo-Japanese conflict, Warder Collection; **p. 948** Riots in Milan, 1898, Based on a photo by Luca Comerio, appearing in *L'Illustrazione Italiana*, 1898, Biblioteca, Milan; **p. 955** Caricature of Bismarck and Pope Leo XIII from *Kladderadatsch*, 1875, Staatsbibliothek, Berlin, Photo courtesy Bildarchiv Preussischer Kulturbesitz; **p. 956** Emperor William II and the Death's Head Hussars, Warder Collection.

Chapter 22: p. 961 Queen Victoria, By courtesy of the National Portrait Gallery, London (P51); **p. 962** Mr. & Mrs. Hutt in Borneo, Popperfoto; **p. 963** Germany and France establish their colonial borders in the Congo, From *Le Petit Journal*, 9 November 1913, © cliché Bibliothèque Nationale de France, Paris; **p. 968** The British fleet anchored off Alexandria, 1882, Mansell Collection; **p. 969** Usambara-Bahn, 1907, Ullstein Bilderdienst; **p. 970** Anton von Werner, *Der Kongreß zu Berlin*, 1881, photo by Klaus Göken, 1993, Bildarchiv Preussischer

Kulturbesitz; **p. 971** Caricatures of Germans in Africa, From *Jugend*, 1896, Warder Collection; **p. 972** Statue of Lord Gordon, Hulton Deutsch Collection Ltd; **p. 973** The charge of the dervishes at the Battle of Omdurman in the Sudan, Mansell Collection; **p. 974** Boer commandos crossing the Orange River, Cape Archives Depot Ref #AG 283; **p. 976** Kimberley diamond fields, 1871, Hulton Deutsch Collection Ltd; **p. 979** IMP/GEH Warder Collection; **p. 980** (left) Lithograph after a drawing by Captain G.F. Atkinson, Courtesy of the Director, National Army Museum, London; (right) The ruins of Lucknow, © the Board of Trustees of the Victoria & Albert Museum/Art Resource, NY; **p. 981** Viceroy Lord Curzon and Lady Curzon enter Delhi, 1903, Mansell Collection; **p. 986** J. Macfarlane from *The Kipling Reader*, 1908, © British Library; **p. 988** Trading ships in Calcutta, India Office Library; **p. 989** Maxim gun crew, Courtesy of the Director, National Army Museum, London; **p. 990** *Simplicissimus* caricature of British imperialism, Warder Collection; **p. 995** Thomas Jones Barker, *Queen Victoria Presenting a Bible at Windsor*, 1861, By courtesy of the National Portrait Gallery, London (#4969).

Chapter 23: p. 1004 *Simplicissimus* cartoon, Warder Collection; **p. 1005** (top) *Simplicissimus* cartoon, Warder Collection; (bottom) Emperor Francis Joseph, Hulton Deutsch Collection Ltd; **p. 1007** Austrian cartoon from *Figaro,* Vienna, Warder Collection; **p. 1013** Postcard commemorating Kaiser William II's launching of the S. S. *Imperator,* Altonaer Museum, Hamburg; **p. 1015** Broadside about Morocco, c. 1906, © cliché Bibliothèque Nationale de France, Paris; **p. 1019** Street scene in Sarajevo, 1908, Warder Collection; **p. 1022** German cartoon about the Balkan Wars, c. 1912, Warder Collection; **p. 1023** David Wilson, *The Vortex: Will the Powers Be Drawn In?*, 1912, The Mansell Collection; **p. 1025** Marshal Joseph Joffre, Canadian War Museum #19810152-012; **p. 1030** Archduke Ferdinand and his wife in Sarajevo, UPI.

Chapter 24: p. 1040 (left) Soldiers depart for war, Warder Collection; (right) Southwark Town Hall, London, December 1915, Hulton Deutsch Collection Ltd; **p. 1043** (top) Refugees flee the battle zone in northern France, Jean-Loup Charmet, Paris; (right) Old combat and new in World War I, Imperial War Museum; **p. 1044** Paul Nash's *We Are Making New World,* Imperial War Museum; **p. 1046** Trench warfare, Hulton Deutsch Collection Ltd; **p. 1047** No-man's-land, northern France, Photograph by Ivor Castle/ National Archives of Canada/ Negative no. PA 786; **p. 1048** (left) French soldiers wearing gas masks, Roger-Viollet; (right) Victims of a German gas attack, National Archives; **p. 1049** Dogfight, Warder Collection; **p. 1051** Attacking a German-owned store in London, 1914, Hulton Deutsch Collection Ltd; **p. 1052** (left) Poster of Lord Kitchener, Canadian War Museum, 56-04-11-078; (right) "Women of Britain say—Go!", Canadian War Museum, 56-04-11-074; **p. 1055** After the Battle of the Somme, Imperial War Museum; **p. 1057** Stopping deserters, 1915, Warder Collection; **p. 1059** Turkish sniper captured in Gallipoli, 1915, Imperial War Museum; **p. 1060** Serbian retreat across the River Dvina, winter 1915, Imperial War Museum; **p. 1063** Battlefield of the Somme, UPI/Bettmann; **p. 1064** Russian sharpshooters, Canadian War Museum; **p. 1067** Italian women workers, Imperial War Museum; **p. 1068** Canadian and German soldiers, Canadian War Museum, 8D#2367; **p. 1071** Citizens of Berlin hunt for food, Ullstein Bilderdienst; **p. 1075** Allied tanks, Canadian War Museum, 0.1568, Acq# 1981-692/3.

Chapter 25: p. 1086 Procession after the coronation of Tsar Nicholas II, VA/Sovfoto; **p. 1087** Young workers in St. Petersburg, Central Archive for Film & Photographic Documentary, St. Petersburg; **p. 1093** Strikers outside the Putilov factory, 1905, RIA-Novosti/Sovfoto; **p. 1094** Bloody Sunday, Roger-Viollet; **p. 1096** A member of the Duma greets a peasant, Warder Collection; **p. 1098** Tsar Nicholas II blessing the troops, 1915, Popperfoto; **p. 1100** Tsar Nicholas II and family, Tass from Sovfoto; **p. 1101** Tsarina Alexandra and Grigori Rasputin, Warder Collection; **p. 1103** Nevsky Prospect, Courtesy George Eastman House; **p. 1104** Russian factory workers, 1917, Warder Collection; **p. 1106** Workers and soldiers guarding a government building, 1917, Bildarchiv Preussischer Kulturbesitz; **p. 1108** A Russian soldier with red flag, Imperial War Museum; **p. 1111** Kerensky with troops, Petrograd, 1917, Sovfoto; **p. 1116** Bolsheviks seize the Winter Palace, October, 1917, Warder Collection; **p. 1120** Lenin addressing troops, 1920, Warder Collection; **p. 1122** White army executes suspected Bolsheviks, UPI/Bettmann; **p. 1123** The Red Army leaving for the southern front, 1919, Warder Collection; **p. 1126** Trotsky reviews the Red Band, Red Square, 1921, Hulton Deutsch Collection Ltd; **p. 1128** (left) Starving refugee children, 1921, Hulton Deutsch Collection Ltd; (right) Free market during NEP, 1921, Warder Collection; **p. 1131** Lenin and Stalin, Photoworld/FPG; **p. 1133** Deportation of kulaks, 1930, The Illustrated London News Picture Library; **p. 1135** *Fighting Lazy Workers*, 1931, The Museum of Modern Art, Gift of Miss Jessie Rosenfeld, Photograph © 1996 The Museum of Modern Art, New York; **p. 1136** Soviet campaign against illiteracy, USIS, Paris.

Chapter 26: p. 1140 Fascist squad, Gruppo Editoriale Fabbri; **p. 1141** The Council of Four, 1919, Imperial War Museum; **p. 1143** Karl Liebknecht, 1919, Photograph by Willy Römer, Berlin, Ullstein Bilderdienst; **p. 1145** Adrien Senechal, *Ville de Reims, Emprunt de la Reconstruciton*, 1921, Paris, Musée d'Histoire Contemporaine, Paris; **p. 1150** Devalued German currency, Archiv für Kunst und Geschichte (Katherine Young); **p. 1159** Irish Republicans in Dublin, Warder Collection; **p. 1168** Apples selling for 30 billion marks per half pound, 1923, Herman Axelbank; **p. 1171** A barricade during the London General Strike, 1926, Warder Collection; **p. 1173** John Heartfield, cover collage for *Der Dada*, No. 3, April 1920, Courtesy Merrill C. Berman Collection; **p. 1175** Max Ernst, *Europe after the Rain (I)*, 1933, private collection; **p. 1179** Mussolini leaving the Quirinale, Centro Anni a Roma, Fratelli Palombi Editori, Roma; **p. 1179** Mussolini and Victor Emmanuel III, Keystone/ Hulton Deutsch Collection Ltd; **p. 1180** Mussolini addressing a crowd in Venice, Editori Laterza; **p. 1181** Italian women mobilized for Mussolini, Gruppo Editoriale Fabbri; **p. 1183** Nazi storm troopers, 1922, Ullstein Bilderdienst; **p. 1184** Hitler in Weimar, 1926, Fotoarchiv Hoffmann, Bayerische Staatsbibliothek; **p. 1185** Plebiscite propaganda, 1934, Photoworld/FPG.

Chapter 27: p. 1187 (left) Mussolini, Hulton Deutsch Collection Ltd; (right) Hitler, British Film Institute Stills, Posters, and Designs; **p. 1190** (left) James N. Rosenberg, *October 29, Dies Irae,* 1929, Philadelphia Museum of Art, Purchased: Lila Dowin Peck Fund; (right) Briton seeks work, 1930, Hulton Deutsch Collection Ltd; **p. 1193** Outside Lords Cricket Ground, 1937, Hulton Deutsch Collection Ltd; **p. 1197** Nazi rally, 1934, Canadian War Museum, 199202050-001; **p. 1209** Communists arrested after Reichstag fire, 1933, Bundesarchiv, Koblenz; **p. 1211** Hitler and Hindenburg, Warder Collection; **p. 1212** German youth meet Hitler, Canadian War Museum, 19920250-001; **p. 1216** Targeting of Jewish-owned shops, Hulton Deutsch Collection Ltd; **p. 1218** Hitler and Mussolini, National Archives; **p. 1223** Spanish peasant, Annabel Davies Collection, London; **p. 1226** Pablo Picasso, *Guernica* (mural), 1937, Museo del Prado; **p. 1227** (top) Nuns murdered by loyalist anticlericals, Annabel Davies Collection, London; (bottom) Abraham Lincoln Brigade, Annabel Davies Collection, London; **p. 1228** Francisco Franco, 1937, Ullstein Bilderdienst; **p. 1229** "La Pasionaria," UPI/Bettmann; **p. 1230** Spanish refugees, 1938, Keystone; **p. 1232** Austria after annexation, 1938, Hulton Deutsch Collection Ltd; **p. 1234** David Low cartoon on British appeasement, 1933, Courtesy Trustees of *The Evening Standard*; **p. 1236** Neville Chamberlain, 1938, Hulton Deutsch Collection Ltd.

Chapter 28: p. 1240 Germany invades Poland, 1939, Warder Collection; **p. 1243** Finland, 1940, Popperfoto; **p. 1245** Hitler in Paris, 1940, Canadian War Museum,19910172-001, Grossdeutschland im Weltgeschehen 1940; **p. 1247** (left) Children evacuated from London, 1940, The Illustrated London News Picture Library; (right) Churchill at St. Paul's Cathedral after the blitz, 1940, Warder Collection; **p. 1251** Rommel in North Africa, 1942, Ullstein Bilderdienst; **p. 1260** Lithuanians slaughtering Jews, 1942, Marx-Verlag GmbH, Allgemeine Wochenzeitung der Juden in Deutschland; **p. 1262** Dutch Jews before transport to a concentration camp, Warder Collection; **p. 1265** Partisan headquarters in Yugoslavia, 1944, Camera Press Ltd, London; **p. 1268** Vichy raid against Maquis, 1944, Roger-Viollet; **p. 1275** Siege of Leningrad, 1942, Novosti (London); **p. 1276** (left) Hamburg after Allied bombing, Ullstein Bilderdienst; (right) Stuttgart after Allied bombing, Ullstein Bilderdienst; **p. 1279** D-Day, June 1944, Maritime Administration; **p. 1280** (top) French resistance sabotaging train tracks, ECPA, Photo Cinéma Vidéo des Armées; (bottom) Liberation of Paris, Imperial War Museum; **p. 1281** Germans flee the Red Army, Hilmar Pabel/Leica Gallery; **p. 1283** Yalta, 1945, National Archives; **p. 1284** Hanging of Mussolini and his mistress, April 1945, Editori Laterza; **p. 1285** Soviet flag mounted on Reichstag, Photograph by Yevgeny Chaldey/ Voller Ernst.

Chapter 29: p. 1292 Displaced persons, 1945, Henri Cartier-Bresson/Magnum Photos, New York; **p. 1294** Potsdam, 1945, U.S. Signal Corps; **p. 1300** Collaborator escorted out of

Cherbourg, 1944, Robert Capa/Magna Photos, New York; **p. 1302** Cast of Picasso's play *Le Desir Attrapé* in his Paris studio, 1944, Photographie Brassai © copyright Gilberte Brassai; **p. 1304** Alexei and Sergei Tkachev, *Between Engagements,* Warder Collection; **p. 1307** Five-Year plan poster, 1950, Warder Collection; **p. 1311** (left) Italian peasant, Warder Collection; (right) Fiat factory in Turin, 1955, Hulton Deutsch Collection Ltd; **p. 1314** Gandhi, Information Service of India; **p. 1318** (left) Russian cartoon of Suez Canal seizure, School of Slavonic and Eastern European Studies, University of London; (right) Sunken ships block the Suez Canal, 1956, Hulton Deutsch Collection Ltd; **p. 1320** (left) French in Vietnam, 1952, L'Illustration/Sygma; (right) French patrol, Vietnam, © 1954 Robert Capa/Magnum Photos, New York; **p. 1321** French in Algeria, © 1959 Sergio Larrain/Magnum Photos, New York; **p. 1323** De Gaulle and Adenauer, 1958. UPI/Bettmann; **p. 1331** Parisians watching TV, © 1963 Marc Riboud/Magnum Photos, New York; **p. 1332** Coca-cola delivery, Venice, © 1950 David Seymour/Magnum Photos, New York; **p. 1334** Housing in Czechoslovakia, Warder Collection; **p. 1338** Berlin airlift, Wide World Photos; **p. 1339** Cult of Mao, Camera Press Ltd.; **p. 1342** Uprising in Hungary, 1956, Keystone Press Agency; **p. 1344** Harold M. Talburt, *Dog Daze,* 1957, Scripps-Howard Newspapers; **p. 1345** (left) Building the Berlin Wall, 1961, German Information Service, New York; (right) Kennedy in Berlin, 1963, AP/Wide World Photos; **p. 1346** (left) Khrushchev and Castro, 1963, Novosti, London; (right) UN Security Council during Cuban Missile Crisis, 1962, Neal Boenzi/NYT Pictures; **p. 1349** May Day Parade, 1963, Camera Press Ltd.

Chapter 30: p. 1352 Germans greet Gorbachev, 1989, AP/Wide World Photos; **p. 1354** (left) Students revolt in Paris, © 1968 Bruno Barbey/Magnum Photos Inc.; (right) Conservatives counter-demonstrate, Roger-Viollet; **p. 1357** Caricature of Thatcher years by Jeff Danziger, *The Christian Science Monitor,* © L.A. Times Syndicate; **p. 1360** Nuclear power plant and windmill, U.N. Photo; **p. 1366** McDonald's, Warder Collection; **p. 1372** Aldo Moro's body discovered, 1978, Hulton Deutsch Collection Ltd; **p. 1373** IRA bombing, Belfast, 1972, © 1995 Abbas/Magnum Photos, New York; **p. 1377** (left) Communist Party summit, 1968, AP/Wide World Photos; (right) Tanks in Prague, 1968, © 1968 Josef Koudelka/Magnum Photos Inc.; **p. 1383** Gorbachev in East Berlin, 1987, AP/Wide World Photos; **p. 1386** Lech Walesa, Daily Herald Photo; **p. 1387** The Berlin Wall falls, ©Alexandra Avakian/Woodfin Camp; **p. 1390** Václav Havel, 1989, AP/Wide World Photos; **p. 1394** (left) Mass grave in Timisoara, © Gilles Saussier/Gamma Liaison; (right) Militiaman watching Ceausescu's execution on the presidential television set, © 1989 David C. Turnley/Black Star; **p. 1397** (left)Yeltsin resisting the coup, 1991, AP/Wide World Photos; (right) Yeltsin and Gorbachev, Photo by Shone/Gamma Liaison; **p. 1401** (left) Requiem in a Sarajevo cemetary, © 1995 Paul Lowe/Network Matrix; (right) Bombing of Croatian civilians by Serbs, 1993 © Jean-Claude Coutausse/Press Images; **p. 1404** (left) Homeless woman in Moscow, 1990, Imre Benko/Wostok Press; (right) Russian fish market, 1992, Markus Jokela/Helsingin Sanomat, Finland; **p. 1406** Pollution in post-Communist Romania, © 1995 Barry Lewis/Network Matrix; **p. 1408** Neo-Nazis in Bavaria, © 1992 Sacha Hartgers/Focus/Matrix; **p. 1409** Berlin 1989, AP/Wide World Photos.

Tables: Table 1-1 (p. 21) European Population in the Sixteenth and Seventeenth Centuries, in Richard MacKenney, *Sixteenth-Century Europe: Expansion and Conflict* (New York: Macmillan, 1993), p. 51; **Table 7-1 (p. 281)** The Size of European Armies, 1690-1814, in Paul Kennedy, *The Rise and Fall of the Great Powers* (New York: Vintage, 1989), p. 99; **Table 9-1 (p. 371)** European Population, 1700-1800, in Paul Kennedy, *The Rise and Fall of the Great Powers* (New York: Vintage, 1989); **Table 16-1 (p. 672)** Estimated Populations of Various European Countries from 1800-1850, in Carlo M. Cipollo, ed., *The Fontana Economic History of Europe: Vol 3, The Industrial Revolution* (London: HarperCollins, 1973), p. 29; **Table 16-2 (p. 680)** Manufacturing Capacity throughout Europe, in Carlo M. Cipolla, ed., *The Fontana Economic History of Europe: Vol. 4(1), The Emergence of Industrial Societies* (London: HarperCollins, 1973), p. 165; **Table 20-1 (p. 847)** Annual Output of Steel, in Carlo M. Cipolla, ed., *The Fontana Economic History of Europe: Vol 4(2), The Emergence of Industrial Societies* (London: HarperCollins, 1973), p. 775; **Table 20-2 (p. 857)** Population Growth in Major States between 1871 and 1911, in Colin Dyer, *Population and Society in Twentieth Century France* (New York: Holmes and Meier, 1978), p. 5; in M. Huber, *La Population de L'Europe Pendant la Guerre* (Paris: P.U.F., 1931), p. 7; **Table 20-3 (p. 858)** The Decline in Family Size (Number of Children) in England and Wales, in E. A. Wrigley, *Popu-*

INDEX

Page number in *italics* refer to illustrations and figures.

1447